KEY NOTATION USED IN THE TEXT

k_d Required return on a bond; Pretax cost of debt; Yield to maturity on a bond

k_e Required return on common stock; Cost of internal equity

k'_e Cost of external equity

k_i After-tax cost of debt

k_j Required return from security j

$\hat{k}_m$ Expected market return

k_p Required return on preferred stock; Cost of preferred stock financing

LBO   Leveraged buyout

LIBOR   London interbank offered rate

LIFO   Last-in, first-out inventory valuation

M   Maturity value of a bond

MACRS   Modified accelerated cost recovery system of depreciation

NAL   Net advantage to leasing

NCF   Net cash flow

NINV   Net investment

NPV   Net present value

P_{net} Net proceeds to a firm from the sale of a security

P_t Price of a security at time period t

PB   Payback period

P/BV   Market price per share/Book value per share

P/E   Market price per share/Current earnings per share

P_f (1) Preferred stock in a firm's capital structure

         (2) Market value of a firm's preferred stock

PI   Profitability index

PV   Present value

PVAN   Present value of an annuity

PVIF   Present value interest factor

PVIFA   Present value of an annuity interest factor

PVPER   Present value of a perpetuity

r Internal rate of return of a project

R_t Cash flow received or paid in period t

RADR   Risk-adjusted discount rate

r_f Risk-free rate of return

SML   Security Market Line

T Marginal tax rate

t Time period indicator

Contemporary
Financial Management

■

FOURTH EDITION

Contemporary
Financial Management

FOURTH EDITION

R. Charles Moyer
WAKE FOREST UNIVERSITY

■

James R. McGuigan
JRM INVESTMENTS

■

William J. Kretlow
UNIVERSITY OF HOUSTON

WEST PUBLISHING COMPANY

Saint Paul ■ New York ■ Los Angeles ■ San Francisco

To Laura, Craig, and Sally   RCM

To the memory of my mother and father   JRM

To Cindy, John, and Jim   WJK

Copyediting: Gnomi Gouldin
Composition: Parkwood Composition
Text Design: Kristen M. Weber
Cover Photo: Steuben

Library of Congress Cataloging-in-Publication Data

Moyer, R. Charles, 1945–
   Contemporary financial management/R. Charles Moyer, James R. McGuigan,
William J. Kretlow.—4th ed.
      p.   cm.
   Includes bibliographical references.
   ISBN 0-314-58059-X
      1. Corporations—Finance. 2. Busines enterprises—Finance.
I. McGuigan, James R. II. Kretlow, William J. III. Title.
HG4026.M68   1990
658.15—dc20

89–37332
CIP

R. Charles Moyer holds the Integon Chair in Finance in the Babcock Graduate School of Management, Wake Forest University. Prior to assuming his present position, Professor Moyer was a Professor of Finance and Chairman of the Department of Finance at Texas Tech University between 1980 and 1988. Professor Moyer previously taught at the University of Houston, Lehigh University and the University of New Mexico. Born in Reading, Pennsylvania, he earned his B.A. in economics (*cum laude*) from Howard University, where he was elected to Phi Beta Kappa. He received his M.B.A. and Ph.D. in Business from the University of Pittsburgh. In addition to his teaching career, Professor Moyer has spent a year at the Federal Reserve Bank of Cleveland and a year as a Sears-AACSB Federal Faculty Fellow at the Maritime Administration, U.S. Department of Commerce, serving as a financial and economic analyst. Professor Moyer has taught extensively in executive education programs, including the Stonier Graduate School of Banking. He also frequently is called upon to provide expert testimony in public utility rate cases across the nation.

Professor Moyer has been a productive scholar. In addition to co-authoring *Contemporary Financial Management*, 4th edition, he has also co-authored *Managerial Economics*, 5th edition (West, 1989), and *Financial Management with Lotus 1-2-3* (West, 1986). Professor Moyer has published extensively in leading finance and economic journals including *Financial Management, Journal of Finan-*

cial and Quantitative Analysis, Journal of Finance, Financial Review, Journal of Financial Research, International Journal of Forecasting, Journal of Economics and Business, Journal of Industrial Organization, and many others. In total he has published over 70 articles. Professor Moyer serves as vice president and member of the Program Committee of the Financial Management Association, and is a past director of the FMA. He is an active reviewer for many finance and economic journals, and an associate editor of the *Financial Review*.

Professor Moyer enjoys athletics and is particularly active as a runner, golfer, and basketball player.

James R. McGuigan currently owns and operates his own numismatic investment firm. Prior to this activity, he was Associate Professor of Finance and Business Economics in the School of Business Administration at Wayne State University, where he taught in the undergraduate and masters programs for ten years. He also has taught at the University of Pittsburgh and Point Park College.

Dr. McGuigan received his undergraduate degree from Carnegie-Mellon University. His graduate degrees are from the Graduate Schools of Business at the University of Chicago (M.B.A.) and the University of Pittsburgh (Ph.D.).

He has published articles dealing with his research on options in the *Journal of Financial and Quantitative Analysis*. In

addition to his interests in financial management, Dr. McGuigan has coauthored books in managerial economics, including *Managerial Economics*, 5th edition (West, 1989), coauthored with R. Charles Moyer.

Dr. McGuigan's other interests include running and traveling.

William J. Kretlow is chair of the Finance Department at the University of Houston. Born and raised in Chicago, he earned his B.S. from the University of Michigan. He received his M.B.A. from the University of Houston and his Ph.D. from Purdue University, where he was a David Ross Fellow. In addition to teaching at UH, he has been a part-time Associate Professor of Economics at Rice University. At UH, he has taught financial management and investments at all levels. He has taught large introductory sections of managerial finance at both Houston and Rice. He currently teaches in both the UH Executive M.B.A. and the Executive Development Programs. In addition, he also teaches at the Stonier Graduate School of Banking of the American Bankers Association.

Professor Kretlow has received several teaching awards, including the University of Houston Teaching Excellence Award and the College of Business Administration Excellence in Teaching Award. He also is a recipient of Rice University's *Magna Cum Laude* Teaching Excellence Award.

In the area of academic research, Professor Kretlow has

published approximately fifteen articles and given several papers at professional society meetings. His research has dealt with the capital asset pricing model, dividend policy, bond ratings and financial planning models.

Professor Kretlow's business experience includes a total of five years with Tenneco and Monsanto, and he has advised various small and medium-sized companies on a variety of financial matters. He also has served as an expert witness in a number of financial cases. He is experienced in the valuation of closely held businesses.

CONTENTS

Appendix 9A ■ Additional Depreciation and Tax Issues   321

Chapter 10 ■ Capital Budgeting Decision Criteria   328

Appendix 10A ■ Mutually Exclusive Investments Having Unequal Lives   360

Chapter 16 ■ Managing Long-Term Funding Sources   546

Appendix 16A ■ Bond Refunding, Stockholder Voting Rights, and Rights Offerings   575

■ PART SEVEN   THE MANAGEMENT OF WORKING CAPITAL   583

Chapter 17 ■ Working Capital Policy   584

Chapter 18 ■ The Management of Cash and Marketable Securities   608

Chapter 19 ■ Management of Accounts Receivable and Inventories   640

Chapter 20 ■ Obtaining Short-Term Funds   680

▬ PART EIGHT SELECTED TOPICS IN CONTEMPORARY FINANCIAL MANAGEMENT 711

Chapter 21 ■ International Financial Management 712

Chapter 22 ■ Corporate Restructuring 728

APPENDIX A ■ AN OVERVIEW OF THE CFM LOTUS DISK 761

REFERENCE MATERIALS 765

The financial management field has witnessed an exciting period of change and growth during the 1970s and 1980s. Substantial fluctuations in inflation rates have caused the cost of a firm's funds to vary significantly, forcing them to be more careful in the allocation of their resources. Corporate and other financial practitioners increasingly employ new financial management techniques and computer resources to aid in their decision making. New financial instruments and transactions such as options, financial futures contracts, options on futures contracts, foreign currency swaps, and interest rate swaps have been developed to help cope with an environment of uncertainty. At the same time financial researchers have been making important theoretical strides.

The decade of the 1990s promises to be an even more exciting time for finance professionals. Spurred on by the activities of "corporate raiders," managers have refocused attention on the basic objective of maximizing shareholder wealth. Managers who act contrary to the interests of shareholders face the prospect of an unfriendly takeover or a corporate restructuring. The high fixed charges that accompany leveraged buyout transactions have disciplined managers to use the firm's resources more efficiently and to generate maximum cash flows. Indeed, the central importance of cash flows in the financial management of a firm has never been more apparent. As firms enter the 1990s carrying significantly more debt than in the past, financial managers will face new challenges during business downturns.

Contemporary Financial Management, fourth edition, incorporates these changes with the increased focus on shareholder wealth maximization and cash flow management into a text designed primarily for an introductory course in financial management. The book also is useful for management development programs and as a reference aid to practicing finance professionals.

Because we recognize that students will enter this course with a wide variety of backgrounds in mathematics, economics, accounting and statistics, the only presumption we make regarding prior preparation is that all students will have had at least one course in accounting.

Distinctive Features

Many financial management texts are well written and provide adequate coverage of the basic topics in financial management. In preparing this fourth edition, we, too, have been concerned with continuing to provide a complete and well-written introduction to the field of financial management. In addition, we have created a text package that fully reflects contemporary financial management developments in the book's organizational design, pedagogical aids to learning, and ancillary materials.

Organizational Design

Contemporary Financial Management (CFM) is organized around the objective of maximizing the value of the firm for its shareholders. This objective is introduced early in the book, and each major financial decision is linked to the impact it has on the value of the firm. The distinctive features designed to complement this objective are:

■ **Emphasis on cash flow, net present value, and risk/return relationships.**
Three primary concepts are central to virtually all financial management

decisions: (1) the importance of cash flows as the relevant source of value to a firm, (2) the significance of the net present value rule for valuing cash flows, and (3) the relationship between risk and returns in the valuation of cash flows. These three concepts are introduced in Chapter 2 and are used extensively in the balance of the text.

■ **Unique treatment of international financial management.** In a world that is increasingly affected by international trade, finance students must be aware of the important dimensions of international finance. Some texts provide a single chapter dealing with a potpourri of international issues, causing most instructors to have a difficult time covering this material. Other texts use a series of short international topic sections scattered throughout the book. This approach is not suited to providing the in-depth coverage needed for some international finance topics, such as hedging exchange rate risk. In the fourth edition of *CFM* we have included *both* a series of "International Concerns" sections that appear in appropriate places throughout the book and a separate chapter on international finance. Chapter 21, "International Financial Management," provides in-depth coverage of foreign currencies, exchange rates, and the financing of foreign trade and investments. Covering international finance in this dual manner assures that all students will be exposed to international dimensions of financial management decisions as required by the AACSB, and provides an opportunity for in-depth coverage of the more important international finance topics.

■ **Early coverage of institutional characteristics and valuation models for financial instruments.** Chapters 6 and 7 deal with the valuation of fixed income securities and common stock, and define all of the important characteristics of each of these security types. This structure provides students with both an institutional understanding of bonds, preferred stock, and common stock, and an understanding of the valuation process for securities in the financial marketplace. In addition, students are introduced early on to the reading and understanding of financial market quotations from sources such as the *Wall Street Journal* (Appendix 1A).

■ **Integration of the capital structure decision.** The tools and theory of capital structure decision making have been fully integrated into Chapter 13 and Appendix 13A; in particular, the role played by business risk, financial risk, and the degrees of operating and financial leverage in establishing an optimal capital structure.

■ **Attention to the financial management problems of small businesses.** In recognition of the growing role of small and medium-sized firms in the American business environment, a number of "Small Business Concerns" sections appear in appropriate places throughout the book to highlight the finance-related problems and concerns unique to small businesses.

■ **Extensive development of the cash flow estimation process in capital budgeting.** Perhaps the most important step in the capital budgeting process, the estimation of cash flows for potential projects is the single topic of Chapter 9. A detailed discussion of the impact of recent tax law changes affecting the capital budgeting decision appears in Appendix 9A.

■ **Detailed treatment of working capital management.** For many small and medium-sized companies, the management of working capital can present more challenges than any other area of financial management. A thorough and up-to-date four chapter section on working capital management is included.

■ **Emphasis on the impact of inflation.** During the 1970s and 1980s finance practitioners were forced to learn how to operate in an inflationary environment. Since these skills undoubtedly will remain important in the 1990s, this text contains frequent discussions on the impact of inflation.

■ **Introduction to new financial instruments and strategies.** Options, interest rate swaps, corporate restructurings, and leveraged buyouts (LBOs), to name but a few, have become increasingly important to contemporary financial managers. These topics are introduced to the student in an applied context that illustrates their value to financial managers.

Pedagogical Aids

CFM has been carefully designed to assist the student in learning and to stimulate student interest. Distinctive pedagogical features include:

■ **Financial Dilemmas.** Each chapter begins with an illustration of a financial management problem faced by a firm or individual. These exciting lead-ins come from actual situations involving RJR Nabisco, Eastern Airlines, J. David & Company, Public Service Company of New Mexico, Texas Air, Dixie Yarns, E. F. Hutton, and other firms. These examples focus on financial problems in the topic area of the chapter and highlight the importance of learning sound financial management principles. The Financial Dilemmas have been extensively revised and updated from the third edition, with many new examples added.

■ **Use of financial policies and problems involving real firms.** Throughout the book we have illustrated financial management concepts using problems facing real firms, and minimized the number of hypothetical situations. By using real data and situations facing actual firms that the students will recognize and can relate to, we have offered a new element of realism and excitement to *CFM*.

■ Many of the Integrative Cases have been changed or revised to make them flexible enough to demonstrate the power of financial spreadsheets, such as the Lotus 1-2-3 templates provided with the book, to perform extensive sensitivity analysis.

■ Many existing problems have been modified and new problems have been added. All problems are now in a "stand-alone" format.

■ **Key Notation Summary.** A handy summary of the key notation used throughout the book is provided inside the front cover.

Ancillary Materials

A complete set of ancillary materials is available to adopters to supplement the text, including the following:

■ A totally new *Test Bank*, co-authored by the text authors and Professor John Dunkelberg of Wake Forest University, offers approximately 1,500 multiple choice questions and problems. This unique test bank is designed with the instructor in mind. Approximately 60 percent of the questions are "fact" questions, taken directly from the discussion in the text. Approximately 30 percent of the questions are "elementary problem" questions that closely parallel problem examples developed in the chapter and easier problems at the end of the chapter. Approximately 10 percent of the questions are "challenging problems" that require the student to apply concepts developed in the chapter to new problem situations.

Following each "fact" question the instructor is provided with: (1) the correct answer, (2) an identification of the question topic and a reference to the major heading and subheading in the text where the correct answer is found, and (3) a place to record the date the problem was used and the percentage of students who answered the question correctly.

Following each problem the instructor is provided with: (1) the correct answer, (2) a detailed solution to the problem, and (3) a place to record the date the problem was used and the percentage of students who answered the question correctly.

■ WESTEST, a computerized version of the test bank, is available in order to simplify the preparation of quizzes and exams.

■ An *Instructor's/Solutions Manual* contains solutions to the end-of-chapter questions and problems. Lotus template solutions to appropriate problems are also included in the manual.

■ A set of 133 *Transparency Acetates* allows display of the most important tables and graphs.

■ A set of *Demonstration Problems* is provided in transparency master format. The problems parallel the major examples developed in the text.

■ *The CFM Lotus Disk*, developed by Professor Phillip Sisneros of Lehigh University and Jesse Reyes, are designed to solve a wide variety of financial management problems. Problems in the text that can be solved using these Lotus-based templates are indicated with a small diskette logo next to the problem. These templates are based on the most popular spreadsheet program used in business and academic institutions—Lotus 1-2-3. The templates require *absolutely no prior knowledge of Lotus 1-2-3*. All input and instructions are menu driven in a clear, concise command menu created by the authors. All of the templates are designed so they can be used to solve actual business financial analysis problems, not just simplified textbook examples. For example, the capital budgeting template uses the powerful macro features of Lotus 1-2-3 to "build" the correct-size worksheet to solve any capital budgeting problem. A brief overview of the *CFM Lotus Disk* is contained in Appendix A at the end of the text.

CFM can be ordered with or without the disk shrinkwrapped with the book. When ordered with the book each disk comes with detailed documentation. The *CFM Lotus Disk* is designed to run on a two floppy drive IBM (or compatible) PC. For users with a hard disk and single floppy drive system, a hard disk version can be provided to professors. This version can then be copied for students who need it.

■ A *Study Guide* written by Professor John D. Stowe of the University of Missouri—Columbia is available for students. The *Study Guide* contains detailed chapter outlines, solved true-false questions, and a large number of solved numerical problems. Illustrative Lotus problem solutions also are included.

Major Changes in the Fourth Edition

The fourth edition of *CFM* has been extensively updated and revised to reflect contemporary developments in finance and the many fine suggestions from third edition users and reviewers. These changes are listed below by chapter.

Chapter 1—The Finance Function: An Overview

- Covers more explicitly social responsibility concerns of corporate managers.
- Expanded agency problem discussion includes agency problems between stockholders and creditors.
- A new section dealing with managerial strategies for maximizing shareholder wealth discusses the value and limitations of the marginal decision rules from economics and the primary determinants of firm value: the magnitude of cash flows, the timing of cash flows, and the risk of cash flows.
- Areas of managerial action to influence firm value are identified.
- Information is provided for students regarding professional finance association opportunities.
- Appendix 1A is new and introduces students to the reading of stock and bond quotations in the *Wall Street Journal*.

Chapter 2—Foundation Concepts for Financial Management

- New chapter.
- Introduces three important foundation concepts for financial managers: cash flow, net present value, and risk-return.
- Looks at the role of financial markets in determining required rates of return on various return streams of corporations and securities.
- Appendix 2A updated to reflect recent changes in federal tax laws.

Chapter 3—Evaluation of Financial Performance

- Includes the use of common size financial statements.
- Provides increased emphasis on balance sheet and earnings statement quality.
- Covers special problems of financial analysis of multinational firms.

Chapter 4—Cash Flow Forecasting

- Important elements of cash flow analysis are developed.
- New "Statement of Cash Flows" is presented and discussed.
- Cash flow forecasting, cash budgeting and cash breakeven analysis techniques are presented.
- Appendix 4A contains a detailed discussion of breakeven analysis.

Chapter 5—Financial Mathematics

- Improved discussion of the present value of uneven cash flows, the present value of deferred annuities, and effective versus nominal rates of interest.
- The interest factor notation has been simplified.

Chapter 6—Characteristics and Valuation of Fixed Income Securities

- Combines discussion of debt and preferred stock valuation with discussion of the characteristics of these securities.

■ Offers students a unified source of information on these securities.
■ Provides contemporary data on bond ratings and debt structure.

Chapter 7—Characteristics and Valuation of Common Stock

■ Combines discussion of common stock valuation with discussion of the characteristics of equity securities.
■ Offers students a unified source of information on these securities.
■ Discusses special valuation problems for small firms.

Chapter 8—Analysis of Risk and Return

■ Expands discussion of portfolio risk and return analysis.
■ The concepts of efficient portfolios and the Capital Market Line are included.
■ Expands discussion of the relationship between inflation, risk aversion, and required returns.
■ Offers brief, intuitive introduction to the Arbitrage Pricing Theory of valuation.
■ Includes new section dealing the techniques of managing risk and uncertainty.

Chapter 9—Capital Budgeting and Cash Flow Analysis

■ New section dealing with the practice of cash flow estimation for capital budgeting has been added.
■ Examples in the chapter use straight-line depreciation in order to simplify the analysis.
■ Contains discussion of Modified Accelerated Cost Recovery System (MACRS) depreciation.
■ Problems are provided using both straight-line and MACRS depreciation.

Chapter 10—Capital Budgeting Decision Criteria

■ Reorganized to place primary emphasis on the net present value model.

Chapter 11—Capital Budgeting and Risk

■ Restructured to place emphasis on "beta" risk in the use of the risk-adjusted discount rate approach.
■ The Hamada leverage adjustment for beta is developed and illustrated.

Chapter 12—The Cost of Capital

■ Includes new material on callable preferred stock and the cost of capital for small firms.
■ Discussion of the determination of break points in the marginal cost of capital schedule has been simplified.

Chapter 13—The Capital Structure Decision

- Ties the capital structure decision to shareholder wealth maximization.
- Extensive discussion of business and financial risk.
- Shortened theoretical discussion of capital structure models.
- Expanded coverage of the role of agency costs, personal taxes, industry effects, signaling effects, and the pecking order theory in the determination of capital structure.
- Cash insolvency analysis added to the section dealing with the practice of capital structure determination.
- International capital structure concerns addressed.
- Appendix 13A covers operating and financial leverage analysis.

Chapter 14—Dividend Policy

- Updated to reflect recent tax law changes and effects, the signaling effects of dividend policy, small firm and multinational firm dividend policy issues, and dividend capture strategies.
- Expanded discussion of share repurchase decisions and effects.

Chapter 15—Managing Intermediate-Term Funding Sources

- Updated to reflect the impact of the Tax Reform Act on leasing.
- Several new examples have been added.

Chapter 16—Managing Long-Term Funding Sources

- New material discussing common stock valuation in an options framework, the role of convertible securities as a funding source, and the increasing importance of financial innovations.

Chapter 17—Working Capital Policy

- Features an expanded discussion and illustration of the operating cycle concept.
- Working capital policies for actual firms have been added.

Chapter 18—Management of Cash and Marketable Securities

- New discussion of speculative motives for holding cash.
- Examples illustrate the practice of liquidity management in various firms.
- Expanded treatment of float management.
- New section on electronic funds transfers.
- Discussion of small business and multinational firm cash management problems.
- New section dealing with ethics and cash management.

Chapter 19—Management of Accounts Receivable and Inventories

- Integrates these two topics and offers an expanded treatment of "just-in-time" inventory management systems.

Chapter 20—Obtaining Short-Term Funds

■ New discussion of the calculation of the cost of short-term funds, distinguishing between the annual financing cost concept and the annual percentage rate concept.

Chapter 21—International Financial Management

■ Updated to include a discussion of currency futures as well as forward currency contracts.

Chapter 22—Corporate Restructuring

■ Updated to reflect recent trends in mergers, LBOs, restructurings, and bankruptcy filings.
■ Many new examples added.

Organization and Intended Use

CFM is organized into eight major parts. Part I defines the finance function, examines the goals of the firm, and considers the role of the financial manager. The basic concepts of cash flows, net present value, and risk/return analysis are introduced. Finally, the institutional environment facing financial managers is discussed. Part II consists of two chapters covering the tools of financial analysis and cash flow forecasting. Part III develops the theory of valuation, risk-return analysis, and the tools of financial mathematics. Part IV presents the capital investment decision, emphasizing both the theoretical and the practical aspects of capital budgeting. Part V deals with the determinants of an optimal capital structure, the cost of capital, and the firm's dividend policy.

Part VI describes the sources of intermediate- and long-term funds. Part VII consists of a four-chapter sequence covering the important area of working capital management. Finally, Part VIII includes chapters dealing with international financial management and corporate restructuring.

Those instructors who wish to cover topics in an order other than that provided in the text will find it quite easy to make adjustments. For example, many instructors prefer to cover working capital management early in the course. They should find no difficulty in moving all or a portion of chapters 17 through 20 to a position following Chapter 4 or 5. Similarly, some instructors may prefer to cover the area of financial analysis later in the course. Accordingly, chapters 3 and 4 can be moved easily to another location that is more consistent with the instructor's teaching style and objectives.

This book is designed for use in a typical 3-semester hour (or the equivalent in the quarter system) course in financial management. Typically, within the constraints of this time limit, it is often not possible to fully cover all topics. Instructors will find it easy to defer more advanced or specialized topics, such as corporate restructuring, warrants, convertibles, bond refunding, and leasing, until a later course.

Acknowledgments

The authors wish to acknowledge the helpful comments provided by many of our first, second and third edition users. We are particularly grateful for the careful reviews and suggestions made by the following professors:

Richard Bauer	George Hettenhouse	Ralph Pope
Carl Beidleman	L. Dean Hiebert	Dwight Porter
Thomas Berry	K. P. Hill	Robert Porter
Don Bowlin	Shalom Hochman	Kelly Price
Robert Chatfield	Thomas Howe	Dennis Proffitt
David Cox	Pearson Hunt	Ramesh Rao
John Crockett	Keith B. Johnson	William J. Regan
Rudolph D'Souza	Charles P. Jones	Jesse Reyes
Bill Dukes	Kee Kim	Charles T. Rini
Fred Ebeid	Thomas Klaasen	Richard Sapp
John W. Ellis	Timothy Koch	Bernard A. Shinkel
Keith W. Fairchild	Keith Laycock	Mark Shrader
Edward Farragher	Joseph J. Levitzky	Phil Sisneros
Mike Ferri	David Lindsley	Rolf K. Tedefalk
Jane Finley	Charles Linke	Richard J. Teweles
Richard Gendreau	Mike Lockett	Niranjan Tripathy
Jim Gentry	Wayne M. Marr	Anthony M. Tuberose
Michael Gombola	Z. Lew Melynk	George Ulseth
Jim Greenleaf	Richard Meyer	David Upton
Kamal Haddad	Edward M. Miller	Howard E. Van Anken
Thomas Hamilton	Robert A. Olsen	John M. Wachowicz, Jr.
Charles Harper	Coleen G. Pantalone	Charlie Wade
Delbert Hastings	Susan M. Phillips	J. Daniel Williams
Pat Hays	Mario Picconi	Richard Zock
Shantaram P. Hedge	Alwyn du Plessis	J. Kenton Zumwalt
Robert Hehre		

and the following business professionals:

Gordon B. Bonfield	Ira G. Kawaller	Robert B. Morris III
Richard H. Brock	Carl J. Lange	T. Boone Pickens
Roy V. Campbell	Martin H. Lange	Jack S. Rader
Norman Dmuchowski	Lewis Lehr	M. W. Ramsey
Stephen H. Grace	C. Londa	William J. Regan
Samuel C. Hadaway	Paul MacAvoy	Albert J. Robison
R. Lee Haney	Frank Mastrapasqua	Julie Salamon
Raymond A. Hay	John H. Maxheim	Kenneth Schwartz
Lawrence Ingrassia	Thomas R. Mongan	Terry J. Winders

For this revision we are particularly greatful for the careful reviews and numerous excellent suggestions made by the following professors:

Scott Besley	Don Fehrs	Walter W. Perlick
Gordon R. Bonner	Harry R. Kuniansky	Jack H. Rubens
William Brunsen	Thomas J. Liesz	Herbert Weinraub
Lynn E. Dellenbarger, Jr.	Inayat U. Mangla	

We are also indebted to Lehigh University, Texas Tech University, University of Houston, University of New Mexico, Wake Forest University, and

Wayne State University for the considerable support they provided. We thank Margaret Williams for her typing assistance. We greatly appreciate the diligent assistance provided by Roberts Bass, Andy Cooney, and Allison Varon. We also owe thanks to our fellow faculty members at these universities for the encouragement and assistance they provided on a continuing basis during the preparation of the manuscript.

Finally, we wish to express our thanks to the members of the West Publishing Company staff. We are particularly appreciative of the total project support provided by Ken Zeigler. Tad Bornhoft, our production editor, did a superb job of supervising the production of a most attractive and technically precise text. Tad was a pleasure to work with. Most of all we would like to thank our editor, Mary Schiller, who has provided a continual flow of excellent ideas for this project. Her high performance standards and in-depth knowledge of publishing have been invaluable in the development of this text.

I

Introduction

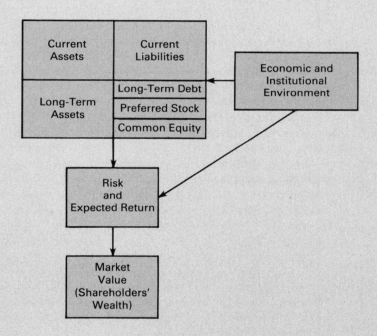

Part I of the text provides an overview introduction to the field of financial management. Chapter 1 discusses the relationship between finance and other business disciplines, the forms of business organization, the organization of the financial management function in a firm, and the history of the financial management field. This chapter also introduces the overall objective of the firm—maximizing shareholder wealth. Appendix 1A develops an understanding of stock and bond market price quotations. Chapter 2 looks at the relationship between the firm and the economic–institutional environment. Economic and institutional factors have a major impact on the expected returns and the risk of these returns generated by the firm. Risk and return are two of the key determinants of the value of a firm and its securities. The important concepts of net present value and cash flows are introduced in this chapter. Appendix 2A highlights elements of federal income tax laws that are relevant to financial management decisions.

1

The Finance Function: An Overview

KEY CHAPTER CONCEPTS

1. *Shareholder wealth* is defined as the present value of the expected future returns to the owners of the firm. It is measured by the market value of the shareholders' common stock holdings.

2. The primary normative goal of the firm is to maximize shareholder wealth.

3. Achievement of the shareholder wealth maximization goal often is constrained by social responsibility concerns and problems arising out of agency relationships.

4. The market value of a firm's stock is determined by the magnitude, risk, and timing of the cash flows the firm is expected to generate. There are many actions that managers can take to influence the magnitude, timing, and risk of the firm's cash flows.

5. The corporate form of business organization has significant advantages over sole proprietorships and partnerships, including
   a. Limited liability
   b. Permanency
   c. Flexibility

6. The finance function usually is headed by a (senior) vice-president or chief financial officer.
   a. Financial management responsibilities often are divided between the controller and treasurer.
   b. The controller normally has responsibility for all activities related to accounting.
   c. The treasurer normally is concerned with the acquisition, custody, and expenditure of funds.

GLOSSARY OF NEW TERMS

Agency relationships occur when one or more individuals (principals) hire another individual (agent) to perform a service on behalf of them. Agency relationships often lead to agency problems and agency costs. Two of the most important agency relationships in finance are the relationship between stockholders (owners) and managers and the relationship between owners and creditors.

Agent In an agency relationship, the party who acts on behalf of the principal.

Book value The accounting value of an asset or firm. The book value per share of common stock is equal to a firm's net worth divided by the total number of shares of outstanding common stock.

Common stock Shares in the ownership of a company. Common stock represents a residual form of ownership in that dividends are paid out only after more senior financial obligations are fulfilled, such as interest on debt.

Corporation A business organization that is created as a "legal person" separate and distinct from the individual or individuals who own the firm's stock. The primary characteristics of and advantages of incorporating include limited liability for the firm's owners, permanency, and flexibility with respect to making changes in ownership.

Discount rate The rate of interest used in the process of finding present values.

Market value The price at which a stock trades in the financial marketplace.

Partnership A business organization in which two or more persons form a business with the intention of making a profit. In a *general partnership* each partner has unlimited liability for the debts of the firm. *Limited partnerships* allow one or more partners to have limited liability.

Preferred stock A form of equity that has a senior claim on earnings—in the form of a (normally) fixed periodic dividend payment—and assets of a firm. This is in contrast to the claims of common stockholders.

Present value The current value of some future payment or stream of payments, evaluated at an appropriate discount rate.

Principal In an agency relationship, the party who employs someone else, the agent, to perform service on behalf of the principal.

Shareholder wealth Present value of the expected future returns to the owners (that is, shareholders) of the firm. It is measured by the market value of the shareholders' common stock holdings.

Sole proprietorship A business owned by one person. The owner of a sole proprietorship has unlimited liability for debts incurred by the business.

Stakeholders The constituent groups in a firm, including stockholders, bondholders, suppliers, customers, employees, community neighbors, and creditors.

Problems in Financial Management

- In 1989, Kohlberg Kravis Roberts & Co. (KKR) acquired RJR Nabisco, Inc., for $109 per share, nearly twice the price that RJR's stock was selling for prior to the takeover.
- In late 1988, several firms, including American Express and Sara Lee announced a plan, engineered by Shearson Lehman Hutton, Inc., that would involve an exchange of up to 20 percent of the common stock for a package of bonds, preferred stock, and equity appreciation units. The new instruments were to be known as *unbundled stock units*. The bonds would pay interest for thirty years at a rate equal to the current common stock dividend rate and would be redeemed at a higher price than the current stock price. The preferred stock would pay a dividend equal to any increases in the common stock dividend over the thirty years, and holders of the equity appreciation certificates would receive all appreciation in the common stock price above the redemption price of the bonds. In early 1989, the unbundled stock unit plan was abandoned.
- In 1984, Federal Express introduced its ZapMail service, which guaranteed delivery of a document to its destination in two hours. After twenty-six months and an operating loss of $317 million, Federal Express discontinued its ZapMail service. Since 1985, Federal Express' international business has lost approximately $75 million. In January 1989, Federal Express received approval for its proposed $880 million acquisition of Tiger International, Inc., the world's largest heavy cargo airline, in order to gain access to its delivery routes and to expand Federal's overseas operations.
- In 1987, the investment banking firm of Graystone Nash, Inc., underwrote an offering of securities for a new firm, WINE, Inc. The securities were brought to the market at $10 per unit and sold for $67 per unit four business days later.
- In 1985, Middle South Utilities, faced with severe cash flow problems, eliminated its dividend, and its stock price plummeted from over $15 per share to nearly $8 per share. In 1988, Middle South's prospects improved and dividend payments were resumed. The stock price rose from a low of $8.50 per share prior to the dividend resumption to a high of over $16 after the dividend payment announcement.
- In 1986, Global Marine, one of the world's largest operators of offshore drilling rigs, filed for bankruptcy under Chapter 11 of the Bankruptcy Act. Earnings per share had declined from a peak level of $2.61 in 1981 to a *negative* $8.67 per share in 1986, and the company's stock price declined from its peak of $36.50 to less than $0.50 per share. In late 1988, Global Marine announced that it had reached agreements with its creditors and that it shortly would be restructured and emerge from bankruptcy proceedings.
- In 1985, E. F. Hutton, one of the nation's largest brokerage firms (now part of Shearson Lehman Hutton) pleaded guilty to 2,000 counts of mail and wire fraud, arising from its elaborate check overdraft scheme, designed to obtain large sums of money from many of its 400 banks without paying interest.

Each of these situations was the direct result of financial decision making. Financial management decisions made within enterprises—small or large, international or local, profit seeking or not for profit—help to determine the kinds of products and services we consume and their prices, availability, and quality. In short, financial decision making has impacts that are felt daily throughout the entire economy.

The situations just described pose many important questions for financial managers. The financial concepts and tools needed to deal with problems such as these and to make you a more effective decision maker are the subject matter of this book. In Chapter 1, we define the goals of the firm that guide financial managers, the organization of the financial management function in a firm, and the relationship between financial management and other subjects in your study of business.

INTRODUCTION

The field of financial management is an exciting and challenging one. Students who choose to major in finance will find a wide range of rewarding job opportunities open in the fields of corporate financial management, investment banking, investment analysis and management, commercial banking, real estate, insurance, and the public sector—to name only a few broad areas of potential career opportunities. Students who choose not to major in finance still will be confronted with important financial decisions—both in their careers and in their personal lives—on a nearly daily basis.

The importance and relevance of the skills that can be learned in this finance course are apparent from the results of a recent survey of graduates of business schools. *By a wide margin, these executives indicated that the courses taken in financial management were the most useful courses in their business school curriculum.*[1]

As is evident regularly in the major business periodicals, such as the *Wall Street Journal*, *Business Week*, *Fortune*, *Forbes*, and *Dunn's*, financial managers are involved in important and challenging tasks. Consider, for example, the challenge of arranging $25 billion of financing for KKR's takeover of RJR Nabisco. Extensive, careful financial analysis had to be done when KKR was deciding on a price to bid for RJR Nabisco and the form (cash plus various securities) that bid would take. Imagine the daily challenges facing the financial managers of Pan American as they seek the funds needed to avert failure. Put yourself in the position of the managers of Texaco, as you struggle to avoid a takeover by Carl Icahn. Think of being the portfolio manager who bought units (stock plus other securities) in a new firm, WINE, Inc., for $10 per unit on Thursday, September 3, 1987, and saw them increase to $67 per unit by the following Tuesday.

Any business—whether large or small, profit seeking or not for profit—has important financial concerns, and as such its success or failure depends in a large part on the quality of its financial decisions. Nearly every key decision made by a firm's managers has important financial implications. Managers daily face questions like the following:

- Will a particular investment be profitable?
- Where will the funds come from to finance the investment?
- Does the firm have adequate cash or access to cash—through bank borrowing agreements, for example—to meet its daily operating needs?
- Which customers should be offered credit, and how much should they be offered?
- How much inventory should be held?
- Is a merger or acquisition advisable?
- How should profits be used or distributed? That is, what is the optimal dividend policy?
- In trying to arrive at the best financial management decisions, how should risk and return be balanced?

This text presents an introduction to the theory, institutional background, and analytical tools essential for proper decision making in these and related areas. As a prospective manager, you will be introduced to the financial management process of typical firms. By learning how the financial man-

[1] John A. Pollock, J. R. Bartol, B. C. Sherony, and G. R. Carnaham, "Executives' Perceptions of Future MBA Programs." *Collegiate News and Views* (Spring 1983): 23–25.

agement process functions, you establish one of the key building blocks for a successful management career.

The remaining sections of this chapter discuss the history of the practice and study of financial management, the goals of the firm, organization of the firm and the financial management-related function, relationship between financial management and other academic disciplines, and organization of the text. Appendix 1A explains the stock and bond quotations that appear in sources such as the *Wall Street Journal.*

A BRIEF HISTORY OF THE FINANCIAL MANAGEMENT FIELD

Prior to the 1930s the field of financial management basically was confined to descriptive discussions of the various financial markets and the securities traded in those markets.[2] Thus, finance as a field of study traditionally focused on the liabilities and stockholders' equity side of the balance sheet and on fund raising.

The field underwent a number of significant changes during the Great Depression, when it became more involved with legal matters of bankruptcy, reorganization, and government regulation. Finance texts written during the 1930s and 1940s often devoted many chapters to bankruptcy-related matters, such as reorganization and liquidation.

Through the 1940s and into the 1950s the teaching of financial management continued to be basically qualitative and descriptive. During the 1950s, however, a number of significant changes took place in the field. First, financial management was expanded to include the asset side of the balance sheet, or the uses of a firm's funds. In addition, the application of discounted cash flow techniques to the problems of capital expenditure analysis was being refined and perfected. Also, financial researchers were making significant breakthroughs in developing techniques for measuring the cost of capital and valuing financial assets. Progress in the areas of both capital budgeting and cost of capital has continued to the present day.

During the 1960s mathematical models using statistical and optimization techniques were applied to the allocation of current assets, such as cash, accounts receivable and inventories, and fixed assets. Throughout the 1960s and 1970s the trend continued toward a more quantitative and precise concept of financial management. Another important emphasis of the last two decades has been the integration of specific finance topics with a risk-adjusted model in an attempt to maximize the value of the firm and shareholder wealth.

During the decade of the 1980s there has been an increasing emphasis on applying computer (and computer-related) technology to assist in financial decision making. In addition, financial managers have become more aggressive in managing the assets of the firm in response to an environment characterized by higher and more volatile interest rates.

In the late 1980s and projected into the 1990s there has been a renewed focus on the goal of shareholder wealth maximization and the creation of organizational structures that will enhance the achievement of this goal. This renewed focus on value creation and managerial efficiency is evident in the debate over corporate takeovers and leveraged buyouts. Also, the

---

[2] The terms *financial management, managerial finance, corporate finance,* and *business finance* are virtually equivalent and are used interchangeably. Most financial managers, however, seem to prefer either *financial management* or *managerial finance.*

decade of the 1980s has witnessed an explosion of new financial instruments, such as options and futures contracts, that can be used to manage risk.

Over the past 50 years financial management has developed into a more rigorous discipline, and today's employers expect business and finance graduates to possess a solid working knowledge of modern finance techniques. Table 1-1 summarizes the most significant developments in the evolution of financial management.

THE PRIMARY GOAL: MAXIMIZING SHAREHOLDER WEALTH

Effective financial decision making requires an understanding of the goal(s) of the firm. What objective(s) *should* guide business decision making? That is, what *should* management try to achieve for the owners of the firm? The most widely accepted objective of the firm is to maximize the value of the firm for its owners; that is, to *maximize shareholder wealth*. Shareholder wealth is represented by the market price of a firm's common stock.

The shareholder wealth maximization goal states that management *should* seek to maximize the *present value* of the *expected future returns* to the owners (that is, shareholders) of the firm. These returns can take the form of periodic dividend payments or proceeds from the sale of the stock. Present value is defined as the value today of some future payment or stream of payments, evaluated at an appropriate discount rate. It takes into account the returns that are available from alternative investment opportunities during a specific (future) time period. As we shall see in Chapter 5, the longer a benefit, such as dividend payments or price appreciation, is deferred into the future, the lower will be the current value placed by investors on that benefit. In addition, the greater the risk associated with receiving a future benefit, the lower will be the value placed by investors on that benefit. Stock prices,

Evolution of Financial Management		TABLE 1-1
Period	**Focus**	
Pre-1930	Descriptive emphasis on financial markets and securities. Little attention to asset management.	
1930s and 1940s	Focus on legal matters dealing with bankruptcy and reorganization and the effects of newly emerging government regulation.	
1950s	Increasing emphasis on asset management. Significant theoretical developments in valuation theory.	
1960s	Application of mathematical models to allocation of current and fixed assets. Additional theoretical developments in valuation theory, cost of capital, dividend policy, and risk analysis.	
1970s	Development of more precise theories and measures of risk. Application of these theories to investment analysis and valuation.	
1980s	Increasing application of computer technology to assist in financial decision making.	
Late 1980s and 1990s	Reemphasis on value maximization concepts, and the role of competitive, efficient, and complete capital markets.	

the measure of shareholder wealth, reflect the magnitude, timing, and risk associated with future benefits expected to be received by stockholders.

Shareholder wealth is measured by the market value of the shareholders' common stock holdings. *Market value* is defined as the price at which the stock trades in the marketplace, such as on the New York Stock Exchange. Thus, total shareholder wealth equals the number of shares outstanding times the market price per share.

The objective of shareholder wealth maximization has a number of distinct advantages. First, as we have seen earlier, this objective explicitly considers the timing and the risk of the benefits expected to be received from stock ownership. Similarly, managers can consider the elements of timing and risk as they make important financial decisions, such as capital expenditures. In this way managers can make decisions that will contribute to increasing shareholder wealth.

Second, it is conceptually possible to determine whether a particular financial decision is consistent with this objective. If a decision made by a firm has the effect of increasing the market price of the firm's stock, it is a good decision. If it appears that an action will not achieve this result, the action should not be taken (at least not voluntarily).

Third, shareholder wealth maximization is an *impersonal* objective. Stockholders who object to a firm's policies are free to sell their shares *under more favorable terms* (that is, at a higher price) *than are available under any other strategy* and invest their funds elsewhere. If an investor who has a consumption pattern or risk preference that is not accommodated by the investment, financing, and dividend decisions of that firm, the investor will be able to sell his or her shares in that firm at the best price and purchase shares in a company that more nearly meets the investor's needs.

For these reasons, the shareholder wealth maximization objective is the primary goal in financial management. Concerns for the social responsibilities of business, the existence of divergent objectives pursued by some managers, and problems that arise from agency relationships may cause some departures from pure wealth maximizing behavior by owners and managers. (These problems are discussed later.) Nevertheless, the shareholder wealth maximization goal provides the standard against which actual decisions can be judged and, as such, is the objective assumed in financial management analysis.

Social Responsibility Concerns

Testifying in 1988 in support of an antitakeover bill sponsored by Senator Proxmire, David Roderick, chairman of USX Corporation, recognized the various constituent groups in a corporation when he complained about "massive abuses by a small group of raiders, arbitrageurs, promoters, and investment bankers, who reap enormous profits serving only their self-interest at the expense of stockholders, employees, creditors, communities, and the nation at large." In a similar vein, NCR Corporation recently ran a series of ads extolling the importance of the interests of other constituent groups in the firm—customers, employees, suppliers, and the worldwide community in which they operate—in addition to the interests of stockholders. NCR sees no conflict between being a good citizen and running a successful business.

The success of the firm often is linked to various constituent groups (stakeholders), including employees, suppliers, customers, and community neighbors. Some have argued that the failure of Eastern Airlines resulted from management's lack of attention to its constituent stakeholders, particularly employees. Likewise, the welfare of many of these groups is closely related to the continued growth and prosperity of the firm. As illustrated earlier in the NCR and USX cases, it often is argued that business should seek to balance the interests of all these constituencies, rather than be concerned with shareholder wealth maximization alone. In many cases these social responsibilities can take on almost as much importance as laws and other formal obligations.

A wide diversity of opinion exists as to what corporate social responsibility actually entails. The concept is somewhat subjective and is neither perceived uniformly nor applied uniformly by all firms. As yet no satisfactory mechanism has been suggested that specifies how these social responsibility commitments can be balanced with the interests of the owners of the firm.

Certainly there are instances where decisions made to maximize shareholder wealth also will be good for the firm's other stakeholders. However, there will be inevitable conflicts between shareholders and these other stakeholders. To the extent that conflicts exist, managers may be constrained in their pursuit of the wealth maximization objective.

Divergent Objectives

The goal of shareholder wealth maximization specifies how financial decisions *should* be made. It has been observed that, in practice, not all management decisions are consistent with this objective. In other words, there often is a divergence between the shareholder wealth maximization goal and the *actual* goals pursued by management. What is the reason for this divergence? The primary reason has been attributed to *separation of ownership and control* (management) in corporations.

Separation of ownership and control has permitted managers to pursue goals more consistent with their own self-interests, subject, of course, to the constraint that they satisfy shareholders sufficiently to maintain control of the corporation. Instead of seeking to maximize some objective (such as shareholder wealth), management is said to "satisfice" or seek acceptable levels of performance, while maximizing their own welfare.

Maximization of their own personal welfare (or utility) may lead managers to be concerned with long-run survival (job security). The concern for long-run survival may lead management to minimize (or limit) the amount of risk incurred by the firm, since unfavorable outcomes can lead to their dismissal or possible bankruptcy for the firm. Likewise, the desire for job security is cited as one reason why management often opposes takeover offers (mergers) by other companies. Giving senior management "golden parachute" contracts to compensate them if they lose their positions as the result of a merger is one approach designed to ensure that they will act in the interests of shareholders in merger decisions, rather than in their own interests.

Agency Problems

The existence of divergent objectives between owners and managers is one example of a class of problems arising from agency relationships. *Agency relationships* occur when one or more individuals (the principals) hire another individual (the agent) to perform a service on behalf of the principals.[3] In an agency relationship, decision-making authority is often delegated to the agent from the principals. In the context of finance, two of the most important agency relationships are the relationship between stockholders (owners) and managers and the relationship between stockholders and creditors.

STOCKHOLDERS AND MANAGERS. Inefficiencies that arise because of agency relationships have been called *agency problems*. These problems occur because each party to a transaction is assumed to act in a manner consistent with maximizing his or her own utility (welfare). The example cited earlier of the concern by management for long-run survival (job security), rather than shareholder wealth maximization, is an example of an agency problem. Another example is the consumption of on-the-job perquisites (such as the use of company airplanes, limousines, and luxurious offices) by managers who have no (or only a partial) ownership interest in the firm. Shirking by managers is also an agency-related problem.

These agency problems give rise to a number of *agency costs*, which are incurred by shareholders to minimize agency problems. Examples of agency costs include

1. Expenditures to structure the organization in such a way as to minimize the incentives for management to take actions contrary to shareholder interests, such as providing a portion of management's compensation in the form of stock of the corporation.
2. Expenditures to monitor management's actions, such as paying for audits of managerial performance and internal audits of the firm's expenditures.
3. Bonding expenditures to protect the owners from managerial dishonesty.
4. The opportunity cost of lost profits arising from complex organizational structures that prevent management from making timely responses to opportunities.

Managerial motivations to act in the interests of stockholders include the structure of their compensation package, the threat of dismissal, and the threat of takeover by a new group of owners. Financial theory has shown that agency problems and their associated costs can be reduced greatly if the financial markets operate efficiently. Some agency problems can be reduced by the use of complex financial contracts. Remaining agency problems give rise to costs that show up as a reduction in the value of the firm's shares in the marketplace.

STOCKHOLDERS AND CREDITORS. Another potential agency conflict arises from the relationship between a company's owners and its creditors. Creditors have a fixed financial claim on the company's resources in the form of long-term debt, bank loans, commercial paper, leases, accounts payable, wages payable, taxes payable, and so on. Because the returns offered to creditors are fixed whereas the returns to stockholders are variable, conflicts may arise between creditors and owners. For example, owners may attempt to increase the riskiness of the company's investments, in hopes of receiving greater returns. When this occurs, bondholders suffer because they do not have an opportunity to share in these higher returns. For example, when

---

[3] See Amir Barnea, R. Haugen, and L. Senbet, *Agency Problems and Financial Contracting.* Englewood Cliffs, N.J.: Prentice-Hall, 1985, for an overview of the agency problem issue.

RJR Nabisco (RJR) was acquired by KKR, the debt of RJR increased from 38 percent of total capital to nearly 90 percent of total capital. This unexpected increase in financial risk caused the value of RJR's bonds to decline by nearly 20 percent.

In order to protect their interests, creditors often insist on certain protective covenants in a company's bond indentures. These covenants take many forms, such as limitations on dividend payments, limitations on the type of investments (and divestitures) the company can undertake, and limitations on the issuance of new debt. The constraints on the owner-managers may reduce the potential market value of the firm. In addition to these constraints, bondholders also will demand a higher fixed return to compensate for risks not adequately covered by bond indenture restrictions.

MAXIMIZATION OF SHAREHOLDER WEALTH: MANAGERIAL STRATEGIES

If the managers of a firm accept the goal of maximizing shareholder wealth, how should they achieve this objective? One might be tempted to argue that managers will maximize shareholder wealth if they maximize the profits of the firm. After all, profit maximization is the predominant objective that emerges from basic microeconomic models of the firm. Unfortunately, the profit maximization objective has too many shortcomings to provide consistent guidance to the practicing manager.

Before discussing some of these shortcomings, it is useful to highlight one important managerial decision rule that emerges from the microeconomic profit maximization model. In order to maximize profits, we learned in microeconomics that a firm should expand output to the point where the marginal (additional) cost (MC) of the last unit produced and sold just equals the marginal revenue (MR) received. To move beyond that output level will result in greater additional costs than additional revenues, and hence lower profits. To fail to produce up to the point where MC = MR results in a lower level of total profits than are possible by following the rule. This fundamental rule, that an economic action should be continued up to the point where the marginal revenue (benefit) just equals the marginal cost, offers excellent guidance for financial managers dealing with a wide range of problems. For example, we shall see that the basic capital expenditure analysis model simply is an adaptation of the MC = MR rule. Other applications appear in the working capital management area and the capital structure area.

Despite the excellent insights it offers financial managers, the profit maximization model is not useful as the central decision-making model for the firm for several reasons. First, the standard microeconomic model of profit maximization is *static;* that is, it lacks a time dimension. Profit maximization as a goal offers no explicit basis for comparing long-term and short-term profits. Major decisions made by financial managers, however, *must* reflect the time dimension. For example, capital expenditure decisions, which are central to the finance function, have a long-term impact on the performance of the firm. Financial managers must make tradeoffs between short-run and long-run returns in conjunction with capital investment decisions.

The second limitation has to do with the definition of profit. Generally accepted accounting principles (as discussed in Chapter 3) result in literally hundreds of definitions of profit for a firm, because of the latitude permitted firms in recognizing and accounting for costs and revenues. Even if we could agree on the appropriate accounting definition of profits, it is not clear whether a firm should attempt to maximize total profit, the rate of profit, or earnings per share (EPS).

Consider a firm with 10 million shares outstanding that currently earns a profit of $10 million after tax. If the firm sells an additional 1 million shares of stock and invests the proceeds to earn $100,000 per year, the total profit of the firm will increase from $10 million to $10.1 million. However, are shareholders better off? Prior to the stock sale, earnings per share were $1 ($10 million profit divided by 10 million shares of stock). After the stock sale, earnings per share decline to $0.92 ($10.1 million in earnings divided by 11 million shares). Although total profit has increased, earnings per share have declined. Stockholders are not better off from this action.

This example might lead one to conclude that managers should seek to maximize earnings per share (for a given number of shares outstanding). This, too, can result in misleading actions. For example, consider a firm with total assets at the start of the year of $10 million. The firm is financed entirely with common equity (1 million shares outstanding). After-tax earnings are $1 million, or a return on common equity of 10 percent ($1 million in earnings divided by $10 million in common equity), and earnings per share are $1. The company decides to retain one-half of this year's earnings (increasing assets and common equity to $10.5 million) and pay out the balance in common stock dividends. Next year the company's earnings total $1.029 million, resulting in earnings per share of $1.029. Are shareholders better off because of the decision by managers to reinvest $500,000 into the firm? In this example, a strong argument can be made that the position of shareholders has deteriorated. Although earnings per share have increased from $1 per share to $1.029 per share, the realized return on common equity actually has declined, from 10 percent to 9.8 percent ($1.029 million divided by $10.5 million of common equity). In essence, the company's managers have reinvested $500,000 of shareholders' money to earn a return of only 5.8 percent ($0.029 million of additional earnings divided by $0.5 million of additional investment). This type of investment is not likely to result in maximum shareholder wealth. Shareholders could do better by investing in risk-free government bonds yielding more than 5.8 percent.

The third major problem associated with the profit maximization objective is that it provides no direct way for financial managers to consider the risk associated with alternative decisions. For example, two projects generating identical future expected cash flows and requiring identical outlays may be vastly different with respect to the risk of the expected cash flows. Similarly, it often is possible for a firm to increase its earnings per share (EPS) by increasing the proportion of debt financing used in the firm's capital structure. However, leverage-induced increases in EPS come at the cost of increased financial risk. The financial marketplace will recognize the increased risk of financial distress that accompanies increases in debt financing and will value the resulting EPS accordingly.

Determinants of Value

If the profit maximization objective does not provide the proper guidance to managers seeking to maximize shareholder wealth, what rules should these managers follow? First, it is important to recognize that the maximization of shareholder wealth is a market concept, not an accounting concept. Managers should attempt to maximize the *market value* of the company's shares, not the accounting or *book value* per share. The book value reflects the historic cost of assets, not the earning capacity of those assets. Also, the book value does not consider the risk associated with the assets.

What factors determine the market value of a company's shares of stock? There are three major factors: the amount of the cash flows expected to be generated for the benefit of stockholders; the timing of these cash flows; and the risk of the cash flows. Consider first the focus on cash flow. Cash flow relates to the actual cash generated or paid by the firm. Only cash can be used to acquire assets and only cash can be used to make valuable distributions to investors. In contrast, the accounting system focuses primarily on a matching over time of the historic cost-based revenues and expenses of a company, resulting in a bottom line earnings figure. But accounting earnings often are misleading because earnings do not reflect the actual cash inflows and outflows of the firm. For example, an accountant records depreciation expense on an asset each period over the depreciable life of that asset. Depreciation is designed to reflect the decline in value of that asset over time. However, depreciation itself results in no cash outflow. The entire cash outflow occurred when the asset originally was purchased.

The market value of a share of stock is influenced not only by the amount of the cash flows it is expected to produce, but also by the timing of those cash flows. If faced with the opportunity of receiving $100 today or $100 three years from today, you would surely choose the $100 today, because you could invest that $100 for three years and accumulate substantially more than $100 in three years. Thus, financial managers must consider both the magnitude of the cash flows they expect to generate and the timing of these cash flows because investors will reflect these dimensions of return in their valuation of the enterprise.

Finally, the market value of a share of stock is influenced by the perceived risk of the cash flows it is expected to generate. Most rational investors will demand a higher rate of return on an investment when greater risk is associated with the expected returns from that investment. Thus, financial managers also must consider the risk of the cash flows expected to be generated by the firm because investors will reflect this risk in their valuation of the enterprise.

Managerial Actions to Influence Value

How can managers influence the magnitude, timing, and risk of the cash flows expected to be generated by the firm in order to maximize shareholder wealth? Many factors ultimately influence the magnitude, timing, and risk of a firm's cash flows and thus the price of the firm's stock. Some of these factors are related to the external economic environment and largely are outside the direct control of managers. Other factors can be directly manipulated by the managers. Figure 1-1 illustrates the factors affecting stock prices. The top panel enumerates some of the factors in the economic environment that have an impact on the strategic decisions managers can make. The economic environment factors largely are outside the direct control of managers, but managers must be aware of how these factors affect the policy decisions under the control of management. The policy decision areas are enumerated in the next panel. Managers make choices regarding

FIGURE 1-1

**Factors Affecting
Stock Prices**

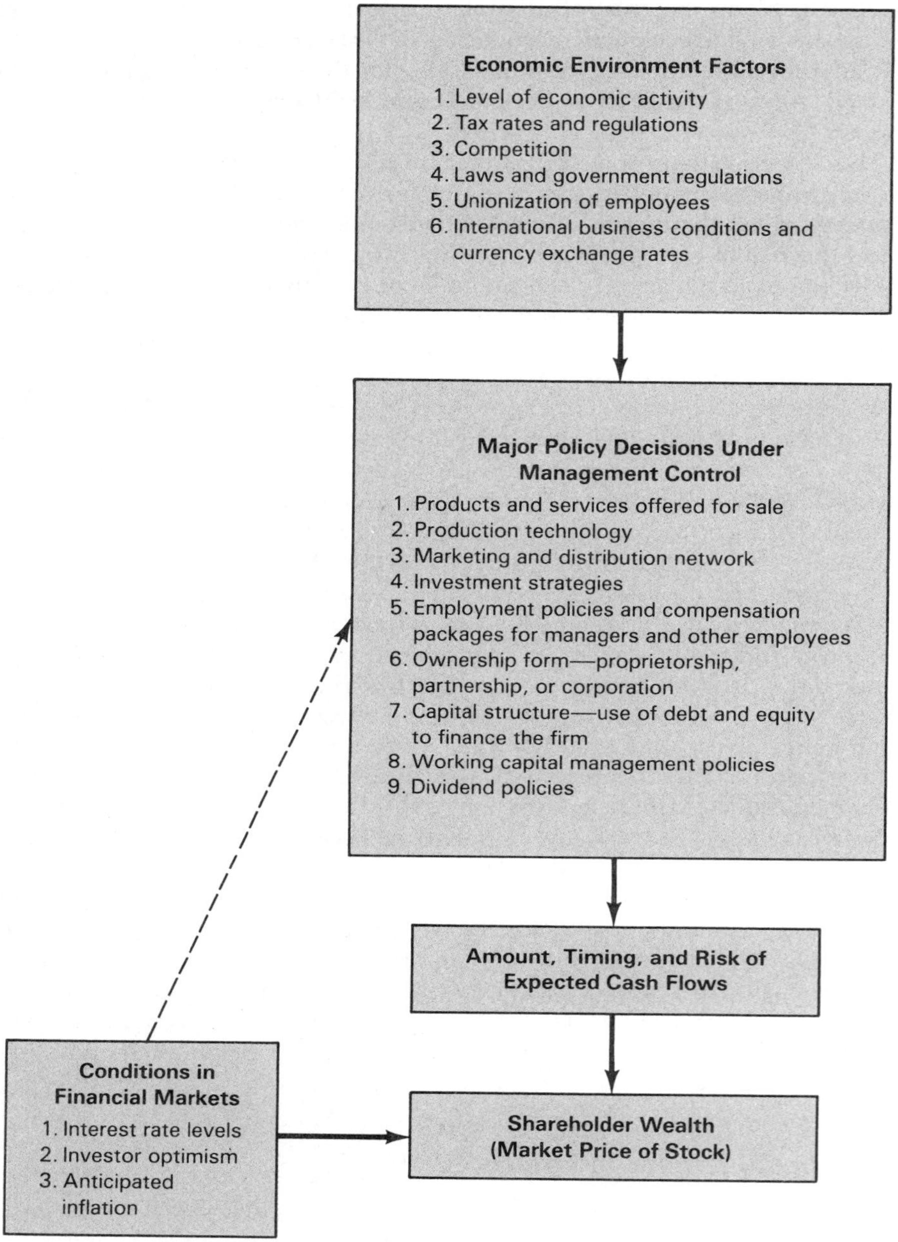

Economic Environment Factors

1. Level of economic activity
2. Tax rates and regulations
3. Competition
4. Laws and government regulations
5. Unionization of employees
6. International business conditions and
   currency exchange rates

**Major Policy Decisions Under
Management Control**

1. Products and services offered for sale
2. Production technology
3. Marketing and distribution network
4. Investment strategies
5. Employment policies and compensation
   packages for managers and other employees
6. Ownership form—proprietorship,
   partnership, or corporation
7. Capital structure—use of debt and equity
   to finance the firm
8. Working capital management policies
9. Dividend policies

**Amount, Timing, and Risk of
Expected Cash Flows**

**Conditions in
Financial Markets**

1. Interest rate levels
2. Investor optimism
3. Anticipated
   inflation

**Shareholder Wealth
(Market Price of Stock)**

the products to be produced, the technology used to produce them, the
marketing effort and distribution channels, and the selection of employees
and their compensation. In addition, managers establish investment policies, the ownership structure of the firm, the capital structure (use of debt)
of the firm, working capital management policies, and dividend policies.
The decisions made in these key policy decision areas determine the amount,
timing, and risk of the firm's expected cash flows. Participants in the financial markets evaluate the cash flows expected by the firm, in relation
to alternative streams of cash flows expected from other firms, and ultimately establish the price of the firm's stock. The value of a firm's stock is

influenced at any point in time by general conditions in the financial markets, including the level of interest rates, anticipated inflation rates, and the level of investor optimism regarding the future. Financial market conditions also affect the major policy decisions made by management.

Accordingly, the focus of this book is on making financial decisions that can improve the amount, the timing, or the risk profile of a firm's cash flow stream, thus leading to increases in shareholder wealth. In the next sections we examine alternative firm structures and the organization of the financial management function in a typical firm. The major areas of responsibility for financial managers also are detailed.

FORMS OF BUSINESS ORGANIZATION

Most businesses are organized into either a *sole proprietorship*, a *partnership*, or a *corporation*.

Sole Proprietorship

A sole proprietorship is a business owned by one person. One of the major advantages of the sole proprietorship business form is that it is easy and inexpensive to establish. A major disadvantage of a sole proprietorship is that the owner of the firm has *unlimited personal liability* for all debts and other obligations incurred by the firm.

Sole proprietorships have another disadvantage in that their owners often have difficulty raising funds to finance growth. Thus, sole proprietorships generally are small. Although approximately 80 percent of all businesses in the United States are of this type, their dollar volume of business activity amounts to only 10 percent of the total business activity in the country. Sole proprietorships are especially important in the retail trade and service industries.

Partnership

A partnership is a business organization in which two or more co-owners form a business, normally with the intention of making a profit. Each partner agrees to provide a certain percentage of the funds necessary to run the business and also agrees to do some portion of the necessary work. In return the partners share in the profit (or losses) of the business.

Partnerships may be either *general* or *limited*. In a *general partnership*, each partner has unlimited liability for all of the obligations of the business. Thus, general partnerships have the same major disadvantage as sole proprietorships. Even so, approximately 90 percent of all partnerships in the United States are of this type.

A *limited partnership* usually involves one or more general partners and one or more limited partners. Although the limited partners may limit their liability, the extent of this liability can vary, as set forth in the partnership agreement. Limited partnerships are common in real estate ventures, and in recent years many corporations have restructured themselves as *master limited partnerships*, where the partnership units trade just like shares of stock. The primary motivation for master limited partnerships was to avoid the double taxation of the firm's income that occurs in a corporation. Tax code changes in 1987 largely eliminated the tax motivation for master limited partnerships.

Partnerships are relatively easy to form, but they must be reformed when there is a change in the makeup of the general partners. Partnerships have a greater capacity to raise capital than sole proprietorships, but they lack the tremendous capital attraction ability of corporations.

Corporation

A corporation is a "legal person" composed of one or more actual individuals or legal entities. It is considered to be separate and distinct from those individuals or entities. Money contributed to start a corporation is called *capital stock* and is divided into *shares;* the owners of the corporation are called *stockholders* or *shareholders.*

The corporate form of business organization has four major advantages over both sole proprietorships and partnerships including the following:

- **Limited Liability** Once stockholders have paid for their shares, they are not liable for any obligations or debts the corporation may incur. They are liable only to the extent of their investment in the shares.
- **Permanency** The legal existence of a corporation is not affected by whether or not stockholders sell their shares. Thus, it is a more permanent form of business organization.
- **Flexibility** It is relatively easy to effect a change of ownership within a corporation; one individual can merely sell shares to another. Even when shares of stock are sold, the corporation continues to exist in its original form.
- **Ability to Raise Capital** The major advantage of the corporate form of business organization is the ability of the firm to raise large amounts of capital. This capital raising ability is due to the limited liability of owners and the easy marketability of shares of ownership.

However, the ability to raise capital comes with a cost. In the typical large corporation there is a separation of ownership from management. This gives rise to the potential conflicts of goals and the agency costs discussed earlier. However, the ability to raise large amounts of capital at a relatively low cost is such a large advantage of the corporate form that a certain level of agency costs are tolerated.

As a "legal person," a corporation can purchase and own assets, borrow money, sue, and be sued. Its officers are considered to be *agents* of the corporation and are authorized to act on the corporation's behalf. For example, only an officer, such as the treasurer, can sign an agreement to repay a bank loan for the corporation.

CORPORATE ORGANIZATION. In most corporations the stockholders elect a *board of directors*, which, in theory, is responsible for managing the corporation. In practice, however, the board of directors usually deals only with broad policy matters, leaving the day-to-day operations of the business to the *officers,* who are elected by the board. Corporate officers normally include a *president, vice-president(s), treasurer,* and *secretary.* In some corporations one person holds more than one office; many small corporations have a person who serves as secretary-treasurer. In most corporations the president and various other officers are also members of the board of directors. These officers are called "inside" board members, whereas other board members, such as the company's attorney or banker, are called "outside" board members. A corporation's board of directors usually contains at least three members.

CORPORATE SECURITIES. In return for the use of their funds, investors in a corporation are issued certificates, or *securities*. Corporate securities represent claims against the assets and future earnings of the firm.

There are two types of corporate securities. Investors who lend money to the corporation are issued *debt securities;* these investors expect periodic interest payments, as well as the eventual return of their principal. Owners of the corporation are issued *equity securities.* Equity securities take the form of either *common stock* or *preferred stock.* Common stock is a residual form of ownership; that is, the claims of common stockholders on the firm's earnings[4] and assets are considered only after all other claims—such as those of the government, debtholders, and preferred stockholders—have been met. Common stockholders are considered to be the true owners of the corporation. Common stockholders possess certain rights or claims, including dividend rights, assets rights, voting rights, and preemptive rights.[5] (Appendix 1A illustrates how to obtain information about a company's common stock and debt securities from sources such as the *Wall Street Journal.*)

Preferred stockholders have priority over common stockholders with regard to the firm's earnings and assets. They are paid cash dividends before common stockholders. In addition, if the corporation goes bankrupt, is reorganized, or is dissolved, preferred stockholders have priority over common stockholders in the distribution of the corporation's assets. However, preferred stockholders are second in line behind the firm's creditors.

Because of the advantages of limited liability, permanency, and flexibility, and because ownership shares in corporations tend to be more liquid (and hence relatively more valuable) than ownership interests in proprietorships and partnerships, it is easy to see why the majority of business conducted in the United States is done under the corporate form of organization.

SMALL BUSINESS CONCERNS: MAXIMIZATION OF SHAREHOLDER WEALTH

Small businesses constitute an important sector of the American economy. Small business firms may be organized as sole proprietorships, partnerships, or corporations. According to criteria used by the Small Business Administration, over 95 percent of all business firms are considered small. These firms account for the majority of private sector employment and nearly all of the net growth in new jobs.

It is difficult to arrive at a precise definition of a small business; however, the characteristics of small business firms can be identified. In general, small businesses are not the dominant firm in the industries in which they compete. Small firms typically grow more rapidly than larger firms. Small firms have limited access to the financial markets. Small firms often do not have the depth of specialized managerial resources available to larger firms. Small firms also have a very high failure rate.

In our discussion of the goals of the firm, we concluded that the predominant goal of financial managers is to maximize shareholder wealth, as measured by the price of the firm's stock. Many small corporations are closely held and their stock trades infrequently, if ever. Other small firms are organized as sole proprietorships or partnerships. In these cases, there is no readily accessible external measure of performance. Consequently,

---

[4] The terms *earnings, income,* and *profits* are used interchangeably throughout this text.

[5] These rights are discussed in more detail in Chapter 7.

small firms must rely more heavily on accounting-based measures of performance to track their progress. Accounting-based measures of performance are discussed in Chapter 3.

As discussed earlier, in the large modern corporation, there is a concern that a firm's managers may not always act in the interests of the owners (the agency problem). This problem is much less severe in many small businesses, because managers and owners are one and the same. An owner-manager who consumes "excessive" perks is merely reducing his or her ability to withdraw profits from the firm. But to the extent that the manager is the owner, there is no owner-manager agency problem. Of course, the potential for agency-related conflicts between owners and lenders still exists and may be greater in the closely held firm. As a consequence, many small firms find it difficult to acquire capital from lenders, without also giving the lender an option on a part of the ownership in the firm or agreeing to an unlimited liability personal loan guarantee from the owner.

In the face of this significant difference in the management-ownership structure of small businesses, it should be kept in mind that small business owner-managers have strong incentives to take actions that will maximize firm value, because the wealth of the owner-manager often is closely tied to the performance of the firm. Also, a firm that is efficiently run and successful makes a tempting target for acquisition by a larger company. A well-run firm will command a much higher takeover price.

Throughout this book we will highlight situations where the financial management of small businesses poses special challenges. The major areas of concern will be tax considerations, the valuation of small firms, risk considerations, access to the money and capital markets, and the management of cash resources. In general, we will find that small firms often lack the depth of managerial talent needed to apply sophisticated financial planning techniques. Also, because significant economies of scale often are associated with using sophisticated financial management techniques, it frequently will be the case that these techniques are not justified on a cost-benefit analysis basis in many small companies.

ORGANIZATION OF THE FINANCIAL MANAGEMENT FUNCTION

Many firms divide the decision-making responsibilities of management among several different officers, which often include manufacturing, marketing, finance, personnel, and engineering. A sample organization chart, emphasizing the finance function, is shown in Figure 1-2. The finance function usually is headed by a (senior) vice-president of finance or *chief financial officer* (CFO), who reports to the president. In addition to overseeing the accounting, treasury, tax, and audit functions, today's CFO often has responsibility for strategic planning, monitoring and trading foreign currencies, managing the risk from volatile interest rates, and monitoring production and inventory levels. CFOs also must be able to convince investors of the company's financial health.

James Wirth, senior vice-president for finance and CFO of Aluminum Company of America was recently honored as one of America's fifty best CFOs. He said, "One of the key elements of the job is that financial markets have become very sophisticated. Financing has to be sought worldwide. It's not just a situation where you deal in U.S. money markets. You have to look at Euro markets and others as well. It's become more complex."

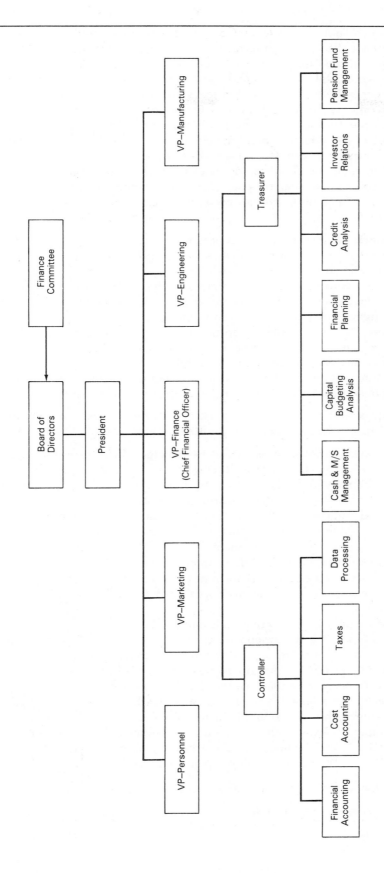

Finance Committee

Board of Directors

President

VP–Personnel

VP–Marketing

VP–Finance (Chief Financial Officer)

VP–Engineering

VP–Manufacturing

Controller

Treasurer

Financial Accounting

Cost Accounting

Taxes

Data Processing

Cash & M/S Management

Capital Budgeting Analysis

Financial Planning

Credit Analysis

Investor Relations

Pension Fund Management

W. Bruce Thomas, vice-chairman for administration and CFO at USX was also among the honored top fifty CFOs. He said, "Financing used to be a relatively simple matter of either borrowing from banks or issuing what are known as plain vanilla bonds, just relatively simple bond or debenture instruments. In the last five or ten years, the variety of financial instruments has become so diversified, and so many new instruments have been invented, that that aspect of the job has become a much more challenging one, and one in which a good financial officer can make a real contribution to his company in terms of imaginative financing."[6]

The chief financial officer often distributes the financial management responsibilities between the *controller* and the *treasurer*.[7] The controller normally has responsibility for all accounting related activities. These include such functions as

- **Financial Accounting** This function involves the preparation of the financial statements for the firm, such as the balance sheet, income statement, and the statement of cash flows.
- **Cost Accounting** This department often has responsibility for preparing the firm's operating budgets and monitoring the performance of the departments and divisions within the firm.
- **Taxes** This unit prepares the reports that the company must file with the various government (local, state, and federal) agencies.
- **Data Processing** Given its responsibilities involving corporate accounting and payroll activities, the controller may also have management responsibility for the company's data processing operations.

The treasurer normally is concerned with the acquisition, custody, and expenditure of funds. These duties often include

- **Cash and Marketable Securities Management** This group monitors the firm's short-term finances—forecasting its cash needs, obtaining funds from bankers and other sources when needed, and investing any excess funds in short-term interest-earning securities.
- **Capital Budgeting Analysis** This department is responsible for analyzing capital expenditures—that is, the purchase of long-term assets such as new facilities and equipment.
- **Financial Planning** This department is responsible for analyzing the alternative sources of long-term funds, such as the issuance of bonds or common stock, that the firm will need to maintain and expand its operations.
- **Credit Analysis** Most companies have a department that is responsible for determining the amount of credit that the firm will extend to each of its customers. Although this group is responsible for performing financial analysis, it sometimes may be located in the marketing area of the firm because of its close relationship to sales.
- **Investor Relations** Many large companies have a unit responsible for working with institutional investors (for example, mutual funds), bond rating agencies, stockholders, and the general financial community.
- **Pension Fund Management** The treasurer may also have responsibility for the investment of employee pension fund contributions. The invest-

---

[6] "CFO Role Broadens beyond Balancing Books," *Pittsburgh Press* (October 7, 1986).

[7] In smaller companies, the owner may supervise the activities of the controller and treasurer, or the chief financial officer may perform both activities under the title of controller, treasurer, or vice-president of finance.

ment analysis and portfolio management functions may be performed either within the firm or through outside investment advisors.

It should be emphasized that *the specific functions of the controller and treasurer shown in Figure 1-2 are illustrative only and that the actual functions performed vary from company to company.* For example, in some companies, the treasurer may have responsibility for tax matters. Also, as shown in Figure 1-2, the board of directors of the company may establish a finance committee, consisting of a number of directors and officers of the firm with substantial financial expertise, to make recommendations on broad financial policy issues.

PROFESSIONAL FINANCE AFFILIATIONS

There are several professional organizations for practicing financial managers. These include the Financial Executives Institute, the Institute of Chartered Financial Analysts, and the Financial Management Association. These organizations provide an opportunity for professional interaction and lifelong learning.

The Financial Management Association (FMA) has a goal of serving as a bridge between the academic study of practical finance and the practice of finance by financial managers. This goal is achieved through the publication of an applied, quarterly journal, *Financial Management.* The FMA also publishes *Financial Management Collection* three times a year. It reprints and abstracts timely articles of interest to financial practitioners and provides insights into various finance career options. The FMA sponsors student chapters at many universities and sponsors the National Honor Society, the only national honorary organization for students of finance. The FMA also holds an annual meeting featuring the presentation of financial research, panel discussions led by leading academic and financial practitioners, and tutorials on new developments in finance. Additional membership information can be obtained from the Financial Management Association, College of Business Administration, University of South Florida, Tampa, Florida 33620.

FINANCIAL MANAGEMENT AND OTHER DISCIPLINES

As you pursue your study of financial management, you should keep in mind that financial management is not a totally independent area in business administration. Instead, it draws heavily on related disciplines and fields of study. The most important of these are *accounting* and *economics;* in the latter discipline, *macroeconomics* and *microeconomics* are of special significance. *Marketing, production,* and the study of *quantitative methods* also have an impact on the financial management field. Each of these is discussed in the following sections.

Accounting

Financial managers often turn to accounting data to assist them in making decisions. Generally a company's accountants are responsible for developing financial reports and measures that assist its managers in assessing the past performance and future direction of the firm and in meeting certain legal obligations, such as the payment of taxes. The accountant's role includes the development of financial statements such as the *balance sheet*, the *income statement*, and the *statement of cash flows*.

Financial managers are primarily concerned with a firm's *cash flows*, because they often determine the feasibility of certain investment and financing decisions. The financial manager refers to accounting data when making future resource allocation decisions concerning long-term investments, when managing current investments in working capital, and when making a number of other financial decisions (for example, determining the most appropriate capital structure and identifying the best and most timely sources of funds needed to support the firm's investment programs).

In many small and medium-sized firms the accounting function and the financial management function may be handled by the same person or group of persons. In such cases the distinctions just identified may become blurred.

Economics

There are two areas of economics with which the financial manager must be familiar: *microeconomics* and *macroeconomics*. Microeconomics deals with the economic decisions of individuals, households, and firms, whereas macroeconomics looks at the economy as a whole.

The typical firm is heavily influenced by the overall performance of the economy and is dependent upon the money and capital markets for investment funds. Thus, financial managers should recognize and understand how monetary policies affect the cost of funds and the availability of credit. Financial managers also should be versed in fiscal policy and how it affects the economy. What the economy can be expected to do in the future is a crucial factor in generating sales forecasts as well as other types of forecasts.

The financial manager uses microeconomics when developing decision models that are likely to lead to the most efficient and successful modes of operation within the firm. Specifically, the financial manager may utilize the basic economic notion from microeconomic theory of setting marginal cost equal to marginal revenue when making long-term investment decisions *(capital budgeting)* and when managing cash, inventories, and accounts receivable *(working capital management)*.

Marketing, Production, and Quantitative Methods

Figure 1-3 depicts the relationship between financial management and its primary supportive disciplines. Marketing, production, and quantitative methods are indirectly related to the key day-to-day decisions made by financial managers.

For example, financial managers should consider the impact of new product development and promotion plans made in the marketing area, because these plans will require capital outlays and have an impact on the firm's projected cash flows. Similarly, changes in the production process may necessitate capital expenditures, which the firm's financial managers must evaluate and then finance. And, finally, the tools of analysis developed in the quantitative methods area frequently are helpful in analyzing complex financial management problems.

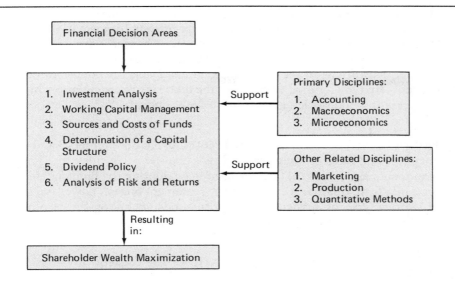

FIGURE 1-3

Impact of Other Disciplines on Financial Management

ORGANIZATION OF THE TEXT

This text provides an introduction to both analytical tools and descriptive materials that are useful in financial management. Because this is an introductory-level text, however, it does *not* attempt to make the reader an expert in every aspect of financial decision making. Instead, it is intended to do the following:

■ Acquaint the reader with the types of decisions faced by financial managers.
■ Develop a framework for analyzing these decisions in a systematic manner.
■ Provide the reader with the background necessary to pursue more advanced readings and courses in financial management.

Although the subject matter in this text is divided into a series of parts, it should be noted that the various types of financial decisions are interrelated and should not be considered in isolation from one another.

Each chapter begins with a Financial Dilemma faced by an actual firm. The dilemma is related to the material covered in the chapter. Also, at the outset, each chapter contains a summary review of the key concepts from the chapter and a glossary defining new terms that will be encountered in the chapter. At the end of each chapter is a point-by-point summary of the chapter, a carefully selected list of additional references, and an extensive set of questions and problems that you can use to test your understanding of the text material. Some chapters also have more complex, integrative case problems. Where appropriate, special small business financial management issues and international financial management issues are discussed. Check answers to selected problems appear at the end of the book. Also, at the end of the book, you will find an overview of the CFM Lotus Disk, a set of Lotus-based templates that are available for solving many of the complex chapter problems and cases.

Parts of the Text

PART I INTRODUCTION. Chapter 1 examines the financial goals of the firm, discusses the various forms of business organization, and considers the role of the financial manager in the decision-making process. The primary financial instruments are defined. Accessing financial information from the *Wall Street Journal* is covered in Appendix 1A. Chapter 2 provides an overview of the business environment in the United States and the role of financial institutions in the economy. Chapter 2 also introduces three basic concepts that are applied throughout the text: risk-return relationships, the net present value model, and the cash flow concept.

PART II FINANCIAL ANALYSIS AND FORECASTING. Chapters 3 and 4 present the basic tools of financial analysis. Chapter 3 considers the financial statements and ratios that can be used in evaluating the financial performance of a firm. Chapter 4 examines the statement of cash flows, and the use of various types of financial planning methods, including the cash budget, pro forma financial statements, and breakeven analysis.

PART III DETERMINANTS OF VALUATION. The concept of valuation is a central theme of the book. Chapter 5 develops the concepts of discounting, compounding, and present value. These concepts are used in the valuation of securities and in the evaluation of capital expenditure projects that are expected to provide benefits over a number of years. Chapter 6 applies the basic valuation model to fixed income securities, such as bonds and preferred stock. Chapter 7 deals with the valuation of common stock. Chapter 8 provides a comprehensive introduction to the concept of risk in finance and the relationship between risk, required returns, and the shareholder wealth maximization goal of the firm.

PART IV THE CAPITAL INVESTMENT DECISION. This portion of the text focuses on capital expenditures; that is, investments in long-term assets. Chapters 9 and 10 present the fundamentals of capital budgeting; namely, the process of investing in long-term assets. Chapter 9 deals with the measurement of the cash flows (benefits and costs) associated with long-term investment projects; Chapter 10 considers various decision-making criteria that can be used when choosing projects that will maximize the value of the firm. Chapter 11 extends the concepts developed in Chapter 10 by considering some of the decision-making techniques that attempt to deal with the problem of the risk associated with a specific project's cash flow.

PART V THE COST OF CAPITAL, CAPITAL STRUCTURE, AND DIVIDEND POLICY. Chapter 12 illustrates the principles of measuring a firm's cost of capital. The cost of funds to a firm is an important input in the capital budgeting process. Chapter 13 addresses the relationship of the cost of capital to the firm's capital structure. Chapter 14 discusses the factors that influence the choice of a dividend policy and the impact of various dividend policies on the value of a firm.

PART VI MANAGING FUNDING SOURCES. This part of the text describes the characteristics of the major sources of intermediate and long-term funds. Specifically, Chapter 15 deals with term loans and leases. Chapter 16 focuses on the management of long-term funding sources.

PART VII THE MANAGEMENT OF WORKING CAPITAL. Chapters 17 through 20 examine the management of a firm's current asset and liability accounts (that is, working capital). Chapter 17 provides an overview of working capital management, with emphasis on the risk-return tradeoffs involved in working capital decision making. Chapter 18 deals with the management of cash and marketable securities, and Chapter 19 with accounts receivable and inventories. Finally, Chapter 20 discusses the management of secured and unsecured short-term credit.

PART VIII SELECTED TOPICS IN CONTEMPORARY FINANCIAL MANAGEMENT. Chapter 21 discusses international financial management. Chapter 22 examines issues associated with corporate restructuring.

SUMMARY

- The primary normative goal of financial management decision making is the *maximization of shareholder wealth* as measured by the price of the firm's stock. This objective permits decision makers explicity to make the needed tradeoffs between risk and return and between long-run versus short-run profits.
- The amount, timing and risk of the cash flows generated by a firm can be influenced by key financial management decisions, including investment decisions, dividend decisions, financing decisions, and ownership structure decisions. These decisions must be made in the context of factors in the broader economic environment.
- The marginal cost equals marginal revenue rule from microeconomics provides a framework for structuring many financial management problems.
- The three principal forms of business organization are the *sole proprietorship*, the *partnership*, and the *corporation*. Corporations have certain advantages over the other two forms of business organization, especially for large businesses; as a result, corporations account for about 85 percent of the dollar volume of business activity in the United States.
- A corporation is defined as a "legal person" composed of one or more actual individuals or legal entities. The owners of a corporation are called *stockholders* or *shareholders*. The stockholders elect a *board of directors* that usually deals with broad policy matters, whereas the day-to-day operations are supervised by the *officers*.
- Corporations issue *debt securities* to investors who lend money to the corporation and *equity securities* to investors who become owners.
- The finance function usually is headed by a (senior) vice-president or *chief financial officer*. The financial management responsibilities are often divided between the *controller* and the *treasurer*. The controller normally has responsibility for all accounting related activities. The treasurer normally is concerned with the acquisition, custody, and expenditure of funds.
- Over the past 50 years financial management has developed into a much more analytically rigorous discipline.
- Financial management is closely related to other areas of business decision making, particularly accounting and economics.

QUESTIONS AND TOPICS FOR DISCUSSION

1. Define *shareholder wealth*. Explain how it is measured.

2. What are the differences between shareholder wealth maximization and profit maximization? If a firm chooses to pursue the objective of shareholder wealth maximization, does this preclude the use of profit maximization decision-making rules? Explain.

3. Which type of corporation is more likely to be a shareholder wealth maximizer—one with wide ownership and no owners directly involved in the firm's management, or one that is closely held?

4. Is the shareholder wealth maximization goal a short- or long-term goal? Explain your answer.

5. It has been argued that shareholder wealth maximization is not a realistic normative goal for the firm, given the social responsibility activities that the firm is "expected" to engage in (such as contributing to the arts, education, etc.). Explain why these social responsibility activities are not necessarily inconsistent with shareholder wealth maximization.

6. Explain why management may tend to pursue goals other than shareholder wealth maximization.

7. Explain what is meant by *agency relationships* and *agency costs*.

8. In the agency relationship between the shareholders (owners) and management of a firm, give some examples of agency costs incurred by shareholders.

9. What is the source of potential agency conflicts between owners and bondholders? Who is the agent and who is the principal in this relationship?

10. Explain the differences in the responsibilities of the treasurer and the controller in a large corporation.

11. Explain the relationship between financial management and (a) microeconomics and (b) macroeconomics.

12. How does financial management in the 1980s differ from financial management in the 1920s and 1930s—both as a profession and as a field of study?

13. Why is earnings per share not a consistently good measure of a firm's performance?

14. In late 1988, Metropolitan Life Insurance Company, Swiss Bank Corporation, and several other holders of RJR Nabisco bonds filed suit against the company to prevent it from completing the leveraged buyout acquisition from Kohlberg Kravis Roberts. Why do you think the bondholders wanted to block this transaction? What arguments can you make against the bondholders' case?

15. What are the major factors that determine the value of a firm's stock?

16. NCNB, a large Southeast regional bank, acquired First Republic Bank of Texas in 1988, after the failure of the Texas bank. What effect do you think this acquisition had on NCNB's stock price, considering each of the three major factors that determine stock prices?

17. In early 1989, Eastern Airlines, a unit of Texas Air Corporation, declared bankruptcy after its machinists and pilots went on strike. How can you reconcile a bankruptcy declaration with a management pledged to maximize shareholder wealth?

18. Compare the potential for agency problems in sole proprietorships, partnerships, and corporations. In light of your analysis, why is the corporate form of organization so popular?

SELECTED REFERENCES

Barnea, Amir, R. Haugen, and L. Senbet. *Agency Problems and Financial Contracting.* Englewood Cliffs, NJ: Prentice-Hall, 1985.

Beranek, William. "Research Directions in Finance." *Quarterly Review of Economics and Business* (Spring 1981): 6–24.

Berle, Adolf, and G. C. Means. *The Modern Corporation and Private Property.* New York: Macmillan, 1932.

Cornell, Bradford, and Alan C. Shapiro. "Corporate Stakeholders and Corporate Finance." *Financial Management* (Spring 1987): 5–14.

Fama, Eugene. "Agency Problems and the Theory of the Firm." *Journal of Political Economy* (April 1980): 288–307.

Findlay, M. Chapman, and G. A. Whitmore. "Beyond Shareholder Wealth Maximization." *Financial Management* (Winter 1974): 25–35.

Jensen, Michael C., and William H. Meckling. "Theory of the Firm: Managerial Behavior, Agency Costs, and Ownership Structure." *Journal of Financial Economics* (October 1976): 305–360.

Rappaport, Alfred. *Creating Shareholder Value.* New York: Free Press, 1986.

Weston, J. Fred. "Developments in Financial Theory." *Financial Management* (June 1981): 5–22.

Understanding Financial Market Quotations

▰▰▰ INTRODUCTION

As a student of finance, it is important that you be able to read and understand the financial information regularly reported in the financial section of newspapers and business magazines. The most comprehensive source of this information is the *Wall Street Journal (WSJ)*. The *WSJ* contains information on all listed bonds and stocks that are traded on any day. The *WSJ* also contains extensive information about interest rates, options, futures contracts for stocks, bonds, commodities, and foreign currencies, plus an extensive array of other relevant financial information. In this appendix we illustrate the information that can be obtained from stock and bond quotations reported in the *WSJ*.

▰▰▰ UNDERSTANDING BOND QUOTATIONS

The majority of existing debt issues (bonds[1]) of U.S. corporations are traded in the over-the-counter (OTC) market. The OTC market is a network of security dealers who buy and sell bonds and stock from each other, either for their own account or for their retail clients. Price information on bonds that are traded over-the-counter is not reported in the *WSJ*. However, some larger issues of corporate bonds are listed and traded on the New York Exchange. Price quotations for these listed bonds are published daily in the *WSJ*. Table 1A-1 shows a selected list of bond quotations.

Bond prices are quoted as a percentage of their par value (usually $1,000). For example, the closing price for the Exxon issue was $807.50. The "6s97" after the Exxon bond name means the bond offers a contract, or coupon, interest rate of 6 percent. Thus a holder of the issue receives $30 in interest per bond every six months for a total of $60 (6.0% × $1,000) each year. This debt issue, or series (the *s* stands for "series"), matures in the year 1997, hence the 97 listing after the coupon interest rate. The current yield is calculated by dividing the annual interest by the day's closing price; for example, $60/$807.50 = 7.4 percent. However, this current yield is only an approximation of the true promised yield on the bond, called the *yield-to-maturity*.[2]

---

[1] In this discussion, the term *bond* includes corporate debt securities that are secured with the pledge of specific assets (mortgage bonds), debt securities that are secured only by the income generating capacity of the firm and a general claim on the company's assets (debentures), and intermediate-term corporate debt securities (notes). The details of the differences between these debt security types is discussed in Chapter 6.

[2] Chapter 6 contains a discussion of yield-to-maturity calculations.

Selected Bond Quotations from the New York Exchange				
Bonds	Cur Yld	Vol	Close	Net Chg.
AlldC zr09	...	275	14	−⅜
Exxon 6s97	7.4	5	80¾	−⅛
Wendy's 7¼10	cv	59	70¼	...

A *cv* in the current yield column, such as appears for the Wendy's bonds, indicates that the bond issue is convertible into common stock under certain conditions. Convertible securities are discussed in Chapter 16. Also, note that the Allied Corporation bond issue (AlldC) has a *zr* before the expiration date of the bond (2009). The *zr* indicates that this is a zero coupon bond; that is, a bond that pays no interest. Rather, it initially is sold at a discount from par value ($1,000), and the purchaser receives a return by holding the bond to maturity, at which point it is redeemed for $1000. You will note that this bond is currently selling for only 14 percent of its par value, or $140.

UNDERSTANDING STOCK QUOTATIONS

Table 1A-2 shows selected stock quotations for stocks traded on the New York Stock Exchange. Beginning at the left-hand side, the first two columns show the stock's price range during the previous 52 weeks. For example, the per-share price of Cincinnati Gas and Electric Company common stock ranged between $29 and $25.125. The column immediately to the right of the stock name shows the ticker symbol used to identify this stock on the exchange's ticker tape. The next column shows the current annual dividend rate; for example, the Cincinnati Gas and Electric Company's (CGE) current annual dividend rate is $2.24 per share of common stock. Dividends are normally paid in four quarterly installments throughout the year. The next column shows the dividend percentage yield. For CGE, the figure is 8.6 (calculated as the annual dividend divided by the closing price, or $2.24/$26.125 = 8.6%).

The price to earnings (P/E) ratio (the current price divided by the last twelve months' earnings) is shown next. The P/E ratio (6) indicates how much investors are willing to pay for $1 of current earnings from the firm. Generally, the greater the risk of the firm, the lower will be its P/E multiple. Similarly, the P/E ratio will tend to be higher the more rapid the expected growth rate in future earnings. The next figure is the sales volume in hundreds of shares; on this day, 40,000 shares of CGE's common stock were traded. The next three columns list the high, low, and closing prices for the day. The final column shows the net change in price per share for the day, or the difference between this day's closing price and the closing price on the

Selected Stock Quotations from the New York Exchange											
52 Weeks		Stock	SYM	Div	Yld %	PE	Vol 100s	Hi	Lo	Close	Net Chg
Hi	Lo										
29	25⅛	CincGE	CIN	2.24	8.6	6	400	26⅛	25⅞	26⅛	+¼
43¾	39	CincGE pf		4.00	9.8	...	320	40¾	40¾	40¾	−1¼

previous business day (or the last day on which a trade took place). For the day, the common stock of CGE gained $0.25 per share.

When a company has preferred stock outstanding that also is traded on the New York Exchange, the different classes of preferred stocks will be listed below the common stock. As can be seen in Table 1A-2, CGE has a preferred stock issue outstanding that pays a set dividend of $4 per share. Unlike common stock dividends, the preferred stock dividend rate normally will not change over the time the issue is outstanding.

Information on stocks that are not traded on an organized exchange, that is, stock traded over-the-counter (OTC), also appears in the *Wall Street Journal*, although the form and amount of the information provided is slightly different. The major difference is that the prices that appear reflect transactions between security dealers rather than the actual prices paid by individual retail investors.

UNDERSTANDING GOVERNMENT BOND PRICE QUOTATIONS

The U.S. government raises funds by selling debt securities. These securities take the form of short-term Treasury bills, intermediate-term Treasury notes, and long-term Treasury bonds. U.S. Treasury bills have an initial maturity of 13, 26, or 52 weeks and pay $10,000 per bill to the holder at maturity. Treasury bills pay no explicit interest; rather, they are sold at a discount from maturity value. An investor who buys a bill at a discount and holds it to maturity will receive as interest the difference between the price paid and $10,000. The quote for a typical Treasury bill follows:

Mat. date	Bid	Asked Discount	Yield
5-11	8.55	8.51	8.82

The bill shown above matures in approximately 3 months. The "bid" and "asked" prices indicate the *annualized* percentage discount from maturity value. An *asked discount* of 8.51 percent translates into a cash discount from $10,000 of approximately $212.75, or a price of $9787.25 (8.51%/4 = 2.1275% discount). The stated *yield* is the annualized yield an investor will receive by purchasing this bill and holding it to maturity.

Longer-term government debt is issued in the form of Treasury notes and bonds. Treasury notes typically have an initial maturity ranging from 1 to 10 years. Treasury bonds typically have initial maturities ranging from 10 to 30 years. Like corporate bonds, Treasury notes and bonds pay a stated coupon rate of interest semiannually. They are issued in denominations of $1,000. There are two major differences between the price quotations of corporate bonds and the price quotations of Treasury notes and bonds. First, Treasury note and bond prices vary in units of $\frac{1}{32}$nd of 1 percent of par value. Thus a price quote of 94-17 means that the bond will sell for 94$\frac{17}{32}$ percent of par, or $945.31. The second difference is that Treasury note and bond quotations indicate the yield to maturity (or the yield to the first call date in the case of bonds that can be called for redemption prior to the maturity date) for the bond at its current price, rather than the current yield shown in the *WSJ* for corporate bonds.

PROBLEMS*

1. Recently, the *Wall Street Journal* reported the following stock quotations:

102¼	78½	Du Pont	DD	4.20	4.3	11	7178	98⅞	97¼	98⅛	−1⅜
44⅜	40	Du Pont pf		3.50	8.7	...	23	40¼	40	40¼	−¾
110¾	98¼	McKesson pf		1.80	1.8	...	1	101	101	101	−1
23⅛	19½	PubSvcCol	PSR	2.00	9.7	10	2834	20¾	20½	20⅝	−⅛
7⅛	5½	Wendys	WEN	.24	3.8	21	5344	6⅜	6⅛	6¼	...
3⅞	2	Zapata	ZOS		...	...	931	3	2⅞	2⅞	−⅛

a. What are the dividend yields on the common stock of Du Pont and Public Service Company of Colorado?
b. What possible explanation can you give for the difference in dividend yields between Du Pont and Public Service Company of Colorado?
c. What is the current price–earnings ratio for Du Pont?
d. Why do you think the dividend yield on Du Pont's preferred stock is so much higher than the dividend yield on McKesson's preferred stock?
e. What was the previous day's closing price for the McKesson preferred stock?
f. Which stock has been most volatile over the past year?
g. What is Wendys' price–earnings ratio? Why do you think it is so much higher than the price–earnings ratio for Du Pont and Public Service Company of Colorado?
h. Which company is currently losing money?

2. The following bond quotations recently appeared in the *Wall Street Journal:*

EKod 8⅝ 16	10.3	194	83¾	...
HollyFar 6s 17	cv	6	104	−¼
Seagrm zr 06	...	36	32½	+¼
Sears 13¼ 92	12.3	5	107⅜	−1¼
TxAir 15¾ 92	16.4	20	96	...

a. What is the coupon rate and year of maturity for each bond?
b. How much would you have had to pay to buy one Seagram bond at the closing trade?
c. Why is the yield on the Texas Air bond so much higher than the yield on the Sears bond?
d. How much did the price of one Seagrams bond change from the prior day's closing price?

3. The yield to maturity on Elsinore Corporation bonds was approximately 20 percent at the same time when Exxon's bonds of a similar maturity were yielding 10 percent. What conclusions can you draw about Elsinore Corporation?

4. The "asked" discount on a 6-month Treasury bill recently was quoted as 8.97 percent. Approximately how much would you have to pay to buy one of these Treasury bills ($10,000 maturity value)?

5. How much would you have to pay for a U.S. government bond ($1,000 maturity value) scheduled to mature in November 2015 and quoted at 105-18 "asked"? The coupon rate on the bond is 9⅞ percent.

* Color numbers denote problems that have check answers provided at the end of the book.

Foundation Concepts for Financial Management

KEY CHAPTER CONCEPTS

1. The cash flow concept is central to the valuation of investments in physical assets and financial assets.
   a. The after-tax operating cash flow concept is used primarily when estimating the cash flows for capital investment analysis purposes.
   b. The free cash flow concept is used in long-range financial planning and in the evaluation of firms for potential acquisition.
2. The net present value rule is the primary decision-making rule used throughout the practice of financial management.
   a. The net present value of an investment is equal to the present value of future returns minus the required initial outlay.
   b. The net present value of an investment made by a firm represents the contribution of that investment to the value of the firm and, accordingly, to the wealth of shareholders.
   c. The net present value of an investment will decline as the perceived risk of the investment increases.
3. In the U.S. financial system, funds flow from net savers (such as households) to net investors (such as businesses) through financial middlemen and financial intermediaries.
   a. Financial middlemen include securities brokers and investment bankers.

b. Financial intermediaries include commercial banks, thrift institutions, investment companies, and finance companies.
4. Financial markets are classified as money or capital markets and primary or secondary markets.
   a. Short-term securities, having maturities of 1 year or less, are traded in money markets, and long-term securities, having maturities of more than 1 year, are traded in capital markets.
   b. New securities are traded in the primary markets and existing securities are traded in the secondary markets.
5. Required rates of return on securities vary because of differences in maturity, default risk, marketability, the business and financial risk of the issuing firm, the seniority of the security, and because of changes in the risk-free rate.
6. There is a positive relationship between the required rate of return on an investment and the perceived risk of the returns expected from that investment.
7. In efficient capital markets, security prices represent an unbiased estimate of the true economic value of the cash flows expected to be generated to the benefit of that security.

GLOSSARY OF NEW TERMS

After-tax operating cash flow Operating cash flows before tax less tax payments. Operating cash flows before tax equal cash revenues minus cash operating costs.

Business risk The variability in a firm's operating earnings over time.

Capital markets Financial markets in which long-term securities are bought and sold.

Cash flow The actual amount of cash collected and paid out by a firm.

Default risk The chance that the interest and principal will not be paid as promised in a bond indenture or loan agreement.

Expected return The benefits (price appreciation and distributions) an individual anticipates receiving from an investment.

Expected value The average of individual possible outcomes from an event, such as an investment, weighted by the probability of each possible outcome.

Financial risk The additional variability in a company's earnings per share caused by the use of fixed-cost sources of funds, such as debt and preferred stock.

Free cash flow After-tax operating cash flow less after-tax interest payments, debt redemptions, preferred stock dividends and redemptions, net working capital increases, and required investment in property, plant, and equipment.

Holding period return The change in price from holding an asset (security) plus distributions received from the asset divided by the initial price at which the asset was acquired.

Investment banker A financial institution that underwrites and sells new securities. In general, investment bankers assist firms in obtaining new financing.

Marketability risk The ability of an investor to buy and sell an asset (security) quickly and without a significant loss of value.

Maturity premium A bond risk premium that is an increasing function of the number of years until the bond matures.

Money markets Financial markets in which short-term securities are bought and sold.

Net present value The present value of expected future returns from an investment minus the required initial outlay, evaluated at the required rate of return on the investment; the contribution of an investment to shareholder wealth.

Primary markets Financial markets in which *new* securities are bought and sold for the first time; investment bankers are active in the primary markets.

Required return The return an individual demands from an investment as compensation for postponing consumption and assuming risk.

Risk The possibility that actual future returns will deviate from expected returns; the variability of returns.

Risk-free rate of return The return required by an investor in a security having no risk of default; equal to the sum of the *real rate of return* and an *inflation* risk premium.

Risk premium The difference between the required rate of return on a risky investment and the rate of return on a risk-free asset (such as a U.S. government Treasury security) having the same maturity.

Secondary markets Financial markets in which *existing* securities are offered for resale. The New York Stock Exchange is a secondary market.

Seniority risk premium The risk of a security that arises because of the claim the security holder has on a firm's cash flows and assets relative to the claims of holders of more senior securities in a firm.

Term structure of interest rates The pattern of interest rate yields for debt securities that are similar in all respects except for their length of time to maturity; the term structure of interest rates usually is represented by a graphic plot called a *yield curve*.

Underwriting A process whereby a group of investment bankers agrees to purchase a new security issue at a set price and then offers it for sale to investors.

O. M. Scott & Sons*

In December 1986, the lawn products company O. M. Scott & Sons was taken private in a leveraged buyout (LBO) transaction. Prior to that time it was a subsidiary of ITT, the large conglomerate. Leveraged buyouts are financed with large amounts of debt, resulting in substantial principal and interest obligations for the owners.

The president of O. M. Scott, Tadd Seitz, recalls the problems immediately following the LBO. "We had a large problem to begin with—we weren't going to have enough cash soon enough to pay the banks and bondholders the $25 million we owed them in the first 12 months." When Scott operated as a subsidiary of ITT it would have simply asked the treasurer at ITT world headquarters for the needed funds. Operating on its own and already heavily in debt, Scott had to look for internal sources of cash. Internal cash had assumed the importance of air in a diver's tank.

Seitz assigned his assistant treasurer, John Wall, to look for additional internal cash. First, Wall suggested that monitoring of inventory levels be changed from a monthly frequency to once an hour. This monitoring was designed to help the company produce its products closer to the time they would be sold. This was particularly true for its seasonal products, such as fertilizer. The result was to free up significant amounts of cash that previously had been invested in inventories. The purchasing department was directed to obtain better terms from its suppliers. In just 2 years, the average level of monthly working capital investment declined from $75 million to $35 million, while sales rose from $160 million to $200 million per year.

Cash flows are extremely important to the survival of a firm. By maximizing its cash flows, a firm also takes a huge step toward maximizing shareholder wealth. LBOs, with their large debt burdens, make a focus on cash flows doubly important for managers. In a typical LBO transaction, there is very little cushion for careless resource management. Managers of LBOs redouble their efforts to improve the immediate and long-term cash flow position of the firm so that debt service obligations can be met.

In this chapter we develop three of the most important foundation concepts in the practice of financial management. The first concept is the importance of cash flows. The second concept is the net present value (NPV) model. The NPV model is used to value the cash flows expected from an investment in a financial asset (security) or a physical asset. Cash flows received at different points in time must be valued at a common point in time. This is accomplished by discounting the cash flows back to the present using an appropriate required rate of return. The third concept is the relationship between risk and return. The required rate of return depends on conditions in the financial markets, such as the general level of interest rates, and the risk of the investment or security. The successful application of these concepts will lead to the maximization of shareholder wealth.

* This financial dilemma is based, in part, on Brett Duval Fromson, "Life After Debt: How LBOs Do It," *Fortune* (March 13, 1989), pp. 91–92.

INTRODUCTION

As we learned in Chapter 1, the objective of financial management is to maximize shareholder wealth, as measured by the market price of a firm's common stock. In Chapter 1, we also learned that the market price of a firm's common stock is determined by the magnitude, timing, and risk of the cash flows expected to be generated by the firm. In this chapter we develop the process by which the financial marketplace values a firm's cash flows.

The first major section of this chapter establishes why cash flows are the relevant source of value, rather than alternative benefit measures, such as net income. Next the basic net present value rule of valuation is introduced.

The net present value rule applied to cash flows is the central decision-making paradigm used throughout this text and in the practice of financial management. The last major section of this chapter integrates the role of financial markets in the resource allocation and valuation process. Concepts of required return, risk, and market efficiency are shown to be of great importance in the operation of financial markets.

THE CASH FLOW CONCEPT

Charles Royce, president of the Pennsylvania Mutual Fund, has said that "Cash flow can be a better measure of an operation than earnings. A company can keep earnings up for awhile by cutting back on spending. But there is nowhere to hide from careful cash flow analysis."[1] Lawrence Sondike, an analyst with Mutual Shares Corporation, says "Earnings count, but it would be folly to look at earnings without looking at cash flow."[2] Takeover specialists, such as Carl Icahn, T. Boone Pickens, and Kohlberg Kravis Roberts focus on the cash flows of a potential acquisition, because the acquired firm's cash flows are relied upon to repay the debt used to finance the acquisition.

The concept of *cash flow* is one of the central elements of financial analysis, planning, and resource allocation decisions. Cash flows are important because the financial health of a firm depends on its ability to generate sufficient amounts of cash to pay its creditors, employees, suppliers, and owners. Only cash can be spent. You cannot spend accounting net income because net income does not reflect the actual cash inflows and outflows of the firm. For example, an accountant records depreciation expense on an asset each period over the depreciable life of that asset in an attempt to recognize the decline in value of the asset over its life. However, depreciation expenses require no cash outlays. The entire cash outflow related to a depreciable asset occurs at the time the asset is purchased.

Consider the situation facing Macintosh Enterprises, a rapidly growing firm in the computer industry. The balance sheet, projected income statement, and projected cash flows for Macintosh are shown in Table 2-1. Macintosh is expected to have an excellent year. Earnings after tax (net income) is expected to be $1.2 million. The company plans to pay the same $800,000 dividend it paid last year. However, as can be seen in the projected cash flow statement of Macintosh, the firm faces a significant cash shortage over the coming year. This cash shortage arises for several reasons. First, not all sales are expected to be for cash or to be credit sales (accounts receivable) collected during the year. In addition, Macintosh has a debt repayment obligation of $1 million. Payment of taxes, interest, and a cash dividend further reduces Macintosh's cash position. In contrast, the depreciation expense reported on the income statement does not represent a required cash outlay. Accordingly, the reported net income understates the firm's operating cash flows by $500,000 (from depreciation). The net effect of projected operations for Macintosh is a cash shortage of $1.1 million over the coming year. The firm's managers will have to arrange to meet this cash shortfall through actions such as borrowing, the sale of new common equity, a reduction in dividend payments, sale of accounts receivable, or increases in accounts payable.

---

[1] Andrew E. Serwer, "Cashing In On Cash Flow," *Fortune* (May 23, 1988), p. 113.
[2] Jeffrey Laderman, "The Savviest Investors Are Going with the Flow," *Business Week* (September 7, 1987), p. 92.

TABLE 2-1

Balance Sheet, Projected Income Statement, and Projected Cash Flows for Macintosh Enterprises

Balance Sheet
(December 31, 19X8)
(thousands)

Assets		Liabilities and stockholders' equity	
Cash	$1,000	Short-term bank debt	$1,000
Inventories	500	Accounts payable	500
Accounts receivable	1,000	Long-term debt	3,000
Other assets	5,000	Stockholders' equity	3,000
Total assets	$7,500	Total liabilities and	
		stockholders' equity	$7,500

*Due for repayment in 10 months.

Projected Income Statement
(Year Ending December 31, 19X9)
(thousands)

Sales (60% for cash or accounts receivable expected to be collected during the coming year)	$5,000
Less: Cash operating expenses	2,000
Less: Depreciation	500
Earnings before interest and taxes	$2,500
Less: Interest expense	500
Earnings before taxes	$2,000
Less: Tax (at 40%)	800
Earnings after tax	$1,200
Anticipated cash dividend	$800

Projected Cash Flows
(Year Ending December 31, 19X9)
(thousands)

Cash Inflows and Available at Beginning of Period:	
Cash sales and collected receivables	$3,000
Beginning cash balance	1,000
Total available cash	$4,000
Cash Outflows:	
Cash operating expenses	$2,000
Interest expense	500
Tax	800
Repayment of short-term bank debt	1,000
Cash dividend	800
Total expected cash outflows	$5,100

Expected Cash Shortfall = Total expected cash outflows − Total available cash
= $5,100 − $4,000 = $1,100

In Chapter 4 we discuss a more complete cash flow statement than the one presented in Table 2-1. This statement, called the "Statement of Cash Flows," is one of the primary financial statements included in the financial reports prepared by a firm's accountants and provided to investors. It gives a financial analyst a comprehensive view of the cash position of a company over time. Chapter 4 also presents a key *pro forma* (projected) cash flow statement called the "Cash Budget." The cash budget is particularly useful in helping a firm plan for its cash needs over some projected time horizon.

Importance of Cash Flows

The value of common stock, bonds, and preferred stock is based upon the present value of the cash flows that these securities are expected to provide to investors.[3] Similarly, the value to a firm of a capital expenditure is equal to the present value of the cash flows that the capital expenditure is expected to produce for the firm. In addition, cash flows are central to the prosperity and survival of a firm. For example, rapidly expanding firms often grow faster than their ability to generate internally the cash flows needed to meet operating and financial commitments. As a result, these firms may be faced with difficult financial decisions regarding the external sources of funds needed to sustain rapid growth. On the one hand, increases in debt to support expansion result in an increase in the firm's financial risk. On the other hand, if new shares of common stock are sold, ownership in the firm may be diluted more than is desired by the firm's controlling group of owners. Therefore, it is important for managers to pay close attention to the projected cash flows associated with investment and firm expansion strategies.

As you learned in your accounting courses and as will be discussed in Chapter 3, generally accepted accounting principles (GAAP) provide considerable latitude in the determination of the net income for a firm. As a consequence, GAAP concepts of net income do not provide a clear indication of the economic performance of a firm. Cash flow concepts are unambiguous and provide the necessary insight for managers making a wide range of financial resource allocation decisions. Investors also find that cash flow concepts provide a clear measure of the performance of a firm. Accordingly, the concept of cash flow assumes great importance in the analysis of a firm's performance and the management of its resources.

Cash Flow Definitions

For financial analysis purposes, two important definitions of cash flows are used. The two most common cash flow definitions are *after-tax operating cash flow* and *free cash flow*.

AFTER-TAX OPERATING CASH FLOW. The after-tax operating cash flow concept is used primarily when estimating cash flows for capital investment analysis purposes. After-tax operating cash flow (CF) is defined as operating cash flows before tax minus tax payments. Operating cash flows before tax equal total cash revenues minus total cash operating costs. Depreciation expenses are not included directly in this calculation because depreciation does not require the outlay of any funds. Rather, the effect of depreciation is to reduce taxable income by the amount of the depreciation and therefore reduce the cash outlay for taxes by an amount equal to the depreciation charge times the firm's marginal tax rate. Thus, CF is equal to the cash flow

[3] The present value concept is formally introduced in the next section. It is covered in detail in Chapter 5.

before tax times one minus the firm's marginal tax rate plus noncash expenses (primarily depreciation) times the firm's marginal tax rate, or

$$CF = (R - O)(1 - T) + Dep(T) \qquad (2.1)$$

where R is total cash revenues, O is cash operating expenses, Dep is depreciation,[4] and T is the firm's marginal tax rate. An equivalent formula for computing operating cash flow is

$$CF = (R - O - Dep)(1 - T) + Dep \qquad (2.2)$$

Equation 2.2 is used in Chapter 9 when the cash flows from an investment project are being estimated.

FREE CASH FLOW. The free cash flow (FCF) concept is particularly important in long-range corporate financial planning and when evaluating companies for the purpose of acquisition. FCF recognizes that part of the funds generated by an ongoing enterprise must be set aside for reinvestment in the firm. Therefore, these funds are not available for distribution to the firm's owners. Free cash flow can be computed as

$$FCF = CF - I(1 - T) - D_p - P_f - B - WC - Y \qquad (2.3)$$

where CF is the after-tax operating cash flow as defined in Equation 2.1 (or 2.2), I is the before-tax interest payments, D_p is the preferred stock dividend payments, P_f is the required redemption of preferred stock, B is the required redemption of debt, WC is the required net investment in working capital (increases [decreases] in inventories and receivables less increases [decreases] in non-interest bearing current liabilities), and Y is the investment in property, plant, and equipment required to maintain cash flows at their current levels. FCF represents the portion of a firm's total cash flow available to service additional debt, to make dividend payments to common stockholders, and to invest in other projects.

The FCF concept is particularly useful when evaluating a firm for potential acquisition. When valuing a takeover prospect it is important to recognize that explicit cash outlays normally are required to sustain or increase the current cash flows of the firm. For example, if one firm were considering the acquisition of an oil production company, it is not correct to project current cash flows into an indefinite future without explicitly recognizing that crude oil reserves are a depleting resource that require continual, significant investment to assure future cash flow streams. The free cash flow concept is encountered in our discussion of corporate restructuring in Chapter 22.

Cash Flows and Shareholder Wealth

In spite of the close tie between cash flow concepts and the objective of shareholder wealth maximization, many managers do not seem to place enough emphasis on this concept. Some managers focus on alternative per-

---

[4] The relevant depreciation number to be used when computing the operating cash flow expected from an investment project is the depreciation amount that will be reported on the company's tax returns. A detailed discussion of depreciation is contained in Chapter 9 and Appendix 9A.

formance measures, including accounting net income, accounting profit ratios (such as the return on equity or the return on assets), the sales growth rate, and market share. The focus on these accounting-based measures of performance may detract from the long-term performance of the company because performance measures that are not based on cash flows are subject to short-term manipulation by managers.

By emphasizing cash flows rather than accounting-based measures of performance when making decisions, a manager is more likely to achieve the objective of shareholder wealth maximization. A firm that takes actions to maximize the present value of expected future cash flows *will* achieve a record of financial performance that will be reflected both in the company's financial statements and the market value of its stock.

In the next section of this chapter we develop the fundamental net present value concept, which is applied when evaluating the cash flows from a firm or from a particular investment.

THE NET PRESENT VALUE RULE

To achieve the objective of shareholder wealth maximization, a set of appropriate decision rules must be specified. In Chapter 1 we saw that the decision rule of setting *marginal cost equal to marginal revenue* (MC = MR) provides a framework for making many important resource allocation decisions. The MC = MR rule is best suited for situations when the costs and benefits occur at approximately the same time. Many financial decisions require that costs be incurred immediately but result in a stream of benefits over several future time periods. In these cases, the *net present value rule* (NPV) provides appropriate guidance for decision makers. Indeed, the NPV rule is central to the practice of financial management. You will find this rule constantly applied throughout this text.

Determining the Net Present Value of an Investment

In order to understand the NPV rule, consider the following situation. You have just inherited $1 million. Your financial advisor has suggested that you use these funds to purchase a piece of land near a proposed new highway interchange. Your advisor, who is also a state road commissioner, is certain that the interchange will be built and that in 1 year the value of this land will increase to $1.2 million. Hence, you believe initially that this is a riskless investment. At the end of one year you plan to sell the land. You are being asked to invest $1 million today in the anticipation of receiving $1.2 million a year from today, or a profit of $200,000. You wonder whether this profit represents a sufficient return on your investment.

You feel it is important to recognize that there is a 1 year difference between the time you make your outlay of $1 million and the time you receive $1.2 million from the sale of the land. A return of $1.2 million received 1 year from today must be worth less than $1.2 million today because you could invest your $1 million today to earn interest over the coming year. *A dollar received in the future is worth less than a dollar in hand today because a dollar today can be invested to earn a return immediately.* Therefore, to compare a dollar received in the future with a dollar in hand today, it is necessary to multiply the future dollar by a *discount factor* that reflects the alternative investment opportunities that are available.

Instead of investing your $1 million in the land venture, you are aware that you could also invest in a U.S. government bond that currently offers a return of 9 percent. The 9-percent return represents the return (the opportunity cost) foregone by investing in the land project. The 9-percent rate also can be thought of as the compensation to an investor who agrees to postpone receiving a cash return for one period. The appropriate discount factor (PVIF), also called the *present value interest factor*, is equal to

$$\text{PVIF} = \frac{1}{1 + i}$$

where i is the compensation for postponing receipt of a cash return for one period. The present value (PV$_0$) of an amount received 1 year in the future (FV$_1$) is equal to that amount times the discount factor, or

$$\text{PV}_0 = \text{FV}_1 \times (\text{PVIF})$$

In the case of the land project, the present value of the promised $1.2 million expected to be received in 1 year is equal to

$$\text{PV}_0 = \$1.2 \text{ million} \left(\frac{1}{1 + 0.09}\right) = \$1,100,917$$

If you invested $1,100,917 today to earn 9 percent for the coming year, you would have $1.2 million at the end of the year. You are clearly better off with the proposed land investment (assuming that it really is riskless like the U.S. government bond investment). How much better off are you?

The answer to this question is at the heart of NPV calculations. The land investment project is worth $1,100,917 today to an investor who demands a 9-percent return on this type of investment. You, however, have been able to acquire this investment for only $1,000,000. Thus your present wealth has increased by undertaking this investment by $100,917 ($1,100,917 present value of the projected investment opportunity payoffs minus the required initial investment of $1,000,000). The net present value (NPV) of this investment is $100,917. In general, the (NPV) of an investment is equal to

NPV = Present value of future returns *minus* Initial outlay   **(2.4)**

This example was simplified by assuming that the returns from the investment were received exactly 1 year from the date of the initial outlay. The NPV rule can be generalized to cover returns received over any number of future time periods. In Chapter 5 the present value concept is developed in considerably more detail so that it can be applied in more complex investment settings.

Net Present Value and Shareholder Wealth Maximization

The net present value of an investment made by a firm represents the contribution of that investment to the value of the firm and, accordingly, to the wealth of shareholders. The net present value concept is used to evaluate the *cash flows* generated from the firm's activities. Hence, the NPV concept plays a central role in the achievement of shareholder wealth maximization.

Risk and the NPV Rule

The land investment example assumed that the investment was riskless. Therefore, the rate of return used to compute the discount factor and the net present value was the riskless rate of return available on a U.S. government bond having a 1 year maturity. What if you do not believe your investment advisor who says that the construction of the new interchange is a certainty or you are not confident about your advisor's estimate of the value of the land in 1 year? To compensate for the perceived risk of this investment, you decide that you require a 19 percent rate of return on your investment. Using a 19-percent required rate of return in calculating the discount factor, the present value of the expected $1.2 million sales price of the land is $1,008,403 [$1.2 million times (1/1.19)]. Thus, the NPV of this investment declines to $8,403. The increase in the perceived risk of the investment results in a dramatic decline in its NPV.

As we shall see throughout the text, a primary problem facing financial managers is the difficulty of evaluating the risk associated with investments and then translating that risk into a discount rate that reflects an adequate level of risk compensation. Later in this chapter we discuss factors that affect investment risk and influence the required rate of return on an investment.

THE U.S. FINANCIAL SYSTEM: AN OVERVIEW

As discussed in the previous sections, the value of an investment, whether it is a physical asset like a piece of machinery or a financial asset like a bond or share of common stock, is equal to the *net present value* of the investment's *cash flows*. To determine the net present value, the investor's required rate of return must be known. Required rates of return are determined in the financial marketplace. Therefore, it is important for financial managers to understand the functioning of the U.S. financial system and the factors that influence required rates of return.

In considering any economy as a whole, the actual savings for a given period of time must equal the actual investments. This phenomenon is called the *saving–investment cycle*.

Table 2-2 presents a summary of the saving–investment cycle in the United States for 1987. Total gross savings for that year equaled $560.4 billion—$104.2 billion from personal savings by individuals, $561.1 billion

TABLE 2-2

U.S. Gross Savings and Investment, 1987 (in billions of dollars)		
Personal savings		$104.2
Gross business savings:		
Undistributed profits	$ 81.1	
Depreciation allowances	480.0	561.1
Government surplus or deficit (−)		− 104.9
Gross savings		$560.4
Gross private domestic investment		$712.9
Net foreign investment		− 160.6
Statistical discrepancy		8.1
Gross investment		$560.4

SOURCE: *Federal Reserve Bulletin* (January, 1989).

FIGURE 2.1

**Flow-of-Funds
Diagram**

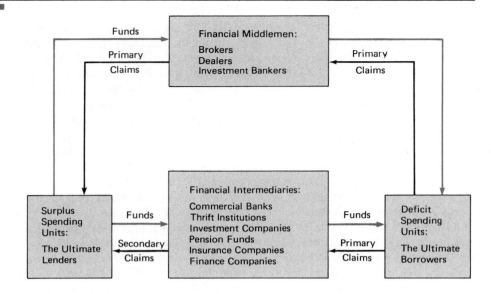

from business, and a government deficit of $104.9 billion. (This last figure is a combination of federal, state, and local deficits, and it may be viewed as dissavings.) Gross investment also totaled $560.4 billion—$712.9 billion in gross private domestic investments less $160.6 billion in net foreign investments. This latter figure indicates that investments of foreign entities in the United States exceeded the investments of U.S. entities abroad by $160.6 billion. (Because these data are not final, there is a statistical discrepancy of $8.1 billion.)

The saving–investment cycle depends on net savers, or *surplus spending units,* and net investors, or *deficit spending units.* The cycle is completed when the surplus spending units transfer funds to the deficit spending units. The main purpose of the U.S. financial system—including the financial markets and all financial institutions—is to facilitate this transfer of funds. Figure 2-1 graphically depicts this continual flow.

Funds flow from surplus spending units, such as households, to deficit spending units, such as businesses, through *financial middlemen* and *financial intermediaries. Financial middlemen* include *brokers,* who buy securities for investors; *dealers,* who sell securities to investors out of an inventory they carry; and *investment bankers,*[5] who assist corporations in selling their securities. These securities are called *primary claims,* because they are sold directly by the borrower and bought directly by the saver (lender).

Financial intermediaries include commercial banks, thrift institutions, investment companies, pension funds, insurance companies, and finance companies. They differ from financial middlemen in that they issue *secondary claims* to the lender instead of primary claims. (A bank savings account is an example of a secondary claim.) A financial intermediary may lend money to a corporation even though there is a small chance that the corporation will default on its loan. In general, individuals or households are unwilling to lend funds to a corporation under these circumstances, but they will allow a commercial bank to use their funds, because the bank can guarantee them both liquidity and safety.

[5] The role of investment bankers in corporate finance is discussed in more detail in Chapter 16.

Thus, financial intermediaries facilitate the transfer of funds. They are compensated for their services by an *interest rate spread*. For example, a bank might loan money to a business at an average of 11 percent interest, pay depositors an average of 8 percent interest, and use the 3 percent difference to pay employee salaries and other expenses, as well as to provide a return to their stockholders. The various financial intermediaries are examined in more detail later in this section.

Financial Assets

Whereas *money* is the most obvious financial asset, there are others as well, including *debt securities* and *equity securities*. Both debt and equity securities represent claims against the assets and future earnings of the corporation. Debt and equity securities are financial *assets* of the investors who own them and, at the same time, these securities appear on the *liabilities* and *stockholders' equity* side of the issuing company's balance sheet.

Financial Markets

Financial markets are the vehicles through which financial assets are bought, sold, and traded. They generally are classified as *money* or *capital markets* and *primary* or *secondary markets*.

MONEY AND CAPITAL MARKETS. *Money markets* deal in *short-term* securities having maturities of 1 year or less. *Capital markets* deal in *long-term* securities having maturities greater than 1 year. (In both cases the 1-year breaking point is somewhat arbitrary.)

Most large corporations participate in the money markets, especially when they have more cash on hand than is needed to run their businesses. For example, Ford Motor Company had over $9 billion in short-term investments at the end of 1988—approximately 43 percent of its current assets. By participating in the money market, the company earned interest, rather than leaving its funds in a non-interest-bearing commercial bank checking account.

Corporations enter the capital markets to obtain long-term funds, either debt or equity. Most large U.S. corporations are unable to generate enough funds *internally* to satisfy their needs, so they raise additional funds *externally* in the capital markets. For example, during 1987 Reynolds Metals made capital expenditures of $176 million, invested an additional $78 million in working capital, paid $32 million of common and preferred stock dividends, and retired $623 million of preferred stock and debt. During the same year Reynolds generated only $371 million of cash flow internally. As a result, Reynolds had to sell substantial amounts of new common stock and long-term debt.

PRIMARY AND SECONDARY MARKETS. An investor who purchases *new* securities is participating in a *primary* financial market. Net proceeds from the sale of new securities go directly to the issuing company. On virtually any given business day the *Wall Street Journal* contains announcements about the issuance of new debt and equity securities. (These are called *tombstones* because of their resemblance to epitaphs.)

An investor who resells existing securities is participating in a *secondary* financial market. Secondary markets are well established in the United States, where stocks can be traded on the "floor" of a security exchange, such as the New York Stock Exchange (NYSE) or the American Stock Exchange (ASE or AMEX). (Some debt securities, such as bonds, also are traded on these exchanges.) Both the New York and the American stock exchanges are located in the Wall Street financial district of New York City. In addition, there are various regional security exchanges around the country, including the Midwest Exchange in Chicago and the Pacific Stock Exchange in San Francisco and Los Angeles.

Most individuals who invest in stocks are involved with secondary financial markets. Participation in these markets is relatively easy. Suppose, for example, that Susan Jones desires to purchase a stock that is traded, or "listed," on the NYSE. She telephones a security or brokerage firm that is a member of (that is, owns a "seat" on) that exchange. The firm wires Jones's order to its representative on the exchange floor, who purchases the stock for her.

Stocks that are not traded on security exchange floors are said to be traded "over-the-counter." The over-the-counter market is normally conducted by telephone and computer reporting of price quotations between brokerage firms that "make a market"; that is, agree to buy and sell a particular security. Appendix 1A provides sample stock and bond price information from the *Wall Street Journal*.

Financial Intermediaries

As indicated earlier in this section, a variety of different financial intermediaries exist to facilitate the flow of funds between surplus spending units and deficit spending units. These different financial intermediaries specialize in the types of deposits they accept (sources of funds) and the types of investments they make (uses of funds).

COMMERCIAL BANKS. Commercial banks accept both demand deposits (in the form of checking accounts) and time deposits (in the form of savings accounts and certificates of deposit). These funds are loaned to individuals, businesses, and governments. They are an important source of short-term loans. Seasonal businesses, such as retailers, certain manufacturers (for example, those who deal in leisure products), some food processors, and builders often require short-term financing to help them through peak periods. Many other types of businesses have a more or less continuing need for short-term financing and make prior arrangements with their banks to borrow on short notice. Thus, banks provide significant amounts of both temporary and "permanent" short-term financing.[6]

Banks are also a major source of *term loans*, or those that have maturities greater than 1 year.[7] The proceeds from term loans can be used to finance current assets, such as inventory or accounts receivable, and to finance the purchase of fixed plant facilities and equipment, as well as to repay other debts.

Through their trust departments, commercial banks also invest their clients' funds in corporate securities.

---

[6] Short-term bank credit is discussed further in Chapter 20.
[7] Term loans are examined in Chapter 15.

THRIFT INSTITUTIONS. Thrift institutions include savings and loan associations, mutual savings banks, and credit unions. These institutions accept both demand and time deposits. Savings and loan associations and mutual savings banks invest most of their funds in home mortgages, whereas credit unions are engaged primarily in consumer loans.

INVESTMENT COMPANIES. Investment companies, such as mutual funds and real estate investment trusts (REITs), pool the funds of many savers and invest these funds in various types of assets. Mutual funds invest in financial assets, such as debt and equity securities of corporations or money market instruments, depending on the objectives of the fund. Mutual funds attempt to achieve superior performance through diversification[8] and professional investment management. REITs, as the name suggests, invest their pooled funds in real estate.

PENSION FUNDS. Private pension funds pool the contributions of employees (and/or employers) and invest these funds in various types of financial assets, such as corporate securities, or real assets, such as real estate. Pension funds are often managed by bank trust departments and life insurance companies.

INSURANCE COMPANIES. Insurance companies receive periodic or lump-sum payments (known as premiums) from individuals or organizations in exchange for agreeing to make certain future contractual payments. Life insurance companies make payments to a beneficiary based on certain events, such as the death or disability of the insured party. Property and casualty insurance companies make payments when a financial loss occurs due to such events as fire, theft, accident, and illness. The premiums received are used to build reserves to pay future claims. These reserves are invested in various types of assets such as corporate securities.

FINANCE COMPANIES. Finance companies obtain funds by issuing their own debt securities and through loans from commercial banks. These funds are used to make loans to individuals and businesses. Some finance companies are formed to finance the sale of the parent company's products. A well-known example is General Motors Acceptance Corporation (GMAC).

Suppliers of Capital

Over the past decade there has been a major shift in the mix of the suppliers of funds in the U.S. capital markets. For example, during the period 1977–1979 funds were loaned through the U.S. capital markets at an annual rate of about $357 billion. During the first half of 1988, this figure had grown to an annual rate of $695 billion. During the early period, private U.S. investors provided 62.7 percent of these funds. Insurance companies and pension funds provided 20.9 percent, foreign banks and investors provided 3.9 percent, and the balance came from miscellaneous sources. By 1988, private investors were providing only 44.7 percent of the total. The share

---

[8] *Diversification* is the act of investing in a set of securities having different risk-return characteristics. The topic is covered in Chapter 8.

provided by foreign banks and investors grew to 20.9 percent, and insurance and pension funds provided 31.8 percent.[9] Thus, it can be seen that the mix of capital suppliers has changed dramatically over the past decade. Proportionately more funds are coming from abroad or are being channeled through insurance companies and pension funds. Thus, the United States is growing increasingly dependent upon international financial markets to supply its capital needs. The role of international financial markets is covered in more detail in Chapter 21.

THE RELATIONSHIP BETWEEN RISK AND RETURN

Understanding the tradeoff between risk and required (and expected) rates of return is integral to effective financial decision making. For example, investors who purchase shares of common stock hope to receive returns that will exceed those that might be earned from alternative investments, such as a savings account, U.S. government bonds, or high-quality corporate bonds. Investors recognize that the expected return from common stock over the long run tends to be higher than the expected return from less risky investments. To receive higher returns, however, investors must be prepared to accept a higher level of risk.

Key Definitions

Before continuing the discussion of risk–return relationships, it is necessary to define some important terms and concepts.

HOLDING PERIOD RETURNS. The return from holding a security can be defined by the following equation:

$$\text{Holding period return (\%)} = \frac{\text{Ending price} - \text{Beginning price} + \text{Distributions}}{\text{Beginning price}} \times 100\% \quad \textbf{(2.5)}$$

Distributions are the interest on debt or the dividends on stock.

To illustrate, suppose you purchased 100 shares of Unisys Corporation for $29 a year ago. During the year you received $1 per share in dividends, and you sold the shares now for $32 each. Your holding period return would be calculated as

$$\text{Holding period return (\%)} = \frac{\$32 - \$29 + \$1}{\$29} \times 100\% = 13.8\%$$

Returns are expressed as a percentage or fraction and usually are quoted on an annual basis.

The return just computed is called a *realized*, or *ex post* (after-the-fact) return. Realized returns differ from *expected*, or *ex ante* (before-the-fact) returns. Although ex ante returns are calculated in the same manner as ex

[9] Vivian Brownstein, "Where All the Money Comes From," *Fortune* (January 2, 1989), pp. 75–80.

post returns, ending prices and distributions for expected returns are *estimated* values, whereas ending prices and distributions for realized returns are *actual* values.

RISK. The term *risk* is used in a broad sense to refer to deviations from expectations. In finance, risk often is measured in terms of the variability of returns. Suppose, for example, that you decide to deposit a sum of money in a passbook savings account at an insured commercial bank that offers to pay an expected annual return of 5.5 percent. Because your deposit is insured by an agency of the U.S. government, deviations from your expected 5.5 percent return would most probably be zero. Thus, the risk associated with a passbook account is considered to be nearly zero.

Now suppose you invest your money in common stock. You hope that the price of your stock will increase, but you also recognize that the price may decrease. Deviations from your expectation of an increased price are likely to be high. Therefore, the risk associated with common stock investments is considered to be high.

EXPECTED RETURNS AND REQUIRED RETURNS. The concept of an *expected return* reflects the benefits (distributions and price appreciation) an investor *anticipates* receiving from an investment. In contrast, the concept of a *required return* reflects the return an investor *demands* as compensation for postponing consumption and assuming risk. As we shall see, required returns are one of the two key determinants of the value of an investment, whether that investment is a physical asset or a financial security. The other key determinant of value is the anticipated cash flows from the investment.

The value of an investment is determined as investors compare the expected (ex ante) returns from the investment with the return required on that investment, given its risk characteristics. When the expected return from an investment is greater than or equal to the required return, an investor will find the investment attractive.

MARKET EFFICIENCY. In an efficiently functioning capital market, security (for example, stock and bond) prices will be bid to a level where the expected return just equals the required return. When new information about the expected returns from a security or the risk of that security is made known to participants in financial markets, the price of the security will adjust quickly to reflect this new information. Security prices also will adjust quickly to reflect changes in the general level of interest rates, because general interest rate changes influence the required returns on all securities.

Market efficiency requires that a large number of wealth maximizing investors continually analyze securities, in an attempt to identify the "true" value of the security. U.S. financial markets have millions of investors and many specialized institutions, such as brokerage firms, that invest substantial resources to uncover the true value of various financial securities.

Many tests have been conducted of the efficiency of U.S. financial markets. The results of these tests indicate that U.S. financial markets are highly efficient, in the sense that they quickly reflect information (risk, expected returns, and interest rate levels) relevant to determining the value of a security. Tests of market efficiency occasionally have found apparent exceptions to the market efficiency concept. However, the market efficiency concept generally has been supported by this research.

Efficient financial markets offer an *unbiased* estimate of the "true" value of a security. Thus, market efficiency has important implications for the practice of financial management. In an efficient capital market, shareholders can measure the performance of a firm's managers by observing the firm's stock price. Managers who take actions that result in increases in the firm's stock price are contributing directly to the goal of maximizing shareholder wealth.

Risk and Required Returns

The relationship between risk and required returns can be defined as follows:

$$\text{Required return} = \text{Risk-free return} + \text{Risk premium} \qquad \textbf{(2.6)}$$

A *risk premium* is a potential "reward" that an investor can expect to receive from making a risky investment. Investors generally are considered to be *risk averse;* that is, they expect, on average, to be compensated for the risk they assume when making an investment. Thus, over the long term, expected returns and required returns from securities will tend to be equal.

Investors who buy bonds receive interest payments and a return of principal as compensation for postponing consumption and accepting risk. Similarly, common stock investors expect to receive dividends and price appreciation from their stock. The rate of return required by these investors represents a *cost of capital* to the firm. This required rate of return is used by a firm's managers when computing the net present value of the cash flows expected to be generated from the company's investments. The required rate of return on a security also is an important determinant of the market value of financial securities, including common stock, preferred stock, and bonds.

The required rate of return on a financial security is determined in the financial marketplace and depends on the supply of loanable funds and the demand for these funds plus a premium to reflect the risk of a security's promised cash flows. In this section we consider some of the important determinants of required rates of return on financial securities.

THE RISK-FREE RATE OF RETURN. The concept of a risk-free rate of return refers to the return available on a security with no risk of default. In the case of debt securities, no default risk means that promised interest and principal payments are guaranteed to be made. The best example of risk-free securities are U.S. government bonds. There is no risk of default on these securities because the U.S. government always can print more money. Of course, if the government recklessly prints money to pay its obligations, the purchasing power of this money will decline. Nevertheless, the buyer of a U.S. government bond always is assured of receiving the promised *dollar* payments.

The risk-free rate of return is composed of two elements. The first, called a *real rate of return*, is the return that investors would require from a security having no risk of default in a period of no expected inflation. It is the amount necessary to convince investors to postpone current, *real*, consumption opportunities. The real rate of return is determined by the interaction of the supply of funds made available by savers and the demand for funds for investment. Historically, the real rate of return has been estimated to average in the range of 2 to 4 percent.

The second component of the risk-free rate of return is an *inflation, or purchasing power loss premium*. Investors also require compensation for expected losses in purchasing power when they postpone current consumption and lend funds. Consequently, a premium for expected inflation also is included in the required return from any security. For example, for the 10 year period from 1978 through 1987, the compound annual rate of return that investors would have achieved from holding short-term, risk-free U.S. Treasury bills was 9.17 percent. Over the same time the average annual inflation rate was 6.39 percent.[10] *Increases in expected inflation rates normally lead to increases in the required rates of return on all securities.*

At any point in time, the required risk-free rate of return from any security can be estimated from the yields on short-term U.S. government securities, such as 90-day Treasury bills.

THE MATURITY RISK PREMIUM. The return required on a security also is influenced by the maturity of that security. The *term structure of interest rates* is the pattern of interest rate yields (required returns) for securities that differ only in the length of time to maturity. Plotting interest rates (percent) on the vertical axis and the length of time to maturity (years) on the horizontal axis results in a *yield curve*. Three yield curves for U.S. government securities are shown in Figure 2-2.[11] Note the different shapes of

---

[10] *Stocks, Bonds, Bills and Inflation, 1988 Yearbook* (Chicago: Ibbotson Associates, 1988), p. 84.

[11] The primary reason for examining U.S. government securities is that we are able to hold many of the factors affecting yields, such as default risk, constant. Corporate debt security issues, even for the same company, often differ significantly with respect to their key provisions, including sinking fund, call, conversion, subordination, and mortgage features. Hence, these bond issues differ with respect to risk. Consequently, it is difficult to use corporate debt securities to make yield versus time-to-maturity comparisons. However, the same general conclusions concerning the term structure of interest rates apply to these securities.

Yield Curves Showing the Term Structure of Interest Rates for U.S. Treasury Securities   FIGURE 2-2
SOURCE: *Federal Reserve Bulletin* (October 1981 and April 1989).

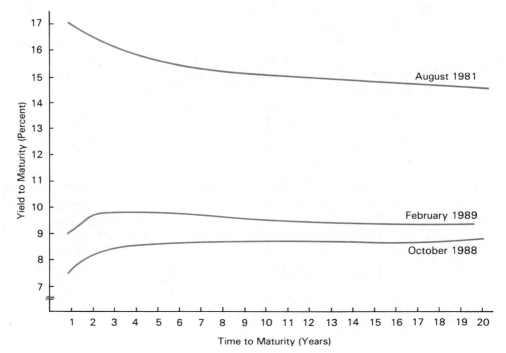

the three yield curves. The yield curve for August 1981 is *downward sloping*, indicating that the longer the time to maturity, the lower is the required return on the security. The yield curve for October 1988 is *upward sloping*, indicating that the longer the time to maturity, the higher is the required return on the security.[12]

In general, the yield curve has been upward sloping more often than it has been downward sloping. For example, between 1985 and the end of 1988, the yield on 3-month U.S. government Treasury bills has averaged approximately 6.6 percent. In contrast, the yield on 10-year U.S. government bonds averaged 8.9 percent, and the yield on 30-year U.S. government bonds averaged 9.1 percent.[13]

A number of theories have been advanced to explain the shape of the yield curve. Yield curves can be viewed as reflecting an *expectation regarding future interest rate levels*. If future short-term interest rates (and inflation rates) are expected to rise, the yield curve will tend to be upward sloping. In contrast, a downward sloping yield curve reflects an expectation of declining future short-term interest rates (and inflation rates).

The yield curve also reflects what is called a *maturity premium*. The maturity premium (often called a liquidity premium) theory of the yield curve holds that required returns on long-term securities tend to be greater the longer the time to maturity. The maturity premium reflects a preference by many lenders for shorter maturities, because the interest rate risk associated with these securities is less than with longer-term securities. As we shall see in Chapter 6, the value of a bond tends to vary more as interest rates change, the longer the term to maturity. Thus if interest rates rise, the holder of a long-term bond will find that the value of her investment has declined substantially more than the holder of a short-term bond. In addition, the short-term bond holder has the option of holding the bond for the short time remaining to maturity and then reinvesting the proceeds from his bond at the new higher interest rate. The long-term bond holder must wait much longer before this opportunity is available. Accordingly, it is argued that whatever the shape of the yield curve, a maturity or liquidity premium is reflected in it. The maturity premium is larger for long-term bonds than for short-term bonds.

The maturity structure of interest rates also changes depending on the relative supply and demand for securities in various maturity ranges. Some investors, such as insurance companies and pension funds, prefer to hold long-term securities. In contrast, commercial banks prefer securities with shorter terms to maturity. Accompanying the fluctuations in the demand and supply for bonds of different maturities by investors and borrowers, there will be fluctuations in the level of interest rates across maturity horizons.

THE DEFAULT RISK PREMIUM. As discussed earlier, U.S. government securities generally are considered to be free of default risk; that is, the risk that interest and principal will not be paid as promised in the bond indenture. In contrast, corporate bonds are subject to varying degrees of default

---

[12] Upward and downward sloping yield curves are not the only possible shapes. At various times in the past, the yield curve has been relatively flat and also has been "hump-shaped"; that is, high intermediate-term yields and low short-term and long-term yields. In February 1989 the curve was hump-shaped, as shown in Figure 2-2.

[13] *Federal Reserve Bulletin* (Washington, D.C.: Board of Governors of the Federal Reserve System, January, 1989).

risk. Investors require higher rates of return on securities subject to default risk. Bond rating agencies, such as Moody's, Standard and Poor's, Duff and Phelps, and Fitch, provide evaluations of the default risk of many corporate bonds in the form of bond ratings. Moody's, for example, rates bonds on a 9-point scale from Aaa, Aa through C, where Aaa-rated bonds have the lowest expected default risk.[14] As can be seen in Table 2-3, the yields on bonds increase as the risk of default increases, reflecting the positive relationship between risk and required returns. Over time, the spread between the required returns on bonds having various levels of default risk varies, reflecting the economic prospects, and the resulting probability of default.

THE SENIORITY RISK PREMIUM. Corporations issue many different types of securities. These securities differ with respect to their claim on the cash flows generated by the company and the claim on the company's assets in the case of default. A partial listing of these securities, from the least senior (that is, from the security having the lowest priority claim on cash flows and assets) to the most senior includes the following: common stock, preferred stock, income bonds, subordinated debentures, debentures, second mortgage bonds, and first mortgage bonds. Generally, the less senior are the claims of the security holder, the greater will be the required rate of return demanded by investors in that security. For example, the holders of bonds issued by Exxon are assured that they will receive interest and principal payments on these bonds except in the highly unlikely event that the company faces bankruptcy. In contrast, common stockholders have no such assurance regarding dividend payments. Also, in the case of bankruptcy, all senior claimholders must be paid before common stockholders receive any proceeds from the liquidation of the firm. Accordingly, common stockholders require a higher rate of return on their investment in Exxon stock than do Exxon bond holders.

BUSINESS AND FINANCIAL RISK PREMIUMS. Within individual security classes, one observes significant differences in required rates of return between firms. For example, the required rate of return on the common stock of Prime Computer is considerably higher than the required rate of return

---

[14] A more detailed discussion of the bond rating process is contained in Chapter 6. The Moody's bond rating system also applies numerical modifiers, 1, 2, and 3, in each generic rating classification from Aa through B. A modifier of 1, such as Aa1, indicates that the bond ranks at the high (better quality) end of the Aa category. A modifier of 2 indicates a mid-range ranking, and a 3 indicates a bond at the low (quality) end of the Aa rating category.

TABLE 2-3

Relationship between Default Risk and Required Returns	
Security	**Yield**
U.S. Treasury Bonds (30 year)	8.88%
Aaa-rated Corporate Bonds	9.44
Aa-rated Corporate Bonds	9.68
A-rated Corporate Bonds	9.97
Baa-rated Corporate Bonds	10.39

SOURCE: Board of Governors of the Federal Reserve System, *Federal Reserve Bulletin* (Washington, D.C.: January 1989), p. A24.

on the common stock of IBM. The difference in the required rate of return on the securities of these two companies reflects differences in their business and financial risk. The *business risk* of a firm refers to the variability in the firm's operating earnings over time. Business risk is influenced by many factors, including variability in sales and operating costs over a business cycle, the diversity of a firm's product line, the market power of the firm, and the choice of production technology. As a much larger, more powerful, and diverse firm, IBM can be expected to have a lower perceived level of business risk and a resulting lower required return on its common stock (all other things held constant).

Financial risk refers to the additional variability in a company's earnings per share that results from the use of fixed-cost sources of funds, such as debt and preferred stock. In addition, as debt financing increases, the risk of bankruptcy increases. For example, Prime Computer had a long-term debt to common equity ratio of 1.2 times in 1988. In comparison, the long-term debt to common equity ratio was approximately 0.12 for IBM in 1988. This difference in financial risk will lead to lower required returns on the common stock of IBM compared to the common stock of Prime.

THE MARKETABILITY RISK PREMIUM. Marketability risk refers to the ability of an investor to buy and sell a company's securities quickly and without a significant loss of value. For example, there is very little marketability risk for the shares of stock of most companies that are traded on the New York or American Stock Exchange or listed on the NASDAQ system for over-the-counter stocks. For these securities there is an active market. Trades can be executed almost instantaneously with low transactions costs at the current market price. In contrast, if you own shares in a rural Nebraska bank, you might find it difficult to locate a buyer for those shares (unless you owned a controlling interest in the bank). When a buyer is found, that buyer may not be willing to pay the price that you could get for similar shares of a larger bank listed on the New York Stock Exchange. The marketability risk premium can be significant for securities that are not regularly traded, such as the shares of many small and medium-size firms.

SECURITY TYPE, RISK, AND REQUIRED (EXPECTED) RETURNS. Figure 2-3 illustrates the relationship between required (and expected) rates of return and risk, as represented by the various risk premiums just discussed. As shown in Figure 2-3 the lowest risk security is represented by short-term U.S. Treasury bills. All other securities have one or more elements of additional risk, resulting in increasing required (expected) returns by investors. The order illustrated in this figure is indicative of the general relationship between risk and required returns of various security types. There will be situations that result in differences in the ordering of risk and required returns. For example, it is possible that the risk of some junk (high risk) bonds may be so great that investors require a higher rate of return on these bonds than they require on high grade common stocks.

The relationship between risk and return can be observed by examining the returns actually earned by investors in various types of securities over long periods of time. Finance professionals believe that investor expectations of the relative returns anticipated from various types of securities are heavily influenced by the returns that have been earned on these securities

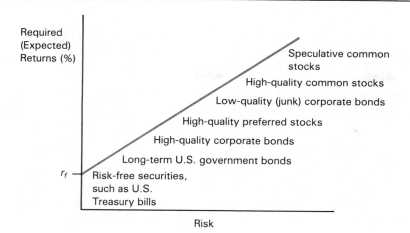

F I G U R E 2-3

**Conceptual Risk–
Return Relationship**

in the past. Table 2-4 shows the returns that have been earned by investors over long periods of time. This table confirms the general positive nature of the relationship between risk and return.

NET PRESENT VALUE, REQUIRED RETURNS, CASH FLOWS, AND STOCK PRICES

This chapter has introduced three of the most important concepts in the study and practice of financial management. In an efficient financial market, stock prices provide an unbiased estimate of the true value of an enterprise. Stock prices reflect a *net present value* estimate of the firm's *expected cash flows*, evaluated at an appropriate *required rate of return*. The required rate of return is determined by conditions in the financial markets, including the supply of funds from savers, the investment demand for funds, and expectations regarding future inflation rates. The required rate of return on a security also depends on the seniority of the security, the maturity of that security, the business and financial risk of the firm issuing the security, the risk of default, and the marketability of the security. In the following chapters the net present value, cash flow, and required rate of return concepts are developed further in the context of determining shareholder wealth maximizing solutions to resource allocation problems facing financial managers.

T A B L E 2-4

Annual Historical Rates of Return: 1926–1987	
Security Type	**Mean Annual Return**
U.S. Treasury Bills	3.5%
Long-Term Government Bonds	4.6
Long-Term Corporate Bonds	5.2
Common Stocks	12.0
Small Company Common Stocks	17.7

SUMMARY

■ The cash flows from investments both in physical assets, such as a building or manufacturing equipment, and financial assets, such as common stock or bonds, are one of the primary determinants of the value of these investments.

■ The *after-tax operating cash flow concept* is equal to operating cash flows before tax less tax payments. Operating cash flows before tax equal total cash revenues minus total cash operating expenses. The after-tax operating cash flow concept is used primarily when estimating cash flows for capital investment analysis purposes.

■ The *free cash flow concept* is used in long-range financial planning and when evaluating potential acquisition candidates. Free cash flow is equal to the after-tax operating cash flow minus after-tax interest payments, minus preferred stock dividends and redemptions, minus debt redemptions, minus required investments in net working capital, minus required investments in property, plant, and equipment.

■ The net present value (NPV) rule is central to financial analysis. The net present value of an investment is equal to the present value of future returns minus the initial outlay. Future outlays are discounted back to the present at a required rate of return that reflects the perceived risk of the investment.

■ The net present value of an investment made by a firm represents the contribution of the investment to the value of the firm and, accordingly, to the wealth of shareholders.

■ The main purpose of an economy's financial system is to facilitate the transfer of funds from *surplus spending units* to *deficit spending units*. *Financial middlemen*, such as investment bankers, bring together the surplus and deficit spending units in the capital markets so that funds can be transferred. *Financial intermediaries*, such as commercial banks, receive *primary claims* from their borrowers and issue *secondary claims* to their lenders. Secondary claims have different risk and liquidity characteristics than primary claims.

■ *Financial assets* consist of *money, debt securities*, and *equity securities*.

■ Financial assets are bought and sold in *financial markets*. Financial markets include *money* and *capital markets*, and *primary* and *secondary markets*. Money markets deal in securities with maturities of approximately 1 year or less, whereas capital markets deal in securities with maturities greater than 1 year. Primary markets are those in which *new* securities are issued; secondary markets are those in which *existing* securities are traded.

■ The *expected rate of return* from a security reflects the distributions an investor *anticipates* receiving from an investment. The *required rate of return* reflects the return an investor *demands* as compensation for postponing consumption and assuming risk. In efficient financial markets, required rates of return and expected rates of return should be approximately equal.

■ The required rate of return on a security is a function of the general level of interest rates, as reflected in the risk-free rate of return, the maturity risk of the security, the default risk of the security, the business and financial risk of the firm that issues the security, the seniority risk of the security, and the marketability risk of the security.

■ The greater the risk associated with the returns from a security or an investment in a physical asset, the greater will be the required rate of return on that investment.

QUESTIONS AND TOPICS FOR DISCUSSION

1. Describe and discuss the saving–investment cycle.
2. What roles do financial middlemen and financial intermediaries play in the operation of the U.S. financial system? How do the two differ?
3. How do money and capital markets differ? How do primary and secondary markets differ? Discuss each type.
4. Describe the various types of financial intermediaries, including the sources of their funds and the types of investments they make.
5. What is the *term structure* of interest rates?
6. What is the *risk structure* of interest rates?
7. How is *risk* defined in a financial sense?
8. Discuss the general relationship between risk and expected return.
9. Distinguish between the terms *after-tax operating cash flow* and *free cash flow*.
10. Is it possible for a firm to report large positive profits and a negative operating cash flow during the same year? Explain why or why not.
11. What is the relationship between the concepts of net present value and shareholder wealth maximization?
12. Describe the concept of market efficiency. In what sense is this concept an important part of the shareholder wealth maximization objective?
13. What factors determine investors' required rates of return on corporate bonds? Common stocks? U.S. government bonds?

PROBLEMS*

1. An investor bought 100 shares of Venus Corporation common stock 1 year ago for $40 per share. She just sold the shares for $44 each, and during the year she received four quarterly dividend checks for $40 each. Calculate the investor's percentage holding period return.
2. An investor bought ten Ellis Industries, Inc. long-term bonds 1 year ago, when they were first issued by the company. He paid $1,000 each for the bonds, and today the bonds are selling at $950 each (long-term interest rates have increased slightly over the past year). The bonds have a stated interest rate of 12 percent per year. The investor received an interest payment equaling $60 per bond 6 months ago and has just received another $60 interest payment per bond. Calculate the investor's percentage holding period return for the 1 year he has held the bonds.
3. a. Suppose a U.S. Treasury bill, maturing in 1 year, can be purchased today for $92,500. Assuming that the security is held until maturity, the investor will receive $100,000 (face amount). Determine the percentage holding period return on this investment.
   b. Suppose a National Telephone and Telegraph (NTT) Company bond, maturing in 1 year, can be purchased today for $975. Assuming that the bond is held until maturity, the investor will receive $1,000 (principal) plus 7

* Colored numbers denote problems that have check answers provided at the end of the book.

percent interest (that is, .07 × $1000 = $70). Determine the percentage holding period return on this investment.

c. Determine the implied risk premium on NTT bonds.

4. a. National Telephone and Telegraph (NTT) Company common stock currently sells for $60 per share. NTT is expected to pay a $4 dividend during the coming year and the price of the stock is expected to increase to $65 a year from now. Determine the *expected* (ex ante) percentage holding period return on NTT common stock.

b. Suppose that 1 year later NTT's common stock is selling for $75 per share. During the 1-year period, NTT paid a $4 common stock dividend. Determine the *realized* (ex post) percentage holding period return on NTT common stock.

c. Repeat Part b given that NTT's common stock is selling for $58 one year later.

d. Repeat Part b given that NTT's common stock is selling for $50 one year later.

5. During 1989 the Viking Corporation reported total sales revenues (all cash) of $10 million. Cash operating expenses were $5.6 million, depreciation was $1.4 million, and Viking's tax rate was 40 percent. Compute Viking's after-tax operating cash flow for 1989.

6. Omni Enterprises is considering the acquisition of Marathon Products. For the coming year, Omni expects Marathon to report after-tax operating cash flows of $100 million. Interest expense is estimated to be $10 million; preferred stock dividend payments are $2 million; preferred stock redemption requirements are $5 million; long-term debt redemption requirements are $14 million; additional working capital investment of $15 million is required; and required investments in property, plant, and equipment total $30 million. The tax rate is 40 percent. Compute Marathon's expected free cash flow.

7. An investment project requires an outlay of $2 million immediately. After 1 year, your firm expects to be able to sell this investment to another firm for $3 million. Given the risk associated with this investment, you determine that you require a 20 percent rate of return. What is the expected contribution of this investment to shareholder wealth of your firm?

8. The real rate of interest has been estimated to be 3 percent, and the expected long-term annual inflation rate is 7 percent.

a. What is the current risk-free rate of return on 1-year Treasury bills?

b. If the yield on 10-year U.S. Treasury bonds is 12 percent, what is the maturity risk premium between a 10-year bond and a 1-year bond?

c. If American Airlines bonds, scheduled to mature in 10 years, currently sell to yield 13 percent, what is the default risk premium on these bonds?

d. If investors in the common stock of American Airlines require a 16-percent rate of return, what is the seniority risk premium on American's common stock?

▅▅▅ SELECTED REFERENCES

Bowden, E. V. *Money Banking and the Financial System.* St. Paul, MN: West Publishing Company, 1989.

Copeland, Thomas E., and J. Fred Weston. *Financial Theory and Corporate Policy*, 3d ed. Reading, MA: Addison-Wesley, 1988.

Hoffman, William H., and Eugene Willis, General Editors. *West's Federal Taxation: Corporations, Partnerships, Estates, and Trusts*, 1989 Annual Edition. St. Paul, MN: West Publishing Company, 1989.

Kaufman, George G. *The U.S. Financial System: Money, Markets, and Institutions,* 4th ed. Englewood Cliffs, NJ: Prentice-Hall, 1989.

Kidwell, David S., and Richard L. Peterson. *Financial Institutions, Markets, and Money,* 3d ed. Hinsdale, IL: Dryden Press, 1987.

Van Horne, James C. *Financial Market Rates and Flows,* 2d ed. Englewood Cliffs, NJ: Prentice-Hall, 1984.

Federal Income Taxes

GLOSSARY OF NEW TERMS

Capital gains Profits on the sale of capital assets.

Capital losses Losses on the sale of capital assets.

Marginal tax rate The tax rate on the last dollar of taxable income earned by an individual or firm.

S corporation A small business that takes advantage of the corporate form of organization while having its income taxed directly to the stockholders at their individual personal income tax rates.

Tax deduction An amount subtracted from taxable income. For a corporation with a 34 percent marginal tax rate, a $100 tax deduction reduces taxable income by $100 and reduces taxes owed by $34.

◼◼◼ INTRODUCTION

Because so many financial decisions are based on after-tax cash flows, finance and business professionals must have a basic understanding of tax matters. Tax knowledge is essential in making a wide variety of business decisions, including what form of business organization to select, what type of securities to issue, whether to lease or buy business equipment, and whether to expense or capitalize a $10,000 piece of equipment in a small business.

In October 1986 Congress passed the Tax Reform Act of 1986. The tax bill represents the most comprehensive tax reform measure since the passage of the 1954 Tax Code. Generally, the Tax Reform Act of 1986 lowers tax rates on income for both individuals and corporations and also decreases the deductions that may be taken.

◼◼◼ CORPORATE INCOME TAXES

In general, the taxable income of a corporation is calculated by subtracting business expenses from revenues. Tax-deductible business expenses normally include the cost of goods sold, selling and administrative expenses, depreciation allowances, and interest expenses.[1] Federal income taxes are

[1] Chapter 9 and Appendix 9A contain a detailed discussion of depreciation methods.

computed on the resulting taxable income. For tax years beginning on or after July 1, 1987, the tax rules imposed on corporations are as follows:

Taxable Income	Rate
$1–$50,000	15%
$50,001–$75,000	25%
Over $75,000	34%

The benefit of the 15 and 25 percent rates is phased out by imposing an additional 5 percent tax on taxable incomes between $100,000 and $335,000. The effect of the additional 5 percent tax is that corporations with taxable incomes of $335,000 or greater pay a flat rate of 34 percent on all taxable income.

The computation of the total tax for three companies (A, B, and C) with taxable incomes of $100,000, $300,000, and $1,000,000, along with the average tax, is shown in Table 2A-1. The *average tax rate* of a corporation is calculated by dividing the total tax by the taxable income. The *marginal tax rate* of a corporation is defined as the tax rate on the last dollar of taxable income. Companies A and C in Table 2A-1 have marginal tax rates of 34 percent; Company B has an effective marginal tax rate of 39 percent. The marginal tax rate is more important than the average tax rate for financial planning purposes. All but the smallest corporations (or firms operating at a loss) are taxed at the 34 percent rate, for tax years beginning on or after July 1, 1987.

Taxable income that is taxed at the 34 percent rate is called *operating* or *ordinary* income. Ordinary income is often contrasted with *capital gains income* and *dividend income*.

Tax Rate Used in the Text

Throughout the text we have used an *assumed* marginal tax rate of 40 percent rather than the *actual* corporate marginal tax rate of 34 percent. There are two reasons for following this convention. First it simplifies many of the calculations. Second, most firms also are subject to state-imposed income taxes. A 40-percent rate is an excellent approximation of the *combined* federal and state income tax rates facing most firms.

Computation of Corporate Income Taxes			T A B L E 2A-1
Taxable Income	**A—$100,000**	**B—$300,000**	**C—$1,000,000**
	$0.15 \times 50,000 = \$ 7,500$ $0.25 \times 25,000 = 6,250$ $0.34 \times 25,000 = 8,500$	$= \$ 22,250$	$= \$ 22,250$
		$0.39 \times 200,000 = \underline{78,000}$	$0.39 \times 235,000 = 91,650$ $0.34 \times 665,000 = \underline{226,100}$
Total Tax	$22,250	$100,250	$340,000*
Average Tax Rate	$\frac{\$ 22,250}{\$100,000} = 22.3\%$	$\frac{\$100,250}{\$300,000} = 33.4\%$	$\frac{\$ 340,000}{\$1,000,000} = 34\%$
Effective Marginal Tax Rate	34%	39%	34%

* For corporations with annual taxable incomes of $335,000 or greater, the total tax can be calculated simply by multiplying taxable income by 34%.

Capital Gains Income

Corporate capital gains income currently (1989) is taxed at the same marginal tax rate as ordinary income. Prior to the enactment of the Tax Reform Act of 1986, capital gains income for most large U.S. corporations was taxed at a lower rate than ordinary income. Corporate capital losses are deductible only against capital gains.

Dividend Income

Dividends received by a corporation normally are entitled to a 70-percent exclusion from federal income taxes. To illustrate, suppose that the Hastings Corporation owns stock in the Fremont Corporation and that Fremont pays $100,000 in dividends in Hastings during 1989. Hastings has to pay taxes on only 30 percent of the $100,000, or $30,000. (The other 70 percent, or $70,000, is excluded; that is, received tax-free. However, Fremont has to pay taxes on its income before paying the $100,000 to Hastings, because dividends are *not* considered tax-deductible expenses.) The $30,000 of taxable dividend income is taxed at ordinary income tax rates.[2] Assuming that Hastings is large enough to have a marginal tax rate of 34 percent, the tax on the dividends is calculated as follows:

$$\$30,000 \times 0.34 = \$10,200$$

For corporations having a marginal tax rate of 34 percent, intercompany dividends are taxed at an effective rate of 10.2 percent; that is, $(1 - 0.7) \times 34\%$.

Loss Carrybacks and Carryforwards

Corporations that sustain net operating losses during a particular year are permitted by tax laws to apply the losses against any taxable income in other years, thereby lowering the taxes owed in those years. If such a loss is applied against a previous year, it is called a *loss carryback;* if it is applied against a succeeding year, it is called a *loss carryforward.*

The tax laws specify that a corporation's net operating loss may be carried back three years and forward fifteen years to offset taxable income in those years. For example, suppose the NOL Corporation incurs a net operating loss totaling $200,000 in 19X6. This loss may be carried back three years to 19X3. If the NOL Corporation had 19X3 taxable income of $125,000, for example, it could receive a tax refund equal to the taxes it paid for that year. The remaining $75,000 portion of the 19X6 net operating loss next could be carried back to 19X4.

SMALL BUSINESS CONCERNS: S CORPORATIONS

The Internal Revenue Code allows certain small businesses to take advantage of the corporate form of organization while having their business in-

---

[2] For corporate shareholders that own 20 percent or more of the voting power and value of the stock of a distributing corporation, there is an 80-percent dividends-received exclusion.

come taxed directly to their shareholders at individual income tax rates. To qualify for S corporation status, a firm may not have more than thirty-five shareholders.

Gains or losses of S corporations are not taxed as corporate income. Rather, they are taxed as individual income to the shareholders regardless of whether the shareholders actually receive any income. For new businesses that incur losses, the S corporation form of organization can be advantageous if the shareholders have other taxable income with which to offset the losses. In addition, S corporations avoid the *double taxation of dividends*, because the corporate income is taxed only once.

TAX RATE IMPLICATIONS FOR FINANCIAL MANAGERS

The existence of corporate income taxes has important implications for financial managers. Although the effect of income taxes on financial decisions are detailed where appropriate throughout the book, in this section a brief overview of some of the critical areas of concern is provided.

Taxes have important implications for capital structure policy because the interest payments associated with debt financing are tax deductible, whereas common stock dividends and preferred stock dividends are not. As a result, a large tax advantage is associated with debt financing. This tax advantage of debt is a prime reason behind leveraged buyouts and financial restructurings.

Dividend policy also is influenced by corporate income taxes. When dividends are paid to common stockholders, these dividends are taxed immediately as income to the stockholder. If, instead of paying dividends, a firm retains and reinvests its earnings, the price of the stock can be expected to increase. Taxes owed on common stock price appreciation are deferred until the stock is sold. The ability to defer taxes on retained earnings influences investor preferences for retention and ultimately capital gains versus dividends. This investor preference has an impact on corporate dividend policy.

Capital expenditure decisions also are influenced by corporate income taxes. Capital expenditures require an outlay of *after-tax* dollars in order to acquire the needed assets. The assets are expected to generate a stream of operating income that is subject to tax. A tax-deductible expense associated with many capital expenditures is depreciation. Depreciation provides a tax deduction equal to a part of the original cost of a depreciable asset, such as machinery or buildings. The tax code details the methods that may be used to depreciate assets. Because depreciation is a noncash expense (the cash outlay was made when the asset was purchased), it simply reduces taxable income and hence reduces the amount of taxes that must be paid. Changes in the tax code that speed up (slow down) the depreciation rate, increase (decrease) the present value of the cash flows from the investment project and make the project a more (less) desirable investment. Therefore, financial managers must pay close attention to expected tax law changes.

Finally, the decision to lease or buy an asset often is motivated by its tax effects. If the lessee (asset user) is losing money or not subject to taxation (a nonprofit enterprise), leasing may be advantageous because the lessor (asset owner) can reflect the tax benefits of the owner in the lease rate charged to the lessee.

These and other tax effects of financial decisions are discussed throughout the text.

QUESTIONS AND TOPICS FOR DISCUSSION

1. What are the differences between the operating income, capital gains income, and dividend income of a corporation? At approximately what rates are these different types of income taxed?
2. What is an *S corporation*?
3. What is meant by the *double taxation of dividends*?

PROBLEMS*

1. Last year, the Connersville Corporation had taxable ordinary income of $2 million and capital gains income of $500,000. The company also had $50,000 in dividend income and paid its stockholders $150,000 in dividends. Based on July 1, 1987, tax rates, calculate the Connersville Corporation's tax bill.
2. Last year the Muncie Corporation had earnings before interest and taxes (operating income) equal to $1 million. It paid $200,000 in dividends to its stockholders and $100,000 in interest to its creditors. During the year the company also repaid a bank loan of $150,000. Assuming a corporate income tax rate of 40 percent on all taxable income, calculate the Muncie Corporation's tax bill.

* Colored numbers denote problems that have check answers provided at the end of the book.

II

Financial Analysis and Forecasting

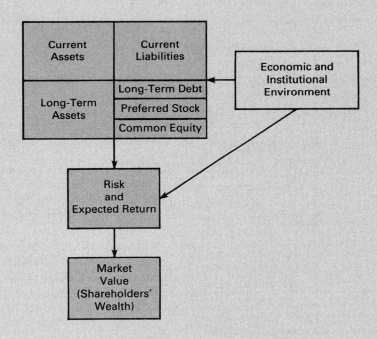

In evaluating the financial performance of a firm, the tools of financial statement analysis can be very helpful. These are discussed in Chapter 3. Chapter 4 looks at the cash flow analysis and forecasting activities of a firm. If the objective of shareholder wealth maximization is to be achieved, the firm must effectively manage and forecast its cash flows. Effective cash flow forecasting also can alert management to potential problem areas well in advance. By carefully evaluating current financial strengths and weaknesses and by managing cash flows effectively, risk and return can be controlled to maximize the value of the firm.

3

Evaluation of Financial Performance

KEY CHAPTER CONCEPTS

1. The evaluation of financial performance involves a series of techniques that can be used to help identify the strengths and weaknesses of a firm.

2. Financial ratios, which use data from a firm's balance sheet, income statement, and certain market data, often are used when evaluating the financial performance of a firm.
   a. *Liquidity ratios* indicate a firm's ability to meet its short-term financial obligations.
   b. *Activity ratios* indicate how efficiently a firm is using its assets to generate sales.
   c. *Financial leverage ratios* indicate a firm's capacity to meet short- and long-term debt obligations.
   d. *Profitability ratios* measure how effectively a firm's management generates profits.
   e. *Market-based ratios* reflect the financial

market's assessment of a company's performance.

3. Common-size financial statements express financial items as percentages (rather than dollar amounts) and are useful in evaluating financial performance.

4. *Trend analysis* evaluates a firm's performance over time, whereas *comparative analysis* evaluates a firm's performance relative to other firms.

5. When evaluating a firm's performance based on its balance sheet, income statement, and a series of financial ratios, a good financial analyst must be aware of the accounting techniques used by the firm and mindful of the quality of the firm's earnings and its balance sheet.

Activity ratios Financial ratios that indicate how efficiently a firm is utilizing its assets to generate sales.

Balance sheet A financial statement that lists a firm's assets, liabilities, and stockholders' equity at a point in time.

Common-size balance sheet A balance sheet in which a firm's assets and liabilities are expressed as a percentage of total assets, rather than as dollar amounts.

Common-size income statement An income statement in which a firm's income and expense items are expressed as a percentage of net sales, rather than as dollar amounts.

Comparative analysis An examination of a firm's performance based on one or more financial ratios, which are compared with the financial ratios of competitive firms or with an industry standard.

Discriminant analysis A statistical technique designed to classify observations (firms) into two or more predetermined groups based on certain characteristics (such as financial ratios) of the observations.

EAT The abbreviation for *earnings after taxes*.

EBIT The abbreviation for *earnings before interest and taxes* (also called *operating earnings*).

EPS The abbreviation for *earnings per share*.

FIFO The abbreviation for the *first-in, first-out* inventory valuation method. The method assumes that a firm uses the oldest items in the inventory first. Thus, they are *priced out* of the inventory based on the oldest inventory acquisition costs rather than the most recent.

Financial analysis The utilization of a group of analytical techniques, including financial ratio analysis, to determine the strengths, weaknesses, and direction of a company's performance.

Financial leverage ratios Financial ratios that measure the degree to which a firm is financing its assets with fixed-charge sources of funds such as debt, preferred stock, or leases.

Financial ratio A statistical yardstick that relates two numbers generally taken from a firm's income statement, balance sheet, or both at a specific point in time.

Generally accepted accounting principles (GAAP) A broad set of accounting rules followed in preparing financial statements.

Income statement A financial statement that indicates how a firm performed during a period of time.

LIFO The abbreviation for the *last-in, first-out* inventory valuation method. The method assumes that a firm uses the most recently acquired items in the inventory first. Thus they are *priced out* of the inventory based on the most recent inventory acquisition costs rather than the oldest.

Liquidity ratios Financial ratios that indicate a firm's ability to meet short-term financial obligations.

Market-based ratios Financial ratios that measure the market's (investors') assessment of the risk and performance of a firm.

Profitability ratios Financial ratios that measure the total effectiveness of a company's management in generating profits.

Stockholders' equity The total of a firm's common stock at par, contributed capital in excess of par, and retained earnings accounts from the balance sheet. It is sometimes called the *book value* of the firm, *owners' equity*, or *net worth*.

Trend analysis An examination of a firm's performance over time. It frequently is based on one or more financial ratios.

Understanding Annual Reports*

The following quote appeared in a *Forbes* article dealing with understanding annual reports and financial statements: "Reading annual reports isn't much fun. Unless you read with a knowing eye, it may not even be enlightening." Annual reports are examined by a company's financial managers and by outsiders such as bankers, security analysts, credit managers, unions, and potential employees. These persons must be able to "go behind" the glossy pictures of the company's products and officers and determine its financial strengths and weaknesses.

The financial statements of most U.S. companies are prepared in accordance with *generally accepted accounting principles* (GAAP). Even though careful financial analysis can provide excellent insights into the direction and relative strength of the firm, the financial analyst must keep in mind that GAAP gives firms considerable latitude in reporting their financial positions. Therefore, the analyst must be aware of the specific accounting conventions that gave rise to the financial statements being analyzed.

In the United States, the Financial Accounting Standards Board issues *Statements of Financial Accounting Standards* (SFAS), which describe accounting rules that companies must follow in preparing their financial statements. For example, SFAS No. 96, "Accounting for Income Taxes," issued in December 1987, requires a company to follow specific new rules in calculating the income tax liabilities it reports to its stockholders. As a direct result of the SFAS No. 96 rule changes, General Electric, a company with a reputation of following conservative accounting practices, was required to report a $577 million increase in net income in 1987. The financial analyst reading the 1987 General Electric Annual Report must understand the reason for the income gain and realize it did not come from increased sales or cost reductions.

This chapter discusses the tools of financial statement analysis. These tools are helpful in evaluating the financial condition and performance of a firm.

* Adapted in part from Penelope Lang, "Annual Obfuscation," *Forbes* (May 2, 1988): 71.

▅▅▅▅ INTRODUCTION

Chapters 3 and 4 develop the tools of financial analysis and cash flow forecasting. This chapter deals with the evaluation of financial performance, using financial statement analysis. A carefully executed financial statement analysis can assist the financial manager in assessing the current financial condition of the firm. Trend analysis and common-size financial statements can assist the financial manager in detecting changes in the firm's financial performance over time.

Once the firm's current financial condition has been assessed, the financial manager is in a position to plan for the future direction of the firm, given the constraints imposed by, and the strengths of, the current financial condition. A key element in planning for the future direction of the firm is cash flow forecasting. With effective cash flow management and forecasting, financial managers can plan for the acquisition and management of both long- and short-term assets (the capital budgeting decision and the working capital management decision). In addition, effective cash flow management and forecasting can assist the financial manager in funding the firm's assets (the capital structure decision). Cash flow analysis and forecasting tools are developed in Chapter 4.

USES OF FINANCIAL ANALYSIS

A *financial analysis* assists in identifying the major strengths and weaknesses of a business enterprise. It indicates whether a firm has enough cash to meet obligations; a reasonable accounts receivable collection period; an efficient inventory management policy; sufficient plant, property, and equipment; and an adequate capital structure—all of which are necessary if the firm is to achieve the goal of maximizing shareholder wealth. Financial analysis also can be used to assess a firm's viability as an ongoing enterprise and to determine whether a satisfactory return is being earned for the risks taken.

When performing a financial analysis, the analyst may discover specific problem areas in time for remedial action. For example, the analyst may find that the firm has unused borrowing power that could finance additional income-producing assets. The results of a financial analysis can indicate certain facts and trends that can aid the financial manager in planning and implementing a course of action consistent with the goal of maximizing shareholder wealth.

Financial analyses also are used by persons other than financial managers. For example, credit managers may examine some basic financial ratios concerning a prospective customer when deciding whether or not to extend credit. Security analysts use financial analysis to assess the investment worth of different securities. Bankers use the tools of financial analysis when deciding whether to grant loans. Financial ratios have been used successfully to forecast such financial events as impending bankruptcy. Unions refer to them when evaluating the bargaining positions of certain employers. Finally, students and other job hunters may perform financial analyses of potential employers to determine career opportunities.

INTERPRETING FINANCIAL RATIOS

A *financial ratio* is a relationship that indicates something about a firm's activities, such as the ratio between the firm's current assets and current liabilities or between its accounts receivable and its annual sales. Financial ratios enable an analyst to make a comparison of a firm's financial condition over time or in relation to other firms. Ratios essentially standardize various elements of financial data for differences in the size of a series of financial data when making comparisons over time or between firms. For example, the total profits of IBM are many times those of Apple Computer, because IBM is a much larger firm than Apple. By computing a ratio such as net profits divided by total assets, the relative performance of the two firms can be assessed more accurately.

Successful financial ratio analysis requires that the analyst keep in mind the following key points:

■ Any discussion of financial ratios is likely to include only a representative sample of possible ratios. Many other ratios can be developed to provide additional insights. In some industries, such as banking, the analyst will use special ratios unique to the activities of the firms in those industries.
■ Financial ratios are only "flags" indicating potential areas of strength or weakness. A thorough analysis requires the examination of other data as well.

■ Frequently a financial ratio must be dissected to discover its true meaning. For example, a low ratio may be caused by either a low numerator or a high denominator. A good financial analyst will examine both the numerator and the denominator before drawing any conclusions.

■ A financial ratio is meaningful only when it is compared with some standard, such as an industry ratio trend, a ratio trend for the specific firm being analyzed, or a stated management objective.

■ When financial ratios are used to compare one firm with another, it is important to remember that differences in accounting techniques may result in substantial differences in financial ratios. Failure to keep this in mind can lead to incorrect conclusions.

BASIC CLASSIFICATIONS OF FINANCIAL RATIOS

Because different groups inside and outside the firm have varying objectives and expectations, they approach financial analysis from different perspectives. For example, suppliers and short-term creditors are likely to be most concerned with a firm's current liquidity and near-term cash-generating capacity. Bond holders and holders of preferred stock, who have long-term claims on a firm's earnings and assets, focus on the firm's cash-generating ability over the long run and on the claims other investors have on the firm's cash flows. Common stockholders and potential investors are especially interested in measures of profitability and risk, because common stock prices are dependent on the amount and stability of a firm's future earnings and dividends. Management is concerned with all aspects of financial analysis on both a short- and a long-term basis, because it is responsible for conducting the firm's day-to-day operations and earning a competitive rate of return for risks taken.

No single financial ratio could begin to answer all these analytical needs. In fact, five different groups of ratios have been developed:

■ *Liquidity ratios* indicate a firm's ability to meet short-term financial obligations.

■ *Activity ratios* indicate how efficiently a firm is using its assets to generate sales.

■ *Financial leverage ratios* indicate a firm's capacity to meet short- and long-term debt obligations.

■ *Profitability ratios* measure how effectively a firm's management generates profits on sales, assets, and stockholders' investments.

■ *Market-based ratios* measure the financial market's evaluation of a company's stock.

Each type is discussed in detail in this chapter.[1] The financial statements of the Drake Manufacturing Company, a medium-sized firm that produces various replacement components for the lawn equipment industry, will be examined to illustrate how ratios are used in financial analysis. Data will be used from Drake's *balance sheet* for the years ending December 31, 19X6 and 19X5 and from its *income statement* for the year 19X6.

The balance sheet shown in Table 3-1 contains information on Drake's *assets, liabilities,* and *stockholders' equity*. The figures provide a "snapshot"

---

[1] The ratios discussed in this chapter are only a representative sample of the total number of financial ratios that may be analyzed.

Drake Manufacturing Company Balance Sheet (in thousands of dollars)					T A B L E 3-1
		December 31, 19X6		December 31, 19X5	

		December 31, 19X6		December 31, 19X5	
ASSETS					
Cash		$ 2,540		$ 2,081	
Marketable securities		1,800		1,625	
Accounts receivable, net		18,320		16,850	
Inventories		27,530		26,470	
Total current assets		$50,190		$47,026	
Plant and equipment	$43,100		$39,500		
Less: Accumulated depreciation	11,400		9,500		
Net plant and equipment		$31,700		$30,000	
Total assets		$81,890		$77,026	
LIABILITIES AND STOCKHOLDERS' EQUITY					
Accounts payable		$ 9,721		$ 8,340	
Notes payable—bank (10%)		8,500		5,635	
Accrued taxes payable		3,200		3,150	
Other current liabilities		2,102		1,750	
Current portion of long-term debt		2,000		2,000	
Total current liabilities		$25,523		$20,875	
Long-term debt (9⅞% mortgage bonds)*		$22,000		$24,000	
Total liabilities		$47,523		$44,875	
Common stock ($10 par value)	$13,000		$13,000		
Contributed capital in excess of par	10,000		10,000		
Retained earnings	11,367		9,151		
Total stockholders' equity		$34,367		$32,151	
Total liabilities and stockholders' equity		$81,890		$77,026	

* Mortgage bonds require a $2,000(000) annual payment to a sinking fund.

view of the firm's financial health on December 31, 19X6, and December 31, 19X5. Drake's assets are recorded on the balance sheet at the price the company paid for them (that is, at historic cost). The liabilities are amounts the firm owes its creditors, and the stockholders' equity (also termed *net worth* or *owners' equity*) is the difference between total assets and total liabilities. The stockholders' equity accounts in Table 3-1 are (1) common stock ($10 par value); (2) contributed capital in excess of par; and (3) retained earnings.

The income statement in Table 3-2 indicates Drake's performance during the year ended December 31, 19X6. The *cost of sales, other operating expenses, interest expenses,* and *taxes* are deducted from the revenues generated, or *net sales,* to arrive at the firm's *net income,* or *earnings after taxes (EAT).* The statement in Table 3-2 also shows how the firm's earnings are distributed between dividend payments to stockholders and earnings reinvested in the firm.

Common-size financial statements also are helpful in financial analysis. A *common-size balance sheet* shows the firm's assets and liabilities as a percentage of total assets, rather than in dollar amounts. Table 3-3 shows the Drake Company's common-size balance sheet at December 31, 19X6, and December 31, 19X5. A *common-size income statement* lists the firm's income

TABLE 3-2

Drake Manufacturing Company Income Statement (in thousands of dollars)

For the Year Ended December 31, 19X6

Net sales		$112,760
Cost of sales		85,300
Gross margin		$ 27,460
Operating expenses:		
Selling	$6,540	
General and administrative*	9,400	
Total operating expenses		15,940
Earnings before interest and taxes (EBIT)		$ 11,520
Interest charges:		
Interest on bank notes	$ 850	
Interest on mortgage bonds	2,310	
Total interest charges		3,160
Earnings before taxes (EBT)		$ 8,360
Federal and state income taxes at a combined 40% rate		3,344
Earnings after taxes (EAT) and available for common stockholders		$ 5,016
OTHER INFORMATION:		
Dividends paid on common stock		$ 2,800
Earnings retained in the firm		$ 2,216
Shares outstanding		1,300
Market price per share		$20
Book value per share		$26.44
Earnings per share		$3.86
Dividends per share		$2.15

* Includes $150(000) in annual lease payments.

and expense items as a percentage of net sales, rather than in dollar amounts. Table 3-4 contains Drake's common-size income statement for the year ended December 31, 19X6. Common-size financial statements allow trends in financial performance to be detected and monitored more easily than with financial statements showing only dollar amounts.

The statement of cash flows is useful in financial analysis, too. It indicates how a firm generated cash flows from its operations, how it used cash in investing activities, and how it obtained cash from financing activities. The statement of cash flows is discussed in Chapter 4.

Liquidity Ratios

A firm that intends to remain a viable business entity must have enough cash on hand to pay its bills as they come due. In other words, the firm must remain *liquid*. One way to determine whether this is the case is to examine the relationship between a firm's current assets and approaching obligations. Liquidity ratios are quick measures of a firm's ability to provide sufficient cash to conduct business over the next few months. *Cash budgets* provide the best assessment of a firm's liquidity position. They are discussed in Chapter 4.

This section discusses two different liquidity ratios—the *current ratio* and the *quick ratio*.

TABLE 3-3

Drake Manufacturing Company Common-Size Balance Sheet

	December 31, 19X6	December 31, 19X5
ASSETS		
Cash	3.1%	2.7%
Marketable securities	2.2	2.1
Accounts receivable, net	22.4	21.9
Inventories	33.6	34.4
Total current assets	61.3%	61.1%
Net plant and equipment	38.7	38.9
Total assets	100.0%	100.0%
LIABILITIES AND STOCKHOLDERS' EQUITY		
Current liabilities	31.2%	27.1%
Long-term debt (9⅝% mortgage bonds)	26.8	31.2
Total liabilities	58.0%	58.3%
Stockholders' equity	42.0	41.7
Total liabilities and stockholders' equity	100.0%	100.0%

TABLE 3-4

Drake Manufacturing Company Common-Size Income Statement

For the Year Ended December 31, 19X6

Net sales	100.0%
Cost of sales	75.7
Gross margin	24.3%
Operating expenses	14.1
Earnings before interest and taxes (EBIT)	10.2%
Interest charges	2.8
Earnings before taxes (EBT)	7.4%
Federal and state income taxes at a combined 40% rate	3.0
Earnings after taxes (EAT) and available for common stockholders	4.4%

CURRENT RATIO. The current ratio is defined as follows:

$$\text{Current ratio} = \frac{\text{Current assets}}{\text{Current liabilities}} \qquad (3.1)$$

Current assets include the cash a firm already has on hand and in the bank, plus any assets that can be converted into cash within a "normal" operating period of 12 months, such as marketable securities held as short-term investments, accounts receivable, inventories, and prepayments. Current liabilities include any financial obligations expected to fall due within the next year, such as accounts payable, notes payable, the current portion of long-term debt due, other payables, and various accruals such as taxes and wages due.

Using data from Table 3-1, Drake's current ratio at year-end 19X6 can be calculated as $50,190/$25,523 = 1.97, or about 2:1. Or, it can be said that Drake's current assets *cover* its current liabilities about two times.

The ratio is interpreted to mean that to satisfy the claims of short-term creditors exclusively from existing current assets, Drake must be able to convert each dollar of current assets into at least $0.51 of cash ($1.00/1.97 = $0.507, or $0.51). The *industry average* for the current ratio is 2.40 times,[2] meaning that the average firm in the industry must convert only $0.42 ($1.00/2.40 = $0.416, or $0.42) of each dollar of current assets into cash to meet short-term obligations.

The fact that Drake's current ratio is below the industry average does *not* mean that the firm would consider closing its doors voluntarily to meet the demands of short-term creditors. Nor does it mean that Drake's creditors are any less well protected than the creditors of competing firms, because no two firms—even those in the same industry—are identical. In fact, ratios that suggest the presence of a problem in one firm may be quite satisfactory for another firm.[3] Drake's current ratio provides only *one* standard for measuring liquidity. The financial analyst must dissect, or "go behind," the ratio to discover why it differs from the industry average and determine whether a serious problem exists.

QUICK RATIO. The quick ratio is defined as follows:

$$\text{Quick ratio} = \frac{\text{Current assets} - \text{Inventories}}{\text{Current liabilities}} \qquad \textbf{(3.2)}$$

This ratio, sometimes called the "acid test," is a more stringent measure of liquidity than the current ratio. By subtracting inventories from current assets, this ratio recognizes that a firm's inventories are often one of its least liquid current assets. Inventories, especially work-in-process, are very difficult to liquidate quickly at, or near, their book value. Referring to the figures on Drake's balance sheet (Table 3-1), the firm's quick ratio at year-end 19X6 is calculated as follows:

$$\frac{\$50,190 - \$27,530}{\$25,523} = \frac{\$22,660}{\$25,523} = 0.89 \text{ times}$$

The industry average is 0.92 times; Drake's quick ratio is nearly equal to that.

The quick ratio is interpreted to mean that Drake's cash and other current assets one step removed from cash—that is, marketable securities and accounts receivable—are equal to 89 percent of the current liabilities.[4] The crucial assumption behind the quick ratio is that a firm's accounts receivable may be converted into cash within the "normal" collection period (and with little "shrinkage"), or within the period of time for which credit was initially granted.

---

[2] Industry averages are obtained from various sources. The "Sources of Comparative Financial Data" section later in this chapter discusses a number of such sources.

[3] Many practitioners view a current ratio of 1.5 times (1.5) as satisfactory for industrial firms. Public utilities, on the other hand, typically function with considerably lower ratios. However, the financial analyst must be very cautious when using any of these "rules of thumb." The safe level of a current ratio is a function of how fast the firm's current assets and liabilities turn over. In the case of a public utility, the accounts receivable turn over on a monthly basis—much faster than in the typical industrial firm. Thus, public utilities are able to safely sustain lower current ratios than industrial firms.

[4] A quick ratio of 1 times (1.0) is considered satisfactory for most industrial firms.

The analyst who doubts the liquidity of a firm's receivables may wish to prepare an *aging schedule*. The following one lists Drake's accounts receivable as of December 31, 19X6:

Days Outstanding	Amount Outstanding (in thousands of dollars)	Percentage of Total
Less than 30	$ 9,450	51.6%
30–59	5,161	28.2
60–89	2,750	15.0
Over 90	959	5.2
Total accounts receivable	$18,320	100.0%

Unfortunately, the data required to prepare an aging schedule normally are not available to outside analysts. Hence, the aging schedule is useful primarily for internal analysis.

To evaluate the figures contained in an aging schedule, the analyst would need to consider Drake's selling terms. If, for example, Drake's customers are expected to pay within 40 days (which, in fact, they are), then the aging schedule indicates that many accounts are past due. However, because only 5.2 percent of the firm's receivables have been outstanding over 90 days, the major problem appears to be with slow-paying rather than uncollectible accounts. Some analysts adjust the quick ratio *downward* if a significant percentage of a firm's receivables are long past due and have not been written off as losses. Adjusting Drake's quick ratio downward involves the following calculation:

$$\frac{\begin{array}{c}\text{(Current assets } - \text{ Inventories)} \\ - \text{ Accounts outstanding over 90 days}\end{array}}{\text{Current liabilities}} = \frac{\$22,660 - \$959}{\$25,523} = 0.85 \text{ times}$$

The 0.04 difference between the quick ratio, 0.89 times, and the adjusted ratio, 0.85 times, probably is insignificant. Therefore, even if Drake's accounts over 90 days old were considered uncollectible, this alone would not indicate any real problem for the firm.

Activity Ratios

One objective of financial management is to determine how a firm's resources can best be distributed among the various asset accounts. If a proper mix of cash, receivables, inventories, plant, property, and equipment can be achieved, the firm's asset structure will be more effective in generating sales revenue.

Activity ratios indicate how much a firm has invested in a particular type of asset (or group of assets) relative to the revenue the asset is producing. By comparing activity ratios for the various asset accounts of a firm with established industry norms, the analyst can determine how efficiently the firm is allocating its resources.

This section discusses several types of activity ratios, including the *average collection period*, the *inventory turnover ratio*, the *fixed-asset turnover ratio*, and the *total asset turnover ratio*.

AVERAGE COLLECTION PERIOD. The average collection period is the average number of days an account receivable remains outstanding. It is usually determined by dividing a firm's year-end receivables balance by the average daily credit sales (based on a 365-day year):[5]

$$\text{Average collection period} = \frac{\text{Accounts receivable}}{\text{Annual credit sales}/365} \qquad \textbf{(3.3)}$$

Using figures from both Drake's balance sheet (Table 3-1) and the income statement (Table 3-2), the average collection period ratio at year-end 19X6 can be calculated as \$18,320/(\$112,760/365) = \$18,320/\$308.93 = 59.3 days. Because the industry average for this ratio is 47 days, Drake's ratio is substantially above the average.

Drake's credit terms call for payment within 40 days. The ratio calculations show that 59.3 days of sales are tied up in receivables, meaning that a significant portion of Drake's customers are not paying bills on time. (This also is indicated by the aging schedule of the firm's accounts receivable.) The analyst would interpret this ratio to mean that Drake has allocated a greater proportion of total resources to receivables than the average firm in the industry. If the company implemented a more vigorous collection program and reduced the collection period to the industry norm of 47 days, some of these funds would be released for investment elsewhere or debt reduction. The released funds of (59.3 days − 47 days) × \$308.93 per day = \$3,800 could be invested in other assets that might contribute more significantly to profitability.[6]

An average collection period substantially above the industry norm usually is not desirable and may indicate too liberal a credit policy. Ultimately the firm must determine if the liberal credit policy generates enough sales and profits to justify the cost.[7] In contrast, an average collection period far *below* the industry norm may indicate that the firm's credit terms are too stringent and are hurting sales by restricting credit only to the very best customers. Although moderate-to-slow paying customers may seem troublesome individually, they can be profitable as a group, and a credit policy that is too tight may drive them to competitor firms.

INVENTORY TURNOVER RATIO. The inventory turnover ratio is defined as follows:

$$\text{Inventory turnover} = \frac{\text{Costs of sales}}{\text{Average inventory}} \qquad \textbf{(3.4)}$$

Whereas the cost of sales usually is listed on a firm's income statement, the average inventory has to be calculated. This can be done in a number of ways. For example, if a firm has been experiencing a significant and continuing rate of growth in sales, the average inventory may be computed by

---

[5] When credit sales figures are not available (which is frequently the case), total sales figures are customarily used in calculating the ratio. This results in an *overstatement* of the average daily sales and an *understatement* of the average collection period.

For firms with seasonal sales, the analyst should calculate an average of the end-of-month receivables balances. When comparing average collection period ratios with industry norms, the analyst must make sure the industry ratios have been computed in the same manner as the particular firm's ratios.
[6] Recall that the analysis for Drake is being done in terms of thousands of dollars. Hence, the actual released funds total approximately \$3.8 million.
[7] Chapter 19 contains an example of this type of analysis.

adding the figures for the beginning and ending inventories for the year and dividing by two. If sales are seasonal or otherwise subject to wide fluctuations, however, it would be better to add the month-end inventory balances for the entire year and divide by twelve.

Some analysts calculate inventory turnover as simply the ratio of annual sales to ending inventory. Although the *sales-to-inventory ratio* is technically inferior and gives different results than more commonly used ratios, it may be satisfactory if used consistently when making comparisons between one firm and the industry as a whole. However, there is a problem with this ratio in that it tends to differ from one firm to another, depending on policies regarding markups on the cost of sales.

Because Drake's sales are spread evenly over the year and its growth rate has been fairly moderate, the average inventory can be calculated by taking the average of the beginning and ending inventory balances, ($27,530 + $26,470)/2 = $27,000. Dividing the cost of sales by this figure, $85,300/ $27,000, gives an inventory turnover ratio of 3.16 times. This is considerably below the industry norm of 3.9 times, indicating that Drake has a larger investment in inventory relative to the sales being generated than the average firm. If the company could increase its inventory turns up to the industry average of 3.9 times, its average inventory investment in 19X6 would be $21,872 ($85,300/3.9). The released funds, $27,000 − $21,872 = $5,128, could be used either for investment in other, potentially more profitable, assets or possibly for debt reduction.[8]

Two factors may be responsible for Drake's allocating an excessive amount of resources to inventory:

■ The firm may be attempting to carry all possible types of replacement parts so that every order can be filled immediately. Drake should carefully examine this policy to determine whether the cost of carrying excessive stocks is justified by the profits earned on additional sales.[9]
■ Some of Drake's inventory may be damaged, obsolete, or slow moving. Stock falling into these categories has questionable liquidity and should be recorded at a value more reflective of the realizable market value.

If a firm's inventory turnover ratio is too high, it may mean the firm is frequently running out of certain items in stock and losing sales to competitors. For inventory to contribute fully to profitability, the firm has to maintain a reasonable balance of inventory levels.

FIXED-ASSET TURNOVER RATIO. The fixed-asset turnover ratio is defined as follows:

$$\text{Fixed-asset turnover} = \frac{\text{Sales}}{\text{Net fixed assets}} \qquad (3.5)$$

It indicates the extent to which a firm is utilizing existing property, plant, and equipment to generate sales.

The balance sheet figures that indicate how much a firm has invested in property, plant, and equipment are affected by several factors, including the following:

---

[8] Recall that the analysis for Drake is being done in terms of thousands of dollars. Hence, the actual released funds total approximately $5.128 million.
[9] The determination of optimal inventory levels is discussed in Chapter 19.

- The cost of the assets when acquired.
- The length of time since acquisition.
- The depreciation policies adopted by the firm.
- The extent to which fixed assets are leased rather than owned.

Because of these factors it is possible for firms with virtually identical plants to have significantly different fixed-asset turnover ratios. Thus, the ratio should be used primarily for year-to-year comparisons within the same company rather than for intercompany comparisons.

Drake's fixed-asset turnover ratio is $112,760/$31,700 = 3.56 times—considerably below the industry average of 4.6 times. However, the financial analyst should acknowledge the shortcomings of the ratio and perform further analyses before concluding that the company makes inefficient use of its property, plant, and equipment.

TOTAL ASSET TURNOVER RATIO. The total asset turnover ratio is defined as follows:

$$\text{Total asset turnover} = \frac{\text{Sales}}{\text{Total assets}} \tag{3.6}$$

It indicates how effectively a firm uses its total resources to generate sales and is a summary measure influenced by each of the activity ratios previously discussed.

Drake's total asset turnover ratio is $112,760/$81,890 = 1.38 times, whereas the industry average is 1.82 times. In view of Drake's other asset turnover ratios, the firm's relatively poor showing with regard to this ratio is not surprising. Each of Drake's major asset investment programs—accounts receivable; inventory; and property, plant, and equipment—has been found apparently lacking. The analyst could look at these various ratios and conclude that Drake is not generating the same level of sales from its assets as other firms in the industry.

Financial Leverage Ratios

Whenever a firm finances a portion of assets with any type of fixed-charge financing—such as debt, preferred stock, or leases—the firm is said to be using financial leverage. Financial leverage ratios measure the degree to which a firm is employing financial leverage, and as such are of interest to creditors and owners alike.

Both long- and short-term creditors are concerned with the amount of leverage a firm employs, because it indicates the firm's risk exposure in meeting debt service charges (that is, interest and principal repayment). A firm that is heavily financed by debt offers creditors less protection in the event of bankruptcy. For example, if a firm's assets are financed with 85 percent debt, the value of the assets can decline by only 15 percent before creditors' funds are endangered. In contrast, if only 15 percent of a firm's assets are debt financed, asset values can drop by 85 percent before jeopardizing the creditors.

Owners are interested in financial leverage because it influences the rate of return they can expect to realize on their investment and the degree of risk involved. For example, if a firm is able to borrow funds at 9 percent and employ them at 12 percent, the owners earn the 3 percent difference and are likely to view financial leverage favorably. On the other hand, if the firm can earn only 3 percent on the borrowed funds, the −6 percent difference (3% − 9%) will result in a lower rate of return to the owners.[10]

Either balance sheet or income statement data can be used to measure a firm's use of financial leverage. The balance sheet approach gives a *static* measure of financial leverage at a specific point in time and emphasizes *total* amounts of debt, whereas the income statement approach provides a more *dynamic* measure and relates required interest payments on debt to the firm's ability to pay. Both approaches are employed widely in practice.

There are several types of financial leverage ratios, including the *debt ratio*, the *debt-to-equity ratio*, the *times interest earned ratio*, and the *fixed-charge coverage ratio*.

DEBT RATIO. The debt ratio is defined as follows:

$$\text{Debt ratio} = \frac{\text{Total debt}}{\text{Total assets}} \qquad (3.7)$$

It measures the proportion of a firm's total assets that is financed with creditors' funds. As used here, the term *debt* encompasses all short-term liabilities and long-term borrowings.

Bond holders and other long-term creditors are among those likely to be interested in a firm's debt ratio. They tend to prefer a low debt ratio, because it provides more protection in the event of liquidation or some other major financial problem. As the debt ratio increases, so do a firm's fixed-interest charges. If the debt ratio becomes too high, the cash flows a firm generates during economic recessions may not be sufficient to meet interest payments. Thus, a firm's ability to market new debt obligations when it needs to raise new funds is crucially affected by the size of the debt ratio and by investors' perceptions about the risk implied by the level of the ratio.

Debt ratios are stated in terms of percentages. Drake's debt ratio as of year-end 19X6 is ($25,523 + $22,000)/$81,890 = $47,523/$81,890 = 0.58, or 58 percent. The ratio is interpreted to mean that Drake's creditors are financing 58 percent of the firm's total assets. This figure is considerably higher than the 47 percent industry average, indicating that Drake has less unused borrowing capacity than the average firm in the industry.

A high debt ratio implies a low *proportionate equity base;* that is, the percentage of assets financed with equity funds. As the proportionate equity base declines, investors are more hesitant to acquire a firm's debt obligations. Whether Drake can continue to finance its assets with 58 percent of "outsiders" money largely depends on the growth and stability of future earnings and cash flows.

DEBT-TO-EQUITY RATIO. The debt-to-equity ratio is defined as follows:

$$\text{Debt-to-equity} = \frac{\text{Total debt}}{\text{Total equity}} \qquad (3.8)$$

[10] The tradeoff between risk and return resulting from the use of financial leverage is discussed in Chapter 13.

It is similar to the debt ratio and relates the amount of a firm's debt financing to the amount of equity financing.

Because most interest costs are incurred on long-term borrowed funds— that is, those having maturities greater than 1 year—some analysts prefer to use a *long-term debt-to-equity ratio.* Many analysts also include a firm's preferred stock with its debt when computing the debt-to-equity ratio, because preferred stock dividends, like interest requirements, are usually fixed.

The debt-to-equity ratio also is stated as a percentage. Drake's debt-to-equity ratio at year-end 19X6 is $47,523/$34,367 = 1.383, or 138.3 percent. Because the industry average is 88.7 percent, Drake's ratio indicates that the firm uses more than the usual amount of borrowed funds to finance its activities. Specifically, it raises nearly $1.38 from creditors for each dollar invested by stockholders. This is interpreted to mean that the firm's debt suppliers have a lower margin of safety than is common in the industry. In addition, Drake has a greater potential for financial distress if earnings do not exceed the cost of borrowed funds.

TIMES INTEREST EARNED RATIO. The times interest earned ratio is defined as follows:

$$\text{Times interest earned} = \frac{\text{Earnings before interest and taxes (EBIT)}}{\text{Interest charges}} \quad \textbf{(3.9)}$$

Often referred to as simply *interest coverage*, this ratio employs income statement data to measure a firm's use of financial leverage. It tells the analyst the extent to which the firm's current earnings are able to meet current interest payments. The EBIT figures are used because the firm makes interest payments out of operating income, or EBIT.

Drake's times interest earned ratio is $11,520/$3,160 = 3.65 times. In other words, it covers annual interest payments 3.65 times; this figure is considerably below the industry norm of 6.7 times. This is further evidence that the company makes extensive use of creditors' funds to finance its operations.

FIXED-CHARGE COVERAGE RATIO. The fixed-charge coverage ratio is defined as follows:

$$\text{Fixed-charge coverage} = \frac{\text{EBIT + Lease payments}}{\text{Interest + Lease payments + Preferred dividends before tax + Before tax sinking fund}} \quad \textbf{(3.10)}$$

It measures the number of times a firm is able to cover total *fixed charges,* which include (in addition to interest payments) preferred dividends and payments required under long-term lease contracts. Many corporations also are required to make *sinking fund* payments on bond issues, which are annual payments aimed at either retiring a portion of the bond obligation each year or providing for the ultimate redemption of bonds at maturity. Under most sinking fund provisions the firm either may make these payments to the bond holders' representative (the *trustee*), who determines through a lottery process which of the outstanding bonds will be retired, or deliver to the trustee the required number of bonds purchased by the firm in the open market. Either way, the firm's outstanding indebtedness is reduced.

In calculating the fixed-charge coverage ratio, the analyst must consider each of the firm's obligations on a *before-tax* basis. However, because sinking fund payments and preferred stock dividends are not tax deductible and therefore must be paid out of after-tax earnings, a mathematical adjustment has to be made. After-tax payments must be divided by $(1 - T)$, where T is the marginal tax rate. This effectively converts such payments to a before-tax basis, or one that is comparable to the EBIT.[11] And, because lease payments are deducted in arriving at the EBIT, they must be added back into the numerator of the ratio, because the fixed charges (in the denominator) also include lease payments.

The fixed-charge coverage ratio is a more severe measure of a firm's ability to meet fixed financial obligations. Using figures from Drake's income statement for 19X6,[12] the fixed-charge coverage ratio can be calculated as follows:

$$\frac{\$11,520 + \$150}{\$3,160 + \$150 + \$2,000/(1 - 0.4)} = \frac{\$11,670}{\$6,643} = 1.76 \text{ times}$$

Because the industry average is 4.5 times, once again it is apparent that Drake provides creditors with a smaller margin of safety—that is, a higher level of risk—than the average firm in the industry. As a result, Drake probably is straining its relations with creditors. If a "tight money" situation developed in the economy, Drake's high debt and low coverage ratios probably would limit the firm's access to new credit sources, and Drake might be forced to curtail operations or borrow on prohibitively expensive and restrictive terms.

Profitability Ratios

More than anything else, a firm's *profits*[13] demonstrate how well the firm is making investment and financing decisions. If a firm is unable to provide adequate returns in the form of dividends and share price appreciation to investors, it may be unable to maintain, let alone increase, its asset base. Profitability ratios measure how effectively a firm's management is generating profits on sales; total assets; and, most importantly, stockholders' investment. Therefore, anyone whose economic interests are tied to the long-run survival of a firm will be interested in profitability ratios.

There are several types of profitability ratios, including the *gross profit margin ratio*, the *net profit margin ratio*, the *return on investment ratio*, and the *return on stockholders' equity ratio*.

[11] The rationale for this computation is as follows:

$$\begin{aligned}
\text{After-tax earnings} &= \text{Before-tax earnings} - \text{Tax} \\
&= (\text{Before-tax earnings}) - (\text{Before-tax earnings}) \times T \\
&= \text{Before-tax earnings } (1 - T)
\end{aligned}$$

$$\frac{\text{After-tax earnings}}{1 - T} = \text{Before-tax earnings}$$

[12] Some analysts exclude preferred dividend payments when computing the fixed-charge coverage ratio. In the calculation that follows, the $150 represents annual long-term lease payments, and the $2,000 represents sinking fund obligations.

[13] The terms *profits, earnings,* and *net income* are used interchangeably in this discussion.

GROSS PROFIT MARGIN RATIO. The gross profit margin ratio is defined as follows:

$$\text{Gross profit margin} = \frac{\text{Sales} - \text{Cost of sales}}{\text{Sales}} \qquad \textbf{(3.11)}$$

It measures the relative profitability of a firm's sales after the cost of sales has been deducted, thus revealing how effectively the firm's management is making decisions regarding pricing and the control of production costs.

Drake's gross profit margin ratio is $27,460/$112,760 = 24.4%. This is just slightly below the industry average of 25.6 percent, indicating that either Drake's pricing policies or production methods are not quite as effective as those of the average firm in the industry. Differences in inventory accounting methods (and, to a lesser extent, depreciation methods) used by Drake and the firms included in the industry average also influence the cost of sales and, by extension, the gross profit margin.

NET PROFIT MARGIN RATIO. The net profit margin ratio is defined as follows:

$$\text{Net profit margin} = \frac{\text{Earnings after taxes (EAT)}}{\text{Sales}} \qquad \textbf{(3.12)}$$

It measures how profitable a firm's sales are after all expenses, including taxes and interest, have been deducted.

Some analysts also compute an *operating profit margin ratio*, defined as EBIT/sales. It measures the profitability of a firm's operations before considering the effects of financing decisions. Because the operating profit margin is computed before considering interest charges, this ratio often is more suitable for comparing the profit performance of different firms.

Drake's net profit margin ratio is $5,016/$112,760 = 4.45%. This is below the industry average of 5.1 percent and is interpreted to mean that the company is earning 0.65 percent less on each dollar of sales than the average firm in the industry. This indicates that Drake may be having difficulty controlling either total expenses (including interest, operating expenses, and the cost of sales) or the prices of its products. In this case the former probably is more accurate, because Drake's financial structure contains a greater proportion of debt, resulting in more interest charges.

RETURN ON INVESTMENT (TOTAL ASSETS) RATIO. The return on investment ratio is defined as follows:

$$\text{Return on investment} = \frac{\text{Earnings after taxes (EAT)}}{\text{Total assets}} \qquad \textbf{(3.13)}$$

It measures a firm's net income in relation to the total asset investment.

Drake's return on investment ratio, $5,016/$81,890, is 6.13 percent—considerably below the industry average of 9.28 percent. This is a direct result of the firm's low activity ratios and low profit margins.

Some analysts also like to compute the ratio of EBIT/total assets. This measures the operating profit rate of return for a firm. An after-tax version of this ratio is earnings before interest and after tax (EBIAT) divided by total assets. These ratios are computed before interest charges. Hence they may be more suitable when comparing the operating performance of two or more firms that are financed differently.

RETURN ON STOCKHOLDERS' EQUITY RATIO. The return on stockholders' equity ratio is defined as follows:

$$\text{Return on stockholders' equity} = \frac{\text{Earnings after taxes (EAT)}}{\text{Stockholders' equity}}$$

It measures the rate of return that the firm earns on stockholders' equity. Because only the stockholders' equity appears in the denominator, the ratio is directly influenced by the amount of debt a firm is using to finance assets.

Drake's return on stockholders' equity ratio is \$5,016/\$34,367 = 14.60%. Again, Drake's ratio is below the industry average of 17.54 percent. The firm's low activity ratios and low profit margins result in profitability ratios inferior to the industry norms, even after the effects of debt financing (financial leverage) are considered.

Market-Based Ratios

The financial ratios discussed in the previous four groups are all derived from accounting income statement and balance sheet information provided by the firm. Analysts also frequently are interested in the financial market's assessment of the performance of a firm. There should be a close parallel between the accounting ratios of a firm and the market-based ratios for that firm. For example, if the accounting ratios of a firm suggest that the firm has more risk than the average firm in the industry and has lower profit prospects, this should be reflected in a lower market price of that firm's stock.

PRICE TO EARNINGS (P/E) RATIO. The price to earnings ratio is defined as follows:

$$\text{P/E} = \frac{\text{Market price per share}}{\text{Current earnings per share}} \tag{3.15}$$

(Some security analysts use projected next year's earnings per share in the denominator. There is nothing wrong with this alternative definition as long as comparisons between firms are done on the same basis.)

In general, a firm's P/E ratio should be higher the lower is the firm's risk. In addition, the better the growth prospects of its earnings, the greater is the P/E multiple. For example, Manufacturers Hanover Corporation, a bank holding company with substantial risk due partly to the uncertainty associated with its loans in developing countries, had a P/E multiple of 2, as of March 1, 1989. In contrast, NCNB Corporation, the largest bank holding company in the southeastern United States, with relatively little problematic foreign debt and better growth prospects than Manufacturers Hanover, enjoyed a P/E multiple of 11, as of March 1, 1989.

Drake's current (19X6) earnings per share are \$3.86 (earnings of \$5,016 divided by 1,300 shares). If Drake's current market price is \$24 per share, its P/E ratio is 6.22 times. This is below the industry average of 8.0 times, and indicates that Drake has either higher risk than the average firm, lower growth prospects, or both.

MARKET (PRICE) TO BOOK (VALUE) (P/BV) RATIO. The market to book ratio is defined as follows:

$$P/BV = \frac{\text{Market price per share}}{\text{Book value per share}} \tag{3.16}$$

Generally, the higher the rate of return a firm is earning on its common equity relative to the return required by investors (the cost of common equity), the higher will be the P/BV ratio.

The book value per share of common stock is determined by dividing the total common stockholders' equity for a firm by the number of shares outstanding. In the case of Drake at year-end 19X6, the book value per share is equal to $26.44 (stockholders' equity of $34,367 divided by 1,300 shares outstanding). With a market price per share of $24, the market to book ratio for Drake is 0.91. This compares unfavorably with the industry average of 1.13.

It should be noted that, because the market to book ratio contains the book value of the common stockholders' equity in the denominator (remember that common stockholders' equity is equal to total assets minus total liabilities), it is affected by the accounting treatments used by a firm in such crucial areas as inventory valuation and depreciation. For this reason, comparisons between firms often can be misleading.

SUMMARY OF FINANCIAL RATIO ANALYSIS

Table 3-5 lists all the financial ratios calculated for the Drake Manufacturing Company, summarizing the comparative financial ratio analysis undertaken for the firm.

The assessment column to the right of the table contains an evaluation of each of Drake's ratios in comparison with the industry averages. For example, the firm's liquidity position is rated fair to satisfactory. Whereas its current ratio is somewhat below the industry norm, its quick ratio is satisfactory, indicating that Drake probably has sufficient liquidity to meet maturing obligations. The firm's asset structure is not generating sufficient sales revenues, however. Drake's activity ratios indicate that the firm is investing too much in receivables and inventories, as well as property, plant, and equipment, relative to the sales volume being generated. Thus, Drake should consider implementing more stringent credit and collection policies as well as better inventory controls. The firm also should evaluate its investment in property, plant, and equipment to determine whether reductions could be made without impairing operations.

Drake's financial leverage ratios indicate that the firm is using significantly more debt to finance operations than the average firm in the industry. Because of its poor coverage ratios, the company will likely have difficulty obtaining debt financing for further asset additions. In the event of an economic slowdown, Drake's creditors probably would reevaluate the firm's borrowing capacity and make less funds available to it. If Drake wants to restore its borrowing capacity, it should take steps to increase its equity base. The market-based ratios confirm the analysis performed using Drake's financial statements.

It should be emphasized that the ratios discussed in this analysis are interrelated. For example, Drake is using more debt and investing more in receivables and inventories than the average firm in the industry. If the company could reduce its investment in receivables and inventories and use the released funds to lower debt, *both* the activity ratios and the financial leverage ratios would be closer to the industry averages.

TREND ANALYSIS

Thus far the analysis of the Drake Manufacturing Company has focused solely on the year 19X6. This has provided a fairly complete, if rather static, picture of the company's situation at that particular point in time in comparison with industry standards. To gain insight into the direction the company is moving, however, a trend analysis should be performed. A trend analysis indicates a firm's performance *over time* and reveals whether its position is improving or deteriorating relative to other companies in the industry.

A trend analysis requires that a number of different ratios be calculated over several years and plotted to yield a graphic representation of the company's performance. Figure 3-1 depicts a trend analysis for the Drake Company for the years 19X0 to 19X6 and indicates the direction the firm has been taking for the last several years. Each of the four different categories of financial ratios is represented in the figure. For example, it is evident that the firm's liquidity position—as measured by the quick ratio—has gradually declined over the 7-year period, falling to slightly below the industry average in 19X6. Unless this downward trend continues, however, liquidity should not be a major problem for the firm.

The trend analysis tells another story about the firm's leverage and profitability. Drake's use of debt has exceeded the industry average since 19X2. The activity ratios—the total asset turnover ratio and the average collection period ratio—indicate that the company has used much of this new debt to finance additional assets, including a buildup in receivables. Unfortunately, the new assets have not produced offsetting increases in profits. As a result, returns on investment have dropped below the industry standards by increasing amounts over the past seven years.

In summary, the comparative financial ratio analysis and the trend analysis combined provide the financial analyst with a fairly clear picture of Drake's performance. It is evident that the firm has employed excessive debt to finance asset additions, which have not been sufficiently productive in generating sales revenues. This has resulted in returns on investment and stockholders' equity that are significantly lower than average. If the firm intends to reverse these trends, it will have to make more effective use of assets and reduce the use of creditors' funds. This will enable the firm to improve relations with creditors and potentially increase profitability and reduce risk for its owners.

RETURN ON INVESTMENT

The preceding discussion on ratios indicates that a firm's return on investment (ROI) is defined as the ratio of earnings after taxes (EAT) to total

Ratio Analysis Summary for the Drake Manufacturing Company

Ratio	Definition
LIQUIDITY	
1. Current ratio	$\dfrac{\text{Current assets}}{\text{Current liabilities}}$
2. Quick ratio (acid test)	$\dfrac{\text{Current assets} - \text{Inventories}}{\text{Current liabilities}}$
ACTIVITY	
3. Average collection period	$\dfrac{\text{Accounts receivable}}{\text{Credit sales}/365}$
4. Inventory turnover	$\dfrac{\text{Cost of sales}}{\text{Average inventory}}$
5. Fixed-asset turnover	$\dfrac{\text{Sales}}{\text{Fixed assets}}$
6. Total asset turnover	$\dfrac{\text{Sales}}{\text{Total assets}}$
FINANCIAL LEVERAGE	
7. Debt ratio	$\dfrac{\text{Total debt}}{\text{Total assets}}$
8. Debt-to-equity	$\dfrac{\text{Total debt}}{\text{Total equity}}$
9. Times interest earned	$\dfrac{\text{Earnings before interest and taxes (EBIT)}}{\text{Interest charges}}$
10. Times fixed-charges earned	$\dfrac{\text{EBIT} + \text{Lease payments}}{\text{Interest} + \text{Lease payments} + \text{Before-tax sinking fund} + \text{Preferred stock dividends before tax}}$
PROFITABILITY	
11. Gross profit margin	$\dfrac{\text{Sales} - \text{Cost of sales}}{\text{Sales}}$
12. Net profit margin	$\dfrac{\text{Earnings after taxes (EAT)}}{\text{Sales}}$
13. Return on investment	$\dfrac{\text{Earnings after taxes (EAT)}}{\text{Total assets}}$
14. Return on stockholders' equity	$\dfrac{\text{Earnings after taxes (EAT)}}{\text{Stockholders' equity}}$
MARKET-BASED	
15. Price to earnings ratio	$\dfrac{\text{Market price per share}}{\text{Current earnings per share}}$
16. Market to book ratio	$\dfrac{\text{Market price per share}}{\text{Book value per share}}$

assets. The ROI ratio can be examined more closely to provide additional insights into its significance.

The ROI also can be viewed as a function of the net profit margin times the total asset turnover, because the net profit margin ratio = EAT/sales, and the total asset turnover ratio = sales/total assets:

$$\frac{\text{EAT}}{\text{Total assets}} = \frac{\text{EAT}}{\text{Sales}} \times \frac{\text{Sales}}{\text{Total assets}} \qquad \textbf{(3.17)}$$

Calculation	Industry Average	Assessment
$\dfrac{\$50,190}{\$25,523} = 1.97$ times	2.40 times	Fair
$\dfrac{\$22,660}{\$25,523} = 0.89$ times	0.92 times	Satisfactory
$\dfrac{\$18,320}{\$112,760/365} = 59.3$ days	47 days	Unsatisfactory
$\dfrac{\$85,300}{(\$27,530 + \$26,470)/2} = 3.16$ times	3.9 times	Unsatisfactory
$\dfrac{\$112,760}{\$31,700} = 3.56$ times	4.6 times	Poor
$\dfrac{\$112,760}{\$81,890} = 1.38$ times	1.82 times	Poor
$\dfrac{\$47,523}{\$81,890} = 58$ percent	47 percent	Poor
$\dfrac{\$47,523}{\$34,367} = 138.3$ percent	88.7 percent	Poor
$\dfrac{\$11,520}{\$3,160} = 3.65$ times	6.7 times	Poor
$\dfrac{\$11,520 + \$150}{\$3,160 + \$150 + \$2,000/(1 - 0.4)} = 1.76$ times	4.5 times	Poor
$\dfrac{\$27,460}{\$112,760} = 24.4$ percent	25.6 percent	Fair
$\dfrac{\$5,016}{\$112,760} = 4.45$ percent	5.10 percent	Unsatisfactory
$\dfrac{\$5,016}{\$81,890} = 6.13$ percent	9.28 percent	Poor
$\dfrac{\$5,016}{\$34,367} = 14.60$ percent	17.54 percent	Poor
$\dfrac{\$24}{\$3.34} = 6.22$ times	8.0 times	Poor
$\dfrac{\$24}{\$26.44} = 0.91$	1.13	Poor

It is important to examine a firm's ROI in terms of "margin" and "turnover," because each plays a major role in contributing to profitability. "Margin" measures the profit earned per dollar of sales but ignores the amount of assets used to generate sales. The ROI relationship brings these two components together and shows that a deficiency in either one will lower a firm's return on investment.

Using the figures from the net profit margin ratio and total asset turnover ratio calculated previously for the Drake Company, the firm's ROI for 19X6

FIGURE 3-1

Trend Analysis of the Financial Ratios for the Drake Manufacturing Company from 19X0 to 19X6

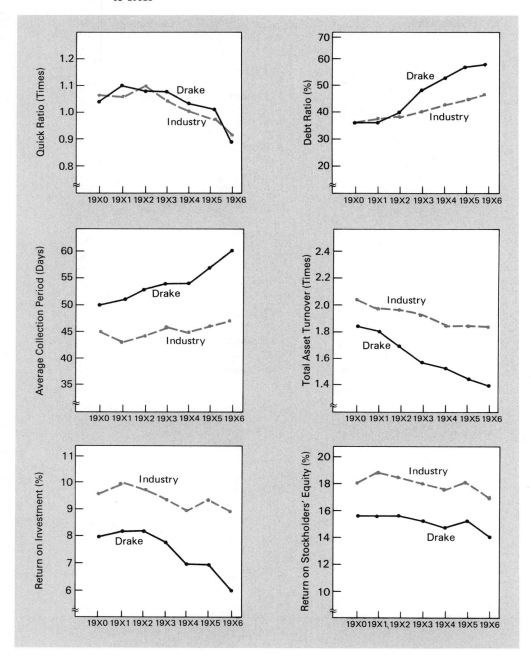

can be computed as 4.45% × 1.377 = 6.13%. Figure 3-2, called a *DuPont chart* because it was developed and is used by the DuPont Corporation, illustrates this relationship. For purposes of comparison, the industry average ROI = 5.10% × 1.82 = 9.28%. The ROI relationship shows Drake to be deficient in both margin and turnover relative to the industry average. Improvement in either area would increase the firm's ROI. To improve its *margin*, for example, Drake must either increase sales revenues more than costs or decrease costs more than sales revenues. To improve its *turnover*, the firm must either increase sales revenue or reduce the asset level required to support the current sales volume. The DuPont chart illustrates the relationship between a firm's ROI and the factors that determine it. By working back through the DuPont chart an analyst can begin to pinpoint potential areas for improvement that will enhance the firm's ROI.

The relative contributions of the net profit margin and the asset turnover ratio in the ROI relationship differ from industry to industry. Specifically, the turnover ratio is largely dependent on a firm's investment in property, plant, and equipment. Firms with large investments in fixed assets tend to have low turnover ratios; public utilities, railroads, and large industrial firms fall into this category. If these companies are to succeed, their relatively low turnover ratios must be offset by correspondingly high margins to produce competitive ROIs. For example, electric and gas utilities typically have net profit margins of 10 to 15 percent. In contrast, other industries require much lower investments in fixed assets, resulting in higher turnover ratios. A typical example is the retail grocery chain industry, which has margins of only 1 or 2 percent. Firms in this industry often achieve turnovers of 10 times or more. If a grocery chain had a lower turnover, its ROI probably would not be sufficient to attract investors.

▰▰▰ RETURN ON STOCKHOLDERS' EQUITY

Figure 3-2 also shows Drake's return on stockholders' equity, which is computed as 14.60 percent. If the firm were financed solely with common equity (stock), the return on stockholders' equity would equal the return on investment. Drake's stockholders have supplied only about 42 percent of the

Determinants of Return on Investment for the Drake Manufacturing Company, 19X6   F I G U R E 3-2

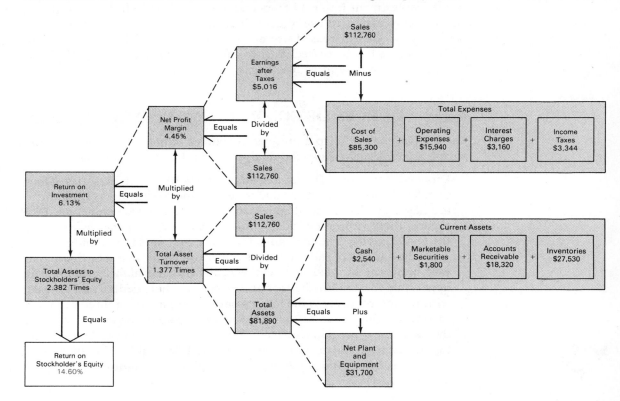

firm's total capital, whereas creditors have supplied the remaining 58 percent. Because the entire 6.13 percent return on investment belongs to the stockholders (even though they only supplied 42 percent of the total capital), Drake's return on common equity is higher than its return on investment.

To better clarify how the return on stockholders' equity is determined, a new ratio, the *equity multiplier ratio*, is defined as follows:

$$\text{Equity multiplier} = \frac{\text{Total assets}}{\text{Stockholders' equity}} \qquad \textbf{(3.18)}$$

Drake's equity multiplier ratio is computed from figures found in Table 3-1 as $81,890/$34,367 = 2.382 times. The industry average for the ratio is 1.89 times. Once again it can be seen that Drake has financed a greater proportion of assets with debt than the average firm in the industry.

The equity multiplier ratio may be used to show how a firm's use of debt to finance assets affects the return on equity, as follows:

$$\begin{array}{c}\text{Return on}\\ \text{stockholders'} =\\ \text{equity}\end{array} \begin{array}{c}\text{Net profit}\\ \text{margin}\end{array} \times \begin{array}{c}\text{Total asset}\\ \text{turnover}\end{array} \times \begin{array}{c}\text{Equity}\\ \text{multiplier}\end{array} \qquad \textbf{(3.19)}$$

$$= \frac{\text{Earnings after taxes}}{\text{Sales}} \times \frac{\text{Sales}}{\text{Total assets}} \times \frac{\text{Total assets}}{\text{Stockholders' equity}}$$

In Drake's case the return on stockholders' equity is 4.45 × 1.377 × 2.382 = 14.60%.

Although this figure is the same as the return on equity computed directly by dividing earnings after tax by stockholders' equity, the calculations shown illustrate more clearly how Drake managed to magnify a 6.13 percent return on total investment into a 14.60 percent return on stockholders' equity by making more extensive use of debt financing than did the average firm in the industry. This increased use of debt has improved Drake's return on equity but also has increased its risk—more likely resulting in a decline in Drake's stock price relative to other, similar firms.

SOURCES OF COMPARATIVE FINANCIAL DATA

The analyst may refer to a number of sources of financial data when preparing a comparative financial analysis, including the following:

■ **Dun and Bradstreet** Dun and Bradstreet (D&B) prepares a series of fourteen key business ratios for 800 different lines of business. These ratios are based on the financial statements of some 400,000 companies. D&B reports three values for each ratio—the *median*, the *upper quartile*, and the *lower quartile*. The median is the figure that falls in the middle when individual ratios of sampled firms are arranged by size. The figure halfway between the median and the ratio with the highest value is the upper quartile, and the figure halfway between the median and the ratio with the lowest value is the lower quartile. By reporting three values for each ratio, D&B enables the analyst to compare a particular firm with the "average" (median) firm, as well as with the "typical" firms in the top and bottom halves of the sample. The D&B publication containing the data is titled *Industry Norms and Key Business Ratios*.

■ **Robert Morris Associates** This national association of bank loan and credit officers uses information provided by loan applications to compile sixteen ratios for over 250 lines of business. Like D&B, Robert Morris Associates reports the median, upper quartile, and lower quartile for each ratio. Data are presented for four categories of firm size. This source is especially useful to the analyst gathering information about smaller firms. The Robert Morris publication containing the data is titled *Statement Studies.*

■ *Quarterly Financial Reports for Manufacturing Companies* The Federal Trade Commission (FTC) and the Securities and Exchange Commission (SEC) cooperate in publishing quarterly reports on balance sheet and income statement data of various manufacturing companies. These include analyses of the firms by industry and asset size, along with presentations of financial statements in ratio form.

■ **Prentice-Hall's** *Almanac of Business and Industrial Financial Ratios* This annual almanac of business and industrial financial ratios reports twenty-two ratios for 162 separate industries. It also includes the number of establishments in the sampled industry, the number without net income, and the total dollar receipts for each of the eleven size groups into which firms in each industry are classified.

■ *Financial Studies of Small Business* This annual publication of Financial Research Associates is particularly valuable for the evaluation of small firms.

■ **Moody's or Standard and Poor's Industrial, Financial, Transportation, and Over-the-Counter Manuals** These contain a large amount of balance sheet and income statement data, as well as other relevant background information about a firm.

■ **Annual reports** Most corporations publish an annual report containing income statement and balance sheet data along with other information of interest.

■ **10K Reports** Every widely held firm is required annually to file a 10K report with the SEC. These reports contain income statement and balance sheet data, plus a wide range of other relevant information dealing with the firm's past and current performance and expected future prospects.

■ **Trade journals** These are published by trade associations and contain a great deal of financial and other types of information on member firms.

■ **Commercial banks** Frequently banks compile financial reports on selected industries. One example is First Chicago's semiannual financial survey of sales finance and consumer finance companies.

■ **Computerized data sources** A number of computerized data bases also are available to assist in financial analysis. The *Compustat* data base is available from Standard and Poor's. It contains complete balance sheet, income statement, stock price, and dividend information for several thousand companies, covering a period of 20 years. The *Compustat* data base is available in a form for both mainframe computers and microcomputers. *Value Line* provides summary financial data and forecasts of future performance for over 1700 firms. The *Value Line* data base is available in both hard copy and in a microcomputer-usable format called *Value Screen.* In addition, many of these data sources can be accessed for a small fee through computer time sharing services such as *Compuserve.* The *Disclosure* data base contains complete financial data for over 10,000 firms. It is available for use on microcomputers and through *Compuserve.*

A WORD OF CAUTION ABOUT FINANCIAL RATIO ANALYSIS

Throughout the analysis of the Drake Manufacturing Company performed in this chapter, it has been emphasized that the analyst must exercise caution when evaluating a firm's financial ratios. Although ratios can provide valuable information, they also can be misleading for a number of reasons.

First, ratios are only as reliable as the accounting data on which they are based. Different firms follow different accounting procedures for inventory valuation, depreciation, reporting long-term leases, pension fund contributions, and mergers and acquisitions, to name just a few. These, in turn, affect reported earnings, assets, and owners' investments. Unless the analyst makes adjustments for accounting reporting differences, ratio comparisons between individual companies and with various industry norms never can be viewed as definitive.

Second, with the exception of disclosing upper and lower quartile values, firms that compile industry norms often do not report information about the *dispersion*, or distribution, of the individual values around the mean ratio. If the reported ratios are widely dispersed, the industry average will be of questionable value, because it may not reflect the "typical" firm in the industry. Furthermore, the standard of comparison probably should not be the "typical" firm, but rather the better performing firms in the industry. Without some measure of dispersion, however, ratios for these better performing firms cannot be determined.

Third, valid comparative analysis depends on the availability of data for appropriately defined industries. Some industry classifications are either too broad or too narrow to be reliable sources of comparative data when an analyst is evaluating a particular firm. Most firms operate in more than one industry, and this makes analysis more difficult.

Fourth, it is important to remember that financial ratios provide a *historic* record of the performance and financial condition of a firm. Further analysis is required before this historic record can be used as a basis for future projections.

Finally, comparisons of a firm's ratios with industry norms may not always be what they seem. Ratios comparing unfavorably with industry norms should be construed as "red flags" indicating the need for further investigation—not signals of impending doom. On the other hand, even if a firm's ratios compare favorably with those of the better performing firms in the industry, it does not necessarily mean the firm is performing adequately. If, for example, the industry itself is experiencing a declining demand for its goods and services, favorable ratio comparisons may simply indicate that a firm is not decaying as rapidly as the typical firm in the industry. Thus, comparisons of selected ratios—particularly those relating to profitability—must be made with *national* industry averages in order to determine whether a particular firm in a particular industry is justified in making further investments.

In summary, ratios should not be viewed as substitutes for sound business judgment. Instead, they are simply tools that can help management make better decisions.

EARNINGS AND BALANCE SHEET QUALITY AND FINANCIAL ANALYSIS

When performing a financial analysis of a firm, it is important to be mindful of the *quality of the earnings* reported by a firm as well as the *quality of the firm's balance sheet.* These two dimensions of financial analysis can have a critical impact on the final assessment of the firm's financial condition.

Earnings Quality

When considering the quality of a firm's earnings, two key factors should be kept in mind. First, high quality earnings tend to be cash earnings. The proportion of a firm's earnings that can be viewed as cash earnings is greatly influenced by the firm's procedures with respect to sales revenue recognition. For example, a firm may recognize a sale at the time a contract is signed, a down payment is made, or when the full proceeds from the sale are actually collected as cash. Generally, the closer the recognition of a sale is to the time the full proceeds from that sale are collected, the higher is the quality of the firm's reported earnings.

Some firms report a large noncash component in their income because of special accounting practices in their industry. For example, utilities generally recognize earnings, for financial reporting purposes, on assets that are under construction but that have not yet been placed in the rate-base of the firm for ratemaking purposes. This component of earnings is frequently called *allowance for funds used during construction* (AFUDC) and it recognizes the return that the firm ultimately will earn on these assets once they are placed in service by the utility. For utilities with large construction programs, the proportion of noncash to total earnings can be very large. For example, for the year ending March 31, 1987, El Paso Electric, which is involved in a large construction program, reported an AFUDC as a percent of net income ratio of 92%, indicating that only a small portion of the firm's earnings represented cash income. In contrast, Consolidated Edison Corporation reported an AFUDC to net income ratio of only 2%, indicating that its earnings were of much higher quality than those of El Paso Electric.

In the banking industry, an analyst must look to the quality of the loans the bank has made and the adequacy of loan loss reserves to determine if reported net income figures accurately reflect the earnings for the period being reviewed. When loan loss reserves are not adequate, future earnings will be adversely affected if the bank must charge off a significant portion of its bad loans. In the same context, an analyst examining any firm must consider the quality of that firm's accounts receivable. If some receivables are not likely to be collected, then the future earnings of the firm will be reduced.

Second, a firm's earnings can be viewed as high quality the greater is the proportion of those earnings derived from regularly recurring transactions. To the extent that reported earnings reflect the impact of nonrecurring transactions, the quality of those earnings is reduced. For example, in 1988 Tenneco sold its oil and gas businesses. Because these businesses were carried on Tenneco's books at an amount less than the total sales price, the company was able to recognize a gain of $892 million on the transaction. This transaction is of a nonrecurring nature and should not be considered when evaluating the earnings capacity of the firm. Other, similar, nonrecurring gains can emerge when a firm repurchases its debt on the open market at a price lower than the face value of that debt. Also, a firm may change its accounting treatment of inventories and record a significant gain from this transaction. General Motors (GM) did this in 1988 and reported a one-time gain of $217 million.[14] Another example of a nonrecurring trans-

[14] Gary Hector, "Cute Tricks on the Bottom Line," *Fortune* (April 24, 1989); p. 193.

action from which gains can occur involves lowering the reported depreciation expense on a company's existing assets. In 1988, GM also did this by increasing the length of time it depreciates auto plants from 35 years to 45 years, the same figure Ford uses. As a result, GM had a nonrecurring earnings increase of $790 million in 1988.[15] These are only a few examples of significant nonrecurring transactions. *The important point to remember is that earnings quality is lower the greater is the proportion of nonrecurring items in a firm's reported earnings figures.*

Balance Sheet Quality

The quality of a firm's balance sheet also should be of concern to a financial analyst. If the assets on a firm's balance sheet have a market value equal to or greater than the book value at which they are being carried, this enhances the quality of the firm's balance sheet. In contrast, if a significant portion of the assets of a firm have a market value substantially below book value, the quality of the firm's balance sheet is reduced. Over the last decade we have seen many firms in the so-called smokestack industries record large losses as significant portions of their assets are abandoned and written off as losses. These firms include Kaiser Aluminum, U.S. Steel (USX), and Bethlehem Steel. Commercial banks regularly write off a portion of their loan portfolios when it becomes clear that particular loans will not be repaid. For example, in May 1987 Citicorp set aside $3 billion against possible losses on its loans to Brazil. Similarly, during the mid-1980s Texas banks had to write off hundreds of millions of dollars of loans because the oil price slump forced oil industry firms to sustain major losses. These actions greatly reduce the equity ratios for the firm. Similarly, if a firm has significant amounts of inventory that cannot be moved (such as the Adam computers that Coleco once produced), the quality of the balance sheet is reduced until the firm charges off this low quality inventory.

In addition to asset quality issues, an analyst should also be aware of hidden liabilities. These liabilities may take the form of such things as long-term lease obligations not appearing on the company's balance sheet or uninsured losses arising from pending lawsuits. When large potential liabilities such as these exist, an analyst must be quite careful before drawing conclusions about the adequacy of a firm's capital structure, based upon an analysis of its reported balance sheet.

In contrast, some firms have significant hidden assets. These assets may be physical assets, such as real property that has appreciated in value but is carried on the firm's books at cost or securities that are carried on the books at cost even though the market value of these securities has increased above the original cost.

This list of balance sheet and earnings quality issues certainly is not all inclusive, but it does give an indication of the extent to which a surface analysis of a firm's financial statements can lead to misleading conclusions about the financial condition of that firm.

USING FINANCIAL RATIOS TO FORECAST FUTURE FINANCIAL PERFORMANCE

Throughout this chapter we have emphasized the caution that a financial analyst must exercise when evaluating a firm's financial ratios. Yet, in spite

---

[15] Ibid.

of this, financial ratios have been used in conjunction with sophisticated statistical techniques to forecast events such as bankruptcy of a firm. This section provides an overview of this area; a detailed discussion is beyond our scope.

One of the primary limitations of traditional financial ratio analysis is that it looks at only one ratio at a time and then relies on the analyst to form a judgment about the overall financial profile of the firm. Recently, more powerful statistical techniques have been applied to assist the analyst in making judgments about the financial condition of the firm.

Discriminant analysis is a statistical technique that helps the analyst classify observations (firms) into two or more predetermined groups based on certain characteristics of the observation. In the context of financial statement analysis, the characteristics typically are financial ratios.

One early application of discriminant analysis in finance was a model developed by Edward Altman to predict bankruptcy of firms.[16] Altman identified five financial ratios that contributed significantly to the predictive accuracy of his model:

- Net working capital/Total assets
- Retained earnings/Total assets
- EBIT/Total assets
- Market value of total equity (common and preferred)/Book value of total debt
- Sales/Total assets

Altman's basic model was developed from a sample of sixty-six manufacturing firms—half of which went bankrupt. On the basis of the analysis, he established a guideline score, which could be used to classify firms as either financially sound or headed toward bankruptcy. The lower the score, the greater was the probability of bankruptcy; the higher the score, the lower was the probability of bankruptcy. In other words, the lower the values of the five ratios just listed, in general, the greater was the probability of bankruptcy.

More recent refinements of Altman's bankruptcy forecasting model have broadened the spectrum of firms to which it can be applied to include retailing as well as manufacturing firms.[17] The newer model is about 70 percent accurate as much as 5 years prior to bankruptcy.

INFLATION AND FINANCIAL STATEMENT ANALYSIS

Inflation can cause a number of problems for the financial analyst who is trying to assess the performance of a firm over time and in comparison with other firms in the industry. In particular, *inventory profits*, or short-lived increased profits that occur as a result of the timing of price increases, can make a significant difference in a firm's reported earnings from year to year.

For example, consider a supply company that buys equipment parts wholesale from the manufacturer for $4.00 each and sells them at a retail price of $5.00 each, realizing a profit of $1.00 per unit. Suppose the manufacturer announces a price increase of $0.50 per unit to $4.50, effective on

[16] Edward I. Altman, "Financial Ratios, Discriminant Analysis, and the Prediction of Corporate Bankruptcy," *Journal of Finance* (September 1968): 589–609.
[17] Edward I. Altman, R. G. Haldeman, and P. Narayanan. "Zeta Analysis: A New Model to Identify Bankruptcy Risk of Corporations," *Journal of Banking and Finance* (June 1977): 29–54.

the first of next month. If the supply company passes the increase on to customers and announces a price increase of its own to $5.50, also effective on the first of next month, it will realize a gross profit of $1.50 on every unit sold, which originally cost $4.00. In other words, the company will make additional profit on the units already in inventory *prior to the price increase*. Once it begins purchasing parts from the manufacturer at the new price of $4.50 per unit, it will revert to its original $1.00 profit. In the meantime, however, the timing of the price increase will allow the company to enjoy short-lived increased profits, or inventory profits.

Most companies do not want to pay income taxes on inventory profits, preferring to use these funds to replenish inventories—especially in inflationary times. Fortunately, there is a way of avoiding or deferring the necessity of reporting these higher profits. The *last-in, first-out* (LIFO) inventory valuation method assumes that the items a firm uses from inventory are those that were acquired most recently. Thus, they can be *priced out* of the inventory based on the most recent inventory acquisition costs. In contrast, the *first-in, first-out* (FIFO) method of inventory valuation, which assumes that the items a firm uses from inventory are the oldest items in inventory, results in the firm's having to show a higher profit and therefore pay higher income taxes.

During the 1960s, most large U.S. corporations were using the FIFO method. Inflation at that time was low to moderate, and the majority of companies thought it desirable to report their net income as high as possible. By 1974, however, inflation rates had risen to about 12 percent, and companies that were experiencing increasing inventory profits began switching to the LIFO method in an attempt to conserve cash by paying less income taxes.

The accounting method used for inventory will affect a firm's profits and its balance sheet. Hence, any financial ratio that contains balance sheet inventory figures (for example, the total asset turnover ratio) or net income will vary from one firm to another, depending on the firm's accounting treatment of inventory. Another effect of inflation on financial statements is the tendency for the value of fixed assets to be understated. Also, to the extent that inflation causes a rise in interest rates, the value of long-term debt outstanding will decline. Thus, a firm will appear to be more financially leveraged in an inflationary period than is actually the case.

Inventory profits and inflation are only two factors that can affect a firm's reported earnings. Differences in the reporting of earnings, the recognition of sales, and other factors also can make comparisons between firms somewhat misleading. Again, the good financial analyst will always "go behind" the figures stated on a firm's income statement or balance sheet to find out what actually is occurring within a company. It should be obvious at this point that financial analysis is no simple matter. At first, it may appear as if all it involves is the evaluation of a certain number of apparently clear-cut ratios. As is evident from this chapter, however, it involves a great deal more.

INTERNATIONAL CONCERNS: FINANCIAL ANALYSIS OF MULTINATIONAL CORPORATIONS

The tools of financial statement analysis developed in this chapter are useful in evaluating the financial performance of purely domestic United States firms as well as firms with small international operations. However, assessing the financial performance and condition of a firm with sizable international operations is generally more complicated than analyzing a firm whose operations are largely domestic.

Part of the complication involves the translation of foreign operating results from the host country's currency to U.S. dollars. To illustrate, suppose IBM's French operations show net earnings of 100 million French francs. IBM reports its results to stockholders denominated in U.S. dollars. Therefore, the French results must be translated into U.S. dollars. The *dollar* amount of IBM's French earnings depends on the exchange rate between dollars and francs.[18] If, for example, the exchange rate between francs and dollars is 8.0 French francs per dollar, the earnings of 100 million French francs are reported as $12,500,000 (100 million francs/8.0 francs per dollar). But, if the exchange rate changes to 10.0 French francs to the dollar, the earnings of 100 million francs translate into only $10,000,000 U.S. dollars (100 million francs/10 francs per dollar). Thus, the earnings reported by a U.S. company with sizable foreign operations depend not only on the earnings stated in the local currency, but on the exchange rates between local currencies and the U.S. dollar.

When the U.S. dollar is relatively "strong" against a foreign currency— that is, when the dollar will "buy" more French francs, for example—foreign earnings translate into fewer dollars than when the dollar is relatively "weak." This is illustrated in the IBM example.[19]

An additional complication in financial analysis of multinational firms arises because of fluctuating exchange rates. What happens to the *dollar* value on the parent (IBM's) balance sheet of IBM's French *assets* and *liabilities* as the exchange rate between francs and dollars changes? According to *Statement of Accounting Standards No. 52*, which deals with international accounting, assets and liabilities normally are translated at the exchange rate in effect on the balance sheet date.[20] However, any gains and losses resulting from the translation of asset and liability accounts are not reflected on the income statement and therefore also are not included in the retained earnings figure on the balance sheet. Instead gains and losses from foreign translation are reported separately on the balance sheet as a part of stockholders' equity, usually under a heading such as "cumulative foreign exchange translation adjustment." For example, during 1988 IBM reported a decrease of $948 million in its translation adjustments account.[21] This decrease did not affect IBM's 1988 earnings, but it did change stockholders' equity on IBM's balance sheet. The decrease occurred because the dollar generally strengthened during 1988 against the currencies in the countries where IBM has most of its overseas assets, and because IBM had substantially more assets than debt employed in its non-U.S. operations in 1988.

Financial managers and analysts in the 1990s will have to be knowledgeable about the complex international aspects of financial statement analysis.

SUMMARY

■ *Financial ratios* are statistical yardsticks that relate two numbers generally taken from a firm's income statements and balance sheets.
■ Financial ratios fall into five categories:

[18] Exchange rates are discussed in detail in Chapter 21.
[19] The effects of exchange rate levels on business conditions are discussed further in Chapter 21.
[20] See Eiteman, David K. and Arthur T. Stonehill, *Multinational Business Finance*, 4th ed. Reading, MA: Addison-Wesley, 1986 for a further discussion of translation procedures.
[21] *Annual Report* (International Business Machines Corporation, 1988), p. 43.

1. *Liquidity ratios,* which measure a firm's ability to meet its maturing obligations.
2. *Activity ratios,* which measure how efficiently a firm is using resources to generate sales.
3. *Financial leverage ratios,* which indicate a firm's capacity to meet short- and long-term debt obligations.
4. *Profitability ratios,* which measure the firm's ability to generate profits on sales, assets, and owners' investment.
5. *Market-based ratios,* which measure the market's (investors') perceptions of a firm's performance and risk.

■ Common-size financial statements, which express financial items in percentages, are helpful in detecting and monitoring financial trends.

■ *Trend analysis* introduces the element of time into financial ratio analysis. It gives the analyst a more dynamic view of a company's situation than does a pure comparative financial ratio analysis alone.

■ The relationship of the return on investment (ROI) to "margin" and "turnover" can be used to determine if one or both of the two is deficient in contributing to the profitability of a firm.

■ To gain further insight into the relative financial position of a firm, the analyst must compare the financial ratios with *industry averages.* The more diversified the firm, the more difficult it will be to make such a comparison. Two major sources of industry ratios are Dun and Bradstreet and Robert Morris Associates.

■ The quality of a firm's earnings is higher the greater the proportion of cash earnings to total earnings and the greater the proportion of recurring income to total income.

■ The quality of a firm's balance sheet is enhanced the greater is the ratio of the market value of the firm's assets to the book value of those assets and the lesser is the amount of "hidden liabilities" that appears on the firm's balance sheet.

■ Financial ratios have been used in conjunction with sophisticated statistical techniques to forecast events such as bankruptcy of a firm.

■ *Inflation* can have a significant impact on a firm's reported earnings. For example, it can influence the firm to choose a different inventory valuation method and cost accounting system. When comparing the performance of two or more firms, the financial analyst should recognize that the firms may use different accounting methods to calculate net income.

■ Financial statements of multinational firms are influenced by fluctuating foreign exchange rates.

QUESTIONS AND TOPICS FOR DISCUSSION

1. What are the primary limitations of ratio analysis as a technique of financial statement analysis?
2. What is the major limitation of the current ratio as a measure of a firm's liquidity? How may this limitation be overcome?
3. What problems may be indicated by an average collection period that is substantially above or below the industry average?
4. What problems may be indicated by an inventory turnover ratio that is substantially above or below the industry average?
5. What factors limit the use of the fixed asset turnover ratio in comparative analyses?

6. What are the three most important determinants of a firm's return on stockholders' equity?

7. What specific effects can the use of alternative accounting procedures have on the validity of comparative financial analyses?

8. How can inflation affect the comparability of financial ratios between firms?

9. What is the relationship between a firm's P/E multiple and that firm's risk and growth potential?

10. Discuss the general factors that influence the quality of a company's reported earnings and its balance sheet.

11. Why would you anticipate a lower P/E ratio for a typical natural gas utility than for a computer technology firm, such as Digital Equipment?

PROBLEMS*

1. Vanity Press, Inc., has annual credit sales of $1,600,000 and a gross profit margin of 35 percent.

   a. If the firm wishes to maintain an average collection period of 50 days, what level of accounts receivable should it carry? (Assume a 365-day year.)

   b. The inventory turnover for this industry averages 6 times. If all of Vanity's sales are on credit, what average level of inventory should the firm maintain to achieve the same inventory turnover figure as the industry?

2. Pacific Fixtures lists the following accounts as part of its balance sheet.

Total assets	$10,000,000
Accounts payable	$ 2,000,000
Notes payable (8%)	1,000,000
Bonds (10%)	3,000,000
Common stock at par	1,000,000
Contributed capital in excess of par	500,000
Retained earnings	2,500,000
Total liabilities and stockholders' equity	$10,000,000

   Compute the return on stockholders' equity if the company has sales of $20 million and the following net profit margin:

   a. 3 percent.
   b. 5 percent.

3. Clovis Industries had sales in 19X1 of $40 million, 20 percent of which were cash. If Clovis normally carries 45 days of credit sales in accounts receivable, what are its average accounts receivable balances? (Assume a 365-day year.)

4. Williams Oil Company had a return on stockholders' equity of 18 percent during 19X1. Its total asset turnover was 1.0 times, and its equity multiplier was 2.0 times. Calculate the company's net profit margin.

5. Using the data in the following table for a number of firms in the same industry, do the following:

   a. Compute the total asset turnover, the net profit margin, the equity multiplier, and the return on equity for each firm.

   b. Evaluate each firm's performance by comparing the firms with one another. Which firm or firms appear to be having problems? What corrective action would you suggest the submarginal firms take? Finally, what additional data would you want to have on hand when conducting your analyses?

* Colored numbers denote problems that have check answers provided at the end of the book.

	Firm			
	A	B	C	D
Sales (in millions of dollars)	20	10	15	25
Net income after tax (in millions of dollars)	3	0.5	2.25	3
Total assets (in millions of dollars)	15	7.5	15	24
Stockholders' equity (in millions of dollars)	10	5.0	14	10

6. Tarheel Furniture Company is planning to establish a wholly owned subsidiary to manufacture upholstery fabrics. Tarheel expects to earn $1 million after tax on the venture during the first year. The president of Tarheel wants to know what the subsidiary's balance sheet would look like. The president believes that it would be advisable to begin the new venture with ratios that are similar to the industry average.

Tarheel plans to make all sales on credit. All calculations assume a 365-day year. In your computations you should round all numbers to the nearest $1,000.

Based upon the industry average financial ratios presented here, complete the projected balance sheet for Tarheel's upholstery subsidiary.

	Industry Averages
Current ratio	2:1
Quick ratio	1:1
Net profit margin ratio	5 percent
Average collection period	20 days
Debt ratio	40 percent
Total asset turnover ratio	2 times
Current liabilities/stockholders' equity	20 percent

Forecasted Upholstery Subsidiary Balance Sheet

Cash	—	Total current liabilities	—
Accounts receivable	—	Long-term debt	—
Inventory	—	Total debt	—
Total current assets	—	Stockholders' equity	—
Net fixed assets	—	Total liabilities and	
Total assets	—	stockholders' equity	—

7. The Sooner Equipment Company has total assets of $100 million. Of this total, $40 million was financed with common equity and $60 million with debt (both long and short term). Its average accounts receivable balance is $20 million, and this represents an 80-day average collection period. Sooner believes it can reduce its average collection period from 80 days to 60 days without affecting sales or the dollar amount of net income after tax (currently $5 million). What will be the effect of this action on Sooner's return on investment and its return on stockholders' equity if the funds received by reducing the average collection period are used to buy back its common stock at book value? What impact will this action have on Sooner's debt ratio?

8. The Jamesway Printing Corporation has current assets of $3.0 million. Of this total, $1.0 million is inventory, $0.5 million is cash, $1.0 million is accounts receivable, and the balance is marketable securities. Jamesway has $1.5 million in current liabilities.

a. What are the current and the quick ratios for Jamesway?

b. If Jamesway takes $0.25 million in cash and pays off $0.25 million of current liabilities, what happens to its current and quick ratios? What happens to its real liquidity?

c. If Jamesway sells $0.5 million of its accounts receivable to a bank and uses the proceeds to pay off short-term debt obligations, what happens to its current and quick ratios?

d. If Jamesway sells $1.0 million in new stock and places the proceeds in marketable securities, what happens to its current and quick ratios?

e. What do these examples illustrate about the current and quick ratios?

9. Gulf Controls, Inc., has a net profit margin of 10 percent and earnings after taxes of $600,000. Its current balance sheet follows:

Current assets	$1,800,000	Current liabilities	$ 600,000
Fixed assets	2,200,000	Long-term debt	1,000,000
Total assets	$4,000,000	Common stock	500,000
		Retained earnings	1,900,000
		Total liabilities and stockholders' equity	$4,000,000

a. Calculate Gulf's return on stockholders' equity.
b. The industry average ratios are as follows:

Net profit margin	6 percent
Total asset turnover	2.5 times
Equity multiplier	1.4 times

Compare Gulf Controls with the average firm in the industry. What is the source of the major differences between Gulf and the industry average ratios?

10. Using the following data for Jackson Products Company, answer parts a through g:

Jackson Products Company's Balance Sheet
December 31, 19X1

Cash	$ 240,000	Accounts payable	$ 380,000
Accounts receivable	320,000	Notes payable (9%)	420,000
Inventory	1,040,000	Other current liabilities	50,000
Total current assets	$1,600,000	Total current liabilities	$ 850,000
Net plant and equipment	800,000	Long-term debt (10%)	800,000
Total assets	$2,400,000	Stockholders' equity	750,000
		Total liabilities and stockholders' equity	$2,400,000

Income Statement
for the Year Ended December 31, 19X1

Net sales (all on credit)		$3,000,000
Cost of sales		1,800,000
Gross profit		$1,200,000
Selling, general, and administrative expenses		860,000
Earnings before interest and taxes		$ 340,000
Interest:		
Notes	$37,800	
Long-term debt	80,000	
Total interest charges		117,800
Earnings before taxes		$ 222,200
Federal income tax (40%)		88,880
Earnings after taxes		$ 133,320

Industry Averages	
Current ratio	2.5 times
Quick ratio	1.1 times
Average collection period (365-day year)	35 days
Inventory turnover ratio	2.4 times
Total asset turnover ratio	1.4 times
Times interest earned ratio	3.5 times
Net profit margin ratio	4.0 percent
Return on investment ratio	5.6 percent
Total assets/stockholders' equity (equity multiplier) ratio	3.0 times
Return on stockholders' equity ratio	16.8 percent
P/E ratio	9.0 times

a. Evaluate the liquidity position of Jackson relative to that of the average firm in the industry. Consider the current ratio, the quick ratio, and the net working capital (current assets minus current liabilities) for Jackson. What problems, if any, are suggested by this analysis?

b. Evaluate Jackson's performance by looking at key activity ratios. Are any problems apparent from this analysis?

c. Evaluate the financial risk of Jackson by examining its times interest earned ratio and its equity multiplier ratio relative to the same industry average ratios.

d. Evaluate the profitability of Jackson relative to that of the average firm in its industry.

e. Give an overall evaluation of the performance of Jackson relative to other firms in its industry.

f. Construct a Du Pont chart analysis for Jackson. What areas appear to have the greatest need for improvement?

g. Jackson's current P/E ratio is 7 times. What factor(s) are most likely to account for this ratio relative to the higher industry average ratio?

11. Given the following data for Profiteers, Inc., and the corresponding industry averages, perform a trend analysis of the return on investment and the return on stockholders' equity. Plot the data and discuss any trends that are apparent. Also, discuss the underlying causes of these trends.

	Years				
	19X1	19X2	19X3	19X4	19X5
Profiteers, Inc.					
Net profit margin	14%	12%	11%	9%	10%
Asset turnover	1.26×	1.22×	1.20×	1.19×	1.21×
Equity multiplier	1.34×	1.40×	1.61×	1.65×	1.63×
Industry Averages					
Net profit margin	12%	11%	11%	10%	10%
Asset turnover	1.25×	1.27×	1.30×	1.31×	1.34×
Equity multiplier	1.42×	1.45×	1.47×	1.51×	1.53×

12. If a company sells additional common stock and uses the proceeds to increase its inventory level and to increase its cash balances, what is the near-term (immediate) impact (increase, decrease, no change) of this transaction on the following ratios?

a. Current ratio

b. Return on stockholders' equity

c. Quick ratio

d. Debt to total assets
e. Total asset turnover

13. Lane Enterprises had sales of $20 million and earnings after tax of $1.6 million. The firm had a total asset turnover of 2.5 times. The industry average was 2.0 times. The equity accounts for Lane are as follows:

Common stock at par	$ 600,000
Contributed capital in excess of par	2,400,000
Retained earnings	3,400,000

The following ratios represent averages for Lane's industry:

Net profit margin	6%
Total asset turnover	2 times
Equity multiplier	2.08 times

a. Use the Du Pont analysis to calculate Lane's return on equity.
b. Compare Lane's performance to the industry average.

14. Keystone Resources has a net profit margin of 8% and earnings after tax of $2 million. Its current balance sheet is as follows:

Current assets	$ 6,000,000	Current liabilities	$ 3,500,000
Fixed assets	10,000,000	Long-term debt	5,500,000
Total assets	$16,000,000	Common stock	2,000,000
		Retained earnings	5,000,000
		Total liabilities and	
		stockholders' equity	$16,000,000

a. Calculate Keystone's return on stockholders' equity.
b. Industry average ratios are

Net profit margin	10%
Total asset turnover	2.0 times
Equity multiplier	1.5 times

What does a comparison of Keystone to these averages indicate about the firm's strengths and weaknesses?
c. Keystone has inventories of $3.2 million. Compute the firm's quick ratio.

15. Palmer Chocolates, a maker of chocolates that specializes in Easter candy, had the following inventories over the past year:

Month	Inventory Amount
January	$25,000,000
February	60,000,000
March	90,000,000
April	30,000,000
May	20,000,000
June	22,000,000
July	25,000,000
August	38,000,000
September	50,000,000
October	60,000,000
November	70,000,000
December	30,000,000

Palmer had sales of $290 million over the past year. Cost of sales constituted 50 percent of sales. Calculate Palmer's inventory turnover using beginning of year inventory, end of year inventory, and a monthly average inventory. Which method do you feel is most appropriate? Why?

16. The stock of Jenkins Corporation, a major steel producer, is currently selling for $50/share. The book value per share is $125. In contrast, the price per share of Dataquest's stock is $40, compared to a book value per share of $10. Dataquest, a leading software developer, has a copyright on the best-selling database management program. Why do these two firms have such dramatically different market to book ratios?

17. Using one (or more) of the sources of comparative financial data mentioned in this chapter, evaluate the performance of Bethlehem Steel Corporation versus the performance of Carpenter Technology. In particular, evaluate the total asset turnover, the fixed asset turnover, the net profit margin, the return on investment, and the return on stockholders' equity for each firm. Then do the following:
    a. Determine which firm seems to be performing better. What criterion did you use in reaching this conclusion?
    b. Point out some problems Bethlehem Steel seems to have had in the past several years.
    c. Using the latest 5 years of data, perform a financial trend analysis on Bethlehem Steel Corporation. Consider such ratios as the current, quick, inventory turnover, average collection period, total asset turnover, net profit margin, return on investment, and return on stockholders' equity ratios. What can you say about the trend in the financial health of Bethlehem Steel?

18. Hoffman Paper Company, a profitable distributor of stationary and office supplies, has an agreement with its banks that allows Hoffman to borrow money on a short-term basis to finance its inventories and accounts receivable. The agreement states that Hoffman must maintain a current ratio of 1.5, or higher, *and* a debt ratio of 50%, or lower. Given the following balance sheet, determine how much additional money Hoffman could borrow at this time to invest in inventory and accounts receivable without violating the terms of its borrowing agreement.

Cash	$ 50,000	Current liabilities	$ 200,000
Accounts receivable	150,000	Long-term debt	300,000
Inventory	250,000	Shareholders' equity	630,000
Fixed assets	680,000	Total liabilities and	
Total assets	$1,130,000	shareholders' equity	$1,130,000

19. Sun Minerals, Inc., is considering issuing additional long-term debt to finance an expansion. At the present time the company has $50 million in 10 percent debt outstanding. Its after-tax net income is $12 million, and the company is in the 40 percent tax bracket. The company is required by the debt holders to maintain its times interest earned ratio at 3.5 or greater.

    a. What is the present coverage (times interest earned) ratio?
    b. How much additional 10 percent debt can the company issue now and maintain its times interest earned ratio at 3.5? (Assume for this calculation that earnings before interest and taxes remains at its present level.)
    c. If the interest rate on additional debt is 12 percent, how much unused "debt capacity" does the company have?

20. The balance sheet and income statement of Eastland Products, Inc., are as follows:

Balance Sheet, December 31, 19X1 (in millions of dollars)

Current assets	$ 40	Current liabilities	$ 30
Fixed assets, net	110	Long-term debt	40
		Common stock ($1 par)	5
		Contributed capital in excess of par value	20
		Retained earnings	55
Total assets	$150	Total liabilities and equity	$150

Income Statement for Year Ended December 31, 19X1
(in millions of dollars)

Sales	$120
Cost of sales	80
EBIT	$ 40
Interest	5
EBT	$ 35
Taxes (40%)	14
Net Income	$ 21

Additional Information

Total dividends	$10 million
Market price of common stock	$32 a share
Number of common shares issued	5 million

Using these data, determine the following:

a. Earnings per share.
b. Price–earnings ratio.
c. Book value per share.
d. Market to book ratio.
e. How much of the retained earnings total was added during 19X1?
f. Show Eastland's new balance sheet after the company sells 1 million new common shares in early 19X2 to net $30 a share. Part of the proceeds, $10 million, is used to reduce current liabilities, and the remainder is temporarily deposited in the company's bank account. Later this remainder (along with additional long-term debt financing) will be invested in new manufacturing facilities.

21. Jefferson Foods Corporation has the following balance sheet and income statement:

Cash	$ 50,000	Current liabilities	$ 200,000
Marketable securities	200,000	Long-term debt	400,000
Other current assets	300,000	Stockholders' equity	800,000
Fixed assets	850,000	Total liabilities and	
Total assets	$1,400,000	stockholders' equity	$1,400,000

Sales and other revenues	$3,000,000
Cost of sales	2,600,000
EBIT	$ 400,000
Interest	50,000
EBT	$ 350,000
Taxes (40%)	140,000
Net income (EAT)	$ 210,000

Additional Information	
Shares outstanding	80,000
Market price per share	$20
Interest rate earned on marketable securities	6 percent

    a. Calculate Jefferson's present return on stockholders' equity, earnings per share, and debt ratio.

    b. Suppose Jefferson's management decides that the company's stock represents a good investment at its present price level. Recalculate the same ratios you calculated in Part a, assuming the company uses a portion of its marketable securities to repurchase 8,000 shares at $20 a share. The repurchased shares will be held as treasury stock.

    c. Explain why the ratio values you calculated in Part a changed after the share repurchase.

22. Thompson Electronics, Inc., is presently 100 percent equity financed and has assets of $100 million. Thompson's present net income is $9 million, and the company's marginal and average tax rates are 40 percent. In addition, Thompson has 4 million common shares outstanding, and its current annual dividend is $0.75 a share. At the present time, the company is able to borrow 10 percent *perpetual* debt; that is, debt that has no maturity date. What amount of 10 percent perpetual debt would Thompson have to borrow in order to increase its return on stockholders' equity to 15 percent?

▰▰▰▰ SELECTED REFERENCES

Altman, Edward I., R. G. Haldeman, and P. Narayanan. "Zeta Analysis: A New Model to Identify Bankruptcy Risk of Corporations." *Journal of Banking and Finance* (June 1977): 29–54.

Chen, Kung H., and Thomas A. Shimerda. "An Empirical Analysis of Useful Financial Ratios." *Financial Management* (Spring 1981): 51–60.

Foster, George. *Financial Statement Analysis*, 3d ed. Englewood Cliffs, NJ: Prentice-Hall, 1986.

Harrington, Diana R., and B. D. Wilson. *Corporate Financial Analysis*, 2d ed. Plano, TX: Business Publications, 1986.

Horrigan, James C. "A Short History of Financial Ratio Analysis." *Accounting Review* (April 1968): 284–294.

Jackobsen, Robert. "The Validity of ROI as a Measure of Business Performance." *American Economic Review* (June 1987): 370–379.

Lev, Baruch. *Financial Statement Analysis: A New Approach*. Englewood Cliffs, NJ: Prentice-Hall, 1974.

Murray, Roger F. "The Penn Central Debacle: Lessons for Financial Analysis." *Journal of Finance* (May 1971): 327–332.

CHAPTER
4
Cash Flow Analysis and Forecasting

KEY CHAPTER CONCEPTS

1. Cash flows are the ultimate source of financial value. Therefore, cash flow analysis and forecasting are important parts of a firm's financial plans.

2. After-tax operating cash flow is equal to earnings after tax plus noncash charges.

3. The statement of cash flows shows the effects of a firm's operating, investing, and financing activities on its cash balance.

4. *Pro forma* financial statements show the results of some assumed event (for example, sales forecast) rather than an actual event.

5. The percentage-of-sales forecasting method is used in estimating the amount of additional financing that the firm will need for a given increase in sales, based on certain assumptions about the relationship between sales and the various asset and liability accounts.

6. A cash budget is the projection of a firm's cash receipts and disbursements over a future time period and is useful in determining the amount of short-term funds the firm will need to borrow.

7. *Breakeven analysis* is a technique used to study the relationships between a firm's sales, fixed operating costs, variable operating costs, and operating income (EBIT) at various levels of output (Appendix 4A).

8. Other important topics include
   a. Deferred taxes
   b. Pro forma statement of cash flows
   c. Cash breakeven point
   d. Trend analysis
   e. Econometric forecasting
   f. Computerized financial planning models

GLOSSARY OF NEW TERMS

After-tax operating cash flow Operating cash flow before tax minus tax payments. Operating cash flow before tax equals revenues minus cash operating costs.

Breakeven analysis A technique used to examine the relationship between a firm's sales, costs, and profits at various levels of output. It sometimes is termed *cost-volume-profit analysis*.

Cash budget A projection of a company's cash receipts and disbursements over some future period of time.

Cash flow The actual amount of cash collected and paid out by a firm.

Cash flow forecasting The projection and estimation of a firm's future cash flows.

Contribution margin The difference between price and variable cost per unit in breakeven analysis.

Deterministic model A financial planning model that projects single number estimates of a financial variable or variables without specifying their probability of occurrence.

Financial forecasting The projection and estimation of a firm's future financial statements.

Financial planning model A computerized representation of some aspect of a firm's financial planning process.

Optimization model A financial planning model that determines the values of financial decision variables that maximize (or minimize) some objective function such as profits (or costs).

Percentage of sales forecasting method A method of estimating the additional financing that will be needed to support a given future sales level.

Probabilistic model A financial planning model that uses probability distributions as inputs and generates a probability distribution for financial variables as output.

Pro forma financial statements Financial statements that project the results of some *assumed* event rather than an *actual* event.

Sensitivity analysis A method of analysis in which a financial planning model is rerun to determine the effect on the output variable(s) (for example, profit) of given changes in the input variable(s) (for example, sales). Sensitivity analysis is sometimes called *what if* analysis.

Statement of cash flows A financial statement showing the effects of a firm's operating, investing, and financing activities on its cash balance.

Trend analysis A method of analysis that estimates the future value of a financial variable on the basis of past actual values of the variable.

Increasing Emphasis on Cash Flow Analysis

Even though financial analysts have stressed the importance of cash flow analysis for many years, there is an increased emphasis on cash flows in the late 1980s. The increased cash flow emphasis is evident in a number of ways.

First, the old, and often ambiguous, sources and uses of funds statement has been replaced by a new, more useful, statement of cash flows. The statement of cash flows shows the effects of a company's operating, investing, and financing activities on its cash balance. It provides relevant information about a company's cash receipts and payments during a particular accounting period.

Cash flow analysis also is being emphasized by security analysts. Increasingly, security analysts seem to be advising investors to disregard reported earnings and focus on cash flow analysis as a basis for selecting stocks to buy.[1] Furthermore, cash flow analysis is reported to represent a major change in sentiment by Wall Street.[2]

Companies reporting their 1988 results to stockholders also seemed to reflect the increased emphasis on cash flows. For example,

Navistar International, a U.S. truck manufacturer, included the following statement about its cash flows in its 1988 annual report:[3] "In the absence of significant unanticipated cash demands, management believes that current cash balances, cash flow generated by operations, and available financing sources will be sufficient to finance truck, engine and service parts operations, capital expenditures, anticipated preferred dividends . . ."

Schlumberger, an oilfield services company, reported a $1.1 billion decrease in its cash and short-term investments in 1988.[4] In its 1988 annual report, Schlumberger explained in detail that the decrease in cash and short-term investments resulted primarily from a $1.2 billion repurchase of its own shares. The company reported that its operating activities generated cash inflows of $900 million, sufficient to pay for capital expenditures of $455 million and to pay dividends of $325 million to stockholders. Schlumberger further advised its stockholders that "current liquidity levels, combined with liquidity provided by ongoing operations, are expected to fully satisfy future business requirements."

This chapter deals with the important cash flow concept. Cash flow analysis methods are discussed, and cash flow forecasting techniques are covered.

[1] Andrew E. Serwer, "Cashing In On Cash Flow," *Fortune* (May 23, 1988), p. 113.
[2] Jeffrey Laderman, "The Savviest Investors Are Going with the Flow," *Business Week* (September 7, 1987), p. 92.
[3] *Annual Report* (Navistar International Corporation, 1988), p. 18.
[4] *Annual Report* (Schlumberger Limited, 1988), p. 10.

═══ **INTRODUCTION**

We already have stressed, in both Chapters 1 and 2, the importance of the cash flow concept in financial decision making. Cash flows are the relevant source of financial value, rather than alternative benefit measures, such as net income. As mentioned earlier, only cash can be spent. The firm cannot spend its accounting net income because net income does not reflect the actual cash inflows and outflows of the firm.

Any firm that hopes to operate successfully within the competitive environment of the 1990s will have to make detailed corporate plans stating its objectives and how it intends to achieve them. The analysis and forecasting of cash flows will play an important role in these plans.

In this chapter we develop two key aspects of the cash flow concept—cash flow analysis and cash flow forecasting. The first section deals with cash flow analysis, and the second section covers cash flow forecasting. In addition, a final section considers several other financial forecasting tools.

This section deals with the analysis of a firm's overall cash flows. Recall that, in Chapter 3, net income, or earnings after tax (EAT), were calculated by deducting the firm's various costs and expenses from its net sales. Table 4-1 shows the Drake Manufacturing Company's income statement for the year ended December 31, 19X6, analyzed in Chapter 3. The income statement in Table 4-1 also shows the calculation of Drake's after-tax operating cash flow, CF. During 19X6, the company had total noncash expenses of $2,000 included in its total expenses. Adding these noncash expenses to the earnings after tax results in an after-tax operating cash flow equal to $7,019, calculated as follows:

$$CF = EAT + \text{Noncash charges} \qquad \textbf{(4.1)}$$
$$= \$5,019 + \$2000 = \$7,019$$

The after-tax operating cash flow can be used to make capital expenditures, to pay dividends, and to repay debt. As a result, it is considered to be a more important number than the net income figure.

Generally a firm has two types of noncash expenses—depreciation and deferred taxes—that are added to earnings after tax to calculate the after-tax operating cash flow.

Depreciation is defined as the systematic allocation of the cost of an asset over more than 1 year.[5] The annual depreciation expense recorded for a particular asset is an allocation of its original cost and does not represent a cash outlay. As a result, a company's annual depreciation expense is added to earnings after tax in calculating after-tax operating cash flow. For example, in 1988 Mobil Corporation had earnings after tax of $2.03 billion.[6] In calculating Mobil's 1988 after-tax operating cash flow, its 1988 depreciation expense of $2.68 billion must be added to the net income amount.

[5] This definition is consistent with the "Cash Flows from Operating Activities" portion of the accounting statement of cash flows. It differs from the definition presented in Chapter 2, principally by including interest expense in its calculation (Table 4-1). The definition from Chapter 2 is used more in finance and will be encountered again in our discussion of capital budgeting.

[6] *Annual Report* (Mobil Corporation, 1988), p. 30.

TABLE 4-1

Drake Manufacturing Company Income Statement (in thousands of dollars)
For the Year Ended December 31, 19X6

Net sales	$112,760
Cost of sales	85,300
Gross margin	$ 27,460
Operating expenses	15,940
Earnings before interest and taxes (EBIT)	$ 11,520
Interest charges	3,160
Earnings before taxes (EBT)	$ 8,360
Federal and state income taxes at a combined 40% rate	3,344
Earnings after taxes (EAT) and available for common stockholders	$ 5,016
Plus Noncash expenses	
Depreciation	1,900
Deferred income taxes	100
After-tax operating cash flow (CF)	$ 7,016

Deferred Taxes

Cash flow also differs from net income by the amount of a company's *deferred taxes*. In accordance with generally accepted accounting principles and specifically in accordance with Statement of Financial Accounting Standards No. 96, a company usually reports a different income tax expense amount to its stockholders than it actually pays in cash during that year. Frequently the income tax amount shown on the company's income statement is larger than the income tax amount paid. The difference between the tax amount reported to stockholders and the cash amount actually paid is referred to as a *deferred tax*, because it is due to be paid by the company sometime in the future. For example, during 1988 General Electric (GE) reported the following earnings amounts to its stockholders:[7]

Earnings before taxes	$4,721 million
Less Income taxes	1,335 million
Earnings after taxes	$3,386 million
Income taxes:	
Current portion	$1,211 million
Deferred	124 million

In calculating GE's 1988 cash flow from operations, the deferred tax amount, $124 million, is added to the earnings after tax, because the deferred taxes were subtracted as an expense in determining earnings but did not constitute a cash payment by GE in 1988.

Deferred taxes generally occur because of temporary differences in the stated amounts of assets and liabilities for financial reporting purposes and for tax purposes. Specifically, even though deferred taxes can occur for a variety of reasons, some of the more common reasons include differences between financial reporting and tax methods regarding accounting for depreciation, inventories, and pensions. The following example specifically shows how deferred taxes occur as a result of different depreciation methods. Many companies use the straight-line depreciation method to calculate the income they report to their stockholders and an accelerated depreciation method to calculate taxable income. As shown in Table 4-2, this usually results in the taxes currently owed being less than they would be if the company used straight-line depreciation methods for tax purposes. Using straight-line depreciation, the company's earnings before taxes are $20 million; using accelerated depreciation, its earnings before taxes are $18 million. Taxes of $6.8 million are calculated on the taxable earnings figure of $20 million, but only $6.12 million in taxes currently is owed, resulting in $0.68 million in taxes that are deferred. The company effectively can continue to defer payment of these taxes as long as it continues to purchase a sufficient amount of new fixed assets. When it ceases purchasing such assets or purchases fewer of them, it will have to pay the deferred taxes.

The cash flow from operations for the company in Table 4-2, $23.88 million, is calculated easily by adding the tax depreciation amount, $12.00 million, to the net earnings amount, $11.88 million. If the tax records are not available, the cash flow from operations is calculated using Equation 4.2, as follows:

---

[7] *Annual Report* (General Electric Company, 1988), p. 24.

(A) Calculation of Taxes for Financial Reporting and Tax Purposes
(in millions of dollars)

	FINANCIAL REPORTING PURPOSES	TAX PURPOSES
Sales	$100.00	$100.00
Expenses, excluding depreciation	70.00	70.00
Depreciation:		
Straight line	10.00	
MACRS*		12.00
Income before taxes	$ 20.00	$ 18.00
Taxes (34%)	6.80	6.12
Net income	$ 13.20	$ 11.88

(B) Partial Income Statement Reported to Stockholders
(in millions of dollars)

Income before taxes	$ 20.00
Federal income taxes:	
Current	$ 6.12
Deferred	0.68
Total federal income tax	$ 6.80
Net income	$ 13.20

* MACRS stands for Modified Accelerated Cost Recovery System and is explained in Appendix 9A.

$$\text{Cash Flow (CF)} = \text{Net Earnings} + \text{Depreciation}$$
$$+ \text{Deferred taxes} \qquad (4.2)$$
$$= \$13.20 \text{ million} + \$10.00 \text{ million}$$
$$+ \$0.68 \text{ million}$$
$$= \$23.88 \text{ million}$$

The Statement of Cash Flows

The statement of cash flows, together with the balance sheet and the income statement, constitute a major portion of a company's financial statements. The *statement of cash flows* shows the effects of a company's *operating*, *investing*, and *financing* activities on its cash balance. The principal purpose of the statement of cash flows is to provide relevant information about a company's cash receipts and cash payments during a particular accounting period.

The procedures for preparing the statement of cash flows are presented in Statement of Financial Accounting Standards No. 95, issued by the Financial Accounting Standards Board (FASB) in November 1987. It requires companies to include a statement of cash flows when issuing a complete set of financial statements for annual periods ending after July 15, 1988.

The FASB encourages companies to prepare their statement of cash flows using the *direct* method of presenting cash flows from operating activities.

111

Table 4-3 shows an example of such a statement using the direct method for the Summit Furniture Company, a retail furniture store. During the year, Summit had $14,600 net cash provided by its operating activities. The company received $142,000 from its customers and received $600 of interest. Summit's operating cash outflows totaled $128,000 ($120,000 paid to suppliers and employees plus $2,000 of interest paid and $6,000 of income taxes paid). Next, Summit's investing activities used net cash of $18,000. The company spent $19,000 on capital expenditures and received $1,000 in proceeds from the sale of an asset. Also, during the year the net cash provided by financing activities equaled $3,600. The $3,600 is calculated as the difference between financing activities that require cash outflows and those that result in cash inflows. Summit had financing cash outflows totaling $3,100 ($2,600 repayment of long-term debt and $500 of dividends paid out) and financing cash inflows totaling $6,700 (bank borrowing of $1,000 plus proceeds from the issuance of long-term debt of $4,000 plus proceeds from the issuance of common stock of $1,700). Next, the overall change in cash is calculated as follows:

Net cash **(4.3)**
increase (decrease) = Net cash provided (used) by operating activities
+ Net cash provided (used) by investing activities
+ Net cash provided (used) by financing activities

Net cash
increase (decrease) = $14,600 − $18,000 + $3,600
= $200

TABLE 4-3

Summit Furniture Company Statement of Cash Flows
For the Year Ended December 31, 19X1

Increase (Decrease) in Cash and Cash Equivalents*

Cash Flows from Operating Activities:		
Cash received from customers	$142,000	
Cash paid to suppliers and employees	⟨120,000⟩	
Interest received	600	
Interest paid (net of amount capitalized)	⟨2,000⟩	
Income taxes paid	⟨6,000⟩	
Net cash provided (used) by operating activities		$14,600
Cash Flows from Investing Activities:		
Proceeds from sale of asset	1,000	
Capital expenditures	⟨19,000⟩	
Net cash provided (used) by investing activities		⟨18,000⟩
Cash Flows from Financing Activities:		
Net borrowings under bank line-of-credit agreement	1,000	
Repayments of long-term debt	⟨2,600⟩	
Proceeds from issuance of long-term debt	4,000	
Proceeds from issuance of common stock	1,700	
Dividends paid	⟨500⟩	
Net cash provided (used) by financing activities		3,600
Net increase (decrease) in cash and cash equivalents		200
Cash and cash equivalents at beginning of year		5,000
Cash and cash equivalents at end of year		$ 5,200

* Cash and cash equivalents includes currency on hand, bank deposits and similar accounts, and short-term (maturities less than 3 months), highly liquid investments.

The statement of cash flows presented in Table 4-3 provides Summit's management, investors, and creditors with a summary of its cash flows for the year. In particular, Summit's operations provided net cash of $14,600; however, the company used a total of $18,000 in its investing activities. As a result, if Summit wanted to keep its cash balance at about $5,000, the company's financing activities would have to provide $3,400 of net cash ($18,000 − $14,600). In fact, Summit's financing activities actually did provide $3,600, causing the ending cash balance to be $5,200, or $200 above the beginning $5,000.

A sampling of 1988 annual reports shows that very few companies presented their statement of cash flows using the direct method. Instead most companies use the *indirect*, or *reconciliation*, method to report the net cash flow from operating activities. The indirect method involves adjusting net income to reconcile it to net cash flow from operating activities. Table 4-4 shows the statements of cash flows using the indirect method for 1988 and 1987 for A. M. Castle and Company, a steel distributor based in Franklin Park, Illinois.

Castle had 1987 net income of approximately $6.6 million. But to convert this amount to a cash flow, first the company added back its noncash expenses, primarily depreciation. Then the company adjusted the net income amount from the accrual method (required by generally accepted accounting principles) to the cash amount by showing the increases or decreases in its various current asset and current liability accounts. After making these adjustments, Castle showed net cash provided from operating activities of about $14.9 million. In 1987, Castle used only $717,000 in its investing activities. As a result, a substantial amount of the cash flow provided by operating activities was available for use in financing activities. The company actually used $13.65 million in financing activities, principally in (1) net repayment of $8 million to its banks under line-of-credit agreements,[8] (2) repayment of long-term debt of $2.816 million, and (3) dividend payments of $3.04 million to stockholders.

The year 1988 was an excellent one for Castle, and the 1988 statement of cash flows provides a good picture of the company's cash flow activities for the year. Net income in 1988 amounted to $13.656 million, more than double the 1987 amount. During 1988 strong demand for its products led Castle to decide to increase inventories by $40.303 million. The inventory increase, combined with the other adjustments to cash flow, resulted in Castle's 1988 operating activities *using* $19.287 million. Also, partly because of the strong demand for its products, Castle decided to increase its warehouse capacity and expand its business. Capital expenditures in 1988 increased to $7.816 million, up from $2.605 million in 1987. This resulted in $7.313 million net cash flow being *used by* investing activities. The use of cash by both operating and investing activities meant that the company's financing activities would have to *provide* cash, if Castle were to maintain its 1988 beginning cash balance of $3.396 million. Financing activities in 1988 provided a net cash flow of $24.763 million primarily because the company incurred new long-term debt of $37 million. Overall, Castle's cash decreased by $1.837 million in 1988 to $1.559 million by December 31, 1988. By analyzing the statement of cash flows, a financial analyst can determine the effect of the company's activities on its cash balance.

---

[8] A line of credit is a form of short-term note payable. Lines of credit are discussed in Chapter 20.

TABLE 4-4

A. M. Castle and Company Statement of Cash Flows
(in thousands of dollars)

	For the Years Ended December 31,	
	1988	**1987**
Cash Flows from Operating Activities:		
Net income	$13,656	$ 6,624
Adjustments to reconcile net income to net cash provided from operating activities		
Depreciation	3,914	3,726
Provision for bad debts	548	621
Gain on sale of facilities or equipment	(296)	(288)
(Increase) decrease in current assets or liabilities		
Accounts receivable	(12,407)	(11,885)
Inventories	(40,303)	(4,051)
Receivables—income tax	—	3,663
Accounts payable	6,754	17,203
Accrued liabilities	6,905	2,590
Current deferred income taxes	618	(131)
Increase (decrease) in deferred taxes and pensions	490	419
(Increase) decrease in prepaid expenses	834	(3,555)
Total adjustments	(32,943)	8,312
Net cash provided from (used by) operating activities	(19,287)	14,936
Cash Flows from Investing Activities:		
Proceeds from sale of facilities or equipment	503	1,888
Capital expenditures	(7,816)	(2,605)
Net cash used by investing activities	(7,313)	(717)
Cash Flows from Financing Activities:		
Net borrowing under line-of-credit agreements	(6,000)	(8,000)
Proceeds from issuance of long-term debt	37,000	—
Repayments of long-term debt	(2,816)	(2,816)
Proceeds from issuance of stock	36	204
Dividends paid	(3,442)	(3,040)
Fractional shares repurchased	(15)	—
Net cash provided from (used by) financing activities	24,763	(13,652)
Net Increase (Decrease) in Cash	(1,837)	567
Cash—Beginning of Year	3,396	2,829
Cash—End of Year	$ 1,559	$ 3,396

SOURCE: *Annual Report* (A. M. Castle and Company, 1988).

CASH FLOW FORECASTING

This section presents an overview of the cash flow forecasting process, with emphasis on the important role of pro forma financial statements. *Pro forma financial statements*, showing the results of some *assumed* event rather than an *actual* event, usually are an integral part of a financial forecast. For example, an operating budget that shows the level of net income that can be expected if sales and expenses are at a given assumed level next year is a pro forma income statement. Short-term forecasts, those that deal with 1 year or less, tend to be rather detailed, whereas long-term forecasts are more general. Cash flow forecasting involves the projection and estimation of a firm's *future* cash needs. This section specifically discusses the percentage of sales forecasting method, cash budgets, the pro forma statement of cash flows, and cash breakeven analysis.

Percentage of Sales Forecasting Method

The percentage of sales forecasting method permits a company to forecast the amount of financing it will need for a given increase in sales. The use of this method is illustrated with the following example of the Industrial Supply Company (ISC).

The present (19X6) ISC balance sheet and income statement are shown in Table 4-5. Management forecasts that sales will increase by 25 percent, or $3,750,000, next year to $18,750,000.

One of management's primary questions is, How much cash will be needed to finance this expected growth? Up to now, the company has financed its growth by using both internally and externally generated cash. The company has reinvested most of its past earnings back into the company, primarily into additional inventory. The company also has used external financing in the form of short-term borrowings from its bank.

To determine the amount of additional financing necessary to reach the expected $18,750,000 annual sales level, the ISC management has made the following observations about the company's various assets and liabilities:

1. **Cash.** Management feels the company's cash balances generally are adequate for the present sales level and would have to increase proportionately as sales increase.
2. **Accounts receivable.** The company's present average collection period is approximately 49 days. Management feels the company's present credit

TABLE 4-5

Industrial Supply Company Financial Statements

Balance Sheet as of December 31, 19X6

ASSETS		LIABILITIES	
Cash	$ 500,000	Accounts payable	$1,500,000
Accounts receivable	2,000,000	Notes payable	1,000,000
Inventories	4,000,000	Total current liabilities	$2,500,000
Total current assets	$6,500,000	Long-term debt	500,000
Fixed assets, net	1,000,000	Stockholders' equity	4,500,000
Total assets	$7,500,000	Total liabilities and equity	$7,500,000

Income Statement for the Year Ended December 31, 19X6

Sales	$15,000,000
Cash expenses, including interest and taxes	14,250,000
After-tax operating cash flow	$ 750,000
Dividends	250,000
Retained earnings	$ 500,000

Selected Financial Ratios

Current ratio	2.60 times
Debt ratio	40%
Ratio of after-tax operating cash flow to stockholders' equity	16.7%

policies are appropriate for its type of business. As a result, they feel that the average collection period will remain approximately constant and that accounts receivable will increase proportionately as sales increase.

3. **Inventory.** Management feels the company's inventory is properly managed at present. Therefore, they feel inventory would have to increase proportionately for sales to increase.

4. **Fixed assets.** The company is a distributor with relatively few fixed assets (delivery trucks, forklifts, office equipment, storage racks, and so forth). Because the company's fixed assets *are being utilized at nearly full capacity,* management feels fixed assets will have to increase as sales grow. For financial planning purposes, management is willing to assume that the *net* fixed asset figure on the balance sheet will increase proportionately as sales increase.

5. **Accounts payable.** The company now maintains good relations with its suppliers. As the company purchases more inventory, its accounts payable balance will increase proportionately as sales increase.

6. **Long-term debt.** Long-term debt and notes payable do not necessarily have a direct relationship to the sales level. For example, a portion of the company's future cash flows may be used to pay off the present debt.

In summary, as the company's sales increase, its assets will increase proportionately to support the new sales. In addition, the current liabilities that vary directly with sales, namely accounts payable, will also increase. The difference between the forecasted asset increase and the forecasted current liability increase is equal to the total financing the company will need. This relationship can be expressed in equation form as follows:

$$
\begin{matrix}
\text{Total} \\ \text{financing} \\ \text{needed}
\end{matrix}
=
\begin{matrix}
\text{Forecasted} \\ \text{asset} \\ \text{increase}
\end{matrix}
-
\begin{matrix}
\text{Forecasted} \\ \text{current} \\ \text{liability} \\ \text{increase}
\end{matrix}
$$

$$
= \frac{A}{S}(\Delta S) - \frac{CL}{S}(\Delta S) \tag{4.4}
$$

where A is the company's present level of assets that vary proportionately with sales, S is the company's present sales, CL is the company's present level of current liabilities that vary proportionately with sales, and ΔS is the forecasted sales increase.

A portion of the total financing needed can be generated internally. Specifically, the internal financing generated during the time period when sales increase from S to $S + \Delta S$ can be expressed in equation form as follows:

$$
\begin{matrix}
\text{Internal} \\ \text{net cash} \\ \text{provided}
\end{matrix}
=
\begin{matrix}
\text{Forecasted} \\ \text{cash} \\ \text{flow (CF)}
\end{matrix}
- \text{Dividends }(D)
$$

$$
= CF - D \tag{4.5}
$$

The additional financing needed can be calculated by subtracting the internal net cash provided from the total financing needed:

$$
\begin{matrix}
\text{Additional} \\ \text{financing} \\ \text{needed}
\end{matrix}
=
\begin{matrix}
\text{Total} \\ \text{financing} \\ \text{needed}
\end{matrix}
-
\begin{matrix}
\text{Internal} \\ \text{net cash} \\ \text{provided}
\end{matrix}
$$

$$
= \left[\frac{A}{S}(\Delta S) - \frac{CL}{S}(\Delta S)\right] - (CF - D) \tag{4.6}
$$

Referring back to the ISC example, the additional financing needed to support a sales increase of $3,750,000 up to the $18,750,000 level now can be calculated. Assume that management forecasts cash expenses to be $17,750,000 and after-tax operating cash flow to be $1,000,000 during the coming year. Assume further that the company plans to maintain its dividend payments at the same level in 19X7 as in 19X6. Substituting this data into Equation 4.6 yields:

$$\text{Additional financing needed} = \left[\frac{7,500,000}{15,000,000} (3,750,000) - \frac{1,500,000}{15,000,000} (3,750,000) \right]$$

$$- (1,000,000 - 250,000)$$

$$= \$750,000$$

The approximate amount of additional financing that will be needed to finance ISC's forecasted growth in sales from $15,000,000 to $18,750,000 is $750,000.[9] Even though the financing will be needed gradually as sales increase, the ISC management has to decide whether to (1) borrow on a short-term basis, (2) borrow on a long-term basis, (3) sell additional common stock, or (4) cut dividends. The factors that influence the debt versus equity decision are discussed in Chapter 13; the factors that influence the short-term versus long-term debt decision are discussed in Chapter 17; and the factors that influence the dividend decision are discussed in Chapter 14. As this example illustrates, *the investment, financing, and dividend decisions of the firm are interdependent.*

Table 4-6 shows ISC's pro forma financial statements for 19X7, *assuming* that all of the additional financing needed is in the form of short-term notes payable. Examination of the selected financial ratios in Tables 4-5 and 4-6 shows that this financing plan will increase the ratio of after-tax operating cash flow to stockholders' equity from 16.7 percent in 19X6 to 19.0 percent in 19X7. However, it also reduces the firm's current ratio (measure of liquidity) from 2.60 to 2.24 and increases its debt ratio (measure of leverage) from 40 percent to 44 percent. ISC management would have to weigh these factors (as well as others) in determining how to obtain the $750,000 of additional financing needed.

The percentage of sales forecasting method for calculating financing needs is a useful and convenient cash flow forecasting technique. However, as with all analytical techniques, the application of this method should be supplemented by any additional factors that are unique to the particular situation.

One such factor is *economies of scale.* Economies of scale may result in nonlinear relationships between sales and certain types of assets. In other words, the relationships may not be strictly proportional, as assumed in the model. For example, a 10 percent increase in sales may only require a 5 percent increase in fixed assets or inventories. Another factor in some industries is that capacity can be added only in *discrete* or *"lumpy"* increments. Once output reaches the capacity of an existing production facility, expansion requires building another facility. This causes fixed assets to increase in a stepwise manner as sales are increased, rather than increasing proportionately.

[9] The $750,000 figure assumes that none of the present notes payable or long-term debt will have to be repaid during the year.

TABLE 4-6

Industrial Supply Company Pro Forma Financial Statements

Pro Forma Balance Sheet as of December 31, 19X7

ASSETS		LIABILITIES	
Cash	$ 625,000	Accounts payable	$1,875,000
Accounts receivable	2,500,000	Notes payable	1,750,000
Inventories	5,000,000	Total current liabilities	$3,625,000
Total current assets	$8,125,000	Long-term debt	500,000
Fixed assets, net	1,250,000	Stockholders' equity	5,250,000
Total assets	$9,375,000	Total liabilities and equity	$9,375,000

Pro Forma Income Statement for the Year Ending December 31, 19X7

Sales	$18,750,000
Cash expenses, including interest and taxes	17,750,000
After-tax operating cash flow	$ 1,000,000
Dividends	250,000
Retained earnings*	$ 750,000

Selected Pro Forma Financial Ratios

Current ratio	2.24 times
Debt ratio	44%
Ratio of after-tax operating cash flow to stockholders' equity	19.0%

*This simplified analysis does not consider directly depreciation effects, thereby resulting in a pro forma overstatement of stockholders' equity.

Cash Budgeting

Cash budgeting plays an important role in the firm's financial forecasting process. Effective cash budgeting can help management identify potential cash flow problems well in advance. Usually cash flow problems are easier to solve when they are anticipated. In addition to a detailed discussion of cash budgets, this section contains a brief overview of budgeting.

AN OVERVIEW OF BUDGETING. *Budgets* are simply pro forma financial statements that detail a firm's financial forecasts. They show how the company's cash will be spent on labor, materials, and capital goods and indicate how cash will be obtained.

Budgets are used to *plan, coordinate*, and *control* a firm's operations. They are essential to *planning* because they represent the company's objectives in numerical terms, such as dollars of sales, units of production, pounds of raw materials, and dollars of financing required from the capital markets. Once a firm has made financial plans, it refers to the budgets when *coordinating* its overall activities. For example, the purchasing department examines the budgets when deciding how best to integrate purchasing activities with monthly production requirements to ensure the availability of sufficient raw materials. The production and marketing departments then work together to guarantee that sufficient finished goods inventories are on hand. Finally, the finance department coordinates the company's need for funds with the requirements of the purchasing, production, and marketing departments.

The projected figures in a firm's budgets also are used as a *control* device against which actual figures are compared. This ensures that the various departments and divisions are functioning properly and working together toward the objectives developed in the planning phase.

A firm's budgets are based on the *assumption* of certain future sales and production levels. As pro forma financial statements, budgets predict what a company's financial statements will look like if specific plans are realized.

CASH BUDGETS. A cash budget is the projection of a company's cash receipts and disbursements over some future period of time. Typically, a cash budget is prepared on an annual basis and subdivided into months. However, more detailed and refined cash budgeting is done on a weekly or even daily basis by some companies that employ good ongoing cash management procedures.

Cash budgets are useful in determining the amount of short-term funds the firm may need to borrow to cover any projected cash shortages. Short-term borrowed funds almost always are easier to obtain when the need for them is anticipated. In addition to planning for any cash shortages, the cash budget also indicates the periods when the firm may have cash surpluses. This information is helpful in managing the firm's marketable securities investments. Thus, the cash budget is one of the most important short-range financial forecasting tools. In addition, cash budgets can be useful for control and coordination purposes.

To explore actual cash budgeting procedures, the Midwestern Manufacturing Company Central Division will be examined. Table 4-7 illustrates a cash budget worksheet for that division for the first quarter of 19X6. Table 4-8 is an actual cash budget for the time period.

The first step in cash budget preparation is the estimation of cash receipts, which results directly from the sales forecast. Midwestern has found that, on the average, about 10 percent of total sales in any given month are cash sales. The remaining 90 percent are credit sales.[10]

[10] Estimated December credit sales are 90 percent of estimated December sales; that is, $0.90 \times \$540,000 = \$486,000$.

TABLE 4-7 **Cash Budget Worksheet**

Midwestern Manufacturing Company—Central Division
Cash Budget Worksheet
First Quarter, 19X6

	DECEMBER	JANUARY	FEBRUARY	MARCH
BUDGET OF RECEIPTS FROM SALES				
Estimated sales	$540,000	$500,000	$550,000	$620,000
Estimated credit sales	486,000	450,000	495,000	558,000
Estimated receipts:				
Cash sales		$ 50,000	$ 55,000	$ 62,000
Collections of accounts receivable:				
70% of last month's credit sales		$340,200	$315,000	$346,500
30% of current month's credit sales		135,000	148,500	167,400
Total accounts receivable collections		$475,200	$463,500	$513,900
BUDGET OF PAYMENTS FOR PURCHASES				
Estimated purchases*	$275,000	$302,500	$341,000	
Estimated payments of accounts payable†		$275,000	$302,500	$341,000

* Purchases are estimated at 55 percent of next month's sales.   † Payments are estimated to lag purchases by one month.

TABLE 4-8 Cash Budget

Midwestern Manufacturing Company—Central Division
Cash Budget*
First Quarter, 19X6

	DECEMBER	JANUARY	FEBRUARY	MARCH
Sales	$540,000	$500,000	$550,000	$620,000
Projected cash balance, beginning of month		$ 61,000	$ 50,700	$ 50,000
Receipts:				
Cash sales		50,000	55,000	62,000
Collection of accounts receivable		475,200	463,500	513,900
Total cash available		$586,200	$569,200	$625,900
Disbursements:				
Payment of accounts payable		$275,000	$302,500	$341,000
Wages and salaries		158,000	154,500	145,500
Rent		17,000	17,000	17,000
Other expenses		4,500	7,000	8,000
Taxes		81,000	—	—
Dividends on common stock		—	—	30,000
Purchase of new equipment (capital budget)		—	70,000	—
Total disbursements		$535,500	$551,000	$541,500
Excess of available cash over disbursements		$ 50,700	$ 18,200	$ 84,400
Cash loans needed to maintain balance of $50,000		—	31,800	—
Loan repayment		—	—	(31,800)
Projected cash balance, end of month		$ 50,700	$ 50,000	$ 52,600

About 30 percent of the company's credit sales are collected during the month in which the sale is made, and all of the remaining 70 percent are collected during the following month. Thus, the total accounts receivable the company can expect to collect during January are equal to 70 percent of the forecasted December credit sales plus 30 percent of the forecasted January credit sales:

$$(0.70 \times \$486,000) + (0.30 \times \$450,000) = \$340,200 + \$135,000$$

$$= \$475,200$$

The forecasted cash receipts for February and March are calculated the same way.

The next step in cash budgeting is the scheduling of *disbursements*, or payments the firm must make to others. Many of these items remain relatively constant from month to month and thus are relatively easy to budget. Others, however, such as the payment of accounts payable for purchases of merchandise, raw materials, and supplies, are more complicated. The key determinants of a firm's schedule of payables are the level of purchases per period and the terms given by suppliers.

Frequently, accounts payable become due before goods are sold and cash is received; this can lead to temporary cash shortages. In fact, many companies experience cash difficulties immediately after a good sales period.

Inventories are depleted and must be replenished, but cash is low because collections from the good sales period have not yet been received. Midwestern's purchases generally are estimated to be 55 percent of next month's sales. This percentage is based on the company's past experience and can vary considerably among industries and companies. (Note that depreciation does not appear as a disbursement in the cash budget, because it is a noncash charge.)

After cash receipts and disbursements have been estimated, the next step in the cash budgeting process is the determination of a desired cash balance at the beginning of each month. This minimum cash balance figure usually is a function of several factors, including the nature of the business, tax laws, and bank requirements. Table 4-8 lists Midwestern's projected cash balances for the beginnings of January, February, and March. In this example, $50,000 is assumed to be the most appropriate minimum cash balance for the first quarter, 19X6.[11]

It can be seen from Table 4-8 that Midwestern expects to need a short-term loan of $31,800 in February to maintain a minimum cash balance of $50,000. This is because the company expects a decrease in the collection of accounts receivable in February, brought about by slightly lower than normal sales expected in January. In addition, the company plans to purchase new equipment in February, which will cost $70,000; this also contributes to the expected need for a short-term loan.

If the company planned to spend much more money than this on new equipment, it might decide to secure longer-term financing at this time instead of the short-term loan. The proceeds from longer-term financing could be budgeted as a separate cash receipt in February, permitting the company to separate short-term and long-term cash needs.

After projecting the need for a short-term loan in February, the cash budget in Table 4-8 shows that the loan probably can be paid at the end of March, because the available cash balance of $84,400 will still be above $50,000 after repayment of $31,800. The company has indicated the repayment on the cash budget by adding another side caption: loan repayment.[12]

Most companies follow this same general format for cash budgeting, yet few companies use *exactly* the same format. A company's actual cash budgeting system will depend on its business and its accounting procedures. Computerized financial spreadsheet models are useful in constructing and analyzing cash budgets. A cash budgeting spreadsheet model is included with the CFM Lotus Disk that has been prepared for use with this text. The cash budgeting template from the CFM Lotus Disk is discussed in Appendix A at the end of the book.

Pro Forma Statement of Cash Flows

The statement of cash flows also can be used to determine how much additional financing a company will need in some future period. Suppose the Summit Furniture Company, whose statement of cash flows for 19X1 is shown in Table 4-3, is preparing a cash flow forecast for 19X2. In the fall of 19X1, the company's management tentatively decides to spend $25,000 in 19X2 for capital expenditures. Also, Summit's financial manager esti-

---

[11] Cash management is discussed further in Chapter 18.
[12] Note that the cash budget does not include any interest payments on this loan (or interest earned on investments of excess cash). These items generally have a relatively small impact on cash flows. However, they can be added to a cash budget if necessary.

mates that the company's 19X2 operating activities will *provide* approximately $21,000 of net cash. This forecast is detailed in Summit's pro forma statement of cash flows, which is shown in Table 4-9.

Next, Summit's financial manager must estimate whether the company's financing activities will need to provide cash in order to maintain its desired cash balance. Because the net cash expected to be *used* by investing activities is greater than the net cash expected to be *provided* by operating activities, the company's financing activities will need to *provide* net cash to maintain the present cash balance. In addition, Summit feels that its cash balance needs to be increased by approximately $1,500. As a result, Summit's financing activities in 19X2 must *provide* net cash of $5,500 (−$21,000 + $25,000 + $1,500). The pro forma statement of cash flows details how Summit expects to achieve $5,500 of net cash provided by financing activities.

Cash Breakeven Analysis

Another concept that sometimes is useful in cash flow forecasting is breakeven analysis. *Breakeven analysis* is a technique used to examine the relationship between a firm's revenues, costs, and operating profits at various output levels.[13] The *breakeven point* is defined as the output level at which

[13] An expanded discussion of breakeven analysis appears in the appendix to this chapter.

TABLE 4-9

**Summit Furniture Company Pro-Forma Statement of Cash Flows
For the Year Ending December 31, 19X2**

Increase (Decrease) in Cash and Cash Equivalents*		
Cash Flows Expected from Operating Activities:		
Cash received from customers	$170,000	
Cash paid to suppliers and employees	⟨140,000⟩	
Interest received	500	
Interest paid (net of amount capitalized)	⟨2,500⟩	
Income taxes paid	⟨7,000⟩	
Expected net cash provided (used) by operating activities		$21,000
Cash Flows Expected from Investing Activities:		
Proceeds from sale of asset	—	
Capital expenditures	⟨25,000⟩	
Expected net cash provided (used) by investing activities		⟨25,000⟩
Cash Flows Expected from Financing Activities:		
Net borrowings under bank line-of-credit agreement	2,000	
Repayment of long-term debt	⟨3,000⟩	
Proceeds from issuance of long-term debt	7,000	
Proceeds from issuance of common stock	—	
Dividends paid	⟨500⟩	
Expected net cash provided (used) by financing activities		5,500
Expected Net Increase (Decrease) in Cash and Cash Equivalents		1,500
Cash and Cash Equivalents at Beginning of Year		5,200
Expected Cash and Cash Equivalents at End of Year		$ 6,700

* Cash and cash equivalents include currency on hand, bank deposits and similar accounts, and short-term (maturities less than 3 months), highly liquid investments.

total revenues equal total operating costs; it is calculated by dividing fixed operating costs, F, by the difference between price, P, and variable cost per unit, V (see Equation 4A.4 in the appendix to this chapter).

The calculation of a *cash breakeven point* may assist a firm in its cash flow forecasting. Some of a firm's fixed operating costs, namely depreciation, are *noncash outlays*. The cash breakeven point is calculated by subtracting the noncash depreciation charges, *Dep*, from the fixed operating costs, F, in the numerator of the breakeven equation (Equation 4A.4):

$$\text{Cash breakeven point} = \frac{F - Dep}{P - V} \qquad \textbf{(4.7)}$$

It measures the volume of output (units) required to cover the firm's fixed cash operating outlays, such as management salaries, rent, and utilities.

Cash breakeven analysis also can be performed in terms of dollar sales. The cash breakeven dollar sales volume can be determined with the following expression:

$$\text{Cash breakeven sales} = \frac{F - Dep}{1 - (V/P)} \qquad \textbf{(4.8)}$$

All other things being equal, a firm with a larger proportion of its fixed costs in the form of noncash outlays will have a lower cash breakeven point and be better able to survive during a business downturn than a firm whose fixed costs consist mainly of cash outlays.

Consider the following example. Victor Rodriguez has been offered a new auto dealership, and the manufacturer has provided him with various sales forecasts. As part of a detailed analysis of the proposed dealership, he would like an estimate of the cash breakeven point for new car sales. He estimates that fixed costs will be $2 million a year, including depreciation expense of $300,000 a year. In addition, the new car sales price is expected to be $10,000 per unit, and the new car variable cost is expected to be $8,000 per unit. The estimated cash breakeven point for new car sales can be calculated using Equation 4.7:

$$\text{Cash breakeven point} = \frac{\$2,000,000 - \$300,000}{\$10,000 - \$8,000}$$

$$= 850 \text{ units}$$

The cash breakeven sales volume is calculated using Equation 4.8:

$$\text{Cash breakeven sales} = \frac{\$2,000,000 - \$300,000}{1 - (\$8,000/\$10,000)}$$

$$= \$8,500,000$$

Rodriguez can now analyze the manufacturer's marketing data to determine the likelihood of exceeding the estimated cash breakeven point for new car sales.

It should be strongly emphasized that the calculation of a firm's cash breakeven output does not constitute a comprehensive method of cash flow analysis. A complete cash flow analysis, which takes account of the timing of all the firm's cash receipts and disbursements, requires the preparation of a detailed cash budget.

OTHER FINANCIAL FORECASTING TOOLS

This section deals with trend analysis, econometric techniques, and computerized financial planning models. Trend analysis and econometric techniques may be useful in estimating the financial variables needed in cash flow forecasting.

Trend Analysis

Trend analysis is the process of estimating the future value of some financial variable on the basis of past actual values of the variable. Both *linear* and *nonlinear* trend analysis can be performed.

To illustrate a linear trend analysis, consider a company that wishes to forecast its 19X6 sales based on known sales figures since 19X0. As shown in Figure 4-1(a), a straight line can be fitted to the data points from 19X0 to 19X5 and then *extrapolated* forward to 19X6. This "best fitting" straight line can be determined either visually or using more sophisticated *least squares* estimation procedures.[14] The visual analysis shown results in a 19X6 sales forecast of $13 million.

In some cases a nonlinear trend analysis is more representative than a linear one. This is especially true for maturing growth companies, or those whose past sales have been growing at a decreasing rate. Assume that one such company wishes to forecast 19X6 sales based on past actual sales figures since 19X0. As Figure 4-1(b) shows, this can be accomplished by plotting the past actual data and, instead of estimating the "best" straight line passing through these points, fitting a smooth curve using visual or least squares estimating techniques and then extending it until 19X6. This visual curve-fitting technique results in an estimate of $9.5 million in sales for the year.

Although trend analysis can be a useful financial forecasting technique, it has limitations. Specifically, it assumes that future trends will simply be

[14] See James R. McGuigan and R. Charles Moyer, *Managerial Economics*, 5th ed. St. Paul, MN: West Publishing, 1989, Ch. 6 for a discussion of least-squares procedures.

Trend Analysis

(a) (b)

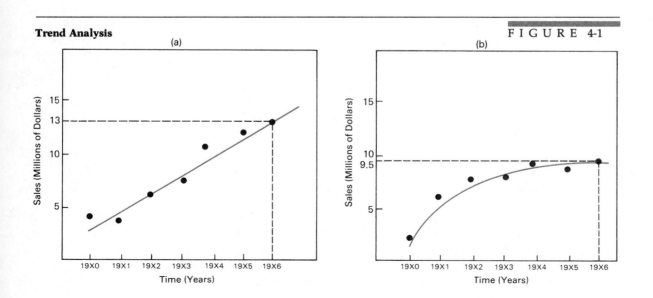

FIGURE 4-1

a continuation of past trends, and this is not always the case. Therefore, the analyst must exercise caution when performing a trend analysis and take into account current information about industry and economic cycles.

Econometric Techniques

Econometric techniques involve the development and empirical measurement of functional relationships between economic variables (for example, sales) and one (or more) explanatory variables.[15] For example, a company might hypothesize that its sales are a linear function of the Gross National Product (GNP). A plot of the company's sales and GNP data for the last six years (19X0–19X5) is shown in Figure 4-2. A linear regression of the form

$$\text{Sales} = a + b \text{ GNP} \tag{4.9}$$

could be used as a model of the relationship. Once the a and b coefficients are estimated, using either visual or least-squares techniques, one can substitute a forecasted value for GNP in 19X6 into Equation 4.9 to obtain an estimate of company sales for 19X6.

More complicated relationships involving two or more explanatory variables and/or nonlinear relationships also can be employed if the simple techniques are not satisfactory.

Computerized Financial Planning Models

In the last 25 years or so, many companies have spent considerable amounts of time and money developing models to represent various aspects of their financial planning process, as well as cash flow forecasting. Today, these representations usually are computerized and generally are called *financial planning models*. A detailed discussion of these models is beyond the scope of this text, because it requires a familiarity with a number of quantitative

[15] Econometric techniques are discussed in more detail in ibid., Chs. 6 and 9.

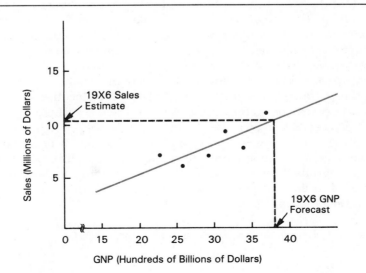

techniques, such as regression analysis and linear programming—topics not covered here. A brief general introduction to the topic can be useful for informational purposes, however.

Financial planning models often are classified according to whether they are *deterministic* or *probabilistic* and whether or not they attempt to *optimize* (that is, achieve the most desirable level of) the value of some objective function, such as net income or stock price.

A *deterministic model* gives a single-number forecast of a financial variable or variables without stating anything about its probability of occurrence. An example of a deterministic model is a computerized representation of a firm's operating budget, or a *budget simulator*. Companies that employ budget simulators enter estimated future revenues and expenses into the computer and receive as output an estimate of various financial variables, such as net income and earnings per share. The model tells the company nothing about the chances of achieving these estimates, nor does it indicate whether the company will be able to manage its resources in such a way as to attain higher levels of these variables.

The main advantage of deterministic models is that they allow the user to perform *sensitivity analyses* quickly and easily. A sensitivity analysis essentially consists of rerunning the model to determine the effect on the output variables of changes in the input variables. For example, a company may want to know *what* the net income will be *if* it discontinues some product line. Thus, sensitivity analysis is also called *what if* analysis.

Some companies prepare different budgets to reflect different assumptions about the type of year they expect to have. For instance, a company may compile three separate budgets to reflect *pessimistic*, *realistic*, and *optimistic* assumptions about the coming year. Whereas these scenario analysis models are essentially deterministic, they represent a first step toward the use of probabilistic models.

Probabilistic models are becoming increasingly popular, because they often provide financial decision makers with more useful information than other models. Whereas deterministic models yield single-point estimates, probabilistic models yield more general probability distributions. To illustrate, suppose a company is planning to build a new plant. Instead of estimating a single sales figure, the company's planners might estimate that there is a 25 percent chance that the firm's sales will be $2 million, a 50 percent chance that they will be $3 million, and a 25 percent chance that they will be $4 million. The use of a probabilistic planning model yields output in the form of a probability distribution, which gives the company's planners more useful information than a deterministic model would. In the case of complex probabilistic models, more input is necessary.[16]

Optimization models determine the values of financial decision variables that optimize (that is, maximize or minimize) some objective function such as profits or costs. For example, consider an oil refinery whose capacity and production costs are known. By combining these known figures with estimates of the sales prices for gasoline and heating fuel, it is possible, with the use of an optimization model, to specify what output product mix will achieve an optimal level of operating income. Optimization models are not widely used in finance, even though various applications have been proposed in the financial literature.

---

[16] Additional examples of probabilistic models are discussed in Chapter 11.

- Two key aspects of the cash flow concept are cash flow analysis and cash flow forecasting.
- After-tax operating cash flow is equal to earnings after tax plus noncash charges. Depreciation and deferred taxes are examples of noncash charges.
- The *statement of cash flows* is a major financial statement showing the effects of a firm's operating, investing, and financing activities on its cash balance.
- A firm's financial manager plays an important role in the cash flow forecasting process. Basically, the cash flow forecasting process involves the development of a set of financial plans for the orderly acquisition and expenditure of cash. Pro forma financial statements usually are an integral part of any financial plan. *Pro forma financial statements* show the results of some *assumed* rather than *actual* events.
- Cash flow forecasting involves the projection and estimation of a firm's future cash flows. The percentage of sales method, cash budgeting, the pro forma statement of cash flows, and cash breakeven analysis are used in cash flow forecasting.
- The *percentage of sales* method is used to estimate the amount of additional financing that will be needed to support a given future sales level.
- *Budgets* are pro forma financial statements that detail a company's future plans regarding the acquisition and spending of funds. Budgets are used for *planning, coordinating,* and *controlling* the operations of the firm.
- *Cash budgets* are projections of cash receipts and disbursements over some future time period. The steps involved in preparing a cash budget include the following:
  1. Estimating cash receipts based on historical information about the collection of receivables.
  2. Scheduling disbursements.
  3. Determining a minimum cash balance.
  4. Calculating the amount of loans required to cover any cash shortages.
- A pro forma statement of cash flows may assist the financial manager in forecasting cash flows.
- *Breakeven analysis* is used to examine the relationship among a firm's revenues, costs, and operating profits (EBIT) at various output levels. Frequently the analyst constructs a breakeven chart based on linear cost–output and revenue–output relationships to determine the operating characteristics of a firm over a limited output range.
- *The cash breakeven point* is defined as the output level at which total revenues equal cash operating costs. In the linear breakeven model, the breakeven point is found by dividing fixed (operating) costs by the difference between price and variable cost per unit.
- Through trend analysis, the future value of a financial variable is estimated by extrapolating historical data. In general, the analyst should exercise caution when using either the percentage of sales method or trend analysis, because the techniques involved in these analytical methods assume that the future simply will be a continuation of the past. Econometric techniques involve the use of explanatory variables to forecast future values of financial variables.
- A *financial planning model* is a computerized representation of some aspect of a firm's financial planning process. Financial planning models

usually are classified according to whether they are *deterministic* or *probabilistic* and whether or not they seek to *optimize* the value of some objective function.

QUESTIONS AND TOPICS FOR DISCUSSION

1. What is the *statement of cash flows*?

2. What are *deferred taxes*?

3. What are *pro forma financial statements*?

4. What is the *percentage of sales* forecasting method? What are some of the limitations financial analysts should be aware of in applying this method?

5. What is a *cash budget*? What are the usual steps involved in preparing a cash budget?

6. Illustrate how the statement of cash flows can be used as a financial planning technique.

7. What is *cash breakeven analysis*?

8. Explain the difference between deterministic and probabilistic financial planning models.

9. Explain the difference between trend analysis and econometric techniques in forecasting company sales.

10. Explain how sensitivity analysis can be used in financial planning.

PROBLEMS*

1. Last year Blue Lake Mines, Inc., had earnings after tax of $650,000. Included in its expenses were depreciation of $400,000 and deferred taxes of $100,000. The company also purchased new capital equipment for $300,000 last year. Calculate Blue Lake's after-tax operating cash flow for last year.

2. Consider the Industrial Supply Company example (Table 4-5) again. Assume that the company plans to maintain its dividend payments at the same level in 19X7 as in 19X6. Also assume that all of the additional financing needed is in the form of short-term notes payable. Determine the amount of additional financing required and pro forma financial statements (that is, balance sheet, income statement, and selected financial ratios) for 19X7 under each of the following conditions:

	Increase in Sales	Increase in Expenses
a.	$3,750,000	$3,750,000
b.	$3,000,000	$2,800,000
c.	$4,500,000	$4,000,000

3. Prepare a cash budget for Atlas Products, Inc., for the first quarter of 19X2, based on the following information.

The budgeting section of the corporate finance department of Atlas Products, Inc., has received the following sales estimates from the marketing department:

---

* Colored numbers denote problems that have check answers printed at the end of the book.

	Total Sales	Credit Sales
December 19X1	$825,000	$770,000
January 19X2	730,000	690,000
February 19X2	840,000	780,000
March 19X2	920,000	855,000

The company has found that, on the average, about 25 percent of its credit sales are collected during the month when the sale is made, and the remaining 75 percent of credit sales are collected during the month following the sale. As a result, the company uses these figures for budgeting.

The company estimates its purchases at 60 percent of next month's sales, and payments for those purchases are budgeted to lag the purchases by 1 month.

Various disbursements have been estimated as follows:

	January	February	March
Wages and salaries	$250,000	$290,000	$290,000
Rent	27,000	27,000	27,000
Other expenses	10,000	12,000	14,000

In addition, a tax payment of $105,000 is due on January 15, and $40,000 in dividends will be declared in January and paid in March. Also, the company has ordered a $75,000 piece of equipment. Delivery is scheduled for early January, and payment will be due in February.

The company's projected cash balance at the beginning of January is $100,000, and the company desires to maintain a balance of $100,000 at the end of each month.

4. Prepare a cash budget for Elmwood Manufacturing Company for the first 3 months of 19X7 based on the following information:

Month	Estimated Sales	Estimated Factory Overhead	Estimated Selling & Administrative Expenses
December	$ 4,600,000	$640,000	$1,250,000
January	6,400,000	650,000	1,275,000
February	11,200,000	670,000	1,285,000
March	8,400,000	670,000	1,310,000
April	7,000,000	680,000	1,300,000

The company has found that approximately 40 percent of sales are collected during the month the sale is made and the remaining 60 percent are collected during the month following the sale. Material purchases are 30 percent of next month's estimated sales and payments lag these purchases by 1 month. Labor costs are 35 percent of next month's sales and are paid during the month incurred. Factory overhead and selling and administrative expenses are paid during the month incurred. In addition, a payment for new equipment of $1.5 million is due in February. Also, a tax payment of $1.6 million and a dividend payment of $650,000 are due in March.

The company's projected cash balance at the beginning of January is $1.5 million. Furthermore, Elmwood desires to maintain a $750,000 cash balance at the end of each month.

5. The Covington Engine Company is considering opening a new plant facility to build truck engines. As part of a detailed analysis of the proposed facility,

Covington's management wants some information on the cash breakeven point. Fixed costs for the facility are expected to be $6 million a year, including depreciation expenses of $800,000 a year. The engines' sales price is expected to be $7,000 per unit, and the variable cost is expected to be $3,000 per unit. Calculate the expected annual cash breakeven point and the expected annual cash breakeven sales.

6. Refer to the Summit Furniture Company example (Table 4-3). Recalculate the cash and cash equivalents at the end of 19X1 assuming that (1) the company had 19X1 capital expenditures of $22,000; (2) it paid dividends of $800; and (3) it did not issue any common stock. Assume that Summit's other cash flows are the same as those shown in Table 4-3.

7. Prepare a statement of cash flows (using the indirect method) for the Midland Manufacturing Corporation for the year ending December 19X2, based on the following comparative balance sheets.

Midland Manufacturing Corporation
Comparative Balance Sheets
(in millions of dollars)*

	December 31, 19X1	December 31, 19X2
ASSETS		
Current assets:		
Cash	$ 4.9	$ 0.8
Accounts receivable	7.2	7.5
Inventories	13.8	14.5
Total current assets	$25.9	$ 22.8
Property and equipment	$80.7	$115.0
Less Accumulated depreciation	16.3	25.8
Net property and equipment	$64.4	$ 89.2
Total assets	$90.3	$112.0
LIABILITIES AND STOCKHOLDERS' EQUITY		
Current liabilities:		
Accounts payable	$ 8.0	$ 9.5
Other current liabilities	6.0	8.2
Total current liabilities	$14.0	$ 17.7
Long-term debt	$18.8	$ 31.8
Deferred federal income taxes	$ 1.2	$ 1.4
Stockholders' equity:		
Common stock	$ 3.0	$ 3.0
Additional paid-in capital	29.0	29.0
Retained earnings	24.3	29.1
Total stockholders' equity	$56.3	$ 61.1
Total liabilities and stockholders' equity	$90.3	$112.0

* Net income for the year ended December 31, 19X2 totaled $8.3 million; dividends paid during the same period totaled $3.5 million; $2.0 million of long-term debt was retired in 19X2; and fixed assets were sold during 19X2 for $1.0 million.

8. The Norfolk Corporation is considering a $200 million expansion (capital expenditure) program next year. The company wants to know approximately how much additional financing (if any) will be required if it decides to go through with the expansion program. Next year the company expects to earn $80 million after interest and taxes. The company also expects to maintain its present level of dividends, which is $15 million. If the expansion

program is accepted, the company expects its inventory and accounts receivable to each increase by approximately $20 million next year. Long-term debt retirement obligations total $10 million for next year, and depreciation is expected to be $80 million. The company does not expect to sell any fixed assets next year. The company maintains a cash balance of $5 million, which is sufficient for its present operations. If the expansion is accepted, the company feels it should increase its year-end cash balance to $8 million because of the increased level of activities. For planning purposes, assume no other cash flow changes for next year.

9. **a.** Using the percentage of sales method, calculate the additional financing needed over the next year for the Baldwin Products Company if a sales level of $6.0 million is expected to be reached in 1 year. The company expects after-tax operating cash flow during the next year to equal $400,000. During the past several years the company has been paying $50,000 in dividends to its stockholders. The company expects to continue this policy for at least the next year. The actual balance sheet and income statement for Baldwin during 19X8 follow. Show the pro forma balance sheet for the company as of December 31, 19X9, assuming a sales level of $6.0 million is reached. Assume that the additional financing needed is obtained in the form of additional notes payable.

Baldwin Products Company
Balance Sheet
as of December 31, 19X8

Cash	$ 200,000	Accounts payable	$ 600,000
Accounts receivable	400,000	Notes payable	500,000
Inventories	1,200,000	Long-term debt	200,000
Fixed assets, net	500,000	Stockholders' equity	1,000,000
Total assets	$2,300,000	Total liabilities and equity	$2,300,000

Income Statement
for the Year Ending December 31, 19X8

Sales	$4,000,000
Cash expenses, including interest and taxes	$3,700,000
After-tax operating cash flow	$ 300,000

b. Consider Part a again. Suppose that the Baldwin Products' management feels that the average collection period on its additional sales—that is, sales over $4 million—will be 60 days instead of the current level. By what amount will this increase in the average collection period increase the financing needed by the company over the next year?

c. Refer to Part a again. Suppose that the Baldwin Products' banker requires the company to maintain a current ratio equal to 1.6 or greater. What is the maximum amount of additional financing that can be in the form of bank borrowings (notes payable)? What other potential sources of financing are available to the company?

10. In the Industrial Supply Company example (Table 4-5) it was assumed that the company's fixed assets were being utilized at nearly full capacity and that net fixed assets would have to increase proportionately as sales increased. Alternatively, suppose that the company has excess fixed assets and that *no increase* in net fixed assets are required as sales are increased. Assume that the company plans to maintain its dividend payments at the same level in 19X7 as in 19X6. Determine the amount of additional financing required for 19X7 under each of the following conditions:

	Increase in Sales	Increase in Expenses
a.	$3,750,000	$3,750,000
b.	$3,000,000	$2,800,000
c.	$4,500,000	$4,000,000

11. Berea Resources is planning a $75 million capital expenditure program for the coming year. Next year, Berea expects to report to the IRS earnings of $40 million after interest and taxes. Dividend payments are expected to increase from the present level of $10 million to $12 million. The company expects its current asset needs to increase from a current level of $25 million to $30 million. Current liabilities, excluding short-term bank borrowing, are expected to increase from $15 million to $17 million. Interest payments are $5 million next year and long-term debt retirement obligations are $8 million next year. Depreciation next year is expected to be $15 million on the company's financial statements, but the company will report depreciation of $18 million for tax purposes.

    How much external financing is required by Berea for the coming year?

Last year (19X6) Midwest Chemicals, Inc. (MCI), undertook a $20 million plant expansion and modernization program. The firm originally had planned to finance the program partially from the sale of new common stock. However, due to depressed stock prices, a stock offering was not feasible at that time. Instead, the firm financed the entire $20 million with a 5-year term loan from a large insurance company. Because of tight money conditions in the economy and the relatively large amount of debt in its capital structure, MCI was required to pay 14 percent interest on the term loan. MCI also has a mortgage loan of $20 million outstanding, which is being repaid in annual installments of $2 million (due on December 30 each year) plus 10 percent interest. The balance sheet and income statement for the current year (19X7), along with some relevant industry ratios, are shown in the tables.

Midwest Chemicals, Inc.
(A) Balance Sheet as of December 31, 19X7
(in thousands of dollars)

ASSETS		
Cash	$ 4,000	
Accounts receivable	22,000	
Inventories	22,000	
Total current assets		$ 48,000
Plant and equipment	$70,000	
Less Accumulated depreciation	30,000	
Net plant and equipment		40,000
Total assets		$ 88,000
LIABILITIES AND STOCKHOLDERS' EQUITY		
Accounts payable	$18,000	
Current portion of mortgage loan ($i = 10\%$)	2,000	
Total current liabilities		$ 20,000
Mortgage loan ($i = 10\%$)		16,000
Term loan		20,000
Stockholders' equity (common stock and retained earnings)		32,000
Total liabilities and stockholders' equity		$ 88,000

(B) Income Statement for the Year Ended
December 31, 19X7
(in thousands of dollars)

Sales		$148,000
Less Raw materials	$76,000	
Labor	10,000	
Depreciation	6,000	
Cost of sales		92,000
Gross profit		$ 56,000
Less Selling and administrative expenses		45,200
Earnings before interest and taxes		$ 10,800
Less Interest expense		4,800
Net income before taxes		$ 6,000
Less Federal and state income tax (40%)		2,400
Net income after taxes		$ 3,600
Less Common stock dividends (1,000,000 × $2.00/share)		2,000
Net additions to retained earnings		$ 1,600

(C) Selected Industry Ratios
19X7

Ratio	Industry Average
Current	2.7 times
Quick	1.7 times
Debt to equity	86%
Times interest earned (EBIT ÷ Interest charges)	5.4 times
Net profit margin on sales	3.77%
Return on stockholders' equity	13.5%

Conditions in the capital markets have improved considerably since last year (that is, the price of MCI common stock has risen and interest rates have fallen). The treasurer of MCI has decided that this would be an opportune time to float (that is, sell) an issue of common stock and use the proceeds to reduce the amount of high-cost debt in the firm's capital structure. Specifically, the firm plans to sell 200,000 shares of new common stock at a net price of $50 per share to yield the firm $10 million. The funds would be used to repay one-half of the term loan, thus reducing its interest expenses and improving its financial position.

The MCI economists have forecast a 10 percent increase in the firm's sales for next year (19X8). Raw material, labor, and selling and administrative expenses also are expected to increase by 10 percent next year. Depreciation expenses next year are anticipated to be $4 million. The firm's (combined) federal and state income tax rate is expected to remain at 40 percent next year. The board of directors of the firm is expected to increase the dividend rate by 10 percent to $2.20 per share.

Receivables and inventories are expected to rise by 10 percent next year as a result of the forecasted sales increase. The treasurer feels that the firm's minimum cash needs can be met with the existing $4 million balance during the coming year. New additions to plant and equipment totaling $2 million are planned during the coming year. The firm has been paying many of its trade creditors beyond the due date and would like to avoid this situation in the future. To accomplish this, the firm wants to hold its accounts payable at $18 million during the coming year, even though its raw material purchases will increase.

1. Prepare a pro forma income statement for MCI for 19X8.

2. Prepare a pro forma balance sheet for MCI as of December 31, 19X8. Use "additional short-term debt" as the balancing account to reflect the need for additional financing. (HINT: First determine MCI's assets and then determine liabilities and net worth. Total assets should equal $90,400[000].)

3. How much additional financing (beyond that generated from operations) is required to meet the needs of the firm? What are some possible sources of these funds?

4. Prepare a pro forma statement of cash flows (using the indirect method) for 19X8.

5. Using a ratio analysis of the firm's pro forma statements for 19X8, evaluate the impact of the proposed financing plan on the financial condition of the firm.

6. What are the reasons why the percentage of sales forecasting method cannot be used in this case?

Carleton, W. T., and J. M. McInnes. "Theory, Models and Implementation in Financial Management." *Management Science* (Sept. 1981):957–978.

Chambers, John C., Satinder K. Mullick, and Donald D. Smith. "How to Choose the Right Forecasting Technique." *Harvard Business Review* 49 (July–Aug. 1971):45–74.

Francis, Jack C., and Dexter R. Powell. "A Simultaneous Equation Model of the Firm for Financial Analysis and Planning." *Financial Management* (Spring 1979):29–44.

Hunt, Pearson. "Funds Position: Keystone in Financial Planning." *Harvard Business Review* 53 (May–June 1975):106–115.

Lee, Cheng F. *Financial Analysis and Planning*. (Reading, MA: Addison-Wesley, 1985).

Maier, Steven F., and James H. Vander Weide. "A Practical Approach to Short-Run Financial Planning." *Financial Management* (Winter 1978):10–16.

Myers, Stewart C., and Gerald A. Pogue. "The Programming Approach to Corporate Financial Management." *Journal of Finance* 29 (May 1974):579–599.

Smith, Gary, and William Brainard. "The Value of A Priori Information in Estimating a Financial Model." *Journal of Finance* 31 (Dec. 1976):1299–1322.

Wheelwright, Steven C., and Daniel G. Clarke. "Corporate Forecasting: Promise and Reality." *Harvard Business Review* (Nov.–Dec. 1976):40–68.

Breakeven Analysis

INTRODUCTION

Many of the forecasting activities that take place within a firm are based on anticipated levels of output. The study of the interrelationships among a firm's sales, operating costs, and EBIT at various output levels is known as *cost-volume-profit analysis*, or *breakeven analysis*.

The term *breakeven analysis* is somewhat misleading, because this type of analysis typically is used to answer many questions besides those dealing with the breakeven output level of a firm. For example, breakeven analysis also is used to forecast the financial profitability of new firms and new product lines. In addition, it is a valuable analytical tool for measuring the effects of changes in selling price, fixed costs, and variable costs on the output level that must be achieved before the firm can realize operating profits.

A breakeven analysis of a firm can be developed graphically, algebraically, or as a combination of the two.

GRAPHIC METHOD

Figure 4A-1 is an example of a basic linear breakeven analysis chart. Costs and revenues (measured in dollars) are plotted on the vertical axis, and output (measured in units) is plotted on the horizontal axis. The *total revenue* function, TR, represents the total revenue the firm will realize at each output level, given that the firm charges a constant selling price, P, per unit of output. Similarly, the *total* (operating) *cost* function, TC, represents the total cost the firm will incur at each output level. Total cost is computed as the sum of the firm's fixed costs, F, which are independent of the output level, plus the variable costs, which increase at the constant rate, V, per unit of output.

The assumptions of a constant selling price per unit, P, and a constant variable cost per unit, V, yield *linear* relationships for the total revenue and total cost functions. However, these linear relationships are valid only over some *relevant range* of output values, such as from Q_1 to Q_2 in Figure 4A-1. (The concept of relevant range is discussed later in this chapter).

The breakeven point occurs at point Q_b in Figure 4A-1, where the total revenue and the total cost functions intersect. If a firm's output level is below this breakeven point—that is, if TR < TC—it incurs *operating losses*, defined as a *negative EBIT*. If the firm's output level is above this breakeven point—that is, if TR > TC—it realizes *operating profits*, defined as a *positive EBIT*.

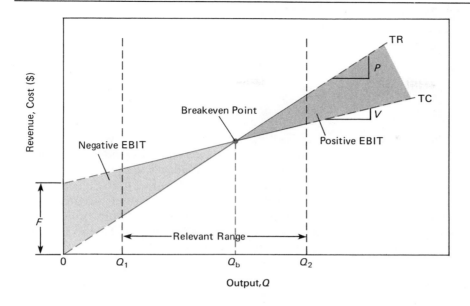

Determining a firm's breakeven point graphically involves three steps:

1. Drawing a line through the origin with a slope of P to represent the TR function.
2. Drawing a line that intersects the vertical axis at F and has a slope of V to represent the TC function.
3. Determining the point where the TR and TC lines intersect, dropping a perpendicular line to the horizontal axis, and noting the resulting value of Q_b.

ALGEBRAIC METHOD

To determine a firm's breakeven point algebraically, it is necessary to set the total revenue and total (operating) cost functions equal to each other and solve the resulting equation for the breakeven volume.

Total revenue is equal to the selling price per unit times the output quantity:

$$TR = P \times Q \qquad \text{(4A.1)}$$

Total (operating) cost is equal to fixed plus variable costs, where the variable cost is the product of the variable cost per unit times the output quantity:

$$TC = F + (V \times Q) \qquad \text{(4A.2)}$$

Setting the total revenue and total cost expressions equal to each other (that is, setting $EBIT = TR - TC = 0$) and substituting the breakeven output Q_b for Q results in the following:

$$TR = TC$$

or

$$PQ_b = F + VQ_b \qquad \text{(4A.3)}$$

137

Finally, solving Equation 4A.3 for the breakeven output Q_b yields the following:

$$PQ_b - VQ_b = F$$

$$(P - V)Q_b = F$$

$$Q_b = \frac{F}{P - V} \qquad \text{(4A.4)}$$

The *difference* between the selling price per unit and the variable cost per unit, $P - V$, sometimes is referred to as the *contribution margin per unit*. It measures how much each unit of output contributes to meeting fixed costs and operating profits. Therefore, it also can be said that the breakeven output is equal to the fixed costs divided by the contribution margin per unit.

Breakeven analysis can also be performed in terms of dollar *sales* rather than units of output. The breakeven dollar sales volume, S_b, can be determined by the following expression:

$$S_b = \frac{F}{1 - (V/P)} \qquad \text{(4A.5)}$$

where V/P is the variable cost ratio (that is, the variable cost per dollar of sales).

Occasionally the analyst is interested in determining the output quantity at which a *target profit* (expressed in dollars) is achieved. An expression similar to Equation 4A.4 can be used to find such a quantity:

$$\text{Target volume} = \frac{\text{Fixed cost} + \text{Target profit}}{\text{Contribution margin per unit}} \qquad \text{(4A.6)}$$

EXAMPLES OF BREAKEVEN ANALYSIS

The equations defined in the preceding section can be used to perform a breakeven analysis for the Allegan Manufacturing Company for the year ending December 31, 19X1. Assume that the firm manufactures one product, which its sells for $250 per unit. The current output, Q, is obtained by dividing total dollars sales ($5 million) by the selling price per unit ($250) to obtain 20,000 units per year. Its variable (operating) costs per unit, V, are determined by dividing total variable costs ($3 million) by current output (20,000) to obtain $150 per unit.

The firm's fixed costs, F, are $1 million. Substituting these figures into Equation 4A.4 yields the following breakeven output:

$$Q_b = \frac{\$1,000,000}{\$250 - \$150}$$

$$= 10,000 \text{ units}$$

Allegan's breakeven output can also be determined graphically, as shown in Figure 4A-2. The breakeven level of dollar sales is also shown in Figure 4A-2 to be $2,500,000.

Because a firm's breakeven output is dependent upon a number of variables—in particular, the price per unit and variable (operating) costs per unit—the firm may wish to analyze the effects of changes in any one of the

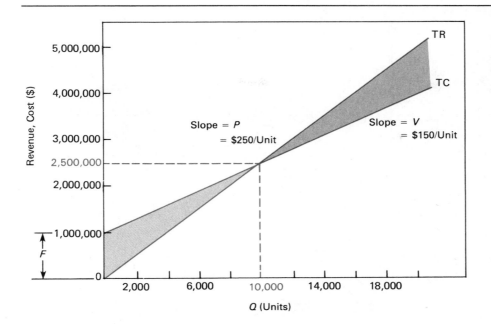

FIGURE 4A-2

Linear Breakeven
Analysis Chart for
the Allegan
Manufacturing
Company

variables on the breakeven output. For example, it may wish to consider either of the following: (1) changing the selling price, or (2) substituting fixed costs for variable costs.

Assume that Allegan increased the selling price per unit by $25 to $275, P'. Substituting this figure into Equation 4A.4 gives a new breakeven output:

$$Q_b' = \frac{\$1,000,000}{\$275 - \$150}$$

$$= 8,000 \text{ units}$$

This also can be seen in Figure 4A-3, in which an increase in the price per unit increases the slope of the total revenue function, TR′, and reduces the breakeven output.

Rather than increasing the selling price per unit, Allegan's management may decide to substitute fixed costs for variable costs in some aspect of the company's operations. For example, as labor wage rates increase over time, many firms seek to reduce operating costs through automation, which in effect represents the substitution of fixed-cost capital equipment for variable-cost labor. Suppose that Allegan determines it can reduce labor costs by $25 per unit by purchasing $1 million in additional equipment. Assume that the new equipment is depreciated over a 10-year life using the straight-line method. Under these conditions, annual depreciation of the new equipment would be $1,000,000/10 = $100,000, and the firm's new level of fixed costs, F', would be $1,000,000 + $100,000 = $1,100,000. Variable costs per unit, V', would be $150 − $25 = $125. Substituting P = $250 per unit, V' = $125 per unit, and F' = $1,100,000 into Equation 4A.4 yields a new breakeven output:

$$Q_b' = \frac{\$1,100,000}{\$250 - \$125}$$

$$= 8,800 \text{ units}$$

139

**Linear Breakeven
Analysis Chart for
the Allegan
Manufacturing
Company Showing
the Effects of a Price
Increase**

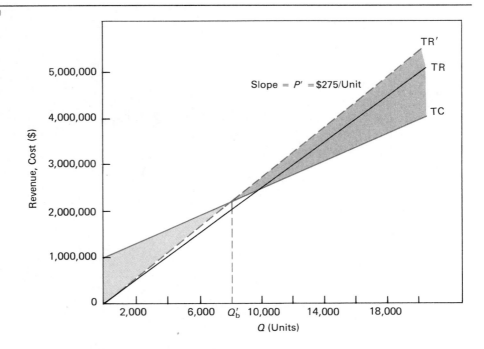

As can be seen in Figure 4A-4, the effect of this change in operations is to raise the intercept on the vertical axis; decrease the slope of the total cost function, TC'; and reduce the breakeven output.

BREAKEVEN ANALYSIS AND RISK ASSESSMENT

The information generated from a breakeven analysis can be used to assess the operating risk to which a firm is exposed. Consider the example represented in Figure 4A-2. With fixed costs of $1 million, a price per unit of $250 and variable costs per unit of $150, the breakeven output was computed to be 10,000 units. If we add to this set of information the *expected* (mean) level of sales (in units) for some future period of time, the standard deviation of the distribution of sales, and the assumption that actual sales are approximately normally distributed, it is possible to compute the probability that the firm will have operating losses (that is, sell fewer units than the breakeven level) and the probability that the firm will have operating profits (that is, sell more units than the breakeven level).

For example, suppose that expected unit sales for Allegan are 15,000 units with a standard deviation of 4,000 units. The probability of having operating losses (that is, the probability of selling fewer than 10,000 units) can be computed by determining the number of standard deviations that this value is from the expected value and using the probability values from Reference Table V.

$$z = \frac{10,000 - 15,000}{4,000} = -1.25$$

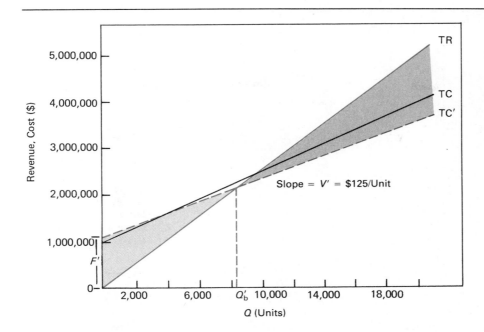

Linear Breakeven
Analysis Chart for
the Allegan
Manufacturing
Company Showing
the Effects of
Substituting Fixed
Costs for Variable
Costs

In other words, a sales level of 10,000 units is 1.25 standard deviations *below* the mean. From Table V it can be seen that the probability associated with −1.25 standard deviations is 10.56 percent. Therefore there is a 10.56 percent chance that the firm will incur operating losses and an 89.44 percent (100 percent minus 10.56 percent chance of losses) chance that the firm will record operating profits (that is, sell more than the breakeven number of units of output).

SOME LIMITATIONS OF BREAKEVEN ANALYSIS

Breakeven analysis as it was just developed has a number of limitations. These arise from the *assumptions* that are made in constructing the model and developing the relevant data. The application of breakeven analysis is of value only to the extent that these assumptions are valid.

Constant Selling Price and Variable Cost Per Unit

Recall that in the graphic breakeven analysis model, the assumptions of a constant selling price and variable cost per unit yield linear relationships for the total revenue and total cost functions. In practice these functions tend to be nonlinear. In many cases a firm can sell additional units of output only by lowering the price per unit. This results in a total revenue function that is curvilinear, as shown in Figure 4A-5, instead of a straight line.

In addition, a firm's total cost function may be nonlinear as variable costs per unit initially decrease and then increase. This also is shown in Figure 4A-5. Decreasing variable costs per unit can occur if, for example, labor specialization results in increased output per labor hour. Increasing variable costs per unit can occur if, for example, a firm uses more costly overtime labor as output approaches production capacity.

141

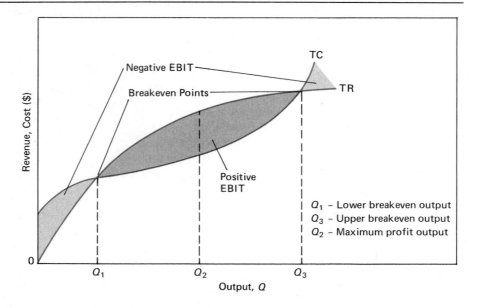

Nonlinear TC and TR functions can result in a firm having more than one breakeven output point. This is shown in Figure 4A-5, where a breakeven situation occurs at both Point Q_1 and Point Q_3. This is interpreted to mean that the firm will incur operating losses *below* an output level of Q_1 and *above* an output level of Q_3. The firm's total operating profits are maximized within the range of $Q_1 - Q_3$ at the point where the vertical distance between the TR and TC curves is greatest; that is, at output level Q_2.

In summary, the assumption of a constant selling price and variable cost per unit is probably valid over some "relevant range" of output levels. However, consideration of output levels outside this range normally will require modifications in the breakeven chart.

Composition of Operating Costs

Another assumption of breakeven analysis is that costs can be classified as either fixed or variable. In fact, fixed and variable costs are dependent on both the time period involved and the output range under consideration. As mentioned earlier, all costs are variable in the long run. In addition, some costs are partly fixed and partly variable. Furthermore, some costs increase in a stepwise manner as output is increased (that is, *semivariable costs*) and are constant only over relatively narrow ranges of output.

Multiple Products

The breakeven model also assumes that a firm is producing and selling either a *single* product or a *constant mix* of different products. In many cases the product mix changes over time, and problems can arise in allocating fixed costs among the various products.

Uncertainty

Still another assumption of breakeven analysis is that the selling price and variable cost per unit, as well as fixed costs, are known at each level of output. In practice these parameters are subject to uncertainty. Thus, the usefulness of the results of breakeven analysis depends on how accurate the estimates of these parameters are.

Short-Term Planning Horizon

Finally, breakeven analysis normally is performed for a planning period of 1 year or less. However, the benefits received from some costs may not be realized until subsequent periods. For example, research and development costs incurred during a specific period may not result in new products for several years. For breakeven analysis to be a dependable decision-making tool, a firm's operating costs must be matched with resulting revenues for the planning period under consideration.

■■■ QUESTIONS AND TOPICS FOR DISCUSSION

1. Explain how a linear breakeven chart is constructed when a firm's selling price, variable costs per unit, and fixed costs are known.

2. What are some of the limitations of breakeven analysis? How can these limitations affect actual financial decision making?

3. Assuming that all other factors remain unchanged, determine how a firm's breakeven point is affected by each of the following:

   a. The firm finds it necessary to reduce the price per unit because of competitive conditions in the market.
   b. The firm's direct labor costs increase as a result of a new labor contract.
   c. The Occupational Safety and Health Administration (OSHA) requires the firm to install new ventilating equipment in its plant. (Assume that this action has no effect on worker productivity.)

■■■ PROBLEMS*

1. East Publishing Company is doing an analysis of a proposed new finance text. Using the following data, answer parts a through e.

FIXED COSTS (PER EDITION):
Development (reviews, class testing, and so on)	$18,000
Copyediting	5,000
Selling and promotion	7,000
Typesetting	40,000
Total	$70,000

VARIABLE COSTS (PER COPY):
Printing and binding	$ 4.20
Administrative costs	1.60
Salespeople's commission (2% of selling price)	.60
Author's royalties (12% of selling price)	3.60
Bookstore discounts (20% of selling price)	6.00
Total	$16.00
PROJECTED SELLING PRICE	$30.00

   a. Determine the company's breakeven volume for this book:
      i. In units.
      ii. In dollar sales.

* Colored numbers denote problems that have check answers provided at the end of the book.

   b. Develop a breakeven chart for the text.

   c. Determine the number of copies East must sell in order to earn an (operating) profit of $21,000 on this text.

   d. Determine total (operating) profits at the following sales levels:
     i. 3,000 units.
     ii. 5,000 units.
     iii. 10,000 units.

   e. Suppose East feels that $30.00 is too high a price to charge for the new finance text. It has examined the competitive market and determined that $24.00 would be a better selling price. What would the breakeven volume be at this new selling price?

2. Jenkins Appliances produces microwave ovens. Jenkins has computed its breakeven level of sales to be 60,000 units. An analysis of the market has led Jenkins to *expect* sales of 75,000 units with a standard deviation of 10,000 units.

   a. What is the probability that Jenkins will incur operating losses?

   b. What is the probability that Jenkins will operate above its breakeven point?

III

Determinants of Valuation

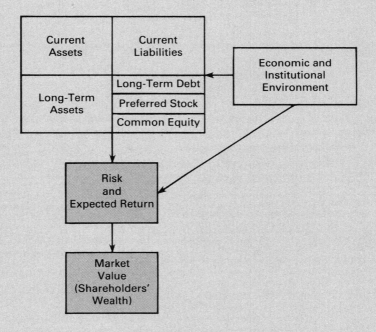

The primary objective of financial management is to maximize the value of the stock of the firm's shareholders. This part discusses the valuation process in detail. Chapter 5 develops the tools of financial mathematics essential for any serious analysis of important financial decisions that have an impact on the firm over a number of years. Chapters 6 and 7 build valuation models for a firm's securities. Chapter 6 focuses on the valuation of fixed-income securities; namely, bonds and preferred stock. Chapter 7 deals with the valuation of common stock. These are important chapters because valuation is the dominant theme carried throughout the text and related to all financial decisions. Chapter 8 explores the determinants of risk and relates risk to the valuation process.

5

Financial Mathematics

KEY CHAPTER CONCEPTS

1. The concept of interest
   a. Simple interest is paid on the principal sum only.
   b. Compound interest is paid on both the initial principal amount *and* on any interest earned, but not withdrawn during earlier periods.

2. Future (compound) value calculations determine the value at some point in time in the future of X dollars invested today, earning some compound rate of interest, i, per period.

3. Present value calculations determine the value today (present value) of some amount to be received in the future.

4. An annuity is a series of equal periodic payments.
   a. Ordinary annuity payments are made at the end of each period.

   b. Annuity due payments are made at the beginning of each period.

5. Future value of an annuity calculations determine the future value of an annuity stream of cash flows.

6. Present value of an annuity calculations determine the present value of an annuity stream of cash flows.

7. Other important topics
   a. Compounding frequency
   b. Determining the present value of perpetuities
   c. Determining the present value of uneven cash flow streams
   d. Determining the present value of deferred annuities

GLOSSARY OF NEW TERMS

Annuity The payment or receipt of a series of equal cash flows per period for a specified amount of time. In an *ordinary annuity*, payments are made at the end of each period; in an *annuity due*, payments are made at the beginning.

Capital recovery problem An annuity amount necessary to recover a capital investment.

Compound interest Interest that is paid not only on the principal, but also on any interest earned but not withdrawn during earlier periods.

Discount rate The rate of interest used in the process of finding present values (discounting).

Effective interest rate The actual rate of interest paid by the borrower or earned by the lender.

Future value (or terminal value) The value at some future point in time of a present payment (or a series of payments) evaluated at the appropriate interest (growth) rate.

Interest The return earned by or the amount paid to an individual who foregoes current consumption or alternative investments and "rents" money to a business, bank, the government, some other form of institution, or another individual.

Nominal interest rate The periodic rate of interest that is stated in a loan agreement or security. Frequently the *effective interest rate* is greater than the nominal rate because of factors like the frequency of compounding and the deduction of interest in advance.

Perpetuity A financial instrument that agrees to pay an equal cash flow per period into the indefinite future (that is, infinity).

Present value The value today of a future payment (or a series of future payments) evaluated at the appropriate discount rate.

Principal An amount of money that has been borrowed or invested.

Simple interest Interest paid or earned on the principal only.

Sinking fund problem An annuity amount that must be invested each period (year) to produce a future value.

Prepaying Your Mortgage Loan

In the early 1980s interest rates were near their historic highs. Home mortgage rates of 16 to 18 percent were not uncommon for conventional new home mortgages. Banks and savings and loan institutions were paying very high costs to attract and retain funds. At the same time, these institutions were burdened with many older mortgages written at low, fixed rates of interest.

In an attempt to free up some funds invested in low interest rate mortgages, a number of financial institutions offered plans designed to encourage people to pay off their low rate mortgages more rapidly. First Federal Savings and Loan Association offered Natalie Mayer the opportunity to increase her monthly principal and interest mortgage payments from $852.39 to $1,691.49. In return, First Federal agreed to reduce the interest rate on the loan from 10.875 percent per annum to 10.00 percent. With the new payment plan, the loan would be paid off in 5 years and 10 months, compared with 27 years and 10 months under the original loan terms. First Federal computed the total (undiscounted) interest savings over the life of the loan to be $166,577.47. The current loan balance is $89,435.61.

If Mayer believes she will have opportunities to invest the funds needed for the early payment plan at a 15 percent annual rate of return over the life of the mortgage, should she accept the First Federal offer?

This type of problem illustrates the value of having a working knowledge of financial mathematics. As we shall see later in the chapter, the difference between the two alternatives is dramatic.

INTRODUCTION

Understanding the concept of compound interest is crucial to effective financial management. In fact, anyone who is involved with money should have some comprehension of compound interest. Consider the following:

- A banker who makes loans and other investments.
- A financial officer whose job includes the consideration of various alternative sources of funds in terms of their cost.
- A corporate planner who must choose among various alternative investment projects.
- A securities analyst who evaluates the securities that the firm sells to investors.
- An individual who is confronted with a host of daily financial problems ranging from personal credit account management to deciding whether to make certain purchases for the home.

Each of these individuals makes frequent use of some form of financial mathematics. However, many people fear that a working knowledge of compound interest might be too difficult to master. Instead, the availability of interest tables and calculators make the subject readily accessible.

Although an understanding of compound interest factors is useful in and of itself, it also is a necessary prelude to the following topics:

- Valuation of securities and other assets.
- Capital budgeting (the analysis of investment projects).
- The cost of capital.
- Working capital (short-term asset and liability) management.
- Lease analysis.

This chapter introduces the concepts and skills necessary to understand compound interest and its applications. The analysis in this chapter assumes that the student will use the interest tables (Tables I through IV) at the end of the book. Many students will have access to financial calculators, such as those made by Texas Instruments and Hewlett-Packard. The last section of this chapter provides a general discussion of the use of financial calculators. That section also compares the capabilities of financial calculators and microcomputers to solve financial problems.

INTEREST

Money can be thought of as having a time value. In other words, an amount of money received today is worth more than the same dollar amount would be if it were received a year from now.[1] The primary reason that a dollar today is worth more than a dollar to be received sometime in the future is that the current dollar can be invested to earn a rate of return. (This holds true even if risk and inflation are not considerations.) Suppose, for example, that you had $100 and decided to put it into a savings account for a year. By doing this, you would temporarily give up, or forego, spending the $100 however you wished, or you might forego the return that the $100 might earn from some alternative investment, such as U.S. Treasury bonds. Or you might forego paying an additional $100 on your mortgage. Similarly, a bank that loans money to a firm foregoes the opportunity to earn a return on some alternative investment.

Interest is the return earned by or the amount paid to someone who has foregone current consumption or alternative investment opportunities and "rented" money in a creditor relationship.[2] The *principal* is the amount of money borrowed or invested. The *term* of a loan is the length of time or number of time periods during which the borrower can use the principal. The *rate of interest* is the percentage on the principal that the borrower pays the lender per time period as compensation for foregoing other investment or consumption opportunities.

Simple Interest

Simple interest is the interest paid (in the case of borrowed money) or earned (in the case of invested money) on the principal only. The amount of simple interest is equal to the product of the principal times the rate per time period times the number of time periods:

$$I = PV_0 \times i \times n \tag{5.1}$$

where I = the simple interest in dollars; PV_0 = the principal amount at time 0, or the present value; i = the interest rate per time period; and n = the number of time periods. The following problems illustrate the use of Equation 5.1:

1. *What is the simple interest on $100 at 10 percent per annum for 6 months?*
   Substituting $100 for PV_0, 10% (0.10) for i, and $\frac{6}{12}$ (0.5) for n yields the following:

[1] The terms *amount of money, cash flow,* and *payment* are used interchangeably throughout the chapter.
[2] Although there are other forms of returns, and these are dealt with throughout the text, this discussion is limited to borrowing–lending situations.

$$I = \$100 \times 0.10 \times 0.5$$
$$= \$5$$

2. *If Gene Smith bought a house and borrowed \$30,000 at a 10 percent annual interest rate, what would be his first month's interest payment?* Substituting \$30,000 for PV_0, 10 percent (0.10) for i, and $1/12$ for n yields the following:

$$I = \$30,000 \times 0.10 \times 1/12$$
$$= \$250$$

3. *Mary Schiller receives \$30 every 3 months from a bank account that pays a 6 percent annual interest rate. How much is invested in the account?* Because PV_0 is the unknown in this example, Equation 5.1 is rearranged:

$$PV_0 = \frac{I}{i \times n} \tag{5.2}$$

Substituting \$30 for I, 0.06 for i, and $1/4$ (0.25) for n yields the following:

$$PV_0 = \frac{\$30}{0.06 \times 0.25}$$
$$= \$2,000$$

It is also useful to be able to calculate the amount of funds a person can expect to receive at some point in the future. In financial mathematics, the *terminal*, or *future* value of an investment is called FV_n and denotes the principal plus interest accumulated at the end of n years. It is written as follows:

$$FV_n = PV_0 + I \tag{5.3}$$

4. *Mr. E. Z. Go borrows \$1,000 for 9 months at a rate of 8 percent per annum. How much will he have to repay at the end of the 9-month period?*
Combining Equations 5.1 and 5.3 to solve for FV_n results in the following new equation:

$$FV_n = PV_0 + (PV_0 \times i \times n)$$

or

$$FV_n = PV_0 [1 + (i \times n)] \tag{5.4}$$

Substituting \$1,000 for PV_0, 0.08 for i, and $3/4$ (9 months = $3/4$ of 1 year) for n yields the following:

$$FV_{3/4} = \$1,000[1 + (0.08 \times 3/4)]$$
$$= \$1,000(1 + 0.06)$$
$$= \$1,060$$

This problem can be illustrated using the following time line:

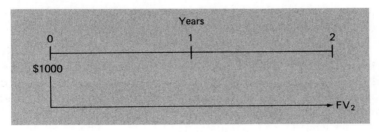

5. *Ms. E. Z. Come agrees to invest $1,000 in a venture that promises to pay 10 percent simple interest each year for 2 years. How much money will she have at the end of the second year?* Using Equation 5.4 and assuming two 10 percent simple interest payments, the future value of Ms. E. Z Come's investment at the end of 2 years is computed as follows:

$$FV_2 = PV_0 + (PV_0 \times i \times 2)$$
$$= \$1,000 + (\$1,000 \times 0.10 \times 2)$$
$$= \$1,000 + \$200$$
$$= \$1,200$$

This problem can be illustrated using the following time line:

In general, in the case of *simple interest*, the future, or terminal, value (FV_n) at the end of n years is given by Equation 5.4.

COMPOUND INTEREST AND FUTURE VALUE

Compound interest is interest that is paid not only on the principal, but also on any interest earned but not withdrawn during earlier periods. For example, if Jerry Jones deposits $1,000 in a savings account paying 6 percent interest compounded annually, the future (compound) value of his account at the end of 1 year (FV_1) is calculated as follows:

$$FV_1 = PV_0 (1 + i) \qquad (5.5)$$
$$= \$1,000 (1 + 0.06)$$
$$= \$1,060$$

This problem can be illustrated using the following time line:

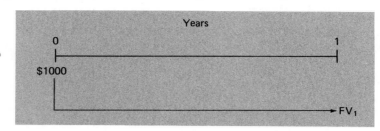

If Jones leaves the $1,000 *plus* the accumulated interest in the account for another year, its worth at the end of the second year is calculated as follows:

$$FV_2 = FV_1(1 + i) \tag{5.6}$$

$$= \$1,060(1 + 0.06)$$

$$= \$1,123.60$$

This problem can be illustrated using the following time line:

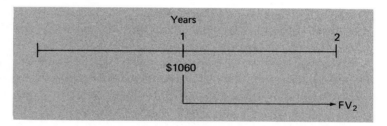

Recall that in the case of compound interest, interest in each period is earned not only on the principal, but also on any interest accumulated during previous periods and not withdrawn. As shown in Figure 5-1, if Jones's account paid simple interest instead of compound interest, its value at the end of 2 years would be $1,120 instead of $1,123.60. The $3.60 difference is the interest on the first year's interest, 0.06 × $60.

If Jones makes no withdrawals from the account for another year, it will total the following at the end of the third year:

$$FV_3 = FV_2(1 + i) \tag{5.7}$$

$$= \$1,123.60(1 + 0.06)$$

$$= \$1,191.02$$

This problem can be illustrated using the following time line:

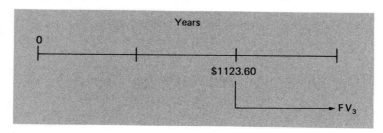

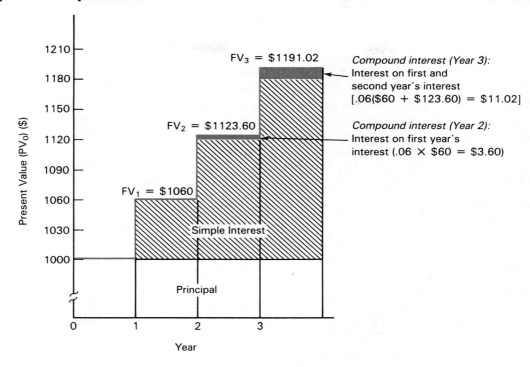

Figure 5-1 illustrates that if the account paid only simple interest, it would be worth only $1,180 at the end of 3 years. The $11.02 difference (i.e., $1191.02–$1180) is the interest on the first and second years' interest, 0.06 × ($60 + $123.60).

A general formula for computing future values can be developed by combining Equations 5.5, 5.6, and 5.7. Substituting Equation 5.6 into Equation 5.7 yields the following equation:

$$FV_3 = FV_1(1 + i)(1 + i)$$

or

$$FV_3 = FV_1(1 + i)^2 \qquad\qquad \textbf{(5.8)}$$

Substituting Equation 5.5 into Equation 5.8 yields the following:

$$FV_3 = PV_0(1 + i)(1 + i)^2$$

or

$$FV_3 = PV_0(1 + i)^3 \qquad\qquad \textbf{(5.9)}$$

153

This equation can be further generalized to calculate the future value at the end of year n for any payment compounded at interest rate i:

$$FV_n = PV_0 (1 + i)^n \qquad (5.10)$$

Although Equation 5.10 is useful for solving future value problems involving 1, 2, 3, or even 4 years into the future, it is rather tedious to use this equation for problems involving longer time periods. For example, solving for 20 years into the future would require calculating $(1 + i)^{20}$. Future *value interest factors* (FVIFs) commonly are used to simplify such computations. Table I at the end of the book provides a listing of future value interest factors for various interest rates covering up to 60 years (or other time periods). Because each future value interest factor is defined as $(1 + i)^n$, Equation 5.10 may be rewritten as follows:

$$FV_n = PV_0(FVIF_{i,n}) \qquad (5.11)$$

where i = the nominal interest rate per annum and n = the number of years.

To better understand Table I, it is helpful to think of each factor as the result of investing or lending $1 for a given number of time periods, n, at interest rate i. The solution for any amount other than $1 is the product of that principal amount times the factor for a $1 principal amount.

A portion of Table I is reproduced as Table 5-1. Table 5-1 can be used to determine the value of $1,000 compounded at 6 percent for 20 years:

$$FV_{20} = PV_0(FVIF_{0.06,20})$$

$$= \$1,000(3.207)$$

$$= \$3,207$$

The 3.207 figure is arrived at by reading the 6 percent, or 0.06, column down and the 20 row under the "Year" heading across to where they meet.

T A B L E 5-1

Future Value Interest Factors (FVIFs) for $1 at Interest Rate i for n Years*

YEAR (n)	Interest Rate (i)				
	1%	5%	6%	8%	10%
1	1.010	1.050	1.060	1.080	1.100
2	1.020	1.102	1.124	1.166	1.210
3	1.030	1.158	1.191	1.260	1.331
4	1.041	1.216	1.262	1.360	1.464
5	1.051	1.276	1.338	1.469	1.611
8	1.083	1.477	1.594	1.851	2.144
9	1.094	1.551	1.689	1.999	2.358
10	1.105	1.629	1.791	2.159	2.594
20	1.220	2.653	3.207	4.661	6.728
25	1.282	3.386	4.292	6.848	10.835

*The values in this and similar tables in this text have been rounded off to three places. When large sums of money are involved, more accurate tables or financial calculators should be used.

As another example, $1,000 compounded at 10 percent for 20 years yields the following:

$$FV_{20} = PV_0(FVIF_{0.10,20})$$

$$= \$1,000(6.728)$$

$$= \$6,728$$

Solving for the Interest Rate

In some compound value problems, the present value (PV_0) and future value (FV_n) are given and the objective is to determine the interest rate *(i)* that solves Equation 5.10. For example, the future value interest factor for an investment requiring an initial outlay of $1,000 and promising a $1,629 return after 10 years is as follows:

$$FVIF_{i,10} = \frac{FV_{10}}{PV_0}$$

$$= \frac{\$1,629}{\$1,000}$$

$$= 1.629$$

Reading across the 10-year row in Table 5-1, 1.629 is found in the 5 percent column. Thus, the investment yields a 5 percent compound rate of return. For values that fall between those found in the interest tables in this book, interpolation can be used. Examples of interpolation are provided in Chapters 6 and 10. Financial calculators can provide accurate answers to all the problems discussed in this chapter. Interpolation is not required when calculators are used.

Solving for the Number of Compounding Periods

The future value interest factor tables also can be used to solve for the number of annual compounding periods *(n)*. For example, to determine how long it would take for $1,000 invested at 8 percent to double, search the 8 percent column to locate a future value interest factor of 2.000. The closest value to this figure is 1.999. Reading to the left of this figure, it can be seen that the original $1,000 would be worth nearly $2,000 in 9 years. This problem also can be solved algebraically:

$$FV_n = PV_0(FVIF_{0.08,n})$$

$$FVIF_{0.08,n} = \frac{FV_n}{PV_0}$$

$$= \frac{\$2,000}{\$1,000}$$

$$= 2.000$$

Referring to Table 5-1, the closest value to FVIF = 2.000 under the 8 percent column is 1.999, which occurs at approximately 9 years.[3]

Compounding also can be illustrated graphically. Figure 5-2 shows the effects of time, n, and interest rate, i, on the growth of a $100 investment. As the figure shows, the higher the compound interest rate, the faster the growth rate of the value of the initial principal. The notion that an interest rate may be thought of as a *growth rate* will be useful during later discussions of valuation and cost of capital.

▬▬ PRESENT VALUE

The compound, or future, value calculations answer the question, What will be the future value of X dollars invested today, compounded at some rate

[3] In a shortcut solution to this type of problem known as the "Rule of 72," the number 72 is divided by the interest rate to determine the number of years it would take for a sum of money to double. In this case, 72/8% = 9. The Rule of 72 also can be used to determine the interest rate required for a sum of money to double in a given number of years: 72/9 = 8%. The Rule of 72 does not yield exact figures, but it can be used to calculate good approximations.

FIGURE 5-2

Growth of a $100 Investment at Various Compound Interest Rates

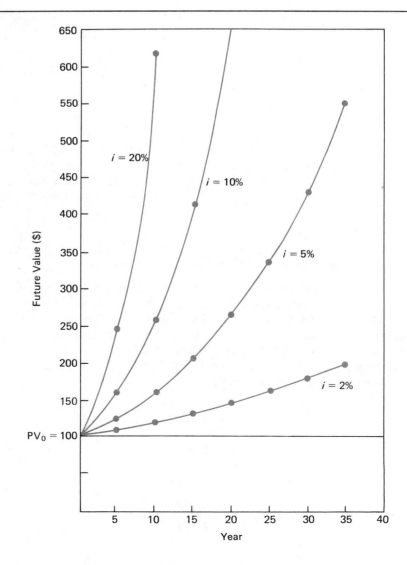

of interest, i? The financial decision maker, however, often is faced with another type of problem: Given some future value, FV_n, what is its equivalent value today? That is, what is its present value, PV_0? The solution requires *present value* calculations, which are used to determine the dollar amount today, PV_0, that is equivalent to some promised *future* dollar amount, FV_n. The equivalence depends upon the rate of interest (return) that can be earned on investments during the time period under consideration.

The relationship between compound value and present value can be shown by rewriting Equation 5.10 to solve for PV_0:

$$FV_n = PV_0 (1 + i)^n \qquad (5.10)$$

or

$$PV_0 = FV_n \left[\frac{1}{(1 + i)^n} \right] \qquad (5.12)$$

where $1/(1 + i)^n$ is the reciprocal of the compound value factor. The process of finding present values is frequently called *discounting*. Equation 5.12 is the basic discounting formula.

To illustrate the use of Equation 5.12, suppose your banker offers to pay you $255.20 in 5 years if you deposit X dollars today at an annual 5 percent interest rate. Whether the investment would be worthwhile depends on how much money you must deposit, or the *present value* of the X dollars. FVIF tables, such as Table 5-1 presented earlier, can be used to solve the problem as follows:

$$PV_0 = FV_5 \left(\frac{1}{FVIF_{0.05,5}} \right)$$

$$= \$255.20 \left(\frac{1}{1.276} \right)$$

$$= \$200$$

This problem can be illustrated with the following time line:

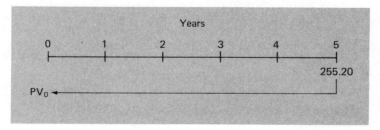

Thus, an investment of $200 today would yield a return of $55.20 in 5 years.

Because determining the reciprocals of the compound value interest factors, $1/(1 + i)^n$, can be a tedious process, *present value interest factors* (PVIFs) are commonly used to simplify such computations. Accordingly, Equation 5.12 can be written in the following form:

$$PV_0 = FV_n(PVIF_{i,n}) \qquad (5.13)$$

Table II at the end of the book provides a number of present value interest factors. A portion of Table II is reproduced here as Table 5-2.

TABLE 5-2

Present Value Interest Factors (PVIFs) for $1 at Interest Rate i for n Years

YEAR (n)	Interest Rate, (i)					
	1%	5%	6%	8%	10%	13%
1	0.990	0.952	0.943	0.926	0.909	0.885
2	0.980	0.907	0.890	0.857	0.826	0.783
3	0.971	0.864	0.840	0.794	0.751	0.693
4	0.961	0.823	0.792	0.735	0.683	0.613
5	0.951	0.784	0.747	0.681	0.621	0.543
8	0.923	0.677	0.627	0.540	0.467	0.376
10	0.905	0.614	0.558	0.463	0.386	0.295
20	0.820	0.377	0.312	0.215	0.149	0.087
25	0.780	0.295	0.233	0.146	0.092	0.047

For example, Table 5-2 can be used to determine the present value of $1,000 received 20 years in the future discounted at 10 percent:

$$PV_0 = FV_{20}(PVIF_{0.10,20})$$

$$= \$1,000(0.149)$$

$$= \$149$$

Thus, $149 invested today at 10 percent interest compounded annually for 20 years would be worth $1,000 at the end of the period. Conversely, the promise of $1,000 in 20 years is worth $149 today, given a 10 percent interest rate.

Solving for Interest and Growth Rates

Present value interest factors also can be used to solve for interest rates. For example, suppose you wish to borrow $5,000 today from an associate. The associate is willing to loan you the money if you promise to pay back $6,802 four years from today. The compound interest rate your associate is charging can be determined as follows:

$$PV_0 = FV_4(PVIF_{i,4})$$

$$\$5,000 = \$6,802(PVIF_{i,4})$$

$$PVIF_{i,4} = \frac{\$5,000}{\$6,802}$$

$$= 0.735$$

Reading across the 4-year row in Table 5-2, 0.735 is found in the 8 percent column. Thus, the effective interest rate on the loan is 8 percent per year, compounded annually.

Another common example of the use of present value tables is the calculation of the compound rate of growth of an earnings or dividend stream. Suppose the Gamma Machine Corporation had earnings of $3.50 per share in 19X1. These earnings grew to $6.45 at the end of 19X6. Over this 5-year period, what was the compound annual rate of growth in Gamma's earnings? The answer to this problem can be obtained by solving for the present value interest factor over the 5-year period as follows:

$$\$3.50 = \$6.45 \ (PVIF_{i,5})$$

$$PVIF_{i,5} = 0.543$$

From Table II or Table 5-2 we find this present value interest factor in the 5-year row under the 13 percent interest, or growth rate, column. Hence the compound annual rate of growth in Gamma's earnings per share is 13 percent.

The discounting process also can be illustrated graphically. Figure 5-3 shows the effects of time, n, and interest rate, i, on the present value of a $100 investment. As the figure shows, the higher the discount rate, the lower the present value of the $100.

ANNUITIES

An *annuity* is the payment or receipt of equal cash flows per period for a specified amount of time.[4] An *ordinary annuity* is one in which the payments or receipts occur at the *end* of each period, as shown in Figure 5-4. An *annuity due* is one in which payments or receipts occur at the *beginning* of each period, as shown in Figure 5-5. Most lease payments, such as apartment rentals, as well as life insurance premiums are annuities due.

[4] This discussion focuses primarily on periods of 1 year.

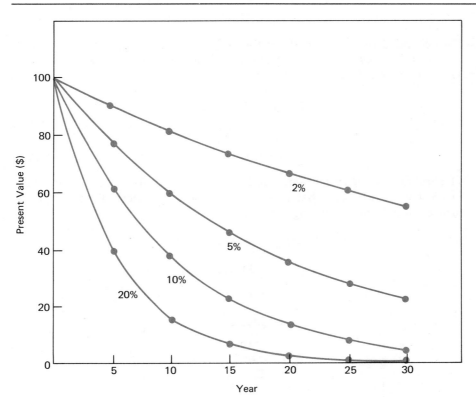

FIGURE 5-3

Present Value of $100 at Various Discount Rates

FIGURE 5-4

Time Line of an
Ordinary Annuity of
$100 per Period for 4
Periods

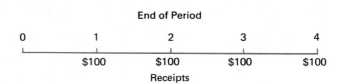

In a 4-year ordinary annuity the last payment is made at the end of the fourth year. In a 4-year annuity due, the last payment is made at the end of the third year (the beginning of the fourth year).

Future Value of an Ordinary Annuity

Future value of an annuity ($FVAN_n$) problems ask the question, If R dollars are deposited in an account at the end of each year for n years, and if the deposits earn interest rate i compounded annually, what will be the value of the account at the end of n years? To illustrate, suppose Ms. Jefferson receives a 3-year ordinary annuity of $1,000 per year and deposits the money in a savings account at the end of each year. The account earns interest at a rate of 6 percent compounded annually. How much will her account be worth at the end of the 3-year period?

The problem involves the calculation of future values. The last deposit, R_3, made at the end of year 3, will earn no interest. Thus, its future value is as follows:

$$FV_{3rd} = R_3(1 + 0.06)^0$$
$$= \$1,000(1)$$
$$= \$1,000$$

The second deposit, R_2, made at the end of year 2, will be in the account for 1 full year before the end of the 3-year period, and it will earn interest. Thus, its future value is as follows:

$$FV_{2nd} = R_2(1 + 0.06)^1$$
$$= \$1,000(1.06)$$
$$= \$1,060$$

The first deposit, R_1, made at the end of year 1, will be in the account earning interest for 2 full years before the end of the 3-year period. Therefore its future value is the following:

$$FV_{1st} = R_1(1 + 0.06)^2$$
$$= \$1,000(1.124)$$
$$= \$1,124$$

FIGURE 5-5

Time Line of an
Annuity Due of $100
per Period for 4
Periods

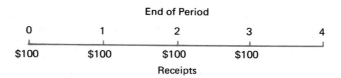

The sum of the three figures is the future value of the annuity:

$$FVAN_3 = FV_{3rd} + FV_{2nd} + FV_{1st}$$
$$= \$1{,}000 + \$1{,}060 + \$1{,}124$$
$$= \$3{,}184$$

The future value of an annuity interest factor (FVIFA) is the sum of the future value interest factors presented earlier in Table I. In this example the future value of an annuity interest factor is calculated as

$$FVIFA_{0.06,3} = FVIF_{0.06,2} + FVIF_{0.06,1} + FVIF_{0.06,0}$$
$$= 1.124 + 1.060 + 1.000$$
$$= 3.184$$

Figure 5-6 illustrates this concept.

Tables of the future value of an ordinary annuity interest factors are available to simplify such computations. Table III at the end of the book provides a number of future value of an annuity interest factors. A portion of Table III is reproduced here as Table 5-3.

The future value of an ordinary annuity ($FVAN_n$) may be calculated by multiplying the annuity amount, R, by the appropriate interest factor, $FVIFA_{i,n}$:[5]

$$FVAN_n = R(FVIFA_{i,n}) \tag{5.14}$$

Table 5-3 can be used to solve the problem involving Jefferson's annuity.

[5] Using summation notation, the future value of an ordinary annuity is equal to

$$FVAN_n = \sum_{t=1}^{n} R(1+i)^{n-t}$$
$$= R \sum_{t=1}^{n} (1+i)^{n-t}$$
$$= R\,(FVIFA_{i,n})$$

where $FVIFA_{i,n} = \sum_{t=1}^{n} (1+i)^{n-t}$. It can be shown that $FVIFA_{i,n} = [(1+i)^n - 1]/i$. This formula can be used in computing FVIFAs other than those shown in Table III.

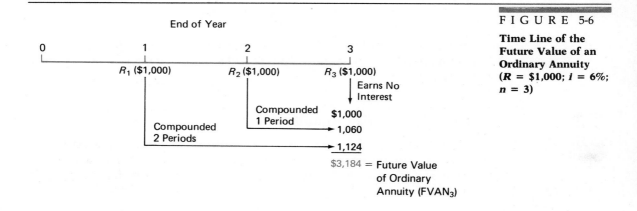

F I G U R E 5-6

**Time Line of the
Future Value of an
Ordinary Annuity
($R = \$1{,}000$; $i = 6\%$;
$n = 3$)**

End of Year

0   1   2   3

R_1 (\$1,000) R_2 (\$1,000) R_3 (\$1,000)

Earns No
Interest

Compounded
1 Period   \$1,000

Compounded
2 Periods   1,060

1,124

\$3,184 = Future Value
of Ordinary
Annuity ($FVAN_3$)

TABLE 5-3

Future Value of an Ordinary Annuity Interest Factors (FVIFA) for $1 per Year at Interest Rate *i* for *n* Years

END OF YEAR, (*n*)	Interest Rate, (*i*)			
	1%	5%	6%	10%
1	1.000	1.000	1.000	1.000
2	2.010	2.050	2.060	2.100
3	3.030	3.152	3.184	3.310
4	4.060	4.310	4.375	4.641
5	5.101	5.526	5.637	6.105
10	10.462	12.578	13.181	15.937
20	22.019	33.066	36.786	57.275
25	28.243	47.727	54.865	98.347

Because $R = \$1,000$, and the interest factor for $n = 3$ years and $i = 6\%$ is 3.184, the future value of an ordinary annuity can be calculated as follows:

$$FVAN_3 = R(FVIFA_{0.06,3})$$

$$= \$1,000(3.184)$$

$$= \$3,184$$

SINKING FUND PROBLEM. Future value of an annuity interest factors also can be used to find the annuity amount that must be invested each year to produce a future value. This is sometimes called a *sinking fund problem*. Suppose the Omega Graphics Company wishes to set aside an equal, annual, end-of-year amount in a "sinking fund account" earning 10 percent per annum over the next 5 years. The firm wants to have $5 million in the account at the end of 5 years in order to retire (pay off) $5 million in outstanding bonds. How much must be deposited in the account at the end of each year?

We know that the future value ($FVAN_5$) is $5 million, and that the appropriate interest factor (FVIFA) from Table 5-5 or Table III is 6.105 (10 percent for 5 years). Using Equation 5.14, we can solve for the annuity amount (that is, the sinking fund deposit) as follows:

$$FVAN_5 = R(FVIFA_{0.10,5})$$

$$\$5,000,000 = R(6.105)$$

$$R = \$819,001$$

By depositing $819,001 at the end of each of the next 5 years in the account earning 10 percent per annum, Omega will accumulate the $5 million needed to retire the bonds.

Future Value of an Annuity Due

Table III at the end of the book (future value of an annuity interest factor) assumes *ordinary* (end-of-year) annuities. For an *annuity due*, in which payments are made at the *beginning* of each year, the interest factors in Table III must be modified.

Consider the case of Jefferson cited earlier. If she deposits $1,000 in a savings account at the *beginning* of each year for the next 3 years and the account earns 6 percent interest, compounded annually, how much will be in the account at the end of 3 years? (Recall that when the deposits were made at the *end* of each year the account totaled $3,184 at the end of 3 years.)

Figure 5-7 illustrates this problem as an *annuity due*. R_1 is compounded for 3 periods, R_2 for 2 periods, and R_3 for 1 period. The correct *annuity due* interest factor may be obtained from Table III by multiplying the FVIFA for 3 years and 6 percent (3.184) by 1 plus the interest rate (1 + 0.06). This yields a FVIFA for an annuity due of 3.375, and the future value of the annuity due ($FVAND_n$) is calculated as follows:

$$FVAND_n = R[FVIFA_{i,n}(1 + i)] \qquad \textbf{(5.15)}$$

and

$$FVAND_3 = \$1,000(3.375)$$

$$= \$3,375$$

Note that this amount is larger than the $3,184 obtained in the ordinary annuity example given previously.

Present Value of an Ordinary Annuity

The present value of an ordinary annuity ($PVAN_0$) is the sum of the present value of a series of equal periodic payments.[6] For example, to find the present value of an ordinary $1,000 annuity received at the end of each year for 5 years discounted at a 6 percent rate, the sum of the individual present values would be determined as follows:

$$PVAN_0 = \$1,000\left[\frac{1}{(1 + 0.06)^1}\right] + \$1,000\left[\frac{1}{(1 + 0.06)^2}\right]$$

$$+ \$1,000\left[\frac{1}{(1 + 0.06)^3}\right] + \$1,000\left[\frac{1}{(1 + 0.06)^4}\right]$$

$$+ \$1,000\left[\frac{1}{(1 + 0.06)^5}\right]$$

[6] This text focuses primarily on annual payments.

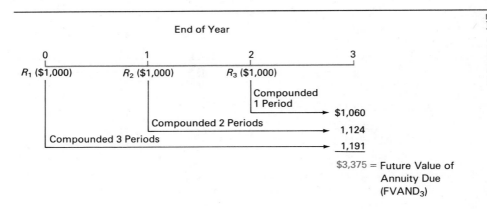

FIGURE 5-7

Time Line of the
Future Value of an
Annuity Due ($R =$
$1,000; $i = 6\%$; $n = 3$)

Referring to the interest factors in Table 5-2 yields the following:

$$PVAN_0 = \$1,000(PVIF_{0.06,1}) + \$1,000 (PVIF_{0.06,2})$$
$$+ \$1,000 (PVIF_{0.06,3}) + \$1,000 (PVIF_{0.06,4})$$
$$+ \$1,000(PVIF_{0.06,5})$$
$$= \$1,000(0.943) + \$1,000(0.890) + \$1,000(0.840)$$
$$+ \$1,000(0.792) + \$1,000(0.747)$$
$$= \$1,000(0.943 + 0.890 + 0.840 + 0.792 + 0.747)$$
$$= \$4,212$$

Figure 5-8 illustrates this concept.

Tables of the present value of an ordinary annuity interest factors (PVIFA) are available to simplify such computations. Table IV at the end of the book provides a number of the present value of an annuity interest factors. A portion of Table IV is reproduced here as Table 5-4.

The present value of an annuity can be determined by multiplying the annuity amount, R, by the appropriate interest factor, $PVIFA_{i,n}$:[7]

$$PVAN_0 = R (PVIFA_{i,n}) \qquad (5.16)$$

Referring to Table 5-4 to determine the interest factor for $i = 6\%$ and $n = 5$, the present value of an annuity in the previous problem can be calculated as follows:

[7] Using summation notation, the present value of an ordinary annuity is equal to

$$PVAN_0 = \sum_{t=1}^{n} \frac{R}{(1+i)^n}$$
$$= R \sum_{t=1}^{n} \frac{1}{(1+i)^n}$$
$$= R (PVIFA_{i,n})$$

where $PVIFA_{i,n} = \sum_{t=1}^{n} \frac{1}{(1+i)^n}$. It can be shown that $PVIFA_{i,n} = [1 - 1/(1+i)^n]/i$. This formula can be used in computing PVIFAs other than those shown in Table IV.

FIGURE 5-8

Time Line of a Present Value of an Ordinary Annuity ($R = \$1,000$; $i = 6\%$; $n = 5$)

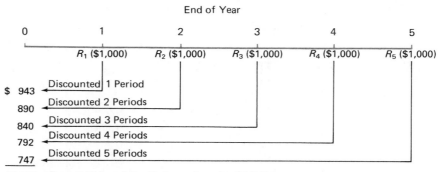

$\$4,212 =$ Present Value of the Ordinary Annuity ($PVAN_0$)

Present Value of an Ordinary Annuity Interest Factors (PVIFA) for $1 per Year at Interest Rate *i* for *n* Years

END OF YEAR, (*n*)	Interest Rate (*i*)			
	1%	5%	6%	10%
1	0.990	0.952	0.943	0.909
2	1.970	1.859	1.833	1.736
3	2.941	2.723	2.673	2.487
4	3.902	3.546	3.465	3.170
5	4.853	4.329	4.212	3.791
10	9.471	7.722	7.360	6.145
20	18.046	12.462	11.470	8.514
25	22.023	14.094	12.783	9.077

$$PVAN_0 = R (PVIFA_{0.06,5})$$

$$= \$1,000 (4.212)$$

$$= \$4,212$$

SOLVING FOR THE INTEREST RATE. Present value of an annuity interest factors also can be used to solve for the rate of return expected from an investment.[8] Suppose the Big Spring Tool Company purchases a machine for $100,000. This machine is expected to generate annual cash flows of $23,742 to the firm over the next 5 years. What is the expected rate of return from this investment?

Using Equation 5.16 we can determine the expected rate of return in this example as follows:

$$PVAN_0 = R (PVIFA_{i,5})$$

$$\$100,000 = \$23,742(PVIFA_{i,5})$$

$$PVIFA_{i,5} = 4.212$$

From the 5-year row in Table 5-4 or Table IV, we see that a PVIFA of 4.212 occurs in the 6 percent column. Hence, this investment offers a 6 percent expected rate of return.

CAPITAL RECOVERY PROBLEM AND LOAN AMORTIZATION. Present value of an annuity interest factors also can be used to find the annuity amount necessary to recover a capital investment, given a required rate of return on that investment. This is called a *capital recovery problem*. Similarly, present value of an annuity interest factors can be used to find the payments necessary to pay off a loan.

Suppose you borrowed $10,000 from the Whisperwood Bank. The loan is for a period of 3 years at an interest rate of 10 percent. It requires that you

[8] This interest rate, or rate of return, is referred to by various names in finance, depending on the type of "investment" under consideration. When evaluating a bond (fixed-income security), this rate is referred to as the *yield-to-maturity* (YTM) (see Chapter 6). In the analysis of capital expenditure decisions, this rate is known as the *internal rate of return* (IRR) (see Chapter 10). Finally, when calculating the cost of bank loans and other types of credit, this rate is known as the *annual percentage rate* (APR) (see Chapter 20).

make three equal, annual, end-of-year payments that include both principal and interest on the outstanding balance. Equation 5.16 and either Table 5-4 or Table IV can be used to solve this problem as follows:

$$PVAN_0 = R \ (PVIFA_{0.10,3})$$

$$\$10,000 = R(2.487)$$

$$R = \$4,020.91$$

By making three annual, end-of-year payments to the bank of \$4,020.91 each, you will completely pay off your loan, plus provide the bank with its 10 percent interest return. This can be seen in the loan amortization table developed in Table 5-5. At the end of each year, you pay the bank \$4,020.91. During the first year, \$1,000 of this payment is interest (0.10 × \$10,000 remaining balance), and the rest (\$3,020.91) is applied against the principal balance owed at the beginning of the year. Hence, after the first payment, you owe \$6,979.09 (\$10,000 − \$3,020.91). Similar calculations are done for years 2 and 3.

Present Value of an Annuity Due

Annuity due calculations also are important when dealing with the present value of an annuity problem. In these cases the interest factors in Table IV must be modified.

Consider the case of a 5-year annuity of \$1,000 each year, discounted at 6 percent. What is the present value of this annuity if each payment is received at the *beginning* of each year? (Recall the example presented earlier, illustrating the concept of the present value of an ordinary annuity, in which each payment was received at the *end* of each year and the present value was \$4,212.) Figure 5-9 illustrates this problem.

The first payment received at the beginning of year 1 (end of year 0) already is in its present value form and therefore requires no discounting. R_2 is discounted for 1 period, R_3 is discounted for 2 periods, R_4 is discounted for 3 periods, and R_5 is discounted for 4 periods.

The correct *annuity due* interest factor for this problem may be obtained from Table IV by multiplying the present value of an ordinary annuity interest factor for 5 years and 6 percent (4.212) by 1 plus the interest rate (1 + 0.06). This yields a PVIFA for an annuity due of 4.465, and the present value of this annuity due ($PVAND_0$) is calculated as follows:

TABLE 5-5

Loan Amortization Table

End of Year	Payment	Interest (10%)	Principal Reduction	Remaining Balance
0	—	—	—	\$10,000.00
1	\$4,020.91	\$1,000.00	\$3,020.91	6,979.09
2	4,020.91	697.91	3,323.00	3,656.09
3	4,020.91	365.61	3,656.09*	0*

*Due to rounding, the remaining balance is not exactly zero. The use of a calculator or more accurate interest tables would eliminate this rounding error.

FIGURE 5-9

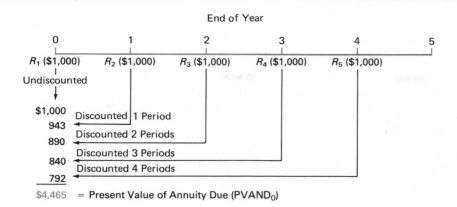

Time Line of a
Present Value of an
Annuity Due (R =
$1,000; i = 6%;
n = 5)

$$PVAND_0 = R[PVIFA_{i,n}(1 + i)] \qquad (5.17)$$

$$PVAND_0 = \$1,000(4.465)$$

$$= \$4,465$$

Note that this amount is larger than the $4,212 obtained in the ordinary annuity example presented above.

Annuity due calculations are especially important when dealing with rental or lease contracts, because it is common for these contracts to require that payments be made at the beginning of each period.

PRESENT VALUE: SOME ADDITIONAL CASH FLOW PATTERNS

The discussion of present value thus far has focused on two cash flow patterns: single payments and annuities. The present value of three additional types of cash flow streams are examined in this section; namely, *perpetuities*, *uneven cash flows*, and *deferred annuities*. Examples of these types of cash flows are encountered in many different areas of financial decision making.

Perpetuities

A *perpetuity* is a financial instrument that promises to pay an equal return (cash flow) per period forever; that is, an infinite series of payments. Therefore a perpetuity may be thought of as an infinite annuity. Some bonds (and some preferred stock) take the form of a perpetuity because these special securities never mature; that is, there is no obligation on the part of the issuer to redeem these bonds at their face value at any time in the future. A financial instrument such as this provides the holder with a series of equal, periodic payments into the indefinite future.

Consider, for example, a financial instrument that promises to pay an infinite stream of equal, annual returns (cash flows) of $R_t = R$ for $t = 1, 2, 3, \ldots$ years; that is, $R_1 = R_2 = R_3 = \ldots = R$. If we wish to find the present value ($PVPER_0$) of this financial instrument, it can be represented as follows:

$$PVPER_0 = \frac{R}{(1 + i)} + \frac{R}{(1 + i)^2} + \frac{R}{(1 + i)^3} + \cdots$$

or, using summation notation, as

$$PVPER_0 = \sum_{t=1}^{\infty} \frac{R}{(1 + i)^t} \tag{5.18}$$

where i equals the rate of return required by an investor in this financial instrument. It should be apparent that Equation 5.18 represents a special type of annuity where the number of periods for the annuity equals infinity. This type of problem cannot be solved using Table IV.

For example, assume that Baltimore Gas and Electric series B preferred stock promises payments of $4.50 per year forever and that an investor requires a 10 percent rate of return on this type of investment. How much would the investor be willing to pay for this security?

An examination of the PVIFA interest factors for 10 percent (in Table IV) indicates that the value in the 10% column increases as the number of years increases, but at a decreasing rate. For example, the PVIFA factor for 10% and 10 years is 6.145, whereas the factor for 10% and 20 years is only 8.514 (much less than twice the 10-year factor). The limiting value in any column of Table IV is 1 divided by the interest rate of that column, i. In the case of a 10 percent perpetuity, the appropriate interest factor is 1/0.10, or 10. Thus Equation 5.18 can be rewritten as follows:

$$PVPER_0 = \frac{R}{i} \tag{5.19}$$

In this example, the value of a $4.50 perpetuity at a 10 percent required rate of return is given as

$$PVPER_0 = \frac{\$4.50}{0.10}$$
$$= \$45$$

In Chapter 6 the concept of a perpetuity is examined in more detail in the specific cases of preferred stock and perpetual bonds. In that chapter, a proof of the relationship expressed as Equation 5.19 is also provided.

Present Value of Uneven Cash Flows

Many problems in finance—particularly in the area of capital budgeting—cannot be solved according to the simplified format of the present value of an annuity because the periodic cash flows are not equal. Consider an investment that is expected to produce a series of unequal cash flows, R_1, R_2, $R_3 \ldots$, R_n, over the next n periods. The present value of this uneven cash flow stream is equal to the sum of the present values of the individual cash flows. Algebraically, the present value can be represented as

$$PV_0 = \frac{R_1}{(1 + i)} + \frac{R_2}{(1 + i)^2} + \frac{R_3}{(1 + i)^3} + \cdots + \frac{R_n}{(1 + i)^n}$$

or, using summation notation, as

$$PV_0 = \sum_{t=1}^{n} \frac{R_t}{(1 + i)^t} \tag{5.20}$$

$$= \sum_{t=1}^{n} R_t(PVIF_{i,t}) \tag{5.21}$$

where i is the interest rate (that is, required rate of return) on this investment and $PVIF_{i,t}$ is the appropriate interest factor from Table II. It should be noted that the cash flows (R_t's) can be either positive (cash *in*flows) or negative (*out*flows).

Consider the following example. Suppose Allied Signal Company is evaluating an investment in new equipment that will be used to manufacture a new product it has developed. The equipment is expected to have a useful life of 5 years and yield the following stream of cash flows over the 5-year period:

End of Year	Cash Flow
t	R_t
1	+ $100,000
2	+ 150,000
3	− 50,000
4	+ 200,000
5	+ 100,000

Note that in year 3 the cash flows are negative. (This is due to a new law that requires the company to purchase and install pollution abatement equipment.) The present value of these cash flows, assuming an interest rate (required rate of return) of 10 percent, is calculated using Equation 5.21 as follows:

$$PV_0 = \$100,000 \, (PVIF_{0.10,1}) + \$150,000 \, (PVIF_{0.10,2})$$

$$- \$50,000 \, (PVIF_{0.10,3}) + \$200,000 \, (PVIF_{0.10,4})$$

$$+ \$100,000 \, (PVIF_{0.10,5})$$

$$= \$100,000 \, (0.909) + \$150,000 \, (0.826)$$

$$- \$50,000 \, (0.751) + \$200,000 \, (0.683) + \$100,000 \, (0.621)$$

$$= \$375,950$$

Figure 5-10 illustrates a time line for this investment. The present value of the cash flows ($375,950) would be compared with the initial cash outlay (that is, net investment in year 0) in deciding whether to purchase the equipment and manufacture the product.

As will be seen later in the text, during the discussion of capital budgeting, calculations of this type are extremely important when making project evaluations.

Present Value of Deferred Annuities

Frequently, in finance, one encounters problems where an annuity begins more than 1 year in the future. For example, suppose that you wish to provide for the college education of your daughter. She will begin college 5 years from now, and you wish to have $15,000 available for her at the beginning of each year in college. How much must be invested today at a 12 percent annual rate of return in order to provide the 4-year, $15,000 annuity for your daughter?

This problem can be illustrated in the time line given in Figure 5-11. Four payments of $15,000 each are required at the end of years 5, 6, 7, and 8. Of

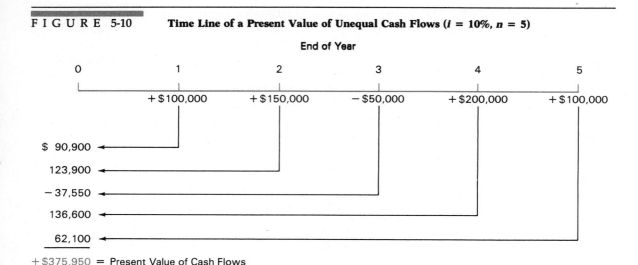

FIGURE 5-10   Time Line of a Present Value of Unequal Cash Flows ($i = 10\%$, $n = 5$)

course, this problem could be solved by finding the sum of the present values of each of the payments as follows:

Year t	Payment R_t	$PVIF_{.12,t}$	Present Value
5	$15,000	0.567	$ 8,505
6	$15,000	0.507	$ 7,605
7	$15,000	0.452	$ 6,780
8	$15,000	0.404	$ 6,060
	Present Value of Deferred Annuity =		$28,950

It should be apparent that this would be an extremely tedious method of calculation in the case of a 10-year deferred annuity, for example. Figure 5-11 illustrates one alternative means of solving this problem. First, you can calculate the present value of the 4-year annuity, evaluated at the end of year 4 (remember that this is the same as the beginning of year 5). This calculation is made by multiplying the annuity amount ($15,000) by the

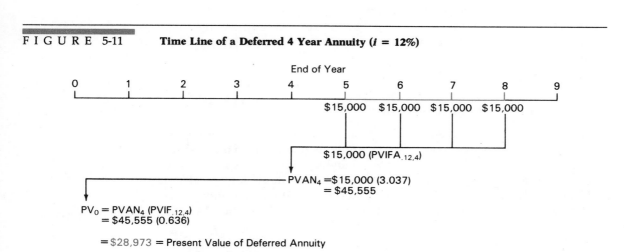

FIGURE 5-11   Time Line of a Deferred 4 Year Annuity ($i = 12\%$)

PVIFA for a 4-year, 12% annuity. This factor is 3.037 and can be obtained from Table IV. Next the present value of the annuity ($45,555), evaluated at the end of year 4 ($PVAN_4$), must be discounted back to the present time (PV_0). Hence we multiply $45,555 by a PVIF for 12% and 4 years. This factor, obtained from Table II, is equal to 0.636. The present value of the deferred annuity is $28,973. (This differs from the amount calculated earlier due to rounding in the tables. No difference will exist if this problem is solved with a calculator or tables that are carried out to more decimal places.)[9]

If you have $28,973 today and invest it in an account earning 12% per year, there will be exactly enough money in the account to permit your daughter to withdraw $15,000 at the beginning of each year in college. After the last withdrawal, the account balance will be zero.

COMPOUNDING PERIODS AND EFFECTIVE INTEREST RATES

The frequency with which interest rates are compounded (for example, annually, semiannually, quarterly, and so on) affects both the present and future values of cash flows as well as the effective interest rates being earned or charged.

Effect of Compounding Periods on Present and Future Values

Thus far it has been assumed that compounding (and discounting) occur annually. Recall the general compound interest equation:

$$FV_n = PV_0(1 + i)^n \qquad (5.10)$$

where PV_0 is the initial deposit, i the annual interest rate, n the number of years, and FV_n the future value that will accumulate from the annual compounding of PV_0. An interest rate of i percent per year for n years is assumed. In the remainder of this section, this *annual nominal interest rate* will be designated i_{nom} to differentiate it from the *annual effective interest rate*, i_{eff}.

In some circumstances, interest on an account is compounded *semiannually* instead of annually; that is, half of the nominal annual interest rate, $i_{nom}/2$, is earned at the end of 6 months. The investor earns additional interest on the interest earned *before* the end of the year, or $(i_{nom}/2) PV_0$. In calculating interest compounded semiannually, Equation 5.10 is rewritten as follows:

$$FV_n = PV_0\left(1 + \frac{i_{nom}}{2}\right)^{2n}$$

The same logic applies to interest compounded *quarterly:*

$$FV_n = PV_0\left(1 + \frac{i_{nom}}{4}\right)^{4n}$$

[9] An alternative way to solve this problem is to multiply the annuity amount ($15,000) by the difference between ($PVIFA_{.12,8}$) and ($PVIFA_{.12,4}$). By subtracting ($PVIFA_{.12,4}$) from ($PVIFA_{.12,8}$) you are viewing this problem as an 8-year annuity that has no payments during the first 4 years. In this case, the calculation yields: PV_0 = $15,000(4.968 − 3.037) = $28,965. (The slight difference from the amount calculated earlier is due to rounding in Table IV.)

In general, the compound interest for any number of periods during a year may be computed by means of the following equation:

$$FV_n = PV_0 \left(1 + \frac{i_{nom}}{m}\right)^{mn} \tag{5.22}$$

where m is the number of times during the year the interest is compounded and n is the number of years. (The limiting case of continuous compounding and discounting is discussed in Appendix 5A.)

Table 5-6 contains the future value, FV_1, of \$1,000 earning a nominal interest of 10 percent for several different compounding frequencies. For example, the future value (FV_1) of \$1,000 compounded *semiannually* ($m = 2$) at a nominal interest rate (i_{nom}) of 10 percent per year by Equation 5.22 is

$$FV_1 = \$1,000 \left(1 + \frac{0.10}{2}\right)^{2 \times 1}$$

$$= \$1,102.50$$

It can be seen that the more frequent the compounding, the greater is the future value of the deposit, and the greater is the *effective* interest rate. Effective interest, in contrast to *nominal* interest, is the *actual* rate of interest earned by the lender and generally is the most economically relevant definition of interest rates.

The relationship between present values and compound values suggests that present values also will be affected by the frequency of compounding. In general, the present value of a sum to be received at the end of year n, discounted at the rate of i_{nom} percent and compounded m times per year, is as follows:

$$PV_0 = \frac{FV_n}{\left(1 + \frac{i_{nom}}{m}\right)^{mn}} \tag{5.23}$$

T A B L E   5-6

Effects of Different Compounding Frequencies on Future Values of \$1,000 at a 10 Percent Interest Rate

Initial Amount	Compounding Frequency	Future Value, FV₁ (End of Year 1)
\$1,000	Yearly	\$1,100.00
1,000	Semiannually	1,102.50
1,000	Quarterly	1,103.81
1,000	Monthly	1,104.71
1,000	Daily	1,105.16
1,000	Continuously*	1,105.17

*For advanced applications, it is useful to know that continuous compounding is obtained by letting m approach infinity in $FV_n = PV_0 (1 + i/m)^{mn}$. In this case, $\lim_{m \to \infty} (1 + i/m)^m = e^i$, and the compound value expression becomes $FV_n = PV_0(e)^{in}$, where e is the exponential number having the approximate value of 2.71828. See Appendix 5A for a complete discussion of continuous compounding and discounting.

Table 5-7 contains a number of present values, PV_0, for $1,000 received 1 year in the future discounted at a nominal interest rate of 10 percent with several different compounding frequencies. For example, the present value (PV_0) of $1,000 compounded *quarterly* ($m = 4$) at a nominal interest rate (i_{nom}) of 10 percent per year by Equation 5.23 is

$$PV_0 = \frac{\$1,000}{\left(1 + \dfrac{0.10}{4}\right)^{4 \times 1}}$$

$$= \$905.95$$

It can be seen that the more frequent the compounding, the smaller the present value of a future amount.

Throughout the text, much of the analysis assumes annual compounding instead of compounding for more frequent periods, because it simplifies matters and because the differences between the two are small. Similarly, unless otherwise stated, cash flows from a security or investment project are assumed to be received in a lump sum at the beginning or end of each period. More frequent compounding periods require more extensive tables or the use of a business calculator programmed to solve financial mathematics problems.

Regardless of the frequency of compounding, it is important to recognize that *effective* rates of interest are the relevant rates to use for financial and economic analysis. The next section considers the calculation of effective interest rates in more detail for those cases where compounding is done more than one time a year.

Effective Rate Calculations

The previous section illustrated the fact that the more frequently an annual *nominal* rate of interest is compounded, the greater is the *effective* rate of interest being earned or charged. Thus, if you were given the choice of receiving (1) interest on an investment, where the interest is compounded annually at a 10 percent rate, or (2) interest on an investment, where the interest is compounded semiannually at a 5 percent rate every six months, you would choose the second alternative, because it would yield a higher effective rate of interest.

Effects of Different Compounding Frequencies on Present Values of $1,000 at a 10 Percent Interest Rate

TABLE 5-7

Amount	Compounding Frequency	Present Value, PV_0
$1,000	Yearly	$909.09
1,000	Semiannually	907.03
1,000	Quarterly	905.95
1,000	Monthly	905.21
1,000	Daily	904.85
1,000	Continuously	904.84

Given the annual *nominal* rate of interest (i_{nom}), the *effective* rate of interest (i_{eff}) can be calculated as follows:

$$i_{\text{eff}} = \left(1 + \frac{i_{\text{nom}}}{m}\right)^m - 1 \qquad (5.24)$$

where m is the number of compounding intervals per year.[10]

For example, suppose a bank offers you a loan at an annual nominal interest rate of 12 percent compounded quarterly. What effective annual interest rate is the bank charging you? Substituting $i_{\text{nom}} = 0.12$ and $m = 4$ into Equation 5.24 yields

$$i_{\text{eff}} = \left(1 + \frac{0.12}{4}\right)^4 - 1$$
$$= 0.1255$$

or 12.55 percent.

There also are situations in finance where one is interested in determining the interest rate during each compounding period that will provide a given annual effective rate of interest. For example, if the annual effective rate is 20 percent and compounding is done quarterly, you may wish to know what quarterly rate of interest will result in an *effective* annual rate of interest of 20 percent.

In general, the rate of interest per period (where there is more than one compounding period per year), i_m, which will result in an effective annual rate of interest, i_{eff}, if compounding occurs m times per year, can be computed as follows:

$$i_m = (1 + i_{\text{eff}})^{1/m} - 1 \qquad (5.25)$$

In this example, the quarterly rate of interest that will yield an annual effective rate of interest of 20 percent is[11]

$$i_m = (1 + 0.20)^{.25} - 1$$
$$= (1.04664) - 1$$
$$= 0.04664 \text{ or } 4.664\%$$

Thus, if you earn 4.664 percent per period and compounding occurs four times per year, the effective annual rate earned will be 20 percent. This concept is encountered in Chapter 6 in the discussion of the valuation of bonds that pay interest semiannually.

---

[10] Note that annual effective interest rates are equivalent to annual nominal interest rates in the case where compounding occurs only one time per year, at year end. This can be shown by substituting $m = 1$ into Equation 5.24:

$$i_{\text{eff}} = \left(1 + \frac{i_{\text{nom}}}{1}\right)^1 - 1$$
$$= 1 + i_{\text{nom}} - 1$$
$$= i_{\text{nom}}$$

[11] Finding the ¼ or 0.25 root of $(1 + 0.20)$ can be done easily with any financial or scientific calculator using the root function on the calculator.

This chapter has assumed values for the compounding and discounting rates that were used in the various problems. What factors determine the appropriate rate to use in a specific situation?

One important factor is the general level of interest rates in the economy. Interest rates are set by the forces of supply and demand for funds in the economy. An important factor that influences the general level of interest rates is the current and expected future level of inflation. When the inflation rate is high, interest rates also tend to be high.

The time frame over which an investment is being considered also influences the choice of a discounting or compounding rate. In general, interest rates tend to be higher on securities having a longer maturity than on securities having a shorter maturity.

Finally, the risk of the investment being considered also determines the appropriate compounding or discounting rate. At any point in time an array of interest rates are available in the market. For example, investors in low risk U.S. government securities might require a 10 percent annual return. Investors in somewhat riskier corporate bonds might require a 13 percent annual return. Finally, investors in common stock might require a 17 percent rate of return. Generally, the higher the risk, the greater is the required return on a security or investment project. The nature of risk and its impact on required returns are discussed in more detail in Chapters 8 and 12.

SOLVING THE FINANCIAL DILEMMA

Recall from the "Financial Dilemma" at the beginning of this chapter that Natalie Mayer has been offered the option of continuing her present mortgage payments of $852.39 over the next 27 years and 10 months to pay off her 10.875 percent home mortgage, or to increase the monthly payments to $1,691.49, receive a reduction in the interest rate to 10 percent, and pay off the loan in 5 years and 10 months. If Mayer has investment opportunities expected to yield a 15 percent rate of return over the life of the mortgage, should she accept the early payoff offer?

This problem can be treated as a present value of an annuity problem.[12] What Mayer wishes to determine is which alternative has the lower present value cost. For simplicity, she will ignore the effects of the tax deductibility of interest in this example. Including the tax effect does not alter the final decision. Under the original mortgage, Mayer would make 334 payments of $852.39 each month. The monthly discount rate is 1.25 percent (15%/12 months per year). The following is the present value of this annuity:

$$PVAN_0 = \$852.39 \ (PVIFA_{0.0125,334})$$

$$= \$67,115$$

Under the First Federal option, Mayer would make seventy payments of

---

[12] The solution to this problem requires either a more complete set of tables than those provided in your text or, preferably, a financial calculator. We have simply set up the problem and indicated the final answer here.

$1,691.49 each month. The monthly discount rate is 1.25 percent. The present value of this annuity follows:

$$PVAN_0 = \$1,691.49 \ (PVIFA_{0.0125,70})$$

$$= \$78,603$$

Thus, given a 15 percent investment opportunity rate for Mayer, the early payment plan is not worth accepting, because its present value cost is more than $11,000 higher than the percent value cost of the original alternative.

USING CALCULATORS AND MICROCOMPUTERS IN FINANCE

The practice of financial management has been revolutionized by the development of powerful and inexpensive calculators and microcomputers. There is a temptation to think of sophisticated financial calculators as an intermediate step in the development of information processing technology that can be used by the financial manager, with the microcomputer representing the current "state of the art." In a sense this perception is correct. However, it is incorrect to conclude that the microcomputer will replace the hand-held calculator as the "tool of choice" by sophisticated financial managers. Rather, the two tools are complementary. Certain types of problems can be solved more efficiently with a hand-held calculator; other problems are more suited to microcomputer solutions. Financial managers and students of finance should develop the skills necessary to use both tools.

Using Financial Calculators

Two basic types of financial calculators are available. One type, represented by the Texas Instruments (TI) family of financial calculators, uses the algebraic entry method. In contrast, some of the calculators produced by Hewlett-Packard use reverse Polish notation (RPN) when sequencing key strokes in solving a problem. Although the algebraic entry method probably is easier to learn, the RPN method is quicker. Financial calculators range in price from $20 to $200. Generally, the calculators from Hewlett-Packard are more expensive (and perform more types of calculations) than the business calculators produced by TI. The choice of a calculator will depend on your personal preference for entry methods, the functions you wish to have the calculator perform, and how much money you can afford to spend.

Calculators generally are more efficient than a microcomputer in solving a number of problems. Generally, the easier the problem, the more likely it is that a calculator can be used to solve it efficiently. To use a calculator you only have to turn it on and enter the appropriate keystrokes. To use a microcomputer you must turn it on, load the appropriate software, and then begin the calculations. This can take more time than is necessary to completely solve many problems with a calculator. The types of problems most amenable to solution using a financial calculator include

1. Making any arithmetic calculation.
2. Calculating the present value of a single future amount or the present value of an annuity (both ordinary annuity and annuity due problems).

3. Calculating the future value of a single present amount or the future value of an annuity (both ordinary annuity and annuity due problems).
4. Calculating the effective rate of interest when the present value, future value, and time period are known.
5. Calculating the effective rate of interest when the present value, annuity amount, and number of periods are known.
6. Calculating the effective rate of interest when the future value, annuity amount, and number of periods are known.
7. Solving any other problems that normally would involve calculations using Tables I through IV at the end of the book.
8. Some financial calculators (generally the more expensive ones) compute the net present value of an investment (see Chapters 9 through 11) and the internal rate of return on an investment if the investment has uneven periodic cash flows.
9. Some financial calculators compute the precise yield to maturity of a bond (see Chapter 6) or the current value of a bond. Calculators can also be used to compute the value of common stock and preferred stock under certain assumptions.

Although other functions can be performed with a hand-held financial calculator, this list is indicative of the problems that will be encountered most frequently throughout your financial management coursework.

Using Computers in Finance

Computers have revolutionized the practice of financial management in many companies. Only about a decade ago the widespread use of computers in the financial management function was limited to relatively large companies that could afford large-scale computers and the costly software required to operate them. This situation has changed dramatically with the advent of powerful and low-cost micro- and minicomputers.

Paralleling the availability of this hardware has been the development of flexible, inexpensive, easy to use, and very powerful software. Foremost among these developments has been the development of electronic spreadsheets. The most popular spreadsheet is *Lotus 1-2-3*. Another popular spreadsheet is *Microsoft Excel*. The electronic spreadsheet incorporates the capabilities of a pencil and eraser, a calculator, and accounting and financial management techniques into an easy-to-use analysis and planning tool. An electronic spreadsheet is similar to a large electronic sheet of paper with rows and columns, like an accountant's blank accounting pad. Formulas can be set up in this worksheet just like a large sheet of paper. Unlike a sheet of paper, however, the formulas stay intact in this electronic worksheet and can be recalculated without having to redo the entire worksheet by hand. For example, if you have a 300-line income statement set up in the spreadsheet, the firm's net income can be calculated in a few seconds. Because the formulas stay intact, you can change an assumption (or correct an error) and see the impact on the bottom line in a few seconds. Imagine how long it would take to recalculate the firm's net income if all you had at your disposal was a calculator and you decided to analyze the effect of an increase in sales and variable costs by 10 percent. The spreadsheet will perform the necessary calculations in a matter of seconds. Furthermore, the analysis and formulas can be saved for future use.

Simply stated, the user of an electronic spreadsheet enters formulas and historic data, such as the relationships found in an income statement, balance sheet, or cash budget. With these formulas and historic data, the spreadsheet has the capability to quickly generate forecasts of future financial relationships in the firm. The analyst is in a position to answer many different "what if" questions regarding the bottom line impact of changes in various assumptions.

One of the disadvantages of spreadsheet analysis is that learning to build (and then actually building) a spreadsheet to analyze a particular problem can be time consuming. If spreadsheets were already programmed to solve particular problems, the financial analyst could spend more time analyzing important financial problems rather than generating instructions for the computer. Financial analysis templates are preprogrammed spreadsheets set up to handle a wide variety of financial problems. Some templates are set up to handle very specific problems. Other, more sophisticated templates are flexible enough to deal with many different problems. For example, a flexible capital budgeting template would be able to analyze all types of investment projects—regardless of the expected economic life of the project, the depreciation schedule being used, or the growth rate in revenues and costs over the project life.

One of the features of *Contemporary Financial Management*, fourth edition, is the availability of a sophisticated, preprogrammed disk containing templates to solve a wide range of complex financial management problems. This disk, the CFM Lotus Disk, is designed to be used in conjunction with the Lotus 1-2-3 electronic spreadsheet program. The CFM Lotus Disk requires *no prior knowledge of Lotus 1-2-3* and is menu driven. A brief overview of each template is provided in Appendix A at the end of the text. Complete documentation accompanies the disk. As part of the problem section of selected chapters we have included problems that can be solved using the financial management templates. These problems are identified by a small computer diskette logo printed next to the problem number. The computer template itself is available from your instructor, or may have been packaged with your text if it was ordered that way.

▬▬ SUMMARY

▪ Financial mathematics plays an important role in many areas of financial decision making.

▪ An understanding of *interest* is crucial to sound financial management. *Simple interest* is interest earned or paid on the principal only. *Compound interest* is interest paid not only on the principal, but also on any interest earned but not withdrawn during earlier periods.

▪ An *annuity* is the payment or receipt of a series of equal cash flows per period for a specified number of periods. In an *ordinary annuity* the cash flows occur at the *end* of each period. In an *annuity due* the cash flows occur at the *beginning* of each period.

▪ Table 5-8 summarizes the equations used to compute the future and present values of the various cash flow streams.

▪ In solving financial mathematics problems it is necessary to answer two questions:
   1. Do we need a future value or a present value?
   2. Are we dealing with a single payment or an annuity?

Once these questions have been successfully answered, the following table can be used to select the appropriate table of interest factors:

	Future Value	Present Value
Single Payment	Table I	Table II
Annuity	Table III	Table IV

- *Sinking fund problems* determine the annuity amount that must be invested each year to produce a future value.
- *Capital recovery problems* determine the annuity amount necessary to recover some initial investment.
- The more frequently compounding occurs during a given period, the higher is the *effective* interest rate on an investment. More frequent compounding results in higher future values and lower present values than less frequent compounding at the same interest rate.
- The appropriate compounding or discount rate to use in a particular problem depends upon the general level of interest rates in the economy, the time frame used for analysis, and the risk of the investment being considered.
- Calculators and microcomputers can assist in solving a wide variety of complex financial management problems.

Summary of Future and Present Value Equations

T A B L E 5-8

Type of Calculation	Equation	Interest Factor Table	Equation Number
Future value of a single payment	$FV_n = PV_0(FVIF_{i,n})$	Table I	5.11
Future value of an (ordinary) annuity	$FVAN_n = R(FVIFA_{i,n})$	Table III	5.14
Future value of an annuity due	$FVAND_n = R[FVIFA_{i,n}(1 + i)]$	Table III	5.15
Present value of a single payment	$PV_0 = FV_n(PVIF_{i,n})$	Table II	5.13
Present value of an (ordinary) annuity	$PVAN_0 = R(PVIFA_{i,n})$	Table IV	5.16
Present value of an annuity due	$PVAND_0 = R[PVIFA_{i,n}(1 + i)]$	Table IV	5.17
Present value of an uneven cash flow stream	$PV_0 = \sum_{t=1}^{n} R_t(PVIF_{i,t})$	Table II	5.21
Present value of a perpetuity	$PVPER_0 = \dfrac{R}{i}$	—	5.19

Definitions:
n = number of time periods of discounting or compounding (usually years).
i = annual rate of interest (i.e., annual nominal interest rate).
R = annuity cash flow (i.e., amount of cash flow paid or received for a specified number of years or forever in the case of a perpetuity). In an ordinary annuity the cash flows are received at the end of each year. In an annuity due the cash flows are received at the beginning of each year.
R_t = cash flow paid or received in year t.

■■■ QUESTIONS AND TOPICS FOR DISCUSSION

1. Which would you rather receive—the proceeds from a 2-year investment paying 5 percent simple interest per year, or from one paying 5 percent compound interest? Why?

2. Which is greater—the future value interest factor (FVIF) for 10 percent and 2 years or the present value interest factor (PVIF) for 10 percent and 2 years?

3. What happens to the present value of an annuity as the interest rate increases? What happens to the future value of an annuity as the interest rate increases?

4. Which would you prefer to invest in—a savings account paying 6 percent compounded annually or a savings account paying 6 percent compounded daily? Why?

5. What type of contract might require the use of annuity due computations?

6. What effect does more frequent compounding have on present values?

7. Why should each of the following be familiar with compounding and present value concepts?
   a. A marketing manager.
   b. A personnel manager.

8. Explain what is meant by the "Rule of 72." How can it be used in finance applications? (See Footnote 3.)

9. What is the relationship between present value and future value?

10. What is the difference between an ordinary annuity and an annuity due? Give examples of each.

11. If the required rate of return increases, what is the impact on the following?
    a. A present value of an annuity.
    b. A future value of an annuity.

12. Explain how future value of an annuity interest factors can be used to solve a sinking fund problem.

13. Describe how to set up a loan amortization schedule.

14. November 21, 1980, was the day of a tragic fire in the MGM Grand Hotel in Las Vegas. At the time of the fire, the hotel had only $30 million of liability insurance. One month after the fire, the hotel bought an extra $170 million of liability coverage for a premium of $37.5 million, retroactive to November 1, 1980 (before the fire). Based on your knowledge of present value concepts, why would insurers be willing to issue insurance to MGM under these conditions?

15. A savings account advertises that "interest is compounded continuously and paid quarterly." What does this mean?

16. Give an example of a perpetuity. How does a perpetuity differ from an annuity?

17. Explain how to determine the present value of an uneven cash flow stream.

18. Evaluate the following statement: "The development of powerful, inexpensive microcomputers have made the hand calculator as obsolete as the slide rule."

■■■ PROBLEMS*

⚠️1. How much will $1,000 deposited in a savings account earning a compound

---

* Colored numbers denote problems that have check answers provided at the end of the book.

annual interest rate of 6 percent be worth at the end of the following number of years?

a. 3 years.
b. 5 years.
c. 10 years.

Handwritten: $Fvn = Pvn(1+K)^n$ $1000(1.06)^3 = 1,191$
$1000(1.06)^5 = 1,338$
$1000(1.06)^{10} = 1,791$

2. If you require a 9 percent return on your investments, which would you prefer?

a. $5,000 today.   *Handwritten:* $PV = 5000$
b. $15,000 five years from today.   *Handwritten:* $15,000 = PV(1.09)^5$ $Pvn = Fvn\left(\frac{1}{(1+K)^n}\right)$
c. $1,000 per year for 15 years.   *Handwritten:* $An = R(PVIFA\ 0.09, 15)$ ∴ Prefer B

3. The Lancer Leasing Company has agreed to lease a hydraulic trencher to the Chavez Excavation Company for $20,000 a year over the next 8 years. Lease payments are to be made at the beginning of each year.

Assuming that Lancer invests these payments at an annual rate of 9 percent, how much will it have accumulated by the end of the eighth year?

Handwritten: $Sn = R\sum_{t=1}^{n}(1+K)^{n-t}$
$Sn = R(FVIFA\ K\%, n)(1+K)$
$= 20,000(11.028)(1.09)$
$= 240,410.40$

4. The Mutual Assurance and Life Company is offering an insurance policy under either of the following two terms:

a. Make a series of twelve $1,200 payments at the beginning of each of the next 12 years (the first payment being made today).
b. Make a single lump sum payment today of $10,000 and receive coverage for the next 12 years.

Handwritten: $An = R(PVIFA\ 8, 12)(1.08)$
$= 1200(7.536)(1.08)$
$= 9,766.67$

If you had investment opportunities offering an 8 percent annual return, which alternative would you prefer?

5. How much must you deposit at the end of each year in an account that pays a nominal annual rate of 20%, if at the end of 5 years you want $10,000 in the account?

Handwritten: $10,000 = R(FVIFA\ 20\%, 5)$

6. A leading broker has advertised money multiplier certificates that will triple your money in 9 years; that is, if you buy one for $333.33 today, it will pay you $1,000 at the end of 9 years. What rate of return will you earn on these money multiplier certificates?

Handwritten: $Fvn = Pv(1+K)^9$
$3Pv = Pv(1+K)^9$
$3 = (1+K)^9$ $\sqrt[9]{3} = 1+K$
rate는 문제 √
∴ $K = 12.98\%$
$\fallingdotseq 13\%$

7. You have $10,000 to invest. Assuming annual compounding, how long will it take for the $10,000 to double if it is invested at the following rates?

a. 8 percent.
b. 10 percent.
c. 14 percent.
d. 20 percent.

8. The Tried and True Corporation had earnings of $0.20 per share in 1973. By 1990, a period of 17 years, they had grown to earnings of $1.01 per share. What has been the compound annual rate of growth in the company's earnings?

9. What is the present value of $800 to be received at the end of 8 years, assuming the following annual interest rate?

a. 4 percent.   *Handwritten:* $PV = 800(PVIF\ 4\%, 8)$ or $Fvn = Pv(1+K)^n$
b. 8 percent.
c. 20 percent.
d. 0 percent.   *Handwritten:* $= 800$

10. Mr. Jones bought a building for $60,000 payable on the following terms: a $10,000 down payment and twenty-five equal annual installment payments to include principal and interest of 10 percent per annum. Calculate the amount of the installment payments. How much of the first year's payment goes toward reducing the principal amount?

Handwritten: 1st interest
$50,000 \times 0.1 = 5,000$
$An = R(PVIFA\ 0.1, 25)$
$50,000 = R(9.077)\ R = 5508.4279$ (per term)

11. A firm purchases 100 acres of land for $200,000 and agrees to remit twenty equal annual end-of-year installments of $41,067 each. What is the true annual interest rate on this loan?

Handwritten: $An = R(PVIFA\ K, n)$
$200,000 = 41,067(PVIFA\ K, 20)$
$K = 20\%$ by table.

12. Thirty years ago, Jesse Jones bought 10 acres of land for $1,000 per acre in what is now downtown Houston. If this land grew in value at an 8 percent per annum rate, what is it worth today?

13. Susan Robinson is planning for her retirement. She is 30 years old today and would like to have $600,000 when she turns 55. She estimates that she will be able to earn a 9 percent rate of return on her retirement investments over time; she wants to set aside a constant amount of money every year (at the end of the year) to help achieve her objective. How much money must Robinson invest at the end of each of the next 25 years to realize her goal of $600,000 at the end of that time? $S_n = R (FVIFA k\%, n)$
$600,000 = R (84.701)$ $R = 7,083.74$

14. What would you be willing to pay for a $1,000 bond paying $70 interest at the end of each year and maturing in 25 years if you wanted the bond to yield the following rates of return?

   a. 5 percent.
   b. 7 percent.
   c. 12 percent.
   (NOTE: At maturity, the bond will be retired and the holder will receive $1,000 in cash. Bonds typically are issued with $1,000 face, or par, values. The actual market value at any point in time will tend to rise as interest rates fall and fall as interest rates rise.)

15. A life insurance company offers loans to its policyholders against the cash value of their policies at a (nominal) annual interest rate of 8 percent, compounded quarterly. Determine the effective annual percentage interest rate on these loans.

16. Two investment opportunities are open to you: Investment 1 and Investment 2. Each has an initial cost of $10,000. Assuming that you desire a 10 percent return on your initial investment, compute the present value of the two alternatives and evaluate their relative attractiveness:

Investment 1 Cash Flows	Year	Investment 2 Cash Flows	Year
$5,000	1	$8,000	1
6,000	2	7,000	2
7,000	3	6,000	3
8,000	4	5,000	4

17. Your great-uncle Claude is 82 years old. Over the years he has accumulated savings of $80,000. He estimates that he will live another 10 years at the most and wants to spend his savings by then. (If he lives longer than that, he figures you will be happy to take care of him.)

   Uncle Claude places his $80,000 into an account earning 10% percent annually and sets it up in such a way that he will be making ten equal annual withdrawals—the first one occurring 1 year from now—such that his account balance will be zero at the end of 10 years. How much will he be able to withdraw each year?

18. You decide to purchase a building for $30,000 by paying $5,000 down and assuming a mortgage of $25,000. The bank offers you a 15-year mortgage requiring annual end-of-year payments of $3,188 each. The bank also requires you to pay a 3 percent loan origination fee, which will reduce the effective amount the bank lends to you. Compute the annual percentage rate of interest on this loan.

19. You purchase a 5-acre vacation property for $10,000. Five years from now you expect to sell the property for $22,550. Your anticipated annual end-of-year tax payments will be $500 for each of the next 5 years. Compute the annual rate of return on this investment. HINT: Try 14 percent.

(a) $6,000 \, (PVIFA \, 12\%, 5) + 4,000 \, (PVIFA \, 12\%, 10 - PVIFA \, 12\% \, 5)$
$= 6000 \, (3.605) + 4,000 \, (5,650 - 3.605) = 21,630 + 8,180 = 29,810$

20. An investment promises to pay $6,000 at the end of each year for the next 5 years and $4,000 at the end of each year for years 6 through 10.

   a. If you require a 12 percent rate of return on an investment of this sort, what is the maximum amount you would pay for this investment?

   b. Assuming that the payments are received at the *beginning* of each year, what is the maximum amount you would pay for this investment, given a 12 percent required rate of return?

21. You are considering investing in a bond that matures 20 years from now. It pays an annual end-of-year coupon rate of interest of 8.75 percent, or $87.50 per year. The bond currently sells for $919. Your marginal income tax rate (applied to interest payments) is 28 percent. Capital gains are taxed at the same rate as ordinary income. What is your *after-tax* rate of return if you buy this bond today and hold it until maturity? (HINT: Try 7 percent).

22. Your parents have discovered a $1000 bond at the bottom of their safe deposit box. The bond was given to you by your late great-aunt Hilda on your second birthday. The bond pays interest at a rate of 5 percent per annum, compounded annually. Interest accumulates and is paid at the time the bond is redeemed. You are now 27 years old. What is the current worth of the bond (principal plus interest)? $FVn = PV \, (1+0.5)^{25}$ or $PV \, (FVIF \, 5\%, 25)$

23. Suppose that a local savings and loan association advertises a 6 percent annual (nominal) rate of interest on regular accounts, compounded monthly. What is the effective annual percentage rate of interest paid by the savings and loan association? $APR = (1 + \frac{Knom}{m})^m - 1.0$ $(1 + \frac{0.06}{12})^{12} - 1.0 = 0.0617$

24. Your mother is planning to retire this year. Her firm has offered her a lump sum retirement payment of $50,000 or a $6,000 lifetime annuity—whichever she chooses. Your mother is in reasonably good health and expects to live for at least 15 more years. Which option should she choose, assuming that an 8 percent interest rate is appropriate to evaluate the annuity? $An = R \, (PVIFA \, 8\%, 15)$ $6000 \, (8.559) = 51,354$

25. A life insurance company has offered you a new "cash grower" policy that will be fully paid up when you turn 45. At that time it will have a cash surrender value of $18,000. When you turn 65 the policy will have a cash surrender value of $37,728. What rate of interest is the insurance company promising you on your investment?

26. Your aunt would like to help you set up your new medical practice when you complete your medical training in 6 years. She wishes to have $250,000 available for your use at that time. How much must she invest in an account at the end of each of the next 6 years in order to reach her goal, if the account offers a 12 percent annual rate of return?

27. Strikler, Inc. has issued a $10 million, 10-year bond issue. The bonds require Strikler to establish a sinking fund and make 10 equal, end-of-year deposits into the fund. These deposits will earn 8 percent annually, and the sinking fund should have enough accumulated in it at the end of 10 years to retire the bonds. What are the annual sinking fund payments?

28. Construct a loan amortization schedule for a 3-year, 11 percent loan of $30,000. The loan requires 3 equal, end-of-year payments.

29. a. What payments are due on a 5-year, 10 percent loan, with an initial outstanding balance of $100,000? (At the end of 5 years, the loan will be paid off. All loan payments are equal and occur at the end of the year.)

   b. What portion of the year 2 payment is principal? Interest?

30. The Nucleo-Robotics Corporation has just issued $10,000,000 of first mortgage bonds, each having a par value of $1,000 and a coupon interest rate of 15%. The bonds have a 25-year maturity and require that the firm establish a sinking fund sufficient to retire *80 percent* of the bonds by the time the bonds are scheduled to mature. The first deposit into the sinking fund will occur at the end of year 6. The firm will make 20 end-of-year deposits.

Money deposited into the sinking fund is expected to earn a 12 percent rate of return over the 20-year life of the fund. How much must the firm deposit into the fund each year in order to meet its sinking fund obligations?

31. Shyster Investments has offered you the following investment opportunity:
    - $6,000 at the end of each year for the first 5 years, plus
    - $3,000 at the end of each year from years 6 through 10, plus
    - $2,000 at the end of each year from years 11 through 20.

    a. How much would you be willing to pay for this investment if you required a 12 percent rate of return?
    b. If the payments were received at the beginning of each year, what would you be willing to pay for this investment?

32. Upon retirement your goal is to spend 5 years traveling around the world. To travel in the style to which you are accustomed will require $250,000 per year at the beginning of each year. If you plan to retire in 30 years, what are the equal, annual, end-of-year payments necessary to achieve this goal? The funds in the retirement account will compound at 10 percent annually.

33. A Baldwin United Company agent has just presented the following offer. If you deposit $25,000 with the firm today, they will pay you $10,000 per year at the end of years 8 through 15. If you require a 15% rate of return on this type of investment, would you make this investment?

34. You deposit $4,500 per year at the end of each of the next 25 years into an account that pays 10% compounded annually. How much could you withdraw at the end of each of the 20 years following your last deposit? (The twenty-fifth and last deposit is made at the beginning of the 20-year period. The first withdrawal is made at the end of the first year in the 20-year period.)

35. Upon retirement you are offered a choice between a $250,000 lump sum payment or a lifetime annuity of $51,300, with annuity payments being made at the end of each year. If you expect to live for 15 years after retirement, at what required rate of return would you be indifferent between the two alternatives (to the nearest whole percent)?

36. You deposit $10,000 at the end of each of the next 4 years into an account that pays 12% annually. What is the account balance at the end of 10 years?

37. Determine the value at the end of 3 years of a $10,000 investment (today) in a bank certificate of deposit (CD) that pays a nominal annual interest rate of 8 percent, compounded

    a. Semiannually.
    b. Quarterly.
    c. Monthly.

38. A bank offers an *effective* annual interest rate of 15 percent, compounded quarterly. What rate of interest is being paid quarterly by the bank?

39. An investment requires an outlay of $100,000 today. Cash inflows from the investment are expected to be $40,000 per year at the end of years 4, 5, 6, 7, and 8. If you require a 20% rate of return on this type of investment, should the investment be undertaken?

40. An investment of $100,000 is expected to generate cash inflows of $60,000 in 1 year and $79,350 in 2 years. Calculate the expected rate of return on this investment to the nearest whole percent.

41. An investment offers the following year-end cash flows:

End of Year	Cash Flow
1	$20,000
2	$30,000
3	$15,000

Using a 15% interest rate, convert this series of irregular cash flows to an equivalent (in present value terms) 3-year annuity.

42. Congratulations! Your have just won the Publishers Corporation Sweepstakes. You have been offered a lump sum of $1,000,000, or a lifetime (end-of-year) annuity of $100,000 per year. If you expect to live for 20 years and can earn 15 percent on your investments, which alternative should you choose (ignoring tax consequences)? If you expect to earn only 7 percent on your investments, how does your answer change?

43. James Street's son, Harold, is 10 years old today. Harold, a studious young fellow, already is making plans to go to college on his eighteenth birthday, and his father wants to start putting money away now for that purpose. Street estimates that Harold will need $18,000, $19,000, $20,000, and $21,000 for his freshman, sophomore, junior, and senior years, respectively. He plans on making these amounts available to Harold at the beginning of each of these years.

   Street would like to make eight annual deposits (the first of which would be made on Harold's eleventh birthday, 1 year from now, and the last on his eighteenth birthday, the day he leaves for college) in an account earning 10 percent annually. He wants the account to eventually be worth enough to *just* pay for Harold's college expenses. Any balances remaining in the account will continue to earn the 10 percent.

   How much will Street have to deposit in this "planning" account each year to provide for Harold's education?

44. How much must you deposit at the end of each quarter in an account that pays a nominal interest rate of 20 percent, compounded quarterly, if at the end of 5 years you want $10,000 in the account. (HINT: In working with the compound interest tables when solving this problem, you need to adjust the interest rate and the number of compounding periods to reflect quarterly, rather than annual, compounding.)

45. IRA Investments develops retirement programs for individuals. You are 30 years old and plan to retire on your sixtieth birthday. You want to establish a plan with IRA that will require a series of equal, annual, end-of-year deposits into the retirement account. The first deposit will be made 1 year from today on your thirty-first birthday. The final payment on the account will be made on your sixtieth birthday. The retirement plan will allow you to withdraw $120,000 per year for 15 years, with the first withdrawal on your sixty-first birthday. Also at the end of the fifteenth year you wish to withdraw an additional $250,000. The retirement account promises to earn 12% annually.

   What periodic payment must be made into the account to achieve your retirement objective?

46. If you deposit $1,000 a year (at the end of each of the next 5 years) in an account paying a nominal 12 percent per year, compounded semiannually, how much will you have in the account at the end of 10 years?

47. Your child will go to college 12 years from now and will require $20,000, $21,000, $22,000, and $23,000 at the beginning of each year in school. In addition you and your spouse plan to retire in 20 years. You want to have $75,000 available for each of your expected 15 years of blissful retirement. These funds will need to be available at the *beginning* of each year. If you now have $15,000 that can be used to meet these obligations, how much must you invest at the end of each of the next 20 years (if all funds earn an 11 percent rate of return) in order to meet your financial objectives?

48. You have just had your thirtieth birthday. You have two children. One will go to college 10 years from now and require four beginning-of-year payments for college expenses of $10,000, $11,000, $12,000, and $13,000. The second child will go to college 15 years from now and require four beginning-of-year payments for college expenses of $15,000, $16,000, $17,000, and $18,000.

In addition, you plan to retire in 30 years. You want to be able to withdraw $50,000 per year (at the end of each year) from an account throughout your retirement. You expect to live 20 years beyond retirement. The first withdrawal will occur on your sixty-first birthday.

What equal, annual, end-of-year amount must you save for each of the next 30 years to meet these goals, if all savings earn a 13 percent annual rate of return?

49. You are currently 30 years of age. You intend to retire at age 60 and you want to be able to receive a 20 year, $100,000 beginning of year annuity with the first payment to be received on your sixtieth birthday. You would like to save enough money over the next 15 years to achieve your objective; that is, you want to accumulate the necessary funds by your forty-fifth birthday.

  a. If you expect your investments to earn 12 percent per year over the next 15 years and 10 percent per year thereafter, how much must you accumulate by the time you reach age 45?

  b. What equal, annual amount must you save at the end of each of the next 15 years to achieve your objective, assuming that you currently have $10,000 available to meet your goal? Assume the conditions stated in Part a.

Continuous Compounding and Discounting

CONTINUOUS COMPOUNDING

In Chapter 5 we assumed that interest was received (or growth in a stream of payments occurred) at discrete points in time, such as at the end of each year, semiannually, quarterly, and so forth. It was shown that a nominal rate of i_{nom} percent per year results in a greater than i_{nom} percent effective rate per year if compounding occurs more frequently than one time at the end of the year. Specifically, the future value (FV_n) of some initial amount (PV_0) is given by Equation 5.22:

$$FV_n = PV_0 \left(1 + \frac{i_{nom}}{m} \right)^{mn}$$

where i_{nom} is the nominal annual rate of interest or growth, m is the number of times per year that compounding occurs, and n is the number of years compounding occurs. (Recall from Footnote 10 in Chapter 5 that an annual nominal interest rate is equivalent to an effective annual rate in the case where compounding occurs one time a year at the end of the year.)

As is shown in Table 5-6, the more often the compounding takes place each year, the greater will be the future value of some present amount. Another way of looking at this is to indicate that the more often that compounding takes place each year, the greater is the *effective* rate of interest (or growth) compared to the stated, annual *nominal* rate.

At the limit, we could accrue, or compound interest *continuously*. In this limiting case, the future value equation for continuous compounding becomes:

$$FV_n = PV_0(e)^{i_{nom}n} \tag{5A.1}$$

where e is approximately equal to the value 2.71828. (This value is the base number in natural logarithms.) If you have a financial or scientific calculator, the value of $e^{i_{nom}n}$ normally can be found by multiplying the nominal rate i by the number of years n and then punching the e^x key.

For example, if $1,000 is invested for 1 year at a nominal rate of 10 percent compounded continuously, the future value at the end of that year is given as follows:

$$FV_1 = \$1,000(e)^{0.10(1)} = \$1,000(2.71828)^{0.10}$$

$$= \$1,105.17$$

187

In the case where the $1,000 is invested at a nominal rate of 10 percent for 3 years, the future value, assuming continuous compounding, is equal to

$$FV_3 = \$1,000(e)^{0.10(3)} = \$1,000(2.71828)^{0.30}$$

$$= \$1,349.86$$

CONTINUOUS DISCOUNTING

Equation 5A.1 can also be modified to reflect continuous discounting. At the limit where compounding takes place continuously, present values can be computed as follows:

$$PV_0 = \frac{FV_n}{(e)^{i_{nom}n}} \tag{5A.2}$$

or equivalently

$$PV_0 = FV_n(e)^{-i_{nom}n} \tag{5A.3}$$

For example, if $1,349.86 is to be received 3 years from now at the continuously compounded rate of 10 percent, the present value can be computed as follows:

$$PV_0 = \frac{\$1,349.86}{(2.71828)^{0.10(3)}}$$

$$= \$1,000$$

EFFECTIVE RATE CALCULATIONS

When a *nominal* rate, i_{nom}, of interest (or growth) is known and compounding occurs continuously, it is easy to compute the *effective* rate using the following expression:

$$\text{Effective (annual) rate} = e^{i_{nom}} - 1.0 \tag{5A.4}$$

For example, if the nominal annual rate is 20 percent and compounding occurs continuously, the effective annual rate is computed as follows:

$$\text{Effective (annual) rate} = 2.71828^{(0.2)} - 1.0$$

$$= 1.2214 - 1.0$$

$$= 0.2214 \text{ or } 22.14\%$$

The effective rate is higher than the nominal rate because, with continuous compounding, the money is working harder; that is, interest is being accumulated more frequently (continuously) and this accumulated interest is available to earn its own interest on an ongoing (continuous) basis.

Alternatively, we may wish to calculate a continuous discount (or compounding) rate that is equivalent to an effective annual rate (when compounding is assumed to occur only one time at the end of the year). In this case, the continuous rate can be computed as follows:

$$\text{Continuous effective rate} = \ln(1 + i_{nom}) \tag{5A.5}$$

where ln represents the natural logarithm (base 2.71828) and i_{nom} represents the annual rate. (The natural logarithm of a number can be easily found using a financial or scientific calculator or a table of natural logarithms.)

For example, we may wish to know what continuously compounded effective rate of interest will yield the same present value of a future cash flow as an annual rate of interest of 10 percent (where compounding occurs only one time a year). This may be computed as follows:

$$\text{Continuous effective rate} = \ln (1 + 0.10)$$
$$= 0.0953 \text{ or } 9.53\%$$

It is logical that this continuous rate will be less than the annual rate, because the money is working harder when compounding occurs continuously (even more frequently than every second) than when it occurs only one time a year.

PROBLEMS*

1. What is the future value of $10,000 invested for 2 years at a nominal interest rate of 15 percent compounded continuously?
2. You expect to receive $5,000 in 5 years. What is the present value of this future receipt at the continuously compounded rate of 12 percent?
3. The nominal rate of interest on a bank CD is 10 percent. If compounding occurs continuously, what is the effective annual rate?
4. What continuously compounded rate of interest will yield the same present value of a $5,000 cash flow to be received 1 year in the future as an annual rate of interest of 9 percent (where compounding occurs one time a year)? Prove your answer by finding the present value of the $5,000 future cash flow under both conditions.

* Colored numbers denote problems that have check answers provided at the end of the book.

C H A P T E R

6

Characteristics and Valuation of Fixed-Income Securities

KEY CHAPTER CONCEPTS

1. The characteristics of fixed income (debt and preferred stock) securities are examined, including
   a. Types of each form of security
   b. Features
   c. Users
   d. Advantages and disadvantages
2. Capitalization-of-income method of valuation
   a. Value of an asset is equal to the present value of the expected future benefits discounted at the appropriate required rate of return.
   b. Required rate of return is a function of the risk or uncertainty associated with the returns from the asset, as well as the risk free rate.
3. Bond valuation
   a. Value of a bond with a finite maturity

date is equal to the present value of the interest payments and principal payment (at maturity) discounted at the investor's required rate of return.
   b. Yield to maturity of a bond is equal to the rate of return that equates the price of the bond to the present value of the interest and principal payments.
4. Preferred stocks often are treated as perpetuities with a value equal to the annual dividend divided by the required rate of return.
5. Other important topics include
   a. Market value of assets and market equilibrium
   b. Valuation of perpetual bonds

GLOSSARY OF NEW TERMS

Bond A long-term debt instrument that promises to pay the lender a series of periodic interest payments in addition to returning the principal at maturity. Most corporate bonds are offered in $1,000 principal amounts (par value).

Bond rating An evaluation of a bond's probability of default. This is performed by an outside rating agency, such as Standard and Poor's or Moody's.

Bond refunding The redemption of a callable bond issue and replacement with a lower interest cost issue.

Book value The accounting value of an asset or a corporation. The book value per share of common stock is equal to the total book value of the company (that is, net worth) divided by the total number of shares of common stock outstanding.

Call feature A provision that permits an issuer of bonds (and sometimes preferred stock) to retire the obligation prior to its maturity.

Call premium The difference between a bond's call price and its par value.

Call price The price at which a bond may be retired, or called, prior to its maturity.

Capitalization of income A method of determining the present value of an asset that is expected to produce a stream of future benefits. This involves *discounting* the stream of expected future benefits at an appropriate rate.

Convertible bond A bond that may be exchanged for common stock at the holder's option.

Coupon rate of interest The interest rate stated on a bond. The coupon rate of interest times the *par*, or principal, value of a bond determines the periodic dollar interest payments received by the bondholder.

Cumulative dividends A typical feature of preferred stock that requires past-due preferred stock dividends to be paid before any common stock dividends can be paid.

Debenture A bond that is *not* secured by a mortgage on any specific asset but instead by the general credit and earning power of the issuing firm.

Going-concern value The value of a firm, assuming that the firm's organization and assets remain intact and are used to generate future income and cash flows.

Income bond A bond that pays interest only if the firm earns sufficient income.

Indenture The contract between the issuing firm and the lenders in a debt obligation.

Interest rate risk The variation in the market price (and hence in the realized rate of return or yield) of a security that arises from changes in interest rates.

Junk bond A high-yield debt security issued by a company with a low credit rating.

Liquidation value The value of a firm, assuming that it sells all its assets and stops using them to generate future income and cash flows.

Mortgage bond A bond that is secured by a pledge of a specific asset or group of assets.

Par value (bond) Represents the amount of principal borrowed (usually $1,000) and due at maturity.

Par value (preferred stock) An arbitrary value assigned by the issuing firm.

Perpetual bond A bond that has no maturity date.

Required rate of return The rate used to value a stream of future benefits from an asset (also called the *discount rate*). The riskier the return from the asset, the higher the required rate of return.

Senior debt Debt that has a higher claim to a firm's earnings and/or assets than junior debt.

Subordinated debenture A bond that has a claim on the issuing firm's assets that is junior to other forms of debt in the event of a liquidation. The claims of subordinated debenture holders can be met only *after* all the claims of senior creditors have been met.

Trustee The bondholder's representative in a public debt offering. The trustee is responsible for monitoring the borrower's compliance with the terms of the indenture.

Yield to maturity The discount rate that equates the present value of all expected interest payments and the repayment of principal from a bond with the present bond price.

Bond Valuation and "Event Risk"*

In the past, bonds of blue-chip corporations were considered ideal investments for investors seeking stable and secure returns on their capital. However, recent events have shown that such an investment strategy may not always work. After management of the RJR Nabisco Company proposed a multibillion dollar leveraged buyout of the company in October 1988, the prices of the company's bonds dropped 20 percent. (In a leveraged buyout transaction, the buyer of a company borrows a large portion of the purchase price, using the purchased assets as partial collateral for the loan.)[1] The bonds of many other industrial companies, which also were possible takeover targets, likewise dropped in value. For example, during the month of October 1988, consumer goods companies' debt had a *negative* 1.04 percent return compared with positive total returns on bonds in every other sector of the bond market. Over a longer time period, from 1985 to the middle of 1988, the bonds of ninety-one investment-grade industrial companies, or approximately 18 percent of the total, experienced losses in market value because of takeover-related events.

This "event risk" has had a significant impact on the bond market. Investors are concerned that the large amount of debt being used to finance a takeover or leveraged buyout will transform a company's existing investment-grade bonds into potentially speculative high-

yield, high-risk junk bonds. As Greta Marshall (former head of the California Public Employees Retirement System) notes, "The lesson is that bondholders who invest in large quality companies can be disenfranchised by managers who have the benefit of inside information." Metropolitan Life Insurance Company (with sizable holdings of RJR Nabisco bonds) filed a lawsuit claiming that management of the company violated its fiduciary responsibility to existing bondholders by initiating a leveraged buyout. This suit seeks to establish the principle that shareholder gains in a restructuring cannot come at the expense of bondholders.

The effect of "event risk" is to make long-term debt financing more costly to companies that are potential restructuring targets. According to one estimate, the debt of a potential takeover target now trades at a price that yields some 1½ percentage points above the level suggested by its blue-chip rating. To make their debt more attractive to investors, some companies are now issuing "poison put" bonds. These bonds allow investors to sell their bonds back to the company at face value if a corporate restructuring lowers the rating of the bonds to less than investment grade.

This chapter focuses on the characteristics and valuation of bonds, such as those of RJR Nabisco, as well as preferred stock.

* Based on articles in the *Wall Street Journal* (November 8, 1988, and November 25, 1988) and *Business Week* (November 14, 1988; December 5, 1988; and February 6, 1989).

[1] See Chapter 22 for a further discussion of these transactions.

INTRODUCTION

Firms issue various types of long-term securities to help meet their needs for funds. These include long-term debt (bonds),[2] preferred stock, and common stock. Long-term debt and preferred stock are classified as *fixed-income securities*, because they involve relatively constant distributions of interest or dividend payments over time to their holders. For example, Baltimore Gas and Electric Company sold $100 million of mortgage bonds in 1986, at which time it agreed to pay its lenders an interest rate of 9⅛ percent or $91.25 per year until 2016 for each $1,000 of debt outstanding. Since then the company has continued to pay this interest rate even though market interest rates have fluctuated. Similarly, USX Corporation issued $250 million of preferred stock in 1987. Investors paid $50 per share and the company

[2] The terms *long-term debt securities*, *debt*, and *bonds* are used interchangeably throughout the chapter.

agreed to pay an annual dividend of $3.50 per share. Since that time, USX has continued to pay this amount, even though common stock dividends have been increased.

Common stock, on the other hand, is a variable-income security. Common stockholders are said to participate in a firm's earnings, because they may receive a larger dividend if earnings increase in the future, or their dividend may be cut if earnings drop.

Fixed-income securities—long-term debt and preferred stock—differ from each other in several ways. For example, the interest paid to bondholders is a tax-deductible expense for the borrowing company, whereas dividends paid to preferred stockholders are not. Legally, long-term debtholders are considered creditors, whereas preferred stockholders are considered owners. Thus a firm is not legally required to pay dividends to its preferred stockholders, and the failure to do so has less serious consequences than the failure to meet interest payment and principal repayment obligations on long-term debt. In addition, long-term debt normally has a specific maturity, whereas preferred stock often is perpetual.

A knowledge of the characteristics of the various types of long-term securities is necessary in developing valuation models for these securities. The valuation of long-term securities is important to a firm's financial managers, as well as to current owners, prospective investors, and security analysts. For example, financial managers should understand how the price or value of the firm's securities (particularly common stock) is affected by its investment, financing, and dividend decisions. Similarly, both current owners and prospective investors should be able to compare their own valuations of the firm's securities with actual market prices to make rational security purchase and sale decisions. Likewise, security analysts use valuation techniques in evaluating long-term corporate securities when making investment recommendations.

This chapter focuses on the characteristics and valuation of fixed income securities; namely, long-term debt and preferred stock. The next chapter contains a similar discussion of variable income securities; namely, common stock.

CHARACTERISTICS OF LONG-TERM DEBT

When a company borrows money in the capital markets, it issues long-term debt securities to investors. These bonds usually are sold in denominations of $1,000 and constitute a promise by the issuing company to repay a certain amount of money (the $1,000 principal) on a particular date (the maturity date) and to pay a specified amount of interest at fixed intervals (usually twice a year). Most debt has a *par value* of $1,000, and debt prices are often expressed as a percentage of that value. For example, a market price listing of "87" indicates that a $1,000 par value bond may be purchased for $870.

There are many different types of long-term debt. The type or types a company chooses to use will depend on its own particular financial situation and the characteristics of the industry as a whole.

Types of Long-Term Debt

Long-term debt generally is classified according to whether or not it is secured by specific physical assets of the issuing company. Secured debt issues usually are called *mortgage bonds*, and issues not secured by specific assets are called *debentures* or, occasionally, *debenture bonds*. The term *bond* is often used to denote any type of long-term debt security.

At the present time, utility companies are the largest users of mortgage bonds. In recent years the use of mortgage bonds relative to other forms of long-term debt has declined, whereas the use of debentures has increased. Because debentures are unsecured, their quality depends on the general credit-worthiness of the issuing company. As a result, they are usually issued by large, financially strong firms.

The yield differential between the mortgage bond and debenture alternatives is another example of the risk-return tradeoff that occurs throughout finance. For example, suppose Midstates Oil Company could issue either mortgage bonds or debentures. If the mortgage bonds could be sold with a 10 percent interest rate, the debentures would have to be sold at a higher rate—for example, 10¼ percent—to attract investors. This is due to the fact that investors require a higher return on debentures, which are backed only by the unmortgaged assets of the company and the company's earning power, than they do on mortgage bonds, which are secured by specific physical assets as well as the company's earning power.

Debt issues also are classified according to whether they are *senior* or *junior*.[3] Senior debt has a higher priority claim to a firm's earnings and/or assets than junior debt. Occasionally the actual name of the debt issue will contain a "junior" or "senior" qualifier. In most instances, however, identification of how a particular company's debt issues are ranked requires an analysis of the restrictions placed on the company by the purchasers of the issue.

Unsecured debt also may be classified according to whether it is *subordinated* to other types of debt. In the event of a liquidation or reorganization, the claims of *subordinated debenture holders* are considered only *after* the claims of *unsubordinated debenture holders*. In general, subordinated debentures are junior to other types of debt, including bank loans, and may even be junior to *all* of a firm's other debt.

Equipment trust certificates are used largely by railroad and trucking companies. The proceeds from these certificates are used to purchase specific assets, such as railroad rolling stock. The certificate holders own the equipment and lease it to the company. Technically, equipment trust certificates are not true bonds, even though they are guaranteed by the issuing company, because the interest and principal are paid by the *trustee* (the financial institution responsible for looking after the investors' interests). Even so, they are classified as debt because they have all of the characteristics of debt.

Collateral trust bonds are backed by stocks or bonds of other corporations. This type of financing is principally of historic interest; it is used today primarily by holding companies. A holding company, for example, may raise needed funds by pledging the stocks and/or bonds of its subsidiaries as collateral. In this arrangement the holding company serves as the *parent* company. The subsidiary borrows from the parent, and the parent borrows from the capital markets. This makes good sense, because the parent company generally can get more favorable terms for its debt in the capital markets than the subsidiary.

---

[3] The senior–junior classification scheme also is used in connection with preferred and common stock. Preferred stock is junior to long-term debt and senior to common stock.

Income bonds also are largely of historic interest, although they still are used occasionally today. Income bonds promise to pay interest only if the issuing firm earns sufficient income; if it does not, no interest obligation exists. These securities rarely are issued directly. Instead, they often are created in reorganizations following bankruptcy and are normally issued in exchange for junior or subordinated issues. Thus, unsecured income bonds generally are considered to be "weak" securities.

Pollution control bonds and *industrial revenue bonds* are issued by local governments rather than corporations. The interest paid to purchasers of municipal bonds is tax exempt, and the interest rate typically is less than what a corporation would have to pay. The interest payments are guaranteed by the corporation for whose benefit the bonds are issued.

Features of Long-Term Debt

Long-term debt has a number of unique features. Several of these are discussed in the following paragraphs.

INDENTURE. An indenture is a contract between a firm that issues long-term debt securities and the lenders. In general, an indenture does the following:

- It thoroughly details the nature of the debt issue.
- It carefully specifies the manner in which the principal must be repaid.
- It lists any restrictions that are placed on the firm by the lenders. These restrictions are called *covenants*, and the firm must satisfy them to keep from defaulting on its obligations.[4] Typical restrictive covenants include the following:
  1. A minimum coverage, or times interest earned, ratio the firm must maintain.
  2. A minimum level of working capital[5] the firm must maintain.
  3. A maximum amount of dividends the firm can pay on its preferred and common stock.
  4. Other restrictions that effectively limit how much leasing and issuing of additional debt the firm may do.

TRUSTEE. Because the holders of a large firm's long-term debt issue are likely to be widely scattered geographically, the Trust Indenture Act of 1939 requires that a trustee represent the debtholders in dealings with the issuing company. A trustee usually is a commercial bank or trust company that is responsible for ensuring that all the terms and convenants set forth in the indenture agreement are adhered to by the issuing company. The issuing company must pay the trustee's expenses.

CALL FEATURE. A call feature is an optional retirement provision that permits the issuing company to redeem, or *call*, a debt issue prior to its maturity

---

[4] A company defaults on its debt when it does not pay interest or required principal on time, or when it violates one or more of the bond's restrictive covenants. When default occurs, the debt is often said to be "triggered," meaning that the entire principal amount comes due immediately. This could result in bankruptcy.

[5] *Working capital*, defined as the firm's investment in current assets less its current liabilities, is discussed in Chapter 17.

date at a specified price termed the *redemption*, or *call*, *price*. Many firms use the call feature because it provides them with the potential flexibility to retire debt prior to maturity if, for example, interest rates decline.

The call price is greater than the par value of the debt, and the difference between the two is the *call premium*. During the early years of an issue the call premium usually is equal to about 1 year's interest. Some debt issues specify *fixed* call premiums, whereas others specify *declining* call premiums. For example, in 1986 the El Paso Natural Gas Company issued $100 million of 9⅝ percent, 25-year sinking fund debentures. During 1987 the company could have retired all or part of this issue at 109.13 percent of par value, and during 1988 the redemption price dropped to 108.67 percent of par. Similar reductions in the redemption price are scheduled for each year up to the year 2011. Many bonds are not callable at all for several years after the initial date. For example, in 1987 Chrysler issued $250 million of 10.40 percent notes due in 1999 that are not callable until 1997. This situation is referred to as a *deferred call*.

Details of the call feature are worked out before the debt is sold in the negotiations between the underwriters and the issuing company. Because a call feature gives the company significant flexibility in its financing plans, while at the same time potentially depriving the lenders of the advantages they would gain from holding the debt until maturity, the issuing company has to offer the investors compensation in the form of the call premium in exchange for the call privilege. In addition, the interest rate on a callable debt issue usually is slightly higher than the interest rate on a similar noncallable issue.

Because of the interest savings that can be achieved, a firm is most likely to call a debt issue when prevailing interest rates are appreciably lower than those that existed at the time of the original issue. When a company calls a relatively high interest issue and replaces it with a lower interest issue, the procedure is called *bond refunding*. This topic is discussed in the appendix to Chapter 16.

SINKING FUND. Usually lenders will require that a borrowing company gradually reduce the outstanding balance of a debt issue over its life instead of having the entire principal amount come due on a particular date twenty or thirty years into the future. The usual method of providing for a gradual retirement is a sinking fund, so called because a certain amount of money is put aside annually, or "sunk," into a *sinking fund account*. For example, with the El Paso 25-year, 9⅝ percent debentures described earlier, the company was required to redeem $4 million of the bonds annually between 1997 and 2010, thus retiring 56 percent of the debt issue prior to maturity. In practice, however, a company also can satisfy its sinking fund requirements either by purchasing a portion of the debt each year in the open market or, if the debt is callable, by using a lottery technique to determine which actual numbered certificates will be called and retired within a given year. The alternative chosen depends on the current market price of the debt issue. In general, if current interest rates are above the issue's coupon rate, the current market price of the debt will be less than $1,000, and the company should meet its sinking fund obligation by purchasing the debt in the open market. If, on the other hand, market interest rates are lower than the issue's coupon rate, and if the market price of the debt is above the call price, the company should use the call procedure.

CONVERSION FEATURE. Some debt issues (and some preferred stock issues) have a conversion feature that allows the holder to exchange the security for the company's common stock at the option of the holder. The features of convertible securities are discussed in Chapter 16.

TYPICAL SIZES OF DEBT ISSUES. Debt issues sold to the public through underwriters are usually in the $25 to $200 million range, although very large firms occasionally borrow up to $500 million or more at one time. Because the use of an underwriting group in a public offering involves considerable expense, it usually is uneconomical for a company to make a public offering of this nature for debt issues less than about $25 million. *Private placements*, however, frequently involve lesser amounts of money— for example, $5 to $10 million—because the entire debt issue is purchased by a single investor, such as an insurance company.

COUPON RATES. The coupon rates on new bonds normally are fixed and set equal to market interest rates on bonds of comparable quality and maturity so that the bonds sell at or near par value. However, during the inflationary period of the early 1980s when interest rates reached record levels and bond prices were quite volatile, highly-rated companies began issuing bonds with *floating* coupon rates.

An example of a floating rate issue is Baltimore Gas and Electric's $100 million in floating rate notes (series II) maturing in 1995. Interest is adjusted and paid quarterly at a rate of 112.5 basis points (that is, 1.125 percentage points) above the applicable 91-day Treasury bill auction rate. The quarterly interest rate is limited to being no greater than 11.90 percent nor less than 7.90 percent. Such a bond protects investors against a rise in interest rates because the market price of the bond does not fluctuate as much as for fixed interest rate bonds.

Another type of bond that was issued in the early 1980s, when inflation and interest rates were relatively high, was *original issue deep discount* (OID) bonds. These bonds have coupon rates that are below prevailing market interest rates at the time of issue, and hence sell at a discount from par value. Some OID bond issues pay no interest and are known as *zero coupon* bonds. The Allied Corporation zero coupon money market multiplier note issue maturing on January 15, 1996, is one such example. One advantage of these types of bonds to the issuing firm is the reduction in (or elimination of) interest payments (a cash outflow) during the life of the bonds. Another advantage is the slightly lower cost (yield to maturity) of these issues compared with bonds that are issued at (or near) par value. The primary disadvantage of these types of bonds is the large cash outflow required by the firm at maturity. OID bonds have decreased in popularity in the last few years, due to changes in the tax laws (which eliminated the tax advantages to companies of these issues over debt issued at par) and the issuance by several brokerage firms of lower risk substitutes. One such substitute is Merill Lynch's "TIGRs"—Treasury Investment Growth Receipts—which are backed by U.S. Treasury bonds. The U.S. Treasury also has issued its own zero coupon bonds. These securities, which pay no interest, are purchased at a discount from face value and then can be redeemed for the full face value at maturity.

MATURITY. The typical maturity on long-term debt is about 20 to 30 years. Occasionally companies borrow money for as long as 40 years. On the other end of the scale, companies in need of financing often are willing to borrow for only about 10 years, especially if they feel that interest rates are temporarily high, as was true in the environment of the late 1970s and until mid-1982—an environment characterized by high rates of inflation and historically high interest rates. By the spring of 1983, many large companies were again issuing fixed-rate debt securities with 25- and 30-year maturities.

Like the floating rate bonds described earlier, which protect investors against interest rate risk, firms also have been issuing bonds that are redeemable at par *at the option of the holder.* These are known as extendable notes or put bonds. If interest rates rise and the market price of the bond falls, the holder can redeem them at par and reinvest the proceeds in higher yielding securities. An example of an extendible note is General Electric Capital Corporation's $200 million of 10⅜ percent extendible notes maturing in 2000. The notes were issued in February 1985 and are redeemable at the option of the holder after February 20, 1990, for the full principal amount.

From an accounting standpoint, debt obligations maturing in more than 1 year are usually classified as long-term debt on the balance sheet.

Bond Ratings

Debt issues are rated according to their relative degree of risk by various financial companies, including Moody's Investors Services and Standard and Poor's (S&P) Corporation. These agencies consider a variety of factors when rating a firm's securities, including earnings stability, coverage ratios, the relative amount of debt in the firm's capital structure, and the degree of subordination, as well as past experience. According to Moody's rating scale, the highest-quality–lowest-risk issues are rated Aaa, and the scale continues down through Aa, A, Baa, Ba, B, Caa, Ca, and C. On the Standard and Poor's ratings scale, AAA denotes the highest-quality issues, and this rating is followed by AA, A, BBB, BB, B, and so on. S&P also has various C and D classifications for high-risk issues; the vast majority of debt issues, however, fall into one of the A or B categories. Figure 6-1 shows Moody's and S&P's bond-rating definitions.

Table 6-1 gives some examples of capital structure and coverage ratios for various companies' debt ratings. In general, as the debt rating decreases from AAA to lower ratings, the percentage of long-term debt in the capital structure increases and the coverage ratio decreases.

As a general rule, "triple A" issues yield the lowest interest rates at any given time. This is another example of the risk–return tradeoff in finance. Because the perceived default risk difference between companies rated A and B usually is less during periods of economic prosperity than during recessionary periods, the interest rate spread between A- and B-rated issues also tends to be smaller during periods of economic prosperity.

Companies with weak financial positions (e.g., highly leveraged balance sheets or low earnings) often issue high-yield debt securities to obtain capital needed for internal expansion or for corporate acquisitions and buyouts. Such debt, also known as *junk bonds,* is rated Ba or lower by Moody's (or BB or lower by Standard and Poor's) and typically yields 3 percent or more than the highest quality corporate debt. For example, Campeau Corporation had to pay over 17 percent in November 1988 to obtain some of the funds it needed to pay for the acquisition of Federated Department Stores. These

MOODY'S CORPORATE RATINGS

FIGURE 6-1

Moody's and Standard & Poor's Bond-Rating Definitions

SOURCE: *Moody's Bond Record* (January 1989). Reprinted by permission of Moody's Investment Service, Inc. *Standard & Poor's Bond Guide* (January 1989). Reprinted by permission of Standard and Poor's. ©Standard and Poor's.

Aaa

Bonds which are rated **Aaa** are judged to be of the best quality. They carry the smallest degree of investment risk and are generally referred to as "gilt edge." Interest payments are protected by a large or by an exceptionally stable margin and principal is secure. While the various protective elements are likely to change, such changes as can be visualized are most unlikely to impair the fundamentally strong position of such issues.

Aa

Bonds which are rated **Aa** are judged to be of high quality by all standards. Together with the **Aaa** group they comprise what are generally known as high grade bonds. They are rated lower than the best bonds because margins of protection may not be as large as in **Aaa** securities or fluctuation of protective elements may be of greater amplitude or there may be other elements present which make the long-term risks appear somewhat larger than in **Aaa** securities.

A

Bonds which are rated **A** possess many favorable investment attributes and are to be considered as upper medium-grade obligations. Factors giving security to principal and interest are considered adequate but elements may be present which suggest a susceptibility to impairment sometime in the future.

Baa

Bonds which are rated **Baa** are considered as medium-grade obligations, i.e., they are neither highly protected nor poorly secured. Interest payments and principal security appear adequate for the present but certain protective elements may be lacking or may be characteristically unreliable over any great length of time. Such bonds lack outstanding investment characteristics and in fact have speculative characteristics as well.

Ba

Bonds which are rated **Ba** are judged to have speculative elements; their future cannot be considered as well assured. Often the protection of interest and principal payments may be very moderate and thereby not well safeguarded during other good and bad times over the future. Uncertainty of position characterizes bonds in this class.

B

Bonds which are rated **B** generally lack characteristics of the desirable investment. Assurance of interest and principal payments or of maintenance of other terms of the contract over any long period of time may be small.

Caa

Bonds which are rated **Caa** are of poor standing. Such issues may be in default or there may be present elements of danger with respect to principal or interest.

Ca

Bonds which are rated **Ca** represent obligations which are speculative in a high degree. Such issues are often in default or have other marked shortcomings.

C

Bonds which are rated **C** are the lowest-rated class of bonds and issues so rated can be regarded as having extremely poor prospects of ever attaining any real investment standing.

Note: Moody's applies numerical modifiers, **1, 2,** and **3** in each generic rating classification from **Aa** through **B** in its corporate bond rating system. The modifier **1** indicates that the security ranks in the higher end of its generic rating category; the modifier **2** indicates a mid-range ranking; and the modifier **3** indicates that the issue ranks in the lower end of its generic rating category.

STANDARD & POOR'S CORPORATE AND MUNICIPAL DEBT RATINGS

AAA

Debt rated **AAA** has the highest rating assigned by Standard & Poor's. Capacity to pay interest and repay principal is extremely strong.

AA

Debt rated **AA** has a very strong capacity to pay interest and repay principal and differs from the higher rated issues only in a small degree.

A

Debt rated **A** has a strong capacity to pay interest and repay principal although it is somewhat more susceptible to the adverse effects of changes in circumstances and economic conditions than debt in higher rated categories.

BBB

Debt rated **BBB** is regarded as having an adequate capacity to pay interest and repay principal. Whereas it normally exhibits adequate protection parameters, adverse economic conditions or changing circumstances are more likely to lead to a weakened capacity to pay interest and repay principal for debt in this category than in higher rated categories.

BB, B, CCC, CC, C

Debt rated **BB, B, CCC, CC** and **C** is regarded, on balance, as predominantly speculative with respect to capacity to pay interest and repay principal in accordance with the terms of the obligation. **BB** indicates the lowest degree of speculation and **C** the highest degree of speculation. While such debt will likely have some quality and protective characteristics, these are outweighed by large uncertainties or major risk exposures to adverse conditions.

CI

The rating **CI** is reserved for income bonds on which no interest is being paid.

Debt rated **D** is in payment default. The **D** rating category is used when interest payments or principal payments are not made on the date due even if the applicable grace period has not expired, unless S&P believes that such payments will be made during such grace period.

Plus (+) or Minus (−)

The ratings from **AA** to **CCC** may be modified by the addition of a plus or minus sign to show relative standing within the major rating categories.

Event Protection

S & P recently has developed an event risk covenant ranking system to supplement traditional ratings. The rankings range from E-1 (strong protection) to E-5 (insignificant or no protection), indicating bondholder protection from a dramatic credit quality decline in the event of a restructuring or takeover.

bonds were rated CCC+ by Standard and Poor's. At the time, the highest quality (AAA rated) corporate debt was yielding less than 10 percent. Junk bonds constitute an increasingly important segment of all corporate debt outstanding, having risen from 13 percent in 1983 to 25 percent in 1988.[6]

Information on Debt Financing Activities

Every business day financial newspapers contain information on debt financing activities. For example, the *Wall Street Journal* devotes at least one page to financing activities in the bond market. This page contains announcements by underwriters concerning the characteristics of the new issues presently being offered.

The *Wall Street Journal* also contains information on the secondary debt markets, including price quotations for the widely traded corporate debt issues listed on the New York Exchange. Appendix 1A contains a discussion of these price quotations.

[6] *Business Week* (February 6, 1989), p. 83.

TABLE 6-1

Company	Standard and Poor's Debt Rating*	Debt to Total Capitalization**	Times Fixed Charges Earned**
IBM Corp.	AAA	8.16%	11.84
General Electric	AAA	21.23	3.29
Ford Motor	AA	7.71	11.50
Dayton-Hudson	A+	41.16	2.50
Monsanto	A−	25.86	3.14
Boise Cascade	BBB+	36.07	2.75
Inland Steel	BBB−	31.33	3.10
FMC Corp.	BB	118.59	1.85
General Host	B	46.14	—†
Mattel	CCC+	73.15	—†

Selected Examples of Capital Structure and Coverage Ratios for Various Debt Ratings

* *Standard & Poor's Bond Guide* (January 1989).
** *Moody's Industrial Manual* (1988).
† Indicates that the company incurred a loss (that is, negative net income after taxes) during the given year.

Users of Long-Term Debt

Most large and medium-sized companies finance some portion of their fixed assets with long-term debt. This debt may be in the form of either secured bonds or unsecured debentures. Utilities rely on debt capital to a large degree and, as a group, are the largest users of secured bonds; the *first mortgage bonds* of a utility are typically a safe, low-risk investment. Manufacturing companies, in contrast, rely on debt capital to varying degrees and generally use unsecured debt more often than secured debt.

Many large companies have virtually continuous capital expenditure programs. Usually a company will plan to finance at least partially any new assets with long-term debt. Because it generally is uneconomical to borrow small amounts of long-term capital, however, companies that have ongoing construction programs often gradually "draw down" on their short-term revolving credit agreements. Then, once every couple of years or so, a firm of this type will enter the capital markets and sell long-term debt. At that time a portion of the proceeds is used to repay the short-term borrowings, and the cycle begins again. This procedure is called *funding* short-term debt; as a result, long-term debt is sometimes referred to as *funded debt*.

Most established companies attempt to maintain reasonably constant proportions of long-term debt and common equity in their capital structures. During the course of a company's normal profitable operations, though, long-term debt is gradually retired as it matures, and the retained earnings portion of common equity is increased. This in turn decreases the debt-to-equity ratio. Thus, to maintain their desired capital structures, companies have to raise long-term debt capital periodically. This gradual refunding of debt, along with the tax deductibility of interest, accounts for the fact that about 85 to 90 percent of the external long-term capital raised in the United States is in the form of debt.

Advantages and Disadvantages of Long-Term Debt Financing

From the issuing firm's perspective, the major advantages of long-term debt include the following:

- Its relatively low after-tax cost due to the tax deductibility of interest.
- The increased earnings per share possible through financial leverage.
- The ability of the firm's owners to maintain greater control over the firm.

The following are the major disadvantages of long-term debt financing, from the firm's perspective:

- The increased financial risk of the firm resulting from the use of debt.
- The restrictions placed on the firm by the lenders.

From the investors' viewpoint, in general, debt securities offer stable returns and therefore are considered relatively low-risk investments compared with common stock investments. Because debtholders are creditors, however, they do not participate in any increased earnings the firm may experience. In fact, during periods of relatively high inflation, holders of existing debt find that their *real* interest payments decrease, because the nominal interest payments remain constant.

Before developing specific models for the valuation of bonds (and preferred stocks) later in the chapter, the following section discusses the general concept of asset valuation, including the capitalization-of-income method and market and book values of assets.

VALUATION OF ASSETS

■■ 203 ■■

CHAPTER 6
Characteristics and
Valuation of Fixed-
Income Securities

The value of any asset is based on the *expected future benefits* the owner will receive over the life of the asset. For example, the value of a *physical asset*, such as a new piece of equipment or production plant, is based on the expected cash inflows the asset will generate for the firm over its useful life. These cash inflows take the forms of increased revenues and/or reduced costs plus any salvage value received from the sale of the asset.[7]

Similarly, the value of a *financial asset*, such as a stock or bond, is based on the expected cash returns the asset will generate for the owner during the *holding period*. These returns take the form of interest or dividend payments over the holding period plus the amount the owner receives when the security is sold.

It is assumed throughout this and the following chapter that the firms under discussion are *going concerns;* that is, their organization and assets will remain intact and be used to generate future income and cash flows. Techniques other than the ones described here must be used to value long-term securities of firms faced with the possibility of bankruptcy. In such cases the *liquidation value* of the firm's assets is the primary determinant of the value of the various types of long-term securities.[8]

Capitalization-of-Income Method

One way of determining the value of an asset is to calculate the present value of the stream of expected future benefits discounted at an appropriate *required rate of return*. This is known as the *capitalization-of-income* method of valuation and is represented algebraically as follows:

$$V_0 = \frac{R_1}{(1 + i)^1} + \frac{R_2}{(1 + i)^2} + \dots + \frac{R_n}{(1 + i)^n} \tag{6.1}$$

or, using summation notation, as follows:

$$V_0 = \sum_{t=1}^{n} \frac{R_t}{(1 + i)^t} \tag{6.2}$$

where V_0 is the value of the asset at time zero, R_t the expected cash return in period t, i the required rate of return or discount rate, and n the length of the holding period.

For example, assume that the cash returns, R_t, of an investment are expected to be an annuity of $1,000 per year for $n = 6$ years, and the required rate of return, i, is 8 percent. Using the capitalization-of-income method, the value of this investment is

$$V_0 = \sum_{t=1}^{6} \frac{\$1,000}{(1 + 0.08)^t}$$

Recognizing this expression as the present value of an annuity (PVAN$_0$) the value of the investment is computed using Equation 5.16 of the previous chapter:

[7] Chapters 9–11 contain a detailed discussion of capital budgeting.
[8] This topic is discussed in Chapter 22.

$$V_0 = \$1,000(\text{PVIFA}_{0.08,6})$$
$$= \$1,000(4.623)$$
$$= \$4,623$$

The *required rate of return, i,* on an asset is a function of the uncertainty, or risk, associated with the returns from the asset as well as the risk-free interest rate.[9] As indicated in the discussion of the determinants of discount rates in the previous chapter, this function is upward sloping, indicating that the higher the risk, the greater is the investor's required rate of return. The measurement of risk and the development of the risk–return tradeoff function is discussed further in Chapter 8.

Market Value of Assets and Market Equilibrium

From Equation 6.1 it can be seen that the value of an asset depends on both the expected cash returns, R_t, and the owner's (or prospective buyer's) required rate of return, i. However, potential buyers and sellers can have different opinions of an asset's value based on their individual assessments of the potential cash returns from the asset and individual required rates of return.

The *market price,* or *market value,* of an asset (such as shares of common stock) is determined in much the same way as the price of most goods and services in a market-oriented economy; namely, by the interaction of supply and demand. This is shown in Figure 6-2. Potential buyers are represented by a *demand* schedule showing the maximum prices they are willing to pay for given quantities of an asset, and potential sellers are represented by a *supply* schedule showing the minimum prices at which they are willing to sell given quantities of the asset. The transaction price, the price at which an asset is sold, occurs at the intersection of the demand and supply schedules. The intersection represents the *market value,* or *market price,* of the asset, P_m, in Figure 6-2.

The market price of an asset is the value placed on the asset by the *marginally satisfied buyer and seller* who exchange assets in the marketplace. A marginally satisfied buyer is one who paid his or her maximum acceptable price for the asset, and a marginally satisfied seller is one who received his or her minimum acceptable price for the asset. Clearly, many owners (potential sellers) will place a higher value on the asset than the current market price; likewise, many investors (potential buyers) will place a lower value on the asset than the current market price.

Market equilibrium exists whenever there is no tendency for the price of the asset to move higher or lower. At this point the *expected* rate of return on the asset is equal to the marginal investor's *required* rate of return. *Market disequilibrium* occurs when investors' required rates of return, i, and/or the expected returns, R_t, from the asset change. The market price adjusts over time—that is, it moves upward or downward—to reflect changing conditions, and a new market equilibrium is established.

Most financial assets are bought and sold in organized markets. The bonds, preferred stock, and common stock of many small, as well as most medium and large, firms are traded in one or more national or regional exchanges or in the over-the-counter market. Because large numbers of competing

---

[9] Recall that risk was defined in Chapter 2 as the possibility that actual future returns will deviate from expected returns.

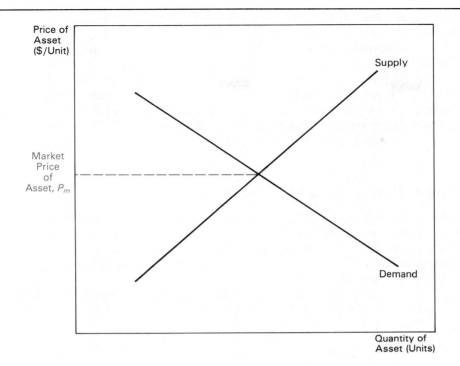

FIGURE 6-2

Market Price of an Asset

buyers and sellers operate in the markets, the market price of a security represents a *consensus* judgment as to the security's value or worth. Although no such market-determined measure of value exists for securities of firms that are not publicly traded, their market values can be approximated using the market price of publicly traded securities of firms having similar operating and financial characteristics.

Book Value of an Asset

The book value of an asset represents the *accounting* value, or the historic acquisition cost minus any accumulated depreciation or other write-offs. Because market value normally is related to expected future returns and book value is based on historic cost, the market value of an asset does not necessarily bear any relationship to the book value. In fact, the market value may be either greater or less than the book value, depending on the changes over time in the market capitalization rate and the asset's expected future returns. For example, prior to the takeover attempt by an investment group headed by T. Boone Pickens in 1983, Gulf Oil common stock was selling for less than $40 per share, which was less than two-thirds of its book value of approximately $60 per share. When the takeover battle ended in early 1984, Chevron (Standard Oil of California) agreed to purchase all of the common stock of Gulf Oil for $80 per share ($13.2 billion), or one and one-third times its book value.

▬ BOND VALUATION

The valuation of bonds is a relatively straightforward process, because future cash returns to the bondholder always are specified ahead of time in a contract. The firm issuing the bonds must meet the interest and principal payments as they come due, or the bonds will go into default. Defaulting on bond payments can have disastrous consequences for the firm and its stockholders, such as possible bankruptcy, reorganization, or both.

Due to default risk, investors normally require a higher rate of return than the risk-free rate before agreeing to hold a firm's bonds. The required rate of return varies among bond issues of different firms, depending on their relative risks of default. All other things being equal, the greater the default risk on a given bond issue, the higher the required rate of return.

Bonds Having Finite Maturity Dates

Bonds that mature within finite periods of time pay the investor two types of returns: interest payments $(I_1, I_2, \ldots, I_n)$ during each of the next n periods and a principal payment (M) in period n. Period n is defined as the bond's *maturity date*, or the time at which the principal must be repaid and the bond issue retired.

The value of a bond can be computed by applying the capitalization-of-income method to the series of cash returns:

$$P_0 = \frac{I_1}{(1 + k_d)^1} + \frac{I_2}{(1 + k_d)^2} + \cdots + \frac{I_{n-1}}{(1 + k_d)^{n-1}} + \frac{I_n + M}{(1 + k_d)^n} \quad (6.3)$$

where P_0 is the present value of the bond at time zero, or its purchase date, and k_d is the investor's required rate of return on this particular bond issue.

Because all of the interest payments on a bond normally are equal (that is, $I_1 = I_2 = \ldots = I_{n-1} = I_n = I$), Equation 6.3 can be simplified as follows:

$$P_0 = \sum_{t=1}^{n} \frac{I}{(1 + k_d)^t} + \frac{M}{(1 + k_d)^n} \quad (6.4)$$

The first term in Equation 6.4, $\sum_{t=1}^{n} I/(1 + k_d)^t$, represents the present value of an *annuity* of I per period for n periods; the second term, $M/(1 + k_d)^n$, represents the present value of a *single payment* of M in period n. Equation 6.4 can be further simplified as follows:

$$P_0 = I(\text{PVIFA}_{k_d,n}) + M(\text{PVIF}_{k_d,n}) \quad (6.5)$$

To illustrate the use of Equation 6.5, consider the following example. American Telephone and Telegraph (AT&T) in 1971 issued $500,000,000 of 7 percent debentures (that is, bonds that are not secured by any specific asset) maturing in 2001. The bonds were issued in $1,000 denominations (par value). For purposes of simplifying this example, assume that the bonds mature at the *end* of 2001 and that interest is paid annually at the end of each year.[10]

An investor who wishes to purchase one of these AT&T bonds at the end (December 31) of 1989 and requires an 8 percent rate of return on this

---

[10] This particular bond issue actually matures on February 15, 2001, and pays interest *semiannually* on February 15 and August 15 each year.

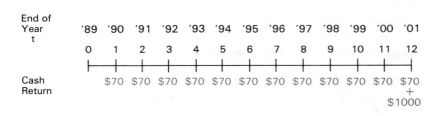

FIGURE 6-3

Cash Returns from an AT&T Bond

particular bond issue would compute the value of the bond as follows.[11] These calculations assume that the investor will hold the bond until maturity and receive twelve annual interest payments of $70 each ($I =$ $1,000 × 0.07) plus a principal payment, M, of $1,000 at the end of the twelfth year, 2001. The cash returns from this bond are shown in Figure 6-3. Substituting these values along with $k_d = 8\%$ (0.08) into Equation 6.4 gives the following value for the bond:[12]

$$P_0 = \sum_{t=1}^{12} \frac{\$70}{(1 + 0.08)^t} + \frac{\$1,000}{(1 + 0.08)^{12}}$$

$$= \$70(\text{PVIFA}_{0.08,12}) + \$1,000(\text{PVIF}_{0.08,12})$$

$$= \$70(7.536) + \$1,000(0.397)$$

$$= \$527.52 + \$397$$

$$= \$924.52(\text{or } \$925)$$

---

[11] A question often arises as to why investors would require an 8 percent rate of return on bonds that pay only 7 percent interest. The answer is that the required rate of return has increased since the bonds originally were issued. At the time of issue, the prevailing rate of interest (that is, the required rate of return) on bonds of this maturity and quality was approximately 7 percent. Hence, the coupon rate was set at 7 percent. Because of such factors as tight credit market conditions, higher inflation, increased firm risk, and so on, investors now require a higher rate of return to induce them to purchase these bonds.

[12] Bond interest normally is paid *semiannually*. With semiannual interest and compounding, the value of this AT&T bond would be calculated as follows:

$$P_0 = \sum_{t=1}^{24} \frac{\$35}{(1 + 0.04)^t} + \frac{\$1,000}{(1 + 0.04)^{24}}$$

$$= \$35(\text{PVIFA}_{0.04,24}) + \$1,000(\text{PVIF}_{0.04,24})$$

$$= \$35(15.247) + \$1,000(0.390)$$

$$= \$533.65 + \$390$$

$$= \$923.65 \text{ (or } \$924)$$

This value differs slightly from the value determined in the example in the text. Note that in the case of semiannual compounding, the annual interest rate is divided by 2(0.08/2 = 0.04), and the number of periods is multiplied by 2(12 × 2 = 24).

It also should be noted that the use of a semiannual discount rate of 4 percent will result in a slightly greater than 8 percent effective annual discount rate. Based on the discussion of "Effective Rate Calculations" in the previous chapter, a semiannual discount rate of (see Equation 5.25):

$$i_2 = (1 + 0.08)^{1/2} - 1$$
$$= 0.03923$$

or 3.923 percent should be used in the bond valuation calculation. However, we will ignore this complication in the remainder of this chapter.

In other words, an investor requiring an 8 percent return on this AT&T bond would be willing to pay approximately $925 for it at the end of 1989.

An investor who desires more than an 8 percent rate of return on this bond would value it at a price less than $925. Similarly, an investor who requires less than 8 percent rate of return would value it at a price greater than $925. This *inverse relationship* between the required rate of return and the corresponding value of a bond to the investor is illustrated for bonds with 3-year and 15-year maturities in Table 6-2 and Figure 6-4. In other words, as the required rate of return increases, the value of the bond decreases, and vice versa.

The relationship between a bond's value and the investor's required rate of return depends on the time remaining before maturity. All other things being equal, the value of a longer-term bond is affected more by changes in required rates of return than the value of a shorter-term bond. As Table 6-2 and Figure 6-4 show, the variation in the value of the 15-year bond is considerably greater than the variation of the 3-year bond over the given range of required rates of return (3 to 11 percent).

Also, as can be seen in Table 6-2, when the required rate of return (prevailing market interest rate) is less than the coupon rate, the bond is valued (sells) at a *premium* over its par value of $1,000. Conversely, when the required rate of return is greater than the coupon rate, the bond is valued at a *discount* under its par value.

Investors who purchase a bond at the price determined by Equation 6.4 and *hold it until maturity* will realize their required rate of return, regardless of any changes in the market price of the bond.[13] However, if the market

[13] This assumes that the investor reinvests all interest received from the bond at a rate equal to the required rate of return on the bond. Otherwise the realized return will differ slightly from the required return.

F I G U R E 6-4

Relationship Between the Value of a Bond and the Required Rate of Return

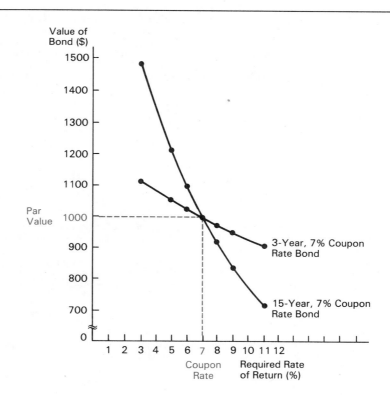

Value of 7 Percent Coupon Rate Bonds at Various Required Rates of Return				TABLE 6-2
Required Rate of Return, k_d	Value of 15-Year Bond	Value of 3-Year Bond	Bond Value Relative to Par Value	
3%	$1,478	$1,113	Premium	
5	1,208	1,055	Premium	
6	1,097	1,027	Premium	
7	1,000	1,000	At Par	
8	914	974	Discount	
9	839	949	Discount	
11	712	902	Discount	

price of the bond declines due to a rise in prevailing interest rates (required rates of return), and if the bond is sold *prior to maturity*, the investors will earn less than their required rate of return and may even incur a loss on the bond. This variation in the market price (and hence in the realized rate of return) of a bond (or any fixed income security) is known as *interest rate risk*.

Perpetual Bonds

A *perpetual bond*, or perpetuity, is a bond issued without a finite maturity date.[14] Perpetual bonds promise to pay interest indefinitely, and there is no contractual obligation to repay the principal; that is, $M = 0$.

The valuation of a perpetual bond is simpler than the valuation of a bond having a finite maturity date. Assuming that the bond pays a fixed amount of interest, I, per period forever, the value is as follows:

$$P_0 = \sum_{t=1}^{\infty} \frac{I}{(1 + k_d)^t} \qquad (6.6)$$

where k_d is the required rate of return. Equation 6.6 can be simplified to obtain the following expression:[15]

$$P_0 = \frac{I}{k_d} \qquad (6.7)$$

---

[14] Perpetual bonds, also referred to as *consuls*, are rare. Some countries, such as Great Britain, and some railroads, such as the Canadian Pacific and the Canadian National, have issued perpetual bonds.

[15] Equation 6.6 is the present value of an infinite series and can be simplified to Equation 6.7 in the following manner. Rewrite Equation 6.6 as follows as follows:

$$P_0 = I\left[\frac{1}{(1 + k_d)^1} + \frac{1}{(1 + k_d)^2} + \frac{1}{(1 + k_d)^3} + \ldots + \frac{1}{(1 + k_d)^n}\right] \qquad (a)$$

Multiply both sides of Equation a by $(1 + k_d)$:

$$P_0(1 + k_d) = I\left[1 + \frac{1}{(1 + k_d)^1} + \frac{1}{(1 + k_d)^2} + \frac{1}{(1 + k_d)^3} + \ldots + \frac{1}{(1 + k_d)^{n-1}}\right] \qquad (b)$$

Subtract Equation a from Equation b:

$$P_0(1 + k_d - 1) = I\left[1 - \frac{1}{(1 + k_d)^n}\right] \qquad (c)$$

(Continued on next page)

Consider, for example, the Canadian Pacific Limited Railroad's perpetual 4 percent debentures. What is the value of a $1,000 bond to an investor who requires an 8 percent rate of return on these Canadian Pacific bonds? Because $I = 0.04 \times \$1,000$, or $40, and $k_d = 8\%$, Equation 6.7 can be used to compute the answer as follows:

$$P_0 = \frac{\$40}{0.08}$$

$$= \$500$$

Thus, the investor would be willing to pay up to $500 for this bond.

Yield to Maturity of a Bond

The *yield to maturity* of a bond is the discount rate that equates the present value of all expected interest payments and the repayment of principal from a bond with the present bond price.[16] If the current price of a bond, P_0, the uniform annual interest payments, I, and the maturity value, or principal, M, are known, the yield to maturity of a bond having a finite maturity date can be calculated by solving Equation 6.4 presented earlier for k_d:

$$P_0 = \sum_{t=1}^{n} \frac{I}{(1 + k_d)^t} + \frac{M}{(1 + k_d)^n}$$

Given values for any three of the four variables in this equation, one can solve for the value of the fourth variable. In the bond valuation calculation illustrated earlier in this section, this equation was used to determine the value of a bond (P_0) when the value of k_d is known (along with the values of I and M). In the yield to maturity calculation, which follows, the equation is used to determine k_d when the value of P_0 is known (along with the values of I and M).[17]

The yield to maturity can be used to compare the risk of two or more bonds that are similar *in all other respects*, including time to maturity. The bond with the higher yield to maturity is the one perceived to be the riskier by investors. Also, the yield to maturity on existing bonds can be used as an estimate of the required returns of investors on any new (and similar) bonds the firm may issue.

---

[15]*Continued* As $n \to \infty$ then $1/(1 + k_d)^n \to 0$ and Equation c approaches the following:

$$P_0(k_d) = I \qquad \text{(d)}$$

or

$$P_0 = \frac{I}{k_d} \quad \text{(Equation 6.7)}$$

[16] In contrast, the *current yield* on a bond having a finite maturity date is defined as the annual interest payment, I, divided by the current price, P_0. The yield to maturity calculation assumes that cash flows from the bond occuring prior to maturity are reinvested at a rate equal to the yield to maturity.

[17] For bonds with a call feature, one also can compute the expected *yield to call*. This is done by replacing the maturity value (M) by the call price and the number of years until maturity (n) by the number of years until the company can call the bond. If present interest rates are significantly below the coupon rate on the (callable) bond, then it is likely that the bond will be called in the future. In such a case, the relevant expected rate of return on the bond is the yield to call rather than the yield to maturity.

There are a number of ways to compute the yield to maturity for a bond. First, special bond tables can be used to directly identify the yield to maturity for any particular bond. Also, many financial calculators currently available are capable of computing yields to maturity. In the absence of these aids it is necessary to use the "trial-and-error" approach in conjunction with the present value tables found at the end of the text.

The steps in the trial-and-error procedure are as follows:

Step 1. Make an approximate estimate of the yield to maturity. Note that if the current price (P_0) of the bond is above (below) the maturity value (M) (i.e., if the bond is selling at a premium [discount]), then the trial rate should be less than (greater than) the coupon rate.

Step 2. Use this rate to compute the present value of the bond's cash flows (that is, purchase price, interest payments, and principal payment).

Step 3. Try a *higher* rate if a positive present value results or a *lower* rate if a negative one results.

Step 4. Repeat the process (attempting to "bracket" the yield to maturity) until a rate is found at which the present value of the cash flows is equal to zero.

To illustrate this procedure, consider a Chevron 7 percent debenture that matures in 1996. The par value of this bond is $1,000. As in the AT&T bond example discussed earlier, assume that the Chevron bonds mature at the end of 1996 and that interest is paid annually at the end of each year.[18] Suppose that the Chevron bonds are selling for $877.50 at the end of 1989 (7 years prior to maturity). Determine the bond's yield to maturity.

Table 6-3 illustrates the use of the trial-and-error procedure to calculate the yield to maturity of the Chevron bonds. Because the bond is selling at a discount—that is, less than its $1,000 par value—the yield to maturity is greater than the 7 percent coupon rate. A trial rate of 9 percent results in a present value for the bond's cash flows of $+21.81 as shown in column 4 of Table 6-3. Because this value is positive, a higher rate must be tried. At a rate of 10 percent, as can be seen in column 6 of Table 6-3, the present value of the bond's cash flows is $-23.74. This indicates that the bond's

---

[18] This particular bond issue actually matures on April 1, 1996, and pays interest *semiannually* on April 1 and October 1 each year.

Trial-and-Error Computation of Yield to Maturity for Chevron Bonds

Year (1)	Cash Flow (2)	k_d = 9% Present Value Interest Factor (3)	k_d = 9% Present Value (4) = (3) × (2)	k_d = 10% Present Value Interest Factor (5)	k_d = 10% Present Value (6) = (5) × (2)
0	$ −877.50	1.000*	$−877.50	1.000*	$−877.50
1–7	70.00	5.033†	352.31	4.868†	340.76
7	1,000.00	0.547*	547.00	0.513*	513.00
		Total	$+ 21.81		$− 23.74

* From Table II at the back of the book.
† From Table IV at the back of the book.

yield to maturity is between 9 and 10 percent. A more exact yield to maturity can be computed by means of interpolation:

$$k_d = 9\% + \frac{21.81}{21.81 + 23.74}(10\% - 9\%)$$

$$= 9.5\%$$

Therefore the yield to maturity on this bond is 9.5 percent.[19]

An *approximate* yield to maturity can be calculated by using the following expression:

$$\text{Approximate yield to maturity} = \frac{\text{Annual interest} + \dfrac{\text{Bond discount or premium}}{\text{Years to maturity}}}{\text{Average investment}}$$

or, after substituting the relevant variables into this equation, as

$$\text{Approximate yield to maturity} = \frac{I + (M - P_0)/n}{(P_0 + M)/2} \tag{6.8}$$

If the bond is selling at a discount (premium), then the term $M - P_0$ is positive (negative). Application of this expression can be illustrated using the Chevron bonds discussed earlier. Substituting $I = \$70$, $M = \$1,000$, $P_0 = \$877.50$, and $n = 7$ into Equation 6.8 yields

$$\text{Approximate yield to maturity} = \frac{\$70 + (\$1,000 - \$877.50)/7}{(\$1,000 + \$877.50)/2}$$

$$= 0.093 \text{ or } 9.3\%$$

compared with the more exact value of 9.5% obtained earlier.

ZERO COUPON BONDS. For zero coupon bonds that pay no interest over their life, the only payment to holders is the principal payment at maturity. Therefore it is not necessary to use the trial-and-error approach just discussed in determining the yield to maturity of zero coupon bonds. To illustrate the calculation of the yield to maturity for such a bond, consider the Allied Corporation zero coupon money multiplier notes (discussed earlier) due January 15, 1996. Suppose these bonds (having a par value of $1,000) were purchased for $512.50 on January 15, 1989 (7 years prior to maturity). Determine the yield to maturity on these bonds.

Figure 6-5 shows cash returns from the purchase of an Allied Corporation zero coupon bond. Because there are no interest payments, the yield to maturity equation (Equation 6.4) can be simplified to

$$P_0 = \frac{M}{(1 + k_d)^n}$$

$$= M \, (\text{PVIF}_{k_d,n})$$

---

[19] The yield to maturity equation implicitly assumes that the annual interest payments are reinvested over the remaining life of the bond at the calculated rate, k_d.

Jan. 15	'89	'90	'91	'92	'93	'94	'95	'96
t	0	1	2	3	4	5	6	7
Cash Return	−$512.50 0	0	0	0	0	0	0	+$1000

Substituting $n = 7$, $P_0 = \$512.50$, and $M = \$1,000$ into this expression yields

$$\$512.50 = \$1,000 \, (\text{PVIF}_{k_d,7})$$

$$(\text{PVIF}_{k_d,7}) = 0.513$$

From Table II at the back of the book, we find this present value interest factor in the 7-year row under the 10 percent interest rate column. Hence the yield to maturity (k_d) on this zero-coupon bond is 10 percent.[20]

PERPETUAL BONDS. The rate of return, or yield to maturity, on a *perpetual* bond can be found by solving the perpetual bond valuation equation presented earlier (Equation 6.7) for k_d:

$$P_0 = \frac{I}{k_d}$$

which gives

$$k_d = \frac{I}{P_0} \tag{6.9}$$

It is not necessary to employ the trial-and-error method (or interpolation) to determine the yield for a perpetual bond.

For example, recall the 4 percent Canadian Pacific Limited Railroad debentures described earlier. If the current price of a bond is $640, what is the yield on the bond? Substituting $P_0 = \$640$ and $I = \$40$ (or 4 percent of $1,000) into Equation 6.9 gives the following:

$$k_d = \frac{\$40}{\$640}$$

$$= 0.0625 \text{ (or 6.25 percent)}$$

CHARACTERISTICS OF PREFERRED STOCK

As a source of capital for a firm, preferred stock occupies an intermediate position between long-term debt and common stock. Like common stock, preferred stock is part of the stockholders' equity. Like long-term debt, it is considered a fixed-income security, although preferred stockholders re-

[20] If the interest factor falls between two values in Table II one can interpolate to get a more exact answer.

ceive dividends instead of interest payments. Because the issuing firm often does not promise repayment at a specific date, preferred stock tends to be a more permanent form of financing than long-term debt. Dividends on preferred stock, like interest payments on long-term debt, normally remain constant over time.

The popularity of preferred stock financing has declined in recent decades. Dividends cannot be deducted from income for corporate income tax purposes, whereas interest payments are tax deductible. This means that for a company paying more than one-third of its income in taxes, the after-tax cost of preferred stock is greater than that of long-term debt, assuming that the pretax preferred stock and long-term debt rates are about the same and that the company makes no change in its capital structure.[21]

Preferred stock bears its name because it usually has preference, or priority, over common stock with regard to the company's dividends and assets. For example, if a company's earnings in a given year are insufficient to pay dividends on preferred stock, the company is not permitted to pay dividends on its common stock. In the event of a liquidation following bankruptcy, the claims on the firm's assets by preferred stockholders are subordinate to those of creditors but have priority over those of common stockholders.

Features of Preferred Stock

Like long-term debt, preferred stock has its own unique distinguishing characteristics. A number are discussed here.

SELLING PRICE AND PAR VALUE. The selling price, or issue price, is the per-share price at which preferred stock shares are sold to the public. Preferred stocks typically are issued at prices of $25, $50, or $100 per share.

The par value is the value assigned to the stock by the issuing company, and it is frequently the same as the initial selling price. No relationship necessarily exists between the two, however. A preferred stock sold at $25 per share may have a $25 par value, $1 par value, or no par value at all. Regardless of what a preferred stock's actual par value is, however, the preferred stockholders are entitled to their issue price plus dividends in the event of liquidation after the claims of creditors have been paid in full.

Preferred stock usually is designated by its dividend amount rather than its dividend percentage. For example, suppose Intermountain Power Company has a series of preferred stock that pays an annual dividend of $2.20, has a $1 par value, and was initially sold to the public at $25 per share. An investor would most likely refer to the stock as "Intermountain Power's $2.20 preferred."

ADJUSTABLE RATE PREFERRED STOCK. This type of preferred stock became popular in 1982. With these issues, dividends are reset periodically and offer returns that vary with interest rates. For example, USX issued

[21] For a given company at a particular time, preferred stock often will cost slightly more than long-term debt, even on a pretax basis, because investors require a higher return to compensate them for the greater risk involved with preferred stock. (See Chapter 12 for a further discussion of this topic.) In contrast, preferred dividends received by corporate investors qualify for a 70 percent intercompany dividend exclusion, whereas interest income does not. Thus, a preferred stock offering that largely is purchased by other corporations may have a lower yield than similar debt offerings. The 1986 tax reform bill made preferred stock financing more appealing because of the lower marginal corporate tax rate.

$200 million of adjustable rate preferred stock on August 25, 1982 with an initial dividend rate of 13.50 percent per annum until December 31, 1982. The quarterly rate thereafter (determined in advance) is to be the "applicable rate." The "applicable rate" is equal to 0.35 percentage points plus the *highest* of (a) the 3-month U.S. Treasury bill rate, (b) the U.S. Treasury 10-year constant maturity rate, and (c) the 20-year constant maturity rate. However, the "applicable rate" for any dividend period is not to be less than 7½ percent nor greater than 15¾ percent.

CUMULATIVE FEATURE. Most preferred stock is cumulative. This means that if, for some reason, a firm fails to pay its preferred dividend, it cannot pay dividends on its common stock until it has satisfied all or a prespecified amount of preferred dividends in arrears. The principal reason for this feature is that investors generally are unwilling to purchase preferred stock that is not cumulative.

PARTICIPATION. Stock is said to be *participating* if the holders share in any increased earnings the company might experience. Virtually all preferred stock, however, is *nonparticipating;* that is, the preferred dividend remains constant, even if the company's earnings increase. Any dividend increases resulting from higher earnings accrue directly to the common stockholders.

MATURITY. Preferred stock technically is part of a firm's equity capital. As such, some firms issue preferred stock that is intended to be *perpetual,* that is, a permanent portion of the stockholders' equity having no specific maturity date. Many preferred stock investors, however, desire sinking fund provisions, which guarantee that the issue will be retired over a specified time period.

CALL FEATURE. Like long-term debt, preferred stock sometimes can be redeemed, or *called,* at the issuing firm's option at some specified price. For example, Xerox issued, at $50 per share, $75 million of $4.125, 20-year sinking fund preferred stock on February 1, 1988. The issue is callable (deferred call) beginning on April 1, 1994 at $54.1250. The call price drops to $53.7125 on April 1, 1995. Similar reductions in the call price occur until 2004 when the call price drops to $50.

Whereas the call feature allows the issuing company a measure of flexibility in its financing plans, the call feature generally is not attractive to investors. Thus, a firm usually must also provide investors with a *call premium,* or the difference between the call price and the original selling price, should it decide to attach a call feature to its preferred stock.

The probability that a firm will exercise the call privilege is likely to increase during times when market interest rates have decreased below those that existed at the time of issue. After calling the original issue, the firm can replace it with a lower cost issue.

VOTING RIGHTS. As a general rule, preferred stockholders are not entitled to vote for the company's board of directors. However, special voting procedures frequently take effect if the company omits its preferred dividends or incurs losses for a period of time. In such a case, the preferred stockholders often vote as a separate group to elect one or more members of the company's board of directors. This ensures that the preferred holders will have direct representation on the board.

Trading of Preferred Shares

Following the initial sale of preferred stock by a firm, investors who purchase the shares may decide to sell them in the secondary markets. Large issues of actively traded preferred stock are listed on the major stock exchanges, such as the New York and the American stock exchanges. However, a majority of preferred stock issues are traded rather thinly, and these are traded over-the-counter.

Users of Preferred Stock

Utility companies are the most frequent users of preferred stock financing, largely because of the regulatory treatment of preferred stock dividend payments. Utilities are permitted by their regulatory agencies to consider preferred dividends as an expense for rate-making purposes, thus reducing the after-tax cost disadvantage of preferred stock that deters non-utility firms from making extensive use of this form of financing.

Within the last 25 years or so, preferred stock (usually convertible) has been used rather widely in mergers and acquisitions. Frequently, acquiring companies issue preferred stock in exchange for the common stock of acquired companies. For example, Chrysler issued (convertible) preferred stock in August 1987 when it acquired American Motors. This, in effect, is another example of financial leverage, and it can cause an increase in the earnings per common share of the acquiring company.[22]

Other occasional users of preferred stock financing are capital-intensive companies undertaking expansion programs. These companies may choose preferred stock as a means of securing long-term financing for the following reasons:

- Their capital structures and various other restrictions prevent the judicious use of additional long-term debt.
- Depressed common stock prices and the potential dilution of per-share earnings may cause them to decide against external common equity financing.

Often these same companies have relatively low marginal tax rates (because of losses and accelerated depreciation) that make the after-tax cost of preferred stock not appreciably different from that of long-term debt. For example, USX (formerly U.S. Steel) and Navistar (formerly International Harvester) have issued preferred stock during the past decade.

Large commercial banks were another group of preferred stock users during the 1980s. These banks, including BankAmerica, Chase Manhattan, and Manufacturers Hanover, issued variable-rate preferred stock, partly to get additional equity into their capital structures.

---

[22] Chapter 22 contains a more detailed discussion of the use of preferred stock in mergers.

Advantages and Disadvantages of Preferred Stock Financing

From the issuing company's perspective, the principal advantage of preferred stock is that preferred dividend payments are potentially flexible. Omitting a preferred dividend in difficult times usually results in less severe consequences than omitting an interest payment on long-term debt.

In addition, preferred stock financing can increase a firm's degree of financial leverage. However, financial analysts may regard the issuance of preferred stock as equivalent to debt. In this case, the company is viewed as having used up a portion of its "debt capacity." Or, in effect, the company has leveraged with preferred stock rather than long-term debt—at a greater after-tax cost.

From the investors' perspective, companies who purchase the preferred stock of other companies accrue certain tax advantages resulting from the 70 percent exclusion of intercompany dividends from federal income taxes. For example, an insurance company in the 34 percent tax bracket can invest in the preferred stock of another company and pay taxes equal to only about 10.2 percent of the preferred dividend income.[23] In contrast, the same insurance company would be required to include all the interest received in its taxable income.

The principal disadvantage of preferred stock financing is its high after-tax cost as compared with long-term debt, because dividends cannot be deducted for income tax purposes. This means that the after-tax cost to the firm for preferred stock is greater than the after-tax cost of long-term debt, assuming that the firm's capital structure remains constant. As a result, most companies considering long-term financing with fixed-income securities choose long-term debt over preferred stock. A complete discussion of the cost of debt and preferred stock is in Chapter 12.

VALUATION OF PREFERRED STOCK

Most preferred stock pays regular, fixed dividends. Preferred dividends per share are normally not increased when the earnings of a firm increase, nor are they cut or suspended unless the firm faces serious financial problems. If preferred stock dividends are cut or suspended for a period of time for whatever reason, the firm usually is required to make up the past due payments before paying any common stock dividends. Thus, the investor's expected cash return from holding most preferred stocks can be treated as a fixed, constant amount per period.

The investor's required rate of return on a preferred stock issue is a function of the risk that the firm will be unable to meet its dividend payments. The higher the risk, the higher the required rate of return. Because bondholders have a prior claim over preferred stockholders on the income and assets of a firm, it is more risky to hold a firm's preferred stock than to hold its bonds. As a result, investors normally require a higher rate of return on preferred stock than on bonds.

Because many preferred stock issues do not have maturity dates, the cash returns (dividend payments) from holding no-maturity preferred stock can be treated as a perpetual stream of payments, or a *perpetuity*. Capitalizing

[23] This 10.2 percent figure is calculated by multiplying the portion of dividends that is subject to taxes, namely, 30 percent, by 34 percent.

the perpetual stream of dividend payments gives the following valuation expression:

$$P_0 = \sum_{t=1}^{\infty} \frac{D_p}{(1 + k_p)^t} \tag{6.10}$$

where D_p is the dividend per period, and k_p is the investor's required rate of return.[24]

Equation 6.10 is similar to Equation 6.7 for a perpetual bond. Like the perpetual bond valuation model, this equation can be simplified into the following valuation model:

$$P_0 = \frac{D_p}{k_p} \tag{6.11}$$

To illustrate the use of Equation 6.11, assume that Gulf and Western pays annual end-of-year dividends on a $5.75 cumulative preferred stock issue. What is the value of this stock to an investor who requires a 9 percent rate of return on the investment? Substituting $5.75 for D_p and 0.09 for k_p yields the following:

$$P_0 = \frac{\$5.75}{0.09}$$

$$= \$63.89$$

SUMMARY

- The value of a long-term security is based on the *expected future returns* the owner will receive in the period during which the asset is held.
- The *capitalization-of-income* method of valuation can be used to determine the value of a security to an investor. This involves calculating the present value of the stream of expected future returns discounted at the investor's required rate of return. The required rate of return is a function of the *risk* associated with the returns from the asset, as well as the risk-free rate.
- The *market price* of a security represents the value placed on it by marginally satisfied buyers and sellers.
- Long-term debt and preferred stock are classified as *fixed-income securities*, because interest (on long-term debt) and dividends (on preferred stock) tend to remain constant over time. Common stock, on the other hand, is a *variable-income security*, because the dividends paid on common stock tend to fluctuate over time.
- Long-term debt generally is classified according to whether or not it is *secured* by specific physical assets of the issuing company. Secured debt issues are *mortgage bonds*, whereas debt issues backed only by unmortgaged assets and the company's earning power are *debentures*.
- Long-term debt usually has the following features:
  1. The *indenture*, or the contract between the issuing company and the debtholders.

---

[24] If an investor is considering purchasing a preferred stock issue that is expected to be called in the future, its value is calculated by capitalizing (that is, discounting) the call price plus the dividend payments to be received before the issue is called.

2. The *trustee*, who represents the debtholders in dealings with the company.
3. The *call feature*, which gives the issuing company the option to retire the debt prior to maturity.
4. The *sinking fund requirement*, which, in practice, means the company must gradually reduce the outstanding balance of the debt issue over its life.

■ Bond *refunding* occurs when a company redeems a callable issue and sells a lower cost issue to take its place.
■ The value of a *perpetual bond* is equal to the interest payment divided by the investor's required rate of return.
■ The major disadvantage of long-term debt financing is the increased financial risk of the firm.
■ The value of a *bond having a finite maturity date* is equal to the present value of the stream of interest and principal payments discounted at the investor's required rate of return.
■ The value of a *perpetual bond* is equal to the interest payment divided by the investor's required rate of return.
■ The *yield to maturity* on a bond is the rate of return the investor expects to earn if the bond is purchased at a given price and held until maturity.
■ Preferred stock occupies an intermediate position between long-term debt and common stock as a source of capital. Like common stock, preferred stock is part of the stockholders' equity, and preferred stockholders receive returns in the form of dividends. Preferred stock is also similar to long-term debt in that preferred dividends, like the interest on long-term debt, usually remain constant over time.
■ Preferred stock usually has the following features:
1. The *selling price*, or *issue price*, is the per-share price at which the shares are sold to the public.
2. The *par value* is an arbitrary value assigned to the stock by the issuing company.
3. Most preferred stock is *cumulative;* that is, dividends on common stock cannot be paid as long as any past or present preferred dividends remain unpaid.
4. Virtually all preferred stock is *nonparticipating;* that is, preferred stock does not share in any increased earnings of the firm.
5. Some preferred stock is *perpetual*, whereas other preferred stock is gradually retired by the firm.
6. Preferred stock often is *callable*.

■ From the issuing company's perspective, preferred stock financing is advantageous due to the potential flexibility of preferred dividend payments.
■ The principal disadvantage of preferred stock financing is that dividends are not tax deductible, which causes the after-tax cost of preferred stock to the firm to be higher than the cost of long-term debt, all other things being equal.
■ The returns from most *preferred stocks* can be treated as perpetuities. Therefore, the value of a preferred stock is equal to the annual preferred dividend divided by the investor's required rate of return.

QUESTIONS AND TOPICS FOR DISCUSSION

1. Define the following terms associated with long-term debt:

   a. Indenture.
   b. Trustee.
   c. Call feature.
   d. Sinking fund.
   e. Conversion feature.
   f. Coupon rate.

2. Describe the basic features of each of the following types of bonds:

   a. Mortgage bonds.
   b. Debentures.
   c. Subordinated debentures.
   d. Equipment trust certificates.
   e. Collateral trust bonds.
   f. Income bonds.

3. Suppose a company simultaneously sold two long-term debt issues at par: 9⅛ percent senior debentures and 9⅜ percent senior subordinated debentures. What risk-return tradeoff would an investor face who was considering one of these issues?

4. What is the relationship between par value, market value, and book value for the following?

   a. Long-term debt.
   b. Preferred stock.

5. Define the following terms associated with preferred stock:

   a. Cumulative feature.
   b. Participation.
   c. Call feature.

6. What variables must be known (or estimated) in applying the capitalization-of-income method of valuation to a physical or financial asset?

7. Define the following:

   a. The market value of an asset.
   b. Market equilibrium.

8. What is the primary difference between the book value and the market value of an asset?

9. Describe the relationship between the coupon rate and the required rate of return that will result in a bond selling at

   a. a discount.
   b. par value.
   c. a premium.

10. How does the yield to maturity on a bond differ from the coupon yield or current yield?

11. Under what conditions will a bond's current yield be equal to its yield to maturity.

12. In what ways is preferred stock similar to long-term debt? In what ways is it similar to common stock?

13. Explain why bondholders often prefer a sinking fund provision in a bond issue.

14. Explain what is meant by *interest rate risk*.

15. Explain how a bond can be classified as a fixed-income security when the yield to maturity can fluctuate significantly over time, depending on the market price of the bond.

16. Describe the basic features of each of the following types of bonds:
    a. Floating-rate bonds.
    b. Original issue deep discount bonds.
    c. Zero coupon bonds.
    d. Extendable notes (put bonds).

PROBLEMS*

1. Determine the value of a $1,000 Canadian Pacific Limited perpetual 4 percent debenture (bond) at the following required rates of return:
   a. 4 percent.
   b. 5 percent.
   c. 6 percent.

2. Canadian Pacific Limited's debentures (see Problem 1) are traded on the New York Exchange. During 1988 the high and low market prices of these bonds were $457.50 and $398.75, respectively. Determine the yield to maturity of one of these debentures if it was purchased under the following conditions:
   a. At the high 1988 market price.
   b. At the low 1988 market price.

3. Consider Allied Signal Corporation's 9⅞ percent bonds that mature on June 1, 2002. Assume that the interest on these bonds is paid and compounded annually. Determine the value of a $1,000 denomination Allied Signal Corporation bond as of June 1, 1990, to an investor who holds the bond until maturity and whose required rate of return is
   a. 7 percent.
   b. 9 percent.
   c. 11 percent.
   d. What would be the value of the Allied Signal Corporation bonds at an 8 percent required rate of return if the interest were paid and compounded *semiannually*?

handwritten:
k = market interest rate
m = par value
I = coupon value
V = value of the bond
n = number of years in maturity

$V = I(PVIFA\ k\%, n) + M(PVIFK\%\ n)$

a. $98.75 \times n.943 + 1000 \times 0.444 = 1228.37$
b. $98.75 \times n.161 + 1000 \times 0.356 = 1,063$
c. $98.75 \times 6.492 + 1000 \times 0.286 = 924$

$98.75 \div 2 = 49.375$ $V = 49.375 \times 15.247 + 1,000 \times 0.39 = 1142.8$

4. Creative Financing, Inc., is planning to offer a $1,000 par value 15-year maturity bond with a coupon interest rate that changes every 5 years. The coupon rate for the first 5 years is 10 percent, 10.75 percent for the next 5 years, and 11.5 percent for the final 5 years. If you require an 11 percent rate of return on a bond of this quality and maturity, what is the maximum price you would pay for the bond? (Assume interest is paid annually at the end of each year.)

5. Public Service Electric and Gas has issued 12 percent bonds that mature at the end of 2004. Assume that interest is paid and compounded annually.
   a. Determine the *exact* yield to maturity (to the nearest tenth of 1 percent) by the trial-and-error method if an investor purchases a $1,000 denomination bond for $1,040 at the end of 1989.

handwritten: $V = 120(PVIFA\ 11\%, 15) + 1,000(PVIF\ 11\%, 15)$
$= 1071.92$
$11\% < yield\ to\ maturity < 12\%$

   b. Determine the *approximate* yield to maturity on the Public Service Electric and Gas bonds. How does the approximate yield compare with the exact yield?

handwritten: $YTM = \dfrac{I + \left(\frac{m-V}{n}\right)}{\frac{m+V}{2}} = \dfrac{120 + \frac{(1000-1040)}{15}}{1020}$

6. American Telephone & Telegraph has issued 7⅛ percent debentures that will mature on December 1, 2003. Assume that interest is paid and compounded annually. If an investor purchases a $1,000 denomination bond for $806.25 on December 1, 1988, determine the following:
   a. The bond's *exact* yield to maturity (to the nearest tenth of 1 percent) using the trial-and-error method.

* Colored numbers denote problems that have check answers provided at the end of the book.

b. The bond's *approximate* yield to maturity.

7. Consider the Allied Corporation zero coupon bonds of 1998. The bonds were issued in 1982 for $125. Determine the yield-to-maturity (to the nearest tenth of 1 percent) if the bonds are purchased at the

    a. Issue price in 1982. (NOTE: To avoid a fractional year holding period, assume that the issue and maturity dates are at the mid-point—July 1— of the respective years).

    b. Market price as of July 1, 1988—$390.

    c. Explain why the returns calculated in Parts a and b are different.

8. If you purchase a zero-coupon bond today for $225 and it matures at $1,000 in 11 years, what rate of return will you earn on that bond (to the nearest tenth of 1 percent)? $1000 = 225(1+K)^{11}$ $(1+K)^{11} = 4.444$ $1+K = \sqrt[11]{4.444}$ $K = 0.1452 = 14.5\%$

9. In 1985 Chrysler issued 13 percent debentures that will mature on March 1, 1997.

    a. If an investor purchases one of these bonds ($1,000 denomination) on March 1, 1989, for $1105, determine the exact yield to maturity (to the nearest tenth of 1 percent). Explain why an investor would be willing to pay $1105 in 1989 for one of these bonds when he or she is going to receive only $1,000 when the bond matures in 1997.

    b. The Chrysler 13 percent debentures are callable by the company any time on or after March 1, 1995, at $1,000. Determine the *yield to call* (see Footnote 17) as of March 1, 1989, assuming that Chrysler calls the bonds on March 1, 1995.

10. What is the value of a share of Litton Industries Series B $2.00 cumulative preferred stock to an investor who requires the following rates of return?

    a. 9 percent

    b. 10 percent

    c. 12 percent

11. Determine the value of a share of Baltimore Gas and Electric 4½ percent cumulative preferred stock, series B, par value $100 to an investor who requires a 9 percent rate of return on this security.

SELECTED REFERENCES

Babcock, Guilford C. "Duration as the Link between Yield and Value." *Journal of Portfolio Management* (Summer 1984): 58–65.

Drexel Burnham Lambert. *1989 High Yield Market Report: Financing America's Future.* Beverly Hills, CA: Drexel Burnham Lambert, 1989.

Dunn, Kenneth B., and Chester S. Spatt. "A Strategic Analysis of Sinking Fund Bonds." *Journal of Financial Economics* 13 (September 1984): 399–424.

Emanuel, David. "A Theoretical Model for Valuing Preferred Stock." *Journal of Finance* 38 (September 1983): 1133–1156.

Fooladi, Iraj, and Gordon S. Roberts. "On Preferred Stock." *Journal of Financial Research* 9 (Winter 1986): 319–324.

Francis, Jack C. *Investments: Analysis and Management,* 5th ed. New York: McGraw-Hill, 1986.

Ho, Thomas, and Ronald F. Singer. "Bond Indenture Provisions and the Risk of Corporate Debt." *Journal of Financial Economics* 10 (December 1982): 375–406.

Rodriguez, Ricardo J. "Default Risk, Yield Spreads, and Time to Maturity." *Journal of Financial and Quantitative Analysis* (March 1988): 111–117.

Sharpe, William, F., *Investment Analysis and Portfolio Management,* 3d ed. Englewood Cliffs, NJ: Prentice-Hall, 1980.

Smith, David B. "A Framework for Analyzing Nonconvertible Preferred Stock Risk." *Journal of Financial Research* 6 (Summer 1983); 127–140.

Williams, J. B. *The Theory of Investment Value*. Cambridge, MA: Harvard University Press, 1938.

7

Characteristics and Valuation of Common Stock

KEY CHAPTER CONCEPTS

1. The characteristics of variable income (common stock) securities, including
   a. Accounting aspects
   b. Stockholder rights
   c. Features
   d. Advantages and disadvantages
2. Common stock valuation
   a. In the general dividend valuation model, the value of a common stock is equal to the present value of all future dividend payments discounted at the investor's required rate of return.
   b. In the constant growth dividend valuation model, the value of a common stock is equal to the next period's dividend divided by the difference between the investor's required rate of return and the dividend growth rate.
3. The valuation of small firm stock requires an explicit consideration of the marketability of that stock, whether the stock represents minority or majority ownership, and whether the stock is voting or nonvoting.
4. Other important topics include
   a. Zero growth dividend valuation model
   b. Above-normal dividend growth valuation model

GLOSSARY OF NEW TERMS

Book value (per share) The total book value of the company (that is, net worth) divided by the total number of shares of common stock outstanding.

Capital gains yield The expected percentage increase in the price of the stock.

Capitalization of income A method of determining the present value of an asset that is expected to produce a stream of future benefits. This involves *discounting* the stream of expected future benefits at an appropriate rate.

Dividend yield The annual dividend payment divided by the price of the stock.

Par value (common stock) An arbitrary value assigned to common stock by the issuing firm.

Perpetuity A financial instrument that agrees to pay an equal cash flow per period into the indefinite future (that is, infinity).

Preemptive right A provision contained in some corporate charters that gives common stockholders the right to buy on a pro rata basis any new common shares sold by the firm.

Required rate of return The rate used to value a stream of future benefits from an asset (also called the *discount rate*). The riskier the return from an asset, the higher is the required rate of return.

Right A short-term option issued by a firm that permits an existing stockholder to buy a specified number of shares of common stock at a specified price (the subscription price), which is below the current market price.

Shareholder wealth Present value of the expected future returns to the owners (that is, shareholders) of the firm. It is measured by the market value of the shareholders' common stock holdings.

Stock dividend A payment of additional shares of common stock to stockholders.

Stockholders' (common) equity The total of a firm's common stock, at par, contributed capital in excess of par, and retained earnings accounts from the balance sheet. It is sometimes called the *book value* of the firm, *owners' equity*, or *net worth*.

Stock split The issuance of a number of new shares in exchange for each old share held by a stockholder.

Treasury stock Common stock that has been reacquired by the issuing company.

Valuation of RJR Nabisco Stock*

In October 1988 RJR Nabisco became the target of a leveraged buyout by a management group led by its president and chief executive officer, F. Ross Johnson. (In a leveraged buyout transaction, the buyer of a company borrows a large portion of the purchase price, using the purchased assets as collateral for the loan.)[1] He proposed buying the publicly owned tobacco and food company for about $75 per share or $17.6 billion. After the announcement, RJR Nabisco's common stock price increased $21.375 per share to $77.50. This price was above the proposed offer of $75 because many stock market analysts thought that the company's true value was in excess of $100 per share and that additional bidders might make higher offers for the company. Shortly after Johnson made his offer, Kohlberg Kravis Roberts & Co. (KKR), an investment firm engaged in buying other companies, offered $90 per share or $20.6 billion. After additional bidding by these two groups (as well as by another group led by the investment banking firm of First Boston Corporation), the RJR Nabisco board of directors accepted a $25.07 billion or $109 per share offer from KKR. The offer consisted of

- $81 per share in cash
- $18 per share in preferred stock
- $10 per share in debentures (bonds), convertible into a total of about 25 percent of

the acquiring company's equity. (A convertible bond is a security that may be exchanged for a firm's common stock at the holder's option.)[2]

It represented the largest corporate takeover in history.

At the time of the proposed takeover, the book value of the company was about $24 per share. The estimated breakup, or sale, value of RJR Nabisco's businesses was $24.6 billion to $26.1 billion—consisting of $12.5 billion to $13.0 billion for its tobacco operations (e.g., Camel, Winston, Salem, etc.) and $12.1 billion to $13.1 billion for its food operations (e.g., Nabisco cookies and crackers, Del Monte canned fruit and vegetables, Shredded Wheat and Cream of Wheat cereals, Planters Peanuts, Life Savers, etc.).

This buyout, as well as many other large restructurings over the past several years, has raised a number of interesting valuation questions. For example, why was RJR Nabisco stock selling before the takeover for about one-half the eventual price paid by KKR? Why was KKR willing to pay over four times the company's book value in order to gain control? Methods used in the valuation of common stock are discussed in this chapter.

---

* Based on articles in *the Wall Street Journal* (October 25, 1988 and December 2, 1988).
[1] See Chapter 22 for a further discussion of these transactions.
[2] See Chapter 16 for a further discussion of convertible securities.

INTRODUCTION

Unlike long-term debt and preferred stock, which are normally fixed-income securities, common stock is a variable-income security. Common stockholders are said to participate in a firm's earnings, because they may receive a larger dividend if earnings increase in the future, or their dividends may be cut if earnings drop. For example, in 1974 Tucson Electric Power Company sold new common stock when annual dividends were $0.84 per share. By 1988 the annual rate was $3.60 per share, having been raised several times during the intervening years.

Common stock also differs from long-term debt and preferred stock in that the market price tends to fluctuate more than the price of bonds and preferred stock, thus causing returns on common stock investments to vary more widely over time than returns on long-term debt or preferred stock.

This chapter describes the various characteristics of common stock and develops various models that can be used in the valuation of these securities.

■■■■ **CHARACTERISTICS OF COMMON STOCK**

■■■ 227 ■■■

CHAPTER 7
Characteristics and
Valuation of
Common Stock

A firm's common stockholders are its true owners. Common stock is a *residual form of ownership* in that the claims of common stockholders on the firm's earnings and assets are considered only *after* the claims of governments, debtholders, and preferred stockholders have been met. Common stock is considered a *permanent* form of long-term financing, because, unlike debt and some preferred stock, common stock has no maturity date.

Common Stock and Accounting

Common stock appears on the right-hand side of a firm's balance sheet as part of the stockholders' equity. This is shown for the Lawrence Company in Table 7-1.

Stockholders' equity includes both preferred stock (if any exists) and common stock. The total equity attributable to the common stock of the Lawrence Company is equal to the total stockholders' equity less the preferred stock:

$$\$117,820,000 - \$37,500,000 = \$80,320,000$$

In other words, the sum of the common stock account, contributed capital in excess of par value account, and retained earnings account equals the total common stockholders' equity.

The *book value* per share of common stock is calculated as follows:

$$\text{Book value per share} = \frac{\text{Total common stockholders' equity}}{\text{Number of shares outstanding}} \quad (7.1)$$

In the case of the Lawrence Company,

$$\text{Book value per share} = \frac{\$80,320,000}{6,675,000}$$

$$= \$12.03$$

A common stock's book value is calculated on the basis of balance sheet figures and does not necessarily have any relationship to the common stock's

Lawrence Company Stockholders' Equity, December 31, 19X5 (in thousands of dollars)		TABLE 7-1
Stockholders' Equity		
Preferred stock; $25 par value; authorized, 2,000,000 shares; issued and outstanding, 1,500,000 shares	$ 37,500	
Common stock; $2 par value; authorized, 10,000,000 shares; issued and outstanding, 6,675,000 shares	13,350	
Contributed capital in excess of par value*	28,713	
Retained earnings	38,257	
Total stockholders' equity	$117,820	

* The *contributed capital in excess of par* account has several other frequently used names, including *capital surplus* and *additional paid-in capital*. Many accountants feel that the expression *capital surplus* is misleading, because it implies that the firm has excess capital.

market value, which is based primarily on expectations concerning general economic conditions and the firm's future earnings.

The balance in the common stock account is calculated by multiplying the number of shares actually outstanding by the *par value,* an arbitrary value assigned to shares of common stock.[3] To continue with this example, the Lawrence Company has 6.675 million shares outstanding and a $2 par value, resulting in a balance of $13.35 million.

To illustrate the nature of the contributed capital in excess of par value account, suppose Lawrence decides to raise an additional $12 million in external equity capital by selling 600,000 common shares at $20 each.[4] The amount credited to the common stock account is $1.2 million (600,000 shares times the $2 par value). The remainder of the $12 million is added to the contributed capital in excess of par value account. In other words, this account represents capital that is paid into the firm in excess of the par value when common stock is issued.

Additions to the retained earnings account occur as a result of earnings retained in the business, as opposed to earnings paid out to the stockholders as dividends. Retained earnings, which are internally generated funds, are the most important source of capital for business.

Stockholder Rights

Common stockholders have a number of general rights, including the following:

- **Dividend rights.** Stockholders have the right to share equally on a per-share basis in any distribution of corporate earnings in the form of dividends.
- **Asset rights.** In the event of a liquidation, stockholders have the right to assets that remain after the obligations to the government (taxes), employees, and debtholders have been satisfied.
- **Voting rights.** Stockholders have the right to vote on stockholder matters, such as the selection of the board of directors.
- **Preemptive rights.** Stockholders may have the right to share proportionately in any new stock sold. For example, a stockholder who owns 20 percent of a corporation's stock may be entitled to purchase 20 percent of any new issue.

Whereas all stockholders have dividend and liquidation rights, in addition to voting rights (unless the stock is specifically nonvoting), preemptive rights exist in a relatively small minority of firms at the present time. (Voting rights and preemptive rights are discussed in detail in Appendix 16A.)

Other Features of Common Stock

This subsection covers other topics related to the ownership of common stock, including *common stock classes, stock splits, stock dividends,* and *stock repurchases.*

[3] At one time par value was considered important for any possible liquidation proceedings, but today it has little, if any, real significance. Par value normally is a low figure and tends to be less than $5 per share. Occasionally companies issue stock with no par value. In these instances the balance in the common stock account is a "stated value."

[4] Before sales of the new shares, a reasonable price level might be about $21 or $22 per share. (This example ignores flotation costs.)

COMMON STOCK CLASSES. Occasionally a firm may decide to create more than one class of common stock. The reason for this may be that the firm wishes to raise additional equity capital by selling a portion of the existing owners' stock while maintaining control of the firm. This can be accomplished by creating a separate class of *nonvoting stock*. Typically so-called Class A common stock is nonvoting, whereas Class B has voting rights; normally the classes are otherwise equal. The Ford Motor Company is an example of a large, widely held company that has more than one class of common stock. Ford's 37.7 million shares of "Class B stock" are held entirely by Ford family interests. This class has 40 percent of the total voting power. Ford's 469.8 million shares of "common stock" are held by the public and have 60 percent of the total voting power. The two classes are otherwise equal. In recent years, General Motors created two new classes of common stock—"E" and "H"—which it used in the acquisition of Electronic Data Systems and Hughes Aircraft Company, respectively.

STOCK SPLITS. If management feels that the firm's common stock should sell at a lower price to attract more purchasers, it can effect a *stock split*. There seems to be a general feeling in the finance community that the optimum price range for a share of common stock should be very roughly $15 to $70. Consequently, if a stock rises above this range, management may decide on a stock split to get the price back to a more desirable trading level.

For example, the per-share price of General Motors common stock rose to the $90 range in early 1989, at which time the board of directors declared a two-for-one stock split. Following the split, the stock traded in the $45 range.

Frequently companies choose to raise their dividend levels at the time of a split. Prior to the split, General Motors regular quarterly dividend was $1.25 per share; after the split, the dividend was raised to $0.75 per share, which amounted to $1.50 per share on the presplit shares.

Many investors believe stock splits are an indication of good financial health. The mere splitting of a stock, however, should not be taken in and of itself as evidence that the stock will necessarily perform well in the future.

From an accounting standpoint, when a stock is split, its par value is changed accordingly. For example, when the split is two for one, the par value is reduced by one-half, and the number of shares is doubled. No changes occur in the firm's account balances or capital structure.

REVERSE STOCK SPLITS. Reverse stock splits are stock splits in which the number of shares is decreased. They are used to bring low-priced shares up to more desirable trading levels. For example, assume the management of Ajax Steel, whose stock has dropped to about $4 per share, is concerned that potential investors might be unwilling to buy the stock because of the relatively large percentage commission on low-priced stocks, as well as the stigma that is attached to them. One alternative it might choose is a one-for-five reverse stock split, which could bring the stock price back up to about $20 per share. It should be obvious, however, that the reverse stock split itself will not cure any ills Ajax might be experiencing.

Many investors feel reverse stock splits indicate poor corporate health. For this reason they are relatively uncommon.

STOCK DIVIDENDS. A stock dividend is a dividend to stockholders that consists of additional shares of stock instead of cash. Normally stock dividends are in the 2 to 10 percent range—that is, the number of shares outstanding is increased by 2 to 10 percent. From an accounting (but not a cash flow) standpoint, stock dividends involve a transfer from the retained earnings account to the common stock and additional paid-in capital accounts.[5]

STOCK REPURCHASES. From time to time companies repurchase some of their own shares (known as *treasury stock*). Figure 7-1 contains an announcement of such a share repurchase by TRW. In addition to undertaking share repurchases as part of the firm's dividend decision, which is discussed in Chapter 14, there are a number of other reasons why a firm may decide to repurchase its own stock. These include:

■ **Investment.** Management may feel that the common stock is undervalued, based on its assessment of the future earnings potential of the firm. By repurchasing shares, the company hopes to raise its earnings per share and future stock price. Many companies, such as USX, Honeywell, and RJR Nabisco, announced stock repurchases after the stock market crash in October 1987, feeling that their stock prices had fallen too low.

[5] Chapter 14 contains a more detailed discussion of stock dividends.

FIGURE 7-1

**Share Repurchase
Announcement**

*Morgan Stanley acted as financial advisor to
TRW, Inc. in this transaction.*

TRW Inc.

has repurchased

7,702,471 shares
of Common Stock

as part of a corporate restructuring

- ■ **Financial restructuring.** By issuing debt and using the proceeds to re-purchase its common stock, the firm can alter its capital structure to gain the benefits of increased financial leverage.
- ■ **Future corporate needs.** Stock can be repurchased for use in future ac-quisitions of other companies, stock option plans for executives, con-version of convertible securities, and the exercise of warrants.[6]
- ■ **Disposition of excess cash.** The company may want to dispose of excess cash that it has accumulated from operations or the sale of assets. These funds are expendable because management may not feel that they can be invested profitably within the company in the foreseeable future.
- ■ **Reduction of takeover risk.** Share repurchases can be used to increase the price of a firm's stock and reduce a firm's cash balance (or increase its debt proportion in the capital structure) and thereby reduce returns to investors who might be considering an acquisition of the firm.

These reasons are not mutually exclusive—a firm may repurchase shares for a combination of reasons.

Advantages and Disadvantages of Common Stock Financing

One of the major advantages of common stock financing is that no fixed-dividend obligation exists, at least in principle. In practice, however, div-idend cuts are relatively uncommon for companies paying a "regular" div-idend, a fact that implies that corporate management generally views a firm's current level of dividends as a minimum for the future.[7] Nevertheless, common stock financing does allow firms a greater degree of flexibility in their financing plans than fixed-income securities. Thus, common stock is less risky to the firm than fixed-income securities. Limits on additional debt and the maintenance of working capital levels are only two of the constraints imposed on a firm when fixed-income security financing is employed.

In addition, common stock financing can be advantageous for a firm whose capital structure contains more than an optimal amount of debt. Under these circumstances, common stock financing can lower the firm's weighted cost of capital.[8]

From the investors' perspective, however, common stock is a riskier in-vestment than debt securities or preferred stock. Because of this, investors in common stock require relatively high rates of return, and this means that the firm's cost for common stock financing is high compared with fixed-income securities.

From another perspective, external common stock financing frequently results in an initial dilution of per-share earnings, particularly if the assets acquired with the proceeds of the financing do not produce earnings im-mediately. Table 7-2, which contains figures for Desert Electric Power Com-pany for 19X6 and 19X5, illustrates this point.

Notice that whereas the firm's net income increased in 19X6 over 19X5, its earnings per share declined because of the new shares issued. Thus, the additional issue of common shares can dilute the original owners' claims on the firm's earnings. If, on the other hand, the new assets earn a higher rate of return than the existing assets, the original owners will benefit from

---

[6] Warrants and convertible securities are examined in Chapter 16.
[7] See Chapter 14 for a discussion of dividend policy.
[8] See Chapters 12 and 13 for a discussion of the measurement of, and the effect of capital structure on, the firm's weighted cost of capital.

TABLE 7-2

Example of Diluted Per-Share Earnings as a Result of Common Stock Financing		
	Year Ended September 30	
	19X6	19X5
Net income available for common stock	$25,821,000	$20,673,000
Average number of common shares outstanding	15,600,000	12,122,007
Earnings per average share of common stock	$1.66	$1.71

the increased earnings. Also, the problem of diluted earnings should be only temporary if the firm is investing wisely and should have no adverse consequences in a well-informed market.

A final disadvantage of external equity financing involves the relatively high flotation[9] costs associated with common stock sold to the public.

VALUATION OF COMMON STOCK

In principle, the valuation of common stock is no different from the valuation of other types of securities, such as bonds and preferred stock. The basic procedure involves capitalizing (that is, discounting) the expected stream of returns received from holding the common stock. This is complicated by several factors, however.

First, the returns from holding a common stock take two forms: the cash dividend payments made during the holding period and/or changes in the price of the stock (capital gains or losses) over the holding period. All the returns paid to the common stockholder are derived from the firm's earnings and can either be paid to shareholders in the current period as cash dividends or reinvested in the firm to (it is hoped) provide higher future dividends and a higher stock price.

Second, because common stock dividends normally are expected to grow rather than remain constant, the relatively simple annuity and perpetuity formulas used in the valuation of bonds and preferred stock generally are not applicable, and more complicated models must be used.

Finally, the future returns from common stock usually are much more uncertain than the returns from bonds and preferred stock. Common stock dividend payments are related to the firm's earnings in some manner, and it can be very difficult to forecast future long-term earnings and dividend payments with a high degree of accuracy.

To better understand the application of the capitalization-of-income valuation method to common stock, it is best to begin by considering the *one*-period dividend valuation model and then move on to consider multiple-period valuation models.

One-Period Dividend Valuation Model

Assume that an investor plans to purchase a common stock and hold it for *one* period. At the end of that period, the investor expects to receive a cash dividend, D_1, and sell the stock for a price, P_1. What is the value of this stock

[9] Flotation costs are discussed in detail in Chapter 16.

to the investor *today* (time 0), given a required rate of return on the investment, k_e?

In the capitalization-of-income valuation method, the discounted present value of the returns on the stock is calculated as follows:

$$P_0 = \frac{D_1}{1 + k_e} + \frac{P_1}{1 + k_e} \qquad (7.2)$$

For example, if Ohio Engineering Company common stock is expected to pay a $1.00 dividend and sell for $27.50 at the end of one period, what is the value of this stock to an investor who requires a 14 percent rate of return? The answer is computed as follows:

$$P_0 = \frac{\$1.00}{(1 + 0.14)} + \frac{\$27.50}{(1 + 0.14)}$$

$$= \$1.00(PVIF_{0.14,1}) + \$27.50 \ (PVIF_{0.14,1})$$

$$= \$1.00(0.877) + \$27.50(0.877)$$

$$= \$24.99 \ (\text{or} \ \$25)$$

Thus, the investor who purchases the stock for $25.00, collects the $1.00 dividend, and sells the stock for $27.50 at the end of one period will receive the 14 percent required rate of return.

Two-Period Dividend Valuation Model

Next, consider an investor who plans to purchase a common stock and hold it for *two* periods. The cash returns to the investor consist of cash dividends—D_1 at the end of the first period and D_2 at the end of the second period—and an amount, P_2, from the sale of the stock at the end of the second period. Capitalizing the returns at the investor's required rate of return, k_e, gives the following valuation equation:

$$P_0 = \frac{D_1}{(1 + k_e)^1} + \frac{D_2}{(1 + k_e)^2} + \frac{P_2}{(1 + k_e)^2} \qquad (7.3)$$

Returning to the example of the Ohio Engineering Company, assume that the company is expected to pay common stock dividends of $1.00 at the end of next year and $1.00 at the end of the second year, and that the market price of the stock is expected to be $30.35 two years from now. What is the current value of the stock if the investor requires a 14 percent rate of return? Substituting $1.00 for D_1, $1.00 for D_2, $30.35 for P_2, and 14 percent, or 0.14, for k_e into Equation 7.3 gives the following value for the stock:

$$P_0 = \frac{\$1.00}{(1 + 0.14)^1} + \frac{\$1.00}{(1 + 0.14)^2} + \frac{\$30.35}{(1 + 0.14)^2}$$

$$= \$1.00(PVIF_{0.14,1}) + \$1.00(PVIF_{0.14,2}) + \$30.35(PVIF_{0.14,2})$$

$$= \$1.00(0.877) + \$1.00(0.769) + \$30.35(0.769)$$

$$= \$24.98 \ (\text{or} \ \$25)$$

n-Period Dividend Valuation Model

The dividend valuation process just described can be generalized to the n-period case. The returns to the investor who purchases a share of common stock and holds it for n periods consist of dividend payments during each of the next n periods—$D_1, D_2, \ldots, D_n$—plus an amount, P_n, from the sale of the stock at the end of the nth period. Capitalizing the returns at the investor's required rate of return, k_e, gives the following valuation equation:

$$P_0 = \frac{D_1}{(1 + k_e)^1} + \frac{D_2}{(1 + k_e)^2} + \cdots + \frac{D_n}{(1 + k_e)^n} + \frac{P_n}{(1 + k_e)^n} \qquad \textbf{(7.4)}$$

which can be summarized as

$$P_0 = \sum_{t=1}^{n} \frac{D_t}{(1 + k_e)^t} + \frac{P_n}{(1 + k_e)^n} \qquad \textbf{(7.5)}$$

Consider again the Ohio Engineering Company common stock. Suppose that the investor is considering purchasing a share of this stock and holding it for 5 years. Assume that the investor's required rate of return is still 14 percent. Dividends from the stock are expected to be $1.00 in the first year, $1.00 in the second year, $1.00 in the third year, $1.25 in the fourth year, and $1.25 in the fifth year. The expected selling price of the stock at the end of 5 years is $41.00.

Using Equation 7.5, the value of the stock to the investor is computed as follows:

$$P_0 = \frac{\$1.00}{(1 + 0.14)^1} + \frac{\$1.00}{(1 + 0.14)^2} + \frac{\$1.00}{(1 + 0.14)^3}$$

$$+ \frac{\$1.25}{(1 + 0.14)^4} + \frac{\$1.25}{(1 + 0.14)^5} + \frac{\$41.00}{(1 + 0.14)^5}$$

$$= \$1.00\,(\text{PVIF}_{0.14,1}) + \$1.00(\text{PVIF}_{0.14,2})$$

$$+ \$1.00(\text{PVIF}_{0.14,3}) + \$1.25(\text{PVIF}_{0.14,4})$$

$$+ \$1.25(\text{PVIF}_{0.14,5}) + \$41.00(\text{PVIF}_{0.14,5})$$

$$= \$1.00(0.877) + \$1.00(0.769) + \$1.00(0.675)$$

$$+ \$1.25(0.592) + \$1.25(0.519) + \$41.00(0.519)$$

$$= \$24.99 \ (\text{or } \$25).$$

Note that the *current* value of a share of Ohio Engineering common stock is the same (that is, $P_0 = \$25.00$) regardless of whether the investor plans to hold it for 1, 2, or 5 years.[10]

A General Dividend Valuation Model

In each of the valuation models described, the current value of the stock, P_0, is dependent upon the expected price of the stock at the end of the

---

[10] The value of a stock at *any* point in time is simply the present value of all dividends expected to be paid from that time forward. Hence, the price, P_5, of $41 reflects the present value of dividends expected in years 6 through infinity.

expected holding period—P_1 in the 1-period case, P_2 in the 2-period case, and P_n in the n-period case. Although this seems straightforward, providing accurate forecasts of stock prices when applying the models to specific stocks can be difficult, if not impossible. A final generalization permits the elimination of P_n from the model while showing that the dividend valuation models discussed are consistent with one another.

First, the value of the stock at the end of the nth period, P_n, must be redefined. Using the capitalization-of-income approach, it can be shown that P_n is a function of all expected *future* dividends that the investor will receive in periods $n + 1$, $n + 2$, and so on. Discounting the stream of dividends at the required rate of return, k_e, gives the value of the stock at the end of the nth period:

$$P_n = \sum_{t=n+1}^{\infty} \frac{D_t}{(1 + k_e)^{t-n}} \qquad (7.6)$$

Substituting Equation 7.6 into Equation 7.5 yields the following:

$$P_0 = \sum_{t=1}^{n} \frac{D_t}{(1 + k_e)^t} + \sum_{t=n+1}^{\infty} \frac{D_t}{(1 + k_e)^t}$$

which can be further simplified into the following *general dividend valuation model:*

$$P_0 = \sum_{t=1}^{\infty} \frac{D_t}{(1 + k_e)^t} \qquad (7.7)$$

Thus, *the value of a firm's common stock to the investor is equal to the discounted present value of the expected future dividend stream.* As was shown, the valuation of a firm's common stock given by the n-period model (Equation 7.5) is equivalent to the valuation given by the general model (Equation 7.7). In addition, the 1- and 2-period valuation models (Equations 7.2 and 7.3) are equivalent to the general model (Equation 7.7).[11] The general dividend valuation model is applicable regardless of whether the stream of dividends over time is fluctuating or constant, increasing or decreasing.

Note that the general dividend valuation model treats the stream of dividends as a *perpetuity* having no finite termination date. Whereas this assumption is reasonable for firms that are going concerns, shorter time horizons must be used when considering firms that might be either acquired by other firms or liquidated in the foreseeable future.

Some profitable firms (such as Digital Equipment and Federal Express) reinvest all their earnings and do not pay current cash dividends. In fact, some profitable firms have *never* paid cash dividends for as long as they have been in existence and are not expected to do so in the near future. How can the general dividend valuation model be applied to the common stock of a firm such as this? It must be assumed that the firm will be able to start making regular, periodic cash dividend payments to its shareholders *at some time in the future.* Or, these returns could consist of the *proceeds from the sale of the firm's outstanding common stock* should the firm be acquired by another company. The value of such a firm's stock according to the general dividend valuation model (Equation 7.7) would be zero only

---

[11] You will be asked to demonstrate these relationships in Problem 12 at the end of this chapter.

if the firm were *never* expected to pay a cash dividend *of any type* to its shareholders.

As stated in Chapter 1, the primary goal of most firms is the *maximization of shareholder wealth*. The general dividend valuation model (Equation 7.7) indicates that shareholder wealth, as measured by the value of the firm's common stock, P_0, is a function of the expected stream of future dividend payments and the investor's required rate of return. Thus, when making financial decisions that are consistent with the goal of maximizing shareholder wealth, management should be concerned with how these decisions affect both the expected future dividend stream and the discount rate that investors apply to the dividend stream. The relationship between financial decision making and shareholder wealth is illustrated in Figure 7-2. A primary emphasis of the financial management function is attempting to define and measure this relationship.

GROWTH MODELS FOR THE VALUATION OF COMMON STOCK

The general dividend valuation model can be simplified if a firm's dividend payments over time are expected to follow one of several fairly straightforward patterns, including *constant growth*, *zero growth*, and *above-normal growth*.

Constant Growth Dividend Valuation Model

If a firm's future dividend payments per share are expected to grow at a *constant* rate, g, per period forever, then the dividend at any future time period t can be forecasted as follows:

$$D_t = D_0(1 + g)^t \tag{7.8}$$

where D_0 is the dividend in the current period ($t = 0$). The expected dividend in period 1 is $D_1 = D_0(1 + g)^1$, the expected dividend in period 2 is $D_2 = D_0(1 + g)^2$, and so on. The constant-growth curve in Figure 7-3 illustrates such a dividend pattern.

Substituting Equation 7.8 for D_t in the general dividend valuation model (Equation 7.7) yields the following:

$$P_0 = \sum_{t=1}^{\infty} \frac{D_0(1 + g)^t}{(1 + k_e)^t} \tag{7.9}$$

FIGURE 7-2

Relationship between Financial Decisions and Shareholder Wealth

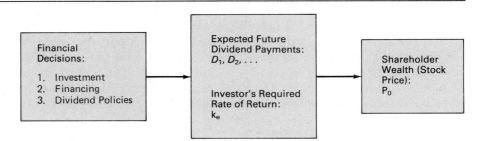

Assuming that the required rate of return, k_e, is greater than the dividend growth rate,[12] g, Equation 7.9 can be transformed algebraically to obtain the following simplified common stock valuation model:[13]

$$P_0 = \frac{D_1}{k_e - g} \qquad (7.10)$$

To apply this valuation model to a specific common stock issue, it is necessary to estimate the expected future dividend growth rate, g, per period for the firm. If the firm's historical dividend growth pattern is expected to continue into the foreseeable future, the growth rate in dividends per share for the past several years can be used to estimate the future compound annual expected dividend growth rate.

The constant growth dividend valuation model can be used to illustrate the two forms of returns an investor can expect to receive from holding a common stock. Solving Equation 7.10 for k_e yields the following:

$$k_e = \frac{D_1}{P_0} + g \qquad (7.11)$$

The investor's required rate of return is equal to the expected dividend yield, D_1/P_0, plus the capital gains yield, g—the expected increase in dividends and, ultimately, in the price of the stock.

---

[12] If this assumption is not satisfied—that is, if the growth rate (g) is greater than or equal to the required rate of return (k_e)—then the market price (P_0) would be infinite.

[13] Equation 7.10 is often referred to in finance literature as the *Gordon model*, for Myron J. Gordon, who pioneered its use. See Myron J. Gordon. *The Investment, Financing, and Valuation of the Corporation.* Homewood, Ill.: Irwin, 1962. Equation 7.10 can be derived from Equation 7.9 in the following manner. Rewrite Equation 7.9 as follows:

$$P_0 = \frac{D_0(1 + g)^1}{(1 + k_e)^1} + \frac{D_0(1 + g)^2}{(1 + k_e)^2} + \ldots + \frac{D_0(1 + g)^n}{(1 + k_e)^n} \qquad \text{(a)}$$

Multiply both sides of Equation (a) by $(1 + k_e)/(1 + g)$:

$$\frac{P_0(1 + k_e)}{(1 + g)} = D_0 + \frac{D_0(1 + g)^1}{(1 + k_e)^1} + \ldots + \frac{D_0(1 + g)^{n-1}}{(1 + k_e)^{n-1}} \qquad \text{(b)}$$

Subtract Equation (a) from Equation (b):

$$\frac{P_0(1 + k_e)}{(1 + g)} - P_0 = D_0 - \frac{D_0(1 + g)^n}{(1 + k_e)^n} \qquad \text{(c)}$$

Given that k_e is greater than g, as the number of time periods (n) approaches infinity, the second term on the right-hand side of Equation (c) approaches zero. Hence,

$$\frac{P_0(1 + k_e)}{(1 + g)} - P_0 = D_0 \qquad \text{(d)}$$

or

$$P_0\left[\frac{1 + k_e - (1 + g)}{(1 + g)}\right] = D_0 \qquad \text{(e)}$$

Multiplying both sides of Equation (e) by $(1 + g)$ yields

$$P_0(k_e - g) = D_0(1 + g) \qquad \text{(f)}$$

Solving Equation (f) for P_0, and recognizing that $D_1 = D_0(1 + g)$ gives

$$P_0 = \frac{D_1}{k_e - g} \qquad \text{(Equation 7.10)}$$

FIGURE 7-3

Dividend Growth Patterns

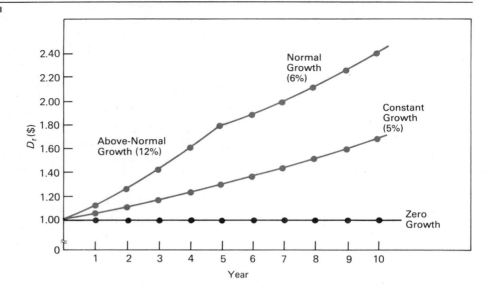

For example, consider the Boston Edison Company, which has estimated its common stock dividend for *next* year to be $1.82 per share. According to estimates provided by security analysts, earnings and dividends are expected to grow at a compound annual rate of 2.5 percent for the foreseeable future. What is the value of a share of this stock to an investor who requires a 14 percent rate of return? Substituting $1.82 for D_1, 2.5 percent (0.025) for g, and 14 percent (0.14) for k_e in Equation 7.10 yields the following value for the Boston Edison Company common stock:

$$P_0 = \frac{\$1.82}{0.14 - 0.025}$$

$$= \$15.83$$

Thus, the investor's 14 percent required rate of return consists of an 11.5 percent dividend yield ($D_1/P_0 = \$1.82/\$15.83$) plus a 2.5 percent capital gains yield.

Zero Growth Dividend Valuation Model

If a firm's future dividend payments per share are not expected to grow over time—that is, if they are expected to remain constant *forever*—then D_t in Equation 7.7, the general dividend valuation model, can be replaced by a constant value D to yield the following:

$$P_0 = \sum_{t=1}^{\infty} \frac{D}{(1 + k_e)^t} \tag{7.12}$$

This equation represents the value of a perpetuity and is analogous to those used for valuing a perpetual bond (Equation 6.7) and a preferred stock

(Equation 6.11) developed in the previous chapter. It can be simplified to obtain

$$P_0 = \frac{D}{k_e} \qquad (7.13)$$

Equation 7.13 really is a special case of the constant growth model in which the dividend growth rate, g, is zero. Substituting 0 for g and D for D_1 in the constant growth dividend valuation formula gives the zero growth dividend valuation expression. Again, this model is valid only when a firm's dividend payments are expected to remain constant *forever*. Although there are few, if any, common stocks that strictly satisfy these conditions, the model still can be used to approximate the value of a stock for which dividend payments are expected to remain constant for a relatively long period into the future. Figure 7-3 also illustrates a zero growth dividend payment pattern.

To illustrate the zero growth dividend valuation model, assume that the Mountaineer Railroad common stock pays an annual dividend of $1.50 per share, which is expected to remain constant for the foreseeable future. What is the value of the stock to an investor who requires a 12 percent rate of return? Substituting $1.50 for D and 12 percent (0.12) for k_e in Equation 7.13 yields the following:

$$P_0 = \frac{\$1.50}{0.12}$$

$$= \$12.50$$

Above-Normal Growth Dividend Valuation Model

Many firms experience growth rates in sales, earnings, and dividends that are *not* constant. Typically, a firm will have a period of above-normal growth as it exploits new technologies, new markets, or both; this generally occurs relatively early in the firm's life cycle. Following this period of rapid growth, earnings and dividends tend to stabilize, or grow at a more normal rate comparable to the overall average rate of growth in the economy. The reduction in the growth rate occurs as the firm reaches maturity and has fewer sizable growth opportunities. Figure 7-3 also illustrates an above-normal growth pattern.[14]

A relatively simple model can be developed to determine the value of a common stock having the dividend pattern just described. If g_1 is defined as the above-normal growth rate over the first m years, and g_2 is the normal growth rate beginning in year $m + 1$ and continuing indefinitely, the current value of the common stock can be computed as follows:

$$P_0 = \sum_{t=1}^{m} \frac{D_0(1 + g_1)^t}{(1 + k_e)^t} + \frac{P_m}{(1 + k_e)^m} \qquad (7.14)$$

[14] The transition between the periods of above-normal and normal, or average, growth usually is not as pronounced as Figure 7-3 indicates. Typically, a firm's growth rate *declines gradually* over time from the above-normal rate to the normal rate. Growth models similar to Equation 7.15 can be developed to handle cases like this.

or

$$P_0 = \sum_{t=1}^{m} \frac{D_0(1 + g_1)^t}{(1 + k_e)^t} + \frac{1}{(1 + k_e)^m}\left(\frac{D_{m+1}}{k_e - g_2}\right) \tag{7.15}$$

where k_e is the investor's required rate of return and D_0 and D_{m+1} are the dividend payments in years 0 and $m + 1$, respectively. Equation 7.15 indicates that the value of a firm's common stock is equal to the discounted present value of the stream of dividends received during the above-normal growth period plus the discounted present value of the stock price at the end of the above-normal growth period.

Because dividends are expected to grow at a constant rate, g_2, beginning in year $m + 1$, the constant growth model, $D_{m+1}/(k_e - g_2)$, can be used to find the value of the stock in year m, P_m.

For example, suppose investors expect the earnings and common stock dividends of NICOR, Inc. (a diversified holding company engaged in the exploration, production, marketing and distribution of natural gas) to grow at a rate of 12 percent per annum for the next 5 years. Following the period of above-normal growth, dividends are expected to grow at the slower rate of 6 percent for the foreseeable future. The firm currently pays a dividend D_0 of $2.00 per share. What is the value of NICOR common stock to an investor who requires a 15 percent rate of return?

Table 7-3 illustrates the step-by-step solution to this problem. First, compute the sum of the present values of the dividends received during the above-normal growth period (years 1–5 in this problem). This equals $9.25. Second, use the constant growth model to determine the value of NICOR common stock at the end of year 5; namely, P_5 equals $41.56. Next, determine the present value of P_5, which is $20.66. Finally, add the present value of the dividends received during the first 5 years ($9.25) to the present value of P_5 ($20.66) to obtain the total value of the common stock of $29.91 per share. A time line showing the expected cash returns (flows) from the purchase of NICOR common stock is given in Figure 7-4.

SMALL BUSINESS CONCERNS: VALUATION OF CLOSELY HELD FIRMS

The ownership of many small firms is closely held. An active market for shares of closely held companies normally does not exist. As a result small business owners occasionally need to have the value of their enterprises estimated by independent appraisers. The reasons for these valuations include mergers and acquisitions, divestitures and liquidations, initial public offerings, estate and gift tax returns, leveraged buyouts, recapitalizations, employee stock ownership plans, divorce settlements, estate valuation, and various other litigation matters.

The principles of valuation developed in this chapter and applied to large publicly traded firms also apply to the valuation of small firms. Small firm valuation poses several unique challenges. When valuing the shares of a closely held corporation, many factors are considered including the nature and history of the business, the general economic outlook and the condition and outlook of the firm's industry, earnings capacity, dividend paying capacity, the book value of the company, and the company's financial con-

Value of the NICOR Common Stock

Year, t	Dividend $D_t = \$2.00(1 + 0.12)^t$	Present Value Interest Factor, $PVIF_{0.15,t}$	Present Value, D_t

Present Value of First 5 Years' Dividends, $\sum_{t=1}^{5} \dfrac{D_0(1 + g_1)^t}{(1 + k_e)^t}$

1	$\$2.00(1 + 0.12)^1 = \$2.24$	0.870	\$1.95
2	$2.00(1 + 0.12)^2 = 2.51$	0.756	1.90
3	$2.00(1 + 0.12)^3 = 2.81$	0.658	1.85
4	$2.00(1 + 0.12)^4 = 3.15$	0.572	1.80
5	$2.00(1 + 0.12)^5 = 3.53$	0.497	1.75
			$\overline{\$9.25}$

Value of Stock at End of Year 5, $P_5 = \dfrac{D_6}{k_e - g_2}$

$$P_5 = \frac{D_6}{0.15 - 0.06}$$

$$D_6 = D_5(1 + g_2)$$

$$= \$3.53(1 + 0.06)$$

$$= \$3.74$$

$$P_5 = \frac{\$3.74}{0.15 - 0.06}$$

$$= \$41.56$$

Present Value of P_5, $PV(P_5) = \dfrac{P_5}{(1 + k_e)^5}$

$$PV(P_5) = \frac{\$41.56}{(1 + 0.15)^5}$$

$$= \$41.56(PVIF_{0.15,5})$$

$$= \$41.56(0.497)$$

$$= \$20.66$$

Value of Common Stock, $P_0 = PV \text{ (first 5 years' dividends)} + PV(P_5)$

$$P_0 = \$9.25 + \$20.66$$

$$= \$29.91$$

dition, whether the shares represent a majority or minority (less than 50 percent) interest, and whether the stock is voting or nonvoting.

Specifically, however, in valuing a company that sells products and services, earnings capacity usually is the most important factor to be considered. Typically, the company as a whole is valued by determining a normal earnings level and multiplying that figure by an appropriate price–earnings multiple. This approach is known as the "capitalization of earnings" approach and results in a "going concern value." If the shares represent a minority interest in the corporation, a discount is taken for the lack of marketability of these shares.

FIGURE 7-4

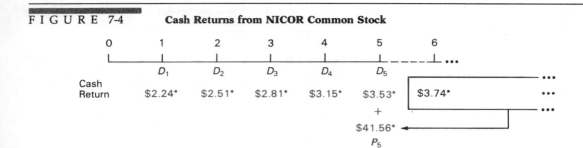

Cash Returns from NICOR Common Stock

Determination of Normal Earnings

The determination of an average, or "normal" earnings figure usually involves either a simple average or some type of weighted average of roughly the last 5 years of operations. For example, if the earnings of the company have been growing, some type of weighted average figure that places greater emphasis on more recent results often is used.

In some cases the reported earnings of the company may not be an appropriate figure for valuation purposes. For example, suppose a portion of the salary paid to the president (and principal stockholder) really constitutes dividends paid as salary to avoid the payment of income taxes. In this situation, it is appropriate to adjust the reported earnings to account for these dividends.

Determination of an Appropriate Price–Earnings Multiple

The next step in the valuation process is to determine an appropriate rate at which to capitalize the normal earnings level. This is equivalent to multiplying the earnings by a price–earnings multiple. Had there been recent arms-length transactions in the stock, the price–earnings multiple would be known and observable in the financial marketplace. However, this situation rarely exists for closely held corporations. As a consequence, the appraiser must examine the price–earnings multiple for widely held companies in the same industry as the firm being valued in an attempt to find firms that are similar to the firm of interest. The price–earnings multiple for these comparable firms is used to capitalize the normal earnings level.

Minority Interest Discount

The owner of a minority interest in a closely held corporation has an investment that lacks control and often marketability. There usually is either no market for the shares or the only buyer is either the other owners or the corporation itself. In addition, the owner of minority interest shares generally receives little, if any, dividends. The minority interest shareholder lacks control and is not able to change his or her inferior position. As a result of these problems, it is a widely practiced and accepted principle of valuation that the value of minority interest shares is discounted.

The usual procedure in valuing minority interest shares is to value the corporation as a whole. Next, this value is divided by the number of shares outstanding to obtain a per-share value. Finally, a discount is applied to this per-share value to obtain the minority interest share value. These discounts have ranged from a low of 6 percent to more than 50 percent.[15]

In conclusion, it can be seen that the basic valuation concepts are the same for small and large firms. However, the lack of marketability of shares for many small firms and the problem of minority interest positions pose special problems for the analyst.

■ SUMMARY

■ The common stockholders are the true owners of the firm; and, as such, common stock is a permanent form of financing. Common stockholders participate in the firm's earnings, potentially receiving larger dividends if earnings rise or smaller dividends if earnings drop.

■ Stockholder rights include the following:
1. The right to dividends.
2. The right to any assets remaining after senior claims are satisfied in a liquidation.
3. Voting rights.
4. The *preemptive right*, or the right to share proportionately in any new stock sold. This right is available in some firms but not in others.

■ If a company's common stock price rises above the price range considered optimal, the company's management can effect a *stock split* to get the price back to a more desirable trading level.

■ A firm may decide to repurchase its own shares for various reasons, including investment, financial restructuring, future corporate needs, disposition of excess cash, and reduction of takeover risk.

■ Common stock permits a firm more flexibility in its financing plans than fixed-income securities, because, in principle, no fixed-dividend obligation exists.

■ The valuation of *common stocks* is considerably more complicated than the valuation of either bonds or preferred stocks for the following reasons:
1. The returns can take two forms, cash dividend payments and capital gains.
2. Common stock dividends normally are expected to grow and not remain constant.
3. The returns from common stocks generally are more uncertain than the returns from other types of securities.

■ In the *general dividend valuation model* the value of a common stock is equal to the present value of all the expected future dividends discounted at the investor's required rate of return. Simpler common stock valuation models can be derived from assumptions concerning the expected growth of future dividend payments.

■ Assuming that dividends continue to grow at a *constant* rate, g, indefinitely, the value of a common stock is equal to the next year's dividend, D_1, divided by the difference between the investor's required rate of return, k_e, and the growth rate, g.

■ The valuation of stock in small corporations poses special challenges because of its limited marketability, lack of liquidity, and the difference between minority interest and controlling interest shares.

[15] See George S. Arneson, "Minority Discounts beyond Fifty Percent Can be Supported," *Taxes: The Tax Magazine* (February 1981): 97–102; and Ruth R. Longenecker, "A Practical Guide to Valuation of Closely Held Stock," *Trusts and Estates* (January 1983): 32–41.

QUESTIONS AND TOPICS FOR DISCUSSION

1. Define the following terms associated with common stock:

   a. Nonvoting stock
   b. Stock split
   c. Reverse stock split
   d. Stock dividend
   e. Book value
   f. Treasury stock

2. Does the retained earnings figure on a company's balance sheet indicate the amount of funds the company has available for current dividends or capital expenditures? Explain fully.

3. Discuss the reasons why a firm may repurchase its own common stock.

4. Explain the differences between par value, book value, and market value per share of common stock.

5. Discuss the various stockholder rights.

6. What factor or factors make the valuation of common stocks more complicated than the valuation of bonds and preferred stocks?

7. According to the general dividend valuation model, a firm that reinvests all its earnings and pays no cash dividends can still have a common stock value greater than zero. How is this possible?

8. Explain the relationship between financial decisions and shareholder wealth.

9. Explain how *each* of the following factors would affect the valuation of a firm's common stock, assuming that all other factors remain constant:

   a. The general level of interest rates shifts upward, causing investors to require a higher rate of return on securities in general.
   b. Increased foreign competition reduces the future growth potential of the firm's earnings and dividends.
   c. Investors reevaluate upward their assessment of the risk of the firm's common stock as the result of increased South American investments by the firm.

10. In the context of the constant growth dividend valuation model, explain what is meant by

    a. Dividend yield
    b. Capital gains yield

11. Explain why the valuation models for a perpetual bond, preferred stock, and common stock with constant dividend payments (zero growth) are virtually identical.

12. Explain how the book value per share of common stock can change over time.

PROBLEMS*

1. General Cereal common stock dividends have been growing at an annual rate of 7 percent per year over the past 10 years. Current dividends are $1.70 per share. What is the current value of a share of this stock to an investor who requires a 12 percent rate of return if the following conditions exist?

   a. Dividends are expected to continue growing at the historic rate for the foreseeable future.

* Colored numbers denote problems that have check answers provided at the end of the book.

$D_1 = D_0 (1+g)^{time \ (1)}$
$(time)$

$g = 0.07$
$D_0 = 1.7$
$K_S = 12\%$

a. $P_0 = \dfrac{D_1}{K_S - g}$

$= \dfrac{(1.70)(1.07)}{0.12 - 0.07} = 36.38$

$$b. \quad P_0 = \frac{D_1}{k_s - g} = \frac{(1.70)(1.09)}{0.12 - 0.09} = \frac{1.853}{0.03} = 61.767$$

$$c. \quad P_0 = \frac{D_1}{k_s - g} = \frac{(1.70)(1.81)}{0.12 - 0.065} = \frac{1.81}{0.055} = 32.918.$$

b. The dividend growth rate is expected to *increase* to 9 percent per year.

c. The dividend growth rate is expected to *decrease* to 6.5 percent per year.

2. The Foreman Company's earnings and common stock dividends have been growing at an annual rate of 6 percent over the past 10 years and are expected to continue growing at this rate for the foreseeable future. The firm currently (that is, as of year 0) pays an annual dividend of $5.00 per share. Determine the current value of a share of Foreman common stock to investors with each of the following required rates of return:

   a. 12 percent
   b. 14 percent
   c. 16 percent
   d. 6 percent
   e. 4 percent

3. The common stock of General Land Development Company (GLDC) is expected to pay a dividend of $1.25 next year and currently sells for $25. Assume that the firm's future dividend payments are expected to grow at a constant rate for the foreseeable future. Determine the implied growth rate for GLDC's dividends (and earnings) assuming that the required rate of return of investors is 12 percent.

4. Cascade Mining Company expects its earnings and dividends to increase by 7 percent per year over the next 6 years and then to remain relatively constant thereafter. The firm currently (that is, as of year 0) pays a dividend of $5.00 per share. Determine the value of a share of Cascade stock to an investor with a 12 percent required rate of return.

5. Over the past 5 years the dividends of the Gamma Corporation have grown from $0.70 per share to the current level of $1.30 per share (D_0). This growth rate (computed to one tenth of 1 percent accuracy) is expected to continue for the foreseeable future. What is the value of a share of Gamma Corporation common stock to an investor who requires a 20 percent return on her investment?

6. Bubba's Doggery currently (D_0) pays a $2.50 dividend per share. Next year's dividend is expected to be $3.00 per share. After next year dividends are expected to increase at a 9 percent annual rate for 3 years and a 6 percent annual rate thereafter.

   a. What is the current value of a share of Bubba's Doggery stock to an investor who requires a 15 percent return on his investment?
   b. If the growth rate over the next 3 years is expected to be only 7 percent and then 6 percent thereafter, what will the new stock price be?

7. The Edgar Corporation currently (D_0) pays a $2.00 per share dividend. This dividend is expected to grow at a 20 percent annual rate over the next 3 years and then to grow at 6 percent per year for the foreseeable future. What would you pay for a share of this stock if you demand a 20 percent rate of return?

8. The Seneca Maintenance Company currently (that is, as of year 0) pays a common stock dividend of $1.50 per share. Dividends are expected to grow at a rate of 11 percent per year for the next 4 years and then to continue growing thereafter at a rate of 5 percent per year. What is the current value of a share of Seneca common stock to an investor who requires a 14 percent rate of return?

9. Ten years ago Video Toys began manufacturing and selling coin-operated arcade games. Dividends are currently $1.50 per share, having grown at a 15 percent compound annual rate over the past 5 years. That growth rate is expected to be maintained for the next 3 years, after which dividends are expected to grow at half that rate for 3 years. Beyond that time, Video Toys'

dividends are expected to grow at 5 percent per year. What is the current value of a share of Video Toys common stock if your required rate of return is 18 percent?

10. During the previous 4 years Spiro Company's common stock dividends have grown from $1.00 (year 0) to $1.36 (year 4) per share.

   a. Determine the compound annual dividend growth rate over the 4-year period. HINT: Refer to the compound value techniques developed in Chapter 5, especially Equation 5.13.
   b. Forecast Spiro's dividends for the next 5 years, assuming that dividends continue to grow at the rate determined in Part a.
   c. Determine the current value of a share of Spiro common stock to an investor who plans to hold it for 5 years, assuming that the stock price *increases at the same rate* as the dividends. The investor's required rate of return is 12 percent.

11. The chairman of Heller Industries told a meeting of financial analysts that he expects the firm's earnings and dividends to double over the next 6 years. The firm's current (that is, as of year 0) earnings and dividends per share are $4.00 and $2.00, respectively.

   a. Estimate the compound annual dividend growth rate over the 6-year period (to the nearest whole percent).
   b. Forecast Heller's earnings and dividends per share for each of the next 6 years, assuming that they grow at the rate determined in Part a.
   c. Based on the constant growth dividend valuation model, determine the current value of a share of Heller Industries common stock to an investor who requires an 18 percent rate of return.
   d. Why might the stock price calculated in Part c not represent an accurate valuation to an investor with an 18 percent required rate of return?
   e. Determine the current value of a share of Heller Industries common stock to an investor (with an 18 percent required rate of return) who plans to hold it for 6 years, assuming that earnings and dividends per share grow at the rate determined in Part a for the next 6 years and then at 6 percent thereafter.

12. Show that the 1-period and 2-period valuation models (Equations 7.2 and 7.3) are equivalent to the general dividend valuation model (Equation 7.7).

13. Piedmont Enterprises currently (D_0) pays a dividend of $1 per share. This dividend is expected to grow at a 20 percent per year rate for the next two years, after which it is expected to grow at 6 percent per year for the foreseeable future. If you require a 15 percent rate of return on an investment of this type, what price do you expect the stock to sell for *at the beginning of year 5?*

14. Over the past 10 years the dividends of Party Time, Inc., have grown at an annual rate of 15 percent. The current (D_0) dividend is $3 per share. This dividend is expected to grow to $3.40 next year, then grow at an annual rate of 10 percent for the following 2 years, and 6 percent per year thereafter. You require a 15 percent rate of return on this stock.

   a. What would you be willing to pay for a share of Party Time stock today?
   b. What price would you anticipate the stock selling for at the beginning of year 3?
   c. If you anticipated selling the stock at the end of 2 years, how much would you pay for it today?

SELECTED REFERENCES

Brealey, Richard A. *An Introduction to Risk and Return from Common Stocks*, 2d ed. Cambridge MA: MIT Press, 1983.

Francis, Jack C. *Investments: Analysis and Management*, 5th ed. New York: McGraw-Hill, 1986.

Fuller, Russell J., and Chi-Cheng Hsia. "A Simplified Common Stock Valuation Model," *Financial Analysts Journal* 40 (September–October 1984): 49–56.

Keim, Donald B., and Robert F. Stambaugh. "Predicting Returns in the Stock and Bond Markets," *Journal of Financial Economics* 17 (December 1986): 357–390.

Lorie, J. H., P. Dodd, and M. Hamilton Kimpton. *The Stock Market: Theories and Evidence*, 2d ed. Homewood, Ill.: Richard D. Irwin, 1985.

Sharpe, William F. *Investment Analysis and Portfolio Management*, 3d ed. Englewood Cliffs, NJ: Prentice-Hall, 1986.

Williams, J. B., *The Theory of Investment Value*. Cambridge, MA: Harvard University Press, 1938.

CHAPTER

8

Analysis of Risk and Return

KEY CHAPTER CONCEPTS

1. *Risk* represents the variability of possible future returns from an investment. Risk tends to increase as one looks farther into the future.

2. A *probability distribution* indicates the percentage chance of occurrence of each of the possible outcomes.
   a. The *expected value* is a measure of the mean or average value of the possible outcomes, each having an associated probability of occurrence.
   b. The *standard deviation* is an important measure of the total risk or variability of possible outcomes, each having an associated probability of occurrence.
   c. The *coefficient of variation* is a useful total risk measure when comparing two investments with different expected returns.

3. Portfolios are composed of two or more assets.
   a. The risk of a portfolio of assets depends on the risk of the individual assets in the portfolio and the correlation of returns between the pairs of assets in the portfolio.
   b. By combining assets that are less than perfectly, positively correlated, portfolio risk can be *reduced* below the level of the weighted average risk of the individual assets.

4. The *Capital Asset Pricing Model (CAPM)* is a theory that can be used to determine re-

quired rates of return on investments in financial assets (securities) or physical assets.
   a. The *systematic* risk of a security refers to that portion of the variability of an individual security's returns caused by factors affecting the security market as a whole, such as interest rate changes.
   b. *Beta*, measured as the slope of a regression line between market returns and a security's returns, commonly is used as a measure of *systematic* risk.
   c. The *unsystematic* risk of a security refers to the portion of the variability of a security's returns caused by factors unique to that security.
   d. The *security market line* expresses the relationship between the required returns from a security and the systematic risk of that security.

5. The *Arbitrage Pricing Theory* (APT) relates required rates of return on investments to multiple risk factors.

6. Other techniques for managing risk include
   a. Acquisition of additional information
   b. Hedging
   c. Purchasing insurance
   d. Gaining control over the operating environment
   e. Limited use of firm-specific assets.

GLOSSARY OF NEW TERMS

Beta A measure of systematic risk. It is a measure of the volatility of a security's returns relative to the returns of a broad-based market portfolio of securities.

Capital Asset Pricing Model (CAPM) A theory that formally describes the nature of the risk-required rate of return relationship on investments in financial assets (securities) or physical assets.

Characteristic line A regression line relating the periodic returns for a specific security to the periodic returns on the market portfolio. The slope of this regression line is an estimate of the *beta* of the security—a measure of its systematic risk.

Coefficient of variation The ratio of the *standard deviation* to the *expected value*. It provides a *relative* measure of risk.

Correlation A relative statistical measure of the degree to which two series of numbers, such as the returns from two securities, tend to move or vary together.

Covariance An absolute statistical measure of how closely two variables (such as securities' returns) move together. It measures the degree to which increases (decreases) in the level of one variable tend to be associated with increases (decreases) in the level of another variable over time.

Diversification The act of investing in a set of financial (securities) or physical assets having different risk–return characteristics.

Expected value A statistical measure of the mean or average value of the possible outcomes. Operationally it is defined as the weighted average of the possible outcomes with the weights being the probability of occurrence.

Hedging A transaction that limits the risk associated with market price fluctuations for a particular investment position.

Portfolio A collection of two or more financial (securities) or physical assets.

Security market line (SML) The relationship between systematic risk and required rates of return for individual securities.

Standard deviation A statistical measure of the dispersion, or variability, of possible outcomes around the expected value, or mean. Operationally it is defined as the square root of the weighted average squared deviations of possible outcomes from the expected value. The standard deviation provides an *absolute* measure of risk.

Systematic risk That portion of the variability of an individual security's returns that is caused by factors affecting the market as a whole. This also is called *nondiversifiable risk.*

Unsystematic risk Risk that is unique to a firm; this also is called *diversifiable risk.*

There Is No Free Lunch—J. David & Company

J. David & Company was established in 1979 in San Diego as a sole proprietorship by J. David Dominelli. By 1983 the firm had grown to 270 employees with offices located in Newport Beach, San Francisco, Chicago, Los Angeles, London, and the Carribean island of Montserrat. The firm operated three major divisions: J. David Municipals and Governments, J. David Securities, and J. David Intercurrency.

The J. David Intercurrency operation ultimately led to the collapse of J. David Dominelli's financial empire. Dominelli employed a well-paid staff of salespersons, including former stockbrokers, lawyers, accountants, and real estate agents. These agents received 10 percent immediately for every dollar of funds they could attract to the firm's foreign currency investment operation. In addition these salespersons received nontaxable gifts, such as cars and computers, from Dominelli.

The lure to investors was extraordinarily high returns. Investors reported monthly returns of 4 to 5 percent, resulting in annual returns of 48 to 60 percent. The minimum investment was $100,000 and investors committed at least $150 million to the foreign exchange arm of J. David & Company. Monthly profits were automati-cally "reinvested" by the firm unless an investor explicitly withdrew the funds. J. David Intercurrency purportedly was offering these investors an opportunity to share the profits from the firm's success in trading in the highly volatile foreign currency market. The operation apparently was run much like a mutual fund. Investors had no way of knowing what their funds were invested in or how monthly profits were computed. All they received was a monthly statement indicating the profits for the month. The venture attracted many prominent and wealthy individuals.

In late 1983, the scheme began to collapse. What started out as a foreign currency trading mutual fund grew into a giant Ponzi scheme in which the early investors were paid with the capital provided by later investors. In early 1984, checks written by J. David & Company began to bounce. Dominelli soon disappeared to the Carribean island of Montserrat, only to be declared an undesirable and sent back to Miami where federal marshalls took him into custody.

Greedy investors, seeking to earn astronomically high returns, lost some $150 million in the venture. They learned one of the most important lessons in finance—HIGH RETURNS NORMALLY CAN BE EARNED ONLY BY ASSUMING HIGH RISKS. IN FINANCE, THERE IS NO FREE LUNCH.

This chapter defines the concepts of risk and return and develops the relationship between these important concepts. This relationship is one of the dominant themes in finance.

INTRODUCTION

Chapters 6 and 7 talked about the investors' *required rate of return* on a bond, preferred stock, and common stock. These required rates of return were used to discount the expected cash flows from each of these securities to determine the value of that security. In Chapter 2 the required rate of return from a security (or other asset) was represented as an increasing function of that security's *risk;* that is, the greater the risk, the greater is the required rate of return.

The major focus of this chapter is on investment diversification and portfolio risk analysis. The chapter defines risk in more precise terms; looks at a number of alternative techniques for measuring risk; and then considers the relationships between risk, required return, and security values. The final section examines various techniques, in addition to investment diversification, for managing risk.

Recall in Chapter 2 that *risk* was defined as the possibility that actual future returns will deviate from expected returns. In other words, it represents the variability of returns. Hence, risk implies that there is a chance for some unfavorable event to occur. From the perspective of security analysis or the analysis of an investment in some project (such as the development of a new product line), risk is the *possibility that actual cash flows (returns) will be different than forecasted cash flows (returns).*

An investment is said to be *risk-free* if the dollar returns from the initial investment are known with certainty. Some of the best examples of risk-free investments are United States Treasury securities. There is virtually no chance that the Treasury will fail to redeem these securities at maturity or that the Treasury will default on any interest payments owed. As a last resort, the Treasury can always print more money.[1]

In contrast, RJR Nabisco bonds constitute a *risky* investment because it is possible that the company will default on one or more interest payments and will lack sufficient funds to redeem the bonds at face value at maturity. In other words, the possible returns from this investment are *variable*, and each potential outcome can be assigned a *probability*.

If, for example, you were considering investing in RJR Nabisco bonds, you might assign the probabilities shown in Table 8-1 to the three possible outcomes of this investment. These probabilities are interpreted to mean that an 80 percent chance exists that the bonds will not be in default over their life and will be redeemed at maturity, a 15 percent chance of interest default during the life of the bonds, and a 5 percent chance that the bonds will not be redeemed at maturity.

Hence, from an investment perspective, risk refers to the chance that returns from an investment will be different than expected. We can define risk more precisely, however, by introducing some probability concepts.

Probability Distributions

The *probability* that a particular outcome will occur is defined as the *percentage chance* (or likelihood) of its occurrence. A *probability distribution* indicates the percentage chance of occurrence of each of the possible outcomes. Probabilities may be determined either objectively or subjectively. An objective determination is based on past occurrences of similar out-

---

[1] Note that this discussion of risk deals with *dollar returns* and ignores other considerations, such as potential losses in purchasing power. In addition, it assumes that securities are held until maturity, which is not always the case. Sometimes a security must be sold prior to maturity for less than face value because of changes in the level of interest rates.

Probability of Default on RJR Nabisco Bonds		TABLE 8-1
Outcome	**Probability**	
No default, bonds redeemed at maturity	0.80	
Default on interest for one or more periods	0.15	
No interest default, but bonds not redeemed at maturity	0.05	
	$\overline{1.00}$	

comes, whereas a subjective one is merely an opinion made by an individual about the likelihood that a given outcome will occur. In the case of projects that frequently are repeated—such as the drilling of developmental oil wells in an established oil field—reasonably good objective estimates can be made about the success of a new well. Similarly, good objective estimates can often be made about the expected returns of an AT&T bond. However, the expected returns from securities of new, small firms often are much more difficult to estimate objectively. Hence, highly subjective estimates regarding the likelihood of various returns are necessary. *The fact that many probability estimates in business are at least partially subjective does not diminish their usefulness.*

Let us consider the concept of probability and risk with a sample probability distribution of the returns available from an investment of $100,000 in the stock of either Wisconsin Public Service (WPS), a public utility firm, or Texas Instruments (TI), a maker of electronic equipment. By investing in the stock of either of these firms, an investor expects to receive dividend payments plus stock price appreciation. We will assume that the investor plans to hold the stock for one year and then sell it. Over the coming year, the investor feels there is a 20 percent chance for an economic *boom*, a 60 percent chance for a *normal* economic environment, and a 20 percent chance for a *recession*. Given this assessment of the economic environment *over the next year*, the investor estimates the probability distribution of returns from the investment in WPS and TI as shown in Table 8-2.

Expected Values

From this information the *expected value* of returns from investing in the stock of WPS and TI can be calculated. The expected value is a statistical measure of the mean or average value of the possible outcomes. Operationally, it is defined as the weighted average of possible outcomes, with the weights being the probabilities of occurrence.

Algebraically the expected value of the returns from a security or project may be defined as follows:

$$\hat{R} = \sum_{j=1}^{n} R_j P_j \qquad (8.1)$$

TABLE 8-2

Probability Distribution of Returns from WPS and TI

State of the Economy	Probability	Rate of Return Anticipated under Each State of the Economy*	
		WPS	TI
Recession	0.2	10%	−4%
Normal year	0.6	18	18
Boom	0.2	26	40
	1.0		

* For example, a 10 percent rate of return for WPS means that the stock value plus dividends total $110,000 at the end of one year. Working with a *discrete* probability distribution, as this example does, indicates that there is no probability of a loss by investing in WPS. This, of course, is unrealistic. In the following discussion of continuous distributions this assumption is relaxed.

where $\hat{R}$ is the expected return; R_j is the outcome for the jth case, where there are n possible outcomes; and P_j is the probability that the jth outcome will occur. The expected returns for WPS and TI are computed in Table 8-3. The expected return is 18 percent for both WPS and TI.

Standard Deviation: An Absolute Measure of Risk

The standard deviation is a statistical measure of the dispersion of possible outcomes about the expected value. It is defined as the *square root of the weighted average squared deviations of possible outcomes from the expected value* and computed as follows:

$$\sigma = \sqrt{\sum_{j=1}^{n}(R_j - \hat{R})^2 P_j} \tag{8.2}$$

where σ is the standard deviation.

The standard deviation can be used to measure the variability of returns from an investment. As such, it gives an indication of the *risk* involved in the asset or security. The larger the standard deviation, the more variable is an investment's returns and the riskier is the investment. A standard deviation of zero indicates no variability and thus no risk. Table 8-4 shows the calculation of the standard deviations for the investments in WPS and TI.

From the calculations in Table 8-4, it can be seen that TI appears riskier than WPS, because possible returns from TI are more variable, measured by its standard deviation of 13.91 percent, than those from WPS, which have a standard deviation of only 5.06 percent.

This example dealt with a *discrete* probability distribution of outcomes (returns) for each firm; that is, a *limited* number of possible outcomes were identified, and probabilities were assigned to them. In reality, however, many different outcomes are possible for the investment in the stock of each firm—ranging from losses during the year to returns in excess of TI's 40 percent return. To indicate the probability of *all* possible outcomes for these investments, it is necessary to construct a *continuous* probability distribution. This is done by developing a table similar to Table 8-2, except that it would have many more possible outcomes and their associated probabilities. The detailed table of outcomes and probabilities can be used to develop the expected value of returns from WPS and TI, and a continuous curve would be constructed to approximate the probabilities associated with each outcome. Figure 8-1 illustrates continuous probability distributions of returns for investments in the stock of WPS and TI.

Expected Return Calculation for Investment in WPS and TI					

TABLE 8-3

WPS			TI		
R_j	P_j	$R_j \times P_j$	R_j	P_j	$R_j \times P_j$
10%	0.2	2.0%	−4%	0.2	−0.8%
18	0.6	10.8	18	0.6	10.8
26	0.2	5.2	40	0.2	8.0
Expected return $= \hat{R} = $ 18.0%			Expected return $= \hat{R} = $ 18.0%		

TABLE 8-4

Computation of Standard Deviations of Returns—WPS and TI

	j	R_j	$\hat{R}$	$R_j - \hat{R}$	$(R_j - \hat{R})^2$	P_j	$(R_j - \hat{R})^2 P_j$
WPS	1 (Recession)	10%	18%	−8%	64	0.2	12.8
	2 (Normal)	18	18	0	0	0.6	0
	3 (Boom)	26	18	+8	64	0.2	12.8

$$\sum_{j=1}^{3} (R_j - \hat{R})^2 P_j = 25.6$$

$$\sigma = \sqrt{\sum_{j=1}^{n} (R_j - \hat{R})^2 P_j} = \sqrt{25.6} = 5.06\%$$

	j	R_j	$\hat{R}$	$R_j - \hat{R}$	$(R_j - \hat{R})^2$	P_j	$(R_j - \hat{R})^2 P_j$
TI	1 (Recession)	−4%	18%	−22%	484	0.2	96.8
	2 (Normal)	18	18	0	0	0.6	0
	3 (Boom)	40	18	+22	484	0.2	96.8

$$\sum_{j=1}^{3} (R_j - \hat{R})^2 P_j = 193.6$$

$$\sigma = \sqrt{\sum_{j=1}^{n} (R_j - \hat{R})^2 P_j} = \sqrt{193.6} = 13.91\%$$

From this figure it can be seen that the WPS possible returns have a tighter probability distribution, indicating a lower variability of returns, whereas the TI possible returns have a flatter distribution, indicating higher variability and, by extension, more risk.

Normal Probability Distribution

The possible returns from many investments tend to follow a *normal* probability distribution. The normal probability distribution is characterized by a symmetrical, bell-like curve. If the expected continuous probability distribution of returns is approximately normal, a table of the *standard normal probability distribution* (that is, a normal distribution with a mean equal to 0.0 and a standard deviation equal to 1.0, such as Table V at the

FIGURE 8-1

Continuous Probability Distributions for the Expected Returns from Investments in the WPS and TI Stocks

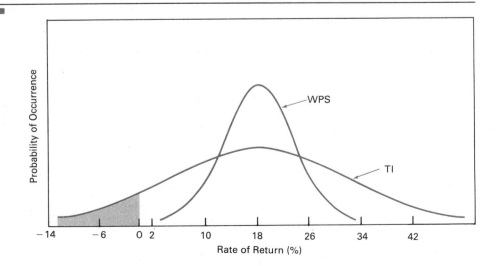

end of the text), can be used to compute the probability of occurrence of any particular outcome. From this table, for example, it is apparent that the actual outcome should be between plus or minus 1 standard deviation from the expected value 68.26 percent of the time,[2] between plus or minus 2 standard deviations 95.44 percent of the time, and between plus or minus 3 standard deviations 99.74 percent of the time. This is illustrated in Figure 8-2.

The number of standard deviations, z, that a particular value of R is from the expected value, $\hat{R}$, can be computed as follows:

$$z = \frac{R - \hat{R}}{\sigma} \qquad (8.3)$$

Equation 8.3, along with Table V, can be used to compute the probability of a return from an investment being less than (or greater than) some particular value.

For example, as part of the analysis of the risk of an investment in TI stock, suppose we are interested in determining the probability of earning a negative rate of return; that is, a return less than 0 percent. This probability is represented graphically in Figure 8-1 as the area to the left of 0 (that is, the shaded area) under the TI probability distribution. The number of standard deviations that 0 percent is from the expected return (18 percent) must be calculated. Substituting the expected return and the standard deviation from Tables 8-3 and 8-4 into Equation 8.3 yields the following:

$$z = \frac{0\% - 18\%}{13.91\%}$$

$$= -1.29$$

[2] For example, Table V indicates that there is a probability of 0.1587 of a value occurring that is greater than $+1\sigma$ from the mean *and* a probability of 0.1587 of a value occurring that is less than -1σ from the mean. Hence, the probability of a value *between* $+1\sigma$ and -1σ is 68.26 percent—that is, $1.00 - (2 \times 0.1587)$.

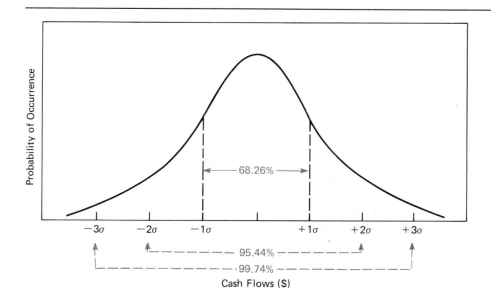

FIGURE 8-2

Sample Illustration of Areas under the Normal Probability Distribution Curve

In other words, the return of 0 percent is 1.29 standard deviations *below* the mean. From Table V the probability associated with 1.29 standard deviations is 0.0985. Therefore there is a 9.85 percent chance that TI will have returns below 0 percent. Conversely, there is a 90.15 percent (100 − 9.85) chance that the return will be greater than 0 percent.

Coefficient of Variation: A Relative Measure of Risk

The standard deviation is an appropriate measure of risk when the investments being compared are approximately equal in expected returns and the returns are estimated to have symmetrical probability distributions. Because the standard deviation is an *absolute* measure of variability, it generally is *not* suitable for comparing investments with different expected returns. In these cases the *coefficient of variation* provides a better measure of risk.

Consider, for example, two assets, T and S. Asset T has expected annual returns of 25 percent and a standard deviation of 20 percent, whereas Asset S has expected annual returns of 10 percent and a standard deviation of 18 percent. Intuition tells us that Asset T is less risky, because its *relative* variation is smaller.

The coefficient of variation, v, considers relative variation and thus is well suited for use when comparing two investments with different expected returns. It is defined as the ratio of the standard deviation, σ, to the expected value, $\hat{R}$:

$$v = \frac{\sigma}{\hat{R}} \qquad \textbf{(8.4)}$$

As the coefficient of variation increases, so does the relative risk of an asset. The coefficients of variation for Assets T and S are computed as follows using Equation 8.4:

$$\text{Asset T:} \qquad v = \frac{20\%}{25\%}$$
$$= 0.8$$

$$\text{Asset S:} \qquad v = \frac{18\%}{10\%}$$
$$= 1.8$$

Asset S's returns have a larger coefficient of variation than Asset T's, and therefore Asset S is the more risky of the two investments.

In general, when comparing two equal-sized investments, the standard deviation is an appropriate measure of total risk. When comparing two investments with different expected returns, the coefficient of variation is the more appropriate measure of total risk.[3]

---

[3] The relationship between the coefficient of variation and several other measures of risk (including the standard deviation) is developed in John M. Wachowicz, Jr., and Ronald E. Shrieves, "An Argument for Generalized Mean-Coefficient of Variation Analysis," *Financial Management* (Winter 1980): 51–58.

Risk as an Increasing Function of Time

Most investment decisions require that returns be *forecasted* several years into the future. The riskiness of these forecasted returns may be thought of as an *increasing function of time*. Returns that are generated early generally can be predicted with more certainty than those that are anticipated further out into the future.

Consider the risk facing a firm that plans to begin producing and marketing a new home computer system. This project is expected to generate cash flows to the firm of $2 million per year over the 7-year life of the project. Even though the expected annual cash flows are equal for each year, it is reasonable to assume that the riskiness of these flows increases over time as more and more presently unknown variables have a chance to affect the project's cash flows. Figure 8-3 illustrates this situation.

The distribution is relatively tight in year 1, because the market conditions affecting that year's cash flows are reasonably well known. By year 7, however, the distribution has become flat, indicating a considerable increase in the standard deviation, caused by increased uncertainty in market conditions.

Some types of cash flows are not subject to increasing variability. These include, for example, contractual arrangements, such as lease payments, in which the expected cash flows remain constant (or change at some predefined rate) over the life of the contract. In spite of the exceptions, it is reasonable to conclude that the riskiness of the cash flows from most investment projects gradually increases over time. Similarly, the riskiness of returns from most securities increases the further into the future these returns are being considered. For instance, the interest return from the purchase of Chrysler Corporation bonds is nearly guaranteed for the next year. However, projecting the interest returns to be received 10 years in the future is much more difficult due to the potential impact of competition, new technology, and other factors.

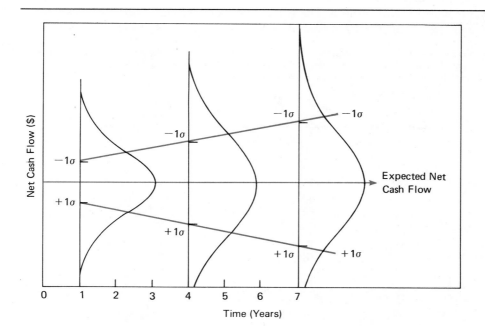

FIGURE 8-3

Sample Illustration of the Risk of a Project over Time

INVESTMENT DIVERSIFICATION AND PORTFOLIO RISK ANALYSIS

The preceding section examined the risk associated with single investments [financial assets (securities) and physical assets]. However, most financial and physical assets are held as parts of portfolios. Banks hold many different loans and many different bonds; individuals hold many different bonds and stocks; and corporations hold many different physical assets. Consequently, it is important to know how the returns from portfolios of investments behave over time—not only how the returns from any individual asset in the portfolio behave. *Portfolio risk*, the risk associated with collections of financial and physical assets, is considered in this and the following two sections. The questions of importance are as follows:

■ What return can be expected to be earned from the portfolio?
■ What is the risk of the portfolio?

Consider the following example. Assume that Alcoa (the aluminum industry's largest producer) is considering diversifying into gold mining and refining. During economic boom periods, aluminum sales tend to be brisk; gold, on the other hand, tends to be most in demand during economic downturns.[4] Thus, the returns from the aluminum business and the gold mining business are inversely, or *negatively*, related. If Alcoa expands into gold mining and refining, its overall return will tend to be less variable than individual returns from these businesses.

This effect is illustrated in Figure 8-4. Panel (a) shows the variation of rates of return in the aluminum industry over time, panel (b) shows the corresponding variation of returns from gold mining over the same time frame, and panel (c) shows the combined rate of return for both lines of business. As can be seen from this figure, when the return from aluminum operations is high, the return from gold mining tends to be low, and vice versa. The *combined* returns are more stable, and therefore less risky.

This *portfolio effect* of reduced variability results because a *negative correlation* exists between the returns from aluminum operations and the returns from gold mining. The *correlation* between any two variables—such as rates of return or net cash flows—is a relative statistical measure of the

---

[4] As investors lose confidence in the economy's performance, many of them turn to gold as an investment. This drives the price of gold up and increases returns to gold mining firms, whose costs of operation are not directly related to the demand for gold.

FIGURE 8-4

Sample Illustration of Diversification and Risk Reduction

Time (Years)

(a) Aluminum

Time (Years)

(b) Gold Mining

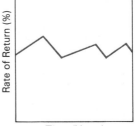

Time (Years)

(c) Aluminum and Gold Mining Combined

degree to which these variables tend to move together. The *correlation coefficient* measures the extent to which high (or low) values of one variable are associated with high (or low) values of another. Values of the correlation coefficient can range from $+1.0$ for *perfectly positively correlated* variables to -1.0 for *perfectly negatively correlated* variables. If two variables are unrelated (that is, uncorrelated), the correlation coefficient between these two variables will be 0.

Figure 8-5 illustrates perfect positive correlation, perfect negative correlation, and zero correlation for different pairs of common stock investments. For perfect positive correlation, panel (a), high rates of return from Stock L always are associated with high rates of return from Stock M; conversely, low rates of return from L always are associated with low rates of return from M. For perfect negative correlation, panel (b), however, the opposite is true; high rates of return from Stock P are associated with low rates of return from Stock Q and vice versa. For zero correlation, panel (c), no perceptible pattern or relationship exists between the rates of return on Stocks V and W.

In practice, the returns from most investments a firm or individual considers are positively correlated with other investments held by the firm or individual. For example, returns from projects that are closely related to the firm's primary line of business have a high positive correlation with returns from projects already being carried out, and thus provide limited opportunities to reduce risk. In the Alcoa example, if Alcoa were to build a new smelter, it would not realize the risk reduction possibilities that investing in gold mining and refining would produce. Similarly, the returns from most common stocks are positively correlated, because these returns are influenced by such common factors as the general state of the economy, the level of interest rates, and so on.

In order to explore further the concepts of diversification and portfolio risk, it is necessary to develop more precise measures of portfolio returns and risk.

Expected Returns from a Portfolio

When two or more securities are combined into a portfolio, the expected return of the portfolio is equal to the weighted average of the expected

Perfect Positive, Perfect Negative, and Zero Correlation for Two Investments   FIGURE 8-5

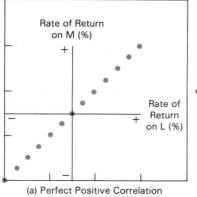

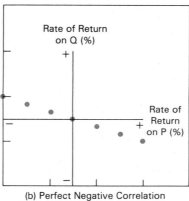

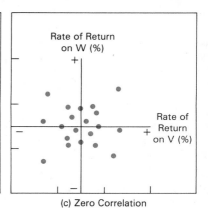

(a) Perfect Positive Correlation   (b) Perfect Negative Correlation   (c) Zero Correlation

returns from the individual securities. If a portion, W_A, of the available funds (wealth) is invested in Security A, and the remaining portion, W_B, is invested in Security B, the expected return of the portfolio R_p is as follows:

$$\hat{R}_p = W_A\hat{R}_A + W_B\hat{R}_B \tag{8.5}$$

where $\hat{R}_A$ and $\hat{R}_B$ are the expected returns for Securities A and B, respectively. Furthermore, $W_A + W_B = 1$, indicating that all funds are invested in either Security A or Security B.

For example, consider a portfolio consisting of the common stock of American Electric Power (A), a public utility company, and Bethlehem Steel (B), an integrated steel producer. The expected returns on the two stocks are 12 percent ($\hat{R}_A$) and 16 percent ($\hat{R}_B$), respectively. A portfolio consisting of 75 percent (W_A) invested in American Electric Power and the remainder or 25 percent (W_B) invested in Bethlehem Steel would yield an expected return, by Equation 8.5, of

$$\hat{R}_p = 0.75 (12\%) + 0.25 (16\%)$$

$$= 13.0\%$$

Table 8-5 (columns W_A and $\hat{R}_p$) and Figure 8-6 illustrate the relationship between the expected return for a portfolio containing Securities A and B and the proportion of the total portfolio invested in each security. For example, when $W_A = 1.0$ (100%) and $W_B = 0$ (because $W_A + W_B = 1.0$), the expected portfolio return is 12 percent—the same as the return for A. When $W_A = 0.5$ (50 percent) and $W_B = 0.5$ (50 percent), the expected portfolio return is 14 percent. As shown earlier, when $W_A = 0.75$ and $W_B = 0.25$, the expected portfolio return is 13 percent. Thus it can be seen that the expected return from a portfolio of securities is simply equal to the weighted average of the individual security returns where the weights represent the proportion of the total portfolio invested in each security. This results in the linear relationship shown in Figure 8-6.

In general, the expected return from any portfolio of n securities or assets is equal to the sum of the expected returns from each security times the proportion of the total portfolio invested in that security:

T A B L E 8-5

Expected Returns and Portfolio Risk from a Portfolio of the Stocks of American Electric Power (A) and Bethlehem Steel (B)

Proportion Invested in Security A W_A (%)	Expected Return on Portfolio $\hat{R}_P$ (%)	Portfolio Risk σ_p (%)		
		$\rho_{AB} = +1.0$	$\rho_{AB} = 0.0$	$\rho_{AB} = -1.0$
0.0%	16.0%	20.0%	20.0%	20.0%
25.0	15.0	17.5	15.0	12.5
33.333	14.67	16.67	13.74	10.0
50.0	14.0	15.0	11.2	5.0
66.667	13.33	13.33	9.43	0.0
75.0	13.0	12.5	9.01	2.5
100.0	12.0	10.0	10.0	10.0

Note: $\hat{R}_A = 12\%$; $\hat{R}_B = 16\%$; $\sigma_A = 10\%$; $\sigma_B = 20\%$.

$$\hat{R}_{\mathrm{p}} = \sum_{i=1}^{n} W_i \hat{R}_i \qquad\qquad (8.6)$$

where $\Sigma W_i = 1$ and $0 \le W_i \le 1$.

Portfolio Risk

Although the expected returns from a portfolio of two or more securities can be computed as a weighted average of the expected returns from the individual securities, it generally is not sufficient merely to calculate a weighted average of the risk of each individual security to arrive at a measure of the portfolio's risk. Whenever the returns from the individual securities are not perfectly positively correlated, the risk of any portfolio of these securities may be reduced through the effects of diversification. Thus, diversification can be achieved by investing in a diverse set of securities that have different risk–return characteristics. The amount of risk reduction achieved through diversification depends on the degree of correlation between the returns of the individual securities in the portfolio. The lower the correlations among the individual securities, the greater the possibilities of risk reduction.

Expected Return from a Portfolio of the Stocks of American Electric Power (A) and Bethlehem Steel (B)   F I G U R E 8-6

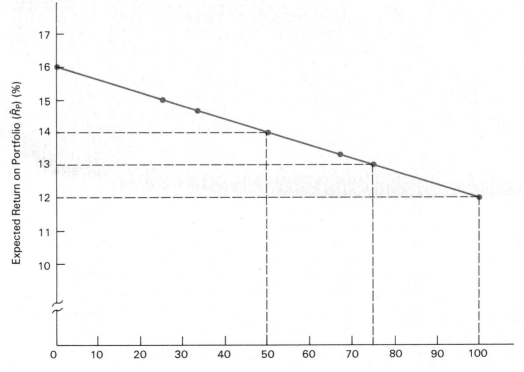

Note: $\hat{R}_{\mathrm{A}} = 12\%$; $\hat{R}_{\mathrm{B}} = 16\%$; $W_{\mathrm{A}} + W_{\mathrm{B}} = 1.0$ (100%). Data points in graph are from Table 8-5.

The risk for a two-security portfolio, measured by the standard deviation of portfolio returns, is computed as follows:

$$\sigma_p = \sqrt{W_A^2\sigma_A^2 + W_B^2\sigma_B^2 + 2W_AW_B\rho_{AB}\sigma_A\sigma_B} \tag{8.7}$$

where W_A is the proportion of funds invested in Security A; W_B is the proportion of funds invested in Security B; $W_A + W_B = 1$; σ_A^2 is the variance of returns from Security A (or the square of the standard deviation for Security A, σ_A); σ_B^2 is the variance of returns from Security B (or the square of the standard deviation for Security B, σ_B); and ρ_{AB} is the correlation coefficient of returns between Securities A and B.[5]

Consider, for example, the portfolio (discussed earlier) consisting of the common stock of American Electric Power (A) and Bethlehem Steel (B). The standard deviation of returns for these two securities are 10 percent (σ_A) and 20 percent (σ_B), respectively. Furthermore, suppose that the correlation coefficient (ρ_{AB}) between the returns on these securities is equal to $+0.50$. Using Equation 8.7, a portfolio consisting of 75 percent (W_A) invested in American Electric Power and 25 percent (W_B) in Bethlehem Steel would yield a standard deviation of portfolio returns of

$$\sigma_p = \sqrt{(.75)^2(10)^2 + (.25)^2(20)^2 + 2(.75)(.25)(+.50)(10)(20)}$$
$$= 10.90\%$$

With the techniques just described for calculating expected portfolio return and risk, we can now examine in more detail the risk versus return tradeoffs associated with investment diversification.

CASE I: PERFECT POSITIVE CORRELATION. Table 8-5 (columns $\hat{R}_p$ and $\rho_{AB} = +1.0$) and panel (a) of Figure 8-7 illustrate the risk–return tradeoffs associated with portfolios consisting of various combinations of American Electric Power (A) and Bethlehem Steel (B) stock when $\rho_{AB} = +1.0$. As can be seen, when the returns from the two securities are perfectly positively correlated, the risk of the portfolio is equal to the weighted average of the risk of the individual securities (10 and 20 percent in this example). Therefore, no risk reduction is achieved when perfectly positively correlated securities are combined in a portfolio.

CASE II: ZERO CORRELATION. Table 8-5 (columns $\hat{R}_p$ and $\rho_{AB} = 0.0$) and panel (b) of Figure 8-7 illustrate the possible trade-offs when $\rho_{AB} = 0.0$. In this case, we see that diversification can reduce portfolio risk below the risk of either of the securities that make up the portfolio. For example, an investment consisting of 75 percent in American Electric Power (A) stock and 25 percent in Bethlehem Steel (B) stock has a portfolio standard deviation of only 9.01 percent, which is less than the standard deviations of either of the two securities (10 and 20 percent, respectively) in the portfolio. In gen-

---

[5] In general, the risk of a portfolio containing n securities, as measured by the standard deviation of portfolio returns, is computed as follows:

$$\sigma_p = \sqrt{\sum_{i=1}^{n}\sum_{j=1}^{n} W_iW_j\rho_{ij}\sigma_i\sigma_j}$$

The double summation sign ($\Sigma\Sigma$) indicates that all possible combinations of i and j should be included in calculating the total value. Problem 19 at the end of the chapter examines the case of a three-security portfolio.

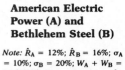

Relationship between Portfolio Expected Return and Risk for the Stocks of American Electric Power (A) and Bethlehem Steel (B)

Note: $\hat{R}_A = 12\%$; $\hat{R}_B = 16\%$; $\sigma_A = 10\%$; $\sigma_B = 20\%$; $W_A + W_B = 1.0$ (100%). Data points in graphs are from Table 8-5.

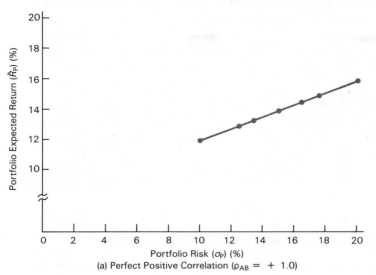

(a) Perfect Positive Correlation ($\rho_{AB} = +\ 1.0$)

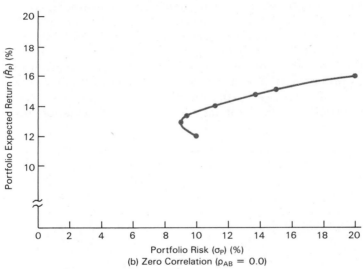

(b) Zero Correlation ($\rho_{AB} = 0.0$)

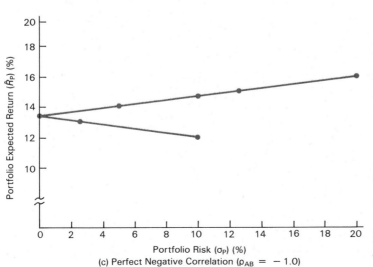

(c) Perfect Negative Correlation ($\rho_{AB} = -\ 1.0$)

263

eral, when the correlation coefficient between the returns on two securities is less than 1.0, diversification can reduce the risk of a portfolio below the weighted average of the total risk of the individual securities. The less positively correlated are the returns from two securities, the greater will be the portfolio effects of risk reduction.

CASE III: PERFECT NEGATIVE CORRELATION. Table 8-5 (columns $\hat{R}_p$ and $\rho_{AB} = -1.0$) and panel (c) of Figure 8-7 show the risk–return relationship when $\rho_{AB} = -1.0$. As illustrated, with perfectly negatively correlated returns, portfolio risk can be reduced to zero. In other words, with a perfect negative correlation of returns between two securities, there always will be some proportion of the securities that will result in the complete elimination of portfolio risk.

Efficient Portfolios and the Capital Market Line

The risk–return relationships just discussed can be extended to analyze portfolios involving more than two securities. For example, consider the graph shown in Figure 8-8. Each dot within the shaded area represents the risk (standard deviation) and expected return for an individual security available for possible investment. The shaded area (or opportunity set) represents all the possible portfolios found by combining the given securities in different proportions. The curved segment from A to B on the boundary of the shaded area represents the set of *efficient portfolios*, or the *efficient frontier*. A portfolio is efficient if, for a given standard deviation, there is no

F I G U R E   8-8

Portfolio Opportunity Set

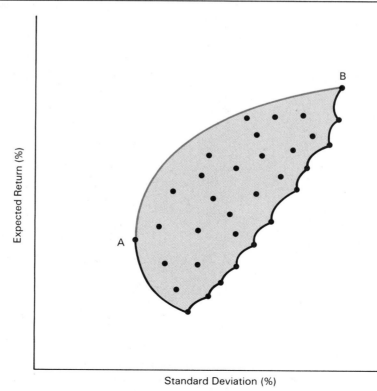

Expected Return (%)

Standard Deviation (%)

other portfolio with a higher expected return, or for a given expected return, there is no other portfolio with a lower standard deviation.

Risk-averse investors, in choosing their optimal portfolios, need only consider those portfolios on the efficient frontier. The choice of an optimal portfolio, whether portfolio A that minimizes risk (standard deviation), or portfolio B that maximizes expected return, or some other portfolio on the efficient frontier, depends on the investor's attitude toward risk (that is, risk aversion). More conservative investors will tend to choose lower-risk portfolios (closer to A); more aggressive investors will tend to select higher-risk portfolios (closer to B).

If investors are able to borrow and lend money at the risk-free rate (r_f), they can obtain any combination of risk (standard deviation) and expected return on the straight-line joining r_f and portfolio m as shown in Figure 8-9. When the market is in equilibrium, portfolio m represents the market portfolio, which consists of all available securities, weighted by their respective market values. The line joining r_f and m is known as the *capital market line*.[6] Any risk–return combination on this line *between* r_f and m can be obtained by investing (i.e., *lending*) part of the initial funds in the risk-free security (such as U.S. Treasury bills) and investing the remainder in portfolio m. Any combination *beyond* m on this line can be obtained by *borrowing* money at the risk-free rate and investing the borrowed funds (as well as the initial funds) in portfolio m (that is, purchasing securities on margin).

[6] In constructing the capital market line, it is assumed that all investors have homogeneous (i.e., identical) expectations about the distributions of returns offered by securities. As a result of this assumption, all investors will perceive the same set of efficient portfolios.

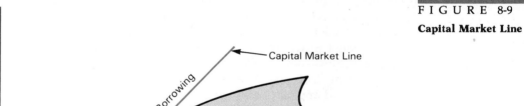

FIGURE 8-9

Capital Market Line

With the ability to borrow and lend at the risk-free rate, the choice of an optimal portfolio for risk-averse investors involves determining the proportion of funds to invest in the market portfolio (m) with the remaining proportion being invested in the risk-free security. More conservative investors will tend to choose portfolios nearer to the r_f point on the capital market line. More aggressive investors will tend to select a portfolio closer to, or possibly beyond, point m on the capital market line.

Finally, note that the slope of the capital market line measures the (equilibrium) market price of risk. In other words, it measures the additional expected return that can be obtained by incurring one additional unit of risk (one percentage point of standard deviation).

PORTFOLIO RISK AND THE CAPITAL ASSET PRICING MODEL

The preceding analysis illustrates the possibilities for portfolio risk reduction when two or more securities are combined to form a portfolio. Unfortunately, when more than two securities are involved—as is usually the case—the number of calculations required to compute the portfolio risk increases geometrically. For example, whereas 45 correlation coefficients are needed for a portfolio containing 10 securities, 4,950 correlation coefficients must be computed for a portfolio containing 100 securities. In other words, a 10-fold increase in securities causes a greater than 100-fold increase in the required calculations.[7] In addition, a substantial computational undertaking is required to find the particular portfolio of securities that minimizes portfolio risk for a given level of return or maximizes return for a given level of risk, even for a portfolio that contains only a few securities. Obviously a more workable method is needed to assess the effects of diversification on a portfolio of assets.

One method that has gained widespread use in analyzing the relationship between portfolio risk and return is the *Capital Asset Pricing Model (CAPM)*. This model provides a strong analytical basis for evaluating risk–return relationships—both in the context of financial management and securities investment decisions. The remainder of this section discusses the development and application of the CAPM.

Systematic and Unsystematic Risk

As illustrated in the previous section, whenever the individual securities in a portfolio are less than perfectly positively correlated, diversification can reduce the portfolio's risk below the weighted average of the total risk (measured by the standard deviation) of the individual securities. Because most securities are positively correlated with returns in the securities market in general, it usually is not possible to totally eliminate risk in a portfolio of securities. As the economic outlook improves, returns on most individual securities tend to increase; as the economic outlook deteriorates, individual security returns tend to decline. In spite of this positive "comovement" among the returns of individual securities, each security experiences some "unique" variation in its returns that is unrelated to the underlying economic factors that influence all securities. In other words, there are two types of risk inherent in all securities:

[7] The number of correlation coefficients needed to evaluate an n-security portfolio is computed as $(n^2 - n)/2$.

■ *Systematic*, or *nondiversifiable*, risk.
■ *Unsystematic*, or *diversifiable*, risk.

Systematic risk refers to that portion of the variability of an individual security's returns caused by factors affecting the market as a whole; as such, it can be thought of as being nondiversifiable. Systematic risk accounts for 25 to 50 percent of the total risk of any security. Some of the sources of systematic risk, which cause the returns from all securities to vary more or less together, include the following:

■ Interest rate changes.
■ Changes in purchasing power (inflation).
■ Changes in investor expectations about the overall performance of the economy.

Because diversification cannot eliminate systematic risk, this type of risk is the predominant determinant of individual security risk premiums.

Unsystematic risk is risk that is unique to the firm. It is the variability in a security's returns that is caused by factors such as the following:

■ Management capabilities and decisions.
■ Strikes.
■ The availability of raw materials.
■ The unique effects of such government regulation as pollution control.
■ The effects of foreign competition.
■ The particular levels of financial and operating leverage the firm employs.

Because unsystematic risk is unique to each firm, an efficiently diversified portfolio of securities can successfully eliminate most of the unsystematic risk inherent in individual securities, as is shown in Figure 8-10. To eliminate effectively the unsystematic risk inherent in a portfolio's individual securities, it is not necessary for the portfolio to include a large number of securities. In fact, randomly constructed portfolios of as few as ten to fifteen securities on average can successfully diversify away a large portion of the unsystematic risk of the individual securities.[8] The risk remaining *after* diversification is market-related risk, often called *systematic risk*, and it cannot be eliminated through diversification. Because unsystematic risk commonly accounts for 50 percent or more of the total risk of most individual securities, it should be obvious that the risk-reducing benefits of efficient diversification are well worth the effort.

Given the small number of securities required for efficient diversification by an individual investor, as well as the dominance of the securities markets by many large institutional investors who hold widely diversified portfolios, it is safe to conclude that the most relevant risk that must be considered for any widely traded individual security is its systematic risk. The unsystematic portion of total risk is relatively easy to diversify away.

Security Market Line (SML)

The return required of any risky asset is determined by the prevailing level of risk-free interest rates plus a risk premium. The greater the level of risk an investor perceives about a security's return, the greater the required risk

[8] W. H. Wagner and S. C. Lau. "The Effect of Diversification on Risk," *Financial Analysts Journal* (November–December 1971): 48–53.

premium will be. In other words, investors require returns that are commensurate with the risk level they perceive. In algebraic terms, the required return from any Security j, k_j, is equal to the following:

$$k_j = r_f + \theta_j \qquad (8.8)$$

where r_f is the risk-free rate and θ_j is the risk premium required by investors.

The security market line (SML) indicates the "going" required rate of return in the market for a given amount of systematic risk, and it is illustrated in Figure 8-11. The SML intersects the vertical axis at the risk-free rate, r_f, indicating that any security with an expected risk premium equal to zero should be required to earn a return equal to the risk-free rate. As risk increases, so do the risk premium and the required rate of return. According to Figure 8-11, for example, a security having a risk level of a' should be required to earn a 10 percent rate of return.

Beta: A Measure of Systematic Risk

Thus far we have not addressed the question of the appropriate risk measure to use when considering the risk–return tradeoffs illustrated by the SML. The previous discussion of risk in a portfolio context suggests that a measure of systematic risk is an appropriate starting point.

The systematic risk of a security is a function of the total risk of a security as measured by the standard deviation of the security's returns, the standard

---

FIGURE 8-10

**Unsystematic Risk
and Portfolio
Diversification**

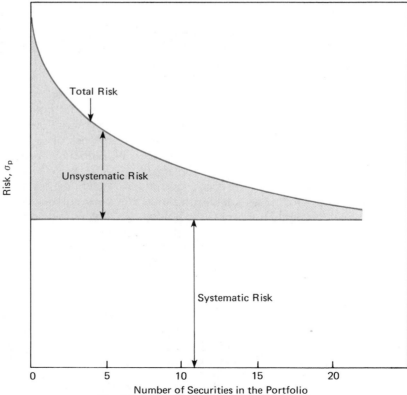

Total Risk = Systematic Risk + Unsystematic Risk

deviation of the returns from the market portfolio, and the correlation of the security's returns with those of all other securities in the market. A broad-based security market index, such as the *Standard and Poor's 500 Market Index* or the *New York Stock Exchange Index*, normally is used as a measure of total market returns.

One useful measure of the systematic risk of a Security j is the value called *beta*. Beta is a measure of the volatility of a security's returns relative to the returns of a broad-based Market Portfolio *m*. It is defined as the ratio of the covariance (or comovement) of returns on Security j and Market Portfolio *m* to the variance of returns on the Market Portfolio:

$$b_j = \frac{\text{Covariance}_{j,m}}{\text{Variance}_m}$$

$$b_j = \frac{\rho_{jm}\sigma_j\sigma_m}{\sigma_m^2} \tag{8.9}$$

where b_j is the measure of systematic risk for Security j, σ_j is the standard deviation of returns for Security j, σ_m is the standard deviation of returns for Market Portfolio *m*, σ_m^2 is the variance of returns for Market Portfolio m, and ρ_{jm} is the correlation coefficient between returns for Security j and Market Portfolio *m*.

In practice, beta may be computed as the slope of a regression line between periodic (usually yearly, quarterly, or monthly) rates of return on the Market Portfolio (as measured by a market index, such as the *Standard and Poor's 500 Market Index*) and the periodic rates of return for Security j, as follows:

$$k_j = a_j + b_j k_m + e_j \tag{8.10}$$

where k_j is the periodic percentage holding period rate of return for Security j, a_j is a constant term determined by the regression, b_j is the computed historical beta for Security j, k_m is the periodic percentage holding period

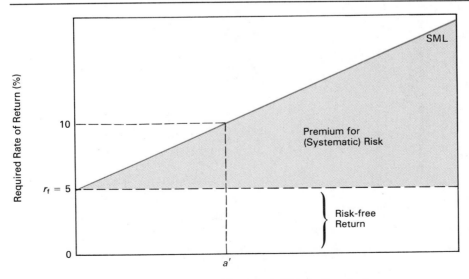

FIGURE 8-11

The Security Market Line (SML)

Measure of Systematic Risk for Security j

rate of return for the market index, and e_j is a random error term. This equation describes a line called Security j's *characteristic line*.

Figure 8-12 shows the characteristic line for General Motors. The slope (and intercept) of this line can be estimated using the least-squares technique of regression analysis. The slope of this line, or beta, is 0.97, indicating that the systematic returns from General Motors common stock are slightly less variable than the returns for the market as a whole.

A beta of 1.0 for any security indicates that the security is of average systematic risk; that is, a security with a beta of 1.0 has the same risk characteristics as the market as a whole when only systematic risk is considered. When beta equals 1.0, a 1 percent increase (decline) in market returns indicates that the *systematic* returns for the individual security should increase (decline) by 1 percent.[9] A beta greater than 1.0—for example, 2.0—indicates that the security has greater than average systematic risk. In this case, when market returns increase (decline) by 1 percent, the security's systematic returns can be expected to increase (decline) by 2 percent. A beta of less than 1.0—for example, 0.5—is indicative of a security of less than average systematic risk. In this case a 1 percent increase (decline) in market returns implies a 0.5 percent increase (decline) in the security's systematic returns. Table 8-6 summarizes the interpretation of selected betas.

[9] Of course, there will also be *unsystematic* components to a security's returns at any point in time. We assume these are diversified away in the portfolio.

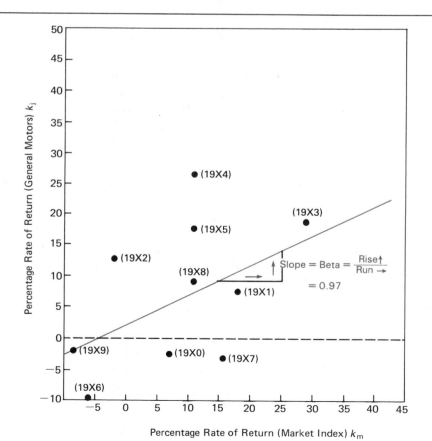

Percentage Rate of Return (Market Index) k_m

TABLE 8-6

Interpretation of Selected Beta Coefficients

Beta Value	Direction of Movement in Returns	Interpretation
2.0	Same as market	Twice as risky (responsive) as market
1.0	Same as market	Risk equal to that of market
0.5	Same as market	Half as risky as market
0	Uncorrelated with market movements	No market-related risk
−0.5	Opposite of market	Half as responsive as market, but in the opposite direction

The beta for the market portfolio as measured by a broad-based market index equals 1.0. This can be seen in Equation 8.10. Because the correlation of the market with itself is 1.0, the beta of the market portfolio must also be 1.0.

Finally, the beta of any portfolio of n securities or assets is simply the weighted average of the individual security betas:

$$b_p = \sum_{j=1}^{n} W_j b_j \qquad (8.11)$$

This concept is particularly useful when evaluating the effects of capital investment projects or mergers on a firm's systematic risk.

Fortunately for financial managers, it is not necessary to compute the beta for each security every time a security's systematic risk measure is needed. Several investment advisory services, including the *Value Line Investment Survey* and Merrill Lynch, regularly compute and publish individual security beta estimates, and these are readily available. Table 8-7 lists the Value Line computed betas for selected stocks.

Security Market Line and Beta

Given the information presented thus far, it is possible to compute risk premiums, θ, that are applicable to individual securities. The SML also may be defined in terms of beta. The risk premium for any Security j is equal to the difference between the investor's required return, k_j, and the risk-free rate, r_f:

$$\theta_j = k_j - r_f \qquad (8.12)$$

If we let $\hat{k}_m$ be the expected rate of return on the overall market portfolio and $\hat{r}_f$ be the expected (short-term) risk-free rate (that is, the rate of return on Treasury bills), then the market risk premium is equal to

$$\hat{\theta}_m = \hat{k}_m - \hat{r}_f$$

Betas for Selected Stocks

Company Name	Value Line Beta
American Electric Power	0.75
AT&T	0.85
Apple Computer	1.35
BankAmerica	1.00
Boeing Company	0.95
Caterpillar	1.20
CBS, Inc.	1.05
Coca-Cola	0.95
Delta Air Lines	1.05
Digital Equipment	1.20
Eastman Kodak	0.90
Exxon	0.80
Federal Express	1.10
Ford Motor	1.20
General Electric	1.10
General Mills	1.00
K Mart Corporation	1.15
Playboy	0.80
Texas Instruments	1.40
Weis Markets	0.90
Wisconsin Public Service	0.60
Zenith Electronics	1.55

SOURCE: *Value Line Investment Survey* (New York: Value Line, Inc., March 3, 1989). ©1989 by Value Line, Inc. Used by permission.

Based on historic stock market data over the time period from 1926 to 1987, the average market risk premium has been 8.3 percent.[10]

For a security with average risk (b_j equal to 1.0), the risk premium should be equal to the market risk premium, or 8.3 percent. A security whose beta is 2.0, however, is twice as risky as the average security, so its risk premium should be twice the market risk premium:

$$\hat{\theta}_j = b_j(\hat{k}_m - \hat{r}_f)$$
$$= 2.0\ (8.3\%)$$
$$= 16.6\%$$

The required return for any security may be defined in terms of its systematic risk (beta), the expected market return, $\hat{k}_m$ and the expected risk-free rate, as follows:

$$k_j = \hat{r}_f + \hat{\theta}_j$$

or

$$k_j = \hat{r}_f + b_j(\hat{k}_m - \hat{r}_f) \tag{8.13}$$

[10] *Stocks, Bonds, Bills and Inflation: 1988 Yearbook* (Chicago: Ibbotson Associates, 1988), p. 81.

For example, if the risk-free rate is 7 percent and $(\hat{k}_m - \hat{r}_f)$ is 8.3 percent, then the required return for Ford Motor Company, which has a beta of 1.20, is computed as follows:

$$k_j = 7\% + 1.20\ (8.3\%)$$
$$= 16.96\%$$

Equation 8.13 provides an explicit definition of the SML in terms of the systematic risk of individual securities. Figure 8-13 illustrates the SML for Equation 8.13. The slope of the SML is shown as being constant throughout. When measured between a beta of 0 and a beta of 1.0, it is equal to $(\hat{k}_m - \hat{r}_f)/(1 - 0)$, or simply $\hat{k}_m - \hat{r}_f$. This slope represents the risk premium on an average risk security. Assuming a risk-free rate of 7 percent and a market risk premium of 8.3 percent, the return required on a low-risk stock (for example, beta equal to 0.5) is 11.15 percent. The return required on a high-risk stock (for example, beta equal to 2.0) is 23.6 percent, and the return required on a stock of average risk (for example, beta equal to 1.0) is 15.3 percent, the same as the market required return.

Also, from Figure 8-13 we can determine what securities (assets) are attractive investments by comparing the *expected* return from a security with the return *required* for that security, given its beta. For example, Security A with a beta of 1.0 and an expected return of 17 percent would be an attractive investment because the expected return *exceeds* the 15.3 percent required return. In contrast, Security B with a beta of 2.0 is not an acceptable investment because its expected return (20 percent) *is less than* its required return (23.6 percent).

The Security Market Line in Terms of Beta

FIGURE 8-13

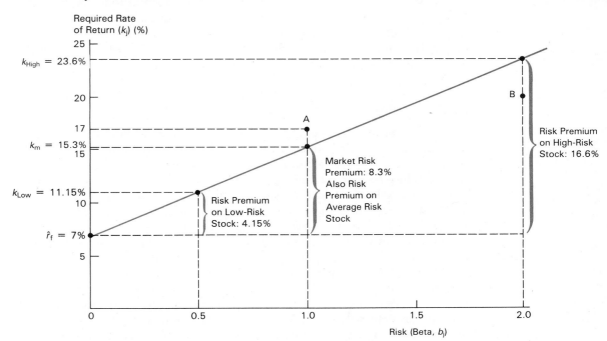

Inflation and the Security Market Line

The risk-free rate of return, r_f, can be thought of as consisting of the following two components:

- A *real* rate of return that is free from the effects of any inflationary expectations.
- A *premium* that is equal to the effects of expected inflation.

Historically the real rate of return on risk-free securities, such as U.S. government bonds, has averaged 2 to 5 percent per annum. The inflation premium normally is equal to investors' expectations about future purchasing power changes. If, for example, inflation is expected to average 4 percent over some future period, the risk-free rate of return on U.S. Treasury bills (assuming a real rate of return of 3 percent) should be approximately the following:

$$\hat{r}_f = \text{Real return} + \text{Expected inflation premium} \qquad (8.14)$$
$$= 3\% + 4\%$$
$$= 7\%$$

By extension, if inflation expectations suddenly increased from 4 to 6 percent, the risk-free rate should increase from 7 to 9 percent (3 percent real return plus 6 percent inflation premium).

Because the required return on any risky security, k_j, is equal to the risk-free rate plus the risk premium, an increase in inflationary expectations effectively increases the required return on all securities. This is shown in Figure 8-14. In the figure, SML' represents the returns required on all securities following a 2 percentage points increase in the expected future inflation rate. The required returns of all securities increase by 2 percentage points—the change in expected inflation. For example, the required rate of return on a security of average risk (that is, beta equal to 1.0) would increase from 15.3 to 17.3 percent. When investors increase their required returns, they become unwilling to purchase securities at existing prices, causing prices to decline. It should come as no surprise, then, that security analysts and investors take a dim view of increased inflation.

Risk Aversion and the Security Market Line

If the average risk premium (measured by the slope of the SML) increases because of an increase in uncertainty regarding the future economic outlook, or because investors as a group have tended to become more averse to risk and therefore require a higher rate of return for any level of risk, the slope of the SML will increase. This, in turn, will increase the risk premium on stocks with greater than average risk (beta greater than 1.0) more than on stocks with less than average risk (beta less than 1.0). This is shown in Figure 8-15. In the figure, SML" represents the returns required on all securities following a one percentage point increase in the market risk premium from 8.3 to 9.3 percent. For example, the required risk premium on a security with a beta of 0.5 increases by only 0.5 percentage points [0.5 × (9.3% − 8.3%)], or an increase in the required return from 11.15 to 11.65 percent. In contrast, the risk premium on a security with a beta of 2.0 experiences a rise in its required risk premium of 2 percentage points (2.0

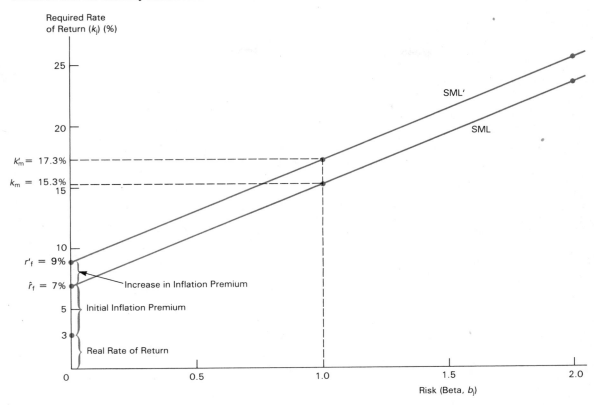

× 1.0%), or an increase in the required rate of return from 23.6 to 25.6 percent.

Uses of the CAPM and Portfolio Risk Concepts

The concepts of portfolio risk and the Capital Asset Pricing Model (CAPM), which relates required returns to systematic risk (beta), are powerful pedagogical tools to explain the nature of risk and its relationship to required returns on securities and physical assets. In Chapter 12 the CAPM is discussed as one technique that can be used to estimate the cost of equity capital. That chapter considers where the necessary data may be obtained to apply the model. Also, Chapter 11 considers the use of CAPM-determined required rates of return as a technique to adjust for risk in the capital budgeting process.

Assumptions and Limitations of the CAPM

The theoretical CAPM and its applications are based upon a number of crucial assumptions about the securities markets and investors' attitudes, including the following:

■ Investors hold well-diversified portfolios of securities. Hence their return

275

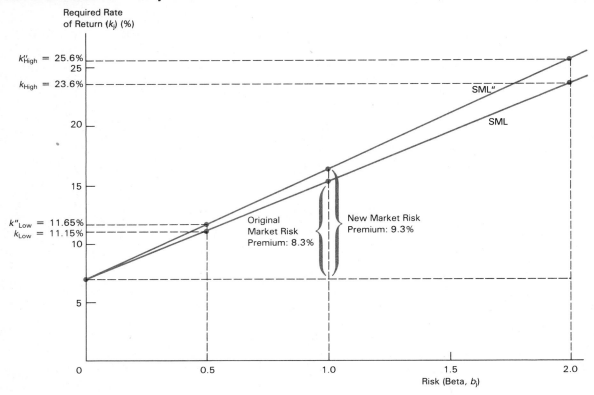

requirements are primarily influenced by the systematic (rather than total) risk of each security.

- Securities are actively traded in a competitive market, where information about a given firm and its future prospects is freely available.
- Investors can borrow and lend at the risk-free rate, which remains constant over time.
- There are no brokerage charges for buying and selling securities.
- There are no taxes.
- All investors prefer the security that provides the highest return for a given level of risk, or the lowest amount of risk for a given level of return.
- All investors have common (homogeneous) expectations regarding the expected returns, variances, and correlations of returns among all securities.

Whereas these assumptions may seem fairly limiting at first glance, extensions of the basic theory presented in this chapter, which relax the assumptions, generally have yielded results consistent with the fundamental theory. In addition, statistical tests of observed behavior in securities markets tend to support the results implied by the model presented here. In spite of these restrictive assumptions, this basic model has been extensively used, both practically and conceptually, to consider the risk–return tradeoff required by investors in the securities market. For example, the CAPM (or a modification thereof) has been used in regulated public utility rate case testimony aimed at determining a reasonable allowed rate of return for the utility's investors.

However, users of this approach also should be aware of some of the major problems encountered in practical applications. These include the following:

- Estimating expected future market returns.
- Determining the most appropriate estimate of the risk-free rate.
- Determining the best estimate of an asset's *future* beta.
- Reconciling the fact that some empirical tests have shown that investors do not totally ignore unsystematic risk, as the theory suggests.
- Measures of beta have been shown to be quite unstable over time, making it difficult to confidently measure the beta *expected* by investors.
- There is an increasing body of evidence to suggest that required returns on most securities are determined by factors in addition to the risk-free rate of interest and the systematic risk of the security.

ARBITRAGE PRICING THEORY[11]

As mentioned earlier, there is empirical evidence to indicate that the expected rate of return on a security is a function of multiple risk factors and not just the expected market return as postulated in the CAPM. A model, known as the *Arbitrage Pricing Theory* (APT), developed by Ross in the mid-1970s, uses multiple risk factors to explain security returns.[12] The APT postulates that the rate of return on a security is a linear function of a set of economic factors common to all securities. It can be expressed as follows:

$$k_j = \hat{k}_j + b_{1j}(\text{Factor 1}) + b_{2j}(\text{Factor 2}) + \ldots + b_{ij}(\text{Factor i}) + e_j \quad \textbf{(8.15)}$$

where

$$
\begin{aligned}
k_j &= \text{actual (realized) return on security j} \\
\hat{k}_j &= \text{expected return on security j} \\
(\text{Factor } i) &= \text{deviation of the } i\text{th factor} \\
&\quad \text{return from its expected value} \\
b_{ij} &= \text{sensitivity of security j returns to factor i} \\
e_j &= \text{random error term for security j} \\
&\quad \text{(with an expected value equal to 0)}
\end{aligned}
$$

In the CAPM the expected return on a security is equal to the risk-free rate plus a single risk premium that is equal to the product of the expected rate of return on the market portfolio less the risk-free rate times the sensitivity of the security's returns to the market return (that is, beta). The APT specifies that the expected return on a security is equal to the risk-free rate plus the sum of several risk premiums. Each of these risk premiums is equal to the product of the expected return on the factor less the risk-free rate times the sensitivity of the security's returns to the corresponding factor. Unlike the CAPM, the APT does not specify what (risk) factors should be used in determining expected security returns.

[11] This section may be omitted without loss of continuity.
[12] Ross, Stephen A. "Arbitrage Pricing Theory," *Journal of Economic Theory* (December 1976): 341–360.

Empirical studies by Roll and Ross suggest that possibly four economic factors can be used in measuring security returns.[13] These are *unanticipated* changes in

1. Industrial production.
2. Inflation.
3. Bond default risk premiums (measured by differences in the yield, or spread, between low-grade and high-grade bonds).
4. Slope of the yield curve (measured by differences in long-term and short-term rates on U.S. government bonds).

Unanticipated changes in the economic factors are used in the model because any anticipated changes already have been incorporated into the expected return on the security.

Because of difficulties with the statistical methodology employed in testing the APT, mixed results have been obtained with respect to determining the appropriate economic factors to use in the model to explain security returns.

OTHER DIMENSIONS OF RISK

This chapter has focused on various measures of variability in returns— either total variability, measured by the *standard deviation* and the *coefficient of variation*, or systematic variability, measured by *beta*. Although variability of returns is very important, it does not adequately consider another important risk dimension—that is, the risk of failure. In the case of an individual investment project, failure is a situation in which a project generates a *negative* rate of return. In the case of the entire firm, failure is the situation in which a firm loses money and ultimately is forced into bankruptcy.

For risk-averse investors, the risk of failure may play a large role in determining the types of investments undertaken. For example, the management of a firm is not likely to be eager to invest in a project that has a high risk of failure and that ultimately may cause the firm to fail if it proves to be unsuccessful. After all, the continued survival of the firm is closely tied to the economic well-being of management.

From a shareholder wealth maximization perspective, failure is a particularly undesirable occurrence. The direct and indirect costs of bankruptcy can be very high. Consequently, this failure risk often is an important determinant of investment risk. The risk and cost of failure can explain, in large part, the desire of many firms to diversify. In addition to reducing the overall risk of a firm, diversification can result in a lower probability of bankruptcy and thus lower *expected* costs incurred during bankruptcy. These costs include the following:

■ The loss of funds that occur when assets are sold at distressed prices during liquidation.
■ The legal fees and selling costs incurred when a firm enters bankruptcy proceedings.
■ The opportunity costs of the funds that are unavailable to investors dur-

[13] Roll, Richard, and Stephen A. Ross. "An Empirical Investigation of the Arbitrage Pricing Theory," *Journal of Finance* (December 1980): 1073–1104 and "The Arbitrage Pricing Theory Approach to Strategic Portfolio Planning," *Financial Analysts Journal* (May–June 1984): 14–26.

ing the bankruptcy proceedings (for example, it took over eight years to settle the Penn-Central bankruptcy).

If, through diversification, a firm can decrease the probability of bankruptcy, it can reduce its *expected* bankruptcy costs. Lower expected bankruptcy costs should increase shareholder wealth, all other things being equal.

Diversification also may reduce a firm's cost of capital. By reducing the overall risk of the firm, diversification will lower the default risk of the firm's debt securities, and the firm's bonds will receive higher ratings and require lower interest payments. In addition, the firm may be able to increase the proportion of low-cost debt relative to equity in its optimal capital structure, further reducing the cost of capital and increasing shareholder wealth.[14]

Although we will focus primarily on return variability as our measure of risk in this book, the risk and cost of failure also should be kept in mind.

MANAGING RISK AND UNCERTAINTY

In addition to investment diversification, there are many other avenues open to the financial manager who wishes to reduce the level of risk associated with a particular resource allocation decision. In this section we briefly consider some of these strategies for managing risk.

Acquisition of Additional Information

In many cases the risk facing a manager arises because of a lack of information. For example, when making the decision to invest in the development and marketing of a new product, there is considerable risk regarding the market's acceptance of this new product. To reduce this risk many firms will "test market" the product in a limited area or present the product to panels of consumers for their evaluation. These tactics provide important information to the company as it seeks to assess the probable success of the new product.

Information also can be purchased from individuals or firms that possess the knowledge the decision maker seeks. For example, a wildcat oil drilling firm will employ the services of petroleum geologists as it attempts to determine where to drill exploratory wells. Similarly, companies that plan to sell new debt securities often pay to have their bonds "rated" by one of the bond rating services, such as Moody's or Standard and Poor's. The ratings applied to the bonds reduce the risk of determining the yield that will have to be offered to investors when the bonds are sold.

Normally, additional information is costly. Hence, the wealth maximizing firm would be willing to invest in additional information as long as the marginal value of that information exceeds its marginal cost.

Hedging

A *hedge* is a transaction that limits the risk associated with market price fluctuations for a particular investment position. A hedge is accomplished by taking offsetting positions in the ownership of an asset or security, such

---

[14] The concept of optimal capital structure is discussed in Chapter 13.

as buying or selling a futures contract (or an option) to offset risk exposure in the cash market. A *futures contract* is a standardized contract, traded on an organized exchange, to buy or sell a fixed quantity of a defined commodity at a set price in the future. Hedging also can be accomplished using *forward contracts*. A forward contract is a contractual agreement between two parties to exchange a commodity at a set price in the future. The primary differences between futures contracts and forward contracts are that forward contracts are not actively traded on an organized exchange, such as the Chicago Board of Trade; normally forward contracts do not deal in standardized goods; and they carry the risk that one party to the contract may not perform as agreed. In contrast, futures contracts carry no such performance risk because they are essentially guaranteed by the exchange on which they are traded.

Futures and forward contracts create the legal obligation for the buyer (or seller) to purchase (or sell) the goods specified in the contract at the agreed upon price at some future point in time. In contrast, an *option* gives the buyer the *right*, but not the obligation, to either buy or sell the underlying commodity. We will confine our discussion of hedging to futures contracts. A complete discussion of hedging using forward contracts, options, and options on futures contracts is provided in several of the references listed at the end of this chapter.

Futures markets exist for many commodities, including materials (such as copper, gold, silver, and crude oil), agricultural commodities (such as corn, wheat, live hogs, cotton, and cattle), and financial instruments (such as Treasury bills, Treasury bonds, foreign currencies, commercial paper, and broad-based common stock indexes like the *Standard and Poor's 500 Stock Index*). Any enterprise that normally buys or sells these commodities (or products closely related to these commodities) or is engaged in borrowing or lending operations can make use of futures contracts, forward markets, and options to eliminate, or at least largely offset, the risk of future price fluctuations.

For example, consider the case of the corporate treasurer of Zenith Electric who projects in late September that the company's cash flows will require a $3 million bank loan in mid-December. This loan is expected to be needed for 3 months. The contractual agreement between the corporate borrower and its bank establishes the rate on loans such as this to be 1.5 percentage points above the 3-month Eurodollar rate (also referred to as LIBOR—London Interbank Offering Rate). The current (September) LIBOR rate is 9.5 percent. The treasurer is concerned that this rate may increase over the next 3 months. Therefore, the treasurer wishes to "lock-in" her company's cost of borrowing in mid-December.

Eurodollar Time Deposit futures contracts are traded on the International Monetary Market (IMM), a division of the Chicago Mercantile Exchange. These Eurodollar contracts are for $1 million of 3-month Eurodollar time deposits. The IMM has a pricing system that quotes these contracts on a discounted percentage basis; that is, the price of a contract is quoted as 100 minus the annualized interest rate on 3-month Eurodollar Time Deposits. For example, a contract price of 91 implies an annualized interest rate of 9 percent (100 minus 91 = 9 percent).

In September, the corporate treasurer observes that the December futures contract, which can be used to "lock-in" the forward borrowing rate, is trading at 90.30, implying a forward Eurodollar rate of 9.7 percent (100.0 − 90.3). If the treasurer sells three December Eurodollar futures contracts

($1 million each) at 90.3, she can assure that Zenith's cost of funds in December will be 11.2 percent (9.7 percent LIBOR rate plus the 1.5 percentage points spread over LIBOR charged by the bank).

By mid-December the current Eurodollar rate has risen to 12.0 percent. The December futures price has declined to 88.00, reflecting the current 12 percent rate. Because of these higher rates, the company's quarterly interest payments to the bank are $101,250 ($3,000,000 × 13.5 percent × 0.25 years). The decline in the futures price, however, produces a profit for Zenith of $17,250 [(90.3 − 88.0) × $2,500 × 3 contracts]. (Each one percentage point increase in the price of a Eurodollar futures contract is equivalent to an increase in the value of that contract of $2,500, (that is, $1,000,000 × .01 × 0.25 years). Recall that the corporate treasurer sold three Eurodollar contracts in September at 90.3. The treasurer can cancel her position in the futures market by buying three contracts in December at the new lower price of 88.0.

Thus, the net interest cost to Zenith is $84,000 ($101,250 interest payment to the bank less $17,250 profit from the futures contracts), giving an effective annual rate of 11.2 percent. In this example, the treasurer has perfectly hedged her borrowing cost position. In practice, it usually is not possible to perfectly hedge one's position because of (1) differences in the size of standard future contracts and the amount of hedging desired by the firm; (2) the inability to find a futures contract in a commodity or financial instrument that has precisely the same pattern of price movements as the commodity or financial instrument in which the firm is dealing; and (3) variations in the difference (called the *basis*) between the spot or cash market price for a commodity or financial instrument and the futures market price. In spite of these shortcomings, hedging can be used in many situations to reduce the risk of future price changes in goods or financial instruments. Over the past decade many new financial futures and option contracts have been developed that permit financial institutions and other firms to control their future financing cost and/or to guarantee their returns on anticipated future investments.

Other Approaches for Managing Risk

In addition to investment diversification, acquiring additional information, and hedging, several other techniques can be used to manage risk, such as purchasing insurance, gaining control over the operating environment, and limiting the use of firm-specific assets.

INSURANCE. When a business firm pays a premium to an insurance company, that firm is exchanging the premium payment for protection against specified losses, up to the limits identified in the policy. Insurance commonly is available for losses due to fires, natural disasters, accidents occurring in the workplace, the death of key employees, fraud, product liability, and theft. Some financial instruments such as corporate bonds are backed by insurance that guarantees the payment of principal and interest. When deciding which risks should be insured externally and which should be self-insured, financial managers are confronted with a tradeoff between a certain, small, periodic cost (the payment of the insurance premium), and the uncertainty of bearing the full cost of a loss from time to time. The willingness of managers to assume some insurable risks, the cost of the insurance, and the severity of the consequences of experiencing an uninsured loss will determine whether insurance is purchased.

GAINING CONTROL OVER THE OPERATING ENVIRONMENT. Some business risks can be reduced by actions designed to gain control over the operating environment. For example, to assure adequate outlets for its products, a firm may invest in a network of exclusive dealerships. If access to raw materials is uncertain, a firm may integrate backwards toward the source of supplies. The use of patents and copyrights can protect a firm against immediate competition. Legal action also can reinforce its rights under patents and copyrights. For example, in early 1988 Apple Computer sued Microsoft because many of the new programs being developed by Microsoft had "the look and feel of the Apple operating environment." This lawsuit has been widely recognized as an attempt to delay the development of operating systems for the IBM personal computer that would compete more directly with the Apple products.

LIMITED USE OF FIRM-SPECIFIC ASSETS. If a firm builds a plant that can be used only to produce its specific product, that firm has effectively limited its options should the product prove unsuccessful. The more general the purpose of the assets employed by a firm, the more flexibility that firm has to redeploy these assets to other uses. A tradeoff exists between the use of firm- or product-specific assets, which are likely to be more efficient, and the use of more general-purpose assets, which give the firm increased future flexibility. When planning new investments, this tradeoff must be carefully evaluated.

SUMMARY

- The *risk* of a security or an investment project generally is defined in terms of the potential *variability* of its returns. When only one return is possible—for example, as with U.S. government securities held to maturity—there is no risk. When more than one return is possible for a particular project, it is risky.
- The *standard deviation*, σ, of the returns from an investment is an *absolute* measure of risk. It is computed as the square root of the weighted average squared deviations of possible outcomes from the expected value.
- When investments with unequal expected returns are being compared, the *coefficient of variation*, v, is a more appropriate measure of risk. The coefficient of variation is the ratio of the standard deviation to the expected value.
- Because cash flow projections and expected returns can be estimated with less certainty further into the future, risk generally is thought to *increase over time*.
- Risk also is influenced by the possibility of investment *diversification*. For example, if a proposed project's returns are not *perfectly correlated* with the returns from the firm's other investments, the total risk of the firm may be reduced by accepting the proposed project. This is known as the *portfolio effect*.
- The *expected return from a portfolio* of two or more securities is equal to the weighted average of the expected returns from the individual securities.

■ The *risk of a portfolio* is a function of both the risk of the individual securities in the portfolio and the correlation among the individual securities' returns.

■ The *Capital Asset Pricing Model* (CAPM) is a theory that can be used to determine required rates of return on financial and physical assets.

■ The *unsystematic* portion of the total risk in a security's return is that portion of return variability unique to the firm. Efficient diversification of a portfolio of securities can eliminate most unsystematic risk.

■ *Systematic risk* refers to the portion of total risk in a security's return caused by overall market forces. This risk cannot be diversified away in a portfolio. Systematic risk forms the basis for the risk premium required by investors in any risky security.

■ The *security market line* (SML) provides an algebraic or graphic representation of the risk–return tradeoff required in the marketplace for risky securities. It measures risk in terms of systematic risk.

■ An index of systematic risk for a security is the security's *beta*. Beta is determined from the slope of a regression line, the *characteristic line*, between the market return and the individual security's return. It is a measure of the volatility of a security's returns relative to the returns of the market as a whole.

■ The required return on common stock consists of the risk-free rate plus a risk premium. This risk premium is equal to a security's beta times the market risk premium, and the market risk premium is equal to the difference between the expected market return and the risk-free rate.

■ The *Arbitrage Pricing Theory* (APT) is a model that relates expected returns on securities to multiple risk factors. Unlike the CAPM, the APT does not specify what risk factor(s) should be used in determining expected returns.

■ In addition to investment diversification, other techniques can be used in managing risk. These include acquisition of additional information, hedging, insurance, gaining control over the environment, and limited use of firm-specific assets.

QUESTIONS AND TOPICS FOR DISCUSSION

1. Define the following terms:
   a. Risk
   b. Probability distribution
   c. Standard deviation
   d. Required rate of return
   e. Coefficient of variation
   f. Efficient portfolio
   g. Efficient frontier
   h. Capital market line
   i. Beta coefficient
   j. CAPM
   k. Correlation coefficient
   l. Portfolio
   m. Characteristic line
   n. Security market line
   o. Covariance
   p. Systematic risk
   q. Unsystematic risk
   r. Arbitrage Pricing Theory (APT)
   s. Hedging

t. Futures contract

u. Option

2. If the returns from a security were known with certainty, what shape would the probability distribution of returns graph have?

3. What is the nature of the risk associated with "risk-free" U.S. government bonds?

4. If inflation expectations increase, what would you expect to happen to the returns required by investors in bonds? What would happen to bond prices?

5. Under what circumstances will the coefficient of variation of a security's returns and the standard deviation of that security's returns give the same relative measure of risk when compared with the risk of another security?

6. Explain how diversification can reduce the risk of a portfolio of assets to below the weighted average of the risk of the individual assets.

7. What are the primary variables that influence the risk of a portfolio of assets?

8. Distinguish between unsystematic and systematic risk. Under what circumstances are investors likely to ignore the unsystematic risk characteristics of a security?

9. What effect do increasing inflation expectations have on the required returns of investors in common stock?

10. The stock of Amrep Corporation has a *beta* value estimated to be 1.4. How would you interpret this beta value? How would you evaluate the firm's systematic risk?

11. How is a security's beta value computed?

12. Under what circumstances can the beta concept be used to estimate the rate of return required by investors in a stock? What problems are encountered when using the CAPM?

13. Explain the difference between forward and futures contracts.

14. Explain the difference between a futures contract and an option contract.

PROBLEMS*

1. You have estimated the following probability distributions of expected future returns for Stocks X and Y:

Stock X		Stock Y	
Probability	Return PR	Probability	Return
0.1	−10% ◡1,0	0.2	2% 0,4
0.2	10 2	0.2	7 1,4
0.4	15 6	0.3	12 3,6
0.2	20 4	0.2	15 3,0
0.1	40 4	0.1	16 1,6
	15%		10,0 %

$b(R - E.R)^2 P + \cdots$

a. What is the expected rate of return for Stock X? Stock Y?

b. What is the standard deviation of expected returns for Stock X? For Stock Y? $\sigma^2 (-10-15)^2 0.1 + (10-15)^2 0.2 + (15-15)^2 0.4$

$CV_x = \dfrac{0.1164}{0.15} \times (106) = 77.6\%$

c. Which stock would you consider to be riskier? Why? $\dfrac{\sigma}{P(R)} \times (100)$

$CV_y = \dfrac{0.0494}{0.10} (100) = 49.40\%$ The return expected from Project number 542 is 22 percent. The standard deviation of these returns is 11 percent. If returns from the project are normally distributed, what is the chance that the project will result in a rate of return above 33 percent? What is the probability that the project will result in losses (negative rates of return)?

3. The expected rate of return for the stock of Cornhusker Enterprises is 20 percent, with a standard deviation of 15 percent. The expected rate of return for the stock of Mustang Associates is 10 percent, with a standard deviation of 9 percent.

   a. Which stock would you consider to be riskier? Why?
   b. If you knew that the beta coefficient of Cornhusker stock is 1.5 and the beta of Mustang is 0.9, how would your answer to Part a change?

4. The current dividend, D_0, of the stock of Sun Devil Corporation is $3 per share. Under present conditions this dividend is expected to grow at a rate of 6 percent annually for the foreseeable future. The beta of Sun Devil's stock is 1.5. The risk-free rate of return is 7 percent, and the expected market rate of return is 14 percent.

   a. At what price would you expect Sun Devil's common stock to sell?
   b. If the risk-free rate of return declines to 6 percent, what will happen to Sun Devil's stock price? (Assume the expected market rate of return remains at 14 percent.)
   c. Sun Devil's management is considering acquisitions in the machine tool industry. Management expects the firm's beta to increase to 1.6 as a result of these acquisitions. The dividend growth rate is expected to increase to 7 percent annually. Would you recommend this acquisition program to management? (Assume the same initial conditions that existed in Part a.)

5. You are considering purchasing a portfolio of securities. The securities available to you have the following expected returns:

Security	Expected Return (%)
A	14
B	9
C	15
D	11

   a. If you invest 20 percent of your funds in Security A, 40 percent in B, 20 percent in C, and 20 percent in D, what is the expected return of the portfolio?
   b. How does the expected return of the portfolio change if you invest 40 percent in A, 10 percent in B, 40 percent in C, and 10 percent in D?
   c. In addition to the portfolio in Part b having a different expected return than the portfolio in Part a, how would you expect the two portfolios to differ with respect to risk?

6. You are considering investing in two securities, X and Y. The following data are available for the two securities: coefficient of variation

	Security X	Security Y
Expected return	0.10	0.07
Standard deviation of returns	0.08	0.04

$$CVx = \frac{0.08}{0.10}(100) = 80\%$$
$$CVy = \frac{0.04}{0.07}(100) = 57.14\%$$

X is risky.

   a. If you invest 40 percent of your funds in Security X and 60 percent in Security Y, and if the correlation of returns between X and Y is +0.5, compute the following:
   i. The expected return from the portfolio.
   ii. The standard deviation of returns from the portfolio.

b. What happens to the expected return and standard deviation of returns of the portfolio in Part a if 70 percent of your funds are invested in Security X and 30 percent of your funds are invested in Security Y?

c. What happens to the expected return and standard deviation of returns of the portfolio in Part a if the following conditions exist?
  i. The correlation of returns between Securities X and Y is +1.0.
  ii. The correlation of returns between Securities X and Y is 0.
  iii. The correlation of returns between Securities X and Y is −0.7.

7. You have the following information on two securities you have invested in:

(a) $CVx = \dfrac{4.5\%}{15\%} = 30\%$

$CVK = \dfrac{3.8\%}{12\%} = 31.6$ Kodak

Kodack is riskyer.

Security	Expected Return	Standard Deviation	Beta	% Invested (W)
Xerox	15%	4.5%	1.2	35%
Kodak	12%	3.8%	0.98	65%

a. Which stock is riskier in a portfolio context? Which stock is riskier if you are considering them as individual assets (not part of a portfolio)?

(b) $Kp = W_1K_1 + W_2K_2 \cdots W_nk_n$

b. Compute the expected return on the portfolio.

$0.35(15\%) + 0.65(12\%) = 13.05\%$

c. If the securities have a correlation of 0.60, compute the standard deviation of the portfolio.

$Bp = W_1B_1 + W_2B_2 \cdots + W_nB_n$

d. Compute the beta of the portfolio $Bp = (35\%)(1.2) + (65\%)(0.98)$

$= 1.057$

$W_T = weights$
$K_T = individual\ rate\ of\ return$
$Kp = potpolio's\ rate\ of\ return$

8. Realizing the benefits of diversification you have invested in the following securities:

	United	Chubb	Chase
Expected return	12%	14%	9%
Standard deviation of return	3%	5%	3%
Beta	1.65	1.2	0.89
Amount invested in each security	$50,000	$125,000	$75,000

a. Compute the expected rate of return on the portfolio.
b. Compute the beta of the portfolio.

9. The SML has been estimated as follows:

$$k_j = 0.06 + 0.083\ b_j$$

This estimate assumes an expected rate of inflation of 4 percent. If inflation expectations increase from 4 to 6 percent, what will be the equation of the new SML?

10. The stock of Pizza Hot, Inc., a Mexican pizza chain, has an estimated beta of 1.5. Calculate the required rate of return on Pizza Hot's stock if the SML is estimated as follows:

$$k_j = 0.06 + 0.083\ b_j$$

based on

a. An inflation expectation of 4 percent.
b. A new inflation expectation of 6 percent.

11. Caledonia Minerals has an estimated beta of 1.6. The company is considering the acquisition of another firm that has a beta of 1.2. Both companies are exactly the same size.

a. What is the expected new beta value for the combined firm?
b. The risk-free rate of return is estimated at 7 percent, and the market return is estimated as 12 percent. What is your estimate of the required return of investors in Caledonia before and after the merger?

Caledonia Minerals is expected to pay a $1 dividend next year ($D_1 = \$1$). This dividend is expected to grow at a rate of 6 percent per year for the foreseeable future if the merger is not completed. The merger is not expected to change the current dividend rate, but future dividends are expected to grow at a 7 percent rate as a result of the merger.

   c. What is the value of a share of stock in Caledonia Minerals prior to the merger?
      HINT: Use the required equity return computed in Part b.
   d. What is the new value of a share of stock, assuming that the merger is completed?
   e. Would you recommend that Caledonia go ahead with the merger?

12. Globe Steel has decided to diversify into the home improvement field. As a result of this expansion, Globe's beta value drops from 1.3 to 0.9, and the expected future, long-term growth rate in the firm's dividends drops from 8 to 7 percent. The expected market return, k_m, is 14 percent; the risk-free rate, r_f, is 7 percent; and the current dividends per share, D_0, are $3. Should Globe undertake the planned diversification?

13. Tucker Manufacturing Company has a beta estimated at 1.0. The risk-free rate is 6 percent, and the expected market return is 12 percent. Tucker expects to pay a $4 dividend next year ($D_1 = \$4$). This dividend is expected to grow at 3 percent per year for the foreseeable future. The current market price for Tucker is $40.

   a. Is the current stock price an equilibrium price, based upon the SML calculation of k_e for Tucker?
   b. What do you think the appropriate equilibrium price is? How will that price be achieved?

14. Using Equation 8.13, suppose you have computed the *required* rate of return for the stock of Bulldog Trucking to be 16.6 percent. Given the current stock price, the current dividend rate, and analysts' projections for future dividend growth, you *expect* to earn a rate of return of 18 percent.

   a. Would you recommend buying or selling this stock? Why?
   b. If your *expected* rate of return from the stock of Bulldog is 15 percent, what would you expect to happen to Bulldog's stock price?

15. You want to construct a portfolio with a 20 percent expected return. The portfolio is to consist of some combination of Security A and Security B:

Security	Expected Return	Beta
A	15%	0.82
B	28	1.75

   a. What percentage of your portfolio should consist of Security A? Of Security B?
   b. What is the beta of the portfolio?

16. a. The stock of Koch Brickyard, Inc., is expected to return 14 percent with a standard deviation of 5 percent. Uptown Potbelly Stove Works' stock is expected to return 16 percent with a standard deviation of 9 percent. If you invest 30 percent of your funds in Koch stock and 70 percent in Uptown stock, what is the expected return on your portfolio?
    b. What is the expected risk of this portfolio if the returns for the two stocks have
       i. A perfect positive correlation ($+1.0$).
       ii. A slightly negative correlation (-0.2).

17. Security A offers an expected return of 15 percent with a standard deviation of 7 percent. Security B offers an expected return of 9 percent with a standard deviation of 4 percent. The correlation between the returns of A and B

is $+0.6$. If an investor puts one-fourth of his wealth in A and three-fourths in B, what is the expected return and risk (standard deviation) of this portfolio?

18. The beta of MacDrive is estimated to be 1.3. The beta of MacWalk is estimated to be 1.1. If these two firms merge, to form MacRun, what will be the beta of the new firm, assuming that MacWalk was two times as large as MacDrive?

19. Equation 8.7 can be modified to compute the risk of a three-security portfolio as follows:

$$\sigma_p = \sqrt{W_A^2\sigma_A^2 + W_B^2\sigma_B^2 + W_C^2\sigma_C^2 + 2W_AW_B\rho_{AB}\sigma_A\sigma_B + 2W_AW_C\rho_{AC}\sigma_A\sigma_C + 2W_BW_C\rho_{BC}\sigma_B\sigma_C}$$

You have decided to invest 40 percent of your wealth in Security A, 30 percent in Security B, and 30 percent in Security C. The following information is available about the possible returns from the three securities:

Security A		Security B		Security C	
Return (%)	**Probability**	**Return (%)**	**Probability**	**Return (%)**	**Probability**
10	0.25	13	0.30	14	0.40
12	0.50	16	0.35	18	0.30
14	0.25	19	0.35	22	0.30

Compute the expected return of the portfolio and the risk of the portfolio if the correlations between returns from the three securities are $\rho_{AB} = 0.70$; $\rho_{AC} = 0.60$; and $\rho_{BC} = 0.85$.

20. Mammouth Mutual Fund of New York has $10 million to invest in certificates of deposit (CDs) for the next 6 months (180 days). It can buy either a Pittsburgh National Bank (PNB) CD with an annual yield of 11 percent or a Frankfurt (West Germany) Bank CD with a yield of 13.5 percent. Assume that the CDs are of comparable default risk. The analysts of the mutual fund are concerned about exchange rate risk. They were quoted the following exchange rates by the international department of a New York City bank:

**West Germany
(deutsche marks)**

Spot	$0.5200
30-day forward	0.5190
90-day forward	0.5170
180-day forward	0.5155

a. If the Frankfurt Bank CD is purchased and held to maturity, determine the net gain (loss) in U.S. dollars relative to the PNB CD assuming that the exchange rate in 180 days equals today's spot rate.

b. Suppose the West German mark declines in value by 5 percent relative to the U.S. dollar over the next 180 days. Determine the net gain (loss) of the Frankfurt Bank CD in U.S. dollars relative to the PNB CD for an uncovered position.

c. Determine the net gain (loss) from a covered position.

21. The return on the Tarheel Corp. stock is expected to be 14 percent with a standard deviation of 8 percent. The beta of Tarheel is 0.8. The risk-free rate is 7 percent and the expected return on the market portfolio is 15

percent. What is the probability that an investor in Tarheel will earn a rate of return less than the required rate of return?

22. The stock of Jones Trucking is expected to return 13 percent annually with a standard deviation of 8 percent. The stock of Bush Steel Mills is expected to return 17% annually with a standard deviation of 14 percent. The correlation between the returns from the two securities has been estimated to be +0.3. The beta of the Jones' stock is 0.9 and the beta of the Bush stock is 1.2. The risk-free rate of return is expected to be 8 percent and the expected return on the market portfolio is 15 percent. The current dividend for Jones is $4. The current dividend for Bush is $6.

   a. What is the expected return from a portfolio containing the two securities if 40 percent of your wealth is invested in Jones and 60 percent is invested in Bush?
   b. What is the expected standard deviation of the portfolio of the two stocks?
   c. Which stock is the better buy in the current market? Why?

SELECTED REFERENCES

Chen, Nai-Fu. "Some Empirical Tests of the Theory of Arbitrage Pricing," *Journal of Finance* 38 (December 1983): 1393–1414.

Copeland, Thomas E., and J. Fred Weston. *Financial Theory and Corporate Policy*, 3d ed. Reading, MA: Addison-Wesley, 1988.

Elton, E. J., and M. J. Gruber. *Modern Portfolio Theory and Investment Analysis*, 2d ed. New York: John Wiley, 1984.

Findlay, M. C., and E. E. Williams. "Better Betas Didn't Help the Boat People," *Journal of Portfolio Management* (Fall 1986): 4–10.

Harrington, Diana R. *Modern Portfolio Theory, the Capital Asset Pricing Model and Arbitrage Pricing Theory: A User's Guide*, 2d ed. Englewood Cliffs, NJ: Prentice-Hall, 1987.

Lintner, J. "The Valuation of Risky Assets and the Selection of Risky Investments in Stock Portfolios and Capital Budgets," *Review of Economics and Statistics* 47 (February 1965): 13–37.

Markowitz, Harry M. "Portfolio Selection," *Journal of Finance* 7 (March 1952): 77–91.

Markowitz, Harry M. *Portfolio Selection: Efficient Diversification of Investments*. New York: John Wiley, 1959.

Mullins, David W., Jr. "Does the Capital Asset Pricing Model Work?" *Harvard Business Review* 60 (January–February 1982): 105–114.

Reilly, Frank K., and D. J. Wright. "A Comparison of Published Betas," *Journal of Portfolio Management* (Spring 1988): 64–68.

Sharpe, William F. "Capital Asset Prices: A Theory of Market Equilibrium under Conditions of Risk," *Journal of Finance* 19 (September 1964): 425–442.

Statman, Meir. "How Many Stocks Make a Diversified Portfolio?" *Journal of Financial and Quantitative Analysis* (September 1985): 353–365.

IV

The Capital Investment Decision

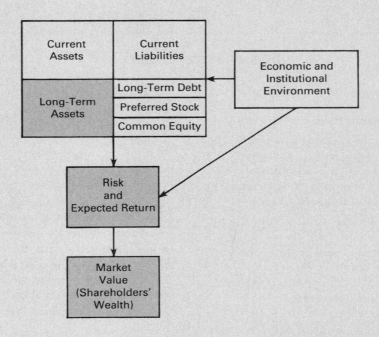

This part of the text looks at the financial management of the long-term asset portion of a firm's balance sheet. Investments in these assets (for example, property, plant, and equipment) have a major impact on a firm's future stream of earnings and the risk of those earnings. As such, the long-term investment (capital budgeting) decision has a significant effect on the value of the firm. Chapter 9 deals with the measurement of cash flows from long-term investments. Chapter 10 analyzes various investment decision criteria in light of the wealth maximization objective of the firm. Chapter 11 extends the analysis to consider techniques to account for differential levels of risk among projects.

9

Capital Budgeting and Cash Flow Analysis

KEY CHAPTER CONCEPTS

1. *Capital budgeting* is the process of planning for purchases of assets whose returns (cash flows) are expected to continue beyond 1 year.

2. The *cost of capital* is defined as the cost of funds supplied to a firm. It represents the required rate of return a firm must earn on its investments, and thus is an important input in the capital budgeting process.

3. There are four key steps in the capital budgeting process,
   a. Generating investment project proposals.
   b. Estimating cash flows.
   c. Evaluating alternatives and selecting projects to be implemented.
   d. Reviewing a project's performance after it has been implemented, and postauditing its performance after termination.

4. Investment projects can be generated by growth opportunities, by cost reduction opportunities, and to meet legal requirements and health and safety standards.

5. The initial outlay required to implement a project is called the *net investment*. It includes

   a. The installed cost of the assets,
   b. Plus any net working capital requirements,
   c. Less any cash inflows from the sale of replacement assets,
   d. Plus or minus the tax consequences associated with the sale of existing assets and/or the purchase of new assets.

6. The *net cash flow* from a project is equal to the change in net income after taxes plus the change in depreciation associated with the adoption of a project. In the last year of a project's life this net cash flow definition may have to be modified to reflect the recapture of the net working capital investment and any after-tax salvage value received.

7. The economic viability of a project can be affected by special tax considerations, such as the use of accelerated depreciation methods, like the Modified Accelerated Cost Recovery System (MACRS) of depreciation.

GLOSSARY OF NEW TERMS

Capital budgeting The process of planning for purchases of assets whose returns (cash flows) are expected to continue beyond 1 year.

Capital expenditure The amount of money spent to purchase a long-term asset, such as a piece of equipment. This cash outlay generally is expected to result in a flow of future cash benefits extending beyond 1 year in time. (Also called *capital investment*.)

Capital rationing The process of limiting the number of capital expenditure projects because of insufficient funds to finance all projects that otherwise meet the firm's criteria for acceptability, or because of a lack of sufficient managerial resources to undertake all otherwise acceptable projects.

Contingent project A project whose acceptance depends on the adoption of one or more other projects.

Depreciation The systematic allocation of the cost of an asset over its expected economic life or some other period of time for financial reporting purposes, tax purposes, or both.

Independent project A project whose acceptance or rejection does not directly result in the elimination of other projects from consideration.

MACRS depreciation The Modified Accelerated Cost Recovery System of depreciation, established in 1986.

Mutually exclusive project A project whose acceptance precludes the acceptance of one or more alternative projects.

Net cash flow Cash inflow minus cash outflow. It often is measured as income after tax plus noncash expenses associated with a particular investment project.

Net investment The net cash outlay required at the beginning of an investment project.

Normal project A project whose cash flow stream requires an initial outlay of funds followed by a series of positive net cash inflows. This sometimes is called a *conventional project*.

Estimating Cash Flows from Corporate Benefits*

In 1987, Union Bank in Los Angeles opened a day-care facility at its operations center. It cost the bank $105,000 to operate the day-care facility in 1988, but the bank estimates that the facility actually saved the bank roughly $185,000 during the year.

The bank estimated that the cash flow savings came from two principal sources:

1. Estimated savings from employee turnover totaled approximately $110,000, based mostly on the fact that turnover among center users was much lower than among the bank's other employees.
2. Savings from lost days' work were estimated to be $35,000, because, on average, center users were absent less than the bank's other employees.

Today, in general, companies require detailed estimates of the expected cash flow benefits from their investments. This applies not only to investments in new plant and equipment, but also to investments in such programs as day-care assistance, maternity leaves, and flexible work schedules.

The analysis of capital investments (that is, projects having economic lives extending beyond a year in time) is a key financial management function. Each year large and small firms spend hundreds of billions of dollars on capital investments. These investments chart the course of a company's future for many years to come. Therefore it is imperative that capital investment analysis be performed correctly. This chapter develops the principles of capital investment analysis—with emphasis on the estimation of cash flows from a project. Chapter 10 considers appropriate decision criteria in the capital budgeting process.

* Adopted from "Companies Try Measuring Cost Savings from New Types of Corporate Benefits," *Wall Street Journal* (December 29, 1988), p. B1.

▰▰▰ INTRODUCTION

This is the first of several chapters that explicitly deal with the financial management of the assets on a firm's balance sheet. In this and the following two chapters we consider the management of long-term assets. Later in the book (Chapters 17 to 19) the emphasis shifts to the management of short-term assets; that is, the working capital decision.

Capital budgeting is the process of planning for purchases of assets whose returns are expected to continue beyond 1 year. A *capital expenditure* is a cash outlay that is expected to generate a flow of future cash benefits lasting longer than 1 year. It is distinguished from a normal operating expenditure, which is expected to result in cash benefits during the coming 1-year period. (The choice of a 1-year period is arbitrary, but it does serve as a useful guideline.)

Several different types of outlays may be classified as capital expenditures and evaluated using the framework of capital budgeting models, including the following:

■ The purchase of a new piece of equipment, real estate, or a building in order to expand an existing product or service line or enter a new line of business.

■ The replacement of an existing capital asset, such as a drill press.

- Expenditures for an advertising campaign.
- Expenditures for a research and development program.
- Investments in permanent increases of target inventory levels or levels of accounts receivable.
- Investments in employee education and training.
- The refunding of an old bond issue with a new, lower interest issue.
- Lease-versus-buy analysis.
- Merger and acquisition evaluation.

Capital expenditures are important to a firm both because they require sizable cash outlays and because they have a long-range impact on the firm's performance. Table 9-1 summarizes the capital expenditures made by U.S. firms during 1985 and 1988. Total capital expenditures of all industries in the United States during 1988 exceeded 487 *billion* dollars. During 1988 Digital Equipment earned about $1.3 billion after taxes and made outlays for new plant facilities and equipment in excess of $1.5 billion. Bethlehem Steel had 1986 losses of $153 million, yet it made $229 million in capital expenditures that year.

A firm's capital expenditures affect its future profitability and, when taken together, essentially plot the company's future direction by determining which products will be produced, which markets will be entered, where production facilities will be located, and what type of technology will be used. Capital expenditure decision making is important for another reason as well. Specifically, it often is difficult, if not impossible, to reverse a major capital expenditure without incurring considerable additional expense. For example, if a firm acquires highly specialized production facilities and equipment, it must recognize that there may be no ready used-equipment market in which to dispose of them if they do not generate the desired future cash flows. For these reasons, a firm's management should establish a number of definite procedures to follow when analyzing capital expenditure projects. Choosing from among such projects is the objective of capital budgeting models.

Capital Expenditures Made by Selected Groups of U.S. Firms (in billions of dollars)			T A B L E 9-1
Industry	1985	1988*	
Manufacturing	153.48	163.56	
Durable goods	73.27	78.06	
Nondurable goods	80.21	85.50	
Mining	15.88	12.62	
Transportation	18.02	21.56	
Railroad	7.08	7.05	
Air	4.79	7.61	
Other	6.15	6.91	
Public utilities	48.81	46.47	
Electric	36.11	32.20	
Gas and other	12.70	14.27	

* Estimated

SOURCE: *Survey of Current Business* (U.S. Department of Commerce), September 1988.

■■■■ KEY TERMS AND CONCEPTS IN CAPITAL BUDGETING

Before proceeding with the discussion of the capital budgeting process, it is necessary to introduce a number of terms and concepts encountered in subsequent chapters.

Cost of Capital

A firm's *cost of capital* is defined as the cost of the funds supplied to it. It also is termed the *required rate of return*, because it specifies the minimum necessary rate of return required by the firm's investors. In this context, the cost of capital provides the firm with a basis for choosing among various capital investment projects. In this and the following two chapters it is assumed that the cost of capital is a known value. Chapter 12 explores the methods used to determine the cost of capital.

How Projects Are Classified

A firm usually encounters several different types of projects when making capital expenditure decisions, including *independent projects, mutually exclusive projects*, and *contingent projects*. As is demonstrated in Chapter 10, project classification can influence the investment decision process.

INDEPENDENT PROJECTS. An independent project is one whose acceptance or rejection does not directly eliminate other projects from consideration. For example, a firm may want to install a new telephone communications system in its headquarters and replace a drill press during approximately the same time. In the absence of a constraint on the availability of funds, both projects could be adopted if they meet minimum investment criteria.

MUTUALLY EXCLUSIVE PROJECTS. A mutually exclusive project is one whose acceptance precludes the acceptance of one or more alternative proposals. Because two mutually exclusive projects have the capacity to perform the same function for a firm, only one should be chosen. For example, General Motors was faced with deciding whether it should locate its Saturn Manufacturing complex in Kalamazoo, Michigan, or Spring Hill, Tennessee. It ultimately chose the Spring Hill site, and this precluded the Kalamazoo alternative.

CONTINGENT PROJECTS. A contingent project is one whose acceptance is dependent on the adoption of one or more other projects. For example, the decision by RJR Nabisco to build a new bakery in North Carolina was contingent upon RJR Nabisco investing in suitable air and water pollution control equipment. When a firm is considering contingent projects, it is best to consider together all projects that are dependent on one another and treat them as a single project for purposes of evaluation.

Availability of Funds

When a firm has adequate funds to invest in all projects that meet some capital budgeting selection criterion, such as has been true for Ford Motor Company in recent years, the firm is said to be operating without a *funds constraint.* Frequently, however, the total initial cost of the acceptable projects in the absence of a funds constraint is greater than the total funds the firm has available to invest in capital projects. This necessitates *capital rationing*, or setting limits on capital expenditures, and results in some special capital budgeting problems.[1]

BASIC FRAMEWORK FOR CAPITAL BUDGETING

According to economic theory, a firm should operate at the point where the marginal cost of an additional unit of output just equals the marginal revenue derived from the output. Following this rule leads to *profit maximization*. This principle also may be applied to capital budgeting decisions. In this context, a firm's marginal revenue is the rates of return earned on succeeding investments, and marginal cost may be defined as the firm's *marginal cost of capital* (MCC); that is, the cost of successive increments of capital acquired by the firm.

Figure 9-1 illustrates a simplified capital budgeting model. This model assumes that all projects have the same risk. This assumption is relaxed in Chapter 11. The projects under consideration are indicated by lettered bars on the graph.

Project A requires an investment of $2 million and is expected to generate a 24 percent rate of return. Project B will cost $1 million ($3 million minus $2 million on the horizontal axis) and is expected to generate a 22 percent rate of return, and so on. The projects are arranged in descending order according to their expected rates of return, in recognition of the fact that no firm has an inexhaustible supply of projects offering high expected rates of return. This schedule of projects often is called the firm's *investment opportunity curve* (IOC). Typically, a firm will invest in its best projects first—such as Project A—before moving on to less attractive alternatives.

The MCC schedule represents the marginal cost of capital to the firm. Note that the schedule increases as more funds are sought in the capital markets. The reasons for this include the following:

[1] These are treated in Chapter 10.

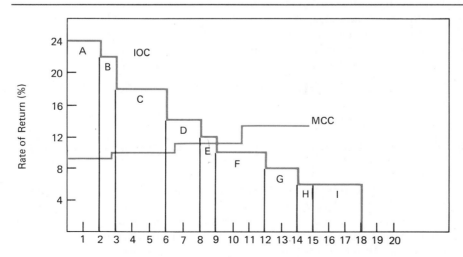

Investment (in millions of dollars)

- Investors' expectations about the firm's ability to successfully undertake a large number of new projects.
- The business risk to which the firm is exposed because of its particular line of business.
- The firm's financial risk, which is due to its capital structure.
- The supply and demand for investment capital in the capital market.
- The cost of selling new stock, which is greater than the cost of retained earnings.

The basic capital budgeting model indicates that, in principle, the firm should undertake Projects A, B, C, D, and E, because the expected returns from each project exceed the firm's marginal cost of capital. Unfortunately, however, in practice financial decision making is not this simple. Some practical problems are encountered in trying to apply this model, including the following:

- At any point in time a firm probably will not know all of the capital projects available to it. In most firms, capital expenditures are proposed continually, based on results of research and development programs, changing market conditions, new technologies, corporate planning efforts, and so on. Thus, a schedule of projects similar to Figure 9-1 will probably be incomplete at the time the firm makes its capital expenditure decisions.
- The shape of the MCC schedule itself may be difficult to determine. (The problems and techniques involved in estimating a firm's cost of capital are discussed in Chapter 12.)
- In most cases a firm can make only uncertain estimates of a project's future costs and revenues (and, consequently, its rate of return). Some projects will be more risky than others. The riskier a project is, the greater the rate of return that is required before it will be acceptable. (This concept is considered in more detail in Chapter 11.)

In spite of these and other problems, all firms make capital investment decisions. This chapter and the following two chapters provide tools that may be applied to the capital budgeting decision-making process.

Briefly, that process consists of four important steps:

1. Generating capital investment project proposals.
2. Estimating cash flows.
3. Evaluating alternatives and selecting projects to be implemented.
4. Reviewing a project's performance after it has been implemented, and postauditing its performance after its termination.

The remainder of this chapter is devoted to a discussion of the first two steps.

GENERATING CAPITAL INVESTMENT PROJECT PROPOSALS

Ideas for new capital investments can come from many sources, both inside and outside a firm. Proposals may originate at all levels of the organization—from factory workers up to the board of directors. Most large and medium-sized firms allocate the responsibility for identifying and analyzing capital expenditures to specific staff groups. These can include cost accounting, industrial engineering, marketing research, research and development, and corporate planning groups. In most firms, systematic procedures are established to assist in the search and analysis steps. For example, many firms provide detailed forms that the originator of a capital expenditure proposal must complete. These forms normally request information on the project's initial cost, the revenues it is expected to generate, and how it will affect the firm's overall operating expenses. These data are then channeled to a reviewer or group of reviewers at a higher level in the firm for analysis and possible acceptance or rejection.

Where a proposal goes for review often depends on how the particular project is *classified*.

Classifying Investment Projects

As noted earlier, there are several types of capital expenditures. These can be grouped into *projects generated by growth opportunities, projects generated by cost reduction opportunities,* and *projects generated to meet legal requirements and health and safety standards.*

PROJECTS GENERATED BY GROWTH OPPORTUNITIES. Assume that a firm produces a particular product that is expected to be in increasing demand during the upcoming years. If the firm's existing facilities are inadequate to handle the demand, proposals should be developed for expanding the firm's capacity. These proposals may come from the corporate planning staff group, from a divisional staff group, or from some other source.

Because most existing products eventually become obsolete, a firm's growth also is dependent on the development and marketing of new products. This involves the generation of research and development investment proposals, marketing research investments, test marketing investments, and perhaps even investments in new plant, property, and equipment. For example, in order for the mineral extraction industries to keep growing, they must continually make investments in exploration and development. Similarly, firms in high technology industries—such as electronics and computers—must undertake continuing programs of research and development to compete successfully.

PROJECTS GENERATED BY COST REDUCTION OPPORTUNITIES. Just as products become obsolete over time, so do plant, property, equipment, and production processes. Normal use makes older plants more expensive to operate because of the higher cost of maintenance and down time (idle time). In addition, new technological developments may render existing equipment economically obsolete. These factors create opportunities for cost reduction investments, which include replacing old, obsolete capital equipment with newer, more efficient equipment.

PROJECTS GENERATED TO MEET LEGAL REQUIREMENTS AND HEALTH AND SAFETY STANDARDS. These projects include investment proposals for such things as pollution control, ventilation, and fire protection equipment. In terms of analysis, this group of projects is best considered as contingent upon other projects.

To illustrate, suppose a firm wishes to build a new steel plant in Cleveland, Ohio. The decision will be contingent upon the investment in the amount of pollution abatement equipment required by state and local laws. Thus, the decision to invest in the new plant must be based upon the *total* cost of the plant, including the pollution abatement equipment, and not just the operating equipment alone.In the case of existing facilities, this type of decision making sometimes is more complex. For example, suppose a firm is told it must install new pollution abatement equipment in a plant that has been in operation for some time. The firm first needs to determine the lowest cost alternative that will meet these legal requirements. "Lowest cost" is normally measured by the smallest present value of net cash out-flows from the project. Then management must decide whether the re-maining stream of cash flows from the plant is sufficient to justify the expenditure. If it appears as though it will not be, the firm may consider building a new facility, or it may decide to simply close down the original plant.

Project Size and the Decision-Making Process

Whereas the classification of a proposed project influences the capital in-vestment decision-making process, there are other factors to consider—in particular, the size of the expenditure required to carry out the project.

Most firms *decentralize* the decision-making function. For example, whereas the approval of the president and the board of directors may be needed for especially large outlays, a divisional vice-president may be the final decision maker in the case of medium-sized outlays. A plant manager may have responsibility for deciding on smaller outlays, and a department head in a particular plant may be authorized to approve small outlays. For example, at Hershey Foods a corporate-level review is required for all projects of more than $500,000. Projects below this amount are evaluated at the op-erating division level only. Hershey is moving toward a system that will require a corporate-level review for all projects of $50,000 or more. This "chain of command" varies with individual companies. In large firms, how-ever, it is impossible for any one person to make every decision regarding proposed capital expenditures, and a decentralized system is usually employed.

PRINCIPLES OF ESTIMATING CASH FLOWS

The capital budgeting process is concerned primarily with the estimation of the *cash flows* associated with a project, not just the project's contribution to accounting profits. Typically, a capital expenditure requires an initial *cash outflow*, termed the *net investment*. Thus, it is important to measure a project's performance in terms of the *net cash inflows* it is expected to generate over a number of future years.

Figure 9-2 shows the estimated cash flows for a particular project. After an initial net investment of $100,000, the project is expected to generate a stream of net cash inflows over its anticipated 5-year life of $50,000 in year 1; $40,000 in year 2; $30,000 in year 3; $25,000 in year 4; and $5,000 in year 5. This type of project is called a *normal* or *conventional project*.

Nonnormal or nonconventional projects have cash flow patterns with more than one sign change. Table 9-2 illustrates the cash flow patterns for three sample projects. Projects X, Y, and Z can cause some analytical problems, as we shall see. Project X might require that certain equipment

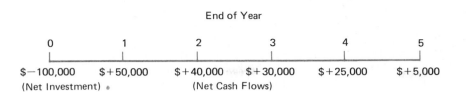

End of Year

0	1	2	3	4	5
$-100,000	$+50,000	$+40,000	$+30,000	$+25,000	$+5,000
(Net Investment)		(Net Cash Flows)			

be shut down and rebuilt in year 3, and Project Y could be an investment in a mining property, with the negative cash flow in year 5 representing abandonment costs associated with closing down the mine after its mineral wealth has been depleted. Finally, Project Z might represent the investment in some pollution control equipment.

Regardless of whether a project's cash flows are expected to be normal or nonnormal, certain basic principles should be applied during their estimation, including the following:

- **Cash flows should be measured on an incremental basis.** In other words, the cash flow stream for a particular project should be estimated from the perspective of how the entire cash flow stream of the firm will be affected if the project is adopted as compared with how the stream will be affected if the project is not adopted. Therefore *all* changes in the firm's revenue stream, cost stream, and tax stream that would result from the acceptance of the project should be included in the analysis. In contrast, cash flows that would not be changed by the investment should be disregarded.
- **Cash flows should be measured on an after-tax basis.** Because the initial investment made on a project requires the outlay of after-tax cash dollars, the returns from the project should be measured in the same units; namely, after-tax cash flows.
- **All the indirect effects of a project should be included in the cash flow calculations.** For example, if a proposed plant expansion requires that working capital be increased for the firm as a whole—perhaps in the form of larger cash balances, inventories, or accounts receivable—the increase in working capital should be included in the *net investment* required for the project. As another example, assume that one division of a firm introduces a new product that competes directly with a product produced by another division. The first division may consider this product desirable, but when the impact on the second division's sales are considered, the project may be much less attractive.
- **Sunk costs should not be considered when evaluating a project.** A *sunk cost* is an outlay that already has been made (or committed to be made).

							TABLE 9-2

Sample Cash Flow Patterns for Nonnormal Projects

	Year					
PROJECT	0	1	2	3	4	5
X	-100,000	+80,000	+60,000	-50,000	+75,000	+60,000
Y	-200,000	+150,000	+50,000	+40,000	+30,000	-20,000
Z	-150,000	-20,000	-20,000	-25,000	-25,000	-30,000

Because sunk costs cannot be recovered, they should not be considered in the decision to accept or reject a project. For example, in 1989 the Chemtron Corporation was considering constructing a new chemical disposal facility. Two years earlier the firm had hired the R.O.E. Consulting Group to do an environmental impact analysis of the proposed site at a cost of $500,000. Because this $500,000 cost cannot be recovered whether the project is undertaken or not, it should not be considered in the accept–reject analysis taking place in 1989. The only relevant costs are the incremental outlays that will be made from this point forward if the project is undertaken.

■ **The value of resources used in a project should be measured in terms of their opportunity costs.** *Opportunity costs* of resources (assets) are the cash flows those resources could generate if they are not used in the project under consideration. For example, suppose that the site Chemtron is considering to use for its disposal facility has been owned by the firm for some time. The property originally cost $50,000, but a recent appraisal indicates that the property could be sold for $1 million. Because Chemtron must forego the receipt of $1 million from the sale of the site if the disposal facility is constructed, the appropriate opportunity cost of this piece of land is $1 million, not the original cost of $50,000.

These five principles of cash flow estimation may be applied to the specific problem of defining and calculating a project's *net investment* and *net cash flows*.

NET INVESTMENT (NINV)

The *net investment* (NINV) in a project is defined as the project's initial net cash outlay. It is calculated using the following steps:

Step 1. The new project cost plus any installation and shipping costs associated with acquiring the asset and putting it into service[2]

PLUS

Step 2. Any increases in net working capital required as a result of the new investment

MINUS

Step 3. The net proceeds from the sale of existing assets when the investment is a replacement decision[3]

PLUS or MINUS

Step 4. The taxes associated with the sale of the existing asset and/or the purchase of the new one[4]

EQUALS

The net investment (NINV).

The calculation of the net investment for two example projects follows. Also discussed in the following sections are some of the tax consequences that can influence the net investment of a project. These tax effects are the treatment of gains and losses from asset sales in the case of replacement decisions.

[2] The asset cost plus installation and shipping costs form the basis upon which depreciation is computed.
[3] This normally is computed as the actual salvage value of the asset being replaced less any costs associated with physically removing or selling it.
[4] These taxes include any taxes associated with the disposal of the old asset. The total tax effect may be either positive or negative; this is why it is either added to or subtracted from the new project cost.

If a project generates additional revenues and the company extends credit to its customers, an additional investment in accounts receivable is required. Moreover, if additional inventories are necessary to generate the increased revenues, then an additional investment in inventory is required, too. This increase in working capital—that is, cash, accounts receivable, and inventories—should be calculated *net* of any automatic increases in current liabilities, such as accounts payable or wages and taxes payable, that occur because of the project. As a general rule, replacement projects require little or no net working capital increase. Expansion projects, on the other hand, normally require an investment in additional net working capital.

Some projects require outlays over more than one year before positive cash inflows are generated. In these cases the NINV for that project will be equal to the present value (at time 0) of this series of outlays, discounted at the firm's cost of capital. For example, the NINV of a project requiring outlays of $100,000 in year 0, $30,000 in year 1, and $20,000 in year 2, assuming a cost of capital of 10 percent, equals $143,790, computed as follows:[5]

Year	Cash Outlay	$PVIF_{0.10, t}$	Present Value of NINV
0	$100,000	1.000	$100,000
1	30,000	0.909	27,270
2	20,000	0.826	16,520
			$143,790

NET CASH FLOWS

Capital investment projects are expected to generate after-tax cash flow streams after the initial net investment has been made. The process of estimating project cash flows is an important part of the capital budgeting process.

In general, cash flows are defined as follows:

$$\text{Cash flow (CF)} = \text{Earnings after taxes (EAT)} + \text{Noncash charges} \quad \textbf{(9.1)}$$

The most significant noncash charge normally found on a firm's income statement is depreciation.[6] Depreciation is the systematic allocation of the cost of an asset with an economic life in excess of 1 year. Depreciation reduces reported profits and it also reduces taxes paid by a firm.

Capital budgeting is concerned primarily with the *incremental, after-tax net cash flows* (NCF) of a particular project, or cash inflows minus cash outflows. For any year during the life of a project, these may be defined as the change in earnings after taxes, ΔEAT, plus the change in depreciation, ΔDep:

$$\text{NCF} = \Delta EAT + \Delta Dep \quad \textbf{(9.2)}$$

---

[5] For tax purposes, the installed cost of this asset would be $150,000—the actual cash outlays required to put the plant or equipment in service.

[6] Depreciation *itself* is not a cash flow. Rather, it reduces earnings before taxes (EBT) and thus reduces income tax payments (a cash outflow). Equation 9.1 provides an easy procedure for reflecting the cash flow impact of depreciation.

ΔEAT is equal to the change in earnings before taxes (ΔEBT) times $(1 - T)$, where T is the marginal tax rate:

$$\Delta EAT = \Delta EBT(1 - T) \tag{9.3}$$

ΔEBT is defined as the change in cash revenues, ΔR, minus the changes in cash operating costs, ΔO, and depreciation, ΔDep:

$$\Delta EBT = \Delta R - \Delta O - \Delta Dep \tag{9.4}$$

Substituting Equation 9.4 into Equation 9.3 yields the following:

$$\Delta EAT = (\Delta R - \Delta O - \Delta Dep)(1 - T)$$

Substituting this equation into Equation 9.2 yields the following definition of net cash flow:

$$NCF = (\Delta R - \Delta O - \Delta Dep)(1 - T) + \Delta Dep \tag{9.5}$$

This equation can be further extended into an *operational* definition of NCF by defining ΔR as $R_2 - R_1$, ΔO as $O_2 - O_1$, and ΔDep as $Dep_2 - Dep_1$, where

R_1 = Cash revenues of the firm *without* the project.
R_2 = Cash revenues of the firm *with* the project.
O_1 = Cash operating costs for the firm *without* the project.
O_2 = Cash operating costs for the firm *with* the project.
Dep_1 = Depreciation charges for the firm *without* the project.
Dep_2 = Depreciation charges for the firm *with* the project.

The definition given in Equation 9.5 can be rewritten as follows:

$$NCF = [(R_2 - R_1) - (O_2 - O_1) - (Dep_2 - Dep_1)](1 - T) \tag{9.6}$$
$$+ (Dep_2 - Dep_1)$$

In the final year of a project's economic life Equation 9.6 must be modified to reflect two additional cash flow items: (1) recovery of the incremental after-tax salvage value of the asset(s) and (2) recovery of the incremental net working capital investment. (It is also possible that a project will require incremental net working capital investments after the year 0 investment. If this occurs, the incremental net working capital investment for each year is deducted from the NCF for that year.[7] There are no tax consequences of net working capital investments.)

Recovery of After-Tax Salvage Value

Whenever an asset is sold that has been depreciated, there are potential tax consequences that may affect the after-tax net proceeds received from the asset sale. These tax consequences are important when estimating the after-tax salvage value to be received at the end of the economic life of any project.

---

[7] If a project requires an incremental net working capital investment, *NWC*, in a given year, the NCF for that year is calculated as follows:

$$NCF = [(R_2 - R_1) - (O_2 - O_1) - (Dep_2 - Dep_1)](1 - T) + (Dep_2 - Dep_1) - NWC$$

As discussed earlier, the tax consequences of asset sales also are important when calculating the net investment required in a replacement investment project. There are four cases that need to be considered.

CASE 1: SALE OF AN ASSET FOR ITS BOOK VALUE. If a company disposes of an asset for an amount exactly equal to the asset's tax book value, there is neither a gain nor a loss on the sale, and thus there are no tax consequences. For example, if Burlington Textile sells for $50,000 an asset with a book value for tax purposes of $50,000, no taxes are associated with this disposal. (In general the tax book value of an asset equals the installed cost of the asset less accumulated tax depreciation.)

CASE 2: SALE OF AN ASSET FOR LESS THAN ITS BOOK VALUE. If Burlington Textile sells for $20,000 an asset having a tax book value of $50,000, Burlington Textile incurs a $30,000 pretax loss. Assuming that this asset is used in business or trade (an essential criterion for this tax treatment), this loss may be treated as an operating loss or an offset to operating income. This operating loss effectively reduces the company's taxes by an amount equal to the loss times the company's marginal tax rate.

Assume that the company's income before taxes is $100,000 (before consideration of the operating loss from the disposal of the asset). Taxes on this income are $100,000 times the company's marginal (40 percent) tax rate, or $40,000. (We use a 40 percent marginal tax rate throughout the book for ease of calculation. Actual current corporate marginal tax rates are discussed in Appendix 2A.) Because of the operating loss incurred by selling the asset for $20,000, the company's taxable income is reduced to $70,000, and the taxes decline to $28,000 (40 percent of $70,000). The $12,000 difference in taxes is equal to the tax loss on the sale of the old asset times the company's marginal tax rate ($30,000 × 40%).

CASE 3: SALE OF AN ASSET FOR MORE THAN ITS BOOK VALUE BUT LESS THAN ITS ORIGINAL COST. If Burlington Textile sells the asset for $60,000—$10,000 more than the current tax book value—$50,000 of this amount constitutes a tax-free cash inflow, and the remaining $10,000 is taxed as operating income. As a result, the firm's taxes increase by $4,000, or the amount of the gain times the firm's marginal tax rate ($10,000 × 40%). (The IRS treats this gain as a recapture of depreciation.)

CASE 4: SALE OF AN ASSET FOR MORE THAN ITS ORIGINAL COST. If Burlington Textile sells the asset for $120,000 (assuming an original asset cost of $110,000), part of the gain from the sale is treated as ordinary income, and part is treated as a long-term *capital gain*. The gain receiving ordinary income treatment is equal to the difference between the original asset cost and the current tax book value, or $60,000 ($110,000 − $50,000). The capital gain portion is the amount in excess of the original asset cost, or $10,000. Under the 1986 Tax Reform Act, both ordinary income and capital gains are taxed at the same corporate rate (34 percent).

Recovery of Net Working Capital

In the last year of a project that has required incremental net working capital investments, this net working capital is assumed to be liquidated and returned to the firm as cash. At the end of a project's life, all net working capital additions required over the project's life are recovered—not just the net working capital outlay occurring at time 0. Hence, the total net working capital must be added to the net cash flows in the last year of the project. Of course, no tax consequences are associated with this transaction.

Interest Charges and Net Cash Flows

Often the purchase of a particular asset is closely tied to the creation of some debt obligation, such as the sale of mortgage bonds or a bank loan. Nevertheless, it generally is considered *incorrect* to deduct the interest charges associated with a particular project from the estimated cash flows. This is true for two reasons.

First, the decision about how a firm should be financed can—and should—be made independently of the decision to accept or reject one or more projects. Instead, the firm should seek some combination of debt, equity (common stock), and preferred stock capital that is consistent with management's wishes concerning the tradeoff between financial risk and the cost of capital. In many cases this will result in a capital structure with the cost of capital at or near its minimum. Because investment and financing decisions normally should be made independently of one another, each new project can be viewed as being financed with the same proportions of the various sources of capital funds used to finance the firm as a whole.

Second, when a discounting framework is used for project evaluation, the discount rate, or cost of capital, already incorporates the cost of funds used to finance a project. Thus, including interest charges in cash flow calculations essentially would result in a double counting of costs.

Depreciation

Depreciation is defined as the systematic allocation of the cost of an asset over more than 1 year. It allows a firm to spread the costs of fixed assets over a period of years to better match costs and revenues in each accounting period. The annual depreciation expense recorded for a particular asset simply is an allocation of historic costs and does not necessarily indicate a declining market value. For example, a company that is depreciating an office building may find the building's market value *appreciating* each year.

There are a number of alternative methods of recording the depreciation of an asset for *financial reporting* purposes. These include straight-line depreciation and various accelerated depreciation methods. Under the straight-line depreciation method, the annual amount of an asset's depreciation is calculated as follows:

$$\text{Annual depreciation amount} = \frac{\text{Installed cost}}{\text{Number of years over which the asset is depreciated}} \quad \textbf{(9.7)}$$

For *tax* purposes, the depreciation rate a firm uses has a significant impact on the cash flows of the firm. This is so because depreciation represents a *noncash* expense that is deductible for tax purposes. Hence, the greater the amount of depreciation charged in a period, the lower will be the firm's taxable income. With a lower reported taxable income, the firm's tax obligation (a cash outflow) is reduced, and the cash inflows for the firm are increased. This can be seen in the following fundamental definition of cash flows:

$$\text{Operating cash flow} = \text{Net income after tax} + \text{Noncash charges} \quad \textbf{(9.8)}$$

For example if the Badger Tool Company has revenues of $1,000, cash operating expenses of $500, straight-line depreciation of $100, and a marginal tax rate of 40 percent, its operating cash flow will be:

Cash revenues		$1,000
Less Cash operating expenses	$500	
Depreciation	100	
Total		600
Net income before taxes		$ 400
Less Taxes (40%)		160
Net income after taxes		$ 240
Plus Depreciation		100
Operating cash flow		$ 340

Now suppose Badger Tool opts to use an accelerated depreciation method for tax purposes rather than the straight-line method. As a result, its depreciation expense is recorded as $150 instead of $100. Its new operating cash flow will be as follows:

Cash revenues		$1,000
Less Cash operating expenses	$500	
Depreciation	150	
Total		650
Net income before taxes		$ 350
Less Taxes (40%)		140
Net income after taxes		$ 210
Plus Depreciation		150
Operating cash flow		$ 360

A comparison of the two cash flow statements shows that the use of accelerated depreciation reduces net income after taxes from $240 to $210 and reduces taxes from $160 to $140, but increases operating cash flow to $360 from $340. Hence, the use of accelerated depreciation for tax purposes is desirable for the firm, because it reduces tax outlays and thereby increases cash flow. In general, a profitable firm will depreciate its assets as quickly as the tax law allows, and it should use whatever allowable method permits the highest percentage depreciation in the early years of an asset's life. The tax method currently used in the United States is the *Modified Accelerated Cost Recovery System (MACRS)* method; it is explained in the appendix to this chapter.

The cash flow examples discussed in this chapter use straight-line depreciation to keep the calculations simple. In actual practice, companies today should use the MACRS method when computing the NCFs from a project.

ASSET EXPANSION PROJECTS

A project that requires a firm to invest funds in additional assets in order to increase sales (or reduce costs) is called an *asset expansion project*. For example, suppose the TLC Yogurt Company has decided to capitalize on the exercise fad and plans to open an exercise facility in conjunction with its main yogurt and health foods store. To get the project underway the company will rent additional space adjacent to its current store. The equipment required for the facility will cost $50,000. Shipping and installation charges for the equipment is expected to total $5,000. This equipment will be depreciated on a straight-line basis over its 5-year economic life to an estimated salvage value of $0. In order to open the exercise facility, TLC estimates that it will have to add about $7,000 to its net working capital in the form of additional inventories of exercise supplies, cash, and accounts receivable for its exercise customers (less accounts payable).

During the first year of operations, TLC expects its total revenues (from yogurt sales and exercise services) to increase by $50,000 above the level that would have prevailed without the exercise facility addition. These incremental revenues are expected to grow to $60,000 in year 2, $75,000 in year 3, decline to $60,000 in year 4, and decline again to $45,000 during the fifth and final year of the project's life. The company's incremental cash operating costs associated with the exercise facility, including the rental of the facility, are expected to total $25,000 during the first year and increase at a rate of 6 percent per year over the 5-year project life. Depreciation will be $11,000 per year ($55,000 installed cost, assuming no salvage value, divided by the 5-year economic life). TLC has a marginal tax rate of 40 percent.

Calculating the Net Investment

First, we determine the net investment required for the exercise facility expansion. TLC must make a cash outlay of $50,000 to pay for the facility equipment. In addition it must pay $5,000 in cash to cover the costs of shipping and installation of the equipment. Finally, TLC must invest $7,000 in net working capital to get the project underway. This net working capital investment will be recovered at the termination of the project. The net investment (NINV) required at time 0 is

Purchase price of exercise equipment	$50,000
Plus Shipping and installation	5,000
Plus Net working capital required	7,000
Equals Net investment	$62,000

Calculating Annual Net Cash Flows

Next we need to calculate the annual net cash flows associated with the project. Using Equation 9.5 these cash flows can be computed as shown in Table 9-3.

The cash flows associated with the exercise facility project can be summarized as follows:

Year	Net Investment and Net Cash Flows
0	−$62,000
1	19,400
2	24,500
3	32,546
4	22,535
5	19,463

Calculation of Annual Net Cash Flows for TLC Exercise Facility

	Year 1	Year 2	Year 3	Year 4	Year 5
Incremental cash revenues (ΔR)	$50,000	$60,000	$75,000	$60,000	$45,000
Minus Incremental cash operating costs (ΔO)	25,000	26,500	28,090	29,775	31,562
Minus Incremental depreciation (ΔDep)	11,000	11,000	11,000	11,000	11,000
Equals Incremental earnings before tax (ΔEBT)	$14,000	$22,500	$35,910	$19,225	$ 2,438
Less Incremental taxes (40%)(T)	5,600	9,000	14,364	7,690	975
Equals Incremental earnings after tax (ΔEAT)	$ 8,400	$13,500	$21,546	$11,535	$ 1,463
Plus Incremental depreciation (ΔDep)	11,000	11,000	11,000	11,000	11,000
Plus After-tax salvage	—	—	—	—	0
Plus Return of net working capital	—	—	—	—	7,000
Equals Net cash flow (NCF)	$19,400	$24,500	$32,546	$22,535	$19,463

In Chapter 10 several different capital budgeting decision models are applied to cash flows such as these to determine the desirability of capital investment projects.

ASSET REPLACEMENT PROJECTS

The previous example of an asset expansion project illustrated the key elements of the calculation of a project's net investment and its annual net cash flows. In this section we consider an *asset replacement* project. Asset replacements involve retiring one asset and replacing it with a more efficient asset.

The Jones Equipment Company purchased an automated drill press 10 years ago that had an estimated economic life of 20 years. The drill press originally cost $150,000 and has been fully depreciated, leaving a current book value of $0. The actual market value of this drill press is $40,000. The company is considering replacing the drill press with a new one costing $190,000. Shipping and installation charges will add an additional $10,000 to the cost. The new machine would be depreciated to zero on a straight-line basis. The new machine is expected to have a 10-year economic life, and its actual salvage value at the end of the 10-year period is estimated to be $25,000. Jones' current marginal tax rate is 40 percent.

Calculating the Net Investment

Steps 1 and 2 of the net investment calculation are easy; the new project cost ($190,000) plus shipping and installation ($10,000) is $200,000. In this case, no new net working capital is required.

In steps 3 and 4 the net proceeds received from the sale of the old drill press have to be adjusted for taxes.

Because the old drill press is sold for $40,000, the gain from this sale is treated as a recapture of depreciation and thus taxed as ordinary income. Table 9-4 summarizes the NINV calculation for Jones Equipment. As can be seen in this table, the NINV is equal to $176,000.

Calculating Annual Net Cash Flows

The Jones Equipment Company expects annual revenues during the project's first year to increase from $70,000 to $85,000 if the new drill press is purchased. (This might occur because the new press is faster than the old one and can meet the increasing demands for more work.) After the first year, revenues from the new project are expected to increase at a rate of $2,000 a year for the remainder of the project life.[8]

Assume further that while the old drill press required two operators, the new drill press is more automated and needs only one, thereby reducing annual operating costs from $40,000 to $20,000 during the project's first year. After the first year, annual operating costs of the new drill press are expected to increase by $1,000 a year over the remaining life of the project.[9] The old machine is fully depreciated, whereas the new machine will be depreciated on a straight-line basis. The marginal tax rate of 40 percent applies.

The first-year net cash flow resulting from the purchase of the new drill press can be computed by substituting $R_2 = \$85,000$, $R_1 = \$70,000$, $O_2 = \$20,000$, $O_1 = \$40,000$, $Dep_2 = \$20,000$, $Dep_1 = \$0$, and $T = 0.40$ into Equation 9.6, as follows:

$$NCF = [(R_2 - R_1) - (O_2 - O_1) - (Dep_2 - Dep_1)] (1 - T) + (Dep_2 - Dep_1)$$

Year 1:

$$NCF_1 = [(\$85,000 - \$70,000) - (\$20,000 - \$40,000) \\ - (\$20,000 - \$0)](1 - 0.4) + (\$20,000 - \$0) \\ = \$29,000$$

[8] For simplicity, we have assumed that the revenue figure of $70,000 without the project remains constant over the life of the project.
[9] For simplicity, we have assumed that the operating cost figure of $40,000 without the project remains constant over the life of the project.

T A B L E 9-4	**Net Investment Calculation for Jones Equipment Company**	
	Cost of new drill press	$190,000
	Plus Shipping and installation charges	10,000
	Equals Installed cost	$200,000
	Plus Increase in net working capital	0
	Less Proceeds from sale of old drill press	40,000
	Equals Net investment before taxes	$160,000
	Plus Tax on gain from sale of old drill press (40% × $40,000)	16,000
	Equals Net investment	$176,000

Using the different expected values for new revenues, R_2, and new operating costs, O_2, the remaining annual net cash flows can be computed as follows:

Year 2:

$$NCF_2 = [(\$87,000 - \$70,000) - (\$21,000 - \$40,000) \\ - (\$20,000 - \$0)](1 - 0.4) + (\$20,000 - \$0) \\ = \$29,600$$

Year 3:

$$NCF_3 = [(\$89,000 - \$70,000) - (\$22,000 - \$40,000) \\ - (\$20,000 - \$0)](1 - 0.4) + (\$20,000 - \$0) \\ = \$30,200$$

Year 4:

$$NCF_4 = [(\$91,000 - \$70,000) - (\$23,000 - \$40,000) \\ - (\$20,000 - \$0)](1 - 0.4) + (\$20,000 - \$0) \\ = \$30,800$$

Year 5:

$$NCF_5 = [(\$93,000 - \$70,000) - (\$24,000 - \$40,000) \\ - (\$20,000 - \$0)](1 - 0.4) + (\$20,000 - \$0) \\ = \$31,400$$

Year 6:

$$NCF_6 = [(\$95,000 - \$70,000) - (\$25,000 - \$40,000) \\ - (\$20,000 - \$0)](1 - 0.4) + (\$20,000 - \$0) \\ = \$32,000$$

Year 7:

$$NCF_7 = [(\$97,000 - \$70,000) - (\$26,000 - \$40,000) \\ - (\$20,000 - \$0)](1 - 0.4) + (\$20,000 - \$0) \\ = \$32,600$$

Year 8:

$$NCF_8 = [(\$99,000 - \$70,000) - (\$27,000 - \$40,000) \\ - (\$20,000 - \$0)](1 - 0.4) + (\$20,000 - \$0) \\ = \$33,200$$

Year 9:

$$NCF_9 = [(\$101,000 - \$70,000) - (\$28,000 - \$40,000) \\ - (\$20,000 - \$0)](1 - 0.4) + (\$20,000 - \$0) \\ = \$33,800$$

In this example, in year 10, the $25,000 estimated salvage from the new drill press must be added along with its associated tax effects.[10] This $25,000 salvage is treated as ordinary income because it represents a recapture of depreciation for tax purposes.

$$
\begin{aligned}
NCF_{10} &= [(\$103,000 - \$70,000) - (\$29,000 - \$40,000) \\
&\quad - (\$20,000 - \$0)](1 - 0.4) + (\$20,000 - \$0) \\
&\quad + \$25,000 \text{ salvage} - \text{tax on salvage } (0.4 \times \$25,000) \\
&= \$34,400 + \$25,000 - \$10,000 \\
&= \$49,400
\end{aligned}
$$

Table 9-5 is a summary worksheet for computing the net cash flows for the Jones Company during the 10-year estimated economic life of the new drill press.

Table 9-6 summarizes the net cash flows for the entire project. This schedule of net cash flows plus the NINV computed in the preceding section form the basis for further analysis. In Chapter 10 several different capital budgeting decision models are applied to similar cash flow streams from other projects to determine the investment desirability of these projects. The cash flows developed in this chapter are an essential input in the capital budgeting decision process.

PROBLEMS IN CASH FLOW ESTIMATION

Because project cash flows occur in the future, there are varying degrees of *uncertainty* about the value of these flows. Therefore it is difficult to predict the actual cash flows of a project. The capital budgeting process assumes the decision maker is able to estimate cash flows accurately enough that these estimates can be used in project evaluation and selection. For this assumption to be realistic, a project proposal should be based on inputs from marketing managers regarding revenue estimates and inputs from the production and engineering staffs regarding costs and achievable levels of performance. Objective inputs from these sources can help reduce the uncertainty associated with cash flow estimation.

In addition, cash flow estimates for different projects may have varying degrees of uncertainty. For example, the returns from asset replacement projects generally are easier to forecast than the returns from new product introduction projects. Chapter 11 discusses some of the techniques used to incorporate risk analysis into capital budgeting decision models.

Another difficulty in the practical application of capital budgeting arises because of the intentional or unintentional introduction of *bias* into cash flow estimates. Specifically, someone who has a vested interest in the adoption of a specific project may find it difficult to be completely objective when estimating the project's cash flows. For this reason it is a good idea to obtain an objective outside evaluation of a proposed project before the project is implemented. In addition, an aggressive project review and post-audit should be conducted once the project is under way. These procedures can indicate areas where bias has slipped into cash flow analysis and where corrective action may be needed.

---

[10] In this example there is no add-back of net working capital in the final year of the project, because no new net working capital was assumed when the project was initiated.

TABLE 9-5 Annual Net Cash Flow Worksheet for the Jones Equipment Company Drill Press Acquisition

	Year									
	1	2	3	4	5	6	7	8	9	10
Change in cash revenues $(R_2 - R_1)$*	$15,000	$17,000	$19,000	$21,000	$23,000	$25,000	$27,000	$29,000	$31,000	$33,000
Less Change in cash operating costs $(O_2 - O_1)$†	−20,000	−19,000	−18,000	−17,000	−16,000	−15,000	−14,000	−13,000	−12,000	−11,000
Less Change in depreciation $(Dep_2 - Dep_1)$‡	20,000	20,000	20,000	20,000	20,000	20,000	20,000	20,000	20,000	20,000
Equals Change in earnings before taxes (EBT)	$15,000	$16,000	$17,000	$18,000	$19,000	$20,000	$21,000	$22,000	$23,000	$24,000
Less Tax (40%)	6,000	6,400	6,800	7,200	7,600	8,000	8,400	8,800	9,200	9,600
Equals Change in earnings after taxes (EAT)	$9,000	$9,600	$10,200	$10,800	$11,400	$12,000	$12,600	$13,200	$13,800	$14,400
Plus Change in depreciation $(Dep_2 - Dep_1)$	20,000	20,000	20,000	20,000	20,000	20,000	20,000	20,000	20,000	20,000
Equals Change in net cash flow before salvage	$29,000	$29,600	$30,200	$30,800	$31,400	$32,000	$32,600	$33,200	$33,800	$34,400
Plus Salvage	0	0	0	0	0	0	0	0	0	25,000
Less Tax on salvage (0.4 × salvage)	0	0	0	0	0	0	0	0	0	10,000
Plus Add-back of net working capital	0	0	0	0	0	0	0	0	0	0
Equals Change in net cash flow	$29,000	$29,600	$30,200	$30,800	$31,400	$32,000	$32,600	$33,200	$33,800	$49,400

* The change in cash revenues from undertaking a project may be either positive or negative.

† The change in cash operating costs may be either positive or negative. In this case, the firm's cash operating costs *decline* by $20,000; that is, the change in cash operating costs is *negative*, indicating a cost saving. This cost saving is *added* to the change in revenues (subtracting a negative number is the same as adding a positive number). If, in another situation, operating costs were to *increase* as a result of a project, the increased costs would be *subtracted* from the change in revenues.

‡ The change in depreciation may be either positive or negative. In this case, it is *positive* and has the effect of reducing the amount of taxable earnings, thus reducing the amount of taxes paid. Hence, this *increases* the cash flow from the project. If the change in depreciation were *negative*, it would have the effect of increasing the taxable earnings, increasing taxes paid, and *reducing* the cash flows from the project.

THE PRACTICE OF CASH FLOW ESTIMATION FOR CAPITAL BUDGETING

The analysis presented in this chapter and throughout the book suggests that generating accurate estimates of the cash flows from investment projects is extremely important to the success of the firm. A recent survey supports this conclusion and provides considerable insight regarding the cash flow estimation procedures used by larger firms (*Fortune* 500).[11]

The majority of the firms responding to the survey had annual capital budgets of more than $100 million. Nearly 67 percent of the firms prepared

[11] Pohlman, Randolph A., E. S. Santiago, and F. L. Markel. "Cash Flow Estimation Practices of Large Firms," *Financial Management* (Summer 1988): 71–79.

TABLE 9-6

Summary Project Cash Flows for the Jones Equipment Company

Year	Net Investment and Net Cash Flows
0	−$176,000
1	29,000
2	29,600
3	30,200
4	30,800
5	31,400
6	32,000
7	32,600
8	33,200
9	33,800
10	49,400

formal cash flow estimates for over 60 percent of their annual capital outlays, and a majority produced detailed cash flow projections for capital investments requiring an initial outlay of $40,000 or more. Firms with high capital intensity and high leverage were more likely to have one or more persons, such as a financial analyst, treasurer, controller, or department manager, designated to oversee the process of cash flow estimation. This result reflects the larger number of projects associated with capital intensive firms and the need to effectively manage the risk associated with high leverage.

When asked about the type of cash flow estimates that were generated, 56 percent indicated that they used single dollar estimates, 8 percent used a range of estimates, and 36 percent used both single dollar estimates and a range of estimates. There was a significant positive correlation between firms that use both types of estimates and measures of operating and financial risk, suggesting that the use of a range of estimates is one procedure for managing high risk.

Forecasting methods employed by the respondent firms included subjective estimates from management, sensitivity analysis, consensus analysis of expert opinions, and computer simulation. Many firms used multiple cash flow forecasting techniques. The longer the forecasting horizon—that is, the longer the economic life of the project—the more likely is a firm to use multiple methods for forecasting future cash flows.

Financial factors that are considered to be important in generating cash flow estimates included working capital requirements, project risk, tax considerations, the project's impact on the firm's liquidity, the anticipated rate of inflation, and expected salvage value. Important marketing factors considered include sales forecasts, the competitive advantages and disadvantages of the product, and product life. Important production factors include operating expenses, material and supply costs, overhead and expenses for manufacturing, capacity utilization, and start-up costs.

Three-fourths of the companies surveyed make comparisons between actual and projected cash flows, with nearly all the firms comparing actual versus projected initial outlays and operating cash flows over the project life; and about two-thirds of these firms make comparisons of actual versus projected salvage values. The most accurate cash flow estimates are reported to be the initial outlay estimates, and the least accurate element of cash flow estimates is the annual operating cash flows. Cash flow forecasts were more accurate for equipment replacement investments, compared with expansion, modernization, and acquisitions of ongoing businesses (mergers) investments. Firms with the information system in place to generate cash flow forecasts tend to produce more accurate forecasts than firms with less sophisticated capital project evaluation procedures.

SUMMARY

- *Capital budgeting* is the process of planning for purchases of assets whose returns are expected to continue beyond 1 year.
- Capital investments have a long-term impact on the performance of a firm. The proper forecasting of capital needs can help to ensure that a firm's productive capacity will meet future requirements.
- Ideally a firm should invest in new projects up to the point at which the rate of return from the last project is equal to the marginal cost of capital.
- Projects may be classified as *independent, mutually exclusive,* or *contingent.* The acceptance of an independent project does not directly eliminate other projects from consideration; the acceptance of a mutually exclusive project precludes other alternatives; and the acceptance of a contingent project depends on the adoption of one or more other projects.
- The *cost of capital* is the cost of funds supplied to a firm. It often is used in conjunction with capital project evaluation techniques as a basis for choosing among various investment alternatives.
- There are four basic steps in the capital budgeting process: *the generation of proposals, the estimation of cash flows, the evaluation and selection of alternatives,* and *the postaudit or review.* The first two steps are detailed in this chapter.
- New projects may be generated by *growth opportunities, cost reduction opportunities,* or by *the need to meet legal requirements and health and safety standards.*
- Project cash flows should be measured on an *incremental after-tax* basis and should include all the indirect effects the project will have on the firm.
- Resources of a firm used in an investment project should be valued at their *opportunity cost* based upon the cash flows these resources could generate in their next best alternative use.
- *Sunk costs* represent outlays that already have been made or committed and that cannot be recovered. Sunk costs should not be considered when evaluating an investment project.
- The *net investment* (NINV) in a project is the net cash outlay required to place the project in service. It includes the project cost *plus* any necessary increases in working capital *minus* any proceeds from the sale of the old asset(s) (in the case of replacement decisions) *plus or minus* the taxes associated with the sale of the old asset(s) and/or the purchase of the new asset(s).
- The *net cash flows* (NCF) from a project are the incremental changes in a firm's cash flows that result from investing in the project. These flows include the changes in the firm's revenues, cash operating costs, and taxes with and without the project.
- An *asset expansion* project requires a firm to invest funds in additional

assets to increase sales or reduce costs. *Asset replacements,* in contrast, involve retiring one asset and replacing it with a more efficient one.
■ Two problems that complicate the estimation of cash flows are the element of *uncertainty* associated with cash flows and the intentional or unintentional introduction of *bias* into the estimation procedure.

QUESTIONS AND TOPICS FOR DISCUSSION

1. Discuss how capital budgeting procedures might be used by each of the following:
   a. Personnel managers.
   b. Research and development staffs.
   c. Advertising executives.

2. What is a mutually exclusive investment project? An independent project? A contingent project? Give an example of each.

3. What effect does capital rationing have on a firm's ability to maximize shareholder wealth?

4. What are the primary types of capital investment projects? Does a project's type influence how it is analyzed?

5. Cash flows for a particular project should be measured on an incremental basis and should consider all the indirect effects of the project. What does this involve?

6. What factors should be considered when estimating a project's NINV?

7. Because depreciation is a noncash expense, why is it considered when estimating a project's net cash flows?

8. What are the potential tax consequences of selling an old asset in an asset replacement investment decision?

9. Why is it generally incorrect to consider interest charges when computing a project's net cash flows?

10. Distinguish between asset expansion and asset replacement projects. How does this distinction affect the capital expenditure analysis process?

11. How is the opportunity cost concept used in the capital budgeting process?

PROBLEMS*

1. The MacCauley Company has sales of $200 million and total expenses (excluding depreciation) of $130 million. Straight-line depreciation on the company's assets is $15 million and the maximum accelerated depreciation allowed by law is $25 million. Assume that all taxable income is taxed at 40 percent.

   a. Calculate the MacCauley Company's after-tax operating cash flow using both straight-line and accelerated depreciation.
   b. Assuming the company uses straight-line depreciation for book purposes and accelerated depreciation for tax purposes, show the income statement reported to the stockholders. What is the after-tax operating cash flow under these circumstances?

2. Calculate the annual straight-line depreciation for a machine that costs $50,000 and has installation and shipping costs that total $1,000. The machine will be depreciated over a period of 10 years. The company's marginal tax rate is 40 percent.

---

* Colored numbers denote problems that have check answers provided at the end of the book.

3. The Cooper Electronics Company has developed the following schedule of potential investment projects that may be undertaken during the next 6 months:

Project	Cost (in millions of dollars)	Expected Rate of Return (%)
A	3.0	20
B	1.5	22
C	7.0	7
D	14.0	10
E	50.0	12
F	12.0	9
G	1.0	44

a. If Cooper requires a minimum rate of return of 10 percent on all investments, which projects should be adopted?

b. In general, how would a capital budgeting constraint on the available amount of investment funds influence these decisions?

c. How would differing levels of project risk influence these decisions?

4. Johnson Products is considering purchasing a new milling machine that costs $100,000. The machine's installation and shipping costs will total $2,500. If accepted, the milling machine project will require a net working capital investment of $20,000. Johnson plans to depreciate the machine on a straight-line basis over a period of 8 years. Johnson's marginal tax rate is 40 percent.

a. Calculate the project's net investment (NINV).

b. Calculate the annual straight-line depreciation for the project.

5. A new machine costing $100,000 is expected to save the McKaig Brick Company $15,000 per year for 12 years before depreciation and taxes. The machine will be depreciated on a straight-line basis for a 12-year period to an estimated salvage value of $0. The firm's marginal tax rate is 40 percent. What are the annual net cash flows associated with the purchase of this machine? Also compute the net investment (NINV) for this project.

6. The Jacobs Chemical Company is considering building a new potassium sulfate plant. The following cash outlays are required to complete the plant:

Year	Cash Outlay
0	$4,000,000
1	2,000,000
2	500,000

Jacobs's cost of capital is 12 percent, and its marginal tax rate is 40 percent.

a. Calculate the plant's net investment (NINV).

b. What is the installed cost of the plant for tax purposes?

7. The Taylor Mountain Uranium Company currently has annual cash revenues of $1.2 million and annual cash expenses of $700,000. Depreciation amounts to $200,000 per year. These figures are expected to remain constant for the foreseeable future (at least 15 years). The firm's marginal tax rate is 40 percent.

A new high-speed processing unit costing $1.2 million is being considered as a potential investment designed to increase the firm's output capacity. This new piece of equipment will have an estimated usable life of 10 years and a $0 estimated salvage value. If the processing unit is bought, Taylor's annual cash revenues are expected to increase to $1.6 million and annual cash expenses will increase to $900,000. Annual depreciation will increase to $320,000.

Compute the project's annual net cash flows for the next 10 years, assuming that the new processing unit is purchased. Also compute the net investment (NINV) for this project.

8. A firm has an opportunity to invest in a new device that will replace two of the firm's older machines. The new device costs $570,000 and requires an additional outlay of $30,000 to cover installation and shipping. The new device will cause the firm to increase its net working capital by $20,000. Both the old machines can be sold—the first for $100,000 (book value equals $95,000) and the second for $150,000 (book value equals $75,000). The original cost of the first machine was $200,000 and the original cost of the second machine was $140,000. The firm's marginal tax bracket is 40 percent. Compute the net investment for this project.

9. Five years ago the Mori Foods Company acquired a bean processing machine. The machine cost $30,000 and was being depreciated using the straight line method over a 10-year period to an estimated salvage value of $0.

A new, improved processor is now available, and the firm is considering making a switch. The firm's marginal tax rate is 40 percent. What are the after-tax cash flow effects of selling the old processing unit if it can be sold for the following prices?

 a. $15,000
 b. $5,000
 c. $26,000
 d. $32,000

10. Cornell, Inc., is considering the purchase of a new computer system (ICX) for $130,000. The system will require an additional $30,000 for installation. If the new computer is purchased it will replace an old system which has been fully depreciated. The new system will be depreciated over a period of 10 years using straight-line depreciation. If the ICX is purchased, the old system will be sold for $20,000. The ICX system, which has a useful life of 10 years, is expected to increase revenues by $32,000 per year over its useful life. Operating costs are expected to decrease by $2,000 per year over the life of the system. The firm is taxed at a 40 percent marginal rate.

 a. What net investment is required to acquire the ICX system and replace the old system?
 b. Compute the annual net cash flows associated with the purchase of the ICX system.

11. Two years ago Agro, Inc., purchased an ACE generator that cost $250,000. Agro had to pay an additional $50,000 for delivery and installation, and the investment in the generator required the firm to increase its net working capital position by $25,000. The generator, which is being depreciated over a period of 5 years using straight-line depreciation, has a current market value of $79,550. The firm's marginal tax rate is 40%. If the firm liquidates the asset for its current market value, compute the after-tax proceeds from the sale of the asset.

12. Benford, Inc., is planning to open a new sporting goods store in a suburban mall. Benford will lease the needed space in the mall. Equipment and fixtures for the store will cost $200,000 and be depreciated over a 5-year period on a straight-line basis to $0. The new store will require Benford to increase its net working capital by $200,000.

First-year sales are expected to be $1 million and to increase at an annual rate of 8 percent over the expected 10-year life of the store. Cash operating expenses (including lease payments) are projected to be $700,000 during the first year and increase at a 7 percent annual rate. The salvage value of the store's equipment and fixtures is anticipated to be $10,000 at the end of 10 years. Benford's marginal tax rate is 40 percent.

a. Compute the net investment required for Benford.

b. Compute the annual net cash flows for the 10-year projected life of the store.

13. A new machine costing $100,000 is expected to save the McKaig Brick Company $15,000 per year for 12 years before depreciation and taxes. The machine will be depreciated as a 7-year class MACRS asset. The firm's marginal tax rate is 40 percent. What are the annual net cash flows associated with the purchase of this machine? Also compute the net investment (NINV) for this project. (HINT: See Appendix 9A for information on MACRS depreciation. This problem is the same as Problem 5 except for depreciation method.)

14. Cornell, Inc., is considering the purchase of a new computer system (ICX) for $130,000. The system will require an additional $30,000 for installation. If the new computer is purchased it will replace an old system which has been fully depreciated. The new system will be depreciated under the MACRS rules applicable to 7-year class assets. If the ICX is purchased, the old system will be sold for $20,000. The ICX system, which has a useful life of 10 years, is expected to increase revenues by $32,000 per year over its useful life. Operating costs are expected to decrease by $2,000 per year over the life of the system. The firm is taxed at a 40 percent marginal rate. (HINT: See Appendix 9A for information on MACRS depreciation. Except for the depreciation method, this problem is the same as Problem 10.)

a. What net investment is required to acquire the ICX system and replace the old system?

b. Compute the annual net cash flows associated with the purchase of the ICX system.

15. Argyl Manufacturing is evaluating the possibility of expanding its operations. This expansion will require the purchase of land at a cost of $100,000. A new building will cost $100,000 and be depreciated on a straight-line basis over 20 years to a $0 salvage. Actual land salvage at the end of 20 years is expected to be $200,000. Actual building salvage at the end of 20 years is expected to be $150,000. Equipment for the facility is expected to cost $250,000. Installation costs will be an additional $40,000 and shipping costs will be $10,000. This equipment will be depreciated as a 7-year MACRS asset. Actual estimated salvage at the end of 20 years is $0. The project will require net working capital of $70,000 initially (year 0, an additional $40,000 at the end of year 1, and an additional $40,000 at the end of year 2. The project is expected to generate increased EBIT (operating income) for the firm of $100,000 during year 1. Annual EBIT is expected to grow at a rate of 4 percent per year until the project terminates at the end of year 20. The marginal tax rate is 40 percent. Compute the initial net investment and the annual net cash flow from the project in year 20.

SELECTED REFERENCES

Bierman, Harold, Jr., and Seymour Smidt. *The Capital Budgeting Decision*, 7th ed. New York: Macmillan, 1988.

Clark, John J., T. J. Hindelang, and R. D. Pritchard. *Capital Budgeting: Planning and Control of Capital Expenditures*, 3d ed. Englewood Cliffs, NJ: Prentice-Hall, 1989.

Cooper, K., and R. M. Richards. "Investing the Alaskan Project Cash Flows: The Sohio Experience." *Financial Management* (Summer 1988): 58–70.

Kim, S. H. and E. J. Farragher. "Current Capital Budgeting Practices." *Management Accounting* (June 1981): 26–30.

McConnell, J. J., and C. J. Muscarella. "Corporate Capital Expenditures and the Market Value of the Firm." *Journal of Financial Economics* (September 1985): 399–422.

Scott, D. F., Jr., and J. W. Petty. "Capital Budgeting Practices in Large American Firms: A Retrospective Analysis and Synthesis." *Financial Review* (March 1984): 111–123.

Statman, M., and T. T. Tyebee. "Optimistic Capital Budgeting Forecasts: An Experiment." *Financial Management* (Autumn 1985): 27–34.

Additional Depreciation and Tax Issues

INTRODUCTION

Prior to the establishment of the MACRS system of depreciation, a number of alternative methods of depreciation were permitted by the IRS. These methods included straight-line depreciation and various accelerated methods such as the sum-of-the-years'-digits. Although recent tax law changes have rendered these techniques out of date for tax purposes, it is still useful to understand them for the following reasons:

1. Most firms will continue to own assets acquired prior to these tax law changes. These assets are being depreciated using one of the alternative depreciation methods.
2. Some firms may continue to use these alternative methods for financial reporting purposes.

In addition to discussing the pre-MACRS depreciation methods, this appendix also includes a ready reference to ACRS depreciation and Investment Tax Credit provisions, which were in effect after 1982 and prior to 1987, when the Tax Reform Act of 1986 took effect. It is important to have a basic understanding of these depreciation rules because replacement decisions involving assets purchased prior to 1987 are affected by the depreciation and tax treatment of those old assets.

Finally, this appendix provides detail about the calculation of depreciation amounts under the Modified ACRS, MACRS, system of depreciation, which is used for assets placed in service after December 31, 1986.

STRAIGHT-LINE DEPRECIATION

Under the pre-ACRS straight-line depreciation method, the annual amount of an asset's depreciation is calculated as follows:[12]

$$\text{Annual depreciation amount} = \frac{\text{Cost} - \text{Estimated salvage value}}{\text{Estimated economic life (years)}} \tag{9A.1}$$

[12] Note that under pre-ACRS depreciation rules, the annual depreciation amount was determined as the cost of the asset less its estimated salvage value divided by the estimated economic life. In comparison, under the Accelerated Cost Recovery System provisions of the 1986 Act, no consideration is given to estimated salvage value in determining the annual depreciation amount. See Steven C. Dilley and James C. Young, *The Tax Reform Act of 1986: The New ACRS Rules.* (Paramus, NJ: Prentice-Hall, 1986) for a discussion of the Accelerated Cost Recovery System and additional detail on the MACRS system.

For example, if a company purchases a machine that costs $12,000 and has an estimated salvage value of $2,000 at the end of a 5-year economic life, the annual depreciation amount is ($12,000 − $2,000)/5 = $2,000.

Straight-line depreciation is an appropriate method to employ when an asset is being used up fairly evenly over its lifetime. Many companies use straight-line depreciation for financial accounting purposes—that is, in their reports to stockholders, because it usually results in a greater reported net income—and an accelerated depreciation method for federal income tax purposes, because accelerated depreciation can result in the deferment of tax payments.

SUM-OF-THE-YEARS'-DIGITS METHOD

In the sum-of-the-years'-digits method, annual depreciation charges are computed by multiplying a decreasing fraction by the asset's original cost (less salvage value). The fraction's denominator is the sum of the digits that represent each year of the asset's expected economic life. For example, the sum-of-the-years'-digits for an asset with an expected 5-year lifetime is 5 + 4 + 3 + 2 + 1, or 15.[13] The numerator of the fraction for the first year is the highest digit—in this case, 5. The second year's numerator is the next highest digit—in this case, 4—and so on.

For example, suppose the company mentioned earlier decides to depreciate its $12,000 asset according to the sum-of-the-years'-digits method. Recall that the asset has a $2,000 expected salvage value and a 5-year expected useful life. The calculations are shown in Table 9A-1.

DECLINING BALANCE METHOD

The declining balance method allows a firm to take a percentage of the depreciation amount greater than the straight-line amount during the first year of an asset's life. During subsequent years the book value, or undepreciated amount, of the asset is multiplied by this percentage to calculate annual depreciation costs.

Two commonly used variations of the declining balance method include the 200 percent declining balance, often termed *double declining balance;*

---

[13] In general, the sum of the years' digits is equal to $n(n + 1)/2$, where n is the number of years.

T A B L E 9A-1

Sample Sum-of-the-Years'-Digits Depreciation Calculations

Year (1)	Depreciable Base (2)	Fraction (3)	Depreciation Amount (4) = (2) × (3)
1	$10,000	5/15	$ 3,333
2	10,000	4/15	2,667
3	10,000	3/15	2,000
4	10,000	2/15	1,333
5	10,000	1/15	667
			$10,000

and the 150 percent declining balance. The MACRS tax laws specify which variation is to be used for each asset class.

In the declining balance method, the annual depreciation amount of an asset is calculated by multiplying the straight-line rate by the declining balance percentage figure to get an accelerated rate. The accelerated rate then is multiplied by the asset's book value at the end of each previous year. As each year's depreciation amount is subtracted from the cost of the asset, the resulting *balance* in the asset's book value *declines*. Thus, the depreciation amount *decreases* as the years pass.

MODIFIED ACCELERATED COST RECOVERY SYSTEM

The Tax Reform Act of 1986 created the Modified Accelerated Cost Recovery System (MACRS) of depreciation. Under this depreciation system, six classes of assets are established. All depreciable assets (new and used), except real estate, are assigned to one of these six classes. Regardless of the expected useful life of an asset, its annual depreciation is computed according to the rules for the class of assets to which it has been assigned.

Table 9A-2 summarizes the MACRS classes and depreciable lives that must be used under the 1986 Tax Act. The vast majority of business equipment, from office furnishings to machinery, is found in the 7-year class.

Depreciation Rate

Annual depreciation charges for each asset class must be computed using the declining balance method of depreciation, switching to straight line at the optimal time. For the 3-, 5-, 7- and 10-year asset classes a 200 percent

MACRS Recovery Periods TABLE 9A-2

Recovery Period and Asset Class*	Property Included In Class
3-Year	A small class of short-lived assets including some special tools, some tractors, and racehorses (over 2 years old)
5-Year	Automobiles, light trucks, heavy general purpose trucks, buses, oil drilling equipment, information systems, certain semiconductor, textile, chemical, electronic, and manufacturing equipment, dairy and breeder cattle
7-Year	Most manufacturing equipment, railroad track, office furniture and equipment, railroad cars and locomotives, airplanes, amusement parks, and mining equipment
10-Year	Vessels, barges, petroleum refining equipment, railroad tank cars, some manufacturing equipment
15-Year	Electric generation and distribution systems, cement manufacturing equipment, nuclear power plants, natural gas pipelines, billboards, sewage treatment plants, telephone distribution plant
20-Year	Most public utility property, sewer pipes, railroad structures

* Most equipment is contained in the 7-year class.

declining balance method is used. A 150 percent declining balance method is used for the 15- and 20-year asset classes. The full installed cost of each asset forms the basis upon which depreciation is computed and charged. *Expected salvage value is not considered* in the depreciation calculations under MACRS.

Table 9A-3 provides the annual depreciation percentages. These percentages are multiplied by the installed cost of the asset when computing annual depreciation for any asset in the six classes. Note that the number of years of depreciation is always one greater than the number indicated in the asset class; for example, for a 5-year class asset, depreciation is spread over a total of 6 years. The reason for this is that the 1986 Tax Act requires that the half-year convention be followed. The half-year convention treats any asset placed in service during year 1 as being placed in service in the middle of the year. Consequently the asset only receives one-half of the first year's depreciation. The half-year convention also applies to the last year of depreciation, thus making the number of years of depreciation 1 year longer than is indicated in the asset class name.

For example, assume the Badger Tool Company acquires a $9,000 piece of machinery, which requires $1,000 for shipping and installation. Under MACRS, this asset would be in the 7-year class. The depreciable basis for the asset is

Asset Cost	$ 9,000
Plus Installation and shipping	1,000
Equals Depreciable basis	$10,000

TABLE 9A-3

Depreciation Rates for MACRS Property Other Than Real Property*

Recovery Year	3-Year	5-Year	7-Year	10-Year	15-Year	20-Year
1	33.33%	20.00%	14.29%	10.00%	5.00%	3.750%
2	44.45	32.00	24.49	18.00	9.50	7.219
3	14.81	19.20	17.49	14.40	8.55	6.677
4	7.41	11.52**	12.49	11.52	7.70	6.177
5		11.52	8.93**	9.22	6.93	5.713
6		5.76	8.92	7.37	6.23	5.285
7			8.93	6.55**	5.90**	4.888
8			4.46	6.55	5.90	4.522
9				6.56	5.91	4.462**
10				6.55	5.90	4.461
11				3.28	5.91	4.462
12					5.90	4.461
13					5.91	4.462
14					5.90	4.461
15					5.91	4.462
16					2.95	4.461
17						4.462
18						4.461
19						4.462
20						4.461
21						2.231

* Assumes the half-year convention applies.
** Switchover to straight-line depreciation over the remaining useful life.

Table 9A-3 provides the depreciation rates applied to this 7-year asset that Badger has acquired. The annual MACRS depreciation for this asset is computed as follows:

Year	MACRS Depreciation Rate	Amount of Depreciation (MACRS Rate × $10,000)
1	14.29%	$ 1,429
2	24.49	2,449
3	17.49	1,749
4	12.49	1,249
5	8.93	893
6	8.92	892
7	8.93	893
8	4.46	446
	100.00%	$10,000

MACRS Recovery Periods and Economic Life of an Asset

With the adoption of the MACRS recovery periods for all assets, there no longer is any direct relationship between the period over which depreciation is taken on an asset and that asset's economic life. Consequently, when estimating the cash flows from a project, there normally will be several years beyond the MACRS recovery period when no depreciation expense will be recorded. It is important to remember that cash flows for all projects (assets) should be projected over the full economic life of the project, not just the MACRS recovery period.

REAL PROPERTY

The Tax Reform Act of 1986 establishes two classes of real property for depreciation purposes. The 27.5-Year Straight-Line Class includes residential rental property. The 31.5-Year Straight-Line Class includes all nonresidential real property, such as office buildings. Depreciation is computed on a straight-line basis. The amount of depreciation taken during the first year depends upon the month property is placed in service. Furthermore, a half-month convention is used; that is, it is assumed that a building is placed in service in the middle of the first month and is therefore eligible for only one-half month's depreciation during month one.

Tables 9A-4 and 9A-5 provide depreciation percentages for real property.

ASSETS ACQUIRED PRIOR TO 1987

Because replacement decisions are influenced by the depreciation and tax treatment of the old asset in addition to the new asset, it is important to know how assets acquired prior to January 1987 were depreciated. Assets acquired between 1981 and the end of 1986 were depreciated under the old ACRS depreciation rules. Old ACRS established four classes of assets in addition to separate real estate classes. The two most important asset classes were the 3-year ACRS class and the 5-year ACRS class. The 3-year class included automobiles, light duty trucks, research and development equipment, and some special tools. The 5-year class included nearly all other

Straight-Line Depreciation Percentages for 27.5-Year Residential Real Property

Month of First Year the Property is Placed in Service	Recovery Years			
	1	2–27	28	29
1	3.48%	3.64%	1.88%	0.00%
2	3.18	3.64	2.18	0.00
3	2.88	3.64	2.48	0.00
4	2.58	3.64	2.78	0.00
5	2.27	3.64	3.09	0.00
6	1.97	3.64	3.39	0.00
7	1.67	3.64	3.64	0.05
8	1.36	3.64	3.64	0.36
9	1.06	3.64	3.64	0.66
10	0.76	3.64	3.64	0.96
11	0.45	3.64	3.64	1.27
12	0.15	3.64	3.64	1.57

equipment and machinery. The 10- and 15-year classes included public utility property and certain other assets. Real estate was generally depreciated over 18 years.

Prior to January 1, 1986 (the ITC was abolished effective January 1, 1986), assets acquired in the 3-, 5-, 10- and 15-year classes were eligible for an Investment Tax Credit (ITC). For 3-year assets the credit was equal to 6 percent of the installed cost of the asset. For other assets the credit equalled 10 percent of the installed cost. Real property was not eligible for the ITC. The credit was treated as a direct reduction of tax liability for the firm that acquired the asset. If an asset is sold prior to the end of 3 years (for 3-year assets) or prior to the end of 5 years for other asset classes, a portion of the

Straight-Line Depreciation Percentages for 31.5-Year Nonresidential Real Property

Month of First Year the Property is Placed in Service	Recovery Years			
	1	2–31	32	33
1	3.04%	3.17%	1.86%	0.00%
2	2.78	3.17	2.12	0.00
3	2.51	3.17	2.39	0.00
4	2.25	3.17	2.65	0.00
5	1.98	3.17	2.92	0.00
6	1.72	3.17	3.18	0.00
7	1.46	3.17	3.17	0.27
8	1.19	3.17	3.17	0.54
9	0.93	3.17	3.17	0.80
10	0.66	3.17	3.17	1.07
11	0.40	3.17	3.17	1.33
12	0.13	3.17	3.17	1.60

Note: Tables 9A-4 and 9A-5 use the midmonth convention, which assumes that an asset is placed in service in the middle of the month. A midmonth convention also is used in the year an asset is disposed of. In the year of disposition, depreciation runs from the beginning of the year until the middle of the month of disposition. Accuracy is to two decimal places with rounding errors corrected in the last year so that depreciation percentage totals 100 percent over 27.5 and 31.5 years, respectively.

ITC is recaptured (i.e., 2 percentage points of the 10 percentage point ITC is earned for each *full* year the asset is held), resulting in an increased tax liability.

PROBLEMS

1. Using the following depreciation methods, calculate the depreciation schedule for an asset that has a $15,000 original cost, an expected useful life of 5 years, and no expected salvage value:

   a. Straight-line depreciation.

   b. Sum-of-the-years'-digits depreciation.

2. **a.** Calculate the annual MACRS depreciation for a machine in the 7-year MACRS asset class, assuming that the asset costs $20,000.

   b. If you knew that the asset had an expected salvage value of $2,000 at the end of its 12-year economic life, would your answer to Part a change?

3. Calculate the annual MACRS depreciation for a $20,000 truck that qualifies as a 5-year MACRS asset. The truck is estimated to have a $7,000 salvage value 6 years from now.

4. Calculate the MACRS depreciation schedule for a drill press that costs $148,000 and has installation and shipping costs of $2,000. The drill press is classified as a 7-year MACRS asset.

5. Calculate the depreciation schedule for a $1 million office building placed in service in October 1989.

CHAPTER

10

Capital Budgeting Decision Criteria

KEY CHAPTER CONCEPTS

1. The *net present value rule* is the primary decision-making rule used throughout the practice of financial management. The *net present value* of an investment project is defined as the present value of the stream of net cash flows from the project minus the project's net investment.
   a. A project is acceptable if its NPV is greater than or equal to zero.
   b. By maximizing the net present value of accepted projects, a firm will also maximize shareholder wealth.

2. The *internal rate of return* (IRR) is defined as the discount rate that equates the present value of net cash flows from a project with the present value of the net investment.
   a. A project is acceptable if it has an internal rate of return that is greater than or equal to the firm's cost of capital.
   b. The net present value and internal rate of return approaches give the same accept–reject signals for independent projects, although the two may be in conflict in the case of mutually exclusive investment alternatives. In these cases, the decision indicated using the net present value technique is preferable.
   c. Another disadvantage of the IRR approach is that it can lead to multiple internal rates of return in some cases, thus complicating the decision process. In these

cases the net present value technique should be used.

3. The *profitability index* (PI) is the ratio of the present value of future net cash flows over the life of the project to the net investment.
   a. If a project has a (PI) equal to or greater than 1.0, it is acceptable.
   b. The PI can be used as a guide to resource allocation in a situation of capital rationing.

4. The *payback period* of an investment is the period of time required for the cumulative cash inflows (net cash flows) from a project to equal the initial cash outlay.
   a. Weaknesses of the payback method include that it is not a measure of profitability; it ignores the timing of cash flows; it ignores cash flows beyond the payback period; and it has no explicit tie to the goal of shareholder wealth maximization.
   b. The payback technique can be used as a project liquidity measure and as a crude risk-screening technique.

5. Project postaudits and reviews can assist management in uncovering biases in the project analysis procedure of a firm. Project reviews also can assist management in making abandonment decisions for projects that are not performing up to expectations.

GLOSSARY OF NEW TERMS

Capital rationing The process of limiting the number of capital expenditure projects because of insufficient funds to finance all projects that otherwise meet the firm's criteria for acceptability, or because of a lack of sufficient managerial resources to undertake all otherwise acceptable projects.

Contingent project A project whose acceptance depends on the adoption of one or more other projects.

Independent project A project whose acceptance or rejection does not directly result in the elimination of other projects from consideration.

Internal rate of return (IRR) The discount rate that equates the present value of net cash flows from a project with the present value of the net investment. It is the discount rate that gives the project a net present value equal to zero. The IRR is used to evaluate, rank, and select from among various investment projects.

Multiple rates of return Two or more internal rates of return from the same project. This situation sometimes arises when the IRR method is being used for project selection. It occurs only with nonnormal projects, or those whose cash flow patterns contain more than one sign change.

Mutually exclusive project A project whose acceptance precludes the acceptance of one or more alternative projects.

Net cash flow Cash inflow minus cash outflow. It often is measured as operating income after tax plus noncash expenses associated with a particular investment project.

Net investment The net cash outlay required at the beginning of an investment project.

Net present value (NPV) The present value of the stream of net cash flows resulting from a project, discounted at the firm's cost of capital, minus the project's net investment. It is used to evaluate, rank, and select from among various investment projects.

Normal project A project whose cash flow stream requires an initial outlay of funds followed by a series of positive net cash inflows. This also sometimes is called a *conventional project*.

Opportunity cost The rate of return that can be earned on funds if they are invested in the *next best* alternative investment.

Payback (PB) period The period of time required for the cumulative cash inflows from a project to equal the initial cash outlay.

Profitability index (PI) The ratio of the present value of net cash flows over the life of a project to the net investment. It is used to evaluate, rank, and select from among various investment projects. Frequently it is used in conjunction with resource allocation decisions in capital rationing situations.

Project postaudit A review of a project that assesses its progress and evaluates its performance after termination.

Reinvestment rate The rate of return at which cash flows from an investment project are assumed to be reinvested from year to year. The reinvestment rate may vary, depending on the investment opportunities available to the firm.

The New Look of Capital Spending*

Fortune reports that "American companies are investing as they never have before" and "that has helped them lift manufacturing productivity faster than in any expansion since World War II." In 1988 capital expenditures of U.S. companies totaled $487 *billion*, a 9.5 percent increase over 1987, after adjusting for inflation. This new wave of capital expenditures differs from previous booms. American companies are trying to manage their factories better and generally are adding more equipment than bricks and mortar. For example, Cincinnati Milacron, the largest U.S. producer of machine tools, is installing new equipment designed to reduce product design and manufacturing times, thereby increasing output with less factory space.

Company managers are trying to improve the capital budgeting process within their companies. In principle, the capital budgeting process is quite simple—if the present value of a project's net cash flows, or benefits, exceeds its cost, the project is acceptable and therefore should be undertaken. In practice, however, benefits and costs are difficult to estimate. In the 1990s companies will be trying to include in their capital budgeting process some benefits that are difficult to quantify, such as improved quality and reduced inventories.

This chapter considers a number of techniques that are of value when analyzing the cash flows expected to be available from capital expenditures. The techniques developed are consistent with the firm's primary objective—the maximization of shareholder wealth.

* Based on "The New Look of Capital Spending," *Fortune* (March 13, 1989), pp. 115–118.

INTRODUCTION

This chapter looks at some widely used capital budgeting decision models, discussing and illustrating their relative strengths and weaknesses. When combined with the cash flow procedures developed in Chapter 9 and the discounting procedures developed in Chapter 5, these models provide the basis for making capital expenditure decisions.

This chapter also examines project review and postaudit procedures and concludes by tracing a sample project through the capital budgeting analysis process.

EVALUATING ALTERNATIVES: DECISION MODELS

As mentioned in Chapter 9, there are four basic steps in the capital budgeting process: the generation of proposals, the estimation of cash flows, the evaluation and selection of alternatives, and the project postaudit and review. This chapter discusses the final two steps in that process.

Four criteria commonly are used for evaluating and selecting investment projects:[1]

- Net present value (NPV).
- Internal rate of return (IRR).
- Profitability index (PI).
- Payback (PB) period.

[1] Another procedure sometimes used is the accounting rate of return (also called the *average rate of return*). It is computed as the ratio of average annual profits after taxes to the average investment in the project. Because this approach has been shown to be generally incorrect as a project selection criterion, it is not discussed here.

Net Present Value

Recall from Chapter 2 that the net present value rule is the primary decision-making rule used throughout the practice of financial management. The net present value—that is, the present value of the future returns minus the initial outlay—of an investment made by a firm represents the contribution of that investment to the value of the firm and, accordingly, to the wealth of firm's shareholders. In this chapter we consider the net present value of capital expenditure projects.

The net present value (NPV) of a capital expenditure project is defined as the present value of the stream of net cash flows from the project minus the project's net investment. (The net present value method sometimes is called the *discounted cash flow* [DCF] technique.) The cash flows are discounted at the firm's required rate of return; that is, its *cost of capital.* A firm's cost of capital is defined as its minimum acceptable rate of return for projects of average risk.

The net present value of a project may be expressed as follows:

$$NPV = PVNCF - NINV \qquad (10.1)$$

where NPV is the net present value; PVNCF, the present value of net cash flows; and NINV, the net investment.

Assuming a cost of capital, k, the net present value for a project with a 5-year expected life would be the following:

$$NPV = \frac{NCF_1}{(1 + k)^1} + \frac{NCF_2}{(1 + k)^2} + \frac{NCF_3}{(1 + k)^3}$$
$$+ \frac{NCF_4}{(1 + k)^4} + \frac{NCF_5}{(1 + k)^5} - NINV \qquad (10.2)$$

where $NCF_1 \ldots NCF_5$ are the net cash flows occurring in years 1 through 5. NCF_5 may be assumed to include any salvage value remaining at the end of the project's life.

As mentioned in Chapter 9, the annual net cash flows for normal projects usually are positive after the initial net investment. Occasionally, however, one or more of the expected net cash flows over the life of a project may be negative. When this occurs, positive numbers are used for years having positive net cash flows (net inflows), and negative numbers are used for years having negative net cash flows (net outflows).

In general, the net present value of a project may be defined as follows:

$$NPV = \sum_{t=1}^{n} \frac{NCF_t}{(1 + k)^t} - NINV$$

$$= \left(\sum_{t=1}^{n} NCF_t \times PVIF_{k,t} \right) - NINV \qquad (10.3)$$

where n is the expected project life, and $\sum_{t=1}^{n} [NCF_t /(1 + k)^t]$ is the arithmetic sum of the discounted net cash flows for each year t over the life of the project (n years); that is, the present value of the net cash flows.

To illustrate net present value calculations, suppose a firm is considering two projects, A and B, having net investments and net cash flows as shown in Table 10-1. The net present value computations for the two projects are presented in Table 10-2. These calculations assume a 14 percent cost of

Sample Project Cash Flows

Year	Project A Net Cash Flow after Taxes	Project B Net Cash Flow after Taxes
1	$12,500	$ 5,000
2	12,500	10,000
3	12,500	15,000
4	12,500	15,000
5	12,500	25,000
6	12,500	30,000
	Net investment = $50,000	Net investment = $50,000

capital. The calculations in these tables also assume that cash flows are received at the end of each year rather than as a flow during the year. This assumption, although a normal one, tends to slightly understate a project's net present value or internal rate of return.

Project A is shown in Table 10-2 to have a negative net present value, and Project B has a positive net present value. What causes some projects to have a negative net present value and others to have a positive net present value? Frequently, product and factor markets have barriers to entry, such as buyer preferences for established brand names, ownership or control of favored distribution systems (e.g., exclusive auto dealerships), patent control of superior product designs or production techniques, or exclusive ownership of superior natural resource deposits. Suppose Project A involves a new soap product to compete with Proctor & Gamble's Tide. Consumers' brand preferences for Tide, as well as Proctor & Gamble's economies of

Sample Net Present Value Calculations

Project A		Project B			
		Year	NCF	$PVIF_{0.14,t}$*	PV of NCF
Present value of an annuity of $12,500 for 6 years at 14 percent:					
PV of NCF = $12,500(PVIFA_{0.14,6})$		1	$ 5,000	0.877	$ 4,385
= $12,500(3.889)†$		2	10,000	0.769	7,690
= $48,612.50		3	15,000	0.675	10,125
		4	15,000	0.592	8,880
Less Net		5	25,000	0.519	12,975
investment	50,000.00	6	30,000	0.456	13,680
Net present					57,735
value	$ − 1,387.50	*Less* Net investment			50,000
		Net present value			$ 7,735

* From the PVIF table (Table II).
† From the PVIFA table (Table IV).

scale for production and distribution could easily cause Project A to have a negative net present value. Suppose Project B is a new baby care product from Johnson & Johnson. Its positive net present value could be the result of buyer preferences due to Johnson & Johnson's established baby care business.

DECISION RULE. In general, a project should be accepted if its net present value is greater than or equal to zero and rejected if its net present value is less than zero. This is so because a positive net present value in principle translates directly into increases in stock prices and increases in shareholders' wealth. In the previous example, Project A would be rejected because it has a negative net present value, and Project B would be accepted because it has a positive net present value.

If two or more *mutually exclusive* investments have positive net present values, the project having the largest net present value is the one selected. Assume, for example, that a firm has three mutually exclusive investment opportunities, G, H, and I, each requiring a net investment of about $10,000. Project G has a net present value of $2,000; H has a net present value of $4,000; and I has a net present value of $3,500. Of the three, H would be preferred to the other two, because it has the highest net present value and therefore is expected to make the largest contribution to the objective of shareholder wealth maximization.

ADVANTAGES AND DISADVANTAGES OF THE NET PRESENT VALUE METHOD. The net present value of a project is the expected number of dollars by which the present value of the firm is increased as a result of adopting the project. Therefore, as we have pointed out, the net present value method is consistent with the goal of shareholder wealth maximization. The net present value approach considers both the magnitude and the timing of cash flows over a project's entire expected life.

A firm can be thought of as a series of projects, and the firm's total value is the sum of the net present values of all the independent projects that make it up. Therefore, when the firm undertakes a new project, the firm's value is increased by the net present value of the new project. The additivity of net present values of independent projects is referred to in finance as the *value additivity principle*.

The net present value approach also indicates whether a proposed project will yield the rate of return required by the firm's investors. The cost of capital (discount rate) represents this rate of return; when a project's net present value is greater than or equal to zero, the firm's investors can expect to earn at least their required rate of return.

The net present value criterion has a weakness in that many people find it difficult to work with a present value dollar return rather than a percentage return. As a result, many firms use another present value–based method that is more easily interpreted; namely, the *internal rate of return* method.

Internal Rate of Return

The *internal rate of return* is defined as the discount rate that equates the present value of the net cash flows from a project with the present value of the net investment.[2] It is the discount rate that causes a project's net present value to equal zero. The internal rate of return for a capital expenditure project is identical to the yield-to-maturity for a bond investment.

A project's internal rate of return can be determined by means of the following equation:

$$\sum_{t=1}^{n} \frac{NCF_t}{(1 + r)^t} = NINV \qquad (10.4)$$

where $NCF_t /(1 + r)^t$ is the present value of net cash flows in period t discounted at the rate r, NINV is the net investment in the project, and r is the internal rate of return.

For a project having a 5-year life, this basic formula can be rewritten as follows:

$$\frac{NCF_1}{(1 + r)^1} + \frac{NCF_2}{(1 + r)^2} + \frac{NCF_3}{(1 + r)^3} + \frac{NCF_4}{(1 + r)^4} + \frac{NCF_5}{(1 + r)^5} = NINV \quad (10.5)$$

Subtracting the net investment, NINV, from both sides of Equation 10.5 yields the following:

$$\frac{NCF_1}{(1 + r)^1} + \frac{NCF_2}{(1 + r)^2} + \frac{NCF_3}{(1 + r)^3} + \frac{NCF_4}{(1 + r)^4} + \frac{NCF_5}{(1 + r)^5} - NINV = 0 \quad (10.6)$$

This essentially is the same equation as that used in the net present value method. The only difference is that in the net present value approach a discount rate, k, is specified and the net present value is computed, whereas in the internal rate of return method the discount rate, r, which causes the project net present value to equal zero, is the unknown.

Figure 10-1 illustrates the relationship between net present value and internal rate of return. The figure plots the net present value of Project B (from Table 10-1) against the discount rate used to evaluate its cash flows. Note that at a 14 percent cost of capital, the net present value of B is $7,735—the same figure that resulted from the computations performed in Table 10-2. The internal rate of return of Project B is approximately equal to 18.2 percent. (The exact calculation will be illustrated algebraically.) Thus, the internal rate of return is a special case of the net present value computation.

The internal rate of return for Projects A and B now can be calculated. Because Project A is an annuity of $12,500 for 6 years requiring a net investment of $50,000, its internal rate of return may be computed directly with the aid of a PVIFA table such as Table IV.

In this case the present value of the annuity, $PVAN_0$, is $50,000, and the annuity R, is $12,500 for $n = 6$ years. The following equation,

$$PVAN_0 = R(PVIFA_{r,n})$$

can be rewritten to solve for the PVIFA:

$$PVIFA_{r,n} = \frac{PVAN_0}{R}$$

---

[2] This also is called the *discounted cash flow* (DCF) rate of return.

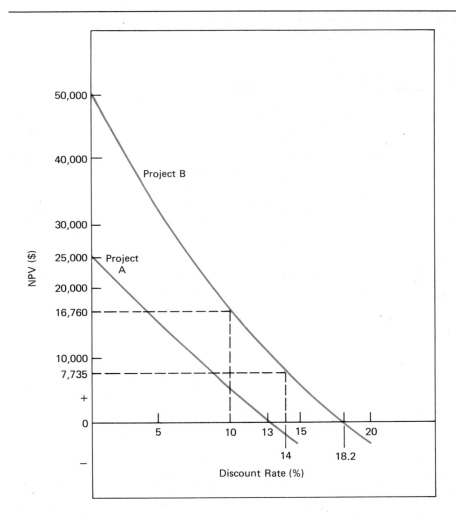

F I G U R E 10-1

**NPV Profiles:
Relationship between
the Net Present
Value and the
Internal Rate of
Return for Projects A
and B**

In this case, PVIFA = $50,000/$12,500 = 4.000. Referring to Table IV and reading across the table for $n = 6$, it can be seen that the interest factor of 4.000 occurs near 13 percent, where it is 3.998. Thus, the internal rate of return for Project A is about 13 percent.

The internal rate of return for Project B is more difficult to calculate, because the project is expected to yield uneven cash flows. In this case, the internal rate of return is computed by trial and error, with the help of a financial calculator, or by using capital budgeting spreadsheet programs such as the one available with this text. The steps in the trial and error procedure are as follows:

■ **Step 1:** Make an approximate estimate of the internal rate of return.
■ **Step 2:** Use this rate to compute the project's net present value.
■ **Step 3:** Try a *higher* rate if a positive net present value results or a *lower* rate if a negative one results.
■ **Step 4:** Repeat the process (attempting to "bracket" the internal rate of return) until a rate is found at which the net present value is equal to zero.

Table 10-3 illustrates this procedure. First, an r of 15 percent is tried, resulting in a net present value of $5,745. Next, a higher discount rate, 19

T A B L E 10-3 Trial-and-Error Computation of the Internal Rate of Return for Project B

Year (1)	Net Cash Flow (2)	PVIF$_{0.15,t}$ (3)	PV Cash Flows (4) = (3) × (2)	PVIF$_{0.19,t}$ (5)	PV Cash Flows (6) = (5) × (2)	PVIF$_{0.18,t}$ (7)	PV Cash Flows (8) = (7) × (2)
1	$ 5,000	0.870	$ 4,350	0.840	$ 4,200	0.847	$ 4,235
2	10,000	0.756	7,560	0.706	7,060	0.718	7,180
3	15,000	0.658	9,870	0.593	8,895	0.609	9,135
4	15,000	0.572	8,580	0.499	7,485	0.516	7,740
5	25,000	0.497	12,425	0.419	10,475	0.437	10,925
6	30,000	0.432	12,960	0.352	10,560	0.370	11,100
			$55,745		$48,675		$50,315
		Less NINV	50,000	Less NINV	50,000	Less NINV	50,000
		NPV =	$ 5,745	NPV =	$−1,325	NPV =	$ 315

percent, is chosen; in this case the net present value is −$1,325. This indicates that the internal rate of return is between 15 and 19 percent. Trying 18 percent results in a net present value of $315, narrowing the range to between 18 and 19 percent.

A more exact internal rate of return can be computed by means of interpolation:

$$r = 18\% + \frac{\$315}{\$315 + \$1,325}(19\% - 18\%)$$

$$= 18\% + 0.19(1\%)$$

$$= 18.19\%$$

DECISION RULE. Generally the internal rate of return method indicates that a project whose internal rate of return is greater than or equal to the firm's cost of capital should be accepted, whereas a project whose internal rate of return is less than the firm's cost of capital should be rejected. In the case of Projects A and B, if the cost of capital were 14 percent B would be acceptable and A would be unacceptable.

When two independent projects are considered under conditions of no capital rationing, the net present value and internal rate of return techniques result in the same accept−reject decision. This can be seen in Figure 10-1. For example, if the firm's cost of capital is 10 percent, Project B has a positive net present value ($16,760). Its internal rate of return is 18.19 percent, exceeding the cost of capital. When two or more mutually exclusive projects are being considered, it *generally* is preferable to accept the project having the highest internal rate of return as long as it is greater than or equal to the cost of capital. In this case, if A and B were mutually exclusive, B would be chosen over A, as can be seen in Figure 10-1. Exceptions to this general rule are considered later in the chapter.

ADVANTAGES AND DISADVANTAGES OF THE INTERNAL RATE OF RETURN METHOD. The internal rate of return method is widely used in industry by firms that employ present value-based capital budgeting techniques. In fact, in a survey of over 100 U.S. firms, nearly 54 percent reported the use of the internal rate of return as their *primary* capital budgeting technique.[3] This popularity may be due to the fact that many people feel more comfortable dealing with the concept of a project's rate of return than with its net present value.[4] Like the net present value approach, the internal rate of return technique takes into account both the magnitude and the timing of cash flows over the entire life of a project in measuring the project's economic desirability.

However, some potential problems are involved in using the internal rate of return technique. The possible existence of *multiple internal rates of return* is one such problem. Whereas equating the net present value of a project to zero will yield only one internal rate of return, *r*, for *normal* investments, there are times when two or more rates may be obtained. Recall that a normal project has an initial cash outlay or outlays (net investment) followed by a stream of positive net cash flows. If for some reason—such as large abandonment costs at the end of a project's life or a major shutdown and rebuilding of a facility sometime during its life—the initial net investment is followed by one or more positive net cash flows (inflows) that then are followed by a negative cash flow,[5] it is possible to obtain more than one internal rate of return.

Whenever a project has multiple internal rates of return, the pattern of cash flows over the project's life contains more than one sign change, for example, $- \uparrow + + \uparrow -$. In this case there are two sign changes (indicated by the arrows)—from minus to plus, and again from plus to minus.

Consider the following investment, which has three internal rates of return—0, 100, and 200 percent:

Year	Net Cash Flows
0	−$ 1,000
1	+$ 6,000
2	−$11,000
3	+$ 6,000

Unfortunately, none of these rates can be compared to the firm's cost of capital to determine the project's acceptability.

Although several techniques have been proposed for dealing with the multiple internal rate of return problem, none provides a simple, complete, and generally satisfactory solution. The best approach is to use the net present value criterion. If a project's net present value is positive, it is acceptable; if it is negative, it is not acceptable. Many computer software packages are available that compute internal rates of return, and they usually will warn the user when a potential multiple internal rate of return problem exists. Whenever this is a possibility, the use of the net present value method is preferred.

Profitability Index

The profitability index (PI), or benefit–cost ratio, is the ratio of the present

---

[3] See Lawrence J. Gitman and John R. Forrester, Jr. "A Survey of Capital Budgeting Techniques Used by Major U.S. Firms," *Financial Management* (Fall 1977): 66–71.

[4] It also is easy to program a computer to perform these calculations, thus eliminating the need for trial-and-error manipulations. Many financial calculators also can solve internal rate of return problems when the periodic cash flows are uneven.

[5] Table 9-2 in Chapter 9 illustrates two such projects, X and Y.

value of future net cash flows over the life of a project to the net investment. It is expressed as follows:

$$PI = \frac{\sum_{t=1}^{n} NCF_t/(1 + k)^t}{NINV} \qquad (10.7)$$

Assuming a 14 percent cost of capital k, and using the data from Table 10-2, the profitability index for Projects A and B can be calculated as follows:

$$PI_A = \frac{\$48,612.50}{\$50,000}$$

$$= 0.97$$

$$PI_B = \frac{\$57,735}{\$50,000}$$

$$= 1.15$$

The profitability index is interpreted as the present value return *for each dollar of initial investment.* In comparison, the net present value approach measures the total present value dollar return.

DECISION RULE. A project whose profitability index is greater than or equal to 1 is considered acceptable, whereas a project having a profitability index less than 1 is considered unacceptable.[6] In this case, Project B is acceptable, whereas Project A is not. When two or more *independent* projects with normal cash flows are considered, the profitability index, net present value, and internal rate of return approaches all will yield identical accept–reject signals; this is true, for example, with Projects A and B.

When dealing with mutually exclusive investments, conflicts may arise between the net present value and the profitability index criteria. This is most likely to occur if the alternative projects require significantly different net investments.

Consider, for example, the following information on Projects J and K. According to the net present value criterion, Project J would be preferred because of its larger net present value. According to the profitability index criterion, Project K would be preferred.

	Project J	Project K
Present value of net cash flows	$25,000	$14,000
Less Net investment	20,000	10,000
Net present value	$ 5,000	$ 4,000
$PI = \dfrac{\text{Present value of net cash flows}}{\text{Net investment}}$	1.25	1.40

When a conflict arises, the final decision must be made on the basis of other factors. For example, if a firm has no constraint on the funds available to it for capital investment—that is, no capital rationing—the net present

---

[6] When a project has a profitability index equal to 1, the present value of the net cash flows is exactly equal to the net investment. Thus, the project has a net present value of zero, meaning that it is expected to earn the investors' required rate of return and nothing more.

value approach is preferred, because it will select the projects that are expected to generate the largest *total dollar* increase in the firm's wealth and, by extension, maximize shareholder wealth. If, however, the firm is in a capital rationing situation, and capital budgeting is being done for only one period,[7] the profitability index approach may be preferred, because it will indicate which projects will maximize the returns *per dollar of investment*—an appropriate objective when a funds constraint exists.

Decision Criteria

Net Present Value versus Internal Rate of Return: The Reinvestment Rate Assumption

As was indicated, both the net present value and the internal rate of return methods result in identical decisions to either accept or reject an *independent* project. This is true because the net present value is greater than (less than) zero if and only if the internal rate of return is greater than (less than) the required rate of return, k. In the case of *mutually exclusive* projects, however, the two methods may yield contradictory results; one project may have a *higher* internal rate of return than another and, at the same time, a *lower* net present value.

Consider, for example, *mutually exclusive* Projects L and M described in the following table. Both require a net investment of $1,000. Using the internal rate of return approach, Project L is preferred, with an IRR of 21.5 percent compared with Project M's IRR of 18.3 percent. Using the net present value approach with a discount rate of 5 percent, Project M is preferred to Project L. Hence, it is necessary to determine which technique is the correct one to use in this situation.

	Project L	Project M
Net investment	$1,000	$1,000
Net cash flows:		
Year 1	$ 667	$ 0
Year 2	$ 667	$1,400
Net present value at 5%	$ 240	$ 270
Internal rate of return	21.5%	18.3%

The outcome depends on what *assumptions* the decision maker chooses to make about the *implied reinvestment rate* for the net cash flows generated from each project. This can be seen in Figure 10.2. For discount (reinvestment) rates below 10 percent, Project M has a higher net present value than Project L and therefore is preferred. For discount rates greater than 10 percent, Project L is preferred using both the net present value and internal rate of return approaches. Hence, a conflict only occurs in this case for discount (cost-of-capital) rates below 10 percent. The net present value method assumes that cash flows are *reinvested at the firm's cost of capital*, whereas the internal rate of return method assumes that these cash flows are *reinvested at the computed internal rate of return*.[8] Generally, the cost of capital

[7] If the firm makes capital budgeting decisions for more than 1 period in the future, it usually is necessary to use some kind of programming model. Footnote 9 lists a number of references for some of these techniques.

[8] A more complete discussion of this problem and the underlying assumptions is found in J. Hirshleifer, "On the Theory of the Optimal Investment Decision," *Journal of Political Economy* 66 (August 1958): 95–103; and James H. Lorie and Leonard J. Savage, "Three Problems in Rationing Capital," *Journal of Business* 23 (October 1955): 229–239.

FIGURE 10-2

**NPV Profiles: Net
Present Value versus
Internal Rate of
Return for Mutually
Exclusive
Alternatives**

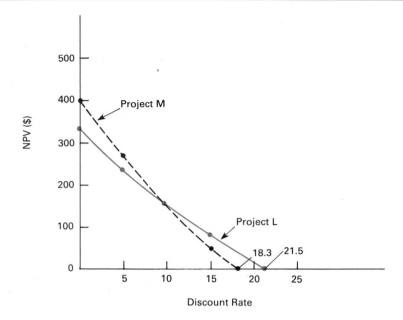

is considered to be a more realistic reinvestment rate than the computed internal rate of return, because this is the rate the next (marginal) investment project can be assumed to earn. This can be seen in Figure 9-1 in Chapter 9. The last project invested in, Project E, offers a rate of return nearly equal to the firm's marginal cost of capital.

Consequently, in the absence of capital rationing, the net present value approach normally is superior to both the profitability index and the internal rate of return when choosing among mutually exclusive investments.

Payback (PB) Period

The payback (PB) period of an investment is the period of time required for the cumulative cash inflows (net cash flows) from a project to equal the initial cash outlay (net investment).

To illustrate, suppose a firm is considering a project that requires a net investment of $50,000 and is expected to generate 6 years of net cash inflows of $12,500 a year. Because the expected net cash inflows are *equal* in each year, the payback period is the ratio of the net investment to the annual net cash inflows:

$$PB = \frac{\text{Net investment}}{\text{Annual net cash inflows}} \qquad \textbf{(10.8)}$$

The payback (PB) period for the preceding example is computed as follows:

$$PB = \frac{\$50,000}{\$12,500}$$

$$= 4 \text{ years}$$

DECISION RULE. Because the payback method has a number of serious shortcomings, it should not be used in deciding whether to accept or reject an investment project.

ADVANTAGES AND DISADVANTAGES OF THE PAYBACK METHOD. The payback method suffers from the following serious disadvantages. First, the payback method gives equal weight to all cash inflows within the payback period, regardless of when they occur during the period. In other words, the technique ignores the *time value of money*.

Assume, for example, that a firm is considering two projects, E and F, each costing $10,000. Project E is expected to yield cash flows over a 3-year period of $6,000 during the first year, $4,000 during the second year, and $3,000 during the third year. Project F is expected to yield cash flows of $4,000 during the first year, $6,000 during the second year, and $3,000 during the third year. Viewed from the payback perspective, these projects are equally attractive, yet the net present value technique clearly indicates that Project E increases the value of the firm more than Project F.

Second, payback generally does not measure the profitability of investment projects and essentially ignores cash flows occurring after the payback period. Thus, payback figures can be misleading.

For example, suppose a firm is considering two projects, C and D, each costing $10,000. It is expected that Project C will generate net cash inflows of $5,000 per year for three years, and that Project D will generate net cash inflows of $4,500 per year forever. The payback period for Project C is two years ($10,000/$5,000), whereas the payback period for Project D is 2.2 years ($10,000/$4,500). If these projects were mutually exclusive, payback would favor C, because it has the lower payback period. Yet Project D clearly has a higher net present value than Project C.

Third, payback provides no *objective* criterion for decision making that is consistent with shareholder wealth maximization. The choice of an acceptable payback period is largely a *subjective* one, and different people using essentially identical data may make different accept–reject decisions about a project.

The payback method is sometimes justified on the basis that it provides a measure of the *risk* associated with a project. Although it is true that less risk may be associated with a shorter payback period than with a longer one, risk is best thought of in terms of the *variability* of project returns. Because payback ignores this dimension, it is at best a crude tool for risk analysis.

A more valid justification for the use of the payback method is that it gives some indication of a project's desirability from a *liquidity* perspective, because it measures the time required for a firm to recover its initial investment in a project. A company that is very concerned about the early recovery of investment funds—such as one investing overseas in a politically unstable area or one expecting a cash shortage in the future—might find this method useful.

In summary, payback is not a satisfactory criterion for investment decision making, because it may lead to a selection of projects that do not make the largest possible contribution to a firm's value. It can be useful as a supplementary decision-making tool, however.

Table 10-4 presents a summary of the four capital budgeting methods discussed in the chapter.

T A B L E 10-4 Summary of the Capital Budgeting Methods

Model	Project Acceptance Criterion	Strengths	Weaknesses
Net present value (NPV)	Accept project if project has a positive or zero NPV; that is, if the present value of net cash flows, evaluated at the firm's cost of capital, equals or exceeds the net investment required.	Considers the timing of cash flows. Provides an objective, return-based criterion for acceptance or rejection. Most conceptually correct approach.	Difficulty in working with a dollar return value, rather than percentage returns.
Internal rate of return (IRR)	Accept project if IRR equals or exceeds the firm's cost of capital.	Same benefits as the NPV. Easy to interpret the meaning of IRR.	Multiple rates of return problem. Sometimes gives decision that conflicts with NPV.
Profitability index (PI)	Accept project if PI is greater than or equal to 1.0.	Same benefits as the NPV. Useful to guide decisions in capital rationing problems.	Sometimes gives decision that conflicts with NPV.
Payback (PB)	PB should not be used in deciding whether to accept or reject an investment project.	Easy and inexpensive to use. Provides a crude measure of project risk. Provides a measure of project liquidity.	No objective decision criterion. Not a measure of profitability. Fails to consider timing of cash flows.

▬▬▬ CAPITAL RATIONING AND THE CAPITAL BUDGETING DECISION

For each of the selection criterion previously discussed, the decision rule is to undertake *all* independent investment projects that meet the acceptance standard. This rule places no restrictions on the total amount of acceptable capital projects a company may undertake in any particular period.

However, many firms do not have unlimited funds available for investment. Rather than letting the size of their capital budget be determined by the number of profitable investment opportunities available, many companies choose to place an upper limit, or *constraint*, on the amount of funds allocated to capital investments. This constraint may be either *self-imposed*—by the firm's management—or *externally imposed*—by conditions in the capital markets.

For example, a very conservative firm may be reluctant to use debt or external equity to finance capital expenditures. Instead, it would limit capital expenditures to cash flows from continuing operations minus any dividends paid. Another firm may feel that it lacks the managerial resources to successfully undertake all acceptable projects in a given year and may choose to limit capital expenditures for this reason.

A number of externally imposed constraints might limit a firm's capital expenditures. For example, a firm's loan agreements may contain restrictive covenants that limit future borrowing. Similarly, a weak financial position, conditions in the securities markets, or both may make the flotation of a new bond or stock issue by the firm impossible or prohibitively expensive. Examples of such market-imposed constraints include depressed stock market prices, unusually high interest rates due to a "tight money" policy on the part of the Federal Reserve, or a reluctance on the part of investors to purchase new securities if the firm has a large percentage of debt in its capital structure.

Several different methods can be used in making capital budgeting decisions under capital rationing. When the initial outlays occur in two (or more) periods, the methods are quite elaborate and require the use of linear, integer, or goal programming.[9] However, when there is a single period capital budgeting constraint, a relatively simple approach employing the profitability index can be used. Briefly, the approach consists of the following steps:

Step 1: Calculate the profitability index for each of a series of investment projects.

Step 2: Rank the projects according to their profitability indexes (from highest to lowest).

Step 3: Beginning with the project having the highest profitability index, proceed down through the list, and accept projects having profitability indexes greater than or equal to 1 until the entire capital budget has been utilized.

At times a firm may not be able to utilize its entire capital budget because the next acceptable project on its list is too large, given the remaining available funds. In this case, the firm's management should choose among the following three alternatives:

Alternative 1: Search for another combination of projects, perhaps including some smaller, less profitable ones that will allow for a more complete utilization of available funds *and* increase the net present value of the combination of projects.

Alternative 2: Attempt to relax the funds constraint so that sufficient resources are available to accept the last project for which funds were not fully available.

Alternative 3: Accept as many projects as possible and either invest any excess funds in short-term securities until the next period,[10] pay out the excess funds to shareholders as dividends, use the funds to reduce outstanding debt, or do a combination of the above.

---

[9] The following references contain information on the use of these more advanced models: James R. McGuigan and R. Charles Moyer, *Managerial Economics*, 5th ed. (St. Paul: West Publishing, 1989, pp. 119–122; or H. Martin Weingartner, *Mathematical Programming and the Analysis of Capital Budgeting Problems*, Englewood Cliffs, NJ: Prentice-Hall, 1963. See also Sang M. Lee and A. J. Lerro, "Capital Budgeting for Multiple Objectives," *Financial Management* 3 (Spring 1974): 58–66; and Richard H. Bernhard, "Mathematical Programming Models for Capital Budgeting: A Survey, Generalization, and Critique," *Journal of Financial and Quantitative Analysis* 4 (June 1969): 111–158.

[10] If a firm does not invest a portion of its available capital resources in projects earning a rate of return at least equal to the cost of capital, an implicit opportunity cost of lost earnings is incurred. For example, suppose a firm cannot invest a portion of its capital budget because the next acceptable project requires a larger net investment than is available in remaining funds. If the firm's after-tax cost of capital is 15 percent and the unutilized funds can be invested only in short-term securities earning 5 percent after taxes, the opportunity cost of this action is a 10 percent difference, representing a loss in potential earnings. Therefore, as long as profitable investment alternatives exist, the firm should seek ways to fully utilize all available capital funds.

The following example illustrates how these alternatives can be applied to an actual capital budgeting decision. Suppose that management of the Old Mexico Tile Company has decided to limit next year's capital expenditures to $550,000. Eight capital expenditure projects have been proposed—P, R, S, U, T, V, Q, and W—and ranked according to their profitability indexes, as shown in Table 10-5. Given the $550,000 ceiling, the firm's management proceeds down the list of projects, selecting P, R, S, and U, in that order. Project T cannot be accepted, because this would require a capital outlay of $25,000 in excess of the $550,000 limit. Projects P, R, S, and U together yield a net present value of $114,750 but require a total investment outlay of $525,000, leaving $25,000 from the capital budget that is not invested in projects. Management is considering the following three alternatives:

Alternative 1: It could attempt to find another combination of projects, perhaps including some smaller ones, that would allow for a more complete utilization of available funds and increase the cumulative net present value. In this case, a likely combination would be Projects P, R, S, T, and V. This combination would fully utilize the $550,000 available and create a net present value of $116,250—an increase of $1,500 over the net present value of $114,750 from projects P, R, S, and U.

Alternative 2: It could attempt to increase the capital budget by another $25,000 to allow Project T to be added to the list of adopted projects.

Alternative 3: It could merely accept the first four projects—P, R, S, and U—and invest the remaining $25,000 in a short-term security until the next period. This alternative is not especially desirable, however, because the return on the short-term investment would surely be less than the firm's cost of capital (required rate of return). Therefore, the difference between the firm's cost of capital and the return on the short-term investment would constitute an *opportunity cost*.

TABLE   10-5   **Sample Ranking of Proposed Projects According to Their Profitability Indexes**

Project (1)	Net Investment (2)	Net Present Value (3)	Present Value of Net Cash Flows (4)	PI = (4) ÷ (2)	Cumulative Net Investment	Cumulative Net Present Value
P	$100,000	$25,000	$125,000	1.25	$100,000	$ 25,000
R	150,000	33,000	183,000	1.22	250,000	58,000
S	175,000	36,750	211,750	1.21	425,000	94,750
U	100,000	20,000	120,000	1.20	525,000	114,750
T	50,000	9,000	59,000	1.18	575,000	123,750
V	75,000	12,500	87,500	1.17	650,000	136,250
Q	200,000	30,000	230,000	1.15	850,000	166,250
W	50,000	−10,000	40,000	0.80	900,000	156,250

In this case, *Alternative 1* seems to be the most desirable of the three. In rearranging the capital budget, however, the firm should never accept a project, such as W, that does not meet the minimum acceptance criterion of a positive net present value (a profitability index greater than 1).

REVIEWING AND POSTAUDITING AN ACCEPTED PROJECT

A final important step in the capital budgeting process is the review of investment projects after they have been implemented. This can provide useful information on the effectiveness of the company's selection process. The postaudit procedure consists of comparing *actual* cash flows from an accepted project with *projected* cash flows that were estimated when the project was adopted. Because projected cash flows contain an element of uncertainty, actual values would not be expected to exactly match estimated values. Instead, a project review should be concerned with identifying systematic biases or errors in cash flow estimation on the part of individuals, departments, plants, or divisions and attempting to determine *why* these biases or errors exist. This type of analysis, when properly performed, can help a company's decision makers better evaluate investment proposals submitted in the future.

The importance of the postaudit process has been highlighted in research by Brown and Miller.[11] They observed that in the common situation where bad projects outnumber good ones, the simple procedure of making unbiased cash flow estimates and choosing projects with positive net present values will result in an upwardly biased acceptance rate for proposed projects (and returns that are, on average, below those that are expected) if there is uncertainty regarding future cash flows. In a situation such as this it is important that the firm correct for this potential bias when projects are being reviewed. The information needed to make this necessary bias-eliminating correction can be gathered from careful project postaudits.

The importance of a good project review and tracking system is illustrated in the following example from Ameritech, a holding company consisting of five telephone companies in the Midwest and several other subsidiaries. Ameritech has a sophisticated tracking system that permits the company to identify the individual responsible for each estimate in a capital project proposal. When the tracking system was announced and initiated, budgets already had been submitted for the coming year. Divisions were permitted to take back their budgets and resubmit them in light of the new tracking system. Seven hundred projects disappeared from the new budgets and many others had reduced estimates of benefits![12]

Another objective of the project review process involves determining whether a project that has not lived up to expectations should be continued or abandoned. The decision to abandon a project requires the company to compare the cost of abandonment with any future cash flows that are ex-

---

[11] Keith C. Brown, "A Note on the Apparent Bias of Net Revenue Estimates for Capital Investment Projects," *Journal of Finance* (September 1974): 1215–1216; K. C. Brown, "The Rate of Return on Selected Investment Projects," *Journal of Finance* (September 1978): 1250–1253; Edward M. Miller, "Uncertainty Induced Bias in Capital Budgeting," *Financial Management* (Autumn 1978): 12–18; E. M. Miller, "The Competitive Market Assumption and Capital Budgeting Criteria," *Financial Management* (Winter 1987): 22–28.

[12] "Capital Budgeting: A Panel Discussion," *Financial Management* (Spring 1989): 10–17.

pected over the project's remaining life. These estimates of future cash flows usually will be more accurate after the project has been in service for a period of time.[13]

A COMPREHENSIVE EXAMPLE OF CAPITAL BUDGETING: OPENING A NEW BANK BRANCH

The First National Bank and Trust Company has a single banking office located in the downtown business district of a medium-sized town. As the population moved to the suburbs, First National has seen its share of both local banking deposits and profits decline. One of the bank's vice-presidents has proposed that First National try to reverse this trend by building a branch in a new, affluent suburban community. He has presented the bank's executive committee with the following information.

The initial cost of the bank building and equipment is $1.1 million. This facility is expected to have a useful life of 20 years. The branch building and its equipment will be depreciated over their 20-year life using straight-line depreciation to a $100,000 salvage value. We have assumed straight-line depreciation for simplicity. As discussed in the appendix to Chapter 9, in actual practice the bank would use MACRS depreciation with a 31.5-year life on the building and a 7-year life on the equipment. The annual straight-line depreciation will be ($1,100,000 − $100,000)/20 = $50,000. The bank building is to be constructed on land leased for $20,000 per year. In addition to the $1.1 million investment for the building and equipment, the parent bank's net working capital must be increased by $100,000 to accommodate the new branch.

Based on customer surveys, population trends, the location of competitor banks, and the experience other area banks have had with their branches, it is estimated that the annual revenues from the new branch will be $400,000. Of this $400,000 in revenues, $50,000 will be drawn away from the bank's main office. (Assume that the main office will not attempt to cut its expenses because of this loss in revenues.)

In addition to the $20,000 annual expense for the land lease, the new branch will incur about $130,000 per year in other expenses, including personnel costs, utilities, and interest paid on accounts. Both expenses and revenues are expected to remain approximately constant over the branch's 20-year life.

The bank's marginal tax rate is 40 percent and its cost of capital (required rate of return) is 9 percent after tax.

Step 1: Computing the Net Investment

New project cost	$1,100,000
Plus Increase in working capital	100,000
Net investment	$1,200,000

The net investment equals the new project cost ($1.1 million) plus the increase in working capital ($100,000).

---

[13] A further discussion of the abandonment question may be found in Gordon Shillinglaw's two articles, "Profit Analysis for Abandonment Decision" and "Residual Values in Investment Analysis," reprinted in Ezra Solomon, ed., *The Management of Corporate Capital* (New York: Free Press, 1959), pp. 269–281 and 259–268, respectively. See also Alexander Robichek and James C. Van Horne, "Abandonment Value and Capital Budgeting," *Journal of Finance* 22 (December 1967): 577–589.

Step 2: Computing Net Cash Flows

Net increase in revenues ($400,000 − $50,000)	$350,000
Less Operating costs of branch ($130,000 + $20,000)	150,000
Less Depreciation	50,000
Net income before taxes	$150,000
Less Tax (40%)	60,000
Net income after taxes	$ 90,000
Plus Depreciation	50,000
Net cash flow	$140,000

Net cash flows are calculated for years 1 through 19 by subtracting branch operating costs and depreciation from the incremental revenues of $350,000. This yields net income before taxes from which taxes (at the 40 percent rate) are deducted to arrive at net income after taxes. By adding back depreciation, the net cash flow equals $140,000 for each year from 1 through 19. Net cash flows in year 20 are computed by adding the $100,000 estimated salvage and the $100,000 return of working capital to the annual net cash flow of $140,000 to equal $340,000.

The $100,000 working capital requirement is added back to the year 20 cash flows because at the end of 20 years, when the project is terminated, there no longer will be a need for this incremental working capital, and thus the working capital of $100,000 can be liquidated and made available to the bank for other uses.

Step 3: Arraying Project Cash Flows and Evaluating Alternatives

Net investment	$1,200,000
Net cash flows:	
Years 1–19	$ 140,000
Year 20	$ 340,000

After the project cash flows have been computed and arrayed, the decision of whether to accept or reject the new branch project must be made. Next, the project is evaluated using the decision criteria discussed in this chapter; namely, net present value, internal rate of return, and profitability index.

■ **Criterion 1: Net Present Value**

$$NPV = PVNCF - NINV$$

$$= \sum_{t=1}^{19} \frac{\$140,000}{(1 + 0.09)^t} + \frac{\$340,000}{(1 + 0.09)^{20}} - \$1,200,000$$

$$= (\$140,000 \times PVIFA_{0.09,19})$$

$$+ (\$340,000 \times PVIF_{0.09,20}) - \$1,200,000$$

The first term in the net present value equation is the present value of an annuity of $140,000 for 19 years at 9 percent, the bank's cost of capital. Using the present value of an annuity table (Table IV), an interest factor of 8.950 may be found. The second term is the present value of $340,000 received in 20 years at 9 percent. From the present value table (Table II), an interest factor of 0.178 is found. Thus, the net present value of this project at a 9 percent cost of capital is as follows:

NPV = $140,000(8.950) + $340,000(0.178) − $1,200,000

= $1,253,000 + $60,520 − $1,200,000

= $113,520

Using the net present value criterion and a cost of capital of 9 percent, this project would be acceptable, because it has a positive net present value.

■ **Criterion 2: Internal Rate of Return**
According to this method, a discount rate that makes the net present value of the project equal to zero must be found:

Present value of net cash flows − Net investment = 0

or

$$\sum_{i=1}^{19} \frac{\$140,000}{(1 + r)^i} + \frac{\$340,000}{(1 + r)^{20}} - \$1,200,000 = 0$$

where r is the internal rate of return.

Because the net present value was positive at an interest rate of 9 percent, only higher rates need be considered, as the higher the rate, the lower is the net present value. Trying $r = 11\%$ yields the following:

NPV = $140,000(7.839) + $340,000(0.124) − $1,200,000

= $1,097,460 + $42,160 − $1,200,000

= −$60,380

Because the net present value is negative, a lower r, such as $r = 10$ percent, should be tried next,

NPV = $140,000(8.365) + $340,000(0.149) − $1,200,000

= $1,171,100 + $50,660 − $1,200,000

= $21,760

Because this figure is positive, the actual internal rate of return falls somewhere between 10 and 11 percent. It is computed by interpolation as follows:

$$IRR = 10\% + \frac{\$21,760}{\$21,760 + \$60,380} (1\%)$$

= 10% + 0.26(1%)

= 10.26%

Because the internal rate of return equals 10.26 percent, which is greater than the cost of capital, the project is acceptable by this criterion.

■ **Criterion 3: Profitability Index**
The profitability index is the ratio of the present value of future net cash flows to the net investment. From the previous net present value cal-

culation, we know that the present value of net cash flows at a 9 percent cost of capital is $1,313,520 ($1,253,000 + $60,520). Thus, the profitability index is computed as follows:

$$PI = \frac{\$1,313,520}{\$1,200,000}$$

$$= 1.09$$

Because the profitability index is greater than 1, the new branch bank project is acceptable according to this criterion.

Based on these calculations, it appears that the new branch proposal will increase shareholder wealth and therefore should be undertaken. The only step remaining is to monitor the performance of the project to see if it meets, falls short of, or exceeds its projected cash flow estimates. Based on the actual results of this project, the bank's management will be able to evaluate other new branch bank proposals in a more knowledgeable manner.

INFLATION AND CAPITAL EXPENDITURES

During inflationary periods the level of capital expenditures made by firms tends to decrease. For example, suppose the Apple Manufacturing Company has an investment opportunity that is expected to generate 10 years of cash inflows of $300 per year. The original cash outflow is $2,000. If the company's cost of capital is relatively low—say, 7 percent—the net present value is positive:

$$NPV = PV \text{ cash inflows} - PV \text{ cash outflows}$$

$$= \$300(PVIFA_{0.07,10}) - \$2,000$$

$$= \$300(7.024) - \$2,000$$

$$= \$107.2$$

According to the net present value decision rule, this project is acceptable.

Suppose, however, that inflation expectations increase and the overall cost of the firm's capital rises to, say, 10 percent. The net present value of the project would then be negative:

$$NPV = PV \text{ cash inflows} - PV \text{ cash outflows}$$

$$= \$300(PVIFA_{0.10,10}) - \$2,000$$

$$= \$300(6.145) - \$2,000$$

$$= -\$156.5$$

Under these conditions, the project would not be acceptable.

The example assumes that expected cash inflows are not affected by inflation. Admittedly, project revenues usually will increase with rising inflation, but so will expenses. As a result, it is somewhat difficult to generalize about net cash inflows. The experience of recent years, however, seems to indicate that cash flow increases often are not sufficient to offset the increased cost of capital. Thus, capital expenditure levels tend to be lower (in real terms) during periods of relatively high inflation than during low inflation times.

Fortunately, it is quite easy to adjust the capital budgeting procedure to take inflationary effects into account. The cost of capital already includes the effects of expected inflation.[14] As the expected future inflation rate increases, the cost of capital also tends to increase. Thus, the financial manager has to estimate future cash flows (revenues and expenses) that reflect the expected inflationary rate. For example, if prices are expected to increase at a rate of 5 percent per year over the life of a project, the revenue estimates made for the project should reflect this rising price trend. Cost or expense estimates also should be adjusted to reflect anticipated inflationary increases, such as labor wage rate increases and raw material price increases.

If these steps are taken, the capital budgeting procedure outlined in this and the preceding chapter will assist the financial manager even in an inflationary environment.

SMALL BUSINESS CONCERNS: CAPITAL BUDGETING

The capital budgeting techniques discussed in this chapter are appropriate for use when evaluating proposed investment projects in both small and large firms. Conceptually, there is no difference between the value maximizing capital investment techniques used by large and small firms. In practice, however, there often are significant differences between the capital budgeting procedures used by small firms and larger firms.

As we have seen, larger firms tend to use the net present value and the internal rate of return approaches to evaluate proposed capital expenditures. A study by Runyon[15] of firms with a net worth under $1 million found that nearly 70 percent used payback or another technically incorrect procedure, such as the accounting rate of return, to evaluate capital expenditures.[16] Several of the firms surveyed reported that they performed no formal analysis of proposed capital expenditures.

Several reasons have been advanced to explain the dramatic differences in the practice of capital expenditure analysis between large and small firms. First, small firm managers simply may lack the expertise needed to implement formal analysis procedures. Or, managerial talent may tend to be stretched to its limits in many small firms, such that the managers simply cannot find the time to implement better project evaluation techniques. Also, one must recognize that implementing and maintaining a sophisticated capital budgeting system is expensive. Large fixed costs are associated with putting a formal system in place, and continuing costs are associated with collecting the data necessary for the system to function effectively. In small firms, investment projects tend to be small, and they may not justify the cost of a complete, formal analysis.

The emphasis on the use of payback techniques by small firms also may reflect the critical cash shortage that faces many small and rapidly expanding firms. Because of their limited access to the capital markets for additional funds, small firms may be more concerned with the speed of cash generation from a project than with the profitability of the project.

[14] This is discussed in Chapter 12.
[15] L. R. Runyon. "Capital Expenditure Decision Making in Small Firms," *Journal of Business Research* (September 1983): 389–397.
[16] See footnote 1 in this chapter for more detail on the accounting rate of return method.

Regardless of these impediments to the use of value maximizing capital budgeting techniques, small firm managers have an excellent opportunity to improve their competitive position by implementing effective managerial control techniques. Managers of small firms that rely on incorrect techniques, such as payback, to make their project accept–reject decisions are more likely to make poor investment decisions than managers who analyze their investment prospects correctly.

SUMMARY

■ The *net present value rule* is the primary decision-making rule used throughout the practice of financial management.

■ The net present value of an investment made by a firm represents the contribution of the investment to the value of the firm and, accordingly, to the wealth of shareholders.

■ The net present value is calculated by subtracting a project's net investment from the net cash flows discounted at the firm's cost of capital.

■ The *internal rate of return* of a project is the discount rate that gives the project a net present value equal to zero.

■ The *profitability index* is the ratio of the present value of net cash flows to the net investment. It gives a measure of the relative present value return per dollar of initial investment. The profitability index is useful when choosing among projects in a *capital rationing* situation.

■ The *payback period* is the number of years required for the cumulative net cash flows from a project to equal the net investment. The payback method has serious weaknesses, including the failure to account for the time value of money or to consider cash flows after the payback period.

■ The net present value and internal rate of return approaches normally yield the same accept–reject decisions for a particular project. However, conflicts may arise when dealing with *mutually exclusive* projects. The reinvestment rate assumption embodied in the net present value approach—namely, that cash flows from a project are reinvested at the cost of capital—generally is more realistic than that underlying the internal rate of return method. For this reason the net present value method is preferred to the internal rate of return method.

■ Project postaudit reviews provide useful information regarding the effectiveness of a company's capital budgeting analysis and selection procedures. If a postaudit uncovers systematic biases in these procedures, corrective action should be taken. Project reviews also may identify whether a project should be abandoned prior to, at, or after its scheduled termination.

■ In general, relatively high levels of inflation tend to reduce the level of capital expenditures in the economy. The general capital budgeting procedures discussed in this text can be applied with equal validity in an inflationary environment as long as the estimates of revenues and costs used in the capital budgeting process include expected price and cost increases.

QUESTIONS AND TOPICS FOR DISCUSSION

1. How does the net present value model complement the objective of maximizing shareholder wealth?

2. When is it possible for the net present value and the internal rate of return approaches to give conflicting rankings of mutually exclusive investment projects?

3. When are multiple rates of return likely to occur in an internal rate of return computation? What should be done when a multiple rate of return problem arises?

4. Describe how the profitability index approach may be used by a firm faced with a capital rationing investment funds constraint.

5. What are the primary strengths and weaknesses of the payback approach as a capital budgeting decision model?

6. What are the primary objectives of the investment project postaudit review?

7. What is the likely effect of inflation on the level of capital expenditures made by private firms? What must the financial manager do to ensure that a firm's capital budgeting procedures will be effective in an inflationary environment?

8. What major problems can you foresee in applying capital budgeting techniques to investments made by public and not-for-profit sector enterprises or organizations?

9. What effect would you expect the use of MACRS depreciation rules to have on the acceptability of a project having a 10-year economic life but a 7-year MACRS classification?

PROBLEMS*

1. Calculate the net present value of a project with a net investment of $20,000 and expected net cash inflows of $3,000 a year for 10 years, if the project's required return is 12 percent. Is the project acceptable?

2. A firm wishes to bid on a contract that is expected to yield the following after-tax net cash flows at the end of each year:

Year	Net Cash Flow
1	$5,000
2	8,000
3	9,000
4	8,000
5	8,000
6	5,000
7	3,000
8	−1,500

To secure the contract, the firm must spend $30,000 to retool its plant. This retooling will have no salvage value at the end of the 8 years. Comparable investment alternatives are available to the firm that earn 12 percent compounded annually. The depreciation tax benefit from the retooling is reflected in the net cash flows in the table.

a. Compute the project's net present value.
b. Should the project be adopted?
c. What is the meaning of the computed net present value figure?

3. A machine that costs $8,000 is expected to operate for 10 years. The estimated salvage value at the end of 10 years is $0. The machine is expected to save the company $1,554 per year before taxes and depreciation. The company depreciates its assets on a straight-line basis and has a marginal tax rate of 40 percent. What is the internal rate of return on this investment?

* Colored numbers denote problems that have check answers provided at the end of the book.

4. Jefferson Products, Inc., is considering purchasing a new automatic press brake, which costs $300,000 including installation and shipping. The machine is expected to generate net cash inflows of $80,000 per year for 10 years. At the end of 10 years, the book value of the machine will be $0 and it is anticipated that the machine will be sold for $100,000. If the press brake project is undertaken, Jefferson will have to increase its net working capital by $75,000. When the project is terminated in 10 years, there no longer will be a need for this incremental working capital, and it can be liquidated and made available to Jefferson for other uses. Jefferson requires a 12 percent annual return on this type of project, and its marginal tax rate is 40 percent.

a. Calculate the press brake's net present value.
b. Is the project acceptable?
c. What is the meaning of the computed net present value figure?
d. What is the project's internal rate of return?
e. For the press brake project, at what annual rates of return do the net present value and internal rate of return methods assume that the net cash inflows are being reinvested?

5. An acre planted with walnut trees is estimated to be worth $12,000 in 25 years. If you want to realize a 15 percent rate of return on your investment, how much can you afford to invest per acre? (Ignore all taxes and assume that annual cash outlays to maintain your stand of walnut trees are nil.)

6. A company is planning to invest $100,000 (before tax) in a personnel training program. The $100,000 outlay will be charged off as an expense by the firm this year (year 0). The returns from the program, in the form of greater productivity and a reduction in employee turnover, are estimated as follows (on an after-tax basis):

Years 1–10:	$10,000 per year
Years 11–20:	$22,000 per year

The company has estimated its cost of capital to be 12 percent. Assume that the entire $100,000 is paid at time 0 (the beginning of the project). The marginal tax rate for the firm is 40 percent.
Should the firm undertake the training program? Why or why not?

7. Two mutually exclusive investment projects have the following forecasted cash flows:

Year	A	B
0	– $20,000	– $20,000
1	+ 10,000	0
2	+ 10,000	0
3	+ 10,000	0
4	+ 10,000	+ 60,000

a. Compute the internal rate of return for each project.
b. Compute the net present value for each project, if the firm has a 10 percent cost of capital.
c. Which project should be adopted? Why?

8. Show that the internal rate of return of the following investment is 0, 100, and 200 percent:

Net investment	– $1,000	Year 0
Net cash flows	+ 6,000	Year 1
	– 11,000	Year 2
	+ 6,000	Year 3

9. Commercial Hydronics is considering replacing one of its larger control devices. A new unit sells for $29,000 (delivered). An additional $3,000 will be needed to install the device. The new device has an estimated 20-year service life. The estimated salvage value at the end of 20 years will be $2,000. The new control device will be depreciated over 20 years on a straight-line basis to $0. The existing control device (original cost = $15,000) has been in use for 12 years, and it has been fully depreciated (that is, its book value equals zero). Its scrap value is estimated to be $1,000. The existing device could be used indefinitely, assuming the firm is willing to pay for its very high maintenance costs. The firm's marginal tax rate is 40 percent. The new control device requires lower maintenance costs and frees up personnel who normally would have to monitor the system. Estimated annual cash savings from the new device will be $9,000. The firm's cost of capital is 12 percent.

Using this information, evaluate the relative merits of replacing the old control device using the net present value approach.

10. A $1,230 investment has the following expected cash returns:

Year	Net Cash Flow
1	$800
2	200
3	400

Compute the internal rate of return for this project.

11. Imperial Systems has $1 million available for capital investments during the current year. A list of possible investment projects, together with their net investments and net present values, is provided in the following table:

Project	Net Investment	Net Present Value
1	$200,000	$20,000
2	500,000	41,000
3	275,000	60,000
4	150,000	5,000
5	250,000	20,000
6	100,000	4,000
7	275,000	22,000
8	200,000	− 18,000

a. Rank the various investment projects in terms of their profitability indexes (computed to three decimal places).
b. In the order of decreasing profitability index values and considering the capital constraints, which projects should be adopted? Are all capital funds expended?
c. Is there another combination that produces a higher aggregate net present value than the one developed in Part b?
d. If less than the entire amount of available funds is invested, what is the opportunity cost of the unused funds?

12. A junior executive is fed up with the operating policies of his boss. Before leaving the office of his angered superior, the young man suggests that a well-trained monkey could handle the trivia assigned to him. Pausing a moment to consider the import of this closing statement, the boss is seized by the thought that this must have been in the back of her own mind ever since she hired the junior executive. She decides to consider seriously replacing the executive with a bright young baboon. She figures that she could argue strongly to the board that such "capital deepening" is necessary for

the cost-conscious firm. Two days later, a feasibility study is completed, and the following data are presented to the president:

- It would cost $12,000 to purchase and train a reasonably alert baboon with a life expectancy of 20 years.
- Annual expenses of feeding and housing the baboon would be $4,000.
- The junior executive's annual salary is $7,000 (a potential saving if the baboon is hired).
- The baboon will be depreciated on a straight-line basis over 20 years to an estimated salvage value of $400.
- The firm's marginal tax rate is 40 percent.
- The firm's current cost of capital is estimated to be 11 percent.

On the basis of the net present value criterion, should the monkey be hired (and the junior executive fired)?

13. The L-S Mining Company is planning to open a new strip mine in western Pennsylvania. The net investment required to open the mine is $10 million. Net cash flows are expected to be +$20 million at the end of year 1 and +$5 million at the end of year 2. At the end of year 3 L-S will have a net cash *outflow* of $17 million to cover the cost of closing the mine and reclaiming the land.

   a. Calculate the net present value of the strip mine if the cost of capital is 5, 10, 15, 30, 71, and 80 percent.
   b. What is unique about this project?
   c. Should the project be accepted if L-S's cost of capital is 10 percent? 20 percent?

14. Fred and Frieda have always wanted to enter the blueberry business. They locate a 50-acre piece of hillside in Maine that is covered with blueberry bushes. They figure that the annual yield from the bushes will be 200 crates. Each crate is estimated to sell for $400 for the next 10 years. This price is expected to rise to $500 per crate for all sales from years 11 through 20.

    In order to get started, Fred and Frieda must pay $150,000 for the land plus $20,000 for packing equipment. The packing equipment will be depreciated on a straight-line basis to a zero estimated salvage value at the end of 20 years. Fred and Frieda believe that at the end of 20 years they will want to retire to Florida and sell their property.

    Annual cash operating expenses, including salaries to Fred and Frieda, are estimated to be $50,000 per year for the first 10 years and $60,000 thereafter. The land is expected to appreciate in value at a rate of 5 percent per year. The couple's marginal tax rate is 30 percent for both ordinary income and capital gains and losses.

    a. If the couple requires at least a 13 percent return on their investment, should they enter the blueberry business?
    b. Assume that the land can be sold for only $50,000 at the end of 20 years (a capital loss of $100,000). Should the couple invest in the land and blueberry business? (Assume that the couple may claim the full amount of their capital loss in the year it occurs—year 20).

15. The Sisneros Company is considering building a chili processing plant in Hatch, New Mexico. The plant is expected to produce 50,000 pounds of processed chili peppers each year for the next 10 years. During the first year, Sisneros expects to sell the processed peppers for $2 per pound. The price is expected to increase at a 7 percent rate per year over the 10-year economic life of the plant. The cash costs of operating the plant, including the cost of fresh peppers, are estimated to be $50,000 during the first year. These costs are expected to increase at an 8 percent rate per year over the next 10 years.

    The plant will cost $80,000 to build. It will be depreciated as a 7-year MACRS asset. The estimated salvage at the end of 10 years is zero. The firm's marginal tax rate is 40 percent. (HINT: See Appendix 9A for information on MACRS depreciation.)

a. Calculate the net investment required to build the plant.
b. Calculate the annual net cash flows from the project.
c. If Sisneros uses a 20 percent cost of capital to evaluate projects of this type, should the plant be built? (Use the net present value criterion.)
d. Calculate the payback period for this project.
e. How many internal rates of return does this project have? Why?

16. Note the following information on two mutually exclusive projects under consideration by Monroe Food Markets, Inc.

	Annual Cash Flows	
Year	A	B
0	$ – 30,000	$ – 60,000
1	10,000	20,000
2	10,000	20,000
3	10,000	20,000
4	10,000	20,000
5	10,000	20,000

Monroe requires a 14 percent rate of return on projects of this nature.

a. Compute the NPV of both projects.
b. Compute the internal rate of return on both projects.
c. Compute the profitability index of both projects.
d. Compute the payback period on both projects.
e. Which of the two projects, if either, should Monroe accept? Why?

17. Channel Tunnel, Inc., plans to build a 23-mile long tunnel under the English Channel for trains. The cost (NINV) of the tunnel is expected to be $3.3 billion. Net cash inflows are expected to equal $651 million per year. How many years must the firm generate this cash inflow stream for investors to earn their required 19 percent rate of return?

18. Commercial Hydronics is considering replacing one of its larger control devices. A new unit sells for $29,000 (delivered). An additional $3,000 will be needed to install the device. The new device has an estimated 20-year service life. The estimated salvage value at the end of 20 years will be $2,000. The new control device will be depreciated as a 7-year MACRS asset. The existing control device (original cost = $15,000) has been in use for 12 years, and it has been fully depreciated (that is, its book value equals zero). Its scrap value is estimated to be $1,000. The existing device could be used indefinitely, assuming the firm is willing to pay for its very high maintenance costs. The firm's marginal tax rate is 40 percent. The new control device requires lower maintenance costs and frees up personnel who normally would have to monitor the system. Estimated annual cash savings from the new device will be $9,000. The firm's cost of capital is 12 percent.

Using this information, evaluate the relative merits of replacing the old control device using the net present value approach. (HINT: See Appendix 9A for information on MACRS depreciation. This problem is the same as Problem 9 except for depreciation method. Comparing the answers you get to Problems 9 and 18, what effect does the use of MACRS depreciation have on the economic desirability of the project?)

19. The Taylor Mountain Uranium Company currently has annual cash revenues of $1.2 million and annual cash expenses of $700,000. Depreciation amounts to $200,000 per year. These figures are expected to remain constant for the foreseeable future (at least 15 years). The firm's marginal tax rate is 40 percent.

A new high-speed processing unit costing $1.2 million is being considered as a potential investment designed to increase the firm's output capacity. This new piece of equipment will have an estimated usable life of 10 years and a $0 estimated salvage value. If the processing unit is bought, Taylor's annual cash revenues are expected to increase to $1.6 million, and annual cash expenses will increase to $900,000. Annual depreciation will increase to $320,000. (NOTE: This problem is the same as Problem 7 in Chapter 9, except for the following questions.)

a. Calculate the processing unit's net present value, using a 12% required return.

b. Should Taylor accept the project?

c. How many internal rates of return does the processing unit project have? Why?

d. Calculate the processing unit's internal rate of return.

20. Benford, Inc., is planning to open a new sporting goods store in a suburban mall. Benford will lease the needed space in the mall. Equipment and fixtures for the store will cost $200,000 and be depreciated to $0 over a 5-year period on a straight-line basis. The new store will require Benford to increase its net working capital by $200,000.

First-year sales are expected to be $1 million and to increase at an annual rate of 8 percent over the expected 10-year life of the store. Cash operating expenses (including lease payments) are projected to be $700,000 during the first year and increase at a 7 percent annual rate. The salvage value of the store's equipment and fixtures is anticipated to be $10,000 at the end of 10 years.

Benford's marginal tax rate is 40 percent. (NOTE: This problem is the same as Problem 12 in Chapter 9, except for the following questions.)

a. Calculate the store's net present value, using an 18% required return.

b. Should Benford accept the project?

c. Calculate the store's internal rate of return.

d. Calculate the store's profitability index.

21. Seco Dame Enterprises (SDE) acquired a robotic saw 6 years ago at a cost of $10 million. The saw was depreciated under the old ACRS rules to its current book value of $0. Actual salvage value today is estimated to be $2 million. SDE's average tax rate is 30 percent, and its marginal tax rate is 40 percent. The weighted cost of capital for SDE is 15 percent.

A new robotic saw will cost $15 million. It will be depreciated under MACRS rules for a 7-year class asset. If SDE acquires the new saw, it estimates that its net working capital investment will decline, due to the reduced need to carry inventories of spare parts for this more reliable machine. Net working capital should decline from a current level of $1 million to a new level of $500,000 as a result of this purchase.

a. Calculate the net investment required to acquire the new saw.

b. The new saw is expected to reduce operating costs for SDE by $800,000 per year over the asset's expected 10-year life. Also, the increased productivity of the new saw is expected to increase SDE's revenue by $2 million per year. Salvage value at the end of 10 years is expected to be $0. Calculate the annual net cash flows for this investment.

c. Compute the NPV for this project.

CAPITAL BUDGETING

First Republic BanCorp is considering the acquisition of a new data processing and management information system. The system, including computer hardware and software, will cost $1 million. Delivery and installation of the system is expected to add $100,000 to this cost. To put this new system in place, the bank expects to have to make an investment of $50,000 in net working capital immediately, and an additional net working capital investment of $25,000 at the end of year 1. The system has an expected economic life of 10 years. It will be depreciated as a 7-year asset under MACRS rules. Actual salvage value at the end of 10 years is expected to be $100,000 and the bank plans to sell the system for its salvage value at that time.

The new data processing system will save the bank the $190,000 fee per year that it currently pays to a computer time-sharing company. Operating, maintenance, and insurance costs for the system are estimated to total $50,000 during the first year. These costs are expected to increase at a rate of 7 percent per year over the 10-year period.

First Republic plans to sell excess computer time to a number of local firms. The demand function for this service during year 1 is estimated to be

$$Q = 20,000 - 200P$$

where

Q = number of units of computer time sold
P = price per unit of computer time sold

Based on an analysis of the local market for computer time, the bank feels that it can charge $14 per unit of computer time. Although the bank does not anticipate changing this charge over the 10-year period, it expects quantity demanded to decline by 5 percent per year after year 1. It is expected that these outside sales of computer time will cost the bank an *additional $40,000 per year* in computer operating costs (including the salary of a computer services representative to handle the new customers). These additional operating costs are expected to increase at a rate of 7 percent annually over the 10-year period.

The bank has a marginal ordinary tax rate of 34 percent. This rate is expected to remain in effect over the life of the project. First Republic uses an after-tax cost of capital of 15 percent to evaluate projects of this risk. This cost of capital was computed based upon the current after-tax cost of equity and debt funds in the bank's capital structure.

Based on the information contained in the case, use the NPV approach to determine if First Republic should acquire the new data processing system.

SELECTED REFERENCES

Bower, Richard S., and Jeffrey M. Jenks. "Divisional Screening Rates." *Financial Management* 4 (Autumn 1975): 42–49.

Cooley, Philip L., Rodney L. Roenfeldt, and It-Keong Chew. "Capital Budgeting Procedures under Inflation." *Financial Management* 4 (Winter 1975): 18–27.

Joy, O. Maurice. "Abandonment Values and Abandonment Decisions: A Clarification." *Journal of Finance* 31 (September 1976): 1225–1228.

Lewellen, Wilbur G., Howard P. Lanser, and John J. McConnell. "Payback Substitutes for Discounted Cash Flow." *Financial Management* 2 (Summer 1973): 17–23.

McDaniel, William R. "Discounted Cash Flows with Explicit Reinvestment Rates: Tutorial and Extension." *Financial Review* (August 1988): 369–385.

Myers, Stewart C. "Notes on an Expert System for Capital Budgeting." *Financial Management* 17 (Autumn 1988): 23–31.

Nelson, Charles R. "Inflation and Capital Budgeting." *Journal of Finance* 31 (June 1976): 923–931.

Ross, Marc. "Capital Budgeting Practices of Twelve Large Manufacturers." *Financial Management* 15 (Winter 1986): 15–22.

Taggert, Robert A. "Allocating Capital among a Firm's Divisions: Hurdle Rate versus Budgets." *Journal of Financial Research* (Fall 1987): 177–191.

Van Horne, James C. "A Note on Biases in Capital Budgeting Introduced by Inflation." *Journal of Financial and Quantitative Analysis* 6 (January 1971): 653–658.

Williams, John Daniel, and Jonathan S. Rakich. "Investment Evaluation in Hospitals." *Financial Management* 2 (Summer 1973): 30–35.

Mutually Exclusive Investments Having Unequal Lives

REPLACEMENT CHAINS

Chapter 10 discussed a number of capital budgeting decision models. When mutually exclusive investments were considered, it was implicitly assumed that the alternative projects had *equal* lives. In actual practice, however, this may not be the case. When two or more mutually exclusive alternatives have *unequal* lives, neither the net present value nor the internal rate of return method yields reliable accept–reject information unless the projects are evaluated for an equal period of time. If, for example, a firm adopts the longer lived of two projects simply on the basis of net present value or internal rate of return data, it essentially ignores any alternative investment opportunities that might have been available at the end of the shorter-lived project.

Suppose a firm is considering two mutually exclusive investments, I and II. Project I requires an initial outlay of $2,000 and is expected to generate a 5-year stream of net cash flows of $600 per year. Project II also requires an initial outlay of $2,000 but is expected to generate a 10-year stream of net cash flows of $375 per year. The firm has a 10 percent cost of capital.

Table 10A-1 shows that the net present value of Project I is $274.60 and the net present value of Project II is $304.37. Therefore, the net present value criterion suggests that Project II should be chosen over Project I.

The expected life of Project II is twice as long as that of Project I. Therefore, the two net present values calculated in Table 10A-1 are not really comparable. At this point the firm also must consider what might happen if Project I were replaced with a similar 5-year life project at the end of 5 years. In other words, it would create a *replacement chain* for the shorter-lived project. Suppose, for example, the firm estimates that replacing Project I with a similar project at the end of 5 years would cost $2,100 and, like Project I, would generate annual net cash flows of $600. This results in a new stream of cash flows for Project I, as shown in Table 10A-2. The new net present value for Project I is higher than that for Project II, thus indicating—correctly—that Project I should be chosen over Project II.

Many times it is not possible to get a series of projects (such as Project I with its replacement at the end of 5 years) that will have an identical time duration to that of the longer-lived project (II). For example, one project might have a life of 15 years, whereas an alternative requires replacement every 8 years. Hence, the shorter-lived project together with its replacement

Cash Flows for Projects I and II

	Project I		Project II	
Year	Net Investment	Net Cash Flow	Net Investment	Net Cash Flow
0	$2,000	—	$2,000	—
1		$600		$375
2		600		375
3		600		375
4		600		375
5		600		375
6		—		375
7		—		375
8		—		375
9		—		375
10		—		375

$$NPV_I = -\$2,000 + \$600(3.791) \qquad NPV_{II} = -\$2,000 + \$375(6.145)$$
$$= \$274.60 \qquad\qquad = \$304.37$$

have a 16-year life, whereas the longer-lived project has a 15-year life. Such a comparison normally will be acceptable, because the discrepancy occurs for only 1 year that is 15 years in the future. In present value terms, this will not have much impact.

The importance of time discrepancies such as these depends on the following:

■ The number of years of the discrepancy. The fewer the years of the discrepancy, the less important it is.

Replacement Chain Cash Flows for Project I Compared with Project II

	Project I with Replacement		Project II	
Year	Net Investment	Net Cash Flow	Net Investment	Net Cash Flow
0	$2,000	—	$2,000	—
1		$600		$375
2		600		375
3		600		375
4		600		375
5	2,100	600		375
6		600		375
7		600		375
8		600		375
9		600		375
10		600		375

$$NPV_I = -\$2,000 + \$600(6.145) - \$2,100(0.621) \qquad NPV_{II} = -\$2,000 + \$375(6.145)$$
$$= \$382.80 \qquad\qquad\qquad\qquad\qquad = \$304.37$$

■ The number of years into the future the discrepancy occurs. The further into the future, the less important the discrepancy is.

■ The relationship between the rate of return on future investments and the cost of capital. When the rate of return on future investments is equal to the cost of capital, these investments have an NPV = 0. Under these circumstances, the discrepancy can be ignored.

EQUIVALENT ANNUAL ANNUITIES

An alternative approach for dealing with the problem of mutually exclusive investments having unequal lives is to use the equivalent annual annuity approach. This technique can solve the problem of time discrepancies often encountered when using the replacement chain approach.

For example, consider the case of a firm that needs to replace an aging piece of machinery. One alternative would be to buy new Machine A having a 9-year life. Another alternative would be to buy new Machine B with a 5-year life. In this case, the time discrepancy between A and B is significant— 4 years. Commonly, this problem is dealt with by developing a string of replacement chains out to a year when both machines would need replacement. The common denominator year in this case is 45 years—indicating nine investments in B and five investments in A.

In cases like this, the equivalent annual annuity approach often is easier to use. In our example, assume the new Machine A will require a net investment of $34,500 and generate net cash flows of $7,000 per year for 9 years. Machine B will require a net investment of $25,000 and generate net cash flows of $8,000 per year for 5 years. The firm's cost of capital is 10 percent. To make our decision on the basis of the equivalent annual annuity criterion, we use the following three steps:

1. First, compute the net present value of each machine over its original expected economic life:

$$NPV_A = -\$34{,}500 + \$7{,}000(PVIFA_{0.10,9})$$

$$= -\$34{,}500 + \$7{,}000(5.759)$$

$$= \$5{,}813$$

$$NPV_B = -\$25{,}000 + \$8{,}000(PVIFA_{0.10,5})$$

$$= -\$25{,}000 + \$8{,}000(3.791)$$

$$= \$5{,}328$$

As these calculations indicate, if the possibility of the replacement of Machine B at the end of 5 years is not considered, Machine A would appear to be the best alternative because of its greater net present value.

2. Next, divide the net present value for each machine computed in Step 1 by the PVIFA factor for the project's original life. This gives the *equivalent annual annuity:*

$$\text{Equivalent annual annuity (A)} = \frac{\$5{,}813}{PVIFA_{0.10,9}}$$

$$= \frac{\$5{,}813}{5.759}$$

$$= \$1{,}009.38$$

$$\text{Equivalent annual annuity (B)} = \frac{\$5,328}{\text{PVIFA}_{0.10,5}}$$

$$= \frac{\$5,328}{3.791}$$

$$= \$1,405.43$$

3. The equivalent annual annuity method assumes that each machine will be replaced an infinite number of times into the future and therefore will provide these annual annuities in perpetuity. As perpetuities, these equivalent annual annuities can be valued (at present) by dividing the annuity amount by the cost of capital:

$$\text{NPV}_A(\text{assuming infinite replacement}) = \frac{\$1,009.38}{0.10}$$

$$= \$10,093.80$$

$$\text{NPV}_B(\text{assuming infinite replacement}) = \frac{\$1,405.43}{0.10}$$

$$= \$14,054.30$$

Machine B should be acquired, because it has the highest net present value when evaluated over an infinite replacement horizon.

In general, the equivalent annual annuity method will give the same decision as the replacement chain technique. Its advantage is that it often is computationally simpler, and it simplifies the handling of the time discrepancies that frequently arise in the replacement chain method.

PROBLEMS*

1. The Smith Pie Company is considering two mutually exclusive investments that would increase its capacity to make strawberry tarts. The firm uses a 12 percent cost of capital to evaluate potential investments. The two projects have the following costs and cash flow streams:

Year	Alternative A	Alternative B
0	−$30,000	−$30,000
1	10,500	6,500
2	10,500	6,500
3	10,500	6,500
4	10,500	6,500
5	—	6,500
6	—	6,500
7	—	6,500
8	—	6,500

a. Using this data, calculate the net present value for Projects A and B.
b. Create a replacement chain for Alternative A. Assume that the cost of replacing A will be $30,000 and that the replacement project will generate cash flows of $10,500 for years 5 through 8. Using these figures, recompute the net present value for Alternative A.
c. Which of the two alternatives should be chosen, A or B? Why?

2. Use the equivalent annual annuity method to solve Problem 1. How does your answer compare with the one obtained in Problem 1?

* Colored numbers denote problems that have check answers provided at the end of the book.

11

Capital Budgeting and Risk

KEY CHAPTER CONCEPTS

1. *Total project risk* refers to the chance that a project will not perform up to expectations. It often is measured by either the standard deviation or the coefficient of variation of cash flows from a project.

2. The *portfolio*, or *beta, risk* of a project refers to the contribution a project makes to the risk of the firm, when the interactions between the cash flows of the project are considered in conjunction with the other cash flows of the firm.

3. When considering the systematic risk of individual projects, the *beta* concept can be used to determine risk-adjusted discount rates for individual projects.

4. The *beta* concept also can be used to compute divisional costs of capital for firms with several operating divisions that differ substantially with respect to the risks of investments that are made.

5. A number of techniques can be used to analyze total project risk. These techniques include
   a. The *net present value/payback approach*
   b. The *simulation analysis approach*
   c. The *sensitivity analysis approach*
   d. The *risk-adjusted discount rate approach*
   e. The *certainty equivalent approach*

GLOSSARY OF NEW TERMS

Beta risk (project) The risk contribution of a project to the systematic risk of the firm.

Certainty equivalent The amount of cash someone would require with certainty in order to make him or her indifferent between that certain amount and an amount expected to be received with risk at the same point in time.

Divisional cost of capital A risk-adjusted discount rate for investments being evaluated by a firm's various divisions. It reflects both the differential required returns of equity investors, estimated from the security market line, and the division's differential debt capacity.

Hurdle rate The minimum acceptable rate of return from an investment project. For projects of average risk, it usually is equal to the firm's cost of capital.

Risk-adjusted discount rate A discount rate that reflects the risk associated with a particular project. In capital budgeting, a higher risk-adjusted rate is used to discount cash flows for riskier projects, whereas a lower risk-adjusted rate is used to discount cash flows for less risky projects.

Sensitivity analysis A procedure used to evaluate the change in some objective, such as net present value, to changes in a variable influencing that objective, such as product price, one of the cash flow elements.

Simulation A financial planning tool that models some event, such as the cash flows from an investment project. A computerized simulation is one technique used to assess the risk associated with a particular project.

The "Smokeless" Cigarette*

The capital budgeting process discussed in the previous two chapters, in reality, is quite simple. If the present value of a project's net cash flows exceeds the outlays required (the net investment), a project is acceptable and should be undertaken. The real difficulty is developing realistic estimates of the costs and benefits from a project. The problems a firm may encounter can stem from an incomplete analysis of a project or from a lack of sufficient concern for the profitability of the firm.

In addition to these problems, it must be recognized that nearly all projects have some element of risk—the chance that the actual cash flows will differ from the forecasted ones. This is the case for Premier, a "smokeless" cigarette developed by RJR Nabisco. On February 28, 1989, RJR Nabisco pulled Premier from the market, 7 years after initiating the project. The *Wall Street Journal* called it "one of the most stunning new product disasters in recent history." Estimates are that RJR spent more than $300 million on Premier. It built a pilot plant and broke ground for an addition to one of its existing cigarette plants. The company even had named a golf tournament after Premier.

The "smokeless" cigarette project met with a number of unforeseen problems. Premier did not taste right when lighted with a match—it had to be lighted with a special kind of butane lighter. Premier was difficult to produce—it required the simultaneous assembly of four parts, instead of the two required in conventional cigarettes. Moreover, antismoking groups called Premier a "drug-delivery device" and argued that it be regulated by the Food and Drug Administration.

This example illustrates one of the painful realities of making capital budgeting decisions—cash flows and costs from a project rarely will meet projections exactly. This is to be expected, because nearly all capital investments contain an element of risk. Although risk cannot be eliminated, a capable financial manager should try to determine at the outset what risks are being assumed when a project is undertaken. What is the worst case outcome? How likely is this outcome? What actions can be taken to reduce this risk? How will investors react to this risk? Given the answers to these questions, risky projects can be properly evaluated. This chapter examines these important questions.

* Adapted from "The Death of Premier," *Wall Street Journal* (March 10, 1989), p. B1.

INTRODUCTION

In Chapter 8 we discussed the nature of risk and its influence on financial decision making. The greater the risk associated with an investment, the greater the return required. This basic principle also applies in the capital budgeting area.

In the previous two chapters, investment projects were evaluated using the firm's weighted cost of capital (required rate of return). This approach implicitly assumes that all projects being considered are of equal risk and that this risk is the same as that for the firm as a whole. When a project has more or less than an average risk level, it is necessary to adjust the analysis to account for this risk level.

TOTAL PROJECT RISK VERSUS PORTFOLIO RISK

When analyzing the risk associated with a capital expenditure, it is important to distinguish between the *total project risk* and the *portfolio*, or *beta*, *risk* of that investment. By total project risk we mean the chance that a project will perform below expectations—possibly resulting in losses from the project and for the firm. In the worst case, these losses could be so severe as to cause the firm to fail.

In contrast, a project that has a high level of total project risk may not affect the portfolio risk of the firm at all. Consider the case of oil and gas exploration companies. The firms know that any wildcat well they drill will cost about $2 million and have only a 10 percent chance of success. Successful wells produce profits of $24 million. Unsuccessful wells produce no profits at all, and the entire investment will be a loss. If each firm only drilled one well, there would be a 90 percent chance the firm would fail (the total project risk would be very high). In contrast, if one firm drilled 100 wildcat wells, the risk of failure from all wells would be very low because of the portfolio risk reduction that results from drilling many wells. In this case the expected return of the firm would be as follows:

$$\text{Expected return} = \frac{\text{Expected profit per well}}{\text{Investment required per well}}$$

$$= \frac{\left(\begin{array}{c}\text{Probability of}\\\text{success}\end{array}\right)\left(\text{Profit}\right) + \left(\begin{array}{c}\text{Probability of}\\\text{failure}\end{array}\right)\left(\text{Loss}\right)}{\text{Investment required per well}}$$

$$= \frac{0.10(\$24\text{ million}) + 0.90(-\$2\text{ million})}{\$2\text{ million}}$$

$$= \frac{\$2.4\text{ million} - \$1.8\text{ million}}{\$2\text{ million}}$$

$$= 0.30\text{ or }30\%$$

This return is achieved with very little risk relative to that facing a firm drilling a single well. As this example illustrates, the risk of drilling any individual well can be diversified away very effectively. Consequently, these risks are not market related, and they should have little, if any, impact on the beta risk of the firm. That risk remains unchanged and approximately equal to the market risk facing other oil and gas exploration companies.

This example has shown that an investment with high total project risk does not necessarily have to possess high beta risk. Of course, it is possible for a project to have both high total project risk and high beta risk. For example, a grocery store chain (which typically has low beta risk) might decide to develop and market a new line of small business computers. Because of the large number of competitors in this business and because of the grocery chain's lack of expertise, this investment can be expected to have a high level of total project risk. At the same time, the beta risk of this investment is likely to be high relative to that of the grocery chain, because business computer sales expand rapidly during boom periods and slow down dramatically during recessions.

From a capital budgeting perspective, the beta risk of a project certainly is important, because the beta of a firm influences the returns required by investors in that firm and hence the value of the firm's shares.

Total project risk also is important to consider in most cases for several reasons. There are a number of relatively undiversified investors, including the owners of small firms, for whom total project and total firm risk are important. Also, the total risk of the firm—not just the beta risk—determines the risk of firm failure and potential bankruptcy. Stockholders, creditors, managers, and other employees all are interested in preventing the tragedy (and avoiding the costs) of total firm failure.

Consequently, in the evaluation of an investment, it is important to consider both the total project risk and the impact of the project on the beta risk of the firm. We continue the chapter with a discussion of techniques to use when evaluating the beta risk of a project. In the final section we examine a number of techniques that can be used to account for total project risk in the capital budgeting process.

ADJUSTING FOR BETA RISK IN CAPITAL BUDGETING

The *beta* concept introduced in Chapter 8 for security risk analysis also can be used to determine risk-adjusted discount rates (RADR) for individual capital budgeting projects. This approach is appropriate for a firm whose stock is widely traded and for whom there is very little chance of bankruptcy. (The probability of bankruptcy is a function of total risk, not just systematic risk.)

Just as the beta (systematic risk) of a portfolio of securities can be computed as the weighted average of the individual security betas, a firm may be considered as a portfolio of assets, each having its own beta. From this perspective the systematic risk of the firm is simply the weighted average of the systematic risk of the individual assets.

The All-Equity Case

For example, consider the security market line shown in Figure 11-1. The firm has a beta of 1.2 and is financed exclusively with internally generated equity capital. The market risk premium is 7 percent. When considering projects of average risk—that is, projects that are highly correlated with the firm's returns on its existing assets and that have a beta similar to the firm's beta (1.2)—the firm should use the computed 13.4 percent cost of equity from Figure 11-1. When considering projects having estimated betas different from 1.2, it should use an equity discount rate equal to the required return calculated from the security market line. For example, if a project's estimated beta is 1.7, and the risk-free rate is 5%, the project's required equity return would be 16.9 percent, or 5% + (1.7 × 7%), and this would be used as the risk-adjusted discount rate for that project, assuming the project is financed with 100 percent equity.

The Equity and Debt Case

Next we develop a procedure for computing the risk-adjusted discount rate for projects financed with both debt and equity. Consider the situation of Vulcan Industries, with a capital structure consisting of 50 percent debt

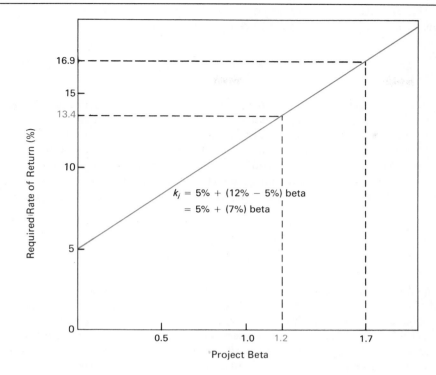

FIGURE 11-1

**Risk-Adjusted
Discount Rates and
the SML**

Required Rate of Return (%)

16.9

15

13.4

10

5

0

$k_j = 5\% + (12\% - 5\%)$ beta
$= 5\% + (7\%)$ beta

0.5   1.0   1.2   1.7

Project Beta

and 50 percent equity. Vulcan is considering expanding into a new line of business and wants to compute the rate of return that will be required on projects in this area. Vulcan has determined that the debt capacity associated with projects in its new business line is such that a capital structure consisting of 40 percent debt and 60 percent common equity is appropriate to finance these new projects. Vulcan's company beta has been estimated to be 1.3, but the Vulcan management does not believe that this beta risk is appropriate for the new business line. Vulcan's managers must estimate the beta risk appropriate for projects in this new line of business, and then determine the risk-adjusted return requirement on these projects.

Because the beta risk of projects in this new business line is not directly observable, Vulcan's managers have decided to rely on surrogate market information. They have identified a firm, Olympic Materials, that competes exclusively in the line of business into which Vulcan proposes expanding. The beta of Olympic has been estimated to be 1.50.

Recall from Chapter 8 that a firm's beta is computed as the slope of its characteristic line and that actual security returns are used in the computations. Accordingly, a firm's computed beta is a measure of both its business risk *and* its financial risk. When a beta is computed for a firm such as Olympic, it reflects both the business and financial risk of that firm. To determine the beta associated with Vulcan's proposed new line of business using the observed beta from another firm (Olympic) that competes exclusively in that business line, it is necessary to convert the observed beta, often called a *leveraged beta*, b_l, into an *unleveraged*, or pure project beta, b_u. This unleveraged beta can then be releveraged to reflect the amount of debt capacity appropriate for this type of project and that will be used by Vulcan

369

to finance it. The following equation can be used to convert a leveraged beta into an unleveraged, or pure project, beta:[1]

$$b_u = \frac{b_l}{1 + (1 - T)(B/E)} \qquad (11.1)$$

where b_u is the unleveraged beta for a project or firm, b_l is the leveraged beta for a project or firm, B is the market value of the firm's debt, E is the market value of the firm's equity, and T is the firm's marginal tax rate.

The use of this equation can be illustrated for the Vulcan Materials example. The beta, b_l, for Olympic has been computed to be 1.50. Olympic has a capital structure consisting of 20 percent debt and 80 percent common equity and a tax rate of 35 percent. Substituting these values into Equation 11.1 yields

$$b_u = \frac{1.50}{1 + (1 - 0.35)(0.25)} = 1.29$$

The unleveraged, or pure project beta for the proposed new line of business of Vulcan is estimated to be 1.29. Vulcan intends to finance this new line of business with a capital structure consisting of 40 percent debt and 60 percent common equity. In addition, Vulcan's tax rate is 40 percent. Equation 11.2 can be used to compute the levered beta associated with this new line of business, given Vulcan's proposed target capital structure for the project.

$$b_l = b_u [1 + (1 - T)(B/E)] \qquad (11.2)$$

$$= 1.29 [1 + (1 - 0.4)(0.667)]$$

$$= 1.81$$

With a risk-free rate of 5 percent and a market risk premium of 7 percent, the required return on the equity portion of the proposed new line of business is computed from the security market line as

$$k_e = 5\% + 1.81 (7\%)$$

$$= 17.7\%$$

If the after-tax cost of debt, k_i, used to finance the new line of business is 8 percent, the risk-adjusted required return, k^*, on the new line of business, given the proposed capital structure of 40 percent debt and 60 percent equity, is a weighted average of the marginal, after-tax debt and equity costs, or[2]

$$k^* = 0.4 (8\%) + 0.6 (17.7\%)$$

$$= 13.8\%$$

---

[1] Robert Hamada. "The Effect of the Firm's Capital Structure on the Systematic Risk of Common Stocks," *Journal of Finance* (May 1972): 435–452.

[2] The concept of a weighted cost of capital is developed extensively in Chapter 12. At this point it is necessary only to recognize that the required return on this project reflects the project's equity return requirement and the debt return requirement for the funds expected to be used to finance the project.

Therefore, the risk-adjusted required rate of return on the proposed new line of business for Vulcan is 13.8 percent. This number reflects both the pure project risk and the financial risk associated with the project as Vulcan anticipates financing it.

Equations 11.1 and 11.2 provide only an approximation of the effect of leverage on beta. Capital market imperfections, such as the existence of risky debt and uncertainty regarding future levels of debt, introduce error into the beta adjustments just presented. Hence, this procedure should be used with caution. This general procedure is used by many different firms, including Digital Equipment and Southwestern Bell Corporation.[3]

Computing the Risk-Adjusted Net Present Value

The net present value (NPV) of a project using the RADR approach, is defined as follows:

$$NPV = \sum_{t=1}^{n} \frac{NCF_t}{(1 + k^*)^t} - NINV \qquad (11.3)$$

where k^* is the risk-adjusted discount rate, NCF_t is the net cash flow in period t, and NINV is the net investment. Suppose a company's weighted cost of capital is 12 percent; and the risk-adjusted discount rate for a new product project the company is considering is 16 percent. If the project's net investment is $50,000 and its expected cash inflows are $10,000 a year for 10 years, the project's NPV is $-$1670 ($10,000 × 4.833 $-$ $50,000), using a 16 percent discount rate, and $6500 ($10,000 × 5.650 $-$ $50,000), using a 12 percent discount rate. Assuming the 16 percent RADR figure has been determined correctly by using the security market line with an accurate beta value, the project should not be accepted even though its NPV, calculated using the company's weighted cost of capital, is positive. This new product project is similar to project 4 in Figure 11-2.

The new product project discussed in the previous paragraph has an internal rate of return of about 15 percent, compared to its 16 percent required return. Therefore the project should be rejected, according to the IRR decision rule. When the IRR technique is used, the RADR given by the SML frequently is called the *hurdle rate*. Some finance practitioners use the term hurdle rate to describe any risk-adjusted discount rate.

Figure 11-2 illustrates the difference between the use of a single discount rate, the weighted cost of capital,[4] for all projects regardless of risk level and a discount rate based on the security market line for each project. In the example shown in Figure 11-2, Projects 1, 2, 3, and 4 are being evaluated by the firm. Using the weighted cost of capital approach, the firm would adopt Projects 3 and 4. However, if the firm considered the differential levels of systematic risk for the four alternatives, it would accept Projects 1 and 3 and reject Projects 2 and 4. In general, *the risk-adjusted discount rate approach is considered preferable to the weighted cost of capital approach when the projects under consideration differ significantly in their risk characteristics.*

---

[3] "Divisional Hurdle Rates and the Cost of Capital," *Financial Management* (Spring 1989): 18–25.
[4] The weighted cost of capital for a firm is defined in more detail in Chapter 12. It is equal to the marginal cost of equity times the proportion of common equity in the firm's target capital structure, plus the after-tax marginal cost of debt times the debt proportion in the firm's target capital structure, plus the after-tax marginal cost of preferred stock times its proportion in the firm's target capital structure. In general, the weighted cost of capital is the appropriate discount rate to use when evaluating projects of average risk.

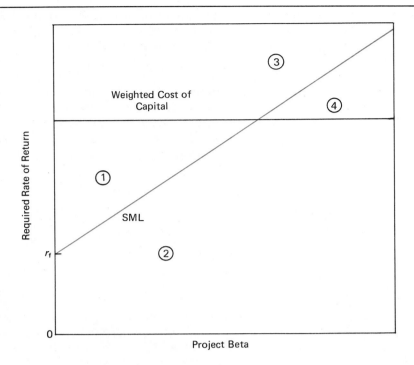

The one problem remaining with this suggested procedure involves the determination of beta values for individual projects. Thus far, the most workable approach available is the use of *surrogate market information* as illustrated in the Vulcan Materials example. For example, if an aluminum firm is considering investing in the leisure time product industry, the beta for this new project could be computed using the average beta for a sample of firms engaged principally in the leisure product industry. Although the beta for the aluminum firm might be 1.3, resulting in a required equity return on projects of average risk of 14.1 percent, or $5\% + (1.3 \times 7\%)$, according to Figure 11-1, this would not be the appropriate rate for leisure product projects. Assuming a beta of 0.9 for leisure product firms, the leisure product projects would be required to earn an equity return of only 11.3 percent or $5\% + (0.9 \times 7\%)$, because of the lower average level of systematic risk associated with leisure product projects. This assumes that the leisure product projects are financed in the same manner as the firms used to generate the surrogate betas. Otherwise, the beta adjustment procedure in Equations 11.1 and 11.2 must be used.

DIVISIONAL COSTS OF CAPITAL

The approach just outlined also can be used to compute the risk-adjusted discount rate (cost of capital) for investments being evaluated by a firm's various divisions. For divisions that have lower (higher) systematic risk than others, the discount rates for projects adopted by these divisions should be lower (higher) than the discount rate for the firm as a whole.

For example, West Coast Power is an electric utility that has a calculated beta of 0.91. The firm has three divisions: the electric power generation and distribution division, which has 70 percent of the firm's assets; an oil and gas exploration division, which has 20 percent of the assets; and a transportation and barge division, which has 10 percent of the assets. Using surrogate market information, the beta for each division is estimated as shown here:[5]

	Estimated Divisional Beta	Proportion of Firm's Assets	Weighted Average Beta
Electric power	0.75	0.70	0.53
Exploration	1.30	0.20	0.26
Transportation	1.20	0.10	0.12
		Weighted average firm beta =	0.91

Note that the weighted average of the divisional betas is equal to the firm's overall beta—in this case, 0.91.

Conglomerate firms that compete in many different product and geographical markets, such as Pacificorp, Litton, or Gulf and Western Industries, often estimate separate divisional costs of capital. These divisional costs of capital reflect both the differential required returns of equity investors, estimated from the security market line, and the differential debt-carrying capacity of each division. For example, the parent company may have a debt-to-total-assets ratio of 60 percent. Individual divisions within the firm may compete against other firms that typically have higher or lower debt-to-total-assets ratios. In computing each divisional cost of capital, many firms try to reflect both the differential divisional risks and the differential normal debt ratios for each division.

ADJUSTING FOR TOTAL PROJECT RISK

The risk adjustment procedures discussed in this section are appropriate when the firm believes that a project's total risk is the relevant risk to consider in evaluating the project, and when it is assumed that the returns from the project being considered are highly positively correlated with the returns from the firm as a whole. Therefore, these methods are appropriate only in the absence of internal firm diversification benefits, which might change the firm's total risk (or the systematic portion of total risk).

Several different techniques are used to analyze total project risk. These include the *net present value/payback approach, simulation analysis, sensitivity analysis*, the *risk-adjusted discount rate approach*, and the *certainty equivalent approach*. In addition, total project risk can be measured by calculating the standard deviation and coefficient of variation. These calculations are discussed in Chapter 8.

Net Present Value/Payback Approach

Many firms combine net present value (NPV) with payback (PB) when analyzing project risk. As noted in Chapter 10, the project payback period is the length of time required to recover the net investment. Because cash flow estimates tend to become more uncertain further into the future, applying a payback cutoff point can help reduce this degree of uncertainty. For ex-

[5] These divisional betas are assumed to have been adjusted for leverage using Equations 11.1 and 11.2.

ample, a firm may decide not to accept projects unless they have positive net present values *and* paybacks of less than some stated number of years.

The net present value/payback method is both simple and inexpensive, yet suffers from some notable weaknesses. First, the choice of which payback criterion should be applied is purely subjective and not directly related to the variability of returns from a project. Some investments may have relatively certain cash flows far into the future, whereas others may not. The use of a single payback cutoff point fails to allow for this. Second, some projects are more risky than others during their start-up periods; the payback criterion also fails to recognize this. Finally, this approach may cause a firm to reject some actually acceptable projects. In spite of these weaknesses, however, some firms have found this approach helpful when screening investment alternatives, particularly investments made overseas in politically unstable countries and investments in products characterized by rapid technological advances.

Simulation Analysis

Computers have made it both feasible and relatively inexpensive to apply simulation techniques to capital budgeting decisions. The simulation approach generally is more appropriate for analyzing larger projects. A simulation is a financial planning tool that models some event. When simulation is used in capital budgeting, it requires that estimates be made of the probability distribution of each cash flow element (revenues, expenses, and so on). If, for example, a firm is considering introducing a new product, the elements of a simulation might include the number of units sold, market price, unit production costs, unit selling costs, the purchase price of the machinery needed to produce the new product, and the cost of capital. These probability distributions then are entered into the simulation model to compute the project's net present value probability distribution.

Recall that net present value is defined as follows:

$$NPV = \sum_{t=1}^{n} \frac{NCF_t}{(1 + k)^t} - NINV$$

where NCF_t is the net cash flow in period t and NINV is the net investment. In any period, NCF_t may be computed as follows:

$$NCF_t = [n(p) - n(c + s) - Dep](1 - T) + Dep \qquad \textbf{(11.4)}$$

where n is the number of units sold; p, the price per unit; c, the unit production cost (excluding depreciation); s, the unit selling cost; Dep, the annual depreciation; and T, the firm's marginal tax rate. Using Equation 11.4, it is possible to simulate the net present value of the project. Based on the probability distribution of each of the elements that influence the net present value, one value for each element is selected at random.

Assume, for example, that the following values for the input variables are randomly chosen: $n = 2,000$; $p = \$10$; $c = \$2$; $s = \$1$; $Dep = \$2,000$; and $T = 50\%$, or 0.50. Inserting these values into Equation 11.4 gives the following calculations:

$$NCF_t = [2,000(\$10) - 2,000(\$2 + \$1) - \$2,000](1 - 0.50) + \$2,000$$

$$= (\$20,000 - \$6,000 - \$2,000)0.50 + \$2,000$$

$$= \$8,000$$

Assuming that the net investment is equal to the purchase price of the machinery ($10,000, in this example), that the net cash flows in each year of the project's life are identical, that $k = 10\%$,[6] and that the project has a 5-year life, the net present value of this particular iteration of the simulation can be computed as follows:

$$
\begin{aligned}
\text{NPV} &= \frac{\$8,000}{(1 + 0.10)^1} + \frac{\$8,000}{(1 + 0.10)^2} + \frac{\$8,000}{(1 + 0.10)^3} + \frac{\$8,000}{(1 + 0.10)^4} \\
&\quad + \frac{\$8,000}{(1 + 0.10)^5} - \$10,000 \\
&= \$8,000 \times 3.791 - \$10,000 \\
&= \$20,328
\end{aligned}
$$

In an actual simulation, the computer program is run a number of different times, using different randomly selected input variables in each instance. Thus, the program can be said to be repeated, or iterated, and each run is termed an *iteration*.[7] In each iteration, the net present value for the project would be computed accordingly. Figure 11-3 illustrates a typical simulation approach.

The results of these iterations then are used to plot a probability distribution of the project's net present values and to compute a mean and a

[6] A strong case can be made for using a risk-free rate to discount the cash flows generated in a simulation analysis, because the simulation technique directly considers risk by generating a probability distribution of the project's NPV or IRR. To use the cost of capital as the discount rate will result in a double-counting of risk. Although this is correct, when a risk-free rate is used as the discount rate, the NPV that results is difficult to interpret. For this reason many practitioners prefer to use the cost of capital when performing simulation analyses.

[7] Often 100 or more iterations of a simulation model are performed.

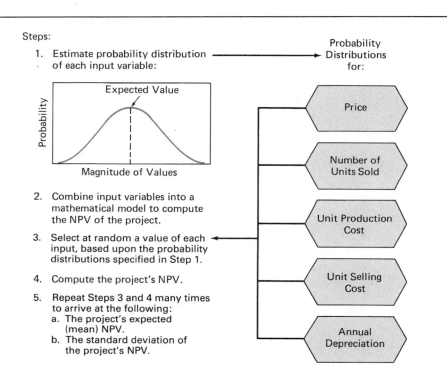

FIGURE 11-3

An Illustration of the
Simulation Approach

Steps:

1. Estimate probability distribution of each input variable: → Probability Distributions for:

2. Combine input variables into a mathematical model to compute the NPV of the project.

3. Select at random a value of each input, based upon the probability distributions specified in Step 1.

4. Compute the project's NPV.

5. Repeat Steps 3 and 4 many times to arrive at the following:
   a. The project's expected (mean) NPV.
   b. The standard deviation of the project's NPV.

Price

Number of Units Sold

Unit Production Cost

Unit Selling Cost

Annual Depreciation

standard deviation of returns.[8] This information provides the decision maker with an estimate of a project's expected returns, as well as its risk. Given this information, it is possible to compute the probability of achieving a net present value that is greater or less than any particular value.

For example, assume that the simulation for the project previously illustrated results in an expected net present value of $12,000, with a standard deviation of $6,000. The probability of the project's having a net present value of $0 or less now can be found. The value of $0 is −2.0 standard deviations below the mean:

$$z = \frac{\$0 - \$12,000}{\$6,000}$$

$$= -2.0$$

where z = the number of standard deviations.

It can be seen from Table V at the back of the book that the probability of a value less than −2.0 standard deviations from the mean is 2.28 percent. Thus, there is a 2.28 percent chance that the actual net present value for this project will be negative. Figure 11-4 shows the probability distribution of this project's net present value. The shaded area under the curve represents the probability that the project will have a net present value of $0 or less.

The simulation approach is a powerful one because it explicitly recognizes all of the interactions among the variables that influence a project's net present value. It provides both a mean net present value and a standard deviation that can help the decision maker analyze tradeoffs between risk

---

[8] Regardless of the shape of the probability distribution for the individual variables used in the simulation, the net present value probability distribution often will be normally, or near normally, distributed.

FIGURE 11-4

A Sample Illustration of the Probability that a Project's Returns Will Be Less than $0

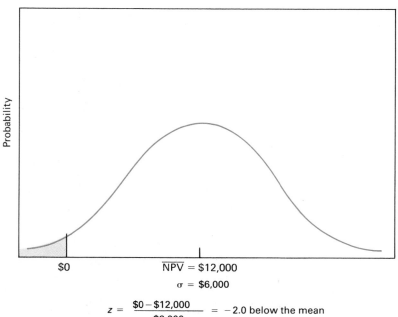

$\sigma = \$6,000$

$z = \dfrac{\$0 - \$12,000}{\$6,000} = -2.0$ below the mean

and expected return.[9] Unfortunately, it can take considerable time and effort to gather the information necessary for each of the input variables and to correctly formulate the model. This limits the feasibility of simulation to very large projects. In addition, the simulation examples illustrated assumed that the values of the input variables were independent of one another. If this is not true—if, for example, the price of a product has a large influence on the number sold—then this interaction must be incorporated into the model, introducing even more complexity.

Sensitivity Analysis

Sensitivity analysis is a procedure by means of which the change in net present value is calculated for a given change in one of the cash flow elements, such as product price. In other words, a decision maker can determine *how sensitive* a project's return is to changes in a particular variable.

Because sensitivity analysis is derived from the simulation approach, it also requires the definition of all relevant variables that influence the net present value of a project. The appropriate mathematical relationships between these variables must be defined, too, in order that the cash flow from the project may be estimated and the net present value computed. Rather than dealing with the entire probability distribution for each of the input variables, however, sensitivity analysis allows the decision maker to use only the "best estimate" of each variable to compute the net present value.

The decision maker then can ask various "what if" questions in which the project's net present value is recomputed under various conditions. For example, the best estimate of a product's price might be $10. The net present value of the project could be computed using this input together with best estimates of all the other variables. The next step would involve asking a question like, What if we cannot charge more than $8 per unit? The net present value could be recomputed using the $8 price and the best estimates for each of the other input variables to determine the effect of the $8 price on the NPV.

Sensitivity analysis can be applied to any variable to determine the effect of changes in one or more of the inputs on a project's net present value. This process provides the decision maker with a formal mechanism for assessing the possible consequences of various scenarios.

It often is useful to construct sensitivity curves to summarize the impact of changes in different variables on the net present value of a project. A sensitivity curve has the project's net present value on the vertical axis and the variable of interest on the horizontal axis. For example, Figure 11-5 shows the sensitivity curves for two variables, sales price and cost of capital for a project.

The steep slope of the price–NPV curve indicates that the net present value is very sensitive to changes in the price for which the product can be sold. If the product price is approximately 8 percent below the base case (or initial analysis) estimate, the net present value of the project drops to $0, and the project becomes unacceptable for further price declines.[10] In

[9] Simulation also may be applied to other decision models, such as the internal rate of return or payback approaches. In these cases the mathematical relationships involved in the simulation have to be respecified.

[10] Notice that sensitivity analysis does not tell the decision maker the actual probability of NPV being negative. The reason for this is that sensitivity analysis uses only the "best estimate" of each variable and not the entire probability distribution. Strictly speaking, sensitivity analysis is not a pure risk-analysis technique, because it does not calculate the probability of a particular NPV value.

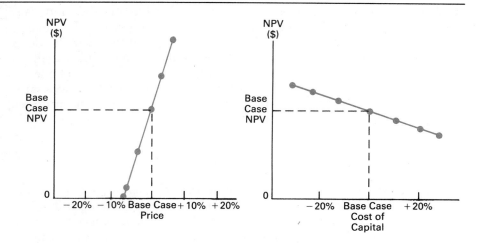

FIGURE 11-5

**Illustrative
Sensitivity Curves**

contrast, the relatively flat cost of capital–NPV curve indicates that the net present value is not very sensitive to changes in the firm's cost of capital. Similar curves could be constructed for project life, salvage value, units sold, operating costs, and other important variables.

USING ELECTRONIC WORKSHEETS FOR SENSITIVITY ANALYSIS. The development of low-cost business and personal microcomputers has revolutionized the application of a number of financial management tools. Sensitivity analysis had been a tool used only by large firms with extensive computer capabilities. Now the availability of computer software that can be used on small business and personal computers has extended the access to these techniques to nearly everyone.

Electronic worksheets, such as the popular Lotus 1-2-3® and Excel, have made the application of sensitivity analysis techniques very simple and inexpensive.[11] Once the base case has been defined and entered in the worksheet, it is very easy to ask hundreds of "what if" type of questions. For example, assume that revenues from a project were expected to be $20,000 in year 1 and to grow by 10 percent annually over the 5-year life of the project. This relationship would be entered into the electronic worksheet along with similar relationships for all other factors that go into the determination of the annual net cash flows from the project. The net present value of the base case is computed by the worksheet. Now, what if the revenues will grow only by 5 percent annually, instead of 10 percent? Only one change must be made on the worksheet (redefine the growth rate to 5 percent), and the worksheet will automatically recompute each period's net cash flows and the net present value of the project. This process can be repeated very rapidly, literally hundreds of times, to develop a profile of how sensitive the project is to changes in the individual components of the project's cash flows. This allows the decision maker to focus his or her analysis on the key variables that are critical to the project's success. (The CFM Lotus Disk accompanying this text can be used very effectively to illustrate the power of spreadsheets in performing sensitivity analyses.)

[11] Lotus 1-2-3 is a registered trademark of the Lotus Development Corporation.

Risk-Adjusted Discount Rate Approach

The risk-adjusted discount rate approach (RADR), as discussed in the section on beta risk, adjusts for risk by varying the rate at which the expected net cash flows are discounted when determining a project's net present value. The RADR approach also can be used in the analysis of projects for which total project risk is the applicable risk measure, rather than beta risk.

In the risk-adjusted discount rate approach, net cash flows for each project are discounted at a risk-adjusted rate, k^*. The magnitude of k^* depends on the relationship between the total risk of the individual project and the overall risk of the firm. To compute k^*, the *risk-free rate*, r_f—that is, a required rate of return associated with investment projects characterized by certain cash flow streams—is used. United States Treasury securities are good examples of risk-free investments, because there is no chance that investors will not get the dollar amount of interest and the principal repayment on schedule. Thus, the yield on U.S. government securities, such as 90-day Treasury bills, is used as the risk-free rate.

Most companies are not in business to invest in risk-free securities; individual investors can do that just as well. Instead, companies assume some amount of risk, expecting to earn higher returns than those available on risk-free securities. The difference between the risk-free rate and the firm's required rate of return (cost of capital) is an *average risk premium* to compensate investors for the fact that the company's assets are risky. This relationship is expressed algebraically as follows:

$$\theta = k - r_f \tag{11.5}$$

where θ is the average risk premium for the firm; r_f, the risk-free rate; and k, the required rate of return for projects of average risk, that is, the firm's cost of capital.

The cash flows from a project having greater than average risk are discounted at a higher rate, k^*—that is, a risk-adjusted discount rate—to reflect the increased riskiness. Total project risk premiums applied to individual projects are commonly established *subjectively*. For example, some firms establish a small number of *risk classes* and then apply a different *risk premium* to each class. Below-average-risk projects, such as straight-forward equipment replacement decisions might be evaluated at 2 percent *below* the firm's cost of capital (a *negative* risk premium, or risk discount). Average-risk projects, such as equipment modification decisions, might be evaluated at the firm's cost of capital; above-average-risk projects, such as facility expansions, might be assigned a risk premium of 3 percent *above* the firm's cost of capital; and high-risk projects, such as investments in totally new lines of business or the introduction of new products, might be assigned a risk premium of 8 percent *above* the firm's cost of capital.

Although the risk-class approach saves time in the analysis stage, it can lead to suboptimal decisions, because the risk premiums themselves usually are subjectively determined, and no explicit consideration is given to the variation in returns of the projects assigned to individual classes. In short, the risk-class approach is most useful when evaluating relatively small projects that are frequently repeated. In these cases, much is known about the projects' potential returns, and it is probably not worth the effort to try to compute more "precise" risk premiums.

Certainty Equivalent Approach

Another approach that can be used to deal with total project risk uses certainty equivalents. The certainty equivalent approach adjusts the net cash flows in the *numerator* of the NPV equation, in contrast to the RADR approach that involves adjustments to the *denominator* of the NPV equation. A certainty equivalent factor is the ratio of the amount of cash someone would require with certainty at a point in time in order to make him or her indifferent between that certain amount and an amount expected to be received with risk at the same point in time. The project is adjusted for risk by converting the expected risky cash flows to their certainty equivalents and then computing the net present value of the project. The risk-free rate, r_f—not the firm's cost of capital, k—is used as the discount rate for computing the net present value. This is done because the cost of capital is a *risky* rate, reflecting the firm's average risk, and using it would result in a double counting of risk.

Certainty equivalent factors range from 0 to 1.0. The higher the factor, the more certain the expected cash flow. For example, one project might offer expected cash flows over its 5-year life as follows:

Year	Expected NCF	Certainty Equivalent Factor (α)	Certainty Equivalent Cash Flows
0	−$10,000	1.0	−$10,000
1	+5,000	0.9	+4,500
2	+6,000	0.8	+4,800
3	+7,000	0.7	+4,900
4	+4,000	0.6	+2,400
5	+3,000	0.4	+1,200

The initial outlay of $10,000 is known with certainty. It might be for the purchase price of a piece of equipment. Hence, the certainty equivalent factor for year 0 is 1.0, and the certainty equivalent cash flow is −$10,000 (−$10,000 × 1.0). The $5,000 cash inflow in year 1 is viewed as being somewhat risky. Consequently, the decision maker has assigned a certainty equivalent factor of 0.9 to the net cash flow in year 1. Multiplying $5,000 times the 0.9 certainty equivalent factor yields a certainty equivalent cash flow of $4,500. This means that the decision maker would be indifferent between receiving the promised, risky $5,000 a year from now or receiving $4,500 with certainty at the same time. A similar interpretation is given to the certainty equivalent factors and certainty equivalent cash flows for years 2 through 5.

Algebraically, the certainty equivalent factors, α, for the cash flows expected to be received during each time period, t, are expressed as follows:

$$\alpha_t = \frac{\text{Certain return}}{\text{Risky return}} \qquad \textbf{(11.6)}$$

The certainty equivalent factors are used to compute a certainty equivalent net present value as follows:

$$\text{NPV} = -\text{NINV}(\alpha_0) + \sum_{t=1}^{n} \frac{\text{NCF}_t \alpha_t}{(1 + r_f)^t} \qquad \textbf{(11.7)}$$

where

α_0 = Certainty equivalent factor associated with the net investment (NINV) at time 0.

n = Expected economic life of the project.

α_t = Certainty equivalent factor associated with the net cash flows (NCF) in each period, t.

r_f = Risk-free rate.

Note in this example that the certainty equivalent factors decline into the future. This reflects the fact that *most* cash flows are viewed as being more risky the further into the future they are projected to occur.[12] This point is discussed in more detail in Chapter 8. In Table 11-1 we have computed the certainty equivalent net present value for this project assuming an 8 percent risk-free rate. It equals $4,753, and the project therefore is acceptable.

The certainty equivalent approach of considering risk is viewed as conceptually sound for the following reasons:

■ The decision maker can adjust separately each period's cash flows to account for the specific risk of those cash flows. This normally is not done when the risk-adjusted discount rate approach is applied.[13]

■ Decision makers must introduce their own risk preferences directly into the analysis. Consequently, the certainty equivalent net present value provides an unambiguous basis for making a decision. A positive net present value means the project is acceptable to that decision maker, and a negative net present value indicates it should be rejected.

INTERNATIONAL CONCERNS: SPECIAL ELEMENTS OF CAPITAL BUDGETING RISK

The techniques of risk analysis presented in this chapter will serve a firm well whether it operates only in the United States or multinationally. How-

---

[12] Different individuals may have different certainty equivalent factors, depending on each individual's relative risk aversion. Risk aversion is a function of many factors, including wealth, age, and the nature of a firm's reward structure.

[13] It is possible, however, to find a risk-adjusted discount rate that will provide results identical (that is, with the same risk-adjusted net present value) to those obtained from the certainty equivalent approach.

Calculation of Certainty Equivalent Net Present Value   T A B L E   11-1

Year	Expected NCF	Certainty Equivalent Factor(α)	Certainty Equivalent Cash Flow	$PVIF_{0.08,t}$	Present Value of Cash Flows
0	− $10,000	1.0	− $10,000	1.000	− $10,000
1	+ 5,000	0.9	+ 4,500	0.926	+ 4,167
2	+ 6,000	0.8	+ 4,800	0.857	+ 4,114
3	+ 7,000	0.7	+ 4,900	0.794	+ 3,891
4	+ 4,000	0.6	+ 2,400	0.735	+ 1,764
5	+ 3,000	0.4	+ 1,200	0.681	+ 817
				Certainty Equivalent NPV =	+ $4,753

ever, managers of multinational firms need to be aware of special elements of risk when investing abroad.

When evaluating a capital expenditure to be made in another country, the parent firm must be concerned with the cash flows that can be expected to be received by the parent—not the cash flows that will accrue to the overseas subsidiary making the investment. There are several reasons for focusing on cash flows to the parent. First, the host country might block the subsidiary from remitting funds back to the parent. Hence, these "captive" funds are not available to the parent for reinvestment in projects offering the highest rate of return. Second, the parent needs to be concerned with the prospect that its assets in foreign subsidiaries could be taken by the host government with no or inadequate compensation. Third, the parent must consider exchange rate risk between the host country's currency and the dollar. (Exchange rate risk and procedures for managing it are discussed in detail in Chapter 21.) Related to exchange rate risk is the higher risk of inflation in many countries, particularly developing countries. Inflation rates well in excess of 100 percent are not uncommon in many South American countries, such as Brazil. The risk of highly volatile inflation and the ability of a firm to protect itself from this risk adds additional uncertainty to investments made abroad. Finally, more uncertainty may be associated with tax rates in the host country than is typical in the United States.

Each of these factors affects the risk of the cash flows that can be expected from investments in other countries. Although multinational firms predominantly use standard capital budgeting procedures, such as NPV and IRR, to evaluate their investments abroad, there is evidence that many multinational firms also use the payback approach to complement their traditional analysis.[14] The use of the payback approach is not surprising in countries where there is a concern about takeovers from the host government.

SUMMARY

- The *risk* of an investment project is defined in terms of the potential *variability* of its returns. When only one return is possible—for example, as with U.S. government securities held to maturity—there is no risk. When more than one return is possible for a particular project, it is risky.
- Risk is also influenced by the possibility of investment *diversification*. If a proposed project's returns are not *perfectly correlated* with the returns from the firm's other investments, the total risk of the firm may be reduced by accepting the proposed project. This is known as the *portfolio effect*.
- When a project differs significantly in its *systematic risk* profile (as measured by *beta*) from the systematic risk of the total firm, a risk-adjusted discount rate appropriate for that project can be computed using the security market line relationship between risk and required return from the capital asset pricing model.
- Multi-industry companies often estimate separate divisional costs of capital, based upon both the differential required returns of equity investors, estimated from the security market line, and the differential debt-carrying capacity of each division.
- There are several ways in which a decision maker can adjust for total project risk in capital budgeting, including the *net present value/payback*

[14] Kim, Suk H., E. J. Farragher, and T. Crick. "Foreign Capital Budgeting Practices Used by the U.S. and Non-U.S. Multinational Companies," *Engineering Economist.* (Spring 1984): 207–215.

approach, *simulation analysis, sensitivity analysis,* the *risk-adjusted discount rate approach,* and the *certainty equivalent approach.*

- The simulation approach is the most expensive of the techniques discussed in this chapter; it normally is applied only when large projects are being analyzed. The widespread availability of inexpensive and powerful computer software such as electronic worksheets has made the use of sensitivity analysis far more accessible to small- and medium-sized firms than was previously possible.

- The risk-adjusted discount rate approach is widely used by firms that attempt to consider differential project risk in their capital budgeting procedures. It requires that a *risk premium* be computed for each project or group of projects so that an appropriate risk-adjusted discount rate can be applied when evaluating a project's cash flows.

- The decision to employ some risk analysis technique to evaluate an investment project depends on the project's size and the additional cost of applying such a technique as compared with the perceived benefits. For small projects, only the simpler risk adjustment techniques should be used; for major projects that have above- or below-normal risk it is worthwhile to analyze the project's risk as precisely as possible. Failure to fully analyze the risk of a large project could result in bad investment decisions and even substantial losses.

- Multinational firms must be concerned with additional risk elements when investing abroad, such as inflation risk, exchange rate risk, and the risk of expropriation.

■■■■ QUESTIONS AND TOPICS FOR DISCUSSION

1. How does the basic net present value model of capital budgeting deal with the problem of project risk? What are the shortcomings of this approach?

2. How would you define *risk* as it is used in a capital budgeting analysis context?

3. Recalling the discussion in Chapter 8, when is the standard deviation of a project's cash flows an appropriate measure of project risk? When is the coefficient of variation an appropriate measure?

4. How does the basic net present value capital budgeting model deal with the phenomenon of increasing risk of project cash flows over time?

5. When should a firm consider the portfolio effects of a new project?

6. Under what circumstances do you think the use of divisional required rates of return (costs of capital) is likely to improve the capital budgeting decision process?

7. What are the primary advantages and disadvantages of applying *simulation* to capital budgeting risk analysis?

8. Computer simulation is used to generate a large number of possible outcomes for an investment project. Most firms invest in a particular project only once, however. How can a computer simulation model be helpful to the typical decision maker who is making a one-time-only investment decision?

9. On average, the expected value of returns from each $1 of premiums paid on an insurance policy is less than $1; this is due to the insurance company's administrative costs and profits. In spite of this fact, why do so many individuals and organizations purchase insurance policies?

10. Describe how certainty equivalent cash flow estimates can be derived for individual project cash flows.

11. Will all individuals apply the same certainty equivalent estimates to the cash flows from a project? Why or why not?

PROBLEMS*

1. Aunt Bessie has discovered an old lithograph of Andrew Johnson at a local flea market. The dealer is asking a price of $20. Recognizing the potential value of this item, Aunt Bessie buys the lithograph. Given the condition of the lithograph, Aunt Bessie has assigned the following probability distribution to the lithograph's ultimate selling price when she offers it to a local dealer:

Probability	Selling Price
0.05	$ 60
0.25	70
0.35	100
0.20	160
0.15	200

a. What is the expected selling price?
b. What is the standard deviation of the selling price?

2. The Topless Auto Company, a maker of convertible cars, has estimated the probability distribution of its annual net cash flows as follows:

Probability	Cash Flows (in thousands of dollars)
0.10	$1,000
0.20	1,500
0.40	2,000
0.20	2,500
0.10	3,000

a. Compute the expected annual cash flow.
b. Compute the standard deviation of annual cash flows.
c. Compute the coefficient of variation of annual cash flows.

3. A new project has expected annual net cash flows of $400,000 with a standard deviation of $250,000. The distribution of annual net cash flows is approximately normal.

a. What is the probability of the project's having negative annual net cash flows?
b. What is the probability that annual net cash flows will be greater than $575,000?

4. Two projects have the following expected net present values and standard deviations of net present values:

Project	Expected Net Present Value	Standard Deviation
A	$50,000	$20,000
B	10,000	7,000

* Colored numbers denote problems that have check answers provided at the end of the book.

a. Using the standard deviation criterion, which project is riskier?
b. Using the coefficient of variation criterion, which project is riskier?
c. Which criterion do you think is appropriate to use in this case? Why?

5. American Steel Corporation is considering two investments. One is the purchase of a new continuous caster costing $100 million. The expected net present value of this project is $20 million. The other alternative is the purchase of a supermarket chain, also costing $100 million. It, too, has an expected net present value of $20 million. The firm's management is interested in reducing the variability of its earnings.

a. Which project should the company invest in?
b. What assumptions did you make to arrive at this decision?

6. The Jacobs Company is financed entirely with equity. The beta for Jacobs has been estimated to be 1.0. The current risk-free rate is 10 percent, and the expected market return is 15 percent.

a. What rate of return should Jacobs require on a project of average risk?
b. If a new venture is expected to have a beta of 1.6, what rate of return should Jacobs demand on this project?
c. The project in question requires an initial outlay of $9.0 million and is expected to generate a 10-year stream of annual net cash flows of $1.9 million. Calculate the NPV of the project using Jacob's required return for projects of average risk.
d. Calculate the NPV of the project using the risk-adjusted rate computed in Part b.

7. Advanced Systems Company is financed one-third with debt and two-thirds with equity. Its market beta has been estimated to be 1.5. The current risk-free rate is 8 percent and the expected market return is 15 percent. Advanced Systems' tax rate is 40 percent. Advanced Systems is planning a major research and development (R and D) investment program. Advanced Systems' management believes that these types of projects should be financed very conservatively. Specifically, the company plans to finance all R and D investments with 90 percent equity and 10 percent debt.

a. If the pure project beta for the R and D investment is the same as the pure project beta for Advanced System's other assets, what rate of return is required on the equity-financed portion of the R and D investment assuming it is financed 90 percent with equity and 10 percent with debt?
b. Advanced Systems' managers believe this project may have more risk than their other investments. Another firm, that invests very heavily in R and D similar to the type proposed by Advanced has been identified. Its capital structure is 80 percent equity and 20 percent debt. Its tax rate is 35 percent and its market beta is 1.6. Using this information, determine the required return on the equity-financed portion of Advanced Systems' R and D project, assuming it is financed 90 percent with equity and 10 percent with debt.

8. Valley Products, Inc., is considering two investments having the following cash flow streams:

Year	Project A	Project B
0	− $50,000	− $40,000
1	+ 20,000	+ 20,000
2	+ 20,000	+ 10,000
3	+ 10,000	+ 5,000
4	+ 5,000	+ 5,000
5	+ 5,000	+ 40,000

Valley uses a combination of the net present value approach and the payback approach to evaluate investment alternatives. It requires that all projects have a positive net present value when cash flows are discounted at 10 percent and that all projects have a payback no longer than 3 years. Which project or projects should the firm accept? Why?

9. Fox Enterprises is considering expanding into the growing laser copier business. Fox estimates that this expansion will cost $1.8 million and will generate a 20-year stream of expected net cash flows amounting to $400,000 per year. The company's weighted cost of capital is 15 percent.

   a. Compute the net present value of the laser copier project using the company's weighted cost of capital and the expected cash flows from the project.

   b. Using the risk-adjusted discount rate approach, management has decided that this project has substantially more risk than average and has decided that it requires a 24 percent expected rate of return on projects like this. Recompute the risk-adjusted net present value of this project.

10. Apple Jacks, Inc., produces wine. The firm is considering expanding into the snack food business. This expansion will require an initial investment in new equipment of $200,000. The equipment will be depreciated on a straight-line basis over a 10-year period to an estimated salvage value of $40,000. The expansion will require an increase in working capital for the firm of $40,000.

   Revenues from the new venture are forecasted at $200,000 per year for the first 5 years and $210,000 per year for years 6 through 10. Cash operating costs from the new venture are estimated at $90,000 for the first 5 years and $105,000 for years 6 through 10. It is assumed that at the end of year 10 the snack food equipment will be sold for its book value.

   The firm's marginal tax rate is 40 percent. The required return for projects of average risk has been estimated as 15 percent.

   a. Compute the project's net present value, assuming that it is an average risk investment.

   b. If management decides that all product line expansions have above average risk and therefore should be evaluated at a 24 percent required rate of return, what will be the risk-adjusted net present value of the project?

11. The Seminole Production Company is analyzing the investment in a new line of business machines. The initial outlay required is $35 million. The net cash flows expected from the investment are as follows:

Year	Net Cash Flow
1	$ 5 million
2	8 million
3	15 million
4	20 million
5	15 million
6	10 million
7	4 million

The firm's cost of capital (used for projects of average risk) is 15 percent.

   a. Compute the net present value of this project assuming it possesses average risk.

   b. Because of the risk inherent in this type of investment, Seminole has decided to employ the certainty equivalent approach. After considerable discussion, management has agreed to apply the following certainty equivalents to the project's cash flows:

Year	α_t
0	1.00
1	0.95
2	0.90
3	0.80
4	0.60
5	0.40
6	0.35
7	0.30

If the risk-free rate is 9 percent, compute the project's certainty equivalent net present value.

c. On the basis of this analysis, should the project be accepted?

12. A simulation model similar to the one described in this chapter has been constructed by the Great Basin Corporation to evaluate the largest of its new investment proposals. After many iterations of the model, Great Basin's management has arrived at an expected net present value for Project A of $1.0 million. The standard deviation of the net present value has been estimated from the simulation model results to be $0.8 million.

a. What is the probability that the project will have a negative net present value?

b. What is the probability that the project will have a net present value greater than $2.2 million?

13. The Buffalo Snow Shoe Company is considering manufacturing radial snow shoes, which are more durable and offer better traction. Buffalo estimates that the investment in manufacturing equipment will cost $250,000 and will have a 10-year economic life. Buffalo will depreciate the equipment on a straight line basis to a $0 estimated salvage value over a 10-year period. The estimated selling price of each pair of shoes will be $50. Buffalo anticipates that it can sell 5,000 pairs a year at this price. Unit production and selling costs (exclusive of depreciation) will be about $25. The firm's marginal tax rate is 40 percent. A cost of capital of 12 percent is thought to be appropriate to analyze a project of this type.

Buffalo has decided to perform a sensitivity analysis of the project before making a decision.

a. Compute the expected net present value of this project.

b. Buffalo's president does not believe that 5,000 pairs of the new snow shoes can be sold at a $50 price. He estimates that a maximum of 3,000 pairs will be sold at this price. How does the change in the estimated sales volume influence the net present value of the project?

14. Project Alpha offers the following net cash flows following an initial (year 0), certain outlay (NINV) of $70,000:

Year	Net Cash Flows	Certainty Equivalent Factor
1	$30,000	0.91
2	30,000	0.79
3	30,000	0.65
4	20,000	0.52
5	20,000	0.40
6	10,000	0.30

a. Compute the NPV of this project at a 17 percent cost of capital.

b. If the risk-free rate is 8 percent, what is the certainty equivalent NPV for Project Alpha?

15. A new project is expected to have an 8-year economic life. The project will have an initial cost of $100,000. Installation and shipping charges for the equipment are estimated at $10,000. The equipment will be depreciated as a 7-year asset under MACRS rules. A working capital investment of $15,000 is required to undertake the project.

The revenues from the project in year 1 are expected to be $60,000. These are expected to increase at a compound annual rate of 6 percent. Operating costs are $15,000. These costs are expected to increase at an 8 percent compound annual rate. The firm's marginal tax rate is 40 percent. The expected salvage value of the equipment at the end of year 8 is $20,000.

a. Compute the project's net investment.
b. Compute the annual net cash flows for the project.
c. If the firm's cost of capital is 19 percent, should the project be undertaken?
d. The managers of the firm have decided also to evaluate this project using the certainty equivalent approach. They have established the following certainty equivalent factors for the cash flows forecasted in each year:

Year	α_t
0	1.00
1	0.95
2	0.90
3	0.80
4	0.60
5	0.50
6	0.45
7	0.40
8	0.35

The risk-free rate is 8 percent. Compute the certainty equivalent NPV for this project.

16. The managers of U.S. Rubber (USR) have analyzed a proposed investment project. The expected net present value (NPV) of the project, evaluated at the firm's weighted cost of capital of 18 percent, has been estimated to be $100,000. The company's managers have determined that the most optimistic NPV estimate of the project is $175,000 and the most pessimistic estimate is $25,000. The most optimistic estimate is a value that is not expected to be exceeded more than 10 percent of the time. The most pessimistic estimate represents a value that the project's NPV is not expected to fall below more than 10 percent of the time. What is the probability that this project will have a negative NPV?

17. U.S. Robotics (USR) has a current (and target) capital structure of 70 percent common equity and 30 percent debt. The beta for USR is 1.4. USR is evaluating an investment in a totally new line of business. The new investment has an expected internal rate of return of 15 percent.

USR wishes to evaluate this investment proposal. If the investment is made, USR intends to finance the project with the same capital structure as its current business. USR's marginal tax rate is 34 percent. USR has identified three firms that are primarily in the line of business that USR proposes expanding into. Their average beta is 1.7 and their average capital structure is 40 percent common equity and 60 percent debt. The marginal tax rate for these three firms averages 40 percent. The risk-free rate is 8 percent and the expected market risk premium is 8.3 percent.

Should USR undertake the project?

CAPITAL BUDGETING AND RISK ANALYSIS

ZeeBancorp is considering the establishment of a contract collection service subsidiary that would provide collection services to small- and medium-sized firms. Compensation would be in the form of a percentage of the amount collected. For amounts collected up to $100 the fee is 55 percent of the amount collected. For amounts collected between $100 and $500 the fee would be 40 percent of the total amount collected on the account. For amounts collected over $500 ZeeBancorp would receive 35 percent of the total amount collected on the account.

ZeeBancorp expects to generate the following amount of business during the first year of operation of the new subsidiary:

Account Class	Number of Collections	Average Amount Collected for Each Account
Up to $100	4,800	$75
Between $100 and $500	2,100	$325
Over $500	1,250	$850

Over the projected 10-year life of this collection venture, the number of accounts in each group is expected to grow at 6 percent per annum. The average amount collected from each account is expected to remain constant.

To establish the collection subsidiary, ZeeBancorp will have to rent office space at a cost of $250,000 for the first year. (Assume the rent is payable at the *end* of each year.) This amount is expected to grow at a rate of 11 percent per year. Other operating expenses (excluding depreciation) are expected to total $350,000 during the first year and grow at an 11 percent annual rate.

ZeeBancorp will have to invest $150,000 in net working capital if it undertakes this venture. In addition, required new equipment will cost $275,000 to purchase and an additional $25,000 to install. This equipment will be depreciated using the MACRS schedule for a 7-year asset. The salvage value for the equipment is estimated to be $50,000 at the end of 10 years.

The firm's *marginal* tax rate is estimated to be 40 percent over the project's life, and its *average* tax rate is projected to be 35 percent over the project's life. The firm requires a 15 percent rate of return on projects of average risk.

1. Compute the net investment required to establish the collection subsidiary.

2. Compute the annual net cash flows over the 10-year life of the project.

3. Compute the net present value of this project assuming it is an average risk investment.

4. Should ZeeBancorp invest in the new subsidiary?

5. ZeeBancorp requires all expansion projects such as this to have a payback of 4 years or less. Under these conditions should ZeeBancorp invest in the new subsidiary?

6. If management decides that this project has above-average risk and hence the required return is 20 percent, should the investment be made?

7. If collections are only 80 percent of projections and the required return is 20 percent, should the investment be made?

8. If operating (excluding depreciation) and lease expenses are expected to increase at an annual rate of 13 percent, should the collection subsidiary be established, assuming a required return of 20 percent and the original revenue projections?

SELECTED REFERENCES

Ang, James S., and W. G. Lewellen. "Risk Adjustment in Capital Investment Project Evaluations," *Financial Management* (Summer 1982): 5–14.

Copeland, T. E., and J. F. Weston, *Financial Theory and Corporate Policy*, 3d ed. Reading, MA: Addison-Wesley, 1988.

"Divisional Hurdle Rates and the Cost of Capital," *Financial Management* (Spring 1989): 18–25.

Harris, Robert S., and J. J. Pringle. "Risk-Adjusted Discount Rates—Extensions from the Average Risk Case," *Journal of Financial Research* (Fall 1985): 237–245.

Hertz, David B. "Risk Analysis in Capital Investment," *Harvard Business Review* 42 (January–February 1964): 95–106.

Lewellen, Wilbur G., and Michael S. Long, "Simulation versus Single-Value Estimates in Capital Expenditure Analysis." *Decision Sciences* 3 (1973): 19–33.

Myers, Stewart C., and S. M. Turnbull. "Capital Budgeting and the Capital Asset Pricing Model: Good News and Bad News," *Journal of Finance* (May 1977): 321–332.

Robichek, Alexander A. "Interpreting the Results of Risk Analysis." *Journal of Finance* 30 (Dec. 1975): 1384–1386.

Shapiro, Alan C., and S. Titman. "An Integrated Approach to Corporate Risk Management," *Midland Corporate Finance Journal* (Summer 1985): 41–56.

V

The Cost of Capital, Capital Structure, and Dividend Policy

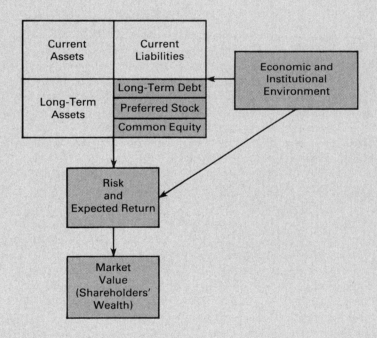

This section considers three closely related topics: the cost of capital (Chapter 12), capital structure (Chapter 13), and dividend policy (Chapter 14). The cost of capital is an important input in the capital budgeting decision process. This market-determined cost of funds also directly influences the value of a firm's securities. The cost of capital cannot be considered in isolation. The capital structure of a firm directly affects its cost of capital. A more debt-laden capital structure at some point will increase the risk of the firm's securities and increase the overall cost of capital to the firm. This results in a reduction in the value of the firm. Chapter 13 looks at the determinants of an "optimal" capital structure—one that is consistent with the objective of shareholder wealth maximization. Finally, the dividend policy of a firm, discussed in Chapter 14, can provide important information to investors that ultimately may affect the firm's risk and cost of capital as perceived by investors.

CHAPTER

12

The Cost of Capital

KEY CHAPTER CONCEPTS

1. The *cost of capital* is the rate of return required by investors in the firm's securities. The cost of capital determines the rate of return that the firm must earn on its new investments (of average risk) to maximize its value.

2. The required return on any security may be viewed as consisting of a risk-free rate of return plus a premium for the risk of that security.

   a. The risk-free rate varies over time and is influenced by the expected rate of inflation and the supply and demand for funds in the overall economy.

   b. The risk premium on a specific security is influenced by the business risk of the firm, the financial risk of the firm, the marketability risk of the security, and the time to maturity of the security.

3. For capital budgeting purposes, the marginal cost of each capital source needs to be calculated.

   a. The after-tax cost of debt is equal to the pretax cost of new debt times one minus the firm's marginal tax rate.

   b. The after-tax cost of a perpetual preferred stock is equal to the dividend rate divided by the net proceeds to the firm from the sale of preferred stock.

   c. The cost of internal equity capital can be computed using a version of the dividend valuation model, the capital asset pricing model, or a risk–premium on debt approach.

   d. The cost of external equity capital exceeds the cost of internal equity capital by the amount of the issuance costs.

4. The weighted cost of capital is equal to the after-tax cost of debt times its proportion in the optimal capital structure, plus the after-tax cost of preferred stock times its proportion in the optimal capital structure, plus the cost of common equity times its proportion in the optimal capital structure.

5. The weighted cost of capital is appropriate for determining the return required on projects of *average* risk.

6. The optimal capital budget can be determined by comparing the expected project returns to the company's marginal cost of capital schedule.

7. The cost of depreciation-generated funds is equal to the firm's weighted (marginal) cost of capital, before considering new stock flotation costs.

GLOSSARY OF NEW TERMS

Beta A measure of a stock's price and total return volatility relative to the volatility of prices and returns in the securities markets as a whole.

Business risk The variability in a firm's operating earnings (EBIT).

Capital Asset Pricing Model (CAPM) A theory that formally describes the nature of the risk-required return tradeoff in finance. It provides one method of computing a firm's cost of equity capital.

Cost of capital The equilibrium rate of return demanded by investors in the securities issued by a firm.

Expected market return (k_m) The return investors expect to earn on stocks with an average beta of 1.0.

Financial risk The additional variability in a company's earnings per share that results from the use of fixed-cost sources of funds, such as debt and preferred stock.

IBES Institutional Brokers Estimate System.

Interest rate risk The variability in the rate of return or yield on securities that arises from changes in interest rates.

Investment opportunity curve A graph or listing showing a firm's investment opportunities (projects) ranked from highest to lowest expected rate of return.

Marginal cost of capital The weighted after-tax cost of the next dollar of capital the firm expects to raise to finance a new investment project.

Marketability risk The ability of an investor to buy and sell an asset (security) quickly and without a significant loss of value.

Optimal capital budget The level of capital spending at which a firm's investment opportunity curve just intersects its marginal cost of capital curve.

Risk-free rate The rate of return on securities that are free of default risk, such as U.S. Treasury bills.

Security market line (SML) A line depicting the risk-required return relationship in the market for all securities.

Cost of Equity Capital for the Gas Company of New Mexico

In 1923, the U.S. Supreme Court issued its landmark decision in the Bluefield Water Works and Improvement Company *v.* Public Service Commission of the State of West Virginia (262 U.S. 679). Among other things this ruling set judicial standards regarding the rate of return a public utility is allowed to earn on its invested capital. The Court stated that:

A public utility is entitled to such rates as will permit it to earn a return on the value of the property which it employs for the convenience of the public equal to that generally being made at the same time . . . in other business undertakings which are attended by corresponding risks and uncertainties; . . . The return should be reasonably sufficient to assure confidence in the financial soundness of the utility and should be adequate, under efficient and economical management, to maintain and support its credit and enable it to raise the money necessary for the proper discharge of its public duties. A rate of return may be reasonable at one time and become too high or too low by changes affecting opportunities for investment, the money market and business conditions generally.

This opinion has been affirmed in many subsequent cases, the most notable one being the Federal Power Commission et al. *v.* Hope Natural Gas Company case (320 U.S. 591) in 1944.

These decisions establish a number of basic principles that are used when a public utility commission is deciding on the rate of return a public utility is to be allowed an opportunity to earn on its equity capital. First, it has been established that the return on equity should be consistent with the opportunity cost principle; that is, the company should be permitted to earn a return equal to that being earned by other companies with similar risks. Second, the return should be sufficient to maintain the financial integrity of the company, maintain its credit, and give it access to the capital markets. Finally, it is recognized that the cost of capital changes depending on business conditions and conditions in the financial markets. The decisions, however, do not establish a methodology for determining the allowed rate of return on common equity to a public utility. In a typical rate case there normally is extensive controversy regarding the cost of common equity.

The Gas Company of New Mexico is the largest natural gas utility operating in New Mexico. It is a wholly owned division of the Public Service Company of New Mexico, which also provides electric service to much of New Mexico and water service to the city of Santa Fe. During 1988, the Gas Company had a major rate case heard before the New Mexico Public Service Commission (NMPSC). In that case four witnesses submitted cost of equity capital testimony. A listing of their recommendations follows:

Witness	Recommended Equity Return	Methodology
Dennis Gee, NMPSC Staff	12.74%	Dividend valuation using Value Line projected growth rates in dividends for a group of "comparable" firms.
Richard Lelash, New Mexico Attorney General's Office	12.50%	Dividend valuation using a combination of historic growth rates in earnings, dividends, and book values, plus growth derived from retention and reinvestment, plus Value Line projected growth rates for a group of "comparable" firms.
George Stolnitz, U.S. Executive Agencies	12.57%	Dividend valuation using historic dividend growth rates and Value Line projected growth rates for a group of "comparable" firms.
R. Charles Moyer, Gas Company of New Mexico	13.6%	Dividend valuation using consensus long-term analyst earnings growth rate forecasts for a group of "comparable" firms. Risk premium on debt analysis.

The cost of equity capital was estimated from a low of 12.5 percent to a high of 13.6 percent. In addition to the disparities in recommended return allowances, many of the parties proposed different "hypothetical" capital structures against which the equity cost would be applied. For example, the company proposed a capital structure of 45 percent common equity, 6 percent preferred stock, and 49 percent long-term debt. The commission staff witness proposed a capital structure containing 50.7 percent common equity, 2.5 percent preferred stock, and 46.8 percent long-term debt. The effect of using a capital structure based on 50.7 percent of common equity, rather than the 45 percent proposed by the company was to increase the return dollars available to the company.

Having considered volumes of conflicting testimony on the issues, the NMPSC was faced with the dilemma of making a final recommendation. The final order in the case permitted the Gas Company to charge rates consistent with its earning a return of 12.74 percent on its common equity capital, assuming a 50.7 percent common equity ratio in its capital structure.

This chapter develops the principles and models that can be used to compute a firm's cost of debt, preferred stock, and common equity. All of the models require the use of some judgment by the analyst. This is particularly true in the case of common equity. The cost of common equity cannot be estimated with the precision possible in the case of debt and preferred stock. However, an analyst who is aware of the basic principles contained in this chapter can make reasonable estimates of the cost of equity capital for any company.

INTRODUCTION

Chapters 9 through 11 considered the capital budgeting decisions of a firm. One of the key variables in capital expenditure analysis is the cost of capital. This chapter discusses the concept of the cost of capital and develops approaches that can be used to measure this important variable.

The *cost of capital* is concerned with what a firm has to pay for the capital—that is, the debt, preferred stock, retained earnings, and common stock—it uses to finance new investments. It also can be thought of as the rate of return required by investors in the firm's securities. As such, the firm's cost of capital is determined in the capital markets and is closely related to the degree of risk associated with new investments, existing assets, and the firm's capital structure. In general, the greater the risk of a firm as perceived by investors, the greater the return investors will require and the greater will be the cost of capital.

The cost of capital also can be thought of as the minimum rate of return required on new investments undertaken by the firm.[1] If a new investment earns an internal rate of return that is greater than the cost of capital, the value of the firm increases. Correspondingly, if a new investment earns a return less than the firm's cost of capital, the firm's value decreases.

This chapter discusses the nature of the tradeoff between risk and required return made by investors in a firm's securities, the measurement of the cost of individual capital components, and the weighted cost of capital and its use in the capital budgeting process. Chapter 13 continues by considering the relationship between capital structure and the cost of capital.

---

[1] Technically, this statement assumes that the risk of the new investments is equal to the risk of the firm's existing assets. Also, when used in this context, the cost of capital refers to a weighted cost of the various sources of capital used by the firm. The computation of the weighted cost of capital is considered later in this chapter.

SUMMARY OF NOTATION

Before beginning our discussion of the cost of capital, it is helpful to summarize the important elements of notation used throughout this chapter.

r_f = riskless (risk-free) rate of return; the return offered on short-term U.S. Treasury securities
k_d = pretax cost of debt
k_i = after-tax cost of debt
k_p = cost of preferred stock
k_e = cost of internal common equity
k_e' = cost of external common equity
k_a = weighted (marginal) cost of capital
P_0 = the current market price of a security
P_{net} = the net proceeds to the firm from the sale of a security
P_f = Market value of a firm's preferred stock
E = Market value of a firm's common equity
B = Market value of a firm's debt in its capital structure

NATURE OF RISK PREMIUMS

Throughout finance, numerous tradeoffs must be made between risk and required return. In capital budgeting, for example, companies require higher returns on projects perceived as "high risk" than on projects considered to be "low risk." The following discussion focuses on the relationship between the risk and required return on a firm's securities.

The required return on any security may be thought of as consisting of a riskless, or risk-free, rate of return, r_f, plus a premium for the risk inherent in that security:

$$\text{Required return} = r_f + \text{Risk premium} \qquad (12.1)$$

The riskless rate of return normally is measured by the rate of return on risk-free securities, such as short-term U.S. Treasury securities. This rate varies over time and consists of two key components:

■ A *real* rate of return that is free from the effects of any inflationary expectations. The real rate of return is determined by the supply and demand for funds in the overall economy.
■ A *premium* that is equal to the effects of expected inflation.

When investors expect a high inflation rate and the implied loss in the purchasing power of their money, they will demand a higher rate of return on their investments—not only in risk-free securities, but in risky securities as well. Similarly, if the anticipated demand for investment funds exceeds the anticipated supply at current interest rates, the rate of return required by investors will increase to create a new, higher equilibrium rate of return. These two factors are the primary determinants of returns on risk-free securities. The returns required on all other securities also are influenced by the risk of those securities.

Four major risk components determine the risk premium on a specific security at any point in time:

■ The business risk of the firm.
■ The financial risk of the firm.

- The marketability risk of the security.
- The length of maturity of the security (interest rate risk).

The *business risk* of a firm refers to the variability in the firm's operating earnings (EBIT). It is determined by the variability in the firm's sales revenues and operating costs and by the amount of operating leverage the firm uses in producing sales. The determinants of business risk are discussed in Chapter 13.

Financial risk refers to the additional variability in a company's earnings per share that results from the use of fixed-cost sources of funds, such as debt and preferred stock. In addition, the financial risk premium includes a premium to compensate for the increased potential risk of bankruptcy that arises from the use of debt financing. The determinants of financial risk are discussed in more detail in Chapter 13.

Marketability risk refers to the ability of an investor to buy and sell a company's securities quickly and without a significant loss of value. For example, AT&T's shares are readily marketable any time at, or very near to, the current market price. Other, less widely owned securities that are not traded on an organized exchange or traded actively in the over-the-counter market usually do not have such a ready market. This may cause time delays in the sale of the securities and necessitate price concessions. Generally the less marketable a security, the higher its required rate of return.

Interest rate risk (also called *maturity risk*) refers to the variability in the rate of return or yield on securities (such as bonds or preferred stocks) that arises from changes in interest rates. As interest rates rise, the prices of fixed-income securities fall, causing current holders of these securities to realize a lower rate of return (than was expected at the time the security was purchased), or yield, when they sell the securities.

Finally, a firm's cost of funds may increase at any point in time with increases in the amount of needed financing. For example, a company might be able to sell 1 million new shares of common stock at $25 per share. If the firm sought to sell an additional 1 million shares, however, it would probably have to offer them at a lower price in order to attract enough buyers. This would, of course, increase the cost of the funds raised by the firm. In addition, as a firm seeks increasing amounts of capital from investors, there is a point at which the investors begin to question the firm's ability to effectively manage the large number of investment projects to be financed with these funds.

Figure 12-1 illustrates the relationship between the riskless rate of return, the risk premium, and the required rate of return on any security.

Although the foregoing concepts provide a useful background for analyzing the cost of a firm's capital, they are not directly applicable to measuring the cost of capital for specific sources of funds. Before considering how the cost of capital may be estimated, it is necessary to examine the relationship between the costs of various capital sources.

RELATIVE COSTS OF CAPITAL

Figure 12-2 illustrates the general risk-return tradeoff between investors' required rates of return and various sources of funds. As was noted, the risk-free rate, r_f, usually is measured as the rate of return on short-term U.S. Treasury securities. Longer-term U.S. government bonds normally com-

**Determinants of the
Required Return of
Any Security**

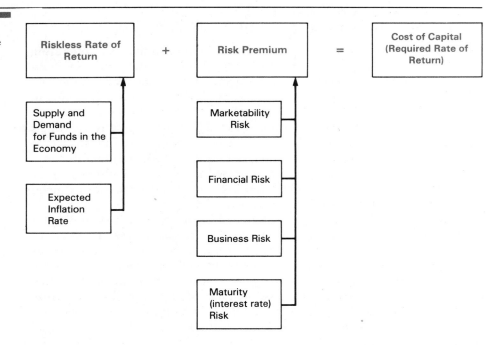

mand a higher rate than shorter-term debt, because bond prices vary more than prices of shorter-term debt securities over time, depending on changes in interest rates. Thus, if interest rates rise, the price of long-term bonds falls, resulting in losses for any investor who must sell the security prior to maturity. Investors normally require a premium to compensate for this *interest rate risk.*

Long-term debt securities of the U.S. government always are less risky than corporate long-term debt securities of the same maturity. The reason, of course, is that there is a finite probability, however small, that the company will default on its obligation to pay interest and principal. Because the government controls the money supply, it can always meet its nominal financial obligations by printing more money. The actual difference in returns, or yields, between government debt and high-quality corporate debt (Aaa rated) is usually less than 1 percent and often less than 0.5 percent. For example, in early 1989 the average yield on Aaa corporate bonds was 9.6 percent, and the average yield on long-term U.S. Treasury bonds was 9.1 percent. Companies with high default risk must offer high coupon interest rates to investors in order to sell their debt issues. This is because the market recognizes that these high default risk companies are more likely to have difficulty meeting their obligations than low default risk companies.

Recently another element of risk has become apparent to owners of corporate bonds. This is the risk that a recapitalization of the firm, such as may occur in a leveraged buyout, may greatly increase the financial risk of the firm. For example, in late 1988 when RJR Nabisco was acquired in a leveraged buyout by a group headed by Kohlberg Kravis Roberts (KKR), the holders of the RJR Nabisco bonds experienced a loss of 20 percent or more in the value of their bonds. The KKR takeover increased the debt ratio of RJR Nabisco substantially. Accordingly, buyers of corporate bonds now require relatively higher returns when the risk of a leveraged buyout is present.

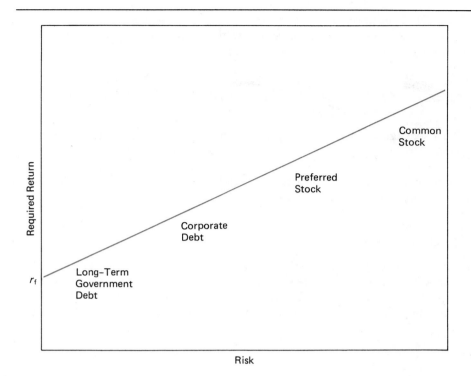

FIGURE 12-2

General Risk-
Required Return
Tradeoff

Preferred stock normally is riskier than debt. The claims of preferred stockholders on the firm's assets and earnings are junior to those of debtholders. Also, dividends on preferred stock are more likely to be cut or omitted than interest on debt. Consequently, investors usually demand a higher return on a company's preferred stock than on its debt.

Common stock is the most risky type of security considered here, because dividends paid to common stockholders are made from cash remaining after interest and preferred dividends have been paid. Thus, the common stock dividends are the first to be cut when the firm encounters difficulties. Because there is a greater degree of uncertainty associated with common stock dividends than with the interest on debt or preferred stock dividends, common stock dividends are judged more risky. In addition, the market price fluctuations of common stocks tend to be wider than those of preferred stocks or long-term debt. As a result of this higher risk, investors' required return on common stock is higher relative to preferred stock and debt. Over the years the differences between returns realized from long-term corporate debt and common stock investments have averaged 6.8 percent.[2]

So far this section has shown that a particular security's risk affects the return required by investors. The analysis must be taken one important step further, however. If capital markets are to clear (that is, supply equals demand), the firm must offer returns consistent with investor requirements. Suppose, for example, that a firm offers a security for sale in the capital markets at a return that is less than investors in general require. Obviously, not enough buyers will come forth. Unless the firm increases the return (by dropping the price, raising the interest or dividend rate, and so on), the securities will remain unsold, and the firm will not be able to raise its

[2] *Stocks, Bonds, Bills, and Inflation: 1988 Yearbook* (Chicago: Ibbotson Associates, 1988).

capital. Therefore, *the cost of capital to the firm is equal to the equilibrium rate of return demanded by investors in the capital markets for securities with that degree of risk.*

■■■ COMPUTING THE COMPONENT COSTS OF CAPITAL

This section develops and applies methods a firm can use to compute the cost of its major component sources of capital: debt, preferred stock, retained earnings, and new common equity. These component costs are then combined into a weighted cost of capital that can be used in making capital budgeting and capital structure decisions.

Cost of Debt

The cost of debt capital to the firm is the rate of return required by investors. For a debt issue, this rate of return, k_d, equates the present value of all expected future receipts—interest, I, and principal repayment, M—with the offering price, P_0, of the debt security (as discussed earlier in Chapter 6):

$$P_0 = \sum_{t=1}^{n} \frac{I}{(1 + k_d)^t} + \frac{M}{(1 + k_d)^n} \qquad (12.2)$$

Most *new* long-term debt issued by companies is sold at or close to par value (normally $1,000 per bond), and the coupon interest rate is set at the rate required by investors. When debt is issued at a price to give the issuing firm net proceeds equal to the par value, the pretax cost of debt, k_d, is equal to the coupon interest rate:[3]

$$k_d = \text{Coupon interest rate} \qquad (12.3)$$

Interest payments made to investors, however, are deductible from the firm's taxable income. Therefore, the *after-tax* cost of debt, k_i, issued at par is computed by multiplying the coupon interest rate by one minus the firm's marginal tax rate, T:[4]

$$k_i = k_d(1 - T) \qquad (12.4)$$

To illustrate the cost of debt computation, suppose that National Telephone and Telegraph sells $100 million of 8.5 percent (k_d) first mortgage bonds at par. Assuming a corporate marginal tax rate (T) of 40 percent, the after-tax cost of debt is computed as follows:

$$k_i = k_d(1 - T) = 8.5(1 - 0.4)$$

$$= 5.1\%$$

---

[3] In general, the pretax cost of debt, k_d, is computed the same way as the yield to maturity, discussed in Chapter 6. When making yield-to-maturity calculations, the price of the bond is the current market price. When computing the pretax cost of debt to a company, the price of the bond is the net proceeds the company receives after considering all issuance costs.

[4] This conversion from a pretax to an after-tax cost of debt is accurate when there are no bond flotation costs. When a bond offering entails flotation costs and the bond is sold either at a discount or premium over face value, there will be a small, insignificant error when using Equation 12.4.

Equation 12.4 assumes that a firm sells the debt to yield *net proceeds*, after the cost of issuance, of $1,000 per bond. However, because of these issue costs, many bonds provide the firm with net proceeds that are less than the $1,000 par value of the bond. In addition, as discussed in Chapter 6, some bonds are sold at prices considerably below par (called *deep discount bonds*). These bonds have coupon rates substantially less than prevailing market rates.

In these cases, the computation of the pretax cost of debt is similar to the calculation of the yield to maturity on a bond as presented in Chapter 6. For example, suppose a firm sells a series of 20-year, $1,000 par value bonds. The price to the public is $755, and the bonds provide a coupon rate of interest of 7 percent ($70 interest per year). (These bonds would be called *deep discount bonds*.) The issue costs per bond are $10 each. Hence, the net proceeds to the firm are as follows:

Net proceeds = $1,000 par value − $245 discount − $10 issue costs

= $745

The pretax cost of debt to this firm is equal to the discount rate that equates the present value of all future interest payments ($70 per year for 20 years) plus the repayment of principal ($1,000) at the end of 20 years with the net proceeds to the firm, or

$$\$745 = \$70(\text{PVIFA}_{k_d,20}) + \$1,000(\text{PVIF}_{k_d,20})$$

By trial and error, try 10 percent:

$$\$745 = \$70(8.514) + \$1,000(0.149)$$

$$= \$745$$

Therefore, the pretax cost of debt is 10 percent. Assuming a 40 percent tax rate, the after-tax cost is as follows:[5]

$$k_i = 10\%(1 - 0.4)$$

$$= 6\%$$

The tax benefits of interest deductibility are available only to firms that are making profits. For a firm losing money, the tax rate in Equation 12.4 is *zero*, and the after-tax cost, k_i, is the same as the pretax cost, k_d.

Cost of Preferred Stock

The cost of preferred stock to the firm is the rate of return required by investors on preferred stock issued by the company. Because many preferred stocks are perpetuities, it is possible to use the simplified preferred stock valuation model developed in Chapter 6:

$$P_0 = \frac{D_p}{k_p} \qquad (12.5)$$

[5] Whether a bond is sold at par or at a discount from par, the calculation of the after-tax cost of debt is the same because discounts and issue costs are amortized over the life of the issue.

where P_0 is the preferred stock price; D_p, the annual preferred dividend; and k_p, the investors' required rate of return. The cost of preferred stock, k_p, is given by the following equation:

$$k_p = \frac{D_p}{P_{net}} \tag{12.6}$$

In calculating preferred stock cost, the price that should be used, P_{net}, is the net proceeds to the firm; that is, the proceeds from the sale of the stock after subtracting *flotation costs*.

To illustrate, suppose Midwestern Airlines just issued 30 million shares of $2.75 cumulative preferred stock at a price to the public of $25 a share. Assuming flotation costs of $1 a share, the cost of preferred stock is calculated as follows:

$$k_p = \frac{\$2.75}{\$25 - \$1}$$

$$= 0.115, \text{ or } 11.5\%$$

Because payments by the firm to preferred stockholders are in the form of dividends, they are not tax deductible; therefore the after-tax cost of preferred stock is equal to the pretax rate.

An increasing number of preferred stock issues are callable, have a sinking fund redemption provision, or have a fixed maturity. In these cases, the computation of the cost of preferred stock financing is similar to that for bonds. For example, Carolina Power plans an offering of $50 par value preferred stock that will pay a $5.00 dividend per year. The preferred stock is expected to yield Carolina net proceeds of $46.40 per share after all issue costs. The preferred stock must be retired at its par value in 15 years. The cost of this preferred stock issue can be computed by solving for k_p in the following valuation model:

$$P_{net} = \$46.40 = \$5(\text{PVIFA}_{k_p,15}) + \$50(\text{PVIF}_{k_p,15})$$

Try

$$k_p = 11 \text{ percent}$$

$$\$46.40 = \$5(7.191) + 50(0.209)$$

$$= \$35.95 + \$10.45$$

$$\$46.40 = \$46.40$$

Therefore, k_p equals 11 percent for Carolina's anticipated preferred stock offering.

Preferred stock is similar to long-term debt in that both types of securities normally involve fixed, uniform payments per period to the holders. In general, investors are required to pay income taxes on both interest and dividends. However, the issuing company can deduct interest only from its taxable income. As a result, in most situations in which a profitable company (with a 34 percent marginal tax rate) is choosing to leverage with either debt or preferred stock, it will prefer to issue debt, because its after-tax cost normally is less than the cost of preferred stock.

Cost of Internal Equity Capital

Like the cost of debt and preferred stock, the cost of equity capital to the firm is the equilibrium rate of return required by the firm's common stock investors.

Firms raise equity capital in two ways:

■ *Internally*, through retained earnings.
■ *Externally*, through the sale of new common stock.

Some analysts and managers incorrectly assume that the cost of internal equity is zero. The opportunity cost concept makes it clear that this is an erroneous assumption. When funds are generated through the earnings of the firm, managers can either pay out these funds as dividends to common stockholders or the funds can be retained and reinvested in the firm. If the funds were paid out to stockholders, they could reinvest the funds elsewhere to earn an appropriate return, given the risk of the investment. Therefore, if managers decide to retain earnings and reinvest them in the firm, there must be investment opportunities in the firm offering a return equivalent to the returns available to common stockholders, on a risk-adjusted basis, in alternative investments.

The cost of internal equity to the firm is less than the cost of new common stock, because the sale of new stock requires the payment of flotation costs. The concept of the cost of internal equity (or simply equity, as it is commonly called) can be developed using several different approaches. The first considered here is based on the dividend valuation model.

Dividend Valuation Model Approach

Briefly reviewing from Chapter 7, the general dividend valuation model (or the dividend capitalization model, as it often is referred to) for common stock valuation is as follows:

$$P_0 = \sum_{t=1}^{\infty} \frac{D_t}{(1 + k_e)^t} \qquad (12.7)$$

where P_0 is the stock's present value or current market price; D_t, the dividend received in period t; and k_e, the return required by investors. This equation shows that in efficient capital markets k_e, the required return and thus the cost of equity capital, equates the present value of all expected future dividends with the current market price of the stock. In principle, the cost of equity capital can be calculated by solving Equation 12.7 for k_e. In practice, however, the expected future dividends are not known and cannot be estimated with the same degree of confidence as preferred stock dividends and debt interest. As a result, the theoretically correct general form of the dividend valuation model is not directly useful in calculating the cost of equity capital.

If the firm's future per-share dividends are expected to grow each period perpetually at a constant rate, g, the dividend valuation model can be written as follows:

$$P_0 = \sum_{t=1}^{\infty} \frac{D_0(1 + g)^t}{(1 + k_e)^t} \qquad (12.8)$$

where D_0 is the dividend in the current period ($t = 0$). Equation 12.8 can be transformed algebraically to the following equation:

$$P_0 = \frac{D_1}{k_e - g} \tag{12.9}$$

where $D_1 = D_0(1 + g)$. Note that, in Equation 12.9, k_e must be greater than g, the expected growth rate. As discussed in Chapter 7, the *constant growth valuation model* assumes that a firm's earnings, dividends, *and* stock price will grow at rate g. Thus g equates to the yearly price appreciation (capital gain). But the total return to stockholders, k_e, is composed of both the price appreciation *and* the dividend yield. Therefore g cannot be greater than or equal to k_e because it is only one of two components making up k_e.

Equation 12.9 can be rearranged to obtain an expression for calculating the cost of equity, assuming that dividends are expected to grow perpetually at a rate g per year:[6]

$$k_e = \frac{D_1}{P_0} + g \tag{12.10}$$

To illustrate the use of Equation 12.10, suppose the Fresno Company's common stock is currently selling at $25 a share. Its present dividend, D_0, is $2 a share, and the expected dividend growth rate is 7 percent. The investor's required return (that is, the firm's cost of equity) is calculated as follows:

$$k_e = \frac{\$2(1.07)}{\$25} + 0.07$$

$$= 0.156, \text{ or } 15.6\%$$

In addition to being used for the constant growth case, the dividend valuation model also can be used to estimate the cost of equity capital for the no-growth case. If a stock pays a current dividend that is expected to remain constant perpetually, the appropriate valuation model follows:

$$P_0 = \frac{D}{k_e} \tag{12.11}$$

and the cost of equity capital is calculated as follows:

$$k_e = \frac{D}{P_0} \tag{12.12}$$

To illustrate, suppose the Mountaineer Railroad pays a dividend of $1.50 that is expected to remain constant forever. The firm's common stock presently is selling at $10 a share. Using these figures, the cost of equity capital is calculated as follows:

[6] The relevant growth rate is the rate expected by investors. This normally is estimated by examining projected future growth rates provided by security analysts such as Value Line, Merrill Lynch, and IBES. A further discussion of this issue is presented at the end of this section.

$$k_e = \frac{D}{P_0}$$

$$= \frac{\$1.50}{\$10}$$

$$= 0.15, \text{ or } 15\%$$

The dividend valuation model also can be used to value common stocks expected to pay dividends that grow at variable rates in the future. For example, a young high technology company could be expected to show a period of relatively rapid growth followed by a continuing period of more normal growth. Using the dividend valuation model and defining g_1 as an above-normal growth rate expected by investors and security analysts over the first m years and g_2 as a normal, perpetual, expected growth rate beginning in year $m + 1$, the current stock price is determined as follows:

$$P_0 = \sum_{t=1}^{m} \frac{D_0(1 + g_1)^t}{(1 + k_e)^t} + \frac{P_m}{(1 + k_e)^m} \qquad (12.13)$$

$$= \sum_{t=1}^{m} \frac{D_0(1 + g_1)^t}{(1 + k_e)^t} + \frac{1}{(1 + k_e)^m} \times \frac{D_{m+1}}{k_e - g_2} \qquad (12.14)$$

The cost of equity capital can be estimated by solving Equation 12.14 for k_e by trial and error.

For example, Avtec Corporation is a rapidly growing producer of microcircuit boards used in the aerospace industry. Its stock is currently selling for $10.95 per share. Current dividends, D_0, are $1.00 per share and are expected to grow at a rate of 10 percent per year over the next 4 years and 6 percent annually thereafter. Avtec's cost of internal equity, k_e, can be found by solving Equation 12.14 as follows:

$$\$10.95 = \sum_{t=1}^{4} \frac{\$1.00(1 + 0.10)^t}{(1 + k_e)^t} + \frac{1}{(1 + k_e)^4} \times \frac{D_5}{k_e - 0.06}$$

$$= \frac{\$1.10}{(1 + k_e)^1} + \frac{\$1.21}{(1 + k_e)^2} + \frac{\$1.33}{(1 + k_e)^3} + \frac{\$1.46}{(1 + k_e)^4} + \frac{1}{(1 + k_e)^4} \times \frac{\$1.55}{k_e - 0.06}$$

$$= \$1.10(\text{PVIF}_{k_e,1}) + \$1.21(\text{PVIF}_{k_e,2}) + \$1.33(\text{PVIF}_{k_e,3}) + \$1.46 (\text{PVIF}_{k_e,4}) + (\text{PVIF}_{k_e,4}) \frac{\$1.55}{k_e - 0.06}$$

A trial value of 17 percent for k_e yields the following:

$$\$10.95 = \$1.10(0.855) + \$1.21(0.731) + \$1.33(0.624)$$

$$+ \$1.46(0.534) + 0.534\left(\frac{\$1.55}{0.17 - 0.06}\right)$$

$$= \$10.95$$

Thus, Avtec's cost of equity is 17 percent.

In principle, the general dividend valuation model approach can be used to estimate the cost of equity capital for any expected dividend pattern. In practice, many stocks not only have exhibited rather constant growth rates in the past, but look as though they will continue to do so in the future. For these stocks the constant growth form of the dividend capitalization model is appropriate, and the expected growth rate often can be estimated in the manner discussed in the next section.

Issues in Implementation

Dividend valuation models (sometimes also referred to as DCF models) frequently are used in the calculation of a firm's cost of equity capital. In implementing these models, the analyst must obtain an estimate of the growth rate(s) in earnings and dividends (and stock price) expected by investors. Where can these investor expectations be obtained?

Investors form expectations about future growth rates based upon past realized growth, current earnings and retention rates, expected future earnings rates (such as the return on equity), and conditions in the markets that the firm serves. These factors often are well summarized in the form of analysts' estimates of future growth rates. Analysts' forecasts may be viewed as the best market- and investor-available summary of all of the factors that determine future growth rates. There are two reasons for this. First, a growing body of research supports the conclusion that analysts' estimates of future earnings growth rates are very accurate—consistently more accurate than estimates provided from any other forecasting model.[7] Second, another body of research has confirmed that analysts' forecasts outperform extrapolative forecasts in explaining share prices.[8]

Analyst forecasts are available from a number of sources. They can be obtained from individual brokerage houses and investment advisory services, such as Merrill Lynch, Salomon Brothers, Shearson Lehman Hutton, Goldman Sachs and Value Line. In addition, the New York brokerage firm of Lynch, Jones and Ryan has developed a service called the Institutional Brokers Estimate System (IBES). IBES summarizes the short- and long-term earnings forecasts made by over 2,400 analysts from more than 130 brokerage firms throughout the United States. IBES covers the stocks of more than 3,400 major firms. IBES reports tell the user how many analysts follow a particular stock, the mean and median earnings per share estimates for the next quarter, the next fiscal year, and the long-term (5-year) expected rate of growth in earnings for the firm. The IBES reports also show the highest and lowest estimate for each period, the number of analysts who have revised their forecasts upward and downward, and the amount of variation that exists among the forecasts provided by the different analysts. IBES reports are readily available at a low cost on computer time sharing services such as Compuserve.

Capital Asset Pricing Model (CAPM) Approach

Another technique that can be used to estimate the cost of equity capital is the *Capital Asset Pricing Model* (CAPM), discussed in Chapter 8. The CAPM formally describes the risk-required return tradeoff for securities. Equation 12.1 illustrates that the rate of return required by investors consists of a

---

[7] See, for example, L. D. Brown and M. S. Rozeff, "The Superiority of Analyst Forecasts as Measures of Expectations: Evidence from Earnings," *Journal of Finance* (March 1978): 1–16; M. S. Rozeff, "Predicting Long-Term Earnings Growth: Comparisons of Expected Return Models, Submartingales and Value Line Analysts," *Journal of Forecasting* (December, 1983): 425–435; R. C. Moyer, R. E. Chatfield, and G. D. Kelley, "The Accuracy of Long-Term Earnings Forecasts in the Electric Utility Industry," *International Journal of Forecasting*, no. 3 (1985): 241–252; and R. C. Moyer, R. E. Chatfield, and P. Sisneros, "The Accuracy of Long-Term Earnings Forecasts for Industrial Firms," *Quarterly Journal of Business and Economics* (Summer 1989).

[8] See, for example, J. G. Cragg and B. G. Malkiel, *Expectations and the Structure of Share Prices* (Chicago: University of Chicago Press, 1982); and R. Harris, "Using Analysts' Growth Forecasts to Estimate Shareholder Required Rates of Return," *Financial Management* (Spring 1986): 58–67.

risk-free return, r_f, plus a premium compensating the investor for bearing the risk. This risk premium varies from stock to stock.

Obviously, less risk is associated with an investment in a stable stock, such as AT&T, than in the stock of a small wildcat oil drilling firm, W. As a result, an investor in the drilling stock requires a higher return than the AT&T investor. Figure 12-3 illustrates the difference in required rates of return (or the cost of internal equity) for the two securities. The relationship illustrated in this figure is the *security market line* (SML). The SML depicts the risk-required return relationship in the market for all securities.

Recall from Chapter 8 that the security market line is defined as follows:[9]

$$k_j = r_f + b_j(k_m - r_f) \qquad \textbf{(12.15)}$$

where k_j = the required rate of return on any security j; r_f = the expected risk-free rate; b_j = the beta (systematic risk) measure for security j; and k_m = the expected return on the market portfolio. Hence, the value $k_m - r_f$ equals the market risk premium (the slope of the SML), or the risk premium applicable to a stock of average (beta = 1.0) risk.

The SML concept is based on investors' expectations regarding a security's risk and return characteristics. Required returns for any individual security also are dependent on expected future levels of interest rates and the expected return on the market as a whole. These expected values are determined as follows:

■ *The risk-free rate (r_f).* The value for r_f that is most frequently used in computing the required return for a security is the 3- or 6-month U.S.

[9] In Chapter 8 we used a hat ($\wedge$) over the r_f and k_m variables to indicate these are *expected* values. For simplicity, the hats are dropped here, but it should be kept in mind that we are still dealing with expected values for these variables.

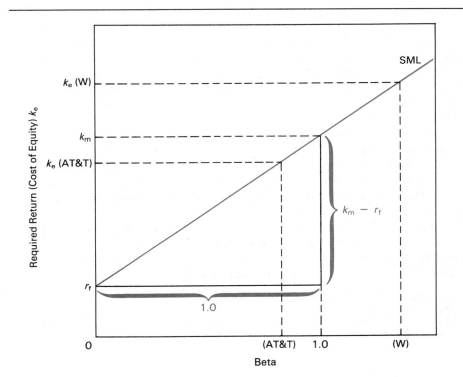

FIGURE 12-3

Security Market Line (SML)

Treasury bill rate. (Some practitioners prefer to use a long-term government bond rate instead.)

■ *The expected market return (k_m).* The expected market return is the return investors expect to earn in the future on stocks with an average beta of 1.0. The average holding period return for stocks during the time period from 1926 to 1987 was about 12.0 percent per year.[10] These actual returns have varied substantially, depending on the holding periods assumed. The average market risk premium measured relative to Treasury bill rates has been 8.3 percent over the past 61 years. The average market risk premium measured relative to long-term government bond yields has been 6.8 percent over the same period.[11] These risk premiums may be used for the market risk premium ($k_m - r_f$) in Equation 12.15. Remember that if the 8.3 percent market risk premium is used, then the risk-free rate (the first term on the right-hand side of Equation 12.15) must be the short-term Treasury bill rate. When the 6.8 percent market risk premium is used, then the risk-free rate must be the long-term government bond rate, such as the yield on 20-year U.S. government bonds.

■ *The firm's beta, b_j* Beta normally is estimated by using historic values of the relationship between a security's returns and the market returns. In Chapter 8 we illustrated the computation of the beta for General Motors. The *Value Line Investment Survey* and brokerage firms such as Merrill Lynch regularly compute and provide betas.[12]

Consider the following example. In early 1989 Value Line reported a beta estimate for Apple Computer of 1.35. If 3-month Treasury bill rates are 8.5 percent, Apple's cost of equity capital may be computed as follows:

$$k_e = r_f + b_j(k_m - r_f)$$

$$= 8.5\% + 1.35(8.3\%)$$

$$= 19.7\%$$

When it seems likely that the basic risk characteristics of a firm will change significantly—perhaps because of a merger or product line expansion or contraction—the historic beta may be of little use as a forecast of the firm's future systematic risk characteristics. Under these circumstances, different methods have to be used to estimate the required future returns for the security.

The SML concept is one more tool that may be used in computing the firm's cost of equity capital, k_e. If all the parameters required of the model are correctly estimated (r_f, $k_m - r_f$, and b_j), the model should give a reasonably accurate estimate of k_e. Many analysts find it useful to compute k_e in more than one way to arrive at a consensus about the rate of return investors require on a security.

Recall from Chapter 8 that the beta measure of risk considers only the systematic risk or market risk of a stock. Poorly diversified investors may be more interested in total risk than in systematic risk. When this is true, the CAPM may understate returns required by those investors.

---

[10] *Stock, Bonds, Bills and Inflation: 1988 Yearbook*, p. 25.

[11] Ibid., p. 81.

[12] Because of statistical biases inherent in the historic computation of betas, these reported betas often are adjusted to provide a better estimate of future betas.

Risk Premium on Debt and Other Approaches for Estimating the Cost of Equity Capital

This subsection begins by considering a shortcut method of estimating the cost of equity capital based on actual historic returns and ends by discussing non-dividend-paying stocks.

Studies analyzing the historical returns earned by common stock investors have found that the holding period returns from average risk common stock investments over the past 61 years have averaged 6.8 percentage points higher than holding period returns on corporate debt issues.[13] Therefore the cost of equity capital for an average risk company (a firm with a beta of about 1.0) can be estimated by adding approximately 6.8 percentage points to the company's current cost of debt. For companies with a less than average level of systematic risk, such as electric utilities (electric utility betas average about 0.7), a risk premium over the company's current cost of long-term debt of 3 to 4 percentage points has been found to be approximately correct. For companies with more than an average level of systematic risk, a risk premium in excess of 6.8 percentage points is warranted. Many analysts use this shortcut method as a reference. Whenever possible, however, the other more precise methods should be used.

For stocks that do not pay dividends, the dividend capitalization model obviously is an inappropriate valuation model and therefore cannot be used directly to determine the cost of equity capital. Investors in non-dividend-paying stocks expect to sell the stock in the future at a higher price than the present price, realizing a capital gain. Investors' expectations about the future price are incorporated into the following valuation model:[14]

$$P_0 = \frac{P_t}{(1 + k_e)^t} \qquad (12.16)$$

where P_t is the expected stock price at time t. In principle, a firm could use this valuation model to determine its cost of equity capital. In practice, however, this would be difficult to do, because the company probably has no way of confidently determining the P_t expectations of investors. Instead, the cost of equity capital for non-dividend-paying stocks normally is determined either by using the Capital Asset Pricing Model, the risk premium on debt approach, or by estimating k_e for comparable dividend-paying stocks in their industry.

For many stocks the cost of equity capital obtained from the dividend capitalization model, the risk premium on debt approach, and the CAPM generally will be in approximate agreement with each other. If substantial differences do exist, further analysis is required. The calculation of the cost of equity capital requires the exercise of good judgment by the financial manager.

Cost of External Equity Capital

The cost of external equity is greater than the cost of internal equity for the following reasons:

[13] *Stock, Bonds, Bills and Inflation*, p. 74.
[14] If investors in a non-dividend-paying stock expected the company to begin paying dividends at some future date, a form of the dividend capitalization model could be constructed to reflect these expectations.

■ Flotation costs associated with new shares usually are high enough that they cannot realistically be ignored.

■ The selling price of the new shares to the public normally is set less than the market price of the stock before the announcement of the new issue. Before any announcement, the current market price of a stock usually represents an equilibrium between supply and demand. If supply is increased (all other things being equal), the new equilibrium price will be lower.

In addition, Masulis and Trueman have argued that retained earnings are a cheaper source of funds than the sale of new equity because retention defers the payment of taxable dividends to shareholders and, therefore, reduces the present value of taxes that must be paid by shareholders.[15]

When a firm's future dividend payments are expected to grow at a constant rate of g per period forever, the cost of external equity, k_e', is defined as follows:

$$k_e' = \frac{D_1}{P_{net}} + g \qquad (12.17)$$

where P_{net} is the net proceeds to the firm on a per-share basis.[16] To illustrate, consider the Fresno Company example used in the "Dividend Valuation Model Approach" section, where $P_0 = \$25$, $D_0 = \$2$, $g = 1.07$, and $k_e = 15.6$ percent.

Assuming that new common stock can be sold at $24 to net the company $23 a share after flotation costs, k_e' is calculated as follows:

$$k_e' = \frac{D_1}{P_{net}} + g$$

$$= \frac{\$2.14}{\$23} + 0.07$$

$$= 0.163, \text{ or } 16.3\%$$

Because of the relatively high cost of newly issued equity, many companies try to avoid this means of raising capital. The question of whether a firm should raise capital with newly issued common stock depends on its investment opportunities.[17]

Table 12-1 summarizes the cost of capital formulas developed in the preceding sections.

■ MARGINAL COSTS ARE THE RELEVANT CAPITAL COSTS

Firms calculate their cost of capital in order to determine a discount rate to use for evaluating proposed capital expenditure projects. Recall that the

[15] Masulis, R. W., and B. Trueman. "Corporate Investment and Dividend Decisions under Differential Personal Taxation," *Journal of Financial and Quantitative Analysis* 23 (1988).
[16] An alternative approach to treat flotation costs is to allocate the dollar amount of these costs to individual projects, thus increasing the project cost. When this procedure is used, no adjustment to capital costs is required. This procedure may be superior (from a theoretical perspective) to the cost of capital adjustment procedure, but it is difficult to implement and not widely used.
[17] This discussion is continued in the section on determining the optimal capital budget.

Formulas for Computing Component Costs		TABLE 12-1

Cost of debt

$k_i = k_d(1 - T)$

where:

k_d = pretax cost of debt

= yield to maturity on a new bond issue when the current price of the bond is set equal to the net proceeds to the issuing company

Cost of preferred stock

$$k_p = \frac{\text{Preferred dividend}}{\text{Net proceeds to the company}} \qquad \text{(for perpetual preferred stock)}$$

$$= \frac{D_p}{P_{net}}$$

Cost of internal common equity

1. Dividend capitalization model approach—the case of perpetual dividends growing at a constant rate:

$$k_e = \frac{\text{Next year's expected dividend}}{\text{Common stock price}} + \text{Expected dividend growth rate}$$

$$= \frac{D_1}{P_0} + g$$

2. Capital Asset Pricing Model Approach:

k_e = Risk-free return + Risk premium

$$= r_f + b_j(k_m - r_f)$$

Cost of external common equity

$$k_e' = \frac{\text{Next year's expected dividend}}{\text{Net proceeds per share to the company}} + \text{Expected dividend growth rate}$$

$$= \frac{D_1}{P_{net}} + g$$

purpose of capital expenditure analysis basically is to determine which *proposed* projects the firm should *actually* undertake. Therefore, it is logical that *the capital whose cost is measured and compared with the expected benefits from the proposed projects should be the next or marginal capital the firm raises.*

As we saw in Chapter 9, the capital budgeting process involves an extension of the marginal analysis principle from economics. The marginal revenue (internal rate of return) from a project is compared with the marginal cost of funds needed to finance the project. The marginal cost of funds is the cost of the next increments of capital raised by the firm. Hence, the costs of the various capital funding components (debt, preferred stock, and common equity) must be their marginal costs. Historic *average* capital costs are not relevant for making new (marginal) resource allocation decisions.

When computing the marginal cost of the various component capital sources, companies typically estimate the component costs they anticipate encountering (paying) during the coming year. If capital costs change significantly during the year, it may be necessary to recompute the new capital costs and use the new estimates when evaluating projects from that time forward. Under most circumstances a semiannual or annual computation of marginal capital costs is sufficient.

SMALL BUSINESS CONCERNS:
THE COST OF CAPITAL

Small firms have a difficult time attracting capital to support their investment programs. Owners of small firms are reluctant to sell common stock because they do not want to lose voting control in the company. When shares are sold, many small firms create two classes of stock, such as Class A and Class B. The Class A stock is the one that is traded most extensively in the capital markets. Class A stock usually receives a higher dividend than Class B. In contrast, Class B stock, often held by the company's founders, has greater voting power than Class A stock. In this way capital can be raised without losing voting control.

Many firms are so small that it is nearly impossible to raise funds by selling common stock. If stock can be sold, investors often will pay much less for these shares than they would for similar firms that are larger and have their stock traded regularly on an organized exchange or over-the-counter. Flotation costs for common stock sales of small firms may exceed 20 percent of the issue size. As a consequence, the cost of equity capital tends to be significantly higher for small firms than it is for larger firms. Because of the limited access to the capital markets for new equity, small firms tend to retain a much larger portion of their earnings to fund future growth than larger firms.

Similarly, the sources of debt capital to small firms also are limited. Bonds and debentures cannot be sold publicly until a firm has grown to a relatively large size. Before reaching a size that will permit it to sell securities publicly the small firm will have to rely upon the following sources for debt funds:

- The owners' own funds and loans from friends.
- Loans from commercial banks and savings and loan associations.
- Small Business Administration loans.
- Commercial finance company loans.
- Leasing companies.
- Venture capital firms that normally demand some equity interest in the firm through conversion features or warrants (discussed in Chapter 17).
- Private placements of debt issues with insurance companies and large corporations, often with a conversion feature or warrants.

Generally, the cost of both debt and equity capital is significantly higher for small firms than larger firms. The high cost of capital puts small firms at a competitive disadvantage relative to large firms in raising funds needed for expansion.

Conceptually, computing the cost of capital for a small, closely held firm is no different than for a large, publicly traded firm. The same models of valuation apply to small firms as for large firms. In practice, however, there often are serious difficulties in developing confident estimates of the cost of capital for small firms. Computing the cost of straight debt and preferred stock (nonconvertible and without attached warrants) is relatively easy. However, when debt and preferred stock securities are convertible or have attached warrants, an analyst must make an estimate about the time and conditions under which these securities will be converted into common stock or when the warrants to purchase common stock will be exercised.

In the case of common stock, there often is no ready market for the stock. Hence, it may not be possible to make confident estimates of the stock price when computing the cost of equity. Also, because many small firms pay little or no dividends, applying the dividend valuation model is more difficult. As a consequence, when computing the cost of equity for small firms, analysts often must compute the cost of equity for a group of larger, publicly traded companies in the same line of business and with a similar financial risk (as measured by the capital structure), and then add an additional risk premium reflective of the perceived increased risk due to reduced marketability and liquidity of the small firm's stock, and any differential in business and financial risk.

WEIGHTED COST OF CAPITAL

Firms usually raise funds in "lumpy" amounts; for example, a firm may sell $50 million in bonds to finance capital expenditures at one point in time, and it may use retained earnings or proceeds from the sale of stock to finance capital expenditures later on. In spite of this tendency to raise funds in lumpy amounts from various sources at different points in time, the weighted (or composite) cost of funds, not the cost of any particular component of funds, is the cost we are interested in for capital budgeting purposes. Another way of saying this is that *it generally is incorrect to associate any particular source of financing with a particular project;* that is, the investment and the financing decisions should be separate.[18]

Consider, for example, the case of a firm that is financed 50 percent with debt and 50 percent with equity. The after-tax cost of equity is 16 percent, and the after-tax cost of debt is 10 percent. The firm has two plants, A and B, which are identical in every respect. The manager of Plant A proposes to acquire a new automated packaging machine costing $10 million. A bank has offered to loan the firm the needed $10 million at a rate that will give the firm a 10 percent after-tax cost. The internal rate of return for this project has been estimated to be 12 percent. Because the rate of return exceeds the cost of funds (debt) used to finance the machine, the manager of Plant A argues that the investment should be made.

The manager of Plant B now argues that she, too, should be allowed to make a similar investment. Unfortunately, she is reminded that the firm has a target capital structure of 50 percent debt and 50 percent equity and that her investment will have to be financed with equity in order for the firm to maintain its target capital structure. Because the cost of equity is 16 percent and the project only offers a 12 percent return, the investment is denied for Plant B.

The point of this illustration is that two economically identical projects were treated very differently, simply because the method of financing the projects was tied to the accept–reject decision. To avoid problems of this type, the capital expenditure decision usually is based on a composite capital cost—that is, each project is assumed to be financed with debt and equity in the proportion in which it appears in the target capital structure. In this case, the composite cost of capital is 13 percent, computed as follows:

---

[18] This statement generally is true; however, there are exceptions. For example, some projects may possess a higher "debt capacity" than is present for the firm as a whole. This may be due to a different level of business risk. The evaluation of mergers frequently considers the debt capacity of the to-be-acquired firm. Hence, the financing of the project may be considered along with the investment decision itself.

Source of Capital	After-Tax Cost	Proportion	Composite Cost
Debt	10%	0.5	5%
Equity	16	0.5	8

Weighted cost of capital = 13%

In this example neither project should be accepted, because the cost of capital exceeds the projects' expected rates of return.

Accordingly, as a firm evaluates proposed capital expenditure projects, it normally does not specify the proportions of debt, preferred stock, and (common) equity financing for each individual project. Instead, each project is presumed to be financed with the same proportion of debt, preferred stock, and equity contained in the company's target capital structure.

Thus, the appropriate after-tax cost of capital figure to be used in capital budgeting not only is based on the next (marginal) capital to be raised but also is weighted by the proportions of the capital components in the firm's long-range target capital structure. Therefore this figure is called the *weighted*, or *overall*, *cost of capital*.

The general expression for calculating the weighted cost of capital, k_a, follows:

$$k_a = \begin{pmatrix} \text{Equity} \\ \text{fraction} \\ \text{of} \\ \text{capital} \\ \text{structure} \end{pmatrix} \begin{pmatrix} \text{Marginal} \\ \text{cost} \\ \text{of} \\ \text{equity} \end{pmatrix} + \begin{pmatrix} \text{Debt} \\ \text{fraction} \\ \text{of} \\ \text{capital} \\ \text{structure} \end{pmatrix} \begin{pmatrix} \text{Marginal} \\ \text{cost} \\ \text{of} \\ \text{debt} \end{pmatrix}$$

$$+ \begin{pmatrix} \text{Preferred} \\ \text{fraction} \\ \text{of} \\ \text{capital} \\ \text{structure} \end{pmatrix} \begin{pmatrix} \text{Marginal} \\ \text{cost} \\ \text{of} \\ \text{preferred} \\ \text{stock} \end{pmatrix} \quad \text{(12.18)}$$

$$= \left(\frac{E}{E + B + P_f}\right)(k_e) + \left(\frac{B}{E + B + P_f}\right)(k_i) + \left(\frac{P_f}{E + B + P_f}\right)(k_p)$$

where B is debt, P_f is preferred stock, and E is equity in the target capital structure.

To illustrate, suppose a company has a current (and target) capital structure of 60 percent equity, 30 percent debt, and 10 percent preferred stock. (The proportions of debt, equity, and preferred stock should be the proportions in which the firm intends to raise funds in the future.) For a firm that is not planning a change in its target capital structure, these proportions should be based on the current *market value weights* of the individual components (debt, preferred stock, and common equity). The company plans to finance next year's capital budget with $60 million of retained earnings (k_e = 15 percent), $30 million of long-term debt (k_d = 10 percent), and $10 million of new preferred stock (k_p = 11 percent). Assume a 40 percent marginal tax rate. Using these figures, the weighted cost of capital being raised to finance next year's capital budget is calculated as follows:

$$k_a = 0.60 \times 15.0\% + 0.30 \times 10.0\% \times (1 - 0.40) + 0.10 \times 11\%$$

$$= 11.9\%$$

Determining the Weighted (Marginal) Cost of Capital Schedule

In the previous section the computation of the weighted (marginal) cost of capital was based on the assumption that the firm would get equity funds only from internal sources, that all debt could be acquired at a 10 percent pretax cost, and that all preferred stock could be acquired at an 11 percent cost. This procedure for computing the weighted (marginal) cost of capital must be modified if the firm anticipates selling new common stock (having a higher component cost) or issuing additional increments of debt securities at successively higher costs to finance its capital budget.

To illustrate, suppose the Major Foods Corporation is developing its capital expenditure plans for the coming year. The company's schedule of potential capital expenditure projects for next year is as follows:

Project	Amount (in millions of dollars)	Internal Rate of Return
A	$4.0	13.8%
B	8.0	13.5
C	6.0	12.5
D	5.0	12.0
E	8.0	11.0
F	4.0	10.0

These projects all are closely related to the company's present business and have the same degree of risk as its existing assets.

The firm's current capital structure (as well as its targeted future capital structure) consists of 40 percent debt, 10 percent preferred stock, and 50 percent common equity measured on the basis of the current market value of debt, preferred stock, and equity in the capital structure. Table 12-2 shows the current balance sheet for Major Foods. Major Foods can raise up to $5 million in debt funds at a pretax cost of 9 percent; debt amounts exceeding $5 million will cost 10 percent. Preferred stock can be sold at an after-tax cost of 10 percent. Major Foods' marginal tax rate is 40 percent.

Major Foods expects to generate $10 million of retained earnings over the coming year. Its present dividend rate, D_0, is $2 per share. The firm's common stock now is selling at $25 per share, and new common stock can be sold to net the firm $24 per share.[19]

Over the past several years Major Foods' earnings and dividends have grown at an average of 7 percent per year, and this growth rate is expected

[19] The net proceeds per share depend on the number of shares sold. As a very general rule, underwriters are reluctant to sell new shares in an amount that exceeds 10 to 15 percent of a company's existing shares.

Balance Sheet for Major Foods (in millions of dollars)

Assets		Liabilities and Equity	
Current assets	$100	Current liabilities	$ 50
Fixed assets	30	Long-term debt	32 (40%)
Total assets	$130	Preferred stock	8 (10%)
		Common equity	40 (50%)
		Total liabilities and equity	$130

to continue for the foreseeable future. The company's dividend payout ratio has been, and is expected to remain, more or less constant.

Given this information, Major Foods' weighted (marginal) cost of capital can be calculated for the coming year:

■ **Step 1: Calculate the cost of capital for each individual component— the cost of debt, the cost of preferred stock, and the cost of equity.**

Cost of debt:

$$k_i = k_d(1 - T) = 9.0 \times 0.6 = 5.4\% \text{ for the first \$5 million of debt}$$
$$k_i = k_d(1 - T) = 10.0 \times 0.6 = 6.0\% \text{ for debt exceeding \$5 million}$$

Cost of preferred stock:

$$k_p = 10\% \text{ (given)}$$

Cost of common equity:

Internal (retained earnings—$10 million):

$$k_e = \frac{D_0 (1 + g)}{P_0} + g$$

$$= \frac{\$2(1.07)}{\$25} + 0.07 = 0.156, \text{ or } 15.6\%$$

External (new common stock—amounts above $10 million):

$$k_e' = \frac{\$2(1.07)}{\$24} + 0.07 = 0.159, \text{ or } 15.9\%$$

■ **Step 2: Compute the weighted (marginal) cost of capital for each increment of capital raised.**

Major Foods should raise funds in proportion to its target capital structure from its lowest cost sources first. In this case, these sources are retained earnings (15.6 percent after-tax cost), preferred stock (10 percent after-tax cost), and the first $5 million in debt (5.4 percent after-tax cost). When these sources are exhausted, the company should consider using the higher cost sources—external equity (15.9 percent after-tax cost) and additional debt (6.0 percent after-tax cost) together with preferred stock.

How much total financing—retained earnings, preferred stock, and debt—can be done before the $5 million in low-cost debt is exhausted and Major must acquire additional debt funds at the higher cost? Because we know that the target capital structure consists of 40 percent debt, the total financing, X, that this will support is equal to the amount of low-cost debt available divided by the debt fraction in the capital structure:

$$X = \frac{\text{Amount of low cost debt available}}{\text{Debt fraction of capital structure}}$$

$$= \frac{\$5 \text{ million}}{0.40}$$

$$= \$12.5 \text{ million}$$

This $12.5 million level represents a break point in the marginal cost of capital schedule. *Break points* delineate the levels of financing where the weighted cost of capital increases due to an increase in the cost of one component source of capital; that is, debt, preferred stock, or common equity.

Break points can be determined by dividing the amount of funds available from each financing source at a fixed cost by the target capital structure proportion for that financing source. Thus, we saw in the Major Foods example that the $5 million of debt, with an after-tax cost of 5.4 percent, would support total financing of $12.5 million. Beyond $12.5 million in total financing, the weighted (marginal) cost of capital will rise, because higher cost debt (6.0 percent) now must be used. Of this $12.5 million in total financing, $5 million will be debt, $1.25 million (10 percent of the total) will be preferred stock, and $6.25 million will be retained earnings. The cost of this first block of funds using Equation 12.18 is as follows:

$$k_a = 0.50 \times 15.6\% + 0.40 \times 5.4\% + 0.10 \times 10\%$$
$$= 10.96\%$$

The amount of available retained earnings also determines a break point. The $10 million of retained earnings will support total financing of $20 million ($10 million / 0.5). Therefore a new break point occurs at a total financing level of $20 million. Beyond that point, the weighted cost of capital increases due to the higher cost (15.9 percent) of external equity. Thus the second block of financing totals $7.5 million ($20 million equity break point minus $12.5 million debt financing break point).

This $7.5 million block of funds represents the size of the second lowest-cost block of funds. Of this $7.5 million in financing, $3.75 million will be retained earnings, $0.75 million will be preferred stock, and $3 million will be debt. The cost of this second block of funds will be as follows:

$$k_a = 0.50 \times 15.6\% + 0.40 \times 6.0\% + 0.10 \times 10\%$$
$$= 11.20\%$$

Beyond the second block, all additional funds raised will be with high-cost debt, new common stock, and preferred stock. The weighted cost of these funds is as follows:

$$k_a = 0.50 \times 15.9\% + 0.40 \times 6.0\% + 0.10 \times 10\%$$
$$= 11.35\%$$

Figure 12-4 provides a graph of the weighted (marginal) cost of capital schedule for Major Foods.

The weighted (marginal) cost of capital schedule can now be used to determine the optimal capital budget for Major Foods. This is illustrated in the next section.

DETERMINING THE OPTIMAL CAPITAL BUDGET

The *optimal capital budget* can be determined by comparing the expected project returns to the company's marginal cost of capital schedule. This is

FIGURE 12-4

**Weighted (Marginal)
Cost of Capital
Schedule for Major
Foods**

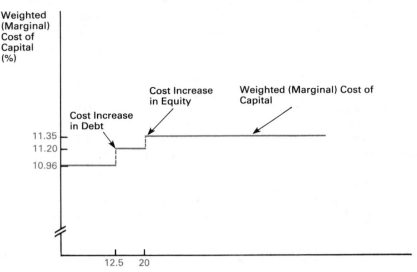

Funds Raised (in Millions of Dollars)

accomplished by first plotting the returns expected from the proposed capital expenditure projects against the cumulative funds required. The resulting graph is called an *investment opportunity curve*. Next, the previously calculated k_a for the three capital "packages" are combined to determine the company's *marginal cost of capital curve*. The optimal capital budget is indicated by the point at which the investment opportunity curve and the marginal cost of capital curve intersect, as shown in Figure 12-5.

Specifically, the Major Foods Corporation's optimal capital budget totals $23 million and includes Projects A, B, C, and D. Projects E and F are excluded, because their returns are expected to be below the 11.35 percent cost of funds. Acceptance of Projects E and F would result in a decrease in the firm's value. In principle, the optimal capital budget maximizes the value of the firm.

▆▆▆▆ RISK AND THE OPTIMAL CAPITAL BUDGET

The procedure for determining the optimal capital budget discussed in the preceding section assumes that all projects being considered are of equal risk with the average risk of the firm. Indeed, whenever the weighted cost of capital is used for capital project evaluation the assumption is being made that the capital project has a level of risk equal to the average risk of the firm. If this is not the case, one of the capital budgeting under risk techniques discussed in Chapter 11 must be incorporated into the procedure described.

▆▆▆▆ THE COST OF DEPRECIATION-GENERATED FUNDS

One large source of funds for many firms is funds generated from depreciation. Of course, depreciation per se does not generate cash. Rather, depreciation simply is a noncash expense charged against income. Therefore

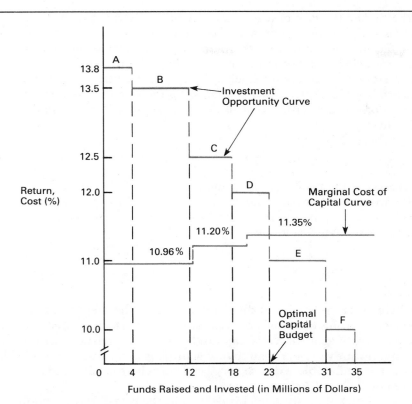

FIGURE 12-5

**Determining the
Optimal Capital
Budget**

Funds Raised and Invested (in Millions of Dollars)

a firm's reported net income normally will understate the amount of cash flow generated by the firm during a given time period. To adjust net income for the cash flow effect of depreciation, the amount of depreciation must be added to net income after taxes. It is in this sense that depreciation represents a source of funds. Also, some firms may generate funds from the sale of assets from time to time. What is the cost of these funds? Because the firm always has the option to either reinvest these funds in the firm or to return them to the stockholders as dividends and to retire outstanding debt, the appropriate opportunity cost of these funds is the firm's weighted (marginal) cost of capital, before considering new stock flotation costs.

With respect to the marginal cost of capital schedule in Figure 12-5, it is generally agreed that these funds have an opportunity cost equal to the first "block" of funds; that is, 10.6 percent. If $10 million in depreciation-generated funds were available, the first block of funds would increase from $12.5 million to $22.5 million, and all other blocks also would be shifted to the right by $10 million.

▬▬ SUMMARY

■ A firm's *cost of capital* is defined as the rate the firm has to pay for the debt, preferred stock, common stock, and/or retained earnings it uses to finance its new investments in assets. The cost of capital is the rate of return required by investors in the firm's securities. Cost of capital also can be thought of as the minimum rate of return required on new investments of average risk undertaken by the firm.

■ The higher the risk of a security, the higher is the return required by investors. In general, common stock is more risky than preferred stock, preferred stock is more risky than corporate debt securities, and corporate debt securities are more risky than government debt securities. Investors' required returns generally decrease in the same order.

■ A firm's pretax *cost of debt capital*, k_d, is the rate of return required by investors. The after-tax cost of debt, k_i, issued at par is calculated as follows:

$$k_i = k_d(1 - T) = \text{Coupon interest rate } (1 - T)$$

where T is the firm's marginal tax rate.

■ A firm's *cost of preferred stock*, k_p, is the rate of return required by the preferred stock investors. In the case of perpetual preferred stock, the cost is calculated as follows:

$$k_p = \frac{D_p}{P_{net}}$$

where D_p is the preferred dividend and P_{net} is the preferred stock price net of flotation costs on new issues. Preferred stock is used relatively infrequently as a source of capital, because its after-tax cost normally is significantly greater than that of debt. This is because interest on debt is a tax-deductible expense for the firm, whereas dividends on stock are not.

■ A firm's *cost of equity capital* is defined as the rate of return required by its common stock investors. Equity capital can be raised *internally* through retained earnings and *externally* through the sale of new common stock.

■ A firm's *cost of internal equity* can be determined by the dividend valuation model, the Capital Asset Pricing Model (CAPM), or the risk premium on debt approach. Using the dividend valuation model and assuming that dividends grow perpetually at a rate of g per year, the following equation for calculating the cost of equity capital, k_e, is obtained:

$$k_e = \frac{D_1}{P_0} + g$$

More complex calculations are required if the constant growth assumption does not hold. Using the CAPM, the cost of equity capital can be calculated as follows:

$$k_e = r_f + b(k_m - r_f)$$

where r_f is the risk-free rate; b (beta) is the relative measure of the stock's return volatility; and $(k_m - r_f)$ is the market risk premium.

■ A firm's *cost of external equity*, k_e', when dividends are expected to grow perpetually at a constant rate, is as follows:

$$k_e' = \frac{D_1}{P_{net}} + g$$

where P_{net} is the net proceeds to the firm on a per-share basis.

■ Firms normally use an after-tax *weighted cost of capital* to evaluate proposed capital expenditure projects. Each project is presumed to be financed with the same proportion of debt, preferred stock, and common equity contained in the company's target capital structure. The general formula for calculating the weighted cost of capital, k_a, is as follows:

$$k_a = \begin{pmatrix} \text{Equity} \\ \text{fraction} \\ \text{of} \\ \text{capital} \\ \text{structure} \end{pmatrix} \begin{pmatrix} \text{Marginal} \\ \text{cost} \\ \text{of} \\ \text{equity} \end{pmatrix} + \begin{pmatrix} \text{Debt} \\ \text{fraction} \\ \text{of} \\ \text{capital} \\ \text{structure} \end{pmatrix} \begin{pmatrix} \text{Marginal} \\ \text{cost} \\ \text{of} \\ \text{debt} \end{pmatrix}$$

$$+ \begin{pmatrix} \text{Preferred} \\ \text{fraction} \\ \text{of} \\ \text{capital} \\ \text{structure} \end{pmatrix} \begin{pmatrix} \text{Marginal} \\ \text{cost} \\ \text{of} \\ \text{preferred} \\ \text{stock} \end{pmatrix}$$

■ The *optimal capital budget* maximizes the value of the firm and occurs at the point where the firm's *investment opportunity curve* and *weighted marginal cost of capital curve* intersect. The investment opportunity curve is obtained by plotting the returns expected from proposed capital expenditure projects against the cumulative funds required.

■ The cost of depreciation-generated funds is equal to the weighted cost of the firm's first "block" of funds.

QUESTIONS AND TOPICS FOR DISCUSSION

1. How do retained earnings differ from other sources of financing?

2. Does the retained earnings figure shown on a firm's balance sheet necessarily have any relationship to the amount of retained earnings the firm can generate in the coming year? Explain.

3. Why is corporate long-term debt more risky than government long-term debt?

4. Why do investors generally consider common stock to be more risky than preferred stock?

5. Should a firm pay cash dividends in a year in which it raises external common equity?

6. Discuss the meaning of an *optimal* capital budget.

7. Evaluate the statement, "Depreciation-generated funds have no explicit cost and therefore should be assigned a zero cost in computing a firm's cost of capital."

8. Describe how to derive the break points in the marginal cost of capital schedule.

9. Discuss the pros and cons of various sources of estimates of future earnings and dividend growth rates for a company.

10. What market risk premium should be used when applying the CAPM to compute the cost of equity capital for a firm if

    a. the risk-free rate is the 90-day Treasury bill rate?
    b. the risk-free rate is the 20-year government bond rate.

11. What factors determine the required rate of return for any security?

12. What are the similarities and differences in preferred stock and debt as sources of financing for a firm?

13. Why is the marginal cost of capital the relevant concept for evaluating investment projects rather than a firm's actual, historic cost of capital?

▬▬▬ PROBLEMS*

1. Calculate the after-tax cost of a $25 million debt issue that Pullman Manufacturing Corporation (40 percent marginal tax rate) is planning to place privately with a large insurance company. This long-term issue will yield 9⅜ percent to the insurance company.

2. Husky Enterprises recently sold an issue of 10-year maturity bonds. The bonds were sold at a deep discount price of $615 each. After flotation costs, Husky received $604.50 each. The bonds have a $1,000 maturity value and pay $50 interest at the end of each year. Compute the after-tax cost of debt for these bonds if Husky's marginal tax rate is 40 percent.

3. Calculate the after-tax cost of preferred stock for Bozeman-Western Airlines, Inc., which is planning to sell $10 million of $6.50 cumulative preferred stock to the public at a price of $50 a share. Flotation costs are estimated to be $2 a share. The company has a marginal tax rate of 40 percent.

4. St. Joe Trucking has sold an issue of $6 cumulative preferred stock to the public at a price of $60 per share. After flotation costs, St. Joe netted $57 per share. The company has a marginal tax rate of 40 percent.

   a. Calculate the after-tax cost of this preferred stock offering assuming this stock is a perpetuity.
   b. If the stock is callable in 5 years at $66 per share, and investors expect it to be called at that time, what is the after-tax cost of this preferred stock offering? (Compute to the nearest whole percent.)

5. The following financial information is available on Fargo Fabrics, Inc.:

Current per-share market price	$20.25
Current per-share dividend	$ 1.12
Current per-share earnings	$ 2.48
Beta	0.90
Expected market risk premium	8.3%
Risk-free rate (Treasury bills)	5.2%

Past 10 years earnings per share:

19X1	$1.39	19X6	$1.95
19X2	1.48	19X7	2.12
19X3	1.60	19X8	2.26
19X4	1.68	19X9	2.40
19X5	1.79	19Y0	2.48

This past earnings growth trend is expected to continue for the foreseeable future. The dividend payout ratio has remained approximately constant over the past 9 years and is expected to remain at current levels for the foreseeable future.

Calculate the cost of equity capital using the following methods:

   a. The dividend capitalization model approach.
   b. The Capital Asset Pricing Model approach.

6. The stock of Alpha Tool sells for $10.25 per share. Its current dividend rate, D_0, is $1 per share. Analysts and investors expect Alpha to increase its

* Colored numbers denote problems that have check answers provided at the end of the book.

dividends at a 10 percent rate for each of the next 2 years. This annual dividend growth rate is expected to decline to 8 percent for years 3 and 4, and then to settle down to 4 percent per year forever. Calculate the cost of internal equity for Alpha Tool.

7. The Hartley Hotel Corporation is planning a major expansion. Hartley is financed 100 percent with equity and intends to maintain this capital structure after the expansion. Hartley's beta is 0.9. The expected market return is 16 percent, and the risk-free rate is 10 percent. If the expansion is expected to produce an internal rate of return of 17 percent, should Hartley make the investment?

8. Wentworth Industries is 100 percent equity financed. Its current beta is 0.9. The expected market rate of return is 14 percent, and the risk-free rate is 8 percent.

   a. Calculate Wentworth's cost of equity.
   b. If Wentworth changes its capital structure to 30 percent debt, it estimates that its beta will increase to 1.1. The after-tax cost of debt will be 7 percent. Should Wentworth make the capital structure change?

9. The Ewing Distribution Company is planning a $100 million expansion of its chain of discount service stations to several neighboring states. This expansion will be financed, in part, with debt issued with a coupon interest rate of 15 percent. The bonds have a 10-year maturity and a $1,000 face value, and they will be sold to net Ewing $990 after issue costs. Ewing's marginal tax rate is 40 percent.

   Preferred stock will cost Ewing 14 percent after taxes. Ewing's common stock pays a dividend of $2 per share. The current market price per share is $15, and new shares can be sold to net $14 per share. Ewing's dividends are expected to increase at an annual rate of 5 percent for the foreseeable future. Ewing expects to have $20 million of retained earnings available to finance the expansion.

   Ewing's target capital structure is as follows:

Debt	20%
Preferred stock	5
Common equity	75

   Calculate the weighted cost of capital that is appropriate to use in evaluating this expansion program.

10. Pacific Intermountain Utilities Company has a present capital structure (which the company feels is optimal) of 50 percent long-term debt, 10 percent preferred stock, and 40 percent common equity. For the coming year the company has determined that its optimal capital budget can be externally financed with $70 million of 10 percent first-mortgage bonds sold at par and $14 million of preferred stock costing the company 11 percent. The remainder of the capital budget will be financed with retained earnings. The company's common stock is presently selling at $25 a share, and next year's common dividend, D_1, is expected to be $2 a share. The company has 25 million common shares outstanding. Next year's net income available to common stock (including net income from next year's capital budget) is expected to be $106 million. The company's past annual growth rate in dividends and earnings has been 6 percent. However, a 5 percent annual growth in earnings and dividends is expected for the foreseeable future. The company's marginal tax rate is 40 percent.

   Calculate the company's weighted cost of capital for the coming year.

11. Panhandle Industries, Inc., currently pays an annual common stock dividend of $2.20 per share. The company's dividend has grown steadily over the past 9 years from $1.10 to its present level; this growth trend is expected

to continue. The company's present dividend payout ratio, also expected to continue, is 40 percent. In addition, the stock presently sells at 8 times current earnings (that is, its "P/E multiple" is 8).

Panhandle Industries' stock has a beta of 1.15, as computed by a leading investment service. The present risk-free rate is 7.0 percent, and the expected return on the stock market is 13.0 percent.

a. Suppose an individual investor feels that 12 percent is an appropriate required rate of return for the level of risk this investor perceived for Panhandle Industries. Using the dividend capitalization model and the Capital Asset Pricing Model approaches, determine whether this investor should purchase Panhandle Industries' stock.

b. Calculate the company's cost of equity capital using both the dividend capitalization model approach and the Capital Asset Pricing Model approach.

12. Colbyco Industries has a target capital structure of 60 percent common equity, 30 percent debt, and 10 percent preferred stock. The cost of retained earnings is 15 percent, and the cost of new equity (external) is 16 percent. Colbyco anticipates having $20 million of new retained earnings available over the coming year. Colbyco can sell $15 million of first-mortgage bonds with an after-tax cost of 9 percent. Its investment bankers feel the company could sell $10 million of debentures with a 9.5 percent after-tax cost. Additional debt would cost 10 percent after tax and be in the form of subordinated debentures. The after-tax cost of preferred stock financing is estimated to be 14 percent.

Compute the marginal cost of capital schedule for Colbyco, and determine the break points in the schedule.

13. The White Corporation makes small Bozo replicas for sale in the growing Austin market. The firm's capital structure consists of 60 percent common equity, 10 percent preferred stock, and 30 percent long-term debt. This capital structure is believed to be optimal. White is planning to raise funds over the coming year to finance expansion plans. The firm expects to have $40 million of retained earnings available. The cost of retained earnings is 18 percent. Additional common equity can be obtained by selling new common stock at a cost of 19.6 percent. The firm can sell a maximum amount of $20 million of preferred stock at a cost of 15 percent. First-mortgage bonds totalling $25 million can be sold at a pretax cost of 14 percent. Beyond $25 million, the firm would have to sell debentures at a pretax cost of 15 percent. The firm's marginal tax rate is 40 percent.

Identify the size of each block of funds and the cost of the funds in each block. Be sure to identify the *maximum* amount of funds White can acquire.

14. Owens Enterprises is in the process of determining its capital budget for the next fiscal year. The firm's current capital structure, which it considers to be optimal, is contained in the following balance sheet:

Balance Sheet

Current assets	$40,000,000	Accounts payable	$20,000,000
Fixed assets	400,000,000	Other current liabilities	10,000,000
Total assets	$440,000,000	Long-term debt	123,000,000
		Common stock at par	15,500,000
		Paid in capital in excess of par	51,000,000
		Retained earnings	220,500,000
		Total liabilities and stockholders' equity	$440,000,000

Through discussions with the firm's investment bankers, lead bank, and financial officers, the following information has been obtained:

- The firm expects net income from this year to total $80 million. The firm intends to maintain its dividend policy of paying 42.25 percent of earnings to stockholders.
- The firm can borrow $18 million from its bank at a 13 percent annual rate.
- Any additional debt can be obtained through the issuance of debentures (at par) that carry a 15 percent coupon rate.
- The firm currently (D_0) pays $4.40 per share in dividends. Dividends have grown at a 5 percent rate in the past. This growth is expected to continue.
- The firm's common stock currently trades at $44 per share. If the firm were to raise any external equity, the newly issued shares would net the company $40 per share.
- The firm is in the 40 percent marginal tax bracket.

Compute Owens' marginal cost of capital schedule.

15. Matsumoto Limited (ML), a large conglomerate firm, has a capital structure that currently consists of 20 percent long-term debt, 10 percent preferred stock, and 70 percent common equity. ML has determined that it will raise funds in the future using 40 percent long-term debt, 10 percent preferred stock, and 50 percent common equity.

ML can raise up to $50 million in the long-term debt market at a pretax cost of 18 percent. Beyond $50 million, the pretax cost of long-term debt is expected to increase to 20 percent. Preferred stock can be raised at a cost of 19 percent. The limited demand for this security permits ML to sell only $20 million of preferred stock. ML's marginal tax rate is 40 percent.

ML's stock currently sells for $40 per share and has a beta of 1.5. ML pays no dividends and is not expected to pay any dividends for the foreseeable future. Investment advisory services expect the stock price to increase from its current level of $40 per share to a level of $99.50 per share at the end of 5 years. New shares can be sold to net the company $38.35. ML expects earnings after tax and available for common stockholders to be $60 million.

Compute the marginal cost of capital schedule for ML, and determine the break points in the schedule.

16. Rolodex, Inc., is in the process of determining its capital budget for the next fiscal year. The firm's current capital structure, which it considers to be optimal, is contained in the following balance sheet:

Rolodex, Inc. Balance Sheet (in millions of dollars)

Current assets	$110	Accounts payable	$ 30
Fixed assets	260	Other current liabilities	20
Total assets	$370	Long-term debt	128
		Preferred stock	32
		Common stock (20 million shares at par)	20
		Contributed capital in excess of par	30
		Retained earnings	110
		Total liabilities and equity	$370

Discussions between the firm's financial officers and the firm's investment and commercial bankers have yielded the following information:

- Rolodex can borrow $40 million from its bank at a pretax cost of 13 percent.

- Rolodex can borrow $80 million by issuing bonds at a net price of $687 per bond. The bonds would carry a 10 percent coupon rate and mature in 20 years.
- Additional debt can be issued at a 16 percent pretax cost.
- Preferred stock can be issued at a pretax cost of 16.5 percent.
- Rolodex expects to generate $140 million in net income and pay $2 per share in dividends.
- The $2 per share dividend ($D_1$) represents a growth of 5.5 percent over the previous year's dividend. This growth rate is expected to continue for the foreseeable future. The firm's stock is currently trading at $16 per share.
- Rolodex can raise external equity by selling common stock at a net price of $15 per share.
- Rolodex's marginal tax rate is 40 percent.

a. Compute Rolodex's marginal cost of capital schedule.
b. Given the following investment opportunity schedule, determine Rolodex's optimal capital budget.

Project	Required Investment	Expected Return on Project
A	$140,000,000	17.0%
B	130,000,000	16.0
C	100,000,000	15.0
D	80,000,000	14.2
E	24,000,000	13.0
F	16,000,000	10.9

Cost of Capital

The Marietta Corporation, a large manufacturer of mufflers, tail pipes, and shock absorbers, presently is carrying out its financial planning for next year. In about 2 weeks, at the next meeting of the firm's board of directors, Frank Bosworth, vice-president of finance, is scheduled to present his recommendations for next year's overall financial plan. He has asked Donna Botello, manager of financial planning, to gather the necessary information and perform the calculations for the financial plan.

The company's divisional staffs, together with corporate finance department personnel, have analyzed several proposed capital expenditure projects. The following is a summary schedule of acceptable projects (defined by the company as projects having internal rates of return greater than 8 percent):

Project	Investment Amount (in millions of dollars)	Internal Rate of Return
A	$10.0	25%
B	20.0	21
C	30.0	18
D	35.0	15
E	40.0	12.4
F	40.0	11.3
G	40.0	10
H	20.0	9

All projects are expected to have 1 year of negative cash flow followed by positive cash flows over the remaining years. In addition, next year's projects involve modifications and expansion of the company's existing facilities and products. As a result, these projects are considered to have approximately the same degree of risk as the company's existing assets.

Botello feels that this summary schedule and detailed supporting documents provide her with the necessary information concerning the possible capital expenditure projects for next year. She now can direct her attention to obtaining the data necessary to determine the cost of the capital required to finance next year's proposed projects.

The company's investment bankers indicated to Bosworth in a recent meeting that they feel the company could issue up to $50 million of 9 percent first-mortgage bonds at par next year. The investment bankers also feel that any additional debt would have to be subordinated debentures with a coupon of 10 percent, also to be sold at par. The investment bankers rendered this opinion after Bosworth gave an approximate estimate of the size of next year's capital budget, and after he estimated that approximately $100 million of retained earnings would be available next year.

Both the company's financial managers and its investment bankers consider the present capital structure of the company, shown in the following table, to be optimal (assume that book value and market value are equal):

Debt	$ 400,000,000
Shareholders' equity:	
Common stock	150,000,000
Retained earnings	450,000,000
	$1,000,000,000

Botello has assembled additional information, as follows:

■ Marietta common stock is presently selling at $21.00 a share.
■ The investment bankers also have indicated that an additional $75 million in new common stock could be issued to net the company $19 a share.
■ The company's present annual dividend is $1.32 a share. However, Bosworth feels fairly certain that the board will increase it to $1.415 a share next year.
■ The company's earnings and dividends have doubled over the past 10 years. Growth has been fairly steady, and this rate is expected to continue for the foreseeable future. The company's marginal tax rate is 40 percent.

Using the information provided, answer the following questions. (NOTE: Disregard depreciation in this case.)

1. Calculate the after-tax cost of each component source of capital.

2. Calculate the marginal cost of capital for the various intervals, or "packages," of capital the company can raise next year. Plot the marginal cost of capital curve.

3. Using the marginal cost of capital curve from Question 2, and plotting the investment opportunity curve, determine the company's optimal capital budget for next year.

4. Should Project G be accepted or rejected? Why?

5. What factors do you feel might cause Bosworth to recommend a different capital budget than the one obtained in Question 3?

6. Assume that a sudden rise in interest rates has caused the cost of various capital components to increase. The pretax cost of first-mortgage bonds has increased to 11 percent; the pretax cost of subordinated debentures has increased to 12.5 percent; the company's common stock price has declined to $18; and new stock could be sold to net Marietta $16 per share.

  a. Recompute the after-tax cost of the individual component sources of capital.
  b. Recompute the marginal cost of capital for the various intervals of capital Marietta can raise next year.
  c. Determine the optimal capital budget for next year at the higher cost of capital.
  d. How does the interest rate surge affect Marietta's optimal capital budget?

SELECTED REFERENCES

Arditti, Fred D., and Haim Levy. "The Weighted Average Cost of Capital as a Cutoff Rate: A Critical Analysis of the Classical Textbook Weighted Average." *Financial Management* (Fall 1977): 24–34.

Copeland, T. E., and J. F. Weston. *Financial Theory and Corporate Policy*, 3d ed. Reading, MA: Addison-Wesley, 1988.

Fama, E. F. "Risk-Adjusted Discount Rates and Capital Budgeting under Uncertainty." *Journal of Financial Economics* (August 1977): 3–24.

Gordon, Myron. *The Investment, Financing, and Valuation of the Corporation.* Homewood, IL: Irwin, 1962.

Harris, Robert S., and John J. Pringle. "Risk-Adjusted Discount Rates—Extensions from the Average-Risk Case." *Journal of Financial Research* (Fall 1985): 237–244.

Makhija, Anil K., and Howard E. Thompson. "Comparison of Alternative Models for Estimating the Cost of Equity Capital for Electric Utilities." *Journal of Economics and Business* 36 (1984): 107–131.

Morin, Roger, A. *Utilities' Cost of Capital.* Arlington, VA: Public Utilities Reports, 1984.

Newbold, P. J., J. K. Zumwalt, and S. Kannan. "Combining Forecasts to Improve Earnings Per Share Prediction: An Examination of Electric Utilities." *International Journal of Forecasting* 3 (1987): 229–238.

Rosenberg, Barr, and Andrew Rudd. "The Corporate Uses of Beta." In *Issues in Corporate Finance*, pp. 45–52. New York: Stern, Stewart, Putnam & Macklis, 1983.

Siegel, Jeremy J. "The Application of the DCF Methodology for Determining the Cost of Equity Capital." *Financial Management* (Spring 1985): 46–54.

13

The Capital Structure Decision

KEY CHAPTER CONCEPTS

1. *Leverage* involves the use of fixed operating costs or fixed capital costs by a firm.

2. The *degree of operating leverage (DOL)* is defined as the percentage change in EBIT resulting from a 1 percent change in sales.
   a. The degree of operating leverage approaches a maximum as the firm comes closer to operating at its breakeven level of output.
   b. All other things being equal, the higher a firm's DOL, the greater is its business risk.
   c. Business risk, the inherent variability of a firm's EBIT, also is influenced by the variability of sales and operating costs over time.

3. The *degree of financial leverage (DFL)* is defined as the percentage change in earnings per share (EPS) resulting from a 1 percent change in EBIT.
   a. The degree of financial leverage approaches a maximum as the firm comes closer to operating at its loss level, the level where EPS = $0.
   b. All other things being equal, the higher a firm's DFL, the greater is its financial risk.

c. Financial risk, the additional variability of a firm's EPS that results from the use of financial leverage, can also be measured by various financial ratios, such as the debt to total assets ratio, and the times interest earned ratio.

4. The *degree of combined leverage (DCL)* is defined as the percentage change in earnings per share resulting from a 1 percent change in sales. It also is equal to the DOL for a company times that company's DFL. The degree of combined leverage used by a firm is a measure of the overall variability of EPS, as sales levels vary, due to the use of fixed operating and capital costs.

5. *Capital structure* is defined as the relative amount of permanent short-term debt, long-term debt, preferred stock, and common equity used to finance a firm. The *optimal* capital structure occurs at the point at which the cost of capital is minimized and firm value is maximized.

6. The value of the firm is *independent* of capital structure given perfect capital markets and no corporate income taxes.

7. The optimal capital structure consists entirely of debt if a corporate income tax exists and there are no bankruptcy or agency costs.

8. Given a corporate income tax, bankruptcy costs, and agency costs, an optimal capital structure consisting of both debt and equity is shown to exist.

9. *EBIT-EPS* analysis is an analytical technique that can be used to help determine the circumstances under which a firm should employ financial leverage. The *indifference point* in EBIT-EPS analysis is that level of EBIT where earnings per share are the same, regardless of which of two alternative capital structures is used.

10. Cash insolvency analysis can be used to evaluate the impact of a proposed capital structure on the cash position of a firm during a major business downturn.

11. Other factors that are considered when establishing a capital structure policy are industry standards, lender requirements, managerial risk aversion, and the desire of owners to retain control of the firm.

GLOSSARY OF NEW TERMS

Agency costs Costs incurred by owners of a firm when the firm is managed by others; includes monitoring costs, bonding costs, and any losses that cannot be economically eliminated by monitoring and bonding.

Arbitrage The process of simultaneously buying and selling the same or equivalent securities in different markets to take advantage of temporary price differences.

Bankruptcy costs Costs related to financial distress, which are incurred by a firm as it increases its debt level.

Business risk The inherent variability or uncertainty of a firm's operating earnings (EBIT).

Capital structure The amount of permanent short-term debt, long-term debt, preferred stock, and common equity used to finance a firm.

Debt capacity The amount of debt contained in a firm's optimal capital structure.

Degree of combined leverage (DCL) The percentage change in a firm's earnings per share (EPS) resulting from a 1 percent change in sales or output. This also is equal to the degree of operating leverage times the degree of financial leverage used by the firm.

Degree of financial leverage (DFL) The percentage change in a firm's EPS resulting from a 1 percent change in EBIT.

Degree of operating leverage (DOL) The percentage change in a firm's EBIT resulting from a 1 percent change in sales or output.

Financial leverage The extent to which a firm is financed by securities having fixed costs or charges, such as debt and preferred stock.

Financial risk The additional variability of a company's earnings per share that results from the use of fixed-cost sources of funds, such as debt and preferred stock. In general, the more financial leverage a firm uses, the greater is its financial risk.

Financial structure The amount of current liabilities, long-term debt, preferred stock, and common equity used to finance a firm.

Indifference point That level of EBIT where the earnings per share of a firm are the same, regardless of which of two alternative capital structures is employed.

Optimal capital structure The capital structure that minimizes a firm's weighted cost of capital and, therefore, maximizes the value of the firm.

Operating leverage The extent to which a firm uses assets having fixed costs.

Target capital structure The proportions of permanent short-term debt, long-term debt, preferred stock, and common equity that a firm *desires* to have in its capital structure.

Total risk The variability of returns to a firm's shareholders.

Regulating Leveraged Buyouts*

A leveraged buyout (LBO) is a transaction in which the buyer of a company borrows a large portion of the purchase price, using the purchased assets as partial collateral for the loans. The buyers of the company frequently are the managers of the company being sold or a group of takeover specialists. Historically, LBOs have involved relatively small firms. During 1986 there were a total of 331 LBO transactions with a total value of over $46 billion. In 1987 the number of LBOs was 259 with a value of more than $35 billion. During 1988 and 1989 the LBO transaction has been used to acquire very large firms, including the 1989 acquisition of RJR Nabisco by Kohlberg Kravis Roberts for $25 billion.

The pace of LBO transactions and other actions taken by managers, often in an attempt to fend off an unfriendly takeover, have resulted in significant increases in the financial leverage used by U.S. corporations. In the 6 years ending in 1988, nonfinancial corporations have nearly doubled their debt, to $1.8 trillion. Over the same period more than $400 billion of equity has been retired. The ratio of operating income to total interest expense for all U.S. nonfinancial corporations has declined from nearly 25 times in 1956 to less than 4 times in 1988. The frenzy of takeover activity, the increase in corporate debt ratios, and the decline in interest coverage ratios has begun to be noticed by Congress and regulators in Washington.

Some of the concerns include the potential for bankruptcy at many of these highly leveraged firms when the economy enters a major recession. With low interest coverage ratios, these firms have only a small margin of protection in a recession. The case of Revco Drug, the largest LBO to fail to date, often is cited as evidence of the potential problem. Many in Congress have expressed a concern that the tax code, which permits deductions for interest expenses but not for common stock dividends, encourages the increased use of leverage, and threatens the tax revenues of the Treasury. Another concern is for the interests of existing bondholders in firms that are taken over in an LBO transaction. These bondholders often see substantial declines in the value of their bonds because of the higher leverage used in the surviving firm. For example, in the RJR Nabisco takeover, the value of RJR Nabisco's bonds declined by as much as 20 percent when the takeover was announced.

Offsetting these concerns is the fact that shareholders in acquired firms reap very large profits, as the acquiring firm bids up the stock price to succeed in the takeover. After most LBO transactions, profit margins have tended to rise substantially. For example, one study found that operating profit margins of LBO companies were 40 percent higher than the median profit margin for their industry 2 years after the buyout. Faced with the enormous debt burden in an LBO, managers (who often have a large ownership stake in the LBO) are disciplined to make very careful use of the firm's resources. In an LBO there is very little leeway for managers to squander resources. Studies of LBOs have found that post LBO employment stays about the same as before the buyout, and that LBOs do not have a significant impact on research and development (R&D) expenditures at companies that require large R&D outlays.

In early 1989, the Congress began an extended series of hearings to consider the pros and cons of LBOs and to decide if legislation or new regulations to restrict LBO takeover activity is warranted. Structuring a package of reforms that balances all of the concerns expressed about LBOs is a financial dilemma of major proportions for the Congress.

* This dilemma is based on J. P. Newport, Jr., "LBOs: Greed, Good Business—or Both," *Fortune*, (January 2, 1989), pp. 66–68; J. Grant, "Corporate Finance, 'Leveraged to the Hilt,' " *Wall Street Journal* (October 25, 1988); and "Learning to Live with Leverage," *Business Week*, (November 7, 1988), pp. 138–143.

INTRODUCTION

This chapter considers how a firm analyzes its capital structure decision. *Capital structure* is defined as the amount of permanent short-term debt,[1]

[1] *Permanent* short-term debt is contrasted with *seasonal* short-term debt. Short-term debt financing policy is discussed in Chapter 17.

long-term debt, preferred stock, and common equity used to finance a firm. In contrast, *financial structure* refers to the amount of total current liabilities, long-term debt, preferred stock, and common equity used to finance a firm. Thus, capital structure is part of the financial structure, representing the permanent sources of the firm's financing. This chapter deals only with the total permanent sources of a firm's financing; the decision about what proportions of debt should be long-term and short-term is considered in Chapter 17.

To illustrate the capital structure concept, suppose that a company currently has $10 million in permanent short-term debt, $40 million in long-term debt outstanding, $10 million in preferred stock, and $40 million in common equity (common stock and retained earnings). In this case the company's current capital structure is said to be "50 percent debt, 10 percent preferred stock, and 40 percent common equity"[2] Thus, the capital structure pertains to the permanent debt, preferred stock, and common equity portion of the balance sheet.

The emphasis of capital structure analysis is on the firm's long-range *target capital structure;* that is, the capital structure at which the firm ultimately plans to operate. For most companies the current and target capital structures are virtually identical, and calculating the target structure is a straightforward process. Occasionally, however, companies find it necessary to change from their current capital structure to a different target. The reasons for such a change may involve a change in the company's asset mix (and a resulting change in its risk), or an increase in competition that may imply more risk. For example, in response to increased risk and competition in the electric utility industry, Standard and Poor's, a bond rating agency reduced the desired proportion of debt in the capital structure of an AA-rated utility from a range of 42 to 47 percent to a range of 39 to 46 percent. As a consequence many utilities have moved toward more conservative capital structures.

In this chapter, both the theoretical and practical aspects of the determination of the optimal capital structure are reviewed. In addition, a number of tools of analysis are introduced that can assist managers in making capital structure decisions.

CAPITAL STRUCTURE DECISIONS AND MAXIMIZATION OF SHAREHOLDER WEALTH

What is meant by a firm's *optimal capital structure?* The optimal capital structure is the mix of debt, preferred stock, and common equity that minimizes the *weighted cost* to the firm *of* its employed *capital.* At the capital structure where the weighted cost of capital is minimized, the total value of the firm's securities (and, hence, the value of the firm) is maximized. As a result, the minimum-cost capital structure is called the *optimal* capital structure.

The amount of debt contained in a firm's optimal capital structure often is referred to as the firm's *debt capacity.* The optimal capital structure and, accordingly, the debt capacity of a firm are determined by factors including the business risk of the firm, the tax structure, the extent of potential bankruptcy and agency costs, and the role played by capital structure policy in

[2] Companies normally do not distinguish in their capital structure between whether common equity is obtained by retained earnings or new common stock. In other words, only the *total* common shareholders' equity is considered, not the *relative* amounts in the common stock, contributed capital in excess of par, and retained earnings accounts.

providing signals to the capital markets regarding the firm's performance. Each of these factors is considered in the following sections.

ASSUMPTIONS OF CAPITAL STRUCTURE ANALYSIS

The analysis that follows is based on some important assumptions. First, it is assumed that a firm's investment policy is held constant when we examine the effects of capital structure changes on firm value and particularly on the value of common stock. This assumption means that the level and variability of operating income (EBIT) is not expected to change as changes in capital structure are contemplated. Therefore, capital structure changes change only the distribution of the operating income between the claims of debtholders, preferred stockholders, and common stockholders.

By assuming a constant investment policy, we also assume that the investments undertaken by the firm do not materially change the debt capacity of the firm. This assumption does not always hold in practice, but for the overwhelming majority of investment projects, it is a realistic assumption that also helps us focus on the key determinants of an optimal capital structure.

BUSINESS RISK

Two elements of firm-specific risk are primary considerations in the capital structure decision: the business risk and the financial risk of a firm. *Business risk* refers to the variability or uncertainty of a firm's operating income (EBIT). *Financial risk* refers to the additional variability of earnings per share *and* the increased probability of insolvency (and ultimately bankruptcy) that occurs when a firm uses fixed-costs sources of funds, such as debt and preferred stock, in its capital structure. As we shall see, generally *the greater is a firm's business risk, the less the amount of financial leverage that will be used in the optimal capital structure*, holding constant all other relevant factors.

Business risk is often measured by the coefficient of variation of EBIT over time. For example, between 1980 and 1988 the mean level of EBIT for American Brands, a cigarette manufacturer and consumer products firm, was $851 million with a standard deviation of $162 million, resulting in a coefficient of variation of 0.19 ($162 million/$851 million). In comparison, the mean level of EBIT for Delta Airlines over the same period was $470 million with a standard deviation of $248 million, or a coefficient of variation of 0.53.[3] In 1988, Delta had a *long-term debt to total capital* ratio of 25 percent compared with 34 percent for American Brands.

Many factors influence a firm's business risk (holding constant the effects of all other important factors) including:

1. *The variability of sales volumes over the business cycle.* Firms such as Delta Airlines, whose sales tend to fluctuate greatly over the business cycle, have more business risk than firms such as American Brands.
2. *The variability of selling prices.* In some industries, prices are quite stable from year to year, or the firm may be able to increase prices regularly

---

[3] A better measure of the coefficient of variation would be the ratio of the standard error of the estimate of a regression line relating EBIT to time divided by the mean value of EBIT from the regression line. This would eliminate much of the bias that results when the simple measure of the coefficient of variation, defined earlier, is computed for a growing firm.

over time. This is true for many consumer products, such as cigarettes and many prepared food items. In contrast, in other industries price stability is much less certain. For example, over the past decade the oil companies such as Exxon, Shell Oil, and Mobil have learned important lessons about the instability of prices as the price of crude oil declined from more than $30 a barrel to less than $10 a barrel.

3. *The variability of costs.* The more variability there is in the cost of the inputs used to produce a firm's output, the greater is the business risk of that firm. For example, airline companies, such as Delta, American, and United have been affected significantly by the volatility in the price of jet fuel.

4. *Existence of market power.* Firms that have greater market power, such as General Motors, because of their size or the structure of the industry in which they compete, often have a greater ability to control their costs and the price of their outputs than firms operating in a more competitive market environment. Therefore, the greater is a firm's market power, the less its business risk. When evaluating a firm's market power, it often is useful to consider not only the current competition facing the firm, but also potential future competition, especially competition that might develop from abroad.

5. *The degree of operating leverage (DOL).* Operating leverage involves the use of assets having fixed costs. The more a firm makes use of operating leverage, the more sensitive EBIT will be to changes in sales. The degree of operating leverage is the multiplier effect resulting from a firm's use of fixed operating costs. Specifically, the DOL is defined as the *percentage change in EBIT* resulting from (divided by) a given *percentage change in sales (output).* Thus, if a firm is subject to considerable sales volatility over the business cycle, the variability of EBIT (business risk) can be reduced by limiting the use of assets having fixed costs in the production process. Similarly, if a firm's sales tend to be stable over the business cycle, using a high percentage of fixed-cost assets in the production process will have little impact on the variability of EBIT. The measurement of DOL is considered in more detail in Appendix 13A.

In a sense, the business risk of a firm is determined by the accumulated investments the firm makes over time. These investments determine the industries in which a firm will compete, the amount of market power the firm will possess, and the extent of fixed costs in the production process. Firms in consumer products industries, such as grocery retailing (Albertsons, for example), brewing (Anheuser Busch), food processing (RJR Nabisco), and electric (Duke Power) and natural gas distribution (Atlanta Gas Light) utilities tend to have low levels of business risk. In contrast, firms in durable goods manufacturing (Chrysler), industrial goods manufacturing (Bethlehem Steel), and airlines (Delta Airlines) tend to have higher levels of business risk.

FINANCIAL RISK AND FINANCIAL LEVERAGE

Financial risk refers to the additional variability of earnings per share *and* the increased probability of insolvency that arises when a firm uses fixed-cost sources of funds, such as debt and preferred stock,[4] in its capital struc-

---

[4] Long-term, noncancelable leases (often called *financial leases*) also represent a significant source of fixed-cost financing for many firms. They are not discussed in this chapter in order to simplify the analysis. See Chapter 15 for a discussion of lease financing.

ture. (Insolvency occurs when a firm is unable to meet contractual financial obligations—such as interest and principal payments on debt, payments on accounts payable, and income taxes—as they come due.) Fixed capital costs represent contractual obligations a company must meet regardless of the EBIT level.[5] The use of increasing amounts of debt and preferred stock raises the firm's fixed financial costs; this, in turn, increases the level of EBIT that the firm must earn in order to meet its financial obligations and remain in business. The reason a firm accepts the risk of fixed-cost financing is to increase the possible returns to stockholders.

The use of fixed-cost financing sources is referred to as the use of *financial leverage*. Financial leverage causes a firm's earnings per share (EPS) to change at a rate greater than the change in operating income (EBIT). For example, if a firm is 100 percent equity financed and EBIT increases (decreases) by 10 percent, EPS also will increase (decrease) by 10 percent. When financial leverage, such as long-term debt, is used, a 10 percent change in EBIT will result in a greater than 10 percent change in EPS. Figure 13-1 illustrates the concept of financial leverage. Line A represents the financial leverage used by a firm financed *entirely with common stock*. A given percentage change in EBIT results in the *same* percentage change in EPS.

---

[5] In financial emergencies, firms are able to omit preferred dividends. Omitting preferred dividends has many undesirable consequences for the firm, however (see Chapter 6). Therefore the payment of preferred dividends is treated here as if it were a contractual obligation similar to interest.

FIGURE 13-1

**Illustration of
Financial Leverage**

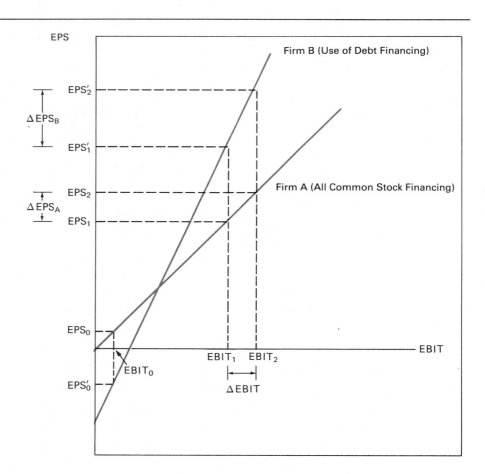

Line B represents a firm that uses debt (or other sources of fixed cost funds) in its capital structure. As a result, the *slope* of the EPS-EBIT line is increased, thus increasing the responsiveness of EPS to changes in EBIT. As can be seen in Figure 13-1, a given change in EBIT yields a larger change in EPS if the firm is using debt financing (ΔEPS_B) than if the firm is financed entirely with common stock (ΔEPS_A).

It is also clear from Figure 13-1 that the use of financial leverage magnifies the returns—both positive and negative—to the shareholder. When EBIT is at a relatively high level, such as $EBIT_2$, Firm B's use of financial leverage *increases* EPS above the level attained by Firm A, which is not using financial leverage. On the other hand, when EBIT is relatively low—for example, at $EBIT_0$—the use of financial leverage *decreases* EPS below the level that would be obtained otherwise; that is, $EPS_0' < EPS_0$. At $EBIT_0$ the use of financial leverage results in negative EPS for Firm B.

Effect of Financial Leverage on Stockholder Returns and Risk

Firms employ financial leverage to increase the returns to common stockholders. Recalling, however, that *there is no free lunch*, these increased returns are achieved at the expense of increased risk. The objective of capital structure management is to find the capital mix that leads to shareholder wealth maximization.

To illustrate the effects of financial leverage on stockholder returns and risk, consider the following example of KMI Technology, Inc. As can be seen in Table 13-1, KMI has total assets of $1 million. KMI expects an operating income (EBIT) of $200,000. If KMI uses debt in its capital structure, the cost of this debt will be 10 percent per annum.[6] Table 13-1 shows the effect of an increase in the debt to total assets ratio (debt ratio) from 0 percent to 40 percent to 80 percent on the return on stockholders' equity. With an all equity capital structure, the return on equity is 12 percent. At a debt ratio of 40 percent, the return on equity increases to 16 percent, and at a debt ratio of 80 percent, the return on equity is 36 percent. KMI is earning 20 percent (pretax) on its assets. The cost of debt is 10 percent pretax. Thus, when KMI uses debt in its capital structure, the difference between the return on its assets and the cost of debt accrues to the benefit of equity holders.

However, this increased equity return is achieved only at the cost of higher risk. For example, if EBIT declines by 25 percent to $150,000, the return on equity for the all equity capital structure also declines by 25 percent to 9.0 percent. In contrast, at a 40 percent debt ratio, the return on equity declines by 31.25 percent to 11 percent. At an 80 percent debt ratio, the return on equity declines by 41.67 percent to 21 percent. The effects of a 60 percent reduction in EBIT to $80,000 are even more dramatic. In this case, the pretax return on assets is *less than* the pretax cost of debt. To pay the prior claims of the debtholders, the equity returns are reduced to a level below those that prevail (4.8 percent) under the all equity capital structure. In the case of a 40 percent debt ratio, the return on equity is only 4.0 percent, and in the case of an 80 percent debt ratio, the return on equity is 0 percent. Thus, it can be seen that the use of financial leverage both increases the

---

[6] In this simplified example, we hold the cost of debt constant as the ratio of debt to total assets increases from 20 percent to 80 percent. In reality as the debt ratio increases, the cost of debt can also be expected to increase.

Effect of Financial Leverage on Stockholder Returns and Risk at KMI Technology, Inc.

Leverage Factor (debt/total assets)	0%	40%	80%
Total assets	$1,000,000	$1,000,000	$1,000,000
Debt (at 10% interest)	$0	$400,000	$800,000
Equity	1,000,000	600,000	200,000
Total liabilities and equity	$1,000,000	$1,000,000	$1,000,000
Expected operating income (EBIT)	$200,000	$200,000	$200,000
Interest (at 10%)	0	40,000	80,000
Earnings before tax	$200,000	$160,000	$120,000
Income tax at 40%	80,000	64,000	48,000
Earnings after tax	$120,000	$96,000	$72,000
Return on equity	12.0%	16.0%	36.0%
Effect of a 25 Percent Reduction in EBIT to $150,000			
Expected operating income (EBIT)	$150,000	$150,000	$150,000
Interest (at 10%)	0	40,000	80,000
Earnings before tax	$150,000	$110,000	$70,000
Income tax at 40%	60,000	44,000	28,000
Earnings after tax	$90,000	$66,000	$42,000
Return on equity	9.0%	11.0%	21.0%
Effect of a 60 Percent Reduction in EBIT to $80,000			
Expected operating income (EBIT)	$80,000	$80,000	$80,000
Interest (at 10%)	0	$40,000	$80,000
Earnings before tax	$80,000	$40,000	$ 0
Income tax at 40%	32,000	16,000	0
Earnings after tax	$48,000	$24,000	$ 0
Return on equity	4.8%	4.0%	0.0%

potential returns to common stockholders and the risk, or variability, of those returns.

Financial Risk Measures

Various financial ratios can be used to measure the financial risk associated with a firm's use of debt and preferred stock in its capital structure. These ratios include the debt-to-total assets ratio, the debt-to-equity ratio, the times interest earned ratio, and the fixed-charge coverage ratio.[7] In particular, the times interest earned ratio and the fixed-charge coverage ratio can help measure the extent to which a firm will be able to meet fixed capital costs out of EBIT. Another measure of the financial risk of a firm is the *degree of financial leverage* (DFL). The DFL is defined as the *percentage change* in earnings per share (EPS) resulting from a given *percentage change* in EBIT:

$$\text{DFL at } X = \frac{\text{Percentage change in EPS}}{\text{Percentage change in EBIT}} \qquad \textbf{(13.1)}$$

[7] These ratios are discussed in detail in Chapter 3.

Because a firm's DFL is different at each EBIT level, it is necessary to indicate the EBIT point, X, at which financial leverage is being measured.

A firm that is 100 percent equity financed would have a DFL of 1.0 for all positive levels of EBIT. In contrast, a firm financed with some long-term debt, would have a DFL of greater than 1.0. If the DFL of Philip Morris, given its current level of EBIT, is equal to 2.5, then for each 1 percent increase (decrease) in EBIT, earnings per share would be expected to increase (decrease) by 2.5 percent. The measurement and interpretation of DFL is considered in more detail in Appendix 13A.

Other Financial Risk Measures

In addition to using various financial ratios and the degree of financial leverage as measures of the financial risk facing a firm, it is possible to make more formal statements about the financial risk facing a company if the probability distribution of future operating income can be estimated. For example, consider the case of the Travco Manufacturing Corporation. Given the current capital structure of Travco, the company has interest payment obligations of $500,000 for the coming year. The company has no preferred stock. The $500,000 in interest represents the *loss level* for Travco. If EBIT falls below $500,000, losses will be incurred (EPS will be negative). At EBIT levels above $500,000, Travco will have positive earnings per share.

Based upon past experience, Travco's managers have estimated that the expected value of EBIT over the coming year is $700,000 with a standard deviation of $200,000, and that the distribution of operating income is approximately normal. With this information, it is possible to compute the probability of Travco having negative earnings per share over the coming year (or, conversely, the probability of having positive earnings per share).

Using Equation 8.3 and the probability values from Table V, the probability of Travco having negative EPS is equal to the probability of having EBIT below the loss level of $500,000, or

$$z = \frac{\$500,000 - \$700,000}{\$200,000} = -1.0$$

In other words, a level of EBIT of $500,000 is 1.0 standard deviation below the mean. From Table V it can be seen that the probability associated with a value that is less than or equal to -1.0 standard deviation from the mean is 15.87 percent. Thus, there is a 15.87 percent chance that Travco will have negative earnings per share with its current capital structure. Conversely, there is an 84.13 percent chance (100 percent less 15.87 percent chance of losses) of having positive earnings per share.

This type of analysis can give a financial manager a better feel for the level of financial risk facing a firm. As we shall see at the end of this chapter, when a financial manager is considering two or more alternative capital structures, this same kind of analysis can be used to help select the most desirable capital structure.

CAPITAL STRUCTURE THEORY

In this section we develop some simplified models of the relationship between capital structure, as measured by the ratio of debt to total assets, and the cost of capital (and the value of the firm). These models help isolate the impact of personal and corporate taxes, bankruptcy costs, and agency costs on the determination of an optimal capital structure. Also, in this section we consider some other factors that influence the choice of long-term financing instruments, including the impact of information asymmetries. We conclude with a brief review of the market reaction to various capital structure altering transactions that firms undertake.

Capital Structure without a Corporate Income Tax

In 1958 two prominent financial researchers, Franco Modigliani and Merton Miller (MM),[8] showed that, under certain assumptions, a firm's overall cost of capital, and therefore its value, is *independent* of capital structure. In particular, assume that the following *perfect* capital market conditions exist:

■ There are no transactions costs for buying and selling securities.
■ A sufficient number of buyers and sellers exists in the market, so no single investor can have a significant influence on security prices.
■ Relevant information is readily available to all investors and is costless to obtain.
■ All investors can borrow or lend at the same rate.

MM also assumed that all investors are rational and have homogeneous expectations of a firm's earnings. Additionally, firms operating under similar conditions are assumed to face the same degree of business risk. This assumption is called the *homogeneous risk class assumption*. Finally, MM assumed that there are no income taxes. MM later relax this no-tax assumption. The results of the tax case follows after the no-tax case discussion.

In the no-tax MM case the cost of debt and the overall cost of capital are constant regardless of a firm's leverage position. As a firm increases its relative debt level, the cost of equity capital, k_e, increases, reflecting the higher return requirement of stockholders due to the increased risk imposed by the additional debt. The increased cost of equity capital exactly offsets the benefit of the lower cost of debt, k_d, so that the overall cost of capital does not change with changes in capital structure. This is illustrated in Figure 13-2. Because the firm's market value is calculated by discounting its expected future operating income by the weighted (marginal) cost of capital, k_a, the market value of the firm is independent of capital structure.

MM support their theory by arguing that a process of arbitrage[9] will prevent otherwise equivalent firms from having different market values simply because of capital structure differences. For example, suppose two firms in the same industry differed only in that one was *levered* (that is, it had some debt in its capital structure) and the other was *unlevered* (that is, it had no debt in its capital structure). If the MM theory did not hold, the unlevered firm could increase its market value by simply adding debt to its capital structure. However, in a perfect capital market without transactions costs, MM argue that investors would not reward the firm for increasing its debt. Stockholders could change *their own* financial debt–equity structure without cost to receive an equal return. Therefore, stockholders would not

[8] Franco Modigliani, and Merton Miller. "The Cost of Capital, Corporation Finance, and the Theory of Investment," *American Economic Review* 48 (June 1958): 261–296.
[9] Arbitrage is the process of simultaneously buying and selling the same or equivalent securities in different markets to make a profit. Arbitrage transactions are risk free.

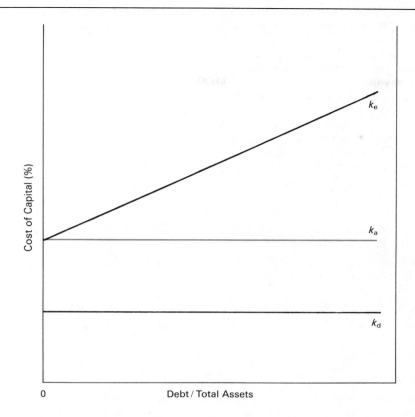

FIGURE 13-2

Weighted Cost of Capital: Miller and Modigliani (No Taxes)

increase their opinion of the market value of an unlevered firm just because it took on some debt.

The MM argument is based on the arbitrage process. If one of two unlevered firms with identical business risk took on some debt and the MM theory did not hold, its value should increase and therefore so would the value of its stock. MM suggest that under these circumstances, investors will sell the overpriced stock of the levered firm. They can then use an arbitrage process of borrowing, buying the unlevered firm's stock, and investing the excess funds elsewhere. Through these costless transactions, investors can increase their return without increasing their risk. Hence, they have substituted their own personal financial leverage for corporate leverage. MM argue that this arbitrage process will continue until the selling of the levered firm's stock drives down its price to the point where it is equal to the unlevered firm's stock price, which has been driven up due to increased buying.

The arbitrage process occurs so rapidly that the market values of the levered and unlevered firms are equal. Therefore MM conclude that *the market value of a firm is independent of its capital structure in perfect capital markets with no income taxes.*

The MM no-tax theory can be illustrated as in the example shown in Table 13-2. Table 13-2 contains financial data on two firms, U and L, that have equal levels of operating risk and differ only in their capital structure. Firm U is unlevered and firm L is levered, with a perpetual debt, B, of $2,000 in its capital structure. For simplicity, we assume that the income of both firms available for stockholders is paid out as dividends. As a result, the

Capital Structure without a Corporate Income Tax: Financial Data on Firms U and L

	Firm U	Firm L
Equity amount in capital structure	$10,000	$8,000
Cost of equity, k_e	10%	11.25%
Debt amount in capital structure, B	—	$2,000
Cost of debt, k_d	—	5%
Net operating income	$ 1,000	$1,000
Less Interest payments to debtholders	—	100
Income available to stockholders (dividend)	$ 1,000	$ 900
Total income available to security holders	$ 1,000	$1,000

expected growth rate of both firms is zero, because no income is available for the firms to reinvest.

The present value of both firms is calculated using the following perpetuity valuation equation:

$$\text{Market value of firm} = \text{Market value of equity}$$
$$+ \text{Market value of debt}$$
$$= \frac{D}{k_e} + \frac{I}{k_d} \quad \textbf{(13.2)}$$

where D is the annual amount of dividends paid to the firm's stockholders, I is the interest paid on the firm's debt, k_e is the return required on common equity, and k_d is the return required on debt. The required return on debt k_d is assumed to equal the coupon rate on the debt, i. For firm U, the present value of the expected future cash flows is $10,000, calculated as follows:

$$\text{Market value of firm U} = \frac{\$1,000}{0.10}$$
$$= \$10,000$$

For firm L, the present value is also $10,000, calculated as follows:

$$\text{Market value of firm L} = \frac{\$900}{0.1125} + \frac{\$100}{0.05}$$
$$= \$8,000 + \$2,000$$
$$= \$10,000$$

Thus, the market values of firms U and L are equal. This example shows that the market value of the firm is independent of capital structure, assuming that the MM theory holds and no corporate income tax exists.

Capital Structure with a Corporate Income Tax

Next, the relationship between capital structure and firm market value is considered, assuming that a corporate income tax exists. Table 13-3 shows

Capital Structure with a Corporate Income Tax: Financial Data on Firms U and L

	Firm U	Firm L
Equity amount in capital structure	$6,000	$4,000
Cost of equity, k_e	10%	11.25%
Debt amount in capital structure, B	—	$2,000
Cost of debt, k_d	—	5%
Net operating income	$1,000	$1,000
Less Interest payments to debtholders	—	100
Income before taxes	$1,000	$ 900
Corporate tax, $T = 40\%$	400	360
Income available to stockholders (dividend)	$ 600	$ 540
Total income available to security holders	$ 600	$ 640

financial data for an unlevered firm, U, and a levered firm, L. The total income available to the security holders of firm U is $600, and assuming a cost of equity capital equal to 10 percent, the value of firm U is calculated, using Equation 13.2, to be $6,000.

Because interest paid to debtholders is a tax-deductible expense, the total income available to the debt and equity security holders of firm L, shown in Table 13-2, is $640. This amount is greater than the $600 available to the firm U equity security holders by $40. The $40 amount is the tax shield caused by the tax deductibility of the interest payments. The annual tax shield amount is calculated using the following equation:

$$\text{Tax shield amount} = i \times B \times T \tag{13.3}$$

$$= (0.05) \times (\$2,000) \times (0.40)$$

$$= \$40$$

The total market value of firm L is obtained using Equation 13.2:

$$\text{Market value of firm L} = \frac{D}{k_e} + \frac{I}{k_d}$$

$$= \frac{\$540}{0.1125} + \frac{\$100}{0.05}$$

$$= \$4800 + \$2000$$

$$= \$6800$$

In this example the value of firm L is greater than firm U's value by an amount equal to $800. This difference in value is caused by the tax shield. In fact, the difference in value between the levered and unlevered firm is equal to the present value of the tax shield from the perpetual debt:

$$\text{Present value of tax shield} = \frac{i \times B \times T}{i}$$

$$= B \times T \tag{13.4}$$

In this equation, the annual tax shield amount, iBT, is discounted at a rate,

443

$i(i = k_d)$. In the case of firm L, the present value of the tax shield is $800, calculated as follows:

$$\text{Present value of tax shield} = \$2,000 \times 0.40$$
$$= \$800$$

We can now state that the market value of the levered firm is equal to the market value of the unlevered firm plus the present value of the tax shield:

$$\begin{array}{ccc}\text{Market value of} \\ \text{levered firm}\end{array} = \begin{array}{c}\text{Market value of} \\ \text{unlevered firm}\end{array} + \begin{array}{c}\text{Present value of} \\ \text{tax shield}\end{array} \qquad \textbf{(13.5)}$$

From this equation we can conclude that the value of the firm increases linearly as the amount of debt in the capital structure increases, as shown in the upper panel of Figure 13-3. This result implies that a firm should increase its level of debt to the point at which the capital structure consists entirely of debt. In other words, the market value of the firm is maximized and its optimal capital structure is achieved when capital structure is all debt. As shown in the lower panel of Figure 13-3, the weighted cost of capital, k_a, declines with increases in the debt-to-total assets ratio. The weighted cost of capital is minimized at a debt-to-total-assets ratio of 100 percent.

In practice, we *normally* do not observe companies with extremely high levels of debt in their capital structures. (The increasing volume of financial restructurings and leveraged buyouts, such as the KKR takeover of RJR Nabisco, which have resulted in debt ratios of 80 to more than 90 percent, suggest that many managers are paying closer attention to the advantages of debt financing.) Even in the face of leveraged buyouts, however, we still do not observe many companies that approach a 100 percent debt-financed capital structure. Hence, other factors must be influencing the determination of an optimal capital structure. Two of the most important factors are bankruptcy and agency costs. These are considered in the following section.

Capital Structure with a Corporate Income Tax, Bankruptcy Costs, and Agency Costs

The capital structure analysis in this section assumes a corporate income tax and assumes bankruptcy and agency costs.

BANKRUPTCY COSTS. From a practical viewpoint, a firm cannot expect to gain the benefits associated with the tax deductibility of interest payments without also increasing certain costs. One significant cost category is the costs of financial distress, or bankruptcy.[10] As a firm increases its debt level, lenders may demand very high interest payments to compensate for the increased financial risk taken on by the firm. The high interest payments constitute a cost to the firm. In the extreme, lenders may choose not to lend at all. Under these conditions, the firm may have to forego acceptable projects. Thus, the firm incurs an opportunity cost. In addition, some customers

---

[10] In this discussion we follow the convention of using the term *bankruptcy* to refer generally to a condition of financial distress. As will be seen in Chapter 22, there also is a more precise legal meaning of the term *bankruptcy*.

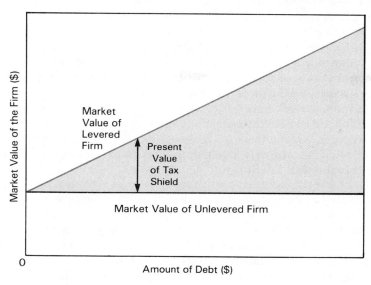

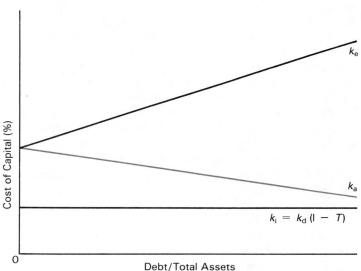

and potential customers may lose confidence in the firm's ability to continue in existence and instead buy from other companies more likely to remain in business. This loss of customer confidence is another bankruptcy cost. As a company experiences cash flow, or insolvency, problems, it may incur legal and accounting costs as it attempts to financially restructure itself. Finally, if the firm is forced to liquidate, assets may have to be sold at less than their market values. These costs also are bankruptcy costs.

Altman[11] has measured the size of bankruptcy costs for industrial firms. He defines *bankruptcy costs* to consist of direct costs (costs paid by debtors in the bankruptcy and restructuring process) and indirect costs (costs associated with the loss of customers, suppliers, and key employees plus the managerial effort expended to manage the firm in its distressed condition).

[11] Edward Altman. "A Further Empirical Investigation of the Bankruptcy Cost Question," *Journal of Finance* 39 (1984): 1067–1089.

Altman found evidence that the direct costs of bankruptcy average about 6 percent of firm value at the time of filing for bankruptcy. Direct plus indirect costs as a percent of firm value averaged 12.1 percent three years prior to filing and 16.7 percent at the time of filing. Thus, it appears that bankruptcy costs are significant, even if one adjusts for the expected time of occurrence and the probability of occurrence. Castanias[12] offers evidence that supports this conclusion when he finds that small firms in industries with high failure rates tend to use less financial leverage.

The likelihood of bankruptcy is not a linear function of a firm's debt ratio. Rather, there is evidence that it increases at an increasing rate beyond some threshold level. Accordingly, bankruptcy costs also become more important beyond this threshold debt ratio.

AGENCY COSTS. As discussed in Chapter 1, in most large firms the security holders (often referred to as the *principals*), both debtholders and common stockholders, are not in a position to actively manage the firm's investment, financing, and daily operational activities. Security holders employ "agents" to carry out these important activities. Under these circumstances conflicts can develop between the interests of the principal and those of the agent. In the case of the choice between debt and common equity financing, the debtholders can be viewed as the principal and the common stockholders can be viewed as the agents. The common stockholders are in a position to direct the investment and financing decisions of the firm through the elected board of directors and the managers hired by the board.

When debt is used in the capital structure of a firm, there are incentives for the common stockholders to undertake actions that may be detrimental to the interests of the debtholders. These actions include investing in extremely risky projects. The higher expected returns from risky investments accrue to the benefit of stockholders. Also, in the absence of restraints, stockholders are inclined to increase the proportions of debt in the capital structure, thus diminishing the protection afforded the earlier bondholders. The higher risk resulting from these actions may lead to a reduction in a firm's bond ratings. Lower bond ratings translate into lower bond values in the marketplace and thus a loss in wealth to the bondholders.

Not surprisingly, bondholders will want to take actions that reduce the prospect of this wealth transfer to stockholders. Agency theory argues that expected agency costs will be borne by the agent. Therefore debtholders can be expected to demand a higher interest rate on the bonds they purchase in order to compensate them for the expected wealth losses. As an alternative, monitoring and bonding expenses can be incurred to reduce the incidence of these agency problems, and thereby reduce the interest rate that will be demanded by bondholders. In the case of bonds, monitoring and bonding expenses take the form of protective covenants in the bond indenture.

Typical protective covenants place restrictions on the payment of dividends, limit the issuance of additional debt, limit the sale of assets, and limit the type of assets that may be acquired. (Protective covenants are discussed in more detail in Chapter 15.) However, the more extensive are the protective covenants, the more costly it is to monitor compliance. In addition, increasingly extensive covenants may restrict the operating free-

---

[12] Richard Castanias. "Bankruptcy Risk and Optimal Capital Structure," *Journal of Finance* 38 (1983): 1617–1635.

dom and efficiency of managers, to the detriment of both stockholders and bondholders.

Thus, the firm can be viewed as having a choice along a continuum. At one extreme, there would be no protective covenants, resulting in high interest rates, low or no monitoring costs, and no restrictions placed on the operating freedom of managers. At the limit, all decisions of the firm would be subject to review by the debtholders. This is obviously not feasible. *Monitoring and bonding activities should be carried out by the firm up to the point that the reduction in the interest rate charged by debtholders is balanced against the cost of additional monitoring and bonding activities.*

At low debt ratios, bondholders do not demand extensive protective covenants and monitoring arrangements, because the risk exposure for the bondholders is viewed as being quite limited.[13] Also, at low debt ratios, the interest cost of debt financing will be low. As the amount of debt increases as a proportion of the total capital structure, bondholders find themselves subject to increased risk that managers (acting on behalf of stockholders) may make investments or take financing actions that could harm the current bondholders. Accordingly, monitoring costs are assumed to increase with increases in a firm's debt ratio, resulting in an increase in the *implicit* cost of debt, including the cost of monitoring and lost operating efficiency. This increase in the cost of debt has the effect of reducing the total value of the firm's securities.

In summary, agency costs are an increasing function of the proportion of debt in the capital structure of a firm. Because of this, agency costs represent another powerful reason, in addition to the increased bankruptcy potential at higher debt ratios, why a firm will choose a value-maximizing capital structure that is less than the 100 percent debt corner solution implied by the MM analysis.

THE VALUE MAXIMIZING CAPITAL STRUCTURE. The preceding discussion of the impact of taxes, bankruptcy costs, and agency costs indicates that the market value of a levered firm can be represented by the following equation:

$$
\begin{array}{l}
\text{Market value} \\
\text{of levered} \quad = \quad
\begin{array}{l}
\text{Market value} \\
\text{of unlevered} \quad plus \quad
\begin{array}{l}
\text{Present} \\
\text{value of} \quad minus \\
\text{tax shield}
\end{array} \\
\text{firm}
\end{array} \\
\text{firm}
\end{array}
$$

$$
\begin{array}{l}
\text{Present value} \\
\text{of bankruptcy} \quad minus \quad
\begin{array}{l}
\text{Present} \\
\text{value of} \\
\text{agency} \\
\text{costs}
\end{array} \\
\text{costs}
\end{array} \qquad \textbf{(13.6)}
$$

Figure 13-4 illustrates this relationship graphically. As indicated in this figure and in Equation 13.6, the present value of expected bankruptcy costs and the agency costs associated with debt financing offset the present value of the tax shield accruing from debt—resulting in an interior optimal (value-maximizing) capital structure.

[13] The recent takeover of RJR Nabisco by KKR appears to have altered this market perception somewhat. RJR's bondholders experienced a wealth loss of 20 percent or more as a result of the high leverage used in the takeover by KKR. This transaction had a significant impact on the corporate bond market as investors in the bonds of the most credit-worthy U.S. firms demanded higher returns to compensate them for this heretofore unexpected risk.

FIGURE 13-4

Value of the Firm as a Function of Capital Structure (with Corporate Income Tax, Bankruptcy Costs, and Agency Costs)

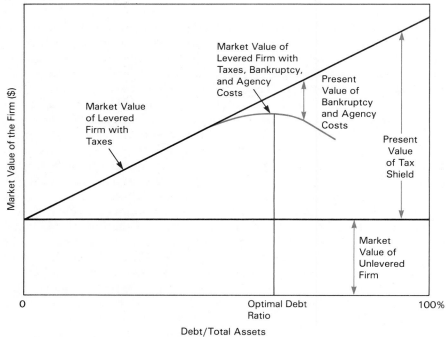

The Cost of Capital and the Optimal Capital Structure

In this section we examine the relationship between the cost of capital and the firm's capital structure when corporate taxes, bankruptcy costs, and agency costs are considered. In the following analysis we assume that capital structure contains only permanent debt and common equity; that is, we assume, for simplicity that no preferred stock financing is used.

The first step in the analysis considers the relationship between the cost of debt and capital structure. All other things being equal, investors in debt consider the debt less risky if the firm has a low, rather than high, proportion of debt in its capital structure. As the proportion of debt in the capital structure increases, investors require a higher return on the more risky debt. And because the firm's cost of capital is the investor's required return, the cost of debt increases as the proportion of debt increases.

The precise relationship between the cost of debt and the debt ratio is difficult to determine. This is because it is impossible to observe the cost of debt at two different capital structures (at the same time) for a single firm. Nevertheless, there is good evidence, as discussed earlier, that the cost of debt increases rather slowly for moderate amounts of debt. There is a point at which the capital markets consider any new debt "excessive" and therefore much more risky. The cost of debt curve, k_i, in Figure 13-5 illustrates such a relationship. The actual region where the cost of debt begins to increase more rapidly varies by firm and industry, depending on the firm's level of business risk.

The next step in this analysis focuses on the relationship between the cost of equity capital and capital structure. When a firm has a low debt ratio, any equity employed is less risky than equity used when the firm is financed with a relatively high proportion of debt. Earlier in this chapter it was shown that the greater the fraction of debt used, the greater is the variability

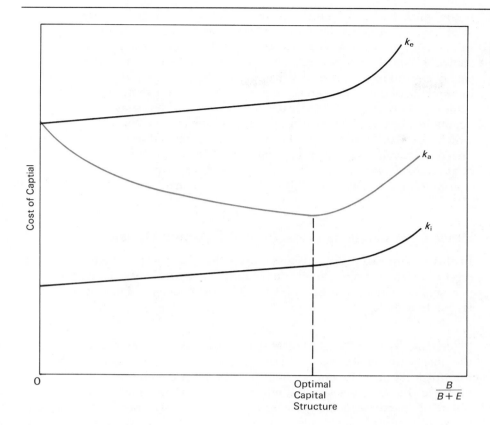

FIGURE 13-5

**Overall Cost of
Capital as a Function
of Capital Structure**

Cost of Capital

k_e

k_a

k_i

0

Optimal
Capital
Structure

$\dfrac{B}{B+E}$

in earnings per common share. In addition, the greater the fraction of debt used, the greater is the risk of bankruptcy. Because the returns expected by stockholders in the form of present and future dividends depend partly on current earnings, it can be concluded that variability in earnings per common share can result in variability of the returns to investors; that is, greater risk. Therefore it can be stated that investors' required returns and the cost of equity capital increase as the relative amount of debt used to finance the firm increases.

Once again, the exact nature of the relationship between the cost of equity and the debt ratio is difficult to determine in practice. However, there is agreement that the cost of equity capital increases at a relatively slow rate as the debt proportion increases up to moderate amounts. Then, in the range where additional debt is viewed as "excessive" and much more risky, the cost of equity increases more rapidly. This is shown in Figure 13-5. As is true in the debt illustration, the region where the cost of equity capital, k_e, begins to increase more rapidly varies by firm and industry.

The relationship between the weighted cost of capital, k_a, and the debt proportion now can be considered. The following equation,

$$k_a = \left(\frac{E}{B + E}\right)(k_e) + \left(\frac{B}{B + E}\right)(k_i)$$

can be used to calculate k_a for any debt ratio, provided that the values of k_e and k_i at the debt ratio are known. (B is the market value of debt and E

449

is the market value of equity in the firm's capital structure.) Because the relationships between the debt ratio and k_i and k_e have been developed, the relationship between k_a and the debt ratio follow accordingly. The k_a curve, shown in Figure 13-5, begins at $k_a = k_e$, because by definition the weighted cost of capital for an all-equity firm equals the cost of equity. As even small increments of debt are used, k_a becomes lower; as the debt proportion continues to increase from moderate to excessive, k_a "bottoms out" and then begins to increase. The resulting saucer-shaped curve contains a point at which the firm's overall cost of capital is minimized and its value maximized. This point is the firm's *optimal capital structure*. If the firm is thought of as a cash flow generator, it can be seen that the lower the discount rate (the weighted cost of capital), the higher is the firm's value.

Other Considerations in the Capital Structure Decision

In this section we briefly discuss some other factors that have an impact on the determination of an optimal capital structure. These factors include personal tax effects, industry effects, signaling effects, and managerial preference effects.

PERSONAL TAX EFFECTS. The MM tax case led to the conclusion that, in the absence of bankruptcy and agency costs, the firm should attempt to minimize its taxes by employing the maximum amount of debt. The MM tax case did not consider the effect of personal income taxes, however. Miller[14] has extended the tax case analysis to include both corporate and personal income taxes. Miller argued that although a firm can save taxes by increasing its debt ratio, individual investors would pay greater taxes on their returns from the firm if these returns were predominantly interest, rather than dividends and capital appreciation on common stock. Historically, the tax code has favored capital gains income from stock over interest income, because capital gains generally have been taxed at a lower rate than ordinary income (including interest income) and because taxes on capital gains are deferred until the capital gain is realized.

Miller concluded that when both personal and corporate income taxes are considered, there is no optimal debt ratio for an individual firm, although there is an optimal amount of total debt in the marketplace, reflecting the difference in corporate and personal tax rates. The Tax Reform Act of 1986, which removed much of the personal tax advantage associated with equity financing, has raised questions about the validity of the Miller model. Under the current tax law there probably is some tax advantage associated with corporate borrowing, as long as the firm is confident that it can use the full amount of the interest tax shield. This debt advantage depends upon corporate tax rates being higher than the tax rates of bondholders. The debt advantage disappears as the probability of being able to use the full amount of the interest tax shield declines.

INDUSTRY EFFECTS. A number of studies have found significant capital structure differences among industries. For example, a study by Kester[15]

[14] M. H. Miller. "Debt and Taxes," *Journal of Finance*, 32 (May 1977): 261–276.
[15] W. C. Kester. "Capital and Ownership Structure: A Comparison of United States and Japanese Manufacturing Corporations," *Financial Management* (Spring 1986): 5–16.

shows a debt to equity ratio for firms in the paper industry of 1.36 times, compared with 0.079 for firms in the pharmaceutical industry. Kester found that the more profitable are firms, the less debt they tend to use. Other studies have found that leverage ratios are negatively related to the frequency of bankruptcy in the industry. Also, there is some evidence that firms generating stable cash flows over the business cycle tend to have higher debt ratios. In general, the studies of industry effects in capital structure tend to conclude that there is an optimal capital structure for individual firms. The market rewards firms that achieve this capital structure.

SIGNALING EFFECTS. When a firm issues new securities, this event can be viewed as providing a signal to the financial marketplace regarding the future prospects of the firm or the future actions planned by the firm's managers.[16] Ross argues that signals provided by capital structure changes are credible because of the potential bankruptcy cost penalty incurred if the implied future cash flows do not occur. In general, studies of capital structure changes have found that new security offerings yield negative stock price responses. Repurchases of common stock have led to large positive announcement returns on the company's common stock. Actions that increase leverage generally have been associated with positive stock returns and actions that decrease leverage are associated with negative stock returns. The results of many studies of capital structure changes are consistent both with direct effects of the change, such as the benefits of greater tax shields, and with indirect information effects. Therefore when a firm makes capital structure changes it must be mindful of the potential signal that the proposed transaction will transmit to the marketplace regarding the firm's current and future earnings prospects and the intentions of its managers.[17]

MANAGERIAL PREFERENCE EFFECTS: A PECKING ORDER THEORY. Myers[18] has suggested that there may be no particular target capital structure. Myer's pecking order theory implies that firms prefer to finance internally. Myers argued that managers modify dividend payouts to avoid the need for external equity sales while avoiding major changes in the dividend amount. If external financing is required, Myers suggested that the safest securities are issued first. Debt tends to be the first security issued and external equity the security of last resort. The preference for internal financing is based on a desire to avoid the discipline and monitoring that occurs when new securities are sold publicly. In addition, Myers argued that the pecking order of financing may reflect the relative issue costs for various security types. The pecking order theory helps to explain why profitable firms tend to have low debt ratios.

Managerial Implications of Capital Structure Theory

The rich body of theoretical and empirical capital structure studies provides important insights for financial managers. First, it is clear that the capital structure decision is one of the centrally important decisions facing financial

---

[16] Stephen Ross. "The Determination of Financial Structure: The Incentive-Signaling Approach," *Bell Journal of Economics* 8 (1977): 23–40.
[17] See Ronald W. Masulis, *The Debt/Equity Choice*, (Cambridge, MA: Ballinger Publishing, 1988) for an excellent discussion and review of the signaling literature as it relates to capital structure decisions.
[18] S. C. Myers. "The Capital Structure Puzzle," *Journal of Finance* 39 (July 1984): 575–592.

managers. There is little doubt that changes in capital structure result in changes in the market value of the firm. Second, the benefits of the tax shield from debt lead to increased firm value, at least up to the point that increased bankruptcy and agency costs begin to offset the debt advantage. Third, the optimal capital structure is influenced heavily by the business risk facing the firm. Fourth, when managers make explicit changes in a firm's capital structure, these actions transmit important information to investors.

■■■ THE PRACTICE OF CAPITAL STRUCTURE MANAGEMENT

In the remainder of this chapter, we consider techniques used by managers seeking an optimal capital structure for their firm. These techniques include EBIT-EPS analysis and cash insolvency analysis.

EBIT-EPS Analysis

Consider the Yuma Corporation with a present capital structure consisting only of common stock (35 million shares). Assume that Yuma is considering an expansion and evaluating two alternative financing plans.[19] Plan 1, equity financing, would involve the sale of an additional 15 million shares of common stock at $20 each. Plan 2, debt financing, would involve the sale of $300 million of 10 percent long-term debt.

If the firm adopts Plan 1, it remains totally equity financed. If, however, the firm adopts Plan 2, it becomes partially debt financed (leveraged). Because Plan 2 involves the use of financial leverage, this financing issue basically is one of whether it is in the best interests of the firm's existing stockholders to employ financial leverage.

An analytical technique called *EBIT-EPS analysis*[20] can be used to help determine when debt financing is advantageous and when equity financing is advantageous. Table 13-4 illustrates the calculation of EPS at two different assumed levels of EBIT for both financing plans. Because the relationship between EBIT and EPS is linear, the two points calculated in Table 13-4 can be used to graph the relationship for each financing plan; this is shown in Figure 13-6.

In this example, earnings per share at EBIT levels less than $100 million are higher using the equity financing alternative. Correspondingly, at EBIT levels greater than $100 million, earnings per share are higher with debt financing. The $100 million figure is called the *EBIT-EPS indifference point*. By definition, the earnings per share for the debt and equity financing alternatives are equal at the EBIT-EPS indifference point:

$$\text{EPS (debt financing)} = \text{EPS (equity financing)} \qquad \textbf{(13.7)}$$

This equation may be rewritten as follows:

$$\frac{(\text{EBIT} - I_d)(1 - T) - D_p}{N_d} = \frac{(\text{EBIT} - I_e)(1 - T) - D_p}{N_e} \qquad \textbf{(13.8)}$$

---

[19] Preferred stock is not included in this example because it merely complicates the matter. Because preferred stock is a fixed-income security, it would be treated much like debt in this example.
[20] To review briefly, EBIT is earnings before interest and taxes, or operating income; EPS is earnings per share.

TABLE 13-4

EBIT-EPS Analysis—Yuma Corporation (all figures except per-share amounts are in millions of dollars)*

	EBIT = $75	EBIT = $125
Equity Financing (Plan 1)		
EBIT	$ 75	$125
Interest	—	—
EBT	$ 75	$125
Taxes @ 40%	30	50
EAT	$ 45	$ 75
Shares outstanding	50	50
EPS	$0.90	$1.50
% change in EBIT		+66.67%
% change in EPS		+66.67%
Debt Financing (Plan 2)		
EBIT	$ 75	$125
Interest	30	30
EBT	$ 45	$ 95
Taxes @ 40%	18	38
EAT	$ 27	$ 57
Shares outstanding	35	35
EPS	$0.77	$1.63
% change in EBIT		+66.67%
% change in EPS		+112%

*EBIT = earnings before interest and taxes; EBT = earnings before taxes; EAT = earnings after taxes; EPS = earnings per share.

where EBIT is earnings before interest and taxes, I_d is the firm's total interest payments if the debt alternative is chosen, I_e is the firm's total interest payments if the equity alternative is chosen, and N_d and N_e represent the

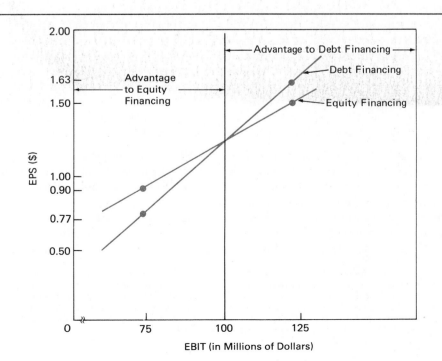

FIGURE 13-6

EBIT-EPS Analysis

EBIT (in Millions of Dollars)

number of common shares outstanding for the debt and equity alternatives, respectively. The firm's effective tax rate is indicated as T, and D_p is the amount of preferred dividends for the firm. This equation may be used to calculate directly the EBIT level at which earnings per share for the two alternatives are equal.[21] The data from the example shown in Table 13-4 yield the EBIT level of $100 million at the indifference point:

$$\frac{(\text{EBIT} - \$30)(1 - 0.4) - 0}{35} = \frac{(\text{EBIT} - \$0)(1 - 0.4) - 0}{50}$$

$$50(0.6 \text{ EBIT} - \$18) = 35(0.6 \text{ EBIT})$$

$$30 \text{ EBIT} - \$900 = 21 \text{ EBIT}$$

$$9 \text{ EBIT} = \$900$$

$$\text{EBIT} = \$100$$

Note that in the equity alternative, a 67 percent increase in EBIT (from $75 million to $125 million) results in a 67 percent increase in earnings per share (from $0.90 to $1.50) or a degree of financial leverage of 1.0. In the debt alternative, a 67 percent increase in EBIT results in a 112 percent increase in earnings per share or a degree of financial leverage of 1.67. A similar magnification of earnings per share will occur if EBIT declines. This wider variation in earnings per share, which occurs with the debt financing alternative, is an illustration of *financial risk*, because *financial risk* is defined as the increased variability in earnings per share due to the firm's use of debt. All other things equal, an increase in the proportion of debt financing is said to increase the financial risk of the firm.

DETERMINING AN OPTIMAL CAPITAL STRUCTURE USING EBIT-EPS ANALYSIS. The tools of EBIT-EPS analysis and the theory of an optimal capital structure can help a firm decide on an appropriate capital structure. This section utilizes an example to develop a five-step procedure designed to assist financial managers in making capital structure decisions.

Balboa Department Stores has been 100 percent financed with equity funds since the firm was founded. While analyzing a major expansion program, the firm has decided to consider alternative capital structures. In particular, it has been suggested that the firm should use this expansion program as an opportunity to increase the long-term debt ratio from the current level of 0 percent to a new level of 30 percent. Interest on the proposed new debt will amount to $100,000 per year.

■ **Step 1: Compute the expected level of EBIT after the expansion.** Based on Balboa's past operating experience and a projection of the impact of the expansion, it estimates its expected EBIT to be $500,000 per year under normal operating circumstances.

■ **Step 2: Estimate the variability of this level of operating income.** Based on the past performance of the company over several business cycles, the standard deviation of operating income is estimated to be $200,000

---

[21] An alternative indifference point measure is defined in terms of uncommitted earnings per share. *Uncommitted earnings per share* are defined as earnings after tax and preferred dividends *minus sinking fund obligations* (which are not tax deductible) *on outstanding debt* divided by the number of shares outstanding. Uncommitted earnings per share recognizes that sinking fund payments must be made if the firm is to remain solvent. The indifference point based on uncommitted EPS always will be at a higher EBIT level than the indifference point based on EPS.

per year. (Operating income is assumed to be normally distributed, or at least approximately so.)

■ **Step 3: Compute the indifference point between the two financing alternatives**—add new debt or maintain the all-equity capital structure. Using the techniques of EBIT-EPS analysis previously discussed, the indifference point is computed to be $300,000.

■ **Step 4: Analyze these estimates in the context of the risk the firm is willing to assume.** After considerable discussion, it has been decided that the firm is willing to accept a 25 percent chance that operating earnings in any year will be below the indifference point, and a 5 percent chance that the firm will have to report a loss in any year. To complete this analysis, it is necessary to compute the probability that operating earnings will be below the indifference point; that is, the probability that EBIT will be less than $300,000. This is equivalent on the standard normal curve to the following:

$$z = \frac{\$300,000 - \$500,000}{\$200,000}$$

$$= -1.0$$

or 1.0 standard deviation below the mean. The probability that EBIT will be less than 1.0 standard deviation below the mean is 15.87 percent; this is determined from Table V at the end of the book. Therefore on the basis of the indifference point criterion, the proposed new capital structure appears acceptable. The probability of incurring losses must now be analyzed. This is the probability that EBIT will be less than the required interest payments of $100,000. On the standard normal curve, this corresponds to the following:

$$z = \frac{\$100,000 - \$500,000}{\$200,000}$$

$$= -2.0$$

or 2.0 standard deviations below the mean. The probability that EBIT will be less than 2.0 standard deviations below the mean is 2.28 percent, as shown in Table V. According to this criterion, the proposed capital structure also seems acceptable.

If either or both of these tests had shown the proposed capital structure to have an unacceptable level of risk, the analysis would have been repeated for lower levels of debt than the proposed 30 percent rate. Similarly, because the proposed capital structure has exceeded the standards set by the firm, management might want to consider even higher levels of debt than the proposed 30 percent.

■ **Step 5: Examine the market evidence** to determine whether the proposed capital structure is too risky in relation to the following: the firm's level of business risk, industry norms for leverage ratios and coverage ratios, and the recommendations of the firm's investment bankers.

This step is undertaken only after a proposed capital structure has met the "internal" tests for acceptability. Financial leverage is a two-edged sword: it enhances expected returns, but it also increases risk. If the increase in perceived risk is greater than the increase in expected returns, the firm's weighted cost of capital may rise instead of fall, and the firm's value will decline.

It is important to note that there is no need for a firm to feel constrained by industry standards in setting its own capital structure. If, for example, a firm traditionally has been more profitable than the average firm in the industry, or if a firm's operating income is more stable than the operating income of the average firm, a higher level of financial leverage probably can be tolerated. The final choice of a capital structure involves a careful analysis of expected future returns and risks relative to other firms in the industry.

FINANCIAL LEVERAGE AND STOCK PRICES. The most important question arising from EBIT-EPS analysis is the impact of financial leverage on the firm's common stock price. Specifically, which financing alternative results in the higher stock price? Suppose the Yuma Corporation (discussed earlier) is able to operate at the $125 million EBIT level. Then, if the company chooses the debt financing alternative, its EPS will equal $1.63, and if it chooses the equity alternative, its EPS will be $1.50. But the stock price depends on the price–earnings (P/E) ratio that the stock market assigns to each alternative. Suppose the stock market assigns a P/E ratio of 10.0 to the company's common stock if the equity alternative is chosen, and a P/E ratio of 9.8 if the debt alternative is chosen. The common stock price, P_0, can be calculated for both alternatives as follows:

$$P_0 = (P/E\ ratio)(EPS)$$

Equity alternative:

$$P_0 = (10.0)(\$1.50) = \$15$$

Debt alternative:

$$P_0 = (9.8)(\$1.63) = \$15.97,\ or\ approximately\ \$16$$

These calculations show that in this case the stock market places a higher value on the company's stock if the debt alternative is chosen rather than the equity alternative. Note that the stock market assigned a slightly lower P/E ratio to the debt alternative. The stock market recognized the increased financial risk associated with the debt alternative, but this increased risk was more than offset by the increased EPS possible with the use of debt.

To carry the Yuma Corporation example one important step further, suppose the company, while operating at the $125 million EBIT level, chooses an even higher debt capital structure, which causes its EPS to increase to $2.25. Suppose further that the stock market feels that this high-debt capital structure significantly increases the company's financial risk—to the point where bankruptcy could occur if EBIT levels turned downward in a recession. If the stock market assigns a P/E ratio of 6.0, for example, the stock price would be $13.50, or $2.25 × 6.0, and it would be clear that this change in capital structure is not desirable.

It is important to emphasize that the P/E ratios in the preceding example simply are assumptions. As an analytical technique, EBIT-EPS analysis does not provide a complete solution to the optimal capital structure question.

In summary, the firm potentially can show increased earnings to its stockholders by increasing its level of financial risk. However, because increases in risk tend to increase the cost of capital (which is analogous to a decrease in the P/E ratio), the firm's management has to assess the tradeoff between the higher earnings per share for its stockholders and the higher costs of capital.

═══ **457** ═══
CHAPTER 13
The Capital
Structure Decision

Cash Insolvency Analysis

In Chapter 3 the *times interest earned* and *fixed-charge coverage* ratios were introduced. These ratios provide an indicator of the ability of a firm to meet its interest and other fixed charge obligations (including lease payments, sinking fund payments, and preferred dividends) out of current operating income. Also, in that chapter liquidity ratios, such as the *current ratio* and the *quick ratio*, were introduced. Liquidity ratios provide a simple measure of a firm's ability to meet its obligations, especially in the near term. In that chapter, we also indicated that the best measure of a firm's cash adequacy can be obtained by preparing a detailed cash budget—as discussed in Chapter 4.

Coverage ratios and liquidity ratios do not provide an adequate picture of a firm's solvency position. A firm is said to be technically insolvent if it is unable to meet its current obligations. We need a more comprehensive measure of the ability of a firm to meet its obligations if this information is to be used to assist in capital structure planning. This measure must consider both the cash on hand and the cash expected to be generated in the future. Donaldson has suggested that a firm's level of fixed financial charges (including interest, preferred dividends, sinking fund obligations, and lease payments), and thus its debt carrying capacity, should depend on the cash balances and net cash flows that can be expected to be available in a worst-case (recessionary environment) scenario.[22] This analysis requires the preparation of a detailed cash budget under assumed recessionary conditions.

Donaldson defines a firm's net cash balance in a recession, CB_R, to be

$$CB_R = CB_0 + NCF_R \qquad \textbf{(13.9)}$$

where CB_0 is the cash (and marketable securities) balance at the beginning of the recession, and NCF_R is the net cash flows expected to be generated during the recession. These *net cash flows* are defined to include expected collections from sales, other cash receipts such as interest income and dividend income, proceeds from the sale of assets, and cash from planned financing transactions such as the sale of new common stock or debt. Subtracted from these cash inflows are required cash outflows such as payroll expenses, payments on accounts payable, cash purchases of materials and supplies, taxes, utilities, asset purchases, interest and sinking fund payments (at the current debt financing level), and dividend payments.

For example in September, 1988 AMAX Corporation, a natural resource company, reported a cash (and marketable securities) balance of approximately $22 million. Suppose that management anticipates net cash flows of $30 million during a projected 1-year recession. These net cash flows reflect both operating cash flows during the recession and current required

[22] See Gordon Donaldson. "New Framework for Corporate Debt Policy," *Harvard Business Review*, 40 (March–April 1962): 117–131; and Gordon Donaldson. "Strategy for Financial Emergencies," *Harvard Business Review*, 47 (November–December 1969): 67–79.

fixed financial charges. Under the current capital structure, consisting of approximately 44 percent debt, the cash balance at the end of the recession would be $52 million ($22 million plus $30 million). Assume that the management of AMAX is considering a change in its capital structure that would add an additional $40 million of annual interest and sinking fund payments. The effect would be a cash balance at the end of the recession of

$$CB_R = \$22 \text{ million} + \$30 \text{ million} - \$40 \text{ million} = \$12 \text{ million}$$

The managers of AMAX must decide if this projected cash balance of $12 million leaves them enough of a cushion in a recession.

This analysis can be enhanced if it is possible to specify the probability distribution of expected cash flows during a recession. For example, if the managers believe, based upon past experience, that the expected cash flows during a 1-year recession are $30 million with a standard deviation of $20 million, they can compute the probability of running out of cash if the new debt is added. The probability of running out of cash is equal to the probability of ending the recession with a cash balance of less than $0. This can be computed as follows:

$$z = \frac{(\$0 - \$12 \text{ million})}{\$20 \text{ million}} = -0.60$$

From Table V, the probability of a z value of -0.60 or less is 27.43 percent. The managers may feel that this is too much risk to assume. If they only want to assume a 5 percent risk of running out of cash during a 1-year recession, they could determine the amount of additional interest and sinking fund payments that could safely be added as

$$z = -1.65 = \frac{(\$0 - x)}{\$20 \text{ million}}$$

$$x = \$33 \text{ million}$$

The -1.65 value is the number of standard deviations to the left of the mean that leaves approximately a 5 percent probability of occurrence in the lower tail of the normal distribution. This value was obtained from Table V. The $33 million represents the expected cash balance needed at the end of a 1-year recession if the risk of running out of cash is to be held to 5 percent. Because AMAX expects to enter the recession with $22 million in cash and generate $30 million during a 1-year recession, it can assume just $19 million in additional fixed financial charges ($52 million less $33 million).

The willingness of management to assume the risk associated with running out of cash depends on several factors including funds available from outstanding lines of credit with banks and the sale of new long-term debt, preferred stock, and common stock, and the potential funds realized by cutting back on expenses during a business downturn, reducing dividends, and selling assets.

Other Factors to Consider in Making Capital Structure Decisions

In addition to a consideration of tax effects, bankruptcy costs, agency costs, the business risk facing the firm, EBIT-EPS analysis, and cash insolvency analysis, there are additional factors normally considered as a firm makes its capital structure decisions. These factors are briefly discussed in this section.

INDUSTRY STANDARDS. Financial analysts, investment bankers, bond rating agencies, common stock investors, and commercial bankers normally compare the financial risk for a firm, as measured by its interest and fixed-charge coverage ratios and its debt ratio, with industry standards or norms. There is considerable evidence that the capital structure of an average firm varies significantly from industry to industry. For example, in 1988 the average long-term debt ratio in the automobile industry was about 27 percent. This ratio was 39 percent for the restaurant industry, 44 percent for the natural gas distribution industry, 49 percent for the electric utility industry, and 20 percent for the computer industry.[23] In general, firms tend to cluster closely around the industry debt ratio, probably reflecting the fact that the business risk facing a firm largely is industry determined. A firm that adopts a capital structure that differs significantly from the industry norms will have to convince the financial markets that its business risk is sufficiently different from that facing the average firm in the industry to warrant this divergent capital structure.

LENDER AND BOND-RATER REQUIREMENTS. Lenders and bond rating agencies often impose restrictions on a firm's capital structure choices as a condition for extending credit or maintaining a bond or preferred stock rating. For example, Standard & Poor's has established the benchmark standards for rating the debt of electric utilities shown in Table 13-5. The ratios shown in Table 13-5 are not the only factors considered when establishing a company's bond rating, but they are very important guidelines that a firm must follow if it wishes to retain or improve its credit rating. A more complete discussion of the factors considered by bond rating agencies is contained in Chapter 6.

MANAGERIAL RISK AVERSION. Management's willingness to assume risk often has a major impact on the capital structure chosen by the firm, although the relative risk aversion of management *does not* influence the firm's optimal capital structure. Some managers adopt unusually risky or unusually low-risk capital structures. When a suboptimal capital structure is chosen, the financial marketplace normally will penalize a firm for this action.

[23] *Value Line Investment Survey* (New York: Value Line, 1989), various issues.

Electric Utility Bond Rating Standards			T A B L E 13-5
Rating Level	**Pretax Interest Coverage**	**Debt Leverage**	
AAA	Greater than 4.5 times	Less than 41%	
AA	3.5 to 5.0 times	39 to 46%	
A	2.5 to 4.0 times	44 to 52%	
BBB	1.5 to 3.0 times	50 to 58%	
BB	Less than 2.0	Greater than 56%	

SOURCE: *Standard and Poor's Creditweek* (February 18, 1985): 2244.

For example, the average debt ratio in the beverage industry during 1988 was 31 percent. The debt ratio for Adolph Coors was 0 percent, because of an extremely conservative owner-manager financing philosophy. Most financial analysts agree that Coors could safely add a significant amount of debt to its capital structure and thereby lower its overall cost of capital and increase the market value of the firm. Coors has been able to sustain this capital structure because the Coors family controls 100 percent of the company's voting shares. If this owner-management control did not exist, it is very likely that Coors would be acquired by new owners who would significantly modify the company's capital structure. Differences in managerial philosophies regarding the appropriate capital structure for a firm are a major driving force behind many leveraged buyout offers (LBOs).

RETENTION OF CONTROL. Some firms use debt or preferred stock financing rather than common stock financing to avoid selling new shares of common stock. When new voting common stock is sold, the relative control position of existing stockholders is diluted.

INTERNATIONAL CONCERNS: CAPITAL STRUCTURE

Multinational firms have a more complex capital structure decision than purely domestic firms. Should each foreign subsidiary maintain the same capital structure as the parent's consolidated structure or should separate capital structures be established for each foreign subsidiary? Most firms tend to pay relatively little attention to establishing uniquely optimal capital structures for their foreign subsidiaries. Rather, the approach normally is one of establishing an optimal capital structure for the multinational firm as a whole, and then adjusting foreign subsidiary capital structures to take advantage of local financing opportunities. The object is to minimize the multinational firm's overall cost of capital.

Factors that determine the specific capital structure that will prevail for each subsidiary include

1. *Exchange rate risk in the host country.* When exchange rate risk is high, there will be a preference to raise more of the subsidiary's capital in the financial markets of the host country.
2. *Local industry standards.* In some countries, it may be common for firms to have higher debt ratios than in others. Subsidiary capital structures normally reflect these traditions.[24]
3. *Host country requirements.* Some governments place restrictions on the capital structure of multinational firms operating in their country.
4. *Risk of expropriation.* The greater is the risk that multinational firm's subsidiary assets may be expropriated without adequate compensation, the greater will be the incentive for the multinational firm to finance that subsidiary with debt capital, especially debt capital raised in the host country and not guaranteed by the parent firm.
5. *Availability of special, low-cost financing in a host country.* Some host countries make low-cost financing available to multinational firms to stimulate additional investment. When this low-cost financing is available, firms normally take advantage of it.

[24] J. M. Collins, and W. S. Sekely. "The Relationship of Headquarters Country and Industry Classification to Financial Structure," *Financial Management* (Autumn 1983): 45–51.

Other factors that determine the optimal capital structure for a multi-national firm as a whole include the increased capital market access for firms operating in several different countries and the extent to which political and economic country risk is diversified by the firm. The diversification of political and economic country risk largely is a function of the number and location of foreign subsidiaries of the multinational firm.

SUMMARY

- *Capital structure* is defined as the relative amount of permanent short-term debt, long-term debt, preferred stock, and common stock used to finance a firm. The capital structure decision is important to the firm, because there exists in practice a capital structure at which the *cost of capital* is minimized. This minimum-cost capital structure is the *optimal* capital structure, because the value of the firm is maximized at this point.
- The *business risk* of a firm refers to the variability of a firm's operating income. It is influenced by the variability of sales volumes, prices, and costs over the business cycle. Business risk also is influenced by a firm's market power and its use of operating leverage.
- The *financial risk* of a firm is the additional variability of earnings per share and the increased probability of insolvency that arises when a firm uses fixed-cost sources of funds, such as debt and preferred stock, in its capital structure.
- The use of financial leverage results in an increase in perceived risk to the suppliers of a firm's capital. To offset this increased risk, higher returns are required.
- Modigliani and Miller show that the value of the firm is *independent* of capital structure given perfect capital markets and no corporate income taxes. MM also show that the optimal capital structure consists entirely of debt if a corporate income tax exists.
- Given a corporate income tax, bankruptcy costs, and agency costs, an optimal capital structure consisting of both debt and equity is shown to exist.
- Capital structure changes often signal important information to investors about a firm's future prospects.
- *EBIT-EPS analysis* is an analytical technique that can be used to help determine the circumstances under which a firm should employ financial leverage. Basically, it involves calculating earnings per share at different levels of EBIT for debt and equity financing plans. This information then may be used to graph earnings per share versus EBIT to determine the EBIT levels at which financial leverage is advantageous to the firm.
- The *indifference point* in EBIT-EPS analysis is that level of EBIT where earnings per share are the same, regardless of which of two alternative capital structures is used. At EBIT levels greater than the indifference level, more financially levered capital structures will produce higher levels of earnings per share; at EBIT levels less than the indifference point, less financially levered capital structures will produce higher levels of earnings per share.
- A firm can analyze its capital structure decision by performing an EBIT-EPS analysis, computing the risk of unfavorable financial leverage at its expected level of operating income, and analyzing financial leverage ratios and coverage ratios for other firms in the industry. A careful evaluation of these facts, together with an analysis of the firm's business risk,

can assist in making the final determination regarding the desirability of a proposed capital structure.

■ *Cash insolvency analysis* can provide additional insights about the appropriate capital structure. Cash insolvency analysis evaluates the adequacy of a firm's cash position in a worst-case (recession) scenario.

QUESTIONS AND TOPICS FOR DISCUSSION

1. Explain the research results of Modigliani and Miller in the area of capital structure.
2. What is the relationship between the value of a firm and its capital structure without a corporate income tax? With a corporate income tax?
3. What is the relationship between the value of a firm and its capital structure, given the existence of a corporate income tax, bankruptcy costs, and agency costs?
4. What are the major limitations of EBIT-EPS analysis as a technique to determine the optimal capital structure?
5. In practice, how can a firm determine whether it is operating at (or near) its optimal capital structure?
6. Under what circumstances should a firm use *more* debt in its capital structure than is used by the "average" firm in the industry? When should it use *less* debt than the "average" firm?
7. Why do public utilities typically have capital structures with about 50 percent debt, whereas major oil companies average about 25 percent debt in their capital structures?
8. What role does "signaling" play in the establishment of a firm's capital structure?
9. What is *cash insolvency analysis*, and how can it help in the establishment of an optimal capital structure?

PROBLEMS*

1. Referring back to Table 13-2, calculate the value of firm L (without a corporate income tax), if the equity amount in its capital structure decreases to $5,000, and the debt amount increases to $5,000. At this capital structure the cost of equity is 15.0 percent.
2. a. Referring back to Table 13-3, calculate the value of firm L (with a corporate income tax), if the equity amount in its capital structure decreases to $3,000, and the debt amount increases to $3,000.
   b. For firm L (with equity = $3,000 and debt = $3,000), calculate the income available to the stockholders and the cost of equity.
3. Piedmont Instruments Corporation has estimated the following costs of debt and equity capital for various fractions of debt in its capital structure:

Debt Fraction	k_i	k_e with Bankruptcy Costs and without Agency Costs	k_e with Bankruptcy and Agency Costs
0.00	—	12.00	12.00
0.10	4.8	12.05	12.05
0.30	4.9	12.10	12.20
0.40	5.0	12.20	12.60
0.45	5.2	12.40	13.40
0.50	5.7	12.80	14.80
0.60	7.0	15.00	18.00

* Colored numbers denote problems that have check answers provided at the end of the book.

a. Based on these data, determine the company's optimal capital structure, (i) with bankruptcy costs and without agency costs, and (ii) with bankruptcy and agency costs.

b. Suppose the company's actual capital structure is 50 percent debt and 50 percent equity. How much higher is k_a at this capital structure than at the optimal value of k_a, with bankruptcy and agency costs?

c. Is it necessary in practice for the company to know precisely its optimal capital structure? Why?

4. Emco Products has a present capital structure consisting only of common stock (10 million shares). The company is planning a major expansion. At this time the company is undecided between the following two financing plans (assume a 40 percent marginal tax rate):

■ *Equity financing.* Under this plan, an additional 5 million shares of common stock will be sold at $10 each.

■ *Debt financing.* Under this plan, $50 million of 10 percent long-term debt will be sold.

One piece of information the company desires for its decision analysis is an EBIT-EPS analysis.

a. Calculate the EBIT-EPS indifference point.

b. Graphically determine the EBIT-EPS indifference point.

HINT: Use EBIT = $10 million and $25 million.

c. What happens to the indifference point if the interest rate on debt increases and the common stock sales price remains constant?

d. What happens to the indifference point if the interest rate on debt remains constant and the common stock sales price increases?

5. Two capital goods manufacturing companies, Rock Island and Davenport, are virtually identical in all aspects of their operations—product lines, amount of sales, total size, and so on. The two companies differ only in their capital structures, as shown here:

	Rock Island	Davenport
Debt (8%)	$400 million	$100 million
Common equity	$600 million	$900 million
Number of common shares outstanding	30 million	45 million

Each company has $1,000 million ($1 billion) in total assets.

Capital goods manufacturers typically are subject to cyclical trends in the economy. Suppose that the EBIT level for both companies is $100 million during an expansion and $60 million during a recession. (Assume a 40 percent tax rate for both companies.)

a. Calculate the earnings per share for both companies during expansion and recession.

b. Which stock is riskier? Why?

c. At what EBIT level are the earnings per share of the two companies identical?

d. Calculate the common stock price for both companies during an expansion if the stock market assigns a price–earnings ratio of 10 to Davenport and 9 to Rock Island.

6. Morton Industries is considering opening a new subsidiary in Boston, to be operated as a separate company. The company's financial analysts expect the new facility's average EBIT level to be $6 million per year. At this time the company is considering the following two financing plans (use a 40 percent marginal tax rate in your analysis):

■ *Plan 1: Equity financing.* Under this plan, 2 million common shares will be sold at $10 each.

■ *Plan 2: Debt–equity financing.* Under this plan, $10 million of 12 percent long-term debt and 1 million common shares at $10 each will be sold.

a. Calculate the EBIT-EPS indifference point.

b. Calculate the expected EPS for both financing plans.

c. What factors should the company consider in deciding which financing plan to adopt?

d. Which plan do you recommend the company adopt?

e. Suppose Morton adopts Plan 2, and the Boston facility initially operates at an annual EBIT level of $6 million. What is the times interest earned ratio?

f. If the lenders require that the new company maintain a times interest earned ratio equal to 3.5 or greater, by how much could the EBIT level drop and the company still be in compliance with the loan agreement if Plan 2 is adopted?

g. Suppose the expected annual EBIT level of $6 million is normally distributed with a standard deviation of $3 million. What is the probability that the EPS will be negative in any given year, if Plan 1 is selected?

7. High Sky, Inc., a hot air balloon manufacturing firm, currently has the following simplified balance sheet:

Assets		Liabilities and Capital	
Total assets	$1,100,000	Bonds (10% interest)	$ 600,000
		Common stock at par ($3), 100,000 shares outstanding	300,000
		Contributed capital in excess of par	100,000
		Retained earnings	100,000
		Total liabilities and capital	$1,100,000

The company is planning an expansion that is expected to cost $600,000. It can be financed with new equity (sold to net the company $4 per share) or with the sale of new bonds at an interest rate of 11 percent. (The firm's marginal tax rate is 40 percent.)

a. Compute the indifference point between the two financing alternatives.

b. If the expected level of EBIT for the firm is $240,000 with a standard deviation of $50,000, what is the probability that the debt financing alternative will produce higher earnings than the equity alternative? (EBIT is normally distributed.)

c. If the debt alternative is chosen, what is the probability that the company will have negative earnings per share in any period?

8. The Anaya Corporation is a leader in artificial intelligence research. Anaya's present capital structure consists of common stock (30 million shares) and debt ($250 million with an interest rate of 15 percent). The company is planning an expansion and wishes to examine alternative financing plans. The firm's marginal tax rate is 40 percent. Two alternatives under consideration are:

■ *Common equity financing.* Under this plan an additional 3 million shares of common stock will be sold at $20 each.

■ *Debt financing.* Under this plan the firm would sell $30 million of first-mortgage bonds with a pretax cost of 14 percent and $30 million of debentures with a pretax cost of 15 percent.

a. Compute the indifference point between these two alternatives.

b. One of Anaya's artificially intelligent financial managers has suggested that the firm might be better off to finance with preferred stock rather than common stock. He suggested that the indifference point be computed between the debt financing alternative and a preferred stock financing alternative. Preferred stock ($60 million) will cost 16 percent after tax. Which option should be selected on an EPS basis? (No calculations are necessary if you set the problem up and think about the implications.)

9. The Bullock Cafeteria Corporation has computed the indifference point between a debt and common equity financing option to be $4 million of EBIT. Expected EBIT is $4.5 million with a standard deviation of $600,000.

   a. What is the probability that the equity financing option will be superior to the debt option?
   b. Under the debt option, Bullock will incur $3 million in interest expenses. What is the chance of Bullock losing money under the debt option?

10. Jenkins Products has a current capital structure that consists of $50 million in long-term debt at an interest rate of 10 percent and $40 million in common equity (10 million shares). The firm is considering an expansion program that will cost $10 million. This program can be financed with additional long-term debt at a 13 percent rate of interest, or preferred stock at a cost of 14 percent, or the sale of new common stock at $10 per share. The firm's marginal tax rate is 40 percent.

   a. Compute the indifference point level of EBIT between the debt financing option and the common stock option.
   b. Compute the indifference point level of EBIT between the common stock option and the preferred stock option.
   c. Is there an indifference point between the debt and preferred stock options? Why or why not?

11. The Oakland Shirt Company has computed its indifference level of EBIT to be $500,000 between an equity financing option and a debt financing option. Interest expense under the debt option is $200,000 and interest expense under the equity option is $100,000. The expected EBIT for the firm is $620,000, with a standard deviation of $190,000.

   a. What is the probability that the equity financing option will be preferred to the debt financing option?
   b. What is the probability that the firm will incur losses under the debt option?

12. Lassiter Bakery currently has 3 million shares of common stock outstanding that sell at a price of $25 per share. Lassiter also has $10 million of bank debt outstanding at a pretax interest rate of 12 percent, and a private placement of $20 million in bonds at a pretax interest rate of 14 percent. Lassiter's marginal tax rate is 40 percent.

    Lassiter is planning entry into a new market area. This project will require Lassiter to raise $30 million. Two alternatives have been proposed:

    ■ *Plan 1:* Sell new stock at a net proceeds price to Lassiter of $20 per share.

    ■ *Plan 2:* Sell a combination of stock at a net proceeds price to Lassiter of $20 per share and $10 million of long-term debt at a pretax interest rate of 15 percent.

    a. Compute the indifference level of EBIT between these two alternatives.
    b. If Lassiter expects to have EBIT of $20 million next year with a standard deviation of $5 million, what is the probability that Plan 2 will result in higher earnings per share than Plan 1?

13. Jackson Asphalt, Inc. (JA), currently has 2 million shares of common stock outstanding and $50 million of 10 percent coupon-rate first-mortgage bonds. JA's marginal tax rate is 40 percent. JA's CFO has made three alternative proposals for financing a planned capital expansion:

    ■ *Plan 1.* Sell $50 million of debentures at a coupon interest rate of 12 percent.

■ *Plan 2.* Sell $50 million of preferred stock paying a dividend at an 11 percent rate.

■ *Plan 3.* Sell 1 million shares of new common stock to raise $50 million.

If JA's only objective is to have the highest possible earnings per share next year, and if EBIT is expected to total $21 million next year, which alternative should be chosen based on an EBIT-EPS indifference point analysis?

14. Bowaite's Manufacturing has a current cash and marketable securities balance of $50 million. The company's economist is forecasting a 2-year recession. Net cash flows during the recession are expected to total $70 million, with a standard deviation of $60 million.

   a. Under these conditions, what is the probability that Bowaite's will run out of cash during the recession?

   b. Bowaite's is considering a major capital expansion project. If the project is undertaken it will be financed initially with debt totaling $200 million. This debt financing will require aftertax cash outflows for debt service during the 2-year recession of $60 million. If Bowaite's is willing to accept a 10 percent chance of running out of cash, should the expansion (with debt financing) be undertaken?

SELECTED REFERENCES

Barnea, A., R. Haugen, and L. Senbet. *Agency Problems and Financial Contracting.* Englewood Cliffs, NJ: Prentice-Hall, 1985.

Billingsley, R. S., R. E. Lamy, and G. R. Thompson. "The Choice among Debt, Equity, and Convertible Bonds." *Journal of Financial Research* (Spring 1988): 43–57.

Hochman, Shalom, and Oded Palmon. "The Impact of Inflation on the Aggregate Debt–Asset Ratio." *Journal of Finance* 40 (September 1985): 1115–1126.

Lee, Wayne Y., and Henry H. Barker. "Bankruptcy Costs and the Firm's Optimal Debt Capacity: A Positive Theory of Capital Structure." *Southern Economic Journal* 43 (April 1977): 1453–1465.

Linn, S. C., and J. M. Pinegar. "The Effect of Issuing Preferred Stock on Common and Preferred Stockholder Wealth." *Journal of Financial Economics* 22 (1988): 155–184.

Miller, M. "Debt and Taxes." *Journal of Finance* 32 (May 1977): 261–275.

Modigliani, F., and M. Miller. "The Cost of Capital, Corporation Finance, and the Theory of Investment." *American Economic Review* (June 1958): 261–297.

Myers, Stewart C. "The Capital Structure Puzzle." *Journal of Finance* (July 1984): 575–592.

Titman, S. "The Effect of Capital Structure on a Firm's Liquidation Decision." *Journal of Financial Economics* 13 (1984): 137–151.

Operating and Financial Leverage

INTRODUCTION

The concepts of operating and financial leverage are useful to financial analysis, planning, and control. In finance, *leverage* is defined as a firm's use of assets and liabilities having fixed costs in an attempt to increase potential returns to stockholders. Specifically, operating leverage involves the use of *assets* having fixed costs, whereas financial leverage involves the use of *liabilities* (and *preferred stock*) having fixed costs.

A firm utilizes operating and financial leverage in the hope of earning returns in excess of the fixed costs of the assets and liabilities (and preferred stock), thereby increasing the returns to common stockholders. Leverage is a two-edged sword, however; because it also increases the *variability* (or risk) of these returns. If, for example, a firm earns returns that are *less* than the fixed costs of assets and liabilities, then the use of leverage actually can *decrease* the returns to common stockholders. Thus, leverage magnifies shareholders' potential losses as well as potential gains. Leverage concepts are particularly revealing to the financial analyst in that they highlight the *risk–return tradeoffs* of various types of financial decisions.

This appendix begins by discussing the relationship between a firm's use of leverage and the income statement. Next, the measurement of operating leverage and its relationship to risk is illustrated. This is followed by an examination of financial leverage and its relationship to risk. And, finally, the chapter concludes with a discussion of the combined effects of operating and financial leverage on a firm's overall level of risk and returns.

LEVERAGE AND THE INCOME STATEMENT

Financial statements of the Allegan Manufacturing Company are referred to throughout this appendix for purposes of illustration. Table 13A-1 contains two types of statements for the firm, a traditional format and a revised format. The traditional format shows various categories of costs as separate entries. *Operating costs* include such items as the cost of sales and general, administrative, and selling expenses. Interest charges and preferred dividends, which represent *capital costs*, are listed separately, as are income taxes.

The revised format is more useful in leverage analysis, because it divides the firm's operating costs into two categories, *fixed* and *variable*.

Traditional and Revised Income Statements, Allegan Manufacturing Company, Year Ending December 31, 19X1

Traditional Income Statement Format

	Sales		$5,000,000
Operating leverage	*Less* Cost of sales	$2,500,000	
	Selling, administrative, and general expenses	1,500,000	
	Total operating costs		4,000,000
	Earnings before interest and taxes (EBIT)		1,000,000
	Less Interest expense		250,000
	Earnings before taxes (EBT)		750,000
Financial leverage	*Less* Income taxes (40% rate)		300,000
	Earnings after taxes (EAT)		450,000
	Less Preferred stock dividends		150,000
	Earnings available to common stockholders		$ 300,000
	Earnings per share (EPS)—100,000 shares		$3.00

Revised Income Statement Format

	Sales		$5,000,000
Operating leverage	*Less Variable* operating costs	$3,000,000	
	Fixed operating costs	1,000,000	
	Total operating costs		4,000,000
	Earnings before interest and taxes (EBIT)		1,000,000
Financial leverage	*Less Fixed* capital costs (interest)		250,000
	Earnings before taxes (EBT)		750,000
	Less Income taxes *(variable)*, 40% rate		300,000
	Earnings after taxes (EAT)		450,000
	Less Fixed capital costs (Preferred stock dividends)		150,000
	Earnings available to common stockholders		$ 300,000
	Earnings per share (EPS)—100,000 shares		$3.00

Short-Run Costs

Over the short run, certain operating costs within a firm vary directly with the level of sales whereas other costs remain constant, regardless of changes in this level. Costs that move in close relationship to changes in sales are called *variable costs*. They are tied to the number of units produced and sold by the firm rather than to the passage of time. They include raw material and direct labor costs, as well as sales commissions.

Over the short run, certain other operating costs are independent of sales or output levels. These, termed *fixed costs*, primarily are related to the passage of time. Depreciation on property, plant, and equipment; rent; insurance; lighting and heating bills; property taxes; and the salaries of management all usually are considered fixed costs. If a firm expects to keep functioning, it must continue to pay these costs, regardless of the sales level.

A third category, *semivariable costs*, also can be considered. Semivariable costs are costs that increase in a *stepwise* manner as output is increased. One cost that sometimes behaves in a stepwise manner is management salaries. Whereas these costs generally are considered fixed, this assumption is not always strictly valid. For example, Public Service Company of New Mexico faced with declining profits in 1988 and 1989, cut the salaries of many of its administrative personnel and reduced its work force by nearly 20 percent.

Panels a, b, and c of Figure 13A-1 show the behavior of variable, fixed, and semivariable costs, respectively, over the firm's output range.

Long-Run Costs

Over the *long run*, all costs are variable. In time, a firm can change the size of its physical facilities and number of management personnel in response to changes in the level of sales. Not all costs can be classified as either completely fixed or variable; some have both fixed and variable components. Costs for utilities, such as water and electricity, frequently fall into this category. Whereas part of a firm's utility costs (such as electricity) are fixed and must be paid regardless of the level of sales or output, another part is variable in that it is tied directly to sales or production levels. In the revised format of Allegan's income statement, these are divided into their fixed and variable components and included in their respective categories of operating costs.

Note that in the revised income statement format, both interest charges and preferred dividends represent fixed capital costs. These costs are contractual in nature and thus are independent of a firm's level of sales or earnings. Also, note that income taxes represent a variable cost that is a function of earnings before taxes.

▓▓▓ OPERATING AND FINANCIAL LEVERAGE

Whenever a firm incurs either fixed operating costs or fixed capital costs, it is said to be using *leverage*. Fixed obligations allow the firm to magnify small changes into larger ones—just as a small push on one end of an actual lever results in a large "lift" at the other end.

Operating leverage has fixed operating costs for its "fulcrum." When a firm incurs fixed operating costs, a change in sales revenue is magnified into a relatively larger change in earnings before interest and taxes (EBIT). The multiplier effect resulting from the use of fixed operating costs is known as the *degree of operating leverage*.

Financial leverage has fixed capital costs for its "fulcrum." When a firm incurs fixed capital costs, a change in EBIT is magnified into a larger change in earnings per share (EPS). The multiplier effect resulting from the use of fixed capital costs is known as the *degree of financial leverage*.

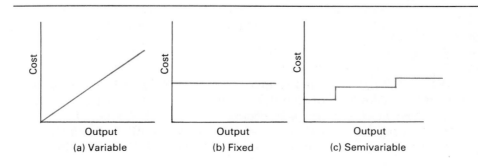

F I G U R E   13A-1

**Behavior of
(a) Variable,
(b) Fixed, and
(c) Semivariable
Costs**

Degree of Operating Leverage

A firm's *degree of operating leverage* (DOL) is defined as the multiplier effect resulting from the firm's use of fixed operating costs. More specifically, DOL can be computed as the *percentage change* in earnings before interest and taxes (EBIT) resulting from a given *percentage change* in sales (output):

$$\text{DOL at } X = \frac{\text{Percentage change in EBIT}}{\text{Percentage change in sales}}$$

This can be rewritten as follows:

$$\text{DOL at } X = \frac{\dfrac{\Delta \text{ EBIT}}{\text{EBIT}}}{\dfrac{\Delta \text{Sales}}{\text{Sales}}} \qquad \textbf{(13A.1)}$$

where ΔEBIT and ΔSales are the changes in the firm's EBIT and sales, respectively. Because a firm's DOL differs at each sales (output) level, it is necessary to indicate the sales (units of output) point X, at which operating leverage is measured. The degree of operating leverage is analogous to the elasticity concept of economics (for example, price and income elasticity) in that it relates percentage changes in one variable (EBIT) to percentage changes in another variable (sales).

The calculation of the DOL can be illustrated using the Allegan Manufacturing Company example discussed earlier. From Table 13A-1, recall that Allegan's variable operating costs were $3 million at the current sales level of $5 million. Therefore the firm's variable operating cost ratio is $3 million / $5 million = 0.60, or 60 percent.

Suppose the firm increased sales by 10 percent to $5.5 million while keeping fixed operating costs constant at $1 million and the variable (operating) cost ratio at 60 percent. As can be seen in Table 13A-2, this would increase the firm's earnings before interest and taxes (EBIT) to $1.2 million. Substituting the two sales figures ($5 million and $5.5 million) and associated EBIT figures ($1 million and $1.2 million) into Equation 13A.1 yields the following:

$$\text{DOL at } \$5,000,000 = \frac{\dfrac{(\$1,200,000 - \$1,000,000)}{\$1,000,000}}{\dfrac{(\$5,500,000 - \$5,000,000)}{\$5,000,000}}$$

$$= \frac{\$200,000}{\$1,000,000} \times \frac{\$5,000,000}{\$500,000}$$

$$= 2.0$$

A DOL of 2.0 is interpreted to mean that each 1 percent change in sales from a base sales level of $5 million results in a 2 percent change in EBIT *in the same direction as the sales change*. In other words, a sales *increase* of 10 percent results in a 10% $\times$ 2.0 = 20% *increase* in EBIT. Similarly, a 10 percent *decrease* in sales produces a 10% $\times$ 2.0 = 20% *decrease* in EBIT.

Effect on Earnings per Share of a 10 Percent Increase in Sales, Allegan Manufacturing Company, Year Ending December 31, 19X1

	(1)		(2)	% Change [(2) − (1)] ÷ (1)
Sales		$5,000,000	$5,500,000	+10%
Less Variable operating costs (0.60 × Sales)	$3,000,000		$3,300,000	+10%
Fixed operating costs	1,000,000		$1,000,000	0%
Total operating costs		4,000,000	4,300,000	+ 8%
Earnings before interest and taxes		$1,000,000	$1,200,000	+20%
Less Interest payments (fixed capital cost)		250,000	250,000	0%
Earnings before taxes		$ 750,000	$ 950,000	+27%
Less Income taxes (variable), 40%		300,000	380,000	+27%
Earnings after taxes		$ 450,000	$ 570,000	+27%
Less Preferred dividends (fixed capital cost)		150,000	150,000	0%
Earnings available to common stockholders		$ 300,000	$ 420,000	+40%
Earnings per share (100,000 shares)		$3.00	$4.20	+40%

The greater a firm's DOL, the greater the magnification of sales changes into EBIT changes.

Equation 13A.1 requires the use of two different values of sales and EBIT. Another equation[1] that can be used to compute a firm's DOL more easily is as follows:

$$\text{DOL at } X = \frac{\text{Sales} - \text{Variable costs}}{\text{EBIT}} \qquad \textbf{(13A.2)}$$

Inserting data from Table 13A-1 on the Allegan Manufacturing Company into Equation 13A.2 gives the following:

$$\text{DOL at \$5 million} = \frac{\$5 \text{ million} - \$3 \text{ million}}{\$1 \text{ million}}$$

$$= 2.0$$

This result is the same as that obtained using the more complex Equation 13A.1.

A firm's DOL is a function of the nature of the production process. If the firm employs large amounts of labor-saving equipment in its operations, it tends to have relatively high fixed operating costs and relatively low variable operating costs. Such a cost structure yields a high DOL, which results in large operating profits (positive EBIT) if sales are high and large operating losses (negative EBIT) if sales are depressed.

[1] Equation 13A.2 is derived from Equation 13A.1. Problem 4 at the end of this appendix asks for an explanation of how this is done.

DOL and Breakeven Analysis

The variables defined in Appendix 4A on breakeven analysis (TR = total revenue, Q = quantity, P = price/unit, V = variable cost per unit, and F = fixed costs) also can be used to develop a formula for determining a firm's DOL at any given output level. Because sales are equivalent to TR (or $P \times Q$), variable cost is equal to $V \times Q$, and EBIT is equal to total revenue (TR) less total (operating) cost, or $(P \times Q) - F - (V \times Q)$, these values can be substituted into Equation 13A.2 to obtain the following:

$$\text{DOL at } Q = \frac{(P \times Q) - (V \times Q)}{(P \times Q) - F - (V \times Q)}$$

or

$$\text{DOL at } Q = \frac{(P - V)Q}{(P - V)Q - F} \qquad \textbf{(13A.3)}$$

Assume that, in the case of Allegan Manufacturing Company, the parameters of the breakeven model are determined as P = \$250/unit, V = \$150/unit, and F = \$1 million. Substituting these values in Equation 13A.3 along with the respective output values yields the DOL values shown in Table 13A-3.

Note that Allegan's DOL is largest (in absolute value terms) when the firm is operating near the breakeven point (that is, where Q_b = 10,000 units). Note also that the firm's DOL is negative below the breakeven output level. A negative DOL indicates the percentage *reduction* in operating *losses* that occurs as a result of a 1 percent *increase* in output. For example, the DOL of -1.50 at an output level of 6,000 units indicates that, from a base output level of 6,000 units, the firm's operating *losses* are *reduced* by 1.5 percent for each 1 percent *increase* in output.

Degree of Financial Leverage

A firm's degree of financial leverage (DFL) is computed as the *percentage change* in earnings per share (EPS) resulting from a given *percentage change* in earnings before interest and taxes (EBIT):

$$\text{DFL at } X = \frac{\text{Percentage change in EPS}}{\text{Percentage change in EBIT}}$$

This also can be written as follows:

$$\text{DFL at } X = \frac{\dfrac{\Delta \text{EPS}}{\text{EPS}}}{\dfrac{\Delta \text{EBIT}}{\text{EBIT}}} \qquad \textbf{(13A.4)}$$

where ΔEPS and ΔEBIT are the changes in EPS and EBIT, respectively. Because a firm's DFL is different at each EBIT level, it is necessary to indicate the EBIT point, X, at which financial leverage is being measured.

Allegan Manufacturing Company: DOL at Various Output Levels

Output, Q	Degree of Operating Leverage, DOL	
0	0	
2,000	−0.25	
4,000	−0.67	
6,000	−1.50	
8,000	−4.00	
10,000	(Undefined)	Breakeven level
12,000	+6.00	
14,000	+3.50	
16,000	+2.67	
18,000	+2.25	
20,000	+2.00	

Using the information contained in Table 13A-4, the degree of financial leverage used by the Allegan Manufacturing Company can be calculated. The firm's EPS level is $3.00 at an EBIT level of $1 million. At an EBIT level of $1.2 million, EPS equals $4.20. Substituting these quantities into Equation 13A.4 yields the following:

$$\text{DFL at } \$1{,}000{,}000 = \frac{\dfrac{(\$4.20 - \$3.00)}{\$3.00}}{\dfrac{(\$1{,}200{,}000 - \$1{,}000{,}000)}{\$1{,}000{,}000}}$$

$$= \frac{\$1.20}{\$3.00} \times \frac{\$1{,}000{,}000}{\$200{,}000}$$

$$= 2.0$$

A DFL of 2.0 indicates that each 1 percent change in EBIT from a base EBIT level of $1 million results in a 2 percent change in EPS *in the same direction as the EBIT change.* In other words, a 10 percent *increase* in EBIT results in a 10% × 2.0 = 20% *increase* in EPS. Similarly, a 10 percent *decrease* in

T A B L E 13A-4 Earnings per Share for Alternative Levels of EBIT, Allegan Manufacturing Company, Year Ending December 31, 19X1

EBIT	$400,000	$800,000	$1,000,000	$1,200,000	$1,600,000
Less Interest expenses	250,000	250,000	250,000	250,000	250,000
Earnings before taxes	$150,000	$550,000	$ 750,000	$ 950,000	$1,350,000
Less Income taxes	60,000	220,000	300,000	380,000	540,000
Earnings after taxes	$ 90,000	$330,000	$ 450,000	$ 570,000	$ 810,000
Less Preferred dividends	150,000	150,000	150,000	150,000	150,000
Earnings available to common stockholders	−$60,000	$180,000	$300,000	$420,000	$660,000
Earnings per share (EPS)	−$0.60	$1.80	$3.00	$4.20	$6.60

EBIT produces a 20 percent *decrease* in EPS. The larger the firm's DFL, the greater is the magnification of EBIT changes into EPS changes.

Measuring a firm's DFL using Equation 13A.4 is somewhat cumbersome, because it necessitates using two EBIT and EPS projections. Computation is simplified when Equation 13A.4 is rewritten as follows:[2]

$$\text{DFL at } X = \frac{\text{EBIT}}{\text{EBIT} - I - D_p / (1 - T)} \tag{13A.5}$$

where I is the firm's interest payments, D_p the firm's preferred dividend payments, T the firm's marginal income tax rate, and X the level of EBIT at which the firm's DFL is being measured.

Unlike interest payments, preferred dividend payments are not tax deductible. Therefore on a comparable tax basis, a dollar of preferred dividends costs the firm more than a dollar of interest payments. Dividing preferred dividends in Equation 13A.5 by $(1 - T)$ puts interest and preferred dividends on an equivalent, *pretax* basis.

Consider again the data presented in Table 13A-1 on the Allegan Manufacturing Company. According to that table, EBIT = $1 million, I = $250,000, D_p = $150,000, and T = 40 percent, or 0.40. Substituting these values into Equation 13A.5 yields the following:

$$\text{DFL at } \$1,000,000 = \frac{\$1,000,000}{\$1,000,000 - \$250,000 - \$150,000 / (1 - 0.40)}$$
$$= 2.0$$

This result is the same as that obtained using Equation 13A.4.

Just as a firm can change its DOL by raising or lowering fixed operating costs, it also can change its DFL by increasing or decreasing fixed capital costs. The amount of fixed capital costs incurred by a firm depends primarily on the mix between debt and common stock equity in the firm's *capital structure*. *Capital structure* is defined as all *permanent sources of capital* available to a firm, including permanent debt, preferred stock, and common stock equity. Thus, a firm that has a relatively large proportion of debt and preferred stock in its capital structure will have relatively large fixed capital costs and a high DFL.

Degree of Combined Leverage

Combined leverage occurs whenever a firm employs *both* operating leverage and financial leverage in an effort to increase the returns to common stockholders. It represents the magnification of sales increases (or decreases) into relatively larger earnings per share increases (or decreases), resulting from the firm's use of both types of leverage. The joint multiplier effect is known as the *degree of combined leverage*.

---

[2] For the firm with no preferred stock, Equation 13A.4 becomes the following:

$$\text{DFL at } X = \frac{\text{EBIT}}{\text{EBIT} - I}$$
$$= \frac{\text{EBIT}}{\text{EBT}}$$

where EBT represents earnings before taxes.

A firm's degree of combined leverage (DCL) is computed as the percentage change in earnings per share resulting from a given percentage change in sales (output)

$$\text{DCL at } X = \frac{\text{Percentage change in EPS}}{\text{Percentage change in sales}}$$

This can be rewritten as follows:

$$\text{DCL at } X = \frac{\dfrac{\Delta\text{EPS}}{\text{EPS}}}{\dfrac{\Delta\text{Sales}}{\text{Sales}}} \qquad \textbf{(13A.6)}$$

where ΔEPS and ΔSales are the changes in a firm's EPS and sales, respectively, and X represents the level of sales at which the firm's combined leverage is measured. The degree of combined leverage also is equal to the product of the degree of operating leverage and the degree of financial leverage.[3]

$$\text{DCL at } X = \text{DOL} \times \text{DFL} \qquad \textbf{(13A.7)}$$

[3] This follows logically from the definitions of DCL, DOL, and DFL:

$$\frac{\text{Percentage change in EPS}}{\text{Percentage change in sales}} = \frac{\text{Percentage change in EBIT}}{\text{Percentage change in sales}} \times \frac{\text{Percentage change in EPS}}{\text{Percentage change in EBIT}}$$

To simplify matters, Equations 13A.2 and 13A.5 can be substituted into Equation 13A.7 to obtain a new formula for determining the DCL in terms of basic income statement quantities:

$$\text{DCL at } X = \frac{\text{Sales} - \text{Variable costs}}{\text{EBIT}} \times \frac{\text{EBIT}}{\text{EBIT} - I - D_p / (1 - T)}$$

or

$$\text{DCL at } X = \frac{\text{Sales} - \text{Variable costs}}{\text{EBIT} - I - D_p / (1 - T)} \qquad \textbf{(13A.8)}$$

These three formulas for calculating DCL can be illustrated using the Allegan Manufacturing Company example developed earlier in the appendix. Equation 13A.6 can be used to calculate Allegan's DCL with the data from Tables 13A-1 and 13A-2. The EPS level was $3.00 at a sales level of $5 million and $4.20 at a sales level of $5.5 million. Substituting these values into Equation 13A.6 yields the following:

$$\text{DCL at } \$5,000,000 = \frac{\dfrac{(\$4.20 - \$3.00)}{\$3.00}}{\dfrac{(\$5,500,000 - \$5,000,000)}{\$5,000,000}}$$

$$= \frac{\$1.20}{\$3.00} \times \frac{\$5,000,000}{\$500,000}$$

$$= 4.0$$

Substituting Sales = $5,000,000; Variable costs = $3,000,000; EBIT = $1,000,000; I = $2,500,000; D_p = $150,000; and T = 40% (0.40) into Equation 13A.8 gives the same value for Allegan's DCL:

$$\text{DCL at } \$5,000,000 = \frac{\$5,000,000 - \$3,000,000}{\$1,000,000 - \$250,000 - \$150,000 / (1 - 0.40)}$$

$$= 4.0$$

Also, recall from the earlier discussion of operating and financial leverage for Allegan that DOL = 2.0, and DFL = 2.0. Substituting these values into Equation 13A.7 yields a DCL value identical to that just calculated:

$$\text{DCL at } \$5,000,000 = 2.0 \times 2.0$$

$$= 4.0$$

This DCL is interpreted to mean that each 1 percent change in sales from a base sales level of $5 million results in a 4 percent change in Allegan's EPS.

OVERALL RISK

The degree of combined leverage used by a firm is a measure of the overall variability of EPS as sales levels vary due to fixed operating and capital costs. These costs can be combined in many different ways to achieve a desired DCL. In other words, a number of possible tradeoffs can be made between operating and financial leverage.

Equation 13A.7 shows that DCL is a function of DOL and DFL. If a firm has a relatively high DOL, for example, and wishes to achieve a certain DCL, it can offset this high DOL with a lower DFL. Or it may have a high DFL, in which case it would aim for a lower DOL. To illustrate, assume that a firm is considering purchasing assets that will increase fixed operating costs. To offset this high DOL, the firm may want to decrease the proportion of debt (and/or preferred stock) in its capital structure, thereby reducing fixed financial costs and the DFL.

The firm is limited in the amount of operating and financial leverage it can use in seeking to increase EPS. As the firm's use of leverage increases, so does its degree of risk, and investors who supply funds to the firm in the form of preferred and common equity and debt will consider this degree of risk when determining their required rates of return. The greater the firm's overall risk, the higher the rates of return investors will require. In other words, a firm that uses "excessive" amounts of leverage will have to pay higher costs for debt and preferred stock. These costs will tend to offset the returns gained from the use of leverage. Finally, "excessive" use of leverage will cause the market value of the firm to decline.

SUMMARY

- *Leverage* refers to a firm's use of assets and liabilities having fixed costs. A firm uses leverage in an attempt to earn returns in excess of the fixed costs of these assets and liabilities, thus increasing the returns to common stockholders.
- *Operating leverage* occurs when a firm uses assets having fixed operating costs. The *degree of operating leverage* (DOL) measures the percentage change in a firm's EBIT resulting from a 1 percent change in sales (or units of output). As a firm's fixed operating costs rise, its DOL increases.
- *Business risk* refers to the variability of a firm's EBIT. It is a function of several factors, including the firm's DOL and the variability of sales. All other things being equal, the higher a firm's DOL, the greater is its business risk.
- *Financial leverage* occurs when a firm makes use of funds (primarily from debt and preferred stock) having fixed capital costs. The *degree of financial leverage* (DFL) measures the percentage change in the firm's EPS resulting from a 1 percent change in EBIT. As a firm's fixed capital costs rise, its DFL increases.
- *Financial risk* refers to the additional variability of a firm's EPS that results from the use of financial leverage.
- The *combined leverage* of a firm is equal to the *product* of the degrees of operating and financial leverage. These two types of leverage can be combined in many different ways to achieve a given degree of combined leverage (DCL). The total variability of the firm's EPS is a combination of business risk and financial risk.

QUESTIONS AND TOPICS FOR DISCUSSION

1. Define *leverage* as it is used in finance.
2. Define and give examples of the following:

a. Fixed costs.
b. Variable costs.

3. Define the following:

a. Operating leverage.
b. Business risk.
c. Financial leverage.
d. Financial risk.

4. What other factors besides operating leverage can affect a firm's business risk?

5. How is a firm's degree of combined leverage (DCL) related to its degrees of operating and financial leverage?

6. Is it possible for a firm to have a high degree of operating leverage and a low level of business risk? Explain.

7. Is it possible for a firm to have a high degree of combined leverage and a low level of total risk? Explain.

PROBLEMS*

1. The Hurricane Lamp Company forecasts that next year's sales will be $6 million. Fixed operating costs are estimated to be $800,000, and the variable cost ratio (that is, variable costs as a fraction of sales) is estimated to be 0.75. The firm has a $600,000 loan at 10 percent interest. It has 20,000 shares of $3 preferred stock and 60,000 shares of common stock outstanding. Hurricane Lamp is in the 40 percent corporate income tax bracket.

a. Forecast Hurricane Lamp's earnings per share (EPS) for next year. Develop a complete income statement using the revised format illustrated in Table 13A-1 of this appendix. Then determine what Hurricane Lamp's EPS would be if sales were 10 percent above the projected $6 million level.

b. Calculate Hurricane Lamp's degree of operating leverage (DOL) at a sales level of $6 million using the following:
   i. The definitional formula (Equation 13A.1).
   ii. The simpler, computational formula (Equation 13A.2).
   iii. What is the economic interpretation of this value?

c. Calculate Hurricane Lamp's degree of financial leverage (DFL) at the EBIT level corresponding to sales of $6 million using the following:
   i. The definitional formula (Equation 13A.4).
   ii. The simpler, computational formula (Equation 13A.5).
   iii. What is the economic interpretation of this value?

d. Calculate Hurricane Lamp's degree of combined leverage (DCL) using the following:
   i. The definitional formula (Equation 13A.6).
   ii. The simpler, computational formula (Equation 13A.8).
   iii. The degree of operating and financial leverage calculated in Parts b and c.
   iv. What is the economic interpretation of this value?

2. The Alexander Company reported the following income statement for 19X1:

Sales	$15,000,000
Less Operating expenses	
Wages, salaries, benefits	$6,000,000
Raw materials	3,000,000
Depreciation	1,500,000
General, administrative, and selling expenses	1,500,000

* Colored numbers denote problems that have check answers provided at the end of the book.

Total operating expenses	12,000,000
Earnings before interest and taxes (EBIT)	$ 3,000,000
Less Interest expense	750,000
Earnings before taxes	$ 2,250,000
Less Income taxes	1,000,000
Earnings after taxes	$ 1,250,000
Less Preferred dividends	250,000
Earnings available to common stockholders	$ 1,000,000
Earnings per share—250,000 shares outstanding	$4.00

Assume that all depreciation and 75 percent of the firm's general, administrative, and selling expenses are *fixed costs* and that the remainder of the firm's operating expenses are *variable costs*.

a. Determine Alexander's fixed costs, variable costs, and variable cost ratio.

b. Based on its 19X1 sales, calculate the following:
  i. The firm's DOL.
  ii. The firm's DFL.
  iii. The firm's DCL.

c. Assuming that next year's sales increase by 15 percent, fixed operating and financial costs remain constant, and the variable cost ratio and tax rate also remain constant, use the leverage figures just calculated to forecast next year's EPS.

d. Show the validity of this forecast by constructing Alexander's income statement for next year according to the revised format.

e. Construct an EPS-EBIT graph based on Alexander's 19X1 income statement.

3. Gibson Company sales for the year 19X1 were $3 million. The firm's variable operating cost ratio was 0.50, and fixed costs (that is, overhead and depreciation) were $900,000. Its average (and marginal) income tax rate is 40 percent. Currently, the firm has $2.4 million of long-term bank loans outstanding at an average interest rate of 12.5 percent. The remainder of the firm's capital structure consists of common stock (100,000 shares outstanding at the present time).

a. Calculate Gibson's degree of combined leverage for 19X1.

b. Gibson is forecasting a 10 percent increase in sales for next year (19X2). Furthermore, the firm is planning to purchase additional labor-saving equipment, which will increase fixed costs by $150,000 and reduce the variable cost ratio to 0.475. Financing this equipment with debt will require additional bank loans of $500,000 at an interest rate of 12.5 percent. Calculate Gibson's expected degree of combined leverage for 19X2.

c. Determine how much Gibson must reduce its debt in 19X2 (for example, through the sale of common stock) to maintain its DCL at the 19X1 level.

4. Show algebraically that Equation 13A.2,

$$\text{DOL at } X = \frac{\text{Sales } - \text{ Variable costs}}{\text{EBIT}}$$

is equivalent to Equation 13A.1,

$$\text{DOL at } X = \frac{\Delta\text{EBIT/EBIT}}{\Delta\text{Sales/Sales}}$$

5. Albatross Airlines' fixed operating costs are $5.8 million, and its variable cost ratio is 0.20. The firm has $2 million in bonds outstanding with a coupon interest rate of 8 percent. Albatross has 30,000 shares of preferred stock outstanding, which pays a $2.00 annual dividend. There are 100,000 shares of common stock outstanding. Revenues for the firm are $8 million, and the firm is in the 40 percent corporate income tax bracket.

a. Compute Albatross's degree of operating leverage.
b. Compute its degree of financial leverage.
c. Compute its degree of combined leverage, and interpret this value.
d. Compute the firm's breakeven dollar sales volume.

6. Given the following information for Computech, compute the firm's degree of combined leverage (dollars are in thousands except EPS):

	19X1	19X2
Sales	$500,000	$570,000
Fixed costs	120,000	120,000
Variable costs	300,000	342,000
Earnings before interest and taxes	80,000	108,000
Interest	30,000	30,000
Earnings per share (EPS)	$1.00	$1.56

7. McGee Corporation has fixed operating costs of $10 million and a variable cost ratio of 0.65. The firm has a $20 million, 10 percent bank loan and a $6 million, 12 percent bond issue outstanding. The firm has 1 million shares of $5 (dividend) preferred stock and 2 million shares of common stock ($1 par). McGee's ordinary tax rate is 40 percent and its capital gains rate is 20 percent. Sales are expected to be $80 million.

a. Compute McGee's degree of operating leverage at an $80 million sales level.
b. Compute McGee's degree of financial leverage at an $80 million sales level.
c. If sales decline to $76 million, forecast McGee's earnings per share.

8. A firm has earnings per share of $2.60 at a sales level of $5 million. If the firm has a degree of operating leverage of 3.0 and a degree of financial leverage of 5.5 (both at a sales level of $5 million), forecast earnings per share for a 2 percent sales decline.

9. Blums, Inc., expects its operating income over the coming year to equal $1.5 million, with a standard deviation of $300,000. Blums must pay interest charges of $700,000 next year and preferred stock dividends of $240,000. Blums' marginal tax rate is 40 percent. What is the probability that Blums will have negative earnings per share next year? (Assume operating income is normally distributed.)

10. A firm has sales of $10 million, variable costs of $5 million, EBIT of $2 million, and a degree of combined leverage of 3.0.

a. If the firm has no preferred stock, what are its annual interest charges?
b. If the firm wishes to reduce its degree of combined leverage to 2.5 by reducing interest charges, what will be the new level of annual interest charges?

SELECTED REFERENCES

Gahlon, J. M., and James A. Gentry. "On the Relationship between Systematic Risk and the Degrees of Operating and Financial Leverage." *Financial Management* (Summer 1982): 15–23.

Gritta, Richard D. "The Effect of Leverage on Air Carrier Earnings: A Breakeven Analysis." *Financial Management* 8 (Summer 1979): 53–60.

Krainer, Robert E. "Interest Rates, Leverage, and Investor Rationality." *Journal of Financial and Quantitative Analysis* 12 (March 1977): 1–16.

Percival, John R. "Operating Leverage and Risk." *Journal of Business Research* 2 (April 1974): 223–227.

Reinhardt, U. E. "Break-Even Analysis for Lockheed's Tri Star: An Application of Financial Theory." *Journal of Finance* 28 (September 1973): 821–838.

Shalit, Sol S. "On the Mathematics of Financial Leverage." *Financial Management* 4 (Spring 1975): 57–66.

14

Dividend Policy

KEY CHAPTER CONCEPTS

1. Dividend policy determines the ultimate distribution of the firm's earnings between retention (that is, reinvestment) and cash dividend payments to shareholders.

2. Factors influencing the firm's choice of a dividend policy are examined.

3. Theories of the effect of dividend policy on the value of the firm include:
   a. Share values are determined solely by investment decisions and *not* by dividend policy.
   b. Share values are influenced by the division of earnings between dividends and retained earnings.

4. Alternative dividend policies include:
   a. Passive residual approach.
   b. Stable dollar dividend approach.
   c. Constant payout ratio approach.
   d. Policy of paying a small, regular dividend plus year-end extras.

5. Other important topics
   a. How dividends are paid.
   b. Stock dividends.
   c. Stock splits.
   d. Share repurchase as a dividend decision.

Agency costs Costs incurred by owners of a firm when the firm is managed by others. It includes monitoring costs, bonding costs, and any losses that cannot be economically eliminated by monitoring and bonding.

Clientele effect The concept that investors will tend to be attracted to companies that have dividend policies consistent with the investors' objectives.

Declaration date The day on which the directors of a company declare a dividend.

Dividend capture strategy Buying a stock shortly before its ex-dividend date to receive the quarterly dividend. Later, after the dividend has been received, the stock is sold.

Dividend reinvestment plan An option that allows shareholders to have their cash dividends automatically reinvested in additional shares of the company's stock.

Ex-dividend date The date on which the right to the most recently declared dividend no longer goes along with the sale of the stock. The ex-dividend date is 4 business days prior to the *record date*.

Informational content The concept that, for a company following a stable dividend policy, changes in dividend payments convey information (i.e., a *signal*) to investors concerning management's expectations about the future profitability of the company.

Insolvency A situation in which either a firm's liabilities exceed its assets or it is unable to pay its creditors as required.

Passive residual theory A theory of dividend policy that suggests that a company should retain its earnings as long as there are investment opportunities available promising a rate of return higher than the required rate of return.

Record date The date on which a company makes a list from its stock transfer books of those shareholders who are eligible to receive the declared dividend.

Stock dividend A payment of additional shares of common stock to stockholders.

Treasury stock Common stock that has been reacquired by the issuing company.

Middle South Utilities Suspends Its Dividend*

As a matter of policy, many firms pay out a relatively stable amount of their earnings to shareholders in the form of dividends. In general, a firm will increase dividend payments only when it is confident that it can sustain the higher rate through increased earnings and cash flows. Likewise, there is a reluctance to reduce the dollar amount of dividends from one period to the next unless the firm is faced with severe financial problems.

In August 1985 Middle South Utilities (MSU), which has revenues of $3 billion, suspended its quarterly dividend payment of $0.445 per share, effectively cutting its annual dividend rate from $1.78 per share to zero. This action resulted from a severe cash flow problem precipitated in part by the refusal of utility regulators to allow MSU's operating subsidiaries to raise rates sufficiently to recover their investments in the large Grand Gulf 1 nuclear plant. MSU was asking for rate increases of 50 percent or $1.5 billion. Without rate relief and some financial belt-tightening, such as reducing dividends, renegotiating (that is, stretching out) debt repayment schedules with its lenders, and cutting construction, the company faced the possibility of bankruptcy. According to financial analysts, MSU needed more than $1 billion in new capital during the coming year, but was expected to generate only about $250 million internally. Even with the possibility of $200 million in short-term rate relief, the company would still be faced with a cash shortage of $500 million.

Cutting the company's dividend would generate over $300 million in annual cash savings. Along with other financial measures, this action would go a long way toward solving the firm's short-term cash flow crisis. However, offsetting the savings associated with a dividend cut, there can be some undesirable effects. As Edwin Lupberger, MSU's chief financial officer, states, "Dividends are the seed corn for all our financing." A dividend cut would put the company in a "Catch 22" situation. The lower dividend payout would make it harder for the company to sell new stock or bonds to finance the estimated $1.5 billion of Grand Gulf costs that would have to be deferred over the next several years. Also, as the company found out, cutting the dividend can have a severe impact on the value of the firm. Over a period of less than 1 month in 1985, MSU's stock price dropped from $14 per share before the dividend suspension announcement to $9 per share after the announcement. This represented a loss of more than $1 billion or about 35 percent of market value.

For the next 3 years, the company did not pay any dividends. With no dividends paid to shareholders and with its long-term future in jeopardy, MSU's stock price fluctuated widely during this period, ranging from a low of $7.75 to a high of $16.25. As one financial analyst for Value Line, Inc., noted, "This stock is not for the typical utility investor." The company eventually received rate relief and averted bankruptcy. Although it still faced large write-offs (possibly $600 million or $3 per share) on a nuclear plant (Grand Gulf 2) whose construction was suspended, MSU began paying a (smaller) dividend ($.20 per share) in the last quarter of 1988.

This chapter discusses the elements of a sound dividend policy and how this policy can contribute to the overall firm objective of maximizing shareholder wealth.

* Based on an article in *Business Week* (September 2, 1985).

■ INTRODUCTION

The value of a firm is influenced by three types of financial decisions:

- ■ Investment decisions.
- ■ Financing decisions.
- ■ Dividend decisions.

Although each is presented as a separate topic in this and most financial management textbooks,[1] it is important to realize that the three are inter-

[1] In this text investment decisions are dealt with in Chapters 9 through 11, and 17 through 19, and financing decisions are discussed in Chapters 6, 7, 13, 15, 16, and 20.

dependent in a number of ways. For example, the investments made by a firm determine the level of future earnings and future potential dividends; capital structure influences the cost of capital, which in turn determines in part the number of acceptable investment opportunities; and dividend policy influences the amount of equity capital in a firm's capital structure (via the retained earnings account) and, by extension, influences the cost of capital. In making these (interrelated) decisions, the goal is to maximize shareholder wealth.

Consider the following dividend decisions:

1. During 1987 IBM paid out $2,654 million ($4.40 per share) in common stock dividends, or about 50 percent of its after-tax earnings of $5,250 million.
2. During 1987, Digital Equipment paid *no* dividends even though it had after-tax earnings of $1,137 million.
3. Also during 1987, Deere & Company (farm equipment manufacturer) paid out $16.962 million ($.25 per share) in common stock dividends even though it had a net after-tax *loss* of $90.019 million ($1.46 per share).
4. Finally, during 1988, Texas Utilities paid out approximately $490 million ($2.80 per share) in common stock dividends (a *decrease* in stockholders' equity) while, during the same period, the company sold $138.125 million in new common stock (an *increase* in stockholders' equity) and incurred the associated flotation costs.[2]

These dividend decisions raise a number of important questions, such as

1. Is IBM's dividend policy more consistent with shareholder wealth maximization than is Digital Equipment's dividend policy? Is one dividend policy necessarily optimal for all firms?
2. Why did Deere pay a common stock dividend when it had negative earnings? Alternatively, would not the elimination of its dividend have been a more prudent strategy, because it would conserve cash (i.e., reduce cash outflows) during this period of economic difficulty?
3. Why did Texas Utilities pay common stock dividends *and* incur the flotation costs of selling new common stock during the same time period? As an alternative to issuing new common stock, why didn't Texas Utilities reduce (or eliminate) its common stock dividend temporarily until it accumulated the amount of equity funds it planned to raise externally?
4. Finally, on a more fundamental level, does it really matter, with respect to the maximization of shareholder wealth, what amount (or percentage of earnings) a firm pays out in dividends?

In this chapter we seek to answer dividend policy questions such as these.

This chapter begins by examining the factors that influence a company's choice of dividend policy. Next, it considers the pros and cons of a number of different dividend policies. And, finally, it discusses the mechanics of dividend payments, along with stock dividends and share repurchase plans.

DETERMINANTS OF DIVIDEND POLICY

Dividend policy determines how the earnings of a company are distributed. Earnings are either retained and reinvested in the company or they are paid out to shareholders. In recent years the retention of earnings has been a

---

[2] See Chapter 16 for a discussion of flotation costs.

major source of equity financing for private industry. In 1987 corporations retained $74 billion in earnings, while issuing $43 billion in new common stock. Although the division between new stock issues and retained earnings tends to vary over time, retained earnings (in the aggregate) are more important than new stock issues as a source of equity.

On the one hand, retained earnings can be used to stimulate growth in future earnings and as a result can influence future share values. On the other hand, dividends provide stockholders with tangible current returns. Many factors combine to determine the dividend policy of a firm.

Legal Constraints

Most states have laws that regulate the dividend payments a firm chartered in that state can make. These laws basically state the following:

- A firm's capital cannot be used to make dividend payments.
- Dividends must be paid out of a firm's present and past *net* earnings.
- Dividends cannot be paid when the firm is insolvent.

The first restriction is termed the *capital impairment restriction*. In some states *capital* is defined as including only the par value of common stock; in others, *capital* is more broadly defined to also include the contributed capital in excess of par account (sometimes called *capital surplus*).

For example, consider the following capital accounts on the balance sheet of Johnson Tool and Die Company:

Common stock ($5 par; 100,000 shares)	$ 500,000
Contributed capital in excess of par	400,000
Retained earnings	200,000
Total common stockholders' equity	$1,100,000

If the company is chartered in a state that defines *capital* as the par value of common stock, then it can pay out a total of $600,000 ($1,100,000 − $500,000 par value) in dividends. If, however, the company's home state restricts dividend payments to retained earnings alone, then Johnson Tool and Die could only pay dividends up to $200,000. Regardless of the dividend laws, however, it should be realized that dividends are paid from a firm's *cash* account with an offsetting entry to the *retained earnings* account.

The second restriction, called the *net earnings restriction*, requires that a firm have generated earnings *before* it is permitted to pay any cash dividends. This prevents the equity owners from withdrawing their initial investment in the firm and impairing the security position of any of the firm's creditors.

The third restriction, termed the *insolvency restriction*, states that an insolvent company may not pay cash dividends. When a company is insolvent, its liabilities exceed its assets. Payment of dividends would interfere with the creditors' prior claims on the firm's assets and therefore is prohibited.

These three restrictions affect different types of companies in different ways. New firms, or small firms with a minimum of accumulated retained earnings, are most likely to feel the weight of these legal constraints when determining their dividend policies, whereas well-established companies with histories of profitable performances and large retained earnings accounts are less likely to be influenced by them.

Restrictive Covenants

Restrictive covenants generally have more impact on dividend policy than the legal constraints just discussed. These covenants are contained in bond indentures, term loans, short-term borrowing agreements, lease contracts, and preferred stock agreements.

These restrictions basically limit the total amount of dividends a firm can pay. Sometimes they may state that dividends cannot be paid at all until a firm's earnings have reached a specified level. For example, the term loan agreement that Atlas Corporation has with the Manufacturers Hanover Trust prohibits the payment of dividends without the prior approval of the bank.

In addition, *sinking fund requirements*, which state that a certain portion of a firm's cash flow must be set aside for the retirement of debt, sometimes limit dividend payments. Also, dividends may be prohibited if a firm's net working capital (current assets less current liabilities) or its current ratio does not exceed a certain predetermined level.

Tax Considerations

Prior to the 1986 Tax Reform Act, the personal marginal tax rates (up to 50 percent) on dividend income were higher than the marginal rates (up to 20 percent) on long-term capital gains income. This was an incentive for corporations to keep dividends low so that shareholders could receive a greater proportion of their pretax returns in the form of capital gains and thus increase their *after-tax* returns. However, the 1986 Tax Reform Act eliminated this differential by taxing both dividend and capital gains income at the same marginal rate (up to 33 percent).[3]

Despite the elimination of the favorable tax treatment of capital gains income, there still is a tax advantage (although smaller) to this form of income compared with dividend income. Dividend income is taxed immediately (in the current year), but capital gains income (and corresponding taxes) can be deferred into the future. Consequently, for most investors, the *present value* of the taxes on (future) capital gains income is less than the taxes on an equivalent amount of (current) dividend income.[4]

Whereas the factors just explained tend to encourage corporations to retain their earnings, the IRS Code—specifically Sections 531 through 537— has an opposite effect. In essence, the code prohibits corporations from retaining an excessive amount of profits to protect stockholders from paying taxes on dividends received. Dividend payments are considered taxable income. If a corporation decides to retain its earnings in anticipation of providing growth and future capital appreciation for its investors, the investors are not taxed until their shares are sold.

If the IRS rules that a corporation has accumulated excess profits to protect its stockholders from having to pay personal income taxes on dividends, the firm has to pay a heavy penalty tax on those earnings. It is the responsibility of the IRS to prove this allegation, however. Some companies are more likely to raise the suspicions for the IRS than others. For example, small closely held corporations whose shareholders are in high marginal

[3] The top marginal rate actually is 28 percent with a *5 percent surcharge* over certain income ranges (for example between $71,900 and $149,250 for married taxpayers).
[4] The exceptions to this rule are institutional investors (such as pension funds) that pay no income taxes and corporations (such as insurance companies) that pay a lower marginal tax rate on dividend income (10.2 percent) than on capital gains income (34 percent). See Appendix 2A for a discussion of corporate income taxes.

tax brackets, firms that pay consistently low dividends, and those that have large amounts of cash and marketable securities are good candidates for IRS review.

Liquidity Considerations

Dividend payments are cash outflows. Therefore the more liquid a firm is, the more able it is to pay dividends. Even if a firm has a past record of high earnings that have been reinvested, resulting in a large retained earnings balance, it may not be able to pay dividends unless it has sufficient liquid assets, primarily cash.[5] (Middle South Utilities, which was discussed in the Financial Dilemma at the beginning of this chapter, is an example of a company that was faced with a liquidity crisis and was forced to suspend its dividend payments.) Liquidity is likely to be a problem during a long business downturn, when both profits and cash flows often decline. Rapidly growing firms with many profitable investment opportunities also often find it difficult to maintain adequate liquidity and pay dividends at the same time.

Borrowing Capacity and Access to the Capital Markets

Liquidity is desirable for a number of reasons. Specifically, it provides protection in the event of a financial crisis. It also provides the flexibility needed to take advantage of unusual financial and investment opportunities. There are other ways of achieving this flexibility and security, however. For example, companies frequently establish lines of credit and revolving credit agreements with banks, allowing them to borrow on short notice.[6] Large well-established firms usually are able to go directly to credit markets with either a bond issue or a sale of commercial paper. The more access a firm has to these external sources of funds, the better able it will be to make dividend payments.

A small firm whose stock is closely held and infrequently traded often finds it difficult (or undesirable) to sell new equity shares in the markets. As a result, retained earnings are the only source of new equity. When a firm of this type is faced with desirable investment opportunities, the payment of dividends is often inconsistent with the objective of maximizing the value of the firm.

Earnings Stability

Most large widely held firms are reluctant to lower their dividend payments, even in times of financial stress. Therefore a firm with a history of stable earnings usually is more willing to pay a higher dividend than a firm with erratic earnings.

A firm whose cash flows have been more or less constant over the years can be fairly confident about its future and frequently reflects this confidence in higher dividend payments.

---

[5] For example, John A. Brittain found that corporate dividend payments are positively related to a firm's liquidity. See John A. Brittain, *Corporate Dividend Policy* (Washington, D.C.: Brookings, 1966), pp. 184–187.

[6] See Chapter 20 for a more detailed discussion of this topic.

Growth Prospects

A rapidly growing firm usually has a substantial need for funds to finance the abundance of attractive investment opportunities. Instead of paying large dividends and then attempting to sell new shares to raise the equity investment capital it needs, this type of firm usually retains larger portions of its earnings and avoids the expense and inconvenience of public stock offerings. Table 14-1 illustrates the relationship between earnings growth rates and dividend payout ratios for selected companies. Note that the companies with the highest dividend payout ratios tend to have the lowest growth rates and vice versa.

Inflation

In an inflationary environment, funds generated by depreciation often are not sufficient to replace a firm's assets as they become obsolete. Under these circumstances a firm may be forced to retain a higher percentage of earnings to maintain the earning power of its asset base.

Inflation also has an impact on a firm's working capital needs. In an atmosphere of rising prices, *actual* dollars invested in inventories and accounts receivable tend to increase to support the same *physical* volume of business.[7] And, because the dollar amounts of accounts payable and other payables requiring cash outlays are high with rising prices, transaction cash balances normally have to be increased. Thus, inflation can force a firm to retain more earnings as it attempts to maintain its same relative preinflation working capital position.

Shareholder Preferences

In a closely held corporation with relatively few stockholders, management may be able to set dividends according to the preferences of its stockholders.

[7] The ultimate impact of inflation on a firm's liquidity depends on whether the firm is able to pass these higher costs on to its customers in the form of higher prices.

T A B L E 14-1

Recent Dividend Payout Ratios and Growth Rates for Selected Companies

Company	1988 Dividend Payout Ratio (%)	10-year EPS Growth Rate (%)
Public Service Co. of New Mexico	100.4	2.0
San Diego Gas & Electric	81.8	4.5
American Electric Power	72.6	−0.5
Potomac Electric Power	64.1	9.5
Sears	52.8	6.0
K-Mart	46.3	7.3
American Brands	41.5	12.0
Westinghouse Electric	34.1	13.0
McDonald's Corp.	16.0	16.5
Tandy	15.5	17.5
Wal-Mart Stores	10.6	36.5
Digital Equipment	0.0	19.0

SOURCE: *Value Line Investment Survey* (New York: Value Line, Inc.), various issues. Copyright © by Value Line, Inc. Used by permission.

For example, assume that the majority of a firm's stockholders are in high marginal tax brackets. They probably favor a policy of high earnings retention, resulting in eventual price appreciation, over a high payout dividend policy. However, high earnings retention implies that the firm has enough acceptable capital investment opportunities to justify the low payout dividend policy. In addition, recall that the IRS does not permit corporations to retain excessive earnings if they have no legitimate investment opportunities. Also, a policy of high retention when investment opportunities are not available is inconsistent with the objective of maximizing shareholder wealth.

In a large corporation whose shares are widely held, it is nearly impossible for a financial manager to take individual shareholders' preferences into account when setting dividend policy. Some wealthy stockholders prefer retention and capital gains, whereas other stockholders, who are in lower marginal tax brackets or who depend upon dividends as a source of current income, prefer a higher dividend rate. Therefore, when a firm's ownership is diverse, management should consider investment opportunities, cash flow needs, access to the financial markets, and other related factors when setting dividend policy. Those stockholders who do not find this policy acceptable can sell their shares and buy stock in other firms that are more attractive to them.

It has been argued that firms tend to develop their own "clientele" of investors. This *clientele effect*, originally articulated by Merton Miller and Franco Modigliani,[8] indicated that investors will tend to be attracted to companies that have dividend policies consistent with the investors' objectives. Some companies, such as public utilities, which pay out a large percentage (typically 70 percent or more) of their earnings as dividends, traditionally have attracted investors who desire a high dividend yield. In contrast, growth-oriented companies, which pay no (or very low) dividends, have tended to attract investors who prefer earnings retention and greater price appreciation. Empirical studies generally support the existence of a dividend clientele effect.[9]

Protection against Dilution

If a firm adopts a policy of paying out a large percentage of its annual earnings as dividends, it may need to sell new shares of stock from time to time to raise the equity capital needed to invest in potentially profitable projects. If existing investors do not or cannot acquire a proportionate share of the new issue, their percentage ownership interest in the firm is *diluted*. Some firms choose to retain more of their earnings and pay out lower dividends rather than risk dilution.

There are alternatives to high earnings retention, however; one of these involves raising external capital in the form of debt. This increases the financial risk of the firm, however, ultimately raising the cost of equity

[8] Merton Miller and Franco Modigliani. "Dividend Policy, Growth and the Valuation of Shares," *Journal of Business* 34 (October 1961): 411–433.

[9] See Edwin J. Elton and Martin J. Gruber, "Marginal Stockholder Tax Rates and the Clientele Effect," *Review of Economics and Statistics* (February 1970): 68–74; Wilbur C. Lewellen, Kenneth L. Stanley, Ronald C. Lease, and Gary C. Schlarbaum, "Some Direct Evidence on the Dividend Clientele Phenomenon," *Journal of Finance* (December 1970): 1385–1399; and R. Richardson Pettit, "Taxes, Transactions Costs and the Clientele Effect of Dividends," *Journal of Financial Economics* (December 1977): 419–436.

capital and at some point lowering share prices.[10] If the firm feels that it already has an optimal capital structure, a policy of obtaining all external capital in the form of debt is likely to be counterproductive, unless sufficient new equity capital is retained or acquired in the capital markets to offset the increased debt.

DIVIDEND POLICY AND FIRM VALUE

There are two major schools of thought among finance scholars regarding the effect dividend policy has on a firm's value. Although Miller and Modigliani argue that dividend policy does not have a significant effect on a firm's value,[11] Myron Gordon, David Durand, and John Lintner argue that it does.[12] Each viewpoint is discussed in this section.

Arguments for the Irrelevance of Dividends

The group led by Miller and Modigliani (MM) contends that a firm's value is determined solely by its investment decisions, and that the dividend payout ratio is a mere detail. They maintain that the effect of any particular dividend policy can be exactly offset by other forms of financing, such as the sale of new common equity shares. This argument depends on a number of key assumptions, however, including the following:

- *No taxes.* Under this assumption, investors are indifferent about whether they receive either dividend income or capital gains income.
- *No transaction costs.* This assumption implies that investors in the securities of firms paying small or no dividends can sell (at no cost) any number of shares they wish in order to convert capital gains into current income.
- *No flotation costs.* If firms did not have to pay flotation costs on the issue of new securities, they could acquire needed equity capital at the same cost, regardless of whether they retained their past earnings or paid them out as dividends. The payment of dividends sometimes results in the need for periodic sales of new stock.
- *Existence of a fixed investment policy.* According to MM, the firm's investment policy is not affected by its dividend policy. Furthermore, MM claim that it is investment policy, *not* dividend policy, that really determines a firm's value.

INFORMATIONAL CONTENT. MM realize that there is considerable empirical evidence indicating that changes in dividend policy influence stock prices. As discussed later in this chapter, many firms favor a policy of reasonably stable dividends. An increase in dividends conveys a certain type of *information* to the shareholders; namely, that management expects future earnings to be higher. Similarly, a cut in dividends is viewed as

---

[10] See Chapters 12 and 13.
[11] Miller and Modigliani, "Dividend Policy, Growth, and the Valuation of Shares."
[12] See Myron Gordon, "The Savings, Investment and Valuation of a Corporation," *Review of Economics and Statistics* (February 1962): 37–51; Gordon, *The Investment, Financing and Valuation of the Corporation*, Homewood, IL: Irwin, 1962; David Durand, "Bank Stocks and the Analysis of Covariance," *Econometrica* (January 1955): 30–45; and John Lintner, "Dividends, Earnings, Leverage, Stock Prices and the Supply of Capital to Corporations," *Review of Economics and Statistics* (August 1962): 243–269.

conveying unfavorable information about the firm's earnings prospects. MM argue that this *informational content* of dividend policy influences share prices, and *not* the pattern of dividend payments per se.

SIGNALING EFFECTS. In effect, changes in dividend payments represent a *signal* to investors concerning management's assessment of the future earnings and cash flows of the company.[13] Management, as an insider, is perceived as having access to more complete information about future profitability than is available to investors outside the company. Dividend changes are thought to provide unambiguous signals about the company's future prospects—information that cannot be fully conveyed through other methods such as annual reports and management presentations before security analysts. The signaling effect of changes in dividends is similar to the signaling effect of changes in capital structure discussed in the previous chapter.

CLIENTELE EFFECT. MM also claim that the existence of clienteles of investors favoring a particular firm's dividend policy should have no effect on share value. They recognize that a firm that changes its dividend policy could lose some stockholders to other firms with a more appealing dividend policy. This, in turn, may cause a temporary reduction in the price of the firm's stock. Other investors, however, who prefer the newly adopted dividend policy will view the firm as being undervalued and will purchase more shares. In the MM world, these transactions occur instantaneously and at no cost to the investor, the net result being that a stock's value remains unchanged.

Arguments for the Relevance of Dividends

Scholars belonging to the second school of thought argue that share values indeed are influenced by the division of earnings between dividends and retention. Basically, they contend that the MM propositions are reasonable—given MM's restrictive assumptions—but that dividend policy becomes important once these assumptions are removed.

RISK AVERSION. Specifically, Gordon asserts that shareholders who are risk averse may prefer some dividends over the promise of future capital gains, because dividends are regular, certain returns, whereas future capital gains are less certain. According to Gordon, dividends reduce investors' uncertainty, causing them to discount a firm's future earnings at a lower rate, thereby increasing the firm's value. In contrast, failure to pay dividends increases investors' uncertainty, which raises the discount rate and lowers share prices. Although there is some empirical evidence to support this argument, it is difficult to decide which is more valid—the MM informational content (or signaling effect) of dividends approach or the Gordon uncertainty resolution approach.

TRANSACTION COSTS. Of course, if the assumption of no transaction costs for investors is removed, then investors care whether they are paid cash

[13] Merton H. Miller and Kevin Rock. "Dividend Policy Under Asymmetric Information," *Journal of Finance* (September 1985): 1031–1051; and Paul M. Healy and Krishna G. Palepu. "Earnings Information Conveyed by Dividend Initiations and Omissions," *Journal of Financial Economics* 21 (1988): 149–175.

dividends or receive capital gains. In the MM world, investors who own stock paying low or no dividends could periodically sell a portion of their holdings to satisfy current income requirements. In actuality, however, brokerage charges and odd-lot differentials make such liquidations expensive and imperfect substitutes for regular dividend payments.

TAXES. Removal of the no-tax assumption also makes a difference to shareholders, because capital gains are not taxed until the stock is sold. In his study of dividend policy from 1920 to 1960, John A. Brittain found evidence in support of this proposition.[14] In general, he found that rising tax rates tend to reduce dividend payout rates.

FLOTATION COSTS. The existence of flotation costs on new equity sales also tends to make earnings retention more desirable. Given a firm's investment policy, the payout of earnings the firm needs for investments requires it to raise external equity. External equity is more expensive, however, because of flotation costs. Therefore, the use of external equity will raise the firm's cost of capital and reduce the value of the firm. In addition, the cost of selling small issues of equity to meet investment needs is likely to be prohibitively high for most firms. Therefore, firms that have sufficient investment opportunities to profitably utilize their retained funds tend to favor retention.[15]

AGENCY COSTS. It also has been argued that the payment of dividends can reduce *agency costs*[16] between shareholders (owners) and management.[17] The payment of dividends (cash outflow) reduces the amount of retained earnings available for reinvestment and requires the use of more external equity funds to finance growth. Raising external equity funds (i.e., selling new common stock) in the capital markets subjects the company to the scrutiny of regulators (such as the SEC) and potential investors, thereby serving as a monitoring function of managerial performance.

CONCLUSIONS REGARDING DIVIDEND RELEVANCE. The empirical evidence as to whether dividend policy affects firm valuation is mixed. Some studies have found that, because of tax effects, investors require higher pretax returns on high-dividend payout stocks than on low-dividend payout stocks.[18] Other studies have found that share prices are unaffected by dividend payout policy.[19]

[14] John A. Brittain, *Corporate Dividend Policy*, especially Chapter 4.
[15] This argument provides the basis for the passive residual or marginal theory of dividends discussed later in this chapter.
[16] Agency costs were discussed in Chapter 1.
[17] See M. Rozeff. "Growth, Beta and Agency Costs as Determinants of Dividend Payout Ratios," *Journal of Financial Research* (Fall 1982): 249–259; and Chinmoy Ghosh and J. Randall Woolridge. "An Analysis of Shareholder Reaction to Dividend Cuts and Omissions," *Journal of Financial Research* (Winter 1988): 281–294.
[18] See Robert H. Litzenberger and Krishna Ramaswamy, "The Effect of Personal Taxes and Dividends on Capital Asset Prices: Theory and Empirical Evidence," *Journal of Financial Economics* (June 1979): 163–196; Litzenberger and Ramaswamy, "Dividends, Short-Selling Restrictions, Tax Induced Investor Clienteles and Market Equilibrium," *Journal of Finance* (May 1980); and Litzenberger and Ramaswamy, "The Effects of Dividends on Common Stock Prices: Tax Effects or Information Effects?" *Journal of Finance* (May 1982): 429–444.
[19] See Fischer Black and Myron Scholes, "The Effects of Dividend Yield and Dividend Policy on Common Stock Prices and Returns," *Journal of Financial Economics* (May 1974): 1–22; and Merton H. Miller and Myron S. Scholes, "Dividends and Taxes: Some Empirical Evidence," *Journal of Political Economy* (December 1983): 1118–1141.

Many practitioners believe that dividends are important, both for their informational content and because external equity capital is more expensive than retained equity.[20] Thus, when establishing an optimal dividend policy, a firm should consider shareholder preferences along with investment opportunities and the relative cost of retained equity versus externally raised equity.

■■■ DIVIDEND POLICIES

It has been shown that there are a number of practical considerations that influence a firm's board of directors in determining an "optimal" dividend policy. Next, several alternative dividend strategies are discussed.

Passive Residual Policy

The passive residual policy suggests that a firm should retain its earnings as long as it has investment opportunities that promise higher rates of return than the required rate. For example, assume a firm's shareholders could invest their dividends in stocks of similar risk with an expected rate of return (dividends plus capital gains) of 18 percent. This 18 percent figure, then, would constitute the required rate of return on the firm's retained earnings.[21] As long as the firm can invest these earnings to earn this required rate or more, it should not pay dividends (according to the passive residual policy), because such payments would require either that the firm forego some acceptable investment opportunities or raise necessary equity capital in the more expensive external capital markets.

Interpreted literally, the residual theory implies that dividend payments will vary from year to year, depending on available investment opportunities. There is strong evidence, however, that most firms try to maintain a rather stable dividend payment record over time. Of course, this does not mean that firms ignore the principles of the residual theory in making their dividend decisions, because dividends can be smoothed out from year to year in two ways.[22] First, a firm can choose to retain a larger percentage of earnings during years when funding needs are large. If the firm continues to grow, it can manage to do this without reducing the dollar amount of the dividend. Second, a firm can borrow the funds it needs, temporarily raise its debt-to-equity ratio, and avoid a dividend cut in this way. Because issue costs are lower for large offerings of long-term debt, long-term debt capital tends to be raised in large, lumpy sums. If many good investment opportunities are available to a firm during a particular year, this type of borrowing is preferable to cutting back on dividends. The firm will need to retain earnings in future years to bring its debt-to-equity ratio back in line. A firm that has many good investment opportunities for a number of years eventually may be forced to cut its dividend and/or sell new equity shares to meet financing requirements and maintain an optimal capital structure.

[20] For a survey of chief financial officers' attitudes on dividend policy, see H. Kent Baker, Gail E. Farrelly, and Richard B. Edelman, "A Survey of Management Views on Dividend Policy," *Financial Management* (Autumn 1985): 78–84.

[21] This is the rate of return that must be earned on the equity-financed portion of new investments. To earn this return on equity, new investments must earn an overall rate of return equal to the weighted cost of capital—reflecting the fact that all investments are made with a mix of debt and equity funds in the proportions of the target capital structure.

[22] Robert C. Higgins. "The Corporate Dividend-Saving Decision," *Journal of Financial and Quantitative Analysis* (March 1972): 1531–1538, provides empirical support for the view that each period's dividends are a function of longer-term trends.

The residual theory also suggests that "growth" firms normally will have lower dividend payout ratios than firms in mature, low-growth industries. As shown earlier in Table 14-1 companies with low growth rates (such as Public Service Company of New Mexico and San Diego Gas & Electric) tend to have rather high payout ratios, whereas firms with high growth rates (such as Digital Equipment and Wal-Mart Stores) tend to have rather low payout ratios.

Stable Dollar Dividend Policy

There is much evidence to indicate that most firms—and stockholders—prefer reasonably stable dividend policies. This stability is characterized by a rather strong reluctance to reduce the dollar amount of dividends from one period to the next. Similarly, increases in the dollar dividend rate normally are not made until the firm's management is satisfied that future earnings will be high enough to justify the larger dividend. Thus, although dividend rates tend to follow increases in earnings, they also tend to lag behind them to a certain degree.

Figure 14-1 illustrates the relationship between corporate dividends and profits since 1950. It is apparent from this chart that aggregate dividend payments fluctuate much less widely than corporate earnings do. There has been a strong upward trend in the amount of dividends paid, with very few years showing significant reductions. This is in sharp contrast to the more erratic record of corporate earnings.

More specifically, Figure 14-2 shows the dividend and earnings history of Northwest Airlines. Once again, it can be seen that there has been an upward trend in dividends over time. It is clear, however, that dividend increases tend to lag earnings increases. Annual dividend payments also are more stable than earnings figures. Note, for instance, the dramatic growth in earnings in 1977 and compare this with the very modest increase in dividends during the year. When earnings declined in 1980, 1981, and 1982, the $0.80 dividend rate was maintained.

There are many reasons why investors prefer stable dividends. For instance, many investors feel that dividend changes possess *informational content*—they equate changes in a firm's dividend levels with profitability. A cut in dividends may be interpreted as a signal that the firm's long-run profit potential has declined. Similarly, a dividend increase is seen as a verification of the expectation that future profits will increase.[23]

In addition, many shareholders need and depend on a constant stream of dividends for their cash income requirements. Although they can sell off some of their shares as an alternative source of current income, associated transaction costs and odd-lot charges make this an imperfect substitute for steady dividend income.

Some managers feel that a stable and growing dividend policy tends to reduce investor uncertainty concerning future dividend streams. They believe investors will pay a higher price for the stock of a firm that pays stable dividends, thereby reducing the firm's cost of equity.

And, finally, stable dividends are legally desirable. Many regulated financial institutions—such as bank trust departments, pension funds, and insurance companies—are limited as to the types of common stock they are

---

[23] Sometimes, however, an increase in a firm's dividend payout ratio may be interpreted to mean the firm no longer has a large number of high-return investment opportunities available to it.

FIGURE 14-1

**Historic Pattern of
Profits and Dividends
for U.S. Corporations**

SOURCE: *Economic Report of
the President*, 1988.

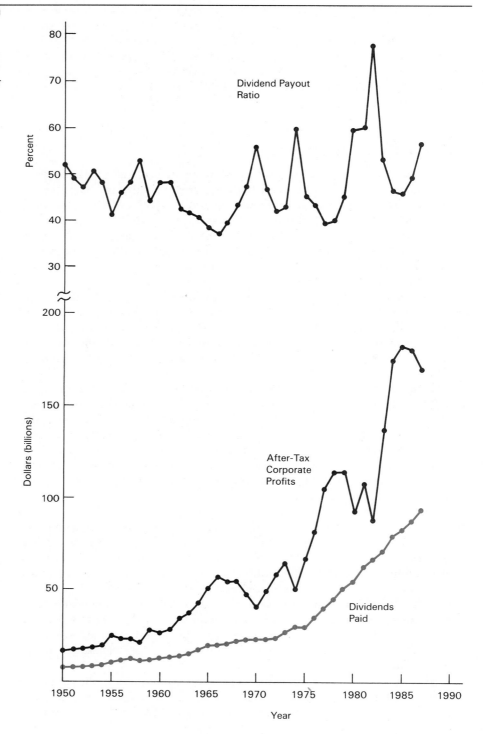

Dividend Payout
Ratio

After-Tax
Corporate
Profits

Dividends
Paid

Year

allowed to own. To qualify for inclusion in these "legal lists," a firm must
have a record of continuous and stable dividends. The failure to pay a
dividend or the reduction of a dividend amount can result in removal from
these lists. This, in turn, reduces the potential market for the firm's shares

Dividends and Earnings for Northwest Airlines
SOURCE: *Value Line Investment Survey* (New York: Value Line, Inc. 1989).

FIGURE 14-2

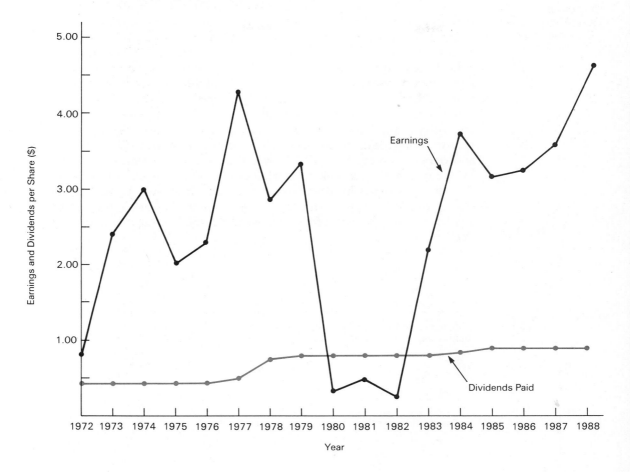

and may lead to price declines. As shown earlier in Figure 14-2, Northwest Airlines maintained its $0.80 per share dividend during the 1980–1982 period even though its earnings per share were less than this amount in each of the years.

Other Dividend Payment Policies

Some firms have adopted a *constant payout ratio* dividend policy. A firm that uses this approach pays out a certain percentage of each year's earnings—for example, 40 percent—as dividends. If the firm's earnings vary substantially from year to year, dividends also will fluctuate. (The late Penn Central Company had adopted this type of dividend payout policy at one time.)

As shown earlier in Figure 14-1, the aggregate dividend payout ratio for U.S. corporations generally has ranged between 40 and 60 percent, although during 1982 it was in excess of 70 percent. This finding supports the notion that firms try to maintain fairly constant payout ratios over time. On a year-to-year basis, however, these payout ratios have varied substantially.

For example, the aggregate payout ratio was 77 percent during 1982, a recession year, and only about 37 percent during 1966, a year of relative prosperity. Because of the reluctance to reduce dividends, payout ratios tend to increase when profits are depressed and decrease as profits increase.

Other firms choose to pay a *small quarterly dividend plus year-end extras.* This policy is especially well suited for a firm with a volatile earnings record, volatile year-to-year cash needs, or both. Even when earnings are low, the firm's investors can count on their regular dividend payments. When earnings are high and there is no immediate need for these excess funds, the firm declares a year-end extra dividend. This policy gives management the flexibility to retain funds as needed and still satisfy investors who desire to receive some "guaranteed" level of dividend payments. U.S. Steel, Du Pont, and General Motors have all followed this policy from time to time. Figure 14-3 shows how this policy has affected General Motors. Although actual dividend payments have varied dramatically from year to year (compare this figure, for example, with Figure 14-2, which shows Northwest Airlines dividends), they have not fallen below $2.40, the "regular" rate in effect in 1975.

FIGURE 14-3   **Dividends and Earnings for General Motors**
SOURCE: *Value Line Investment Survey* (New York: Value Line, Inc. 1989).

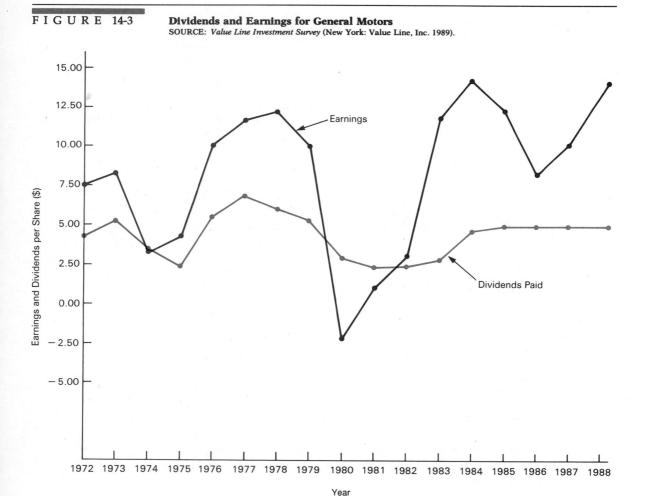

SMALL BUSINESS CONCERNS: DIVIDEND POLICY

Small firms typically differ significantly from larger, more mature firms in terms of the dividend policies they follow. For example, one study of the financial differences between small and large firms found that the average dividend payout ratio for large firms was in excess of 40 percent whereas the average dividend payout ratio for small firms was less than 3 percent.[24] The study found that the majority of small firms that were planning an initial public stock offering paid no dividends at all in the year prior to their stock offering.

What are the reasons for this dramatic difference in dividend policies between large and small firms? First, it is likely that many small firms are in the rapid growth phase of their business development. During this early phase, the firm often is short of funds needed to finance planned investments and increases in working capital. Related to the growth phase argument is the fact that small firms typically have restricted access to capital markets, relative to larger firms. A small, closely held firm has no easy way to raise equity capital other than the retention of earnings. If new shares of stock can be sold, the owners risk a loss of control. In addition stock offerings for small firms are extremely expensive, both in terms of transactions costs and minority interest (as well as marketability) discounts that investors demand.

Another reason for the difference in dividend policies between small and large firms stems from the fact that many small firms are closely held by only one or a few owners, and the dividend policy of these firms frequently reflects the income preferences of these individuals. If funds are retained in the firm, taxes are postponed until a distribution is made at some time in the future or until the firm is sold.

As firms mature, their need for funds to support rapid growth declines, and their access to capital markets improves, there is a tendency to begin or increase dividend payouts. For example, in 1978 Apple Computer had sales of $7.9 million and earnings of 2 cents a share. By 1986 sales had grown to over $1.9 billion and earnings per share were $1.20. During this period of rapid growth Apple paid no dividends. However, as the company entered the maturing stage of its life cycle, the need for internally generated cash flow to support expansion declined and Apple began paying dividends. In 1987 dividends totalling $0.20 per share were paid. In 1988 a $0.34 per share dividend was paid, and in 1989 dividends were being paid at the rate of $0.40 per share.

It is clear that there are significant differences between the dividend policies of small and large firms. Small firms often pay out a smaller percentage of their earnings than larger firms because small firms tend to be growing rapidly and have limited access to the capital markets for other sources of funds to support their growth.

INTERNATIONAL CONCERNS: DIVIDEND POLICIES FOR MULTINATIONAL FIRMS

Dividend payments from foreign subsidiaries represent the primary means of transferring funds to the parent company. Many factors determine the

[24] Ernest W. Walker and J. W. Petty, II. "Financial Differences between Large and Small Firms," *Financial Management* (Winter 1978): 61–68.

dividend payments that are made back to the parent, including tax effects, exchange risk, political risk, the availability of funds, the financing requirements of the foreign subsidiary, and the existence of exchange controls.[25]

Taxes in the host country play a significant role in determining a multinational firm subsidiary's dividend policy. For example, in West Germany the tax rate on earnings paid out as dividends is much lower than the tax rate on retained earnings. When the parent is located in a country with a strong currency and the subsidiary is located in a country with a weak currency, there will be a tendency to rapidly transfer a greater portion of the subsidiary's earnings to the parent to minimize the exchange rate risk. In the face of high political risk, the parent may require the subsidiary to transfer all locally generated funds to the parent except for those funds necessary to meet the working capital and planned capital expenditure needs of the subsidiary. As is true for domestic enterprises, large and more mature foreign subsidiaries tend to remit a greater proportion of their earnings to the parent, reflecting the reduced growth opportunities and needs for funds that exist in larger firms. Also, when the foreign subsidiary has good access to capital within the host country, there is a tendency to pay larger dividends to the parent, because funds needed for future expansion can be obtained locally. Finally, some countries with balance-of-payments problems often restrict the payment of dividends from the subsidiary back to the parent.

Many firms require that the payout ratio for foreign subsidiaries be set equal to the payout ratio of the parent. The argument in favor of this strategy is that it requires each subsidiary to bear an equal proportionate burden of the parent's dividend policy. However, even when this strategy is adopted, it often is modified on a country-by-country basis to reflect the considerations just identified.

HOW DIVIDENDS ARE PAID

In most firms, the board of directors holds quarterly or semiannual meetings to evaluate the firm's past performance and decide the level of dividends to be paid during the next period. Changes in the amount of dividends paid tend to be made rather infrequently—especially in firms that follow a stable dividend policy—and only after there is clear evidence that the firm's future earnings are likely to be either permanently higher or permanently lower than previously reported levels.

Most firms follow a dividend declaration and payment procedure similar to that outlined in the following paragraphs. This procedure usually revolves around a *declaration date*, an *ex-dividend date*, a *record date*, and a *payment date*.

Figure 14-4 is a time line that illustrates the Pennzoil Company's dividend payment procedure. The firm's board of directors meets on the *declaration date*—February 24—to consider future dividends. They *declare* a dividend on that date, that will be payable to *shareholders of record* on the *record date* March 3. On that date, the firm makes a list from its stock transfer books of those shareholders who are eligible to receive the declared dividend.

The major stock exchanges require 4 *business days* prior to the record date for recording ownership changes. The day that begins this 4-day period

[25] This section is based primarily on Alan C. Shapiro, *Multinational Financial Management*, 3d ed. (Boston: Allyn and Bacon, 1989), Chapter 15.

February 24	February 27	March 3	March 15
Declaration Date	Ex-Dividend Date	Record Date	Payment Date

is called the *ex-dividend date*—in this case, February 27 as long as March 3 occurs on a Friday. Investors who purchase stock prior to February 27 are eligible for the March 3 dividend; investors who purchase stock on or after February 27 are not entitled to the dividend. On February 27, the ex-dividend date, one would expect the stock price to decline by the amount of the dividend, because this much value has been removed from the firm. Empirical evidence indicates that, on average, stock prices decline by less than the amount of the dividend on the ex-dividend day.[26]

The *payment date* is normally 2 to 4 weeks after the record date; in this case, March 15. On this date, Pennzoil mails dividend payments to the holders of record.

Dividend Capture Strategies

A *dividend capture strategy* involves buying a stock shortly before its ex-dividend date in order to receive the quarterly dividend. Later, after the dividend has been received, the stock is sold. Hedging, using options and futures contracts, can be employed by investors to minimize the risk of a decline in the stock price during the holding period.[27] Dividend capture programs have been used by certain Japanese investors to convert capital gains income into dividend income.[28] Dividend capture strategies also have been used by U.S. corporations with idle cash to invest for short-term periods. Such strategies attempt to increase after-tax returns by taking advantage of the lower (corporate) tax rate on dividend income.[29] For example, at one point during 1987, Duke Power (located in North Carolina) had $125 million in corporate funds invested in various dividend capture strategies.[30]

Dividend Reinvestment Plans

In recent years many firms have established *dividend reinvestment plans*. Under these plans, shareholders can automatically have their dividends reinvested in additional shares of the company's common stock. There are two types of dividend reinvestment plans—one type involves the purchase

[26] See Edwin J. Elton and Martin J. Gruber. "Marginal Stockholder Tax Rates and the Clientele Effect," *Review of Economics and Statistics* (February 1978): 68–74; Avner Kalay. "The Ex-Dividend Behavior of Stock Prices: A Re-examination of the Clientele Effect," *Journal of Finance* (September 1983): 1059–1070; and Kenneth M. Eades, Patrick J. Hess, and E. Han Kim. "On Interpreting Security Returns during the Ex-Dividend Period," *Journal of Financial Economics* (March 1984): 3–34.

[27] Options are discussed in Chapter 16.

[28] Certain Japanese insurance and trust companies can pay distributions to their shareholders only from current income (e.g., dividends). Capital gains must be retained in the company. A dividend recapture program allows such companies, with large capital gains on their security holdings, to convert these capital gains to current income that can be paid out to shareholders.

[29] Recall from Appendix 2A that dividends received by a corporation are entitled to a 70 percent deduction, making the effective rate only 10.2 percent. To receive this lower rate, U.S. corporations are required to hold the stock for a minimum of 46 days.

[30] *Wall Street Journal* (November 3, 1987); p. 6.

of *existing* stock and the other type involves the purchase of *newly issued* stock. The first type of plan is done through a bank that, acting as a trustee, purchases the stock on the open market and then allocates it on a pro rata basis to the participating shareholders. In the second type of plan, the cash dividends of the participants are used to purchase, often at a small discount (up to 5 percent) from the market price, newly issued shares of stock.

This second type of plan enables the firm to raise substantial amounts of new equity capital over time as well as reduce the cash outflows required by dividend payments.[31] The advantage of a dividend reinvestment plan to shareholders is that it represents a convenient method for them to purchase additional shares of the company's common stock while saving brokerage commissions. The primary disadvantage is that shareholders must pay taxes on the cash dividends reinvested in the company, even though they never receive any cash.[32]

STOCK DIVIDENDS AND STOCK SPLITS

A *stock dividend* is the payment of additional shares of stock to common stockholders. It involves making a transfer from the retained earnings account to the other stockholders' equity accounts.

For example, the Colonial Copies Company has the following common stockholders' equity:

**Pre-Stock Dividend Common
Stockholders' Equity**

Common stock ($5 par, 100,000 shares)	$ 500,000
Contributed capital in excess of par	1,000,000
Retained earnings	5,000,000
Total common stockholders' equity	$6,500,000

Suppose the firm declares a 10 percent stock dividend and existing shareholders receive 10,000 (10% × 100,000) new shares. Because stock dividend accounting usually is based on the predividend market price, a total of $200,000 (10,000 shares × an assumed market price of $20 per share) is transferred from the firm's retained earnings account to the other stockholders' equity accounts. Of this $200,000, $50,000 ($5 par × 10,000 shares) is added to the common stock account and the remaining $150,000 is added to the contributed capital in excess of par account. Following the stock dividend, Colonial has the following common stockholders' equity:

**Post-Stock Dividend Common
Stockholders' Equity**

Common stock ($5 par, 110,000 shares)	$ 550,000
Contributed capital in excess of par	1,150,000
Retained earnings	4,800,000
Total common stockholders' equity	$6,500,000

The net effect of this transaction is to increase the number of outstanding shares and to redistribute funds among the firm's capital accounts. The

---

[31] See *Moody's Annual Dividend Record* (December 31, 1988) for a list of the approximately 650 New York and American Stock Exchange companies offering dividend reinvestment plans.
[32] See Richard H. Pettway and R. Phil Malone. "Automatic Dividend Reinvestment Plans of Nonfinancial Corporations," *Financial Management* (Winter 1973): 11–18, for a more detailed discussion of these plans.

firm's total stockholders' equity remains unchanged, and each shareholder's proportionate claim to the firm's earnings remains constant. For example, if Colonial Copies Company has 100,000 shares outstanding prior to a 10 percent stock dividend, and its total earnings are $200,000 ($2 per share), a stockholder who owns 100 shares has a claim on $200 of the firm's earnings. Following the 10 percent stock dividend, earnings per share decline to $1.82 ($200,000/110,000 shares). The stockholder who originally owned 100 shares now has 110 shares but continues to have a claim on only $200 (110 shares × $1.82 per share) of the firm's earnings.

Because each shareholder's proportionate claim on a firm's net worth and earnings remains unchanged in a stock dividend, the market price of each share of stock should decline in proportion to the number of new shares issued. This relationship can be expressed as follows:

$$\text{Post-stock dividend price} = \frac{\text{Pre-stock dividend price}}{1 + \text{Percentage stock dividend rate}} \quad \textbf{(14.1)}$$

In the Colonial Copies example, a $20 pre-stock dividend price should result in a post-stock dividend price of

$$\text{Post-stock dividend price} = \frac{\$20}{1 + 0.10}$$

$$= \$18.18$$

If a stockholder's wealth prior to the dividend is $2,000 (100 shares × $20 per share), post-dividend wealth also should remain at $2,000 (110 shares × $18.18 per share).

In essence, all a stock dividend does is increase the number of pieces of paper in the stockholders' hands. Nevertheless, there are a number of reasons why firms declare stock dividends. First, a stock dividend may have the effect of broadening the ownership of a firm's shares, because existing shareholders often sell their stock dividends.[33] Second, in the case of a firm that already pays a cash dividend, a stock dividend results in an effective increase in cash dividends, providing that the per-share dividend rate is not reduced. (It is rare for a firm to declare a stock dividend and reduce its cash dividend rate at the same time.) And, finally, the declaration of stock dividends effectively lowers the per-share price of a stock, thereby possibly broadening its investment appeal. Investors seem to prefer stocks selling in approximately the $15 to $70 price range, because more investors will be financially able to purchase 100-share round lots.[34] Round lots of 100 shares are more desirable for investors to own because lower transactions costs are associated with their purchase and sale.

Stock splits are similar to stock dividends in that they have the effect of increasing the number of shares of stock outstanding and reducing the price of each outstanding share. From an accounting standpoint, stock splits are accomplished by reducing the par value of existing shares of stock and

[33] See C. Austin Barker. "Evaluation of Stock Dividends," *Harvard Business Review* (July–August 1958): 99–114, for an empirical confirmation of this point.
[34] For an empirical view of the effects of stock dividends and splits on share values, see C. Austin Barker, ibid.; Keith B. Johnson. "Stock Splits and Price Change," *Journal of Finance* (December 1966): 675–686; W. H. Hausman, R. R. West, and J. A. Langay. "Stock Splits, Price Changes and Trading Profits: A Synthesis," *Journal of Business* (January 1971): 69–77; and E. Fama, R. Fisher, M. Jensen, and R. Roll. "The Adjustment of Stock Prices to New Information," *International Economic Review* (February 1969): 1–21.

increasing the number of shares outstanding. For example, in a two-for-one stock split, the number of shares would be doubled. Although stock splits have an impact similar to stock dividends, they normally are not considered an element of a firm's dividend policy. They are discussed in more detail in Chapter 7.

SHARE REPURCHASES AS DIVIDEND DECISIONS

In addition to the reasons discussed in Chapter 7 for repurchasing stock, share repurchases can be undertaken as part of the firm's dividend decision. According to the passive residual dividend policy, a firm that has more funds than it needs for investments should pay a cash dividend to shareholders. In lieu of (or in addition to) cash dividends, some firms also repurchase outstanding shares from time to time.

Procedures for Repurchasing Shares

Firms carry out share repurchase programs in a number of ways. For example, a company may buy directly from its stockholders in what is termed a *tender offer*, or it may purchase the stock in the open market, or it may privately negotiate purchases from large holders, such as institutions.

Repurchased shares become known as *treasury stock*. Treasury stock often is used to facilitate mergers and acquisitions; to satisfy the conversion provisions of some preferred stock and debentures, as well as the exercise of warrants; and to meet the need for new shares in executive stock options and employee stock purchase plans. From the stockholders' perspective, share repurchases increase earnings per share for the remaining outstanding shares and also increase stock prices, assuming that investors continue to apply the same *price to earnings (P/E) ratio* to the earnings per share before and after repurchase.[35] Recall from Chapter 3 that the P/E *ratio* is equal to the price per share divided by the earnings per share. For example, if a stock sells for $40 per share and earns $8 per share, its P/E multiple is 5 times (40/8). The P/E multiple indicates the value placed by investors on a dollar of a firm's earnings. It is influenced by a number of factors, including earnings prospects and investors' perceptions regarding a firm's risk.

Normally a firm will announce its intent to buy back some of its own shares so that investors will know why there is sudden additional trading in the stock. An announcement of repurchase also is useful to current shareholders, who may not want to sell their shares before they have had an opportunity to receive any price appreciation expected to result from the repurchase program.

Share Repurchase Example

Suppose that the Hewlett-Packard (H-P) Company (electronic equipment manufacturer) plans to distribute to its shareholders $750 million in the form of either a (one-time) extra cash dividend or a share repurchase. The company has expected earnings of $625 million during the coming year and

---

[35] If a stock repurchase results in a substantial increase in the debt-to-equity ratio, the new P/E ratio may be lower because of increased financial risk.

approximately 250 million shares currently outstanding. The current (ex-dividend) market price of H-P stock is $50 per share. The company can pay a (one-time) extra cash dividend of $3 per share ($750 million divided by 250 million shares). Alternatively, it can make a tender offer at $53 per share for 14,150,943 shares ($750 million divided by $53 per share).

If H-P decides to declare a (one-time) extra cash dividend of $3 per share, shareholder wealth would be $53 per share, consisting of the $50 (ex-dividend) share price plus the $3 dividend. The effect on shareholder wealth before and after the stock repurchase is shown in Table 14-2, assuming that the price-earnings (P/E) ratio remains the same at 20 ($50 stock price per share divided by $2.50 earnings per share). If H-P repurchases $750 million worth of its common stock (at $53 per share), then shareholder wealth is $53 per share, with $3 of this value representing price appreciation. Note that the pretax returns to shareholders are the same under each alternative.

Ignoring taxes, transaction costs, and other market imperfections, shareholders should be indifferent between equivalent returns from cash dividends and share repurchases. In other words, the value of the firm should not be affected by the manner in which returns (cash dividends versus capital gains) are paid to shareholders. However, empirical studies suggest that share repurchases do increase stock prices (i.e., value of the firm).[36] Some reasons why this occurs are examined in the remainder of this section.

Tax Considerations

In the context of dividend decisions, tax considerations historically have been the primary reason why firms decided to repurchase their own stock in lieu of (or in addition to) payment of cash dividends. As discussed earlier in the chapter, prior to passage of the 1986 Tax Reform Act, long-term capital gains income was taxed at lower rates than dividend income. However, the new law eliminated the tax rate differentials between capital gains and dividend income. Despite this change in the tax law, there still is a tax advantage (although smaller) to share repurchases compared with cash dividends because the taxes on capital gains income can be deferred into the future (when the stock is sold), whereas taxes on an equivalent amount of dividend income have to be paid in the current year.

[36] See Larry Y. Dann. "Common Stock Repurchases: An Analysis of Returns to Bondholders and Stockholders," *Journal of Financial Economics* (June 1981): 113–138; and Theo Vermaelen. "Common Stock Repurchases and Market Signaling: An Empirical Study," *Journal of Financial Economics* (June 1981): 139–183.

Hewlett-Packard Company Share Repurchase			T A B L E 14-2
	Before Repurchase	**After Repurchase**	
Expected Net Earnings	$625,000,000	$625,000,000	
Shares outstanding	250,000,000	235,849,057	
Expected earnings per share	$2.50	$2.65	
Price-earnings (P/E) ratio	20×	20×	
Expected share price (ex-dividend)	$50	$53	
Expected dividend	$3	$0	

Although a stock repurchase program seems like a desirable way of distributing a firm's earnings, repurchases are deterred to a large degree by the IRS. Specifically, the IRS will not permit a firm to follow a policy of regular stock repurchases as an alternative to cash dividends, because repurchase plans convert cash dividends to capital gains. The IRS looks upon regular repurchases as essentially equivalent to cash dividends and requires that they be taxed accordingly.

Signaling Effects

Like the signaling effects of cash dividend increases, share repurchases also can have a positive impact on shareholder wealth. A share repurchase may represent a signal to investors that management expects the firm to have higher earnings and cash flows in the future.[37]

SUMMARY

■ *Dividend policy* determines the ultimate distribution of a firm's earnings between retention (reinvestment) and cash dividend payments to stockholders. Retained earnings provide investors with a source of potential future earnings growth, whereas dividends provide them with a current distribution.

■ A number of factors influence a firm's choice of dividend policy. These include the following:

1. Legal constraints prohibiting dividends that impair capital.
2. Restrictive covenants in bond indentures and other financing agreements.
3. Tax considerations.
4. The need for liquidity.
5. Borrowing capacity and access to the capital markets.
6. Earnings stability.
7. Capital expansion (growth) opportunities.
8. Inflation.

Shareholders' preferences *(clientele effect)* also may influence a firm's choice of dividend policy. These are determined by stockholders' tax positions and their desire to maintain control of the firm. Some of these factors favor high dividends, whereas others imply a lower payout policy. The board of directors should weigh these factors in each instance and arrive at the best possible dividend policy.

■ Under a restrictive set of assumptions articulated by Miller and Modigliani (MM), the value of the firm is solely dependent on its investment decisions. They claim that any observed changes in firm value as a result of dividend decisions are due only to the *informational content* or *signaling effects* of dividend policy. Under these conditions, dividend policy does not affect the value of the firm. After the MM assumptions are removed, dividend policy may affect firm value because of

1. Risk averse behavior of investors.
2. Shareholder transaction costs.
3. Personal taxes.

[37] See Vermaelen, ibid.; and Paul Asquith and David W. Mullins, Jr. "Signaling with Dividends, Stock Repurchases, and Equity Issues," *Financial Management* (Autumn 1986): 27–44.

4. Flotation costs.
5. Agency costs.

■ There are a number of alternative dividend policies, including the following:
1. The passive residual approach.
2. The stable dollar dividend approach.
3. The constant payout ratio approach.
4. The policy of paying a small, regular dividend plus year-end extras.

There is ample evidence to indicate that many firms favor a stable dividend policy.

■ Small firms tend to pay out a smaller percentage of their earnings as dividends than large firms, reflecting the critical funding needs of many small firms and their limited access to capital markets.

■ Multinational firms establish dividend policies for their subsidiaries reflecting factors such as foreign tax rates, political and exchange rate risk, currency controls, the subsidiary's need for funds, and access to host country capital markets for funds.

■ *Stock dividends* sometimes are used in lieu of (and in conjunction with) cash dividends. The net effect of stock dividends is to leave the total book value of the firm unchanged while increasing the number of shares outstanding and broadening the ownership base.

■ Some firms employ *share repurchase plans* in lieu of (or in addition to) cash dividends. Stock repurchases convert shareholder benefits from ordinary income (dividends) to capital gains income. Theoretically, ignoring taxes, transaction costs, and other market imperfections, share repurchases should have the same effect on shareholder wealth as the payment of cash dividends. However, possibly due to tax considerations (that is, the ability to defer taxes on capital gain income) and signaling effects, share repurchases (via tender offers) are observed to have a positive effect on shareholder wealth.

QUESTIONS AND TOPICS FOR DISCUSSION

1. What legal constraints limit the amount of cash dividends that may be paid by a firm?
2. What aspects of U.S. tax laws tend to (a) encourage and (b) discourage large dividend payments by corporations? Explain how.
3. What other "external" factors limit a firm's ability to pay cash dividends?
4. What is the likely impact of a highly inflationary economy on a firm's ability to pay dividends? Would you expect this impact to be greater or smaller for a rapidly expanding firm? Why?
5. Explain what is meant by the *clientele effect*.
6. Explain what is meant by the *informational content* of dividend policy.
7. Explain what is meant by the *signaling effects* of dividend policy.
8. In the theoretical world of Miller and Modigliani, what role does dividend policy play in the determination of share values?
9. What role do most practitioners think dividend policy plays in determining share values?
10. How can the "passive residual" view of dividend policy be reconciled with the tendency of most firms to maintain a constant or steadily growing dividend payment record?

11. Why do many managers prefer a stable dollar dividend policy to a policy of paying out a constant percentage of each year's earnings as dividends?

12. Under what circumstances would it make sense for a firm to borrow money to make its dividend payments?

13. Some people have suggested that it is irrational for a firm to pay dividends and sell new stock in the same year, because the cost of newly issued equity is greater than the cost of retained earnings. Do you agree? Why or why not?

14. What is a *dividend reinvestment plan*? Explain the advantages of a dividend reinvestment plan to the firm and to shareholders.

15. Why do many firms choose to issue stock dividends? What is the value of a stock dividend to a shareholder?

16. What are the tax limitations on the practice of share repurchases as a regular dividend policy?

17. What effect do share repurchases (undertaken as part of the firm's dividend decision) have on the value of the firm?

18. You are the holder of common stock in the G. Lewis Apartment Renovation Company. Historically the firm has paid generous cash dividends. The firm has recently announced that it would replace its cash dividend with a 20 percent annual stock dividend. Is this good news, bad news, or is it impossible to tell from the information provided? Explain the reason for your answer.

■■■ PROBLEMS*

1. Jacobs Corporation earned $2 million after tax. The firm has 1.6 million shares of common stock outstanding.

   a. Compute the earnings per share of Jacobs.
   b. If Jacobs' dividend policy calls for a 40 percent payout ratio, what are the dividends per share?

2. Drew Financial Associates currently pays a quarterly dividend of 50 cents per share. This quarter's dividend will be paid to stockholders of record on Friday, February 22, 19X1. Drew has 200,000 common shares outstanding. The retained earnings account has a balance of $15 million before the dividend, and Drew holds $2.5 million in cash.

   a. What is the ex-dividend date for this quarter?
   b. Drew's stock traded for $22 per share the day prior to the ex-dividend date. What would you expect the stock price to open at on the ex-dividend date? Give some reasons why this might not occur.
   c. What is the effect of the dividend payment on Drew's cash, retained earnings, and total assets?

3. Winkie Baking has just announced a 100 percent stock dividend. The annual cash dividend per share was $2.40 before the stock dividend. Winkie intends to pay $1.40 per share on each of the new shares. Compute the percentage increase in the cash dividend rate that will accompany the stock dividend.

4. Wolverine Corporation plans to pay a $3 dividend per share on each of its 300,000 shares next year. Wolverine anticipates earnings of $6.25 per share

---

* Colored numbers denote problems that have check answers provided at the end of the book.

over the year. If the company has a capital budget requiring an investment of $4 million over the year and it desires to maintain its present debt to total assets (debt ratio) of 0.40, how much external equity must it raise? Assume Wolverine's capital structure includes only common equity and debt and that debt and equity will be the only sources of funds to finance capital projects over the year.

5. Tulia Dairy pays a $2.50 cash dividend and earns $5 per share. The cash dividend has recently been increased to $2.65 per share, *and* a 3 percent stock dividend has been declared. What is the effective rate of increase in the dividends for Tulia as a result of this action?

6. The Mori Egg Noodle Company has the following equity accounts on its balance sheet:

Common stock ($10 par, 300,000 shares)	$3,000,000
Contributed capital in excess of par	1,500,000
Retained earnings	6,000,000
Total common stockholders' equity	$10,500,000

   a. What is the maximum amount of dividends that may be paid by the Mori Company if the capital impairment provisions of state law are limited to the following?
      i. The par value of common stock.
      ii. The par value and the capital in excess of par accounts.
   b. What other factors may limit Mori's ability to pay dividends?

7. Champoux Hair Factory, Inc., has earnings before interest and taxes of $200,000. Annual interest amounts to $80,000, and annual depreciation is $80,000. Taxes are computed at a 40 percent rate. Existing bond obligations require the payment of $40,000 per year into a sinking fund.
   Champoux wishes to pay a $2 per-share dividend on the existing 20,000 shares. The firm's bond indenture prohibits the payment of dividends unless the cash flow (before dividends and sinking fund payments) is greater than the total of dividends, interest, and sinking fund obligations.

   a. Can Champoux pay the proposed dividend?
   b. What is the maximum dividend per share that may be paid?

8. Lenberg Lens Company believes in the "dividends as a residual" philosophy of dividend policy. This year's earnings are expected to total $10 million. A very conservative company, Lenberg is financed solely with common stock. The required rate of return on retained earnings is 12 percent, whereas the cost of newly raised capital is 14 percent because of flotation costs.

   a. If Lenberg has $6 million of investment projects having expected returns greater than 12 percent, what total amount of dividends should Lenberg pay?
   b. If Lenberg has $12 million of investment projects having expected returns greater than 14 percent, what total amount of dividends should Lenberg pay?
   c. What factors, other than its belief in the residual theory of dividends, should Lenberg consider in setting its dividend policy in Part b?

9. Phoenix Tool Company and Denver Tool Company have had a very similar record of earnings performance over the past 8 years. Both firms are in the same industry and, in fact, compete directly with each other. The two firms have nearly identical capital structures. Phoenix has a policy of paying a constant 50 percent of each year's earnings as dividends, whereas Denver has sought to maintain a constant dollar dividend policy, with changes in the dollar dividend payment occurring infrequently. The record of the two companies follows:

	Phoenix			Denver		
Year	EPS	Dividend	Average Market Price	EPS	Dividend	Average Market Price
19X1	$2.00	$1.00	$20	$2.10	$0.75	$18
19X2	2.50	1.25	24	2.40	0.75	22
19X3	1.50	1.25	15	1.60	0.75	17
19X4	1.00	0.50	10	0.90	0.75	14
19X5	0.50	0.25	8	0.50	0.50	10
19X6	−1.25	nil	8	−1.10	0.50	10
19X7	1.00	0.50	10	1.10	0.75	14
19X8	1.50	0.75	14	1.45	0.75	17

The president of Phoenix wonders what accounts for Denver's current (19X8) higher stock price, in spite of the fact that Phoenix currently earns more per share than Denver and frequently has paid a higher dividend.

a. What factors can you cite that might account for this phenomenon?

b. What do you suggest as an optimal dividend policy for both Phoenix and Denver that might lead to increases in both of their share prices? What are the limitations of your suggestions?

10. The Emco Steel Company has experienced a slow (3 percent per year) but steady increase in earnings per share. The firm has consistently paid out an average of 75 percent of each year's earnings as dividends. The stock market evaluates Emco primarily on the basis of its dividend payout, because growth prospects are modest.

Emco's management presents a proposal to the board of directors that would require the outlay of $50 million to build a new plant in the rapidly expanding Florida market. The expected annual return on the investment in this plant is estimated to be in excess of 30 percent, more than twice the current company average. To finance this investment, a number of alternatives are being considered. They include the following:

a. Finance the expansion with externally raised equity.

b. Finance the expansion with 50 percent externally generated equity and 50 percent internally generated equity. This alternative would necessitate a dividend cut for this year only.

c. Finance the expansion with a mix of debt and equity similar to their current relative proportions in the capital structure. Under this alternative, dividends would not be cut. Rather, any equity needs in excess of that which could be provided internally would be raised through a sale of new common stock.

Evaluate these various financing alternatives with reference to their effects on the dividend policy and common stock values of the company.

11. The Sweet Times Candy Company has the following equity accounts on its balance sheet:

Common stock ($1 par, 500,000 shares)	$ 500,000
Contributed capital in excess of par	2,000,000
Retained earnings	13,000,000
Total common stockholders' equity	$15,500,000

The current market price of the firm's shares is $50.

a. If the firm declares a 10 percent stock dividend, what will be the impact on the firm's equity accounts?

b. If the firm currently pays no cash dividend, what is the impact of a 10 percent stock dividend on the wealth position of the firm's existing stockholders?

c. If the firm currently pays a cash dividend of $1 per share, and this per-share dividend rate does not change after the 10 percent stock dividend, what impact would you expect the stock dividend to have on the wealth position of existing shareholders?

12. Striker's Match Company reports the following financial data:

Net earnings	$3,000,000
Shares outstanding	1,000,000
Earnings per share	$3
Market price per share (ex-dividend)	$40
Expected dividend per share	$2

Striker is considering distributing $2 million to existing stockholders, either as cash dividends or through the repurchase of outstanding shares. The repurchase plan is favored by some of the company's wealthiest and most influential stockholders.

If the shares are repurchased, the company would make a tender offer for 47,619 shares at a price of $42. Alternatively, the firm could pay a $2 dividend, after the payment of which each share would sell for $40.

a. Ignoring taxes, what impact does the choice of a dividend payment or share repurchase plan have on the wealth position of the firm's shareholders?
b. If most shareholders are in a very high marginal tax bracket, which alternative is favored?
c. What are the limitations on the repurchase alternative as an element of the firm's dividend policy?

SELECTED REFERENCES

Brickley, James A. "Shareholder Wealth, Information Signaling and the Specially Designated Dividend: An Empirical Study." *Journal of Financial Economics* 12 (August 1983): 187–210.

Eades, Kenneth M., Patrick J. Hess, and E. Han Kim. "On Interpreting Security Returns during the Ex-Dividend Period." *Journal of Financial Economics* 13 (March 1984): 3–34.

Feldstein, Martin, and Jerry Green. "Why Do Companies Pay Dividends?" *American Economic Review* 73 (March 1983): 17–30.

Haugen, Robert A., and Lemma W. Senbet, "Corporate Finance and Taxes: A Review." *Financial Management* 15 (Autumn 1986): 5–21.

Lakonishok, Josef, and Baruch Lev. "Stock Splits and Stock Dividends: Why, Who, and When?" *Journal of Finance* 42 (September 1987): 913–932.

Lamoureux, Christopher G., and Percy Poon. "The Market Reaction to Stock Splits." *Journal of Finance* 42 (December 1987); 1347–1370.

Miller, Merton H., and Franco Modigliani, "Dividend Policy, Growth, and the Valuation of Shares." *Journal of Business* 34 (October 1961): 411–433.

Offer, Aharon R., and Daniel R. Siegel, "Corporate Financial Policy, Information and Market Expectations: An Empirical Investigation of Dividends." *Journal of Finance* 42 (September 1987): 889–912.

Penman, Steven H. "The Predictive Content of Earnings Forecasts and Dividends," *Journal of Finance* 38 (September 1983): 1181–1199.

Richardson, Gordon R., and Stephen E. Sefcik. "A Test of Dividend Irrelevance Using Volume Reactions to a Change in Dividend Policy." *Journal of Financial Economics* 17 (December 1986): 313–333.

Shefrin, Hersh M., and Meir Statman. "Explaining Investor Preferences for Cash Dividends." *Journal of Financial Economics* 13 (June 1984): 253–282.

Woolridge, J. Randall, and Donald R. Chambers. "Reverse Splits and Shareholder Wealth." *Financial Management* 12 (Autumn 1983): 5–15.

P A R T

VI

Managing Funding Sources

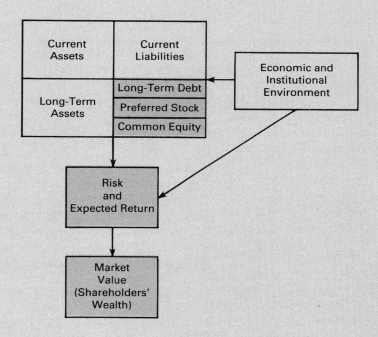

The decision to acquire long-term assets requires arranging sources of financing to fund these asset acquisitions. In this part of the book, the major sources of intermediate- and long-term financing are discussed. Chapter 15 deals with intermediate-term funding sources; namely, term loans and leasing. Chapter 16 looks at long-term funding sources, including the role of the investment banker in obtaining funds. It also covers options, convertible securities, and warrants. Choosing the right mix of financing alternatives can help a firm balance risk, increase returns, and thereby maximize shareholder wealth.

CHAPTER

15

Managing Intermediate-Term Funding Sources

KEY CHAPTER CONCEPTS

1. Term loans are debt obligations having an initial maturity between 1 and 10 years.
   a. The major suppliers of term loans are banks, insurance companies, pension funds, and equipment suppliers.
   b. Term loans usually are amortized over the life of the loan.
   c. The interest rate on term loans obtained from commercial banks normally is greater than the bank's prime rate.
   d. Some term loans from banks require that a compensating balance be maintained at the bank. Other term loans contain a provision that gives the lender an equity participation in the borrowing company.
   e. Most term loans are secured. The loan agreement contains affirmative, negative, and restrictive covenants. In addition the conditions that determine when a default on the loan has occurred are detailed in the loan agreement.

2. Equipment financing loans are commonly made for equipment that is readily marketable. These loans are normally secured with a *conditional sales contract* or a *chattel mortgage.*

3. A *lease* is a contract that allows an individual or a firm to make economic use of an asset for a stated period of time without obtaining an ownership interest in the asset.

4. The major parties to a lease are the *lessor* and the *lessee.*
   a. The lessor is the owner of the asset and the party who receives the lease payments.
   b. The lessee is the user of the asset and the party who makes the lease payments.

5. There are several different classifications of leases.
   a. *Operating leases* are cancelable, period-by-period leases.
   b. *Financial or capital leases* are not cancelable. The lease payments under a financial lease are sufficient to fully amortize the cost of the asset plus provide a return to the lessor.
   c. *Leveraged leases* are special financial leases involving three parties: the lessor, the lessee, and a group of lenders. Leveraged leases are especially important to firms that cannot take advantage of the tax benefits of ownership.

6. An asset should be leased rather than owned if the present value cost of leasing is less than the present value cost of owning.

7. Leasing decisions often are influenced by the tax and accounting treatment of the transaction.

GLOSSARY OF NEW TERMS

Affirmative loan covenant A portion of a loan agreement that outlines actions a firm's management *agrees to take* as conditions for receiving the loan.

Amortization schedule A schedule of periodic payments of interest and principal owed on a debt obligation.

Balloon loan A loan that requires a large final payment greater than each of the periodic (principal and interest) payments.

Bullet loan A loan that requires only the periodic payment of interest during the term of the loan, with a final single repayment of principal at maturity.

Chattel mortgage A lien on personal property, such as machinery, as security for the repayment of a loan.

Compensating balance A certain percentage of a loan balance that the borrower keeps on deposit with a bank as a requirement of a loan provided by the bank.

Conditional sales contract A financing agreement in which the seller of a piece of equipment retains title until all payments have been made.

Direct lease A lease that is initiated when a firm acquires the use of an asset that it did not previously own.

Financial lease A *noncancelable* agreement that obligates the lessee to make payments to the lessor for a predetermined period of time. These payments usually are sufficient to amortize the full cost of the asset plus provide the lessor with a reasonable rate of return on the investment in the asset.

Lease A contract that allows an individual or a firm to make economic use of an asset for a stated period of time without obtaining an ownership interest in it.

Lessee The user and renter of the property in a lease transaction.

Lessor The property owner who collects rental payments from the lessee in a lease transaction.

Leveraged lease A type of financial lease in which the lessor borrows up to 80 percent of the cost of the leased asset on a nonrecourse basis from a group of lenders. The lessor receives the full tax benefits of ownership. This also sometimes is called a *third-party equity lease* or a *tax lease*.

Negative loan covenant A portion of a loan agreement that outlines actions a firm's management *agrees not to take* during the term of the loan.

Operating lease A *cancelable* lease agreement that provides the lessee with the use of an asset on a period-by-period basis. This sometimes is called a *service* or *maintenance lease*, especially if the lessor provides maintenance services as part of the lease contract.

Restrictive loan covenant A portion of a loan agreement that limits the scope of certain actions a firm may take during the term of the loan.

Sale and leaseback A lease that is initiated when a firm sells an asset it owns to another firm and simultaneously leases the asset back for its own use.

Term loan Any debt obligation having an initial maturity between 1 and 10 years. This often is referred to as *intermediate-term credit*.

Leasing a Power Plant*

Leasing is a method employed in separating property use from ownership. A lease is a contract under which one party, the lessor or owner of an asset, agrees to give another party, the lessee, the right to use the asset in exchange for periodic rental payments. Traditionally, leasing has been a popular method of financing business equipment, such as computers and office machines, airplanes, ships, and motor vehicles (automobiles and trucks).

However, more recently, a number of public utility firms have engaged in leasing on a much larger scale, with the sale and leaseback of entire power plants valued in excess of several hundred million dollars. (A sale and leaseback occurs when one party sells an asset to another party and immediately leases it back for its own use.) The following table shows some examples of these lease transactions:

Seller (plant sold)	Buyer	Price
Deseret Generation (44% interest in Bonanza coal plant)	Shell Leasing	$664 million
Basin Electric Power Cooperative (Antelope Valley Station Unit 2)	Beatrice Financing Services, Chrysler Financial, Dart & Kraft Financial, First Chicago Leasing, JC Penney, Saks	$623 million
Oglethorpe Power (60% interest in Scherer Coal Plant Unit 2)	Chrysler Financial, Ford Motor Credit, HEI Investment, IBM	$395 million
Public Service of New Mexico (10.2% interest in Palo Verde Nuclear Plant Unit 1)	Chrysler Financial, Drexel Burnham Leasing, Mellon Financial Services	$325 million
Montana Power (30% interest in Colstrip Unit 4 Plant)	Drexel Burnham Leasing, General Electric Credit, Shell Leasing	$292 million

Why would these utilities, with the ability to raise debt and/or equity funds in the capital markets, use the sale and leaseback of their facilities to finance capital expenditures? The primary reason is that the buyers of these power plants can make better use of the tax benefits than the utility. The buyers lease these generating plants back to the utility firms at rental rates that reflect the value of the tax savings they receive. For example, Deseret Generation (a small Utah-based cooperative) expects to save an average of $45 million per year in principal and interest payments for the next 35 years as the result of its sale and leaseback arrangement with Shell Leasing. This effectively lowers its cost of capital on the power plant from 11 percent to 6 percent. The cooperative estimates that it will have to raise electricity rates by only 7 to 8 percent annually instead of 30 to 40 percent without the sale and leaseback arrangement. Although there are benefits to a utility from a sale and leaseback transaction, there also are costs, because selling a plant means that the company must sacrifice the long-term tax benefits associated with ownership.

In a typical sale and leaseback deal, the buyer has to come up with only a portion of the purchase price, but gets all the tax benefits associated with the purchase price. For example, Shell Leasing, the buyer of the Deseret power plant, expects an annual pretax return of about 25 percent. The balance of the purchase price is raised by issuing long-term, high-yield mortgage bonds backed by the generating plant.

The second part of this chapter examines the costs and benefits of leasing, rather than purchasing, assets.

* Based on an article in *Business Week* (February 3, 1986), pp. 76–77.

INTRODUCTION

The primary sources of intermediate-term funding for companies are term loans and leases. Term loans are discussed in the next four sections. Following that discussion, leases are examined.

TERM LOANS

A *term loan*, or *intermediate-term credit*, is defined as any debt obligation having an initial maturity between 1 and 10 years. It lacks the permanency characteristic of long-term debt.

Term loans constitute the major source of intermediate-term financing. They are made available by a wide variety of financial intermediaries (such as commercial banks), government agencies, and equipment suppliers.

Term loans are well suited for financing small additions to plant facilities and equipment, such as a new piece of machinery. Term loans also can be used to finance a moderate increase in working capital when

- The cost of a public offering of bonds or stock is too high.
- The firm intends to use the term debt only until its earnings are sufficient to amortize the loan.
- The desired increase is relatively long term but not permanent.

Term loans often are preferable to short-term loans, because they provide the borrower with a certain degree of security. Rather than having to be concerned about whether a short-term loan will be renewed, the borrower can have a term loan structured in such a way that the maturity coincides with the economic life of the asset being financed. Thus, the cash flows generated by the asset can service the loan without putting any additional financial strain on the borrower.

Term loans also offer potential cost advantages over long-term sources of financing. Because term loans are privately negotiated between the borrowing firm and the lending institution, they are less expensive than public offerings of common stock or bonds. The issuing firm in a public offering must pay the registration and issue expenses necessary to sell the securities. For small- to moderate-sized offerings these expenses can be large in relation to the funds raised.[1]

Repayment Provisions

A term loan agreement usually requires that the principal be *amortized* over the life of the loan. This means that the firm is required to pay off the loan in installments rather than in one lump sum. This has the effect of reducing the risk to the lender that the borrower will be unable to retire the loan in one lump sum when it comes due. Amortization of principal also is consistent with the idea that term loans are not a permanent part of a firm's capital structure.

The amortization schedule of a term loan might require the firm to make equal quarterly, semiannual, or annual payments of principal and interest.

---

[1] For example, one study indicated that the total flotation cost as a percentage of the gross proceeds for a $500,000 debt issue was 8 percent; for a $500,000 common stock issue, it was about 16 percent. These costs dropped to 1.4 percent for a $10 million debt issue and 6.9 percent for a $10 million common stock issue. For further information on issue costs, see Securities and Exchange Commission, *Cost of Flotation of Registered Equity Issues,* 1963–1965 (Washington, D.C.: GPO, 1979), and Irwin Friend, *Investment Banking and the New Issues Market* (Cleveland: World Publishing, 1967). See also Chapter 16 of this text.

For example, assume a firm borrows $100,000 payable over 8 years, with an interest rate of 9 percent per annum on the unpaid balance. The repayment schedule calls for eight equal annual payments, the first occurring at the end of year 1.

Equation 5.16 from Chapter 5 can be rewritten as follows:

$$PVAN_0 = R(PVIFA_{i,n})$$

$$R = \frac{PVAN_0}{PVIFA_{i,n}}$$

Given the present value of the annuity $(PVAN_0) = \$100,000$, the interest rate $(i) = 9$ percent, the number of time periods $(n) = 8$, and the $PVIFA_{0.09,8}$ from Table IV, the annual payment, R, is computed as follows:

$$R = \frac{\$100,000}{5.535}$$

$$= \$18,067$$

By making eight annual payments of $18,067 to the lender, the borrower will just pay off the loan and provide the lender with a 9 percent return. Table 15-1 shows the principal and interest for each year's annuity payment.

Over the life of this loan the firm will make total payments of $144,536. Of this, $100,000 is the repayment of the principal, and the other $44,536 is interest. It is important to know what proportions of a loan payment are principal and interest, because interest payments are tax deductible.

In this example the repayment schedule calls for equal periodic payments to the lender consisting of both principal and interest. Other types of repayment schedules are also possible, including the following:

■ The borrower might be required to make equal reductions in the prin-

TABLE 15-1

Sample Loan Amortization Schedule*

End of Year (1)	Annual Annuity Amount (2)	Interest[†] (3)	Principal Repayment[‡] (4)	Remaining Balance (5)
0	$ 0	$ 0	$ 0	$100,000
1	18,067	9,000	9,067	90,933
2	18,067	8,183	9,884	81,049
3	18,067	7,294	10,773	70,276
4	18,067	6,324	11,743	58,533
5	18,067	5,267	12,800	45,733
6	18,067	4,116	13,951	31,782
7	18,067	2,860	15,207	16,575
8	18,067	1,492	16,575	0
	$144,536	$44,536	$100,000	

* Figures in the table have been rounded. Rounding is done to yield a zero ending loan balance. If the table reported payments in terms of both dollars *and* cents, and if fractional cents were permitted, no rounding would be necessary.
† Interest each period is equal to 0.09 times the remaining balance from the previous period; for example, interest in year 1 equals 0.09 × $100,000 = $9,000, and interest in year 2 equals 0.09 × $90,933 = $8,183.
‡ The principal repayment each period equals the annual annuity amount ($18,067) minus the per-period interest from Column 3.

cipal outstanding each period, with the interest being computed on the remaining balance for each period.

- The borrower might be required to make equal periodic payments over the life of the loan that only partially amortize the loan, leaving a lump sum payment that falls due at the termination of the loan period (this is called a *balloon loan*).
- The borrower might be required to make a single principal payment at maturity while making periodic (usually quarterly) interest payments only over the life of the loan (this is called a *bullet loan*).[2]

Interest Costs

The interest rate charged on a term loan depends on a number of factors, including the general level of interest rates in the economy, the size of the loan, the maturity of the loan, and the borrower's credit standing. Generally, interest rates on intermediate-term loans tend to be slightly higher than interest rates on short-term loans because of the higher risk assumed by the lender. Also, large term loans tend to have lower rates than small term loans, because the fixed costs associated with granting and administering a loan do not vary proportionately with the size of the loan. In addition, large borrowers often have better credit standings than small borrowers. An interest rate between 0.25 and 2.5 percentage points above the prime rate is common for term loans obtained from banks.

The interest rate on a small term loan is sometimes the same throughout the loan's lifetime. In contrast, most larger term loans specify a *variable* interest rate, which depends on the bank's prime lending rate. For example, if a loan is initially made at 0.5 percentage points above the prime rate, the loan agreement might specify that the interest charged on the remaining balance will continue to be 0.5 percentage points above the prevailing rate. Thus, whenever the prime rate is increased, the loan rate also increases; if the prime rate declines, so does the interest rate on the loan.

COMPENSATING BALANCES. It is not uncommon for a bank to require a borrowing firm to keep a percentage of its loan balance—for example, 10 percent—on deposit as a compensating balance. If this balance is greater than the amount the firm would normally keep on deposit with the bank, this requirement effectively increases the firm's cost of the loan. Compensating balance requirements and their effect on the cost of a loan are discussed in detail in Chapter 20.

EQUITY PARTICIPATIONS. The interest rate charged on a term loan also may be influenced by a desire on the part of the lending institution to take an equity position (often called a "kicker") in the company as an additional form of compensation. This usually is accomplished through the issuance of a *warrant* by the borrower to the lender. A warrant is an option to purchase a stated number of shares of a company's common stock at a specified price sometime in the future. If the company prospers, the lending institution shares in this prosperity on an equity basis. The issuance of warrants in conjunction with a term loan is common when the loan has an above-normal level of risk but the lending institution feels the borrower has promising

---

[2] These three repayment patterns are illustrated in the "Problems" section at the end of this chapter.

growth potential. Alternatively, the borrower may issue warrants to secure a more favorable lending rate. Warrants are discussed in detail in Chapter 16.

SECURITY PROVISIONS AND PROTECTIVE COVENANTS OF TERM LOANS

The security provisions and protective covenants specified by a term loan agreement often are determined by the borrower's credit standing: the weaker the credit standing, the more restrictive the protective covenants.

Security Provisions

In general, security requirements apply more often to intermediate-term loans than to short-term loans. This is due to the fact that longer-term loan contracts tend to have more default risk. Security provisions also are dependent on the size of the borrowing firm. For example, term loans to small firms tend to be secured more often than term loans to large firms, although there is an increasing tendency for all bank-originated term loans to be secured.

The sources of security for a term loan include the following:

- An assignment of payments due under a specific contract.
- An assignment of a portion of the receivables or inventories.
- The use of a floating lien on inventories and receivables.
- A pledge of marketable securities held by the borrower.
- A mortgage on property, plant, or equipment held by the borrower.
- An assignment of the cash surrender value of a life insurance policy held by the borrower for its key executives.

Affirmative Covenants

An affirmative covenant is a portion of a loan agreement that outlines actions the borrowing firm *agrees to take* during the term of the loan. Typical affirmative covenants include the following:

- The borrower agrees to furnish periodic financial statements to the lender, including a balance sheet, income statement, and a statement of cash flows. These may be furnished monthly, quarterly, or annually and frequently are required to be audited. Pro forma cash budgets and projections of the costs needed to complete contracts on hand also may be required.
- The borrower agrees to carry sufficient insurance to cover insurable business risk.
- The borrower agrees to maintain a minimum amount of net working capital (current assets less current liabilities).
- The borrower agrees to maintain management personnel who are acceptable to the financing institution.

Negative Covenants

A negative covenant outlines actions that the borrowing firm's management *agrees not to take* without prior written consent of the lender. Typical negative covenants include the following:

The borrowing firm agrees not to pledge any of its assets as security to other lenders, as well as not to factor (sell) its receivables. This type of agreement, called a *negative pledge clause*, is found in nearly all unsecured loans. It is designed to keep other lenders from interfering with the immediate lender's claims on the assets of the firm.

The borrower is prohibited from making mergers or consolidations. In addition, it may not sell or lease a major portion of its assets without written approval of the lender.

The borrower is prohibited from making or guaranteeing loans to others that would impair the lender's security.

Restrictive Covenants

Rather than requiring or prohibiting certain actions on the part of the borrower, *restrictive covenants* merely *limit their scope*. These are typical restrictive covenants:

Limitations on the amount of dividends a firm may pay.

Limitations on the level of salaries, bonuses, and advances a firm may give to employees.

These restrictions, in essence, force the firm to increase its equity capital base, thereby increasing the security for the loan.

Other restrictive covenants might include the following:

Limitations on the total amount of short- and long-term borrowing the firm may engage in during the period of the term loan.

Limitations on the amount of funds the firm may invest in new property, plant, and equipment. (This restriction usually applies only to those investments that cannot be financed from internally generated funds.)

And, finally, a firm that has outstanding long-term debt may be restricted as to the amount of debt it can retire without also retiring a portion of the term loan.

These restrictions are quite common, but the list is not all-inclusive. For example, a standard loan agreement checklist published by a large New York City bank lists thirty-four commonly used covenants. In general, covenants included in a loan agreement are determined by the particular conditions surrounding the granting of the term loan, including the credit record of the borrower and the maturity and security provisions of the loan.

Default Provisions

All term loans have *default provisions* that permit the lender to insist that the borrower repay the entire loan immediately under certain conditions. The following are examples:

The borrower fails to pay interest, principal, or both as specified by the terms of the loan.

The borrower materially misrepresents any information on the financial statements required under the loan's affirmative covenants.

The borrower fails to observe any of the affirmative, negative, or restrictive covenants specified within the loan.

A borrower who commits any of these common acts of default will not necessarily be called on to repay a loan immediately, however. Basically, a lender will use a default provision only as a last resort, seeking in the meantime to make some agreement with the borrower, such as working out an acceptable modified lending plan with which the borrower is more able to comply. Normally, a lender will call a loan due only if no reasonable alternative is available or if the borrower is facing near-certain failure.

SUPPLIERS OF TERM LOANS

There are numerous sources of term loans, including commercial banks, insurance companies, pension funds, commercial finance companies, government agencies, and equipment suppliers. Many of these sources are discussed in the following subsections.

Commercial Banks and Savings and Loan Associations

Many commercial banks and some savings and loan associations are actively involved in term lending. For example, about one-third of all commercial and industrial loans made by commercial banks are term loans.

In spite of this level of activity, banks generally tend to favor loans having relatively short maturities—that is, less than 5 years—although some banks will make loans having lifetimes as long as 10 years or more. In addition, some banks limit their term lending to existing customers. Often banks will form *syndicates* to share large term loans. This not only limits the risk exposure for any one bank, but also complies with laws that limit the size of *unsecured* loans made to single customers.

Life Insurance Companies and Pension Funds

Whereas commercial banks tend to prefer shorter-term loans, insurance companies and pension funds are most interested in longer-term commitments, for example, 10 to 20 years. As a result, it is common for a bank and an insurance company to share a term loan commitment. Under this type of arrangement, the bank might agree to finance the first 5 years of a loan, with the insurance company financing the loan for the remaining years. This also can be advantageous to the borrower, because banks generally can charge a lower rate of interest for loans having shorter maturities.

From the borrowing firm's perspective, term loan agreements with pension funds and insurance companies have one significant limitation. If a firm decides to retire a term loan with a bank, it usually may do so without penalty. Because insurance companies are interested in having their funds invested for longer periods of time, however, prepayment of an insurance company term loan may involve some penalties.

Term loans from insurance companies and pension funds usually are secured, often with a mortgage on an asset such as a building. These mortgage-secured loans rarely are made for amounts greater than 65 to 75 percent of the value of the collateral, however.

And, finally, term loans from life insurance companies and pension funds tend to have slightly higher stated rates of interest than bank term loans. This is because (1) they generally are made for longer maturities and (2) there are no compensating balance requirements.

Small Business Administration (SBA)

The Small Business Administration (SBA), an agency of the federal government, was established in 1953 to make credit available to small businesses that cannot reasonably obtain financing from private sources.

Normally an SBA loan is secured by a mortgage on the firm's plant and equipment, third-party guarantees, or an assignment of accounts receivable and/or inventories.

The SBA makes three major types of loans:

- Direct loans.
- Participation loans.
- Economic opportunity loans.

Direct loans are financed by the SBA, and because funds are quite limited, these loans usually are made only when the applicant firm cannot borrow from private sources at reasonable rates.

A *participation loan* is obtained from a local bank, with the SBA guaranteeing up to 90 percent of it. The SBA prefers participation loans over direct loans. Typical SBA loans range between $20,000 and $40,000 and have a maximum 10-year maturity. In addition, they usually carry an interest rate that is considerably below the rate that would be charged for a similar non-SBA loan. A rate about 1 percentage point higher than the U.S. Treasury bond rate is common. Like other term loans, SBA loans normally must be amortized; that is, paid off in periodic (usually monthly) installments.

Economic opportunity loans have been made available since 1970 to assist economically and socially disadvantaged individuals who own their own firms.

Small Business Investment Companies (SBICs)

Small business investment companies (SBICs) are licensed by the government to make both equity and debt investments in small firms. They raise their capital by borrowing from the SBA and other sources.

The SBICs take an equity interest in the small firms they loan funds to, hoping to profit from their growth and prosperity. Unlike SBA loans, which are made to any eligible credit-worthy small business, SBICs specialize in providing funds to firms that have above-average growth potential. Naturally, these firms often have above-average risk as well. Thus, the interest charge on an SBIC loan generally is somewhat higher than that on a normal bank term loan. SBIC loans have maturities as long as 10 to 20 years.

Industrial Development Authorities (IDAs)

Many states and municipalities have organized industrial development authorities (IDAs) to encourage new firms to locate in their area or to assist existing firms with expansion plans. In a typical financing plan, a local IDA sells tax-exempt municipal revenue bonds and uses the proceeds to build a firm's new facility. It then leases the plant to the firm, collecting lease payments from the firm that are large enough to pay the principal and interest on the municipal revenue bonds. Because bonds of this nature are tax exempt, the interest on them generally is lower than the interest on bonds issued directly by a private corporation. As a result, an IDA can charge a firm an attractively low lease rate.

The growing need to finance pollution control expenditures has led to the development of *pollution control revenue bonds*, which are issued by municipalities. Proceeds from these bonds are used to acquire pollution control equipment, which is then sold or leased to local industries. Because interest payments on pollution control revenue bonds are tax-free to investors, a firm's cost is much lower than it would be if these investments had to be financed with conventional debt or equity. For example, in February 1986 the Public Service Company of New Hampshire sold $100 million of 30-year pollution control revenue bonds through the Industrial Development Authority of the State of New Hampshire. The interest cost on these bonds was 10.5 percent compared to a return requirement in excess of 12.0 percent had the bonds not been tax-exempt.

EQUIPMENT LOANS

When a firm procures a loan to finance new equipment, it may use the equipment itself as collateral for an intermediate-term loan. These loans are called *equipment financing loans*. Equipment financing loans are commonly made for readily marketable equipment. These loans normally are made for somewhat less than the market value of the equipment, and the difference provides a margin of safety for the lender. This difference may range between 20 and 30 percent for readily marketable and mobile equipment, such as trucks or cars. The amortization schedule for an equipment financing loan usually is tied closely to the asset's economic life.

There are several potential sources of equipment financing, including commercial banks, sales finance companies, equipment sellers, insurance companies, and pension funds. Commercial banks often are the least expensive source of such financing—especially when compared with sales finance companies. The equipment seller may provide financing either directly or through a captive finance subsidiary (that is, the seller's own financing subsidiary). Although at first glance, an equipment seller may appear to charge a very modest interest rate, it often is difficult to make a meaningful comparison between the rates charged by a supplier and other financing sources such as commercial banks. This is because the selling firm might price the equipment in such a way as to conceal part of the cost of carrying its credit customers; that is, noncash customers may pay relatively higher prices than cash customers.

There are two primary security instruments used in connection with equipment financing loans: the *conditional sales contract* and the *chattel mortgage*. Each of these is discussed in the following subsections.

Conditional Sales Contract

When a conditional sales contract (sometimes called a *purchase money mortgage*) is used in an equipment financing transaction, the seller retains title until the buyer has made all payments required by the financing contract. Conditional sales contracts are used almost exclusively by equipment sellers. At the time of purchase, the buyer normally makes a down payment to the seller and issues a promissory note for the balance of the purchase price. The buyer then agrees to make a series of periodic payments (usually monthly or quarterly) of principal and interest to the seller until the note has been paid off. When the last payment has been made, the title to the equipment passes to the buyer. In the case of default, the seller may repossess the asset.

Chattel Mortgage

A chattel mortgage is a lien on property other than real estate. Chattel mortgages are most common when a commercial bank or sales finance company makes a direct equipment financing loan. It involves the placement of a lien against the property by the lender. Notification of the lien is filed with a public office in the state where the equipment is located. Given a valid lien, the lender may repossess the equipment and resell it if the borrower defaults on the loan payment.

INTRODUCTION TO LEASING

A promotional brochure from the Warner and Swasey Financial Corporation states, "The value of a machine is in the use, not its ownership." This is true in the sense that whereas a firm may wish to acquire the *use* of an asset needed in the production of goods and the providing of services, it is not absolutely necessary to acquire legal title to the asset. Leasing is a means of obtaining economic use of an asset for a specific period of time without obtaining an ownership interest in the asset. In the lease contract, the property owner *(lessor)* agrees to permit the property user *(lessee)* to make use of the property for a stated time. In return, the lessee agrees to make a series of periodic payments to the lessor.

Leasing as a source of intermediate- and long-term financing has become increasingly popular since World War II. Prior to that time most lease contracts were written for real estate and farm property. Today few major firms are not involved in leasing. Leased assets range from transportation equipment (such as railroad rolling stock, trucks, automobiles, airplanes, and ships) to computers, medical equipment, specialized industrial equipment, energy transmission equipment, and mining equipment. Some firms lease entire power-generating plants and aluminum reduction mills. In the hotel and motel industry, leases may even include bathroom fixtures, paintings, furniture, and bedding.

The volume of leasing activity expanded greatly during the 1980s—growing at an estimated rate of 16 percent per year.[3] Equipment leasing by companies has risen to over $100 billion per year. Leasing accounts for close to 30 percent of all business investment in equipment.

The Tax Reform Act of 1986 had both positive and negative impacts on the volume of leasing. By eliminating the investment tax credit and reducing depreciation allowances for equipment and property, the tax law diminished the tax advantages of leasing (or owning) such assets. However, the alternative minimum tax (AMT) provisions of the tax law encouraged the use of leasing when acquiring assets. Profitable companies that are subject to the AMT can use leasing to reduce their taxes and financing costs.

Many types of firms originate leases: commercial banks, savings and loan institutions, finance companies, insurance companies, investment banks, equipment manufacturing companies (often through captive leasing subsidiaries), and independent leasing companies. Independent leasing companies and banks (and bank-related firms) account for the largest volume of leasing.

Because of the growing importance and widespread acceptance of lease financing, the contemporary financial manager should have a good under-

---

[3] McAdams, M. Bruce. "Equipment Leasing: An Integral Part of Financial Services," *Business Economics* (July 1988): 43–47.

standing of this financing method. The following sections discuss the characteristics of various types of leases and develop a lease analysis model from
the perspective of the lessor. Later sections consider the tax and accounting
treatment of leases and the advantages and disadvantages of leases. Finally,
a lease analysis model is developed from the perspective of the lessee.

TYPES OF LEASES

Leases are classified in a number of ways. "True leases," which are the
primary focus of this chapter, are traditional leases in which the lessor is
considered to hold the legal title to the leased asset. The asset user, the
lessee, has no ownership interest in the asset. *Operating leases* and various
types of *financial*, or *capital, leases* are subcategories of true leases.

Operating Leases

An *operating lease*, sometimes called a *service* or *maintenance lease*, is an
agreement that provides the lessee with use of an asset on a period-by-
period basis. Normally the payments under an operating lease contract are
insufficient to recover the full cost of the asset for the lessor. As a result,
the contract period in an operating lease tends to be somewhat less than
the usable economic life of the asset, and the lessor expects to recover the
costs (plus a return) from renewal rental payments, or the sale of the asset
at the end of the lease period, or both.

The most important characteristic of an operating lease is that it may be
canceled at the option of the lessee as long as the lessor is given sufficient
notice. Even though the lessee may be required to pay a penalty to the lessor
upon cancelation, this is preferable to being compelled to keep an asset that
is expected to become obsolete in the near future. For example, many firms
lease their computers under an operating lease arrangement. (Of course,
the lessor charges a rental that is consistent with expectations of the asset's
economic life.)

Most operating leases require the lessor to maintain the leased asset. In
addition, the lessor normally is responsible for any property taxes owed on
the asset and for providing appropriate insurance coverage. The costs of
these services are built into the lease rate.

Financial, or Capital Leases

A *financial lease*, also termed a *capital lease*, is a noncancelable agreement.[4]
The lessee is required to make payments throughout the lease period, whether
or not the asset continues to generate economic benefits. Failure to make
payments eventually could force the lessee into bankruptcy.

With financial leases, the lessee generally is responsible for maintenance
of the asset. The lessee may also have to pay insurance and property taxes.
The total payments over the lease period are sufficient to amortize the
original cost of the asset and provide a return to the lessor. Some financial
leases provide for a renewal or repurchase option at the end of the lease;
these are limited by the IRS.

[4] This chapter focuses primarily on financial leases rather than operating leases, because financial
leases represent more permanent obligations. The analysis techniques discussed at the end of this
chapter, however, are equally applicable to both operating and financial leases.

A financial lease may originate either as a *sale and leaseback* or as a *direct lease*.

SALE AND LEASEBACK. A sale and leaseback occurs when a company sells an asset to another firm and immediately leases it back for its own use. In this transaction the lessor normally pays a price close to the asset's fair market value. The lease payments are set at a level that will return the full purchase price of the asset to the lessor, plus provide a reasonable rate of return. The sale and leaseback is advantageous to the lessee for the following reasons:

- The lessee receives cash from the sale of the asset, which may be reinvested elsewhere in the firm or used to increase the firm's liquidity.
- The lessee can continue using the asset, even though it is owned by someone else.

A good illustration of a sale and leaseback transaction was Public Service of New Mexico's decision in 1985 to sell and leaseback its (partial) interest in Palo Verde Nuclear Plant Unit 1 for $325 million.[5] This transaction reduced its annual mortgage payments by one-half to $40 million per year for the next 15 years and its total cost by $375 million.

DIRECT LEASE. A direct lease is initiated when a firm acquires the use of an asset that it did not previously own. The lessor may be the manufacturer of the asset or a financial institution. In the latter instance, the user-lessee first determines the following:

- What equipment will be leased.
- Which manufacturer will supply the equipment.
- What options, warranties, terms of delivery, installation agreements, and service agreements will have to be made.
- What price will be paid for the asset.

The lessee then contacts a financial institution and works out the terms of the lease, after which the institution (which then becomes the lessor) acquires the asset for the lessee and the lessee starts making the lease payments. Under this arrangement the lessee usually is responsible for taxes, insurance, and maintenance.

Leveraged Leases

Approximately 85 percent of all financial leases currently written in the United States are leveraged leases. Also known as *third-party equity leases* and *tax leases*, leveraged leases are designed to provide financing for assets that require large capital outlays (generally greater than $300,000) and have economic lives of 5 years or more. Leveraged leases usually are tax motivated because the asset-user (lessee) is not in a tax position where it can make use of the accelerated depreciation tax shields if the asset is owned instead of leased.

A leveraged lease is a three-sided agreement among the lessee, the lessor, and the lenders. The *lessee* selects the leased asset, receives all the income generated from its use, and makes the periodic lease payments. The *lessor*

[5] *Business Week* (February 3, 1986), p. 78.

(normally a financial institution, such as a leasing company or a commercial bank) acts either for itself or as a trustee for an individual or a group of individuals to provide the equity funds needed to purchase the asset. The *lenders* (usually banks, insurance companies, trusts, pension funds, or foundations) lend the funds needed to make up the asset's full purchase price. Specifically the lessor normally supplies 20 to 40 percent of the purchase price, and the lenders provide the remaining 60 to 80 percent. For example, in the Public Service of New Mexico sale and leaseback of the Palo Verde Nuclear Plant discussed earlier, the lessors (Chrysler Capital, Drexel Burnham Leasing, and Mellon Financial Services) borrowed approximately 80 percent of the purchase price of the facilities.

Figure 15-1 is an announcement of a leveraged lease that was arranged by Salomon Brothers for Kansas City Southern Lines. In this case, the Ford Motor Credit Company acted as the lessor and provided equity funds of $4,728,974 to acquire 450 boxcars, which were leased to Kansas City Southern Lines. Debt funds of $10,072,198 were provided by a number of institutional lenders.

In a leveraged lease the long-term money is supplied to the lessor by the lenders on a nonrecourse basis; that is, the lenders cannot turn to the lessor for repayment of the debt in the event of default. Normally the lender receives mortgage bonds secured by the following:

- A first lien on the asset.
- An assignment of the lease.

F I G U R E 15-1

Announcement of a Leveraged Lease Financing Arrangement

This announcement appears as a matter of record only.

$14,801,172

Kansas City Southern Lines

15 Year Leveraged Lease of 450 Boxcars
Equity Funds of $4,728,974 were provided by

Ford Motor Credit Company

Debt Funds of $10,072,198 were provided by
various institutional lenders.

The undersigned arranged the financing for
this leveraged lease transaction.

Salomon Brothers   **ITEL** CORPORATION

- An assignment of the lease rental payments.
- Occasionally, a direct guarantee from the lessee or a third party (such as the government, in the case of merchant vessel financing).

Referring again to the Public Service of New Mexico nuclear plant sale and leaseback example, the public debt used to finance the transaction was indirectly secured by the facilities and was payable from rental payments due by the utility under the leases. The debt was structured to have principal and interest payments that correspond to the receipt of rental payments. Because the lenders do not have recourse to the lessor in the event of default, the lessor's risk exposure is limited to the 20 to 40 percent equity contribution.

As the owner of the asset, the lessor reports the lease payments as gross income. The lessor receives benefits from the tax-deductible interest and accelerated depreciation. As a result, the lessor incurs large tax losses and receives large cash inflows during the early years of the lease.

Because the lessor receives the entire accelerated depreciation tax shield although making a relatively small equity investment, the lessor can provide an attractive lease rate to the lessee. Lease rates of 4 to 6 percent are not uncommon when AAA-rated bonds are yielding from 9 to 10 percent. Figure 15-2 is a diagram of a typical leveraged lease arrangement.

Lessees who anticipate that their taxable income will not be sufficient to allow them to take advantage of the tax benefits of ownership are most likely to use leveraged leases for large transactions. These include firms with low profit levels, large tax loss carryforwards, or large amounts of tax-

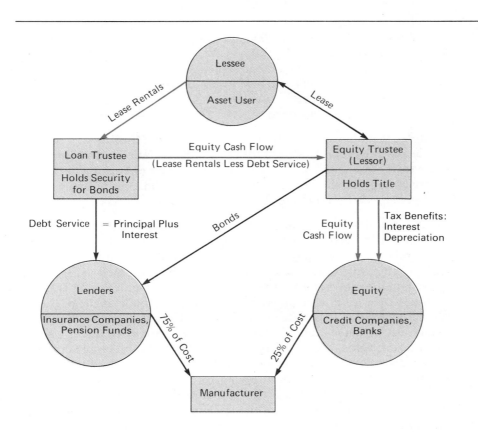

FIGURE 15-2

Diagram of a Typical Leveraged Lease

exempt income. The lessee effectively gives up the tax benefits of ownership in exchange for more favorable lease rates.

DETERMINING THE LEASE PAYMENTS: THE LESSOR'S PERSPECTIVE

Suppose that the Dole Company (lessee) desires to lease a piece of farm equipment valued at $100,000 from the Deere & Company (lessor) for a period of 5 years. Under the terms of the lease, payments are to be made at the beginning of each of the 5 years. Deere expects to depreciate the asset on a straight-line basis of $20,000 per year down to a book salvage value of $0. Actual salvage value is expected to be $10,000 at the end of 5 years. This salvage value will be treated as a recapture of depreciation and taxed at Deere's marginal tax rate of 40 percent. Thus the after-tax salvage value will be $6,000 ($10,000 actual salvage less $4,000 tax on depreciation recapture). If Deere requires an 11 percent after-tax rate of return on the lease, what will be the annual lease payments?

■ **Step 1: Compute the lessor's amount to be amortized.** In this case, it is the $100,000 initial outlay minus the present value of the after-tax salvage at the end of year 5 minus the present value of the after-tax depreciation tax shield for each year. (Recall that depreciation reduces taxable income by the amount of the depreciation and thus reduces a firm's cash outflow for tax payments by an amount equal to the depreciation times the company's marginal ordinary tax rate.)

Initial Outlay	$100,000
Less Present value of $6,000 after-tax salvage at 11% ($6,000 × 0.593)	3,558
Less Present value of annual depreciation tax shield ($20,000 × 0.4 × PVIFA$_{0.11,5}$) = $8,000 × 3.696	29,568
Amount to be amortized	$ 66,874

(If an accelerated depreciation method, such as MACRS, was used by the lessor, the present value of the annual depreciation tax shield would have to be done using a series of Table II PVIF factors, because the annual depreciation tax shield normally will change most years under accelerated depreciation methods.)

■ **Step 2: Compute the annual *after-tax* lease income.** This is the income that the lessor must receive in order to earn the needed 11 percent return. Remember that lease payments received by a lessor are treated as taxable, ordinary income. These payments can be computed using the appropriate interest factor for the present value of an annuity (PVIFA from Table IV). Because lease payments normally are made at the beginning of each year, they constitute an *annuity due*. Thus, the last four payments, which occur at the ends of years 1 through 4, are discounted, whereas the present value of the first payment, made at the *beginning* of year 1, is not discounted. Recall from Chapter 5 that taking the PVIFA for 11 percent and 5 years and multiplying by (1 + 0.11) gives the required PVIFA for an annuity due. If R is the annual after-tax lease income to the lessor, the present value of the lease income may be set equal to the amount to be amortized to determine the required R, as follows:

$$\text{Amount to be amortized} = \text{R (PVIFA}_{0.11,5})\ (1 + 0.11)$$

$$\$66{,}874 = \text{R (3.696) (1.11)}$$

$$\$66{,}874 = \text{R (4.103)}$$

$$\text{R} = \$16{,}299$$

Therefore Deere & Company needs to receive five beginning-of-the-year, after-tax lease income amounts of $16,299 in order to earn an 11 percent after-tax return on the lease.

■ **Step 3: Convert the lease income requirement of the lessor to a lease payment requirement of the lessee.** Recalling that lease payments received by the lessor from the lessee are taxed as ordinary income, we can convert the after-tax lease income requirement of the lessor into a lease payment requirement for the lessee as follows:

$$\begin{aligned}
\text{Lease payment required from the lessee} &= \frac{\text{Lease income required by lessor (after-tax)}}{1 \text{ minus lessor's marginal tax rate}} \\
&= \frac{\$16{,}299}{1 - 0.4} \\
&= \$27{,}165
\end{aligned}$$

Therefore the Dole Company will have to make an annual lease payment of $27,165 to Deere & Company at the beginning of each year.

TAX AND ACCOUNTING ASPECTS OF LEASES

Leasing assets involves a number of tax and accounting considerations. These are examined in this section.

Tax Status of True Leases

Annual lease payments are tax deductible for the lessee if one crucial criterion is met; namely, the IRS must agree that a contract truly is a lease and not just an installment loan called a lease. Before embarking on a lease transaction, all involved parties should obtain an opinion from the IRS regarding the tax status of the proposed lease. The opinion of the IRS normally revolves primarily around the following general rules:

■ The remaining useful life of the equipment at the end of the lease term must be the greater of 1 year or 20 percent of its originally estimated useful life.
■ Leases in excess of 30 years are *not* considered to be leases for tax purposes.
■ The lease payments must provide the lessor with a reasonable return on the investment. At this point in time, a range of 8 to 16 percent would probably be viewed as reasonable. This profit potential must exist apart from the transaction's tax benefits.
■ Renewal options must be reasonable; that is, the renewal rate must be closely related to the economic value of the asset for the renewal period.

■ If the lease agreement specifies a purchase option at the end of the lease period, the purchase price must be based on the asset's fair market value at that time.

■ In the case of a leveraged lease, the lessor must provide a minimum of 20 percent equity.

■ Limited use property (valuable only to the lessee) may not be leased.

If the IRS does not agree that a contract is truly a lease, taxes are applied as if the property had been sold to the lessee and pledged to the lessor as security for a loan. The reason for the IRS restrictions previously cited is that the IRS wants to prohibit lease transactions set up purely to speed up tax deductions. For example, a building normally would be depreciated over 31.5 years under MACRS depreciation rules. It would be possible to set up a lease over a 3-year period that allowed the lessee to effectively write off the cost of the building for tax purposes over 3 years. This would increase tax deductions for the lessee at the expense of tax receipts to the U.S. Treasury. These IRS guidelines are designed to prevent this type of abuse.

Leases and Accounting Practices

In recent years firms have tended to disclose more information regarding lease obligations.

In November 1976 the Financial Accounting Standards Board (FASB) issued *Statement No. 13*, which *requires* lessees to capitalize certain types of leases, primarily financial or capital leases. The capitalized value of a lease is determined by computing the present value of all required lease payments, discounted at a rate equal to the lessee's incremental borrowing rate for a secured loan over a term similar to the lease.[6] Table 15-2 illustrates this procedure.

In addition to making these balance sheet adjustments, a firm must show the following in the footnotes to the financial statements:[7]

■ *For financial leases:*
   1. The gross amount of assets reported under financial leases as of the date of the balance sheet by major classes according to nature or use.

[6] In certain circumstances it is possible for a firm to use a lower rate. See FASB *Standard No. 13* for a more detailed discussion.
[7] The requirements presented here are not inclusive; they merely summarize the most significant disclosures.

TABLE 15-2

Accounting Treatment of Leases

Assets		Liabilities	
Lease property under capital leases less accumulated amortization	$1,500	Current: Obligations under capital leases*	$ 150
		Long term: Obligations under capital leases*	1,350
	$1,500		$1,500

* The $150 represents lease payments due during the next year. The $1,350 represents the present value of lease payments due beyond one year in the future.

2. The amount of accumulated lease amortization.
3. Future minimum lease payments as of the date of the latest balance sheet presented, in total and for each of the next five fiscal years.

■ *For operating leases:*
1. Future minimum rental payments required as of the date of the latest balance sheet presented, in total and for each of the following 5 fiscal years.
2. The rental expense for each period for which an income statement is presented.

The lessee also must indicate in the notes to the financial statements the existence and terms of renewal or repurchase options and escalation clauses, any restrictions imposed by leases (such as restrictions on dividends, additional debt, or further leasing), and any contingent rental obligations.

The effect of these new disclosure requirements is to lower a firm's reported return on investment and to increase the reported debt-to-equity ratios of those firms that have acquired portions of their assets through leasing. In the past some analysts argued that one of the advantages of leasing was that it provided "off-balance sheet" financing and tended to increase a firm's capacity to borrow. Whether or not this was true, the lease-reporting requirements help to eliminate this distortion, facilitate clearer analysis of a firm's financial condition, and make it easier to make comparisons among firms.

ADVANTAGES AND DISADVANTAGES OF LEASING

There are a number of potential advantages to leasing. However, the prudent financial manager also should be aware of the disadvantages.

Advantages

Perhaps the major advantage of leasing is that it provides *flexible financing.* Most lease arrangements tend to have fewer restrictive covenants than loan agreements. In addition, leasing is well suited to piecemeal financing. A firm that is acquiring assets over time may find it more convenient to lease them than to negotiate term loans or sell securities each time it makes a new capital outlay.

In the case of real estate leasing, the lessee may *effectively be able to depreciate land.* Because the lease payments will reflect both the lessor's investment in any buildings *and* the cost of the land, the lessee is able to effectively depreciate the land by deducting the full amount of the lease payment for tax purposes. To keep this benefit in perspective, however, it should be noted that the lessee also loses any salvage value associated with the property at the end of the lease.

The lessee also may be able to make *lower payments* because of the tax benefits enjoyed by the lessor. This is especially important in the case of a leveraged lease, when the lessee is a firm with insufficient taxable income to take advantage of the tax benefits of ownership. In fact, the majority of lease transactions made are tax motivated.

In addition, it *may* be possible for the lessee to *avoid some of the risks of obsolescence* associated with ownership. The lessor will charge a lease rate intended to provide a specified return on the required net investment. The net investment is equal to the cost of the asset minus the present value of the expected salvage value at the end of the lease. If the actual salvage is less than originally expected, the lessor bears the loss.

For the small or marginally profitable firm, *leasing is often the only available source of financing*, because the title to leased property remains with the lessor and reduces the lessor's risk in the event of failure. If the lessee does fail, the lessor can recover the leased property more quickly than a secured lender.

Leasing tends to *smooth out expenses* for the lessee. Because lease payments are a constant annual outlay, whereas MACRS depreciation expenses are large in the early years of ownership and less in later years, earnings tend to appear more stable when assets are leased rather than owned. In addition, reported earnings per share normally are higher in the early years of a lease as compared with ownership because of the use of MACRS depreciation when the asset is owned.

Leasing is said to provide *100 percent financing*, whereas most borrowing requires a down payment. Because lease payments normally are made in advance of each period, this 100 percent financing benefit is diminished by the amount of the first required lease payment.

From the lessee's perspective, leases can *increase a firm's liquidity*. For example, a sale and leaseback transforms some of a firm's fixed assets into cash in exchange for an obligation to make a series of fixed future payments.

And, finally, leasing gives some plant or divisional managers additional *flexibility in acquiring assets* if lease agreements are not subject to internal capital expenditure constraints. In recent years local school districts, municipalities, and the Department of the Navy, among other organizations, have used leasing to circumvent capital outlay restrictions.

Disadvantages

The primary disadvantage of leasing is *cost*. For a firm with a strong earnings record, good access to the credit markets, and the ability to take advantage of the tax benefits of ownership, leasing often is a more expensive alternative. Of course, the actual cost difference between ownership and leasing depends on a number of factors and varies from case to case.

Another disadvantage of leasing is the *loss of the asset's salvage value*. In real estate this loss can be substantial. A lessee may also have *difficulty getting approval to make property improvements* on leased real estate. If the improvements substantially alter the property or reduce its potential range of uses the lessor may be reluctant to permit them.

In addition, if a leased asset (with a financial lease) becomes obsolete or if the capital project financed by the lease becomes uneconomical, *the lessee may not cancel the lease without paying a substantial penalty*.

LEASE–BUY ANALYSIS: THE LESSEE'S PERSPECTIVE

Financial theorists and model builders have devoted a substantial amount of time and effort to developing an analytical framework within which the differential costs associated with leasing versus buying can be compared. At least fifteen different approaches to the problem have been suggested, and there is considerable disagreement as to which one is the best.[8] In spite of this abundance of models, the perplexed financial manager can take some comfort in the fact that the practical effects resulting from the differences in the models tend to be small, because few real-world decisions are changed as a result of which lease–buy model is chosen.[9]

One of the most commonly used approaches to the analysis of a lease versus purchase decision assumes that the appropriate comparison should be between *leasing* and *borrowing to buy*. Advocates of this approach argue that a financial lease is much like a loan in that it requires a series of fixed payments. Failure to make lease payments, like failure to make loan payments, may result in bankruptcy.

The basic approach of the lease–buy analysis model is to compute the *net advantage to leasing* (NAL). The net advantage to leasing compares the present value cost of leasing with the present value cost of owning the asset. If the cost of owning the asset is greater than the cost of leasing the asset, the NAL is positive and the model indicates that the asset should be leased.

The *net advantage to leasing* calculation is as follows:

	Installed cost of the asset
Less	Present value of the after-tax lease payments
Less	Present value of depreciation tax shield
Plus	Present value of after-tax operating costs incurred if owned but not if leased
Less	Present value of the after-tax salvage value
Equals	Net advantage to leasing

The installed cost of the asset equals the purchase price plus installation and shipping charges. The installed cost forms the basis on which depreciation is computed.

The present value of the after-tax lease payments that are made if the asset is leased reduce the NAL; hence they are subtracted when computing the NAL. These lease payments are discounted at the firm's after-tax marginal cost of borrowing to reflect the fact that lease payments are contractually known in advance and thus are not subject to much uncertainty. The present value of the depreciation tax shield is equal to the depreciation claimed each year if the asset is owned times the firm's marginal tax rate. The depreciation tax shield reduces the cost of ownership and hence is subtracted when computing the NAL. Because the depreciation amounts also are known with relative certainty, they also are discounted at the firm's after-tax marginal cost of borrowing.[10]

Sometimes operating costs are incurred if the asset is owned but not if it is leased. These may include property tax payments, insurance, or some maintenance expenses. If these do exist they represent a benefit of leasing and increase the NAL. Hence the after-tax amount of these costs is added in the NAL calculation. These operating cost savings also are discounted at the after-tax marginal cost of borrowing, reflecting their relative certainty. Finally, if the asset is owned the owner will receive the after-tax salvage

---

[8] Basically, the various models differ as to which discount rate should be used to evaluate various components of the cash flows and as to which cash flows should be considered.

[9] Evidence of this is presented in a paper by Arthur Gudikunst and Gordon Roberts. "Empirical Analysis of Lease-Buy Decisions," presented at the 1975 Meeting of the Eastern Finance Association.

[10] The depreciation amounts are known with certainty, but the tax shield from depreciation may not be certain. For example, in 1986 Congress passed a major tax reform plan that lowered the marginal corporate tax rate, thereby reducing the value of the tax shield. Also, there always is the chance that a company will not have sufficient taxable income to take advantage of the depreciation tax shield.

value. This is lost if the asset is leased. Hence the after-tax salvage reduces the NAL and must be subtracted when calculating the NAL. Because asset salvage values generally are subject to substantial uncertainty, they normally are discounted at a rate equal to the firm's weighted (marginal) cost of capital.

Consider the following example to illustrate the procedure just described. Suppose that the Alcoa Corporation is trying to decide whether it should purchase or lease a new heavy duty GMC truck. (The firm already has computed the net present value of this proposed asset acquisition and found the project to be acceptable.) The truck can be purchased for $50,000, including delivery. Alternatively, the truck can be leased from General Motors Acceptance Corporation for a 6-year period at a beginning-of-the-year lease payment of $10,000. If purchased, Alcoa could borrow the needed funds from the Mellon Bank at an annual interest rate of 10 percent. If the truck is purchased, Alcoa estimates that it will incur $750 per year of expenses to cover insurance and a maintenance contract. These expenses would not be incurred if the truck is leased. The truck will be depreciated under MACRS guidelines as a 5-year asset. Alcoa expects the actual salvage value to be $20,000 at the end of 6 years. Alcoa's marginal tax rate is 40 percent, and its weighted after-tax cost of capital is 15 percent. Which alternative— leasing or buying—should be chosen? In order to answer this question we need to compute the NAL. This is shown in Table 15-3. The calculation in Table 15-3 indicates a net advantage to leasing of −$1296. Because the NAL is negative, the asset should be owned rather than leased.[11]

This general procedure can be used to evaluate any lease versus buy decision once it has been determined by standard capital budgeting techniques that an asset should be acquired.

SUMMARY

■ *Terms loans*, or *intermediate-term credit*, include any debt obligation having an initial maturity between 1 and 10 years.

■ Term loans, being privately negotiated between the borrower and the lender, tend to be cheaper than public security offerings, because flotation costs on small to medium-sized public offerings are high. Therefore term loans are a good source of funds for financing small and medium-sized increases in working capital or for financing the acquisition of a piece of equipment.

■ Term loans usually are amortized by a series of installments. The interest rate normally ranges between 0.25 and 2.5 percent above the prime rate. Many term loan agreements require that some specific asset be pledged as *security*. In addition, the borrowing firm may have to agree to certain *affirmative, negative*, and *restrictive covenants* governing its actions during the loan period.

■ Term loans are supplied by several institutions, including commercial banks (frequently the cheapest supplier of term funds), life insurance companies and pension funds (who prefer making loans having longer maturities), the Small Business Administration, small business invest-

---

[11] The lease–buy analysis procedure used here implicitly assumes that the leasing alternative and the borrowing-to-buy alternative have the same impact on the company's debt capacity. This is desirable because leasing and borrowing both represent fixed obligations that are treated by financial analysts as equivalent to debt. Lease-buy analysis also assumes that the asset satisfies the lessee's normal capital investment criteria, such as NPV.

Calculation of the Net Advantage to Leasing for Alcoa

End of Year (1)	Installed Asset Cost (2)	Lease Payment After-tax[1] (3)	Depreciation[2] (4)	Depreciation Tax Shield[3] (5)	Additional Operating Costs If Owned After-Tax[4] (6)
0	$50,000	$6,000	—	—	—
1	—	6,000	$10,000	$4,000	$450
2	—	6,000	16,000	6,400	450
3	—	6,000	9,600	3,840	450
4	—	6,000	5,760	2,304	450
5	—	6,000	5,760	2,304	450
6	—	—	2,880	1,152	450

NAL Cash Flows Except Salvage[5] (7) = (2) − (3) − (5) + (6)	PVIF @ 6%[6] (8)	Present Value[7] (9) = (7) × (8)	After-tax Salvage[8] (10)	PVIF @ 15% (11)	Present Value Salvage[9] (12) = (10) × (11)	NAL[10] (13) = (9) − (12)
$44,000	1.000	$44,000	—	—	—	$44,000
−9,550	0.943	−9,006	—	—	—	−9,006
−11,950	0.890	−10,636	—	—	—	−10,636
−9,390	0.840	−7,888	—	—	—	−7,888
−7,854	0.792	−6,220	—	—	—	−6,220
−7,854	0.747	−5,867	—	—	—	−5,867
−702	0.705	−495	$12,000	0.432	$5,184	−5,679
					Net Advantage to Leasing =	−$1,296

[1] The after-tax lease payment equals the total lease payment ($10,000) times 1 minus Alcoa's marginal tax rate (40 percent). The benefit of the tax deductibility of lease payments is assumed to be received at approximately the same time the lease payments are made, reflecting the quarterly payment of taxes.
[2] MACRS depreciation is computed using the 5-year MACRS rates times the asset cost. The MACRS rates are 20%, 32%, 19.2%, 11.52%, 11.52%, and 5.76%, respectively over the 6 years.
[3] The depreciation tax shield is equal to the depreciation in column (4) times Alcoa's marginal tax rate (40 percent).
[4] Column (6) is equal to $750 pretax cost times 1 minus Alcoa's marginal tax rate (40 percent).
[5] Column (7) is the total of the cash flows needed to compute the NAL that are discounted at the after-tax cost of debt for Alcoa. It is equal to the asset cost (2), less the after-tax lease payments (3), less the depreciation tax shield (5), plus the additional after-tax operating costs incurred if the asset is owned (6).
[6] The after-tax cost of debt is 6 percent (10 percent pretax cost times 1 minus Alcoa's marginal tax rate [40 percent]).
[7] The present value of column (9) is equal to the cash flows in column (7) times the PVIF factors in column (8).
[8] The after-tax salvage is equal to the pretax salvage ($20,000) times 1 minus Alcoa's marginal tax rate (40 percent).
[9] The present value of the salvage is equal to the after-tax salvage times the PVIF for 15 percent and 6 years, where the 15 percent represents Alcoa's weighted cost of capital.
[10] The NAL is equal to the sum of the present value cash flows from column (9) minus the present value of the after-tax salvage from column (12).

ment companies, municipal or state industrial development authorities, and equipment suppliers.

■ Term loans that are secured by a lien on a piece of equipment are called *equipment financing loans*. They are made by the lending institutions previously named, as well as by equipment sellers or their *captive finance subsidiaries*. The two primary security instruments used in equipment financing are the *conditional sales contract* and the *chattel mortgage*.

■ A *lease* is a written agreement that permits the *lessee* to use a piece of property owned by the *lessor* in exchange for a series of periodic lease or rental payments.

■ An *operating lease* provides the lessee with the use of an asset on a period-by-period basis. An operating lease *may be canceled* at the lessee's option. Most operating leases are written for a relatively short period of time, normally less than 5 years.

■ A *financial lease* is a *noncancelable* agreement that obligates the lessee to make payments to the lessor for a predetermined period of time. There are two major types of financial leases: *sale and leaseback* agreements and *direct leases. Leveraged leases*, also called *tax leases*, have become increasingly common. Approximately 85 percent of the financial leases written today are leveraged leases.

■ Subject to a series of IRS guidelines, firms that lease a portion of their assets may deduct the full amount of the lease payment for tax purposes.

■ Decisions by the Financial Accounting Standards Board (FASB) require that many financial leases be capitalized and shown on the lessee's balance sheet.

■ Leasing offers a number of potential advantages, including flexibility, the effective depreciation of land, and tax benefits (in some cases). It also may be the only source of financing available to many marginally profitable firms. It has a number of potential disadvantages, too, however. For example, leasing tends to be more costly than ownership for a firm with a good earnings record and good access to the capital markets.

■ A number of analytical models are available to assist the lessor in determining what lease payments to charge. Other models are available to assist the lessee in determining which is the less expensive source of financing—leasing or borrowing to buy.

QUESTIONS AND TOPICS FOR DISCUSSION

1. Under what circumstances might a firm prefer intermediate-term borrowing to either long- or short-term borrowing?

2. Discuss the advantages and disadvantages of the following types of term loans:

    a. Those that require equal periodic payments.
    b. Those that require equal periodic reductions in outstanding principal.
    c. Balloon loans.
    d. Bullet loans.

3. What are the major factors that influence the effective cost of a term loan?

4. Define the following and give an example of each:

    a. Affirmative covenants.
    b. Negative covenants.
    c. Restrictive covenants.

5. What institutions are the primary suppliers of business term loans?

6. Define the following:

    a. A conditional sales contract.
    b. A chattel mortgage.

7. Under what conditions would a firm prefer the following?

    a. A "fixed-rate" term loan from a bank.
    b. A "floating-rate" term loan, with the rate tied to the bank's prime rate?

8. What are the primary differences between operating leases and financial leases?

9. How does a leveraged lease differ from a nonleveraged financial lease? What type of firm or organization is most likely to take advantage of the leveraged lease financing option? What type of individual or financial institution is most likely to act as the lessor in a leveraged lease?

10. From a tax perspective, what primary requirements in a lease transaction must be met in order for the IRS to consider the transaction a genuine

lease? Why is a favorable IRS ruling regarding the tax status of a lease important to both the lessor and the lessee?

11. One advantage that often has been claimed of lease financing is that it creates "off-balance sheet" financing. Evaluate this benefit in light of FASB Statement No. 13.

12. How can leasing allow a firm to effectively "depreciate" land?

13. What effect does leasing have on the stability of a firm's reported earnings?

14. It has been argued that leasing is almost always more expensive than borrowing and owning. Do you think this is true? Why or why not? Under what circumstances is leasing likely to be more desirable than direct ownership?

▬▬ PROBLEMS*

1. Lobo Banks normally provides term loans that require repayment in a series of equal annual installments. If a $10 million loan is made, what would be the annual end-of-year payments, assuming the following?

   a. A 10 percent loan for 12 years.
   b. A 10 percent loan for 9 years.
   c. A 6 percent loan for 8 years.

2. Set up the amortization schedule for a 5-year, $1 million, 9 percent term loan that requires equal annual end-of-year payments. Be sure to distinguish between the *interest* and the *principal* portion of each payment. What is the *effective* interest cost of this loan?

3. Set up the amortization schedule for a 5-year, $1 million, 9 percent loan that requires equal annual end-of-year principal payments plus interest on the unamortized loan balance. What is the *effective* interest cost of this loan?

4. Set up the amortization schedule for a 5-year, $1 million, 9 percent bullet loan. How is the principal repaid in this type of loan? What is the *effective* interest cost of this loan?

5. A firm receives a $1 million, 5-year loan at a 10 percent interest rate. The loan requires annual payments of $125,000 per year (at the end of each year) for years 1 to 4.

   a. What payment is required at the end of year 5?
   b. What would you call this type of loan?
   c. How does it differ from the loan in Problem 2?
   d. What is the *effective* interest cost of this loan?

6. A $10 million, 5-year loan bears an interest rate of 7 percent. The loan repayment plan calls for five annual end-of-year payments. Each payment is to include an equal amount of principal repayment ($2 million per year) plus accrued interest. Set up the amortization schedule for this loan. Be sure to distinguish between the *interest* and the *principal* portions of each annual payment. What is the *effective* interest cost of this loan?

7. Huskie Bank has provided the Mucklup Manufacturing Company with a 2-year term loan for $200,000 at a stated annual rate of interest of 10 percent. Interest for the entire 2-year period must be prepaid; that is, the loan's total interest payments must be made at the same time the loan is granted. Mucklup is required to repay the entire $200,000 principal balance at the end of the 2-year period.

   Compute the *effective* annual percentage rate of the loan.

8. The James Company has been offered a 4-year loan from its bank in the amount of $100,000 at a stated interest rate of 10 percent per year. The loan

will require four equal end-of-year payments of principal and interest plus a $30,000 balloon payment at the end of the fourth year.

   a. Compute the amount of each of the end-of-year payments.

   b. Prepare a loan amortization schedule detailing the amount of principal and interest in each year's payment.

   c. What is the effective interest rate on this loan? Prove your answer.

      HINT: Each year's payment may be computed by solving for the annuity payment of a 4-year, 10 percent annuity that has a present value of $70,000—the amount of the loan that is amortized by the four yearly payments—and adding to that amount the interest on the unpaid balloon portion of the loan.

9. A $1 million loan requires five end-of-year equal payments of $284,333.

   a. Calculate the *effective* interest rate on this loan.

   b. How much interest (in dollars) is paid over the life of this loan?

10. U.S. Fax has been granted a loan from a commercial finance company for $1 million at a stated interest rate of 10 percent. The loan requires that interest only payments be made at the end of each of the next 5 years. At the end of 5 years, the entire loan balance must be repaid. The finance company requires Fax to pay a $25,000 loan processing fee at the time the loan is approved. What is the *effective* cost of this loan?

11. A $10 million principal amount, 3 year, term loan carries an interest rate of 10 percent. All interest payments (which would normally be due at the end of each year) are deferred until the end of 3 years. The unpaid interest amount compounds at a 10 percent annual rate during the period(s) it remains unpaid. At the end of 3 years, the borrower must repay the principal amount, the deferred interest, plus interest on the deferred interest. The lender also charges a front end loan origination fee on this loan of $100,000.

   Compute the *effective* cost of this loan.

12. MacKenzie Corp. is considering leasing a new asset. The lease would run for 8 years and require 8 *beginning-of-year* payments of $100,000 each. If MacKenzie capitalizes this lease for financial reporting purposes at a 10 percent rate, what asset amount will be reported initially on its balance sheet? What liability amount will be reported on its balance sheet? (Remember, lease payments are made at the beginning of each year, making them an annuity due.)

13. Ajax Leasing Services has been approached by Gamma Tools to provide lease financing for a new automated screw machine. The machine will cost $220,000 and will be leased by Gamma for 5 years. Lease payments will be made at the *beginning* of each year. Ajax will depreciate the machine on a straight-line basis of $44,000 per year down to a book salvage value of $0. Actual salvage value is estimated to be $30,000 at the end of 5 years. Ajax's marginal tax rate is 40 percent. Ajax desires to earn a 12 percent, after-tax rate of return on this lease. What are the required annual beginning-of-year lease payments.

14. The First National Bank of Springer has established a leasing subsidiary. A local firm, Allied Business Machines, has approached the bank to arrange lease financing for $10 million in new machinery. The economic life of the machinery is estimated to be 20 years. The estimated salvage value at the end of the 20-year period is $0. Allied Business Machines has indicated a willingness to pay the bank $1 million per year at the *end* of each year for 20 years under the terms of a financial lease.

   a. If the bank depreciates the machinery on a straight-line basis over 20 years to a $0 estimated salvage value, and has a 40 percent marginal tax rate, what *after-tax* rate of return will the bank earn on the lease?

   b. In general, what effect would the use of MACRS depreciation by the bank have on the rate of return it earns from the lease?

15. Jenkins Corporation wants to acquire a $200,000 computer. Jenkins has a 40 percent marginal tax rate. If owned, the computer would be depreciated on a straight-line basis to a *book* salvage value of $0. The actual cash salvage value is expected to be $20,000 at the end of 10 years. If the computer is purchased Jenkins could borrow the needed funds at an annual pretax interest rate of 10 percent. If purchased, Jenkins will incur annual maintenance expenses of $1,000. These expenses would not be incurred if the computer is leased. The lease rate would be $28,000 per year, payable at the beginning of each year. Jenkins' weighted after-tax cost of capital is 12 percent.

   a. Compute the *net advantage to leasing*.
   b. In general, what effect would the use of accelerated depreciation, such as MACRS, have on the answer to part a?
   c. Which alternative, leasing or owning, should be chosen?

16. The following stream of after-tax cash flows are available to you as a potential equity investor in a leveraged lease:

End of Year	Cash Flow (after tax)	End of Year	Cash Flow (after tax)
0	$ −50	6	$ 0
1	+30	7	−5
2	+20	8	−10
3	+15	9	−15
4	+10	10	+10
5	+ 5		

   The cash flow in year 0 represents the initial equity investment. The high positive cash flows in years 1 to 5 result from the tax shield benefits from accelerated depreciation and interest deductibility on the nonrecourse debt. The negative cash flows in years 7 to 9 are indicative of the cash flows generated in a leveraged lease after the earlier-period tax shields have been utilized. The positive cash flow occurring in year 10 is the result of the asset's salvage value.

   a. What problems would you encounter in computing the equity investor's rate of return on this investment?
   b. If, as a potential equity investor, you require an 8 percent after-tax rate of return on investments of this type, should you make this investment?

17. The Jacobs Company desires to lease a numerically controlled milling machine costing $200,000. Jacobs has asked both First Manufacturers Bank Leasing Corp. and Commercial Associates, Inc. (a commercial finance company), to quote an annual lease rate. Both leasing companies now require a 20 percent *pretax* rate of return on this type of lease. Suppose First Manufacturers estimates the machine's salvage value at the end of the lease to be $30,000, and Commercial Associates estimates salvage to be $80,000. Based on this information, what annual (beginning-of-year) lease payments will each leasing company require, if the lease term is 5 years? (Note: Because the required rate of return of both the bank and the finance company is stated on a pretax basis, you need not consider depreciation or the tax effects of salvage.)

18. The First National Bank of Great Falls is considering a leveraged lease agreement involving some mining equipment with the Big Sky Mining Corporation. The bank (40 percent tax bracket) will be the lessor; the mining company, the lessee (0 percent tax bracket); and a large California pension fund, the lender. Big Sky is seeking $50 million, and the pension fund has agreed to lend the bank $40 million at 10 percent. The bank has agreed to repay the pension fund $4 million of principal each year plus interest. (The

remaining balance will be repaid in a balloon payment at the end of the fifth year.) The equipment will be depreciated on a straight-line basis over a 5-year estimated useful life with no expected salvage value. Assuming Big Sky has agreed to annual lease payments of $10 million, calculate the bank's initial cash outflow and its first 2 years of cash inflows.

19. As a financial analyst for Muffin Construction you have been asked to recommend the method of financing the acquisition of new equipment needed by the firm. The equipment has a useful life of 8 years. If purchased, the equipment, which costs $700,000, will be depreciated under MACRS rules for 7-year class assets. If purchased, the needed funds can be borrowed at a 10 percent pretax annual rate. Muffin's weighted after-tax cost of capital is 12 percent. The *actual* salvage value at the end of 8 years is expected to be $50,000. Muffin's marginal ordinary tax rate is 40 percent. Annual, beginning-of-year lease payments would be $160,000.

    a. Compute the net advantage to leasing.

    b. Should Muffin lease or own the equipment?

20. Darling Leasing is considering the lease of a piece of equipment costing $100,000 to Major State University. The period of the lease will be 8 years. The equipment will be depreciated under MACRS rules for 7-year class assets. Darling's marginal tax rate is 40 percent. Annual (end-of-year) lease payments will be $20,000. Estimated salvage is $10,000. If Darling requires a 20 percent after-tax return on equipment it leases, should the lease be made?

LEASE AND TERM LOAN ANALYSIS

Suppose that Kinko's Copy Centers has decided to install personal computers and printers in its Pittsburgh store, which will be rented to customers on an hourly basis. Kinko's management has called in consultants from a number of computer suppliers to assist it in designing a system. After considering a number of alternatives, Kinko's decided that an Apple Computer company system consisting of 8 Macintosh II computers and two Laser Writer printers best meets its current and projected future needs. Kinko's evaluated the desirability of the acquisition of the Apple computer system using its normal capital budgeting procedures. It found that the computer system has a large positive expected net present value.

Jim Horn, a new management trainee in the financial planning office, has recently been reading about the boom in the leasing industry. He feels that if leasing is growing as rapidly as it seems, there must be some significant advantages of the leasing alternative to ownership.

If purchased, the new computer system will cost $50,000 installed. The computer system has an estimated economic life of 6 years. Kinko's would depreciate the computer system as a 5-year class asset under MACRS rules to a $0 estimated salvage value. If purchased, Kinko's could borrow the needed funds from Pittsburgh National Bank (PNB) at a 10 percent pre-tax annual percentage rate of interest.

If Kinko's decides to lease the computer system it will be required to make six beginning-of-year lease payments of $11,000 each. Kinko's weighted cost of capital is 12 percent (after-tax). Kinko's marginal tax rate is 40 percent.

Under both the lease alternative and the borrow-and-buy alternative, Kinko's will contract with a computer service company to handle the estimated annual service and maintenance costs.

1. Compute the net advantage to leasing.

2. Which alternative should Kinko's accept? What other factors might be considered?

3. If the computer system is owned and Kinko's borrows the needed funds from PNB in the form of a bullet loan carrying a 10 percent interest rate instead of an equal payment loan at 10 percent, what effect would this have on the decision to lease or buy?

4. What effect would the use of straight-line depreciation have on the lease–buy decision? (Answer verbally; no calculations are needed. Ignore the bullet loan assumption in Question 3.)

5. If, at the end of 6 years, the computer system is expected to have an actual salvage value of $5,000, what would be the impact on the net advantage to leasing?

SELECTED REFERENCES

Ang, James, and Pamela P. Peterson. "The Leasing Puzzle." *Journal of Finance* 39 (September 1984): 1055–1066.

Hochman, S., and R. Rabinovitch. "Financial Leasing under Inflation." *Financial Management* (Spring 1984): 17–26.

Hull, John C. "The Bargaining Positions of the Parties to a Lease Agreement." *Financial Management* 11 (Autumn 1982): 71–79.

McConnell, J. J., and J. S. Schalheim. "Valuation of Asset Leasing Contracts." *Journal of Financial Economics* (August 1983): 237–261.

Schall, L. D. "Analytic Issues in Lease versus Purchase Decisions." *Financial Management* 16 (Summer 1987): 17–20.

Smith, C. W., Jr., and L. M. Wakemen. "Determinants of Corporate Leasing Policy." *Journal of Finance* 30 (July 1985): 896–908.

Weingartner, H. Martin. "Leasing, Asset Lives, and Uncertainty: Guides to Decision Making." *Financial Management* 16 (Summer 1987): 5–12.

16

Managing Long-Term Funding Sources

KEY CHAPTER CONCEPTS

1. To effectively manage long-term funding sources, financial managers must understand both the different types of securities the firm can issue and the process of raising funds in the capital markets.

2. An *option* is a security giving the right to buy or sell an asset at a set price during a specified time period.
   a. A *call* option is an option to *buy* an asset at a set price.
   b. A *put* option is an option to *sell* an asset at a set price.

3. The value of a call option is dependent upon four variables:
   a. The relationship between the option's exercise price and the price of the underlying stock.
   b. The time remaining until the option expires.
   c. The level of interest rates.
   d. The expected volatility of the underlying stock's price.

4. A convertible security is a fixed-income security, such as a debenture or a share of preferred stock, that may be exchanged for the company's common stock at the holder's option.

5. A warrant is an option issued by a company to purchase shares of the company's common stock for a particular price during a specified period of time.

6. The owner of either a convertible security or a warrant has a choice of whether or not to obtain the company's common stock.

7. The process of raising funds in the capital markets (that is, selling securities) and the role of the investment banker are discussed.

8. Methods of selling securities in the primary capital markets include
   a. Public cash offering.
   b. Direct placement.
   c. Rights offering to shareholders.

9. Other important topics include
   a. Functioning of the securities markets.
   b. Regulation of the securities markets.
   c. Financial innovations.
   d. Bond refunding (appendix).
   e. Stockholder voting rights (appendix).
   f. Rights offerings (appendix).

GLOSSARY OF NEW TERMS

Bond refunding A situation that occurs when a firm redeems a callable bond issue and sells a generally lower interest cost issue to take its place.

Call option An option to *buy* an asset at a set price. Also referred to as a *call*.

Competitive bidding The process of selling a new security offering to the highest bidding underwriting syndicate.

Contingent claim A security whose payoffs depend on the value of another security.

Conversion premium The amount by which the market value of a convertible security exceeds the higher of its conversion value or straight-bond (preferred) value.

Conversion price The effective price an investor pays for common stock when the stock is obtained by converting a convertible security.

Conversion ratio The number of common shares an investor obtains by converting a convertible security.

Conversion (stock) value The value of a convertible security, based on the value of the underlying shares of common stock.

Convertible security A fixed-income security that may be exchanged for a firm's common stock at the holder's option. The two most common types of convertible securities are *convertible preferred stock* and *convertible debentures*.

Direct placement The sale of an entire security offering to one or more institutional investors rather than the general public. This also is termed a *private placement*.

Exercise price The price at which an option holder can purchase or sell a company's stock. This also is termed the *strike price*.

Flotation cost The cost of issuing new securities. This includes both underwriting expenses and other issue expenses, such as printing and legal fees.

Interest rate swap An agreement between two companies (and/or financial institutions) whereby one party's floating rate debt obligation is traded for another party's fixed rate obligation.

Investment banker A financial institution that underwrites and sells new securities. In general, investment bankers assist firms in obtaining new financing.

Listed security exchanges Organized secondary security markets that operate at designated places of business. The New York Stock Exchange (NYSE) is an example of a listed security exchange.

Negotiated underwriting A process whereby a firm wishing to sell new securities to the public negotiates the terms of the underwriting with the investment banker or bankers.

Option A security that gives its holder the right to buy or sell an asset at a set price during a specified time period.

Over-the-counter (OTC) securities markets A network of security dealers connected by a communications system of telephones and computer terminals that provides price quotations on individual securities.

Prospectus A document that contains a vast amount of information about a company's legal, operational, and financial position. It is prepared for the benefit of prospective investors in a new security issued by the firm.

Purchasing syndicate A *group* of investment bankers who agree to underwrite a new security issue in order to spread the risk of underwriting.

Put option An option to *sell* an asset at a set price. Also referred to as a *put*.

Right A short-term option issued by a firm that permits an existing stockholder to buy a specified number of shares of common stock at a specified price (the subscription price), which is below the current market price.

Rights offering The sale of new shares of common stock by distributing stock purchase *rights* to a firm's existing shareholders. This is also termed a *privileged subscription*.

Securities and Exchange Commission (SEC) The government regulatory agency responsible for administering federal securities legislation.

(Continued on next page)

Straight-bond, or investment, value The value a convertible debt security would have if it did not possess the conversion feature.

Underwriting A process whereby a group of investment bankers agrees to purchase a new security issue at a set price and then offer it for sale to the general public.

Underwriting spread The difference between the selling price to the public of a new security offering and the proceeds received by the offering firm. This is also termed an *underwriting discount.*

Warrant A company-issued long-term option to purchase a specified number of shares of the firm's stock at a particular price during a specified time period.

A FINANCIAL DILEMMA

Securities Innovation*

By now you are aware that firms raise long-term funds to finance their operations by issuing common stock, preferred stock, and bonds. Today the common stock, preferred stock, and bonds discussed in Chapters 6 and 7 frequently are called "plain vanilla" financing. In addition, for years many firms have used two other security types—convertibles and warrants—to raise funds. At one time convertibles and warrants were new and considered innovative. Today, however, most financial managers seem to understand convertibles and warrants reasonably well.

The problem for financial managers in the early 1990s will be to keep abreast of and understand the explosion of new securities being offered. For example, a number of companies (Transamerica Financial and Tenneco, to name two) recently have issued *put bonds*—that is, bonds that investors may sell back to the issuer at par under certain circumstances, regardless of the movement in interest rates. An example of an equity innovation is the creation of an additional class of common stock whose dividends are based on the earnings of a specified subsidiary. General Motors (GM) has done this for its Electronic Data Systems (EDS) and Hughes Electronics subsidiaries. The dividends and performance of GM's Class E and H common stock are based on the earnings and performance of GM's EDS and Hughes subsidiaries, respectively.

Why do financial managers issue innovative securities (other than to make studying finance more difficult)? In this chapter we offer some answers to this question. The proper management of long-term funding sources can help a firm balance risk, increase returns, and thereby maximize shareholder wealth.

* Based in part on John D. Finnerty, "Financial Engineering in Corporate Finance: An Overview." *Financial Management* (Winter 1988): 14–33.

INTRODUCTION

The effective management of long-term funding sources can help a firm achieve its goal of maximizing shareholder wealth by balancing risk and increasing returns. To effectively manage long-term funding sources, financial managers must understand both the different types of securities the firm can issue and the process of raising funds in the capital markets.

In addition to long-term debt, preferred stock, and common stock, a firm has two other primary forms of long-term financing available to it: *convertible securities* and *warrants.* Both convertible securities and warrants are forms of options. An option is a security giving the right to buy or sell an asset under specified conditions. Specifically, a convertible security is a fixed-income security, such as a debenture or a share of preferred stock, that may be exchanged for the company's common stock at the holder's option. By giving the fixed-income security holder an opportunity to share in any increase in its common stock value, the firm is able to reduce potential conflicts between the fixed-income security holders and stockholders. This results in lower agency costs. A warrant is an option issued by a company to purchase shares of the company's common stock at a particular price during a specified period of time. Warrants are frequently sold to investors as part of a *unit* that consists of a fixed-income security with a warrant attached. As a result, warrants are issued by firms basically for the same reasons as convertible securities.

This chapter describes the features and characteristics of options, warrants, and convertible securities. An understanding of these features and characteristics is necessary to evaluate the impact on shareholder wealth of issuing such securities. Next capital markets and the role of investment bankers are considered. The remaining section is devoted to financial innovations.

OPTIONS

Financial managers today need to understand options for the following reasons:

1. A firm's common stock can be better understood using an options framework.
2. Securities such as convertibles, warrants, rights, and executive stock options are all examples of options.

An *option* is a security that gives its holder the right, but not the obligation, to buy or sell an asset at a set price during a specified time period. Options are classified as either *call* or *put* options. A call is an option to *buy* a particular asset whereas a put is an option to *sell* it. Examples of options include calls and puts on common stock, warrants, and convertible securities. A call option on a particular common stock is an option to buy shares (usually 100) at a set price during a specified time period, and a put option is an option to sell shares. A *warrant* is a call option issued by a company on its securities, usually stock. A *convertible security* is a fixed-income security with a call option on common stock. Another common example of an option is the redemption (call) feature of debt securities that permits a company to call, or redeem, its debt prior to maturity.[1] In addition, as discussed in this chapter's Financial Dilemma, some debt issues also contain a put option that gives investors the right to sell the debt back to the issuing company at par value prior to maturity.

Option Valuation Concepts

Suppose an investor is offered an opportunity to purchase a call option on one share of XYZ stock. Consider the following sets of conditions:

1. The option's exercise price is $25, the XYZ stock price is $30 a share, and the option's expiration date is today. Under these conditions, the

[1] The redemption, or call feature, of debt securities is discussed in Chapter 6.

investor is willing to pay $5 for the option. In other words, the value of a call option is equal to the stock price minus the exercise price, or

$$\text{Value of a call option at expiration} = \text{Stock price} - \text{Exercise price} \qquad \textbf{(16.1)}$$

2. The option's exercise price is $25, the XYZ stock price is $30 a share, and the option expires in 6 months. Given these conditions, the investor is willing to pay more than $5 for the option because of the chance that the stock price will increase, thereby causing the option also to increase in value. Therefore,

$$\text{Value of a call option prior to expiration} > \text{Stock price} - \text{Exercise price} \qquad \textbf{(16.2)}$$

3. The option's exercise price is $0.01, the XYZ stock price is $30, and the option expires in 6 months. Under these somewhat unusual conditions, the option investor is willing to pay *almost as much as the stock price*. However, under no conditions should the investor be willing to pay more than the stock price. Therefore,

$$\text{Maximum value of a call option} = \text{Stock price} \qquad \textbf{(16.3)}$$

4. The option's exercise price is $25, the XYZ stock price is $0.01, and the option expires today. The investor most likely is willing to pay nothing for the option given these conditions, but the investor also is not willing to pay someone to take the option "off his hands," because it is an option and can be allowed to expire with no additional cost. Therefore,

$$\text{Minimum value of a call option} = 0 \qquad \textbf{(16.4)}$$

The results of these sets of conditions are shown in Figure 16-1.[2]

Variables Affecting Call Option Valuation

The examples in the previous section illustrate that the value of a call option is dependent on (1) the relationship between the option's exercise price and the price of the underlying stock and (2) the length of time before the option's expiration date.

Two other variables influence the value of a call option: the level of interest rates and the expected volatility of the underlying stock's price. These four variables are discussed in the following subsections.

THE RELATIONSHIP BETWEEN THE EXERCISE PRICE AND THE STOCK PRICE. The effect of the exercise, or strike price, on option value is seen by examining Table 16-1, which lists a number of options quotations for McDonald's. At the time the McDonald's stock was selling at $56 a share.

[2] Figure 16-1 shows a $25 exercise price. Technically Figure 16-1 shows only the results of conditions 1, 2, and 4.

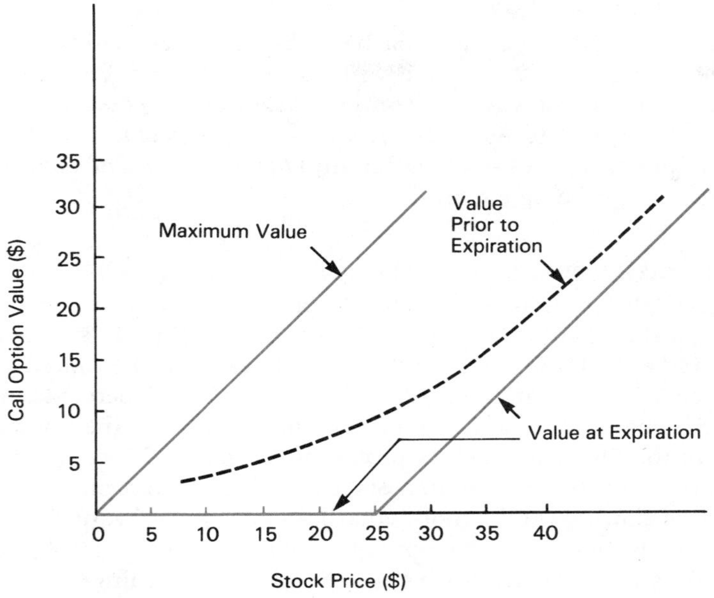

FIGURE 16-1

Call Option
Valuation at
Different Stock
Prices*

* Exercise price = $25.

For options expiring in June, the call option with a $50 exercise price sold at a higher price than the option with a $55 exercise price. This is because buyers have to pay more money to exercise options with higher exercise prices, and thus these options have less value to potential buyers. Therefore, *the higher the exercise price, given the stock price, the lower is the call option value*, all other things being equal.

Because an option's value (payoffs) is dependent, or *contingent*, on the value of another security (in this case, the underlying stock), an option is said to be a *contingent claim*.

TIME REMAINING UNTIL EXPIRATION DATE. The figures in Table 16-1 show that an option expiring in September has a higher value than an option with a June expiration date. This is because investors realize that Mc-Donald's stock has a greater chance to increase in value with three additional months before expiration. Thus, *the longer the time remaining before the option expires, the higher the option value*, all other things being equal. Because of this, an option is sometimes referred to as a "wasting asset."

INTEREST RATES. The buyer of common stock incurs either interest expense (explicit cost) if the purchase funds are borrowed or lost interest

Selected Call Option Prices for McDonald's			T A B L E 16-1
Exercise Price	Expiration Month		
	June	Sept.	
50	6¼	8	
55	2¼	4	

Note: McDonald's stock was selling at $56 a share. The date of the option prices is May 10.

income (implicit cost) if existing funds are used for purchase. In either case, an interest cost is incurred.[3]

Buying a call option is an alternative to buying stock, and by buying an option the interest cost associated with stock is avoided. Because options are an alternative to ownership, option values are affected by the stock ownership interest costs. As a result, *the higher the level of interest rates* (and, hence, the interest cost of stock ownership) *the higher the call option's value is*, all other things being equal.

EXPECTED STOCK PRICE VOLATILITY. Suppose an investor has a choice of buying a call option on either stock S or stock V. Both stocks currently sell at $50 a share, and the exercise price of both options is $50. Stock S is expected to be the more stable of the two—its value at the time the option expires has a 50 percent chance of being $45 and a 50 percent chance of being $55 a share. In valuing the call option on stock S, the investor considers only the $55 price and its probability, because if the stock goes to $45 a share, the call option with a $50 exercise price becomes worthless.

Stock V is expected to be more volatile—its expected value at the time of option expiration has a 50 percent probability of being $30 and a 50 percent probability of being $70 a share. Similarly, in valuing the call option on stock V, the investor considers only the $70 price and its probability.

The investor now has sufficient information to conclude that the call option on stock V is more valuable than the call option on stock S because a greater return can be earned by investing in an option that has a 50 percent chance of being worth $20 (stock price − exercise price = $70 − $50 = $20) at expiration than an option that has a 50 percent probability of being worth $5 (stock price − exercise price = $55 − $50 = $5) at expiration. Therefore, the *greater the expected stock price volatility, the higher the call option value is*, all other things being equal.

Common Stock in an Options Framework

Any firm with debt can be analyzed in an options framework.[4] Suppose a start-up firm raises equity capital and also borrows $7 million, due 2 years from now. Then, suppose further that the firm undertakes a risky project to develop new computer parts. In 2 years the firm must decide whether or not to default on its debt repayment obligation.

Consider this example in an options context. The stockholders can be viewed as having sold the firm to the debtholders for $7 million when they borrowed the $7 million. But the stockholders retained an option to buy back the firm. The stockholders have the right to exercise their option by paying off the debt claim at maturity. Whether they do depends on the value of the firm at the time the debt is due. If the value of the firm is greater than the debt claim, the stockholders will exercise their option by paying off the debt. But, if the value of the firm is less than the debt claim, the stockholders will let their option expire, by not repaying the debt.

This simplified example has interesting implications. Earlier in the options discussion we showed that the greater the expected stock price vol-

---

[3] The interest cost is offset by any dividends received.
[4] The following discussion is based on Scott P. Mason and Robert C. Merton. "The Role of Contingent Claims Analysis in Corporate Finance," in *Recent Advances in Corporate Finance*, Edward I. Altman and Marti G. Subrahmanyam, eds. (Homewood, IL: Richard D. Irwin, 1985).

atility, the higher will be the call option value. Therefore, if the stockholders choose high-risk projects with a chance of very large payoffs, they increase the value of their option. But, at the same time, they also increase the likelihood of defaulting on the debt, thereby decreasing its value. Thus, it is easy to see how potential conflicts between stockholders and debtholders can occur. These potential conflicts are discussed further in the next section on convertible securities. In fact, we shall see that giving the bondholders an equity stake in the firm decreases the potential for conflicts between stockholders and debtholders.

CONVERTIBLE SECURITIES

Both debentures and preferred stock can have convertibility or conversion features. When a company issues convertible securities, its usual intention is the future issuance of common stock. To illustrate, suppose the Beloit Corporation issues 2 million shares of convertible preferred stock at a price of $50 a share. After the sale, the company receives gross proceeds of $100 million. Because of the convertibility feature, the company can expect to issue shares of common stock in exchange for the redemption of the convertible preferred stock over some future time period. As a result, convertibles are sometimes described as a deferred equity offering. In the case of Beloit's convertible preferred, each $50 preferred share can be exchanged for two shares of common stock; that is, the holder has a call option to buy two shares of the company's common stock at an exercise price of $25 a share. Therefore if all the preferred shares are converted, the company in effect will have issued 4 million new common shares, and the preferred shares no longer will appear on Beloit's balance sheet. No additional funds are raised by the company at the time of conversion.

Features of Convertible Securities

As an introduction to the terminology and features of convertible securities, consider a $100 million, 25-year issue of 6⅛ percent convertible subordinated debentures recently sold by Cray Research, Inc., a computer manufacturer. Convertible securities are exchangeable for common stock at a stated *conversion price*. In the case of the Cray issue, the conversion price is $84. This means that each $1,000 debenture is convertible into common stock at $84 a share.

The number of common shares that can be obtained when a convertible security is exchanged is determined by the conversion ratio, which is calculated as follows:

$$\text{Conversion ratio} = \frac{\text{Par value of security}}{\text{Conversion price}} \qquad \textbf{(16.5)}$$

In the case of Cray Research's convertible subordinated debentures, the conversion ratio is the following:

$$\text{Conversion ratio} = \frac{\$1,000}{\$84}$$

$$= 11.9$$

Thus, each $1,000 Cray debenture can be exchanged for 11.9 shares of common stock. Although the conversion ratio may change one or more times during the life of the conversion option, it is more common for it to remain constant.

Normally, the conversion price is set about 15 to 30 percent above the common stock's market price prevailing at the time of issue. For example, at the time Cray issued its convertible debentures, the market price of its common stock was about $65 a share. The $19 difference between the conversion price and the market price represents a 29 percent premium.

Holders of convertible securities are protected against dilution by the company. For example, suppose Cray were to split its common stock two for one. The conversion price (and therefore the conversion ratio) would be adjusted so that the holders would not be disadvantaged by the split. Specifically, in the Cray case the new conversion price would be $42, and the new conversion ratio would be 23.8.

Managing Long-Term Funding with Convertibles

As a general rule, relatively small, risky companies, whose common stock is publicly traded, are the principal issuers of convertibles. These companies, for the most part, are rapidly growing and in need of funds to finance their growth. Investors, on the other hand, frequently are reluctant to lend money to small, risky companies without promises of high interest payments and assurances from the company that it will properly manage the debt.

Recall in Chapter 1 that we introduced agency problems and discussed the conflicts that can occur between a firm's stockholders and its creditors. We said that creditors, to protect their interests, often insist on certain protective convenants in the company's bond indentures. The agency costs to properly implement and monitor the covenants can be high, particularly for small, risky companies. As a result, because of potential conflicts between shareholders and bondholders, and the associated agency costs, it usually is easier and cheaper to offer the bondholders an equity stake in the company—that is, a convertible security. With an equity stake, the bondholders are less concerned about any company attempts to increase the returns to the shareholders by means of risky projects.

In addition to agency costs, several other reasons for issuing convertibles are often cited.

Cash flow benefits accrue to the issuing company in the form of lower interest payments or dividends. This occurs because investors are willing to accept the conversion privilege as part of their overall return. As an example, consider again the Cray Research 6⅛ percent convertible subordinated debentures. At the time Cray sold these convertibles, the company would have had to pay about 9 percent interest on any nonconvertible debt it issued. Thus, the convertibility feature is saving Cray about $2.9 million a year ([0.09 − 0.06125] × $100 million) in interest expense. Typically, firms can issue convertible securities with interest rates or dividend yields about 3 percentage points below similar, nonconvertible issues, that is, issues without convertibility features.

Another reason firms issue convertible securities effectively is to sell common stock at a higher price than the market price prevailing at the time of issue. Suppose a company needs additional equity financing because of a relatively high proportion of fixed-income securities in its capital structure. If the company's management feels the price of its common stock is temporarily depressed, one alternative is to consider issuing a convertible security. With the conversion price typically set about 15–30 percent above the market price at the time of issue, the use of a convertible security effectively gives the issuing company the potential for selling common stock above the existing market price. However, for the sale to be successful, conditions in the future must be such that investors will want to exercise their conversion option. Also, if the market price rises considerably above the conversion price, it may turn out that the company would have been better off to wait and sell common stock directly rather than sell the convertible issue at all.

Another reason for issuing convertible securities centers around the fact that the earnings resulting from projects funded by a particular external financing issue may not begin for some time after financing occurs. For example, the construction and start-up period for a major expansion may be several years. During this period the company may desire debt or preferred stock financing. Eventually, once the expansion is fully operational and producing income, the company may want to achieve its original goal of additional common stock financing. The deferred issue of common stock minimizes the dilution in earnings per share that results from the immediate issuance of common stock.

Valuation of Convertible Securities

Because convertible securities possess certain characteristics of both common stock and fixed-income securities, their valuation is more complex than that of ordinary nonconvertible securities. The actual market value of a convertible security is a function of both the *common stock value*, or *conversion value*, and the value as a fixed-income security, or *straight-bond* or *investment value*. Each of these is discussed here.[5]

CONVERSION VALUE. The conversion value, or stock value, of a convertible bond is defined as the conversion ratio times the common stock's market price:

$$\text{Conversion value} = \text{Conversion ratio} \times \text{Stock price} \quad \textbf{(16.6)}$$

To illustrate, assume a firm offers a convertible bond that can be exchanged for forty shares of common stock. If the market price of the firm's common stock is $20 per share, the conversion value is $800. If the market price of the common stock rises to $25 per share, the conversion value becomes $1,000. And if the stock price rises to $30 per share, the conversion value becomes $1,200. In the case of Cray's convertible bonds, the conversion value was 11.9×65, or $774, at the time of issue.

STRAIGHT-BOND VALUE. The straight-bond value, or investment value, of a convertible debt issue is the value it would have if it did not possess the conversion feature. Thus, it is equal to the sum of the present value of the interest annuity plus the present value of the expected principal repayment:

$$\text{Straight-bond value} = \sum_{t=1}^{m} \frac{\text{Interest}}{(1 + k_d)^t} + \frac{\text{Principal}}{(1 + k_d)^m} \quad \textbf{(16.7)}$$

[5] For simplicity, only convertible debt is considered in this discussion, although the principles apply to convertible preferred stock as well.

where k_d is the current yield to maturity for *nonconvertible* debt issues of similar quality and maturity; t, the number of years; and m, the time to maturity.

Considering again Cray Research's 6⅛ percent, 25-year convertible debentures, the bond value at the time of issue is calculated as follows, assuming that 9 percent is the appropriate discount rate (and that interest is paid annually):

$$\text{Straight-bond value} = \sum_{t=1}^{25} \frac{\$61.25}{(1.09)^t} + \frac{\$1,000}{(1.09)^{25}}$$

$$= \$61.25(\text{PVIFA}_{0.09,25}) + \$1,000(\text{PVIF}_{0.09,25})$$

$$= \$61.25(9.823) + \$1,000(0.116)$$

$$= \$601.66 + \$116$$

$$= \$717.66$$

MARKET VALUE. The market value of a convertible debt issue usually is somewhat above the higher of the conversion or the straight-bond value. This is illustrated in Figure 16-2.

The difference between the market value and the higher of the conversion or the straight-bond value is the *conversion premium* for which the issue sells. This premium tends to be largest when the conversion value and the

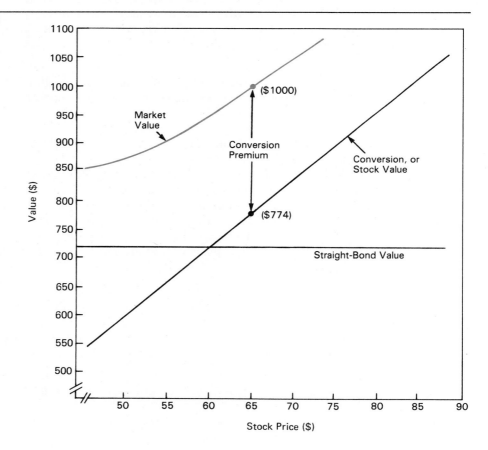

FIGURE 16-2

Convertible Debenture Valuation at Different Stock Prices*

* Conversion ratio = 11.9; straight-bond value = $718.

straight-bond value are nearly identical. This set of circumstances allows investors to participate in any common stock appreciation while having some degree of downside protection, because the straight-bond value can represent a "floor" below which the market value will not fall.[6] The Cray convertible debentures described in this section were offered to the public at $1,000 per bond and quickly were bought up by investors. In this case, investors were willing to pay $1,000 for an issue having a conversion value of approximately $774 and a bond value of about $718. The $1,000 market value contained a premium of $226 over the conversion value (which was higher than the bond value).

Converting Convertible Securities

Conversion can occur in one of two ways:

■ It may be *voluntary* on the part of the investor.
■ It can be effectively *forced* by the issuing company.

Whereas voluntary conversions can occur at any time prior to the expiration of a conversion feature, forced conversions occur at specific points in time.

The method most commonly used by companies to force conversion is the exercise of the *call* privilege on the convertible security. For example, consider the Compaq Computer convertible bonds maturing in 2012, which the company decided to call for redemption in 1988. The bonds had a conversion ratio of 25.22, and the market price of the Compaq common stock at the time of the call was $61.25 per share. Therefore the conversion value was approximately $1,545 per bond. The call price—which was set and agreed upon by both the borrower and the lender at the time of the original issue—was $1047.25 per bond.

Holders of the Compaq convertibles had two alternatives under these circumstances:

■ Conversion, in which case the holder would receive common stock having a market value of $1545 per bond.
■ Redemption, in which case the holder would receive $1047.25 in cash for each bond.

The conversion alternative was the obvious choice, because even those investors who did not wish to hold the common stock could sell it upon conversion for more money than they would receive from redemption. By calling the bonds, Compaq was able to remove $150 million in long-term debt from its balance sheet without having to redeem the bonds for cash, and to save $7.9 million a year in interest expense.

Another way in which a company effectively can force conversion is by raising its dividend on common stock to a high enough level that holders of convertible securities are better off converting them and receiving the higher dividend.

■■■■ WARRANTS

As mentioned earlier in this chapter, a warrant is a company-issued option to purchase a specific number of shares of the issuing company's common

---

[6] The straight-bond value may fall if long-term interest rates rise, however.

stock at a particular price during a specified time period. Warrants frequently are issued in conjunction with an offering of debentures or preferred stock. In these instances, like convertibles, warrants tend to lower agency costs.

In addition, during the 1980s, the various ways in which warrants were used as a financing device seemed to expand. For example, warrants were used in conjunction with bond swaps, equity offerings, and debt restructurings. Also, a small, high-risk company in need of additional financing may offer warrants to prospective lenders in order to give the potential for high expected returns as compensation for the loan's high risk.

Features of Warrants

To illustrate some of the features of financing with warrants, consider Federal National Mortgage Association ("Fannie Mae"), which recently sold 500,000 units, consisting of a $1,000 debenture and twenty-three 5-year warrants, to raise approximately $500 million (less flotation costs). Each warrant allowed the purchase of one common share at $44.25.

The *exercise price* of a warrant is the price at which the holder can purchase common stock of the issuing company. The exercise price—which normally remains constant over the life of the warrant—usually is between 10 and 35 percent above the market price of the common stock prevailing at the time of issue. The exercise price of the Fannie Mae warrants is $44.25, approximately 34 percent above the $33 per-share market price of the common stock at the time of issue. Typically, the life of a warrant is between 5 and 10 years, although on occasion the life can be longer or even perpetual.

The management of Fannie Mae hopes that the common share price will rise above the $44.25 level and remain there, especially until after the warrants expire, because this would mean that the company could reasonably expect holders to exercise their warrants. If this happened, Fannie Mae would receive funds totaling approximately $509 million (500,000 units times twenty-three warrants per unit times $44.25 per warrant) at expiration. Thus, the company would realize its goal of raising additional capital at the time of exercise. This is in contrast to a convertible bond or preferred stock, because with convertible securities the company does not receive additional funds at the time of conversion.

If a warrant is issued as part of a unit with a fixed-income security, the warrant usually is *detachable* from the debenture or preferred stock. This means that purchasers of the units have the option of selling the warrants separately and continuing to hold the debenture or preferred stock.[7] As a result, other investors can purchase and trade warrants.

Prior to 1970, warrants usually were not used as a financing vehicle by large, established firms. In April of that year, however, AT&T sold $1.6 billion of 30-year debentures with warrants to buy 31.4 million common shares at $52 each through May 15, 1975. The use of warrant financing by AT&T undoubtedly caused other large, established firms to consider warrants. Also before 1970, warrants normally were listed either on the American Stock Exchange or traded over the counter, because the New York Stock Exchange would not list them. However, with the AT&T warrants the NYSE changed its policy and began to list warrants of NYSE companies

---

[7] It normally is illogical to consider selling the fixed-income security immediately after purchase unless economic conditions change. An investor who desires only the warrant could purchase it separately.

if the warrants met certain requirements, including a life greater than 5 years. For example, Pan Am, Eli Lilly, and Navistar, among others, have warrants that are traded on the NYSE.

Holders of warrants do not have the rights of common stockholders, such as the right to vote for directors or receive dividends, until they exercise their warrants.

Reasons for Issuing Warrants

The primary reason for issuing warrants with a fixed-income security offering is to lower agency costs. In addition, just as with convertible securities, warrants can permit a company to sell common stock at a price above the price prevailing at the time of original issue. Warrants also allow a company to sell common stock in the future without incurring underwriting costs at the time of sale.

Valuation of Warrants

In general, the value of a warrant is dependent upon the same variables that affect call option valuation. Because a warrant's value is dependent upon the price of the issuing company's stock, it is a contingent claim, just like an option. In this connection, the formula value of a warrant is defined by the following equation:

$$\begin{aligned}
\text{Formula value of a warrant} = \text{Max} \left\{ \$0; \left(\begin{array}{cc} \text{Common stock} & \text{Exercise} \\ \text{market price} & - & \text{price} \\ \text{per share} & \text{per share} \end{array} \right) \right. \\
\left. \times \begin{array}{c} \text{Number of shares} \\ \text{obtainable with} \\ \text{each warrant} \end{array} \right\}
\end{aligned}$$

$$(16.8)$$

At the time of issue, a warrant's exercise price is greater than the common stock price. Even though the calculated formula value may be negative, it is considered to be zero, because securities cannot sell for negative amounts. For example, the Fannie Mae warrants had an exercise price of $44.25 when the firm's common stock price was $33 per share. Each warrant entitled the holder to 1 share, and the formula value was zero:

$$\text{Formula value} = \text{Max} \{\$0; (\$33 - \$44.25)(1)\}$$

$$= 0$$

Suppose later, however, that the price of the Fannie Mae common stock reaches $50 per share. The formula value at this time is calculated as follows:

$$\text{Formula value} = \text{Max} \{\$0; (\$50 - \$44.25)(1)\}$$

$$= \$5.75$$

Prior to the warrant's expiration, the market price of the warrant will be greater than the formula value, just as we discussed in the case of options.

■■■■ **SELECTED CAPITAL MARKET TOPICS**

Financial managers must understand capital markets if they are to effectively manage their firm's long-term funding sources. This section presents several capital market topics. As learned in Chapter 2, capital markets usually are classified as either *primary* or *secondary* markets. New securities are issued in the primary markets, and the firms issuing these securities receive the proceeds from their sale, thus raising new capital. Outstanding securities are traded in the secondary markets, where owners of these securities may sell them to other investors. The corporations whose securities are traded in the secondary markets do not share in the proceeds from these sales.

Although primary and secondary markets are separate, they are closely related. Smoothly functioning secondary markets aid the primary markets, because investors tend to be more willing to purchase new securities when they know they can sell them in the secondary market. In fact, the potential liquidity available in the secondary markets may make investors more willing to accept slightly lower returns on their investments, thereby lowering the cost companies have to pay for their funds.

Security Exchanges and Stock Market Indexes

Secondary markets can be further classified as either listed security exchanges or over-the-counter (OTC) markets. Listed security exchanges operate at designated places of business and have requirements governing the types of securities they can list and trade. The OTC security markets do not have centralized places of business, but rather exist as networks of security dealers connected by a communications system of telephones and terminals with price quotations.

LISTED SECURITY EXCHANGES. The New York Stock Exchange (NYSE), sometimes called the *Big Board,* is the oldest and largest stock exchange in the United States. Over 2,000 common and preferred stocks and over 800 bonds are listed on the NYSE. For a company's stock to be listed and traded on the NYSE, the company must meet certain minimum requirements with regard to the number of shares of stock outstanding, the number of shareholders, the geographical distribution of shareholders, the value of assets, the market value of shares, and the net income level. As a result, only the largest U.S. companies tend to be listed on the NYSE.

The NYSE is composed largely of security firms that purchase memberships, or *seats.* The cost of these seats varies, depending on the securities industry outlook. The other organized national exchange is the American Stock Exchange (ASE or AMEX), which, like the NYSE, is located in New York City. The companies listed on the AMEX are smaller on average than those listed on the NYSE.

In addition to the national exchanges, there are a number of *regional* exchanges located around the country. The two largest are the Midwest Stock Exchange in Chicago and the Pacific Stock Exchange in San Francisco and Los Angeles. In general, regional exchanges list stocks of companies located in their geographical areas. Many large companies are listed on both the NYSE and one or more regional exchanges.

Trading activities on the NYSE and several of the regional exchanges—including the Midwest, Pacific, Philadelphia, Boston, and Cincinnati exchanges—are listed together and reported in the financial press as the *NYSE Composite Transactions.*

OVER-THE-COUNTER MARKETS. Securities that are not listed on exchanges are said to be traded "over-the-counter" (OTC). In general, these include stocks of small and relatively unknown companies, although many bank and insurance company stocks, a majority of corporate bonds and preferred stocks, and most U.S. Treasury and municipal bonds are traded in OTC markets. Security firms that deal in OTC stocks and actually carry inventories in certain stocks play an important role in the smooth functioning of OTC markets, and they are said to "make a market" in the securities they inventory.

On each business day the *Wall Street Journal* contains price quotations on OTC stocks having some national interest. These quotations are from the NASDAQ tape, the automated quotation system of the National Association of Security Dealers. This system has helped to more fully integrate the OTC market at the national level.

In addition to the listings contained in the *Wall Street Journal*, the financial pages of newspapers around the country contain price quotations on OTC stocks of companies located in their areas.

STOCK MARKET INDEXES. Stock market indexes give a broad indication of how the stock market, or a segment of the stock market, performed during a particular day. The most frequently quoted stock market index is the Dow Jones Industrial Average (DJIA), which is based on the stock prices of thirty large, well-established industrial corporations.[8] The DJIA is calculated by adding the prices of the thirty stocks and dividing by a number that reflects stock dividends and splits. When a radio announcer says, "The market was up five points today," the announcer means the DJIA was up five points. A one-point movement in the DJIA is equal to about a 7¢ per share movement in the price of an average stock.

The Dow Jones Transportation Average is based on twenty major railroad, airline, and trucking stocks, and the Dow Jones Utility Average is derived from fifteen major utility stocks. The DJIA is combined with the transportation and the utility averages to form the Dow Jones Composite Average.

The *Standard and Poor's 500* Stock Price Index (S&P 500), another frequently quoted stock market index, is significantly broader than the DJIA. It is compiled from the stock prices of 400 leading industrial firms, twenty transportation firms, forty utilities, and forty financial institutions. The S&P 500 is a *market value–weighted index.* This means, for example, that a stock whose total market value is $20 million influences the index twice as much as a stock whose total market value is $10 million.

Regulation of the Security Markets

Both the individual states and the federal government regulate the securities business. Beginning with Kansas in 1911, each of the fifty states (with the exception of Delaware) has passed so-called blue sky laws. The term *blue*

[8] Dow Jones and Company is a financial company that publishes the *Wall Street Journal*. The *Wall Street Journal* lists the companies that make up the Dow Jones averages. Every day the values of all the major stock market indexes are listed in the *Wall Street Journal* and in the financial section of most major newspapers.

sky came about when some risky securities were called nothing more than "pieces of blue sky." In spite of these state laws, many investors received incomplete and even fraudulent security information during the 1920s. This fact, combined with the 1929 stock market crash and the general reform spirit of the 1930s, led to the enactment of two principal pieces of security legislation—the Securities Act of 1933 and the Securities Exchange Act of 1934. This federal legislation has been aimed primarily at ensuring full disclosure of security information.

The Securities Act of 1933 requires any firm offering *new* securities to the public to make a complete disclosure of all pertinent facts regarding these securities; the Securities Exchange Act of 1934 expanded the coverage to include trading in *existing* securities. The 1934 act also created the Securities and Exchange Commission (SEC), which is responsible for administering the federal securities legislation. These federal laws make no judgments regarding the quality of securities issues; they simply require full disclosure of the facts.[9]

Any company that plans to sell an interstate security issue totaling over $500,000 and having a maturity greater than 270 days is required to register the issue with the SEC.[10] The procedure involves the preparation of a *registration statement* and a *prospectus*. The registration statement contains a vast amount of information about the company's legal, operational, and financial position; the prospectus summarizes the information contained in the registration statement and is intended for the use of potential investors.

After a company has filed a registration statement and prospectus, there normally is a waiting period of 20 days before the SEC approves the issue and the company can begin selling the securities. During the waiting period the company may use a preliminary prospectus in connection with the anticipated sale of securities. This preliminary prospectus often is called a "red herring" because it contains a statement, usually marked in red, saying that the prospectus is "not an offer to sell."

The Securities Exchange Act of 1934 also made it possible for the government to regulate "insider" trading. Any time a director, officer, or major stockholder—that is, an "insider"—of a large corporation trades in that corporation's securities, this fact must be reported to the SEC. This information is available to the public and is used by some investors in deciding which stocks to buy or sell. This aspect of the 1934 act attempts to prevent insiders from secretly trading securities on the basis of private information.

ROLE OF THE INVESTMENT BANKER

Investment bankers are financial middlemen who bring together suppliers and users of long-term funds in the capital markets. Whenever a large corporation is considering raising funds in the capital markets, it almost always will enlist the services of an investment banker. In fact, most large industrial corporations have ongoing relationships with their investment bankers.

The investment banker is well qualified to advise the corporation on a variety of matters, including the following:

■ Long-range financial planning.
■ The timing of security issues.

---

[9] In recent years some states have prohibited the sale of certain securities on the grounds of poor quality rather than any problems associated with the disclosure of information.

[10] Security issues of the federal government and nonprofit organizations do not have to be registered with the SEC. Bank and railroad issues also are exempt, because these industries are regulated by other government agencies.

- The purchase of securities.
- The marketing of securities.
- The arrangement of private loans and leases.
- The negotiation of mergers.

In summary, the investment banker is an important source of financial market expertise.

How Securities Are Sold

Firms can sell securities in the primary capital markets in one of three ways:

- By selling securities through investment bankers to the public in a *public cash offering*.
- By placing a debt or stock issue with one or more large investors in a *private*, or *direct, placement*.
- By selling common stock to existing stockholders through a *rights offering*.

Investment bankers usually assist firms in all three methods of sale. Figure 16-3 is a flowchart that outlines the various methods and steps for the sale of corporate securities.

PUBLIC CASH OFFERINGS. Normally, when a corporation wishes to issue new securities and sell them to the public, it makes an arrangement with an investment banker whereby the investment banker agrees to purchase the entire issue at a set price. This is called *underwriting*. The investment banker then resells the issue to the public at a higher price.

Underwriting can be accomplished either through *negotiations* between the underwriter and the issuing company or by *competitive bidding*. A *negotiated underwriting* simply is an arrangement between the issuing firm and its investment bankers. Most large industrial corporations turn to investment bankers with whom they have had ongoing relationships. In competitive bidding the firm sells the securities to the underwriter (usually a group) that bids the highest price. Many regulated companies, such as utilities and railroads, are required by their regulatory commissions (for example, the Federal Energy Regulatory Commission, the Interstate Commerce Commission, and state regulatory bodies) to sell new security issues in this way.

An investment banker who agrees to underwrite a security issue assumes a certain amount of risk and, in turn, requires compensation in the form of an *underwriting discount* or *underwriting spread*, computed as follows:

Underwriting spread = Selling price to public − Proceeds to company

Examples of underwriting spread amounts are shown in Table 16-2.

It is difficult to compare underwriting spreads for negotiated and competitive offerings, because rarely are two offerings brought to market at the same time that differ only in the ways in which they are underwritten. Generally underwriters receive lower spreads for competitively bid utility issues than for negotiated industrial offers. This primarily is because utilities have tended to have a lower level of risk than industrial companies.

Security issues sold to the public through underwriters normally exceed $25 million in size; amounts totaling $250 million are not uncommon. Due to the size of these issues, individual investment bankers usually do not

FIGURE 16-3   **How Securities Are Sold: A Flowchart**

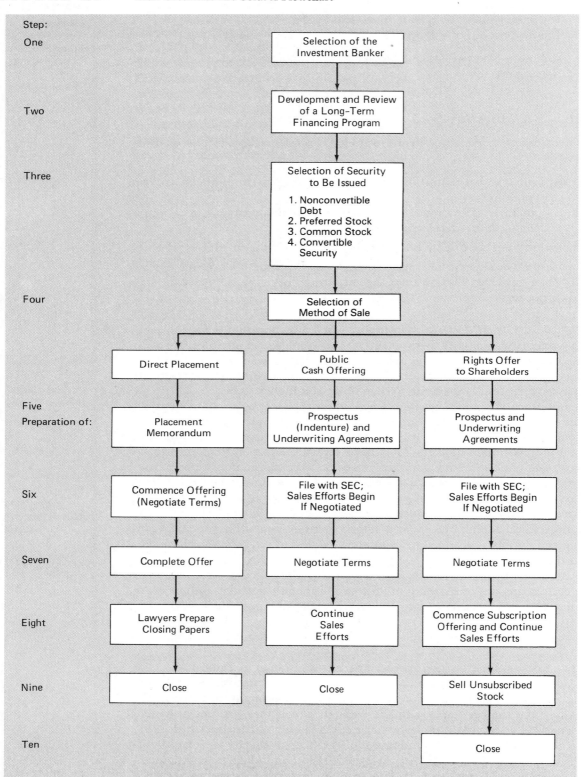

Sample Underwriting Spreads for Selected Issues

Company	Issue Size (in millions of dollars)	Underwriting Spread (%)	S&P Rating*
Debt Issues			
First Interstate Bancorp.	$100	0.63	AA
CIGNA Corporation†	100	1.00	AA
Corning Glass Works†	100	1.00	A
U.S. Leasing International†	30	2.00	BBB
Jerrico, Inc.	40	1.88	BB
Petro-Lewis	85	3.35	B
Sunshine Mining Company	30	3.68	B
Common Stock Issues			
El Paso Electric Company	$ 57.5	3.26	
Ryder System, Inc.	83.4	3.88	
Southwest Airlines	34.7	3.89	
Service Corporation International	48.26	4.48	
Adage, Inc.	10.0	6.26	
Atlantic Southeast Airlines	5.2	8.00	

* Standard and Poor's (S&P) bond-rating scale is AAA (for the highest quality issues), AA, A, BBB, BB, B, CCC, CC, C.
† Convertible issues.

want to underwrite an entire issue by themselves. Normally a group of underwriters, called a *purchasing syndicate,* agrees to underwrite the issue in order to spread the risk.[11] Sometimes the purchasing syndicate can sell an entire issue to large institutional investors;[12] this often is true with high-quality debt issues. On other occasions—particularly with large debt issues or equity issues—the underwriters organize a *selling group* of security firms to market the issue to the public. It is not uncommon for a selling group responsible for marketing a large issue to number over 100 security firms.

An important part of the negotiations between the issuing firm and the investment banker is the determination of the security's selling price. It is in the best interests of both the issuing firm and the underwriter to have the security "fairly priced." If the security is underpriced, the issuing firm will not raise the amount of capital it could have, and the underwriter may lose a customer. If the security is overpriced, the underwriter may have difficulty selling the issue, and investors who discover that they paid too much may choose not to purchase the next issue offered by either the corporation or the underwriter.

Occasionally, with smaller company issues, the investment banker agrees to help market the issue on a "best efforts" basis rather than underwriting it. Under this type of arrangement the investment banker is under no further obligation to the issuing company if some of the securities cannot be sold. The investment banker functions as a *dealer* in an underwriting situation and as a *broker* in a best efforts situation. In a best efforts offering the investment banker does not assume the risk that the securities will not be sold at a favorable price.

[11] In most cases one to three underwriters agree to manage an issue, handling all legal matters, advertising, and so on. These firms are the *managing underwriters.*
[12] Institutional investors include life insurance companies, pension funds, mutual funds, and commercial banks.

PRIVATE PLACEMENTS. Many industrial companies choose to *directly*, or *privately, place* debt or preferred stock issues with one or more institutional investors instead of having them underwritten and sold to the public. In these cases, investment bankers who act on behalf of the issuing company receive a "finder's fee" for finding a buyer and negotiating the terms of the agreement. The private market is an important source of long-term debt capital, especially for smaller corporations.

Private security placements have a number of advantages:

■ They can save on flotation costs by eliminating underwriting costs.
■ They can avoid the time delays associated with the preparation of registration statements and with the waiting period.
■ They can offer greater flexibility in the writing of the terms of the contract (called the *indenture*) between the borrower and the lender.

An offsetting disadvantage is that, as a very general rule, interest rates for private placements are about one-eighth of a percentage point *higher* than they are for debt and preferred issues sold through underwriters. For small-sized debt and preferred stock issues—that is, those that are less than about $20 million—the percentage cost of underwriting becomes fairly large. Because of this, these smaller-sized issues frequently are placed privately with institutional investors.

RIGHTS OFFERINGS AND STANDBY UNDERWRITINGS. Firms may sell their common stock directly to their existing stockholders through the issuance of *rights*, which entitle the stockholders to purchase new shares of the firm's stock at a *subscription price* below the market price. (Rights offerings are also called *privileged subscriptions*.) Each stockholder receives one right for each share owned; in other words, if a firm has 100 million shares outstanding and wishes to sell an additional 10 million shares through a rights offering, each right entitles the holder to purchase 0.1 shares, and it takes ten rights to purchase one share.[13]

When selling stock through a rights offering, firms usually enlist the services of investment bankers, who urge rights holders to purchase the stock. In an arrangement called a *standby underwriting*, the investment banker agrees to purchase—at the subscription price—any shares that are not sold to rights holders. The investment banker then resells the shares. In a standby underwriting the investment banker bears risk and is compensated by an underwriting fee.

FLOTATION COSTS. Flotation costs are the costs involved in issuing new securities. The total flotation cost of a security issue sold through underwriters is calculated as follows:

Total flotation cost = Underwriting spread + Company's issue expenses

The company's issue expenses usually are considerably less than the underwriting spread. For example, when Service Corporation International recently sold 1.35 million shares of common stock, the underwriting spread was $2,160,000, and the issue expenses were $280,564.

Flotation costs can vary widely, depending on the type of the security being offered, the quality of the security, and the size of the issue. Common

[13] Rights and rights offerings are discussed in greater detail in the appendix to this chapter.

stock flotation costs range from about 2 percent to as high as 20 percent or more, whereas flotation costs on good quality debt issues fall into roughly the 0.5 to 3 percent range. Table 16-2 shows the underwriting spreads for several issues.

Generally, flotation costs are higher for common stock than for preferred stock issues, and flotation costs of preferred stock are higher than those of debt issues. One reason for this is the amount of risk each type of issue involves. Common stocks usually involve more risk for underwriters than preferred stock, and preferred stock involves more risk than debt. Stock prices are subject to wider price movements than debt prices. Another reason for these differences in flotation costs is that investment bankers usually incur greater marketing expenses for common stock than for preferred stock or debt issues. Common stock is customarily sold to a large number of individual investors, whereas debt securities are frequently purchased by a much smaller number of institutional investors.

Flotation costs also depend on the quality of the issue. Low-quality debt issues, for example, tend to have higher percentage flotation costs than high-quality issues, because underwriters bear more risk with low-quality issues and therefore require greater compensation. And, finally, flotation costs are dependent on the size of the issue—costs tend to be a higher percentage of small-sized issues, all other things being equal, because underwriters have various fixed expenses (such as advertising expenses, legal fees, registration statement costs, and so on) that are incurred regardless of the issue's size.

FINANCIAL INNOVATIONS

The Financial Dilemma at the beginning of this chapter presented some examples of new and innovative securities being used by firms in their financing.[14] We said we would attempt to answer the question of why firms use these securities later in the chapter. The answer in part deals with the net present value of financial transactions. In Chapter 10 we commented that positive net present value capital expenditure projects can occur because of barriers to entry in product and factor markets. Financial transactions, in general, tend to be zero net present value projects, because financial markets are more efficient than product and factor markets. Consider the example of the Cray Research convertible debentures discussed earlier in this chapter. Cray's financial managers worked with the well-known investment banking firm of Morgan Stanley to determine the interest rate, conversion price, and other features of this convertible issue. Had Cray or Morgan Stanley felt that the convertible issue did not represent a fair deal for them, they would not have attempted to issue the security. On the other hand, apparently a sufficient number of the professional financial analysts who analyzed the Cray convertible issue from the standpoint of a possible investment felt it also was fair enough for them to cause the issue to sell out on the same day it came to market. This is not unusual for financial transactions. The analyses performed by well-trained, knowledgeable financial professionals possessing reasonably complete information about a particular financial transaction tend to cause financial transactions to be zero net present value projects.

We can now state the purpose of financial innovation—to create positive net present value transaction projects and thereby increase the firm's value

[14] This section is based on John D. Finnerty. "Financial Engineering in Corporate Finance: An Overview," *Financial Management* (Winter 1988): 14–33.

for its shareholders. If a financial transaction, for example, possesses features that allow a firm to achieve a lower risk-adjusted after-tax cost of capital than had been possible before the new security and without adversely affecting investors, it can give the firm's shareholders increased value.

Securities innovations can be classified as either debt or equity. The following are examples of debt innovations:

1. *Adjustable Rate Notes.* The interest rate varies and is based on changes in an index, such as the 3-month Treasury bill rate. The issuing firm is exposed to interest rate risk, but the initial interest rate is lower than for a fixed-rate issue.

2. *Bonds Linked to a Commodity Price.* The interest and/or principal is adjusted to changes in the price of a commodity, such as silver. The issuing firm is exposed to commodity price risk, but the initial interest rate is lower than for a conventional debt issue.

3. *Extendible Notes.* The interest rate is adjusted every 2–3 years, at which time the holders can decide whether to put (i.e., sell) the notes back to the issuer at par. Extendible notes are reissued without additional underwriting fees.

4. *Interest Rate Reset Notes.* The interest rate is reset, for example, 3 years after issuance to a rate sufficient to give the notes a predetermined market value such as 101 percent of their face amount. The rate cannot be lowered, however. The issuing firm benefits from a lower initial interest rate due to a reduction in agency costs.

5. *Interest Rate Swaps.* An *interest rate swap* is an agreement between two companies in which one company's floating rate debt repayment obligation is traded for another company's fixed-rate obligation. If a company with floating rate debt feels that interest rates are headed higher, it can execute a swap agreement to obtain the equivalent of fixed-rate debt. The other party to the swap agrees to pay the interest costs in excess of the specified rate. Interest rate swaps are an effective means of shifting interest rate risk from one company to another.

6. *Puttable Bonds.* With a puttable bond, the investor has a put option to sell the bond back to the issuing company at par. The put protects the investor against increases in interest rates or a deterioration of the company's credit quality. As a result, the company benefits from a reduction in agency costs.

The following are examples of equity innovations:

1. *Adjustable Rate Preferred Stock.* The quarterly dividend rate is reset each quarter and usually is based on Treasury issues. The issuing firm is exposed to interest rate risk, but its cost of capital is lowered. Adjustable rate preferred stock is designed to allow short-term corporate investors to take advantage of the intercompany dividend tax exclusion.

2. *Additional Class(es) of Common Stock.* Companies can create an additional class of common stock whose dividends are based upon the earnings of a specified subsidiary. A separate market value for the subsidiary is established, and at the same time, the parent company maintains 100 percent voting control.

3. *Master Limited Partnership.* A business is set up as a partnership, but is publicly owned and traded, as if it were a corporation. The benefit of a master limited partnership is due to lower taxes—a partnership itself is not taxed, just the partners. This tax benefit now is being phased out for most master limited partnerships.

▰▰ SUMMARY

Options

- ▪ An *option* is a security that gives its holder the right to buy or sell an asset at a set *exercise price* until a specified *expiration date*. A *call* is an option to *buy*, and a *put* is an option to *sell*.
- ▪ The value of a call option is dependent upon four variables:
  1. The relationship between the exercise price and the stock price.
  2. The time remaining until the option's expiration date.
  3. The level of interest rates.
  4. The expected stock price volatility.

- ▪ An option is a *contingent claim;* that is, its value depends upon the value of another security.

Convertible Securities

- ▪ *Convertible* debt or preferred stock securities are exchangeable for a company's common stock at the option of the holder.
- ▪ Convertible securities tend to reduce potential conflicts between fixed-income security holders and stockholders, resulting in reduced agency costs.
- ▪ The price at which a convertible security is exchangeable for common stock is the *conversion price*.
- ▪ The number of common shares that can be obtained when a convertible security is exchanged is the *conversion ratio*, which is calculated by dividing the par value of the security by the conversion price.
- ▪ At the time of issue, the conversion price normally exceeds the market price of the common stock by about 15 to 30 percent.
- ▪ Convertible securities possess characteristics of both common stock and fixed-income securities. Their market value is a function of both their stock, or conversion, value and their value as a fixed-income security. The *conversion value* is calculated by multiplying the conversion ratio by the current stock price.

Warrants

- ▪ A *warrant* is an option issued by a company to purchase shares of the company's common stock at a particular price during a specific time period. Warrants frequently are issued as part of a fixed-income security offering. Warrants also are issued as part of more "creative" financing packages.
- ▪ The *exercise price* of a warrant is the price at which the holder can purchase common stock of the issuing company.
- ▪ The primary reason for issuing a warrant with a fixed-income security offering is that warrants tend to lower agency costs.
- ▪ The *formula value* of a warrant depends on the number of common shares each warrant is entitled to receive when exercised and the difference between the common stock market price and the warrant exercise price. Warrants normally sell at a premium over their formula value.

Table 16-3 summarizes the similarities among and differences between convertibles and warrants.

TABLE 16-3	Summary Comparison of Convertibles and Warrants (When Warrants Are Issued as Part of a Fixed-Income Security Offering)

Similarities

1. Both convertibles and warrants tend to lessen potential conflicts between fixed-income security holders and stockholders, thereby reducing agency costs.
2. The intention is the deferred issuance of common stock at a price higher than that prevailing at the time of the convertible or warrant issue.
3. Both the convertibility option and the attachment of warrants result in interest expense or preferred dividend savings for the issuing company, thereby easing potential cash flow problems.

Differences

1. The company receives additional funds at the time warrants are exercised, whereas no additional funds are received at the time convertibles are converted.
2. The fixed-income security remains on the company's books after the exercise of warrants; in the case of convertibles, the fixed-income security is exchanged for common stock and taken off the company's books.
3. Because of the call feature, convertible securities potentially give the company more control over when the common stock is issued.

Capital Markets and Investment Banking

■ Listed exchanges, such as the New York and American stock exchanges, have designated places of business, as well as various trading regulations and listing requirements. The over-the-counter markets do not have a centrally designated place of business, but instead exist through a telephone and computer communications network.

■ The Securities Act of 1933 and the Securities Exchange Act of 1934 are the principal pieces of securities legislation in the United States. The 1933 act requires complete disclosure of information on *new* securities, and the 1934 act expands this coverage to include *existing* securities. The Securities Exchange Act of 1934 also created the Securities and Exchange Commission (SEC), which is responsible for administering federal securities legislation.

■ *Investment bankers* are financial middlemen that bring together suppliers and users of long-term funds in the capital markets. The principal service provided by investment bankers is the *underwriting* of securities. Underwriting is an insurance function whereby an investment banker agrees to purchase an entire issue at a specified price. The underwriters, usually a group called a *purchasing syndicate*, then resell the issue to the public at a slightly higher price. Because they assume a certain amount of risk when they agree to underwrite a security issue, underwriters earn the difference between the proceeds to the company and the selling price; this is called the *underwriting spread*, or the *underwriting discount*.

■ Industrial corporations usually sell their securities through *negotiated underwritings*, whereas utilities and railroads frequently are required by law to sell their new security issues to the highest bidder in *competitive bidding*.

■ Some security issues are *privately*, or *directly*, *placed* with institutional investors instead of being sold to the public through underwriters. The private market is an important source of debt financing for smaller firms.

■ Firms also may choose to sell their common stock to their existing stockholders through a *rights offering*, or *privileged subscription*. Rights entitle stockholders to purchase new shares at a *subscription price* that is below the market price. Underwriters usually assist in rights offerings by agreeing to purchase any unsold shares; this is called *standby underwriting*.

■ *Flotation costs* are the cost of issuing new securities. They generally are higher for common stock issues than for preferred stock issues, which, in turn, are higher than those for debt issues. Flotation costs tend to be inversely proportional to the issue's quality, because underwriters bear more risk with lower quality issues and therefore require greater compensation.

QUESTIONS AND TOPICS FOR DISCUSSION

1. Define the following terms:
   a. Option
   b. Call
   c. Put
   d. Contingent claim
   e. Listed security exchanges
   f. Over-the-counter markets
   g. Stock market index

2. What are the similarities and differences between options and warrants?

3. What variables are important in determining call option prices?

4. Will option values in general be higher at a time when interest rates are relatively high, compared with a time when interest rates are relatively low, all other things being equal?

5. How does a stock's expected price volatility affect the value of a call option on it?

6. In what ways are convertible securities and warrants similar? Dissimilar?

7. Why do companies issue convertible securities?

8. What is the relationship between conversion value, bond value, and market value for a convertible security?

9. How can a company effectively force conversion of a convertible security?

10. Suppose an associate of yours (who has just lost money in the stock market) comments that the stock exchanges should be shut down because "all people do is lose money in the stock market." What would be your response?

11. What is the general purpose of federal and state regulation of security markets?

12. What are the basic provisions of the Securities Act of 1933 and the Securities Exchange Act of 1934?

13. What is an *interest rate swap?* How can swaps be used in raising funds?

14. What are the ways in which firms can sell their securities in the primary capital markets?

15. What factors influence the flotation cost percentage on security issues?

PROBLEMS*

1. The BWS Corporation stock is selling at $50 a share today.
   a. Calculate the value of a BWS call option if its exercise price is $40, and it expires today.

* Colored numbers denote problems that have check answers provided at the end of the book.

b. What can you say about the value of a BWS call option if its exercise price is $40, and it expires in 6 months?

c. Calculate the value of a BWS call option if its exercise price is $60, and it expires today.

d. What can you say about the value of a BWS call option if its exercise price is $60, and it expires in 6 months.

2. The BWS Corporation stock is selling at $50 a share today.

   a. Calculate the value of a BWS put option if its exercise price is $40, and it expires today.

   b. What can you say about the value of a BWS put option if its exercise price is $40, and it expires in 6 months?

   c. Calculate the value of a BWS put option if its exercise price is $60, and it expires today.

   d. What can you say about the value of a BWS put option if its exercise price is $60, and it expires in 6 months.

3. The LeMonde Corporation had debentures outstanding (par value = $1,000) that are convertible into the company's common stock at a price of $25 per share. The convertibles have a coupon interest rate of 6 percent and mature 20 years from now. In addition, the convertible debenture is callable at 107 percent of par value. The company has a marginal tax rate of 40 percent.

   a. Calculate the conversion value if LeMonde's common stock is selling at $25 a share.

   b. Calculate the bond value, assuming that straight debt of equivalent risk and maturity is yielding 9 percent.

   c. Using the answers from Parts a and b, what is a realistic estimate of the market value of the convertible debentures? (No calculation is necessary for this part of the problem.)

   d. What is the conversion value if the company's common stock price increases to $35 a share?

   e. Given the situation presented in Part d, what is a realistic estimate of the market value of the convertible debenture? (No calculation is necessary for this part of the problem.)

   f. What is the minimum common stock price that will allow the LeMonde management to use the call feature of the debentures to effectively force conversion?

   g. Suppose that increased expectations concerning inflation cause the yield on straight debt of equivalent risk and maturity to reach 10 percent. How will this affect the bond value of the convertible?

4. Automatic Data Processing recently issued $150 million of 6½ percent convertible debentures maturing in 2011. The debentures are convertible into common stock at $83.45 a share. The company's common stock was trading at about $67 a share at the time the convertibles were issued.

   a. How many shares of common stock can be obtained by converting one $1,000 par value debenture; that is, what is the conversion ratio?

   b. What was the conversion value of this issue at the time these debentures were originally issued?

   c. By what percentage was the conversion price above the stock price at the time these debentures were originally issued?

5. The Manchester Corporation has warrants presently outstanding, and each warrant entitles the holder to purchase 1 share of the company's common stock at an exercise price of $20 a share. If the market price of the warrants is $8 and the common stock price is $24 a share, what is the premium over the formula value for the warrants?

6. Horizon Corporation has warrants to purchase common stock outstanding. Each warrant entitles the holder to purchase 1 share of the company's common stock at an exercise price of $20 a share. Suppose the warrants

expire on September 1, 1995. One month ago, when the company's common stock was trading at about $21.50 a share, the warrants were trading at $5 each.

   a. What was the formula value of the warrants 1 month ago?

   b. What was the premium over the formula value 1 month ago?

   c. What are the reasons investors were willing to pay more than the formula value for these warrants 1 month ago?

   d. Suppose that in August 1995, the Horizon common stock is still trading at $21.50 a share. What do you think the warrant price would be then? Why?

   e. Horizon paid an annual dividend of $1 a share, as of one month ago, to its common shareholders. Do warrant holders receive dividends?

7. Shaw Products Company, whose present balance sheet is summarized here, is considering issuing $100 million of 6 percent subordinated debentures (par value = $1,000), which are convertible into common stock at a price of $40.

Balance Sheet
(in millions of dollars)

Current assets	$200	Current liabilities	$100
Fixed assets, net	300	Long-term debt	150
Total assets	$500	Common equity	250
		Total liabilities and equity	$500

   a. Show the pro forma balance sheet for the issuance of the convertibles prior to conversion. Assume the proceeds are invested in new plant and equipment, and disregard flotation costs.

   b. Show the pro forma balance sheet, assuming conversion of the entire issue.

   c. How much additional money will the company raise at the time of conversion?

8. The capital structure of Whitefield Mills, Inc., is as follows:

Long-term debt	$250 million
Common stock, $1 par	25 million
Contributed capital in excess of par value	150 million
Retained earnings	350 million
	$775 million

The company had decided to raise additional capital by selling $75 million of 8 percent debentures with warrants attached. Each $1,000 debenture will have 25 warrants attached, and each warrant will entitle the holder to purchase 1 share of common stock at $30.

   a. Show the company's new capital structure after the sale of debentures and the exercise of all the warrants. Assume that no other changes in capital structure occur between now and the time the warrants are exercised.

   b. What condition is necessary in order for the warrants to be exercised?

   c. How much total money will the company raise as a result of this security issue, if all warrants are exercised?

9. You own ten Bitterroot Industries, Inc., 8-percent convertible debentures maturing in 2010. The conversion ratio of the debentures is 30, and the debentures are callable at $1,070 each. You bought the debentures when they originally were issued in 1980 for $1,000 each. At that time, Bitterroot common stock was selling at $28.50 a share, and now it is up to $44 a share. The convertible debentures are now selling at $1,320 each.

Last week you received a notice from Bitterroot Industries stating that the company is calling the debentures.

a. What are your alternatives?

b. Which alternative should you choose?

10. Calculate the after-tax component cost of capital, k_c, for a 7.5 percent convertible debenture sold at par and due to mature in 25 years. The conversion ratio is 25, and conversion is expected to occur at the end of 10 years, when the common stock price is expected to be $54 a share. The company has a 40 percent marginal tax rate.

HINT: Try $k_c = 7.0\%$.

SELECTED REFERENCES

Arnold, Tanya S. "How to do Interest Rate Swaps." *Harvard Business Review* (September–October 1984): 96–101.

Bicksler, James, and Andrew H. Chen. "An Economic Analysis of Interest Rate Swaps." *Journal of Finance* (July 1986): 645–655.

Black, Fischer, and Myron Scholes. "The Pricing of Options and Corporate Liabilities." *Journal of Political Economy* 81 (May–June 1973): 637–654.

Finnerty, John D. "Financial Engineering in Corporate Finance: An Overview." *Financial Management* (Winter 1988): 14–33.

Hansen, R. S., and J. M. Pinkerton. "Direct Equity Financing: A Resolution of a Paradox." *Journal of Finance* (June 1982): 651–666.

Smith, Clifford W., Jr., Charles W. Smithson, and Lee Macdonald Wakeman. "The Market for Interest Rate Swaps." *Financial Management* (Winter 1988): 34–44.

Bond Refunding, Stockholder Voting Rights, and Rights Offerings

---

GLOSSARY OF NEW TERMS

Cumulative voting A voting procedure by which stockholders may cast multiple votes for a single board of directors candidate. Cumulative voting makes it easier for stockholders with minority views to elect sympathetic board members.

Ex-rights A stock sells ex-rights when stock purchasers no longer receive the *rights* along with the shares purchased.

Rights-on A stock sells rights-on when purchasers receive the *rights* along with the shares purchased.

▨ INTRODUCTION

This appendix considers three additional topics related to managing long-term funding sources:

- ▨ Bond refunding analysis.
- ▨ Stockholder voting rights.
- ▨ Analysis of rights offerings.

▨ BOND REFUNDING ANALYSIS

Bond refunding occurs when a company redeems a callable issue and sells a lower cost issue to take its place.[15] The decision of whether to refund a particular debt issue usually is based on a capital budgeting (present value) analysis. The principle benefit, or cash inflow, is the present value of the after-tax interest savings over the life of the issue. The principal investment, or cash outflow at the time of refunding, consists primarily of the call premium and the flotation cost of the new debt.

Bond refunding differs from other capital expenditure projects in one very important way: the cash inflows are known with considerably more

---

[15] Callable preferred stock also can be refunded. The same considerations and analysis apply to both debt and preferred stock.

certainty than the cash flows from a typical capital expenditure project and thus are less risky. As a result, the weighted cost of capital is not used. Instead, the *after-tax cost of the new debt* is believed to be a more appropriate discount rate for bond refunding analysis.

Bond refunding becomes an important decision facing many firms whenever interest rates decline substantially from earlier levels. For example, firms that had issued bonds with coupon rates of 13 percent or more during the period of high inflation and high interest rates in the early 1980s found that they could refund these issues at rates under 10 percent during the mid- and late 1980s.

As an illustration of bond refunding, consider the following example. The APCO Company issued $100 million of 30-year, 13 percent debt 5 years ago. In the meantime, interest rates have declined, and the firm's management feels the decline has bottomed out. The debt issue is now callable at 107 percent of par. The company could refund the old issue with a new 25-year, 10 percent, $100 million issue. Flotation costs on the new issue would be 0.5 percent, or $500,000, whereas the unamortized flotation costs on the old issue are $450,000. If APCO decided to call the old issue and refund it, both issues would be outstanding for a 3-week period, resulting in overlapping interest payments. The company's marginal tax rate is 40 percent. For purposes of discounting, the after-tax cost of new debt is $0.10 \times (1 - 0.4) = 0.06$.

To determine whether APCO should refund the old issue, a bond refunding analysis is carried out.

■ Step 1: Calculate the interest savings (cash inflows):[16]

Annual interest, after tax $\quad$ = Issue size × Interest rate × (1 − Tax rate)

Annual interest, old issue $\quad$ = $100 million × 13% × 0.6 = $7.8 million
Annual interest, new issue = $100 million × 10% × 0.6 = $6.0 million
Annual after-tax interest savings $\qquad\qquad\qquad\qquad\quad$ $1.8 million

Present value of interest savings = Annual after-tax interest × $\text{PVIFA}_{0.06,25}$
$\qquad\qquad\qquad\qquad\qquad\qquad\qquad$ = $1.8 million × 12.783
$\qquad\qquad\qquad\qquad\qquad\qquad\qquad$ = $23.009 million

■ Step 2: Calculate the net investment (*net cash* outflow at time 0). This involves computing the after-tax call premium, the flotation cost of the new issue, the flotation cost of the old issue, and the overlapping interest. The after-tax call premium is calculated as follows:

Call premium, after-tax = $7 million × (1 − 0.4)
$\qquad\qquad\qquad\qquad\quad$ = $4.2 million

The call premium is a cash outflow.

The flotation cost on the new issue is 0.5 percent, or $500,000. This amount cannot be deducted from APCO's current period income for tax purposes. Instead, it must be capitalized and amortized over the life of the debt issue, because the benefits that accrue to a firm as a result of a flotation cost expenditure occur over the life of the issue. Thus,

---

[16] This calculation assumes that interest is received once a year at year-end. Actually, interest is paid every 6 months. However, the two results are not materially different.

Present value of
flotation cost = Flotation cost − Present value tax effect
of new issue

577
APPENDIX 16A
Bond Refunding,
Stockholder
Voting Rights,
and Rights
Offerings

$$= \text{Flotation cost} - \left(\begin{array}{c} \text{Annual after-tax} \\ \text{savings from} \\ \text{amortization} \end{array} \times \text{PVIFA}_{0.06,25} \right)$$

$$= \text{Flotation cost} - \left(\frac{\text{Flotation cost}}{\text{Number of years}} \times \text{Tax rate} \right.$$

$$\left. \times \text{PVIFA}_{0.06,25} \right)$$

$$= \$500,000 - \left(\frac{\$500,000}{25} \times 0.4 \times 12.783 \right)$$

$$= \$500,000 - \$102,264$$

$$= \$397,736$$

The present value of the flotation cost of the *new* issue is a net cash outflow.

APCO has been amortizing the flotation cost of the old issue over its life. If it refunded the issue, the company no longer would receive the benefits from the old issue's flotation cost and therefore could write off the remaining unamortized flotation cost at the time of refunding. Because of the write-off, however, APCO would lose the benefits of the old flotation cost over the remaining life of the issue. Thus,

Present value of Present value, Present value,
flotation cost of = lost benefits, − write-off of old
old issue old flotation cost, flotation cost,
after tax after tax

$$= \left(\frac{\text{Old flotation cost}}{\text{Number of years}} \times \text{Tax rate} \times \text{PVIFA}_{0.06,25} \right)$$

$$- (\text{Old flotation cost} \times \text{Tax rate})$$

$$= \left(\frac{\$450,000}{25} \times 0.4 \times 12.783 \right) - (450,000 \times 0.4)$$

$$= \$92,038 - \$180,000$$

$$= - \$87,962$$

The flotation cost effect of the old issue is a net cash inflow at the time of refunding.

In most bond refundings it is necessary for a firm to sell the new issue and receive the proceeds before paying off the old lenders. Both issues usually are outstanding for less than a month. Thus, the interest expense on the old issue during the overlapping period is considered a cost, or part of the refunding investment. In APCO's case, this expense is calculated as follows:

Overlapping Size of Annual interest rate Fraction of year
interest = issue × of old issue, × both issues
after tax outstanding

$$= \$100 \text{ million} \times 0.078 \times \frac{3}{52}$$

$$= \$450,000$$

The overlapping interest is a cash outflow.[17]

In summary, the net investment is calculated as follows:

Call premium	$4,200,000
Present value of flotation cost, new issue	397,736
Present value of flotation cost, old issue	−87,962
Overlapping interest	450,000
Net investment (cash outflow)	$4,959,774

■ **Step 3: Finally, calculate the net present value of refunding as follows:**

$$\text{Net present value of refunding} = \frac{\text{Present value,}}{\text{interest savings}} - \frac{\text{Present value,}}{\text{net investment}}$$

$$= \$23.009 \text{ million} - \$4.960 \text{ million}$$

$$= \$18.049 \text{ million}$$

Because the net present value is positive, APCO should call its old issue and refund it with the new one.[18]

STOCKHOLDER VOTING RIGHTS

A firm's stockholders elect its board of directors by means of either a *majority* or a *cumulative* voting procedure. Majority voting is similar to the voting that takes place in political elections; namely, if two slates of people are running for the board, the one that receives more than 50 percent of the votes wins. With majority voting it is possible that a group of stockholders with a minority viewpoint will have no representation on the board.

Cumulative voting, in contrast, makes it easier for stockholders with minority views to elect sympathetic board members. In spite of this, cumulative voting is rare among major corporations. In cumulative voting, each share of stock represents as many votes as there are directors to be elected. For example, if a firm is electing seven directors, a particular holder of 100 shares would have 700 votes and could cast all of them for *one* candidate, thereby increasing that candidate's chances for being elected to the board. The following formula can be used to determine the minimum number of shares or votes necessary to elect a certain number of directors:

$$\text{Number of shares} = \frac{\text{Number of directors desired} \times \text{Number of shares outstanding}}{\text{Number of directors being elected} + 1} + 1$$

[17] Normally, during the period of the overlap, the proceeds from the sale of the new issue temporarily are invested in short-term securities. The interest earned will offset part of the overlapping interest expense. For simplification, this offset against the overlapping interest expense has not been considered in this example.
[18] Financial analysts normally can determine the *approximate* net present value of refunding by comparing the present value of the interest savings with the after-tax cost of the call premium. However, as is true with any shortcut method, caution should be exercised.

Of course, it is possible that not all the shareholders will vote their shares. In this case, the calculation is based on the number of shares actually voting rather than the number of shares outstanding.

Consider the following example. The Markham Company has eleven members on its board and 1 million shares of common stock outstanding. If seven members were up for reelection in a given year and all the shares were voted, the number of shares necessary to elect one director would be as follows:

$$\frac{1 \times 1,000,000}{7 + 1} + 1 = 125,001$$

579
APPENDIX 16A
Bond Refunding,
Stockholder
Voting Rights,
and Rights
Offerings

In addition to electing the board of directors, a firm's stockholders may vote from time to time on various other matters, such as whether to retain a particular auditing firm or increase the number of shares authorized.

The election of directors and other voting normally occurs at the annual stockholders' meeting. Because it usually is not possible for all stockholders to attend, management—or anyone else—can solicit votes by *proxy*. Normally, a stockholder can expect to receive a single proxy statement from the firm's management requesting that stockholders follow management's recommendations. In the rather unlikely event that another group of stockholders sends out its own proxy statement, a *proxy fight* is said to occur. Proxy fights are most common when a company is performing poorly.

ANALYSIS OF RIGHTS OFFERINGS

In addition to the sale of new common stock through underwriters, new equity capital can be raised through a *rights offering*. In a rights offering the firm's existing stockholders are given an opportunity to purchase a fraction of the new shares equal to the fraction they currently own. For example, if a company has 10 million shares outstanding and decides to sell 1 million additional shares through a rights offering, each shareholder is entitled to purchase 0.1 new share for each share presently owned. (The *rights* themselves really are the documents describing the offer. Each stockholder receives one right for each share currently held.)

In a rights offering, shareholders have the opportunity to maintain their original ownership percentage. Hence, rights offerings are used in equity financing by companies whose charters contain the *preemptive right*. In addition, rights offerings *may* be used as a means of selling common stock in companies in which preemptive rights do not exist. The number of rights offerings has gradually declined over the years.

The following example illustrates what a rights offering involves. The Miller Company has 10 million shares outstanding and plans to sell an additional 1 million shares via a rights offering. In this case, each right entitles the holder to purchase 0.1 share, and it takes ten rights to purchase one share. The company has to decide on a *subscription price;* that is the price the rightholder will have to pay per new share. The subscription price has to be less than the market price, or rightholders will have no incentive to subscribe to the new issue. As a general rule, subscription prices are 5 to 20 percent below market prices. If the Miller Company's stock is selling at $40 per share, a reasonable subscription price might be $35 per share.

Valuation of Rights

Because a right represents an opportunity to purchase stock below its market value, the right itself has a certain value, which is calculated under two sets of circumstances:

■ The *rights-on* case.
■ The *ex-rights* case.

A stock is said to "trade with rights-on" when the purchasers receive the rights along with the shares they purchase. In contrast, a stock is said to "trade ex-rights" when the stock purchasers no longer receive the rights.

For example, suppose the Miller Company announced on May 15 that shareholders of record as of Friday, June 20, will receive the rights. This means that anyone who purchased stock on or before Monday, June 16, will receive the rights, and anyone who purchased stock on or later than June 17 will not.[19] The stock trades with rights up to and including June 16 and goes ex-rights on June 17, the *ex-rights date*. On that date the stock's market value falls by the value of the right, all other things being equal.

The theoretical, or formula, value of a right for the rights-on case can be calculated using the following equation:

$$R = \frac{M_o - S}{N + 1}$$

where R is the theoretical value for the right; M_o, the rights-on market price of the stock; S, the subscription price of the right; and N, the number of rights necessary to purchase one new share. In the Miller Company example, the right's theoretical value is

$$R = \frac{\$40 - \$35}{10 + 1}$$

$$= \$0.455$$

The theoretical value of a right when the stock is trading ex-rights can be calculated by using the following equation:

$$R = \frac{M_e - S}{N}$$

where M_e is the ex-rights market price of the stock; S, the subscription price of the right; and N, the number of rights necessary to purchase 1 new share. If the Miller stock were trading ex-rights, the theoretical value of a right would be as follows:

$$R = \frac{\$39.545 - \$35}{10}$$

$$= \$0.455$$

(Note that M_e is lower than M_o by the amount of the right; that is, from \$40 to \$39.545.)

---

[19] A stock purchaser becomes a "shareholder of record" four *trading* days after purchase.

Some shareholders may decide not to use their rights because of lack of funds or some other reason. These stockholders can sell their rights to other investors who wish to purchase them. Thus, a market exists for the rights, and a market price is established for them. Generally, the market price is higher than the theoretical value, because investors who are optimistic about the stock's short-run performance often "bid up" the price of the right. Investors can earn a higher return by purchasing the rights than by purchasing the stock because of the leverage rights provide. In general, the premium of market value over theoretical value decreases as the rights expiration date approaches. A right is worthless after its expiration date.

One can demonstrate that there is no net gain or loss to shareholders either from exercising the rights or from selling the right at the theoretical formula value.[20] For example, suppose an investor owns 100 shares of the Miller Company common stock discussed earlier. The investor is entitled to purchase 10 (.10 × 100) additional shares at $35 per share. Prior to the rights offering, the 100 shares of Miller Company are valued at $4,000 (100 shares × $40 per share). *Exercise* of the rights will give the investor ten additional shares at a cost of $35 per share or a total of $350. These 110 shares will be valued at $4,350 (110 × $39.545). Deducting the cost of these additional shares ($350) from the total value of the shares ($4,350), one obtains the same value ($4,000) as before the rights offering. *Sale* of the rights will yield $45.50 (100 × $.455) to the investor. Combining this value with the $3,954.50 (100 × $39.545) value of the 100 shares still owned, one also obtains the same value ($4,000) as before the rights offering.

QUESTIONS AND TOPICS FOR DISCUSSION

1. What is *bond refunding*? At what relative level of interest rates is bond refunding most likely to occur? Explain.
2. What is the difference between majority voting and cumulative voting?
3. What is the *preemptive right* of common stockholders? In what type of company is the preemptive right important? Unimportant?

PROBLEMS*

1. The Springfield Gas and Electric Company is considering refunding $50 million of 11 percent debt with an 8 percent, 20-year debt issue. The existing, or old, issue also matures in 20 years and now is callable at 108 percent of par. The unamortized flotation cost on the old issue is $400,000 and the flotation cost of the new issue is 0.875 percent. The company estimates that both issues will be outstanding for 4 weeks, resulting in overlapping interest. The company has a weighted cost of capital of 10.0 percent and a 40 percent marginal tax rate. In addition, the company's financial management feels as though the present interest rate decline has nearly bottomed out. Calculate the net present value of the refunding, and make a recommendation to management on whether or not to refund.
2. Suppose you have accumulated a sizable investment (100,000 common shares) in Alpine Land and Development Company. You are dissatisfied with the performance of the present management and are considering running for the board of directors. The company has a nine-member board and a total of 1.5

[20] This analysis ignores any brokerage fees incurred in the sale of the rights.
* Colored numbers denote problems that have check answers provided at the end of the book.

million common shares outstanding. Assume that all shares will be voted in the upcoming election and that four of the nine board members are up for reelection.

    a. If the voting procedure is cumulative, what is the minimum number of shares necessary to ensure your election to the board? Is it possible for you to be elected with fewer votes? Explain.

    b. Suppose a close friend of yours also owns a good deal of Alpine and shares your feelings about the present management. If the voting procedure is cumulative, how many shares are necessary to elect both you and your friend to the board?

    c. If the voting procedure is majority, how many votes are necessary for election in Parts a and b of this problem? Explain your answer.

3. Oswego Manufacturing Company has decided to sell additional common stock through a rights offering. The company has 50 million shares outstanding and plans to sell an additional 5 million shares through the rights offering. Each shareholder will receive 1 right for each share currently held, and thus each right will entitle shareholders to purchase 0.1 share. Oswego's common stock is currently selling at $50 a share, and the subscription price of the rights will be $45 a share.

    a. Calculate the theoretical value of the right for both the *rights-on* and the *ex-rights* cases.

    b. How much is the market price of the company's stock expected to drop on the *ex-rights* date, all other things being equal? Why?

    c. If the market price of Oswego's common stock increases to $52 a share, what will the theoretical value of the right be (rights-on)?

    d. Discuss the trend of the right's market price over its life, assuming the company's common stock continues to trade in the $50 range. (No numerical calculations are necessary for this part of the problem.)

PART

VII

The Management of Working Capital

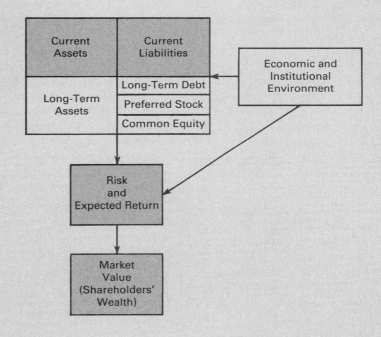

This part of the book considers the financial management of a firm's current assets and current liabilities. This is called *working capital management*. Chapter 17 deals with working capital policy, with emphasis on the risk–return tradeoffs that are implied. Chapter 18 deals with the management of cash and marketable securities; Chapter 19, with accounts receivable and inventories. Chapter 20 looks at current liabilities and the sources of short-term credit. Working capital management influences both the risk of a firm and its expected returns. As such, it is an important determinant of firm value.

CHAPTER

17

Working Capital Policy

KEY CHAPTER CONCEPTS

1. Examination of a firm's operating cycle and cash conversion cycle are important in analyzing its liquidity.

2. Working capital policy decisions include
   a. Investment—level of working capital.
   b. Financing—proportions of short-term and long-term debt.

3. Determination of the optimal level of working capital investment involves profitability versus risk tradeoff analysis:
   a. Higher levels of working capital reduce profitability.
   b. Higher levels of working capital reduce the risk of financial difficulties.

4. Determination of the optimal proportions of short- and long-term debt involves profitability versus risk tradeoff analysis:
   a. Higher proportions of short-term debt increase profitability because of generally lower interest costs.
   b. Higher proportions of short-term debt increase the risk of financial difficulties.

5. Overall working capital policy involves analyzing the *joint* impact of the working capital investment decision and the working capital financing decision on the firm's risk and profitability.

GLOSSARY OF NEW TERMS

Cash conversion cycle The net time interval between the collection of cash receipts from product sales and the cash payments for the company's various resources. The cash conversion cycle is calculated by subtracting the payables deferral period from the operating cycle.

Fluctuating current assets Current assets affected by the seasonal or cyclical nature of the company's sales.

Inventory conversion period The length of time required to produce and sell the product.

Liquidity The ability of a firm to meet its cash obligations as they come due.

Matching approach A financing plan in which the maturity structure of a firm's liabilities is made to correspond exactly to the life of its assets.

Net working capital The difference between a firm's current assets and current liabilities. The term *net working capital* is used interchangeably with *working capital*.

Operating cycle For a typical company it consists of three primary activities: purchasing resources, producing the product, and distributing (selling) the product. The operating cycle is calculated by summing the inventory conversion period and the receivables conversion period.

Payables deferral period The length of time the firm is able to defer payment on its resource purchases.

Permanent current assets Current assets held to meet the company's long-term minimum needs.

Receivables conversion period The length of time required to collect sales receipts. Receivables conversion period is another name for the average collection period.

Working capital The difference between a firm's current assets and current liabilities. The term *working capital* is used interchangeably with *net working capital*.

Going Broke while Making a Profit*

At the beginning of the year, George Mills was in good spirits. He was president of CAM Products, a firm that manufactured computer connectors for $6 each and sold them for $8 each. Demand was strong in this segment of the computer market. Mills kept a 30-day inventory, paid his bills promptly, and billed his customers on terms of net 30 days (that is, payments were due in 30 days). Sales forecasts had been accurate, and a steady increase was anticipated over the next year.

On January 1, the firm's books read as follows:

Cash = $8,000
Inventory = $6,000
Receivables = $8,000

In January Mills sold 1,000 connectors, produced at a cost of $6,000, and collected receivables of $8,000. January's profits totaled $2,000.

On February 1 the firm's books read as follows:

Cash = $10,000
Inventory = $6,000
Receivables = $8,000

February sales increased to an expected 1,500 units. To maintain a 30-day inventory, production was increased to 2,000 units at a cost of $12,000. All January receivables were collected, and profits through February totaled $5,000.

On March 1 the account balances were as follows:

Cash = $6,000
Inventory = $9,000
Receivables = $12,000

March sales increased to 2,000 units. Collections from February were made on time. Production was increased to 2,500 units to maintain a 2,000-unit inventory. Profits for the month totaled $4,000 ($9,000 year to date).

On April 1 the books read as follows:

Cash = $3,000
Inventory = $12,000
Receivables = $16,000

Sales increased to 2,500 units in April; Mills was overjoyed. Customers continued to pay on time. Production was increased to 3,000 units to maintain a 2,500-unit inventory. Profits for the month totaled $5,000 ($14,000 year to date). Mills headed for a long-deserved vacation in the islands.

On May 1 the books read as follows:

Cash = $1,000
Inventory = $15,000
Receivables = $20,000

In May sales exploded to new records—3,000 units—and production was increased to 3,500. Profits for the first 5 months of the year were $20,000. Then Mills got an unexpected call from his accountant, telling him to come home as quickly as possible. The firm was out of cash.

On June 1 CAM Products' accounts had the following balances:

Cash = $0
Inventory = $18,000
Receivables = $24,000

Mills came home, confused and perplexed, and immediately arranged a meeting with his banker.

This example illustrates the importance of proper planning and management of a firm's working capital. This chapter is the first of four chapters dealing with this important area.

* Adapted from "How to Go Broke . . . While Making a Profit." *Business Week* (April 28, 1956), pp. 46–54.

INTRODUCTION

Working capital policy involves decisions about a company's current assets and current liabilities—what they consist of, how they are used, and how their mix affects the risk versus return characteristics of the company. Both the terms *working capital,* and *net working capital* normally denote the *difference* between the company's current assets and current liabilities. The two terms frequently are used interchangeably.

Working capital policies, through their effect on the firm's expected future returns and the risk associated with these returns, ultimately have an impact on shareholder wealth. Effective working capital policies are crucial to a firm's long-run growth and survival. If, for example, a company lacks the working capital needed to expand production and sales, it may lose revenues and profits. A firm needs to maintain high enough working capital levels that it remains *liquid;* that is, it meets its cash obligations as they come due. Otherwise, it may incur the costs associated with a deteriorating credit rating, a potential forced liquidation of assets, and possible bankruptcy.

Working capital management is a continuing process that involves a number of day-to-day operations and decisions that determine the following:

- The firm's level of current asset investment.
- The proportions of short-term and long-term debt the firm will use to finance its assets.
- The level of investment in each type of current asset.
- The specific sources and mix of short-term credit (current liabilities) the firm should employ.

Working capital differs from *fixed* capital in terms of the time required to recover the investment in a given asset. In the case of fixed capital, or long-term assets (such as land, buildings, and equipment), a company usually needs several years or more to recover the initial investment. In contrast, working capital is turned over, or circulated, at a relatively rapid rate. Investments in inventories and accounts receivable usually are recovered during a firm's normal operating cycle, when inventories are sold and receivables are collected.

This chapter, which is the first of four dealing with this important area of finance, considers the *aggregate* level of current assets and current liabilities a firm may employ. The next two chapters detail the optimal level of investment in the major current asset accounts—specifically, Chapter 18 deals with cash and marketable securities; and Chapter 19 covers accounts receivable and inventories. Finally, Chapter 20 discusses the specific sources and appropriate mixes of short-term credit.

━━ OPERATING CYCLE ANALYSIS

A company's operating cycle typically consists of three primary activities: purchasing resources, producing the product, and distributing (selling) the product. These activities create funds flows that are both unsynchronized and uncertain. They are unsynchronized because cash disbursements (for example, payments for resource purchases) usually take place before cash receipts (for example, collection of receivables). They are uncertain because future sales and costs, which generate the respective receipts and disbursements, cannot be forecasted with complete accuracy. If the firm is to maintain liquidity and function properly, it has to invest funds in various short-term assets (working capital) during this cycle. It has to maintain a *cash balance* to pay the bills as they come due. In addition, the company must invest in *inventories* to fill customer orders promptly. And, finally, the company invests in *accounts receivable* to extend credit to its customers.

Figure 17-1 illustrates the operating cycle of a typical firm.[1] The *operating cycle* is equal to the length of the inventory and receivables conversion periods:

$$\text{Operating cycle} = \text{Inventory conversion period} + \text{Receivables conversion period} \quad \textbf{(17.1)}$$

The *inventory conversion period* is the length of time required to produce and sell the product. It is defined as follows:

$$\text{Inventory conversion period} = \frac{\text{Average inventory}}{\text{Cost of sales/365}} \quad \textbf{(17.2)}$$

The *receivables conversion period*, or average collection period, represents the length of time required to collect the sales receipts. It is calculated as follows:

$$\text{Receivables conversion period} = \frac{\text{Accounts receivable}}{\text{Annual credit sales/365}} \quad \textbf{(17.3)}$$

The *payables deferral period* is the length of time the firm is able to defer payment on its various resource purchases (for example, materials, wages, and taxes). Equation 17.4 is used to calculate the payables deferral period:

$$\text{Payables deferral period} = \frac{\text{Accounts payable} + \text{Salaries, benefits, and payroll taxes payable}}{(\text{Cost of sales} + \text{Selling, general and administrative expense}) / 365} \quad \textbf{(17.4)}$$

Finally, the *cash conversion cycle* represents the net time interval between the collection of cash receipts from product sales and the cash payments for the company's various resource purchases. It is calculated as follows:

$$\text{Cash conversion cycle} = \text{Operating cycle} - \text{payables deferral period} \quad \textbf{(17.5)}$$

[1] The following discussion is based on Verlyn D. Richards and Eugene J. Laughlin. "A Cash Conversion Cycle Approach to Liquidity Analysis," *Financial Management* 9 (Spring 1980): 32–38.

F I G U R E 17-1   **Operating Cycle of a Typical Company**

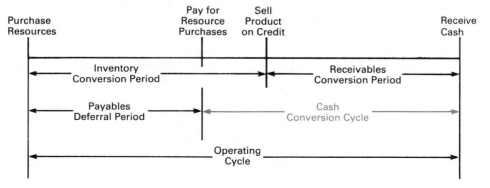

The cash conversion cycle shows the time interval over which additional nonspontaneous sources of working capital financing must be obtained to carry out the firm's activities.[2] An increase in the length of the operating cycle, without a corresponding increase in the payables deferral period, lengthens the cash conversion cycle and creates further working capital financing needs for the company.

Table 17-1 shows an actual cash conversion cycle analysis for Sysco Corporation, the largest distributor of food service products in the United States. Sysco's liquidity, as measured by the current and quick ratios, appears to have deteriorated in 1988, compared to 1987. However, analysis of the cash conversion cycle shows that the company's liquidity position remained about the same in both 1988 and 1987. In 1988, the increase in length of the operating cycle is offset by a roughly equal increase in the length of the payables deferral period, causing the length of the cash conversion cycle to remain about 30 days.

IMPORTANCE OF WORKING CAPITAL

It already has been noted that a firm must have working capital to operate and survive. In many industries, working capital (current assets) constitutes a relatively large percentage of total assets. In the manufacturing sector, for example, current assets comprise about 40 percent of the total assets of all U.S. manufacturing corporations. Among the wholesaling and retailing sectors, the percentages are even higher—in the 50 to 60 percent range.

Table 17-2 shows the distribution of aggregate assets for several large companies. For the six companies shown, current assets as a percentage of total assets range from 20.0 to 55.3 percent. Exxon, with its relatively high percentage of fixed assets, has a relatively low percentage of current assets. In contrast, Merck, a health products company, has a relatively high percentage of current assets, because of its high level of cash. Dayton Hudson, a diversified retailer that owns both Target and Mervyn's stores, has about 25 percent of its assets in inventories. IBM has about 25 percent of its assets in receivables. Because current assets constitute a relatively high percentage

[2] Spontaneous sources of financing (such as trade credit offered by suppliers) automatically expand (contract) as the company's volume of purchases increases (decreases). Nonspontaneous sources of financing (such as bank loans), in contrast, do not automatically expand or contract with the volume of purchases. This concept is discussed further in Chapter 20, which deals with sources of short-term funds.

Cash Conversion Cycle Analysis for Sysco Corporation	1988	1987
Liquidity ratios:		
Current ratio	1.87	2.03
Quick ratio	1.07	1.12
Cash conversion cycle:		
Inventory conversion period	28 days	26 days
Receivables conversion period	29 days	30 days
Operating cycle	57 days	56 days
Less payables deferral period	27 days	26 days
Cash conversion cycle	30 days	30 days

TABLE 17-1

SOURCE: Sysco Corporation, *Annual Report*, 1988, 1987.

Distribution of Aggregate Assets in Selected Companies

	Dayton Hudson	Exxon	General Motors	IBM	Merck	3M
Cash and marketable securities	0.8%	3.2%	7.8%	8.4%	25.3%	10.1%
Receivables—net	18.8	8.2	23.3	24.8	16.7	19.4
Inventories—net	25.6	7.0	8.8	13.1	10.7	20.5
All other current assets	0.6	1.6	4.0	2.1	2.6	3.1
Total current assets	45.8%	20.0%	43.9%	48.4%	55.3%	53.1%
Fixed assets—net	51.8	72.8	35.2	32.1	33.4	34.4
All other noncurrent assets	2.4	7.2	20.9	19.5	11.3	12.5
Total assets	100.0%	100.0%	100.0%	100.0%	100.0%	100.0%

SOURCES: 1988 *Annual Reports:* Dayton Hudson Corporation; Exxon Corporation; General Motors Corporation; International Business Machines Corporation; Merck & Co., Inc.; Minnesota Mining and Manufacturing Company.

of total assets in most businesses, it is important to have effective working capital policies.

In a survey of large industrial corporations, it was found that about 30 percent of the companies have a formal policy for the management of their working capital and another 60 percent have an informal policy.[3] A significantly greater percentage of the larger companies within the sample have a formal policy than do the smaller companies. In almost one-half of the companies that responded to the survey, the financial vice-president has responsibility for establishing the company's overall working capital policy. The president and treasurer are the next most frequently mentioned positions as having responsibility for working capital policy. There is considerable variation in the frequency with which companies review their working capital policy. Annual, quarterly, and monthly reviews are mentioned with about the same relative frequency (approximately 14 to 18 percent), whereas approximately one-half of the companies review working capital policy "whenever necessary."

A firm's net working capital position not only is important from an internal standpoint; it also is widely used as one measure of the firm's *risk*. *Risk*, as used in this context, deals with the probability that a firm will encounter financial difficulties, such as the inability to pay bills on time. All other things being equal, the more net working capital a firm has, the more likely that it will be able to meet current financial obligations. Because net working capital is one measure of risk, a company's net working capital position affects its ability to obtain debt financing. Many loan agreements with commercial banks and other lending institutions contain a provision requiring the firm to maintain a minimum net working capital position. Likewise, bond indentures also often contain such provisions.

LEVELS OF WORKING CAPITAL INVESTMENT

The remainder of this chapter deals with a firm's overall working capital policy. The overall policy considers *both* the level of working capital investment and its financing. In practice, the firm has to determine the *joint*

[3] Keith V. Smith and Shirley B. Sell, "Working Capital Management in Practice," in *Readings in the Management of Working Capital* 2d ed, Keith V. Smith, ed. (St. Paul, MN: West Publishing Company, 1980).

impact of these two decisions upon its profitability and risk. However, to permit a better understanding of working capital policy, the working capital investment decision is discussed in this section, and the working capital financing decision is discussed in the following section. In the final section of the chapter, the two decisions are considered together.

The size and nature of a firm's investment in current assets is a function of a number of different factors, including the following:

- The type of products manufactured.
- The length of the operating cycle.
- The sales level (because higher sales require more investment in inventories and receivables).
- Inventory policies (for example, the amount of safety stocks maintained; that is, inventories needed to meet higher than expected demand or unanticipated delays in obtaining new inventories).
- Credit policies.
- How efficiently the firm manages current assets. (Obviously, the more effectively management economizes on the amount of cash, marketable securities, inventories, and receivables employed, the smaller the working capital requirements.)

For the purposes of discussion and analysis, these factors are held constant for the remainder of this chapter. Instead of focusing on these factors, this section examines the risk–return tradeoffs associated with alternative levels of working capital investments.

Profitability versus Risk Tradeoff for Alternative Levels of Working Capital Investment

Before deciding on an appropriate level of working capital investment, a firm's management has to evaluate the tradeoff between expected profitability and the risk that it may be unable to meet its financial obligations. Profitability is measured by the rate of (operating) return on total assets; that is, EBIT/total assets. As mentioned earlier in this chapter, the risk that the firm will encounter financial difficulties is related to the firm's net working capital position.

Figure 17-2 illustrates three alternative working capital policies.[4] Each curve in the figure demonstrates the relationship between the firm's investment in current assets and sales for that particular policy.

Policy C represents a *conservative* approach to working capital management. Under this policy the company holds a relatively large proportion of its total assets in the form of current assets. Because the rate of return on current assets normally is assumed to be less than the rate of return on fixed assets,[5] this policy results in a *lower expected profitability* as measured by the rate of return on the company's total assets. Assuming that current liabilities remain constant, this type of policy also increases the company's

---

[4] The relationship between current assets and sales is drawn as a concave, *curvilinear* function, because it is assumed that economies of scale exist in the holding of current assets. In other words, increases in sales normally should require less than proportionate increases in current assets, particularly for cash and inventories. The amount of the company's *fixed* assets is held constant in the following discussion.
[5] This assumption is based on the principle that the lower an asset's risk, the lower its expected return. Current assets normally are less risky than fixed assets, because they can be converted into cash more easily and with less potential loss in value. Therefore, current assets should have lower expected returns.

FIGURE 17-2

**Three Alternative
Working Capital
Investment Policies**

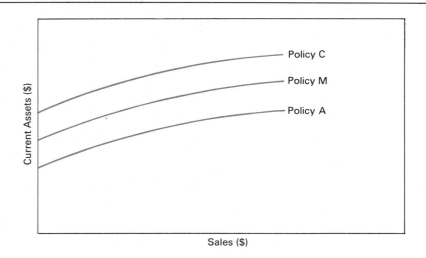

net working capital position, resulting in a *lower risk* that the firm will encounter financial difficulties.

In contrast to Policy C, Policy A represents an *aggressive* approach. Under this policy the company holds a relatively small proportion of its total assets in the form of lower yielding current assets and thus has relatively less net working capital. As a result, this policy yields a *higher expected profitability* and a *higher risk* that the company will encounter financial difficulties.

Finally, Policy M represents a *moderate* approach, because expected profitability and risk levels fall between those of Policy C and Policy A.

These three approaches may be illustrated with the following example. Burlington Northern Inc., a Seattle-based railroad and natural resources company, formed Burlington Resources, Inc., a new subsidiary, in 1988. Then Burlington Northern sold off a portion of the newly created subsidiary in an initial public offering. The proceeds from the stock offering were added to Burlington Resources' working capital. As a result, the management of Burlington Resources faced working capital decisions of the types discussed in this section. In addition, the numbers used in this section probably are typical of the numbers used by Burlington Resources in its working capital policy discussions. Suppose Burlington Resources has forecasted sales next year to be $100 million and EBIT to be $10 million. The company has fixed assets of $30 million and current liabilities totaling $20 million.

Burlington Resources is considering three alternative working capital investment policies:

■ An *aggressive* policy consisting of $35 million in current assets.
■ A *moderate* policy consisting of $40 million in current assets.
■ A *conservative* policy consisting of $45 million in current assets.

Assume that sales and EBIT remain constant under each policy.[6] Table 17-3 contains the results of the three proposed policies.

[6] In practice, however, this assumption may not be completely realistic, because a firm's sales usually are a function of its inventory and credit policies. Higher levels of finished goods inventories and a more liberal credit extension policy—both of which increase a firm's investment in current assets— also may lead to higher sales. This effect can be incorporated into the analysis by modifying the sales and EBIT projections under the various alternative working capital policies. Although changing these projections would affect the numerical values contained in Table 17-3, it should not affect the general conclusions concerning the profitability versus risk tradeoffs.

TABLE 17-3

Profitability and Risk of Alternative Working Capital Investment Policies for Burlington Resources (in millions of dollars)

	Aggressive	Moderate	Conservative
	Relatively *Small* Investment in Current Assets	Moderate Investment in Current Assets	Relatively *Large* Investment in Current Assets
Current assets (C/A)	$ 35	$ 40	$ 45
Fixed assets (F/A)	30	30	30
Total assets (T/A)	$ 65	$ 70	$ 75
Current liabilities (C/L)	$ 20	$ 20	$ 20
Forecasted sales	$100	$100	$100
Expected EBIT	$ 10	$ 10	$ 10
Expected rate of return on total assets (EBIT ÷ T/A)	15.38%	14.29%	13.33%
Net working capital position (C/A − C/L)	$ 15	$ 20	$ 25
Current ratio (C/A ÷ C/L)	1.75	2.0	2.25

The aggressive policy would yield the highest expected rate of return on total assets, 15.38 percent, whereas the conservative policy would yield the lowest rate of return, 13.33 percent. The aggressive policy also would result in a lower net working capital position ($15 million) than would the conservative policy ($25 million).

Using net working capital as a measure of risk, the aggressive policy is most risky, and the conservative policy is the least risky. The current ratio is another measure of a firm's ability to meet financial obligations as they come due. The aggressive policy would yield the lowest current ratio, and the conservative policy would yield the highest current ratio.

Optimal Level of Working Capital Investment

The optimal level of working capital investment is the level expected to maximize shareholder wealth. It is a function of several factors, including the variability of sales and cash flows and the degree of operating and financial leverage employed by the firm. Therefore no single working capital investment policy is necessarily optimal for all firms.

▬ PROPORTIONS OF SHORT-TERM AND LONG-TERM FINANCING

Not only does a firm have to be concerned about the *level* of current assets; it also has to determine the *proportions* of short- and long-term debt to use in financing these assets. This decision also involves tradeoffs between profitability and risk.

Sources of debt financing are classified according to their *maturities*. Specifically, they can be categorized as being either *short-term* or *long-term*, with short-term sources having maturities of 1 year or less and long-term sources having maturities of greater than 1 year.[7]

Cost of Short-Term versus Long-Term Debt

Recall from Chapter 2 that the *term structure of interest rates* is defined as the relationship among interest rates of debt securities that differ in their length of time to maturity. Historically long-term interest rates normally have exceeded short-term rates.

Also, because of the reduced flexibility of long-term borrowing relative to short-term borrowing, the *effective* cost of long-term debt may be higher than the cost of short-term debt, even when short-term interest rates are equal to or greater than long-term rates. With long-term debt, a firm incurs the interest expense even during times when it has no immediate need for the funds, such as during seasonal or cyclical downturns. With short-term debt, in contrast, the firm can avoid the interest costs on unneeded funds by paying off (or not renewing) the debt. In summary, the cost of long-term debt generally is higher than the cost of short-term debt.

Risk of Long-Term versus Short-Term Debt

Borrowing companies have different attitudes toward the relative risk of long-term versus short-term debt than lenders. Whereas lenders normally feel that risk increases with maturity, borrowers feel that there is more risk associated with short-term debt. The reasons for this are twofold.

First, there is always the chance that a firm will not be able to refund its short-term debt. When a firm's debt matures, it either pays off the debt as part of a debt reduction program or arranges new financing. At the time of maturity, however, the firm could be faced with financial problems resulting from such events as strikes, natural disasters, or recessions that cause sales and cash inflows to decline. Under these circumstances the firm may find it very difficult or even impossible to obtain the needed funds. This could lead to operating and financial difficulties. The more frequently a firm must refinance debt, the greater is the risk of its not being able to obtain the necessary financing.

Second, short-term interest rates tend to fluctuate more over time than long-term interest rates. As a result, a firm's interest expenses and expected earnings after interest and taxes are subject to more variation (risk) over time with short-term debt than with long-term debt.

Profitability versus Risk Tradeoff for Alternative Financing Plans

A company's need for financing is equal to the sum of its fixed and current assets.[8] Current assets can be divided into the following two categories:

- *Permanent* current assets.
- *Fluctuating* current assets.

Fluctuating current assets are those affected by the seasonal or cyclical nature of company sales. For example, a firm must make larger investments

---

[7] In this discussion the term *long-term financing* includes any *intermediate-term financing*.
[8] The following discussion assumes a constant amount of equity financing.

in inventories and receivables during peak selling periods than during other periods of the year. Permanent current assets are those held to meet the company's minimum long-term needs (for example, "safety stocks" of cash and inventories). Figure 17-3 illustrates a typical firm's financing needs over time. The fixed assets and permanent current assets lines are upward sloping, indicating that the investment in these assets and, by extension, financing needs tend to increase over time for a firm whose sales are increasing.

One way in which a firm can meet its financing needs is by using a *matching approach* in which the maturity structure of the firm's liabilities is made to correspond exactly to the life of its assets. This is illustrated in Figure 17-4. As can be seen, fixed and permanent current assets are financed with long-term debt and equity funds, whereas fluctuating current assets are financed with short-term debt.[9] Application of this approach is not as simple as it appears, however. In practice the uncertainty associated with the lives of individual assets makes the matching approach difficult to implement.

Figures 17-5 and 17-6 illustrate two other financing plans. Figure 17-5 shows a *conservative* approach, which uses a relatively high proportion of long-term debt. The relatively low proportion of short-term debt in this approach reduces the risk that the company will be unable to refund its debt, and it also reduces the risk associated with interest rate fluctuations. At the same time, however, this approach cuts down on the expected returns

[9] This analysis does not consider "spontaneous" sources of short-term credit, such as accounts payable. Because spontaneous short-term credit is virtually cost-free when used within reasonable limits, a company normally will employ this type of credit to the fullest extent possible before using "negotiated" sources of short-term credit, such as bank loans. Because none of the conclusions concerning the tradeoff between profitability and risk are affected by ignoring spontaneous sources of short-term credit, it need not be considered here.

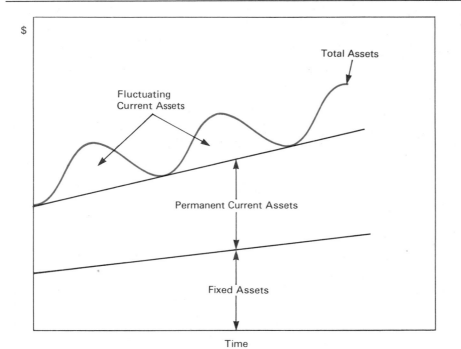

Time

FIGURE 17-3

Financing Needs over Time

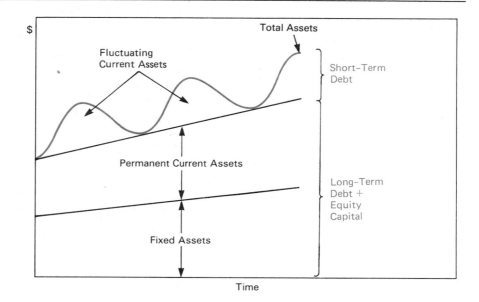

FIGURE 17-4

Matching Approach to Asset Financing

available to stockholders, because the cost of long-term debt is generally greater than the cost of short-term debt.

Figure 17-6 illustrates an *aggressive* approach, which uses a relatively high proportion of short-term debt. A firm that uses this particular approach must refund debt more frequently, and this increases the risk that it will be unable to obtain new financing as needed. In addition, the greater possible fluctuations in interest expenses associated with this financing plan also add to the firm's risk (variability in earnings). These higher risks are

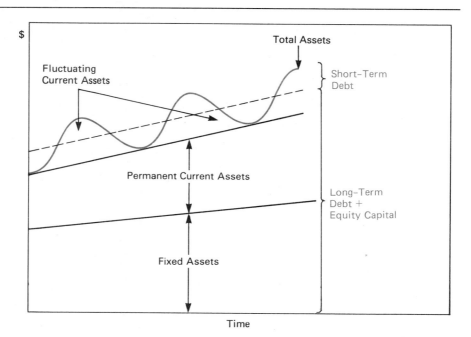

FIGURE 17-5

Conservative Approach to Asset Financing

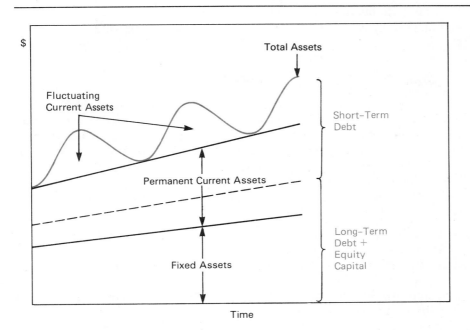

FIGURE 17-6

Aggressive Approach to Asset Financing

offset by the higher expected after-tax earnings that result from the lower costs of short-term debt.

Table 17-4 shows two years of actual working capital data for Dayton Hudson, a diversified retailer that owns both Target and Mervyn's stores. The company's total current assets and inventories fluctuate during the year, peaking during autumn as the holiday shopping season approaches. Its notes payable and accounts payable also fluctuate and peak in autumn. This suggests that the company is using more or less a matching approach

TABLE 17-4 **Working Capital Data for Dayton Hudson Corporation (in millions of dollars)**

	January 31, 1987	May 2, 1987	August 1, 1987	October 31, 1987	January 30, 1988	April 30, 1988	July 30, 1988	October 29, 1988
Cash and marketable securities	$ 224	$ 116	$ 102	$ 89	$ 175	$ 138	$ 109	$ 91
Accounts receivable	1,053	896	843	907	1,074	940	901	994
Inventories	1,313	1,559	1,594	2,147	1,623	1,884	1,767	2,239
Total current assets (C/A)*	$2,617	$2,594	$2,563	$3,167	$2,908	$2,996	$2,810	$3,366
Notes payable	$ -	$ 162	$ 109	$ 631	$ 353	$ 431	$ 306	$ 584
Accounts payable	842	864	843	1,241	1,055	1,073	947	1,288
Total current liabilities (C/L)*	$1,425	$1,508	$1,437	$2,392	$1,986	$2,007	$1,738	$2,429
Net working capital (C/A − C/L)	$1,192	$1,086	$1,126	$ 775	$ 922	$ 989	$1,072	$ 937

* The totals differ from the sums of individual entries because other current assets and other current liabilities are omitted from this table.

SOURCE: Dayton Hudson Corporation, *Annual* and *Quarterly Reports: 1987, 1988.*

to finance its fluctuating current assets. In addition, the company's cash and marketable securities reaches a maximum in January after the holiday shopping season. This suggests that Dayton Hudson also is using a conservative approach, to some extent. Overall, Dayton Hudson seems to have chosen an approach that is between the matching and conservative approaches.

Consider again Burlington Resources, which has total assets of $70 million and common shareholders' equity of $28 million on its books, thus requiring $42 million in short- or long-term debt financing. Forecasted sales for next year are $100 million and expected EBIT is $10 million. Interest rates on the company's short-term and long-term debt are 8 and 10 percent respectively, due to an upward sloping yield curve.

Burlington Resources is considering three different combinations of short-term and long-term debt financing:

- An *aggressive* plan consisting of $30 million in short-term debt (STD) and $12 million in long-term debt (LTD).
- A *moderate* plan consisting of $20 million in short-term debt and $22 million in long-term debt.
- A *conservative* plan consisting of $10 million in short-term debt and $32 million in long-term debt.

Table 17-5 shows the data for each of these alternative proposed financing plans. From the standpoint of profitability, the aggressive financing plan would yield the highest expected rate of return to the stockholders—13.6 percent—whereas the conservative plan would yield the lowest rate of return—12.9 percent. In contrast, the aggressive plan would involve a greater degree of risk that the company will be unable to refund its debt, because it assumes $30 million in short-term debt and the conservative plan assumes only $10 million in short-term debt. This is further substantiated by the fact that the company's net working capital position and current ratio would be lowest under the aggressive plan and highest under the conservative plan—indicating that the degree of risk that the company will be unable to meet financial obligations would be greater with the aggressive plan. The moderate financing plan represents a middle-of-the-road approach, and the expected rate of return and risk level are between the aggressive and the conservative approaches. In summary, both expected profitability and risk increase as the proportion of short-term debt increases.[10]

Optimal Proportions of Short-Term and Long-Term Debt

As it is the case with working capital investment policy, no one combination of short- and long-term debt is necessarily optimal for all firms. In choosing a financing policy that maximizes shareholder wealth, a firm's financial manager also must take into account various other factors, such as the variability of sales and cash flows, that affect the valuation of the firm.

---

[10] This example assumes that the costs of short-term and long-term debt would be the same for each of the three financing policies. In practice, however, this would probably not be the case, because lenders generally require higher interest rates before making loans involving higher risks. Thus, a company following an aggressive financing policy probably will have to pay slightly higher interest rates on debt than a company following a conservative policy. This effect can be incorporated into the analysis by modifying the interest rates on short-term and long-term debt under the various financing policies. This would affect the numerical values in the example, but it should not affect the general conclusions concerning the profitability versus risk tradeoffs.

TABLE 17-5 **Profitability and Risk of Alternative Financing Policies for Burlington Resources (in millions of dollars)**

	Aggressive	Moderate	Conservative
	Relatively *Large* Amount of Short-Term Debt	Moderate Amount of Short-Term Debt	Relatively *Small* Amount of Short-Term Debt
Current assets (C/A)	$ 40	$ 40	$ 40
Fixed assets (F/A)	30	30	30
Total assets (T/A)	$ 70	$ 70	$ 70
Current liabilities (STD)(C/L) (interest rate, 8%)	$ 30	$ 20	$ 10
Long-term liabilities (LTD) (interest rate, 10%)	12	22	32
Total liabilities (60% of T/A)	$ 42	$ 42	$ 42
Common equity	28	28	28
Total liabilities and common equity	$ 70	$ 70	$ 70
Forecasted sales	$100	$100	$100
Expected EBIT	10	10	10
Less Interest: STD, 8% / LTD, 10%	2.4 } 3.6 / 1.2 }	1.6 } 3.8 / 2.2 }	0.8 } 4.0 / 3.2 }
Taxable income	$ 6.4	$ 6.2	$ 6.0
Less Taxes (40%)	2.6	2.5	2.4
Net income after taxes	$ 3.8	$ 3.7	$ 3.6
Expected rate of return on common equity	13.6 %	13.2%	12.9%
Net working capital position (C/A − C/L)	$ 10	$ 20	$ 30
Current ratio (C/A ÷ C/L)	1.33	2.0	4.0

▄▄▄ OVERALL WORKING CAPITAL POLICY

Until now this chapter has analyzed the working capital investment and financing decisions independent of one another in order to examine the profitability–risk tradeoffs associated with each, assuming that all other factors are held constant. Effective working capital policy, however, also requires the consideration of the *joint* impact of these decisions on the firm's profitability and risk.

Referring to Burlington Resources again, assume that the company is 60 percent debt financed (both short-term and long-term) and 40 percent financed with common stock. Also, it is evaluating three alternative working capital investment and financing policies. The *aggressive* policy would require a relatively *small* investment in current assets, $35 million, and a relatively *large* amount of short-term debt, $30 million. The *conservative* policy would require a relatively *large* investment in current assets, $45 million, and a relatively *small* amount of short-term debt, $10 million. The firm also is considering a middle-of-the-road approach, which would involve a *moderate* investment in current assets, $40 million, and a *moderate* amount of short-term debt, $20 million.

Table 17-6 shows the data for each approach. The aggressive working capital policy is expected to yield the highest return on shareholders' equity, 15.4 percent, whereas the conservative policy is expected to yield the lowest return, 11.3 percent. The net working capital and current ratio are lowest under the aggressive policy and highest under the conservative policy, indicating that the aggressive policy is the most risky. The moderate policy yields an expected return and risk level somewhere between the aggressive and the conservative policies.

Whereas this type of analysis will not directly yield the optimal working capital investment and financing policies a company should choose, it can give the financial manager some insight into the profitability–risk tradeoffs of alternative policies. With an understanding of these tradeoffs, the financial manager should be able to make better decisions concerning the working capital policy that will lead to a maximization of shareholder wealth.

T A B L E 17-6 Alternative Working Capital Investment and Financing Policies for Burlington Resources (in millions of dollars)

	Aggressive	Moderate	Conservative
	Relatively *Small* Investment in Current Assets; Relatively *Large* Amount of Short-term Debt	Moderate Investment in Current Assets; Moderate Amount of Short-term Debt	Relatively *Large* Investment in Current Assets; Relatively *Small* Amount of Short-term Debt
Current assets (C/A)	$ 35	$ 40	$ 45
Fixed assets (F/A)	30	30	30
Total assets (T/A)	$ 65	$ 70	$ 75
Current liabilities (STD)(C/L) (interest rate, 8%)	$ 30	$ 20	$ 10
Long-term liabilities (LTD) (interest rate, 10%)	9	22	35
Total liabilities (60% of T/A)	$ 39	$ 42	$ 45
Common equity	26	28	30
Total liabilities and common equity	$ 65	$ 70	$ 75
Forecasted sales	$100	$100	$100
Expected EBIT	10	10	10
Less Interest: STD, 8% LTD, 10%	2.4⎫ 0.9⎭ 3.3	1.6⎫ 2.2⎭ 3.8	0.8⎫ 3.5⎭ 4.3
Taxable income	$ 6.7	$ 6.2	$ 5.7
Less Taxes (40%)	2.7	2.5	2.3
Net income after taxes	$ 4.0	$ 3.7	$ 3.4
Expected rate of return on common equity	15.4 %	13.2%	11.3%
Net working capital position (C/A − C/L)	$ 5	$ 20	$ 35
Current ratio (C/A ÷ C/L)	1.17	2.0	4.5

SUMMARY

- *Working capital* is the difference between current assets and current liabilities. The term *working capital* is used interchangeably with the term *net working capital.*

- *Working capital policy* is concerned with determining the *aggregate amount* and *composition* of a firm's current assets and current liabilities.

- Working capital decisions affect both the *expected profitability* and the *risk* of a firm. In this context, *risk* refers to the probability that the firm will encounter financial difficulties, such as the inability to meet current financial obligations.

- When the level of working capital is increased, both the expected profitability and the risk are lowered. Similarly, when the level of working capital is decreased, both the expected profitability and the risk are increased.

- When the proportion of short-term debt used is increased, both the expected profitability and the risk are increased. Similarly, when the proportion of short-term debt used is decreased, both the expected profitability and the risk are lowered.

- Effective working capital policy requires that the working capital investment and financing decisions be analyzed simultaneously so that their *joint* impact on the firm's expected profitability and risk can be evaluated.

- No single working capital investment and financing policy is necessarily *optimal* for all firms. To select the working capital policy that maximizes shareholder wealth, a financial manager should consider additional factors, including the inherent variability in sales and cash flows and the degree of operating and financial leverage employed.

QUESTIONS AND TOPICS FOR DISCUSSION

1. Why does the typical firm need to make investments in working capital?

2. Define and describe the difference between the operating cycle and cash conversion cycle for a typical manufacturing company.

3. Discuss the profitability versus risk tradeoffs associated with alternative levels of working capital investment.

4. Describe the difference between permanent current assets and fluctuating current assets.

5. Why is it possible for the effective cost of long-term debt to exceed the cost of short-term debt, even when short-term interest rates are higher than long-term rates?

6. Describe the matching approach for meeting the financing needs of a company. What is the primary difficulty in implementing this approach?

7. Discuss the profitability versus risk tradeoffs associated with alternative combinations of short-term and long-term debt used in financing a company's assets.

8. As the difference between the costs of short- and long-term debt becomes smaller, which financing plan, aggressive or conservative, becomes more attractive?

9. Why is no single working capital investment and financing policy necessarily optimal for all firms? What additional factors need to be considered in establishing a working capital policy?

10. **a.** Which of the following working capital financing policies subjects the
firm to a greater risk?
  i. Financing permanent current assets with short-term debt.
  ii. Financing fluctuating current assets with long-term debt.
b. Which policy will produce the higher expected profitability?

PROBLEMS*

1. The Fisher Apparel Company balance sheet for the year ended 19X6 follows:

December 31, 19X6
(in thousands of dollars)

Assets

Cash		$ 3,810
Marketable securities		2,700
Accounts receivable		27,480
Inventories		41,295
Plant and equipment	$64,650	
Less Accumulated depreciation	17,100	
Net plant and equipment		47,550
Total assets		$122,835

Liabilities and Stockholders' Equity

Accounts payable	$ 14,582
Current portion of long-term debt	3,000
Accrued wages	1,200
Accrued taxes	3,600
Other current liabilities	2,200
Long-term debt	33,000
Common stock ($10 par)	19,500
Capital contributed in excess of par	15,000
Retained earnings	30,753
Total liabilities and stockholders' equity	$122,835

a. What is Fisher's investment in current assets?
b. Determine Fisher's working capital investment.
c. Determine Fisher's current ratio.
d. Determine Fisher's return on stockholders' equity, if its 19X6 earnings
after tax is $10,000(000).

2. Consider again the comprehensive example involving Burlington Resources
(Table 17-6). In this example it was assumed that forecasted sales and expected EBIT, as well as the interest rates on short-term and long-term debt,
were independent of the firm's working capital investment and financing
policies. However, these assumptions are not always completely realistic in
practice. Sales and EBIT generally are a function of the firm's inventory and
receivables policies. Both of these policies, in turn, affect the firm's level of
investment in working capital. Likewise, the interest rates on short-term and
long-term debt normally are a function of the riskiness of the firm's debt as
perceived by lenders and, hence, are affected by the firm's working capital
investment and financing decisions. Recompute Burlington's rate of return

---

* Colored numbers denote problems that have check answers provided at the end of the book.

on common equity under the following set of assumptions concerning sales, EBIT, and interest rates for each of the three different working capital investment and financing policies.

Policy	Forecasted Sales (in millions of dollars)	Expected EBIT (in millions of dollars)	Interest Rate	
			STD (%)	LTD (%)
Aggressive	$ 98	$ 9.8	8.5	10.5
Moderate	100	10.0	8.0	10.0
Conservative	102	10.2	7.5	9.5

3. The Garcia Industries balance sheet and income statement for the year ended 19X5 are as follows:

Balance Sheet
(in millions of dollars)

Assets		Liabilities and Stockholders' Equity	
Cash	$ 6.0	Accounts payable	$10.0
Accounts receivable	14.0	Salaries, benefits, and	
Inventories	12.0	payroll taxes payable	2.0
Fixed assets, net	40.0	Other current liabilities	10.0
	$72.0	Long-term debt	12.0
		Stockholders' equity	38.0
			$72.0

Income Statement
(in millions of dollars)

Net sales	$100.0
Cost of sales	60.0
Selling, general, and administrative expenses	20.0
Other expenses	15.0
Earnings after tax	$ 5.0

The average inventory over the past 2 years also equals $12.0 million.

a. Determine the length of the inventory conversion period.
b. Determine the length of the receivables conversion period.
c. Determine the length of the operating cycle.
d. Determine the length of the payables deferral period.
e. Determine the length of the cash conversion cycle.
f. What is the meaning of the number you calculated in Part e?

4. Wilson Electric Company, a manufacturer of various types of electrical equipment, is examining its working capital investment policy for next year. Projected fixed assets and current liabilities for next year are $20 million and $18 million, respectively. Sales and EBIT are partially a function of the company's investment in working capital—particularly its investment in

inventories and receivables. Wilson is considering the following three different working capital investment policies:

Working Capital Investment Policy	Investment in Current Assets (in millions of dollars)	Projected Sales (in millions of dollars)	EBIT (in millions of dollars)
Aggressive (small investment in current assets)	$28	$59	$5.9
Moderate (moderate investment in current assets)	30	60	6.0
Conservative (large investment in current assets)	32	61	6.1

a. Determine the following for each of the working capital investment policies:
   i. Rate of return on total assets (that is, EBIT/total assets).
   ii. Net working capital position.
   iii. Current ratio.
b. Describe the profitability versus risk tradeoffs of these three policies.

5. Reynolds Equipment Company is investigating the use of various combinations of short-term and long-term debt in financing its assets. Assume that the company has decided to employ $30 million in current assets, along with $35 million in fixed assets, in its operations next year. Given this level of current assets, anticipated sales and EBIT for next year are $60 million and $6 million, respectively. The company's income tax rate is 40 percent. Stockholders' equity will be used to finance $40 million of its assets, with the remainder being financed by short-term and long-term debt. Reynolds is considering implementing one of the following financing policies:

Financing Policy	Amount of Short-Term Debt (in millions of dollars)	Interest Rate	
		LTD (%)	STD (%)
Aggressive (large amount of short-term debt)	$24	8.5	5.5
Moderate (moderate amount of short-term debt)	18	8.0	5.0
Conservative (small amount of short-term debt)	12	7.5	4.5

a. Determine the following for each of the financing policies:
   i. Expected rate of return on shareholders' equity.
   ii. Net working capital position.
   iii. Current ratio.
b. Evaluate the profitability versus risk tradeoffs of these three policies.

6. Superior Brands, Inc., wishes to analyze the *joint impact* of its working capital investment and financing policies on shareholder return and risk. The company has $40 million in fixed assets. Also, the firm's financial structure consists of short-term and long-term debt and common equity. Superior wishes to maintain a debt to total assets ratio of 50 percent, where debt consists of both short-term and long-term sources. The company's tax rate is 40 percent.

The following information was developed for three different policies under consideration:

Working Capital Investment and Financing Policy	Investment in Current Assets (in millions of dollars)	Amount of STD (in millions of dollars)	Projected Sales (in millions of dollars)	EBIT (in millions of dollars)	Interest Rate LTD (%)	STD (%)
Aggressive	$56	$48	$118	$11.8	9.5	6.5
Moderate	60	36	120	12.0	9.0	6.0
Conservative	64	24	122	12.2	8.5	5.5

a. Determine the following for each of the three working capital investment and financing policies:
  i. Expected rate of return on shareholders' equity.
  ii. Net working capital position.
  iii. Current ratio.
b. Evaluate the profitability versus risk tradeoffs associated with these three policies.

7. Educational Toys, Inc. (ETI), has highly seasonal sales and financing requirements. The company's balance sheet on December 31, 19X0, (*now*) is as follows:

Assets (in millions of dollars)		Liabilities (in millions of dollars)	
		Short-term debt	$ x
Current assets	$20	Long-term debt	y
Fixed assets	34	Net worth (equity)	30
Total assets	$54	Total liabilities and equity	$54

ETI has made the following projections of its asset needs and net additions to retained earnings (that is, equity) for the next 3 years:

Year	Quarter	Fixed Assets (in millions of dollars)	Current Assets (in millions of dollars)	Net Additions to Retained Earnings (in millions of dollars)
19X1	1 (March 31)	$36	$20	$0
	2 (June 30)	36	24	0
	3 (Sept. 30)	36	30	1
	4 (Dec. 31)	36	24	1
19X2	1 (March 31)	38	24	0
	2 (June 30)	38	28	0
	3 (Sept. 30)	38	36	1
	4 (Dec. 31)	38	28	2
19X3	1 (March 31)	40	28	0
	2 (June 30)	40	32	0
	3 (Sept. 30)	40	38	1
	4 (Dec. 31)	40	30	2

Assuming that ETI does not plan to sell any preferred or new common stock over the next 3 years:

a. Determine ETI's quarterly total assets and *total* (short-term and long-term) *debt requirements* for the next 3 years.

b. Plot the firm's *fixed, current,* and *total* assets over time on a graph.

c. Assume that ETI follows a *matching* approach in financing its assets. In other words, long-term debt will be used to finance its fixed and permanent current assets, and short-term debt will be used to finance its fluctuating current assets. The costs of short-term and long-term debt to ETI under this plan are 6 and 8 percent per annum (that is, 1.5 and 2 percent per quarter), respectively. Using this information, determine the following:

   i. The amount of short-term and long-term debt outstanding each quarter.

  ii. ETI's total interest costs over the 3-year period under this approach.

d. ETI also is considering other financing plans. One plan under consideration is a *conservative* policy. Under this policy the company would determine its *maximum* debt requirements for the coming year and finance this entire amount with long-term debt at an interest rate of 8 percent per annum on December 31 of each year. Any funds in excess of its seasonal (quarterly) needs would be invested in short-term interest-bearing securities to yield a 4 percent per annum rate of return. Using this information, determine the following:

   i. The amount of long-term debt ETI would have to borrow each year.

  ii. ETI's *net* interest costs over the 3-year period under this conservative policy.

e. Finally, ETI also is considering an *aggressive* policy. Under this policy the company would determine its *minimum* debt requirements for the coming year on December 31 of each year and finance one-half of this amount with long-term debt, with the remainder being financed by short-term debt. The costs of short-term and long-term debt under this policy are 6 and 8 percent per annum, respectively. Using this information, determine the following:

   i. The amount of short-term and long-term debt outstanding each quarter.

  ii. ETI's total interest costs over the 3-year period under this aggressive policy.

8. Greenwich Industries has forecasted its monthly needs for working capital (net of spontaneous sources such as accounts payable) for 19X3 as follows:

Month	Amount	Month	Amount
January	$7,500,000	July	$6,000,000
February	6,000,000	August	7,500,000
March	3,000,000	September	8,500,000
April	2,500,000	October	9,000,000
May	3,500,000	November	9,500,000
June	4,500,000	December	9,000,000

Short-term borrowing (that is, a bank line of credit) costs the company 10 percent, and long-term borrowing (that is, term loans) costs the company 12 percent. Any funds in excess of its monthly needs can be invested in interest-bearing marketable securities to yield 8 percent per annum.

a. Suppose the company follows a *conservative* policy by financing the *maximum* amount of its working capital requirements for the coming year with long-term borrowing and investing any excess funds in short-term marketable securities. Determine Greenwich's *net* interest costs during 19X3 under this policy.

b. Suppose the company follows an *aggressive* policy by financing *all* its working capital requirements for the coming year with short-term borrowing. Determine Greenwich's interest costs during 19X3 under this policy.

c. Discuss the profitability versus risk tradeoffs associated with these conservative and aggressive working capital financing policies.

9. Gooding Enterprises is considering two alternative working capital investment and financing policies. *Policy A* requires the firm to keep its current assets at 65 percent of forecasted sales and to finance 70 percent of its debt requirements with long-term debt (and 30 percent with short-term debt.) *Policy B*, on the other hand, requires the firm to keep its current assets at 40 percent of forecasted sales and to finance 40 percent of its debt requirements with long-term debt (and 60 percent with short-term debt). Forecasted sales for next year are $20 million. Earnings before interest and taxes are projected to be 15 percent of sales. The firm's corporate income tax rate is 40 percent. Its fixed assets total $10 million. The firm desires to maintain its existing financial structure which consists of 50 percent debt and 50 percent equity. Interest rates on short- and long-term debt are 12 and 15 percent respectively.

a. Determine the expected rate of return on equity next year for Gooding under each of the working capital policies.

b. Which policy is riskier? Cite specific evidence to support this contention.

SELECTED REFERENCES

Bierman, H., K. Chopra, and J. Thomas. "Ruin Considerations: Optimal Working Capital and Capital Structure." *Journal of Financial and Quantitative Analysis* 10 (March 1975): 119–128.

Carleton, Willard T., and Ian A. Cooper. "Estimation and Uses of the Term Structure of Interest Rates." *Journal of Finance* 31 (September 1976): 1067–1083.

Gentry, James A. "State of the Art of Short-Run Financial Management." *Financial Management* (Summer 1988): 41–57.

Gilmer, R. H. "The Optimal Level of Liquid Assets: An Empirical Test." *Financial Management* (Winter 1985): 39–43.

Kallberg, Jarl G. *Current Asset Management*. New York: Wiley, 1984.

Kroll, Yoram. "On the Difference between Accrual Accounting Figures and Cash Flows: The Case of Working Capital." *Financial Management* (Spring 1985): 75–82.

Lippman, Steven A., and J. J. McCall. "An Operational Measure of Liquidity." *American Economic Review.* (March 1986); 43–56.

Richards, Verlyn, and Eugene J. Laughlin. "A Cash Conversion Cycle Approach to Liquidity Analysis." *Financial Management* 9 (Spring 1980): 32–38.

Scherr, Frederick C. *Modern Working Capital Management: Text and Cases*. Englewood Cliffs, NJ: Prentice-Hall, 1989.

Smith, Keith V., and George W. Gallinger. *Readings on Short-Term Financial Management*, 3d ed. St. Paul, MN: West Publishing, 1988.

Vander Weide, James. *Managing Corporate Liquidity*. New York: Wiley, 1985.

18

The Management of Cash and Marketable Securities

KEY CHAPTER CONCEPTS

1. Companies hold liquid asset balances for several reasons, including
   a. To conduct transactions.
   b. For precautionary reasons.
   c. To meet future requirements.
   d. For speculative reasons.
   e. To compensate banks for various services provided to the firm.

2. The optimal liquid assets balance reflects risk and return tradeoffs and is a function of the following
   a. Holding costs, which are the opportunity returns the company could earn on these funds in their next best alternative use.
   b. Shortage costs, which include possible lost cash discounts, deterioration of the company's credit rating, higher interest expenses, and financial insolvency.

3. Manufacturing firms tend to hold higher liquid asset balances than utilities and service firms. Small firms tend to hold higher liquid asset balances as a proportion of total assets than large firms.

4. The primary objective in controlling cash collections is to reduce the delay between when the customer mails the payment and when it becomes a collected balance in the firm's bank account.

5. Methods for reducing collection time include
   a. Decentralized collection centers and concentration banks.
   b. Lockboxes.
   c. Wire transfers and depository transfer checks (DTC).
   d. Special handling of large remittances.
   e. Preauthorized checks (PAC).

6. The primary objective in controlling cash disbursements is to slow payments and keep the firm's funds in the bank as long as possible.

7. Methods of slowing disbursements include
   a. Scheduling and centralizing payments (zero-balance systems).
   b. Use of drafts rather than checks.
   c. Maximizing check clearing float.
   d. Stretching payables.

8. Electronic funds transfer systems, including wire transfers, the use of automated clearinghouses, and customer-directed computer movements of funds from one ac-

count to another have the potential to greatly reduce the float in financial transactions.

9. Aggressive financial managers need to avoid overstepping the bounds of legal and ethical behavior.

10. The primary criteria the firm should use in selecting marketable securities include
a. Default risk.
b. Marketability (or liquidity).
c. Maturity date.
d. Rate of return.

GLOSSARY OF NEW TERMS

Bank draft An order to pay, similar to a check, except that it is not payable on demand. Instead, a bank draft is payable when the issuing firm accepts it.

Banker's acceptance A short-term debt instrument issued by a firm as part of a commercial transaction. Payment is guaranteed by a commercial bank.

Commercial paper Short-term, unsecured promissory notes. Commercial paper generally is issued by large, well-known corporations and finance companies.

Concentration banking The use of decentralized collection centers and local banks to collect customer payments. This speeds up a firm's collections.

Default risk The risk that a borrower will fail to make interest payments, principal payments, or both on a loan.

Depository transfer check (DTC) An unsigned, nonnegotiable check used to transfer funds from a local collection bank to a concentration bank.

Float The difference between an account balance as shown on the bank's books and as shown on the firm's books. Float represents the net effect of the delays in the payment of checks the firm writes and the collection of checks the firm receives.

Lockbox A post office box maintained by a bank to speed up the collection of payments from customers.

Misdirected funds Funds that cross an international border unintentionally.

Multilateral netting A process of international cash management designed to minimize the cost associated with misdirected funds.

Preauthorized check (PAC) Similar to an ordinary check except that it does not require the signature of the person (or firm) on whose account it is being drawn. PACS are useful for firms that receive a large volume of payments of a fixed amount each period.

Repurchase agreement An arrangement with a bank or securities dealer in which an investor acquires certain short-term securities subject to a commitment that the securities will be repurchased by the bank or securities dealer on a specified date.

Wire transfer The process of electronically sending funds from one bank to another through the Federal Reserve System or private bank wire systems.

Zero-balance system A payment system that uses a master disbursing account that services all other disbursing accounts. A zero balance is maintained in all but the master account until payments must be made.

E. F. Hutton's Interest-Free "Loans"*

In May 1985 E. F. Hutton & Company, a large securities brokerage firm (now part of Shearson Lehman Hutton), pleaded guilty to federal fraud charges involving the operation of a massive check-writing scheme to obtain money from many of its 400 banks without paying interest. The firm pleaded guilty to 2,000 counts of mail and wire fraud and agreed to pay more than $10 million in criminal fines and restitution to the banks. According to the Justice Department, Hutton systematically overdrew hundreds of its own accounts in banks throughout the country and intentionally moved money between banks to artificially delay the collection of funds. The scheme involved checks totaling more than $4 billion written between July 1980 and February 1982. By doing this, Hutton was able to use as much as $250 million in interest-free money on some days.

According to Justice Department documents, Hutton officials frequently misused bank ac-counts of its branches by writing checks for amounts in excess of the volume of customer funds deposited in these accounts. For example, during 1981 Hutton deposited $33.5 million in valid customer receipts in United Virginia Bank while withdrawing more than $640 million from the same account that year. Hutton also pleaded guilty to extending the "float" time during which checks are cleared by setting up a chain of transfers between branch accounts. These transactions, according to the Justice Department, resembled a check kiting scheme and were carried out illegally without the prior agreement or consent of the banks involved. Indeed, the banks generally didn't realize they were victims until they were told by officials from the government.

Although many firms employ techniques to aggressively manage their bank balances and minimize their idle cash, Hutton went from being aggressive to actively defrauding the banks. This chapter examines various *legal* methods for controlling the collection and disbursement of cash.

* Based on articles from the *Wall Street Journal* (May 3, 1985 and May 6, 1985) and *Business Week* (May 20, 1985).

INTRODUCTION

Cash and marketable securities are the most liquid of a company's assets. *Cash* is the sum of the currency a company has on hand and the funds on deposit in bank checking accounts. Cash is the medium of exchange that permits management to carry on the various functions of the business organization. In fact, the survival of a company can depend on the availability of cash to meet financial obligations on time. *Marketable securities* consist of short-term investments a firm makes with its temporarily idle cash. Marketable securities can be sold quickly and converted into cash when needed. Unlike cash, however, marketable securities provide the firm with interest income.

As interest rates have risen, effective cash and marketable securities management has become increasingly important in contemporary companies, government agencies, and not-for-profit enterprises. Corporate treasurers aggressively have sought ways to increase the yields on their liquid cash and marketable security reserves. Traditionally, these liquid reserves were invested almost exclusively in jumbo certificates of deposit, Treasury bills, commercial paper, and repurchase agreements (short-term loans backed by Treasury securities). Many treasurers have shown an eagerness to take some additional risks to increase the return on liquid assets. For example, William Glynn, chief financial officer for MDU Resources, a $400 million utility and natural resources firm, says, "One of the resources a financial officer has is cash—and you have to take risks, just like the operating side of the business."[1] By foregoing instant access to all of these resources, Glynn has been able to earn nearly twice the yield on Treasury bills by aggressively managing MDU's marketable security investments. Managers such as Glynn have invested in money market preferred stocks and variable rate preferred stocks in order to benefit from the 70 percent dividend exclusion treatment for intercorporate dividend payments. At the same time, after-tax yields have increased dramatically.

Aggressive management of cash and marketable securities balances is important because of the high opportunity cost of not investing successfully in a period of high interest rates. In addition, many firms hold significant cash and marketable securities balances. In late 1988 IBM's cash balances topped the $5.4 billion mark; Ford Motor's cash balances exceeded $9.2 billion; Exxon had $2.2 billion; and Boeing had over $4.2 billion. Some firms, such as Dart Group, ICN, PACO Pharmaceuticals, Price Communications, Maxxam Group, and Centronics, hold cash balances substantially in excess of their firm's market value.[2] These cash balances give the firm a cushion to handle economic downturns, and the ability to make investments in other firms when the price is attractive. Large cash balances also have made many firms attractive takeover targets for corporate raiders, who seek to redeploy these surplus funds in more productive ways.

In addition to managing the cash and marketable securities already in possession of a firm, financial managers also aggressively seek to speed up cash collections from customers and to slow down disbursements to suppliers. For example, when Alaska sold its oil leases for $900 million, the state was paid with checks that had to physically reach New York before the state could collect and invest the funds. The state chartered a plane to take the checks to New York, thus saving one day in transit over commercial carriers. The daily interest on these funds was nearly $200,000, and the plane charter cost only $15,000, resulting in $185,000 of additional returns to the state. Cash managers continually look for ways to reduce the collection and clearing time for checks received by the firm so that the funds can be put to work earning a return.

Cash management involves much more than simply paying bills and receiving payments for goods and services. The cash management function is concerned with determining

- The optimal size of a firm's liquid asset balance.
- The most efficient methods of controlling the collection and disbursement of cash.
- The appropriate types and amounts of short-term investments the firm should make.

Cash management decisions require the firm's managers to explicitly consider the *risk versus expected return* tradeoffs from alternative policies. Because cash and marketable securities generally earn low rates of return relative to the firm's other assets, a firm can increase its expected return on assets and on common equity by minimizing its investment in cash and marketable securities. However, a firm that carries a bare minimum of liquid assets exposes itself to the risk that it will run out of cash needed to keep the business operating. Also, a firm with extremely low cash balances

[1] "Wringing More Profits from Idle Corporate Cash," *Business Week* (May 12, 1986), pp. 85–86.
[2] "Wall Street's New Pet: The Big Corporate Kitty," *Business Week* (December 7, 1986), pp. 109–112.

may not be able to take advantage of unique investment opportunities when they arise.

In this chapter we review the various cash management decisions that must be made by financial managers. Our analysis considers the risk versus expected return tradeoffs characteristic of these decisions.

LIQUID ASSET BALANCE

There are a number of reasons why firms hold liquid asset balances, including:

- First, because cash inflows and outflows of the day-to-day operations of the firm are not perfectly synchronized, liquid asset balances are necessary to serve as a buffer between these flows. This reason is the *transactions motive*.[3] Liquid asset balances help the firm handle seasonal fluctuations in cash flows. For example, a firm may wish to hold a large amount of liquid assets during surplus months and "draw down" on them during deficit months.

- Second, because future cash flows and the ability to borrow additional funds on short notice often are uncertain, liquid asset balances are necessary to meet unexpected requirements for cash. This is the *precautionary motive*.

- Third, liquid asset balances are held to meet *future requirements*. These include fixed outlays required on specific dates, such as quarterly dividend and tax payments, capital expenditures, and repayments of loans or bond issues. The firm also may hold as liquid assets the proceeds from a new debt or equity securities offering prior to using these funds for expansion.

- Fourth, firms often hold liquid assets for *speculative* reasons. Some firms have built up large cash balances in preparation for major acquisitions. Both Ford Motor and Boeing have built up very large liquid asset balances. Security analysts expect each of these firms to make major future acquisitions, particularly if they can identify attractively priced firms to acquire. The large cash balances give Ford and Boeing great timing flexibility in pursuing acquisitions.

  In contrast, Schlumberger recently bought back over $1 billion (in market value) of its common stock through a tender offer. In undertaking this transaction Schlumberger's CEO, Evan Baird, said "The decision to make this tender offer came as a result of a five-year strategy plan. . . . The plan indicated that we have ample scope for growth by focusing on our main businesses, and, therefore, we saw no reason to keep our present level of excess liquidity."[4] When Schlumberger's management saw no valid business purpose for holding liquid assets, it distributed cash to shareholders through the stock repurchase plan.

- Finally, a firm generally has to hold cash balances to compensate the bank (or banks) for the services provided. These are called *compensating balances*.

The following sections consider the importance of cash from a number of perspectives.

[3] In *The General Theory of Employment, Interest and Money* (New York: Harcourt, Brace, 1935), economist John Maynard Keynes identified three primary reasons why people hold cash: the transactions motive, the precautionary motive, and the speculative motive. Within the *business firm*, the first two motives for holding cash are much more important than the last one.

[4] Schlumberger Limited, "Letter From the Chairman" (October 24, 1988).

Cash Flows and the Cash Budget

Virtually every activity within a firm generates cash flows. As shown in Figure 18-1, the firm's cash balance is affected by every transaction that involves either a cash inflow or a cash outflow. Cash inflows, or *receipts*, occur when customers pay for their purchases, when the firm obtains bank loans, when it sells new issues of debt and equity securities, and when it sells (or collects interest on) marketable securities. Cash outflows, or disbursements, occur when the firm makes payments to suppliers, when the firm pays wages to employees, taxes to governments, interest and principal to bondholders, and cash dividends to shareholders, and when the firm repays bank loans and purchases marketable securities. Therefore the cash balance at the end of any given period is the result of many interrelated activities.

Cash flows differ with respect to their degree of *certainty*. In general, future outflows are more certain than future inflows. Most expenditures (outflows) are directly controllable by the firm and, as a result, can be forecasted more easily. For example, outflows for such items as raw materials, labor, dividends, debt repayments, and capital equipment are determined primarily by management decisions and usually are known in advance of their occurrence. Inflows, in contrast, occur partly as a result of decisions made outside the firm and thus are usually more difficult to control and forecast. For example, cash inflows from sales depend primarily on the buying decisions of customers, as well as on when they make their payments.

The first step in efficient cash management is the development of a *cash budget* showing the forecasted cash receipts and disbursements over the planning horizon of the firm.[5] A complete cash budget also contains a forecast of any cumulative cash shortages or surpluses expected during each of

[5] Chapter 4 contains a discussion of how cash budgets are developed.

613

CHAPTER 18
The Management
of Cash
and Marketable
Securities

Cash Flows within a Typical Firm*

FIGURE 18-1

* Arrows indicate the *direction* of cash flows.

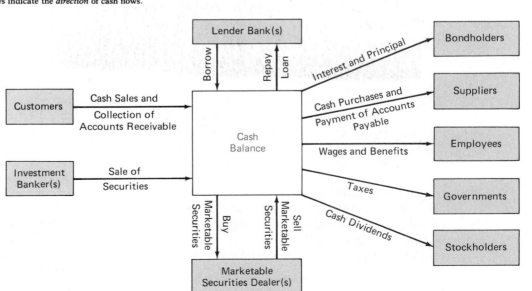

the budgeting subperiods—which is the kind of information needed in making cash management decisions. Many larger firms prepare a series of cash budgets, each covering a different time period. For example, a firm may prepare daily cash budgets for the next 5 working days, weekly cash budgets for the next 10 weeks, and monthly cash budgets for the next 12 months. The daily and weekly forecasts are used in making short-term decisions, such as determining the amount of marketable securities the firm should purchase or sell. The monthly projections are used in longer range planning, such as determining the amount of bank loans the firm will need. A survey of medium- and large-size companies found that over 80 percent of the respondents relied on cash budgets as a cash forecasting technique.[6]

Knowledge of a potential cash shortage ahead of time gives a financial manager ample opportunity to investigate alternative sources of financing and to choose the least costly one. All other things being equal, lending institutions prefer to make loans to firms that have demonstrated an ability to anticipate their future cash needs. Firms that seem to be faced with frequent cash "emergencies" generally have more difficulty getting loans. Similarly, advance knowledge of a cash surplus allows the financial manager to invest in appropriate marketable securities.

Corporate–Bank Relations

A firm's bank provides it a variety of both tangible and intangible services. The most significant tangible services include the following:

- Disbursement, wire transfer, direct deposit, and payroll checking accounts.
- Collection of deposits—including lockbox, automated collections, depository transfers, and vault services.
- Cash management.
- Lines of credit, term loans, or both.
- Handling of dividend payments.
- Registration and transfer of a firm's stock.

The most important intangible banking service is the availability of future credit if and when the need arises. Other intangible services include the following:

- Supplying credit information.
- Providing consulting advice on such matters as economic conditions, mergers, and international business.

A bank is compensated for the services it provides by charging the firm explicit fees and/or requiring the maintenance of a minimum cash balance, or *compensating balance*, in its checking account. The bank can use this compensating balance to make other loans or investments, and the interest income realized is *compensation* for the various services rendered to the firm. Although some banks require firms to maintain *absolute* minimum compensating balances, most stipulate minimum *average* balances.

The monthly account fee that the bank charges a business customer usually is determined by calculating various service charges and then deducting an earnings credit on the account balance. The service charges are computed by multiplying the number of each type of transaction the firm makes per

[6] R. Kamath, S. Khaksari, H. Meier, and J. Winklepleck. "Management of Excess Cash: Practices and Developments," *Financial Management* (Autumn 1985): 70–77.

period (such as payroll checks, vendor checks, customer payments, and other deposits) by the bank's charge per item. The earnings credit is computed by multiplying the available balance during the month (which often includes various deductions, such as the bank's reserve requirement) by the earnings credit rate (that is, some specified interest rate). When the total service charges exceed the earnings credit, the bank collects a fee from the customer. Due to competition among banks and differences in the methods used to compute account income and costs, service fees and compensating balance requirements for a given level of account activity vary from bank to bank. As a result, a firm should occasionally do some "comparison shopping" to determine whether its present bank is offering the best fee schedule and compensating balance requirement currently available.

615

CHAPTER 18
The Management
of Cash
and Marketable
Securities

Optimal Liquid Asset Balance

When a firm holds liquid asset balances, whether in the form of currency, bank demand deposits, or marketable securities, it is in effect investing these funds. To determine the optimal investment in liquid assets, the firm must weigh the benefits and costs of holding these various balances. The determination of an optimal liquid asset balance reflects the classic *risk versus return* tradeoff facing financial managers. Because liquid assets earn relatively low rates of return, a firm can increase its profitability in relation to its asset base by minimizing liquid asset balances. However, low liquid asset balances expose a firm to the risk of not being able to meet its obligations as they come due. Effective cash management calls for a careful balancing of the risk and return aspects of cash management.

A minimum compensating balance requirement on the part of the bank essentially imposes a *lower limit* on the firm's optimal level of liquid asset balances. When the firm holds liquid assets in excess of this lower limit, it incurs an *opportunity cost*. The opportunity cost of excess liquid assets, held in the form of bank deposits, is the return the firm could earn on these funds in their next best use, such as in the expansion of other current or fixed assets. The opportunity cost of liquid asset balances, held in the form of marketable securities, is the income that could be earned on these funds in their next best alternative use *less* the interest income received on the marketable securities.

Given the opportunity cost of holding liquid asset balances, why would a firm ever maintain a bank balance exceeding the compensating balance requirements? The answer is that these balances help the firm avoid the "shortage" costs associated with inadequate liquid asset balances.[7]

Shortage costs can take many different forms, including the following:

- Foregone cash discounts.
- Deterioration of the firm's credit rating.
- Higher interest expenses.
- Possible financial insolvency.

Many suppliers offer customers a cash discount for prompt payment. Having to forego this cash discount can be quite costly to the firm. In addition, the credit-worthiness of a firm is determined at least partially by the current and quick ratios—both of which can be affected by an inadequate liquid asset balance. This, in turn, can cause the firm's credit rating to deteriorate

[7] See William Beranek. *Analysis for Financial Decisions.* Homewood, IL: Irwin, 1963, Chapter 11.

and make loans on favorable terms more difficult for the firm to secure in the future. The credit rating also can fall if the firm fails to pay bills on time because of inadequate cash. This can make future credit difficult to obtain from suppliers. If the firm has inadequate liquid asset reserves, it may have to meet unforeseen needs for cash by short-term borrowing, and it may be unable to negotiate for the best terms—including the lowest possible interest rate—if its credit rating is questionable. Inadequate liquid asset balances may cause a firm to incur high transactions costs when converting illiquid assets to cash. Finally, an inadequate liquid asset balance increases the firm's risk of insolvency, because a serious recession or natural disaster would be more likely to reduce the firm's cash inflows to the point where it could not meet contractual financial obligations.

An inverse relationship exists between a firm's liquid asset balance and these shortage costs: the larger a firm's liquid asset balance, the smaller its associated shortage costs. The opportunity holding costs, in contrast, increase as a firm's liquid asset balance is increased. As shown in Figure 18-2, the optimal liquid asset balance occurs at the point where the sum of the opportunity holding costs and the shortage costs is minimized. Admittedly, many of these shortage costs are difficult to measure. Nevertheless, a firm should attempt to evaluate the tradeoffs among these costs in order to economize on cash holdings.

Gilmer has performed empirical tests to determine if firms actually do face a total cost function similar to Figure 18-2 associated with the maintenance of liquid asset balances. His results were consistent with the concept of an optimal liquid asset balance as shown in Figure 18-2.[8]

The Practice of Liquidity Management

In practice, a wide variety of liquidity policies are found to exist among firms. Table 18-1 offers a sample of the liquidity policies practiced by different firms in several industries. As can be seen in the table, liquidity practices, as measured by the ratio of cash and marketable securities to total assets, vary significantly among industries and among firms within

[8] R. H. Gilmer, Jr. "The Optimal Level of Liquid Assets: An Empirical Test," *Financial Management* (Winter 1985): 39–43.

FIGURE 18-2

Optimal Liquid Asset Balance

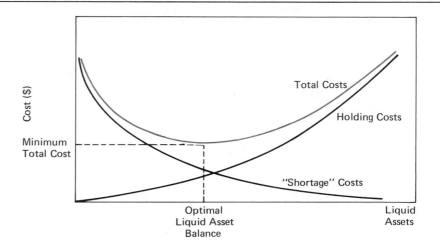

Ratio of Cash and Marketable Securities to Total Assets		TABLE 18-1
Firm	**Ratio**	
Aerospace-defense industry:		
Boeing	27.30%	
General Dynamics	3.50	
Lockheed	0.60	
Martin Marietta	0.60	
Automotive industry:		
Chrysler	12.10%	
Ford	22.50	
General Motors	5.40	
Computer industry:		
Apple Computer	26.20%	
Hewlett-Packard	32.50	
IBM	10.90	
Unisys	0.50	
Electric utility industry:		
FPL Group	0.60%	
Long Island Lighting	2.30	
Pennsylvania Power and Light	0.10	
Real estate development industry:		
AMREP	1.80%	
Horizon Corporation	0.10	
Rouse Company	11.30	
Restaurant industry:		
Dunkin Donuts	5.50%	
McDonald's	2.60	
Shoney's	3.20	
Retailing industry:		
K-Mart	4.00%	
Lands End	26.40	
May Department Stores	2.80	
JC Penney	1.00	

SOURCE: *ValueScreen* Data Base, 1989. Copyright © 1989 by Value Line, Inc. Used by permission.

an industry. Utility firms, real estate developers, and service industry establishments, such as restaurants, tend to hold low liquid asset balances as a proportion of total assets.

Although this table does not provide data on small to medium-sized firms, in general it can be observed that larger firms tend to hold lower liquid asset balances (relative to total assets) than smaller firms. This is because larger firms tend to have better access to "backup" short-term financing should they need it from commercial banks or from their ability to sell commercial paper. Because smaller firms have more limited credit access, they tend to hold greater liquid asset balances as a cushion against the unexpected.

CONTROLLING THE COLLECTION AND DISBURSEMENT OF CASH

The cash collection and disbursement processes provide a firm two areas in which to attempt to economize on cash holdings. For example, the sales of Briggs and Stratton average about $5 million per business day. If the company can speed up collections by only *one day*, the cash balance will increase by $5 million, and these released funds can be invested in other current assets or in fixed assets. If this additional cash can be invested in projects yielding a 10 percent return, it will generate added income of $500,000 per year (10% × $5 million).

Cash collection and disbursement policies are designed to reduce a firm's liquid asset balances (cash and marketable securities) by exploiting imperfections in the collection and payment process. The objective is to speed up collections and slow down disbursements. Financial managers should be aware that policies designed to speed up collections and slow down disbursements are highly competitive. If all firms were to employ the same procedures, the net benefit would be zero. Thus, incremental benefits associated with procedures designed to control collections and disbursements will accrue only to the most aggressive and progressive firms. Similarly, cash managers who do not do at least as much as the average firm in speeding up collections and slowing disbursements will find their firms at a competitive disadvantage.

The primary objective of cash collection involves expediting collections and reducing the lag between the time customers pay their bills and the time the checks are collected. In contrast, the primary objective of cash disbursement is to slow payments so that the firm can keep the funds invested or in the bank as long as possible. Expediting collections and slowing disbursements helps increase the firm's cash balance and provide it with funds to use for other profitable investments. Policies designed to control collections and disbursements take advantage of the *float* present in the payment and disbursement system.

Float

A firm's cash balance as shown on the bank's books generally differs from that shown on the firm's own books. This difference is known as *float* and represents the net effect of the delays in the payment of checks a firm writes and the collection of checks a firm receives. Checks written by a firm result in *disbursement*, or *positive*, float; that is, an excess of bank net collected balances over the balances shown on a firm's books. In contrast, *collection float*, or *negative*, float arises from the delay between the time a customer writes a check to a supplier or other payee and the time the payee actually receives these funds as collected balances (which are spendable). Action being taken by the Federal Reserve System and the rapid progress being made with electronic payment systems mean that float will be less important over time. Until these developments virtually eliminate float, financial managers must understand the sources of float so that they can take legal actions to benefit from it.

There are three primary components, or sources, of float:

1. *Mail float:* the delay between the time a payment is sent to the payee through the mail and the time that payment arrives at the payee's office.
2. *Processing float:* the delay between receipt of payment from a payer and the deposit of that receipt in the payee's account.
3. *Check-clearing float:* the delay between the time a check is deposited in the payee's account and the time the funds are available to be spent. Checks processed through the Federal Reserve System are "cleared" in

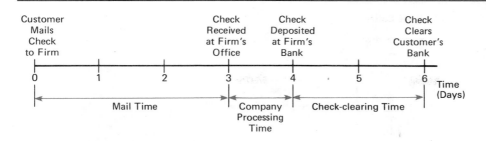

FIGURE 18-3

Cash Collection Process

2 days or less, although the depositor's bank may not make the funds available quite that fast.

Expediting Collections

Figure 18-3 illustrates the main steps in the cash collection process. The total time involved in this process is a combination of mailing (float) time, company processing (float) time, and check-clearing (float) time, each of which may vary depending on where the firm's customers and their respective banks are located.[9] Some methods available for reducing the collection float are discussed in the following paragraphs.

DECENTRALIZED COLLECTION CENTERS AND CONCENTRATION BANKS. Figures 18-4 and 18-5 illustrate two alternative cash collection systems. In the centralized system (Figure 18-4), customers are instructed to send their payments to the firm's headquarters. In the *decentralized* system (Figure 18-5), customers mail their payments to a nearby collection center, which is strategically located to minimize mail delay. The collection center then deposits the checks in a local bank and reports this information to the firm's headquarters. Because most of the checks are drawn on banks that are located in the same geographical area as the collection center,

[9] The particular times shown in Figure 18-3 are merely illustrative. Actual times will vary. (This is also true for Figure 18-7.)

Centralized Collection System

FIGURE 18-4

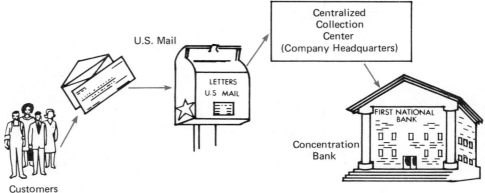

FIGURE 18-5 **Decentralized Collection System**

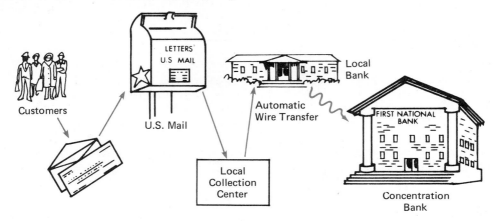

check-clearing float is reduced. Each business day, funds in excess of the amount necessary to compensate the local bank for its services are transferred to an account in a *concentration bank*, where the firm maintains a disbursement account upon which checks are written.

A tradeoff exists between the number of collection centers and the potential savings realized. The more collection centers used, the less time is required to convert customers' checks into collected balances. However, these savings from faster collections are offset by the direct fees involved, the opportunity costs of the compensating balances the firm must maintain at each local bank, or both. The financial manager must weigh the tradeoffs involved in both savings and costs in deciding on the appropriate number and location of collection centers.

LOCKBOXES. Figure 18-6 illustrates a lockbox collection system. A lockbox is a post office box maintained by a local bank for the purpose of receiving

FIGURE 18-6 **Lockbox Collection System**

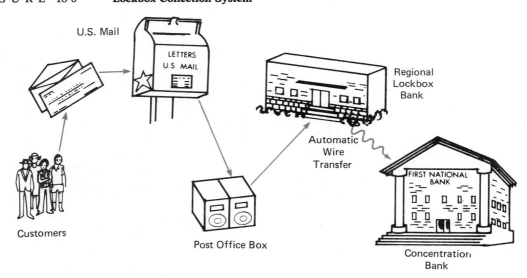

a firm's remittances. Customers mail payments to this post office box, which is usually no more than a few hundred miles away.[10] For example, ITT Corporation, a large conglomerate firm, maintains eleven lockboxes around the country.[11] The bank empties the box several times each working day, deposits the payments in the firm's account, puts the checks into the clearing system, and sends the firm a list of the payments received each day. Not only does the lockbox reduce mailing time, it also eliminates company processing time, because the checks are deposited and begin the clearing process *before* the company's accounting department processes the payments received rather than after processing them. The bank normally charges a fee for this service, requires a compensating balance, or both. Funds in excess of the bank's compensating balance requirement are transferred each day to a master collection account in a concentration bank.

The decision to establish a lockbox collection system requires a comparison of the associated benefits and costs. If the earnings on the funds released by the acceleration of collections exceed the foregone returns on the required compensating balances, the service fees charged by the lockbox bank, or both, the establishment of a lockbox collection system is profitable.

If the number of checks handled is small and the dollar amount of each check is large, a lockbox arrangement is very beneficial to the firm. Under these conditions the bank's work load is light, and the associated service fees, compensating balances, or both, are small. However, when large numbers of checks with small dollar amounts are involved—for example, in the case of oil company credit cards—a lockbox system may not be profitable. Under these conditions the opportunity costs on the required compensating balances, the service fees, or both may exceed the earnings the firm realizes from having the funds available a few days earlier.

The lockbox decision can be illustrated with the following example. The Pacific Company, located in Los Angeles, currently receives and processes all customer payments at its corporate headquarters (that is, a *centralized* system). The firm is considering establishing a bank lockbox collection system for seven southeastern states—Florida, North Carolina, South Carolina, Tennessee, Alabama, Georgia, and Mississippi—that would be located in Atlanta. The lockbox would reduce average mailing time for customer payments from 3 days to 1½ days, check processing time from 2 days to 1 day, and clearing time from 3 days to 1½ days.

Annual collections from the southeastern region are $91.25 million, and the average number of payments received total 550 per day (assume 365 days per year). A bank in Atlanta has agreed to process the payments for an annual fee of $15,000 plus $0.10 per payment received. This bank would not require a compensating balance. Assuming an 8 percent opportunity cost for released funds, should Pacific use the lockbox collection system?

Table 18-2 shows an analysis of this decision. In Step A the amount of funds released ($1 million) is found by multiplying average daily collections ($250,000) by the reduction in collection time (4 days). The annual (pretax) earnings on the released funds ($80,000) are found in Step B by multiplying the amount of funds released ($1 million) by the opportunity cost of funds (.08). The annual bank processing fee ($35,075) is computed in Step C as

---

[10] Determining the optimal location of lockboxes is a complex problem. For some solutions, see Ferdinand K. Levy, "An Application of Heuristic Problem Solving to Accounts Receivable Management," *Management Science* 12 (February 1966): B-236–B-244; and Alan Kraus, et al., "The Lock-Box Location Problem," *Journal of Bank Research* (Autumn 1970): 51–58.

[11] See Ralph E. Jones, "ITT's Cash Management System," *Journal of Cash Management* (May–June 1984): 24–29.

Pacific Company's Analysis of the Decision to Establish a Lockbox Collection System for the Southeastern Region

Step A: Reduction in collection time = Reduction in mailing time + Reduction in processing time + Reduction in check-clearing time

$$= (3 - 1.5) + (2 - 1) + (3 - 1.5)$$

$$= 4 \text{ days}$$

Average daily collections = Annual collections ÷ 365

$$= \$91,250,000 \div 365$$

$$= \$250,000$$

Amount of funds released = Average daily collections × Reduction in collection time

$$= \$250,000 \times 4 \text{ days}$$

$$= \$1,000,000$$

Step B: Annual (pretax) earnings on released funds = Amount of funds released × Interest rate

$$= \$1,000,000 \times 0.08$$

$$= \$80,000$$

Step C: Annual bank processing fee = Fixed cost + Number of payments per year × Variable cost per payment

$$= \$15,000 + (550 \times 365) \times \$0.10$$

$$= \$15,000 + \$20,075$$

$$= \$35,075$$

Step D: Net (pretax) benefits = Annual (pretax) earnings on released funds − Annual bank processing fee

$$= \$80,000 - \$35,075$$

$$= \$44,925$$

the sum of fixed costs ($15,000) and variable costs ($20,075). Finally, in Step D, the net (pretax) benefits of establishing a lockbox system ($44,925) are computed by deducting the annual bank processing fee ($35,075) from the earnings on the released funds ($80,000). Because the net (pretax) benefits are positive, Pacific should employ the lockbox collection system.

WIRE TRANSFERS AND DEPOSITORY TRANSFER CHECKS. Once deposits enter the firm's banking network, the objective is to transfer surplus funds (that is, funds in excess of any required compensating balances) from its local (collection) bank accounts to its concentration (disbursement) bank account or accounts. Two methods used to perform this task are *wire transfers* and *depository transfer checks*.

With a *wire transfer*, funds are sent from a local bank to a concentration bank electronically through the Federal Reserve System or a private bank wire system. Wire transfers are the fastest way of moving funds between banks, because the transfer takes only a few minutes and the funds become *immediately available* (that is, they can be withdrawn) by the firm upon

■■■■ **623** ■■■■

CHAPTER 18
The Management
of Cash
and Marketable
Securities

receipt of the wire notice at the concentration bank. Wire transfers eliminate the mailing and check-clearing times associated with other funds transfer methods. Some firms leave standing instructions with their local (collection) banks to automatically wire surplus funds on a periodic basis (for example, daily, twice a week, and so on) to their concentration bank. Also, some firms specify in their sales contracts that customers must wire their payments on the due dates.

Wire transfer of funds is available to member banks of the Federal Reserve System and to nonmember banks through their correspondent banks. The cost to corporate customers to send a wire transfer at most banks ranges from $10 to $15. A similar change is made to receive and process a domestic wire transfer. For a firm with multiple collection centers that use wire transfers on a daily basis, the annual costs can be substantial. Consequently, this method of transferring funds should be used only when the incremental value of having the funds immediately available exceeds the additional cost, relative to alternatives, such as depository transfer checks.

A *mail depository transfer check* (DTC) is an unsigned, nonnegotiable check drawn on the local collection bank and payable to the concentration bank. As it deposits customer checks in the local bank each day, the collection center mails a depository transfer check to the concentration bank authorizing it to withdraw the deposited funds from the local bank. Upon receipt of the depository transfer check, the firm's account at the concentration bank is credited for the designated amount. Depository transfer checks are processed through the usual check-clearing process. Although the use of depository transfer checks does not eliminate mailing and check-clearing time, it does ensure the movement of funds from the local collection center banks to the concentration bank in a timely manner. Also, the cost of this method of transferring funds is low; often the only cost involved is postage.

An *electronic depository transfer check* (EDTC) also can be used to move funds from a local bank to a concentration bank. The process of transmitting deposit information to a concentration bank is similar to that for mail DTCs just described, except that the information is sent electronically through an automated clearinghouse such as the Automated Clearing House (ACH) system of the Federal Reserve (Fedwire) or the Clearing House Interbank Payments System (CHIPS). These systems eliminate the mail float in moving funds from the local bank to a concentration bank. Funds transferred through an automated system are available for use by the firm in 1 day (or less).

SPECIAL HANDLING OF LARGE REMITTANCES. Firms that receive individual remittances in the multimillion-dollar range may find it more profitable to use special courier services to pick up these checks from customers (rather than having their customers mail the checks) and present them for collection to the banks upon which they are drawn.

USE OF PREAUTHORIZED CHECKS. A *preauthorized check* (PAC) resembles an ordinary check except that it does not require the signature of the person (or firm) on whose account it is being drawn. This system is especially useful for firms that receive a large volume of payments of a fixed amount each period. Insurance companies, savings and loans, charitable institutions, and leasing firms make extensive use of this collection procedure. Preauthorized checks are used extensively in the brewing industry between brewers and beer wholesalers. By 1983, over 85 percent of Heileman's wholesale customers were using its preauthorized payment system. When preauthorized checks are used, the payer agrees to allow the payee (the firm that is owed the money) to write a check on the payer's account and deposit that check immediately for collection at an agreed-upon time. Preauthorized checks have the advantages of completely eliminating the mail float, reducing billing and collecting expenses, and making the cash flows for both parties highly predictable. Many payers like preauthorized check systems because they do not have to bother to write a check each month.

Slowing Disbursements

Figure 18-7 illustrates the principle steps involved in the cash disbursement process. Several ways in which a firm can slow disbursements and keep funds in the bank for longer periods of time are discussed in the following paragraphs.

SCHEDULING AND CENTRALIZING PAYMENTS. A firm should pay bills *on time*—not before or after they are due. Payments made ahead of time lower the firm's average cash balance, whereas late payments can impair the firm's credit rating or fail to qualify for a cash discount.

Centralizing payments from disbursement accounts maintained at a concentration bank helps minimize the amount of idle funds a firm must keep in local field offices and divisional bank accounts. A number of firms have set up *zero-balance* systems to use disbursement float more effectively. In a zero-balance system a *master*, or *concentration*, *account* is set up to receive all deposits coming into the zero-balance system. As checks clear through the zero-balance accounts on which they are issued, funds are transferred to these accounts from the master account. These disbursement accounts are called "zero-balance accounts" because exactly enough funds are transferred into them daily to cover the checks that have cleared, leaving a zero balance at the end of the day. In general, all disbursements for accounts payable, payroll, and whatever other purposes the firm desires are issued from these zero-balance accounts. For a zero-balance system to operate effectively, the firm must have a well-developed network for reporting deposits and disbursements, as well as a close working relationship with its bank.

DRAFTS. A draft is similar to a check, except it is not payable on demand. Instead, when a draft is transmitted to a firm's bank for collection, the bank must present the draft to the firm for acceptance before making payment.

FIGURE 18-7

Cash Disbursement Process

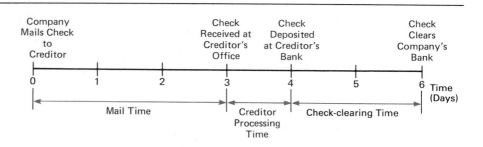

In practice, individual drafts are considered to be legally paid automatically by the bank on the business day following the day of presentation to the firm, unless the firm returns a draft and explicitly requests that it not be paid. Once the draft has been presented, the firm must immediately deposit the necessary funds to cover the payment.

625

CHAPTER 18
The Management
of Cash
and Marketable
Securities

The use of drafts rather than checks permits a firm to keep smaller balances in its disbursement accounts, because funds do not have to be deposited in them until the drafts are presented for payment. Normally, drafts are more expensive to use than checks. The lower account balances and higher processing costs cause banks to impose services charges on firms using drafts; this cost must be included in the analysis of the benefits and costs of using drafts to pay bills.

Drafts now are used primarily to provide for centralized control over payments authorized in field offices, *rather than as a means of slowing disbursements*. For example, a claims agent for Nationwide Insurance might issue a draft to provide for quick settlement of an insurance claim. The claims agent does not have the authority to write a check against Nationwide's checking accounts. By issuing a draft, centralized control can be maintained over these disbursements. The Federal Reserve System requires a firm to transfer funds to the bank *through which* payment is to be made as soon as the drafts are presented to the firm.

MAXIMIZING CHECK-CLEARING FLOAT. Some firms make payments to suppliers from checking accounts located a long distance from the supplier. For example, an East Coast supplier might be paid with checks drawn on a West Coast bank. This increases the time required for the check to clear through the banking system. Some firms maintain an intricate network of disbursing accounts. Checks are issued from the account most distant from the payee, thereby maximizing check-clearing float.

STRETCHING PAYABLES. Many firms pay their accounts payable before they are due. There is no significant benefit to be received by paying these accounts before they are actually due, unless a cash discount is offered for early payment.[12] For example, if Campbell Soup Company makes payments on its accounts payable averaging $10 million per day, and if Campbell found that it made these payments an average of 3 days early, Campbell could gain substantial benefits by slowing its disbursements by 3 days. This would result in an increase in available cash balances of $30 million, which could be invested by Campbell. In making the decision to put a more efficient cash disbursement system in place, Campbell's financial managers would compare the return that can be earned on the $30 million of released funds against the costs of implementing the system.

ELECTRONIC FUNDS TRANSFER[13]

The previous discussion of methods to speed up collections and slow disbursements assumes that virtually all transactions involve the transfer of

---

[12] The cost of not taking cash discounts is discussed in Chapter 20.
[13] This section is based, in part, on Bernell K. Stone, "Electronic Payment Basics," *Economic Review* (March 1986): 9–18; "The Automated Clearinghouse: How Do We Get There From Here," *Economic Review* (April 1986): entire issue; and Robert Guenther, "U.S. Treasury Pays Suppliers Electronically," *Wall Street Journal* (August 24, 1987).

paper (checks) between the payer and the payee. These methods to control collections and disbursements are designed to reduce the float involved in financial transactions. In a sense, the total float in the financial system can be viewed as a measure of inefficiency in the financial system. In an idealized world, the total float would be reduced to zero. Payments would be made and received as usable funds instantaneously. Although the financial system has a long way to go before this ideal is realized, in the past 5 years tremendous progress has been made.

Many consumers now have automatic teller cards which give them access to cash 24-hours a day, seven days a week. In addition, banking customers can use automatic tellers to transfer funds between accounts. Special credit cards, called "debit cards," are used by some consumers. When a debit card is used, funds are transferred from the consumer's bank account electronically to the account of the retailer. The retailer no longer must be concerned whether a check will be good when it is deposited. Increasingly, small and large businesses are using microcomputer links to manipulate funds between interest bearing accounts and non-interest bearing disbursement accounts.

Large payments can be made by wire transfers or through an *automated clearinghouse*. Automated clearinghouse (ACH) systems are computer-based alternatives to the paper check collection and clearing system. The ACH sorts checklike electronic images and exchanges electronic records of payment and receipt. Although acceptance of electronic checking initially was slow, growth has increased dramatically in recent years. In 1987, the U.S. Treasury, which writes 22 million checks a year for $325 billion, announced a system, called "Vendor Express," to begin paying some of its customers electronically. The Treasury's goal is to be "checkless" in about 3 years. RJR Tobacco gives a discount to distributors that pay electronically. General Motors is in the process of converting to a system of electronically paying its 5,500 suppliers, who receive nearly 300,000 checks per month. In 1983 the Ohio Lottery Commission converted to a 100 percent electronic funds transfer (EFT) system for its sales network. In one year the commission estimates it increased revenues by $1.8 million through a greater use of interest income and better use of its employees. The bad debt rate from sales agents dropped from $150,000 per month to $4,000 per month.

EFT mechanisms are profoundly changing the nature of the cash management function. Although paper checks, with their associated mail and processing float, will not completely disappear for some time (if ever), as increased volumes of payments are made electronically, the importance of developing elaborate mechanisms to manage float will be reduced greatly. Increased reliance on EFT as the mechanism for payment will free up some of the cash invested in accounts receivable for more productive uses in the firm. The Ohio Lottery Commission example also suggests that EFT payment systems have the potential to reduce bad debt expenses for many firms. Contemporary financial managers will be challenged in the years ahead to stay current with a fast changing, high technology system of receiving payments and making disbursements.

ETHICS AND CASH MANAGEMENT

Financial managers are confronted with legal and ethical issues as they make cash collection and disbursement decisions. For example, a large firm, such as General Motors (GM) might be tempted to systematically be a few days late in making payments to a small supplier. GM managers may be confident that the small firm will not risk damaging its supply relationship with GM over payment delays of a few days. Similarly, a cash manager may take advantage of weak control mechanisms in its banks and make short-term investments using uncollected funds. As discussed in the chapter opening Financial Dilemma, this type of action got E. F. Hutton's managers into a lot of trouble.

627

CHAPTER 18
The Management
of Cash
and Marketable
Securities

A good financial manager should be mindful of the legal and ethical effects of the firm's actions. Legal violations can result in costly fines, embarrassment, and in some cases prison. Violations of business contracts and the trust built in business transactions may be very costly to a firm's reputation and its future business relationships.

SMALL BUSINESS CONCERNS: CASH MANAGEMENT

Following efficient cash management policies is important for all firms, government agencies, and not-for-profit enterprises. However, effective cash management is particularly important for small firms for several reasons. First, small businesses do not have the same, extensive access to the capital markets as do larger firms. The major source of capital funds to small firms is commercial banks. Bankers require borrowers to present detailed analyses of their anticipated cash needs. To do this, the firm must have efficient cash management procedures in place. Second, because of their limited access to capital, a cash shortage problem is both more difficult and more costly for a small firm to rectify than for a large firm. Third, because many small firms are growing rapidly, they have a tendency to run out of cash. Growing sales require increases in inventories and accounts receivable, thereby using up the firm's cash resources. This problem is illustrated in the Financial Dilemma at the start of Chapter 17. Finally, small firms frequently operate with only a bare minimum of cash resources because of the high cost of, and limited access to, capital. As a result, it is imperative that financial managers of the small firms use the scarce cash resources of the firm in the most efficient way possible.

INVESTING IN MARKETABLE SECURITIES

Rather than let their cash reserves build up in excess of daily cash requirements, many firms invest in interest-bearing short-term marketable securities. Given the higher interest rates (and yields) of recent years, firms have become much more conscious of the sizable opportunity costs (that is, lost income) of idle cash balances. Determining the level of liquid assets that should be invested in marketable securities depends on several factors, including these:

■ The interest to be earned over the expected holding period.
■ The transaction costs involved in buying and selling the securities.
■ The variability of the firm's cash flows.

Various quantitative models have been developed for determining the optimal division of a firm's liquid asset balance between cash and marketable securities.[14] These models vary in complexity, depending partly on the assumptions made about the firm's cash flows. The simpler *deterministic* models assume that cash payments occur at a *uniform certain rate* over time. The more complex *probabilistic* or *stochastic* models assume that cash balances fluctuate from day to day in a *random* or unpredictable manner. Although these models provide the financial manager with useful insights into the cost tradeoffs involved in effective cash management, they have not been widely implemented in actual decision-making situations.

Choosing Marketable Securities

A firm may choose among many different types of securities when deciding where to invest excess cash reserves. In determining which securities to include in its portfolio, the firm should consider a number of criteria, including the following:

- Default risk.
- Marketability.
- Maturity date.
- Rate of return.

Each of these is discussed in this section.

DEFAULT RISK. Most firms invest only in marketable securities that have little or no default risk. U.S. Treasury securities have the lowest default risk, followed by securities of other U.S. government agencies and, finally, by corporate and municipal securities. Various financial reporting agencies, including Moody's Investors Service and Standard and Poor's, compile and publish information concerning the safety ratings of the various corporate and municipal securities. Given the positive relationship between a security's expected return and risk and the desire to select marketable securities having minimal default risk, the firm has to be willing to accept relatively low expected yields on its marketable securities investments.

MARKETABILITY. A firm usually buys marketable securities that can be sold on short notice without a significant price concession. Thus, there are two dimensions to a security's marketability; namely, the time required to sell the security and the price realized from the sale relative to the last quoted price. If a long period of time, a high transaction cost, or a significant price concession is required to dispose of a security, the security has poor marketability and generally is not considered suitable for inclusion in a marketable securities portfolio. Naturally, a tradeoff is involved here between risk and return. Generally, a highly marketable security has a small degree of risk that the investor will incur a loss, and consequently it usually has a lower expected yield than one with limited marketability.

MATURITY DATE. Firms usually limit their marketable securities purchases to issues that have relatively short maturities. Recall that prices of

[14] Inventory models were first applied to cash management by William J. Baumol in "The Transactions Demand for Cash: An Inventory Theoretic Approach," *Quarterly Journal of Economics* 66 (November 1952): 545–556. See Dileep R. Mehta, *Working Capital Management*, Englewood Cliffs, NJ: Prentice-Hall, 1974, Chapter 6, for a further discussion of cash management models.

debt securities decrease when interest rates rise and increase when interest rates fall. For a given change in interest rates, prices of long-term securities fluctuate more widely than short-term securities with equal default risk. Thus, an investor who holds long-term securities is exposed to a greater risk of loss if the securities have to be sold prior to maturity. This is known as *interest rate risk*. For this reason, most firms generally do not buy marketable securities that have more than 180 to 270 days remaining until maturity, and many firms restrict most of their temporary investments to those maturing in less than 90 days. Because the yields on securities with short maturities often are lower than the yields on securities with longer maturities, a firm has to be willing to sacrifice yield to avoid interest rate risk.

629

CHAPTER 18
The Management
of Cash
and Marketable
Securities

RATE OF RETURN. Although the rate of return, or yield, also is given consideration in selecting securities for inclusion in the firm's portfolio, it is less important than the other three criteria just described. The desire to invest in securities that have minimal default and interest rate risk and that are readily marketable usually limits the selection to those having relatively low yields.

Types of Marketable Securities

Firms normally confine their marketable securities investments to "money market" instruments; that is, those high-grade (low default risk) short-term debt instruments having original maturities of 1 year or less. Money market instruments that are suitable for inclusion in a firm's marketable securities portfolio include U.S. Treasury issues, other federal agency issues, municipal securities, negotiable certificates of deposit, commercial paper, repurchase agreements, bankers' acceptances, Eurodollar deposits, money market preferred stocks, money market mutual funds, and bank money market accounts. Each of these will be discussed. (In some cases, firms also will use long-term bonds having 1 year or less remaining to maturity as "marketable" securities and treat them as money market instruments.)

Table 18-3 lists the characteristics and yields of these various money market instruments. As can be seen in the last three columns of the table, yields on these securities vary considerably over time. Yields are a function of a number of factors, including the state of the economy, the rate of inflation, and government monetary and fiscal policies.

UNITED STATES TREASURY ISSUES. United States Treasury bills are the most popular marketable securities. They are sold at weekly auctions through Federal Reserve Banks and their branches and have standard maturities of 91 days, 182 days, and 1 year. Treasury bills are issued at a discount and then redeemed for the full face amount at maturity. Once they are issued, Treasury bills can be bought and sold in the secondary markets through approximately forty government securities dealers. There is a large and active market for Treasury bills, which means that a firm can easily dispose of them when it needs cash. The smallest denomination of Treasury bills is $10,000 of maturity value.

The advantages of Treasury issues include short maturities, a virtually default-free status, and ready marketability. Their primary disadvantage

T A B L E 18-3 Characteristics and Yields of Selected Money Market Instruments

Instrument	Denominations	Maturities	Marketability		Yields* (%) AUG. 1981	OCT. 1985	DEC. 1988
U.S. Treasury bills	Various denominations from $10,000 to $1,000,000	91 days, 182 days, 52 weeks	Highly organized secondary market	(3 months) (6 months) (1 year)	15.51 15.52 14.70	7.16 7.33 7.45	8.09 8.24 8.45
Federal agency issues	Numerous denominations from $5,000 to $1,000,000	Wide variation in maturities from several days to more than 10 years	Well-established secondary market for short-term securities of "big five" agencies		—		
Short-term municipal securities	$5,000 to $5,000,000	1 month to 1 year	Not as good as U.S. Treasury and federal agency issues		—		
Negotiable certificates of deposit	$100,000 to $1,000,000	7 days to 18 months or more	Fairly good secondary market	(1 month) (3 months) (6 months)	17.91 17.96 17.98	7.85 7.88 7.97	9.37 9.25 9.28
Commercial paper	$100,000 or more	2 or 3 days to 270 days	Weak secondary market	(1 month) (3 months) (6 months)	17.58 17.23 16.62	7.81 7.80 7.79	9.31 9.11 8.97
Repurchase agreements	Varying amounts; no standard denominations	1 day to several months	Limited, but borrower agrees to repurchase securities at a fixed price on a fixed date				
Bankers' acceptances	Varying amounts, depending on the size of the commercial transaction	30 to 180 days	Good, although less extensive than for most other instruments	(3 months) (6 months)	17.22 16.56	7.76 7.75	8.96 8.83
Eurodollar deposits	$1,000,000	1 day to 6 months (or more)	Developing a secondary market	(3 months)	18.79	8.08	9.30
Money market preferred stock	$100,000 to $500,000 depending on issue	—	Saleable at auction every 49 days		—		
Money market mutual funds	Minimum of $1,000 is usually required; no standard denominations	Redeemable at any time	Good, because the fund agrees to redeem shares at any time		Yields vary from fund to fund, but they usually exceed the yield available on Treasury bills.		
Bank money market accounts	Minimum of $2,500 required	Normally redeemable at any time (by law, banks reserve the right to require 7 days' written notice for withdrawals)	Excellent, but not available to business firms		Yields vary significantly from bank to bank, but they usually are below Treasury bill yields.		

* SOURCE: *Federal Reserve Bulletin*, Table 1:35, various issues.

lies in the fact that their yields normally are the lowest of any marketable security.

631

CHAPTER 18
The Management
of Cash
and Marketable
Securities

The Treasury also issues notes that have original maturities of from 2 to 10 years and bonds that have maturities over 10 years. As these securities approach their maturity dates, they become, in effect, short-term instruments that are then suitable for inclusion in a firm's marketable securities portfolio. Treasury bonds and notes pay interest semiannually. Minimum Treasury bond denominations are $1,000.

OTHER FEDERAL AGENCY ISSUES. A number of federal government-sponsored agencies issue their own securities, including the "big five": the Federal Home Loan Bank, the Federal Land Banks, the Federal Intermediate Credit Bank, the Bank for Cooperatives, and the Federal National Mortgage Association. Although each of these agencies guarantees its own securities, they do not constitute a legal obligation on the part of the U.S. government. Nevertheless, most investors consider them to be very low risk securities, and they sell at yields slightly above U.S. Treasury securities but below other money market instruments. Because these securities are traded in the secondary markets through the same dealers who handle U.S. Treasury securities, they are readily marketable should a firm need to dispose of them before maturity. Minimum denominations generally are $5,000.

MUNICIPAL SECURITIES. State and local governments and their agencies issue various types of interest-bearing securities. Short-term issues are suitable for inclusion in a firm's marketable securities portfolio. The yields on these securities vary with the credit-worthiness of the issuer. The pretax yields on these securities generally are lower than the yields on Treasury bills because the interest is exempt from federal (and some state) income taxes. The secondary market for municipal issues is not as strong as that for Treasury and other federal agency issues. Municipal (tax-exempt) money market mutual funds also are available.

NEGOTIABLE CERTIFICATES OF DEPOSIT. Commercial banks are permitted to issue certificates of deposit (CDs), which entitle the holder to receive the amount deposited plus accrued interest on a specified date. At the time of issue, maturities on these instruments range from 7 days to 18 months or more. Once issued, CDs become *negotiable*, meaning they can be bought and sold in the secondary markets. Because CDs of the largest banks are handled by government securities dealers, they are readily marketable and thus are suitable for inclusion in a firm's marketable securities portfolio. Yields on CDs generally are above the rates on federal agency issues having similar maturities.

COMMERCIAL PAPER. Commercial paper consists of short-term unsecured promissory notes issued by large, well-known corporations and finance companies. Some finance companies, such as General Motors Acceptance Corporation (GMAC) and C.I.T. Financial Corporation, which issue large amounts of commercial paper regularly, sell it directly to investors. Industrial, utility, and transportation firms and smaller finance companies, which issue commercial paper less frequently and in smaller amounts, sell their commercial paper through commercial paper dealers. Maturities on commercial paper at the time of issue range from 2 or 3 days to 270 days.

The secondary market for commercial paper is weak, although it sometimes is possible to make arrangements with the issuer or commercial paper dealer to repurchase the security prior to maturity. This weak secondary market combined with a somewhat higher default risk results in higher yields on commercial paper than on most other money market instruments.

REPURCHASE AGREEMENTS. A repurchase agreement, or "repo," is an arrangement with a bank or securities dealer in which the investor acquires certain short-term securities subject to a commitment from the bank or dealer to repurchase the securities on a specified date. Securities used in this agreement can be government securities, CDs, or commercial paper. Their maturities tend to be relatively short, ranging from 1 day to several months, and are designed to meet the needs of the investor.

The yield on a repo is slightly less than the rate that can be obtained from outright purchase of the underlying security. The repo rate approximates the rate on federal funds, which is the rate used when banks borrow from other banks. Although repos generally are considered very safe investments, a number of investors did incur losses when several small government securities dealers (which were active in the repo market) failed.

BANKERS' ACCEPTANCES. A bankers' acceptance is a short-term debt instrument issued by a firm as part of a commercial transaction. Payment is guaranteed by a commercial bank. Bankers' acceptances are commonly used financing instruments in international trade, as well as in certain lines of domestic trade.

These instruments vary in amount, depending on the size of the commercial transactions. A secondary market exists in which these acceptances can be traded should a bank or investor choose not to hold them until maturity, which usually ranges between 30 and 180 days at the time of issue. Bankers' acceptances are relatively safe investments, because both the bank and the borrower are liable for the amount due at maturity. Their yields are comparable to the rates available on CDs.

EURODOLLAR DEPOSITS. Eurodollar deposits are dollar-denominated deposits in banks or bank branches located outside the United States. These deposits usually have slightly higher yields than on corresponding deposits in domestic banks because of the additional risks. Eurodollar CDs issued by London banks are negotiable and a secondary market is developing for them.

MONEY MARKET PREFERRED STOCKS. In 1984, Shearson Lehman (a large brokerage firm) began issuing, on behalf of some of its client companies, a new type of preferred stock, known as money market preferred, which is a suitable short-term investment for excess corporate funds. The dividend yield on this type of security is adjusted every 49 days through an auction process, where investors can exchange their stock for cash. As a result, the price of the stock stays near par. Because 70 percent of the dividends received are exempt from corporate income taxes, the after-tax yields often are above the yields on other marketable securities such as CDs or commercial paper. The stock is sold in minimum denominations of $100,000 to $500,000, depending on the issue. Since its original introduction, other investment bankers also have begun offering similar auction rate preferred stock.

633

CHAPTER 18
**The Management
of Cash
and Marketable
Securities**

MONEY MARKET MUTUAL FUNDS. Many of the higher yielding marketable securities described earlier are available only in relatively large denominations. For example, negotiable CDs usually come in amounts of $100,000 or more. As a result, a smaller firm that has limited funds to invest at any given time is often unable to obtain the higher yields offered on these securities. An alternative is a *money market mutual fund* that pools the investments of many other small investors and invests in large-denomination money market instruments. By purchasing shares in a money market fund, such as Dreyfus Liquid Assets or Merrill Lynch Ready Assets, a smaller firm can approach the higher yields offered on large-denomination securities. In addition, most of these funds offer check-writing privileges, which provides liquidity and enables firms to earn interest on invested funds until their checks clear.

BANK MONEY MARKET ACCOUNTS. Early in 1983 banks were permitted to offer checking accounts with yields comparable to those on money market mutual accounts with limited check-writing privileges. These accounts provide yields that are comparable to those on money market mutual funds; however, their use is limited to individuals, nonprofit organizations, and governments.

INTERNATIONAL CONCERNS: CASH MANAGEMENT

The goals of cash management in a multinational company (MNC) parallel the cash management goals of purely domestic corporations. That is, MNCs attempt to speed up collections, slow disbursements, and make the most efficient use of the firm's cash resources by minimizing excess balances and investing balances to earn the highest possible return, consistent with liquidity and safety constraints. However, there are some unique elements of cash management for an MNC.

First, cash management is complicated by difficulties and costs associated with moving funds from one country (and currency) to another. It is costly to convert cash from one currency to another. Second, there is a general lack of integrated international cash transfer facilities such as exist in the United States and most other Western nations. The absence of this capability makes it difficult to move funds quickly from one country to another. Third, investment opportunities for temporary excess cash balances are much broader for an MNC than for a domestic firm. MNCs must consider short-term investment options in many different countries—a process further complicated by exchange rate risk. Fourth, the host government may place restrictions on the movement of cash out of the country.

Practicing MNC cash managers have developed a number of techniques designed to optimize the process of international cash management in the face of these difficulties. First, there is general agreement that the cash management function for an MNC should be centralized with respect to the information gathering and decision-making process. The parent normally maintains an international cash manager who has the expertise and responsibility to keep track of the firm's cash balances around the world and to identify the best sources for short-term borrowing and lending.

Second, many MNCs have instituted a process called *multilateral netting*. Multilateral netting is designed to minimize the cost associated with *misdirected* funds. Misdirected funds are funds that cross a border unnecessarily. It is costly to convert funds from one currency to another, hence it is desirable to minimize unnecessary transactions. For example, consider an MNC that has subsidiaries operating in Spain, West Germany, and Italy. Each subsidiary purchases supplies from the other subsidiaries. If the West German unit purchases $10 million from the unit in Spain and Spanish unit purchases $8 million from the West German unit, the transaction cost associated with transferring funds from the West German unit to the Spanish unit can be reduced if these payments are *netted out* against each other. Thus, instead of the West German unit converting $10 million in funds to send to the Spanish unit, it will net out the Spanish unit's purchases from the West German unit and simply send a $2 million payment. The greater the number of subsidiaries an MNC has, the more complex is the process of managing a multilateral netting system. At the same time the potential cost savings are greatly increased.

SUMMARY

- A firm holds liquid asset balances for the following primary reasons:
    1. To conduct transactions.
    2. For precautionary purposes.
    3. To meet future requirements.
    4. For speculative reasons.
    5. To compensate its bank or banks for various services rendered.

- To manage cash effectively, a firm must first develop a *cash budget* showing all of the forecasted cash inflows and outflows over the planning horizon.
- A firm's optimal liquid asset balance reflects risk and return tradeoffs and depends on both the opportunity cost of holding excess balances and the "shortage" costs associated with not having enough needed cash available.
- The primary objective in controlling cash collections is to reduce the delay between the time when the customer mails the payment and when it becomes a collected balance. Methods for reducing collection time include decentralized collection centers and concentration banks, lockboxes, wire transfers, depository transfer checks, special handling of large remittances, and the use of preauthorized checks.
- The primary objective in controlling cash disbursements is to slow payments and keep the firm's funds in the bank as long as possible. Techniques for slowing disbursements include scheduling and centralizing payments (zero-balance systems), using drafts rather than checks, maximizing check clearing float, and stretching payables.
- Electronic funds transfer mechanisms, including the use of wire transfers and automated check clearinghouses, increasingly will reduce the importance of float management techniques.
- The primary criteria a firm should use in selecting *marketable securities* include *default risk, marketability* (or *liquidity*), *maturity date*, and *rate of return*. The most commonly used marketable securities include U.S.

Treasury issues, other federal agency issues, municipal securities, negotiable certificates of deposit, commercial paper, repurchase agreements, bankers' acceptances, Eurodollar deposits, money market preferred stocks, money market funds, and bank money market accounts.

QUESTIONS AND TOPICS FOR DISCUSSION

1. Define the following terms:
   a. Demand deposits.
   b. Compensating balance.
   c. Disbursement float.
   d. Deposit float.
   e. Lockbox.
   f. Wire transfer.
   g. Depository transfer check.
   h. Zero-balance system.
   i. Draft.
   j. Automated clearinghouse.

2. What are the primary reasons why a firm holds a liquid asset balance?

3. Describe the cost tradeoffs associated with maintaining the following:
   a. Excessive liquid asset balances.
   b. Inadequate liquid asset balances.

4. Define *float* and describe the difference between *disbursement* float and *deposit* float.

5. Describe the primary services a bank provides to a firm. How is the bank compensated for these services?

6. Describe the methods available to a firm for expediting the collection of cash.

7. Describe the techniques available to a firm for slowing disbursements.

8. Explain the tradeoffs involved in determining the number of collection centers that a firm should use.

9. What factors should the firm consider in deciding whether to establish a lockbox collection system?

10. What are the primary criteria in selecting marketable securities for inclusion in a firm's portfolio?

11. What types of marketable securities are most suitable for inclusion in a firm's portfolio? What characteristics of these securities make them desirable investments for temporarily idle cash balances?

12. What is multilateral netting? Give an example of how this would work for a multinational firm.

PROBLEMS*

NOTE: **When converting annual data to daily data or vice versa in these problems, assume there are 365 days per year.**

1. Dexter Instrument Company's sales average $3.0 million per day.
   a. If Dexter could reduce the time between customers' mailing their payments and the funds' becoming collected balances by 2.5 days, determine the increase in firm's average cash balance.

* Colored numbers denote problems that have check answers provided at the end of the book.

   b. Assuming that these additional funds can be invested in marketable securities to yield 8.5 percent per annum, determine the annual increase in Dexter's (pretax) earnings.

2. Exman Company performed a study of its billing and collection procedures and found that an average of 8 days elapses between the time when a customer's payment is received and when the funds become usable by the firm. The firm's *annual* sales are $540 million.

   a. Assuming that Exman could reduce the time required to process customer payments by 1.5 days, determine the increase in the firm's average cash balance.

   b. Assuming that these additional funds could be used to reduce the firm's outstanding bank loans (current interest rate is 8 percent) by an equivalent amount, determine the annual pretax savings in interest expenses.

3. Great Lakes Oil Company currently processes all its credit card payments at its domestic headquarters in Chicago. The firm is considering establishing a lockbox arrangement with a Los Angeles bank to process its payments from ten western states (California, Nevada, Arizona, Utah, Oregon, Washington, Montana, Wyoming, Colorado, and Idaho). Under the arrangement, the average mailing time for customer payments from the western region would be reduced from 3.0 days to 1.5 days, whereas check-processing and -clearing time would be reduced from 6.0 days to 2.5 days. Annual collections from the western region are $180 million. The total number of payments received annually is 4.8 million (an average of 400,000 credit card customers × 12 payments per year). The Los Angeles bank will process the payments for an annual fee of $75,000 plus $0.05 per payment. No compensating balance will be required. Assume that the funds released by the lockbox arrangement can be invested elsewhere in the firm to yield 10 percent before taxes. The establishment of a lockbox system for the western region will reduce payment-processing costs at the Chicago office by $50,000 per year. Using this information, determine the following:

   a. The amount of funds released by the lockbox arrangement.

   b. The annual (pretax) earnings on the released funds.

   c. The annual fee Great Lakes Oil must pay to the Los Angeles bank for processing the payments.

   d. The annual *net* (pretax) benefits Great Lakes Oil will receive by establishing this lockbox arrangement with the Los Angeles bank.

   Great Lakes Oil also has received a proposal from a Salt Lake City bank to set up a lockbox system for the firm. Average mailing time for checks in the western region would be reduced to 2 days under the proposal from the Salt Lake City bank, and check-processing and clearing time would average 2.5 days. The Salt Lake City bank would not charge any fees for processing the payments, but it would require Great Lakes Oil to maintain a $1.5 million average compensating balance with the bank—funds that normally would be invested elsewhere in the firm (yielding 10 percent) and not kept in a non-interest-bearing checking account.

   e. Determine the annual *net* (pretax) benefits to Great Lakes Oil of establishing a lockbox system with the Salt Lake City bank.

   f. Which of the two lockbox systems (if any) should the firm select?

4. Japanese Motors, a major importer of foreign automobiles, has a subsidiary (Japanese Motor Credit Company, or JMCC) that finances dealer inventories, as well as retail installment purchases of the company's cars. With respect to the financing of retail purchases, JMCC currently employs a centralized billing and collection system. Once a customer's credit has been approved at one of the subsidiary's 50 local branch offices, the information is forwarded to JMCC headquarters (located in Los Angeles), and the customer is issued a book of payment coupons. Each month during the life of the installment

contract, the customer mails a coupon stub along with the payment to the Los Angeles office. The average mailing, processing, and check-clearing time with the present collection system is 8 days.

637

CHAPTER 18
The Management
of Cash
and Marketable
Securities

In an effort to reduce this collection time, JMCC is considering establishing a decentralized collection system. Under this system customers would be instructed to mail their payments to the nearest local branch office, which would then deposit the checks in a local bank and report this information to JMCC headquarters in Los Angeles. As the checks cleared in the local banks, funds would be sent each day to JMCC's central bank in Los Angeles. This decentralized collection system would reduce both mailing time and check-clearing time and reduce the average collection time to 5 days.

JMCC's annual installment collections are $900 million. Implementation of the decentralized collection system is expected to reduce collection costs at the Los Angeles headquarters by $100,000 a year compared with the currently employed centralized collection system. However, branch office collection costs are expected to *rise* by $225,000 if the decentralized system is implemented. JMCC's Los Angeles bank currently requires the firm to maintain a $250,000 balance as compensation for depositing customer payments. Compensating balances at the 50 local banks that JMCC would employ with the decentralized collection system are expected to total $500,000. Any funds released under the decentralized collections system would be used to reduce the firm's debt, which currently carries an interest rate of 7.5 percent.

Using this information, determine the annual *net* pretax benefits JMCC would realize by implementing a decentralized collection system.

5. J-Mart, a nationwide department store chain, processes all its credit sales payments at its suburban Detroit headquarters. The firm is considering the implementation of a lockbox collection system with an Atlanta bank to process monthly payments from its southeastern region. Annual credit sales collections from the region are $60 million. The establishment of the lockbox system would reduce mailing, processing, and check-clearing time from 8 days currently to 3.5 days, reduce company processing costs by $25,000 per year, and reduce the compensating balance of its Detroit bank by $200,000. The Atlanta bank would not charge any fee for the lockbox service but would require J-Mart to maintain a $500,000 compensating balance. Funds released by the lockbox arrangement could be invested elsewhere in the firm to earn 15 percent before taxes. Determine the following:

   a. The amounts of funds released by the lockbox arrangement.
   b. The annual (pretax) earnings on the released funds.
   c. The annual *net* (pretax) benefits to J-Mart of establishing the lockbox system with the Atlanta bank.

6. Peterson Electronics uses a decentralized collection system whereby customers mail their payments to one of six regional collection centers. The checks are deposited each working day in the collection center's local bank, and a depository transfer check for the amount of the deposit is *mailed* to the firm's concentration bank in New York. An average of 5 days elapse between the time the checks are deposited in the local bank and the time the funds become collected funds (and available for disbursements) at the concentration bank. Peterson is considering using wire transfers instead of depository transfer checks in moving funds from the six collection centers to its concentration bank. Wire transfers would reduce the elapsed time *by* 3 days. Depository transfer checks cost $0.50 (including postage), and wire transfers cost $10. Assume there are 250 working days per year. Peterson can earn 7 percent before taxes on any funds that are released through more efficient collection techniques. Determine the net (pretax) benefit to Peterson of using wire transfers if annual sales are

   a. $15 million.
   b. $75 million.

Suppose Peterson is considering using *electronic* depository transfer checks rather than mail depository transfer checks to move funds from its six collection centers to its concentration bank. Electronic depository transfer checks would *reduce* collection time by 2 days and would cost $2.50 each. Determine the net (pretax) benefit to Peterson of using electronic depository transfer checks if annual sales are

c. $15 million.

d. $75 million.

7. Wisconsin Paper Company is considering establishing a zero-balance system for its payroll account. The firm pays its employees every 2 weeks on Friday (that is, 26 pay periods per year). Currently the firm deposits the necessary funds in the payroll account on Friday to cover the total amount of the checks written each pay period, which averages $1 million. However, the firm has found that the majority of the checks did not clear the payroll account until the following week. A typical distribution of when the checks clear the payroll account is as follows:

Day	Amount of Funds Clearing Payroll Account
Friday	$ 300,000
Monday	450,000
Tuesday	150,000
Wednesday	100,000
Total	$1,000,000

Assume that the firm can earn 6 percent on any funds released from its payroll account using a zero-balance system.

a. Determine the annual pretax returns the firm would realize from the use of a zero-balance system for its payroll account.

b. What additional information is necessary to make a decision concerning the desirability of establishing such a system?

8. The High-Rise Construction Company, located in Houston, receives large remittances (that is, progress payments) from customers with whom it has contracts. These checks are frequently drawn on New York City banks. If the checks are deposited in High-Rise's Houston bank, the funds will not become collected balances and usable by the firm until 2 *business* days later. In other words, deposits made on Monday become available for use on Wednesday, and deposits made on Friday become available to the firm on the following Tuesday. However, if High-Rise sends an employee to New York with the check and she presents it for payment at the bank upon which it is drawn, the funds will be available immediately (that is, the same day) to the firm. Assuming that High-Rise can earn 6 percent on short-term investments and that the cost of sending an employee to New York to present the check for payment is $350, determine the following:

a. The net (pretax) benefit to the firm of using this special handling procedure for a $1 million check received on the following days:

  i. Monday.

  ii. Friday.

  Why do the answers to Parts i and ii differ?

b. The amount of a check on which the firm just "breaks even" (that is, the net pretax benefit equals zero) using the special handling procedure, assuming that the check is received on the following days:

  i. Monday.

  ii. Friday.

639

CHAPTER 18
The Management
of Cash
and Marketable
Securities

9. Jackson's Thriftway currently processes all of its credit sales at its Seguin, Texas, headquarters. The firm is considering establishing a lockbox arrangement with a Chicago bank to process payments from customers in twelve midwestern states. Average mailing time for customers from this region is currently 4 days. It is expected that the system will reduce this to 2.5 days. Check processing and clearing time would be reduced from 4 days to 1.5 days with the lockbox arrangement. Annual collections from this region are $200 million. The lockbox arrangement would reduce the compensating balance requirement at the firm's Seguin bank by $400,000 and reduce annual payment processing costs at the Seguin office by $25,000. Funds released by the lockbox arrangement can be invested elsewhere in the firm to earn 14 percent before taxes.

   a. The Chicago bank has agreed to process Jackson's customer payments for an annual fee of $130,000. Determine the annual net pretax benefits to Jackson's of establishing a lockbox system with the Chicago bank.

   b. The Chicago bank has agreed to process Jackson's customer payments "free of charge" if the firm maintains a minimum compensating balance of $2 million in its account at the bank. Determine the annual net pretax benefits to Jackson's of establishing the lockbox system under these conditions.

▬▬▬▬ SELECTED REFERENCES

Batlin, C. A., and Susan Hinko. "Lockbox Management and Value Maximization." *Financial Management* 10 (Winter 1981): 39–44.

Driscoll, Mary C. *Cash Management: Corporate Strategies for Profit*. New York: Wiley, 1983.

Gallinger, George W., and P. B. Healey. *Liquidity Analysis and Management*. Reading, MA: Addison-Wesley, 1987.

Hartley, W. C. F., and Yale L. Meltzer. *Cash Management*. Englewood Cliffs, NJ: Prentice-Hall, 1979.

Kallberg, Jarl G., and Kenneth Parkinson. *Current Asset Management*. New York: Wiley, 1984.

Maier, Steven F., and James H. Vander Weide. "What Lockbox and Disbursement Models Really Do." *Journal of Finance* (May 1983): 361–371.

Morris, James R. "The Role of Cash Balances in Firm Valuation." *Journal of Financial and Quantitative Analysis* (December 1983): 533–545.

Nauss, Robert M., and Robert E. Markland. "Solving Lockbox Location Problems." *Financial Management* 8 (Spring 1979): 21–31.

Smith, Keith V. *Readings on Short-Term Financial Management*, 3d. ed. St. Paul, MN: West Publishing Company, 1988.

Stone, Bernell K. "The Design of a Company's Banking System." *Journal of Finance* (May 1983): 373–385.

Stone, Bernell K., and T. W. Miller. "Daily Cash Forecasting with Multiplicative Models of Cash Flow Patterns." *Financial Management* (Winter 1987): 45–55.

19

Management of Accounts Receivable and Inventories

KEY CHAPTER CONCEPTS

1. *Accounts receivable management* refers to the decisions a business makes regarding its overall credit and collection policies and the evaluation of individual credit applicants.

2. In formulating an optimal credit policy, a company's financial managers must analyze the marginal benefits and costs associated with changes in each of the following variables:
   a. Credit standards.
   b. Credit terms.
   c. Collection efforts.

3. The evaluation of individual credit applicants consists of the following three principal steps:
   a. Gathering relevant information on the credit applicant.
   b. Analyzing the information obtained to determine the applicant's creditworthiness.

   c. Deciding whether to extend credit to the applicant and, if so, determining the amount of the line of credit.

4. The determination of the optimal level of inventory investment requires that the benefits and costs associated with alternative levels be measured and compared.

5. Inventory-related costs include
   a. Ordering costs.
   b. Carrying costs.
   c. Stockout costs.

6. The use of inventory control models can aid in efficiently managing a company's level of inventory investment.

7. The economic order quantity model permits determination of the quantity of an inventory item that should be ordered to minimize total inventory costs.

GLOSSARY OF NEW TERMS

ABC inventory classification A method of dividing inventory items into three groups—those with a relatively large dollar value but a small percentage of the total items, those with a small dollar value but a large percentage of the total items, and those items in between.

Average collection period The average number of days between when a credit sale is made and when the customer's payment is received.

Bad-debt loss ratio The proportion of the total receivables volume that is never collected by a business.

Carrying costs All costs associated with holding items in inventory for a period of time.

Cash discount A discount offered for early payment of an invoice.

Credit period The length of time a credit customer has to pay the account in full.

Discount period The length of time a credit customer has to pay the account and still be eligible to take any cash discount offered.

Economic order quantity The quantity of an inventory item that should be ordered to minimize total inventory costs.

Inventory cycle The time between placement of successive orders of an item.

Just-in-time inventory and production concept An approach to inventory and production management in which required inventory items are supplied exactly as needed by production.

Lead time The time between when an order is placed for an item and when the item actually is received in inventory.

Ordering costs All costs associated with placing and receiving an order.

Reorder point The inventory level at which an order should be placed for replenishment of an item.

Seasonal datings Credit terms under which the buyer of seasonal merchandise is encouraged to take delivery well before the peak sales period. Payment on the purchase is deferred until after the peak sales period.

Stockout costs The cost of lost sales associated with the inability to fill orders from inventory.

Variable cost ratio Variable production, administrative, and marketing costs per dollar of sales.

Factories of the Future and Inventory Management*

According to many futurists, factories of the future will be totally automated, consisting of robots that perform the various tasks along with a few technicians to deal with any problems that might occur. Although a few factories may follow this approach, the vast majority of production facilities in the 1990s will be more efficient versions of those in the 1970s; namely, partnerships of workers and machines. Instead of massive investments in fully automated production systems, most companies will use a combination of new production methods, innovative management techniques, a more cooperative work environment, and *some* computer-controlled equipment in their existing plants.

One area in which significant improvements have been made (and will continue to be made) is in inventory management. By reducing the production cycle and employing just-in-time inventory systems, a firm can significantly reduce its inventory investment and associated costs. (With a just-in-time inventory management system, suppliers furnish parts and materials precisely when they are needed.)[1] In the past, many companies tried to lower costs and protect themselves against shortages by purchasing items in large quantities. However, many firms now use computerized production planning and electronic communications between themselves and their suppliers to eliminate the need for large stockpiles of materials. For example, Huffy's bicycle plant at Celina, Ohio, receives daily shipments of steel from Armco's Middletown, Ohio, plant. Approximately 1 week after the steel comes into the plant it goes out as a bicycle, compared with 3 weeks in the past. The number of bins used to store and move parts throughout the bicycle plant has been reduced from 3,000 bins 5 years ago to 700 today, despite an increase in output from 10,000 to 15,000 bicycles per day. Likewise the combination of just-in-time inventory management and a faster process time has permitted Unisys (a maker of computers and office equipment) to reduce inventories at its Flemington, New Jersey plant to a 1.3 month supply today compared with a 7 month supply back in 1981.

Techniques for determining the firm's optimal inventory and accounts receivable investment are developed in this chapter.

* Adapted from the *Wall Street Journal* (November 30, 1987), p. 1.

[1] Just-in-time inventory management systems are discussed further in this chapter.

INTRODUCTION

Accounts receivable and inventories constitute important investments for most companies. As we saw earlier in Table 17-2, these two current assets represent sizeable proportions of the total assets of firms in a wide variety of industries. Among firms engaged in wholesale and retail trade, the proportions for each asset often are 25 percent or more of total assets in many companies. The management of accounts receivable is discussed in the next four sections. Inventory management is examined in the remainder of the chapter.

ESTABLISHING CREDIT AND COLLECTION POLICIES

Accounts receivable consist of the credit a business grants its customers when selling goods or services.[2] They take the form of either *trade credit*, which

[2] From the *customer's* perspective, credit represents a form of short-term financing known as *accounts payable*. This is discussed in more detail in Chapter 20.

the company extends to other companies, or *consumer credit*, which the company extends to its ultimate consumers.[3] The effectiveness of a company's credit policies can have a significant impact on its total performance. For example, Monsanto's credit manager has estimated that a reduction of only *1 day* in the average collection period for the company's receivables increases its cash flow by $10 million and improves profits by $1 million.

For a business to grant credit to its customers, it has to do the following:

- Establish credit and collection policies.
- Evaluate individual credit applicants.

The establishment of optimal credit and collection policies is developed in the next two sections. Procedures for evaluating individual credit applicants are discussed later in the chapter.

643

CHAPTER 19
Management of
Accounts
Receivable and
Inventories

SHAREHOLDER WEALTH AND OPTIMAL INVESTMENTS IN ACCOUNTS RECEIVABLE

When a company decides to extend credit to customers, it is making an investment decision; namely, an investment in accounts receivable, a *current asset*. Like the decision to invest in *long-term assets* (that is, a capital budgeting decision), the primary goal is the maximization of shareholder wealth. Recall from the discussion of the basic framework for capital budgeting decisions in Chapter 9 that the optimal capital budget is determined by accepting all investment projects whose marginal returns, as measured by the internal rate of return, are greater than or equal to the marginal costs of the funds invested in the projects, as measured by the marginal cost of capital. Such a decision rule maximizes shareholder wealth because the projects accepted will earn a return greater than or equal to cost of the funds to the owners of the firm. Following similar reasoning, a company will maximize shareholder wealth by investing in accounts receivable as long as the expected marginal returns obtained from each additional dollar of receivables investment exceed the associated expected marginal costs of the investment, *including the cost of the funds invested*.

The establishment of an *optimal credit extension policy* requires the company to examine and attempt to measure the *marginal costs* and *marginal returns* (benefits) associated with alternative policies. What are the marginal returns and costs associated with a more liberal extension of credit to a company's customers? With respect to returns, a more liberal extension presumably stimulates sales and leads to increased gross profits, assuming that all other factors (such as economic conditions, prices, production costs, and advertising expenses) remain constant. Offsetting these increased returns are several types of credit-related marginal costs, including the opportunity costs of the additional capital funds employed to support the higher level of receivables. Checking new credit accounts and collecting the higher level of receivables also results in additional costs. And finally, a more liberal credit policy frequently results in increased bad-debt expenses, because a certain number of new accounts are likely to fail to repay the credit extended to them.

[3] Some companies use their accounts receivable to obtain short-term financing. For example, a company that is somewhat weak financially might be unable to borrow short-term funds without putting up collateral for the loan. In such a case the company might use its accounts receivable as the collateral by *pledging* them to the bank. Alternatively the company might consider selling, or *factoring*, its accounts receivable to obtain cash. Accounts receivable pledging and factoring are discussed in Chapter 20.

CREDIT POLICY VARIABLES

In determining an optimal credit extension policy, a company's financial managers must consider a number of major controllable variables that can be used to alter the level of receivables, including the following:

■ Credit standards.
■ Credit terms.
■ Collection effort.

The remainder of this section discusses each of these variables in more detail.

Credit Standards

Credit standards are the criteria a company uses to screen credit applicants in order to determine which of its customers should be offered credit and how much. The process of setting credit standards allows the firm to exercise a degree of control over the "quality" of accounts accepted.[4] The quality of credit extended to customers is a multidimensional concept involving the following:

■ The time a customer takes to repay the credit obligation, *given that it is repaid.*
■ The probability that a customer will fail to repay the credit extended to it.

The *average collection period* serves as one measure of the promptness with which customers repay their credit obligations. It indicates the average number of days a company must wait after making a credit sale before receiving the customer's cash payment. Obviously, the longer the average collection period, the higher a company's receivables investment and, by extension, its cost of extending credit to customers.

The likelihood that a customer will fail to repay the credit extended to it is sometimes referred to as *default risk*. The *bad-debt loss ratio*, which is the proportion of the total receivables volume a company never collects, serves as an overall, or aggregate, measure of this risk. A business can estimate its loss ratio by examining losses on credit that has been extended to similar types of customers in the past.[5] The higher a firm's loss ratio, the greater is the cost of extending credit.

For example, suppose that Bassett Furniture Industries is considering making a change in its credit standards. Before reaching any decision, the company must first determine whether such a change would be profitable. The first step in making this decision involves an evaluation of the overall credit-worthiness of the company's existing and potential customers (retailers) using various sources of information.[6] Table 19-1 illustrates the

---

[4] *Complete* control over the quality of accounts accepted is generally impossible due to uncertainty about future events (for example, a recession or a strike) that could make it difficult or even impossible for a customer to repay its account.

[5] This estimation procedure assumes that the loss ratio does not change significantly over time because of changing economic conditions. Otherwise, the loss ratio should be adjusted to take account of expected future economic changes. This procedure also assumes that credit extension and repayment information is available on a sufficiently large sample of accounts to provide a company with a reliable estimate of its loss ratio. Without this information, the financial manager simply has to make an "educated guess" as to the size of the loss ratio.

[6] Some of these sources of information are described later in this chapter.

Credit Evaluation Data Compiled by Bassett Furniture Industries				T A B L E 19-1

Credit Risk Group	Credit Sales ($)	Average Collection Period (Days)	Bad-Debt Loss Ratio (%)
1	900,000	25	—
2	1,100,000	30	0.5
3	400,000	45	3
4	300,000*	60	7
5	100,000*	90	13

* Estimated lost sales due to the fact that no credit is extended to customers in these risk categories.

credit sales, average collection period, and loss ratio data for various credit risk groups of the company's customers in its northwest region.

Under its current credit policy, Bassett extends unlimited credit to all customers in Credit Risk Groups 1, 2, and 3 and no credit to customers in Groups 4 and 5, meaning that the customers in these latter two groups must submit payment along with their orders. As a result of this policy, Bassett estimates that it "loses" $300,000 per year in sales from Group 4 customers and $100,000 per year in sales from Group 5 customers.

Bassett also estimates that its *variable* production, administrative, and marketing costs (including credit department costs) are approximately 75 percent of total sales;[7] that is, the *variable cost ratio* is 0.75. Thus, the profit contribution ratio per dollar of sales is as follows:

$$1.00 - 0.75 = 0.25$$

The company's required pretax rate of return (that is, the opportunity cost) on its receivables investment is 20 percent.

One alternative Bassett is considering is to relax credit standards by extending full credit to Group 4 customers. In evaluating this alternative, the financial manager has to analyze how this policy would affect pretax profits. If the marginal returns of this change in credit standards exceed the marginal costs, pretax profits would increase, and the decision to extend full credit to the Group 4 customers would increase shareholder wealth.

Table 19-2 contains the results of this analysis. In Step A, the marginal profitability of the additional sales, $75,000, is calculated. Next, the cost of the additional investment in receivables, $9,863, is calculated in Step B.[8]

[7] This analysis assumes that the collection costs for Credit Risk Group 4 customers are the same as for customers in the other groups and are included in credit department costs.

[8] Note that we have chosen to use sales value in determining the (opportunity) cost of the additional receivables investment. Disagreement exists in the finance literature concerning the measurement of the incremental investment in accounts receivable (and its associated opportunity cost) arising from a change in credit standards. Some authors contend that the relevant measure of investment is the dollar *cost* the firm has tied up in the new accounts receivable rather than the total *sales value.* The rationale for this approach is that the "profit" on the sale—that is, the difference between the amount of the accounts receivable and their associated cost—would be nonexistent without the change in credit standards. Hence, no opportunity cost is incurred on this uncollected "profit." Advocates of this approach use variable cost or total cost as a measure of the amount of funds invested in accounts receivable. Other authors claim that the total sales value of the new accounts receivable is indeed the relevant measure of investment in accounts receivable. The rationale for this approach is that the opportunity cost of the increased level of accounts receivable is the return a company could earn if it reduced accounts receivable back to its original level. In other words, considerations of symmetry

(Continued on next page)   **645**

Bassett Furniture Industries' Analysis of the Decision to Relax Credit Standards by Extending Full Credit to Customers in Credit Risk Group 4

Step A: Additional sales $300,000

Marginal profitability of additional sales
= Profit contribution ratio × Additional sales
= 0.25 × $300,000 $75,000

Step B: Additional investment in receivables
= Additional average daily sales* × Average collection period

$$= \frac{\text{Additional annual sales}}{365} \times 60$$

$$= \frac{\$300,000}{365} \times 60 \qquad \$ 49,315$$

Cost of the additional investment in receivables
= Additional investment in receivables × Required pretax rate of return
= $49,315 × 0.20 $ 9,863

Step C: Additional bad-debt loss
= Bad-debt loss ratio × Additional sales
= 0.07 × $300,000 $21,000

Step D: Net change in pretax profits
= Marginal returns − Marginal costs
= A − (B + C)
= $75,000 − ($9,863 + $21,000) + $44,137

* Standard practice is to assume that there are 365 days per year.

In Step C, the additional bad-debt loss, $21,000, is computed. Finally, in Step D, the net change in pretax profits is determined by deducting the marginal costs computed in Steps B and C from the marginal returns found in Step A. Because this net change is a positive $44,137, the analysis indicates that Bassett should relax its credit standards by extending full credit to the Group 4 customers. (However, in actual practice a company should recheck carefully the accuracy of its estimates before implementing a decision of this type.)

This analysis contains a number of both explicit and implicit assumptions of which the financial manager also must be aware. One assumption is that *the company has excess capacity* and thus could produce the additional output at a *constant variable cost ratio* of 0.75. If the company currently is operating at or near full capacity, and additional output could be obtained only by paying more costly overtime rates and/or investing in new facilities,

(Continued from previous page)

require that the opportunity cost of increasing accounts receivable by a given amount should be equal to the returns that could be earned on the funds released from decreasing accounts receivable by the same amount. The interested reader should consult the following references for a more complete discussion of the issues involved: John S. Oh, "Opportunity Cost in the Evaluation of Investment in Accounts Receivable," *Financial Management* 5 (Summer 1976): 32–35; Edward A. Dyl, "Another Look at the Evaluation of Investment in Accounts Receivable," *Financial Management* 6 (Winter 1977): 67–70; Joseph C. Atkins and Yong H. Kim, "Comment and Correction: Opportunity Cost in the Evaluation of Investment in Accounts Receivable," *Financial Management* 6 (Winter 1977): 71–74; Tirlochan S. Walia, "Explicit and Implicit Cost of Changes in the Level of Accounts Receivable and the Credit Policy Decision of the Firm," *Financial Management* 6 (Winter 1977): 75–80; and J. Fred Weston and Pham D. Tuan, "Comment on Analysis of Credit Policy Changes," *Financial Management* 9 (Winter 1980): 59–63.

this analysis would have to be modified to take account of these incremental costs. This analysis also assumes that the average collection period of the customers in Groups 1, 2, and 3 would *not increase* once the company began extending credit to Group 4 customers. If it became known that the Group 4 customers had 60 days or more to pay their bills with no penalty involved, the Group 1, 2, and 3 customers, who normally pay their bills promptly, might also start delaying their payments. If this occurred, the analysis would have to be modified to account for such shifts. It also was assumed that the required rate of return on the investment in receivables for Group 4 *does not change* as a result of extending credit to these more risky accounts. A case can be made for increasing the required rate of return to compensate for the increased risk of the new accounts. Finally, this example (and subsequent examples in this chapter) assumes that *no change* in inventory investment takes place as a result of changes in the firm's credit policies. We should recognize that this assumption may not always be correct; that is, the management of accounts receivable and inventories cannot always be considered independent of each other. Often a higher level of sales, which results from more liberal credit standards, can occur only if a company increases its investment in inventories. In summary, for this type of analysis to be valid and to lead to the correct decision, it must include *all* the marginal costs and benefits that result from the decision.

647

CHAPTER 19
Management of
Accounts
Receivable and
Inventories

Credit Terms

A company's *credit terms*, or terms of sale, specify the conditions under which the customer is required to pay for the credit extended to it. These conditions include the *length of the credit period* and the *cash discount* (if any) given for prompt payment plus any special terms, such as *seasonal datings*.

CREDIT PERIOD. Table 19-3 contains some examples of "typical" credit terms offered by various industries. For example, credit terms of "net 30" mean that the customer has 30 days from the invoice date within which to pay the bill and that no discount is offered for early payment. A firm's credit terms frequently are determined by industry customs, and thus they tend to vary among different industries. The credit period may be as short as 7 days or as long as 6 months. Variation appears to be positively related to the length of time the merchandise is in the purchaser's inventory. For example, manufacturers of goods having relatively low inventory turnover periods such as jewelry, tend to offer retailers longer credit periods than distributors of goods having higher inventory turnover periods, such as food products.

A company's credit terms can affect its sales. For example, if the demand for a particular product depends in part on its credit terms, the company may consider lengthening the credit period to stimulate sales. For example, in 1984 IBM apparently tried to stimulate declining sales of its PCjr home computer by extending the length of the credit period in which dealers had to pay for the computers. In making this type of decision, however, a company also must consider its closest competitors. If they lengthen their credit periods, too, every company in the industry may end up having about the same level of sales, a much higher level of receivables investments and costs, and a lower rate of return.

TABLE 19-3

Typical Credit Terms in Various Industries

Industry/Product	Credit Terms
Canned goods (general)	1½/10, net 60
Cigars (wholesaler)	Net 7
Decorations (interior)	6/10, net 60
Drugs (manufacturer)	2/10, net 60; 1/10, net 30
Fruits and produce (fresh)	Net 7
Furniture (upholstered)	2/30, net 60; 2/10, net 30
Groceries (wholesaler)	Net 7; C.O.D.; 1/10, net 30
Implements (agricultural)	2/10, net 60 with seasonal dating
Jewelry	5/30, net 4 months
Lumber and building materials (wholesaler)	2/10, net 30
Motors (electric, fractional horsepower)	Net 30
Petroleum (gasoline and lubricating oils)	1/10, net 30
Plumbing and heating (wholesaler)	2/10, net 30
Seeds (vegetable and flower)	1½/10, net 60; 2/10, net 60
Silverware	2/30, net 4 months
Stationery	2/10, net 60
Teas (importer)	3/10, net 4 months
Teas (wholesaler)	2/10, net 120
Textiles (velvet)	6/10, 60 days' dating with dating as of April 15 and October 15

SOURCE: Adapted from Theodore Beckman and Robert Bartels, *Credits and Collections: Management and Theory,* 8th ed. (New York: McGraw-Hill, 1969), pp. 697–704. Used with permission of McGraw-Hill Book Company.

Analyzing the possible effects of an increase in a company's credit period involves comparing the profitability of the increased sales that are expected to occur with the required rate of return on the additional investment in receivables. Additional bad-debt losses also must be considered. If a company continues to accept the same quality of accounts under its lengthened credit terms, no significant change in the bad-debt loss ratio should occur.

For example, suppose that Nike, a distributor of athletic shoes and sportswear, is considering changing its credit terms from "net 30" to "net 60" in its western Michigan sales territory. The company expects sales (all on credit) to increase by about 10 percent from a current level of $2.2 million and it expects its average collection period to increase from 35 days to 65 days. The bad-debt loss ratio should remain at 3 percent of sales. The company's variable cost ratio is 0.75, which means that its profit contribution ratio (per dollar of sales) is $1.00 - 0.75 = 0.25$. Nike's required pretax rate of return on investments in receivables is 20 percent.

Table 19-4 contains an analysis of Nike's decision. Many of the calculations in this table are similar to those in Table 19-2, which analyzed the effects of a change in credit standards. As in Table 19-2, no account has been taken of any increase in inventory that may be necessary to support this increased level of sales. If inventory investment were increased as a result of this decision, it would be necessary to add an additional cost to the analysis of the effects of a change in credit terms. Specifically, the cost of the additional investment in inventory (computed as the additional inventory investment times the required pretax rate of return) would have to be determined.

The marginal returns ($55,000) computed in Step A represent the marginal profitability of the additional sales generated by the longer credit

Step A: Additional sales

 = Percent increase × Present sales

 = 0.10 × \$2,200,000 · \$220,000

 Marginal profitability of additional sales

 = Profit contribution ratio × Additional sales

 = 0.25 × \$220,000 · \$55,000

Step B: Additional investment in receivables

 = New average balance − Present average balance

 $= \dfrac{\text{New annual sales}}{365} \times$ New average collection period $- \dfrac{\text{Present annual sales}}{365}$

 × Present average collection period

 $= \dfrac{\$2,420,000}{365} \times 65 - \dfrac{\$2,200,000}{365} \times 35$

 = \$430,959 − \$210,959 · \$220,000

 Cost of the additional investment in receivables

 = Additional investment in receivables × Required pretax rate of return

 = \$220,000 × 0.20 · \$44,000

Step C: Additional bad-debt loss

 = Bad-debt loss ratio × Additional sales

 = 0.03 × \$220,000 · \$ 6,600

Step D: Net change in pretax profits

 = Marginal returns − Marginal costs

 = A − (B + C)

 = \$55,000 − (\$44,000 + \$6,600) · · · · · · · · · · · · · · +\$ 4,400

period. The marginal costs (obtained in Steps B and C) consist of the cost of the additional receivables investment (\$44,000) and the additional bad-debt losses (\$6,600). The net increase in pretax profits (Step D) that would result from the decision to lengthen the credit period would be + \$4,400. Therefore the decision would appear to be worthwhile.

CASH DISCOUNTS. A *cash discount* is a discount offered on the condition that the customer will repay the credit extended within a specified period of time. A cash discount normally is expressed as a percentage discount on the net amount of the cost of goods purchased (usually excluding freight and taxes). The length of the discount period also is specified when discount terms are offered. For example, credit terms of "2/10, net 30" mean that the customer can deduct 2 percent of the invoice amount if payment is made within 10 days from the invoice date. If payment is not made by this time, the full invoice amount is due within 30 days from the invoice date. (In some cases the discount period may begin with the date of shipment or the date of receipt by the customer.) Like the length of the credit period, the cash discount varies among different lines of business.

Cash discounts are offered (or increased) to speed up the collection of accounts receivable and, by extension, reduce a company's level of receivables investment and associated costs.[9] Offsetting these savings or benefits is the cost of the discounts that are taken, which is equal to the lost dollar revenues from the existing unit sales volume.

For example, suppose that the CBS Record Company is considering instituting a cash discount. The company currently sells to record distributors on credit terms of "net 30" and wants to determine the effect on pretax profits of offering a 1 percent cash discount on terms of "1/10, net 30" to record distributors in its southwest region. The company's average collection period is now 50 days and is estimated to decrease to 28 days with the adoption of the 1 percent cash discount policy. It also is estimated that approximately 40 percent of the company's customers will take advantage of the new cash discount. CBS's annual credit sales in their southwest region are $2.5 million, and the company's required pretax rate of return on receivables investment is 20 percent.

Table 19-5 contains an analysis of CBS's proposed cash discount policy. The marginal returns ($30,137) computed in Step A represent the earnings CBS expects to realize on the funds released by the decrease in receivables. The marginal costs ($10,000) found in Step B represent the cost of the cash discount. Subtracting the marginal costs from the marginal returns (Step C) yields a net increase in pretax profits of $20,137, indicating that CBS

---

[9] The offering of a cash discount also may increase demand and sales, because some potential customers may view it as a form of price cut and be willing to purchase the product at this new, "lower" price. Throughout the ensuing analysis it is assumed that the cash discount is *not* perceived as a price cut and that there is no resulting increase in demand. It also is assumed that offering cash discounts will not reduce bad-debt losses by any measurable amount.

T A B L E 19-5   **CBS Record Company's Analysis of the Decision to Offer a 1 Percent Cash Discount**

Step A: Decrease in average receivables balance
= Present average balance − New average balance

$$= \frac{\text{Annual sales}}{365} \times \text{Present average collection period} - \frac{\text{Annual sales}}{365}$$

$\times$ New average collection period

$$= \frac{\$2,500,000}{365} \times 50 - \frac{\$2,500,000}{365} \times 28$$

= $342,466 − $191,781   **$150,685**

Earnings on the funds released by the decrease in receivables
= Decrease in receivables × Required pretax rate of return
= $150,685 × 0.20   **$30,137**

Step B: Cost of cash discount
= Annual sales × Percentage taking discount × Percentage discount
= $2,500,000 × 0.40 × 0.01   **$10,000**

Step C: Net change in pretax profits
= Marginal returns − Marginal costs
= A − B
= $30,137 − $10,000   **+$20,137**

should offer the proposed 1 percent cash discount, if it is confident about the accuracy of the estimates used in this analysis.

651

CHAPTER 19
Management of
Accounts
Receivable and
Inventories

SEASONAL DATINGS. Seasonal datings are special credit terms that sometimes are offered to retailers when sales are highly concentrated in one or more periods during the year. Under a seasonal dating credit arrangement, the retailer is encouraged to order and accept delivery of the product well ahead of the peak sales period and then to remit payment shortly after the peak sales period. The primary objective of seasonal dating is to increase sales to retailers who are unable to finance the buildup of inventories in advance of the peak selling period because of a weak working capital position, limited borrowing capacity, or both.

For example, O. M. Scott and Sons, manufacturers of lawn and garden products, has used a seasonal dating plan that is tied to the growing season. Payments for winter and early spring shipments are due at the end of April and May, depending on the geographical area, and payments for shipments during the summer months are due in October or November. Payments for purchases made outside the two main selling seasons are due on the 10th of the second month following shipment. A cash discount of 0.6 percent per month is offered to encourage payments in advance of these seasonal dates. The arrangement enables and encourages dealers of lawn and garden products to be fully stocked with Scott products in advance of the peak selling periods.

Seasonal datings also can be used to reduce the manufacturer's inventory storage costs. With a seasonal sales pattern and a uniform production rate throughout the year, large inventory buildups normally occur prior to each selling period. By encouraging retailers to order in advance of these peak periods, a seasonal dating arrangement reduces these inventory buildups and lowers the manufacturer's warehouse storage costs by passing them on to the retailer. A company considering this type of arrangement, however, should note that seasonal datings probably will not appreciably reduce the required investment. Approximately the same amount of working capital is invested in either case—consisting of receivables investment if seasonal datings are offered and inventory investment if seasonal datings are not offered. Thus, the decision to offer a seasonal dating credit plan involves a comparison of the profitability of the expected increased sales plus any savings in inventory investment and warehouse storage costs versus the required return on the additional investment in receivables.

Collection Effort

The collection effort consists of the methods a business employs in attempting to collect payment on past-due accounts. Some commonly used methods include the following:

■ Sending notices or letters informing the customer of the past-due status of the account and requesting payment.
■ Telephoning and/or visiting the customer in an effort to obtain payment.
■ Employing a collection agency.
■ Taking legal action against the customer.

Another approach, which also is effective in some cases, is for the firm to refuse to make new shipments to the customer until the past-due bills are paid. Although the objectives of the collection effort are to speed up past-due payments and reduce bad-debt losses, a company also must avoid antagonizing normally credit-worthy customers who may be past due for some good reason; for example, because of temporary liquidity problems. A collection effort that is too aggressive may reduce future sales and profits if customers begin buying from other businesses whose collection policies are more lenient.

When determining which methods to use in its collection effort, a company has to consider the amount of funds it has available to spend for this purpose. If the firm has a relatively small amount of money available for collecting past-due accounts, it must confine itself to less costly (and less effective) methods, such as sending letters and making telephone calls. If it has a larger budget, the firm can employ more aggressive (and, it is hoped, more effective) procedures, such as sending out representatives to personally contact past-due customers. In general, the larger a company's collection expenditures, the shorter its average collection period and the lower its level of bad-debt losses. The benefits of additional collection efforts, however, are likely to diminish rapidly at extremely high expenditure levels.

The marginal benefits of the decision to increase collection expenditures consist of the earnings on the funds released from the receivables investment as a result of the shorter average collection period, plus the reduction in bad-debt losses. A business should increase its collection expenditures only if these marginal benefits are expected to exceed the amount of the additional collection expenditures.

Monitoring Accounts Receivable

For a company to effectively control its receivables investment, the credit manager must monitor the status and composition of these accounts. An *aging of accounts* is a useful monitoring technique.[10] In an aging analysis, a company's accounts are classified into different categories based on the number of days they are past due. These classifications show both the aggregate amount of receivables and the percentage of the total receivables outstanding in each category. Aging of accounts receivable provides more information than such summary ratios as, for example, the average collection period. Comparing aging schedules at successive points in time (for example, monthly, quarterly, or semiannually) can help the credit manager monitor any changes in the "quality" of the company's accounts.

EVALUATING INDIVIDUAL CREDIT APPLICANTS

Once a company has established its credit and collection policies, it can use them as a basis for evaluating individual credit applicants.[11] In general, the credit evaluation process consists of these main steps:

■ Gathering relevant information on the credit applicant.
■ Analyzing the information obtained to determine the applicant's credit-worthiness.

[10] Aging schedules also are discussed in Chapter 3.
[11] Once these policies are established, however, they do not have to remain static over time. The credit manager should review them periodically, making appropriate modifications as dictated by changing economic conditions (for example, rising interest rates) or other circumstances.

- Deciding whether to extend credit to the applicant and, if so, determining the amount of the line of credit.

653

CHAPTER 19
Management of
Accounts
Receivable and
Inventories

The credit evaluation process is limited by both time and cost. Often a business may have only a few days—or, in some cases, only a few hours—in which to evaluate a credit request. Delaying this decision too long may result in the loss of a potential customer's order.

The credit evaluation process also is limited by the amount of resources the credit department has. The amount of time and money a company spends on evaluating a customer's request for credit should depend on the size of the losses the company would experience if it made an incorrect decision. These potential losses stem from either denying credit to a credit-worthy customer or offering credit to a customer who is not credit-worthy. The larger the potential losses, the more time and money a business should spend on evaluating the credit applicant.

Gathering Information on the Credit Applicant

Information for evaluating the credit-worthiness of a customer is available from a variety of sources, including the following:

- Financial statements submitted by the customer.
- Credit reporting organizations.
- Banks.
- The company's own prior experience with the customer.

These sources differ with respect to their costs and the reliability of the information they provide.

FINANCIAL STATEMENTS. A company can ask a credit applicant to supply various kinds of financial information, such as income statements and balance sheets (preferably audited ones), and possibly even a forecasted budget. This information can be used to evaluate the applicant's financial strength—and the applicant's ability to repay credit obligations. Unwillingness on the part of the applicant to supply financial statements may indicate financial weakness and suggest the need for more detailed checking, the outright refusal to extend credit, or both.

CREDIT REPORTING ORGANIZATIONS. A number of national and local organizations collect information on the financial position and credit standing of businesses. Other companies and lending institutions that are considering extending credit to a company may obtain information about it from these organizations, usually for a fee. The most widely known organization of this type is Dun and Bradstreet Credit Services, which provides its subscribers with a credit reference book and written credit reports on individual businesses. D&B's reference book is published bimonthly and contains the names and ratings of over 3 million businesses located in the United States, including manufacturers, wholesalers, retailers, business services, and other types of businesses.

Figure 19-1 is a sample of the type of listing contained in the D&B reference book. The D&B rating, shown in the far right column, consists of two parts—the firm's estimated financial strength and its composite credit appraisal—and is based on the rating system shown in Figure 19-2.

F I G U R E 19-1

Sample Listings from the Dun and Bradstreet Reference Book

SOURCE: Reprinted by permission, Dun and Bradstreet Credit Services, Inc.

ABBOTT 312 HILL 71		
07 24	Farmers Gin & Grain Co Inc.	FF2P
	326-7300	
72 12	S And S Co.	ER3P
	326-7300	
58x12	Tufts Gilbert & Sons Inc.	––P
	326-7300	
ABERFOYLE (SEE WOLFE CITY)		

For example, the FF2P rating shown for Farmers Gin & Grain Co., Inc., in Figure 19-1 indicates that the firm has an estimated financial strength, or net worth, of $10,000–19,999 (Category FF in Figure 19-2) and a good composite credit appraisal (Category 2 in Figure 19-2). The letter *P* following the listing indicates that a D&B Payment Analysis Report is also available on that company. The ER3 is an Employee Range designation and indicates that S and S Co.'s number of employees is in the range of 100–499 employees (see Key to Employee Range Designations in Figure 19-2).

A D&B credit report provides far more detailed information about a company's financial position than the reference book does. Figure 19-3 shows an example of the first page of a credit report for Gorman Manufacturing Co., Inc. The report contains a summary of trade credit payments to existing suppliers, which can be extremely valuable to companies that are considering extending credit to Gorman Manufacturing Co., Inc. Also included in a typical report are financial data from the firm's balance sheet and income statement, a review of its banking relationships, historical information about the owners, and a description of its operations, including the location of facilities and the kinds of products sold.[12]

The National Association of Credit Management also fills requests for information on the repayment patterns of specific companies. In addition, a number of other organizations collect and disseminate credit information within given industries, such as the toy and furniture industries, as well as within given geographical areas, such as Chicago and New York.

BANKS. Many banks will assist their business customers in obtaining information on the credit-worthiness of other businesses. Through its contacts with other banks, a customer's bank often can obtain detailed information on the payment patterns and financial status of the company under investigation and pass this information on to a customer.

PRIOR EXPERIENCE WITH THE CUSTOMER. A company's experience with a credit customer can be extremely useful when deciding whether to continue extending credit, increase the amount of credit it currently grants to the customer, or both. If for example the customer tends to remit payments well beyond the due date and/or if the company must employ expensive collection methods in obtaining payments, the credit analyst should weigh this unfavorable information in making the credit extension decision.

---

[12] The reliability and comprehensiveness of this type of report depend in part on how willing a business is to supply D&B with pertinent information.

FIGURE 19-2

Dun and Bradstreet Rating System

SOURCE: Reprinted by permission, Dun and Bradstreet Credit Services, Inc.

Estimated Financial Strength / **Composite Credit Appraisal**

			High	Good	Fair	Limited
5A	$50,000,000	and over	1	2	3	4
4A	$10,000,000 to	$49,999,999	1	2	3	4
3A	1,000,000 to	9,999,999	1	2	3	4
2A	750,000 to	999,999	1	2	3	4
1A	500,000 to	749,999	1	2	3	4
BA	300,000 to	499,999	1	2	3	4
BB	200,000 to	299,999	1	2	3	4
CB	125,000 to	199,999	1	2	3	4
CC	75,000 to	124,999	1	2	3	4
DC	50,000 to	74,999	1	2	3	4
DD	35,000 to	49,999	1	2	3	4
EE	20,000 to	34,999	1	2	3	4
FF	10,000 to	19,999	1	2	3	4
GG	5,000 to	9,999	1	2	3	4
HH	Up to	4,999	1	2	3	4

General Classification based on Estimated Strength and Composite Credit Appraisal

Estimated Financial Strength / **Composite Credit Appraisal**

		Good	Fair	Limited
1R	$125,000 and over	2	3	4
2R	$50,000 to $124,999	2	3	4

Explanation

When the designation "1R" or "2R" appears, followed by a 2, 3 or 4, it is an indication that the Estimated Financial Strength, while not definitely classified, is presumed to be in the range of the ($) figures in the corresponding bracket, and while the Composite Credit Apprasial cannot be judged precisely, it is believed to fall in the general category indicated.

"INV" shown in place of a rating indicates that Dun & Bradstreet is currently conducting an investigation to gather information for a new report. It has no other significance.

"FB" (Foreign Branch). Indicates that the headquarters of this company is located in a foreign country (including Canada). The written report contains the location of the headquarters.

Absence of a Rating -- The Blank Symbol

A blank symbol (--) should not be interpreted as indicating that credit should be denied. It simply means that the information available to Dun & Bradstreet does not permit us to classify the company within our rating key and that further inquiry should be made before reaching a credit decision.

Absence of a Listing

The absence of a listing in the Dun & Bradstreet Business Information File or in the Reference Book is not to be construed as meaning a concern is non-existent or has discontinued business. Nor does it have any other meaning. The letters "NQ" on any written report mean "not listed in the Reference Book." The letters "FBN" on any written report also mean that the business is not listed in the Reference Book and that the headquarters is located in a foreign country.

Employee Range Designation (ER)

Certain businesses do not lend themselves to a Dun & Bradstreet rating. Instead, reports on these businesses carry an Employee Range Designation (ER) which is indicative of size based on number of employees. No other significance should be attached to this classification. The ER listings in the Reference Book represent those businesses on which there has been subscriber interest in the past year. Additional ER Listings are stored and updated in the D&B Business Information File.

Key to Employee Range Designation

ER 1	1000 or more	Employees
ER 2	500-999	Employees
ER 3	100-499	Employees
ER 4	50- 99	Employees
ER 5	20- 49	Employees
ER 6	10- 19	Employees
ER 7	5- 9	Employees
ER 8	1- 4	Employees
ER N		Not Available

Analyzing Credit-Worthiness and Making the Credit Decision

Credit analysts ideally should obtain information about an applicant from as many sources as possible, but they also should consider the time and costs involved. Specifically, analysts should weigh the expected returns to be derived from any additional information against the cost involved in obtaining it.

A good way to structure information collection is to proceed *sequentially*, beginning with the least costly and least time-consuming sources. If the results of this initial check indicate that more information is needed, the analyst can proceed to additional sources. For example, the analyst may begin by consulting the customer's past credit history with the company. If further information is needed, the analyst then can check the D&B reference book and/or ask the applicant to supply financial statements and a list of companies that have extended trade credit to it in the past. Finally,

FIGURE 19-3 **Dun and Bradstreet Credit Report for Gorman Manufacturing Co., Inc.**
SOURCE: Reprinted by permission, Dun and Bradstreet Credit Services, Inc.

Dun & Bradstreet Inc.

This report has been prepared for:

BE SURE NAME, BUSINESS AND ADDRESS MATCH YOUR FILE	ANSWERING INQUIRY	

THIS REPORT MAY NOT BE REPRODUCED IN WHOLE OR IN PART IN ANY MANNER WHATSOEVER

```
DUNS: 00-007-7743                    DATE PRINTED          SUMMARY
GORMAN MANUFACTURING CO INC          AUG 23, 198_    RATING   3A3
GORMAN PRINTING
(Subsidiary of Gorman Holding Companies Inc)  COMMERCIAL PRINTING  STARTED    1965
492 KOLLER ST                        SIC NO.          PAYMENTS   SEE BELOW
(formerly 400 KOLLER ST)             27 51            SALES F    $18,931,956
(and Branches and Divisions)                          WORTH F    $3,482,600
SAN FRANCISCO, CA  94110-0012                         EMPLOYS    500 (150 here)
   TEL: 415 872-9664                                  HISTORY    CLEAR
                                                      FINANCING  SECURED
CHIEF EXECUTIVE: LESLIE SMITH, PRES                   CONDITION  FAIR
                                                      TREND      DOWN
```

SPECIAL EVENTS 8/20/8_   On August 19, 198_, subject experienced a fire due to an electrical short in one of their printing machines. Damages amounted to $35,000, which was fully covered by their insurance company.

PAYMENTS (Amounts may be rounded to nearest figure in prescribed ranges)

RECORDED	PAYING RECORD	HIGH CREDIT	NOW OWES	PAST DUE	SELLING TERMS	LAST SALE WITHIN
07/8_	Ppt	1500	-0-	-0-	N30	1 Mo
07/8_	Ppt	500	-0-	-0-	N30	2-3 Mos
07/8_	Ppt	750	-0-	-0-	N30	2-3 Mos
07/8_	Slow-15	17000	6000	-0-	2 10 N30	1 Mo
07/8_	Slow-15	10000	500	-0-	2 10 N30	1 Mo
07/8_	Slow-30	3000	500	-0-	2 10 N30	1 Mo
07/8_	Slow-60	3000	3000	3000	N30	2-3 Mos
07/8_	Slow-60	2000	2000	2000	N30	2-3 Mos
06/8_	Ppt	7000	300	-0-	N30	2-3 Mos
06/8_	Ppt	5000	2500	-0-	N30	1 Mo
05/8_	Ppt	1000	-0-	-0-	EOM	2-3 Mos
05/8_	Slow-30	12000	2500	2500	N30	2-3 Mos
05/8_	Slow-30	2500	1000	1000	N30	2-3 Mos

Payment experiences reflect how bills are met in relation to the terms granted. In some instances payment beyond terms can be the result of disputes over merchandise, skipped invoices, etc.

CHANGES 03/17/8_   Subject moved from 400 KOLLER ST to 492 KOLLER ST on March 11, 198_.

UPDATE 08/17/8_   On August 17, 198_, KEVIN J. HUNT, Sec-treas stated for the six months ended June 30, 198_, profits were up compared to same period last year.

FINANCE 03/17/8_

	Fiscal Dec 31, 198_	Fiscal Dec 31, 198_	Fiscal Dec 31, 198_
Curr Assets	7,151,675	7,005,442	6,770,968
Curr Liabs	3,379,403	4,015,903	4,192,046
Other Assets	1,354,469	1,336,009	1,309,375
Worth	4,056,901	3,893,231	3,482,600
Sales	26,577,608	20,432,522	18,931,956
Net Income	767,364	64,451	32,892

Fiscal statement dated Dec 31, 198_

Cash	$ 212,597	Accts Pay	$ 1,921,028
Acct Rec	1,733,380	Bank Loans	1,795,000
Inventory	4,439,597	Other Curr Liabs	476,018
Prepaid Exp	385,394		
	-----		-----
Current Assets	6,770,968	Curr Liabs	4,192,046
Fixt & Equip	1,271,811	L.T. Liab-Other	405,697
Other Assets	37,564	CAPITAL STOCK	50,000
		RETAINED EARNINGS	3,432,600
	-----		-----
Total Assets	8,080,343	Total	8,080,343 (Continued)

if still more information is needed, the credit analyst can request a D&B credit report on the applicant and/or request credit checks through banks and the applicant's trade creditors.

Because a great deal of information usually is available about a credit applicant, the credit manager must be able to sort through this information and extract the key elements that will enable a reliable overall assessment of the applicant's credit-worthiness to be made. There are no magic formulas for making unerring credit decisions, but there are some traditional guidelines available that can serve as a framework for analysis. These guidelines are called the "five Cs of credit";

- Character.
- Capacity.
- Capital.
- Collateral.
- Conditions.

Character refers to the applicant's willingness or desire to meet credit obligations. Past payment patterns are useful in gauging this aspect of credit-worthiness.

Capacity refers to the applicant's ability to meet financial obligations. A reasonable estimate of an applicant's capacity usually can be obtained by examining its liquidity position and projected cash flows.

Capital refers to the applicant's financial strength, particularly with respect to net worth. Evidence about a company's capital usually can be obtained by evaluating the balance sheet using financial ratios.

Collateral represents the assets that the applicant may pledge as security for the credit extended to it. However, collateral often is not a critical consideration, because the primary concern for the company offering trade credit is the timely repayment of the credit, not foreclosing on the pledged assets.

Conditions refer to the general economic climate and its effect on the applicant's ability to pay. A good credit risk in prosperous times might be unable to make payments during a recession.

Many credit analysts feel that the first two Cs, character and capacity, are the most important insofar as they help to ensure that the firm considering extending credit will not leave anything important out of the analysis.

Numerical credit scoring systems are another technique that has been found useful, particularly in the area of consumer credit. This technique allows the credit granting business to quantitatively rate various financial and personal characteristics of the applicant, such as the length of the time in business, its D&B credit rating, and its current ratio. The total credit score then can be computed based on the characteristics thought to be related to credit-worthiness. The applicant's credit score next is compared with those of other applicants, or with a minimally acceptable cutoff score. Although numerical credit scoring systems can be beneficial in credit screening, they can be difficult and expensive to install.

Guidelines and techniques such as these can aid in the analysis of an applicant's credit-worthiness; the ability to make sound credit decisions, however, ultimately depends on the decision maker's experience and judgment in evaluating the available information.

■ TYPES AND FUNCTIONS OF INVENTORIES

In a manufacturing firm, *inventories* serve as a buffer between the various phases of the procurement-production-sales cycle.[13] They uncouple the various phases by giving the firm flexibility with respect to timing the purchase of raw materials, scheduling production facilities and employees, and meeting fluctuating and uncertain demand for the finished product. Inventories also serve similar purposes in the procurement-sales cycle of a wholesaling or retailing firm.

The remainder of this chapter explores the various types of inventories and their functions, along with the different categories of inventory-related costs. It also develops some models and procedures that can be used in efficiently managing a firm's level of inventory investment. Although financial managers usually do not have primary responsibility for managing a company's inventories, they are responsible for seeing that funds are invested in a manner consistent with shareholder wealth maximization. (Normally, production and/or marketing management has primary responsibility for determining the specific quantities of the various types of inventories that the firm holds.) To perform this function, financial managers must have a good working knowledge of inventory control techniques.

Manufacturing firms generally hold three types of inventories:

- Raw materials inventories.
- Work-in-process inventories.
- Finished goods inventories.

Like any other asset, the holding of inventories constitutes an investment of funds. Determining the optimal level of inventory investment requires that the benefits and costs, *including the opportunity cost of the funds invested*, associated with alternative levels be measured and compared. To do this, it is necessary to determine the specific benefits associated with holding the various types of inventories.

Raw Materials Inventories

Raw materials inventory consists of items a business purchases for use in its production process. It may consist of basic materials (for example, iron ore for a steel-making operation), manufactured goods (for example, memory chips for a computer assembly operation), or both. Maintaining adequate raw materials inventories provides a company with advantages in both purchasing and production. Specifically, the purchasing department benefits by being able to buy needed items in large quantities and take advantage of *quantity discounts* offered by suppliers. In addition, if rising prices, shortages of specific items, or both are forecasted for the future, maintaining a large stock of raw materials ensures that the company will have adequate supplies at reasonable costs.

Knowing that adequate stocks of raw materials will be available when needed permits the production department to meet production schedules and make the most efficient use of its personnel and facilities. Therefore there are a number of valid reasons why a company's purchasing and production departments will want to maintain large inventories of raw materials.

[13] Inventories are sometimes used as collateral for short-term loans. This topic is discussed in detail in Chapter 20.

Work-in-Process Inventories

659

CHAPTER 19
Management of
Accounts
Receivable and
Inventories

Work-in-process inventory consists of all items that presently are in the production cycle at some intermediate stage of completion. For example, they currently may be undergoing some type of operation (such as assembly or painting); they may be in transit between operations; or they may be stored somewhere, awaiting the next step in the production cycle.

Work-in-process inventories are a necessary part of modern industrial production systems, because they give each operation in the production cycle a certain degree of independence. This, in turn, aids in the efficient scheduling of the various operations and helps minimize costly delays and idle time. For these reasons a company's production department will want to maintain reasonable work-in-process inventories. In general, the longer a firm's production cycle, the larger its work-in-process inventory.

Finished Goods Inventories

Finished goods inventory consists of those items that have completed the production cycle and are available for sale. With the exception of large-scale, specialized types of equipment—such as industrial machinery, military armaments, jet airplanes, and nuclear reactors, which normally are contracted for *before* they are produced—most consumer and industrial products are manufactured and stored in inventory to meet forecasted future sales.

Keeping enough finished goods inventories on hand provides significant benefits for both the marketing and the production departments. From marketing's perspective, large finished goods inventories enable it to fill orders promptly, minimize lost sales, and avoid shipment delays due to stockouts. From production's standpoint, maintaining a large finished goods inventory permits items to be manufactured in large production runs, which helps keep unit production costs low by spreading fixed set-up expenses over large volumes of output.

INVENTORY-RELATED COSTS

At the same time that a number of benefits are to be realized from holding inventories, a number of costs also must be considered, including the following:

- Ordering costs.
- Carrying costs.
- Stockout costs.

Ordering Costs

Ordering costs represent all the costs of placing and receiving an order. They are stated in dollars per order. When a company is ordering from an external source, these include the costs of preparing the purchase requisition, expediting the order (for example, long distance calls and follow-up letters), receiving and inspecting the shipment, and handling payment. Factors such as an item's price and engineering complexity also affect its ordering costs. When an order is placed for an item that is manufactured *internally* within a company, ordering costs consist primarily of *production set-up* costs, which are the expenses incurred in getting the plant and equipment ready for a production run.

In practice, the cost per order generally contains both fixed and variable components, because a portion of the cost—such as that of receiving and inspecting the order—normally varies with the quantity ordered. However, many simple inventory control models, such as the EOQ model (which is described later in this chapter), treat cost per order as fixed by assuming that these costs are independent of the number of units ordered.

Carrying Costs

Carrying costs constitute all the costs of holding items in inventory for a given period of time. They are expressed either in dollars per unit per period or as a percentage of the inventory value per period. Components of this cost include the following:

■ Storage and handling costs.
■ Obsolescence and deterioration costs.
■ Insurance.
■ Taxes.
■ The cost of the funds invested in inventories.

Storage and handling costs include the cost of warehouse space. If a company leases warehouse space, this cost is equal to the rent paid. If a company owns the warehouse, this cost is equal to the value of the space in its next-best alternative use (that is, the opportunity cost). These costs also include depreciation on the inventory handling equipment, such as conveyors and forklift trucks, and the wages and salaries paid to warehouse workers and supervisors.

Inventories are valuable only if they can be sold. *Obsolescence costs* represent the decline in inventory value caused by technological or style changes that make the existing product less salable. *Deterioration costs* represent the decline in value caused by changes in the physical quality of the inventory, such as spoilage and breakage.

Another element of carrying cost is the *cost of insuring* the inventory against losses due to theft, fire, and natural disaster. In addition, a company must pay any *personal property taxes* and *business taxes* required by local and state governments on the value of its inventories.

The *cost of funds invested in inventories* is measured by the *required rate of return* on these funds. Because inventory investments are likely to be of "average risk," the overall weighted cost of capital should be used to measure the cost of these funds. If it is felt that inventories constitute an investment with either above-average or below-average risk, some adjustment in the weighted cost of capital may be necessary to account for this difference in risk.[14]

Some firms incorrectly use the rate of interest on borrowed funds as a measure of this cost. This tends to understate the true cost, because a given amount of lower-cost debt must be balanced with additional higher-cost equity financing. Inventory investment cost constitutes an opportunity cost in that it represents the return a firm foregoes as a result of deciding to invest its limited funds in inventories rather than in some other asset. There-

[14] Chapters 8 and 11 discuss the determination of risk-adjusted discount rates.

fore for most inventory decisions, the appropriate opportunity cost is the firm's weighted cost of capital.

Apple Computer was made painfully aware of the risks associated with inventory investment early in 1989.[15] To protect itself against an industry-wide shortage of computer memory chips, the company paid as much as $38 each for 2 million chips, just as the shortage was easing. To recoup these costs, the company increased prices as much as 29 percent on its computers, which shifted demand to its less profitable models that required fewer memory chips. Subsequently, computer chip prices declined to $23 each, which reduced Apple's March quarter pretax profits by $27 million. The shift in demand to less profitable computers cost Apple an additional $23 million in lost profits.

The cost of carrying inventories can represent a significant cost of doing business. Table 19-6 contains some ranges on annual inventory carrying costs, expressed as a percentage of inventory value. This study found that *total* annual carrying costs were in the range of 20 to 45 percent for most of the businesses surveyed.

Like ordering costs, inventory carrying costs contain both fixed and variable components. Most carrying costs vary with the inventory level, but a certain portion of them—such as warehouse rent and depreciation on inventory handling equipment—are relatively fixed over the short run. Most of the simple inventory control models, such as the EOQ model, treat the entire carrying cost as variable.

Stockout Costs

Stockout costs are incurred whenever a business is unable to fill orders because the demand for an item is greater than the amount currently available in inventory. When a stockout in raw materials occurs, for example, stockout costs include the expenses of placing special orders (backordering) and expediting incoming orders, in addition to the costs of any resulting production delays. A stockout in work-in-process inventory results in additional costs of rescheduling and speeding production within the plant, and it also may result in lost production costs if work stoppages occur. Finally, a stockout in finished goods inventory may result in the immediate loss of profits if customers decide to purchase the product from a competitor, and in potential long-term losses if customers decide to order from other companies in the future.

[15] *Business Week* (February 13, 1989), pp. 30–31.

661

CHAPTER 19
**Management of
Accounts
Receivable and
Inventories**

Inventory Carrying Costs (as a percentage of inventory value)			T A B L E 19-6
Cost Category	**Low**	**High**	
Storage costs	1.0%	4.0%	
Obsolescence and physical loss	5.0	10.0	
Insurance costs	1.0	3.0	
Property taxes	1.0	3.0	
Cost of money	12.0	25.0	

SOURCE: W. E. Dollar, *Effective Purchasing and Inventory Control for Small Business.* Boston, MA: Inc./CBI Publications, 1983, p. 71.

■■■ INVENTORY CONTROL MODELS

Given the significance of the benefits and costs associated with holding inventories, it is important that the firm efficiently control the level of inventory investments. A number of inventory control models are available that can help in determining the optimal inventory level of each item. These models range from the relatively simple to the extremely complex. Their degree of complexity depends primarily on the assumptions made about the demand or use for the particular item and the lead time required to secure additional stock.

A related question involves the extent of control and the type of inventory model that should be applied to different inventory items. A technique called *ABC inventory classification* can be helpful in this regard. The ABC method divides a company's inventory items into three groups. Group A consists of those items with a relatively large dollar value but a relatively small percentage of the total items, whereas group C contains those items with a small dollar value but a large percentage of the total items. Group B contains the items which are in between groups A and C. A typical result of an ABC analysis is that group A contains roughly 1 to 10 percent of the total number of items carried in inventory, but these items may represent as high as 80 to 90 percent of the total dollar value of the inventory. On the other hand, group C may contain about 50 percent of the total number of items, but these items may constitute less than 10 percent of the inventory's total dollar value. Group B contains the remaining items. Even though the actual cutoff between the groups is somewhat arbitrary, the ABC method provides management with information that can be used to determine how closely different inventory items should be controlled.

As an example, consider the Toro Company, which manufactures lawn mowers. It purchases gasoline motors from another company for use in these mowers. Because of their cost, the motors might be classified as group A items. As a result, Toro management might determine the inventory costs associated with the motors and use a detailed model to calculate the economic order quantity. On the other hand, Toro might classify all nuts and bolts it uses as a group C item. As a result, the company's policy on nuts and bolts might consist of little more than simply keeping an ample supply on hand.

In the "classic" inventory models, which include both the simpler *deterministic* models and the more complex *probabilistic* models, it is assumed that demand is either uniform or dispersed and *independent* over time.[16] In other words, demand is assumed either to be *constant* or to fluctuate over time due to *random* elements. These types of demand situations are common in retailing and some service operations.

The simpler deterministic inventory control models, such as the *economic order quantity* (EOQ) *model*, assume that both demand and lead times are *constant* and known with *certainty*. Thus, deterministic models eliminate the need to consider stockouts. The more complex probabilistic inventory

---

[16] *Dependent* demand models, in contrast, assume that demand tends to be "lumpy," or to occur at specific points in time. Dependent demand tends to occur when products are manufactured in lots, because all the items required to produce the lot are usually withdrawn from inventory at the same time rather than unit by unit. Dependent demand is a direct result of the demand for a "higher level" item. Material requirements planning (MRP) models have been developed to deal with the case of dependent demand. See J. Evans, D. Anderson, D. Sweeney, and T. Williams, *Applied Production and Operations Management* (St. Paul, MN: West Publishing Co., 1984), Chapter 14, for a discussion of MRP.

control models assume that demand, lead time, or both are *random variables with known probability distributions.*[17]

663

CHAPTER 19
Management of
Accounts
Receivable and
Inventories

Basic EOQ Model

In its simplest form, the EOQ model assumes the annual demand or usage for a particular item is known with certainty. It also assumes that this demand is stationary or uniform throughout the year. In other words, seasonal fluctuations in the rate of demand are ruled out. Finally, the model assumes that orders to replenish the inventory of an item are filled instantaneously. Given a known demand and a zero lead time for replenishing inventories, there is no need for a company to maintain additional inventories, or safety stocks, to protect itself against stockouts.

The assumptions of the EOQ model yield the saw-toothed inventory pattern shown in Figure 19-4. The vertical lines at the 0, T_1, T_2, and T_3 points in time represent the instantaneous replenishment of the item by the amount of the order quantity, Q, and the negatively sloped lines between the replenishment points represent the use of the item. Because the inventory level varies between 0 and the order quantity, average inventory is equal to one-half of the order quantity, or $Q/2$.

This model assumes that the costs of placing and receiving an order are the same for each order and independent of the number of units ordered. It also assumes that the annual cost of carrying 1 unit of the item in inventory is constant regardless of the inventory level. Total annual inventory costs, then, are the sum of ordering costs and carrying costs.[18] The primary objective of the EOQ model is to find the order quantity, Q, that minimizes total annual inventory costs.

ALGEBRAIC SOLUTION. In developing the algebraic form of the EOQ model, the following variables are defined:

Q = The order *quantity*, in units
D = The annual *demand* for the item, in units

---

[17] Rather than survey all the various inventory control models in depth, this chapter develops the deterministic EOQ model to illustrate the cost tradeoffs involved in determining the optimal inventory level. It then examines the factors that must be considered and the cost tradeoffs involved in developing a probabilistic model, without using mathematical analysis or formal solution techniques.

[18] The *actual cost* of the item (that is, the price paid for items purchased externally or the production cost for items manufactured internally) is excluded from this analysis, because it is assumed to be constant regardless of the order quantity. This assumption is relaxed later when quantity discounts are considered.

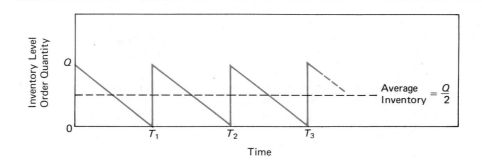

F I G U R E   19-4

Certainty Case of the Inventory Cycle

S = The cost of placing and receiving an order, or *set-up* cost

C = The annual cost of *carrying* 1 unit of the item in inventory

Ordering costs are equal to the number of orders per year multiplied by the cost per order, S. The number of orders per year is equal to annual demand, D, divided by the order quantity, Q. Carrying costs are equal to average inventory, $Q/2$, multiplied by the annual carrying cost per unit, C.

The total annual cost equation is as follows:

$$\text{Total costs} = \text{Ordering costs} + \text{Carrying costs} \qquad \textbf{(19.1)}$$

By substituting the variables just defined into Equation 19.1, the following expression is obtained:

$$\text{Total costs} = (\text{Number of orders per year}$$
$$\times \text{ cost per order}) + (\text{Average inventory} \qquad \textbf{(19.2)}$$
$$\times \text{ Annual carrying cost per unit})$$

or, in algebraic terms,

$$\text{Total costs} = \left(\frac{D}{Q} \times S\right) + \left(\frac{Q}{2} \times C\right) \qquad \textbf{(19.3)}$$

The EOQ is the value of Q that minimizes the total costs given in Equation 19.3. The standard procedure for finding this value of Q involves calculus.[19] The optimal solution, or EOQ, is equal to the following:

$$Q^* = \sqrt{\frac{2SD}{C}} \qquad \textbf{(19.4)}$$

Another item of information that sometimes is useful for planning purposes is the optimal length of one inventory cycle; that is, the time between placements of orders for the item. The optimal length of one inventory cycle, T^*, measured in days, is equal to the economic order quantity, Q^*, divided by the average daily demand, $D/365$ (assuming 365 days per year), as follows:

$$T^* = \frac{Q^*}{D/365} \qquad \textbf{(19.5)}$$

This equation can be rewritten as follows:

$$T^* = \frac{365 \times Q^*}{D} \qquad \textbf{(19.6)}$$

The following example illustrates the use of the EOQ model. Suppose that the Dayton Hudson Company sells Simmons mattresses through its Hudson's department stores located in the Detroit metropolitan area. All inventories are maintained at the firm's centrally located warehouse. Annual demand for the Simmons standard-sized mattress is 3,600 units and is spread evenly throughout the year. The cost of placing and receiving an order is $31.25.

[19] Specifically, the first derivative of Equation 19.3 with respect to Q is set equal to 0, and the equation is solved for Q.

Dayton Hudson's annual carrying costs are 20 percent of the inventory value. Based on a wholesale cost of $50 per mattress, the annual carrying cost per mattress is $0.20 \times \$50 = \$10$. Because Simmons maintains a large regional distribution center in Detroit, Dayton Hudson can replenish its inventory virtually instantaneously. The company wishes to determine the number of standard-sized mattresses it should periodically order from Simmons in order to minimize the total annual inventory costs. Substituting $D = 3,600$, $S = \$31.25$, and $C = \$10$ into Equation 19.4 yields the following EOQ:

665

CHAPTER 19
Management of
Accounts
Receivable and
Inventories

$$Q^* = \sqrt{\frac{2 \times \$31.25 \times 3,600}{\$10}}$$

$$= 150 \text{ mattresses}$$

Using Equation 19.3, we can calculate the total annual inventory costs of this policy:

$$\text{Total costs}^* = \frac{3,600}{15} \times \$31.25 + \frac{150}{2} \times \$10$$

$$= \$1,500$$

Finally, Equation 19.6 can be used to determine Dayton Hudson's optimal inventory cycle for these mattresses:

$$T^* = \frac{365 \times 150}{3,600}$$

$$= 15.2 \text{ days}$$

Thus, the EOQ of 150 mattresses and the optimal inventory cycle of 15.2 days for this item indicate that Dayton Hudson should place an order for 150 mattresses every 15.2 days.

GRAPHIC SOLUTION. The order quantity that minimizes total annual inventory costs can be determined graphically by plotting inventory costs (vertical axis) as a function of the order quantity (horizontal axis). As can be seen in Figure 19-5, annual ordering costs, DS/Q, vary *inversely* with the order quantity, Q, because the number of orders placed per year, D/Q, decreases as the size of the order quantity increases. Carrying costs, $CQ/2$, vary *directly* with the order quantity, Q, because the average inventory, $Q/2$, increases as the size of the order quantity increases.

The total inventory cost curve is found by vertically summing the heights of the ordering cost and carrying cost functions. The order quantity corresponding to the lowest point on the total cost curve is the optimal solution—that is, the economic order quantity, Q^*.

Extensions of the Basic EOQ Model

The basic EOQ model just described makes a number of simplifying assumptions, including those pertaining to the demand for the item, replenishment lead time, the behavior of ordering and carrying costs, and quantity discounts. In practical applications of inventory control models, however,

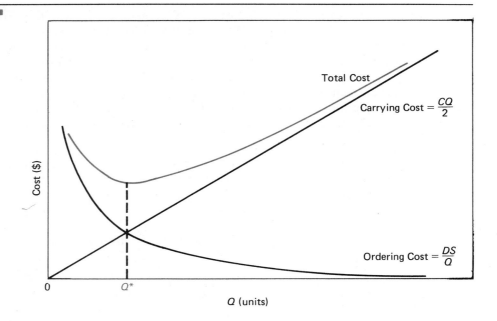

some of these assumptions may not be valid. Thus, it is important to understand how different assumptions affect the analysis and the optimal order quantity. The following discussion examines what occurs when some of these assumptions are altered.

NONZERO LEAD TIME. The basic EOQ model assumes that orders to replenish the inventory of an item are filled instantaneously; that is, the lead time is zero. In practice, however, some time usually elapses between when a purchase order is placed and when the item actually is received in inventory. This lead time consists of the time it takes to manufacture the item, the time it takes to package and ship the item, or both.

If the lead time is *constant* and *known with certainty*, the optimal order quantity, Q^*, is not affected, although the time when an order should be placed is. Specifically, a company should not wait to reorder until the end of the inventory cycle, when the inventory level reaches zero—such as at points T_1, T_2, and T_3 in Figure 19-6. Instead, it should place an order *n days prior* to the end of each cycle, n being equal to the replenishment lead time measured in days. The *reorder point* is defined as the inventory level at which an order should be placed for replenishment of an item. Assuming that demand is constant over time, the reorder point, Q_r, is equal to the lead time, n (measured in days), multiplied by daily demand:

$$Q_r = n \times \frac{D}{365} \qquad\qquad (19.7)$$

where $D/365$ is daily demand (based on 365 days per year).

For example, if the lead time for standard-sized mattresses ordered by Dayton Hudson (discussed earlier in this section) is 5 days, and annual demand is 3,600 mattresses, an order for 150 mattresses (that is, the economic order quantity) should be placed when the inventory level reaches the following:

666

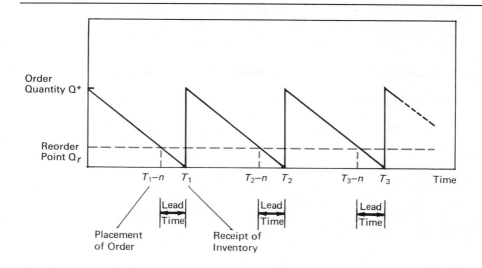

FIGURE 19-6

Nonzero
Replenishment Lead
Time Case of an
Inventory Cycle

$$Q_r = 5 \times \frac{3,600}{365}$$

$$= 49.3 \text{ mattresses}$$

which occurs during the 10th day of each inventory cycle. Five days later, during the 15th day of the inventory cycle—when the inventory level falls to zero—Dayton Hudson will receive the order, and the inventory level will again rise to 150.

QUANTITY DISCOUNTS. Large orders often permit a company to realize substantial per-unit savings (that is, economies of scale) in manufacturing, order processing, and shipping. Many companies encourage their customers to place large orders by passing on to them a portion of these savings in the form of *quantity discounts*. With a quantity discount, the cost per unit to the customer is variable and depends on the quantity ordered. The following approach can be used to determine the effect of a quantity discount on the optimal order quantity.

First, the EOQ is determined, using Equation 19.4. Next, the annual *net* returns when the order quantity is increased from the EOQ level up to the order size necessary to receive the discount are calculated.[20] The annual net returns are equal to the discount savings on the annual demand less any increase in annual inventory costs, as defined in Equation 19.3. If the annual net returns are *positive*, the optimal order quantity is the order size necessary to receive the discount; if they are not, the optimal order quantity is the smaller EOQ value.

For example, in the Dayton Hudson example discussed earlier, suppose Simmons offers a 2 percent, or $1, quantity discount per mattress on orders of 600 or more standard-sized mattresses. Dayton Hudson wishes to determine the optimal order quantity under these conditions. Dayton Hudson's

---

[20] It is assumed that the order quantity necessary to receive a discount is *above* the EOQ level. If this were not the case, the firm would receive the discount automatically when placing an order for the amount of the EOQ.

EOQ is 150 mattresses. Thus, the annual net returns of increasing the order quantity from 150 to 600 need to be calculated.

The discount savings on annual demand are defined as follows:

$$\text{Discount savings} = \text{Discount per unit} \times \text{Annual demand} \quad \textbf{(19.8)}$$

In Dayton Hudson's case, this is calculated as follows:

$$\text{Discount savings} = \$1 \times 3,600$$

$$= \$3,600$$

If Dayton Hudson were to order the discount order quantity, Q', of 600 mattresses, the carrying cost per unit, C', would be reduced to $9.80 ($49 × 0.20). Substituting the appropriate quantities into Equation 19.3 yields the following total annual inventory costs:

$$\text{Total costs}' = \frac{3,600}{600} \times \$31.25 + \frac{600}{2} \times \$9.80$$

$$= \$187.50 + \$2,940$$

$$= \$3,127.50$$

As calculated earlier, the total annual inventory costs at the EOQ of 150 are $1,500. The *change* in annual inventory costs, Δ Total costs, resulting from the increased order quantity, is calculated as follows:

$$\Delta \text{ Total costs} = \text{Total costs}' - \text{Total costs}^*$$

$$= \$3,127.50 - \$1,500$$

$$= + \$1,627.50$$

The annual net returns are equal to the discount savings less the increased inventory costs, or $3,600 − $1,627.50 = $1,972.50. Because the annual net returns in this analysis are positive, Dayton Hudson should increase its order quantity from 150 to 600 mattresses and take advantage of the quantity discount.

Probabilistic Inventory Control Models

Thus far the analysis has assumed that demand or usage is uniform throughout time and known with certainty, as well as that the lead time necessary to procure additional inventory is also a fixed, known value. However, in most practical inventory management problems either (or both) of these assumptions may not be strictly correct. Typically, demand fluctuates over time due to seasonal, cyclical, and "random" influences, and imprecise forecasts of future demands often are all that can be made. Similarly, lead times are subject to uncertainty because of such factors as transportation delays, strikes, and natural disasters. Under these conditions, the possibility of stockouts exists. To minimize the possibility of stockouts and the associated stockout costs, most companies use a standard approach of adding a *safety stock* to their inventory. A safety stock is maintained to meet unexpectedly high demand during the lead time, unanticipated delays in the lead time, or both.

Figure 19-7 shows the inventory pattern characterized by these more realistic assumptions. During the first inventory cycle ($0 - T_2$), an order to replenish the inventory is placed at T_1, when the inventory level reaches the predetermined order point. The order then is received at T_2. The second ($T_2 - T_4$) is similar to the first, except that demand exceeds the normal inventory of the item, and part of the safety stock is consumed during the lead time prior to receipt of the order at T_4. During cycle 3 ($T_4 - T_6$), demand exceeds the normal inventory plus the safety stock and, as a result, a stockout occurs during the lead time prior to receipt of the order at T_6.

Determining the optimal safety stock and order quantities under these more realistic conditions is a fairly complex process that lies beyond the scope of this text.[21] However, the factors that have to be considered in this type of analysis can be identified briefly. All other things being equal, the optimal safety stock increases as the uncertainty associated with the demand forecasts and lead times increases. Likewise, all other things being equal, the optimal safety stock increases as the cost of stockouts increases. Determining the optimal safety stock involves balancing the *expected* costs of stockouts against the cost of carrying the additional inventory.

Just-In-Time Inventory Management Systems

Just-in-time inventory management systems are part of a manufacturing approach that seeks to reduce the company's operating cycle and associated costs by eliminating wasteful procedures. Just-in-time inventory systems are based on the idea that all required inventory items should be supplied to the production process at exactly the right time and in exactly the right quantities. This approach was first developed by the Toyota Motor Company

[21] See any of the following books for a discussion of these more complex models: H. M. Wagner, *Principles of Operations Research: With Applications to Managerial Decisions*, 2d ed. (Englewood Cliffs, NJ: Prentice-Hall, 1975); J. Evans, D. Anderson, D. Sweeney, and T. Williams, *Applied Production and Operations Management* (St. Paul, MN: West Publishing Co., 1984); and Richard I. Levin and Charles A. Kirkpatrick, *Quantitative Approaches to Management*, 4th ed. (New York: McGraw-Hill, 1978).

Uncertainty Case of the Inventory Cycle　　　　　　　　　　　　　　　　F I G U R E　19-7

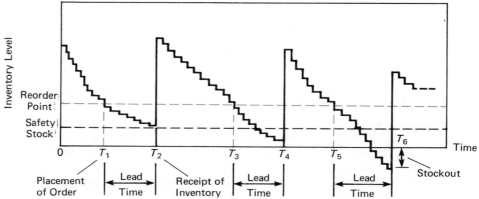

in the 1950s. In contrast, inventory models used in many plants, which rely on safety stocks, sometimes are referred to as "just-in-case" models.

The just-in-time approach works best for companies engaged in repetitive manufacturing operations. A key part of just-in-time techniques is the replacement of production in large batches with a continuous flow of smaller quantities. The use of a just-in-time inventory system requires close coordination between a company and its suppliers, because any disruption in the flow of parts and materials from the supplier can result in costly production delays and lost sales.

Reductions in production time and inventory costs resulting from the use of just-in-time techniques have been reported by large as well as small businesses. Two examples (Huffy and Unisys) were discussed in the Financial Dilemma at the beginning of the chapter. Another example is AT&T's Shreveport, Louisiana, plant that produces office communication systems. The use of just-in-time manufacturing techniques reduced the production cycle from 3½ weeks to 2½ hours. Also, the U.S. Repeating Arms Company in New Haven, Connecticut, used just-in-time techniques to reduce the time required to make wooden shotgun stocks from 5 to 2 weeks. The minimum economic lot size also was lowered from 500 to 100 units.

SUMMARY

- For a business to extend credit to its customers, it must invest a certain amount of funds in *accounts receivable*.
- A company should change its credit extension policy only if the expected *marginal benefits* of the change will exceed the expected *marginal costs*. A more liberal credit policy normally leads to increased sales and generates marginal benefits in the form of higher gross profits. The marginal costs of this type of policy, however, include the cost of the additional funds invested in accounts receivable, any additional credit checking and collection costs, and increased bad-debt expenses.
- A financial manager can exercise control over the company's level of receivables investment through three credit policy variables: *credit standards*, *credit terms*, and the *collection effort*. All three variables can be used to control the average collection period and bad-debt loss ratio.
  1. Credit standards are the criteria a business uses to screen its credit applicants.
  2. Credit terms are the conditions under which customers are required to repay the credit extended to them. Credit terms specify the length of the credit period and the cash discount (if any) given for early payment.
  3. The collection effort represents the methods used in attempting to collect payment from past-due accounts.

- Evaluating individual credit applicants involves *gathering information* about the applicant, *analyzing this information* to determine the applicant's credit-worthiness, and then *making the credit decision*.
- The amount of information a business can collect on a credit applicant is limited by both time and cost considerations. In deciding whether to seek more information about an applicant, the credit analyst should weigh the expected returns from more information against the cost of obtaining it.

- Possible sources of relevant information about a credit applicant include financial statements submitted by the applicant, credit reporting organizations (such as Dun and Bradstreet), banks, and the company's own prior experience with the customer.

- The "five Cs of credit," which include *character, capacity, capital, collateral*, and *conditions*, can be used as credit screening guidelines to help ensure that a company will consider most of the relevant factors in the analysis and decision-making process.

- Inventories serve as a *buffer* between the various stages of the manufacturing firm's procurement-production-sales cycle. By uncoupling the various phases of the firm's operations, inventories provide the firm with *flexibility* in timing purchases, scheduling production, and meeting fluctuating, uncertain demand for the finished product.

- Inventory-related costs include *ordering costs, carrying costs*, and *stockout costs*. Ordering costs include all the costs of placing and receiving an order. Carrying costs include the various costs of holding items in inventory, including the cost of funds invested in inventory. Stockout costs are the costs incurred when demand exceeds available inventory, such as lost profits.

- ABC inventory classification is a method of dividing inventory items into three groups: those with a relatively large dollar value but a small percentage of the total items (A), those with a small dollar value but a large percentage of the total items (C), and items in between (B). Group A items should be more closely controlled than group B or C items.

- Inventory control models usually are classified into two types: *deterministic*, if demand and lead time are known with *certainty*, and *probabilistic*, if demand and/or lead time are *random variables* with known probability distributions.

- The objective of the deterministic *economic order quantity* (EOQ) *model is to find the order quantity that minimizes total inventory costs*.

- The economic order quantity is equal to $\sqrt{2SD/C}$, where D is the annual demand; S, the fixed cost per order; and C, the annual carrying cost per unit.

- Some of the assumptions made in the basic EOQ model do not necessarily apply in practice. In the event of a nonzero lead time or quantity discounts, for example, the model must be modified.

- Probabilistic inventory control models require consideration of the possibility of *stockouts*. One approach used to handle this problem is to add a *safety stock* to the inventory.

- *Just-in-time inventory models* are based on the concept that required inventory items are supplied exactly as needed by production. Successful implementation of just-in-time models can reduce inventory investment.

671

CHAPTER 19
Management of
Accounts
Receivable and
Inventories

QUESTIONS AND TOPICS FOR DISCUSSION

1. What are the marginal returns and costs associated with a more liberal extension of credit to a firm's customers?

2. What are the major credit policy variables a firm can use to control its level of receivables investment?

3. Define the following terms:
   a. Average collection period.
   b. Bad-debt loss ratio.

    c. Aging of accounts.

    d. Stockout.

    e. Deterministic inventory control models.

    f. Probabilistic inventory control models.

    g. Safety stock.

    h. Lead time.

    i. Quantity discount.

4. Discuss at least two reasons why a firm might want to offer seasonal datings to its customers.

5. Describe the marginal costs and benefits associated with each of the following changes in a firm's credit and collection policies:

    a. Increasing the credit period from 7 to 30 days.

    b. Increasing the cash discount from 1 to 2 percent.

    c. Offering a seasonal dating credit plan.

    d. Increasing collection expenditures (and effort).

6. Describe the three steps involved in evaluating credit applicants.

7. What are the primary sources of information about the credit-worthiness of credit applicants?

8. Describe the "five Cs of credit" used in evaluating the credit-worthiness of a credit applicant.

9. How does a firm's required rate of return on investment enter into the analysis of changes in its credit and collection policies?

10. A firm is currently selling on credit terms of "net 30," and its accounts receivable average 30 days past due (that is, the firm's average collection period is 60 days). What credit policy variables might the firm consider changing to reduce its average collection period?

11. "The objective of the firm's credit and collection policies should be to minimize its bad-debt losses." Do you agree or disagree with this statement? Explain.

12. Discuss how each of the following factors would tend to affect a firm's credit extension policies:

    a. A shortage of working capital.

    b. An increase in output to the point where the firm is operating at full production capacity.

    c. An increase in the firm's profit margin (that is, its profit contribution ratio).

    d. An increase in interest rates (that is, borrowing costs).

13. Describe the benefits of holding the following:

    a. Raw materials inventories.

    b. Work-in-process inventories.

    c. Finished goods inventories.

14. Describe the components of carrying costs.

15. How do ordering costs for items purchased externally differ from ordering costs for items manufactured internally within the firm?

16. Describe the nature of stockout costs associated with a stockout in the following:

    a. Raw materials inventories.

    b. Work-in-process inventories.

    c. Finished goods inventories.

17. What is ABC inventory classification? How can this method be useful to a business?

18. Describe the assumptions underlying the basic EOQ model.

19. In general terms, describe how to deal with each of the following conditions when determining the optimal inventory level:

  a. Constant (nonzero) replenishment lead time known with certainty.
  b. Quantity discounts.
  c. Demand and replenishment lead time subject to uncertainty.

20. How does the firm's required rate of return on investment enter into inventory decisions?

21. What are just-in-time inventory models?

673

CHAPTER 19
Management of
Accounts
Receivable and
Inventories

▬▬ PROBLEMS*

NOTE: **Assume 365 days per year when converting from annual to daily amounts or vice versa.**

1. Miranda Tool Company sells to retail hardware stores on credit terms of "net 30." Annual credit sales are $18 million and are spread evenly throughout the year. The company's variable cost ratio is 0.70, and its accounts receivable average $1.9 million. Using this information determine the following for the company:

  a. Average daily credit sales.
  b. Average collection period.
  c. Average investment in receivables.

2. Drake Paper Company sells on terms of "net 30." The firm's variable cost ratio is 0.80.

  a. If annual credit sales are $20 million and its accounts receivable average 15 days *overdue*, what is Drake's investment in receivables?
  b. Suppose that, as the result of a recession, annual credit sales decline by 10 percent to $18 million, and customers delay their payments to an average of 25 days *past the due date*. What will be Drake's new level of receivables investment?

3. Looking back at Tables 19-1 and 19-2, evaluate the impact on Bassett's pretax profits of extending full credit to the customers in Credit Risk Group 5.

4. Once again, consider the Bassett Furniture Industries example. Assume that rising labor and interest costs have increased Bassett's variable cost ratio from 0.75 to 0.80 and its required pretax rate of return on receivables investment from 20 to 25 percent. Reevaluate the effect on Bassett's pretax profits of extending full credit to the customers in Credit Risk Group 4.

5. In evaluating the extension of credit to customers in Credit Risk Group 4 in the chapter (Tables 19-1 and 19-2), it was assumed that no increase in inventory investment was required to support the additional $300,000 in annual sales. Suppose instead that an additional inventory investment (that is, raw materials, work-in-process, and finished goods) of $120,000 is required to expand sales by $300,000. Furthermore, assume that Bassett's required (pretax) rate of return on inventory investment is 20 percent. Reevaluate the decision to extend credit to Group 4 customers under these new conditions.

6. Baker Company, a wholesale distributor of jewelry, sells to retail jewelry stores on terms of "net 120." Its average collection period is 150 days. The company is considering the introduction of a 4 percent cash discount if customers pay within 30 days. Such a change in credit terms is expected to reduce the average collection period to 108 days. Baker expects 30 percent of its customers to take the cash discount. Annual credit sales are $6 million.

* Colored numbers denote problems that have check answers provided at the end of the book.

Baker's variable cost ratio is 0.667, and its required pretax return on receivables investment is 15 percent. Determine the following:

a. The funds released by the change in credit terms.
b. The net effect on Baker's pretax profits.

7. In an effort to speed up the collection of receivables, Hill Publishing Company is considering increasing the size of its cash discount by changing its credit terms from "1/10, net 30" to "2/10, net 30." Currently, the company's collection period averages 43 days. Under the new credit terms it is expected to decline to 28 days. Also, the percentage of customers who will take advantage of the cash discount is expected to increase from the current 50 percent to 70 percent with the new credit terms. Bad-debt losses currently average 4 percent of sales and are not expected to change significantly if Hill changes its credit policy. Annual credit sales are $3.5 million, the variable cost ratio is 60 percent and the required pretax rate of return (that is, the opportunity cost) on receivables investment is 14 percent. Assuming that Hill does decide to increase the size of its cash discount, determine the following:

a. The earnings on the funds released by the change in credit terms.
b. The cost of the additional cash discounts taken.
c. The net effect on Hill's pretax profits.

8. The North Carolina Furniture Company (NCFC) manufactures upholstered furniture, which it sells to various small retailers in the Northeast and Midwest on credit terms of "2/10, net 60." The company currently does not grant credit to retailers with a 3 (fair) or 4 (limited) Dun and Bradstreet Composite Credit Appraisal. If NCFC were to extend credit to retailers in the "fair" category, an estimated additional $1.2 million per year in sales could be generated. The estimated average collection period for these customers is 90 days, and the expected bad-debt loss ratio is 6 percent. Approximately 20 percent of these customers are expected to take the cash discount. NCFC's variable cost ratio is 0.70, and its required pretax rate of return on receivables investment is 20 percent. Determine the net change in NCFC's pretax profits from extending credit to retailers in the "fair" category.

9. Michigan Pharmaceuticals, Inc., a wholesale distributor of ethical drugs to local pharmacies, has been experiencing a relatively long average collection period, because many of its customers face liquidity problems and delay their payments well beyond the due date. In addition, its bad-debt loss ratio is high, because a number of pharmacies have closed due to financial difficulties. To avoid these problems in the future, Michigan Pharmaceuticals is considering a plan to *institute more stringent credit standards* to keep the average collection period and bad-debt losses from rising beyond acceptable limits. Specifically, the firm plans to refuse to grant additional credit to any current customers more than 15 days past due on their payments. Such a change in credit policy is expected to reduce current annual sales of $6.5 million by 20 percent, *reduce* the average collection period from 110 days to 75 days, and lower bad-debt losses from 8 to 4 percent. The firm's variable cost ratio is 0.75, and its required pretax return on receivables investment is 15 percent. Determine the net effect of this plan on the pretax profits of Michigan Pharmaceuticals.

10. Madison Electric Company sells on terms of "net 30." Given the following information on its receivables, construct an aging of accounts schedule as of September 1, showing the percentage of accounts that are current, 1 to 30 days past due, 31 to 60 days past due, 61 to 90 days past due, and over 90 days past due. (Assume 30 days in each month.)

Account Number	Invoice Date	Amount Due
1311	August 15	$1,315
1773	July 14	721
1217	July 25	677
1319	August 14	1,711
1814	April 10	325
1713	August 5	917
1443	May 8	493
1144	June 28	211
1972	May 5	755
1011	April 21	377
1619	August 28	1,550
1322	August 13	275
1173	March 5	675
1856	August 12	695
1317	June 10	720

11. Creole Industries, Inc. estimates that if it spent an additional $20,000 to hire another collection agent in its credit department, it could lower its bad-debt loss ratio to 3.5 percent from a current rate of 4 percent and also reduce its average collection period from 50 to 45 days. (Assume that sales remain unchanged if the agent is hired.) Creole's annual credit sales are $5 million, and its variable cost ratio is 0.75. The firm's required pretax rate of return on receivables investment (that is, the opportunity cost) is 18 percent. Determine the net effect on Creole's pretax profits of hiring the additional collection agent.

12. Jenkins Supply Corp. sells $120 million of its products to wholesalers on terms of "net 50." Currently, the firm's average collection period is 65 days. In order to speed up the collection of receivables, Jenkins is considering offering a 1 percent cash discount if customers pay their bills within 15 days. The firm expects 40 percent of its customers to take the discount and its average collection period to decline to 40 days. The firm's required pretax return on receivables investments is 20 percent.

    Determine the net effect on Jenkins' pretax profits of offering a 1 percent cash discount.

13. The Bimbo Corporation has been experiencing a decline in sales relative to its major competitors. Because Bimbo is confident about the quality of its products, it suspects that this sales loss may reflect its relatively stringent credit standards and terms. The firm currently has credit sales of $50 million annually. With current credit terms of "net 20," its average collection period is now 25 days. Bad debt losses are 2 percent of credit sales. The firm's variable cost ratio is 0.80, and its required pretax return on receivables investments is 20 percent.

    Bimbo plans to change its credit terms to "2/10, net 30." It expects 20 percent of its customers to take advantage of the cash discount. Bimbo also plans to relax credit standards and take on more risky accounts. This action is expected to increase credit sales by 30 percent. Bad-debt losses are expected to increase to 3 percent of credit sales, and the average collection period is expected to become 30 days.

    Determine the net effect of this plan on the pretax profits of Bimbo.

14. Allied Apparel Company received a large order from Websters Department Stores, which operates a chain of approximately 300 popular-priced department stores located primarily in the New England–Middle Atlantic states area. Allied is considering extending trade credit to Websters. As part

of its credit check, Allied obtained Websters' balance sheets and income statements (which follow) for the last 3 years. Websters' Dun and Bradstreet rating is 5A3. A check of several of Websters' trade creditors has revealed that the firm generally takes any cash discounts when they are offered but averages about 30 days overdue on its payments to two suppliers whose credit terms are "net 30."

A Dun and Bradstreet publication entitled *Key Business Ratios* yielded the following information concerning the "average" financial ratios for firms in the same line of business as Websters:

Current assets to current liabilities	2.82
Net income after taxes to sales	1.89%
Net income after taxes to net worth	5.65%
Total liabilities to net worth	1.48

Websters Department Stores, Balance Sheet (in thousands of dollars)

	19X1	19X2	19X3
Assets			
Current assets:			
Cash and marketable securities	$ 9,283	$ 13,785	$ 23,893
Accounts receivable (net)	162,825	179,640	140,543
Inventories	119,860	135,191	129,707
Other	1,994	2,190	1,956
Total current assets	$293,962	$330,806	$296,099
Long-term assets:			
Building and equipment (net)	$ 27,426	$ 30,295	$ 30,580
Other	11,821	14,794	16,687
Total long-term assets	$ 39,247	$ 45,089	$ 47,267
Total assets	$333,209	$375,895	$343,366
Liabilities and net worth			
Current liabilities:			
Accounts payable	$ 23,637	$ 21,861	$ 15,020
Notes payable	117,010	135,929	165,299
Other	49,273	49,229	29,653
Total current liabilities	$189,920	$207,019	$209,972
Long-term liabilities:			
Debentures	$ 38,001	$ 36,101	$ 35,201
Term loan	—	28,440	29,701
Other	4,986	853	655
Total long-term liabilities	$ 42,987	$ 65,394	$ 65,557
Net worth:			
Common stock	$ 5,576	$ 5,576	$ 5,576
Preferred stock	2,580	2,580	2,580
Retained earnings	92,146	95,326	59,681
Total net worth	100,302	103,482	67,837
Total liabilities and net worth	$333,209	$375,895	$343,366

Websters Department Stores, Income Statement (in thousands of dollars)

	19X1	19X2	19X3
Sales	$494,550	$556,132	$529,857
Cost of sales	337,580	384,899	390,980
Gross profit	$156,970	$171,233	$138,877
Selling, general and administrative expenses	133,330	155,494	187,926
Earnings before taxes	$ 23,640	$ 15,739	$ -49,049
Income taxes	7,715	6,222	-14,741
Earnings after taxes	$ 15,925	$ 9,517	$ -34,308
Dividends	6,343	6,337	1,337
Additions to retained earnings	$ 9,582	$ 3,180	$ -35,645

In evaluating Websters' application for trade credit, answer the following questions:

a. What positive financial factors would lead Allied to decide to extend credit to Websters?

b. What negative financial factors would lead Allied to decide *not* to extend credit to Websters?

c. What additional information about Websters would be useful in performing the analysis?

15. Willoughby Industries, Inc., is considering whether to discontinue offering credit to customers who are more than 10 days overdue on repaying the credit extended to them. Current annual credit sales are $10 million on credit terms of "net 30." Such a change in policy is expected to reduce sales by 10 percent, cut the firm's bad-debt losses from 5 to 3 percent, and reduce its average collection period from 72 days to 45 days. The firm's variable cost ratio is 0.70 and its required pretax return on receivables investments is 25 percent. Determine the net effect of this credit-tightening policy on the pretax profits of Willoughby Industries.

16. Allstar Shoe Company produces a wide variety of athletic-type shoes for tennis, basketball, and running. Although sales are somewhat seasonal, production is uniform throughout the year. Allstar's production and sales average 1.92 million pairs of shoes per year. The company purchases shoelaces for its entire product line. Shoelaces are bought in lots of 10,000 pairs at a price of $800 per lot. Ordering costs are $20, including the cost of preparing the purchase order and inspecting the shipment when it arrives at the company's warehouse. Annual inventory carrying costs average 15 percent of the inventory value. Assuming that the shoelace manufacturer is located nearby and that orders are filled on the same day they are placed (that is, virtually instantaneously), determine the following:

a. The EOQ for shoelaces.

b. The total annual inventory costs of this policy.

c. The frequency with which Allstar should place its orders for shoelaces.

17. Quick-Copy Duplicating Company uses 110,000 reams of standard-sized paper a year at its various duplicating centers. Its current paper supplier charges $2.00 per ream. Annual inventory carrying costs are 15 percent of inventory value. The costs of placing and receiving an order of paper are $41.25. Assuming that inventory replenishment occurs virtually instantaneously, determine the following:

a. The firm's EOQ.

b. The total annual inventory costs of this policy.

c. The optimal ordering frequency.

d. Compute and plot ordering costs, carrying costs, and total inventory costs for order quantities of 2,000, 4,000, 5,000, 5,500, 6,000, 7,000, and 9,000 reams. Connect the points on each function with a smooth curve, and determine the EOQ from the graph (and the table used in constructing the graph).

e. Suppose Quick-Copy's paper supplier offers a 1 percent discount on orders of 10,000 or more reams. Determine the net annual pretax returns to Quick-Copy of taking the discount.

f. Suppose another paper supplier offers Quick-Copy the following price discount schedule:

Quantity (reams)	Price per Ream
0–9,999	$2.000
10,000–19,999	1.985
20,000 and up	1.975

677

CHAPTER 19
Management of
Accounts
Receivable and
Inventories

Assuming that Quick-Copy places its order with this other supplier, determine its optimal order quantity.

18. East Publishing Company employs a high-speed printing press in its operations. A typical production run of 5,000 to 50,000 copies of a textbook can be produced in less than 1 day. The manager of the business textbook division is attempting to determine the optimal number of copies of the fifth editions of its financial management and managerial economics textbooks to produce. Expected annual demand for the two books are 50,000 and 22,500 copies, respectively. Furthermore, the manager does not want to produce more than a 3-year supply of either book, because these textbooks normally are revised after the third year. Setup costs of getting the printing press (and bindery) ready for a production run of a given textbook are $2,500 and $2,000, respectively, for the two books. Annual carrying costs are $0.80 per copy (16 percent annual carrying charge times the $5.00 production cost per copy). For each textbook, determine the following:

a. The economic order quantity.
b. The total annual inventory costs.
c. The optimal ordering frequency.

19. Arizona Instruments uses integrated circuits (ICs) in its business calculators. Its annual demand for ICs is 120,000 units. The ICs cost Arizona Instruments $10 each. The company has determined that the EOQ is 20,000 units. It takes 18 days between when an order is placed and when the delivery is received. Carrying costs are 20 percent of the inventory value. Determine the following:

a. The optimal ordering frequency.
b. The average inventory and annual carrying costs.
c. The reorder point.

Suppose Arizona Instruments decides to maintain a 3-month safety stock of ICs to meet unexpected demand and possible shipment delays (due to strikes, shortages, and so on) from its supplier. Determine the following:

d. The amount of safety stock, in units.
e. The average inventory and annual carrying costs.
f. The reorder point.

▆▆▆ SELECTED REFERENCES

Ben-Horim, Moshe, and Haim Levy. "Management of Accounts Receivable Under Inflation." *Financial Management* 12 (Spring 1983): 42–48.

Brick, Ivan E., and W. K. H. Fung. "The Effect of Taxes on the Trade Credit Decision." *Financial Management* 13 (Summer 1984): 24–30.

Emery, Gary W. "A Pure Financial Explanation for Trade Credit." *Journal of Financial and Quantitative Analysis* 19 (September 1984): 271–286.

Gentry, James A., and Jesus M. De La Garza. "A Generalized Model for Monitoring Accounts Receivable." *Financial Management* 14 (Winter 1985): 28–38.

Halloran, John A., and Howard P. Lanser. "The Credit Policy Decision in an Inflationary Environment." *Financial Management* 10 (Winter 1981): 31–38.

Kallberg, Jarl G., and Kenneth L. Parkinson. *Current Asset Management: Cash, Credit, and Inventory.* New York: Wiley Interscience, 1984.

Sartoris, William, and Ned C. Hill. "A Generalized Cash Flow Approach to Short-Term Financial Decisions." *Journal of Finance* 38 (May 1983): 349–360.

Stowe, John D. "An Integer Programming Solution for the Optimal Credit Investigation/Credit Granting Sequence." *Financial Management* 14 (Summer 1985): 66–76.

Walleigh, Richard C. "What's Your Excuse for Not Using JIT?" *Harvard Business Review* 64 (March–April 1986): 38–54.

CHAPTER

20

Obtaining Short-Term Funds

KEY CHAPTER CONCEPTS

1. *Trade credit*, or *accounts payable*, is the principal source of *spontaneous* short-term credit.

2. *Bank loans, commercial paper, accounts receivable loans*, and *inventory loans* are the major sources of negotiated short-term credit.

3. The cost of trade credit is dependent on the size of any cash discount offered and the lengths of the credit and discount periods.

4. The types of short-term bank credit include *single loans, lines of credit*, and *revolving credit agreements*.

5. Commercial paper is a short-term unsecured credit instrument issued by major corporations with good credit ratings.

6. A company can use its accounts receivable to obtain short-term financing. It can either *pledge* the accounts receivable as collateral for a loan or sell (*factor*) the receivables to obtain cash.

7. A company also can use its inventory as collateral for a short-term loan.

GLOSSARY OF NEW TERMS

Annual financing cost (AFC) The simple, annual interest rate for a short-term credit source.

Annual percentage rate (APR) The true annual interest rate paid on a loan. Also called the *effective rate* of a loan.

Commercial paper Short-term unsecured promissory notes issued by major corporations with good credit ratings.

Discount loan A loan in which the bank deducts the interest in advance at the time the loan is made.

Factoring The sale of a firm's accounts receivable to a financial institution known as a *factor*.

Field warehouse financing agreement A loan agreement in which the inventory being pledged as collateral is segregated from the company's other inventories and stored on its premises under the control of a field warehouse company.

Floating lien An inventory loan in which the lender receives a security interest or general claim on all of a company's inventory.

Line of credit An agreement that permits a firm to borrow funds up to a predetermined limit at any time during the life of the agreement.

London interbank offered rate (LIBOR) Interest rate at which banks in the Eurodollar market lend to each other.

Pledging of accounts receivable A short-term borrowing arrangement with a financial institution in which a loan is secured by the borrower's accounts receivable.

Prime rate The lowest rate normally charged by banks on loans made to their most creditworthy business customers.

Promissory note A formal short-term credit obligation that states the amount to be paid and the due date.

Revolving credit agreement A binding agreement that commits a bank to make loans to a company up to a predetermined credit limit. To obtain this type of commitment from a bank, a company usually pays a *commitment fee* based on the unused portion of the pledged funds.

Terminal warehouse financing agreement A loan agreement in which the inventory being pledged as collateral is stored in a bonded warehouse operated by a public warehousing company.

Trust receipt A security agreement under which the borrower holds the inventory and proceeds from the sale of the inventory in trust for the lender. This is also known as *floor planning*.

Dixie Yarns and Delta Woodside

Dixie Yarns and Delta Woodside Industries are two textile companies with a number of similarities. Dixie Yarns, headquartered in Chattanooga, Tennessee, had 1987 sales of $580 million and Delta Woodside, headquartered in Greenville, South Carolina, had fiscal 1988 sales of $489 million.

In spite of their similarities, the two companies use different sources of short-term financing. Dixie Yarns relies upon short-term bank borrowing, in addition to trade credit from its suppliers. Delta Woodside, on the other hand, raises short-term funds by selling its customers' receivables to a *factor*, a financial institution that specializes in purchasing receivables. Delta Woodside, like most businesses, also uses trade credit as a short-term financing source.

Dixie Yarns has a $45 million unsecured revolving credit agreement with its bankers.[1] Under the terms of the agreement, Dixie Yarns may borrow at any time up to the $45 million limit. Dixie Yarns, in turn, pays the lender an annual commitment fee of 0.25 percent on the unborrowed portion of the $45 million. In addition, Dixie Yarns also has credit arrangements with its bankers that permit the company to borrow up to $25.5 million for seasonal needs.

Delta Woodside sells a substantial portion of its accounts receivable to a factor.[2] The factor then pays Delta Woodside for the receivables as they are collected by the factor. In addition, Delta Woodside can, and usually does, borrow from the factor even before the receivables are collected; this is called *advance factoring*.

Delta Woodside is more highly leveraged than Dixie Yarns and, therefore, is financially riskier than Dixie Yarns. The higher risk of Delta Woodside shows up in the company's borrowing terms. Dixie Yarns can borrow unsecured and its borrowing costs are at or below the prime rate. Delta Woodside effectively uses its receivables as collateral and its borrowing costs are above the prime rate.

This chapter considers the characteristics, advantages, and disadvantages of various sources of short-term credit. As these two examples illustrate, even companies in the same industry may choose different means of obtaining short-term financing.

[1] Dixie Yarns, Inc., *Annual Report*, 1987, p. 20.
[2] Delta Woodside Industries, Inc., *Annual Report*, 1988, p. 23.

INTRODUCTION

A company normally employs a combination of short-term credit and long-term debt and equity in financing its current and fixed assets. The various sources of long-term financing already have been discussed. The focus of this chapter is on the major sources of short-term credit.

Short-term credit includes all of a company's debt obligations that originally were scheduled for repayment within 1 year.[3] Short-term credit may be either *unsecured* or *secured*.[4] In the case of unsecured short-term debt, a firm obtains credit from the lender without having to pledge any specific assets as collateral, and the lender depends primarily on the cash-generating ability of the firm to repay the debt. If the firm becomes insolvent and declares bankruptcy, the unsecured lender usually stands little chance of recovering all or even a significant portion of the amount owed.

[3] Short-term credit does *not* always correspond exactly to the current liabilities shown on the firm's balance sheet. Current liabilities also include that portion of long-term debt (such as term loans and mortgages) scheduled for repayment during the next year.
[4] Long-term debt also may be either unsecured or secured.

In the case of secured short-term debt, the borrower pledges certain specified assets—such as accounts receivable, inventory, or fixed assets—as collateral.[5] The Uniform Commercial Code, which was adopted by all states during the 1960s, outlines the procedures that must be followed in order for a lender to establish a valid claim on a firm's collateral.

The first step in this process involves the execution of a *security agreement*, which is a contract between the lender and the firm specifying the collateral held against the loan. The security agreement then is filed at the appropriate public office within the state where the collateral is located. Future potential lenders can check with this office to determine which assets the firm has pledged and which are still free to be used as collateral. Filing this security agreement legally establishes the lender's security interest in the collateral. If the borrower defaults on the loan or otherwise fails to honor the terms of the agreement, the lender can seize and sell the collateral to recover the amount owed. Thus, the lender in a secured short-term debt agreement has *two* potential sources of loan repayment: the firm's cash-generating ability and the collateral value of the pledged assets.

Short-term lenders can be classified as either *cash-flow lenders or asset-based lenders*, depending upon how they view the two potential sources of loan repayment. Cash-flow lenders look upon the borrower's future cash flows as the *primary* source of loan repayment and the borrower's assets as a *secondary* source of repayment. Asset-based lenders tend to make riskier loans than cash-flow lenders, and as a result, they place much greater emphasis on the value of the borrower's collateral. Generally, large, low-leveraged companies with good expected cash flows are able to borrow from cash-flow lenders, such as commercial banks, at relatively low rates. Smaller, highly leveraged businesses with more uncertain future cash flows, often have to borrow on a secured basis from asset-based lenders, such as commercial finance companies, at relatively high rates.

In general, companies prefer to borrow funds on an unsecured basis, because the added administrative costs involved in pledging assets as security raise the cost of the loan to the borrower. In addition, secured borrowing agreements can restrict a company's future borrowing. Many companies, particularly small ones, are not able to obtain unsecured credit, however. For example, a company may be financially weak or too new to justify an unsecured loan, or it may want more credit than the lender is willing to give on an unsecured basis. In any of these circumstances, the company either must provide collateral or it will not receive the loan.

The short-term credit sources available to a company can be either *spontaneous* or *negotiated*. Spontaneous sources, which include *trade credit, accrued expenses*, and *deferred income*, are discussed in the sections following the next section on the cost of the short-term credit. Later sections of this chapter consider the various negotiated sources, such as *bank credit, commercial paper, receivables loans*, and *inventory loans*.

COST OF SHORT-TERM FUNDS

The firm needs a model to calculate the financing cost for the various sources of short-term financing available to it. Equation 5.1 from Chapter 5 gives

---

[5] As an alternative to pledging specific assets as collateral for a loan, a company may get a third party to *cosign*, or *guarantee*, the loan. If the borrower defaults, the third party becomes responsible for repayment. Lenders usually will accept only financially sound third parties, such as a stockholder, supplier, or customer who has a vested interest in the company's success.

the amount of interest paid, I, on borrowed money:

$$I = PV_0 \times i \times n \qquad (20.1)$$

where I = the simple interest in dollars; PV_0 = the principal amount at time 0, or the present value; i = the interest rate per time period; and n = the number of time periods. Solving for i, we obtain

$$i = \frac{I}{PV_0} \times \frac{1}{n} \qquad (20.2)$$

The interest rate, i, is equal to the fractional interest cost per period, I/PV_0, times one divided by the number of time periods, or $1/n$.

The equation we use to calculate the *annual financing cost*, AFC, for short-term financing sources is a variation of Equation 20.2:

$$AFC = \frac{\text{Interest costs} + \text{fees}}{\text{Usable funds}} \times \frac{365}{\text{Maturity (days)}} \qquad (20.3)$$

Short-term financing sources may involve fees in addition to the interest costs. Also, the term *usable funds* is used in place of present value, because some of the money from a particular short-term financing source actually may not be available for a company to use. The term, 365/maturity (days) converts the financing cost to an annual rate.

The annual financing cost calculated using Equation 20.3 is only an approximation to the true (effective) *annual percentage rate*, or APR, of a loan. Equation 20.3 does not consider compounding and slightly understates the true APR. Also, Equation 20.3 normally is used for financing sources of 1 year or less. The following equation gives the true APR for a short-term financing source:

$$APR = \left(1 + \frac{\text{Interest costs} + \text{fees}}{\text{Usable funds}}\right)^m - 1 \qquad (20.4)$$

where m is the number of times per year compounding occurs. Equation 20.4 is a variation of Equation 5.25 from Chapter 5. In addition, the APR of a loan is the internal rate of return between the funds received and the funds paid back.

To illustrate the use of Equations 20.3 and 20.4, consider a 6-month, $10,000 loan that has $500 of interest. If we assume that principal is paid only at maturity, and there are 182 days in the 6-month period, the annual financing cost is calculated, using Equation 20.3, as follows:

$$AFC = \frac{\$500}{\$10,000} \times \frac{365}{182}$$

$$= 0.1003 \text{ or } 10.03\%$$

The loan's APR is determined as follows, using Equation 20.4:

$$APR = \left(1 + \frac{\$500}{\$10,000}\right)^{365/182} - 1$$

$$= 0.1028 \text{ or } 10.28\%$$

The annual financing cost percentage closely approximates the true APR, unless the number of compounding periods is large.

Equation 20.3 is used throughout this chapter to calculate the annual financing cost of the various short-term financing sources available to the firm.

▰▰▰ TRADE CREDIT

Whenever a business receives merchandise ordered from a supplier and then is permitted to wait a specified period of time before having to pay, it is receiving *trade credit*.[6] In the aggregate, trade credit is the most important source of short-term financing for business firms. Smaller businesses in particular usually rely heavily on trade credit to finance their operations, because they often are unable to obtain funds from banks or other lenders in the financial markets.

Most trade credit is extended on an *open account* basis. A firm sends a purchase order to a supplier, who then evaluates the firm's credit-worthiness using various information sources and decision criteria.[7] If the supplier decides to extend the firm credit, it ships the ordered merchandise to the firm, along with an invoice describing the contents of the shipment, the total amount due, and the terms of sale. When the firm accepts the merchandise shipped by the supplier, it in effect agrees to pay the amount due as specified by the terms of sale on the invoice. Once it has been established, trade credit becomes almost automatic and is subject to only periodic reviews by the supplier. Open account trade credit appears on the balance sheet as *accounts payable*.

Promissory notes sometimes are used as an alternative to the open account arrangement. When a company signs a promissory note, which specifies the amount to be paid and the due date, it is formally recognizing an obligation to repay the credit. A supplier may require a company to sign a promissory note if it questions the company's credit-worthiness. Promissory notes usually appear on the balance sheet as *notes payable*.

Credit Terms

Credit terms, or terms of sale, specify the conditions under which a business is required to repay the credit that a supplier has extended to it. These conditions include the *length* and the *beginning date* of the credit period, the *cash discount* (if any) given for prompt repayment, and any *special terms*, such as *seasonal datings*.[8]

Cost of Trade Credit

Trade credit is considered a *spontaneous* source of financing, because it normally expands as the volume of a company's purchases increases. For example, suppose a company experiences increased demand for its products. As a result, the company increases purchases from suppliers by 20 percent

[6] If the supplier does not feel the firm is credit-worthy, it can require that payment be made either before the goods are shipped (cash before delivery, or CBD) or upon delivery of the merchandise (cash on delivery, or COD). These are cash sales and do not involve an extension of credit.

[7] These sources and criteria are discussed in Chapter 19.

[8] This topic is discussed in Chapter 19.

from an average of $10,000 per day to an average of $12,000 per day. Assuming that these purchases are made on credit terms of "net 30" and that the company waits until the last day of the credit period to make payment, its average accounts payable outstanding (trade credit) automatically will increase by 20 percent from $300,000 ($10,000 × 30) to $360,000 ($12,000 × 30).

Because the use of trade credit is flexible, informal, and relatively easy to obtain, it is an attractive source of financing for virtually all firms, especially new and smaller firms. To make intelligent use of trade credit, however, a firm should consider the associated costs. Unlike other sources of financing, such as bank loans and bonds, which include explicit interest charges, the cost of trade credit is not always readily apparent. It may appear to be "cost-free" because of the lack of interest charges, but this reasoning can lead to incorrect financing decisions.

Obviously, someone has to bear the cost of trade credit. In extending trade credit, the supplier incurs the cost of the funds invested in accounts receivable, plus the cost of any cash discounts that are taken. Normally, the supplier passes on all or part of these costs to its customers implicitly as part of the purchase price of the merchandise, depending on market supply and demand conditions. If a company is in a position to pay cash for purchases, it may consider trying to avoid these implicit costs by negotiating lower prices with suppliers.

If the terms of sale include a cash discount, the firm must decide whether or not to take it. If the firm *takes the cash discount*, it forgoes the credit offered by the supplier beyond the end of the discount period. Assuming that the firm takes the cash discount and wants to make maximum use of the credit offered by suppliers, it should pay its bills on the last day of the discount period. Under these conditions trade credit does represent a "cost-free" source of financing to the firm (assuming that no additional discounts are available if the firm pays cash on delivery or cash before delivery).

If a company *forgoes the cash discount* and pays bills after the end of the discount period, a definite opportunity cost of trade credit is incurred. In calculating the cost of not taking the cash discount, it is assumed that the company will make maximum use of extended trade credit by paying on the last day of the credit period. Paying after the end of the credit period, or *stretching accounts payable*, subjects the company to certain other costs; these are considered below.

The annual financing cost of forgoing a cash discount is calculated using Equation 20.5. In this application, the AFC is equal to the fractional interest cost per period times the number of borrowing periods per year:

$$\text{AFC} = \frac{\text{Percentage discount}}{100 - \text{Percentage discount}} \times \frac{365}{\text{Credit period} - \text{Discount period}} \qquad \textbf{(20.5)}$$

For example, suppose the Benson Company has extended $150 of trade credit on terms of "2/10, net 30." As shown in Figure 20-1, the company can either pay the discounted amount ($147) by the end of the discount period (day 10) or the full amount of the invoice ($150) by the end of the credit period (day 30).

By *not* paying on the tenth day—that is, by forgoing the cash discount— the company has the use of $147 (98 percent of the invoice amount) for an

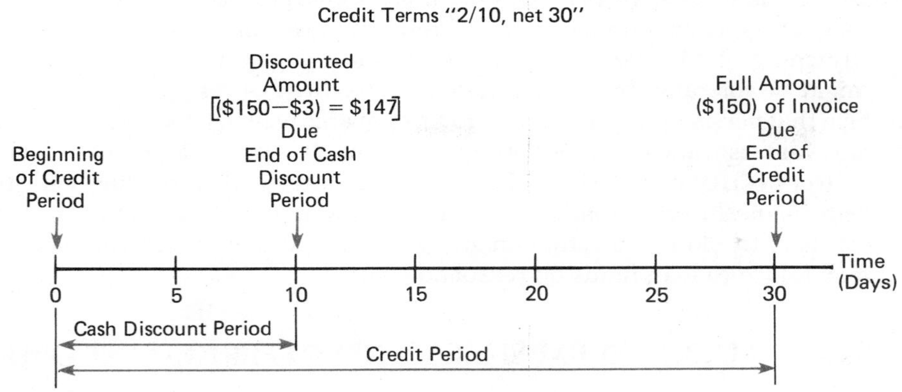

FIGURE 20-1

Benson Company's Cost of Forgoing the Cash Discount

Credit Terms "2/10, net 30"

Discounted
Amount
[($150−$3) = $147]
Due
End of Cash
Discount
Period

Beginning
of Credit
Period

Full Amount
($150) of Invoice
Due
End of
Credit
Period

Time
(Days)

0   5   10   15   20   25   30

Cash Discount Period

Credit Period

additional 20 days and effectively pays $3 in interest. Substituting this information into Equation 20.5 yields the following:

$$\text{AFC} = \frac{2}{100 - 2} \times \frac{365}{30 - 10}$$

$$= \frac{2}{98} \times \frac{365}{20}$$

$$= 37.2\%$$

As this example shows, the annual cost of forgoing cash discounts can be quite high. Therefore, when making financing decisions, a company should compare this cost to the costs of other sources of credit.

Also, the company that offers credit terms of "2/10, net 30" should consider the annual financing cost of having the use of funds for an additional 20 days. As the preceding calculation illustrates, the annual financing cost of offering cash discounts when the credit terms are "2/10, net 30" is about 37 percent. Accordingly, a company may want to consider other less expensive methods of encouraging prompt payment of trade credit. However, other benefits may accrue to a company that offers cash discounts. For example, a company actually may increase its sales by offering cash discounts. Or, a company may find that its bad-debt loss ratio is lowered if it offers a discount.

Abuses of cash discounts also exist; for example, a purchaser may deduct the discount amount even when payment is made after the discount period has passed. As a result, the seller has to decide whether simply to accept the lower payment or attempt to collect the unearned cash discount amount. With either alternative the seller incurs costs.

Stretching Accounts Payable

Rather than pay suppliers within the credit period specified in the terms of sale, a firm can postpone payment of the amount due to beyond the end of the credit period. *Stretching* payments in this manner generates additional short-term financing for the firm, but this credit is not cost-free. Not only does the firm incur the costs of forgoing any cash discounts, but its credit rating also may deteriorate, along with its ability to obtain future credit. Late payment penalties or interest charges also may be added to these costs, depending on specific industry practices. Although occasional stretching of payables—for example, to meet a seasonal need for funds— might be tolerated by suppliers and involve little or no cost to the firm, a firm that persistently stretches accounts payable well beyond their due dates may find its trade credit cut off by suppliers, who may adopt a cash before delivery (CBD) or a cash on delivery (COD) policy when dealing with the firm in the future. Finally, when a firm develops a reputation for being consistently slow in meeting financial obligations, banks and other lenders may refuse to loan funds on reasonable terms.

ACCRUED EXPENSES AND DEFERRED INCOME

Accrued expenses and deferred income are additional spontaneous sources of unsecured short-term credit.

Accrued Expenses

Accrued expenses—such as *accrued wages*, *taxes*, and *interest*—represent liabilities for services rendered to the firm that have not yet been paid for by the firm. As such, they constitute an interest-free source of financing.

Accrued wages represent the money a business owes to its employees. Accrued wages build up between paydays and fall to zero again at the end of the pay period, when the employees receive their paychecks. A company can increase the average amount of accrued wages by lengthening the period between paydays. For example, changing from a 2-week pay cycle to a 4-week pay cycle would effectively double a firm's average level of accrued wages. Also, a company can increase accrued expenses by delaying the payment of sales commissions and bonuses. Legal and practical considerations, however, limit the extent to which a company can increase accrued wages in this manner.

The amounts of *accrued taxes and interest* a firm may accumulate also is determined by the frequency with which these expenses must be paid. For example, corporate income tax payments normally are due quarterly, and a firm can use accrued taxes as a source of funds between these payment dates. Similarly, accrued interest on a bond issue requiring semiannual interest payments can be used as a source of financing for periods as long as 6 months. Of course, a firm has no control over the frequency of these tax and interest payments, so the amount of financing provided by these sources depends solely on the amounts of the payments themselves.

Deferred Income

Deferred income consists of payments received for goods and services that the firm has agreed to deliver at some future date. Because these payments increase the firm's liquidity and assets—namely, cash—they constitute a source of funds.

Advance payments made by customers are the primary sources of deferred income. These payments are common on large, expensive products, such as jet aircraft. Because these payments are not "earned" by the firm until delivery of the goods or services to the customers, they are recognized on the balance sheet as a liability called *deferred income*.

SHORT-TERM BANK CREDIT

■■■■ **689** ■■■■

CHAPTER 20
Obtaining
Short-Term
Funds

Commercial banks are an important source of both secured and unsecured short-term credit. In terms of the aggregate amount of short-term financing they provide to business firms, they rank second behind trade credit. Although trade credit is a primary source of *spontaneous* short-term financing, bank loans represent the major source of *negotiated* short-term funds.

A major purpose of short-term bank loans is to meet the firm's seasonal needs for funds—such as financing the buildup of inventories and receivables. Bank loans used for this purpose are regarded as self-liquidating, because sale of the inventories and collection of the receivables are expected to generate sufficient cash flows to permit the firm to repay the loan prior to the next seasonal buildup.

When a firm obtains a short-term bank loan, it normally signs a promissory note specifying the amount of the loan, the interest rate being charged, and the due date. The loan agreement also may contain various protective covenants.[9] Short-term bank loans appear on the balance sheet under *notes payable*.

The interest rate charged on a bank loan usually is related to the *prime rate*, which is the rate banks historically have charged on loans made to their most credit-worthy, or *prime*, business customers. The prime rate fluctuates over time with changes in the supply of and demand for loanable funds. During the 1970s and 1980s, for instance, the prime rate ranged from as low as 4.5 percent to as high as 21.5 percent. In recent years, however, many large, highly profitable companies have been able to borrow at less than the prime rate. Subprime borrowing is partially the result of increased competition among large banks for especially credit-worthy borrowers.

As an alternative to borrowing funds in the United States, large, well-established multinational corporations can borrow short-term funds in the Eurodollar market.[10] The interest rate in the Eurodollar market usually is related to the *London interbank offered rate*, or *LIBOR*. LIBOR is the interest rate at which banks in the Eurodollar market lend to each other. For example, large well-established multinational corporations usually can borrow at about 0.5 percentage points over LIBOR. Because LIBOR frequently is about 1.5 percentage points below U.S. bank prime rates, large companies can often borrow in the Eurodollar market at subprime rates. For example, in 1988, Browning-Ferris, a large multinational corporation in the solid waste business, borrowed $30 million at a rate of LIBOR plus 0.25 percentage points from two foreign banks.[11]

Short-term bank financing is available under three different arrangements:

■ Single loans (notes).
■ Lines of credit.
■ Revolving credit agreements.

Single Loans (Notes)

Businesses often need funds for short time periods to finance a particular undertaking. In such a case they may request a bank loan. This type of loan is often referred to as a *note*. The length of this type of loan can range from 30 days to 1 year, with most being for 30 to 90 days.

---

[9] The section on term loans in Chapter 15 discusses these protective covenants.
[10] The Eurodollar market is discussed in Chapter 21.
[11] Browning-Ferris Industries, Inc., *Annual Report*, 1988, p. 47.

The interest rate a bank charges on an individual loan at a given point in time depends on a number of factors, including the borrower's credit-worthiness relative to prime (lowest) credit risks. The interest rate often includes a premium of 1 to 2 or more percentage points above the prime rate, depending on how the bank officer perceives the borrower's overall business and financial risk. If the borrower is in a weak financial position and has overall risk that is thought to be too high, the bank may refuse to make an unsecured loan, regardless of the interest rate. When making the loan decision, the loan officer also considers the size of the checking account balance the company maintains at the bank, the amount of other business it does with the bank, and the rates that competitive banks are charging on similar loans.

The annual financing cost of a bank loan is also a function of when the borrower must pay the interest and whether the bank requires the borrower to maintain a compensating balance.

INTEREST PAYMENTS. If the interest on a note is paid at *maturity*, the annual financing cost is equal to the stated annual interest rate. In the case of a *discounted loan*, however, the bank deducts the interest at the time the loan is made, and thus the borrower does not receive the full loan amount. In other words, the borrower pays interest on funds it does not receive, and the annual financing cost of the loan is greater than the stated annual interest rate.

For example, suppose a company receives a 6-month (183 day), $5,000 discounted loan at a stated annual interest rate of 8 percent. The firm pays $201 interest in advance (0.08 × $5,000 × 183/365) and receives only $4799 ($5,000 − $201). Using Equation 20.3, the annual financing cost is calculated as follows:

$$\text{AFC} = \frac{\$201}{\$4799} \times \frac{365}{183}$$

$$= 8.4\%$$

Discounted bank loans today are relatively uncommon; however, other securities—commercial paper and Treasury bills, for example—are sold on a discount basis.

COMPENSATING BALANCES. A compensating balance is a certain percentage, usually 5 to 20 percent, of a loan balance that the borrower keeps on deposit with a bank as a requirement of a loan made by the bank. The compensating balance requirement is stated either in terms of an *absolute minimum* balance or an *average* balance over some stipulated period; borrowers prefer average balances to minimum balances. A compensating balance increases the return the bank earns on the loan and also provides the bank with a small measure of protection ("right of offset") in the event that the borrower defaults. Compensating balances tend to diminish in importance during periods of slack loan demand.

If the required compensating balance is *in excess* of the amount of funds that normally would be maintained in the company's checking account, the annual financing cost of the loan is greater than the stated interest rate. It can be calculated using Equation 20.3. When a compensating balance is required, the *usable funds* amount in the denominator is the *net* amount of the loan that the company can spend after taking into account the amount borrowed, any required compensating balance, and the balance normally maintained in the bank account.

For example, suppose the Cutler Company obtains a 1-year (365 day) $200,000 bank loan at 9 percent interest but is required to maintain a 20 percent average compensating balance. In other words, the company must maintain a $40,000 (0.20 × $200,000) average compensating balance to obtain the loan. If Cutler currently maintains a $30,000 average balance that can be used to meet the compensating balance requirement, it needs to keep an additional $10,000 in the account, and thus the loan generates $190,000 in usable funds. The interest charges on the loan are $18,000 ($200,000 × 0.09). Substituting these values into Equation 20.3 yields the following:

$$\text{AFC} = \frac{\$18,000}{\$190,000} \times \frac{365}{365}$$

$$= 9.5\%$$

However, if Cutler currently has no balances in its bank account that can be used to meet the average compensating balance requirement, it has to keep $40,000 of the $200,000 loan in the checking account, and the amount of usable funds is reduced to $160,000. In this case, the annual financing cost becomes significantly higher:

$$\text{AFC} = \frac{\$18,000}{\$160,000} \times \frac{365}{365}$$

$$= 11.3\%$$

Lines of Credit

A firm that needs funds periodically throughout the year for a variety of purposes may find it useful to negotiate a line of credit with its bank. A line of credit is an agreement that permits the firm to borrow funds up to a predetermined limit at any time during the life of the agreement. The major advantage of this type of borrowing agreement, as compared with single loans, is that the firm does not have to renegotiate with the bank every time funds are required. Instead, it can obtain funds on short notice with little or no additional justification. Another advantage to establishing a line of credit is that the firm can plan for its future short-term financing requirements without having to anticipate exactly how much it will have to borrow each month.

A line of credit usually is negotiated for a 1-year period, with renewals being subject to renegotiation each year. In determining the size of a credit line, a bank will consider a company's credit-worthiness, along with its projected financing needs. As part of the application for a line of credit, the company normally is required to provide the bank with a cash budget for the next year, along with current and projected income statements and balance sheets. The interest rate on a line of credit usually is determined by adding to the prime rate a premium based on the borrower's credit-worthiness. Because the prime rate normally fluctuates over time, the interest rate charged varies during the life of the agreement.

To illustrate, suppose a company has a $500,000 line of credit at 1 percent above the bank's prime rate.[12] During the year the company borrows, or "draws down," $200,000 on the line, and no compensating balances are in effect during the year. The bank's prime rate is 8.0 percent from January 1 to March 31, and on April 1 the bank raises its prime rate to 8.25 percent, where it remains for the rest of the year. The annual financing cost is calculated as follows using Equation 20.3.

Interest costs (January 1–March 31):

$$I = \$200,000 \times 0.09 \times \frac{90}{365}$$

$$= \$4,438.36$$

Interest costs (April 1–December 31):

$$I = \$200,000 \times 0.0925 \times \frac{275}{365}$$

$$= \$13,938.36$$

$$\text{Total interest costs} = \$4,438.36 + \$13,938.36$$

$$= \$18,376.72$$

$$\text{AFC} = \frac{\$18,376.72}{\$200,000.00} \times \frac{365}{365}$$

$$= 9.19\%$$

A line of credit agreement normally includes certain protective covenants. In addition to possibly including a compensating balance requirement, the loan agreement usually contains an annual "clean-up" provision requiring that the company have no loans outstanding under the line of credit for a certain period of time each year, usually 30 to 90 days. This type of policy helps reassure the bank that the company is using the line of credit to finance seasonal needs for funds and not to finance permanent capital requirements. Finally, a line of credit agreement also may contain provisions (similar to those in a term loan agreement) that require the firm to maintain a minimum working capital position, limit total debt and lease financing, and restrict dividend payments.

Revolving Credit Agreements

Although a line of credit agreement does not legally commit the bank to making loans to the firm under any and all conditions, the bank normally will feel morally obligated to honor the line of credit. Some banks, however, have chosen not to provide financing to a firm when the firm's financial position has deteriorated significantly or when the bank lacks sufficient loanable funds to satisfy all its commitments. If the firm desires a guaranteed line of credit, it must negotiate a revolving credit agreement.

Under a revolving credit agreement, or "revolver," the bank is *legally committed* to making loans to a company up to the predetermined credit

---

[12] Finance professionals often refer to this rate as "prime plus one," or "one over prime." In addition, they often write it as "P + 1."

limit specified in the agreement. Revolving credit agreements differ from line of credit agreements in that they require the borrower to pay a *commitment fee* on the unused portion of the funds. This fee typically is in the range of 0.25 to 0.50 percent. Revolving credit agreements are frequently made for a period of 2 to 3 years.

Calculating the annual financing cost of funds borrowed under a revolving credit agreement is slightly more complex than with either a single loan or a line of credit. In addition to the interest rate, commitment fee, compensating balance, and the firm's normal account balance, the annual financing cost of a revolving credit loan also depends on the amount borrowed and the credit limit of the agreement. The annual financing cost can be calculated based on Equation 20.3, as follows:

$$\text{AFC} = \frac{\text{Interest costs} + \text{Commitment fee}}{\text{Usable funds}} \times \frac{365}{\text{Maturity (days)}} \qquad \textbf{(20.6)}$$

For example, suppose the Kalamazoo Company has a $4 million revolving credit agreement with its bank to borrow at the prime rate. The agreement requires the company to maintain a 10 percent average compensating balance on any funds borrowed under the agreement, as well as to pay a 0.5 percent commitment fee on the unused portion of the credit line. The prime rate during the year is expected to be 8 percent. Kalamazoo's average borrowing under the agreement during the year is expected to be $2 million. The company maintains an average of $100,000 in its account at the bank, which can be used to meet the compensating balance requirement.

To calculate the annual financing cost of the revolving credit agreement, Kalamazoo must determine the amount of usable funds generated by the loan, the total interest costs, and the commitment fees. Given average borrowing of $2 million during the year, Kalamazoo is required to maintain an average compensating balance of $200,000 (0.10 × $2 million). Because the company currently maintains an average balance of $100,000, $100,000 of the loan is needed to meet the compensating balance requirement. Therefore, the amount of usable funds is $1.9 million. Interest costs on the average amount borrowed are $160,000 (0.08 × $2 million), and the commitment fee on the unused portion of the credit line is $10,000 (0.005 × [$4 million − $2 million]). Substituting these figures into Equation 20.6 yields the following annual financing cost of the loan:

$$\text{AFC} = \frac{\$160,000 + \$10,000}{\$1,900,000} \times \frac{365}{365}$$

$$= \frac{\$170,000}{\$1,900,000} \times \frac{365}{365}$$

$$= 8.95\%$$

Thus, the annual financing cost of the revolving credit agreement is higher than the stated interest rate.

Many financially sound companies view revolving credit agreements as a form of financial insurance, and, as a result, these companies frequently have little or no borrowings outstanding against the agreements. For example, at the end of fiscal 1988 Digital Equipment Corporation had revolving credit agreements totaling $582 million, and all but $2 million were unused at the time.[13]

COMMERCIAL PAPER

Commercial paper consists of short-term unsecured promissory notes issued by major corporations. Only companies with good credit ratings are able to borrow funds through the sale of commercial paper. Purchasers of commercial paper include corporations with excess funds to invest, banks, insurance companies, pension funds, money market mutual funds, and other types of financial institutions.

Large finance companies, such as General Motors Acceptance Corporation (GMAC) and CIT Financial Corporation, issue sizable amounts of commercial paper on a regular basis, selling it directly to investors like those just mentioned. Large industrial, utility, and transportation firms, as well as smaller finance companies, issue commercial paper less frequently and in smaller amounts; they sell it to dealers who, in turn, sell the commercial paper to investors.

Maturities on commercial paper at the time of issue range from several days to a maximum of 9 months. Companies usually do not issue commercial paper with maturities beyond 9 months, because these issues must be registered with the Securities and Exchange Commission. The size of an issue of commercial paper can range up to several million dollars. It is usually sold to investors in multiples of $100,000 or more. Large issuers of commercial paper normally attempt to tailor the maturity and amounts of an issue to the needs of investors.

Commercial paper represents an attractive financing source for large, financially sound firms, because interest rates on commercial paper issues tend to be below the prime lending rate. To successfully market commercial paper (and get an acceptable rating from Moody's, Standard and Poor's, or both), however, the company must normally have unused bank lines of credit equal to the amount of the issue.

The primary disadvantage of this type of financing is that it is not always a reliable source of funds. The commercial paper market is impersonal. A firm that suddenly is faced with temporary financial difficulties may find that investors are unwilling to purchase new issues of commercial paper to replace maturing issues. In addition, the amount of loanable funds available in the commercial paper market is limited to the amount of excess liquidity of the various purchasers of commercial paper. During tight money periods there may not be enough funds available to meet the aggregate needs of corporate issuers of commercial paper at reasonable rates. As a result, a company should maintain adequate lines of bank credit and recognize the risks of relying too heavily on commercial paper. Finally, a commercial paper issue usually cannot be paid off until maturity. Even if a company no longer needs the funds from a commercial paper issue, it still must pay the interest costs.

Commercial paper is sold on a discount basis. This means that the firm receives less than the stated amount of the note at issue and then pays the investor the full face amount at maturity. The annual financing cost of commercial paper depends on the maturity date of the issue and the prevailing short-term interest rates. In addition to the interest costs, borrowers

[13] Digital Equipment Corporation, *Annual Report*, 1988, p. 57.

also must pay a *placement fee* to the commercial paper dealer for arranging the sale of the issue. The annual financing cost can be computed as follows, based on Equation 20.3:

$$\text{AFC} = \frac{\text{Interest costs} + \text{Placement fee}}{\text{Usable funds}} \times \frac{365}{\text{Maturity (days)}} \quad \textbf{(20.7)}$$

The usable funds are equal to the face amount of the issue less the interest costs and placement fee.

For example, suppose Midland Steel Company is considering issuing $10 million of commercial paper. A commercial paper dealer has indicated that Midland could sell a 90-day issue at an annual interest rate of 9.5 percent. The placement fee would be $25,000. Using Equation 20.7 the annual financing cost of this commercial paper issue is calculated as follows:

$$\text{Interest costs} = \$10,000,000 \times 0.095 \times \frac{90}{365}$$

$$= \$234,247$$

$$\text{AFC} = \frac{\$234,247 + \$25,000}{\$10,000,000 - \$234,247 - \$25,000} \times \frac{365}{90}$$

$$= 10.79\%$$

ACCOUNTS RECEIVABLE LOANS

Accounts receivable are one of the most commonly used forms of collateral for *secured* short-term borrowing. From the lender's standpoint, accounts receivable represent a desirable form of collateral, because they are relatively liquid and their value is relatively easy to recover if the borrower becomes insolvent. In addition, accounts receivable involve documents representing customer obligations rather than cumbersome physical assets. Offsetting these advantages, however, are potential difficulties. One disadvantage is that the borrower may attempt to defraud the lender by pledging nonexistent accounts. Also, the recovery process in the event of insolvency may be hampered if the customer who owes the receivables returns the merchandise or files a claim alleging that the merchandise is defective. Finally, the administrative costs of processing the receivables can be high, particularly when there is a large number of invoices involving small dollar amounts.

Nevertheless, many companies use accounts receivable as collateral for short-term financing by either *pledging* their receivables or *factoring* them.

Pledging Accounts Receivable

The pledging process begins with a loan agreement specifying the procedures and terms under which the lender will advance funds to the firm. When accounts receivable are pledged, the firm retains title to the receivables and continues to carry them on its balance sheet. However, the pledged status of the firm's receivables should be disclosed in a footnote to the financial statements. (Pledging is an accepted business practice, particularly with smaller businesses.) A firm that has pledged receivables as collateral is required to repay the loan, even if it is unable to collect the pledged receivables. In other words, the borrower assumes the default risk, and the lender has *recourse* back to the borrower. Both commercial banks and finance companies make loans secured by accounts receivable.

Once the pledging agreement has been established, the firm periodically sends the lender a group of invoices along with the loan request. Upon receipt of the customer invoices, the lender investigates the credit-worthiness of the accounts to determine which are acceptable as collateral. The percentage of funds that the lender will advance against the collateral depends on the quality of the receivables and the company's financial position. The percentage normally ranges from 50 to 80 percent of the face amount of the receivables pledged. The company then is required to sign a promissory note and a security agreement, after which it receives the funds from the lender.

Most receivables loans are made on a *nonnotification basis*, which means the customer is not notified that the receivable has been pledged by the firm. The customer continues to make payments directly to the firm. To protect itself against possible fraud, the lender usually requires the firm to forward all customer payments in the form in which they are received. In addition, the borrower usually is subject to a periodic audit to ensure the integrity of its receivables and payments. Receivables that remain unpaid for 60 days or so usually must be replaced by the borrower.

The customer payments are used to reduce the loan balance and eventually repay the loan. Receivables loans can be a continuous source of financing for a company, however, provided that new receivables are pledged to the lender as existing accounts are collected. By periodically sending the lender new receivables, the company can maintain its collateral base and obtain a relatively constant amount of financing.

Receivables loans can be an attractive source of financing for a company that does not have access to unsecured credit. As the company grows and its level of receivables increases, it normally can obtain larger receivables loans fairly easily. And, unlike line of credit agreements, receivables loans usually do not have compensating balance or "clean-up" provisions.

The annual financing cost of a loan in which receivables are pledged as collateral includes both the interest expense on the unpaid balance of the loan and the service fees charged for processing the receivables. Typically, the interest rate ranges from 2 to 5 percentage points over the prime rate, and service fees are approximately 1 to 2 percent of the amount of the pledged receivables. The services performed by the lender under a pledging agreement can include credit checking, keeping records of the pledged accounts and collections, and monitoring the agreement. This type of financing can be quite expensive for the firm.

Port City Plastics Corporation is considering pledging its receivables to finance a needed increase in working capital. Its commercial bank will lend 75 percent of the pledged receivables at 2 percentage points above the prime rate, which is currently 10 percent. In addition, the bank charges a service fee equal to 1.0 percent of the pledged receivables. Both interest payments and the service fee are payable at the end of each borrowing period. Port City's average collection period is 45 days, and it has receivables totaling $2 million that the bank has indicated are acceptable as collateral. Table 20-1 calculates the annual financing cost for the pledged receivables (22.8 percent).

Cost of Pledging Receivables for Port City Plastics Corporation

$$\text{Usable funds} = 0.75 \times \text{Pledgeable receivables}$$
$$= 0.75 \times \$2,000,000$$
$$= \$1,500,000$$

$$\text{Interest costs} = \$1,500,000 \times 0.12 \times \frac{45}{365}$$
$$= \$22,192$$

$$\text{Service fee} = \$2,000,000 \times 0.01$$
$$= \$20,000$$

$$\text{AFC} = \frac{\$22,192 + \$20,000}{\$1,500,000} \times \frac{365}{45}$$
$$= 22.8\%$$

Factoring Accounts Receivable

Factoring receivables involves the outright sale of the firm's receivables to a financial institution known as a *factor*. A number of so-called old-line factors, in addition to some commercial banks and finance companies (asset-based lenders), are engaged in factoring receivables. When receivables are factored, title to them is transferred to the factor, and the receivables no longer appear on the firm's balance sheet.

Traditionally, the use of factoring was confined primarily to the apparel, furniture, and textile industries. In other industries the factoring of receivables was considered an indication of poor financial health. Today, factoring seems to be gaining increased acceptance in other industries.

The factoring process begins with an agreement that specifies the procedures for factoring the receivables and the terms under which the factor will advance funds to the firm. Under the normal factoring arrangement, the firm sends the customer order to the factor for credit checking and approval *before* filling it. The factor maintains a credit department to perform the credit checking and collection functions. Once the factor decides that the customer is an acceptable risk and agrees to purchase the receivable, the firm ships the order to the customer. The customer usually is notified that its account has been sold and is instructed to make payments directly to the factor.

Most factoring of receivables is done on a *nonrecourse* basis; in other words, the factor assumes the risk of default.[14] If the factor refuses to purchase a given receivable, the firm still can ship the order to the customer and assume the default risk itself, but this receivable does not provide any collateral for additional credit.

In the typical factoring agreement, the firm receives payment from the factor at the normal collection or due date of the factored accounts. This is called *maturity factoring*. If the firm wants to receive the funds prior to this date, it usually can obtain an advance from the factor; this is referred to as *advance factoring*. Therefore, in addition to credit checking, collecting receivables, and bearing default risk, the factor also performs a lending function and assesses specific charges for each service provided. The maximum advance the firm can obtain from the factor is limited to the amount

---

[14] If the receivables are sold to the factor on a *recourse* basis, the firm is liable for losses on any receivables that are not collected by the factor.

of factored receivables *less* the factoring commission, interest expense, and reserve that the factor withholds to cover any returns or allowances by customers. The reserve is usually 5 to 10 percent of the factored receivables and is paid to the firm after the factor collects the receivables.

The factor charges a factoring commission, or service fee, of 1 to 3 percent of the factored receivables to cover the costs of credit checking, collection, and bad-debt losses. The rate charged depends on the total volume of the receivables, the size of the individual receivables, and the default risk involved. The factor normally charges an interest rate of 2 to 5 percentage points over the prime rate on advances to the firm. These costs are somewhat offset by a number of internal savings that a business can realize through factoring its receivables. A company that factors all its receivables does not need a credit department and does not have to incur the administrative and clerical costs of credit investigation and collection or the losses on uncollected accounts. In addition, the factor may be better able to control losses than a credit department in a small or medium-sized company due to its greater experience in credit evaluation. Thus, although factoring receivables may be a more costly form of credit than unsecured borrowing, the net cost may be below the stated factoring commission and interest rates because of credit department and bad-debt loss savings.

For example, the Masterson Apparel Company is considering an advance factoring agreement because of its weak financial position and because of the large degree of credit risk inherent in its business. The company primarily sells large quantities of apparel to a relatively small number of retailers, and if even one retailer does not pay, the company could experience severe cash flow problems. By factoring, Masterson transfers the credit risk to the factor, Partners Credit Corporation, an asset-based lender. Partners requires a 10 percent reserve for returns and allowances, charges a 2 percent factoring commission, and will advance Masterson funds at an annual interest rate of 4 percentage points over prime. Assume the prime rate is 10 percent. Factoring receivables will allow the company to eliminate its credit department and save about $2,000 a month in administrative and clerical costs. Factoring also will eliminate bad-debt losses, which average about $6,000 a month. Masterson's average collection period is 60 days, and its average level of receivables is $1 million.

Table 20-2 calculates the amount of funds Masterson can borrow from the factor and the annual financing cost of these funds.[15] As can be seen in the table, Masterson can obtain an advance of $859,748, and the annual financing cost is 28.5 percent *before* considering cost savings and elimination of bad-debt losses. *After* considering savings and loss eliminations, the annual financing cost drops to 17.2 percent. Masterson can compare the cost of this factoring arrangement with the cost of other sources of funds in deciding whether or not to factor its receivables. This example calculates the factoring cost for a single 60-day period. In practice, if Masterson did enter into a factoring agreement, it most likely would become a continuous procedure.

INVENTORY LOANS

Inventories are another commonly used form of collateral for secured short-term loans. Like receivables, many types of inventories are fairly liquid.

---

[15] Although the reserve for returns is deducted when figuring the amount of usable funds advanced by the factor, it is not part of the cost of factoring, because the factor will return it to Masterson provided that the company's customers make no returns or adjustments.

TABLE 20-2

Cost of Factoring Receivables for Masterson Apparel Company

Calculation of usable funds:

Average level of receivables		$1,000,000
Less Factoring commission	$0.02 \times \$1,000,000$	−20,000
Less Reserve for returns	$0.10 \times \$1,000,000$	−100,000
Amount available for advance before interest is deducted		$880,000
Less Interest on advance	$(0.14 \times \$880,000 \times 60/365)$	−20,252
Amount of funds advanced by factor, or *usable funds*		$859,748

Interest costs and fees:

Interest costs	$20,252
Fee, or factoring commission	20,000
Total	$40,252

Calculation of annual financing cost, *before* considering cost savings and bad-debt losses:

$$AFC = \frac{\$40,252}{\$859,748} \times \frac{365}{60}$$
$$= 28.5\%$$

Calculation of annual financing cost, *after* considering cost savings and bad-debt losses:

Credit department savings, per 60-day period	$ 4,000
Average bad-debt losses, per 60-day period	12,000
Total	$16,000

$$AFC = \frac{\$40,252 - \$16,000}{\$859,748} \times \frac{365}{60}$$
$$= 17.2\%$$

Therefore lenders consider them a desirable form of collateral. When judging whether a firm's inventory would be suitable collateral for a loan, the primary considerations of the lender are the type, physical characteristics, identifiability, liquidity, and marketability of the inventory.

Firms hold three types of inventories: *raw materials, work-in-process,* and *finished goods.* Normally, only raw materials and finished goods are considered acceptable as security for a loan. The physical characteristic with which lenders are most concerned is the item's *perishability.* Inventory subject to significant physical deterioration over time usually is not suitable as collateral.

Inventory items also should be *readily identifiable* by means of serial numbers or inventory control numbers. This helps protect the lender against possible fraud and also aids the lender in establishing a valid title claim to the collateral if the borrower becomes insolvent and defaults on the loan. The ease with which the inventory can be *liquidated* and the stability of its *market price* are other important considerations. In the event that the borrower defaults, the lender wants to be able to take possession, sell the collateral, and recover the full amount owed with minimal expense and difficulty.

Both commercial banks and asset-based lenders make inventory loans. The percentage of funds that the lender will advance against the inventory's book value ranges from about 50 to 80 percent and depends on the inventory's characteristics. Advances near the upper end of this range normally are made only for inventories that are standardized, nonperishable, easily identified, and readily marketable. To receive an inventory loan, the borrower must sign both a promissory note and a security agreement describing the inventory that will serve as collateral.

In making a loan secured with inventories, the lender can either allow the borrower to hold the collateral or require that it be held by a third party. If the borrower holds the collateral, the loan may be made under a *floating lien* or *trust receipt* arrangement. If a third party is employed to hold the collateral, either a *terminal warehouse* or a *field warehouse* financing arrangement can be used.

Floating Liens

Under a floating lien arrangement, the lender receives a security interest or general claim on *all* of the firm's inventory; this may include both present and future inventory. This type of agreement often is employed when the average value of the inventory items is small, the inventory turns over frequently, or both. Specific items are not identified. Thus, a floating lien does not offer the lender much protection against losses from fraud or bankruptcy. As a result, most lenders will not advance a very high percentage of funds against the book value of the borrower's inventory.

Trust Receipts

A trust receipt is a security agreement under which the firm holds the inventory and proceeds from the sale in trust for the lender. Whenever a portion of the inventory is sold, the firm is required to immediately forward the proceeds to the lender; these then are used to reduce the loan balance.

Some companies engage in inventory financing on a continuing basis. In these cases, a new security agreement is drawn up periodically, and the lender advances the company additional funds using recently purchased inventories as collateral.

All inventory items under a trust receipt arrangement must be readily identified by serial number or inventory code number. The lender makes periodic, unannounced inspections of the inventory to make sure that the firm has the collateral and has not withheld payment for inventory that has been sold.

Businesses that must have their inventories available for sale on their premises, such as automobile and appliance dealers, frequently engage in trust receipt financing. This is also known as *floor planning*. Many "captive" finance companies that are subsidiaries of manufacturers, such as General Motors Acceptance Corporation (GMAC), engage in floor planning for their dealers.

Terminal Warehouse and Field Warehouse Financing Arrangements

Under a *terminal warehouse* financing arrangement, the inventory being used as loan collateral is stored in a bonded warehouse operated by a public warehousing company. When the inventory is delivered to the warehouse, the warehouse company issues a warehouse receipt listing the specific items received by serial or lot number. The warehouse receipt is forwarded to the lender, who then advances funds to the borrower.

Holding the warehouse receipt gives the lender a security interest in the inventory. Because the warehouse company will release the stored inventory to the firm only when authorized to do so by the holder of the warehouse receipt, the lender is able to exercise control over the collateral. As the firm repays the loan, the lender authorizes the warehouse company to release appropriate amounts of the inventory to the firm.

Under a *field warehouse* financing agreement, the inventory that serves as collateral for a loan is segregated from the firm's other inventory and stored on its premises under the control of a field warehouse company. The field warehouse company issues a warehouse receipt, and the lender advances funds to the firm. The field warehouse releases inventory to the firm only when authorized to do so by the lender.

Although terminal warehouse and field warehouse financing arrangements provide the lender with more control over the collateral than it has when the borrower holds the inventory, fraud or negligence on the part of the warehouse company can result in losses for the lender. The fees charged by the warehouse company make this type of financing more expensive than floating lien or trust receipt loans. In a terminal warehouse arrangement, the firm incurs storage charges, in addition to fees for transporting the inventory to and from the public warehouse. In a field warehouse arrangement, the firm normally has to pay an installation charge, a fixed operating charge based on the overall size of the warehousing operation, and a monthly storage charge based on the value of the inventory in the field warehouse.

Overall warehousing fees are generally 1 to 3 percent of the inventory value. The total cost of an inventory loan includes the service fee charged by the lender and the warehousing fee charged by the warehousing company, plus the interest on the funds advanced by the lender. Any internal savings in inventory handling and storage costs that result when the inventory is held by a warehouse company are deducted in computing the cost of the loan.

SUMMARY

- Short-term credit may be either *secured* or *unsecured*. In the case of secured credit, the borrower pledges certain assets (such as inventory, receivables, or fixed assets) as collateral for the loan. In general, firms prefer to borrow on an unsecured basis, because pledging assets as security generally raises the overall cost of the loan and also can reduce the firm's flexibility by restricting future borrowing.
- *Trade credit, accrued expenses,* and *deferred income* are the primary sources of spontaneous short-term credit. *Bank loans, commercial paper, accounts receivable loans,* and *inventory loans* represent the major sources of *negotiated* short-term credit.
- The *annual financing cost, AFC,* for a short-term credit source is calculated as follows:

$$AFC = \frac{\text{Interest costs + fees}}{\text{Usable funds}} \times \frac{365}{\text{Maturity (days)}}$$

■ Trade credit is extended to a firm when it makes purchases from a supplier and is permitted to wait a specified period of time before paying for them. It normally is extended on an *open-account* basis, which means that once a firm accepts merchandise from a supplier, it agrees to pay the amount due as specified by the terms of sale on the invoice.

■ *Stretching accounts payable,* or postponing payment beyond the end of the credit period, can be used to obtain additional short-term financing. The costs of stretching accounts payable include foregone cash discounts, penalties, and interest, as well as possible deterioration of the firm's credit rating and ability to obtain future credit.

■ *Accrued expenses,* such as accrued wages, taxes, and interest, are liabilities for services provided to the firm that have not yet been paid for by the firm.

■ *Deferred income* consists of payments received for goods and services a company will deliver at a future date.

■ Short-term *bank credit* can be extended to the firm under a *single loan,* a *line of credit,* or a *revolving credit agreement.* A line of credit permits the firm to borrow funds up to a predetermined limit at any time during the life of the agreement. A revolving credit agreement legally commits the bank to provide the funds when the firm requests them.

■ *Commercial paper* consists of short-term unsecured promissory notes issued by major corporations with good credit ratings.

■ *Accounts receivable loans* can be obtained by either *pledging* or *factoring* receivables. In the case of a pledging arrangement, the firm retains title to the receivables, and the lender advances funds to the firm based on the amount and quality of the receivables. With factoring, receivables are sold to a factor, who takes the responsibility for credit checking and collection of the accounts. With pledging, the lender does not assume credit risk and has *recourse* back to the borrower if payment is not made, whereas factoring is normally a nonrecourse form of financing.

■ Several types of *inventory loans* are available. In a *floating lien* or *trust receipt* arrangement, the borrower holds the collateral. In a floating lien arrangement, the lender has a general claim on all of the firm's inventory. In a trust receipt arrangement, the inventory being used as collateral is specifically identified by serial or inventory code numbers. In a *terminal warehouse* and a *field warehouse* arrangement, a third party holds the collateral; in the case of a terminal warehouse arrangement, collateral is stored in a public warehouse, whereas in a field warehouse arrangement, collateral is stored in a field warehouse located on the borrower's premises.

■ No one source (or combination of sources) of short-term financing is necessarily optimal for all firms. Many other factors, in addition to cost of financing, need to be considered when choosing the optimal source or sources of short-term financing. Some of these factors include the availability of funds during periods of financial crisis or tight money, restrictive covenants imposed on the firm, and the nature of the firm's operations and funds requirements.

■ QUESTIONS AND TOPICS FOR DISCUSSION

1. Define and discuss the function of *collateral* in short-term credit arrangements.

2. How is the annual financing cost for a short-term financing source calculated? How does the annual financing cost differ from the true annual percentage rate?

3. Explain the difference between *spontaneous* and *negotiated* sources of short-term credit.

4. Under what condition or conditions is trade credit *not* a "cost-free" source of funds to the firm?

5. Define the following:
   a. Accrued expenses.
   b. Deferred income.
   c. Prime rate.
   d. Compensating balance.
   e. Discounted loan.
   f. Commitment fee.

6. Explain the differences between a line of credit and a revolving credit agreement.

7. What are some of the disadvantages of relying too heavily on commercial paper as a source of short-term credit?

8. Explain the differences between pledging and factoring receivables.

9. Explain the difference between a floating lien and a trust receipts arrangement.

10. Explain why the annual financing cost of secured credit frequently is higher than that of unsecured credit.

11. Explain why banks normally include a "clean-up" provision in a line of credit agreement.

12. What savings are realized when accounts receivable are factored rather than pledged?

13. Determine the effect of each of the following conditions on the annual financing cost for a line of credit arrangement (assuming that all other factors remain constant):
    a. The bank raises the prime rate.
    b. The bank lowers its compensating balance requirements.
    c. The firm's average bank balance increases as the result of its instituting more stringent credit and collection policies.

14. Under what condition or conditions, if any, might a firm find it desirable to borrow funds from a bank or other lending institution in order to take a cash discount?

PROBLEMS*

NOTE: **Assume that there are 365 days per year when converting from annual to daily amounts or vice versa.**

1. The Milton Company currently purchases an average of $22,000 per day in raw materials on credit terms of "net 30." The company expects sales to increase substantially next year and anticipates that its raw material purchases will increase to an average of $25,000 per day. Milton feels that it may need to finance part of this sales expansion by *stretching* accounts payable.

   a. Assuming that Milton currently waits until the end of the credit period to pay its raw material suppliers, what is its current level of trade credit?
   b. If Milton stretches its accounts payable an extra 10 days beyond the due date next year, how much *additional* short-term funds (that is, trade credit) will be generated?

* Colored numbers denote problems that have check answers provided at the end of the book.

2. Van Buren Resources, Inc., is considering borrowing $100,000 for 182 days from its bank. Van Buren will pay $6,000 of interest at maturity, and it will repay the $100,000 of principal at maturity.

   a. Calculate the loan's annual financing cost.
   b. Calculate the loan's annual percentage rate.
   c. What is the reason for the difference in your answers to parts a and b?

3. Determine the *annual financing cost* of forgoing the cash discount under each of the following credit terms:

   a. 2/10, net 60.
   b. 1½/10, net 60.
   c. 2/30, net 60.
   d. 5/30, net 4 months (assume 122 days).
   e. 1/10, net 30.

4. Calculate the *annual percentage rate* of forgoing the cash discount under each of the following credit terms:

   a. 2/10, net 60.
   b. 2/10, net 30.

5. Determine the *annual financing cost* of forgoing the cash discount if the credit terms are "1/10, net 30," and the invoice is not paid until it is 20 days past due.

6. Determine the annual financing cost of a 1-year (365 day), $10,000 discounted bank loan at a stated annual interest rate of 9.5 percent. Assume that no compensating balance is required.

7. The Pulaski Company has a line of credit with a bank under which it can borrow funds at an 8 percent interest rate. The company plans to borrow $100,000 and is required by the bank to maintain a 15 percent compensating balance. Determine the annual financing cost of the loan under each of the following conditions:

   a. The company currently maintains $7,000 in its account at the bank that can be used to meet the compensating balance requirement.
   b. The company currently has no funds in its account at the bank that can be used to meet the compensating balance requirement.

8. Determine the annual financing cost of a 6-month (182 day), $20,000 discounted bank loan at a stated annual interest rate of 10 percent. Assume that no compensating balance is required.

9. Pyramid Products Company has a revolving credit agreement with its bank. The company can borrow up to $1 million under the agreement at an annual interest rate of 9 percent. Pyramid is required to maintain a 10 percent compensating balance on any funds borrowed under the agreement and to pay a 0.5 percent commitment fee on the unused portion of the credit line. Determine the annual financing cost of borrowing each of the following amounts under the credit agreement:

   a. $250,000.
   b. $500,000
   c. $1,000,000.

10. Wellsley Manufacturing Company has been approached by a commercial paper dealer offering to sell an issue of commercial paper for the firm. The dealer indicates that Wellsley could sell a $5 million issue maturing in 182 days at an interest rate of 8.5 percent per annum (deducted in advance). The fee to the dealer for selling the issue would be $8,000. Determine Wellsley's annual financing cost of this commercial paper financing.

11. The Brandt Company has been approached by two different commercial paper dealers offering to sell an issue of commercial paper for the company. Dealer A offered to market an $8 million issue maturing in 90 days at an

interest cost of 8.5 percent per annum (deducted in advance). The fee to Dealer A would be $12,000. Dealer B has offered to sell a $10 million issue maturing in 120 days at an interest rate of 8.75 percent per annum (deducted in advance). The fee to Dealer B would be $15,000. Assuming that Brandt wishes to minimize the annual financing cost of issuing commercial paper, which dealer should it choose?

12. Ranger Enterprises is considering pledging its receivables to finance a needed increase in working capital. Its commercial bank will lend 75 percent of the pledged receivables at 1.5 percentage points above the prime rate, which is currently 12 percent. In addition, the bank charges a service fee equal to 1.0 percent of the pledged receivables. Both interest and the service fee are payable at the end of the borrowing period. Ranger's average collection period is 50 days, and it has receivables totaling $5 million that the bank has indicated are acceptable as collateral. Calculate the annual financing cost for the pledged receivables.

13. Designer Textiles, Inc., is considering factoring its receivables. The company's average collection period is 60 days, and its average level of receivables is $2.5 million. Designer's bad-debt losses average $15,000 a month. If the company factors its receivables, it will save $4,000 a month by eliminating its credit department. The factor has indicated that it requires a 10 percent reserve for returns and allowances and charges a 2.5 percent factoring commission. The factor will advance Designer funds at 4 percent over prime, which is currently 8 percent.

   a. Determine the annual financing cost, *before* considering cost savings and bad-debt losses.
   b. Determine the annual financing cost, *after* considering cost savings and bad-debt losses.

14. The Eaton Company needs to raise $250,000 to expand its working capital and has been unsuccessful in attempting to obtain an unsecured line of credit with its bank. The firm is considering *stretching* its accounts payable. Eaton's suppliers extend credit on terms of "2/10, net 30." Payments beyond the credit period are subject to a 1½ percent per month penalty. Eaton purchases $100,000 per month from its suppliers and currently takes cash discounts. For this problem assume that a year consists of twelve 30-day months. Assuming that Eaton is able to raise the $250,000 it needs by stretching its accounts payable, determine the following:

   a. The firm's annual lost cash discounts.
   b. Annual penalties.
   c. The annual financing cost of this source of financing.

15. Which of the following credit terms would you prefer as a customer?

   a. 2/10 net 30.
   b. 1/10 net 40.
   c. 2/10 net 40.
   d. 1/10 net 25.
   e. Indifferent between all options.

   Explain your choice.

16. The Odessa Supply Company is considering obtaining a loan from a sales finance company secured by inventories under a field warehousing arrangement. Odessa would be permitted to borrow up to $300,000 under such an arrangement at an annual interest rate of 10 percent. The additional cost of maintaining a field warehouse is $16,000 per year. Determine the annual financing cost of a loan under this arrangement if Odessa borrows the following amounts:

   a. $300,000.
   b. $250,000.

17. Harpo Music Mart needs to raise $300,000 to increase its working capital. The bank, mindful of Harpo's strained financial condition, has refused to loan the firm the needed funds. Harpo is considering *stretching* its accounts payable in order to raise the funds. Current credit terms are "3/10, net 30." Payments beyond the credit period are subject to a 1 percent per month penalty. Harpo purchases $125,000 per month from its suppliers and currently takes cash discounts. If Harpo is able to raise the $300,000 it needs by stretching its accounts payable, determine the annual financing cost of this source of financing. For this problem, assume that a year consists of twelve 30-day months.

WORKING CAPITAL MANAGEMENT

Anderson Furniture Company manufactures furniture and sells its products to department stores, retail furniture stores, hotels, and motels throughout the United States and Canada. The firm has nine manufacturing plants located in Virginia, North Carolina, and Georgia. The company was founded by Edward G. Anderson in 1906 and has been managed by members of the Anderson family since that time. E. G. Anderson III currently is chairman and president of the company. The treasurer and controller of the company is Claire White, who was hired away from a competing furniture company a few years ago. Anderson owns 35 percent of the common stock of the company and (along with the shares of the firm owned by relatives and employees) has effective control over all of the firm's decisions.

Financial data relating to last year's (19X1) operations, along with relevant industry comparisons, are shown in Table 1. The firm's overall rates of return on equity and total assets have been around the industry average over the past several years—sometimes slightly above average and sometimes slightly below average. The company currently is operating its plants near full capacity and would like to build a new plant in Georgia at a cost of approximately $7.5 million. White has been exploring various alternative methods of financing this expansion and has been unsuccessful thus far in developing an acceptable plan. The sale of new common stock is not feasible at this time because of depressed stock market prices. Likewise, Anderson's banker has advised the firm that the use of additional long-term debt or lease financing is not possible at this time, given the firm's large amount of long-term debt currently outstanding and its relatively low times interest earned ratio. Anderson has ruled out a cut in the firm's dividend as a means of accumulating the required financing. The only other possible sources of financing available to the firm at this time, according to White, appear to be a reduction in working capital (current assets), an increase in short-term liabilities, or both.

Upon learning of these proposed financing methods, Anderson expressed concern about the effect these plans might have on the liquidity and risk of the firm. White replied that the firm currently follows a very conservative working capital policy and that these financing methods would not increase shareholder risk significantly. As evidence, she cited the firm's relatively high current and quick ratios. Anderson was unconvinced and asked White to provide additional information on the effects of these financing plans on the firm's financial status.

1. Anderson's bank requires a compensating balance of $3 million. How much additional funds can be freed up for investment in fixed assets if the firm reduces its cash balance to the minimum required by the bank?

2. How much additional financing can be obtained from receivables if Anderson institutes more stringent credit and collection policies and is able to reduce its average collection period to the industry average? (Assume that credit sales remain constant at $75 million.)

3. How much additional financing can be obtained for fixed-asset expansion if Anderson is able to increase its inventory turnover ratio to the industry average through tighter control of its raw materials, work-in-process, and finished goods inventories? (Assume that the cost of goods sold remains constant at $60.75 million.)

4. Anderson's suppliers extend credit to the firm on terms of "net 30." Anderson normally pays its bills on the last day of the credit period. How much additional financing could be generated if Anderson were to *stretch* its payables 10 days beyond the due date?

5. Prepare a pro forma balance sheet (dollars and percentages) as of December 31, 19X2, assuming that Anderson has instituted *all* actions described in

TABLE 1

Anderson Furniture Company's Financial Data (in Thousands of Dollars)

December 31, 19X1

BALANCE SHEET			INDUSTRY AVERAGE
Assets			
Cash	$ 3,690	6.5%	5.0%
Receivables, net	15,000	26.3	21.6
Inventories	20,250	35.5	33.4
Total current assets	$38,940	68.3%	60.0%
Net fixed assets	18,060	31.7	40.0
Total assets	$57,000	100.0%	100.0%
Liabilities and stockholders' equity			
Accounts payable	$ 3,000	5.3%	7.0%
Notes payable (8%)	3,750	6.6	10.0
Total current liabilities	$ 6,750	11.8%	17.0%
Long-term debt (10%)	18,000	31.6	28.0
Stockholders' equity	32,250	56.6	55.0
Total liabilities and equity	$57,000	100.0%	100.0%

Income Statement for the Year Ended December 31, 19X1

Net sales (all on credit)	$75,000	100.0%
Cost of sales	60,750	81.0
Gross profit	$14,250	19.0
Selling and administrative expenses	7,500	10.0
Earnings before interest and taxes	$ 6,750	9.0
Interest expense	2,100	2.8
Earnings before taxes	$ 4,650	6.2
Income taxes (45.16%)	2,100	2.8
Earnings after taxes	$ 2,550	3.4%

Significant Ratios	Anderson	Industry Average
Current	5.76	3.50
Quick	2.77	1.60
Average collection period (days)	73.00	58.803
Inventory turnover (Cost of sales/ inventory)	3.00	3.50
Sales to total assets	1.30	1.60
Debt to equity	0.80	0.90
Times interest earned	3.20	4.70
Earnings after tax/sales	3.40%	2.40%
Earnings after tax/equity	7.90%	7.90%

Questions 1, 2, 3, and 4, and that the funds generated have been used to build a new plant. (Assume that long-term debt and stockholders' equity at the end of 19X2 remain the same as at the end of 19X1. In other words, no new long-term debt is issued or old long-term debt retired, and all net income after taxes is paid out in common stock dividends. Also assume that net fixed assets, *except for the new plant*, remain unchanged during 19X2. Finally assume that notes payable remain unchanged during 19X2). HINT: The *total* amount of funds generated from the reduction of current assets and the increase in current liabilities determined in Questions 1, 2, 3, and 4 is $7.5 million (rounded to the nearest $1,000). Round all figures to the nearest $1,000.

6. Prepare a pro forma income statement for 19X2. Assume that sales increase to $87 million as a result of the plant expansion. Also assume that the cost of sales and selling and administrative expense ratios (as a percentage of sales) remain constant. Finally, assume that interest expense and the firm's tax rate remain the same in 19X2.

7. Calculate the firm's current, quick, times interest earned, and rate of return on equity ratios based on the pro forma statements determined in Questions 5 and 6. How do these ratios compare with the actual values for 19X1 and the industry averages?

8. What considerations might lead Anderson and White to disagree about the desirability of using short-term sources of funds to finance the plant expansion?

9. What other sources of short-term funds might the firm consider using to finance the plant expansion?

SELECTED REFERENCES

Bartter, Brit J., and Richard J. Rendleman, Jr. "Fee-Based Pricing of Fixed Rate Bank Loan Commitments." *Financial Management* 8 (Spring 1979): 13–20.

MacPhee, William A. *Short-Term Business Borrowing: Sources, Terms, and Techniques.* Homewood, IL: Dow Jones-Irwin, 1984.

Moskowtiz, Louis A. *Modern Factoring and Commercial Finance,* New York: Crowell, 1977.

Stone, Bernell K. "The Design of a Company's Banking System." *Journal of Finance* (May 1983): 373–385.

Stone, Bernell K. "Allocating Credit Lines, Planned Borrowing and Tangible Services over a Company's Banking System." *Financial Management* (Summer 1975): 65–83.

Stone, Bernell K. "The Cost of Bank Loans." *Journal of Financial and Quantitative Analysis* 7 (1972): 2077–2086.

VIII

Selected Topics in Contemporary Financial Management

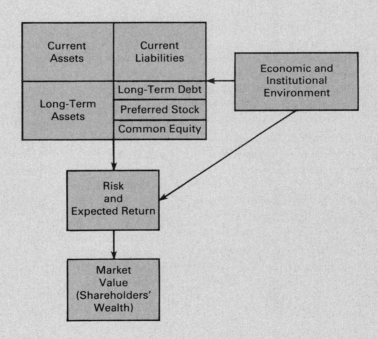

Part Eight looks at a number of additional topics that are important for the financial manager. Chapter 21 covers some important aspects of international financial management that have not been covered in the "International Concerns" sections, including techniques for managing ex-change rate risk. Chapter 22 focuses on corporate restructuring, with emphasis on mergers, liquidations and spinoffs, and failure and reorganization. Each of the decision areas covered in this part offers significant opportunities for maximizing shareholder wealth.

21

International Financial Management

KEY CHAPTER CONCEPTS

1. Companies engaged in international financial transactions face such problems as political and exchange rate risk in addition to those risks encountered in domestic transactions.

2. The exchange rate is the rate at which a currency can be converted into another currency.
   a. The spot rate is the present exchange rate for immediate delivery.
   b. The forward rate is the present exchange rate for deliveries of currencies in the future.

3. The theory of *interest rate parity* states that the annual percentage differential in the forward market for a currency quoted in terms of another currency is equal to the approx-imate difference in interest rates in the two countries.

4. A hedge is an offsetting transaction designed to reduce or prevent risk. Forward and futures exchange hedges and money market hedges are used to reduce transaction exposure. Financing with debt denominated in the same currency as foreign assets is a means of hedging against translation exposure.

5. International financing sources include
   a. Letters of credit
   b. Eurocurrency markets
   c. Eurobonds
   d. National and international development bonds.

GLOSSARY OF NEW TERMS

Eurobond An international bond issued outside the country in whose currency the bonds are denominated.

Eurodollars U.S. dollars deposited in European banks or European branches of U.S. banks.

European currency unit (ECU) A composite currency whose value is based on the weighted value of ten European currencies.

Exchange rate The rate at which a currency can be converted into another currency.

Foreign bond An international bond denominated in the currency of the country in which it is issued.

Forward rate The rate of exchange between two currencies being bought and sold for delivery at a *future* date.

Futures contract A contract calling for the delivery of a standardized quantity and quality of some item, such as a foreign currency, crude oil, or government securities, at a future point in time at a price set at the present time.

Interest rate parity The theory that the annual percentage differential in the forward market for a currency quoted in terms of another currency is equal to the approximate difference in interest rates in the two countries.

International bond A bond issued outside the country of the borrower.

Letter of credit A document issued by a bank guaranteeing payment for a particular shipment of goods.

London interbank offered rate (LIBOR) Interest rate at which banks in the Eurodollar market lend to each other.

Multinational corporation A firm that has direct investments in more than one country.

Spot rate The rate of exchange between two currencies being bought and sold for *immediate* delivery.

Europe 1992*

The twelve members of the European Community (EC) currently are embarked upon an ambitious plan to remove all regulations that have prevented free and open markets for goods and services between their countries. The outcome, if successful, will be a single economic market for the 320 million people of the EC countries. Many of the needed changes already have taken place. For example, it is now possible for truck drivers hauling goods to cross multiple borders with only one document, instead of the pounds of paperwork previously needed. Unified driver's licenses, passports, and phone systems are on the way. Cross border mergers will be simplified under rules recently approved by the EC countries. The prospect of a single European currency appears likely in the foreseeable future.

These dramatic changes have created challenges for nearly all multinational firms. It is impossible to ignore a unified market the size of the EC. At present, many American multinational firms are weighing their options in dealing with this new economic powerhouse. The free movement of capital among nations will permit firms to locate in those areas where the costs of doing business are minimized. This makes investment in Europe a more appealing option for many multinational firms. In 1988, American firms invested over $19 billion in new plant and equipment in EC countries, a 39-percent increase from the previous year.

Large European-based multinational firms will offer increased competition to their American counterparts. Many of these firms are cash rich and many have been on a U.S. buying spree. In 1987, American firms bought $2.4 billion worth of European firms. In contrast, European companies purchased U.S. firms with a value over $37 billion.

The competitive response to a single European market has varied among U.S. multinationals. H. J. Heinz plans to spend $1 billion on acquisitions, plant modernization, and product promotion between 1989 and 1992 in order to improve its competitive position against European rivals Unilever and Nestlé. Caterpillar recently closed a large, high cost plant in Scotland so that it could concentrate on reinvestment in its five other European plants. Digital Equipment is investing heavily in new plants to increase its presence in the European market. Ford plans further integration among its already highly competitive and integrated European operations. Other firms remain on the fence regarding decisions to invest directly in Europe. Smaller firms, such as Gerber Scientific and Menlo Tool Company, feel confident that they can compete successfully in the new Europe from their relatively low-cost domestic bases, as long as the value of the dollar remains low. A significant increase in the value of the dollar could cause these firms to rethink their stay-at-home strategies.

Finally, an economically unified Europe will undoubtedly lead to a stronger and more dominant European banking community that can compete aggressively against American and Japanese financial institutions.

The prospect of a unified Europe highlights the increasing international interdependency facing business firms and their financial managers. Capital investments overseas need to be evaluated, considering the business risk of the investment, and the potential financial risk of fluctuating exchange rates. European and Far East capital markets will need to be tapped to provide the resources necessary to fund these investments. Cash management strategies are becoming increasingly complex as international investment options become more accessible to many firms. This chapter addresses many of the important international dimensions of financial management.

* Adapted from "Writing the New Rules for Europe's Merger Game," *Business Week* (February 6, 1989: 48–49; and "Reshaping Europe," *Business Week* (December 12, 1988): 48–73.

▰▰▰ INTRODUCTION

A growing number of companies engage in various types of international financial transactions. These transactions can take many different forms. At one end of the spectrum are companies that *export* finished goods for sale in a foreign country and/or *import* raw materials or products from abroad for use in a domestic operation. In 1987 U.S. exports and imports totaled over $254 billion and $424 billion, respectively. The difference between exports and imports is the merchandise trade balance. In 1987, the U.S. had a trade deficit of $170 billion (imports of $424 billion minus exports of $254 billion), a record deficit up to that time.

At the other end of the spectrum are the *multinational corporations* that have direct investments in manufacturing or distribution facilities in more than one country. Between these extremes are various other degrees of involvement in international financial transactions, including foreign branch sales offices, licensing arrangements, and joint ventures with foreign firms.

Firms that are engaged in international financial transactions face unique problems and risks not encountered by firms that operate in only one country. First, there are difficulties associated with doing business in different currencies. Financial transactions between U.S. firms and firms (or individuals) in foreign countries normally involve foreign currency that has to be converted into U.S. dollars at some point. Therefore firms that do business on an international basis are concerned with the *exchange rate* between U.S. dollars and foreign currencies. Second, problems are associated with the different government regulations, tax laws, business practices, and political environments in foreign countries. Some of the more important aspects of these problems are considered in this chapter.[1] Finally, we consider some unique factors affecting financial decision making for multinational firms.

FOREIGN CURRENCIES AND EXCHANGE RATES

Whenever a U.S. firm purchases goods or services from a firm in another country, two currencies normally are involved. For example, when a U.S. company purchases materials from a British supplier, the British firm usually prefers payment in British pounds, whereas the U.S. company prefers to make payment in U.S. dollars. If the sales agreement requires that payment be made in pounds, the U.S. company will have to exchange (that is, *sell*) dollars to obtain the required number of pounds. The exact amount of dollars the U.S. company will have to sell depends on the *exchange rate* between the two currencies.

Suppose, for example, that the exchange rate at the time of the transaction is $1.69 per pound.[2] Furthermore, assume that the British supplier and the U.S. firm have agreed on a price of £2 million for the materials. Therefore, the U.S. firm will have to exchange $3.38 million (that is, £2,000,000 × $1.69/pound) to obtain the British currency to pay for the purchase.

The exchange rate can be expressed either in terms of dollars per pound or in terms of pounds per dollar. If the exchange rate from dollars to pounds is $1.69/pound, the exchange rate from pounds to dollars is £0.5917/dollar (that is, 1 ÷ $1.69/pound). Thus, a *reciprocal* relationship exists between the two exchange rates.

[1] Space limitations make it impossible to consider the entire scope of these problems in this text. For a more complete discussion of these issues, see the following references: David K. Eiteman and Arthur T. Stonehill, *Multinational Business Finance*, 4th ed. (Reading, MA: Addison-Wesley, 1986); Rita M. Rodriguez and E. Eugene Carter, *International Financial Management*, 3d ed. (Englewood Cliffs, NJ: Prentice-Hall, 1984); Alan C. Shapiro, *International Corporate Finance*, 2d ed. (Cambridge, MA: Ballinger, 1988); Jeff Madura, *International Financial Management*, 2d ed. (St. Paul, MN: West, 1989); and Alan Shapiro, *Multinational Financial Management*, 3d ed. (Boston: Allyn and Bacon, 1989).
[2] This was the approximate exchange rate in May 1989.

716

PART VIII
Selected Topics in
Contemporary
Financial
Management

Foreign currency that is needed for international financial transactions usually can be exchanged for domestic currency in most countries either at large commercial banks or at a central bank operated by the government. Banks normally charge a small fee for this service. Exchange rates between U.S. dollars and the currencies of most countries are reported daily in the *Wall Street Journal*. Table 21-1 lists the exchange rates between U.S. dollars and various currencies as of March 3, 1986, and April 27, 1989. These are known as *spot rates*. Spot rates represent the rate of exchange for currencies being bought and sold for *immediate delivery*.

Currencies also can be bought and sold today for delivery at some future time, usually 30, 90, or 180 days from today. In these cases, *forward rates* are used rather than spot rates. Forward exchange rates between U.S. dollars and the currencies of several of the major industrial countries also are reported daily in the *Wall Street Journal*. Table 21-2 lists some forward exchange rates as of April 27, 1989.

Forward exchange rates can be either higher or lower than the spot rates; higher rates are termed *premiums,* and lower rates are termed *discounts.* A comparison of the spot and forward rates in Table 21-1 and 21-2 shows that the forward exchange rates of British pounds and Canadian dollars are below their respective spot exchange rates, whereas the forward exchange rates of Japanese yen, Swiss francs, French francs, and West German marks are above their respective spot rates.

The premium between the spot rate and the 180-day forward rate can be expressed on an annual percentage basis using the following equation:

$$\text{Premium} = \left(\frac{\text{Forward} - \text{Spot}}{\text{Spot}}\right)\left(\frac{12}{n}\right)(100\%) \qquad \textbf{(21.1)}$$

where n is the number of months forward. If the result calculated using Equation 21.1 is negative, an annual percentage discount instead of a premium exists.

TABLE 21-1

Sampling of Spot Foreign Exchange Rates

Country	Currency	Exchange Rate (U.S. dollars)	
		MARCH 3, 1986	APRIL 27, 1989
Australia	Dollar	0.6955	0.7947
Britain	Pound	1.4465	1.6910
Canada	Dollar	0.7015	0.8389
China	Yuan	0.3125	0.2687
France	Franc	0.1467	0.1575
India	Rupee	0.0810	0.6345
Italy	Lira	0.000664	0.000728
Japan	Yen	0.005571	0.007570
Netherlands	Guilder	0.3987	0.4727
South Africa	Rand	0.5020	0.3916
Sweden	Krona	0.1395	0.1571
Switzerland	Franc	0.5330	0.6033
West Germany	Mark	0.4517	0.5330
—	ECU	0.9667	1.1088

SOURCE: *Wall Street Journal* (March 4, 1986 and April 28, 1989).

TABLE 21-2

Sampling of Forward Foreign Exchange Rates

	Exchange Rate (U.S. dollars)—April 27, 1989		
CURRENCY	30-DAY FORWARD	90-DAY FORWARD	180-DAY FORWARD
Pound	1.6870	1.6788	1.6676
Canadian dollar	0.8370	0.8338	0.8298
French franc	0.1577	0.1579	0.1584
Yen	0.007605	0.007667	0.007757
Swiss franc	0.6050	0.6083	0.6136
Mark	0.5346	0.5376	0.5417

SOURCE: *Wall Street Journal* (April 28, 1989).

Using the exchange rates listed in Tables 21-1 and 21-2, the following premium involving the West German mark is calculated:

$$\text{Premium} = \left(\frac{0.5417 - 0.5330}{0.5330}\right)\left(\frac{12}{6}\right)(100\%)$$

$$= 3.26\%$$

Similarly, the following British pound calculation is performed:

$$\text{Premium} = \left(\frac{1.6676 - 1.6910}{1.6910}\right)\left(\frac{12}{6}\right)(100\%)$$

$$= -2.77\%$$

These calculations show that the 180-day forward West German mark (quoted in U.S. dollars) is trading at a 3.26 percent annual premium compared to the spot rate, whereas the 180-day forward British pound is trading at a 2.77 percent discount. This means that the spot rate for West German marks is expected to increase in the future, whereas the spot rate for British pounds is expected to decrease in the future.

As will be shown later in this chapter, firms engaged in international transactions can use the forward foreign exchange market to hedge against adverse fluctuations in exchange rates.

Interest Rate Parity

The theory of *interest rate parity* states that the annual percentage forward premium for a currency quoted in terms of another currency, calculated in Equation 21.1, is equal to the approximate difference in interest rates prevailing in the two countries. For example, interest rate parity between Britain (U.K.) and the U.S. is said to exist if the following equation holds:

$$\left(\frac{\text{Forward} - \text{Spot}}{\text{Spot}}\right)\left(\frac{12}{n}\right) = \frac{i_{US} - i_{UK}}{1 + i_{UK}} \qquad \textbf{(21.2)}$$

where i_{US} is the U.S. interest rate and i_{UK} is the comparable U.K. rate.[3]

[3] When interest rates are relatively low, the Equation 21.2 denominator approaches 1.0 and the interest rate difference in the numerator is a good approximation of the fraction's value.

718

PART VIII
Selected Topics in
Contemporary
Financial
Management

When interest rate parity does not hold, arbitrage opportunities exist.[4] Suppose a particular British interest rate is 14 percent and the comparable U.S. rate is 8 percent when the annual discount on forward pounds is 4 percent. Suppose also that a U.S. trader using the foreign exchange market sells U.S. dollars and buys spot British pounds and invests the pounds to earn 14 percent. Simultaneously, the trader sells forward pounds at the prevailing 4 percent annual discount. At the end of the forward period, the trader converts pounds back to dollars. The overall result is that the U.S. trader earns 10 percent instead of the 8 percent available in the U.S. domestic money markets. Because the overall transaction in this example is riskless, the trader is said to be perfectly hedged, or covered. As a result, the procedure carried out in this example by the U.S. trader is referred to as *covered interest arbitrage*. Interestingly, the existence of foreign exchange traders and the opportunities to gain profits by covered interest arbitrage transactions causes approximate interest rate parity to exist between countries.[5]

Factors that Affect Exchange Rates

Exchange rates between currencies vary over time, reflecting supply and demand considerations for each currency. For example, the demand for British pounds comes from a number of sources, including foreign buyers of British exports who must pay for their purchases in pounds, foreign investors who desire to make investments in physical or financial assets in Britain, and speculators who expect British pounds to increase in value relative to other currencies. The British government also may be a source of demand if it attempts to keep the value of the pound (relative to other currencies) from falling by using its supply of foreign currencies or gold to purchase pounds in the market.

Sources of supply include British importers who need to convert their pounds into foreign currency to pay for purchases, British investors who desire to make investments in foreign countries, and speculators who expect British pounds to decrease in value relative to other currencies.

Exchange rates also are affected by economic and political conditions that influence the supply of, or demand for a country's currency. Some of these conditions include differential inflation and interest rates among countries, the government's trade policies, and the government's political stability. A high rate of inflation within a country tends to lower the value of its currency with respect to the currencies of other countries that are experiencing lower rates of inflation. The exchange rate will tend to decline as holders sell or exchange the country's currency for other currencies whose purchasing power is not declining at as high a rate. In contrast, relatively high interest rates within a country tend to increase the exchange rate as foreign investors seek to convert their currencies and purchase these higher yielding securities.

Government trade policies that limit imports—such as the imposition of tariffs, import quotas, and restrictions on foreign exchange transactions— reduce the supply of the country's currency in the foreign exchange market. This, in turn, tends to increase the value of the country's currency with respect to other currencies and thus increase exchange rates.

---

[4] Arbitrage is discussed in Chapter 13. It is a simultaneous buying and selling of equivalent goods in different markets.

[5] This discussion disregards transaction costs such as commissions charged by foreign exchange dealers.

Finally, the political stability of the government will affect the risks perceived by foreign investors and companies doing business in the country. These risks include the possible expropriation of investments or restrictions on the amount of funds (such as returns from investments) that may be taken out of the country.

Effects of Exchange Rate Levels on Business Conditions and Practices

The exchange rate between two currencies can affect the way competing companies in the two countries do business and can have an impact on business conditions in the two countries. Consider the exchange rate data in Table 21-1 between the Japanese yen (JY) and the U.S. dollar. In April 1989 $1 equaled about JY132 (1 ÷ 0.007570), and in March 1986 $1 equaled about JY180 (1 ÷ 0.005571). In relative terms, the dollar was "weak" and the yen was "strong" in April 1989, whereas in March 1986 the dollar was "strong" and the yen was "weak."

Suppose Eastman Kodak makes a camera in the United States for $20 and sells it both in the United States for $25 and in Japan. Fuji makes essentially the same camera in Japan for JY2880 and sells it both in Japan for JY3600 and in the United States.[6] When the dollar is relatively strong, that is, $1 equals JY180, the following will occur:

1. Fuji can sell its camera in the United States at $20 each and maintain the same profit margin it earns in Japan, or it can improve its margin by raising the price.
2. To compete with the Japanese import, Kodak must consider cutting its price in the U.S. market. It also has to control its costs rigidly, thereby helping to keep the U.S. inflation rate low.
3. Kodak cannot compete effectively in Japan. If it tries to maintain the yen equivalent of the $25 U.S. price, Kodak has to price its camera at JY4500, compared to the JY3600 price charged by Fuji.
4. For every JY1000 that Kodak is able to earn in Japan when the exchange rate is JY180 = $1, it reports $5.56 in earnings to its stockholders.

When the dollar is relatively weak, that is, $1 = JY132, the following occur:

1. Kodak can sell its camera in Japan at a price of JY3300 and maintain the same profit margin it earns in the United States. It should be able to compete effectively with Fuji's JY3600 price.
2. Fuji cannot compete effectively in the United States. If it tries to maintain the dollar equivalent of a JY3600 price, Fuji must price its cameras at $27.27, compared to the $25 price charged by Kodak.
3. For every JY1000 that Kodak earns in Japan when the exchange rate is JY132 = $1, it reports $7.58 in earnings to its stockholders.

This example shows that a relatively weak U.S. dollar tends to help U.S. exports and can improve the dollar earnings of U.S. companies doing business outside the United States, both by lowering the prices quoted in foreign currencies and by translating the foreign earnings into more U.S. dollars. Over the past several years, the United States has adopted a weak dollar strategy in an attempt to increase exports and reduce imports. This strategy had begun to work in 1988 and 1989.

---

[6] This example disregards transportation costs between the United States and Japan.

■ 720 ■

PART VIII
Selected Topics in
Contemporary
Financial
Management

Managing Exchange Rate Risk

Because exchange rates between currencies fluctuate over time, companies engaged in international business are exposed to *exchange rate risk*. International companies can lower exchange rate risk exposure by *hedging*. In general, a hedge is an offsetting transaction designed to reduce or prevent risk. Examples of hedging techniques are illustrated in the following sections for both *transaction* and *translation* exposure.

FOREIGN TRADE. Consider again the situation described earlier in which a U.S. company purchases materials from a British supplier. Because the amount of the transaction (£2 million) is stated in pounds, the U.S. company bears the exchange risk. This example of transaction exposure is illustrated in Table 21-3. Assume that the British supplier extends 90-day trade credit to the U.S. company and that the value of the pound increases from $1.69/pound on the purchase date to $1.74/pound on the payment date. If the U.S. firm takes the trade credit extended to it, the cost of the purchase effectively increases from $3.38 million to $3.48 million (that is, £2,000,000 × $1.74/pound).[7]

There are two basic hedging techniques that the U.S. company can use to protect itself against transaction exchange risk:

■ Execute a contract in the forward exchange market, or in the foreign exchange futures market.[8]
■ Borrow U.S. funds and invest in interest-bearing British securities.

Both methods are examined in the paragraphs that follow.

First, the U.S. firm could execute a contract in the forward exchange market to buy £2 million at the *known* 90-day forward rate rather than at the *uncertain* spot rate prevailing on the payment date. This is referred to

[7] In this and the following discussion of exchange rate risk, we are ignoring the brokerage fees involved in executing foreign exchange contracts. Due to these costs, some firms choose not to protect themselves against exchange rate risk.

[8] Currency contracts for future delivery are traded on several organized futures exchanges, including the International Monetary Market (IMM) of the Chicago Mercantile Exchange, the Financial Instrument Exchange, and the MidAmerica Commodity Exchange. Futures contracts are standardized with respect to the amount of a foreign currency to be delivered to the buyer from the seller and with respect to the time of delivery. In contrast, forward contracts can be set for any specific amount (usually above $1 million) and any future time of delivery, although they normally are set for 30, 60, or 90 days in the future.

Alternatively, a hedge can be set by using options on futures contracts. Options on futures give the buyer the right, but not the obligation (as in a futures or forward contract) to buy (or sell) a futures contract at some future point in time. The advantage of options on foreign currency futures contracts is that the buyer (seller) has an opportunity to benefit from favorable movements in currency rates, while protecting the buyer (seller) from unfavorable currency rate movements. This potential for gain and protection from loss is reflected in the "option premium" charged for the option.

TABLE 21-3

Example of Transaction Exchange Rate Risk

Date	Exchange Rate	Amount of Transaction	
		U.S. DOLLARS	BRITISH POUNDS
Purchase date	$1.69/pound	$3,380,000	£2,000,000
Payment date	$1.74/pound	$3,480,000	£2,000,000

as a *forward market hedge*. Assume, for example, that the 90-day forward rate is $1.70/pound. Based on this rate, the U.S. firm effectively would be able to exchange $3.4 million (that is, £2,000,000 × $1.70/pound) 90 days later on the payment date when it is required to pay for the materials. Thus, the U.S. firm would be able to take advantage of the trade credit and, at the same time, hedge against foreign exchange risk.

A second hedging technique, called a *money market hedge*, involves the U.S. firm borrowing the funds from its bank, exchanging them for pounds at the spot rate, and investing them in interest-bearing British securities. By investing in securities that mature on the same date as the payment is due to the British supplier (that is, 90 days after the purchase date), the U.S. firm will have the necessary amount of pounds available to pay for the materials. The net cost of this money market hedge to the U.S. firm will depend on the interest rate on the funds it borrows from its bank relative to the interest rate on the funds it invests in securities. For example, if the bank charges 10 percent per annum and the securities yield 8 percent per annum, the net cost to the U.S. firm would be approximately $16,900; that is, $(0.10 - 0.08) \times (90/360) \times \$3,380,000$.

FOREIGN INVESTMENT. Firms with direct investments in foreign subsidiaries also face exchange rate risk in the form of translation exposure. Changes in the exchange rate affect the value of the subsidiary's assets and liabilities and, ultimately, the income of the multinational parent company. Under current accounting procedures, the following general rules apply when the balance sheets of foreign subsidiaries are translated into the parent company's balance sheet:[9]

- Current assets, unless covered by forward exchange contracts, and fixed assets are translated into dollars at the rate of exchange prevailing on the date of the balance sheet.
- Current and long-term liabilities payable in foreign currency are translated into dollars at the rate of exchange prevailing on the date of the balance sheet.

A decline in the value of a foreign currency relative to the U.S. dollar reduces the conversion value of the foreign subsidiary's liabilities, as well as its assets. Therefore, the parent company's risk exposure depends on the foreign subsidiary's net equity position (that is, assets minus liabilities). Thus, on the books of the parent company, the subsidiary's creditors in effect bear part of the decline in the value of the subsidiary's assets. Present accounting rules require that these translation losses (as well as gains) be reported on the balance sheet as a separate adjustment to stockholders' equity and not on the income statement of the parent company. Revenue and expense items are translated at existing exchange rates and are reported on the parent company's income statement.

The impact of a decrease in the exchange rate on the firm's balance sheet can be illustrated with the following example. American Products has a subsidiary, Canadian Products, with total assets of $12 million (Canadian) and total liabilities of $8 million (Canadian). Based on an exchange rate of $0.80 (U.S.) per dollar (Canadian), the net equity position of the Canadian subsidiary on American Products' balance sheet as shown in Table 21-4 is

[9] The present U.S. accounting rules for foreign currency translation are set forth in *Statement of Financial Accounting Standards Number 52*, issued by the Financial Accounting Standards Board.

Effect of a Decrease in the Exchange Rate on American Products' Balance Sheet

| | Exchange Rate | | | |
| | $0.80 (U.S.) = $1.00 (Canadian) | | $0.75 (U.S.) = $1.00 (Canadian) | |
	$(Canadian)	$(U.S.)	$(Canadian)	$(U.S.)
Assets	$12,000,000	$9,600,000	$12,000,000	$9,000,000
Liabilities	8,000,000	6,400,000	8,000,000	6,000,000
Net equity position	$ 4,000,000	$3,200,000	$ 4,000,000	$3,000,000

$3.2 million (U.S.). Suppose now that the exchange rate declines to $0.75 (U.S.) per dollar (Canadian) and all other things remain the same. As can be seen in the table, the net equity position of the Canadian subsidiary on American Products' balance sheet declines to $3 million (U.S.), resulting in a $200,000 currency exchange loss.

In general, when a foreign subsidiary's assets are greater than (less than) its liabilities, currency exchange losses (gains) will occur when the exchange rate decreases. The opposite effects are true for increases in the exchange rate. A company can hedge against translation exposure by financing its foreign assets with debt denominated in the same currency.

For example, in March, 1985, Hercules Incorporated, a Wilmington, Delaware–based chemicals and plastics manufacturer, issued 10.125 percent 7-year notes. Instead of being denominated in U.S. dollars, as is usual for securities of U.S. companies, these notes are denominated in European Currency Units (ECU). The ECU is a composite currency whose value is based on the weighted value of ten European currencies.[10] The Hercules debt issue totaled ECU 50 million or about $33 million, based on the exchange rate between the U.S. dollars and the ECU at the time of issuance.

The Hercules financial managers apparently had a choice between whether to issue ECU-denominated– or U.S.-dollar–denominated debt. They chose the ECU-denominated debt in order to hedge the company's European assets. For example, if the value of the ECU drops compared to the U.S. dollar value, presumably the U.S. dollar value of Hercules' European assets also decreases. However, if this happens the U.S. dollar amount of both the interest and principal that Hercules has to pay decreases. The Hercules management stated that although the weight of the various currencies in the ECU did not exactly match the relationship of Hercules' European assets, the ECU-denominated debt issue did make a reasonably good hedge overall.

A multinational company also can minimize its exchange rate risk, as well as the risk of expropriation or nationalization of its assets by a foreign government, by developing a *portfolio* of foreign investments. Rather than making all its direct investments in foreign subsidiaries that are located in one particular country, the firm can spread its foreign investments among a number of different countries, thus limiting the risk of incurring large losses within any one country.

[10] "Hercules Issues Notes Denominated in ECUs to Domestic Investors," *Wall Street Journal* (March 18, 1985), p. 53.

Firms engaged in foreign trade and investment have a variety of sources of financing that may not be available to domestic firms. This section examines some of these sources.

Foreign Trade

Firms that import goods into their countries often can arrange an import *letter of credit* to finance the transaction. Basically, a letter of credit is a document issued by a bank guaranteeing payment for a particular shipment of goods. A letter of credit substitutes the credit-worthiness of the bank for that of the importer, thereby greatly reducing the credit risk to the seller.

To illustrate the use of a letter of credit, consider again the example discussed earlier in the chapter of the U.S. company that is purchasing materials from a British supplier. Suppose the British supplier agrees to ship the materials upon receipt of an irrevocable letter of credit from the U.S. firm's bank, with payment to be made in 90 days. The U.S. firm then would arrange with its bank for the letter of credit. By issuing a letter of credit, the bank agrees to pay drafts drawn on the firm's account when they are presented by the British supplier's bank. Upon shipment of the materials, the British firm presents a draft to its bank for payment in 90 days. The draft then is sent to the U.S. firm's bank for acceptance. Once the draft has been accepted by the U.S. bank, it becomes a *bankers' acceptance*—a form of marketable security. If the British firm does not wish to wait 90 days for payment, it can sell the draft at a discount from the face amount to the bank or another investor.

Foreign Investment

For a number of reasons, U.S. firms frequently find it desirable to finance a substantial portion of their foreign investments with funds raised abroad. First, the U.S. government at various times has imposed restrictions, or *quotas*, on the amount of funds U.S. firms can invest abroad. As a result, non-U.S. sources of financing must be used in part to finance foreign investments. Second, firms often find it desirable to obtain part of their financing in the foreign countries in which they are making their investments. This helps minimize any losses the firms might incur if the foreign currencies are devalued or if the foreign governments impose restrictions on the outflow of funds from their countries. Third, by borrowing funds abroad, U.S. firms can avoid the disclosure requirements (and associated costs) imposed by the SEC on debt securities issued in the United States. Fourth, the different banking practices abroad often lead to advantageous borrowing arrangements for U.S. firms. For example, European banks are willing to lend for a longer term than many American banks. Also, many loans made by foreign banks are handled on an overdraft basis; that is, the loan balance always is equal to the checks the borrowing firm writes against the loan account, thereby avoiding paying interest for temporarily unneeded funds.

EURODOLLAR BORROWING. As an alternative to borrowing funds in the United States, large, well-established multinational corporations can bor-

724

PART VIII
Selected Topics in
Contemporary
Financial
Management

row funds either in the international financial markets or in the domestic financial markets of countries where subsidiaries are located. Within the international financial markets are the Eurodollar market and the international bond market. *Eurodollars* are U.S. dollars that have been deposited in foreign (primarily "European") banks or foreign branches of U.S. banks. They are created, for example, when a U.S. firm transfers funds (that is, dollars) from its U.S. bank to a foreign bank where it has an account. The foreign bank then can lend these dollar deposits in the form of *Eurodollar loans* to other companies (such as foreign subsidiaries of U.S. multinational corporations). The interest rate in the Eurodollar market usually is related to the *London interbank offered rate*, or *LIBOR*. LIBOR is the interest rate at which banks in the Eurodollar market lend to each other. For example, large well-established multinational corporations usually can borrow at about 0.5 percentage points over LIBOR. Because LIBOR frequently is about 1.5 percentage points below U.S. bank prime rates, large companies often can borrow in the Eurodollar market at subprime rates.

EUROBOND FINANCING. An international bond is a bond issued outside the country of the borrower. Bonds issued in the international bond markets are either *Eurobonds* or *foreign bonds*. A Eurobond is a bond issued outside the country in whose currency the bonds are denominated, and a foreign bond is denominated in the currency of the country in which it is issued. For example, in 1986 Chrysler Financial Corporation issued 10-year bonds in London denominated in West German marks. This issue is a Eurobond issue or, more specifically, a Euromark bond issue. Had Chrysler Financial issued the bonds in West Germany, they would have been classified as foreign bonds.

The Eurobond market has grown rapidly in recent years. In 1987, for example, $140 billion of Eurobonds were offered.[11] The Eurobond market is characterized by relatively low capital costs for borrowers. For example, in 1986 when Amoco Corp. issued $200 million of 9¾ percent Eurodollar bonds, it was estimated that the company saved about 25 to 30 basis points over what it would have cost to raise the capital in the United States.[12] At the same time, investors were attracted to the Amoco bonds because the yield was 83 basis points over U.S. Treasury issues.[13]

In addition to Eurobonds denominated in a single currency, the number of Eurobond offerings, such as the Hercules, Inc. bonds discussed earlier, denominated in *European currency units*, or ECUs, is growing rapidly. An ECU is a composite currency whose value is based on the weighted value of ten European currencies. For multinational companies with direct investments in several major European countries, ECU-denominated debt provides a convenient means of hedging against translation exposure.

A foreign subsidiary also may be able to obtain loans from international agencies, such as the World Bank and the Inter-American Development Bank. In addition, a number of governments have established national banks that provide financing for projects that promote economic development within their countries.

Thus, a wide variety of sources of funds is available for financing foreign investments. In determining the most appropriate mix of financing for a

---

[11] *OECD Financial Statistics Monthly* (February 1988).
[12] A *basis* point is 0.01 percent. Therefore, 100 basis points equals 1 percent.
[13] *Wall Street Journal* (February 19, 1986), p. 54.

given overseas investment, the firm should consider many other factors besides interest rates.

SUMMARY

■ Firms engaged in international financial transactions face risks and problems not faced in domestic transactions, including difficulties encountered in doing business in different currencies and problems associated with different government regulations, tax laws, business practices, and political environments.

■ The *exchange rate* is the rate at which one currency can be converted into another. The *spot rate* is the rate of exchange for currencies being bought and sold for *immediate delivery today*. The *forward rate* is the rate of exchange between currencies to be delivered at a future point in time— usually 30, 90, and 180 days from today. The *futures rate* also is a rate of exchange between currencies to be delivered at a future point in time. In contrast to forward contracts, futures contracts are standardized with respect to size and delivery date and are traded on organized exchanges, such as the International Monetary Market.

■ The theory of *interest rate parity* states that the annual percentage differential in the forward market for a currency quoted in terms of another currency is equal to the approximate difference in interest rates in the two countries.

■ Firms engaged in international transactions incur *exchange rate risk* because of fluctuations over time in the exchange rates among currencies. *Forward exchange* hedges and *money market* hedges can be used to minimize some of the effects of unfavorable changes in exchange rates.

■ A wide variety of sources of funds is available for financing foreign trade and investments, including letters of credit, the Eurodollar market, the international bond market, and both national and international development banks.

QUESTIONS AND TOPICS FOR DISCUSSION

1. Define the following terms:
    a. Multinational corporation.
    b. Spot exchange rate.
    c. Forward exchange rate.
    d. Futures exchange rate.
    e. Letter of credit.
    f. LIBOR.
    g. ECU.

2. What is the theory of interest rate parity?

3. What is covered interest arbitrage?

4. Describe two techniques that a company can use to hedge against transaction exchange risk.

5. Describe the factors that cause exchange rates to change over time.

6. How can a firm with direct investments in foreign subsidiaries hedge against translation exposure?

7. What are the advantages to a U.S. firm of financing its foreign investments with funds raised abroad?

726

PART VIII
Selected Topics in
Contemporary
Financial
Management

8. What is the difference between the Eurodollar market and the Eurobond market?
9. What is the difference between a Eurobond and a foreign bond?

PROBLEMS*

1. Japanese Motors exports cars and trucks to the U.S. market. On March 3, 1986, its most popular model was selling (wholesale) to U.S. dealers for $7,500. What price must Japanese Motors charge for the same model on April 27, 1989, to realize the same amount (of Japanese yen) as it did 3 years earlier? Refer to Table 21-1.

2. Valley Stores, a U.S. department store chain, annually negotiates a contract with Alpine Watch Company, located in Switzerland, to purchase a large shipment of watches. On March 3, 1986, Valley purchased 10,000 watches for a total of 1.26 million Swiss francs. Refer to Table 21-1 and determine the following:
   a. The total cost and cost per watch in U.S. dollars.
   b. The total cost and cost per watch in U.S. dollars of 12,000 watches purchased on April 27, 1989, assuming that Alpine's price per watch (in Swiss francs) remains unchanged.

3. Determine the percentage change in the value of the U.S. dollar between March 3, 1986, and April 27, 1989, relative to the value of the following currencies (refer to Table 21-1):
   a. China.
   b. Britain.
   c. Japan.
   d. ECU.
   e. West Germany.

4. If the U.S. Treasury bill rate is 7.0 percent, the spot rate between U.S. dollars and British pounds is £1 = $1.69, and the 90-day forward rate is £1 = $1.68, what rate of interest is expected on British Treasury bills, assuming interest rate parity between the dollar and pound exists?

5. Suppose that British short-term interest rates are 13 percent, and the corresponding U.S. rate is 8 percent. Suppose at the same time that the discount on forward pounds is 3 percent per year. Do these conditions present an opportunity for covered interest arbitrage? If so, what steps should a trader in New York take? What annual rate will the trader earn?

6. Mammouth Mutual Fund of New York has $5 million to invest in certificates of deposit (CDs) for the next 6 months (180 days). It can buy either a Philadelphia National Bank (PNB) CD with an annual yield of 10 percent or a Cologne (West Germany) Bank CD with a yield of 12.5 percent. Assume that the CDs are of comparable default risk. The analysts of the mutual fund are concerned about exchange rate risk. They were quoted the following exchange rates by the international department of a New York City bank:

West Germany (deutsche marks)	
Spot	$0.4200
30-day futures	0.4190
90-day futures	0.4170
180-day futures	0.4155

* Colored numbers denote problems that have check answers at the end of the book.

a. If the Cologne Bank CD is purchased and held to maturity, determine the net gain (loss) in U.S. dollars relative to the PNB CD assuming that the exchange rate in 180 days equals today's spot rate.

b. Suppose the West German mark declines in value by 5 percent relative to the U.S. dollar over the next 180 days. Determine the net gain (loss) of the Cologne Bank CD in U.S. dollars relative to the PNB CD for an uncovered position.

c. Determine the net gain (loss) from a covered position.

d. What other factor or factors should be considered in the decision to purchase the Cologne Bank CD?

7. Last year, the French marketing subsidiary of International Pharmaceuticals Corp. (IPC), a New Jersey–based drug manufacturer, earned 700,000 French francs. This year, partly due to a weaker U.S. dollar, the French subsidiary will earn 900,000 French francs. Last year, the exchange rate was 10 francs per dollar, and this year it is 7 francs per dollar. Calculate how many U.S. dollars the French subsidiary contributes to IPC's earnings in each year.

▬ SELECTED REFERENCES

Block, Stanley B., and T. J. Gallagher. "Managing Corporate Exchange and Interest Rate Exposure." *Financial Management* (Autumn 1986): 64–73.

Boyer, R. S., and F. C. Adams. "Forward Premia and Risk Premia in a Simple Model of Exchange Rate Determination." *Journal of Money, Credit, and Banking* (November 1988): 631–644.

Eiteman, David K., and Arthur T. Stonehill. *Multinational Business Finance*, 4th ed. Reading, MA: Addison-Wesley, 1986.

Grabbe, J. Orlin. *International Financial Markets.* New York: Elsevier, 1986.

Kidwell, David S., M. Wayne Marr, and G. Rodney Thompson. "Eurodollar Bonds: Alternative Financing for U.S. Companies." *Financial Management* 14 (Winter 1985): 18–27.

Madura, Jeff. *International Financial Management.* 2d ed. St. Paul, MN: West Publishing, 1989.

Shapiro, Alan C. *International Corporate Finance.* Cambridge, MA: Ballinger Publishing, 1988.

Shapiro, Alan C. *Multinational Financial Management*, 3d ed. Boston: Allyn and Bacon, 1989.

Stockman, A. C., and A. Hernández D. "Exchange Controls, Capital Controls, and International Financial Markets." *American Economic Review* (June 1988): 362–378.

CHAPTER

22

Corporate Restructuring

KEY CHAPTER CONCEPTS

1. Reasons why a company may choose external growth by merger over internal growth can include the following:
   a. The availability of lower cost assets.
   b. Greater economies of scale.
   c. The availability of more secure raw material supplies and additional end-product markets.
   d. The possibility of more rapid growth.
   e. Greater diversification.
   f. Tax considerations.

2. The valuation of merger candidates involves application of capital budgeting principles. A merger is an acceptable project if the present value of its expected free cash inflows exceeds the acquisition cost.

3. The acquisition of a company with a higher P/E ratio causes the earnings per share figure of the acquiring company to decrease if the exchange ratio is based on current stock market prices and no synergy exists. Similarly the acquisition of a company with a lower P/E ratio causes the earnings per share figure of the acquiring company to increase.

4. In the pooling of interests method of accounting for mergers, the acquired assets are

recorded at their cost when acquired. In the purchase method, acquired assets are recorded at their fair market values, and any additional amount paid is listed as goodwill, which then must be amortized.

5. In a financial context, a firm is
   a. *Technically insolvent* when it is unable to meet its current obligations as they come due, even though the value of its assets exceeds its liabilities.
   b. *Legally insolvent* if the recorded value of its assets is less than the recorded value of its liabilities.
   c. *Bankrupt* if it is unable to pay its debts and it files a bankruptcy petition in accordance with the federal bankruptcy laws.

6. The primary causes of business failures are economic factors and lack of experience on the part of the owners of the business.

7. A failing company can either
   a. Attempt to resolve its difficulties with its creditors on a voluntary, or informal, basis; or
   b. Petition the courts for assistance and formally declare bankruptcy.

8. In a bankruptcy proceeding, if the going-concern value of the firm is greater than its liquidation value, it is reorganized; otherwise it is liquidated.
  a. A reorganization plan is carried out under Chapter 11 of the Bankruptcy Reform Act.
  b. A liquidation is carried out under Chapter 7 of the Bankruptcy Reform Act.
9. Other important topics include
  a. Leveraged buyouts.
  b. Divestitures and restructuring.
  c. Antitakeover measures.

GLOSSARY OF NEW TERMS

Assignment The process of informally liquidating a business. Assignment occurs outside the jurisdiction of the bankruptcy courts.

Bankruptcy A situation in which a firm is unable to pay its debts, and its assets are turned over to the court for administration.

Bankruptcy Reform Act of 1978 A U.S. bankruptcy act that significantly changed certain aspects of the federal bankruptcy laws.

Chapter 7 The liquidation chapter of the Bankruptcy Reform Act. Under Chapter 7, a company's assets are sold off, and the proceeds are distributed to creditors.

Chapter 11 The reorganization chapter of the Bankruptcy Reform Act. Under Chapter 11, a company continues to operate while it attempts to work out a reorganization plan.

Composition A situation in which a failing business is permitted to discharge its debt obligations by paying less than the full amounts owed to creditors.

Conglomerate merger A combination of two or more companies in which neither competes directly with the other and no buyer–seller relationship exists.

Exchange ratio The number of shares an acquiring company must give, or *exchange*, for each share of an acquired company in a merger.

Extension A situation in which a failing business is permitted to lengthen the amount of time it has to meet its obligations with creditors.

Goodwill An intangible asset equal to the premium over fair market value of the acquired assets that is paid for a company in a merger.

Holding company A corporation that controls the voting power of one or more other companies.

Horizontal merger A combination of two or more companies that compete directly with each other.

Legal insolvency A situation in which the recorded value of a firm's assets is less than its liabilities.

Leveraged buyout A transaction in which the buyer of a company borrows a large portion of the purchase price, using the purchased assets as partial collateral for the loans.

Merger A combination of two or more companies into one surviving company. Mergers are also called *acquisitions* or *consolidations*.

Pooling of interests method A method of accounting for mergers in which the acquired company's assets are recorded on the acquiring company's books at their cost when originally acquired. No goodwill account is created under the pooling method.

Purchase method A method of accounting for mergers in which the total value paid or exchanged for the acquired firm's assets is recorded on the acquiring firm's books. Any difference between the acquired assets' fair market value and their purchase price is recorded as goodwill.

Technical insolvency A situation in which a firm is unable to meet its current obligations as they come due, even though the value of its assets may exceed its liabilities.

Tender offer A public announcement by a company or individual indicating that it will pay a price above the current market price for the shares "tendered" of a company it wishes to acquire.

Vertical merger A combination of two or more companies that have a buyer–seller relationship with one another.

Texas Air Corporation and the Bankruptcy Laws*

In September 1983 Continental Airlines, a loss-plagued subsidiary of Texas Air Corporation, filed for bankruptcy. This move was designed to eliminate its high-cost labor contracts. The company reduced its route structure, laid off almost two-thirds of its 12,000 employees, and reduced the wages of its remaining workers by more than 50 percent in many cases. It then began building a "new" low-cost airline.

Continental was quite successful in using the bankruptcy laws to reduce labor costs. Two years later in 1985, while still in bankruptcy and operating under court protection, the company earned a record $62.2 million profit. Continental also filed a reorganization plan in which it promised to fully repay creditors, who were owed nearly $900 million.

This action taken by Continental (and other companies) to reduce labor costs was subsequently curtailed by Congress, partly as a result of an intensive lobbying campaign by organized labor. In 1984, after the Supreme Court ruled (in a similar case involving Wilson Foods) that companies could abrogate existing labor contracts as soon as they filed for bankruptcy, a bankruptcy reform law was enacted that makes it more difficult for companies to void labor

contracts. The new rules for trying to reduce labor costs in a reorganization bid require the company to attempt to work out an agreement with the union before it asks for help from the bankruptcy court. The bankruptcy judge then has to weigh the fairness to all parties of the company's offer.

In March 1989, Eastern Airlines, another loss-plagued subsidiary of Texas Air Corporation, filed for bankruptcy when almost all of its pilots refused to cross the picket lines set up by the striking machinists' union. Eastern was attempting to cut labor costs by reducing wage rates paid to the machinists. (The flight attendants and pilots previously had agreed to wage concessions.)

Will this strategy of reducing labor costs through the declaration of bankruptcy, which was used successfully at Continental, work at Eastern? Probably not, according to many analysts. The changes in the bankruptcy laws just described, as well as different economic conditions today (e.g., a shortage of replacement pilots compared with a surplus in 1983), make it much less likely that Texas Air can use the bankruptcy laws to reduce labor costs at Eastern.

The second half of this chapter discusses the alternatives available to companies facing financial failure.

* Based on articles in the *Wall Street Journal* (January 22, 1986), p. 32; (March 14, 1986), p. 1; (March 10, 1989), p. 1; and *Business Week* (July 16, 1984), p. 27.

INTRODUCTION

Corporate restructuring encompasses a broad array of activities that include changes in the ownership, asset structure, and/or capital structure of a company. The goal of any corporate restructuring should be to maximize shareholder wealth. Some aspects of corporate restructuring have already been examined, such as share repurchases discussed in Chapter 7. This chapter focuses on a number of other forms of corporate restructuring. These include external expansion (mergers) and business failure (bankruptcy). The next three sections examine mergers and the final two sections discuss bankruptcy.

MERGERS

Businesses grow *externally* by acquiring, or combining with, other ongoing businesses. This is in contrast to *internal* growth, which is achieved by purchasing individual assets, such as those evaluated in the discussion of capital expenditures in Chapters 9 through 11. When two companies combine, generally the acquiring company pays for the acquired business either with cash or with its own securities, and the acquired company's liabilities and assets are transferred to the acquiring company.

Mergers Defined

A *merger* technically is a combination of two or more companies in which all but one of the combining companies legally cease to exist and the surviving company continues in operation under its original name. A *consolidation* is a combination in which all of the combining companies are dissolved and a new firm is formed. The term *merger* generally is used to describe both of these types of business combinations. *Acquisition* also is used interchangeably with *merger* to describe a business combination. In the following discussion, the term *merger* is used, and it is assumed that only two companies are involved—the acquiring company and the merger candidate.[1]

Merger Statistics

Merger activity has expanded greatly during the 1980s. In 1988 there were almost 3,500 merger transactions valued at $1 million or more involving U.S. corporations.[2] The aggregate value of these transactions was over $225 billion. Approximately one-sixth of these transactions were international in scope; that is, involving both U.S. and foreign companies. Table 22-1 contains a listing of the largest mergers involving U.S. companies. Four of the acquisitions involved the purchase of U.S. companies by foreign companies, namely, British Petroleum, Campeau, Grand Metropolitan, and Royal Dutch Shell.

Types of Mergers

Mergers generally are classified according to whether they are *horizontal*, *vertical*, or *conglomerate*. A *horizontal merger* is a combination of two or more companies that compete directly with one another; the acquisition in 1985 of American Hospital Supply by Baxter Travenol Laboratories, both large health care products companies, for example, was a horizontal merger. The U.S. government has vigorously enforced antitrust legislation in an attempt to stop large horizontal combinations, and this effort has been effective. However, horizontal combinations in which one of the firms is failing often are viewed more favorably. Also, mergers that allow the companies to compete effectively in world markets are viewed more favorably—the acquisition of RCA by General Electric for $6.0 billion in 1985 was an example of this type of horizontal merger.

A *vertical merger* is a combination of companies that may have a buyer–seller relationship with one another. For example, if Sears were to acquire one of its appliance suppliers, this would constitute a vertical merger. This

---

[1] In some instances, merger candidates may be referred to as *takeover candidates, to-be-acquired companies, acquired companies,* or *target companies.*
[2] *Mergers and Acquisitions* (May–June 1989): 53.

Largest Mergers and Acquisitions (U.S. Companies)

Purchaser	Company Acquired	Cost (in billions of dollars)	Year
Kohlberg Kravis Roberts (LBO)*	RJR Nabisco	$25.1	1988
Chevron	Gulf Oil	13.3	1984
Philip Morris	Kraft	13.1	1988
Texaco	Getty Oil	10.1	1984
Dupont	Conoco	8.0	1981
British Petroleum	Standard Oil Ohio (remaining 45% interest)	7.8	1987
U.S. Steel	Marathon Oil	6.6	1981
Campeau	Federated Department Stores	6.5	1988
Kohlberg Kravis Roberts (LBO)	Beatrice	6.2	1985
General Electric	RCA	6.0	1985
Grand Metropolitan	Pillsbury	5.75	1988
Mobil	Superior Oil	5.7	1984
Philip Morris	General Foods	5.6	1985
Royal Dutch Shell	Shell Oil (remaining 30.5% interest)	5.5	1984

SOURCE: *Wall Street Journal* (October 21, 1988; October 31, 1988; and December 2, 1988). Reprinted by permission of the *Wall Street Journal* © Dow Jones and Co., Inc. (1988). All rights reserved worldwide.

* LBO = leveraged buyout.

type of business combination has gradually declined in importance in recent years.

A *conglomerate merger* is a combination of two or more companies in which neither competes directly with the other and no buyer–seller relationship exists. For example, the Phillip Morris acquisition of General Foods in 1985 for $5.6 billion in cash was a conglomerate merger.

Form of Merger Transactions

A merger transaction may be a stock purchase or an asset purchase. In a *stock purchase*, the acquiring company buys the stock of the to-be-acquired company and assumes its liabilities. In an *asset purchase*, the acquiring company buys only the assets (some or all) of the to-be-acquired company and does not assume any of its liabilities.

Normally, the buyer of a business prefers an asset purchase rather than a stock purchase, because unknown liabilities, such as any future lawsuits against the company, are not incurred. In addition, an asset purchase frequently allows the acquiring company to depreciate its new assets from a higher basis than is possible in a stock purchase. As a result of the unknown liability question, many large companies that acquire small companies refuse to negotiate on any terms other than an asset purchase.

Holding Companies

One form of business combination is the *holding company*, in which the acquiring company simply purchases all or a controlling block of another

Joint Ventures

Another form of business combination is a *joint venture*, in which two (unaffiliated) companies contribute financial and/or physical assets, as well as personnel, to a new company formed to engage in some economic activity, such as the production or marketing of a product. The Diamond-Star Motor Company is an example of a joint venture established by Chrysler Motors and Mitsubishi Motors to produce automobiles at a plant in Bloomington, Illinois.

Leveraged Buyouts

One frequently used method to buy a company or a division of a large company is a leveraged buyout, or LBO. In a typical LBO, the buyer borrows a large amount of the purchase price, using the purchased assets as collateral for a large portion of the borrowings. The buyers frequently are the managers of the division or company being sold. It is anticipated that the earnings (and cash flows) of the new company will be sufficient to service the debt and permit the new owners to earn a reasonable return on their investment. In some cases, sales of assets are used to help pay off the debt. The LBO of a publicly held company is sometimes referred to as *going private*, because the entire equity in the company is purchased by a small group of investors and is no longer publicly traded.

The majority of LBOs involve relatively small companies. However, a number of LBOs involving large companies have occurred. For example, in the largest merger or acquisition ever undertaken up to that time, the investment firm of Kohlberg Kravis Roberts used an LBO to purchase RJR Nabisco for $25.1 billion in 1988.

In addition to LBOs undertaken by investment bankers and managers, workers sometimes take over their division or company through an Employee Stock Ownership Plan (ESOP). Significant tax advantages make ESOPs a useful instrument for financing LBOs. In an ESOP transaction, lenders can offer below market interest rates because 50 percent of the interest income they receive from these loans is excluded from taxable income. This often allows employees to pay more than other bidders that don't qualify for these tax breaks. In the past, ESOPs were used to buy either larger companies faced with financial difficulties or smaller companies. However, ESOPs are increasingly being used to finance (either in whole or in part) large, healthy companies such as Avis and J.C. Penney.

Divestitures and Restructurings

Divestitures and *restructurings* can be an important part of a company's merger and acquisition strategy. After an acquiring company completes an acquisition, it frequently examines the various assets and divisions of the recently acquired company to determine whether or not all the acquired

734

PART VIII
Selected Topics in
Contemporary
Financial
Management

company's pieces "fit" into the acquiring company's future plans. If not, the acquiring company may sell off, or *divest*, a portion of the acquired company. In so doing, the acquiring company is said to be *restructuring* itself.

Divestitures and restructurings, however, frequently are not associated directly with a company's acquisitions. A company may divest itself of certain assets because of a change in overall corporate strategy. For example, in 1985 Warner-Lambert, a drug and consumer products manufacturer, decided to get out of the hospital supply business. The company used the proceeds from the sale of its hospital supply assets to buy back some of its stock. As a result, Warner-Lambert changed, or restructured, the asset side of its balance sheet; this is called an *operational restructuring*. In addition, the company changed its capital structure and thereby carried out a *financial restructuring*.

Instead of selling a part of the company for cash, divestures can be accomplished through a *spinoff* or an *equity carve-out*. In a spinoff, common stock in a division or subsidiary is distributed to shareholders of the parent company on a pro rata basis. The subsidiary or division becomes a separate company. Owners of the parent company who receive common stock in the new company can keep the shares or sell them to other investors. An example of such a divestiture was the break up of AT&T in 1984 where AT&T shareholders received one share of stock in each of the seven regional telephone companies for every ten shares of AT&T they owned. In an equity carve-out, common stock in the subsidiary or division is sold directly to the public, with the parent company usually retaining a controlling interest in the shares outstanding. Southmark sold a minority interest in its Integon Insurance subsidiary in the late 1980s.

Tender Offers

Although many mergers are the result of a friendly agreement between the two companies, a company may wish to acquire another company even when the combination is opposed by the management (or board of directors) of the merger candidate company. In such a case, the acquiring company makes a *tender offer* for common shares of the merger candidate. In a tender offer, the acquiring company effectively announces that it will pay a certain price above the then existing market price for any of the merger candidate's shares that are "tendered" (that is, offered to it) before a particular date.

Anti-takeover Measures

In recent years many companies have taken various measures designed to discourage unfriendly takeover attempts. The financial press has described these anti-takeover measures as "shark repellents." One such measure involves staggering the terms of the board of directors over several years instead of having the entire board come up for election at one time. Thus, the acquiring firm will have difficulty electing its own board of directors to gain control. Another measure is to give key executives "golden parachute" contracts, under which the executives would receive large benefits if they were terminated without sufficient cause after a merger. A third measure is to put in the corporate charter voting rules that require a supermajority of shares (e.g., 80 percent) to approve any takeover proposals.

Still another measure used by some companies to discourage takeover attempts involves the issuing of "poison pills"; namely, securities that become valuable only when an unfriendly bidder obtains control of a certain percentage of a company's shares. One example is a bond that contains a put option (called a "poison put") that can be exercised only if an unfriendly takeover occurs. The issuing company hopes that the cashing in by bondholders of a portion of its debt will make the takeover unattractive.

Institutional investors, who often control a significant block of a company's stock, have become increasingly active participants in battles for control in many firms. Some institutional investors have used what is called "boardmail" to fight anti-takeover devices such as poison pills and staggered elections of board members. Boardmail consists of requiring the board of directors to adopt weaker anti-takeover measures in exchange for voting support from the institutional owners. In some cases institutions have been successful in placing sympathetic members on boards of companies in which the institution has a significant ownership interest.

If an unfriendly takeover attempt has been initiated, the merger candidate's management frequently tries to find another, more friendly acquiring company (called a "white knight") that would be willing to enter into a bidding war with the first acquiring company. A second measure is to attempt to negotiate a "standstill agreement" with the bidder, whereby the bidder agrees to limit its holdings in the target company. Another measure is the "Pacman" defense, where the target company makes a takeover bid for the stock of the bidder. Additional measures include litigation to delay the takeover attempt and asset and/or liability restructuring to make the target company less attractive to the bidder. On some occasions, either if the takeover candidate cannot find a white knight, or if it simply does not want to be taken over, the takeover candidate can attempt to buy back its shares from the company or investor who initiated the unfriendly takeover attempt. If the shares are bought back at a premium over the shares' market price, the amount of the premium is referred to as "greenmail."

Reasons for Mergers

The following are some of the reasons why a firm might consider acquiring another firm rather than choosing to grow internally:

- A firm may be able to acquire certain desirable assets at a lower cost by combining with another firm than it could if it purchased the assets directly. In this context, when the *market* value of a company's common stock is below its *book* value (or, more important, below the replacement value of the firm's net assets), this company frequently is referred to as a possible "takeover candidate."
- A firm may be able to achieve greater economies of scale by merging with another firm; this is particularly true in the case of a horizontal merger. When the net income for the combined companies after merger exceeds the sum of the net incomes prior to the merger, *synergy* is said to exist.
- A firm that is concerned about its sources of raw materials or end-product markets might acquire other firms at different stages of its production or distribution processes. These are vertical mergers. For example, in 1984 Mobil Corp., a major international oil company considered strong in refining and marketing but somewhat "crude poor," acquired Superior

736

PART VIII
Selected Topics in
Contemporary
Financial
Management

Oil Company, which owned large oil and gas reserves and had no refining and marketing operations. The acquisition resulted in Mobil becoming a better balanced oil company.

■ A firm may wish to grow more rapidly than is possible through internal expansion. Acquiring another company may allow a growing firm to move more rapidly into a geographic or product area in which the acquired firm already has established markets, sales personnel, management capability, warehouse facilities, and so on, than would be possible by starting from scratch.

■ A firm may desire to diversify its product lines and businesses in an attempt to reduce its business risk by smoothing out cyclical movements in its earnings. For example, a capital equipment manufacturer might achieve steadier earnings by expanding into the replacement parts business. During a recession, expenditures for capital equipment may slow down, but expenditures on maintenance and replacement parts may increase. This reason is of questionable benefit to the company's shareholders because most investors can diversify their holdings (through the securities markets) more easily and at a lower cost than the company can.

■ A firm that has suffered losses and has a tax-loss carryforward may be a valuable merger candidate to a company that is generating taxable income. If the two companies merge, the losses can be deducted from the profitable company's taxable income and hence lower the combined company's income tax payments.

This list, although not exhaustive, does indicate the principal reasons why a firm may choose external expansion over internal growth.

A number of empirical studies have examined the returns to the stockholders of the merger candidate and the acquiring company in a takeover.[3] Because the acquiring company must pay a premium over the current market price to obtain the merger candidate, one would expect to see positive returns to the acquired firm's shareholders. This is the case, with average returns of 20 percent or more in successful mergers.[4] For the acquiring company's shareholders the returns are not as good—averaging 5 percent or less in successful mergers.[5]

Accounting Aspects of Mergers

Two basic methods can be used to account for mergers: the *purchase method* or the *pooling of interests method*. In the purchase method, the total value paid or exchanged for the acquired firm's assets is recorded on the acquiring company's books. The tangible assets acquired are recorded at their fair market values, which may or may not be more than the amount at which they were carried on the acquired firm's balance sheet prior to the merger. Any difference between the total value paid and the fair market value of the acquired assets is termed *goodwill*.[6]

---

[3] See Thomas E. Copeland and J. Fred Weston. *Financial Theory and Corporate Policy*, 3d ed. (Reading, MA: Addison-Wesley, 1988), Chapter 20, for a summary of the empirical studies relating to the returns associated with corporate restructuring.

[4] Ibid., p. 745.

[5] Ibid., p. 745.

[6] The expression *goodwill* rarely appears on the balance sheet; instead, we often find "investment in consolidated subsidiaries in excess of net assets at date of acquisition, less amortization."

In the pooling of interests method, the acquired company's assets are recorded on the acquiring company's books at their cost (net of depreciation) when originally acquired. Thus, any difference between the purchase price and the book value is not recorded on the acquiring company's books, and no goodwill account is created.

The pooling of interests method has certain advantages over the purchase method. All other things being equal, reported earnings will be higher under the pooling method, primarily because depreciation will not be more than the sum of the depreciation charges prior to the merger. In addition, because goodwill is not created on the balance sheet in a pooling, it cannot appear as an amortization charge on the acquiring firm's income statement. Finally, because goodwill is not recognized as a deduction for income tax purposes, it has to be deducted from net income *after taxes*.

For example, suppose that Company B acquires Company A's outstanding common stock for $10 million. The book value of the acquired shares is $7 million. Table 22-2 shows the results of this merger, according to both the purchase and pooling of interests methods.

In the pooling of interests method, the two balance sheets are combined, and the $3 million difference between the purchase price and the book value of Company A's stock is not considered. In the purchase method, in contrast, the $3 million difference between the purchase price and the book value is recorded on both sides of Company B's postmerger balance sheet as an increase in total assets and as stockholders' equity.

The book value of Company A's *assets* is $10 million. Suppose that the market value of Company A's assets at the date of acquisition is $11 million. Company B paid $3 million above the book value of *stockholders' equity*. Of this $3 million, the $1 million difference between the assets' market value and book value is recorded on the balance sheet in the appropriate tangible assets accounts. The other $2 million is recorded as goodwill.

The present accounting rules pertaining to mergers limit use of the pooling of interests method to mergers which essentially combine the entire existing interests of *common* stockholders in independent companies. Otherwise, the purchase method must be used. As a result, most mergers are accounted for using the purchase method.

T A B L E 22-2

Comparison of the Purchase and the Pooling of Interests Methods of Accounting for Mergers*

	Before Acquisition		Company B (after acquisition of Company A)	
	COMPANY A	COMPANY B	PURCHASE METHOD	POOLING OF INTERESTS METHOD
Total assets, book value	$10	$50	$63	$60
Liabilities, book value	3	15	18	18
Stockholders' equity, book value	7	35	45	42

* Terms of merger: Company B acquires common stock of Company A for $10 million.

738

PART VIII
Selected Topics in
Contemporary
Financial
Management

Tax Aspects of Mergers

Taxes can play an important role in determining how an acquired company's shareholders receive compensation for their shares. Merger transactions that are effected through the use of voting equity securities (either common stock or *voting* preferred stock) are tax-free. For example, if an acquired company's stockholders have a gain on the value of their shares at the time of the merger, the gain is not recognized for tax purposes if these shareholders receive voting equity securities of the acquiring company; any gains are not recognized until the newly acquired shares are sold.

In contrast, if the acquired company's shareholders receive cash or *nonvoting* securities (such as debt securities, *nonvoting* preferred stock, or warrants) in exchange for their shares, any gains are taxable at the time of the merger. When a partial cash down payment is made, however, the exchange can be treated as an installment purchase, and the seller can spread the tax liability that is created over the payment period.

VALUATION OF MERGER CANDIDATES

In principle, the valuation of merger candidates is an application of the capital budgeting techniques described in Chapters 9 through 11. The purchase price of a proposed acquisition is compared to the present value of the expected future cash inflows from the merger candidate. If the present value of the cash inflows exceeds the purchase price, the merger project has a positive net present value and is acceptable.

In the case of an acquisition candidate whose common stock is actively traded, the market value of the stock is a key factor in the valuation process. To induce the stockholders of the acquisition candidate to give up their shares for the cash and/or securities of the acquiring firm, they have to be offered a premium over the market value of the stock (prior to the merger announcement). Generally, a 10 to 20 percent premium is considered a minimum offer. Even then, in many situations, stockholders may hold out for much better offers—either from the company making the initial offer or from other interested companies.

Valuation Techniques

Three major methods typically are used to value merger candidates: the comparative price–earnings ratio method, the adjusted book value method, and the discounted cash flow method.

The *comparative price–earnings ratio method* examines the recent prices and price–earnings (P/E) ratios paid for other merger candidates that are comparable to the company being valued. For example, if two companies in a specific industry recently were acquired at P/E ratios of 10, the comparative P/E ratio method suggests that a P/E ratio of 10 may be reasonable for other, similar companies. Financial analysts who use this method should exercise caution and determine whether the companies being compared really are similar. This method, which focuses on the current income statement, may not be useful if the P/E ratios of recent, similar mergers vary widely.

The *adjusted book value method* involves determining the market value of the company's underlying assets. For example, suppose a company has equipment fully depreciated on its books but still in use. The market value of this equipment is determined, and the company's shareholders' equity (book value) is adjusted by the difference between the asset's book value and its market value. Financial analysts who use this method should exercise caution, because the determination of the market value of the merger candidate's assets may be difficult.

The *discounted cash flow method* for valuing merger candidates calculates the present value of the company's expected future free cash flows and compares this figure to the proposed purchase price to determine the proposed acquisition's net present value. Recall from Chapter 2 that *free cash flow* represents the portion of a firm's total cash flow available to service additional debt, to make dividend payments, and to invest in other projects. Also, the free cash flows from a merger should include any effects of synergy because we are interested in the marginal impact of the merger on the acquiring firm.

Consider the following example. Suppose the annual after-tax free cash flow from a merger is calculated to be $2 million and is expected to continue for fifteen years. If the appropriate risk-adjusted discount rate is 14 percent, for example, the present value of the expected cash inflows is as follows:

Present value of an annuity of $2 million for 15 years at 14%

$$= \$2,000,000 \ (PVIFA_{0.14,15})$$

$$= \$2,000,000 \ (6.142)$$

$$= \$12,284,000$$

Therefore, if the merger candidate's purchase price is less than $12,284,000, the proposed merger has a positive net present value and is an acceptable "project."

In principle, the discounted cash flow method is the most correct of the three methods discussed in this section, because this method compares the present value of the cash flow benefits from the merger with the present value of the merger costs. However, in practice, the future cash inflows from a merger can be quite difficult to estimate.

Most financial analysts who work on proposed mergers use all of these methods to attempt to value merger candidates. In addition, they consider a large number of other factors in valuing merger candidates. These factors include the merger candidate's management, products, markets, distribution channels, production costs, expected growth rate, debt capacity, and reputation.

Analysis of a Merger

The following merger examples illustrate some of the steps and considerations involved in typical mergers. Diversified Industries, Inc., is considering acquiring either High-Tech Products, Inc., or Stable Products, Inc. High-Tech Products has a high expected growth rate and sells at a higher P/E ratio than Diversified. Stable Products, on the other hand, has a low expected growth rate and sells at a lower P/E ratio than Diversified. Table 22-3 contains financial statistics on Diversified and the two merger candidates.

The possible merger of Diversified with Stable Products is considered first. To entice Stable Products' present stockholders to tender their shares,

Selected Financial Data: Diversified Industries and Two Merger Candidates

	Diversified Industries	Stable Products	High-Tech Products
Sales	$1,200 million	$130 million	$100 million
Net earnings, E	$ 120 million	$ 12 million	$ 16 million
Number of shares outstanding, NS	40 million	4 million	4 million
Earnings per share, EPS	$3.00	$3.00	$4.00
Dividends per share, D_0	$1.65	$1.50	$0.80
Common stock market price	$30.00	$21.00	$52.00
Price–earnings (P/E) ratio	10.0	7.0	13.0
Expected annual growth rate, g	7%	5%	14%

Diversified probably would have to offer them a premium of at least 10 to 20 percent above Stable Products' present stock price. Suppose Diversified decides to offer a price of $24 per share, and Stable Products accepts. The exchange is on a stock-for-stock basis. As a result, because Diversified's stock price is $30 a share, Stable Products' shareholders receive 0.8 shares of Diversified common stock for every share of Stable Products stock they hold; in other words, the *exchange ratio* is 0.8. The exchange ratio, ER, is the number of acquiring company shares received per share of acquired company stock owned.

Next, the possible merger of Diversified with High-Tech Products is considered. If Diversified decides to offer $60 a share and High-Tech Products accepts, the High-Tech Products' shareholders would receive two shares of Diversified common stock for every share of High-Tech Products stock they hold; in other words, the exchange ratio would be 2.0.

The pro forma financial statement summary is shown in Table 22-4 for Diversified, assuming separate mergers with each of the merger candidates. The following equation is used to calculate the postmerger earnings per share for the combined companies, EPS_c:

$$EPS_c = \frac{E_1 + E_2 + E_{12}}{NS_1 + NS_2(ER)} \qquad (22.1)$$

Diversified Industries: Pro Forma Financial Statement Summary Assuming Separate Mergers*

	Before Merger	After Merger with Stable Products	After Merger with High-Tech Products
Sales	$1,200 million	$1,330 million	$1,300 million
Net income	$ 120 million	$ 132 million	$ 136 million
Common shares outstanding	40 million	43.2 million	48 million
Earnings per share	$ 3.00	$ 3.06	$ 2.83

* The exchange ratio is 0.8 shares of Diversified common stock for each 1.0 share of Stable Products and 2.0 shares of Diversified for each 1.0 share of High-Tech Products. The net income figure for Diversified Industries (after merger) assumes that no economies of scale or synergistic benefits are realized as a result of either proposed merger.

where E_1 and E_2 are the net earnings of the acquiring and acquired companies respectively, E_{12} is the immediate synergistic earnings from the merger, and NS_1 and NS_2 are the number of shares outstanding of the acquiring and acquired companies respectively. For the acquisition of Stable Products by Diversified, EPS_c is calculated as follows:

$$EPS_c = \frac{\$120 \text{ million} + \$12 \text{ million} + 0}{40 \text{ million} + [(4 \text{ million})(0.8)]}$$

$$= \$3.06$$

As a result of a merger with Stable Products, Diversified has earnings per share of $3.06, as compared with $3.00 without the merger. In other words, the merger transaction can cause Diversified's earnings to change, due to P/E differences between merging companies. Specifically, if the exchange ratio is based on current stock market prices and no synergy exists, *the acquisition of a company with a lower P/E ratio causes the earnings per share figure of the acquiring company to increase.* Similarly, *the acquisition of a company with a higher P/E ratio causes the earnings per share figure to decrease.* This short-term earnings per share change is caused solely by the merger transaction, and a rational stock market does not perceive this change to be *real* growth or *real* decline.

A more important question remains, What will happen to the price and the P/E ratio of Diversified's stock after a merger has been accomplished? Obviously, it can go up, stay the same, or go down. Normally the stock market seems to view mergers rationally, recognizing that the postmerger P/E ratio is a weighted average of the two premerger P/E ratios. As a result, the postmerger share price of the acquiring company usually is in the same range as prior to the merger, unless significant economies of scale or synergistic benefits are achieved in the merger.

With regard to a possible merger with Stable Products, suppose Diversified's management is not willing to incur an initial dilution in its earnings per share. What is the maximum price and exchange ratio Diversified should agree to under this criterion? The maximum price is calculated using the following equation:

$$P_{max} = (P/E)_1(EPS_2) \tag{22.2}$$

where P_{max} is the maximum offering price without incurring an initial EPS dilution, $(P/E)_1$ is the price to earnings ratio of the acquiring company, and EPS_2 is the earnings per share for the to-be-acquired company. Diversified can offer up to $30 a share for Stable Products without diluting its EPS:

$$P_{max} = (10)(\$3.00)$$

$$= \$30$$

A price of $30 a share in this example results in an exchange ratio of 1.0, because Diversified's stock also is selling at $30 a share.

Suppose Diversified Industries merges with High-Tech Products and initially dilutes its EPS to $2.83 from its present $3.00 level, assuming no immediate synergy. Diversified's managers may want to know how long it will take the expected EPS of the combined companies to equal the expected EPS of Diversified without the acquisition. To answer this question, we

742

PART VIII
Selected Topics in
Contemporary
Financial
Management

have to consider the expected growth rates of the individual companies given in Table 22-3. Without a merger, Diversified's earnings, dividends, and assets are expected to grow at an annual rate of 7 percent, and High-Tech Products' earnings are expected to grow at 14 percent a year. Assume that the combined companies grow at 9 percent a year. The expected EPS growth for Diversified with and without merger is shown in Figure 22-1. Based on the expected growth rates, the EPS of Diversified with the merger will be equal to its EPS without the merger in about 3 years.[7] This information will be used by the Diversified management in its decision whether or not to acquire High-Tech Products.

ANALYSIS OF A LEVERAGED BUYOUT

The following example illustrates some of the steps and considerations involved in typical LBOs. Suppose that, as a part of a corporate restructuring,

[7] The number of years, n, for the two alternatives to produce equal EPS levels is calculated using the following equation:

$$EPS_1(1 + g_1)^n = EPS_2(1 + g_2)^n$$

where EPS_1 and EPS_2 are the initial EPS values for each alternative, and g_1 and g_2 are the expected annual growth rates for each alternative.

FIGURE 22-1

Diversified Industries' Expected EPS Growth with and without the High-Tech Products Acquisition

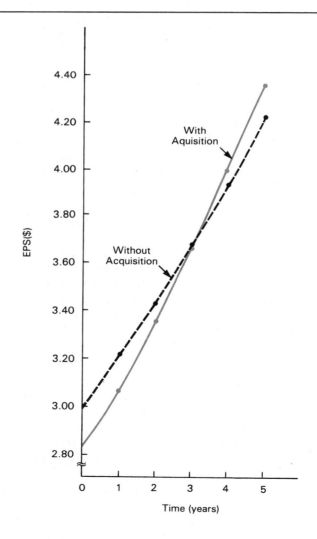

Universal Industries, Inc., recently has decided to sell its Gray Manufacturing Division, a manufacturer of industrial products. The Gray division's top management, together with several private investors, are considering buying Gray and operating it as a separate company. As is fairly typical of LBO candidates, Gray is in a mature industry and its products have a low probability of becoming obsolete. In addition, Gray's fixed assets have a present market value greater than their book value.

The Gray division's financial statements listed in Table 22-5 show that the division presently has an annual pretax loss of $1 million, and therefore its return on stockholders' equity is negative. The Gray management group intends to return Gray to profitability by various cost-cutting and other measures. Gray's parent company, Universal Industries, also could have initiated cost-cutting measures to attempt to return Gray to profitability. However, partly because of Universal's new corporate strategy to get out of the industrial products business, it has chosen instead to sell Gray. Following negotiations between the Gray management group and Universal Industries, the management group agreed to purchase all of the assets of the Gray division for $30 million.

The Gray management group plans to take the following steps to complete the LBO transaction.

1. The management group has put together equity totaling $5 million. Some of these funds will come from liquidated Universal Industries retirement and employee benefit plans. In LBO terminology, equity is sometimes referred to as "ground floor financing."
2. The management group has arranged for short-term commercial bank financing, agreeing to pledge Gray's accounts receivable and inventory

Leveraged Buyout of Gray Manufacturing Division

Balance Sheet
(in millions of dollars)

	BEFORE LBO	PRO FORMA AFTER LBO
Current assets	$22	$22
Fixed assets, net	8	16
Total assets	$30	$38
Current liabilities	$15	$15
Long-term debt	—	18
Stockholders' equity	15	5
Total liabilities and equity	$30	$38

Annual Income Statement
(in millions of dollars)

	BEFORE LBO	PRO FORMA AFTER LBO
Revenues	$30	$30
Cash operating expenses	29	21
Interest expense	1	5
Depreciation	1	3
Earnings before tax	$(1)	$ 1

744

PART VIII
Selected Topics in
Contemporary
Financial
Management

as collateral. This level of financing is called either "second floor" or "top floor" financing.

3. The management group also has arranged to finance the remaining portion of the buyout with subordinated long-term debt financing from an investment banking firm, such as Drexel Burnham Lambert, specializing in providing financing for LBOs. This subordinated debt is called "mezzanine" financing because of its position between the ground floor and the second floor financing. Mezzanine financing is high-risk capital because the company's fixed assets do not provide sufficient collateral for the debt. In addition, Gray's cash flow forecast for its early years as a separate entity indicates that it may experience some difficulty in servicing its debt obligations. As a result, the investment bankers providing the mezzanine financing have insisted that the debentures include attached warrants to provide additional opportunities for return other than the debt's interest payments. Because these debentures are highly risky, they are referred to as "junk bonds." (Recall from Chapter 6 that the term *junk bond* frequently is applied to a debt issue rated Ba or lower by Moody's or BB or lower by Standard & Poors.)[8]

4. The management group intends to initiate a major cost-cutting program as soon as Gray becomes a separate company. They plan to cut unnecessary personnel at all levels, and for the remaining employees they plan to cut salaries and employee benefits. In return, however, they do plan to offer key employees stock options, and all employees will participate in a bonus plan.

   In addition, Gray personnel no longer will have to provide reports to Universal, which in turn reports to its stockholders and the Securities and Exchange Commission. Also, the Gray managers themselves will no longer be spending time talking to security analysts.

5. The management group has determined that Gray's fixed assets (real estate and equipment) have a market value of approximately $16 million, or about twice their present book value. As a result of the LBO, the fixed assets will be written up to their market value and depreciated on the basis of the higher value. The increased depreciation charge will shelter a greater portion of Gray's cash flow from federal income taxes, all other things being equal.

This example illustrates many of the steps a buyer usually takes an LBO.

BUSINESS FAILURE

The remainder of this chapter considers what happens when businesses experience severe and extended problems that might cause failure. The purpose is to present an overview of business failure and the alternatives available to the failing firm. In this section we define business failure and discuss its frequency and causes. The following section examines the various alternatives available to failing firms including the procedures involving the federal bankruptcy laws.

Definitions of Business Failure

Business failure can be considered from both an *economic* and a *financial* viewpoint. In an economic sense, *business success* is associated with firms

---

[8] In the case of privately placed debt, a *junk bond* is a debt issue whose characteristics would cause it to be rated Ba, BB, or lower if it were rated.

that earn an adequate return (equal to or greater than the cost of capital) on their investments. Similarly, *business failure* is associated with firms that earn an inadequate return on their investments. An important aspect of business failure involves the question of whether the failure is *permanent* or *temporary*. For example, suppose a company has $1 million invested in assets and only generates operating earnings of $10,000. Obviously, this 1 percent return on investment is inadequate. However, the appropriate course of action depends to some extent on whether this business failure is judged to be permanent or temporary. If it is permanent, the company probably should be liquidated. If failure is temporary, the company probably should attempt "to ride out the storm," especially if steps can be taken to speed the company's return to business success. From an economic standpoint, business failure also is said to exist when a firm's revenues are not sufficient to cover the costs of doing business.

It is more common, however, for business failure to be viewed in a *financial context*, either as a *technical insolvency*, a *legal insolvency*, or a *bankruptcy*. A firm is said to be *technically insolvent* if it is unable to meet its current obligations as they come due, even though the value of its assets exceeds its liabilities.[9] A firm is *legally insolvent* if the recorded value of its assets is less than the recorded value of its liabilities. A firm is *bankrupt* if it is unable to pay its debts and it files a bankruptcy petition in accordance with the federal bankruptcy laws.

Business Failure Statistics

During the later part of the 1980s approximately 60,000 businesses failed each year in the United States—a failure rate of slightly over 1 percent of all listed businesses.[10] The average liability per failure was about $650,000.[11] As shown in Table 22-6, almost two-thirds of the businesses that failed in 1986 had liabilities under $100,000. Only about 6 percent involved companies with liabilities exceeding $1 million.

Table 22-7 lists the largest bankruptcy filings through 1988. A number of these companies, such as Penn Central and Wickes, have successfully re-

[9] A firm that is *technically insolvent* also can be said to be *illiquid*.
[10] *Business Failure Record* (New York: Dun and Bradstreet, 1987). Dun and Bradstreet defines *business failures* as "businesses involved in court proceedings or voluntary actions involving losses to creditors. In contrast, businesses that discontinue operations for reasons such as loss of capital, inadequate profits, ill health, retirement, etc., are not recorded as failures by Dun and Bradstreet if creditors are paid in full."
[11] Ibid., p. 2.

Distribution of Business Failures in 1986 by Liability Size

T A B L E 22-6

Liabilities	No. of Firms	Percentage of Firms
Under $5,000	21,694	35.2%
$5,000–25,000	4,579	7.4
$25,000–100,000	12,635	20.5
$100,000–1 million	19,013	30.9
Over $1 million	3,695	6.0
Total	61,616	100.0%

SOURCE: Dun and Bradstreet, *Business Failure Record: 1987–1988*, p. 3.

TABLE 22-7 **Largest Bankruptcy (Chapter 11) Filings**

Company	Total Assets	Date Filed	Outcome
Texaco, Inc.	$35.9 billion	April 1987	Emerged April 1988
Baldwin-United	9.4 billion	September 1983	Emerged November 1986
Penn Central Corp.	6.9 billion	June 1970	Emerged October 1978
LTV Corp.	6.3 billion	July 1986	Pending
Public Service Co. of New Hampshire	3.0 billion	January 1988	Pending
Manville Corp.	2.3 billion	August 1982	Emerged November 1988
McLean Industries, Inc.	1.82 billion	November 1986	Pending
Charter Oil Co.	1.81 billion	April 1984	Emerged March 1987
Wickes Cos.	1.6 billion	April 1982	Emerged January 1985
Global Marine, Inc.	1.6 billion	January 1986	Emerged February 1989
Itel Corp.	1.4 billion	January 1981	Emerged September 1983
Storage Technology Corp.	1.3 billion	October 1984	Emerged July 1987
Wheeling-Pittsburgh Steel Corp.	1.22 billion	April 1985	Pending
Revco Drug Stores	1.2 billion	July 1988	Pending
W. T. Grant Co.	1.2 billion	October 1975	Liquidated
Continental Airlines	1.2 billion	September 1983	Emerged September 1986
Smith International	817 million	March 1986	Emerged December 1987
Allegheny International	735 million	February 1988	Pending
A. H. Robbins Co.	706 million	August 1985	Pending
Kaiser Steel Co.	692 million	February 1987	Pending

SOURCE: *Turnarounds and Workouts*, Washington, D.C. Reprinted with permission

organized themselves while in bankruptcy and have emerged to become profitable again. One company, W. T. Grant, was liquidated and ceased to exist. For a number of companies, such as LTV and Public Service Company of New Hampshire, the outcome is pending and may not be known for some time. In the case of Penn Central (the largest U.S. railroad), it took over 8 years for the company to emerge from bankruptcy.

Another interesting characteristic involves the ages of failed businesses. Almost 40 percent of all the companies that failed during 1986 had been in business 3 years or less and over 50 percent had been in business 5 years or less.[12] Only a little more than 20 percent had been in business more than 10 years.

Causes of Business Failure

Table 22-8 shows the causes of business failure for companies that failed during 1986. Although there are a number of reasons why businesses fail, most failures seem to be due at least in part to economic factors and lack of experience on the part of the owners of the businesses. Inadequate sales and heavy operating expenses were also important causes of business failure.

When businesses experience problems such as inadequate sales and heavy operating expenses, they frequently encounter cash flow problems as well. As a result of the cash flow problems, these businesses often increase their short-term borrowings. If the problems persist, the cash flow difficulties can become more acute, and the business may not be able to meet its obligations to its creditors on a timely basis.

[12] Ibid., p. 17.

Causes of Business Failures		TABLE 22-8
Underlying Causes	**Percentage***	
Economic Factors (e.g., insufficient profits, loss of market)	70.2%	
Experience (e.g., incompetence, unbalanced experience, lack of line or managerial experience)	20.4	
Sales (e.g., inadequate sales, competitively weak, economic decline)	11.5	
Expenses (e.g., heavy operating expenses)	7.5	
Neglect (e.g., bad habits, lack of interest, poor health)	1.8	
Customer (e.g., too few customers, receivables difficulties)	0.7	
Disasters (e.g., fire, death of owner)	0.5	
Capital (e.g., excessive withdrawals, burdensome contracts)	0.4	
Fraud (e.g., irregular disposal of assets, embezzlement)	0.3	
Assets (e.g., overexpansion, excessive fixed assets)	0.3	

* Note that because some failures are attributed to a combination of causes, the total of all the categories exceeds 100.0 percent.
SOURCE: Dun and Bradstreet, *Business Failure Record*: 1987–1988, p. 18.

Many of these characteristics of failing firms were measured by the financial ratios used in the Altman bankruptcy prediction model discussed in Chapter 3. Such financial variables as sales, operating expenses (through its effect on EBIT), short-term borrowings (debt), and cash flow (through its effect on net working capital) were all components of one or more of the ratios used to forecast failure.

ALTERNATIVES FOR FAILING BUSINESSES

Once a firm begins encountering these difficulties, the firm's owners and management have to consider the alternatives that are available to failing businesses. In general, a failing company has two alternatives:

- It can attempt to resolve its difficulties with its creditors on a *voluntary*, or *informal*, basis.
- It can petition the courts for assistance and *formally* declare *bankruptcy*.

A company's creditors also may petition the courts, and this may result in the company's being involuntarily declared bankrupt.

Regardless of whether a business chooses informal or formal methods to deal with its difficulties, eventually the decision has to be made whether to *reorganize* or *liquidate* the business. Before this decision can be made, both the business's liquidation value and its going-concern value have to be determined. *Liquidation value* equals the proceeds that would be received from the sale of the business assets minus liabilities. *Going-concern value* equals the capitalized value of the company's operating earnings minus its liabilities. Basically, if the going-concern value exceeds the liquidation value, the business should be reorganized; otherwise, it should be liquidated. However, in practice, the determination of the going-concern and liquidation values is not an easy matter. For example, problems may exist in estimating the price the company's assets will bring at auction. In addition, the company's future operating earnings and the appropriate discount rate at which to capitalize the earnings may be difficult to determine. Also, management is understandably not in a position to be completely objective about these values.

■ 748 ■

PART VIII
Selected Topics in
Contemporary
Financial
Management

Informal Alternatives for Failing Businesses

Regardless of the exact reasons why a business begins to experience difficulties, the result is often the same; namely, cash flow problems.

Frequently, the first steps taken by the troubled company involve stretching its payables. In some cases, this action can buy the troubled company up to several weeks of needed time before creditors take action.

If the difficulties are more than just minor and very temporary, the company may next turn to its bankers and request additional working capital loans. In some situations, the bankers may make the additional loans, especially if they perceive the situation to be temporary. Another possible action the company's bankers and creditors may take is to restructure the company's debt.

Debt restructuring by bankers and other creditors can be quite complex. However, debt restructuring basically involves either *extension*, *composition*, or a combination of the two. In an *extension*, the failing company tries to reach an agreement with its creditors that will permit it to lengthen the time it has to meet its obligations. In a *composition*, the firm's creditors accept some percentage amount less than their actual original claims, and the company is permitted to discharge its debt obligations by paying less than the full amounts owed. The percentage a company's creditors will agree to in the event of a composition usually is greater than the percentage they could net if the company had to sell its assets to satisfy their claims. If a company's creditors feel that the company can overcome its financial difficulties and become a valuable customer over the long run, they may be willing to accept some form of composition.

Debt restructuring by lenders can involve deferment of both interest and principal payments for a time. Before lenders will agree to these deferments, they often require the troubled company's suppliers to also make various concessions. In addition, the lenders frequently demand and receive *warrants* in return for making their deferment concessions.

Large companies that experience cash flow difficulties often sell off real estate, various operating divisions, or both to raise needed cash. For example, Pan American Airlines, which incurred over $1 billion in losses during the 1980s, sold its New York headquarters building, Intercontinental Hotels subsidiary, Pacific route system, and various aircraft during this period to raise the cash needed to stay in business.

Another method often used by failing companies to raise needed cash involves the sale and leaseback of its land and buildings. Some companies also resort to more unusual methods of conserving cash, such as offering preferred stock to certain employees in exchange for a portion of their salary.

Frequently, failing companies voluntarily form a *creditors' committee* that meets regularly and attempts to help the company out of its predicament. The creditors usually are requested to accept deferred payments, and in return the creditors usually request that the company cut various expenditures. If the company and its creditors are able to reach an agreement on the appropriate actions to take, the legal and administrative expenses associated with formal bankruptcy procedures are not incurred. Accordingly, both the company and creditors may be better off as a result.

Liquidation also can occur outside the bankruptcy courts. The process is called an *assignment*. Usually a trustee, who is probably one of the major creditors, is assigned the assets. The trustee then has the responsibility of selling the assets and distributing the proceeds in the best interest of the creditors.

Formal Alternatives for Failing Businesses under the Bankruptcy Laws

The Bankruptcy Reform Act of 1978 states the basic mechanics of the bankruptcy procedure.[13] Either the failing company or its unsecured creditors may initiate bankruptcy procedures by filing a claim in bankruptcy court. When the debtor company files for bankruptcy, it is termed a *voluntary* petition. A bankruptcy proceeding also may be initiated by a group of three or more of the company's unsecured creditors that have aggregate claims of at least $500. The unsecured creditors filing the claim must assert that the debtor company is not paying its present debts as they come due. Such a claim is termed an *involuntary* petition.

After the initial bankruptcy petition has been filed, both the failing company and its creditors receive protection from the courts. The company itself is protected from any further actions on the part of the creditors while it attempts to work out a *plan of reorganization*. The debtor company has 120 days to work out a plan of reorganization. After that, the creditors may file a plan of their own. The court has considerable latitude in a bankruptcy case. For example, depending on the nature of the case, it may decide to appoint a *trustee*, who will be responsible for running the business and protecting the creditors' interests. Normally, the troubled company is allowed to continue operations. If there is reason to believe that continuing operations will result in further deterioration of the creditors' position, however, the court can order the firm to cease operating.

An important aspect of the bankruptcy procedures involves what to do with the failing firm. Just as in the case of the informal alternatives, a decision has to be made about whether a firm's value as a *going concern* is greater than its *liquidation* value. Generally, if this is the case and a suitable plan of reorganization can be formulated, the firm is reorganized; otherwise, it is liquidated.

Reorganization

During Chapter 11 proceedings, the failing company presents its current financial status and its proposed plan of reorganization. This plan of reorganization normally is similar to either composition or extension.

The bankruptcy court and the Securities and Exchange Commission (SEC) review the plan of reorganization for *fairness* and *feasibility*. The term *fairness* means that the claims are to be settled in the order of their priority. The priority of claims is discussed in detail in the next section on liquidation. A *feasible* plan of reorganization is one that gives the business a good chance of reestablishing successful operations. For example, the plan must provide an adequate level of working capital, a reasonable capital structure and debt-to-equity ratio, and an earning power sufficient to reasonably cover interest and dividend requirements. Often a recapitalization may result in fewer fixed charges for the reorganized company and thereby afford it a better chance of succeeding. The reorganization also may involve an extension of the debt maturities, which would help the company's funds flow by causing the debt's principal retirement to occur at later dates.

[13] The Bankruptcy Reform Act of 1978, in general, streamlined the U.S. bankruptcy procedures and increased the number of bankruptcy courts. The Reform Act contains eight odd-numbered chapters, 1 through 15, which are labeled with arabic numerals instead of the roman numerals used in the old Bankruptcy Act.

750

PART VIII
Selected Topics in
Contemporary
Financial
Management

After the bankruptcy court and the SEC have reviewed the reorganization plan, it is submitted to the firm's creditors for approval. Creditors vote by class (e.g., unsecured creditors, secured creditors, common stockholders) on the reorganization plan (or plans in the case where more than one plan is submitted for approval). The plan must be approved by a simple majority (i.e., 50 percent) of the creditors voting in each class and by creditors representing two-thirds (i.e., 66.7 percent) of the total amount of claims voting in each class. Once the bankrupt company obtains approval from the bankruptcy court and its creditors, it can leave Chapter 11. At this point, the court appointed trustee's task is to implement the plan.

A recent example of a company that went through a Chapter 11 reorganization is Global Marine, an offshore oil drilling company.[14] Faced with reduced revenues because of the decline in oil prices and with $1.3 billion in debt, the company filed for bankruptcy in January 1986. Over the next 3 years, under the supervision of the bankruptcy court, Global cut its work force from a high of 3,047 to 1,506 employees. It reduced its yearly overhead from $59 million to $25 million. In February 1989 Global Marine emerged from bankruptcy. Since 1984 the company has lost $807 million and expects to lose an additional $113.6 million through 1992, when it expects to earn its first profits in 8 years.

The reorganization plan is shown in Table 22-9. About forty senior creditors received a combination of cash, debt securities, and 90 percent of the common stock of the reorganized company. Subordinated debt holders received 7.5 percent of the common stock. Global's negative net worth of $116 million virtually wiped out preferred and common shareholders. They received only 2.5 percent of the common stock of the reorganized company, valued at about $3.7 million, plus warrants.

Liquidation

If for some reason reorganization is judged unfeasible, a legally declared bankrupt company may be liquidated. The liquidation procedures are described in Chapter 7 of the Bankruptcy Reform Act. In the liquidation procedure, a *referee* normally is appointed to handle the administrative aspects

[14] *Business Week* (March 13, 1989), p. 44.

TABLE 22-9   **Reorganization of Global-Marine, Inc.**

Creditor Group	Amount Owed	Amount Received
Secured creditors	$700 million	$95 million in cash $400 million in debt 60% of the common stock
Senior unsecured creditors	$154 million	$17 million in debt 30% of the common stock
Subordinated bondholders	$400 million	7.5% of the common stock
Preferred shareholders	—	0.7% of the common stock
Common shareholders	—	1.8% of the common stock

of the bankruptcy procedure. The referee then arranges for a meeting of the creditors, and they in turn select a *trustee*, who liquidates the business and pays the creditors' claims according to the priority of claims set forth in Chapter 7.

The priority of claims states that, in general, secured debts are satisfied first from the sale of the secured assets. The following list specifies the order of priority in which unsecured debts must be paid:

1. The expenses involved in the administration of the bankruptcy.
2. Business expenses incurred after an involuntary petition has been filed, but before a trustee has been appointed.
3. Wages owed for services performed during the 3 months prior to the bankruptcy proceedings, not to exceed $2,000 per employee.
4. Certain unpaid contributions to employee benefit plans (limited to $2,000 per employee).
5. Certain customer layaway deposits, not to exceed $900 per individual.
6. Taxes owed to federal, state, and local governments.
7. Claims of general and unsecured creditors.
8. Preferred stockholders—they receive an amount up to the par value or stated value of the preferred stock.
9. Common stockholders—they share any remaining funds equally on a per-share basis.

To illustrate the priority of claims in a liquidation, consider the balance sheet prior to liquidation of Failures Galore, Inc., shown in Table 22-10.[15] Suppose that the total proceeds of the liquidation are $6.8 million. The distribution of these proceeds is shown in Table 22-11. The proceeds have been distributed in accordance with the priority of claims. Each general and unsecured creditor receives a settlement percentage of the funds owed after priority claims have been settled. As shown in Table 22-11, these priority claims are bankruptcy administration expenses, wages, and taxes owed. In addition, mortgage bondholders receive $1.5 million from the sale of secured assets; this leaves the mortgage bondholders as general creditors

[15] Assume that this liquidation is a voluntary petition, that no unpaid contributions to employee benefit plans exist, and that no customer layaway deposits are involved. In other words, items 2, 4, and 5 in the priority of claims do not apply to this example.

Balance Sheet, Failures Galore, Inc.*

TABLE 22-10

Assets		Liabilities and Equity	
Current assets	$ 6,000,000	Accounts payable	$ 2,000,000
Fixed assets, net	6,500,000	Bank notes payable	2,000,000
		Accrued wages	200,000
		Accrued taxes	300,000
		Mortgage bonds	2,000,000
		Debentures	2,000,000
		Subordinated debentures	2,000,000
		Preferred stock	1,000,000
		Common equity	1,000,000
Total assets	$12,500,000	Liabilities and equity	$12,500,000

* The subordinated debentures are subordinate to the bank notes payable. Assume that all the accrued wages can be paid out of the liquidation proceeds.

TABLE 22-11

Distribution of the Proceeds from the Liquidation of Failures Galore, Inc.

Total liquidation proceeds	$6,800,000
1. Bankruptcy administration expenses	$ 550,000
2. Wages owed to employees	200,000
3. Taxes owed to governments	300,000
Total priority claims	$1,050,000
Funds available for claims of creditors	$5,750,000
4. Payment to mortgage bondholders (proceeds from sale of secured assets)	1,500,000
Funds available for claims of general and unsecured creditors	$4,250,000

$$\text{Settlement percentage for general and unsecured creditors} = \frac{\text{Funds available for general and unsecured creditors}}{\text{Total claims of general and unsecured creditors}}$$

$$= \frac{\$4,250,000}{\$8,500,000}$$

$$= 50\%$$

	Total Claim	Settlement, 50% of Claim (before Subordination Adjustment)	Settlement, 50% of Claim (after Subordination Adjustment)
Accounts payable	$2,000,000	$1,000,000	$1,000,000
Bank notes payable	2,000,000	1,000,000	2,000,000
Mortgage bonds	500,000	250,000	250,000
Debentures	2,000,000	1,000,000	1,000,000
Subordinated debentures	2,000,000	1,000,000	0
	$8,500,000	$4,250,000	$4,250,000

Funds available for preferred and common stockholders	$0

for the balance of their claim ($500,000). After these priority claims have been met, there is $4.25 million in assets remaining to meet the remaining creditor claims of $8.5 million. Each general creditor receives 50 percent of the claim, except bank notes. Because the subordinated debentures are subordinate to bank notes, the bank notes receive the proportionate claim of the subordinated holders ($1 million in this case) in addition to the $1 million directly due the bank notes. Hence, because of the subordination provision in the debentures, the bank notes are paid off in full.

■ SUMMARY

■ Technically, a *merger* is a combination of two or more companies in which all but one of the companies legally cease to exist, and the surviving company continues operation under its original name. A *consolidation* is a combination in which all the companies are dissolved and a new company is formed. The term merger is used to describe both of these types of business combinations.

■ *Mergers are classified according to whether they are horizontal, vertical,* or *conglomerate.* In a horizontal merger, the combining companies are direct competitors. In a vertical merger, the companies have a buyer–seller relationship. In a conglomerate merger, neither company competes directly with the other, and no buyer–seller relationship exists.

■ A *holding company* owns controlling interest in another legally separate company, and the relationship between these affiliated companies is called a *parent–subsidiary* relationship.

■ In a *leveraged buyout* the buyer of a company borrows a large portion of the purchase price, using the purchased assets as partial collateral for the loans.

■ There are a number of reasons why companies choose external growth over internal growth, including the following:
1. The availability of lower cost assets.
2. Greater economies of scale.
3. The availability of more secure raw material supplies and additional end-product markets.
4. The possibility of more rapid growth.
5. Greater diversification.
6. Tax considerations.

■ In the *pooling of interests* method of accounting for mergers, the acquired assets are recorded at their cost when acquired. In the *purchase* method, acquired assets are recorded at their fair market values, and any additional amount paid is listed as *goodwill*, which then must be amortized.

■ Three major methods are used to value merger candidates: the *comparative price–earnings ratio method, the adjusted book value method,* and *the discounted cash flow method.* The discounted cash flow method, which is an application of capital budgeting techniques, is the most theoretically correct valuation method.

■ The acquisition of a company with a higher P/E ratio causes the earnings per share figure of the acquiring company to decrease if the exchange ratio is based on current stock market prices and no synergy exists. Similarly the acquisition of a company with a lower P/E ratio causes the earnings per share figure of the acquiring company to increase.

■ A firm is *bankrupt* if its total liabilities exceed the value of its total assets. A firm is *technically insolvent* if it cannot meet its current obligations as they come due, even though the value of its assets exceeds its liabilities.

■ Economic factors and lack of experience on the part of business owners are generally considered to be the primary causes of most business failures.

■ Failing firms have two basic alternatives:
1. They can attempt to resolve the difficulties with their creditors on an *informal*, voluntary basis.
2. They can petition the courts for assistance and *formally* declare *bankruptcy.*

In addition, the creditors may petition the courts, and the firm involuntarily may be declared bankrupt.

■ Legal bankruptcy proceedings focus on the decision of whether the failing firm should be *reorganized* or *liquidated.* If its going-concern value is greater than its liquidation value, the business will usually be reorganized; otherwise, it will be liquidated.

■ The Bankruptcy Reform Act contains two chapters that outline different bankruptcy procedures. In a Chapter 11 proceeding, the troubled company seeks court protection from its creditors while it works out a *re-*

754

PART VIII
Selected Topics in
Contemporary
Financial
Management

organization plan. If reorganization is judged not feasible, the bankrupt company is liquidated. The liquidation procedures are set forth in Chapter 7 of the Bankruptcy Reform Act.

QUESTIONS AND TOPICS FOR DISCUSSION

1. Define the following terms:
   a. Merger.
   b. Consolidation.
   c. Holding company.

2. Describe some of the measures used by companies to discourage unfriendly takeover attempts.

3. What is the difference between an asset purchase and a stock purchase?

4. What is the difference between an operational restructuring and a financial restructuring?

5. Discuss the differences between the following types of mergers:
   a. Horizontal mergers.
   b. Vertical mergers.
   c. Conglomerate mergers.

6. What are some of the reasons why firms merge with other firms?

7. What methods do financial analysts use to value merger candidates? What are the limitations of each method?

8. Explain what happens to the postmerger earnings per share figure when a company with a relatively high P/E ratio acquires a company with a lower P/E ratio, assuming the exchange ratio is based on current stock market prices and no synergy exists.

9. What are the differences between the *purchase* method and the *pooling of interests* method of accounting for mergers?

10. What is a *leveraged buyout?* What is *mezzanine financing?*

11. What is a *tax-free merger?*

12. Explain the difference between the economic and financial definitions of business failure.

13. Explain the differences among the following terms related to financial failure:
    a. Technical insolvency.
    b. Legal insolvency.
    c. Bankruptcy.

14. What alternatives are available to the failing firm?

15. Basically, what determines whether a bankrupt company is reorganized or liquidated?

16. In a debt reorganization, explain the difference between a *composition* and an *extension.*

17. Explain why an informal settlement may be preferable to declaring bankruptcy for both the failing firm and its creditors.

18. What are the differences between Chapter 7 and Chapter 11 of the Bankruptcy Reform Act?

19. In connection with reorganization plans, what do *fairness* and *feasibility* mean?

20. Explain how a firm that has failed can be reorganized to operate successfully.

21. Rank in order of priority (highest to lowest) the following claims on the proceeds from the liquidation of a bankrupt firm:
    ■ Taxes owed to federal, state, and local governments.

- Preferred stockholders.
- Common stockholders.
- Expenses of administering the bankruptcy.
- Secured creditors.
- Unsecured creditors.
- Wages in 3 months before bankruptcy (up to $2,000 per employee).
- Customer deposits (up to $900 each).
- Expenses incurred after the bankruptcy petition is filed and before a trustee is appointed.
- Contributions to employee benefit plans (up to $2,000 per employee).

PROBLEMS*

1. The Blue Oil Corporation and the Grey Plastics Company have agreed to a merger. The Grey Plastics stockholders will receive 0.75 shares of Blue for each share of Grey held. Assume that no synergistic benefits are expected.

   a. Complete the following table:

	Blue Oil	Grey Plastics	Combined Companies
Sales (millions)	$500	$125	————
Net income (millions)	$ 60	$ 13	————
Common shares outstanding (millions)	16	4	————
Earnings per share	$ 3.75	$ 3.25	————
Common stock (price per share)	$ 41.25	$ 26	————
Price–earnings ratio	————	————	10.0

   b. Calculate the premium percentage received by the Grey stockholders.

   Assume *both* that immediate synergistic earnings of $3 million per year will occur as a result of the merger and the P/E ratio of the combined companies is 10.5.

   c. Rework Part a.
   d. Rework Part b.

2. The McPherson Company is considering acquiring the McAlester Company. Selected financial data for the two companies are shown here:

	McPherson	McAlester
Sales (millions)	$250	$30
Net income (millions)	$ 20	$ 2.25
Common shares outstanding (millions)	5	1
Earnings per share	$ 4.00	$ 2.25
Dividends per share	$ 1.20	$ 0.40
Common stock (price per share)	$ 40.00	$18.00

   Both companies have 40 percent marginal tax rates. Assume that no synergistic benefits are expected.

   a. Calculate the McPherson Company's postmerger earnings per share if the McAlester stockholders accept an offer of $20 a share in a stock-for-stock exchange. (The expression *stock-for-stock exchange* means that the common stock of one company is exchanged for the common stock of another company.)

* Colored numbers denote problems that have check answers provided at the end of the book.

756

PART VIII
Selected Topics in
Contemporary
Financial
Management

b. Recalculate Part a, assuming that the McPherson common stock price is $42 a share. (All other figures remain constant.)

c. Calculate McPherson's earnings per share if the McAlester stockholders accept one $6 convertible preferred share (stated value, $100) for each five shares of McAlester stock held.

d. Calculate McPherson's earnings per share if each group of fifty shares of McAlester stock is exchanged for one 8-percent, $1,000 debenture.

e. Compare the premerger expected dividend return on the McAlester stock with the expected postmerger dividends or interest available with the exchanges described in Parts a, c, and d. (Undoubtedly, at the time of acquisition, McPherson would have pointed out these expected increases in yield to the McAlester stockholders.) Assume that an investor initially holds 100 shares of McAlester stock.

f. What can be said about comparing the expected total premerger return (dividends plus price appreciation) on the McAlester stock versus the expected total postmerger return on the McPherson securities?

3. Ball Industries is considering acquiring the Keyes Corporation in a stock-for-stock exchange. Selected financial data on the two companies follow:

	Ball	Keyes
Sales (millions)	$600	$75
Net income (millions)	$ 30	$10
Common shares outstanding (millions)	6	4
Earnings per share	$ 5.00	$ 2.50
Common stock (price per share)	$ 50	$20

Assume that no synergistic benefits are expected.

a. What is the maximum exchange ratio Ball should agree to if one of its acquisition criteria is no initial dilution in earnings per share?

b. Suppose an investor had purchased 100 shares of Keyes common stock 5 years ago at $12 a share. If the Keyes stockholders accept an offer of $24 a share in a stock-for-stock exchange, how much capital gains tax would this investor have to pay at the time the Keyes shares are exchanged for the Ball shares? (Assume a capital gains tax rate of 28 percent for this investor.)

c. Calculate the postmerger earnings per share if the Keyes stockholders accept an offer by Ball of $24 a share in a stock-for-stock exchange. Assume that immediate synergistic earnings of $4 million will occur as a result of the acquisition.

4. Looking back at Tables 22-3 and 22-4 assume that Diversified Industries acquires High-Tech Products in a stock-for-stock transaction and no immediate synergistic benefits are expected. How long will it take the expected EPS of the combined companies to equal the expected EPS of Diversified without the merger if Diversified is expected to grow at an annual rate of 7 percent without the merger and the combined companies are expected to grow at 8 percent a year?

5. Consider Failures Galore, Inc. (Tables 22-10 and 22-11), discussed in this chapter.

a. If total liquidation proceeds are $5.95 million, determine the distribution of these proceeds among the various creditors of Failures Galore.

b. If total liquidation proceeds are $7.65 million, determine the distribution of these proceeds among the various creditors of Failures Galore.

6. Go-for-Broke Company is being liquidated under Chapter 7 of the bankruptcy code. When it filed for bankruptcy, its balance sheet was as follows:

Assets		Liabilities and Equity	
Current assets	$14,500,000	Accounts payable	$12,145,000
Fixed assets		Accrued wages*	2,030,000
Land and buildings		Accrued taxes	1,160,000
(net)	6,525,000	Notes payable (bank)†	1,350,000
Equipment	7,975,000	Total current	
Total assets	$29,000,000	liabilities	$16,685,000
		Mortgage bonds‡	4,775,000
		Debentures	2,450,000
		Stockholders' equity	5,090,000
		Total liabilities	
		and equity	$29,000,000

* All accrued wages must be paid out of the liquidation proceeds.
† The bank loan is unsecured.
‡ Mortgage bonds are secured by land and buildings.

Assume that the liquidation is a voluntary petition, that no unpaid contributions to employee benefit plans exist, and that no customer layaway deposits are involved. The proceeds from the liquidation of the company's assets are as follows:

Current assets	$ 9,425,000
Land and buildings	3,045,000
Equipment	4,130,000
Total	$16,600,000

Bankruptcy administration charges are $643,750.

a. Determine the distribution (dollar amount and percentage) of these proceeds among the various creditors of Go-For-Broke.

b. Assume that the debentures ($2.45 million) are subordinated to (bank) notes payable. Determine the distribution (dollar amount and percentage) of these proceeds among the various creditors of Go-for-Broke.

MERGERS AND ACQUISITIONS

Admiral Foods Corporation is a diversified food processing and distributing company that has shown excellent growth over the past 10 years as a result of a balanced program of acquisitions and internal growth.

One segment of the food business in which Admiral only recently has begun to compete, however, is the fast-food business. The present top management of Admiral Foods feels that good future growth in the fast-food business still is possible, regardless of the rapid expansion of the 1980s. During the past year, members of the Admiral staff have examined and analyzed a number of independent fast-food firms.[16] One company that the analysis indicated as potentially suitable for acquisition by Admiral is Favorite Food Systems, Inc.

Favorite Food Systems, Inc., which was founded by John Favorite in 1964, is a West Coast chain with current annual sales of approximately $75 million. Favorite's history can best be described as up and down, with the general trend up. The company survived several brief shaky periods during the late 1960s. In 1973 the company went public. (The Favorite family now controls about 57 percent of the common stock.) By 1976 Favorite Foods was recommended by two brokerage firms and was touted by one investment service as "another potential McDonald's." This and other predictions never came true. In fact, Favorite Food Systems' growth rate has slowed appreciably during the past 5 years. One reason frequently given in the trade for Favorite's growth slowdown is Mr. Favorite's apparent indecision regarding expansion. As a result, the competition has increasingly gotten the jump on Favorite with the best locations in new residential growth areas.

The following table shows last year's balance sheets and income statements for both Admiral and Favorite.

Admiral Foods Corporation Balance Sheet
(in millions of dollars)

Current assets	$225.0	Current liabilities	$101.0
Fixed assets, net	307.0	Long-term debt	106.0
		Common equity	
		(10,000,000 shares)	325.0
		Total liabilities	
Total assets	$532.0	and equity	$532.0

Admiral Foods Corporation Income Statement
(in millions of dollars)

Sales	$1261.0
Expenses, excluding depreciation	1118.2
Depreciation	36.0
Earnings before interest and taxes	$ 106.8
Interest	12.8
Earnings before taxes	$ 94.0
Taxes (40%)	37.6
Net income	$ 56.4

[16] Many of the fast-food and restaurant chains are divisions of larger firms. For example, Burger King and Steak and Ale are part of Pillsbury, and Red Lobster is part of General Mills.

Favorite Food Systems, Inc., Balance Sheet
(in millions of dollars)

Current assets	$10.6	Current liabilities	$ 6.5
Fixed assets, net	12.1	Long-term debt	2.2
		Common equity	
		(2,000,000 shares)	14.0
		Total liabilities and	
Total assets	$22.7	equity	$22.7

Favorite Food Systems, Inc., Income Statement
(in millions of dollars)

Sales	$75.2
Expenses, excluding depreciation	65.4
Depreciation	1.4
Earnings before interest and taxes	$ 8.4
Interest	0.4
Earnings before taxes	$ 8.0
Taxes (40%)	3.2
Net income	$ 4.8

Additional Information

	Admiral Foods Corporation	Favorite Food Systems
Dividends per share	$ 2.50	$ 0.60
Common stock (price per share)	$50.00	$15.00

Marie Harrington received her B.B.A. degree in finance 3 years ago and went
to work for Admiral Foods as a financial analyst in the corporate budget department. Recently she became a senior financial analyst responsible for analyzing mergers and major capital expenditures. One of her first assignments is
to prepare a financial analysis of the proposed Favorite acquisition. It is the
conservative policy of Admiral Foods to analyze acquisitions assuming that no
synergistic benefits will occur. Admiral Foods has found that the amount of
synergy in a merger is relatively difficult to forecast. During Harrington's discussions with her supervisor, the following questions came up.

1. Calculate the exchange ratios, based on the common stock market value and
   earnings per share.
2. Mr. Favorite has suggested an exchange ratio based on a 25 percent increase
   over Favorite's current market price. Calculate this exchange ratio.
3. What is the maximum exchange ratio Admiral Foods should agree to if one
   of its acquisition criteria specifies no initial dilution in earnings per share?
   What per-share price for Favorite Food Systems does this exchange ratio
   represent?
4. Even though Harrington's assignment is primarily financial in nature, what
   other considerations are important in a merger such as this?
5. Calculate the Admiral Foods postmerger earnings per share assuming each
   share of Favorite stock is exchanged for 0.40 shares of Admiral stock.

760

PART VIII
Selected Topics in
Contemporary
Financial
Management

6. In discussions with Admiral, Mr. Favorite has stated that he would prefer to exchange his Favorite shares for either Admiral common stock or a convertible preferred rather than cash or debentures. Why?

7. If Admiral Foods is concerned about the possibility that Mr. Favorite will sell his new Admiral shares relatively soon after the merger (and thereby put downward pressure on the price of Admiral's stock), what can Admiral do to effectively prevent such a sale?

8. If Mr. Favorite is unsuccessful in his negotiations with Admiral, two of his key managers, together with a group of private investors, have expressed a willingness to take the company private in a leveraged buyout transaction. How do you think such a transaction would be structured?

9. Based on the information given in the case and your analysis, what do you feel is a fair exchange ratio?

▬▬ SELECTED REFERENCES

Altman, Edward I. *Corporate Financial Distress.* New York: Wiley, 1983.

Ang, James S., and Alan L. Tucker. "The Shareholder Wealth Effects of Corporate Greenmail." *Journal of Financial Research* (Winter 1989): 265–281.

Baldwin, Carliss Y., and Scott P. Mason. "The Resolution of Claims in Financial Distress: The Case of Massey-Ferguson." *Journal of Finance* (May 1983): 505–516.

Bierman, Harold, Jr. "A Neglected Tax Incentive for Mergers." *Financial Management* 14 (Summer 1985): 29–32.

Castagna, A. D., and Z. P. Matolcsy. "The Market Characteristics of Failed Companies: Extensions and Further Evidence." *Journal of Business Finance and Accounting* (Winter 1981): 467–483.

Clark, Truman A., and Mark I. Weinstein. "The Behavior of Common Stock of Bankrupt Firms." *Journal of Finance* (May 1983): 489–504.

Gombola, Michael J., M. E. Haskins, J. E. Ketz, and D. D. Williams. "Cash Flow in Bankruptcy Prediction." *Financial Management* (Winter 1987): 55–66.

Jemison, David B., and Sam B. Sitkin. "Acquisitions: The Process Can Be a Problem." *Harvard Business Review* 64 (March–April 1986): 107–116.

Jensen, M. C. "Takeovers, Folklore and Science," *Harvard Business Review* (November/December 1984): 109–120.

Kim, E. Han, and J. D. Schatzberg. "Voluntary Corporate Liquidations." *Journal of Financial Economics* 19 (1987): 311–328.

Lewellen, Wilbur G., and Michael G. Ferri. "Strategies for the Merger Game: Management and the Market." *Financial Management* 12 (Winter 1983): 25–35.

Malatesta, Paul H., and Rex Thompson. "Partially Anticipated Events: A Model of Stock Price Reactions with an Application to Corporate Acquisitions." *Journal of Financial Economics* 14 (June 1985): 237–250.

Scherer, F. M. "Corporate Takeovers: The Efficiency Arguments." *Journal of Economic Perspectives* (Winter 1988): 69–82.

White, Michelle J. "The Corporate Bankruptcy Decision." *Journal of Economic Perspectives* (Spring 1989): 129–151.

White, Michelle J. "Bankruptcy Costs and the New Bankruptcy Code." *Journal of Finance* (May 1983): 477–488.

An Overview of the CFM Lotus Disk

▰▰▰ INTRODUCTION

The Fourth Edition of *Contemporary Financial Management* has an accompanying diskette, the CFM Lotus Disk, (either shrinkwrapped with your text or available from your instructor) with a set of finance templates that can be used to solve a large number of selected problems and cases in the book. These problems are identified with a computer diskette logo in the margin. The templates are designed to be used in conjunction with the popular spreadsheet program Lotus 1-2-3 (versions 2.00 and 2.01). *The templates are menu-driven, extremely user-friendly, and require no prior knowledge of Lotus 1-2-3.* Lotus 1-2-3 is available in most microcomputer labs. Lotus 1-2-3 and the accompanying templates run on any IBM-PC machine and on all true IBM-compatibles.

This appendix provides a brief overview of the templates. Full documentation for using the CFM Lotus Disk is packaged with the templates if your text was ordered with the templates shrinkwrapped. If your text was not ordered with the templates, your instructor can get a copy of the templates and documentation from West Publishing Co.

▰▰▰ OVERVIEW OF THE TEMPLATES

The eight templates provided with this book can handle a wide range of problems. Detailed information on each template is provided in the documentation. In this appendix we briefly discuss the capabilities of the eight templates.

Loan Amortization Template

The Loan Amortization Template calculates periodic payments on conventional and adjustable rate loans. The template can handle constant principal payment loans and fixed payment loans. The template creates a loan amortization schedule for any loan, identifying the principal and interest components of each payment, and summarizes these over the entire period of the loan. The template also computes the effective rate of interest on adjustable rate loans. The template handles up to 360 payments on a loan.

Stock Valuation Template

The Stock Valuation Template computes the value of a share of stock under: (1) the assumption that the stock's dividends do not grow (such as the valuation of perpetual preferred stock or no-growth common stock), (2) the assumption that the stock's dividends grow at a constant rate in perpetuity, and (3) the assumption that the stock's dividends experience one or more periods of above- (or below-) normal growth followed by a period of constant growth.

Capital Budgeting Template

The Capital Budgeting Template can analyze capital investments with lives ranging from 3 to 30 years. It can analyze projects involving equipment, real estate, or both. Replacement and expansion decisions can be evaluated. The template contains built-in MACRS depreciation schedules (and straight-line rates) for all assets, and pre-1987 ACRS depreciation schedules in the case of old assets being replaced. The template computes a project's net present value, internal rate of return, payback period, profitability index, the terminal value of a project, the net present value adjusted for reinvestment, and internal rate of return adjusted for reinvestment, the infinite chain net present value, the certainty-equivalent net present value, and the risk-adjusted net present value.

Marginal Cost of Capital Template

The Marginal Cost of Capital Template develops a firm's weighted marginal cost of capital schedule. The template computes the after-tax cost of various capital components. It also identifies the break points in the marginal cost of capital schedule, and the weighted marginal cost of capital for each increment of capital, assuming that the firm raises all capital in accordance with its target capital structure.

Indifference Point Template

The Indifference Point Template computes the level of operating income where earnings per share are the same under two financing alternatives. The template also computes the probability that a firm's operating income will be less (greater) than the indifference point level, assuming that operating income is normally distributed. The template also computes the probability that the firm's operating income will be less than the interest payment under both financing alternatives.

Leverage Analysis Template

The Leverage Analysis Template allows you to analyze the impact the firm's use of operating and financial leverage has on the expected risk and return of the firm. This template computes the breakeven dollar level of sales, generates a revised income statement highlighting operating and financial leverage, computes the degrees of operating, financial, and combined leverage, and analyzes the impact of a change in sales on the firm's earnings per share.

Cash Budgeting Template

The Cash Budgeting Template prepares a cash budget for a two-to-twelve-period planning horizon. The template prepares a detailed cash worksheet and a cash budget which identifies the financing required each period. The template is extremely flexible and allows you to model various payment and collection patterns.

Analysis of Credit Terms Template

The Analysis of Credit Terms Template summarizes the results of the firm's current credit policy (including the cost of the current credit policy and the marginal profitability of sales), estimates the cost (benefit) of the firm's average collection period being greater (less) than the credit period, and computes the impact of a change in credit terms on the pre-tax profits of the firm.

Reference
Materials

TABLE I Future Value Interest Factor (FVIF) ($1 at $i\%$ for n years); $FVIF = (1 + i)^n$; $FV_n = PV_0(FVIF_{i,n})$

Period, n	1%	2%	3%	4%	5%	6%	7%	8%	9%	10%	11%	12%	13%
0	1.000	1.000	1.000	1.000	1.000	1.000	1.000	1.000	1.000	1.000	1.000	1.000	1.000
1	1.010	1.020	1.030	1.040	1.050	1.060	1.070	1.080	1.090	1.100	1.110	1.120	1.130
2	1.020	1.040	1.061	1.082	1.102	1.124	1.145	1.166	1.188	1.210	1.232	1.254	1.277
3	1.030	1.061	1.093	1.125	1.158	1.191	1.225	1.260	1.295	1.331	1.368	1.405	1.443
4	1.041	1.082	1.126	1.170	1.216	1.262	1.311	1.360	1.412	1.464	1.518	1.574	1.630
5	1.051	1.104	1.159	1.217	1.276	1.338	1.403	1.469	1.539	1.611	1.685	1.762	1.842
6	1.062	1.126	1.194	1.265	1.340	1.419	1.501	1.587	1.677	1.772	1.870	1.974	2.082
7	1.072	1.149	1.230	1.316	1.407	1.504	1.606	1.714	1.828	1.949	2.076	2.211	2.353
8	1.083	1.172	1.267	1.369	1.477	1.594	1.718	1.851	1.993	2.144	2.305	2.476	2.658
9	1.094	1.195	1.305	1.423	1.551	1.689	1.838	1.999	2.172	2.358	2.558	2.773	3.004
10	1.105	1.219	1.344	1.480	1.629	1.791	1.967	2.159	2.367	2.594	2.839	3.106	3.395
11	1.116	1.243	1.384	1.539	1.710	1.898	2.105	2.332	2.580	2.853	3.152	3.479	3.836
12	1.127	1.268	1.426	1.601	1.796	2.012	2.252	2.518	2.813	3.138	3.498	3.896	4.335
13	1.138	1.294	1.469	1.665	1.886	2.133	2.410	2.720	3.066	3.452	3.883	4.363	4.898
14	1.149	1.319	1.513	1.732	1.980	2.261	2.579	2.937	3.342	3.797	4.310	4.887	5.535
15	1.161	1.346	1.558	1.801	2.079	2.397	2.759	3.172	3.642	4.177	4.785	5.474	6.254
16	1.173	1.373	1.605	1.873	2.183	2.540	2.952	3.426	3.970	4.595	5.311	6.130	7.067
17	1.184	1.400	1.653	1.948	2.292	2.693	3.159	3.700	4.328	5.054	5.895	6.866	7.986
18	1.196	1.428	1.702	2.026	2.407	2.854	3.380	3.996	4.717	5.560	6.544	7.690	9.024
19	1.208	1.457	1.754	2.107	2.527	3.026	3.617	4.316	5.142	6.116	7.263	8.613	10.197
20	1.220	1.486	1.806	2.191	2.653	3.207	3.870	4.661	5.604	6.728	8.062	9.646	11.523
24	1.270	1.608	2.033	2.563	3.225	4.049	5.072	6.341	7.911	9.850	12.239	15.179	18.790
25	1.282	1.641	2.094	2.666	3.386	4.292	5.427	6.848	8.623	10.835	13.585	17.000	21.231
30	1.348	1.811	2.427	3.243	4.322	5.743	7.612	10.063	13.268	17.449	22.892	29.960	39.116
40	1.489	2.208	3.262	4.801	7.040	10.286	14.974	21.725	31.409	45.259	65.001	93.051	132.782
50	1.645	2.692	4.384	7.107	11.467	18.420	29.457	46.902	74.358	117.391	184.565	289.002	450.736
60	1.817	3.281	5.892	10.520	18.679	32.988	57.946	101.257	176.031	304.482	524.057	897.597	1,530.05

Period, n	14%	15%	16%	17%	18%	19%	20%	24%	28%	32%	36%	40%
0	1.000	1.000	1.000	1.000	1.000	1.000	1.000	1.000	1.000	1.000	1.000	1.000
1	1.140	1.150	1.160	1.170	1.180	1.190	1.200	1.240	1.280	1.320	1.360	1.400
2	1.300	1.322	1.346	1.369	1.392	1.416	1.440	1.538	1.638	1.742	1.850	1.960
3	1.482	1.521	1.561	1.602	1.643	1.685	1.728	1.907	2.067	2.300	2.515	2.744
4	1.689	1.749	1.811	1.874	1.939	2.005	2.074	2.364	2.684	3.036	3.421	3.842
5	1.925	2.011	2.100	2.192	2.288	2.386	2.488	2.932	3.436	4.007	4.653	5.378
6	2.195	2.313	2.436	2.565	2.700	2.840	2.986	3.635	4.398	5.290	6.328	7.530
7	2.502	2.660	2.826	3.001	3.185	3.379	3.583	4.508	5.629	6.983	8.605	10.541
8	2.853	3.059	3.278	3.511	3.759	4.021	4.300	5.590	7.206	9.217	11.703	14.758
9	3.252	3.518	3.803	4.108	4.435	4.785	5.160	6.931	9.223	12.166	15.917	20.661
10	3.707	4.046	4.411	4.807	5.234	5.695	6.192	8.594	11.806	16.060	21.647	28.925
11	4.226	4.652	5.117	5.624	6.176	6.777	7.430	10.657	15.112	21.199	29.439	40.496
12	4.818	5.350	5.926	6.580	7.288	8.064	8.916	13.215	19.343	27.983	40.037	56.694
13	5.492	6.153	6.886	7.699	8.599	9.596	10.699	16.386	24.759	36.937	54.451	79.372
14	6.261	7.076	7.988	9.007	10.147	11.420	12.839	20.319	31.961	48.757	74.053	111.120
15	7.138	8.137	9.266	10.539	11.974	13.590	15.407	25.196	40.565	64.359	100.712	155.568
16	8.137	9.358	10.748	12.330	14.129	16.172	18.488	31.243	51.923	84.954	136.969	217.795
17	9.276	10.761	12.468	14.426	16.672	19.244	22.186	38.741	66.461	112.139	186.278	304.914
18	10.575	12.375	14.463	16.879	19.673	22.901	26.623	48.039	85.071	148.023	253.338	426.879
19	12.056	14.232	16.777	19.748	23.214	27.252	31.948	59.568	108.890	195.391	344.540	597.630
20	13.743	16.367	19.461	23.106	27.393	32.429	38.338	73.864	139.380	257.916	468.574	836.683
24	23.212	28.625	35.236	43.297	53.109	65.032	79.497	174.631	374.144	783.023	1,603.00	3,214.20
25	26.462	32.919	40.874	50.658	62.669	77.388	95.396	216.542	478.905	1,033.59	2,180.08	4,499.88
30	50.950	66.212	85.850	111.065	143.371	184.675	237.376	634.820	1,645.50	4,142.07	10,143.0	24,201.4
40	188.884	267.864	378.721	533.869	750.378	1,051.67	1,469.77	5,455.91	19,426.7	66,520.8	219,562	700,038
50	700.233	1,083.66	1,670.70	2,566.22	3,927.36	5,988.91	9,100.44	46,890.4	229,350	*	*	*
60	2,595.92	4,384.00	7,370.20	12,335.4	20,555.1	34,105.0	56,347.5	402,996				

*These interest factors exceed 1,000,000.

T A B L E II Present Value Interest Factor (PVIF) ($1 at i% for n years); $PVIF = \dfrac{1}{(1+i)^n}$; $PV_o = FV_n(PVIF_{i,n})$

Period, n	1%	2%	3%	4%	5%	6%	7%	8%	9%	10%	11%	12%	13%
0	1.000	1.000	1.000	1.000	1.000	1.000	1.000	1.000	1.000	1.000	1.000	1.000	1.000
1	0.990	0.980	0.971	0.962	0.952	0.943	0.935	0.926	0.917	0.909	0.901	0.893	0.885
2	0.980	0.961	0.943	0.925	0.907	0.890	0.873	0.857	0.842	0.826	0.812	0.797	0.783
3	0.971	0.942	0.915	0.889	0.864	0.840	0.816	0.794	0.772	0.751	0.731	0.712	0.693
4	0.961	0.924	0.889	0.855	0.823	0.792	0.763	0.735	0.708	0.683	0.659	0.636	0.613
5	0.951	0.906	0.863	0.822	0.784	0.747	0.713	0.681	0.650	0.621	0.593	0.567	0.543
6	0.942	0.888	0.838	0.790	0.746	0.705	0.666	0.630	0.596	0.564	0.535	0.507	0.480
7	0.933	0.871	0.813	0.760	0.711	0.665	0.623	0.583	0.547	0.513	0.482	0.452	0.425
8	0.923	0.853	0.789	0.731	0.677	0.627	0.582	0.540	0.502	0.467	0.434	0.404	0.376
9	0.914	0.837	0.766	0.703	0.645	0.592	0.544	0.500	0.460	0.424	0.391	0.361	0.333
10	0.905	0.820	0.744	0.676	0.614	0.558	0.508	0.463	0.422	0.386	0.352	0.322	0.295
11	0.896	0.804	0.722	0.650	0.585	0.527	0.475	0.429	0.388	0.350	0.317	0.287	0.261
12	0.887	0.788	0.701	0.625	0.557	0.497	0.444	0.397	0.356	0.319	0.286	0.257	0.231
13	0.879	0.773	0.681	0.601	0.530	0.469	0.415	0.368	0.326	0.290	0.258	0.229	0.204
14	0.870	0.758	0.661	0.577	0.505	0.442	0.388	0.340	0.299	0.263	0.232	0.205	0.181
15	0.861	0.743	0.642	0.555	0.481	0.417	0.362	0.315	0.275	0.239	0.209	0.183	0.160
16	0.853	0.728	0.623	0.534	0.458	0.394	0.339	0.292	0.252	0.218	0.188	0.163	0.141
17	0.844	0.714	0.605	0.513	0.436	0.371	0.317	0.270	0.231	0.198	0.170	0.146	0.125
18	0.836	0.700	0.587	0.494	0.416	0.350	0.296	0.250	0.212	0.180	0.153	0.130	0.111
19	0.828	0.686	0.570	0.475	0.396	0.331	0.276	0.232	0.194	0.164	0.138	0.116	0.098
20	0.820	0.673	0.554	0.456	0.377	0.312	0.258	0.215	0.178	0.149	0.124	0.104	0.087
24	0.788	0.622	0.492	0.390	0.310	0.247	0.197	0.158	0.126	0.102	0.082	0.066	0.053
25	0.780	0.610	0.478	0.375	0.295	0.233	0.184	0.146	0.116	0.092	0.074	0.059	0.047
30	0.742	0.552	0.412	0.308	0.231	0.174	0.131	0.099	0.075	0.057	0.044	0.033	0.026
40	0.672	0.453	0.307	0.208	0.142	0.097	0.067	0.046	0.032	0.022	0.015	0.011	0.008
50	0.608	0.372	0.228	0.141	0.087	0.054	0.034	0.021	0.013	0.009	0.005	0.003	0.002
60	0.550	0.305	0.170	0.095	0.054	0.030	0.017	0.010	0.006	0.003	0.002	0.001	0.001

Period, n	14%	15%	16%	17%	18%	19%	20%	24%	28%	32%	36%	40%
0	1.000	1.000	1.000	1.000	1.000	1.000	1.000	1.000	1.000	1.000	1.000	1.000
1	0.877	0.870	0.862	0.855	0.847	0.840	0.833	0.806	0.781	0.758	0.735	0.714
2	0.769	0.756	0.743	0.731	0.718	0.706	0.694	0.650	0.610	0.574	0.541	0.510
3	0.675	0.658	0.641	0.624	0.609	0.593	0.579	0.524	0.477	0.435	0.398	0.364
4	0.592	0.572	0.552	0.534	0.516	0.499	0.482	0.423	0.373	0.329	0.292	0.260
5	0.519	0.497	0.476	0.456	0.437	0.419	0.402	0.341	0.291	0.250	0.215	0.186
6	0.456	0.432	0.410	0.390	0.370	0.352	0.335	0.275	0.227	0.189	0.158	0.133
7	0.400	0.376	0.354	0.333	0.314	0.296	0.279	0.222	0.178	0.143	0.116	0.095
8	0.351	0.327	0.305	0.285	0.266	0.249	0.233	0.179	0.139	0.108	0.085	0.068
9	0.308	0.284	0.263	0.243	0.225	0.209	0.194	0.144	0.108	0.082	0.063	0.048
10	0.270	0.247	0.227	0.208	0.191	0.176	0.162	0.116	0.085	0.062	0.046	0.035
11	0.237	0.215	0.195	0.178	0.162	0.148	0.135	0.094	0.066	0.047	0.034	0.025
12	0.208	0.187	0.168	0.152	0.137	0.124	0.112	0.076	0.052	0.036	0.025	0.018
13	0.182	0.163	0.145	0.130	0.116	0.104	0.093	0.061	0.040	0.027	0.018	0.013
14	0.160	0.141	0.125	0.111	0.099	0.088	0.078	0.049	0.032	0.021	0.014	0.009
15	0.140	0.123	0.108	0.095	0.084	0.074	0.065	0.040	0.025	0.016	0.010	0.006
16	0.123	0.107	0.093	0.081	0.071	0.062	0.054	0.032	0.019	0.012	0.007	0.005
17	0.108	0.093	0.080	0.069	0.060	0.052	0.045	0.026	0.015	0.009	0.005	0.003
18	0.095	0.081	0.069	0.059	0.051	0.044	0.038	0.021	0.012	0.007	0.004	0.002
19	0.083	0.070	0.060	0.051	0.043	0.037	0.031	0.017	0.009	0.005	0.003	0.002
20	0.073	0.061	0.051	0.043	0.037	0.031	0.026	0.014	0.007	0.004	0.002	0.001
24	0.043	0.035	0.028	0.023	0.019	0.015	0.013	0.006	0.003	0.001	0.001	0.000
25	0.038	0.030	0.024	0.020	0.016	0.013	0.010	0.005	0.002	0.001	0.000	0.000
30	0.020	0.015	0.012	0.009	0.007	0.005	0.004	0.002	0.001	0.000	0.000	0.000
40	0.005	0.004	0.003	0.002	0.001	0.001	0.001	0.000	0.000	0.000	0.000	0.000
50	0.001	0.001	0.001	0.000	0.000	0.000	0.000	0.000	0.000	0.000	0.000	0.000
60	0.000	0.000	0.000	0.000	0.000	0.000	0.000	0.000	0.000	0.000	0.000	0.000

TABLE III Future Value of an Annuity Interest Factor (FVIFA) ($1 per year at $I\%$ for n years); $FVIFA = \dfrac{(1+i)^n - 1}{i}$;

$$FVAN_n = R(FVIFA_{i,n})$$

Period, n	1%	2%	3%	4%	5%	6%	7%	8%	9%	10%	11%	12%	13%
1	1.000	1.000	1.000	1.000	1.000	1.000	1.000	1.000	1.000	1.000	1.000	1.000	1.000
2	2.010	2.020	2.030	2.040	2.050	2.060	2.070	2.080	2.090	2.100	2.110	2.120	2.130
3	3.030	3.060	3.091	3.122	3.152	3.184	3.215	3.246	3.278	3.310	3.342	3.374	3.407
4	4.060	4.122	4.184	4.246	4.310	4.375	4.440	4.506	4.573	4.641	4.710	4.779	4.850
5	5.101	5.204	5.309	5.416	5.526	5.637	5.751	5.867	5.985	6.105	6.228	6.353	6.480
6	6.152	6.308	6.468	6.633	6.802	6.975	7.153	7.336	7.523	7.716	7.913	8.115	8.323
7	7.214	7.434	7.662	7.898	8.142	8.394	8.654	8.923	9.200	9.487	9.783	10.089	10.405
8	8.286	8.583	8.892	9.214	9.549	9.897	10.260	10.637	11.028	11.436	11.859	12.300	12.757
9	9.369	9.755	10.159	10.583	11.027	11.491	11.978	12.488	13.021	13.579	14.164	14.776	15.416
10	10.462	10.950	11.464	12.006	12.578	13.181	13.816	14.487	15.193	15.937	16.722	17.549	18.420
11	11.567	12.169	12.808	13.486	14.207	14.972	15.784	16.645	17.560	18.531	19.561	20.655	21.814
12	12.683	13.412	14.192	15.026	15.917	16.870	17.888	18.977	20.141	21.384	22.713	24.133	25.650
13	13.809	14.680	15.618	16.627	17.713	18.882	20.141	21.495	22.953	24.523	26.212	28.029	29.985
14	14.947	15.974	17.086	18.292	19.599	21.051	22.550	24.215	26.019	27.975	30.095	32.393	34.883
15	16.097	17.293	18.599	20.024	21.579	23.276	25.129	27.152	29.361	31.772	34.405	37.280	40.417
16	17.258	18.639	20.157	21.825	23.657	25.673	27.888	30.324	33.003	35.950	39.190	42.753	46.672
17	18.430	20.012	21.762	23.698	25.840	28.213	30.840	33.750	36.974	40.545	44.501	48.884	53.739
18	19.615	21.412	23.414	25.645	28.132	30.906	33.999	37.450	41.301	45.599	50.396	55.750	61.725
19	20.811	22.841	25.117	27.671	30.539	33.760	37.379	41.446	46.018	51.159	56.939	63.440	70.749
20	22.019	24.297	26.870	29.778	33.066	36.786	40.995	45.762	51.160	57.275	64.203	72.052	80.947
24	26.973	30.422	34.426	39.083	44.502	50.816	58.117	66.765	76.790	88.497	102.174	118.155	136.831
25	28.243	32.030	36.459	41.646	47.727	54.865	63.249	73.106	84.701	98.347	114.413	133.334	155.620
30	34.785	40.568	47.575	56.085	66.439	79.058	94.461	113.283	136.308	164.494	199.021	241.333	293.199
40	48.886	60.402	75.401	95.026	120.080	154.762	199.635	259.057	337.882	442.593	581.826	767.091	1,013.70
50	64.463	84.572	112.797	152.667	209.348	290.336	406.529	573.770	815.084	1,163.91	1,668.77	2,400.02	3,459.51
60	81.670	114.052	163.053	237.991	353.584	533.128	813.520	1,253.21	1,944.79	3,034.82	4,755.07	7,471.64	11,761.9

Period, n	14%	15%	16%	17%	18%	19%	20%	24%	28%	32%	36%	40%
1	1.000	1.000	1.000	1.000	1.000	1.000	1.000	1.000	1.000	1.000	1.000	1.000
2	2.140	2.150	2.160	2.170	2.180	2.190	2.200	2.240	2.280	2.320	2.360	2.400
3	3.440	3.473	3.506	3.539	3.572	3.606	3.640	3.778	3.918	4.062	4.210	4.360
4	4.921	4.993	5.066	5.141	5.215	5.291	5.368	5.684	6.016	6.362	6.725	7.104
5	6.610	6.742	6.877	7.014	7.154	7.297	7.442	8.048	8.700	9.398	10.146	10.846
6	8.536	8.754	8.977	9.207	9.442	9.683	9.930	10.980	12.136	13.406	14.799	16.324
7	10.730	11.067	11.414	11.772	12.142	12.523	12.916	14.615	16.534	18.696	21.126	23.853
8	13.233	13.727	14.240	14.773	15.327	15.902	16.499	19.123	22.163	25.678	29.732	34.395
9	16.085	16.786	17.518	18.285	19.086	19.923	20.799	24.712	29.369	34.895	41.435	49.153
10	19.337	20.304	21.321	22.393	23.521	24.709	25.959	31.643	38.592	47.062	57.352	69.814
11	23.044	24.349	25.733	27.200	28.755	30.404	32.150	40.238	50.399	63.122	78.998	98.739
12	27.271	29.002	30.850	32.824	34.931	37.180	39.580	50.985	65.510	84.320	108.437	139.235
13	32.089	34.352	36.786	39.404	42.219	45.244	48.497	64.110	84.853	112.303	148.475	195.929
14	37.581	40.505	43.672	47.103	50.818	54.841	59.196	80.496	109.612	149.240	202.926	275.300
15	43.842	47.580	51.660	56.110	60.965	66.261	72.035	100.815	141.303	197.997	276.979	386.420
16	50.980	55.717	60.925	66.649	72.939	79.850	87.442	126.011	181.868	262.356	377.692	541.988
17	59.118	65.075	71.673	78.979	87.068	96.022	105.931	157.253	233.791	347.310	514.661	759.784
18	68.394	75.836	84.141	93.406	103.740	115.266	128.117	195.994	300.252	459.449	700.939	1,064.70
19	78.969	88.212	98.603	110.285	123.414	138.166	154.740	244.033	385.323	607.472	954.277	1,491.58
20	91.025	102.444	115.380	130.033	146.628	165.418	186.688	303.601	494.213	802.863	1,298.82	2,089.21
24	158.659	184.168	213.978	248.808	289.494	337.010	392.484	723.461	1,322.66	2,443.82	4,450.00	8,033.00
25	181.871	212.793	249.214	292.105	342.603	402.042	471.981	898.092	1,706.80	3,226.84	6,053.00	11,247.2
30	356.787	434.745	530.321	647.439	790.948	966.712	1,181.88	2,640.92	5,873.23	12,940.9	28,172.3	60,501.1
40	1,342.03	1,779.09	2,360.76	3,134.52	4,163.21	5,529.83	7,343.86	22,728.8	69,377.5	207,874	609,890	*
50	4,994.52	7,217.72	10,435.6	15,089.5	21,813.1	31,515.3	45,497.2	195,373	819,103	*	*	*
60	18,535.1	29,220.0	46,057.5	72,555.0	114,190	179,495	281,733	*	*	*	*	*

*These interest factors exceed 1,000,000.

T A B L E IV **Present Value of an Annuity Interest Factor (PVIFA) ($1 per year at I% for n years); PVIFA = $$\frac{1 - \dfrac{1}{(1+I)^n}}{I}$$;**

$$PVAN = R(PVIFA_{I,n})$$

Period, n	1%	2%	3%	4%	5%	6%	7%	8%	9%	10%	11%	12%	13%
1	0.990	0.980	0.971	0.962	0.952	0.943	0.935	0.926	0.917	0.909	0.901	0.893	0.885
2	1.970	1.942	1.913	1.886	1.859	1.833	1.808	1.783	1.759	1.736	1.713	1.690	1.668
3	2.941	2.884	2.829	2.775	2.723	2.673	2.624	2.577	2.531	2.487	2.444	2.402	2.361
4	3.902	3.808	3.717	3.630	3.546	3.465	3.387	3.312	3.240	3.170	3.102	3.037	2.974
5	4.853	4.713	4.580	4.452	4.329	4.212	4.100	3.993	3.890	3.791	3.696	3.605	3.517
6	5.795	5.601	5.417	5.242	5.076	4.917	4.766	4.623	4.486	4.355	4.231	4.111	3.998
7	6.728	6.472	6.230	6.002	5.786	5.582	5.389	5.206	5.033	4.868	4.712	4.564	4.423
8	7.652	7.325	7.020	6.733	6.463	6.210	5.971	5.747	5.535	5.335	5.146	4.968	4.799
9	8.566	8.162	7.786	7.435	7.108	6.802	6.515	6.247	5.995	5.759	5.537	5.328	5.132
10	9.471	8.983	8.530	8.111	7.722	7.360	7.024	6.710	6.418	6.145	5.889	5.650	5.426
11	10.368	9.787	9.253	8.760	8.306	7.887	7.499	7.139	6.805	6.495	6.207	5.938	5.687
12	11.255	10.575	9.954	9.385	8.863	8.384	7.943	7.536	7.161	6.814	6.492	6.194	5.918
13	12.134	11.348	10.635	9.986	9.394	8.853	8.358	7.904	7.487	7.103	6.750	6.424	6.122
14	13.004	12.106	11.296	10.563	9.899	9.295	8.745	8.244	7.786	7.367	6.982	6.628	6.302
15	13.865	12.849	11.938	11.118	10.380	9.712	9.108	8.559	8.061	7.606	7.191	6.811	6.462
16	14.718	13.578	12.561	11.652	10.838	10.106	9.447	8.851	8.312	7.824	7.379	6.974	6.604
17	15.562	14.292	13.166	12.166	11.274	10.477	9.763	9.122	8.544	8.022	7.549	7.120	6.729
18	16.398	14.992	13.754	12.659	11.690	10.828	10.059	9.372	8.756	8.201	7.702	7.250	6.840
19	17.226	15.678	14.324	13.134	12.085	11.158	10.336	9.604	8.950	8.365	7.839	7.366	6.938
20	18.046	16.351	14.877	13.590	12.462	11.470	10.594	9.818	9.128	8.514	7.963	7.469	7.025
24	21.243	18.914	16.936	15.247	13.799	12.550	11.469	10.529	9.707	8.985	8.348	7.784	7.283
25	22.023	19.523	17.413	15.622	14.094	12.783	11.654	10.675	9.823	9.077	8.422	7.843	7.330
30	25.808	22.397	19.600	17.292	15.373	13.765	12.409	11.258	10.274	9.427	8.694	8.055	7.496
40	32.835	27.355	23.115	19.793	17.159	15.046	13.332	11.925	10.757	9.779	8.951	8.244	7.634
50	39.196	31.424	25.730	21.482	18.256	15.762	13.801	12.233	10.962	9.915	9.042	8.304	7.675
60	44.955	34.761	27.676	22.623	18.929	16.161	14.039	12.377	11.048	9.967	9.074	8.324	7.687

Period, n	14%	15%	16%	17%	18%	19%	20%	24%	28%	32%	36%	40%
1	0.877	0.870	0.862	0.855	0.847	0.840	0.833	0.806	0.781	0.758	0.735	0.714
2	1.647	1.626	1.605	1.585	1.566	1.547	1.528	1.457	1.392	1.332	1.276	1.224
3	2.322	2.283	2.246	2.210	2.174	2.140	2.106	1.981	1.868	1.766	1.674	1.589
4	2.914	2.855	2.798	2.743	2.690	2.639	2.589	2.404	2.241	2.096	1.966	1.849
5	3.433	3.352	3.274	3.199	3.127	3.058	2.991	2.745	2.532	2.345	2.181	2.035
6	3.889	3.784	3.685	3.589	3.498	3.410	3.326	3.020	2.759	2.534	2.399	2.168
7	4.288	4.160	4.039	3.922	3.812	3.706	3.605	3.242	2.937	2.678	2.455	2.263
8	4.639	4.487	4.344	4.207	4.078	3.954	3.837	3.421	3.076	2.786	2.540	2.331
9	4.946	4.772	4.607	4.451	4.303	4.163	4.031	3.566	3.184	2.868	2.603	2.379
10	5.216	5.019	4.833	4.659	4.494	4.339	4.193	3.682	3.269	2.930	2.650	2.414
11	5.453	5.234	5.029	4.836	4.656	4.486	4.327	3.776	3.335	2.978	2.683	2.438
12	5.660	5.421	5.197	4.988	4.793	4.611	4.439	3.851	3.387	3.013	2.708	2.456
13	5.842	5.583	5.342	5.118	4.910	4.715	4.533	3.912	3.427	3.040	2.727	2.469
14	6.002	5.724	5.468	5.229	5.008	4.802	4.611	3.962	3.459	3.061	2.740	2.478
15	6.142	5.847	5.575	5.324	5.092	4.876	4.675	4.001	3.483	3.076	2.750	2.484
16	6.265	5.954	5.669	5.405	5.162	4.938	4.730	4.033	3.503	3.088	2.758	2.489
17	6.373	6.047	5.749	5.475	5.222	4.990	4.775	4.059	3.518	3.097	2.763	2.492
18	6.467	6.128	5.818	5.534	5.273	5.033	4.812	4.080	3.529	3.104	2.767	2.494
19	6.550	6.198	5.877	5.584	5.316	5.070	4.844	4.097	3.539	3.109	2.770	2.496
20	6.623	6.259	5.929	5.628	5.353	5.101	4.870	4.110	3.546	3.113	2.772	2.497
24	6.835	6.434	6.073	5.746	5.451	5.182	4.937	4.143	3.562	3.121	2.776	2.499
25	6.873	6.464	6.097	5.766	5.467	5.195	4.948	4.147	3.564	3.122	2.776	2.499
30	7.003	6.566	6.177	5.829	5.517	5.235	4.979	4.160	3.569	3.124	2.778	2.500
40	7.105	6.642	6.233	5.871	5.548	5.258	4.997	4.166	3.571	3.125	2.778	2.500
50	7.133	6.661	6.246	5.880	5.554	5.262	4.999	4.167	3.571	3.125	2.778	2.500
60	7.140	6.665	6.249	5.882	5.555	5.263	5.000	4.167	3.571	3.125	2.778	2.500

TABLE V

Normal Distribution (Area of the Normal Distribution that is to the right *or* left of z Standard Deviations from the Mean)

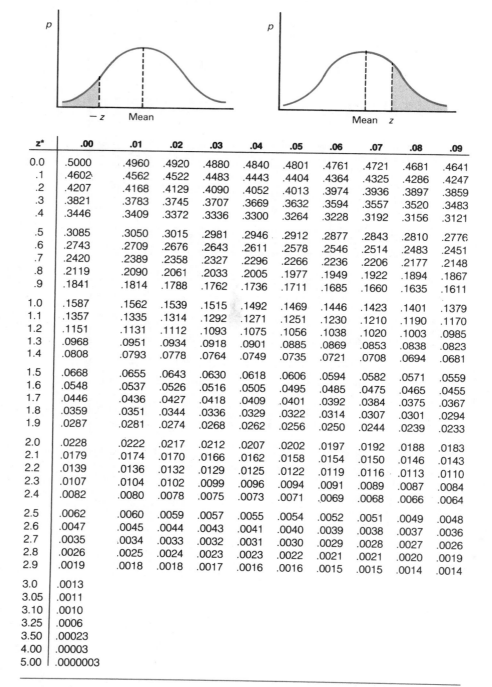

z*	.00	.01	.02	.03	.04	.05	.06	.07	.08	.09
0.0	.5000	.4960	.4920	.4880	.4840	.4801	.4761	.4721	.4681	.4641
.1	.4602	.4562	.4522	.4483	.4443	.4404	.4364	.4325	.4286	.4247
.2	.4207	.4168	.4129	.4090	.4052	.4013	.3974	.3936	.3897	.3859
.3	.3821	.3783	.3745	.3707	.3669	.3632	.3594	.3557	.3520	.3483
.4	.3446	.3409	.3372	.3336	.3300	.3264	.3228	.3192	.3156	.3121
.5	.3085	.3050	.3015	.2981	.2946	.2912	.2877	.2843	.2810	.2776
.6	.2743	.2709	.2676	.2643	.2611	.2578	.2546	.2514	.2483	.2451
.7	.2420	.2389	.2358	.2327	.2296	.2266	.2236	.2206	.2177	.2148
.8	.2119	.2090	.2061	.2033	.2005	.1977	.1949	.1922	.1894	.1867
.9	.1841	.1814	.1788	.1762	.1736	.1711	.1685	.1660	.1635	.1611
1.0	.1587	.1562	.1539	.1515	.1492	.1469	.1446	.1423	.1401	.1379
1.1	.1357	.1335	.1314	.1292	.1271	.1251	.1230	.1210	.1190	.1170
1.2	.1151	.1131	.1112	.1093	.1075	.1056	.1038	.1020	.1003	.0985
1.3	.0968	.0951	.0934	.0918	.0901	.0885	.0869	.0853	.0838	.0823
1.4	.0808	.0793	.0778	.0764	.0749	.0735	.0721	.0708	.0694	.0681
1.5	.0668	.0655	.0643	.0630	.0618	.0606	.0594	.0582	.0571	.0559
1.6	.0548	.0537	.0526	.0516	.0505	.0495	.0485	.0475	.0465	.0455
1.7	.0446	.0436	.0427	.0418	.0409	.0401	.0392	.0384	.0375	.0367
1.8	.0359	.0351	.0344	.0336	.0329	.0322	.0314	.0307	.0301	.0294
1.9	.0287	.0281	.0274	.0268	.0262	.0256	.0250	.0244	.0239	.0233
2.0	.0228	.0222	.0217	.0212	.0207	.0202	.0197	.0192	.0188	.0183
2.1	.0179	.0174	.0170	.0166	.0162	.0158	.0154	.0150	.0146	.0143
2.2	.0139	.0136	.0132	.0129	.0125	.0122	.0119	.0116	.0113	.0110
2.3	.0107	.0104	.0102	.0099	.0096	.0094	.0091	.0089	.0087	.0084
2.4	.0082	.0080	.0078	.0075	.0073	.0071	.0069	.0068	.0066	.0064
2.5	.0062	.0060	.0059	.0057	.0055	.0054	.0052	.0051	.0049	.0048
2.6	.0047	.0045	.0044	.0043	.0041	.0040	.0039	.0038	.0037	.0036
2.7	.0035	.0034	.0033	.0032	.0031	.0030	.0029	.0028	.0027	.0026
2.8	.0026	.0025	.0024	.0023	.0023	.0022	.0021	.0021	.0020	.0019
2.9	.0019	.0018	.0018	.0017	.0016	.0016	.0015	.0015	.0014	.0014
3.0	.0013									
3.05	.0011									
3.10	.0010									
3.25	.0006									
3.50	.00023									
4.00	.00003									
5.00	.0000003									

*Absolute values of z

*The number in parentheses indicates the chapter or appendix
in which the term is discussed.

1A

1. a. DuPont: 4.3%; Public
Service Co. of Colorado: 9.7%
   c. P/E = 11 times
   e. $102
2. b. $325
   d. +$2.50
5. $1,055.625

2

1. 14%
3. b. 9.74%
4. a. 15%
6. $28 million
7. $0.5 million

2A

1. $855,100

3

1. a. $219,178
2. a. 15%
2. $3,945,205
5. a. Firm A: ROE = 30% Equity
      multiplier = 1.5
8. b. Current ratio = 2.2
13. a. ROE = 25%
14. a. 28.57%
19. a. 5.0 times
20. c. $16
22. $66.7 million

4

1. $1,150,000
2. b. $500,000
3. Cash loans needed at end of
     January = $40,000
6. $200
8. $108 million
10. b. $300,000

4A

1. a. i. 5,000
   d. ii. $0

5

1. a. $1,191
3. $240,410.40
5. $1,343.72
6. 13%

7. a. 9 years
9. a. $584.80
11. 20%
14. a. $1,281.58
17. $13,018.71
20. a. $29,806
22. $3,386
24. $51,354
26. $30,807
27. $690,274
30. $111,031
31. a. $31,401
34. $51,980.44
36. $94,337
38. $3.6%
41. $21,879
43. $5,907.83
48. $3,890

5A

2. $2,744
4. 8.62%

6

1. b. $800
3. a. $1,228
4. $964
5. a. 11.4%
7. a. k_d = 13.9%
10. a. $22.22

7

2. a. $88.33
4. $57.36
7. $21.15
8. $21.34
9. $16.21
14. a. $40.36

8

1. a. X: 15%
   b. σ_X = 11.62%
2. p(loss) = 2.28%
4. a. $27.65
5. a. 11.6%
6. a. $E(R_p)$ = 8.2%
   σ_p = 4.87%
7. b. 13.05%
   c. 3.64%
11. a. 1.4
15. a. w_A = 61.54%

16. b. i. 7.8%
    ii. 6.18%
21. 47%

9

2. $5,100
4. a. $122,500
8. $402,000
11. $144,730
13. NCF_1 = $14,716
     NCF_2 = $18,796

10

1. $-3,050
2. a. $158
3. 9.11%
5. $364.53
9. $13,844
10. 8%
12. $4,230
14. a. NPV = $19,031
17. $n \approx 19$
19. a. $-250,800
21. b. NCF_1 = $2,537,400
     NCF_3 = $2,729,400

10A

1. a. NPV_A = $1,888.50
    NPV_B = $2,292

11

1. a. $117.50
   b. $47.10
3. a. 5.48%
6. a. 15%
9. a. $703,600
10. a. $138,061
11. b. $-0.1795 million
13. a. $230,250
15. c. $29,599

12

2. 7.2%
4. b. 13%
5. a. 12.5%
8. a. 13.4%
9. 17.3%
12. First break = $33.33 million
    Cost of first block of funds
      = 13.10%

14. First break = $60 million
   Cost of first block of funds
   = 13.19%

13

1. $10,000
3. a. i. 45% debt; 55% equity
4. a. $15 million
6. a. $2.4 million
7. a. $170,000
8. a. $133.2 million
11. a. 26.43%
12. a. $17.5 million
14. a. 2.28%

13A

1. a. EPS @ $6 million sales =
$5.40
   d. i. 2.778
2. b. i. 1.875
   ii. 1.67
   iii. 3.13
5. a. 10.67
   b. 1.765
9. 9.18%

14

1. b. $0.50
3. 16.7%
4. $1,425,000
7. b. $1.60

15

1. a. $1,467,567
5. a. $972,373
7. 11.8%
8. a. Year 1 = $25,083

9. a. 13%
14. a. 4.96%
15. a. $10,624
18. CF$_1$ = $3.6 million

16

1. c. $0
2. c. $10
3. a. $1,000
   b. $726
4. a. 11.98 shares
6. a. $1.50
   b. $3.50
7. c. $0
8. c. $131.25 million

16A

1. $8,486,832

17

1. b. $50,703,000
2. Aggressive: ROE = 14.55%
3. c. 124.1 days
   e. 69.35 days
4. a. i. Aggressive: ROA =
      12.29%
5. a. iii. Aggressive: CA/CL =
      1.25
6. a. i. Aggressive: 10.85%
7. c. ii. $7.79 million
8. a. $889,980

18

1. a. $7,500,000
3. d. $-18,424
4. $411,044
5. c. $90,959

7. a. $10,471.50
9. a. $257,849

19

1. b. 38.5 days
3. $7,068
5. $20,137
7. c. $-11,363
9. $120,562
11. $17,329
12. $1,163,836
16. a. 80,000
18. a. Fin. Mgmt. = 17,678

20

1. b. $340,000
2. b. 12.40%
3. a. 14.9%
7. a. 8.7%
9. a. 11.67%
12. 23.23%
14. c. 20.4%
17. 22%

21

1. $10,191
2. a. $67.158/watch
3. a. +14%
6. a. $62,500

22

1. b. 19%
2. a. $4.045
   d. $4.258
3. a. 0.50 shares Ball for 1 share
   Keyes